KV-026-782

THE

ALL ENGLAND

LAW REPORTS

2001

Volume 2

Editor

CRAIG ROSE Barrister

Butterworths
A Member of the LexisNexis Group

Members of the LexisNexis Group worldwide

United Kingdom	Butterworths Tolley, a Division of Reed Elsevier (UK) Ltd, Halsbury House, 35 Chancery Lane, LONDON, WC2A 1EL, and 4 Hill Street, EDINBURGH EH2 3JZ
Argentina	Abeledo Perrot, Jurisprudencia Argentina and Depalma, BUENOS AIRES
Australia	Butterworths, a Division of Reed International Books Australia Pty Ltd, CHATSWOOD, New South Wales
Austria	ARD Betriebsdienst and Verlag Orac, VIENNA
Canada	Butterworths Canada Ltd, MARKHAM, Ontario
Chile	Publitecsa and Conosur Ltda, SANTIAGO DE CHILE
Czech Republic	Orac sro, PRAGUE
France	Editions du Juris-Classeur SA, PARIS
Hong Kong	Butterworths Asia (Hong Kong), HONG KONG
Hungary	Hvg Orac, BUDAPEST
India	Butterworths India, NEW DELHI
Ireland	Butterworths (Ireland) Ltd, DUBLIN
Italy	Giuffré, MILAN
Malaysia	Malayan Law Journal Sdn Bhd, KUALA LUMPUR
New Zealand	Butterworths of New Zealand, WELLINGTON
Poland	Wydawnictwa Prawnicze PWN, WARSAW
Singapore	Butterworths Asia, SINGAPORE
South Africa	Butterworths Publishers (Pty) Ltd, DURBAN
Switzerland	Stämpfli Verlag AG, BERNE
USA	LexisNexis, DAYTON, Ohio

A CIP Catalogue record for this book is available from the British Library.

Printed and bound in Great Britain by Williams Clowes Ltd, Beccles and London

ISBN for the complete set of volumes: 0 406 85159 X
for this volume:

ISBN 0-406-93443-6

9 780406 934437

House of Lords

The Lord High Chancellor of Great Britain: Lord Irvine of Lairg

Lords of Appeal in Ordinary

Lord Bingham of Cornhill
Lord Slynn of Hadley
Lord Nicholls of Birkenhead
Lord Steyn
Lord Hoffmann
Lord Hope of Craighead
Lord Clyde
Lord Hutton
Lord Saville of Newdigate
Lord Hobhouse of Woodborough
Lord Millett
Lord Scott of Foscote

Court of Appeal

The Lord High Chancellor of Great Britain

The Lord Chief Justice of England: Lord Woolf
(President of the Criminal Division)

The Master of the Rolls: Lord Phillips of Worth Matravers
(President of the Civil Division)

The President of the Family Division: Dame Elizabeth Butler-Sloss

The Vice-Chancellor: Sir Robert Andrew Morritt

Lords Justices of Appeal

Sir Paul Joseph Morrow Kennedy (Vice-President of the Queen's Bench Division)
Sir Simon Denis Brown
Sir Christopher Dudley Roger Rose (Vice-President of the Criminal Division)
Sir Peter Leslie Gibson
Sir Denis Robert Maurice Henry
Sir Robin Ernest Auld
Sir Malcolm Thomas Pill
Sir William Aldous
Sir Alan Hylton Ward
Sir Konrad Hermann Theodor Schiemann
Sir Mathew Alexander Thorpe
Sir Mark Howard Potter
Sir Henry Brooke
Sir Igor Judge (Senior Presiding Judge for England and Wales)
Sir George Mark Waller
Sir John Frank Mummery
Sir Charles Barrie Knight Mantell
Sir John Murray Chadwick
Sir Robert Walker
Sir Richard Joseph Buxton
Sir Anthony Tristram Kenneth May
Sir Simon Lane Tuckey
Sir Anthony Peter Clarke
Sir John Grant McKenzie Laws
Sir Stephen John Sedley
Sir Jonathan Hugh Mance
Dame Brenda Marjorie Hale
Sir David Nicholas Ramsey Latham
Sir John William Kay
Sir Bernard Anthony Rix
Sir Jonathan Frederic Parker
Dame Mary Howarth Arden
Sir David Wolfe Keene
Sir John Anthony Dyson
Sir Andrew Centlivres Longmore

High Court of Justice

The Lord High Chancellor of Great Britain

The Lord Chief Justice of England

The President of the Family Division

The Vice-Chancellor

The Senior Presiding Judge for England and Wales

The puisne judges of the High Court

Chancery Division

The Lord High Chancellor of Great Britain

The Vice-Chancellor

Sir Francis Mursell Ferris
Sir John Edmund Frederic Lindsay
Sir Edward Christopher Evans-Lombe
Sir Robin Raphael Hayim Jacob
Sir William Anthony Blackburne
(Vice–Chancellor of the County Palatine of Lancaster)
Sir Gavin Anthony Lightman
Sir Robert John Anderson Carnwath
Sir Colin Percy Farquharson Rimer
Sir Hugh Ian Lang Laddie
Sir Timothy Andrew Wigram Lloyd
Sir David Edmund Neuberger
Sir Andrew Edward Wilson Park
Sir Nicholas Richard Pumfrey
Sir Michael Christopher Campbell Hart
Sir Lawrence Anthony Collins
Sir Nicholas John Patten
Sir Terrence Michael Elkan Barnet Etherton

Queen's Bench Division

The Lord Chief Justice of England

Sir Patrick Neville Garland
Sir Michael John Turner
Sir Francis Humphrey Potts
Sir Richard George Rougier
Sir Stuart Neil McKinnon
Sir Thomas Scott Gillespie Baker
Sir Douglas Dunlop Brown
Sir Michael Morland
Sir Roger John Buckley
Sir Anthony Brian Hidden
Sir John Michael Wright
Sir John Christopher Calthorpe Blofeld
Sir Peter John Cresswell
Dame Ann Marian Ebsworth
Sir Christopher John Holland
Sir Richard Herbert Curtis
Dame Janet Hilary Smith
Sir Anthony David Colman
Sir John Thayne Forbes
Sir Michael Alexander Geddes Sachs
Sir Stephen George Mitchell
Sir Rodger Bell
Sir Michael Guy Vicat Harrison
Dame Anne Heather Steel
Sir William Marcus Gage
Sir Thomas Richard Atkin Morison
Sir Andrew David Collins
Sir Maurice Ralph Kay
Sir Anthony Hooper
Sir Alexander Neil Logie Butterfield
Sir George Michael Newman
Sir David Anthony Poole
Sir Martin James Moore-Bick
Sir Gordon Julian Hugh Langley
Sir Roger John Laugharne Thomas
Sir Robert Franklyn Nelson
Sir Roger Grenfell Toulson
Sir Michael John Astill
Sir Alan George Moses
Sir Timothy Edward Walker

[*continued on next page*]

Queen's Bench Division *(continued)*

Sir David Eady
Sir Jeremy Mirth Sullivan
Sir David Herbert Penry-Davey
Sir Stephen Price Richards
Sir David William Steel
Sir Rodney Conrad Klevan
Sir Charles Antony St John Gray
Sir Nicolas Dusan Bratza
Sir Michael John Burton
Sir Rupert Matthew Jackson
Dame Heather Carol Hallett
Sir Patrick Elias
Sir Richard John Pearson Aikens
Sir Stephen Robert Silber
Sir John Bernard Goldring
Sir Peter Francis Crane
Dame Anne Judith Rafferty
Sir Geoffery Douglas Grigson
Sir Richard John Hedley Gibbs
Sir Richard Henry Quixano Henriques
Sir Stephen Miles Tomlinson
Sir Andrew Charles Smith
Sir Stanley Jeffrey Burnton
Sir Patrick James Hunt
Sir Christopher John Pitchford
Sir Brian Henry Leveson
Sir Duncan Brian Walter Ouseley
Sir Richard George Bramwell McCombe
Sir Raymond Evan Jack
Sir Robert Michael Owen
Sir Colin Crichton Mackay
Sir John Edward Mitting (appointed 3 April 2001)
Sir David Roderick Evans (appointed 23 April 2001)

Family Division

The President of the Family Division

Sir Robert Lionel Johnson
Dame Joyanne Winifred Bracewell
Sir Michael Bryan Connell
Sir Jan Peter Singer
Sir Nicholas Allan Roy Wilson
Sir Nicholas Peter Rathbone Wall
Sir Andrew Tristram Hammett Kirkwood
Sir Hugh Peter Derwyn Bennett
Sir Edward James Holman
Dame Mary Claire Hogg
Sir Christopher John Sumner
Sir Anthony Philip Gilson Hughes
Sir Arthur William Hessin Charles
Sir David Roderick Lessiter Bodey
Dame Jill Margaret Black
Sir James Lawrence Munby
Sir Paul James Duke Coleridge

Official Judgment Numbers and Paragraph References

Since 11 January 2001, official judgment numbers have been given to all judgments delivered in the House of Lords, Privy Council, both divisions of the Court of Appeal and the Administrative Court. All such judgments have fixed paragraph numbering, as do judgments delivered on or after 11 January 2001 in divisions of the High Court which have not yet adopted the system of official judgment numbers (see Practice Note (judgments: neutral citation) [2001] 1 All ER 192 for the Court of Appeal and the High Court). We have adopted the following practice in respect of judgments with official judgment numbers and official paragraph numbering:

- The official judgment number is inserted immediately beneath the case name;
- Official paragraph numbers are in bold in square brackets;
- Holding references in the headnotes, and any other cross-references, are to an official paragraph number, not to a page of the report;
- When such a judgment is subsequently cited in another report,

  (i) the official judgment number is inserted before the usual report citations in the case lists and on the first occasion when the case is cited in the text. Thereafter, only the report citations are given;

  (ii) All 'at' references are to the official paragraph number rather than to a page of a report, with the paragraph number in square brackets but not in bold;

  (iii) The 'at' reference is only given in conjunction with the first report cited; eg [2001] 4 All ER 159 at [16], [2001] AC 61. If an 'at' reference is included on the first occasion when the case is cited, it also appears alongside the official judgment number.

For the avoidance of doubt, these changes do not apply to reports of judgments delivered before 11 January 2001 or to the citation of such cases in other reports.

CITATION

These reports are cited thus:

[2001] 2 All ER

REFERENCES

These reports contain references to the following major works of legal reference described in the manner indicated below.

Halsbury's Laws of England

The reference 14 *Halsbury's Laws* (4th edn) para 185 refers to paragraph 185 on page 90 of volume 14 of the fourth edition of *Halsbury's Laws of England.*

The reference 15 *Halsbury's Laws* (4th edn reissue) para 355 refers to paragraph 355 on page 283 of reissue volume 15 of the fourth edition of *Halsbury's Laws of England.*

The reference 7(1) *Halsbury's Laws* (4th edn) (1996 reissue) para 9 refers to paragraph 9 on page 24 of the 1996 reissue of volume 7(1) of the fourth edition of *Halsbury's Laws of England.*

Halsbury's Statutes of England and Wales

The reference 26 *Halsbury's Statutes* (4th edn) 734 refers to page 734 of volume 26 of the fourth edition of *Halsbury's Statutes of England and Wales.*

The reference 40 *Halsbury's Statutes* (4th edn) (1997 reissue) 269 refers to page 269 of the 1997 reissue of volume 40 of the fourth edition of *Halsbury's Statutes of England and Wales.*

Halsbury's Statutory Instruments

The reference 14 *Halsbury's Statutory Instruments* (1999 issue) 201 refers to page 201 of the 1999 issue of volume 14 of the grey volumes series of *Halsbury's Statutory Instruments.*

Cases reported in volume 2

Digest of cases reported in volume 2

House of Lords petitions

This list, which covers the period 15 March 2001 to 24 May 2001 , sets out all cases which have formed the subject of a report in the All England Law Reports in which an Appeal Committee of the House of Lords has, subsequent to the publication of that report, refused leave to appeal. Where the result of a petition for leave to appeal was known prior to the publication of the relevant report a note of that result appears at the end of the report.

Stewart v Engel [2000] 3 All ER 518. Leave to appeal refused 26 March 2001 (Lord Nicholls of Birkenhead, Lord Clyde and Lord Hobhouse of Woodborough).

Rosen v Trustees of Camden Charities [2001] 2 All ER 399. Leave to appeal refused 26 March 2001 (Lord Nicholls of Birkenhead, Lord Clyde and Lord Hobhouse of Woodborough).

Coflexip SA v Stolt Comex Seaway MS Ltd (Note) [2001] 1 All ER 952. Leave to appeal refused 4 April 2001 (Lord Steyn, Lord Millett and Lord Scott of Foscote).

R v Crown Court at Leeds, ex parte Wardle

[2001] UKHL/12

c HOUSE OF LORDS

LORD SLYNN OF HADLEY, LORD NICHOLLS OF BIRKENHEAD, LORD HOPE OF CRAIGHEAD, LORD CLYDE AND LORD SCOTT OF FOSCOTE

29, 30 NOVEMBER 2000, 8 MARCH 2001

d *Criminal law – Committal – Remand in custody – Custody time limits – Police charging appellant with murder – Prosecution producing no evidence in relation to murder charge on day custody time limit expiring and instead laying fresh information charging appellant with manslaughter – Whether laying of information in respect of manslaughter charge giving rise to new custody time limit – Whether new custody time limit compatible with right to liberty – Criminal Law Act 1967, s 6 – Human Rights Act* e *1998, Sch 1, Pt I, art 5 – Prosecution of Offences (Custody Time Limits) Regulations 1987, reg 4(4).*

The appellant, W, appeared before the magistrates' court on 8 January 1999 on an information charging him with murder. Under reg 4(4)[a] of the Prosecution of f Offences (Custody Time Limits) Regulations 1987, there was a maximum custody period, in the case of 'an offence' triable on indictment exclusively, of 70 days between the accused's first appearance and the decision on whether or not to commit him to the Crown Court for trial. Accordingly, in respect of the charge of murder against W, the custody time limit was due to expire on 19 March 1999. When W appeared before the magistrates' court on that day, the prosecution g offered no evidence on the murder charge but laid a charge of manslaughter. The stipendiary magistrate granted the prosecution's application to extend the custody time limit, but held that in any event the new charge of manslaughter attracted its own custody time limit under reg 4(4) so that W's 70-day custody time limit began to run as of new. On W's appeal to the Crown Court, the judge concluded that the h old custody time limit ought not to have been extended. He nevertheless ruled that, as manslaughter was a different offence from murder, W's custody time limit ran de novo from the preferment against him of the new offence of manslaughter. The judge therefore dismissed the appeal, and W applied for judicial review of that decision. The Divisional Court dismissed the application, but certified that a point of law of general public importance was involved in its decision, namely when, in j a magistrates' court, did the charging of an offence cause a fresh custody time limit to run? On appeal to the House of Lords, W submitted that, for the purposes of reg 4(4), the original charge of murder should be regarded as including a new charge of manslaughter because, on an indictment for murder, a person found not

---

a Regulation 4, so far as material, is set out at [10], post

guilty of that offence could be found guilty of manslaughter by virtue of s 6(2)[b] of the Criminal Law Act 1967. Alternatively, he contended that the prosecution's decision to change the charge in the magistrates' court, in circumstances where an extension of the existing custody time limit could not be justified, was an abuse of process if, contrary to his primary argument, the effect of that decision was to subject him to a new custody time limit. Finally, he contended that if reg 4(4) did have the effect of making him subject to a new custody time limit, that provision was incompatible with the right to liberty and the associated rights under art 5[c] of the European Convention for the Protection of Human Rights and Fundamental Freedoms 1950 (as set out in Sch 1 to the Human Rights Act 1998).

Held – (Lord Nicholls and Lord Scott dissenting) On the true construction of reg 4(4) of the 1987 regulations, each offence which was the subject of an information laid before a magistrates' court attracted its own custody time limit. The word 'offence' in that provision referred to the offence for which the person was charged in the information which had been laid against him in the magistrates' court. It could not be read as including any other offence of which a person could be found guilty in the Crown Court by virtue of s 6 of the 1967 Act. That section did not apply to proceedings in the magistrates' court, and the sole function of that court was to examine the question whether there was sufficient evidence to put the accused on trial for the offence charged in the information. Furthermore, the concern of the justices in those proceedings was essentially with questions of fact rather than with questions of law. The operation of custody time limits was linked to the same process and reg 4(4) was designed to fit in with that procedure. Nor was that provision incompatible with art 5 of the convention. Domestic law provided that a person could only be detained in the custody of a magistrates' court while awaiting the completion of a preliminary stage of the proceedings under a procedure which had been laid down by statute. The effect of reg 4 was that any such detention was subject to strictly defined custody time limits. Detention under the statutory scheme was lawful under domestic law and complied with the general requirements of the convention. Accordingly, the fact that reg 4(4) enabled the accused to be subjected to a fresh time limit when a new offence was alleged against him did not give rise to any incompatibility with art 5 of the convention. However, there would be no fresh custody time limit under reg 4(4) if the new charge was simply a restatement of the other offence with different particulars. The offence charged had to be a different offence in law if it was to attract a fresh custody time limit. Moreover, the bringing of a new charge would be an abuse of process if the prosecution could not demonstrate, on the facts of the case, that the bringing of the new charge was justified and the magistrates were satisfied that it had been brought solely for the arbitrary and improper purpose of substituting a new custody time limit. In the instant case there had been no such abuse of process, and the preferring of the manslaughter charge had resulted in the creation of a new custody time limit. Accordingly, the appeal would be dismissed (see [20], [24]–[29], [32]–[38], [66]–[68], [72], [73], [77], [88], [90], [98]–[100], [104]–[107], [112], [114] and [116], post).

R v Waltham Forest Justices, ex p Lee (1992) 97 Cr App R 287, *R v Wolverhampton Justices, ex p Uppal* (1994) 159 JP 86 and *R v Burton on Trent Justices, ex p Nicholson* [1998] COD 262 considered.

---

b Section 6, so far as material, is set out at [65], post

c Article 5, so far as material, is set out at [31], post

a

Notes

For the right to liberty and for custody time limits in magistrates' courts, see respectively 8(2) *Halsbury's Laws* (4th edn reissue) para 127 and 11(2) *Halsbury's Laws* (4th edn reissue) para 852.

For the Criminal Law Act 1967, s 6, see 12 *Halsbury's Statutes* (4th edn) (1997 reissue) 320.

b For the Human Rights Act 1998, Sch 1, Pt I, art 1, see 7 *Halsbury's Statutes* (4th edn) (1999 reissue) 522.

For the Prosecution of Offences (Custody Time Limits) Regulations 1987, see 6 *Halsbury's Statutory Instruments* (2000 issue) 107.

c

Cases referred to in opinions

Amuur v France (1996) 22 EHRR 533, ECt HR.

Bozano v France (1986) 9 EHRR 297, ECt HR.

Bratty v A-G for Northern Ireland [1961] 3 All ER 523, [1963] AC 386, [1961] 3 WLR 965, HL.

d *Brogan v UK* (1988) 11 EHRR 117, ECt HR.

Carter v Bradbeer [1975] 3 All ER 158, [1975] 1 WLR 1204, HL.

Cutter v Eagle Star Insurance Co Ltd, Clarke v Kato [1998] 4 All ER 417, [1998] 1 WLR 1647, HL.

DPP v Schildkamp [1969] 3 All ER 1640, [1971] AC 1, [1970] 2 WLR 279, HL; *affg*

e [1969] 2 All ER 835, [1969] 1 WLR 819, CA.

Guardian Newspapers Ltd, Ex p [1999] 1 All ER 65, [1999] 1 WLR 2130, CA.

Inco Europe Ltd v First Choice Distribution (a firm) [2000] 2 All ER 109, [2000] 1 WLR 586, HL.

Jemmison v Priddle [1972] 1 All ER 539, [1972] 1 QB 489, [1972] 2 WLR 293, DC.

f *Litster v Forth Dry Dock and Engineering Co Ltd* [1989] 1 All ER 1134, [1990] 1 AC 546, [1989] 2 WLR 634, HL.

Marleasing SA v La Comercial Internacional de Alimentaciòn SA Case C-106/89 [1990] ECR I–4135, ECJ.

R v Acott [1997] 1 All ER 706, [1997] 1 WLR 306, HL.

R v Burton on Trent Justices, ex p Nicholson [1998] COD 262, DC.

g *R v Crown Court at Manchester, ex p McDonald, R v Crown Court at Leeds, ex p Forbes, R v Crown Court at Leeds, ex p Wilson* [1999] 1 All ER 805, [1999] 1 WLR 841, DC.

R v Fyffe [1992] Crim LR 442, CA.

R v Governor of Brockhill Prison, ex p Evans (No 2) [2000] 4 All ER 15, [2000] 3 WLR 843, HL.

h *R v Great Yarmouth Magistrates, ex p Thomas* [1992] Crim LR 116, DC.

R v Waltham Forest Justices, ex p Lee (1992) 97 Cr App R 287, DC.

R v Wirral District Magistrates' Court, ex p Meikle (1990) 154 JP 1035, DC.

R v Wolverhampton Justices, ex p Uppal (1994) 159 JP 86.

j *Robertson and Baxter v Inglis* (1897) 24 R 758, CS (IH); *affd* sub nom *Inglis v Robertson and Baxter* [1898] AC 616, HL.

Ross v H M Advocate 1990 SCCR 182.

W v Switzerland (1993) 17 EHRR 60, ECt HR.

Wemhoff v Germany (1968) 1 EHRR 55, ECt HR.

X v UK (1981) 4 EHRR 188, ECt HR.

Yagci and Sargin v Turkey (1995) 20 EHRR 505, ECt HR.

Appeal

Michael John Wardle appealed with leave of the Appeal Committee of the House of Lords given on 12 June 2000 from the decision of the Divisional Court (Kennedy LJ and Mitchell J) on 26 April 1999 dismissing his application for judicial review of the decision of the Crown Court at Leeds (Judge Hoffman) on 22 March 1999 dismissing his appeal from the decision of a stipendiary magistrate at Leeds Magistrates' Court on 19 March 1999 allowing, inter alia, a new custody time period to commence in respect of an information laying a charge of manslaughter against the appellant after the prosecution had produced no evidence in support of a charge of murder laid against him in an earlier information. The Divisional Court certified that a point of law of general public importance was involved in its decision, set out at [1] post. The facts are set out in the opinion of Lord Slynn of Hadley.

Alistair MacDonald QC and *Nicholas Johnson* (instructed by *Grahame Stowe & Bateson,* Leeds) for the appellant.

David Perry and *Sarah Whitehouse* (instructed by the *Crown Prosecution Service*) for the prosecution.

Their Lordship took time for consideration.

8 March 2001. The following opinions were delivered.

LORD SLYNN OF HADLEY. My Lords,

[1] The certified point of law on this appeal is: 'When, in a Magistrates' Court, does the charging of an offence cause a fresh custody time limit to run?' It presumes that a custody time limit is already running in respect of one offence charged and that, to put it neutrally, a second charge of an offence is brought.

[2] What happened here was that the appellant on 17 August 1998 was arrested for a murder committed on 20 July of that year in the course of a violent burglary. The appellant was released but subsequently arrested again and he was charged with murder on 7 January 1999. He appeared before the Leeds Magistrates' Court on the following day.

[3] The police had two statements from a Home Office pathologist which concluded that the victim's death occurred because of minor injuries in the course of a physical struggle and the fear for his safety which that engendered. It was plainly a case in which the police had difficulty in concluding whether murder was the appropriate charge.

[4] By virtue of reg 4 of the Prosecution of Offences (Custody Time Limits) Regulations 1987, SI 1987/299 the time during which the appellant could be detained in custody on the murder charge expired on 19 March 1999. On 11 March the defendant's solicitor received 66 witness statements and 1,600 pages of documents including police statements. The Crown Prosecution Service said in a letter of 10 March: 'Whilst the charge of murder is to be discharged at this stage we reserve counsel's right to reinstate the same should he feel it appropriate on his perusal of the documents after committal.'

[5] When the appellant appeared before the magistrates' court on 19 March 1999 the prosecution offered no evidence on the murder charge but laid a charge of manslaughter. They sought an extension of time for the appellant to be kept in custody on the murder charge. The stipendiary magistrate acceded to the application

and extended the custody time limit on the murder charge and further held that a new custody time limit was to be applied to the manslaughter charge.

[6] On appeal, the Crown Court judge, on 22 March 1999, held that the original time limit should not be extended since the prosecution had not acted with reasonable expedition but he accepted that a new time limit applied to the manslaughter charge. The judge said:

> '... the question is whether any new or amended charge is in substance a different offence, and there is no doubt that manslaughter is a different offence ... carrying a different mens rea, and ... significantly different consequences might flow in terms of length of sentence ... [I]t must follow that the time limit runs de novo from the preferment of the new offence of manslaughter.'

[7] On 23 April the appellant was committed for trial and on 18 May the Crown Court considered a new indictment charging (a) manslaughter, (b) wounding with intent and (c) aggravated burglary. The appellant pleaded not guilty but at the trial on 22 September he pleaded guilty to manslaughter, the other charges remaining on the file and on 24 September he was sentenced to ten years imprisonment.

[8] The Prosecution of Offences Act 1985 in s 22 provides:

> '(1) The Secretary of State may by regulations make provision, with respect to any specified preliminary stage of proceedings for an offence, as to the maximum period—(a) to be allowed to the prosecution to complete that stage; (b) during which the accused may, while awaiting completion of that stage, be—(i) in the custody of a magistrates' court: or (ii) in the custody of the Crown Court; in relation to that offence ...'

[9] Section 22(3) provides that the court may at any time before the expiry of the time limit imposed by the regulations extend, or further extend, that limit. The court is not empowered to do so unless it is satisfied as to certain matters. At the relevant time these were: '(a) that there is good and sufficient cause for doing so; and (b) that the prosecution has acted with all due expedition'. By s 43 of the Crime and Disorder Act 1998 the requirement from 1 June 1999 was that the court should be satisfied that the prosecution 'has acted with all due diligence and expedition'; and by s 22(11ZA) of the 1985 Act it was provided that:

> 'For the purposes of this section, proceedings for an offence shall be taken to begin when the accused is charged with the offence or, as the case may be, an information is laid charging him with the offence.'

[10] By the regulations to which I have referred, made pursuant to s 22 of the 1985 Act, it was provided:

> '4.—(1) ... the maximum period during which a person accused of an indictable offence other than treason may be in the custody of a magistrates' court in relation to that offence while awaiting completion of any preliminary stage of the proceedings specified in the following provisions of this Regulation shall be as stated in those provisions ...
>
> (4) In the case of an offence triable on indictment exclusively the maximum period of custody between the accused's first appearance and the time when the court decides whether or not to commit the accused to the Crown Court for trial, shall be 70 days ...'

[11] Time limits are provided for offences triable either on indictment or summarily and for offences triable summarily. Thus as to the former the period between the accused's first appearance and the start of the summary trial or the time when the magistrates' court decides whether or not to commit to the Crown Court is to be 70 days; when the court decides within 56 days of the accused's first appearance to proceed to summary trial, the time limit between the accused's first appearance and the date of the start of the summary trial must not exceed 56 days. As to offences triable summarily the period of detention between the accused's first appearance and the date of the start of the summary trial must not exceed 56 days.

[12] Regulation 5 provides for custody time limits in the Crown Court. The wording of these provisions is different and nothing specifically turns on them in the present appeal but it is to be noted that in reg 5(2) where a person is accused of an indictable offence other than treason and is committed to the Crown Court for trial—

> 'the maximum period during which he may be in the custody of the Crown Court in relation to that offence, or any other offence included in the indictment preferred against him, while awaiting the preliminary stage of the proceedings specified in the following provisions of this Regulation shall be as stated in those provisions.'

[13] By para 5(4) it is provided:

> 'Where, following a committal for trial, the bill of indictment preferred against the accused (not being a bill preferred under the said section 2(2)(b)) contains a count charging an offence for which he was committed for trial at that committal together with a count charging an offence for which he was committed for trial on a different occasion, paragraph (3) above applies in relation to each offence separately.'

Paragraph (3) provides the maximum periods of custody.

[14] By s 4 of the Bail Act 1976 a person who is accused of an offence must be granted bail when he appears or is brought before a magistrates' court or the Crown Court in the course of or in connection with proceedings for the offence except as provided in Sch 1 to the Act. It is thus plain that at the conclusion of the custody time limit, bail must be granted subject to one of the exceptions in the schedule.

[15] In the Divisional Court, Mitchell J, with whom Kennedy LJ agreed, considered that although it was technically not necessary to have introduced a new charge of manslaughter since even on the murder charge the magistrate could have committed on the charge of manslaughter, this was 'none the less a thoroughly desirable course to take, because accused persons should only be charged, committed and tried for offences which are reflected in the available evidence' even if there was a risk of 'avoiding the statutory consequence of thoroughly dilatory preparation'. No question arises before your Lordships as to whether refusal to extend the time on the earlier charge was justified. Mitchell J then considered in detail five cases where the problem as to whether fresh time limits applied to a substituted or an additional offence arose. I refer to the facts and rulings in those cases as set out in his judgment without repeating them. He did, however, lay particular emphasis on the judgment of Lord Bingham of Cornhill CJ in *R v Burton on Trent Justices, ex p Nicholson* [1998] COD 262 (17 December 1997) in which he said:

a 'The question whether a charge is new so as to attract a new custody time limit must be a question of substance rather than form. The legislative intention underlying the introduction of custody time limits is clear. It would defeat that purpose if relatively minor or unimportant amendments to charges were to enable the authorities to remand a defendant in custody for extended periods. On the other hand, if there is a substantial difference b between one charge and another then it may indeed be just that that result should follow. But whether the difference between one charge and another is substantial must in my judgment depend, as I say, on more than a superficial comparison of the wording and may in a case of any doubt involve some consideration of underlying materials ... It would deprive the applicant of his rights at law if there were to be any prolonged or protracted c delay before this question is resolved if it be the case that on proper analysis these are found to be the old charges in revised form rather than new charges in substance.'

[16] Mitchell J rejected the argument that the difference between murder and manslaughter was one of form and not of substance. In the light of the decided d cases he said: 'I ... have no doubt that the preferring of the manslaughter charges in this case properly resulted in the creation of a new custody time limit.' Although abuse of process is not alleged in this case he added that he could not see how such an allegation could succeed because 'it is desirable that where the evidence only warrants an allegation of manslaughter then manslaughter should e be charged and murder withdrawn'. He expressed concern, however, that since it was difficult to establish 'abuse of process' since bad faith must be established, new time limits could be adopted which would defeat the purpose of the regulations.

[17] It is of course important to bear in mind the purpose of the statute and the f regulations. In *R v Crown Court at Manchester, ex p McDonald* [1999] 1 All ER 805 at 808–809, [1999] 1 WLR 841 at 846 Lord Bingham of Cornhill CJ said:

'The 1985 Act and the 1987 regulations as amended have three overriding purposes: (1) to ensure that the periods for which unconvicted defendants are held in custody awaiting trial are as short as reasonably and practically g possible; (2) to oblige the prosecution to prepare cases for trial with all due diligence and expedition; and (3) to invest the court with a power and duty to control any extension of the maximum period under the regulations for which any person may be held in custody awaiting trial. These are all very important objectives. Any judge making a decision on the extension of h custody time limits must be careful to give full weight to all three.'

[18] It is thus plain that Parliament intended that there should be limits to the period during which a person could be detained. The Secretary of State has imposed those limits by the regulations at the expiry of which bail must be granted. No question arises on this appeal as to the meaning of the regulations j where only one charge is brought and whether or not it includes one or several offences. The question is whether when an offence is subsequently charged whether by alteration of an existing charge or the addition or substitution of a new charge a new limitation period arises in respect of the altered or new charge. It is clear that the additional substitution of a new charge does not affect the limitation period for the original offence charged. That can only be extended by an order under s 22(3) of the 1985 Act if the prescribed conditions are satisfied. The courts

have also clearly recognised that a new period does not begin where the additional or substituted charges are sought to be added in circumstances which constitute an abuse of the process of the court though it is not clear what is the ambit of that exception.

[19] On existing authorities of the Divisional Court, with which I agree, the mere change in the details of the charge which is necessary, eg because of new evidence, does not in itself mean that time begins to run again. The offence is still the same to which the accused first appeared in court even if the details have been changed. If it were otherwise, the prosecution could endlessly add or change detailed particulars of the offence even if with an intention related only to the proper presentation of the case and time would begin to run again. That is not the situation in the present appeal.

[20] It is also common ground that where the first and second offences are plainly distinct, a charge of the second offence attracts its own separate time limit. Detention in the custody of the magistrates' court on a charge of rape added to a charge of burglary committed on the same occasion is to be measured by the period of 70 days from the accused's first appearance on the rape charge. Although the section does not specifically deal with the addition to or substitution of offences to or for an existing offence charged, this seems to me plainly to be right. A separate offence has a separate time limit.

[21] On this appeal the appellant concedes that the charging of a new offence would cause a fresh time to run unless the original offence charged necessarily includes or amounts to, whether expressly or impliedly, the new offence charged or where the prosecution in charging the new offence is 'solely or substantially' influenced by a desire to cause a fresh custody time to run. The latter it is said would be inconsistent with the purpose of s 22 of the 1985 Act and contrary to art 5 of the European Convention for the Protection of Human Rights and Fundamental Freedoms (Rome, 4 November 1950; TS 71 (1953); Cmd 8969) (set out in Sch 1 to the Human Rights Act 1998) and an abuse of process.

[22] It is to be noticed that s 22 empowers the Secretary of State to lay down periods for any stage of proceedings for an offence or time in custody 'in relation to *that offence*'. By sub-s (11ZA) proceedings for '*an offence* shall be taken to begin when the accused is charged *with the offence*'. By reg 4(1) the maximum period of custody 'in relation to *that offence* while awaiting completion of any preliminary stage of the proceedings' is as stated in the regulations. For an offence triable only on indictment the period is from the accused's first appearance and the time when the court decides whether or not to commit him to the Crown Court—that must mean that the period prima facie runs for the offence on which he appears before the magistrate, ie for each offence from the date of his appearance in relation to that offence. The emphasis is on the particular offence in each case.

[23] Reliance is placed however by the appellant on s 6(2) and (3) of the Criminal Law Act 1967. The former provides that on an indictment for murder a person found not guilty of murder may be found guilty inter alia of manslaughter or of causing grievous bodily harm with intent or with an attempt to do so. Subsection (3) provides:

> 'Where, on a person's trial on indictment for any offence except treason or murder, the jury find him not guilty of the offence specifically charged in the indictment, but the allegations in the indictment amount to or include (expressly or by implication) an allegation of another offence falling within the jurisdiction of the court of trial, the jury may find him guilty of that other

a offence or of an offence of which he could be guilty on an indictment specifically charging that other offence.'

[24] I do not consider that these provisions conclude the present question. They simply list the other offences of which the accused may be convicted. They do not make or deem them the same offence. Section 6(2) expressly treats the alternative convictions as being of a distinct offence and s 6(3) recognises that there b may be conviction of 'that other offence'. If it had been intended to read 'offence' in s 22 of the 1985 Act or reg 4 as including other offences of which he might be convicted, it could have said so. It is not surprising that it did not do so. Section 6 is concerned with what happens at the end of a trial. Regulation 4 is concerned with the preliminary stages of the proceedings up to the time when a decision to c commit is taken where the court is concerned with the offences charged rather than with the offence proved. Magistrates are in relation to indictable offences looking to see if there is evidence of an offence justifying his being committed to trial. That is an exercise they carry out separately in relation to the initial offence charged and to the proposed additional or substituted offence. The offences charged in the two informations are separate offences and it is to them separately d and solely that reg 4(4) is directed. Magistrates are not concerned under that regulation with what options would be available on the evidence as it turns out at the trial if the accused is found not guilty of the initial offence charged. They are concerned only with 'that offence' charged in the information (see reg 2(2)(c)).

[25] The appellant has submitted that a new custody time limit does not begin e if 'the original offence charged necessarily includes or amounts to, whether expressly or impliedly, the new offence charged'. This at first sight has its attractions, but the question whether one offence 'impliedly' or 'necessarily includes' the other, may not be an easy one for magistrates to answer when a new information is laid. I also think that it may widen the exceptions to the general rule that each offence is to be taken as a separate offence under the regulation f beyond what is intended or justified. Subject to the power of the court to control improper applications as being an abuse of process, it is in my view only where the constituent elements of the new offence are in substance the same as those of the original offence, so that it can be said that the offences are substantially the same, that a new custody time limit does not begin. That is not so in the g comparison of murder and manslaughter for reasons which it is unnecessary to elaborate. The mens rea is wider, the effect of establishing self-defence or provocation are sufficient examples. It may not be so clear in many other cases and I recognise the restrictions on preventing a new custody time limit from beginning which that produces but in my view it flows from the structure and wording of the h Regulations. As Buxton J said in *R v Wolverhampton Justices, ex p Uppal* (1994) 159 JP 86 at 92:

> '... it is quite clear from the cases that this Court has cited that these regulations are to be construed to say what they say, and they say that each offence shall be taken separately. If the charge is properly justified, then j properly a new custody time limit must run.'

[26] This may or may not be an undesirable result but in my view it is a clear consequence of the language of the statute. I decline to dismiss as absurd the opinion of judges experienced in criminal law and procedure in the cases in the Divisional Court to which we have been referred and the views of the stipendiary magistrate, the Crown Court judge and the Divisional Court in the present case.

It is not in my view right in any event to say that the result is so absurd that the court must be driven to find some other meaning applicable in all cases coming before the magistrates' court which may well not be so clear cut as in the present case. If the result is thought to be unreasonable (and I accept Mitchell J's comments) it is for Parliament to change the provision of the statute and the Secretary of State to reconsider his regulation.

[27] It is accepted that where to add or substitute a new charge amounts to an abuse of process, a new custody time limit does not begin. It has been said that where the new charge is brought in bad faith or dishonestly, that would amount to an abuse of process. In my view the ambit of 'abuse of process' is not so limited. If a new charge is brought simply to keep the accused in custody for a longer period, that is clearly contrary to the intention of the legislation and constitutes an abuse of process. As Professor J C Smith said in his commentary to *R v Great Yarmouth Magistrates, ex p Thomas* [1992] Crim LR 116 at 117:

> 'Perhaps the more specific question to be asked is whether the charges of possession with intent were brought solely for the purpose of retaining the applicants in custody.'

[28] Equally if the court is satisfied that the way in which and the time at which the new charge is added or substituted, indicates that it is not done for the genuine purpose of introducing a new charge on a revised assessment of the case, but is done primarily to keep the accused in custody on the initial charge, then this will constitute an abuse of process. Of course, on the other hand, if the purpose is genuinely to introduce a new charge on such a revised assessment the fact that the accused begins a new custody period does not in itself constitute an abuse of process.

[29] It was not contended below that there was an abuse of process here and on my view of the construction of the section and the regulation such a matter does not fall for consideration on the present appeal.

[30] Though he did not do so in the courts below, before your Lordships the appellant has relied on art 5 of the European Convention for the Protection of Human Rights and Fundamental Freedoms as incorporated in the Human Rights Act 1998. He says further that, pursuant to s 3 of that Act, s 22 of the 1985 Act and the regulations must be read and given effect to in a way compatible with convention rights so far as it is possible to do so.

[31] Article 5 provides so far as relevant:

> '1. Everyone has the right to liberty and security of the person. No one shall be deprived of his liberty save in the following cases and in accordance with a procedure prescribed by law … (c) the lawful arrest or detention of a person effected for the purpose of bringing him before the competent legal authority on reasonable suspicion of having committed an offence or when it is reasonably considered necessary to prevent his committing an offence or fleeing after having done so …
>
> 3. Everyone arrested or detained in accordance with the provisions of paragraph 1(c) of this Article shall be brought promptly before a judge or other officer authorised by law to exercise judicial power and shall be entitled to trial within a reasonable time or to release pending trial. Release may be conditioned by guarantees to appear for trial …'

a [32] On the view which I have formed of the relevant legislation the appellant was deprived of his liberty in accordance with a procedure prescribed by law. It was detention effected for the purpose of bringing him before a competent legal authority on reasonable suspicion of having committed an offence. He was brought promptly before a court and was entitled to trial within a reasonable time.

b [33] To show that procedures of domestic law have been complied with is necessary but it is not enough. Those procedures must themselves respect the objectives of art 5 of the convention. It has been said by the European Court that the purpose of art 5 is 'to protect the individual from arbitrariness' (see *X v UK* (1981) 4 EHRR 188, *Bozano v France* (1986) 9 EHRR 297, *Brogan v UK* (1988) 11 EHRR 117 and *Amuur v France* (1996) 22 EHRR 533). Moreover, it is necessary not c merely that the appellant should have access to a court under precise rules, but his detention should be justified as a matter of public interest and then only during a reasonable time (see *W v Switzerland* (1993) 17 EHRR 60 and *Wemhoff v Germany* (1968) 1 EHRR 55).

[34] Full weight must be given to these cases relied on by the appellant. In my d view, however, it has not been shown that his detention was arbitrary. No complaint can be made for the first 70-day period: the second is justified because a new charge is brought on the basis of a very substantial body of evidence delivered to the defence shortly before the second charge was laid. It was right to change the charge to the lesser offence of manslaughter in the light of the reconsideration of the case. For the serious offences involved here, I do not consider that the periods e prescribed in the regulations can be said to be unreasonable.

[35] Moreover there was an opportunity to challenge the laying of the second charge and the second detention period as an abuse of the process of the court. That was not done, understandably. There existed a procedure by which the decision of the magistrate could be challenged by way of judicial review. That was f done in this case. During the period when the appellant was in the custody of the magistrates' court, the provision of s 128(6) of the Magistrates' Court Act 1980 requires that 'a magistrates' court may not remand a person for a period exceeding 8 clear days …'

[36] Moreover in this case the time spent in custody on remand counts as time served by him as part of the sentence of ten years imprisonment after conviction g (see s 9(3) of the Crime (Sentences) Act 1997).

[37] In all these circumstances I do not consider that there was here a violation of art 5 of the convention. Section 3 of the Human Rights Act 1998 therefore does not fall for consideration.

[38] Accordingly, I would dismiss the appeal.

h

LORD NICHOLLS OF BIRKENHEAD. My Lords,

[39] Read literally, regs 2(2) and 4 of the Prosecution of Offences (Custody Time Limits) Regulations 1987, SI 1987/299 permit of only one interpretation. Manslaughter and murder are different offences. They are different offences even j if they are based on the same facts. But the literal interpretation of the regulations produces a result which is, frankly, absurd. It produces a result which cannot have been the intention of Parliament.

[40] Take the case of a person charged with the offence of murder. He is remanded in the custody of a magistrates' court. The maximum period he may be detained in custody, between the date of his first appearance and the decision on whether or not to commit him to the Crown Court for trial, is 70 days.

This maximum period may be extended, but only in carefully defined circumstances. After some weeks the prosecution decides, wholly properly, that the evidence is not adequate for a charge of murder but that it is adequate for the lesser charge of manslaughter. So the prosecution takes the proper step of substituting the lesser charge of manslaughter for the more serious charge of murder. No new facts are involved. According to the respondent's argument, that substitution sets in motion a new custody time limit.

[41] The absurdity of this contention is that the accused person could have been committed to trial on a charge of manslaughter, and if tried could have been convicted of manslaughter, even if the sole charge had remained a charge of murder. Throughout, once charged with murder, the accused was implicitly facing also the lesser charge of manslaughter. Throughout he was at risk of being convicted of manslaughter. In that sense, a charge of the more serious offence of murder always carried with it a charge of the lesser offence of manslaughter. To my mind it would be nothing short of a nonsense if making explicit what is already implicit were to set in motion a fresh custody time limit. That would be irrational. But this is all that happens when the more serious charge of murder is dropped, and the less serious charge of manslaughter is substituted: one charge is abandoned, and another charge, of which the accused was already at risk, is made explicit. The substitution introduces nothing new. The facts involved in the lesser charge are included within the embrace of the facts involved in the more serious charge. Why should the substitution give rise to a new custody time limit?

[42] The power of the court to grant bail does not provide a meet response to this absurdity. Parliament intended that accused persons should have the benefit of fixed maximum periods of detention in custody, extendable only in certain circumstances. If a new custody time limit is set in motion, an accused person loses that intended benefit.

[43] Nor does the court's ability to prevent abuse of its process provide the answer. The example I have given assumes that throughout the prosecution exercised its powers and discharged its responsibilities properly and conscientiously.

[44] For these reasons I agree with the views and conclusion of my noble and learned friend Lord Scott of Foscote. The literal interpretation, producing an absurd result, must yield to an interpretation which gives effect to the intention properly to be attributed to Parliament. For custody time limit purposes a charge of an offence is to be regarded as including also a charge of a lesser offence of which the person charged could, by virtue of s 6 of the Criminal Law Act 1967, be found guilty. Regulations 2(2) and 4 are to be interpreted accordingly. I would allow this appeal.

LORD HOPE OF CRAIGHEAD. My Lords,

[45] This appeal has been brought with a view to obtaining an answer to the following question of law: 'When, in a Magistrates' Court, does the charging of an offence cause a fresh custody time limit to run?' The answer to this question depends upon the proper interpretation of reg 4 of the Prosecution of Offences (Custody Time Limits) Regulations 1987, SI 1987/299 in which the provisions as to custody time limits in magistrates' courts are to be found.

Background

[46] Prior to the coming into force of s 22 of the Prosecution of Offences Act 1985 there were no statutory rules which obliged the criminal courts in England and Wales to complete the various stages in the criminal process within a fixed number

a of days from the date when a person was remanded in custody before trial. In 1981 the Home Affairs Committee of the House of Commons observed that, quite apart from the deleterious consequences of a large remand population for the prisons and of long waiting times for individual prisoners, there was widespread agreement that excessive delay was harmful in a more general way to the criminal justice system: see the *Fourth Report from the Home Affairs Committee: the Prison Service* (HC b Paper (1980–81) no 412-I, para 55). Those who gave evidence to the committee expressed different views on the merits of imposing a time limit on criminal trials. But the committee concluded that on balance it would be advantageous for legislation to be introduced to extend to England and Wales the 110-day rule that had long been in force in Scotland (see para 58). The current provisions relating to the 110-day overall time limit are set out in s 65 of the Criminal Procedure c (Scotland) Act 1995. Section 65(4)(b) of that Act provides that if the trial of the case is not commenced within that period the accused shall be liberated forthwith and that thereafter he shall be for ever free from all question or process for that offence. The committee's recommendation that this rule be extended to England and Wales was rejected by the government. The reasons which were given for its d rejection were that the Scottish rule operated in a very different context, and that delays in the commencement of trials in England and Wales were not usually attributable to the fault of the prosecutor but to the fact that the backlog of work was too large for available court capacity to handle within the time limit of eight weeks laid down by r 19 of the Crown Court Rules 1971, SI 1971/1292: see *The Government Reply to the Fourth Report from the Home Affairs Committee: the* e *Prison Service* (Cmnd 8446 (1981)) pp 13–14.

[47] The Home Affairs Committee returned to this issue in 1983: see the *First Report from the Home Affairs Committee: Remands in Custody* (HC Paper (1983–84) no 252-I). The committee noted that the situation which had been observed in 1981 had grown much worse, as the number of prisoners held on remand had f increased considerably (see para 3). There was renewed concern that the length of time spent on remand by a great many accused persons was unacceptable and that there were excessive delays in bringing cases to trial (see para 9). After taking evidence from various witnesses, including the Lord Chancellor, Lord Hailsham of St Marylebone, and the Solicitor General for Scotland, Peter Fraser QC, the committee came up with a different solution to the problem which it was thought g would be more acceptable. It recommended that the government should commit itself in principle to introducing statutory time limits for the period from arrest to trial, and that it should embark upon a series of experiments designed to demonstrate what kind of time limits would be feasible in summary and indictable cases respectively (see para 31). On this occasion the committee's recommendations h were favourably received by the government: see *The Government Reply to the First Report from the Home Affairs Committee: Remands in Custody* (Cmnd 9322 (1984)). The legislation with which this case is concerned is the product of the studies which were then carried out in order to determine what kind of statutory time limits would be feasible.

j

The facts

[**48**] The appellant appeared before the Leeds Magistrates' Court on 8 January 1999 on an information charging him with the murder of John Nutter. Mr Nutter had collapsed and died during a burglary which was being carried out at his home in Pudsey, West Yorkshire on 20 July 1998. Expert opinion as to the cause of his death had previously been sought and obtained from a pathologist. The pathologist's

opinion was that Mr Nutter had been suffering from a long-term hypertensive heart disease, and that a combination of minor injuries and the accompanying fear during the attack would have been sufficient to cause his death. On 4 March 1999 the pathologist produced a second opinion to the same effect, namely that Mr Nutter's death occurred when it did due to the combination of minor injuries and the fear in which he had been placed during the burglary. When the appellant appeared in Leeds Magistrates' Court on 19 March 1999 the Crown offered no evidence on the murder charge, but a fresh charge was laid against the appellant for manslaughter.

[**49**] The 70-day custody time limit in terms of reg 4(4) of the 1987 regulations began to run when the appellant first appeared on 8 January 1999. It was due to expire on 19 March 1999. When he appeared in Leeds Magistrates' Court on that date, the charge having been changed from murder to manslaughter, the Crown sought an extension of the custody time limit. The stipendiary magistrate granted the Crown an extension. He found that the prosecution had acted with all due expedition and that there was good and sufficient cause for an extension. But he also held that the new charge of manslaughter attracted its own custody time limit under reg 4(4). The effect of his decision was that the appellant's 70-day custody time limit began to run as of new from 19 March 1999.

[**50**] The appellant appealed against this decision to the Crown Court on 22 March 1999. In the Crown Court Judge Hoffman held that the Crown had not acted with due expedition and that the old custody time limit ought not to have been extended. But he also held that, as manslaughter was a different offence from murder, the appellant's custody time limit ran de novo from the preferment against him of the new offence of manslaughter. An application for judicial review of that decision was dismissed by the Divisional Court (Kennedy LJ and Mitchell J) on 26 April 1999 on the ground that the preferring of the manslaughter charge properly resulted in the creation of a new custody time limit. Mitchell J expressed concern at the end of his judgment about the considerable measure of latitude which had been extended to prosecutors to bypass controls on the extension of the prescribed time limit by introducing new or different charges based on the same evidential material. In his concurring judgment Kennedy LJ said that he agreed, not least with the sentiments expressed at the end of Mitchell J's judgment.

[**51**] On 18 May 1999 the appellant appeared before the Recorder of Leeds at a plea and directions hearing. A new indictment was preferred against him which contained three counts. These were manslaughter, wounding with intent and aggravated burglary. The appellant pleaded not guilty to all three counts, and the case against him was set down for trial on 22 September 1999. On the date of the trial he pleaded guilty to manslaughter. The charges of wounding with intent and aggravated burglary were left on the file. He was sentenced to ten years' imprisonment.

[**52**] In terms of s 9(3) of the Crime (Sentences) Act 1997, the court is required to direct that the number of days for which an offender has been remanded in custody in connection with the offence or a related offence for which he is being sentenced shall count as time served by him as part of the sentence. In the result the appellant has not been prejudiced by the decision that a new custody time limit began to run against him when the charge of manslaughter was brought on the date when the original custody time limit was due to expire. Nevertheless his case raises an important issue of principle. He would have been entitled to be released on bail immediately on the expiry of the original custody time limit, which

a Judge Hoffman held ought not to have been extended, if the correct view was that no new custody time limit was introduced by the bringing of the charge of manslaughter.

The statutory provisions

[53] The Secretary of State was given power by s 22 of the 1985 Act to set time b limits with respect to the preliminary stages of proceedings for an offence. Subsection (1) of that section provides:

> 'The Secretary of State may by regulations make provision, with respect to any specified preliminary stage of proceedings for an offence, as to the maximum period—(a) to be allowed to the prosecution to complete that c stage; (b) during which the accused may, while awaiting completion of that stage, be—(i) in the custody of a magistrates' court; or (ii) in the custody of the Crown Court …'

[54] No regulations have yet been made as to overall time limits. But regulations have been made which govern the period of time an accused may be d kept in the custody of the magistrates' court and the Crown Court. These are contained in the 1987 regulations, as amended: for a list of the amending regulations, see *Archbold's Criminal Pleading, Evidence and Practice* (2001 edn), p 233, para 3-56. Custody time limits in the magistrates' court are governed by reg 4, which so far as relevant to this case provides:

> e '(1) … the maximum period during which a person accused of an indictable offence other than treason may be in the custody of a magistrates' court in relation to that offence while awaiting completion of any preliminary stage of the proceedings specified in the following provisions of this Regulation shall be as stated in those provisions.
>
> f (2) Except as provided in paragraph (3) below, in the case of an offence triable either way the maximum period of custody between the accused's first appearance and the start of summary trial or, as the case may be, the time when the court decides whether or not to commit the accused to the Crown Court for trial shall be 70 days.
>
> g (3) In the case of an offence triable either way if, before the expiry of 56 days following the day of the accused's first appearance, the court decides to proceed to summary trial in pursuance of sections 19 to 24 of the [Magistrates' Courts Act 1980] the maximum period of custody between the accused's first appearance and the start of the summary trial shall be 56 days.
>
> h (4) In the case of an offence triable on indictment exclusively the maximum period of custody between the accused's first appearance and the time when the court decides whether or not to commit the accused to the Crown Court for trial, shall be 70 days …
>
> (5) The foregoing provisions of this regulation shall have effect as if any reference therein to the time when the court decides whether or not to j commit the accused to the Crown Court for trial were a reference—(a) where a court proceeds to inquire into an information as examining justices in pursuance of section 6(1) of the 1980 Act, to the time when it begins to hear evidence for the prosecution at the inquiry …'

[55] Custody time limits in the Crown Court are governed by reg 5, which so far as relevant provides:

'(2) Where—(a) a person accused of an indictable offence other than treason is committed to the Crown Court for trial; or (b) a bill of indictment is preferred against a person under section 2(2)(b) of the Administration of Justice (Miscellaneous Provisions) Act 1933, the maximum period during which he may be in the custody of the Crown Court in relation to that offence, or any other offence included in the indictment preferred against him, while awaiting the preliminary stage of the proceedings specified in the following provisions of this Regulation shall be as stated in these provisions.

(3) The maximum period of custody—(a) between the time when the accused is committed for trial and the start of the trial; or (b) where a bill of indictment is preferred against him under the said section 2(2)(b), between the preferment of the bill and the start of the trial, shall, subject to the following provisions of this Regulation, be 112 days.

(4) Where, following a committal for trial, the bill of indictment preferred against the accused (not being a bill preferred under the said section 2(2)(b)) contains a count charging an offence for which he was committed for trial at that committal together with a count charging an offence for which he was committed for trial on a different occasion, paragraph (3) above applies in relation to each offence separately ...

(6) Where, following a committal for trial, the bill of indictment preferred against the accused (not being a bill preferred under the said section 2(2)(b)) contains a count charging an offence for which he was not committed for trial, the maximum period of custody—(a) between the preferment of the bill and the start of the trial, or (b) if the count was added to the bill after its preferment, between that addition and the start of the trial, shall be 112 days less any period, or the aggregate of any periods, during which he has, since the committal, been in the custody of the Crown Court in relation to an offence for which he was committed for trial ...'

[56] If the charge against the appellant from the outset of the proceedings against him had been one of manslaughter and not murder, the effect of these provisions would have been as follows. Manslaughter is triable only on indictment. So the maximum period during which the appellant could have been detained in the custody of the magistrates' court between his first appearance in that court and the time when the court decided whether or not to commit him to the Crown Court for trial would have been 70 days (see reg 4(4)). The maximum period during which he could have been detained in the custody of the Crown Court between the time when he was committed to that court for trial and the start of the trial would have been 112 days (see reg 5(3)(a)). The fact that the indictment which was preferred against him in the Crown Court included the two other offences of wounding with intent and aggravated burglary would, in this case, have made no difference to the length of the period (see reg 5(6)(a)). The position would have been different if the appellant had been committed for trial on a different occasion on those other two charges. Regulation 5(3) would then have applied in relation to the offences for which he had been committed for trial on different occasions separately (see reg 5(4)). It may be noted in passing that it has also been held in Scotland, in regard to the operation of the 110-day rule, that each offence has to be looked at separately in relation to the date when the committal took place: see *Ross v H M Advocate* 1990 SCCR 182.

[57] It has not been suggested in this case that the provisions of reg 5 of the 1987 regulations regarding the custody time limits in the Crown Court give rise

a to any difficulty. The question which the appellant has raised is directed only to the provisions of reg 4. This is because no express provision is made in reg 4 for cases where additional charges are preferred against the accused while he is in the custody of the magistrates' court. It is to be noted that reg 4 must be read in the light of reg 2(2)(c), which provides:

> b 'In these Regulations, a reference to a person's first appearance in relation to proceedings in a magistrates' court for an offence is ... (c) ... a reference to the time when first he appears or is brought before the court on an information charging him with that offence.'

[**58**] The wording of reg 2(2)(c) reflects that of s 1(1) of the Magistrates' Courts c Act 1980. Criminal proceedings in magistrates' courts are started by the appearance of the accused following arrest and charge or by the laying before the court of an information with a view to commencing a prosecution against him. Section 1(1) prescribes the procedure for the issuing of a summons to a person against whom an information has been laid to appear before the magistrates' court 'to answer to the information'. In the Crown Court the bill of indictment may contain a d count charging an offence for which the accused has not been committed for trial in the magistrates' court. But the preliminary procedure in the magistrates' court is concerned exclusively with the offence which has been described in the information, summons or other document which has been laid before the court (see reg 2(2)(c)). The basis upon which reg 4 appears to proceed is that each e information charging the accused with an offence attracts its own custody time limit.

[**59**] To complete this review of the statutory provisions, it is necessary to mention the provision which deals with extension of the custody time limits. This is s 22(3) of the 1985 Act which, as amended by s 43 of the Crime and Disorder Act 1998 with effect from 1 June 1999, is in these terms:

> f 'The appropriate court may, at any time before the expiry of a time limit imposed by the regulations, extend, or further extend, that limit; but the court shall not do so unless it is satisfied—(a) that the need for the extension is due to—(i) the illness or absence of the accused, a necessary witness, a judge or a magistrate; (ii) a postponement which is occasioned by the g ordering by the court of separate trials in the case of two or more accused or two or more offences; or (iii) some other good and sufficient cause; and (b) that the prosecution has acted with all due diligence and expedition.'

[**60**] At the time when the present case was in the magistrates' court, paras (a) and (b) of that subsection provided simply that in the exercise of its power to h extend the time limit the court had to be satisfied '(a) that there is good and sufficient cause for doing so; and (b) that the prosecution has acted with all due expedition'. Guidance as to the tests laid down in s 22(3) was provided by Lord Bingham of Cornhill CJ in *R v Crown Court at Manchester, ex p McDonald* [1999] 1 All ER 805, [1999] 1 WLR 841. He said, with reference to the condition j in s 22(3)(b), that what the court must require is 'such diligence and expedition as would be shown by a competent prosecutor conscious of his duty to bring the case to trial as quickly as reasonably and fairly possible' (see [1999] 1 All ER 805 at 809, [1999] 1 WLR 841 at 847). Mitchell J said that he regarded it as unsatisfactory that reg 4 gave such latitude to prosecutors to subject persons to new time limits in the magistrates' court by bringing fresh charges against them. He said that this was inconsistent with the purpose of the regulation as it enabled

the prosecution, in effect, to bypass the requirement in s 22(3)(b) that any extension of the time limit had to be justified by showing that all due diligence and expedition had been exercised.

The argument in outline

[**61**] For the appellant Mr MacDonald QC submitted that the charging of a new offence in the magistrates' court will cause a fresh custody time limit to run unless: (a) the new offence is the same as the original offence charged but with different particulars; (b) the original offence charged necessarily includes or amounts to the new offence charged, whether expressly or impliedly; or (c) in charging the new offence the prosecuting authority is committing an abuse of process. As to abuse of process, he submitted that the test to be applied was in need of reconsideration in view of dicta in the Divisional Court which indicated that in this context the test was that of bad faith or dishonesty. He also submitted that, now that the Human Rights Act 1998 is in force, s 3 of that Act requires reg 4 to be read and given effect to in a way that is compatible with art 5 of the European Convention for the Protection of Human Rights and Fundamental Freedoms (the convention) which guarantees to the individual the right to liberty.

[**62**] Applying these arguments to the facts of this case, he submitted that for the purposes of reg 4(4) the original charge of murder should be regarded as including the new charge of manslaughter. This was because on an indictment for murder a person found not guilty of murder may be found guilty of manslaughter: see the Criminal Law Act 1967, s 6(2)(a). He submitted in the alternative that the Crown's decision to change the charge in the magistrates' court from one of murder to one of manslaughter in circumstances where an extension of the existing custody time limit could not be justified was an abuse of process if, contrary to his primary argument, the effect of that decision was to subject the appellant to a new custody time limit.

[**63**] Mr Perry for the respondent accepted that a new custody time limit would not run if the new information consisted simply of an amendment to the particulars of the offence in the original information which had been laid before the court. In that event the offence in the new information would be in law the same offence as the original. He also accepted that a new custody time limit would not run if the laying of the new information could be said to be an abuse of process, as to which bad faith or dishonesty ought no longer to be regarded as the criterion. Where he parted company with Mr MacDonald was in regard to his proposition that a new custody time limit would not run if the original offence charged amounted to or included the new offence, either expressly or impliedly. He also parted company with him in regard to the question whether reg 4, on his construction of it, was incompatible with art 5 of the convention.

The meaning of 'offence'

[**64**] The first question is whether, according to ordinary canons of construction, the word 'offence' when it appears in reg 4(4) of the 1987 regulations can be read as including those other offences of which the accused could be convicted at trial under s 6(2) and (3) of the 1967 Act. In other words, can the reference in the opening words of reg 4(4) to 'an offence triable on indictment' be read as including any other offence of which the accused could be convicted in the Crown Court if the jury were to find him not guilty of the offence with which he has been charged in the information before the magistrates?

a [65] Section 6(2) and (3) of the 1967 Act, which the appellant says should be read in to reg 4(4) of the 1987 regulations, provide:

> '(2) On an indictment for murder a person found not guilty of murder may be found guilty—(a) of manslaughter, or of causing grievous bodily harm with intent to do so; or (b) of any offence of which he may be found guilty under an enactment specifically so providing, or under section 4(2) of this Act; or (c) of an attempt to commit murder, or of an attempt to commit any other offence of which he might be found guilty; but may not be found guilty of any offence not included above.
>
> (3) Where, on a person's trial on indictment for any offence except treason or murder, the jury find him not guilty of the offence specifically charged in the indictment, but the allegations in the indictment amount to or include (expressly or by implication) an allegation of another offence falling within the jurisdiction of the court of trial, the jury may find him guilty of that other offence or of an offence of which he could be found guilty on an indictment specifically charging that other offence.'

d [66] Two points emerge from an examination of the wording of these subsections. The first is that the original offence and the alternative offences of which the person may be found guilty in the circumstances referred to are regarded as being in law different offences: see the words 'of any offence not included above' in sub-s (2) and 'that other offence' in sub-s (3). The second is that these provisions only apply where the trial is on indictment. Section 6 does not apply to proceedings in the magistrates' court.

[67] As to the first point, the alternative offences mentioned in s 6(2) and (3) are not treated by the statute, either expressly or by implication, as forming part of the same offence as that which has been specifically charged in the indictment. This approach reflects a concept which is followed consistently throughout the entire scheme relating to committal proceedings and custody time limits in the magistrates' courts. In terms of s 1(1) of the 1980 Act the justice may issue a summons requiring a person to appear before the magistrates' court to answer to an information that he has, or is suspected of having, committed 'an offence'. The function of the magistrates' court, as described in ss 4 to 6 of that Act, is to inquire into 'an offence as examining justices': see s 5(1) and s 6(1) and (2). If a magistrates' court is satisfied that there is sufficient evidence to put the accused on trial by jury 'for any indictable offence', the court must commit him for trial: see s 6(1). The implication is that it will take that step with regard to 'the offence under inquiry': see the concluding words of the subsection. Alternatively, the court may commit him for trial 'for the offence' if it is satisfied that all the evidence before the court consists of written statements tendered under the 1980 Act without consideration of their contents. Regulation 2(2)(c) of the 1987 regulations defines a reference to a person's first appearance in relation to proceedings in a magistrates' court for an offence as being a reference to the time when he first appears or is brought before the court 'on an information charging him with that offence'. Regulation 4(5)(a) refers, where a court proceeds 'to inquire into an information as examining justices', to the time when it begins to hear evidence for the prosecution 'at the inquiry'.

[68] Thus the scope of the inquiry is determined by the information which has been laid before the magistrates' court. The guiding principle is that the offence should be described in the information clearly and definitely, without duplicity or uncertainty: see *Stone's Justices' Manual* (132nd edn, 2000) vol 1, p 41, para 1-420. The

court's function is to inquire into the offence charged in the information as examining justices. I do not think that there is any ambiguity about what is meant in reg 4(4) by the word 'offence' in these circumstances. It means the offence with which the person is charged in the information which has been laid against him in that court.

[69] It is normal and proper practice for the prosecution to review the charge or charges in the information which was initially laid before the court as further inquiries are conducted into the state of the evidence. This may lead to the bringing against the accused of what are undoubtedly fresh charges, with the consequence that these new charges will attract their own custody time limit. But the question may be raised, as it has been in this case, as to whether the new charges truly are fresh charges or whether they are simply the old charges in a revised form and are thus subject to the original custody time limit.

[70] In *R v Burton on Trent Justices, ex p Nicholson* [1998] COD 262 (17 December 1997) the applicant was charged with a number of offences of dishonesty. When he was charged with three further offences of dishonesty he was refused bail. A draft indictment was prepared which contained a number of new counts. The prosecutor applied to the magistrates' court for the new counts to be put to the applicant, for the old charges to be discharged and for the applicant to be remanded in custody. He also asked the court to note that, since there were new charges, there were correspondingly new custody time limits. The applicant applied for judicial review on the ground that the so-called new charges were simply the old charges with amendments which amounted to changes of detail only. The Divisional Court remitted this matter to the magistrates to consider. Lord Bingham of Cornhill CJ said:

> 'The legislative intention underlying the introduction of custody time limits is clear. It would defeat that purpose if relatively minor or unimportant amendments to charges were to enable the authorities to remand a defendant in custody for extended periods. On the other hand, if there is a substantial difference between one charge and another then it may indeed be just that that result should follow. But whether the difference between one charge and another is substantial must in my judgment depend, as I say, on more than a superficial comparison of the wording and may in a case of any doubt involve some consideration of underlying materials.'

[71] But the question whether the difference between one charge and another is substantial would seem to be capable of only one answer if they involve two offences which are in law distinct or separate offences. As Lord Widgery CJ said in *Jemmison v Priddle* [1972] 1 All ER 539 at 544, [1972] 1 QB 489 at 495, it is legitimate to charge in a single charge one activity even though that activity may involve more than one act. Questions as to whether, if a person stabs another person several times or steals several different chattels from several different rooms in the same dwelling house, he has committed one offence or several are best answered by applying common sense and deciding what is fair in the circumstances: see *R v Fyffe* [1992] Crim LR 442 per Russell LJ. But the general rule is that not more than one offence may be charged in one charge or, where the offence is charged in an indictment, in one count: see the Indictments Act 1915, Sch 1, r 4. The purpose of s 6(2) and (3) of the 1967 Act is to enable alternative verdicts to be returned by juries under certain circumstances in the Crown Court. In the magistrates' court, to which s 6 of the 1967 Act does not apply, no relaxation is permitted against the rule against duplicity.

a [72] As to the second point, it is not part of the function of the magistrates' court in the case of an information charging an offence triable on indictment to consider whether a jury would be entitled to find the person guilty of another offence in the event of its finding him not guilty of the offence which has been specifically charged against him. The court's sole function is to examine the question whether there is sufficient evidence to put the accused on trial for the offence charged in b the information. Furthermore, the concern of the justices in these proceedings is essentially with questions of fact rather than with questions of law. The operation of the custody time limits is linked to the same process. Regulation 4(4) is designed to fit in with that procedure. The maximum period of 70 days begins to run when the accused first appears or is brought before the court 'on an information charging him with that offence': see reg 2(2)(c). It ends, where the court proceeds to inquire c into the information as examining justices, when it begins to hear evidence for the prosecution at the inquiry: see reg 4(5)(a). If the words 'an offence triable on indictment' in reg 4(4) were to be read as extending to the alternative offences of which the accused might be convicted after trial on indictment, this would introduce questions of law into the custody time limit regime which would greatly d complicate the justices' function as examining magistrates. I would regard this as introducing an amendment to the regime which, if it is to be made, ought to be left to the legislature.

[73] For these reasons I would hold that there is no basis, if the ordinary canons of construction are to be applied, for reading in these additional words into reg 4(4). In my opinion each offence which is the subject of an information e which is laid before a magistrates' court attracts its own custody time limit.

[74] There remains the question whether this interpretation produces an absurd result which cannot have been intended by Parliament. I see the force of the objection to the introduction of a new custody time limit, in a case which does not involve any new facts, simply because the prosecution has decided after some f weeks to depart from the more serious charge of murder and substitute for it the less serious charge of manslaughter. But I would be reluctant to hold, on the basis of this example, that Parliament must have intended *in every case* that, for the purposes of the custody time limits laid down in reg 4, the offence charged is to be regarded as including also a charge of a lesser offence of which the person could, by virtue of s 6 of the 1967 Act, be found guilty. The regulation cannot mean g one thing in one case and something else in another. We cannot pick and choose according to the facts of each case. It seems to me that, unless your Lordships can be confident that an absurd result will be produced in *all* cases, the proper conclusion is that the regulation must be applied according to the ordinary meaning of the words used by Parliament.

h [75] Section 6(2) of the 1967 Act deals with the alternative offences which are available to the jury on an indictment for murder. It is sufficient for present purposes to consider the alternative offence of manslaughter. One of the features of this offence is that, for a verdict of manslaughter to be returned instead of murder, the jury normally needs to be in possession of facts which are additional j to those which are needed to prove murder. Provocation reduces murder to manslaughter, but a jury is not entitled to consider this matter unless there is some evidence of a specific act or words of provocation resulting in loss of self-control by the accused: see *R v Acott* [1997] 1 All ER 706, [1997] 1 WLR 306. This may involve the consideration of further information which was not, for the purposes of the murder charge, before the justices. Then there is the case of persons suffering from diminished responsibility. Section 2 of the Homicide Act 1957 provides that a person who is suffering from diminished responsibility who would be liable, but for that section, to be convicted of murder is liable instead to be convicted of manslaughter. The prosecutor does not normally have to lead evidence as to the accused's mental state on a murder charge. This is because the presumption of mental capacity is normally sufficient to prove that he acted consciously and voluntarily: see *Bratty v A-G for Northern Ireland* [1961] 3 All ER 523 at 531, [1963] AC 386 at 407 per Viscount Kilmuir LC. But a prosecutor who, after further investigation, decides to reduce a charge of murder to one of manslaughter on the ground of diminished responsibility will have to undertake the additional burden of leading evidence as to the accused's mental state. This may give rise to the need to bring further information before the justices, as the issue may then be raised as to whether the accused lacked the necessary intention because he was truly suffering not from diminished responsibility but from insanity. I do not think that it would be right in cases of that kind to regard the murder charge and the manslaughter charge as based on the same facts. They relate, of course, to the same incident of homicide. But there are additional facts in the one case which are not present in the other, and it is those additional facts which justify the reduced charge. I would not, speaking for myself, regard it as absurd that where manslaughter is substituted for murder in such a case by the prosecutor there should, for the purposes of reg 4(4), be a new custody time limit.

[76] Then there is the fact that s 6 of the 1967 Act refers to a variety of other offences of which the accused may be found guilty by a jury: see sub-s (2) in regard to an indictment for murder and sub-s (3) in regard to an indictment for any offence except treason or murder. In neither case however is a precise list given of these alternatives. They are to be determined either by reference to other legislation (see sub-s (2)), or by reference to what is included either expressly or by implication 'in the indictment' (see sub-s (3)). The problem here, as I see it, is that these provisions are not apt for consideration at the stage of committal proceedings in the magistrates' court. There is no indictment at that stage, and there are at least some grounds for thinking that the justices ought not to have to consider the questions of law which may be raised by consideration of the available alternatives. Here again I would not, speaking for myself, regard it as absurd to suppose that Parliament did not intend to bring these alternative offences into consideration in that court for custody time limit purposes.

[77] For these reasons I am not persuaded that the ordinary meaning of the words used in reg 4(4) should be departed from and that there should be read into it a reference to the alternative offences of which the person could be found guilty by virtue of s 6 of the Criminal Law Act 1967 after trial in the Crown Court.

Compatibility with art 5

[78] The next question is whether, in the light of the meaning which I would give to the word 'offence' in reg 4(4) according to its ordinary construction, there is an incompatibility with art 5 of the convention which ought to be removed by applying to the regulation the approach to construction which the court is directed to take by s 3(1) of the Human Rights Act 1998.

[79] Sections 3(1) of the 1998 Act provides that, so far as it is possible to do so, primary legislation and subordinate legislation must be read and given effect in a way which is compatible with convention rights. This means that, if according to its ordinary construction reg 4(4) is incompatible with any of the convention rights, a possible meaning for reg 4(4) must be found that will prevent the need for a a declaration of incompatibility. But one must first be satisfied that the ordinary construction of the regulation gives rise to an incompatibility.

[80] Article 5 of the convention, so far as relevant to this case, provides:

> '1. Everyone has the right to liberty and security of person. No one shall be deprived of his liberty save in the following cases and in accordance with b a procedure prescribed by law ... (c) the lawful arrest or detention of a person effected for the purpose of bringing him before the competent legal authority on reasonable suspicion of having committed an offence or when it is reasonably considered necessary to prevent his committing an offence or fleeing after having done so ...
>
> 3. Everyone arrested or detained in accordance with the provisions of c paragraph 1 (c) of this article shall be brought promptly before a judge or other officer authorised by law to exercise judicial power and shall be entitled to trial within a reasonable time or to release pending trial. Release may be conditioned by guarantees to appear for trial.'

d **[81]** Mr MacDonald submitted that the central purpose of art 5 was to protect the individual from a detention which was arbitrary. In *Bozano v France* (1986) 9 EHRR 297 at 313 (para 54) the European Court said:

> 'The main issue to be determined is whether the disputed detention was "lawful," including whether it was in accordance with "a procedure prescribed e by law". The Convention here refers essentially to national law and establishes the need to apply its rules, but it also requires that any measure depriving the individual of his liberty must be compatible with the purpose of Article 5, namely to protect the individual from arbitrariness.'

In *Brogan v UK* (1988) 11 EHRR 117 at 134 (para 58) the court said again that the f fundamental right enshrined by art 5 was the protection of the individual against arbitrary interferences by the state with his right to liberty. To the same effect was the following passage in the court's judgment in *Amuur v France* (1996) 22 EHRR 533 at 559 (para 50):

> g 'Where the "lawfulness" of detention is in issue, including the question whether "a procedure prescribed by law" has been followed, the Convention refers essentially to national law and lays down the obligation to conform to the substantive and procedural rules of national law, but it requires in addition that any deprivation of liberty should be in keeping with the purpose of Article 5, namely to protect the individual from arbitrariness.'

h

[82] In the light of these authorities Mr MacDonald submitted that it was not enough that the provisions of the 1987 regulations relating to a person's detention while he was in the custody of the magistrates' court were precise and accessible. They had also to be so framed as to protect him against decisions which were j arbitrary. The regulations were defective in this respect because they left it open to the prosecution, during the running of the period of 70 days referred to in reg 4(4), to subject the accused to a fresh period of 70 days simply by charging him with a different offence based on the same facts as those in the original information. The custody time limit could be extended several times over by this means. Unless an abuse of process could be established, decisions to that effect by the prosecutor were not subjected to any judicial control. To the extent to which the system which the regulations laid down was open to decisions by the prosecutor which were arbitrary, it was incompatible with art 5 of the convention.

The scheme of art 5

[83] Article 5(1) guarantees liberty and security of person. In this context the concepts of liberty and security are linked together, with the broad aim of protecting the person against an arrest or detention which is arbitrary: see *Bozano v France* (1986) 9 EHRR 297 at 313 (para 54); *Amuur v France* (1996) 22 EHRR 533 at 559 (para 50). As the European Court said in *W v Switzerland* (1993) 17 EHRR 60 at 79 (para 30), continued detention can be justified in a given case only if there are specific indications of a genuine requirement of public interest which, notwithstanding the presumption of innocence, outweighs the rule of respect for individual liberty. To this end art 5(1) provides a right to liberty, which is subject to six specified exceptions and to two overriding requirements. The first requirement is that any deprivation of liberty must be in accordance with a procedure prescribed by law. The second requirement is that it must be lawful. To be lawful in this context, the detention must not only be lawful under domestic law. It must satisfy the requirements of the convention that the domestic law on which the decision is based must be sufficiently accessible to the individual and must be sufficiently precise to enable the individual to foresee the consequences of the restriction: see *R v Governor of Brockhill Prison, ex p Evans (No 2)* [2000] 4 All ER 15 at 29–30, [2000] 3 WLR 843 at 857–858. It is the latter of these two overriding requirements that is in issue in this case.

[84] Paragraphs (2) to (5) of art 5 provide a set of distinct procedural rights for persons who have been arrested or are being detained. We are concerned in this case with para (3), which comprises three distinct rights. These are (1) the right to be brought promptly before a judge or other officer authorised by law to exercise judicial power; (2) the right to be released on bail, except where continued detention can be justified; and (3) the right to be tried within a reasonable period.

[85] Two points in particular require to be noted about art 5(3) in the present context. The first is that the right to be released on bail is not absolute. But if bail is to be refused, the refusal must be justified on the facts of each case to the satisfaction of the judge or other officer. The second is that the purpose of the right to be tried within a reasonable period in art 5(3) is to ensure that no one spends too long in detention before trial. In *Wemhoff v Germany* (1968) 1 EHRR 55 at 74 (para 5) the European Court said that the concern of art 5(3) was to minimise the period of provisional detention of the accused rather than to avoid prolongation of the trial. In this regard it may be regarded as laying down a more exacting requirement than the art 6(1) right to a fair and public hearing within a reasonable time. In *Yagci and Sargin v Turkey* (1995) 20 EHRR 505 at 525–526 (para 50) the court said:

> 'It falls in the first place to the national judicial authorities to ensure that, in a given case, the detention of an accused person pending trial does not exceed a reasonable time. To this end they must examine all the facts arguing for or against the existence of a genuine requirement of public interest justifying, with due regard to the principle of presumption of innocence, a departure from the rule of respect for individual liberty and set them out in their decisions on the applications for release.'

a *Is reg 4(4) incompatible?*

[**86**] The question whether the system which reg 4 of the 1987 regulations lays down for limiting the periods during which a person can be detained while in the custody of the magistrates' court is open to the criticism that it is arbitrary contrary to the right to liberty in art 5(1), or is incompatible with the art 5(3) right to trial within a reasonable time, must be examined in the context in which the regulation b is intended to operate.

[**87**] The primary means for controlling the detention of a person while he is in the custody of the magistrates' court are to be found in the provisions of the Bail Act 1976. The function of the 1987 regulations made under s 22 of the 1985 Act is to set maximum custody time limits. If a custody time limit expires before the completion of the stage of the proceedings in question, the accused must be c granted bail. It is also open to the justices to grant bail at any time before the expiry of the time limit, bearing in mind that s 4(1) of the 1976 Act gives a general right to bail except in certain specified circumstances: see Sch 1 to that Act. Furthermore, the accused, if remanded in custody, must be brought again before the magistrates' court to enable his case to be reviewed at regular intervals, as the d general rule is that a magistrates' court may not remand a person for a period exceeding eight clear days: see s 128(6) of the 1980 Act. His detention is thus subject to judicial control in the magistrates' court throughout the period while he is in the custody of that court. Decisions which are taken in magistrates' courts are amenable to judicial review. And if a magistrates' court decides to extend, or further extend, a custody time limit the accused may appeal against that decision e to the Crown Court: see s 22(7) of the 1985 Act.

[**88**] The effect of these provisions can, I think, be summarised in this way. A person can only be detained in the custody of a magistrates' court while awaiting the completion of a preliminary stage of the proceedings under a procedure which has been laid down by statute, and the effect of reg 4 of the 1987 f regulations is that any such detention is subject to strictly defined custody time limits. As to the complaint that this procedure is not precise or accessible because of the possibility of the substitution of fresh custody time limits, I would reject it. The provisions of the 1976 Act and of the 1980 Act, as amended, deal with the procedure for remands in custody in considerable detail with a view to ensuring that every situation is provided for. It is a procedure which is prescribed by law. g Detention under this procedure is lawful under domestic law, and it complies with the general requirements of the convention. If a fresh custody time limit is to be substituted, the procedure under which this is to be done is laid down by statute and the regulation defines the length of the substituted time limit.

[**89**] The complaint that the procedure is open to abuse as a result of decisions h by the prosecutor which are arbitrary and may result in the person's detention for a time that is more than can be described as reasonable is, at first sight, a more substantial one. It is the case, as I have said, that reg 4(4) has the effect that each offence which is charged in the magistrates' court attracts its own custody time limit. This aspect of the regulation has a legitimate purpose, which is to give j sufficient time to the prosecutor to prepare the evidence relating to each offence for examination by the justices. Like any other procedure prescribed by law, it is vulnerable to abuse if it is used for improper purposes. But this is a matter which is subject to judicial control by the justices or the stipendiary magistrate. On the one hand it is open to the court, applying the approach which was indicated by Lord Bingham of Cornhill CJ in *R v Burton on Trent Justices, ex p Nicholson* [1998] COD 262, to hold that the new charge is simply a reproduction of the old charge

with amendments which are minor or unimportant, and on this ground to refuse to accept that the new charge has given rise to a fresh custody time limit. On the other it is open to the court to refuse to inquire into the information relating to the new charge on the ground that to do so would be an abuse of the process of the court. That would not prevent the same charge being brought again in the Crown Court if the justices were to decide to commit the accused to the Crown Court for trial on the information relating to charges which are already before them. But it would prevent the substitution of a new custody time limit while the case remains in the magistrates' court.

[90] Against that background I would hold that the fact that reg 4(4) of the 1987 regulations, construed according to the ordinary canons of construction in the manner which I favour, enables the accused to be subjected to a fresh time limit when a new offence is alleged against him does not give rise to an incompatibility either with art 5(1) or with art 5(3). I see no need therefore in this case to resort to the new rule of construction laid down by s 3(1) of the 1998 Act.

Abuse of process

[91] The question to which I now turn is the meaning to be given to the concept of abuse of process in the context of a complaint that the Crown has acted in the magistrates' court in a manner which conflicts with the purpose for which the custody time limit has been laid down in reg 4(4) of the 1987 regulations.

[92] In my opinion the essence of abuse of process in the context of criminal proceedings is that the prosecutor has sought to take advantage of a procedural rule for a purpose which can be described as improper or as arbitrary. Difficulty has arisen because it has been suggested in some of the authorities that a complaint of abuse of process has to contain an allegation of bad faith. Before I discuss this issue I must first refer to the relevant authorities.

[93] In *R v Wirral District Magistrates' Court, ex p Meikle* (1990) 154 JP 1035 a fresh charge of theft was preferred against the accused, who had originally been charged with murder and conspiracy to blackmail, which had the effect of activating a fresh custody time limit. This was done by the Crown on the mistaken view that the existing custody time limit had expired. An application for judicial review was made on the ground that the applicant had been a victim of an abuse of the court's process. Watkins LJ said (at 1040), that it was accepted by counsel that there was no authority for the proposition that justices are entitled to reject a new charge merely because they regard that as a device to defeat their obligation to release an accused under the regulations. He then said (at 1041):

> 'Each offence undoubtedly attracts its own custody time limit. As to abuse of process, in the absence as here of *mala fides*, the effect of which it is unnecessary for present purposes to consider, there is no authority for the proposition that the doctrine can apply to decisions made on ancillary matters such as bail on the charge facing the accused.'

[94] In *R v Great Yarmouth Magistrates, ex p Thomas* [1992] Crim LR 116 (29 July 1991) the applicants, who had been charged with being knowingly concerned in the illegal importation of cannabis, were released from custody on the expiry of the custody time limit which the justices had refused to extend. They were then immediately re-arrested and charged with a fresh offence of possession of cannabis with intent to supply. An application for judicial review was made on the ground a of abuse of process. When he was giving the court's reasons for remitting the case to the justices Watkins LJ said:

> 'Here the magistrates' court was confronted with an allegation of mala fides because the defence alleged that they had been victims of a rather unpleasant trick which deprived them of their liberty. The basis for that is not in fact a matter for this court. It is a matter which can be determined only b in the magistrates' court upon whatever evidence is put before it, and the effect of that must then be put into perspective. The justices will have to bear in mind that the burden of establishing dishonesty lies fairly and squarely on the defence, and it is a heavy burden. If the court is satisfied that it is truly a consequence of dishonesty which brought about the further charge and there c is in substance no difference whatsoever between this and the first charge, plainly in my view there has been an abuse of the process. If the court comes to that conclusion, then it seems to me that it has no alternative but to admit these people to bail.'

[95] In *R v Waltham Forest Justices, ex p Lee* (1992) 97 Cr App R 287 the applicants d were charged with attempted murder and remanded in custody. The charge of attempted murder was later withdrawn and charges of offences against s 18 of the Offences against the Person Act 1861 were preferred in their place. The applicants indicated that in relation to these new charges they required the attendance at the committal proceedings of witnesses. A date was fixed for these proceedings which was outside the original custody time limit. The justices refused to extend that e time limit. But they subsequently took the view that the s 18 offences attracted a new custody time limit and the applicants were remanded in custody. The main question which was raised in an application for judicial review was whether the justices were right in concluding that a new custody time limit started to run when the applicants were charged with the s 18 offences. Rose LJ (at 292) said in f regard to this matter that it seemed to him that, on the authorities and as a matter of principle, the regulations applied so as to permit the running of a new custody time limit from the date of preferment of charge of a new offence. He then said (at 292–293):

> 'So far as the question of bad faith and abuse of process is concerned, there g will no doubt be an abuse of process if the Crown Prosecution Service prefer new charges, whether more or less serious alternatives, in relation to the same facts, or charges based on different facts, solely for the purpose of defeating custody time limits. *Mala fides* of that kind, if it occurs, is not to be tolerated. But there is, in this case ... not a scrap of evidence that there was some improper motive or improper conduct on the part of the prosecution.'

h

Pill J said (at 293):

> 'The burden of proving bad faith is upon the defendant. The prosecution must, however, in my view, be expected to provide the justices, who have to make the relevant decision, with information and with the reasons for the j withdrawal of one charge and the preferring of another, or the preferring of an additional charge. This will enable the justices to make an informed decision.'

[96] In *R v Wolverhampton Justices, ex p Uppal* (1994) 159 JP 86 the applicant was charged with rape. The prosecution decided that an additional charge of false imprisonment should be brought. This charge was included in a draft indictment which was served on the applicant's solicitors. The magistrate declined to extend the custody time limit on the rape charge. But when the case returned to the court the next day the applicant was charged with false imprisonment and the magistrate accepted that this had the effect of creating a new custody time limit. In the application for judicial review two arguments were advanced on behalf of the applicant. The first was that the charge of false imprisonment was not a new offence so as to create a new statutory time limit. The second was that the circumstances in which the charge of false imprisonment was preferred amounted to an abuse of process. The Divisional Court held that the false imprisonment charge was clearly a charge of a new offence which attracted a new custody time limit. Buxton J (at 92) said that, if there is a separate offence in law, then it attracts a separate custody time limit. He said:

> '... it is quite clear from the cases that this Court has cited that these regulations are to be construed to say what they say, and they say that each offence shall be taken separately. If the charge is properly justified, then properly a new custody time limit must run.'

However, he went on to say:

> 'This court, however, has not ignored the possibility that that construction of the regulation could produce unfairness to an applicant, because it has made clear that in circumstances where a new count is preferred simply for the purpose of avoiding a custody time limit, then this court will review the matter, from the point of view of abuse of process.'

The decision of the magistrate that there had been no abuse of process was however held to have been one which he was entitled to reach on the evidence.

[**97**] I do not think that it can be doubted that, where dishonesty or mala fides can be established, that will be sufficient to show that there has been an abuse of process. But the concept of abuse of process is not to be confined to cases where there is proof of conscious dishonesty or of an improper motive of that kind. To the extent that the authorities to which I have referred may be taken as indicating the contrary, I would be inclined not to follow them. It seems to me that a broader and simpler test is, in this context, more appropriate. That would be more in keeping with the purpose of art 5(1) of the convention, which is to protect the individual from arbitrariness when he is deprived of his liberty.

[**98**] The true question, as Buxton J indicated in *Uppal*'s case, is whether the new charge has been brought solely for the purpose of avoiding a custody time limit. The issue can best be tested by requiring the prosecutor to demonstrate why, on the facts of the case, the bringing of the new charge is necessary. If the necessity of bringing the new charge can be demonstrated, the substitution of a new custody time limit will follow according to the rules which reg 4(4) has laid down. But if the prosecutor is unable to satisfy this test, it will be open to the court to infer that there is an abuse of process because the charge has been brought solely for the arbitrary and improper purpose of substituting a new custody time limit.

Answer to the question

[**99**] I would therefore answer the question of law which I set out at the outset of this judgment in these terms. The principle upon which reg 4 proceeds is that each offence attracts its own custody time limit. But this principle is subject to two qualifications. First, the bringing of a new charge will not result in the replacement

a of the existing custody time limit by a fresh custody time limit if the offence in the new charge is simply a restatement of the old offence with different particulars. The offence charged must be a different offence in law if it is to attract a fresh custody time limit. Second, the bringing of a new charge will be an abuse of process if the bringing of that charge in the magistrates' court cannot be justified on the facts of the case by the prosecutor and the court is satisfied that it has been brought b solely with a view to obtaining the substitution of a fresh custody time limit.

Conclusion

[100] I agree with Divisional Court that on a proper construction of reg 4(4) of the 1987 regulations the preferring of the manslaughter charge in this case, where abuse of process is not alleged, resulted in the creation of a new custody time limit. c While I recognise the concerns which Mitchell J expressed in his judgment about the measure of latitude which has been extended to prosecutors to charge new offences which may have the effect of prolonging the period of detention in custody, I do not consider that regulation in its present form is incompatible with art 5 of the convention. Any revision of the system to meet these concerns must be a matter for Parliament. I would dismiss the appeal.

d

LORD CLYDE. My Lords,

[101] This appeal concerns the construction of the terms of reg 4(4) of the Prosecution of Offences (Custody Time Limits) Regulations 1987, SI 1987/299. Those regulations have been subject to successive amendments and the version with e which we are concerned includes the amendments made up to the Prosecution of Offences (Custody Time Limits) (Modification) Regulations 1998, SI 1998/3037. Regulation 4(1) explains the scope of reg 4 in these terms:

> '... the maximum period during which a person accused of an indictable offence other than treason may be in the custody of a magistrates' court in f relation to that offence while awaiting completion of any preliminary stage of the proceedings specified in the following provisions of this Regulation shall be as stated in those provisions.'

Regulation 4(4) provides:

> g 'In the case of an offence triable on indictment exclusively the maximum period of custody between the accused's first appearance and the time when the court decides whether or not to commit the accused to the Crown Court for trial, shall be 70 days.'

[102] The meaning to be given to the expression 'the accused's first appearance' h is prescribed in reg 2(2). For present purposes it is sufficient to note that it states:

> 'In these Regulations, a reference to a person's first appearance in relation to proceedings in a magistrates' court for an offence is ... (c) in any other case, a reference to the time when first he appears or is brought before the court on j an information charging him with that offence.'

[103] It is useful also to note the terms of the provision which empowered the making of the regulations. This was s 22 of the Prosecution of Offences Act 1985. Section 22(1) provides:

> 'The Secretary of State may by regulations make provision, with respect to any specified preliminary stage of proceedings for an offence, as to the

maximum period—(a) to be allowed to the prosecution to complete that stage; (b) during which the accused may, while awaiting completion of that stage, be—(i) in the custody of a magistrates' court; or (ii) in the custody of the Crown Court; in relation to that offence.'

[104] The scheme of these time limits is plainly based upon the identification of an offence. Moreover, the scheme is looking to a particular offence. One can see that in the words in reg 4(1), 'to that offence', which refer to the earlier words 'a person accused of an indictable offence'. One can see it also in reg 2(2) where again the reference to a person's first appearance 'for an offence' is to be understood as referring to his first appearance 'on an information charging him with that offence'. So the scheme is one which proceeds upon an identification of the particular offence with which he was charged on the information whereby he first appeared or was brought before the court.

[105] In the present case the appellant was brought before the court on 8 January 1999 on an information charging him with murder. On 19 March 1999 when the 70-day period in respect of his custody on the murder charge was about to expire, he appeared before the court for the first time on an information charging him with manslaughter. It is common ground that murder and manslaughter each constitute a distinct offence in the context of the regulations. It follows from the wording of the regulations that a new custody time limit then began to run in respect of the offence then charged. Bail was refused and the appellant remained in custody.

[106] It seems to me that there is no evident ambiguity or lack of clarity in the wording of the regulation. The construction which I have given to it accords with the construction adopted in a succession of past cases, which have established a recognised and acceptable understanding of the provisions and one with which I would not lightly interfere. Moreover, the contrast with the terms of reg 5 seems to me significant. No doubt for sound reasons of practice and practicability the regulations have made a clear distinction between the position in the magistrates' court and the Crown Court. In the latter express provision is made in the calculation of the time limit not only in relation to 'that offence' but also in relation to any other offence included in the indictment. If it had been intended to build into the time limits the addition or substitution of other offences, that could have been done in terms corresponding with those used in reg 5. But it is said that the result is unfair to the accused and indeed that it constitutes a breach of his rights under art 5 of the European Convention for the Protection of Human Rights and Fundamental Freedoms.

[107] I am not persuaded that the regulation as I have construed it is incompatible with art 5 of the convention. The regulation is clear, precise and accessible. There are safeguards for the accused in the recognition by both parties that the court can intervene in the event of the prosecution acting in a way which would constitute an abuse of process. The regulation prescribes relatively short periods for the completion of the relevant stage of the proceedings and the court has a discretion whether or not an extension to the period is or is not to be allowed. Moreover, the accused has remedies in law, including that of judicial review. Finally, the whole scheme of the regulation has to be seen in the context of the Bail Act 1976 which gives, subject to certain exceptions, a general right to bail.

[108] The appellant has sought to found upon the purpose of the regulations and has argued for a purposive construction. The idea of a purposive construction is in a sense nothing new. It has long been recognised that in construing legislation a one should endeavour to give effect to the intention of the legislator. But, as was noted a considerable time ago by Lord Diplock in *Carter v Bradbeer* [1975] 3 All ER 158 at 161, [1975] 1 WLR 1204 at 1206–1207, there has been a trend away from a purely literal towards a purposive construction of statutory provisions. Essentially this trend marks a change from an insistence on a literalism which fails to give effect to the intention of the legislation. More particularly, through the influence b of European community law greater attention has been paid to the idea of the purpose of the legislation in the domestic context. National courts are bound to comply with the objects and purposes of provisions of community law and where the matter is governed by community law domestic courts must where it is possible interpret national law in light of the purposes as well as the words of the community legislation (see *Marleasing SA v La Comercial Internacional de* c *Alimentación SA* Case C-106/89 [1990] ECR I-4135). An example of the practice of such an approach can be found in *Litster v Forth Dry Dock and Engineering Co Ltd* [1989] 1 All ER 1134, [1990] 1 AC 546. In the context of community law a strained interpretation is acceptable in order to secure a compliance with the law of Europe. The desire to avoid any conflict between a national measure and a d directive leads easily to a situation where the purpose may be preferred to a precise reading of the words. But in the present case we are not concerned with the application of European legislation and a strained interpretation cannot be justified on that ground. The resort to a strained approach, which may be seen as readily acceptable in the context of Community law, is not so readily available in the purely domestic context, particularly if there is no ambiguity in the provision e in question. While it may well be available as an approach to construction where there is no ambiguity, it is more difficult to apply it in domestic legislation where the words are clear. In such a case a clear understanding of the precise purpose of the legislation would be required.

[109] In order to adopt a purposive construction it is, of course, essential to f ascertain the purpose of the legislation. If the purpose cannot be ascertained, or there is doubt about the precise purpose, then the court can only look for some reasonable and sensible meaning from the words themselves. The purpose may be discovered from the legislation itself. It may on occasion be expressly set out in the legislation. Or it may be ascertained by the court from the substance of the legislation. But the interpretation cannot itself provide the purpose. The purpose g must be identified first and then be applied in the process of interpretation.

[110] In the present case the long title of the 1985 Act includes the words 'to provide for the imposition of time limits in relation to preliminary stages of criminal proceedings'. That broad statement does not point to any precise purpose such as might have thrown light on the present problem. Behind the h broad statement is obviously the purpose of putting limits upon the period of time which the prosecution may take in the course of the preliminary stages, and the period of time in which an accused has to wait, including a waiting in custody, for his trial. The more particular purpose of restricting the periods of custody lies behind the express empowering provisions in s 22 of the Act. Plainly the j regulations seek to achieve this purpose. But once the purpose has been identified, the way in which Parliament has chosen to achieve the purpose, by a scheme related to an offence, and the way in which accordingly the regulations have been framed, is matter for Parliament and the executive. It is not for the court to ignore the method selected.

[111] I certainly accept that the purpose includes the desirability of putting limits upon the permissible period of incarceration of an accused person in the course of the proceedings prior to committal and thereafter prior to trial and the corresponding desirability of requiring the prosecution to act with all due diligence and expedition. But I have not been persuaded that it is necessary in order to satisfy these purposes that any other construction of the regulations has to be adopted than that which naturally follows from the clear wording. This seems to me to be a case where the purposive and the literal approaches arrive at the same result.

[112] This is not a case where the solution is to be found by expanding the meaning given to a particular word, as was the position, for example, in *Cutter v Eagle Star Insurance Co Ltd, Clarke v Kato* [1998] 4 All ER 417, [1998] 1 WLR 1647, or in *Ex p Guardian Newspapers Ltd* [1999] 1 All ER 65, [1999] 1 WLR 2130. It is common ground that murder and manslaughter each constitute an 'offence', and the problem raised in the present case cannot then be resolved by the suggestion that the 'offence' is homicide. The argument starts from the recognition that the offence charged is the offence of murder. What the appellant has suggested is that in addition to the word 'offence' one should add some phrase which would cover other offences which could be charged on the same information as that on which the earlier offence proceeded. That seems to me to be going beyond the legitimate scope of construction. It requires one to ignore the express word 'that' which limits the identification of the offence and excludes other offences. It does not simply expand the meaning of the word 'offence' itself, but makes a significant extension to the scope of the regulation by adding new words to it. This seems to me to be a matter of legislation, not of construction.

[113] Furthermore, it is not altogether certain what the substance of the suggested addition should be. It may be that it should encompass any offence which can be based upon the material in the information. It may be that it should comprise any offence of which the accused could be convicted on the charge in question. It may be that it should comprise any offence included in or amounting to the original offence. Various formulations of the proposed addition were proposed during the course of the argument and that very difference to my mind points to the absence of any clear need to adopt the kind of construction sought by the appellant. The court can correct obvious drafting errors by adding, or omitting or substituting words, as was done recently by this House in *Inco Europe Ltd v First Choice Distribution (a firm)* (see [2000] 2 All ER 109 at 115, [2000] 1 WLR 586 at 592 per Lord Nicholls of Birkenhead), but this is not a case of an obvious drafting error. But even in that kind of case it is necessary to know the substance of the provisions which the legislator must have intended to express. In the present case even if the exact words are not essential the precise substance of the proposed extended meaning should be clear. There seems to me also to be force in the contention that at least some of the formulations proposed might well create difficulties in the application of the regulation in the magistrates' court. If a criterion was to be adopted by reference to the law relating to the alternative verdicts which may be permitted by statute or by the common law there might be room at least for debate before the magistrate particularly in relation to more complex cases than the reduction of murder to manslaughter. Even trial judges have erred in deciding whether a jury could or could not convict of a lesser charge (see *Archbold's Criminal Pleading, Evidence and Practice* (2001 edn) p 936, para 7-97).

[114] The construction which I prefer does not require to be applied with a complete rigidity. As Lord Bingham of Cornhill CJ pointed out in *R v Burton on Trent Justices, ex p Nicholson* [1998] COD 262 (17 December 1997), the test to be applied is one of the substance of the charge rather than its form. An amendment to a charge of armed robbery which simply added one further item to the things a which had been taken would not constitute a new offence. But a radical rewriting might in its substance constitute a new offence. Where there is a new offence in law it does not seem to me to be possible by a process of interpretation to treat it as the same as the offence earlier charged for the purpose of reg 4.

[115] It was suggested that the proposed addition of the words is to be justified by s 3 of the Human Rights Act 1998. But if the regulations are already b compatible with the convention, as I believe they are, then there is no need to adopt the ambitious construction which has been suggested. I should also record one area for dispute which may have to be resolved in the future, namely whether s 3 requires reading in or only reading down. The point is one on which different views have been expressed, for example by Richard A Edwards on the one c hand ('Reading down legislation under the Human Rights Act' (2000) 20 LS 353) and Richard Clayton and Hugh Tomlinson *The Law of Human Rights* (2000) vol 1, p 163, para 4.20, on the other. But there is no need to explore that issue in the present case.

[116] Since preparing the foregoing I have had the opportunity of reading in draft the speech which has been prepared by my noble and learned friend d Lord Hope of Craighead. I am in agreement with all that he has said and I do not believe that there is any difference between us in the views which have been expressed. I agree with him that the appeal should be dismissed.

LORD SCOTT OF FOSCOTE. My Lords,

e [117] On 20 July 1998 the appellant, Wardle, and two associates embarked on a violent burglary that went wrong. The victims of the burglary were Mr John Nutter and his sister-in-law who lived together at the address in Leeds where the burglary took place. In the course of the burglary they were roughly manhandled. Mr Nutter died. His sister-in-law suffered wounds. The medical evidence, stated in f layman's terms, was that Mr Nutter died from a heart attack brought about by the manhandling he had been subjected to.

[118] On 17 August 1998 the appellant was arrested on suspicion of having been involved in the incident but was released after interview without being formally charged. He was re-arrested on 5 January 1999 and charged with murder g on 7 January. In the period between August 1998 and January 1999 the police had kept him under surveillance and had thereby obtained evidence, including video recordings, which they believed showed that he had participated in the burglary. The appellant made his first appearance in the magistrates' court on 8 January 1999, and was remanded in custody. The statutory 70-day custody time limit began to h run from that date (see reg 4(4) of the Prosecution of Offences (Custody Time Limits) Regulations 1987, as amended). The custody time limit was due to expire on 19 March 1999.

[119] By 19 March the case was not in a state of readiness for the committal proceedings to commence. It appears that important evidence, including the j evidence that the prosecution relied on as demonstrating that the appellant had been a participant in the burglary, had been supplied to the defence only shortly before 19 March. The defence needed more time to consider the evidence than a commencement of the committal hearing on 19 March would have allowed. It appears, also, that the evidence in question had been in the possession of the prosecution for some considerable time and ought to have been supplied to the defence much earlier.

[120] Upon the expiry of a custody time limit an accused is normally entitled to be released on bail, unless some other custody time limit for some other offence is still unexpired (see s 4(8A) of the Bail Act 1976).

[121] Section 22(3) of the Prosecution of Offences Act 1985, as originally enacted, conferred power on a magistrates' court to extend a custody time limit if satisfied '(a) that there is good and sufficient cause for doing so, and (b) that the prosecution has acted with all due expedition'. In *R v Crown Court at Manchester, ex p McDonald* [1999] 1 All ER 806, [1999] 1 WLR 841 it was held that the court could extend a custody time limit only if both those criteria were satisfied. Lord Bingham of Cornhill CJ, giving the judgment of the court, said ([1999] 1 All ER 806 at 809, [1999] 1 WLR 841 at 847):

> 'What the court must require is such diligence and expedition as would be shown by a competent prosecutor conscious of his duty to bring the case to trial as quickly as reasonably and fairly possible.'

Under an amendment made to s 22(3) by the Crime and Disorder Act 1998, the criteria that had to be satisfied for an extension to be granted were modified. A particular change was that, in place of the original para (b), the court, in order to extend a custody time limit, had to be satisfied 'that the prosecution [had] acted with all due diligence and expedition'. This amendment did not come into effect until 1 June 1999.

[122] When the appellant was brought before the Leeds Magistrates' Court on 19 March 1999, the prosecution preferred a charge of manslaughter against him, in substitution for the original charge of murder. The defence had been notified on 10 March that this would be done. The prosecution gave as their reason for making this change that additional medical evidence had been received from their pathologist, Dr Milroy, on 4 March and had shown that the case against the appellant should be pursued as one of manslaughter rather than murder. There was, however, no material difference between Dr Milroy's report of 4 March and the reports he had earlier made in October and November 1998. He had consistently attributed Mr Nutter's death to heart failure brought about by the manhandling suffered in the course of the burglary and the stress thereby caused.

[123] The prosecution contended that the charge of manslaughter, being a charge of a new offence, attracted a fresh 70-day custody time limit commencing on 19 March 1999, the date on which the appellant first appeared before the magistrates' court on that offence. No doubt in well-founded anticipation that the defence would contest that that was so, the prosecution applied for an extension of the original custody time limit.

[124] The magistrate granted the extension but also expressed himself as satisfied that in any event a new 70-day period had been attracted by the manslaughter charge.

[125] The appellant appealed to the Crown Court. The appeal was heard by Judge Hoffman on 22 March 1999. He disagreed with the magistrate on the extension. He said: 'In the circumstances, I have no hesitation in finding that the prosecution in relation to Wardle did not act with all due expedition.' But, on the question whether the substitution of manslaughter for murder had caused a new 70-day custody time limit to run, he agreed with the magistrate. He held that manslaughter was a new and distinct offence which attracted its own custody time limit. He considered, also, whether the substitution had been made in bad faith for an improper motive, namely for the purpose of preventing the release of the appellant from custody on the expiry of the original custody time limit. As to that,

a there seems to have been no evidence before the court from anyone on the prosecution side explaining the reasons why the manslaughter charge had been substituted and what, if any, part the imminent expiry of the original 70-day period had played. It was counsel appearing for the prosecution who attributed the change to the contents of the medical report of 4 March. But that seems an insubstantial reason since it appears to have been common ground that there was b nothing significant in that report that had not been in the earlier reports. Be that as it may, and notwithstanding the absence of any evidence from the prosecution as to its reasons, the judge expressed himself as satisfied that there was nothing from which bad faith on the prosecution's part could be implied. What the consequence would have been if bad faith had been found is not clear and is something to which I shall have to return.

c **[126]** The appellant sought to challenge, by way of judicial review, Judge Hoffman's decision. The Divisional Court, on 26 April 1999, gave leave but dismissed the substantive application. The judgment was given by Mitchell J with whose judgment Kennedy LJ agreed. Mitchell J reviewed a number of authorities and concluded, as had Judge Hoffman, that the preferring of the manslaughter d charge had attracted a new custody time limit. As to the prosecution's reasons for introducing the manslaughter charge, Mitchell J said:

> 'Abuse of process is not alleged. It is difficult to see how such an allegation could succeed because, as I have said, it is desirable that, where the evidence only warrants an allegation of manslaughter, then manslaughter should be e charged and murder withdrawn.'

and:

> 'For the claim "abuse of process" to succeed, bad faith must be established. That is a heavy burden to discharge. It is not altogether clear on the authorities whether the charging of an offence justified on the evidence, but f solely for the purpose of creating a new custody time limit, itself amounts without more to bad faith. If it does not, then it is difficult to see how there could be any effective challenge to these practices. This considerable measure of latitude which has been extended to prosecutors seems to me to be wholly inconsistent with the purpose of reg 4, because, in effect, it enables g the prosecution to bypass the requirement in s 22(3)(b) that any extension of the time limit has to be justified by showing, under the amendment to s 22(3)(b) introduced by [s] 43 of the Crime and Disorder Act 1998 (which appears not yet to be in force), not only all due expedition but also due diligence.'

h **[127]** Kennedy LJ expressly associated himself with the sentiments expressed by Mitchell J in the passages I have cited.

[128] I share the concern expressed by Mitchell J and Kennedy LJ. The legislative intention which led to s 22 of the 1985 Act and the regulations made thereunder seems to me quite clear. It is to provide a maximum period during which an j accused can be held in custody awaiting trial. Extensions of that period are strictly controlled and can be allowed only if the prosecution can show that it has acted with all due diligence and expedition (see s 22(3)(b) as originally enacted and as amended). If, in the period following an accused's first appearance before the magistrates, new facts emerge which the prosecution need to consider and which may lead to the formulation of a new charge against the accused, I find no difficulty in accepting that an extension of the original 70-day custody time limit may be necessary. And a statutory scheme which allows a further 70 days from the accused's first appearance before the magistrates on a new charge based at least to more than a trivial extent on new facts is not necessarily inconsistent with the legislative intention to which I have referred. But where the new charge is based not on any new facts but on the facts on which the original charge was based, and is simply a lesser charge than that originally preferred, the proposition that the preferment of the new charge attracts a new 70-day custody time limit seems to me to be one that defeats the legislative intention.

[129] In the present case the prosecution did not act with all due diligence and expedition. Judge Hoffman so found and refused the application for an extension. It has not been suggested that he was in error. And yet, by introducing the manslaughter charge on the day of expiry of the original custody time limit, the prosecution procured a further 70 days during which the appellant could be kept in custody. It is, of course, true that it was open to the appellant on 19 March to make an application for bail, and indeed he did so. But the new custody time limit defeated his absolute right to the grant of bail under s 4(8A) of the 1976 Act and his bail application was, in the event, refused.

[130] If the committal hearing had taken place on 19 March, as it would have done if the prosecution had not failed to act with all due diligence and expedition, the prosecution could at the same time have substituted the manslaughter charge for the murder charge and the appellant would have been committed to the Crown Court for trial on the manslaughter charge. If the proceedings had taken that course, the period during which he would have been in custody before the committal would not have exceeded the original 70 days.

[131] On this appeal, the critical question for your Lordships, in my opinion, is whether there is a permissible application of s 22 and reg 4 of the 1987 regulations that would prevent, in a case such as this, the substituted charge from attracting a fresh 70-day custody time limit. There is no doubt, I believe, that if that result can be reached it ought to be reached.

[132] This conclusion is fortified by the impact in a case such as the present of the convention rights to be found in art 5 of the European Convention and of s 3 of the Human Rights Act 1998. Section 3(1) requires primary and subordinate legislation 'So far as it is possible to do so .... [to] be read and given effect in a way which is compatible with the Convention rights.' The words 'and given effect' are of significance. Section 3(1) is directed to the *effect* of legislation as well as to its construction. One of the convention rights to be found in art 5 is 'the right to liberty and security of person' (art 5(1)). The article goes on to provide for exceptions: 'No one shall be deprived of his liberty save in the following cases and in accordance with a procedure prescribed by law…'

[133] One of the 'cases' relates to the detention pending trial of a person suspected of having committed an offence (see para (c)).

[134] In *Bozano v France* (1986) 9 EHRR 297 at 313 (para 54) the Strasbourg court said that 'any measure depriving the individual of his liberty must be compatible with the purpose of Article 5, namely to protect the individual from arbitrariness'. The same point was made in *Brogan v UK* (1988) 11 EHRR 117 at 134 (para 58): '… [article 5] enshrines a fundamental human right, namely the protection of the individual against arbitrary interferences by the State with his right to liberty', and in *Amuur v France* [1996] 22 EHRR 533 at 559 (para 50): '… any deprivation of liberty should be in keeping with the purpose of Article 5, namely to protect the individual from arbitrariness.'

a [135] A construction and application of s 22(1) of the 1985 Act and reg 4(4) of the 1987 regulations that enable the prosecution, by preferring a new charge, to withhold from the accused the release from custody to which he would otherwise have been entitled, in a case where there were no new facts and the new charge was and always had been comprehended within the original charge, would subject the accused to arbitrariness. Section 3(1) of the 1998 Act requires your Lordships, b if it is possible to do so, to avoid allowing s 22(1) and reg 4 to produce that result. Section 22(1) empowers the Secretary of State:

> 'by regulations [to] make provision, with respect to any specified preliminary stage of proceedings for an offence, as to the maximum period—(a) to be allowed to the prosecution to complete that stage; (b) during c which the accused may, while awaiting completion of that stage, be—(i) in the custody of a magistrates' court; or (ii) in the custody of the Crown Court; in relation to that offence.'

[136] The 'provision' referred to by s 22(1) is made by the 1987 regulations. Regulation 4 makes the 'provision' regarding custody time limits in magistrates' d courts. Paragraph (1) provides:

> '... the maximum period during which a person accused of an indictable offence other than treason may be in the custody of a magistrates' court in relation to that offence while awaiting completion of any preliminary stage of the proceedings specified in the following provisions of this Regulation e shall be as stated in those provisions.'

[137] Paragraph (4) of reg 4 deals specifically with offences triable on indictment exclusively. This, therefore, is the particular provision that applied in the present case. It provides:

> f 'In the case of an offence triable on indictment exclusively the maximum period of custody between the accused's first appearance and the time when the court decides whether or not to commit the accused to the Crown Court for trial, shall be 70 days.'

The expression 'first appearance' is defined in reg 2(2):

> g 'In these Regulations, a reference to a person's first appearance in relation to proceedings in a magistrates' court for an offence is ... (c) in any other case, a reference to the time when first he appears or is brought before the court on an information charging him with that offence.'

h [138] Regulations 2(2)(c) and 4(4), literally construed, and subject to abuse of process if it be shown to have been present, make it impossible, in my opinion, to resist the conclusion that a new 70-day custody time began on 19 March when the appellant first appeared in court on the manslaughter charge. Manslaughter may be comprehended within a murder charge but it is, none the less, a separate j offence. If murder by striking the victim with an axe or a bludgeon is charged, it must follow that the alleged acts that constitute the offence would include the facts necessary to constitute also, apart from manslaughter, the offence of unlawful wounding. But no one would describe unlawful wounding as the same offence as murder, or, for that matter, as manslaughter. Each is a separate offence albeit that the facts alleged to constitute the most serious of them, ie murder, would include the facts necessary to constitute each of the others.

[139] If, for the purposes of reg 2(2)(c), the relevant offence is the offence of manslaughter, the reference in the opening sentence to 'an offence' is a reference to the offence of manslaughter and the words 'that offence' at the end of para (c) must also be read as a reference to manslaughter. On that footing, for the purposes of reg 4(4), the appellant's 'first appearance' in relation to the offence of manslaughter was 19 March 1999 and a 70-day custody time limit began on that date. There is, in my opinion, no literal construction that can avoid this result.

[140] So could a purposive construction and purposive application of s 22 and reg 4(4) do so? In the debate before your Lordships various suggestions were made as to words that might be added to, or substituted for, words in reg 2(2) and in reg 4(4) in order to produce a result that accorded with the legislative intention.

[141] Mr MacDonald QC, counsel for the appellant, suggested that the words 'that offence' in reg 4(1) and in reg 2(2)(c) could be expanded so as to read 'that offence or any other offence arising out of the same facts'. An alternative formulation might be 'that offence or any other offence arising out of the allegations in the information or charge'. A number of difficulties arise out of these suggested formulations. The expression 'the same facts' prompts the question 'the same facts as what facts?' The facts as known on the date of the original charge? Or the facts as known by some subsequent, and if so, what, date? Or the facts comprised in the information or charge? As to the information or charge, the contents may be of the sketchiest character at the time the accused makes his first appearance. A third suggested formulation, namely 'that offence or any offence for which the magistrates could commit the accused for trial', seems to me now, although I believe I suggested it, equally unsatisfactory. Under s 6(1) of the Magistrates' Courts Act 1980, magistrates can commit an accused for trial in the Crown Court on any indictable offence disclosed by the evidence before them. The offence does not have to be that with which the accused was originally charged and may depend on new facts which have emerged since the accused's first appearance before the magistrates.

[142] The difficulties which these alternative formulations would be likely to give rise to have led me to conclude that the problem posed by the present case cannot be satisfactorily solved by a purposive reformulation of the statutory language to be found in reg 4. I believe, however, that it could be solved by a judicial limitation on the effect to be given to reg 4 in the case of a new charge.

[143] In my opinion, it is open to your Lordships to rule that if an accused, having appeared or been brought before a magistrates' court on an information charging him with an offence, is then charged with a new offence of which he might, if tried on the original offence, have been convicted (see s 6 (2), (3) and (4) of the Criminal Law Act 1967), a new custody time limit will not be attracted by the new offence and the accused's 'first appearance' in relation to the new offence will be the date on which he first appeared or was brought before the magistrates' court on the information or charge relating to the original offence.

[144] If the addition, or substitution, of the new offence has the consequence that the prosecution is not ready to proceed with the committal hearing within the original 70-day custody time limit, it is always open to the prosecution to apply for an extension. Whether the prosecution would obtain an extension would depend on their showing they had acted 'with all due diligence and expedition'. The end result would thus be in accordance with the legislative intention.

[145] This result can be produced by giving a purposive effect to the statutory provisions notwithstanding that a satisfactory grammatical reformulation of the

a provisions may not be possible. There is authority from your Lordships' House that this is a permissible technique of statutory interpretation.

[146] *DPP v Schildkamp* [1969] 3 All ER 1640, [1971] AC 1 raised a point about s 332(3) of the Companies Act 1948. Schildkamp had been charged with a number of offences in connection with the conduct of the business of a company. One of the offences charged was 'carrying on the business of a company with intent to defraud b creditors contrary to section 332(3) of the Companies Act 1948'. Schildkamp was convicted on this charge. He appealed on the ground, among others, that the company in question, Fiesta Tours Ltd, had never been wound up and that before a prosecution could be initiated for fraudulent trading under s 332(3) the company had to be in liquidation. The Court of Appeal, Criminal Division ([1969] 2 All ER 835, [1969] 1 WLR 819) agreed and allowed the appeal but certified that c a point of law of general public importance was involved, namely 'what, if any, words of limitation must be imported in subsection (3) of section 332 of the Companies Act 1948?' The appeal to your Lordships' House was dismissed. Lord Guest and Viscount Dilhorne, dissenting, took the view that since the words of sub-s (3) were clear and unambiguous they should be given effect to d without speculating about Parliament's intentions. Lord Upjohn ([1969] 3 All ER 1640 at 1652, [1971] AC 1 at 22–23), however, while accepting that 'The subsection plainly applies as a matter of language to the case where there has been no subsequent winding-up', emphasised:

> 'The task of the court is to ascertain the intention of Parliament; one e cannot look at a section, still less a subsection, in isolation, to ascertain that intention: one must look at all the admissible surrounding circumstances before starting to construe the Act.'

[147] So Lord Upjohn examined the whole of the 1948 Act and took into account its legislative history and concluded that it was not Parliament's intention f that sub-s (3) should be of general application while the company was a going concern. He then said ([1969] 3 All ER 1640 at 1654, [1971] AC 1 at 25):

> 'If the Crown's argument to the effect that to limit the effect of sub-s. (3) to prosecutions after the commencement of the winding-up you must virtually rewrite the subsection was correct, I should see much force in his argument, g for it would be very difficult to rewrite the subsection so that in grammatical terms one confined it to prosecutions after winding-up, but I do not think this is necessary for reasons which I will give later.'

[148] The reasons to which Lord Upjohn referred were, in short, that since it was clear that Parliament had not intended sub-s (3) to apply to cases where the h company had not gone into liquidation, the court could, and should, simply limit the application of the subsection accordingly. The following passage is in point ([1969] 3 All ER 1640 at 1654, [1971] AC 1 at 26):

> 'But in my opinion no alteration to the phraseology of sub-s. (3) is required; it stands as it is, plain and unambiguous, but the context in which it is found j requires a limitation in its application to cases where the company has subsequently gone into liquidation.'

[149] Lord Upjohn found support for his approach in a Scottish case, *Robertson and Baxter v Inglis* (1897) 24 R 758, in which the scope of s 3 of the Factors Act 1889 had had to be considered. The question was whether s 3, which stated that a pledge of documents of title to goods should be deemed to be a pledge of the goods, was of general application or was limited to dealings by mercantile agents. The Inner House held that it was so limited. Lord Upjohn commented on the case ([1969] 3 All ER 1640 at 1655, [1971] AC 1 at 26):

> 'Perhaps the opinion of LORD TRAYNER ((1897) 24 R 758 at 816) is most in point. The Inner House did not reach this conclusion by construing s. 3 as a matter of language as so limited but by limiting its scope and ambit to cases where the pledge was by a mercantile agent.'

[150] Lord Reid expressed his agreement with Lord Upjohn. Lord Hodson came to the same conclusion. He, too, found support from *Inglis v Robertson and Baxter*. He said ([1969] 3 All ER 1640 at 1643, [1971] AC 1 at 11): 'I am not impressed by the argument that some rewriting of sub-s. (3) is necessary to make it correspond in terms with sub-s. (1) mutatis mutandis.'

[151] *DPP v Schildkamp* shows that where in order to give effect to Parliament's intention it is necessary to restrict the effect of a statutory provision, it is not a necessary pre-condition that a suitable reformulation of the provision be devised, nor is it necessarily fatal that the statutory provision is clear and unambiguous. It is, of course, essential that Parliament's intention should be clear.

[152] The facts of the present case have, in my opinion, demonstrated that Parliament's intention that there should be a maximum period during which an accused can be kept in custody pending a committal hearing will be frustrated if it is open to the prosecution, by charging a lesser offence, of which the accused was already at risk under the originally charged offence, to produce a fresh custody time limit. A purposive application of reg 4(4), and reg 2(2)(c), to cases where new offences of that character are charged would enable Parliament's intention to be achieved. I would, therefore, allow the appeal.

[153] In concluding, I wish to say a word or two about abuse of process. Your Lordships have been referred to a number of cases in which consideration has been given to the consequences for custody time limits if a new charge is preferred against an accused for an improper purpose.

[154] In *R v Wirral District Magistrates' Court, ex p Meikle* (1990) 154 JP 1035 new offences had been charged but mala fides on the part of the prosecution in preferring the new charges had not been alleged. None the less it was argued for the accused that the new charges were a procedural device designed to circumvent the custody time limit regulations and an abuse of process. Watkins LJ would have none of it. He said (at 1041):

> 'As to abuse of process, in the absence as here of *mala fides*, the effect of which it is unnecessary for present purposes to consider, there is no authority for the proposition that the doctrine can apply to decisions made on ancillary matters such as bail on the charge facing the accused.'

In *R v Great Yarmouth Magistrates, ex p Thomas* [1992] Crim LR 116 (29 July 1991), Watkins LJ reiterated his view that dishonesty or mala fides in preferring the new charges would have to be shown if abuse of process were to be made out. He said, however, that if abuse of process were made out the court would have 'no alternative but to admit these people to bail'.

[155] In my opinion, the requirement of dishonesty or mala fides distracts attention from the true requirements if an allegation of abuse of process is to be made out. The concept of abuse of process is no different in criminal cases from the like concept in civil cases. It involves a use of court process for a purpose other than that for which the purpose in question was intended. It is in that sense that a one may speak of some procedural step being taken for an improper purpose and, therefore, constituting an abuse of process. The procedural step will often be accompanied by bad faith or dishonesty in that a legitimate purpose, not being the true purpose, may be put forward as the true purpose. But bad faith or dishonesty are not essential. What is essential is that court process has been used for some ulterior purpose.

b [156] There will be difficulty where the purpose is mixed. The present case may well be an example. There was every reason, it being clear that the known facts did not support a murder charge but only manslaughter, for the withdrawal of the former and the substitution of the latter as soon as practicable. But the timing of the substitution suggests very strongly, to my mind, that it was done in order to forestall the automatic release of the appellant from custody. There was c no evidence at all from the prosecution as to its reasons for formally substituting manslaughter for murder on 19 March. The prosecution could simply have informed the defence that the murder charge would not be proceeded with and that they would be seeking a committal on manslaughter. In my opinion, however, if a step in litigation is taken for a legitimate reason, whether or not it is d also taken for an illegitimate one, the step cannot be categorised as an abuse of process. The legitimate reason must, of course, be more than merely makeweight or trivial. If abuse of process can be shown, the procedural step taken should, strictly, be regarded as a nullity. This was a point made more than once in the course of the hearing of the appeal by my noble and learned friend, Lord Nicholls of Birkenhead. It is, in my respectful opinion, unanswerable and obviously right. e If a new charge is preferred, not with any genuine intention that the accused should be tried on that charge, but simply in order to attract a new custody time limit, the preferring of the new charge is an abuse of process and the new charge should be struck out as soon as that has become apparent.

[157] If there is a genuine intention that the new charge should be proceeded f with to trial and it is simply the timing of the new charge that appears to be motivated by an intention to avoid the consequences of the expiry of the original custody time limit, the court cannot, in my opinion, strike out the new charge as an abuse of process. But the circumstances in which the substitution of the new charge took place can, and should, in my opinion, be taken into account in considering whether the accused should be released on bail. This, in my view, is g what Watkins LJ had in mind in the remark he made about bail in *R v Great Yarmouth Magistrates, ex p Thomas*.

[158] If I am right in the present case that the substituted charge of manslaughter should not have been treated as giving rise to a fresh custody time limit, the abuse of process point does not arise. If I am wrong, however, and I h understand a majority of your Lordships to take a different view on that point, this was not a case in which the manslaughter charge could have been set aside on abuse of process grounds. However, it was a case in which, on the bail application made to Judge Hoffman, the circumstances in which the substituted charge was preferred should have been taken into account. The fact that the prosecution had j failed to act with all due diligence and expedition was relevant. So was the fact that there was nothing new which explained why the substitution was being made when it was made. The judge should, in my view, have inferred that a substantial reason for the change was that the prosecution wanted to avoid the custody time limit consequences of their own dilatoriness. A decision to award bail in those circumstances would have reflected Parliament's intention in introducing the custody time limit statutory provisions.

[159] But my Lords, for the reasons already expressed, I would allow the appeal. a

Appeal dismissed.

Dilys Tausz Barrister.

a

White v White and another

[2001] UKHL/9

HOUSE OF LORDS

b LORD NICHOLLS OF BIRKENHEAD, LORD MACKAY OF CLASHFERN, LORD COOKE OF THORNDON, LORD HOPE OF CRAIGHEAD AND LORD SCOTT OF FOSCOTE

11–13 DECEMBER 2000, 1 MARCH 2001

Motor insurance – Motor Insurers' Bureau – Liability of bureau to satisfy judgment against uninsured driver – Bureau agreeing with Secretary of State to satisfy awards of damages made c *against uninsured drivers – Agreement intended to give effect to European Community directive – Agreement absolving bureau from liability in respect of claims by passengers who 'knew or ought to have known' that vehicle uninsured – Directive providing for exception from liability where passenger 'knew' driver was uninsured – Whether exclusion covering negligence or carelessness on part of passenger as to driver's insurance status – Second* d *Council Directive (EEC) 84/5, art 1(4) – Motor Insurers' Bureau (Compensation of Victims of Uninsured Drivers) Agreement (1988), cl 6(1)(e)(ii).*

The appellant, W, was seriously injured in a car crash while travelling as a passenger in a car driven by his brother. The brother, whose negligence had caused the accident, was an unlicensed driver and therefore uninsured. At the e time of the accident, W was unaware that his brother was unlicensed, but he had known in the past that his brother had driven without a licence. Since his brother was unable to meet his claim for damages, W looked to the Motor Insurers' Bureau (MIB) to satisfy that claim. Under an agreement with the Secretary of State, made in 1988, MIB was obliged to satisfy any unsatisfied judgment in respect of a liability f which was the subject of a compulsory insurance obligation under the Road Traffic Acts. That agreement was intended to give effect to the Second Council Directive (EEC) 84/5, on the approximation of the laws of the member states relating to insurance against civil liability in respect of the use of motor vehicles. MIB denied liability, relying on cl 6(1)(e)(ii)[a] of the agreement which absolved it from liability where the injured passenger 'knew or ought to have known' that the g vehicle was uninsured. At trial, the judge concluded that W had given no thought to the question of insurance, that he had not actually known that his brother was uninsured, but that he ought to have known. He nevertheless held that cl 6(1)(e)(ii) was incompatible with, and had to yield to, the exception to art 1(4)[b] of the directive which entitled member states to exclude the payment of h compensation for damage or injury to a person who had 'voluntarily' entered an uninsured vehicle only if that person 'knew' that the vehicle was uninsured. He therefore allowed W's claim, but his decision was reversed by the Court of Appeal. W appealed to the House of Lords.

j **Held** – (Lord Scott dissenting) The word 'knew' in art 1(4) of the directive included both actual knowledge and cases where the passenger deliberately refrained from asking questions lest his suspicions that the driver was uninsured be confirmed. It did not, however, extend to cases of carelessness or negligence, such as cases

a Clause 6, so far as material, is set out at [9], post

b Article 1, so far as material, is set out a [12], post

where a passenger gave no thought to the question of insurance, even though an ordinary prudent passenger, in his position and with his knowledge, would have made inquiries. That interpretation of the exception to art 1(4) was consistent with the principle, repeatedly stressed by the Court of Justice of the European Communities, that exceptions to a general rule were to be construed strictly. A strict and narrow interpretation of what constituted knowledge for the purpose of art 1 was reinforced by the subject matter, namely compensation for damage to property or personal injuries caused by vehicles. Proportionality required that a high degree of personal fault had to exist before it would be right for an injured passenger to be deprived of compensation. Moreover, the need for the passenger to have entered the vehicle 'voluntarily' served to confirm that the exception was aimed at persons who consciously colluded in the use of an uninsured vehicle. As the MIB agreement was intended to give effect to that directive, the phrase 'knew or ought to have known' in cl 6(1)(e)(ii) bore, on conventional principles of interpretation, the same meaning as 'knew' in art 1. In the instant case, the judge's finding was no more than a finding of carelessness, assessed by the standard of the ordinary prudent passenger having the knowledge possessed by W. Thus the accident fell outside the circumstances in which the directive permitted a member state to exclude payment of compensation, and was not excepted from the MIB agreement. Accordingly, the appeal would be allowed (see [14]–[20], [23], [28], [29], [34], [36] and [37], post).

Per Lord Nicholls. The principle of European Community law which obliges the English courts to interpret domestic legislation, as far as possible, in a way which gives effect to a directive cannot be stretched to the length of requiring contracts to be interpreted in a manner that would impose on one or other of the parties obligations that the contract does not otherwise impose. That was so even in the case of a contract where one of the parties is an emanation of government. The citizen's obligations are those to which he agreed, as construed in accordance with normal principles of interpretation (see [22], post).

Notes

For the liability of the Motor Insurers' Bureau to satisfy claims for damages against uninsured drivers, see 25 *Halsbury's Laws* (4th edn reissue) para 759.

Cases referred to in opinions

Cia Maritima San Basilio SA v Oceanus Mutual Underwriting Association (Bermuda) Ltd, The Eurysthene [1976] 3 All ER 243, [1977] QB 49, [1976] 3 WLR 265, CA.

Duke v GEC Reliance Systems Ltd [1988] 1 All ER 626, [1988] AC 618, [1988] 2 WLR 359, HL.

Faccini Dori v Recreb Srl Case C-91/92 [1995] All ER (EC) 1, [1994] ECR I-3325, ECJ.

Francovich v Italy Joined cases C-6/90 and C-9/90 [1991] ECR I-5357.

Hardy v Motor Insurers' Bureau [1964] 2 All ER 742, [1964] 2 QB 745, [1964] 3 WLR 433, CA.

Litster v Forth Dry Dock and Engineering Co Ltd [1989] 1 All ER 1134, [1990] 1 AC 546, [1989] 2 WLR 634, HL.

Manifest Shipping Co Ltd v Uni-Polaris Shipping Co Ltd [2001] UKHL/1, [2001] 1 All ER 743, [2001] 2 WLR 170, HL; *affg* [1997] 1 Lloyd's Rep 360, CA; *rvsg* [1995] 1 Lloyd's Rep 651.

Marleasing SA v La Comercial Internacional de Alimentación SA Case C-106/89 [1990] ECR I-4135.

Prenn v Simmonds [1971] 3 All ER 237, [1971] 1 WLR 1381, HL.

a *River Wear Comrs v Adamson* (1877) 2 App Cas 743, [1874–80] All ER Rep 1, HL.
Wagner Miret v Fondo de Garantía Salarial Case C-334/92 [1993] ECR I-6911.
Webb v EMO Air Cargo (UK) Ltd [1992] 4 All ER 929, [1993] 1 WLR 49, HL.

Appeal

The claimant, Brian White, appealed with permission of the Appeal Committee b of the House of Lords given on 14 July 1999 from the order of the Court of Appeal (Hobhouse, Swinton Thomas and Schiemann LJJ) on 30 September 1998 ([1999] 1 CMLR 1251) allowing an appeal by the second defendant, the Motor Insurers' Bureau (MIB), from the order of Judge Potter, sitting as a judge of the High Court on 12 March 1998, that it was liable to satisfy Mr White's claim for damages against c the first defendant, his brother, Shane White, for injuries suffered by him in a road traffic accident caused by his brother's negligence. The Secretary of State for the Environment, Transport and the Regions was granted permission to intervene on the appeal. The facts are set out in the opinion of Lord Nicholls of Birkenhead.

d *Geoffrey Tattersall QC* and *Conor Quigley* (instructed by *Hugh Potter & Co*, Manchester) for Brian White.

Dermod O'Brien QC, Fergus Randolph and *Anna de Chassiron* (instructed by *Greenwoods*) for MIB.

Peter Roth QC and *Helen Davies* (instructed by the *Treasury Solicitor*) for the Secretary of State.

e

Their Lordships took time for consideration.

1 March 2001. The following opinions were delivered.

f **LORD NICHOLLS OF BIRKENHEAD.** My Lords,

[1] Shortly after midnight, in the early moments of 5 June 1993, Brian White was going to a late-night party. He was a front seat passenger in a Ford Capri. The car was being driven by his brother Shane along a country road a few miles outside Hereford. The car crashed and rolled over violently. Brian was very seriously injured. The accident happened at a quiet time of night, and no other g vehicle was involved. Shane's driving was at fault. He lost control of the car coming out of a bend through not driving safely and properly.

[2] Shane was at fault in another respect: neither he nor the car was insured. Indeed, he had not passed a driving test and, moreover, he was disqualified from driving. At the time of the accident Brian did not know his brother was unlicensed h and, hence, uninsured, but he had known in the past that his brother was driving without a licence. The trial judge, Judge Potter sitting as a judge of the High Court, said that while it would be going too far to say that Brian knew Shane was uninsured, it 'stands out a mile' that he ought to have known. He ought to have made sure one way or the other, and he made no effort to do so.

j [3] These simple facts have given rise to this appeal to the House.

Compulsory insurance

[4] Compulsory insurance in respect of the driving of motor vehicles was first introduced in 1930. Before then, most motorists chose to insure themselves against third party risks. But there were cases of serious hardship where the person inflicting the injury was devoid of financial means and, being uninsured, was not

able to pay the damages for which he was liable. It was primarily to meet these cases of hardship that the Road Traffic Act 1930 was enacted. a

[5] The 1930 Act gave no protection to an innocent road user where the motorist failed to comply with his statutory obligation to insure. In 1937 a committee under the chairmanship of Sir Felix Cassel KC recommended that, in cases of failure to insure as required, an injured third party who had obtained a judgment against the person responsible should be able to recover from a central fund: *Report of the Committee on Compulsory Insurance* (Cmd 5528) (1937). The fund should be set up and financed by insurers licensed to transact compulsory motor vehicle insurance business. b

[6] At the end of the war the insurers set up the Motor Insurers' Bureau, which for brevity I will refer to as MIB. MIB is a company incorporated under the Companies Acts. Its primary object is to satisfy judgments in respect of any liability required to be covered by contracts of insurance under the Road Traffic Acts. Its members comprise all insurers which are for the time being transacting compulsory motor vehicle insurance in this country. MIB is funded by levies payable by its members. The amount of the levy is based on the premium income of the members. Ultimately, therefore, the funds of MIB come from the pockets of law abiding motorists who have complied with their statutory insurance obligations. c d

[7] The obligations of MIB are not to be found in an Act of Parliament. Instead, they are the subject of agreement with the appropriate minister. The first agreement was made on 17 June 1946, between the Minister of Transport and MIB. From time-to-time this has been brought up to date with supplemental agreements. The latest supplemental agreement is dated 13 August 1999, made between the Secretary of State for the Environment, Transport and the Regions and MIB. The version of the agreement in force at the time of Brian White's accident was dated 21 December 1988 (Motor Insurers' Bureau (Compensation of Victims of Uninsured Drivers) Agreement). I shall refer to this as 'the 1988 MIB agreement' or simply 'the MIB agreement'. e f

[8] In these proceedings Brian White is looking to MIB to satisfy his claim for damages against his brother Shane. The amounts involved may be very substantial, and there is no question of Shane being able to meet the claim. Before your Lordships' House Brian White's claim was presented primarily as a claim based on the terms of the MIB agreement. I shall consider this claim first. Under the MIB agreement the basic obligation undertaken by MIB relates to any judgment in respect of a liability which is the subject of a compulsory insurance obligation under the Road Traffic Acts. If such a judgment is obtained against any person in any court in this country, and the judgment is not satisfied within seven days, MIB will satisfy the judgment. MIB will do so, regardless of whether the person against whom judgment was obtained was in fact covered by any contract of insurance. g h

[9] MIB's basic obligation is subject to some exceptions. The success or failure of Brian White's claim, so far as it is based on the terms of the MIB agreement, depends on the proper interpretation of one of these exceptions, set out in cl 6(1)(e) of the 1988 MIB agreement. MIB's obligations do not apply in a case where the injured passenger 'knew or ought to have known' that the vehicle had been stolen or was uninsured. Clause 6(1) reads: j

> 'M.I.B. shall not incur any liability under Clause 2 of this Agreement in a case where … (e) at the time of the use which gave rise to the liability the

a person suffering death or bodily injury ... was allowing himself to be carried in or upon the vehicle and ... before the commencement of his journey in the vehicle ... he—(i) knew or ought to have known that the vehicle had been stolen or unlawfully taken, or (ii) knew or ought to have known that the vehicle was being used without there being in force in relation to its use such a contract of insurance as would comply with Part VI of the Road Traffic Act 1972.'

b The crucial phrase for the purposes of this case is 'knew or ought to have known'.

The motor insurance directive

[10] When interpreting any document it is always important to identify, if possible, the purpose the provision was intended to achieve. This makes it necessary, c in the present case, to go to the Second Council Directive (EEC) 84/5 of 30 December 1983, on the approximation of the laws of the member states relating to insurance against civil liability in respect of the use of motor vehicles (OJ 1984 L8, p 17). It is necessary to do so because the purpose of the 1988 MIB agreement was to give effect to the terms of this directive.

d [11] The main purpose of the directive was to improve guarantees of compensation for victims of motor accidents by ensuring a minimum level of protection for them throughout the community. One aspect of this was the need, as stated in the preamble, 'to make provision for a body to guarantee that the victim will not remain without compensation where the vehicle which caused the accident is uninsured or unidentified'. Member states, however, were to have the e opportunity of applying certain 'limited exclusions'.

[12] Article 1 of the directive requires each member state to have compulsory motor insurance covering third party liability for both personal injury and damage to property. It sets minimum standards of protection up to which compensation must be available for the victims of accidents throughout the community. Article 1(4) makes provision regarding unidentified and uninsured vehicles:

f 'Each Member State shall set up or authorize a body with the task of providing compensation, at least up the limits of the insurance obligation, for damage to property or personal injuries caused by an unidentified vehicle or a vehicle for which the insurance obligation provided for in paragraph 1 has g not been satisfied.'

The permitted exception is then stated in these terms:

'However, Member States may exclude the payment of compensation by that body in respect of persons who voluntarily entered the vehicle which h caused the damage or injury when the body can prove that they knew it was uninsured.'

Thus, member states may exclude compensation for damage or injury caused by the driver of an uninsured vehicle if the person who suffered damage or injury 'voluntarily' entered the vehicle and 'knew' it was uninsured. It should be noted j that, unlike the corresponding exception in the MIB agreement ('knew or ought to have known'), the exception permitted by the directive uses the word 'knew' without any adornment. It is this difference in language which gives rise to the issues arising on this appeal.

[13] What is meant by 'knew' in the context of the directive? The interpretation of the directive is a matter governed by community law. If the meaning of 'knew' in art 1 is doubtful, and it is necessary to resolve the doubt in order to decide this

appeal, then a reference to the Court of Justice of the European Communities must be made. Rightly so, because it is important that the provisions of this directive are applied uniformly throughout the community. So I turn to consider what 'knew' means in the directive and whether there is any relevant ambiguity.

[14] The context is an exception to a general rule. The Court of Justice has stressed repeatedly that exceptions are to be construed strictly. Here, a strict and narrow interpretation of what constitutes knowledge for the purpose of art 1 is reinforced by the subject matter. The subject matter is compensation for damage to property or personal injuries caused by vehicles. The general rule is that victims of accidents should have the benefit of protection up to specified minimum amounts, whether or not the vehicle which caused the damage was insured. The exception, therefore, permits a member state, contrary to the general rule, to make no provision for compensation for a person who has suffered personal injury or damage to property. Proportionality requires that a high degree of personal fault must exist before it would be right for an injured passenger to be deprived of compensation. A narrow approach is further supported by the other prescribed limitation on the permissible ambit of any exclusion: the person claiming compensation must have entered the vehicle voluntarily. The need for the passenger to have entered the vehicle voluntarily serves to confirm that the exception is aimed at persons who were consciously colluding in the use of an uninsured vehicle. And it can be noted that the directive emphasises the exceptional nature of the exclusion of compensation by placing the burden of proving knowledge on the party who seeks to invoke the exception, namely, the institution responsible for paying compensation.

[15] This, then, is the context in which 'knew' is used in this directive. In this context, knowledge by a passenger that a driver is uninsured means primarily possession of information by the passenger from which the passenger drew the conclusion that the driver was uninsured. Most obviously and simply, this occurs where the driver told the passenger that he had no insurance cover. Clearly, information from which a passenger drew the conclusion that the driver was uninsured may be obtained in many other ways. Another instance would be when the passenger was aware, from his family or other connections with the driver, that the driver had not passed his driving test ('if he'd taken the test, I would have known'). Knowledge of this character is often labelled actual knowledge, thereby distinguishing other types of case where a person, although lacking actual knowledge, is nevertheless treated by the law as having knowledge of the relevant information.

[16] There is one category of case which is so close to actual knowledge that the law generally treats a person as having knowledge. It is the type of case where, as applied to the present context, a passenger had information from which he drew the conclusion that the driver might well not be insured but deliberately refrained from asking questions lest his suspicions should be confirmed. He wanted not to know ('I will not ask, because I would rather not know'). The law generally treats this state of mind as having the like consequences as would follow if the person, in my example the passenger, had acted honestly rather than disingenuously. He is treated as though he had received the information which he deliberately sought to avoid. In the context of the directive that makes good sense. Such a passenger as much colludes in the use of an uninsured vehicle as a passenger who actually knows that the vehicle is uninsured. The principle of equal treatment requires that these two persons shall be treated alike. The directive is to be construed accordingly.

a [17] Thus far I see no difficulty. I consider that it is acte clair that these two categories of case fall within the scope of the exception permitted by the directive. Conversely, I am in no doubt that 'knew' in the directive does not include what can be described broadly as carelessness or 'negligence'. Typically this would cover the case where a passenger gave no thought to the question of insurance, even though an ordinary prudent passenger, in his position and with his b knowledge, would have made inquiries. He 'ought' to have made inquiries, judged by the standard of the ordinary prudent passenger. A passenger who was *careless* in this way cannot be treated as though he *knew* of the absence of insurance. As Lord Denning MR said in *Cia Maritima San Basilio SA v Oceanus Mutual Underwriting Association (Bermuda) Ltd, The Eurysthene* [1976] 3 All ER 243 at 251, [1977] QB 49 at 68, negligence in not knowing the truth is not equivalent to c knowledge of it. A passenger who was careless in not knowing did not collude in the use of an uninsured vehicle, and he is not to be treated as though he did. To decide otherwise would be to give a wide, rather than a narrow, interpretation to the exception permitted by the directive. This also seems to me to be acte clair.

[18] I pause to note that, on this basis, there is no occasion to refer a question d of interpretation to the Court of Justice in the present case. The circumstances of Brian White's accident come within this last category of case. The judge, having heard oral evidence from Brian White, rejected the idea that on the night in question any one of those involved 'so much as bothered his head about such a matter as insurance'. In the past both brothers had been accustomed to drive while uninsured. In 1990, three years before the accident, they agreed that it e would be better to put themselves in a position where they could drive cars legally. The judge observed that much can happen in three years. So it was going too far to say that, because of what had happened in the past, Brian knew Shane was still driving without insurance in 1993. But Brian ought not to have got into a car driven by his brother without making sure his brother 'had carried out the f good resolution and really had made himself a legal driver'.

[19] This finding by the judge is no more than a finding of carelessness, assessed by the standard of the ordinary prudent passenger having the knowledge possessed by this particular passenger. Thus, this accident falls outside the circumstances in which the directive permits a member state to exclude payment of compensation.

g *The interpretation of the MIB agreement*

[20] Against this background I turn to the interpretation of the phrase 'knew or ought to have known' in cl 6(1)(e) of the 1988 MIB agreement. This question of interpretation is governed by English law. 'Ought' imports a standard by reference to which conduct is measured. Such is the prevalence of negligence in h English law that the phrase immediately prompts the thought that the standard imported by 'ought' is the standard of the reasonable person. In cases of professional negligence the standard is that of the reasonably competent and careful professional in the relevant discipline. But this is not necessarily the standard. The meaning of the phrase depends upon its context. Here the context j is the directive. The MIB agreement was entered into with the specific intention of giving effect to the directive.

[21] Had the MIB agreement been embodied in legislation, whether primary or secondary, the English court would have been under an obligation to interpret its provisions, as far as possible, in a way which gives effect to the directive (see *Marleasing SA v La Comercial Internacional de Alimentación SA* Case C-106/89 [1990] ECR I-4135). As Lord Oliver of Aylmerton observed in *Litster v Forth Dry Dock and*

Engineering Co Ltd [1989] 1 All ER 1134 at 1140, [1990] 1 AC 546 at 559, a purposive construction will be applied to legislation even though, perhaps, it may involve some departure from the strict and literal application of the words which the legislature has elected to use.

[22] The present case does not involve legislation. Despite the contrary argument submitted to your Lordships, I do not see how the *Marleasing* principle, as such, can apply to the interpretation of the MIB agreement. Article 5 of the EC Treaty obliges member states to take all appropriate measures to ensure fulfilment of their obligations arising out of the treaty. The rationale of the *Marleasing* case is that the duty of member states under art 5 is binding on all the authorities of member states, including the courts. The courts must apply national law accordingly, whenever the law was enacted or made. But it is one matter to apply this principle to national law. Whatever form it may take, law is made by authorities of the state. It is quite another matter to apply this principle to contracts made between citizens. The *Marleasing* principle cannot be stretched to the length of requiring contracts to be interpreted in a manner that would impose on one or other of the parties obligations which, the *Marleasing* case apart, the contract did not impose. This is so even in the case of a contract where one of the parties is an emanation of government, here, the Secretary of State. The citizen's obligations are those to which he agreed, as construed in accordance with normal principles of interpretation.

[23] So the *Marleasing* principle must be put on one side. Even so, I consider that the application of conventional principles of interpretation of documents arrives at the same result. The purpose for which the MIB agreement was made furnishes a compelling context. The exception spelled out in cl 6(1)(e)(ii) of the MIB agreement was intended by the parties to carry through the provisions of the directive. The phrase 'knew or ought to have known' in the MIB agreement was intended to be co-extensive with the exception permitted by art 1 of the directive. It was intended to bear the same meaning as 'knew' in the directive. It should be construed accordingly. It is to be interpreted restrictively. 'Ought to have known' is apt to include knowledge which an honest person who enters the vehicle voluntarily would have. It includes the case of a passenger who deliberately refrains from asking questions. It is not apt to include mere carelessness or negligence. A mere failure to act with reasonable prudence is not enough. Hence it does not embrace the present case. Brian White's claim is not excepted from the MIB agreement. On this I respectfully differ from the view of the Court of Appeal (sub nom *Mighell v Reading, Evans v Motor Insurers' Bureau, White v White* [1999] 1 CMLR 1251).

[24] Precisely where the boundary is drawn between the states of mind within the scope of cl 6(1)(e) and those outside it is not a matter which arises on this appeal. This question, should it ever arise, is better pursued on an occasion when the facts make it necessary to obtain guidance from the Court of Justice on the precise scope of the exemption permitted by art 1(4) of the directive. As already noted, a reference for this purpose is not a course open to the House on this appeal.

[25] Mr O'Brien QC, appearing for MIB, objected to the appellant being permitted to advance a case based on this interpretation of the MIB agreement. This interpretation was not advanced at the trial. At the trial the case put forward on behalf of Brian White was that the exemption in the MIB agreement was wider than that permitted by the directive. He should not now be permitted to put forward an interpretation of the MIB agreement which, had it been advanced at the trial, might have led to different findings of fact.

a [26] I am unable to accept this objection. It was for MIB to establish the facts upon which MIB sought to rely to bring the case within cl 6(1)(e). In the course of his submissions to your Lordships, Mr O'Brien expressly disclaimed any wish to have the matter remitted so that the judge's findings of fact could be clarified or amplified on this point.

[27] This conclusion suffices to decide this appeal. Mr Tattersall QC presented b an alternative argument, should he fail on the question of interpretation of the MIB agreement. He submitted that the directive gives rights which are directly enforceable against MIB as an emanation of the state. Since Brian White's claim against MIB based on the MIB agreement itself has succeeded, it is not necessary to pursue, or express any opinion on, this alternative formulation of Brian White's case.

c

LORD MACKAY OF CLASHFERN. My Lords,

[28] I have had the advantage of reading in draft the speech prepared by my noble and learned friend Lord Nicholls of Birkenhead. For the reasons he gives, I agree this appeal should be allowed.

d

LORD COOKE OF THORNDON. My Lords,

[29] I have had the advantage of reading in draft the speeches prepared by the other members of the Appellate Committee who sat in this case. For the reasons given by my noble and learned friend Lord Nicholls of Birkenhead, I would allow e this appeal.

[30] The reasons to the contrary given by my noble and learned friend Lord Scott of Foscote command respect and I acknowledge their force. But I do not see them as so forceful as to override the desirability that, where it is possible without distortion, legal instruments entered into by the government of the United f Kingdom should be construed compatibly with relevant European Community law.

[31] It is an established rule that, even where a community directive does not have direct effect, it is for a United Kingdom court to construe domestic legislation in any field covered by the directive so as to accord with the interpretation of the directive as laid down by the Court of Justice of the European Communities, if that g can be done without distorting the meaning of the domestic legislation: *Webb v EMO Air Cargo (UK) Ltd* [1992] 4 All ER 929 at 939, [1993] 1 WLR 49 at 59, per Lord Keith of Kinkel, citing *Duke v GEC Reliance Systems Ltd* [1988] 1 All ER 626 at 636, [1988] AC 618 at 639–640, per Lord Templeman. Similarly the Court of Justice has held that when applying provisions of national law the national court must h interpret them as far as possible in the light of the wording and purpose of any relevant directive, even if it does not have direct effect (see *Faccini Dori v Recreb Srl* Case C-91/92 [1995] All ER (EC) 1 at 21, [1994] ECR I-3325 at 3357 (para 26)). A helpful discussion and further authorities may be found in *Bennion on Statutory Interpretation* (3rd edn, 1997) pp 1004–1010.

j [32] In relation to enactments the established rule is linked with s 2(4) of the European Communities Act 1972. It may be, however, that the rule is properly to be given wider scope extending to contracts entered into by the United Kingdom government which are manifestly intended to give effect to a European directive. Whether or not that is so, I think that a relevant directive must be at least an aid to the interpretation of such a contract. This can conveniently be called the principle of European compatibility.

[33] In a general sense the MIB agreement of 21 December 1988 was clearly intended by the minister, to the knowledge of the MIB, to give effect to the Second Council Directive (EEC) 84/5 of 30 December 1983, on the approximation of the laws of the member states relating to insurance against civil liability in respect of the use of motor vehicles (OJ 1984 L8, p 17). It is possible, though, as Lord Scott suggests, that one or both of the parties intended 'ought to have known' to include merely negligent ignorance and did so either misapprehending the meaning of 'knew' in art 1(4) of the directive or without properly considering the point.

[34] But what was in fact in the minds of the parties is speculative, nor is an inquiry into it the usual approach. As normally with questions of contractual interpretation at common law, the approach here should be, in my view, objective. Reading cl 6(1)(e)(ii) of the agreement in the light of the background and the principle of European compatibility, can 'knew or ought to have known' fairly be interpreted so as not to extend beyond actual knowledge or a state of mind, such as wilful blindness, so close thereto as not to be justly and realistically distinguished? I think that the answer is 'yes'. In this particular context a negative answer is not compelled by the undoubted fact that, in ordinary cases where Community law has no bearing, an interpretation including mere negligence is commonly applied.

[35] The principle of European compatibility may have little or no weight in interpreting a contract between private parties only, especially if there is no ground for attributing to them a common intention to contract with reference to European law. The MIB agreement is not in that category. Indeed, if it were, Brian White might not have been able to sue on it successfully: see 9(1) *Halsbury's Laws of England* (4th edn reissue) para 764, n 16 and the authorities there collected. Rather it is what is called in Wade and Forsyth *Administrative Law* (8th edn, 2000) p 777 'an administrative device in order to enforce some policy'. That work lists the MIB agreement among the specific examples given. Lord Denning MR said that the MIB agreement was 'as important as any statute' (see *Hardy v Motor Insurers' Bureau* [1964] 2 All ER 742 at 744, [1964] 2 QB 745 at 757). The increasing employment by government at all levels of contractual techniques to achieve regulatory aims is a development well recognised in the courts and by legal writers: see too, for instance, De Smith, Woolf and Jowell, *Judicial Review of Administrative Action* (5th edn, 1995) pp 315–316 (para 6-036). Inevitably, it seems to me, this development will have some influence on the interpretation of relevant contracts. The present case may be placed in that setting also.

[36] In short, contractual interpretation is governed generally by the precepts of Lord Wilberforce and Lord Blackburn (see *Prenn v Simmonds* [1971] 3 All ER 237 at 239–240, [1971] 1 WLR 1381 at 1383–1384 citing *River Wear Comrs v Adamson* (1877) 2 App Cas 743 at 763, [1874–80] All ER Rep 1 at 11). Consideration is given to the matrix of facts; the circumstances with reference to which the words were used; and the object, appearing from those circumstances, which the persons using them had in view. When to those considerations there is added as an aid to interpretation the principle of compatibility with European Community law, I think that there is full justification for holding 'ought to have known' in the MIB agreement to be limited to a state of mind tantamount to actual knowledge.

LORD HOPE OF CRAIGHEAD. My Lords,

[37] I have had the advantage of reading in draft the speech of my noble and learned friend Lord Nicholls of Birkenhead. I agree with it, and for the reasons which he has given I too would allow the appeal.

a **LORD SCOTT OF FOSCOTE.** My Lords,

[**38**] In 1993 the appellant, Brian White, was a passenger in a car being driven by his brother, Shane White. It is not entirely clear to whom the car belonged but it probably belonged to Shane. The car was uninsured. Shane White was uninsured. An accident was caused by the negligence of Shane White. Brian White suffered very serious injuries. He seeks compensation for his injuries from the b Motor Insurers' Bureau (the MIB).

[**39**] Under an agreement dated 21 December 1988 (Motor Insurers' Bureau (Compensation of Victims of Uninsured Drivers) Agreement) between the Secretary of State for Transport and the MIB, the MIB agreed to provide compensation to persons who suffered personal injuries or damage to property arising out of motor car accidents where the offending vehicle, or the offending driver, was c uninsured. The MIB has never put to the test whether its liability under the MIB agreement, or any predecessor agreement, is enforceable against it by the injured third party. It has always honoured its contractual commitment. But it denies that, on the true construction of the MIB agreement, it has any contractual commitment to compensate Brian White.

d [**40**] The MIB agreement contains, in cl 6, an important exception. It is on the true construction of this exception that the MIB's obligation to compensate Brian White depends.

> '(1) M.I.B. shall not incur any liability under Clause 2 of this Agreement in a case where … (e) at the time of the use which gave rise to the liability the e person suffering death or bodily injury or damage to property was allowing himself to be carried in or upon the vehicle and … (ii) knew or ought to have known that the vehicle was being used without there being in force in relation to its use such a contract of insurance as would comply with Part VI of the Road Traffic Act 1972.'

f In other words, if the injured passenger 'knew or ought to have known' that the vehicle was being driven while uninsured, the MIB is not obliged to compensate him for his injuries.

[**41**] Brian White's compensation claim was tried by Judge Potter. He gave judgment on 13 March 1997. He held, notwithstanding a good deal of evidence from which a contrary conclusion might have been drawn and mainly on the g strength of a conversation between the two brothers in 1990 at which they had agreed that their practice of illegal driving should stop and that 'it would be very much better for both of them to put themselves into a position where they could drive motor cars legally', that it would be 'going too far to say that when he [ie Brian] embarked on this journey with [Shane] he knew that [Shane] at that h time was not covered by insurance'. But the judge held that Brian ought to have known 'because he ought not to have got into a vehicle driven by his brother without making sure that his brother had carried out the good resolution and really had made himself a legal driver.' So the action against MIB appeared to be heading towards failure, not because Brian had known his brother was uninsured j but because he ought to have known that that was the position. The judge said:

> 'So I find that I cannot say that the plaintiff knew the first defendant had not done that; [but] he ought to have known, because he ought to have made sure one way or the other, and he certainly made no effort to do so.'

[**42**] It is clear that the judge's conclusion was based on a construction of the phrase 'ought to have known' in the MIB agreement that included something less

than actual knowledge: 'he ought to have known, because he ought to have made sure ...' *a*

[43] Judge Potter's judgment on 13 March 1997 did not dispose of the case. Although his finding that Brian White 'ought to have known' the vehicle was uninsured appeared to bring the case within the cl 6(1)(e)(ii) exception, a point on Community law was raised. The point was based on the Second Council Directive (EEC) 84/5 of 30 December 1983, on the approximation of the laws of the member *b* states relating to insurance against civil liability in respect of the use of motor vehicles (OJ 1984 L8, p 17).

[44] The purpose of the directive was to remove, or obtain the removal of, disparities between the laws of different member states regarding compulsory insurance cover for damage to persons or property arising out of motor vehicle accidents. Article 1(4) of the directive provided, so far as relevant for present *c* purposes:

> 'Each Member State shall set up or authorize a body with the task of providing compensation, at least up to the limits of the insurance obligation for damage to property or personal injuries caused by an unidentified vehicle *d* or a vehicle for which the insurance obligation provided for in paragraph 1 has not been satisfied ... However, Member States may exclude the payment of compensation by that body in respect of persons who voluntarily entered the vehicle which caused the damage or injury when the body can prove that they knew it was uninsured.'

e

[45] A similar exclusion relating to 'persons who voluntarily entered the vehicle which caused the damage or injury, when the insurer can prove that they knew the vehicle was stolen' is to be found in art 2(1) of the directive.

[46] The agreement of 21 December 1988 was not the first agreement between the Secretary of State and the MIB. There had been a succession of agreements, starting with one dated 17 June 1946, under which the MIB had agreed to provide *f* compensation for third parties injured in motor vehicle accidents where there was no insurance cover. But the agreement of 21 December 1988 was intended to implement the requirements of the directive. The notes to the MIB agreement make that clear. Paragraph 3 of the notes, referring to the requirement that compulsory insurance should cover not only personal injuries but also damage to *g* property, said that:

> 'This provision gives effect to Article 1.1 of Council Directive (84/5/EEC) of 30 December 1983 on the approximation of the laws of Member States relating to insurance against civil liability in respect of the use of motor vehicles ...' *h*

There is nothing in the notes to explain the difference between 'knew' in art 1(4) of the directive and 'knew or ought to have known' in cl 6(1)(e)(ii) of the MIB agreement.

[47] The point taken before Judge Potter was that since he had found that *j* Brian did not know that the vehicle and the driver, his brother Shane, were uninsured, and notwithstanding that Brian ought to have known, the terms of art 1(4) of the directive covered the case. Article 1(4), it was argued, was capable of direct enforcement by victims of motor vehicle accidents, the MIB was an emanation of the state and, accordingly, Brian White could enforce art 1(4) against the MIB and claim compensation for his injuries.

a [48] Judge Potter accepted this argument. In a judgment given on 12 March 1998, nearly a year after his judgment on the facts, he found in favour of Brian White. Some of his remarks in the 1998 judgment elucidate the nature of the factual findings in his 1997 judgment. He said:

> '... "ought to have known" very clearly includes cases where one did not, in fact, know. I am quite satisfied that in this respect the directive and the b MIB agreement are incompatible and the MIB agreement must yield to the directive. "Or ought to have known" embraces cases of mere negligence which cannot be equated with knowledge. There would be more to be said, of course, if one were discussing knowledge and how knowledge can be imputed, but if one merely says that somebody ought to have known one is c not even imputing knowledge. One is finding something quite separate and distinct.'

It seems clear from this passage that the judge's finding that Brian White 'ought to have known' was a finding inconsistent with actual knowledge or imputed knowledge.

d [49] The MIB appealed (sub nom *Mighell v Reading, Evans v Motor Insurers' Bureau, White v White* [1999] 1 CMLR 1251) on the issue of Community law and, also, on the judge's failure to find actual knowledge. As to the latter point, Schiemann LJ (at 1258) said: 'Many a judge would I suspect have drawn different inferences from the facts but I am not persuaded that it was not legally open to the judge to draw the inferences which he did draw.' Hobhouse LJ (at 1269) said:

e

> 'Although the finding that White believed his brother was insured and did not know that he was not was somewhat surprising, it was based upon the acceptance of White's oral evidence given at the trial and no adequate basis was shown for the conclusion that the judge was not entitled to accept that evidence if he chose to do so. The judge's finding that White ought to have f known that his brother was not [insured] was clearly of the character of a finding of contributory negligence and no more; it did not amount to a finding which could amount to a finding of knowledge however widely that word was construed.'

g [50] As to the Community law issue, the Court of Appeal held: (i) first, that although the terms of the directive were to be taken into account in construing the MIB agreement, none the less cl 6(1)(e)(ii) of that agreement effected a wider exclusion than was authorised by art 1(4) of the directive, and that it followed that the United Kingdom government had failed fully to implement the directive; (ii) second, that the terms of the directive did not permit direct enforcement. h *Francovich v Italy* Joined cases C-6/90 and C-9/90 [1991] ECR I-5357 and *Wagner Miret v Fondo de Garantía Salarial* Case C-334/92 [1993] ECR I-6911 were relied on.

[51] On the second of these points I am in full agreement with the Court of Appeal. The terms of the directive were not such as to permit direct enforcement. The 'body' to be given the task of providing the compensation is not identified in j the directive. Each member state is given the alternative either to set up a new body or to identify an existing body to provide the compensation. There is nothing in the language of the article to prevent a member state from entrusting the provision of the compensation to more than one body. An example suggested in the course of the hearing by my noble and learned friend Lord Mackay of Clashfern was one body to provide compensation for personal injuries and another body to provide compensation for damage to property. The directive has

left the form of the arrangements to the member states. In *Francovich v Italy*, the Court of Justice of the European Communities said that: *a*

> '... wherever the provisions of a directive appear, as far as their subject-matter is concerned, to be unconditional and sufficiently precise, those provisions may, in the absence of implementing measures adopted within the prescribed period, be relied upon as against any national provision which is incompatible with the directive ...' (See [1991] ECR I-5357 at 5408 (para 11).) *b*

And that:

> '... even though the provisions of the directive in question are sufficiently precise and unconditional as regards the determination of the persons entitled to the guarantee and as regards the content of that guarantee, those *c* elements are not sufficient to enable individuals to rely on those provisions before the national courts. Those provisions do not identify the person liable to provide the guarantee, and the State cannot be considered liable on the sole ground that it has failed to take transposition measures within the prescribed period.' (See [1991] ECR I-5357 at 5412 (para 26).) *d*

[52] In the present case it is not the United Kingdom government that is the defendant. It is the MIB. But the MIB is not identified in the directive and the extent of its liability depends upon arrangements made between the United Kingdom government and itself. If those arrangements do not impose liability on it, then it is not liable. Direct effect cannot, in my opinion, be given to the directive *e* as against the MIB.

[53] Returning to the first community law point, the construction point, a sustained argument has been addressed to your Lordships in support of the proposition that, since the MIB agreement of December 1988 was intended by both parties to implement the directive, the meaning to be attributed to 'knew or *f* ought to have known' in cl 6(1)(e)(ii) of the MIB agreement should be the same as the meaning to be attributed to 'knew' in art 1(4) of the directive. It is, of course, commonplace to say that an agreement should be construed so as to give effect to the intentions, objectively ascertained, of the parties to it. But the proposition that that commonplace principle of construction can resolve the apparent difference between 'knew' and 'knew or ought to have known' is not one that I find myself *g* able to accept. I would accept that 'knew' in art 1(4) can, and should, be construed so as to cover not only actual knowledge but also imputed knowledge. In a very recent case in your Lordships' House, *Manifest Shipping Co Ltd v Uni-Polaris Shipping Co Ltd* [2001] UKHL/1, [2001] 1 All ER 743, [2001] 2 WLR 170, there was an issue as to the meaning of 'with the privity of the assured' in s 39(5) of the *h* Marine Insurance Act 1906. The trial judge ([1995] 1 Lloyd's Rep 651) did not find that there had been any actual knowledge on the part of the assured but he found there had been 'blind-eye' knowledge, in that the assured 'did not want to know'. The Court of Appeal ([1997] 1 Lloyd's Rep 360) reversed the finding and were upheld in this House. My noble and learned friend Lord Hobhouse of Woodborough ([2001] 1 All ER 743 at [26], [2001] 2 WLR 170) agreed with the *j* Court of Appeal that 'A finding of negligence to a very high degree did not suffice for a finding of privity'. In my own judgment, I tried to express the essentials of 'blind-eye' knowledge:

> '... blind-eye knowledge requires, in my opinion, a suspicion that the relevant facts do exist and a deliberate decision to avoid confirming that they

a exist ... The deliberate decision must be a decision to avoid obtaining confirmation of facts in whose existence the individual has good reason to believe.' (See [2001] 1 All ER 743 at [116], [2001] 2 WLR 170.)

[54] Whatever else may be comprehended in the word 'knew' in art 1(4) of the directive on its correct construction, the word must surely comprehend b blind-eye knowledge as described.

[55] At the other extreme, I would regard it as clear that 'knew' does not cover inadvertence. As Lord Hobhouse said in the *Manifest Shipping* case, a finding of negligence cannot suffice. What then is the meaning of 'knew or ought to have known' in the MIB agreement? Can the expression 'ought to have known' be construed so as to exclude negligence? In my opinion, it cannot. It is the deliberate c contrast between 'knew' and 'ought to have known' that seems to me to be conclusive. The phrase is contrasting actual knowledge on the one hand with a state of mind involving the absence of actual knowledge on the other hand. The expression 'ought to have known' is a very common one in our law. It is used time and time again in a great variety of factual situations and legal claims. I do not think it is in d the least ambiguous. It is always, in my experience, taken to connote negligence. Judge Potter took it to mean that. So did the Court of Appeal. A construction of 'ought to have known' that excludes negligence would, I respectfully suggest, be incomprehensible to the lawyers up and down the land who have to make our law work. The justification for the construction would be that the MIB agreement was intended to implement the directive and that 'knew' in the directive did not include e negligence. It would be more apt, I suggest, to infer that the parties intended, by using the expression 'ought to have known', to include negligence and did so either under a misapprehension as to the meaning to be attributed to 'knew' in art 1(4) or without properly directing their minds to the point.

[56] For these reasons I am unable to concur in a construction of the MIB f agreement that would allow Brian White, notwithstanding the finding that he ought to have known the vehicle was uninsured, to recover against the MIB.

[57] I would dismiss this appeal.

Appeal allowed.

Dilys Tausz Barrister.

R v P and others

a

HOUSE OF LORDS

LORD HUTTON, LORD GOFF OF CHIEVELEY, LORD BROWNE-WILKINSON, LORD COOKE OF THORNDON AND LORD HOBHOUSE OF WOODBOROUGH

22–24 MAY, 8 JUNE, 11 DECEMBER 2000

b

Criminal evidence – Interception of communications – Telephone intercepts – Use of telephone intercepts as evidence – Authorities in foreign jurisdiction lawfully carrying out telephone intercepts in that jurisdiction – Prosecution wishing to use intercepts in trial of defendants in England for drugs offence – Whether use of evidence infringing rights to fair hearing and respect for private life – Whether policy of English law prohibiting use of intercepts in evidence regardless of where intercepts carried out – Police and Criminal Evidence Act 1984, s 78 – Interception of Communications Act 1985 – European Convention for the Protection of Human Rights and Fundamental Freedoms 1950, arts 6, 8.

c

d

The defendants were charged with three counts of assisting in the United Kingdom in the commission of drug offences in two other European Union countries. The prosecution alleged, inter alia, that the defendants had been involved with X, a national of one of those countries, in smuggling a large quantity of a Class A drug into and out of that country. In support of that allegation, the prosecution intended to call X as a witness and proposed to put in evidence intercepts of telephone calls made by him on his mobile phone. All those intercepts had been made in X's country, by the appropriate authorities, in accordance with both the law of that country and the European Convention for the Protection of Human Rights and Fundamental Freedoms 1950. The intercepts were admissible in evidence in that country, and had already been used there in a successful prosecution of X. The defendants nevertheless contended, at a preparatory hearing, that the intercepts would be inadmissible at their trial. That contention was rejected by the judge who also declined to exercise his discretion to exclude the evidence under s 78[a] of the Police and Criminal Evidence Act 1984. The judge's decision was affirmed by the Court of Appeal, and the defendants appealed to the House of Lords. They contended that, although the intercept evidence had been properly obtained in accordance with the convention and the law of X's country, its use in their trial would infringe art 6[b] of the convention, which guaranteed the right to a fair hearing, and art 8[c], which prohibited 'interference' by a public authority with the exercise of a person's right to respect for his private life save where it was in accordance with the law and necessary in a democratic society for, inter alia, the prevention of crime. The defendants further contended that there was a rule of policy of English law that intercept and surveillance evidence should not be used at criminal trials, regardless of where and by whom the interception had been carried out.

e

f

g

h

j

Held – (1) Although it was not in dispute that the use made of an intercept could amount to an 'interference' for the purposes of art 8 of the convention, there was

---

a Section 78, so far as material, is set out at p 67 *b* to *d*

b Article 6, so far as material, is set out at p 64 *a*, post

c Article 8 is set out at p 63 *j*, post

a no breach of that article in the instant case. The relevant information, having been lawfully obtained for the purpose of assisting the prosecution of alleged smugglers of Class A drugs, had not been used for any other purpose and had not been kept for longer than was necessary for that purpose. Everything had been done pursuant to statutory authority and subject to judicial supervision, and no qualitative criticism could be made of the statutory provisions. The defendant's b arguments under art 6 also failed. The criterion of fairness under that article was the same as that to be applied by a judge under s 78 of the 1984 Act. The fair use of intercept evidence at a trial was not a breach of art 6 even if the evidence was unlawfully obtained, and it was a cogent factor in favour of the admission of intercept evidence that one of the parties to the relevant conversation was going to be a witness at the trial and give evidence of what was said during it. c A defendant was not entitled to have the unlawfully obtained evidence excluded simply because it had been so obtained. Rather he was entitled to an opportunity to challenge its use and admission in evidence and a judicial assessment of the effect of its admission upon the fairness of the trial, such as that provided for by s 78 (see p 60 *g* to p 61 *a*, p 66 *h j*, p 67 *b*, p 69 *f* and p 70 *c* to *e* post); *R v Aujla* [1998] d 2 Cr App R 16 approved; *Amann v Switzerland* (16 February 2000, unreported) distinguished; *Schenk v Switzerland* (1988) 13 EHRR 242 and *Khan v UK* (2000) 8 BHRC 310 considered.

(2) There was no principle of exclusion of intercept evidence in English law independent of the Interception of Communications Act 1985. Where, as in the instant case, the intercept was made in a foreign country by the authorities of that e country, and the 1985 Act accordingly had no application, there was no basis for the argument that there was a rule of English public policy which made that evidence, which was admissible in the country in which it had been obtained, inadmissible in England. Accordingly, the appeals would be dismissed (see p 60 *g* to p 61 *a*, p 73 *f* to *h* and p 74 *d e*, post); *R v Preston* [1993] 4 All ER 638 and *Morgans* f *v DPP* [2000] 2 All ER 522 considered.

Notes

For the right to a fair hearing and the right to respect for private life, see 8(2) *Halsbury's Laws* (4th edn reissue) paras 134, 149, and for interception of communications, see 11(1) *Halsbury's Laws* (4th edn reissue) paras 270–275.

g For the Police and Criminal Evidence Act 1984, s 78, see 17 *Halsbury's Statutes* (4th edn) (1999 reissue) 236.

For the Interception of Communications Act 1985, see 45 *Halsbury's Statutes* (4th edn) (1999 reissue) 289.

For the European Convention for the Protection of Human Rights and h Fundamental Freedoms 1950, arts 6, 8 (as set out in the Human Rights Act 1998, Sch 1), see 7 *Halsbury's Statutes* (4th edn) (1999 reissue) 523, 524.

Cases referred to in opinions

Amann v Switzerland (16 February 2000, unreported), ECt HR.

j *Khan v UK* (2000) Times, 23 May, ECt HR.

Klass v Federal Republic of Germany (1978) 2 EHRR 214, ECt HR.

Malone v Comr of Police of the Metropolis (No 2) [1979] 2 All ER 620, [1979] Ch 344, [1979] 2 WLR 700.

Malone v UK (1984) 7 EHRR 14, ECt HR.

Morgans v DPP [2000] 2 All ER 522, [2000] 2 WLR 386, HL.

R v Aujla [1998] 2 Cr App R 16, CA.

R v Effik (1992) 95 Cr App R 427, CA; *affd* [1994] 3 All ER 458, [1995] 1 AC 309, [1994] 3 WLR 583, HL.

R v Governor of Belmarsh Prison, ex p Martin [1995] 2 All ER 548, [1995] 1 WLR 412, DC

R v Khan [1996] 3 All ER 289, [1997] AC 558, [1996] 3 WLR 162, HL.

R v Owen [1999] 1 WLR 949, CA.

R v Preston [1993] 4 All ER 638, [1994] 2 AC 130, [1993] 3 WLR 891, HL.

R v Rasool [1997] 4 All ER 439, [1997] 1 WLR 1092, CA.

Schenk v Switzerland (1988) 13 EHRR 242, ECt HR.

Sunday Times v UK (1979) 2 EHRR 245, ECt HR.

Teixeira de Castro v Portugal (1998) 28 EHRR 101, ECt HR.

Appeals

The defendants, P, Q and R, appealed with leave of the Court of Appeal from its decision dismissing their appeals from a ruling of a Crown Court judge that transcripts of telephone intercepts lawfully made in a foreign jurisdiction were admissible in their trial on charges of drug offences contrary to s 20 of the Misuse of Drugs Act 1971. The Court of Appeal certified that two questions of law of general public importance were involved in its decision, namely: '1. Is evidence obtained as a result of a telephone intercept made in a European jurisdiction in accordance with the law of that jurisdiction in respect of a call in which one or both parties make or receive such call within the United Kingdom admissible in criminal proceedings in the United Kingdom? 2. Should the trial judge in this case, in the exercise of his discretion under section 78 of the Police and Criminal Evidence Act 1984 or the court's general jurisdiction to achieve fairness, have excluded the evidence of the contents of the telephone intercept?' The facts are set out in the opinion of Lord Hobhouse of Woodborough.

8 June 2000. Their Lordships announced that the appeals would be dismissed for reasons to be given later.

11 December 2000. The following opinions were delivered.

LORD HUTTON. My Lords, I have had the advantage of reading in draft the speech prepared by my noble and learned friend, Lord Hobhouse of Woodborough. I agree with it and it was for the reasons which he gives that I dismissed these appeals.

LORD GOFF OF CHIEVELEY. My Lords, I have had the opportunity of reading in draft the opinion prepared by my noble and learned friend, Lord Hobhouse of Woodborough. I agree with the reasons given by him for dismissing the appeals.

LORD BROWNE-WILKINSON. My Lords, I have had the advantage of reading in draft the speech prepared by my noble and learned friend, Lord Hobhouse of Woodborough. I agree with it and it was for the reasons he gives that I dismissed the appeals.

a **LORD COOKE OF THORNDON.** My Lords, having had the advantage of reading in draft the speech of my noble and learned friend Lord Hobhouse of Woodborough, I agree with the reasons given by him for the dismissal of these appeals.

LORD HOBHOUSE OF WOODBOROUGH. My Lords, in March of this year b a Crown Court judge sitting in London held a preparatory hearing under s 29 of the Criminal Procedure and Investigations Act 1996 at the request of the parties to decide a question of the admissibility of evidence in connection with a prosecution of three defendants for serious alleged offences contrary to s 20 of the Misuse of Drugs Act 1971. The indictment contained three counts each charging all three defendants with assisting in the United Kingdom in the commission of c drug offences in European Union countries A and B contrary to the laws of those countries.

The Crown case is that the defendants (who are British citizens) had, together with X, a national of country A, and Y, a national of country B, (and presumably others) been concerned in the smuggling of a substantial quantity of a Class A d drug of a high purity into and out of country A, it is said with a view to its later being smuggled into the United Kingdom. The defendant P was alleged to have been the ringleader in the United Kingdom using the defendants Q and R as his 'employees'. Between October 1998 and January 1999 all three defendants made separate visits to country A and met (among others) X. Towards the end of January Q and R, it is alleged on P's instructions, collected the drugs from X in e country A and Q took it to country B and gave it to Y who worked on a ship so that he could bring it into England. Y was arrested in country B before he could leave and X was arrested in country A. The defendants were arrested in England.

The authorities in country A had suspected X of being concerned in drug trafficking for some time and in October 1998 the public prosecutor in country A f had lawfully obtained from an examining magistrate in country A an order authorising the interception of X's telephone calls on certain identified telephones which he was known to use. One of these was a mobile telephone which used a network in country A. The result was that, when he made or received calls on this telephone, they could be monitored by the country A authorities in that country even though he might at the time be in England or g elsewhere outside country A. The authorities in country A were thus able to record in that country telephone calls made or received by X anywhere using his mobile telephone or using one of the other identified land lines in country A which was covered by the order. Under the law of country A such orders were valid for four weeks and after the expiry of that period had to be renewed on fresh h applications to the magistrate. The prosecutor thereafter duly applied for and obtained the requisite renewals.

The intercepts from country A resulted in recordings being made of various telephone conversations between X and each of the defendants. The telephone calls were made from country A to the United Kingdom, or from the United j Kingdom to country A, or when X was using his mobile telephone while visiting England and both parties to the recorded conversation were in England, or when the relevant defendant was visiting country A and both parties were in that country. But in all cases the intercepts and recordings were made in country A in accordance with the law of that country.

Since these recorded conversations involved persons who appeared to be English and X had also been observed by the police of country A meeting persons whom they could not identify, the Prosecutor, with the approval of the magistrate, authorised the police to seek the assistance of the United Kingdom authorities. This co-operative approach paid off, ultimately leading to the arrests to which I have already referred and the seizure of the cocaine. The exchange of information was formalised in an exchange of requests between the English prosecuting authorities and the prosecuting authorities in country A in January 1999. The English request was sent pursuant to the provisions of the Criminal Justice (International Co-operation) Act 1990. By a document dated simply 'May 1999' addressed to 'The Competent Judicial Authorities of [country A]' and sent by a designated Crown prosecutor, he requested, inter alia, that officers of the National Crime Squad should be allowed to travel to country A and obtain all the interception material and evidence relating to the case of X which concerned the three defendants. The relevant recordings could not under the law of country A be lawfully released to the British authorities without an order of a judge of the relevant district court in country A. On 29 June 1999 a judge of that court made the requisite order and the recordings were then handed over. These recordings were included in the material disclosed to the defence in the English prosecutions and the Crown proposed to put them in evidence as part of the Crown case at the trial of the defendants.

It was in these circumstances that the question of the admissibility of these recordings was raised before the Crown Court judge. He heard evidence of how the intercepts had been authorised and the recordings made, of the law of country A and of the part played by the British police and how the recordings and transcripts had come into the possession of the Crown Prosecution Service. He rejected the defendants' submission that the recordings were inadmissible in English law and should be excluded from the evidence at the trial. He held that they were not made inadmissible by the Interception of Communications Act 1985 since that Act only applied to interceptions in this country. He followed the case of *R v Aujla* [1998] 2 Cr App R 16. He declined to exercise his discretion to exclude the evidence under s 78 of the Police and Criminal Evidence Act 1984.

As regards the law of country A, he found that 'the European Convention on Human Rights has been part of the law of country "A" for some years'; that the intercepts had been made with the prescribed judicial authority; and that—

> 'Intercepts of this kind are known to [the law of country A] as coercive measures and notwithstanding that they represent an invasion of privacy have been acceptable to the European Court in Strasbourg who have expressed themselves satisfied with the domestic remedies available to protect the individual in [country A] even though under [the law of country A] the content of the intercepted calls is admissible evidence in a criminal case.'

There had been no infringement of the requirements of the Convention for the Protection of Human Rights and Fundamental Freedoms (Rome, 4 November 1950; TS 71 (1953); Cmd 8969) (the convention). The intercepts had been lawful under the law of country A.

As regards the question of fairness under s 78, he referred to the fact that there was no criticism of the role of the police forces in either country, that the evidence was admissible in country A and had already been used in support of the successful prosecution of X and that it was intended to call X as a prosecution witness at the defendants' trial. He concluded that:

a 'The telephone transcripts provide important relevant probative and admissible evidence which the jury could and should consider in coming to their conclusions and to deprive them of that material would almost certainly result in a miscarriage of justice.'

He gave the defendants leave to appeal because he had considered himself bound by the decision in *R v Aujla* and the Court of Appeal (Criminal Division) might b wish to review that case.

In the Court of Appeal the defendants accepted that the law of country A complied with the convention but challenged the judge's finding that the intercepts had been in accordance with that law. The Court of Appeal considered the evidence and the arguments of counsel in support of this ground of appeal: c the Court of Appeal upheld the judge's finding. The defendants also submitted that whatever may have been the position under the law of country A it was contrary to the public policy of the United Kingdom as evidenced by the 1985 Act to admit evidence of intercepts in English proceedings no matter where the intercepts had been made. This overlapped with an argument presented by another counsel in support of the appeals that the protection provided by the d convention extended also to the use of private material lawfully obtained and that its use in English proceedings without express authorisation by English law constituted an infringement of the defendants' rights. The defendants submitted that *R v Aujla* should not be followed.

The Court of Appeal rejected these arguments. They reviewed the authorities, e applied what had been said by your Lordships' House in *R v Khan* [1996] 3 All ER 289, [1997] AC 558 and approved and followed *R v Aujla*. They upheld the judge's exercise of his discretion under s 78. They dismissed the appeals but, before they had delivered their reasons, the Court of Human Rights published its judgment in *Khan v UK* (2000) Times, 23 May. The Court of Appeal considered that what the Court of Human Rights had there said provided further support for their f approach to the interrelation of the convention and s 78. The Court of Appeal certified questions of general public importance and the defendants have, with leave, appealed to your Lordships' House.

Before your Lordships the defendants have accepted (as they were in practical terms bound to) the findings of fact of the judge upheld by the Court of Appeal; g similarly they were not in a position further to challenge the judge's exercise of his discretion under s 78 unless they could establish that it was vitiated by some error of principle or mistake of law. The defendants have thus argued their appeals upon the basis that, although the intercept evidence was properly obtained in accordance with the convention and the law of country A, its use in h the English trial of the defendants will be contrary to the policy of English law and to the convention. In relation to the policy of English law, they relied particularly upon *R v Preston* [1993] 4 All ER 638, [1994] 2 AC 130 and *Morgans v DPP* [2000] 2 All ER 522, [2000] 2 WLR 386. In relation to the convention, arguments are advanced under both arts 8 and 6. These articles provide:

j '*Article 8*

1. Everyone has the right to respect for his private and family life, his home and his correspondence.

2. There shall be no interference by a public authority with the exercise of this right except such as is in accordance with the law and is necessary in a democratic society in the interests of national security, public safety or the economic well-being of the country, for the prevention of disorder or crime,

for the protection of health or morals, or for the protection of the rights and freedoms of others.' a

'Article 6

1. In the determination of his civil rights and obligations or of any criminal charge against him, everyone is entitled to a fair and public hearing within a reasonable time by an independent and impartial tribunal established by law.' b

Paragraphs 2 and 3 of art 6 give more specific rights to those charged with criminal offences but do not impinge upon the question which your Lordships have to consider. The defendants also relied upon art 13 and ss 6 and 7 of the Human Rights Act 1998. These further arguments were dependent upon their establishing breaches of arts 8 or 6. The hearing, like that in the Court of Appeal, c was conducted on the basis that the 1998 Act had come fully into force since it was to be anticipated that the criminal proceedings would not have been concluded before it did.

At the conclusion of the hearing, at the request of all the parties and so that the criminal trial of the defendants could proceed without further adjournment, your d Lordships announced that they would report to the House that the appeals should be dismissed and the judgment of the Court of Appeal upheld. It remains for your Lordships to give their reasons for this conclusion. I will take the convention points first.

e

The convention: art 8

Before the passing of the 1985 Act, the power to intercept postal and telephone communications in this country was effectively without substantive legal regulation. Intercepts were carried out on the warrant of the Home Secretary. His power to authorise such intercepts was recognised in successive statutes but not otherwise defined. From time to time the interception of communications was the f subject of Parliamentary report as, for example, the Report of the Committee of Privy Councillors appointed to inquire into the interception of communications (1957)(Cmnd 283) under the chairmanship of Lord Birkett. They were impressed by the value of the work done by those carrying out the interceptions in safeguarding the security of the realm and the frustration of the activities of criminals. But they also accepted the view of 'all the authorities' that any disclosure g of the extent of the use of interceptions would impair their effectiveness and be contrary to the public interest (see, for example, para 119). Thus, the culture was that maintaining secrecy was the paramount consideration. This had the consequence that the intercepts were not used in criminal prosecutions nor disclosed in any other way. h

In 1977 an antique dealer, Mr James Malone, was prosecuted for receiving stolen goods. After two trials at which the jury could not agree, he was acquitted. But at his first trial there were found in one of the police witnesses' notebooks a note which appeared to be (and was) a transcript of a telephone intercept. Mr Malone then started civil proceedings in the Chancery Division to establish j the extent of the tapping which had taken place and obtain a declaration that it was unlawful (see *Malone v Comr of Police of the Metropolis (No 2)* [1979] 2 All ER 620, [1979] Ch 344). He failed to obtain the declaration he was seeking but Megarry V-C was openly critical of the lack of any statutory regulation of the power. Mr Malone then made a claim against the United Kingdom government in the Court of Human Rights alleging breaches of arts 8 and 13 (see *Malone v UK* a (1984) 7 EHRR 14). The court held that there had been a breach of art 8 because English law did not satisfy the qualitative test necessary to meet the requirement that any interference with the right of privacy must be 'in accordance with the law' (see (1984) 7 EHRR 14 at 45, 47 (paras 80 and 87)). The court (at 39–40 (para 66)) applied what it had said in *Sunday Times v UK* (1979) 2 EHRR 245 at 271 (para 49):

b '"First, the law must be adequately accessible: the citizen must be able to have an indication that it is adequate in the circumstances of the legal rules applicable to a given case. Secondly, a norm cannot be regarded as a 'law' unless it is formulated with sufficient precision to enable the citizen to regulate his conduct: he must be able—if need be with appropriate c advice—to foresee, to a degree that is reasonable in the circumstances, the consequences which a given action may entail."'

Rejecting the government's arguments, the court said:

'The Court would reiterate its opinion that the phrase "in accordance with d the law" does not merely refer back to domestic law but also relates to the quality of the law, requiring it to be compatible with the rule of law, which is expressly mentioned in the preamble to the Convention. The phrase thus implies—and this follows from the object and purpose of Article 8—that there must be a measure of legal protection in domestic law against arbitrary interferences by public authorities with the rights safeguarded by paragraph e 1. Especially where a power of the executive is exercised in secret, the risks of arbitrariness are evident. Undoubtedly, as the Government rightly suggested, the requirements of the Convention, notably in regard to foreseeability, cannot be exactly the same in the special context of interception of communications for the purposes of police investigations as they are where the object of the relevant law is to place restrictions on the conduct of f individuals. In particular, the requirement of foreseeability cannot mean that an individual should be enabled to foresee when the authorities are likely to intercept his communications so that he can adapt his conduct accordingly. Nevertheless, the law must be sufficiently clear in its terms to give citizens an adequate indication as to the circumstances in which and the conditions g on which public authorities are empowered to resort to this secret and potentially dangerous interference with the right to respect for private life and correspondence.' (See (1984) 7 EHRR 14 at 40–41 (para 67).)

This conclusion made it unnecessary for the court to rule upon the other points raised under art 8(2). However, it specifically accepted that in Great Britain h the increase in crime and particularly the growth in organised crime, the increasing sophistication of criminals and the ease and speed with which they can move about had made telephone interception an indispensable tool in the investigation and prevention of serious crime. But it was open to abuse.

j 'This being so, the resultant interference can only be regarded as "necessary in a democratic society" if the particular system of secret surveillance adopted contains adequate guarantees against abuse.' (See (1984) 7 EHRR 14 at 45 (para 81), citing *Klass v Federal Republic of Germany* (1978) 2 EHRR 214 at 232–233 (paras 49–50).)

This decision made it clear that the enactment of a statutory provision which was sufficiently accessible and precise was essential if the United Kingdom government was to comply with its obligations under the convention. Telephone interception was justifiable but must be based on legal provisions of the requisite quality which would preclude abuse. The 1985 Act was the government's response.

A similar decision was arrived at by the Court of Human Rights in relation to covert surveillance devices planted by the police on private property in the case of *Khan v UK* (2000) Times, 23 May. English law failed the qualitative test.

As explained earlier, it is now accepted that interception of the calls received and made by X on his mobile did not involve any breach of art 8. The intercepts were made in country A by the authorities of that country. The law of country A satisfied the requirements of the convention. The intercepts and the use made of them were subject to judicial supervision. Judicial authority to hand them over to the British prosecuting authorities was sought and given. Any criticisms which may be made of the telephone tapping laws of the United Kingdom are irrelevant. They do not apply to anything occurring in country A nor do they need to be invoked in order to justify what occurred there.

The defendants therefore based their argument upon what occurred in the United Kingdom, that is to say, the use made of the intercepts in the United Kingdom. The defendants relied upon the decision of the Court of Human Rights in *Amann v Switzerland* (16 February 2000, unreported). In October 1981 a telephone call was intercepted by a woman at the Soviet Embassy in Berne to Mr Amann ordering a depilatory device from him. It was the practice of the Swiss authorities at that time to carry out counter-intelligence surveillance measures in relation to the Soviet Embassy. This was legitimate. Mr Amann was investigated and the authorities were satisfied that his activities were wholly innocent; he had been involved fortuitously in a telephone conversation recorded in the course of surveillance measures directed against others. The grievance of Mr Amann arose because notwithstanding his non-involvement in any material activity, his name and some details were placed upon a card and stored in the national security index. Nine years later the existence of this card index became public knowledge and led to his making a claim against the Swiss government, first unsuccessfully in the Federal Court and then successfully in the Court of Human Rights. The Court of Human Rights held, in para 67 of its judgment, that the details on the card related to his private life and, in para 69, that—

> 'the storing by a public authority of data relating to the private life of an individual amounts to an interference within the meaning of art 8. The subsequent use of the stored information has no bearing on that finding …'

Neither the creation of the card nor its storage were 'in accordance with the law' (see para 80).

It is not in dispute that the use made of an intercept can amount to an 'interference' for the purposes of art 8. But it will be appreciated that what has occurred in the present case is very different from what occurred in *Amann v Switzerland*. In the present case the relevant information, having been lawfully obtained for the purpose of assisting the prosecution of alleged smugglers of Class A drugs, has not been used for any other purpose and has not been kept for longer than is necessary for that purpose. All that has been done has been done pursuant to statutory authority and subject to judicial supervision. No qualitative criticism can be made of the relevant statutory provisions. No breach of art 8 has been shown. The Court of Appeal's conclusion was correct.

a It will be necessary to refer to a further argument which was advanced by the defendants in relation to art 8(2). It supported a submission that it is not 'necessary' for the intercepts to be used for these prosecutions because equivalent intercepts obtained in England under English law would not be used for prosecutions (see *R v Preston* [1993] 4 All ER 638, [1994] 2 AC 130 and *Morgans v DPP* [2000] 2 All ER 522, [2000] 2 WLR 386). I will revert to this point when b discussing those authorities and the policy argument.

The convention: art 6

The right in issue is the right to a fair trial—a fair hearing. This involves the same criterion as is applied in s 78 of the 1984 Act:

c '*Exclusion of unfair evidence.*—(1) In any proceedings the court may refuse to allow evidence on which the prosecution proposes to rely to be given if it appears to the court that, having regard to all the circumstances, including the circumstances in which the evidence was obtained, the admission of the evidence would have such an adverse effect on the fairness of the d proceedings that the court ought not to admit it.

(2) Nothing in this section shall prejudice any rule of law requiring a court to exclude evidence.'

As was observed by your Lordships' House in agreeing with the speech of Lord Nolan in *R v Khan* [1996] 3 All ER 289, [1997] AC 558, s 78 requires the judge, e when he exercises his discretion, to have regard to, among other things, the circumstances in which the evidence was obtained. The judge must take into account that the evidence was obtained by intercepting telephone conversations but he must base his decision upon the effect the admission of the evidence would have on the fairness of the trial.

f The Court of Human Rights has explained the inter-relation of arts 8 and 6 in the same way. The leading authority is *Schenk v Switzerland* (1988) 13 EHRR 242. The allegation against Mr Schenk was that he hired a man to kill his wife. Part of the evidence against him was a tape recording of a telephone conversation between Mr Schenk and the man he had hired. The tape recording had been made by the man. The Swiss courts admitted the evidence. Mr Schenk argued g that the evidence had been obtained unlawfully and its admission made his trial unfair in breach of art 6. The Swiss government did not dispute that the recording had been obtained unlawfully. The Court of Human Rights said (at 265–266):

h '46. While Article 6 of the Convention guarantees the right to a fair trial, it does not lay down any rules on the admissibility of evidence as such, which is therefore primarily a matter for regulation under national law. The Court therefore cannot exclude as a matter of principle and in the abstract that unlawfully obtained evidence of the present kind may be admissible. It has only to ascertain whether Mr. Schenk's trial as a whole was fair.

j 47. Like the Commission it notes first of all that the rights of the defence were not disregarded. The applicant was not unaware that the recording complained of was unlawful because it had not been ordered by the competent judge. He had the opportunity—which he took—of challenging its authenticity and opposing its use, having initially agreed that it should be heard. The fact that his attempts were unsuccessful makes no difference.'

The Court of Human Rights also emphasised the fact that the Swiss courts, besides having the recording, had the man as a witness to give evidence of what Mr Schenk had said during the telephone conversation. The Court of Human Rights also rejected an argument that the *use* made of the recording, that is to say the use of it as evidence at Mr Schenk's trial, was contrary to art 8 (see (1998) 13 EHRR 242 at 268 (paras 52–53)). The Court of Human Rights said that that question was subsumed in the answer it had given to the complaint under art 6. Mr Schenk's complaints failed.

This decision of the Court of Human Rights therefore provides a highly persuasive authority in favour of the Crown. The critical question is the fairness of the trial. Questions of the admissibility of evidence are not governed by art 8. The fair use of intercept evidence at a trial is not a breach of art 6 even if the evidence was unlawfully obtained. It is a cogent factor in favour of the admission of intercept evidence that one of the parties to the relevant conversation is going to be a witness at the trial and give evidence of what was said during it.

Later judgments of the Court of Human Rights contain statements to the same effect. In *Teixeira de Castro v Portugal* (1998) 28 EHRR 101, an *agent provocateur* case, the court said (at 114–115):

> '34. The court reiterates that the admissibility of evidence is primarily a matter for regulation by national law and as a general rule it is for the national courts to assess the evidence before them. The court's task under the Convention is not to give a ruling as to whether statements of witnesses were properly admitted as evidence, but rather to ascertain whether the proceedings as a whole, including the way in which evidence was taken, were fair.'

Khan v UK (2000) Times, 23 May was the Court of Human Rights judgment which followed on from the decision of your Lordships' House in *R v Khan* [1996] 3 All ER 289, [1997] AC 558. Three relevant complaints were made by Mr Khan. Firstly he said that the United Kingdom government had breached his rights under art 8. The police had installed covert listening devices on private property without the knowledge or consent of the owner. The Court of Human Rights held that this had not been done 'in accordance with the law' as the relevant law lacked the requisite clarity and therefore qualitatively failed to meet the *Malone* test (see *Malone v UK* (1984) 7 EHRR 14). The complaint under art 8 was therefore upheld. This complaint had not been seriously contested by the government and, indeed, your Lordships' House had proceeded on the basis that there had been a breach of art 8.

Secondly, Mr Khan complained that there had been a breach of art 6 as a tape recording obtained in breach of art 8 had been admitted in evidence against him at his trial. This complaint was rejected. Mr Khan recognised that the fact that the evidence had been obtained in breach of art 8 did not require the conclusion that it should be excluded at the trial but argued that there must be an effective procedure during the trial by which the defendant can challenge its admissibility, that the trial court should have regard to the nature of the violation and that, in distinction to *Schenk v Switzerland* (1988) 13 EHRR 242, the obtaining of the conviction was effectively based upon the unlawfully obtained evidence. In para 34 of the judgment the Court of Human Rights repeated what it had said in previous judgments. The admissibility of evidence was primarily a matter for regulation under national law.

a 'It is not the role of the court to determine, as a matter of principle, whether particular types of evidence—for example, unlawfully obtained evidence—may be admissible or, indeed, whether the applicant was guilty or not. The question which must be answered is whether the proceedings as a whole, including the way in which the evidence was obtained, were fair. This involves an examination of the "unlawfulness" in question and, where b violation of another convention right is concerned, the nature of the violation found.'

Having recognised the differences between the case before it and *Schenk v Switzerland*, the Court of Human Rights continued:

c '38. The central question in the present case is whether the proceedings as a whole were fair. With specific reference to the admission of the contested tape recording, the court notes that, as in the *Schenk* case, the applicant had ample opportunity to challenge both the authenticity and the use of the recording. He did not challenge its authenticity, but challenged its use at the "*voire dire*" and again before the Court of Appeal and the House of Lords. d The court notes that at each level of jurisdiction the domestic courts assessed the effect of admission of the evidence on the fairness of the trial by reference to s 78 of the 1984 Act, and the courts discussed, amongst other matters, the non-statutory basis for the surveillance. The fact that the applicant was at each step unsuccessful makes no difference (see the judgment in *Schenk v* e *Switzerland* (1988) 13 EHRR 242 at 266 (para 47)).

39. The court would add that it is clear that, had the domestic courts been of the view that the admission of the evidence would have given rise to substantive unfairness, they would have had a discretion to exclude it under s 78 of the 1984 Act.

f 40. In these circumstances, the court finds that the use at the applicant's trial of the secretly taped material did not conflict with the requirements of fairness guaranteed by art 6(1) of the convention.'

It should be noted that the Court of Human Rights again emphasised that the defendant is not entitled to have the unlawfully obtained evidence excluded g simply because it has been so obtained. What he is entitled to is an opportunity to challenge its use and admission in evidence and a judicial assessment of the effect of its admission upon the fairness of the trial as is provided for by s 78.

Mr Khan's third complaint was that his right to an effective remedy under art 13 had been violated. The Court of Human Rights upheld this complaint h because the remedy provided—complaint to the Police Complaints Authority—was not a right of recourse to an independent body and therefore was not an *effective* remedy. The Court of Human Rights emphasised that this was a separate question from anything which happened at the criminal trial. It was not within the power of the criminal courts to provide such a remedy. Section 78 was j concerned with the fairness of the trial not with providing a remedy for a breach of art 8. The court's decision on the complaint under art 13 further confirms and reinforces its decision and reasoning in relation to art 6.

The decision of the Court of Human Rights is accordingly to the like effect to that of your Lordships' House when it was considering the appeal of Mr Khan (see *R v Khan* [1996] 3 All ER 289, [1997] AC 558). An assessment and adjudication under s 78 is the appropriate and right way in which to respond to an application to exclude evidence on the ground of a breach of a right to privacy. Lord Nicholls of Birkenhead was right to conclude his speech by saying: a

> '... the discretionary powers of the trial judge to exclude evidence march hand in hand with art 6.1 of the [convention]. Both are concerned to ensure that those facing criminal charges receive a fair hearing ... In the present case the decision of the European Court of Human Rights in *Schenk v Switzerland* (1988) 13 EHRR 242 confirms that the use at a criminal trial of material obtained in breach of the rights of privacy enshrined in art 8 does not of itself mean that the trial is unfair. Thus the European Court of Human Rights case law on this issue leads to the same conclusion as English law.' (See [1996] 3 All ER 289 at 302–303, [1997] AC 558 at 583.) b

The decision of your Lordships' House was arrived at at a time before the 1998 Act had been enacted let alone introduced into Parliament. Therefore the convention did not then have the place it now has in English law. The importance of the Court of Human rights decision is that it confirms that the direct operation of arts 8 and 6 does not invalidate their Lordships' conclusion or alter the vital role of s 78 as the means by which questions of the use of evidence obtained in breach of art 8 are to be resolved at a criminal trial. The criterion to be applied is the criterion of fairness in art 6 which is likewise the criterion to be applied by the judge under s 78. Similarly, the Court of Human Rights decision that any remedy for a breach of art 8 lies outside the scope of the criminal trial and that art 13 does not require a remedy for a breach of art 8 to be given within that trial shows that their Lordships were right to say that a breach of art 8 did not require the exclusion of evidence. Such an exclusion, if any, would have to come about because of the application of art 6 and s 78. c d e

The defendants' argument under art 6 also fails and does so independently of their argument under art 8.

f

The policy of English law

The other way in which the defendants put their case was to submit that there is a rule of policy of English law as demonstrated by legislation and the decisions in *R v Preston* [1993] 4 All ER 638, [1994] 2 AC 130 and *Morgans v DPP* [2000] 2 All ER 522, [2000] 2 WLR 386 that intercept and surveillance evidence should not be used at criminal trials. This rule applies, it is submitted, wherever the interception takes place and regardless of by whom it was carried out. It is accepted that none of the United Kingdom Acts has a relevant extraterritorial application or itself precludes the use of this evidence at the defendants' trial. The decision of the Divisional Court in *R v Governor of Belmarsh Prison, ex p Martin* [1995] 2 All ER 548, [1995] 1 WLR 412 that foreign intercept evidence may be used in support of extradition proceedings is very much in point. The 1985 Act did not apply to the relevant intercepts; therefore the exclusionary provision, s 9, did not apply either. The Divisional Court also rejected the argument that it was a rule of English law derived from the Act and *R v Preston* that intercept evidence was not admissible in an English court. g h j

Any developed society has to have a scheme for the surveillance of those who are liable to attack or prey upon the society or its members. Such schemes have throughout history included the interception of communications and in modern times this has included telecommunications. This in turn has led on to the need for laws to limit and control such interceptions particularly where publicly provided or sponsored means of communication are involved. Since the Royal

Mail came into existence it has been a criminal offence to interfere with the mail. The primary purpose of the 1985 Act, despite the apparent universality of its title, was to update and revise in statutory form laws which prohibited the interference with communications by post and public telecommunications systems and the exceptions to that prohibition. This then leads on to the question: on what basis is the government to be permitted to carry out the surveillance necessary for the health and survival of the society in which we live? Section 2 of the Act accordingly provided for the Secretary of State to issue warrants authorising and requiring interceptions of communications by post or public telecommunication systems to be carried out. This section limits the grounds upon which the Home Secretary can do so. One ground to which it will be necessary to refer again is s 2(2)(b): 'for the purpose of preventing or detecting serious crime'.

But then a further question arises. If the interception results, as no doubt will not infrequently be the case, in the obtaining of evidence which will assist in the conviction of criminals, are the authorities going to use that evidence in court to assist in the prosecution of the criminals concerned? Other things being equal all relevant and probative evidence is admissible. But where surveillance evidence is concerned the use of the evidence comes at a price. If the fairness of the trial is to be preserved the defendant must be permitted to probe the evidence and question the witnesses who come to court to provide the proof. This means that disclosure has to be made and the secrecy of the means and extent of the surveillance have to be sacrificed. This is a real problem for those involved in the prevention and detection of crime as the cases involving informers and concealed cameras have shown. The solution traditionally adopted by the authorities has been to elect for the maintenance of secrecy and to prefer this to the use of covertly obtained material in court. This was the choice made in the 1985 Act. Section 9 of the Act prevents any questions being asked in court which tend to suggest that an official may or may not have had authority under the Act to intercept a communication. In making this choice the government were following the same approach, making secrecy the paramount consideration, as they had urged upon the Birkett Committee in 1957 and was accepted by that committee. Other provisions of the Act, most notably s 6 limiting the dissemination and requiring the destruction of intercept material, are also designed to preserve secrecy.

The oblique wording of s 9 is clearly directed to preserving the secrecy of any surveillance operation covered by the Act. Section 9 does not as such say that the intercept evidence may not be used. It was this oblique method of drafting which gave rise to the two cases on which the defendants rely and to which I must now refer. The first was *R v Preston* decided in 1993 in relation to a telephone intercept in 1989 which together with information supplied by an informer had led to the arrest of the defendants. At their trial the *defendants* demanded the disclosure of the identity of the informer and the contents of the intercept. Both requests were refused by the prosecution, as regards the intercept information on the ground that the relevant material had been destroyed as was required by s 6 of the Act. The defendants then submitted that they could not have a fair trial without having such disclosure. This submission was not accepted and the defendants were convicted. Their appeals failed.

There had been an earlier decision of the Court of Appeal in *R v Effik* (1992) 95 Cr App R 427 which had in effect held that intercept evidence was admissible in criminal trials, giving a restricted interpretation to s 9 and declining to infer from the oblique wording of that section that to admit the evidence would be contrary to the scheme of the Act. In *R v Preston* [1993] 4 All ER 638, [1994] 2 AC 130 your Lordships' House overruled *R v Effik*. As Lord Templeman said, ss 6 and 9 of the Act make it—

> 'impossible for a record of a telephone conversation to be given in evidence and … impossible for evidence to be given that a warrant was issued for a telephone conversation to be intercepted.' (See [1993] 4 All ER 638 at 643, [1994] 2 AC 130 at 140.)

Accordingly it was accepted that the drafting of the Act necessarily had the result that the prosecution could not rely upon the intercept evidence; but the House also held that although not admissible in evidence the material would still have had to have been disclosed if it were not for s 6 and the fact that it had been destroyed. The leading speech was that of Lord Mustill. He recognised:

> 'Those who perform the interceptions wish to minimise the dissemination of the fact that they have been performed, since it is believed that this would diminish the value of activities which are by their nature clandestine. We need not consider to what extent this preoccupation with secrecy at all costs is soundly based for it has been treated as axiomatic for decades, if not longer.' (See [1993] 4 All ER 638 at 648, [1994] 2 AC 130 at 146.)

He came back to what he described as the plain intent and wording of the Act:

> 'The need for surveillance and the need to keep it secret are undeniable. So also is the need to protect to the feasible maximum the privacy of those whose conversations are overheard without their consent. Hence ss 2 and 6. These policies are in flat contradiction to current opinions on the "transparency" of the trial process. Something has to give way, and the history, structure and terms of the statute leave me in little doubt that this must be the duty to give complete disclosure of unused materials.' (See [1993] 4 All ER 638 at 669, [1994] 2 AC 130 at 168–169.)

The argument had included different submissions as to the construction of s 2(2)(b): 'preventing or detecting serious crime'. Did this include obtaining evidence for use at a trial? Construing the Act as a whole, in particular having regard to ss 6 and 9 and parliamentary material, Lord Mustill concluded that a narrow reading of s 2(2)(b) must be adopted:

> 'If the purpose of Parliament was to allow the intercept materials to become part of the prosecution process it is hard to see any point in a provision which would make it wholly or at least partially (according to how [s 9] is read) impossible to use them in that process … The narrower reading of s 2 is strongly supported by the history of the Act. I need not repeat this. The criticisms in *Malone v UK* (1984) 7 EHRR 14 which prompted the government to change its mind and legislate were directed not to the long-established practice but to its inaccessibility, imprecision and lack of formal safeguards. The Act was plainly designed to put these matters right, and I can see no reason to suppose that the government had suddenly and spontaneously decided to go much further and overturn the practice which had persisted for decades of separating the process of surveillance from the prosecution of offenders.' (See [1993] 4 All ER 638 at 667, [1994] 2 AC 130 at 167.)

a This then was a decision upon material specifically falling within the scope of the 1985 Act—an interception of a telephone conversation. The construction of the Act adopted by your Lordships' House was that the dominant principle guiding the interpretation of the provisions of the Act was the policy of preserving the secrecy of the surveillance operations to which the Act applied and, to that end, preventing as far as possible any evidence relating to such b operations ever reaching the public domain. The speech of Lord Mustill does not support the submission that there is a policy that defendants should be protected from having incriminated themselves in intercepted telephone calls. The decision by the House of Lords that 'metering' evidence, that is to say evidence of what calls were made to what numbers as opposed to what was said during such calls, is admissible confirms the true scope of the decision. As Lord Mustill ([1993] 4 All ER c 638 at 670, [1994] 2 AC 130 at 170) put it: 'Parliament has grasped the nettle and put the interests of secrecy first.'

In *R v Preston,* the telephone intercept was expressly covered by the 1985 Act. Where the Act did not apply surveillance evidence was in principle admissible subject to s 78 and the ordinary safeguards. *R v Effik* continued to be treated as an d authority and the clear effect of the speeches in *R v Preston* was overlooked. The matter was brought back before your Lordships' House in *Morgans v DPP* [2000] 2 All ER 522, [2000] 2 WLR 386. There was a further complication. The cases (*R v Rasool* [1997] 4 All ER 439, [1997] 1 WLR 1092 and *R v Owen* [1999] 1 WLR 949) which had appeared to reinstate *R v Effik* had concerned intercepts of conversations where it was the Crown case that one of the parties to the e intercepted conversation had (or, at least, was reasonably believed to have) given his consent to the intercept so taking the intercept outside the scope of s 1 of the 1985 Act. Those cases had held that the evidence was admissible even though there was an issue about the existence of the consent (or reasonable belief). Your Lordships' House held that s 9 and the speeches in *R v Preston* [1993] 4 All ER 638, f [1994] 2 AC 130 meant that the evidence could not be given because questions could not be asked about the consent and belief without tending to suggest that an offence had been committed under s 1 of the Act. Therefore, just as intercepts under a warrant were inadmissible, so also were intercepts said to have been by consent. *R v Rasool* and *R v Owen* were overruled. The broad interpretation of s 9 in *R v Preston* and its implication for the exclusion of intercept evidence falling g with the scope of the Act were confirmed.

Neither *R v Preston* nor *Morgans v DPP* support any principle of exclusion of evidence independently of the 1985 Act. Where as here, the intercept was made in a foreign country by the authorities of that country and the 1985 Act accordingly has no application, the reasoning of *R v Preston* and *Morgans v DPP* h does not apply either. The law of country A under which these intercepts were made does not treat secrecy as paramount; it permits, subject to judicial supervision, the use of intercepts in evidence. There is no basis for the argument that there is a rule of English public policy which makes this evidence, which is admissible in country A, inadmissible in England.

j There remains the point to which I said I would revert. It was argued that if it was not necessary in our democratic society for intercept evidence obtained under the 1985 Act to be admissible, it could not be necessary for intercept evidence obtained abroad to be admissible. There are two answers to this argument. First, the conclusion does not follow. In this country it is, in the judgment of the government, the necessity to have a fully effective interception system which creates the necessity for secrecy and consequently the need to keep the evidence of it out of the public domain. But where secrecy is not required, the necessity is that all relevant and probative evidence be available to assist in the apprehension and conviction of criminals and to ensure that their trial is fair. The latter necessity exists in both cases but in the former case it is trumped by the greater necessity for secrecy, as the speeches in *R v Preston* explain. Secondly, art 8(2) is concerned with justifiable and unjustifiable interferences with the exercise of the art 8(1) right. It is not an abstract question. In the present case it is necessary that, the evidence having been obtained, it be used in England as it has been in country A. This is further demonstrated by the fact that, other things being equal, it is necessary that the evidence be disclosed to the defence (as it has been) and that it be available to be referred to when X comes to give evidence. The tape recordings and transcripts (about the accuracy of which, be it said, there is no dispute) will be the best evidence of what was said. The fairness of the trial of these defendants requires that the evidence be admissible.

There is a related point which should also be referred to. Section 2(2)(b) of the 1985 Act uses the expression 'for the purpose of preventing or detecting serious crime'. In *R v Preston* that expression was construed as not extending to the obtaining of evidence for use in the prosecution of criminals. A similar expression is used in art 8(2)—'for the prevention of disorder or crime'. The expression used in the convention is wider and is not limited by its context as is the statutory expression. The breadth of the expression in the convention is confirmed by the Court of Human Rights judgments to which I have referred, particularly that in the case of *Khan v UK* (2000) Times, 23 May.

My Lords, it follows from what I have said that the appeals had to be dismissed. The case of *R v Aujla* [1998] 2 Cr App R 16 was rightly decided. The decision of the Court of Human Rights in *Khan v UK* shows that the coming into effect of the 1998 Act does not invalidate in the relevant respects the decision of your Lordships' House in that case and that s 78 is an appropriate safeguard of the fairness of the trial.

Appeals dismissed.

Kate O'Hanlon Barrister.

a

Ashurst v Pollard and another

COURT OF APPEAL, CIVIL DIVISION
KENNEDY, POTTER AND JONATHAN PARKER LJJ
27 OCTOBER, 21 NOVEMBER 2000

b

Conflict of laws – Jurisdiction – Title to foreign immovables – Bankrupt owning land in Portugal – English court ordering sale of Portuguese land on application by trustee in bankruptcy – Whether proceedings bankruptcy proceedings for purposes of jurisdiction convention – Whether proceedings falling within exclusive jurisdiction of Portuguese courts as c *proceedings concerning rights in rem in immovable property – Civil Jurisdiction and Judgments Act 1982, Sch 1, arts 1, 16.*

The appellants, a husband and wife, jointly owned a property in Portugal. After the husband was made bankrupt in England, his trustee in bankruptcy sought an order for the sale of the property with vacant possession. The district judge d granted the order, and the bankrupt and his wife appealed. They contended that the proceedings fell within the exclusive jurisdiction of the Portuguese courts since they had 'as their object rights in rem in immovable property' within the meaning of art 16(1)[a] of the Brussels Convention on Jurisdiction and the Enforcement of Judgments in Civil and Commercial Matters 1968 (as set out in Sch 1 to the Civil Jurisdiction and Judgments Act 1982). For his part, the trustee contended that the e proceedings were bankruptcy proceedings within the meaning of art 1[b] of the convention, and therefore fell outside the convention's scope. The judge rejected that contention and held that the order for sale was precluded by art 16(1) since it purported to have effect against the whole world. He nevertheless concluded that art 16(1) was no bar to the enforcement of an English trust over land held f abroad, and that accordingly it did not preclude the court from compelling the bankrupt to complete the trustee's title by an appropriately-drafted order in personam, requiring the appellants to sell the Portuguese property at the best price reasonably obtainable or requiring the bankrupt to convey the property to the trustee. The judge therefore dismissed the appeal, and the bankrupt and his wife appealed to the Court of Appeal. The trustee cross-appealed from the judge's g decision that the proceedings did not fall within the bankruptcy exception to the convention.

Held – (1) Proceedings fell within the bankruptcy exception in art 1 of the convention only if bankruptcy was the principal subject matter of those proceedings. h The mere fact that the claimant happened to be a trustee in bankruptcy could not be sufficient to bring the proceedings within the exception. It followed that the proceedings in the instant case did not fall within the bankruptcy exception, and that accordingly the convention applied (see p 81 *a* to *e* and p 87 *f*, post); *Re Hayward (decd)* [1997] 1 All ER 32 approved.

j (2) In deciding whether art 16 applied in a particular case, the court had to give that article a restrictive interpretation since its effect was to override the parties' choice of forum. Consideration had to be given to the rationale underlying art 16, namely the proper administration of justice, on the footing that the courts of the

a Article 16, so far as material, is set out at p 77 *j* to p 78 *a*, post
b Article 1, so far as material, is set out at p 77 *j*, post

contracting state in which the property was situated would be best placed to conduct any factual investigation which might be required, and to apply local law and practice. It was therefore material to consider whether the proceedings involved a factual investigation which was best carried out by the courts of the state in which the property was situated, and/or whether questions of local law and practice were raised. Moreover, the expression 'which have as their object' in art 16(1) was synonymous with 'which have as their principal subject matter', and 'subject matter' was not to be confused with 'aim' or 'purpose'. In the instant case, in so far as the court was minded to make orders in personam along the lines suggested by the judge, the rationale underlying art 16(1) did not apply since no issue arose as to the factual situation in Portugal, and the proceedings involved no question of Portuguese law or practice. Nor did the proceeding seek to assert any property right against third parties. Rather, they raised personal issues as between the trustee on the one hand and the appellants on the other. Moreover, it was irrelevant that the trustee's ultimate aim or purpose in prosecuting the proceedings was to effect a change in the ownership of the property by achieving its sale. What had to be looked at was the subject matter of the proceedings. The fact that the resolution of a dispute as to personal rights might impact upon property rights enforceable against third parties did not lead to the conclusion that the subject matter of the proceedings for the purposes of art 16(1) was rights in rem. It followed that the proceedings fell outside that provision, and that therefore they were not subject to the exclusive jurisdiction of the Portuguese courts. There was no jurisdictional or other objection to making the orders, and accordingly the appeal would be dismissed (see p 85 *g* to p 86 *d*, p 87 *b* and *d* to *f*, post); *Webb v Webb* Case C-294/92 [1994] 3 All ER 32 applied; *Re Hayward (decd)* [1997] 1 All ER 32 distinguished.

Decision of Jacob J [2000] 2 All ER 772 affirmed.

Notes

For the scope of the Brussels Convention and for jurisdiction under the convention in respect of immovable property, see 8(1) *Halsbury's Laws* (4th edn reissue) paras 626–627.

For the Civil Jurisdiction and Judgments Act 1982, Sch 1, arts 1, 16, see 11 *Halsbury's Statutes* (4th edn) (2000 reissue) 1183, 1188.

Cases referred to in judgments

Duijnstee v Goderbauer Case 288/82 [1983] ECR 3663.
Gourdain v Nadler Case 133/78 [1977] ECR 733.
Hayward (decd), Re [1997] 1 All ER 32, [1997] Ch 45, [1996] 3 WLR 674.
Reichert v Dresdner Bank Case C-115/88 [1990] ECR I-27.
Sanders v Van der Putte Case 73/77 [1977] ECR 2383.
Webb v Webb Case C-294/92 [1994] 3 All ER 911, [1994] QB 696, [1994] 3 WLR 801, [1994] ECR I-1717, ECJ.

Case also cited or referred to in skeleton arguments

Singh v Official Receiver [1997] BPIR 530.

Appeal

By notice dated 10 March 2000 David Charles Pollard and Mary Louisa Pollard appealed with permission of Jacob J from his decision on 3 February 2000 ([2000] 2 All ER 772) dismissing their appeal from the order of District Judge Lay made at a the Brighton County Court on 4 October 1999 on an application by Christopher R Ashurst, Mr Pollard's trustee in bankruptcy, that a property in Portugal owned by the appellants be sold with vacant possession, that the conduct of the sale be given to the trustee, that the appellants concur with the trustee in such a sale, that they do all things necessary to procure the sale of the property with vacant possession and that they give vacant possession forthwith. The facts are set out in b the judgment of Jonathan Parker LJ.

Sebastian Prentis (instructed by *Harkavys*) for Mr and Mrs Pollard.
David Marks (instructed by *Lita Gale*) for the trustee.

c *Cur adv vult*

21 November 2000. The following judgments were delivered.

JONATHAN PARKER LJ (giving the first judgment at the invitation of Kennedy LJ).

d *Introduction*

1. Mr David Pollard and his wife Mrs Mary Pollard jointly owned a property in Portugal. On 26 October 1993 a bankruptcy order was made against Mr Pollard. On 31 August 1994 Mr Christopher Ashurst, a licensed insolvency practitioner, was appointed as Mr Pollard's trustee in bankruptcy (the trustee). On 20 September 1999 e the trustee issued an application in the Brighton County Court in bankruptcy, joining Mr and Mrs Pollard as respondents and seeking an order for the sale of the Portuguese property with vacant possession, and consequential relief. On 4 October 1999 District Judge Lay made the order sought.

2. Mr and Mrs Pollard appealed against the District Judge's order, on the ground that by virtue of art 16(1) of the Convention on Jurisdiction and the Enforcement of f Judgments in Civil and Commercial Matters (Brussels, 27 September 1968 (Cmnd 7395)) (the convention), which was incorporated into United Kingdom domestic law by s 2(1) of the Civil Jurisdiction and Judgments Act 1982, the Portuguese courts have exclusive jurisdiction to hear and determine the trustee's claim.

3. On 3 February 2000 Jacob J handed down judgment dismissing the appeal g ([2000] 2 All ER 772). Mr and Mrs Pollard now appeal to this court, pursuant to permission granted by Jacob J.

4. It is common ground that nothing turns for present purposes on the fact that the property is in joint ownership.

h *The convention*

5. The only articles of the convention which are material for present purposes are arts 1 and 16.

6. Article 1 provides that the convention applies in civil and commercial matters, subject to a number of exceptions including:

j '... bankruptcy, proceedings relating to the winding-up of insolvent companies or other legal persons, judicial arrangements, compositions and analogous proceedings ...'

7. Article 16 is in the following terms (so far as material):

'The following courts shall have exclusive jurisdiction, regardless of domicile:

(1)(a) in proceedings which have as their object rights in rem in immovable property ... the courts of the Contracting State in which the property is situated; (b) [exception in relation to certain tenancies of immovable property] ...

(3) in proceedings which have as their object the validity of entries in public registers, the courts of the Contracting State in which the register is kept ...'

The Insolvency Act 1986

8. Section 283(1)(a) of the 1986 Act provides that the bankrupt's estate for bankruptcy purposes includes 'all property belonging to or vested in the bankrupt at the commencement of the bankruptcy'.

9. 'Property' is defined in s 436 as including: 'money, goods, things in action, land and every description of property *wherever situated*' (my emphasis).

10. Section 306 of the 1986 Act provides as follows (so far as material):

'(1) The bankrupt's estate shall vest in the trustee immediately on his appointment taking effect ...

(2) Where any property which is ... comprised in the bankrupt's estate vests in the trustee ... it shall so vest without any conveyance, assignment or transfer.'

11. Thus, under the 1986 Act Mr Pollard's joint ownership interest in the Portuguese property formed part of his estate for bankruptcy purposes and vested automatically in the trustee on his appointment, without the need for any further formalities. However, the vesting provisions of the 1986 Act plainly cannot effect a change in the Portuguese register of title, which continues to record Mr and Mrs Pollard as the joint owners of the property.

The judgment of Jacob J

12. Two issues were raised before Jacob J. The first issue was whether (as the trustee contended) the proceedings were excepted from the application of the convention by virtue of the inclusion of 'bankruptcy' among the exceptions in art 1. The second and more substantial issue was, as already indicated, whether (as Mr and Mrs Pollard contended) the Portuguese courts have exclusive jurisdiction to hear and determine the trustee's claim. On this second issue it was Mr and Mrs Pollard's case that art 16(1) applies to the proceedings, alternatively that under domestic law the English court has no jurisdiction to make orders relating to trust property held abroad.

13. On the first issue, Jacob J held that the proceedings did not fall within the 'bankruptcy' exception in art 1. He expressed his reasons as follows:

'These are proceedings consequential upon the bankruptcy—not proceedings about whether or not the debtor should be made bankrupt. The question of bankruptcy has already been determined. Moreover the claim made is not a special bankruptcy remedy—it is just a property claim.' (See [2000] 2 All ER 772 at 776 (para 13).)

14. In support of that conclusion, Jacob J cited passages from the judgment of Rattee J in *Re Hayward (decd)* [1997] 1 All ER 32, [1997] Ch 45 and of the Court of Justice of the European Communities in *Gourdain v Nadler* Case 133/78 [1977] ECR 733.

a 15. Jacob J accordingly held in favour of Mr and Mrs Pollard on the first issue. The trustee has served a respondent's notice in respect of the judge's conclusion on the first issue.

16. On the second issue, Jacob J concluded that the order for sale sought by the trustee purported to have effect against all the world, and as such was precluded by art 16(1). However, he went on to conclude, relying on the decision of the b Court of Justice in *Webb v Webb* Case C-294/92 [1994] 3 All ER 911, [1994] ECR I-1717, that the case did not turn on the form of the relief sought; and that where an English trust exists over land held abroad, art 16(1) is no bar to enforcement of that trust. On that basis, he held that art 16(1) did not prevent the bankrupt being compelled to complete the trustee's title. He said (at 777 (para 18)):

c 'There is no doubt that English law regards the Portuguese landholding as vested in the trustee. To the extent that the trustee's title has not been perfected, the bankrupt is, by English law, holding it for the trustee. So the bankrupt can be compelled to complete the trustee's title or do any other act in relation to the land at the trustee's direction. Any such order, provided it is in personam, is an order which the English court can make having, as it does, d jurisdiction over the bankrupt who is domiciled here.'

17. Jacob J then went on to conclude that an order in personam against Mr and Mrs Pollard directing them to sell the Portuguese property at the best price reasonably obtainable would not be within art 16(1). The judge also canvassed the possibility of an order being made against Mr Pollard directing him to convey e the property to the trustee (by which I take the judge to mean an order directing Mr Pollard to effect a transfer of the property according to Portuguese law), commenting that if that were done the trustee could effect his own sale in Portugal under Portuguese law.

18. The judge then turned to the alternative submission made on behalf of f Mr and Mrs Pollard to the effect that the court has no jurisdiction to make orders in relation to trust property held abroad. It was submitted that although s 14 of the Trusts of Land and Appointment of Trustees Act 1996 confers jurisdiction on the court to regulate the performance by trustees of their functions, the Act extends only to England and Wales (see s 27(3)). The judge accepted that that was self-evidently so, but concluded that it was irrelevant. He continued (at 778 (para 20)):

g 'What the 1996 Act does not say is that the court cannot act in relation to trust property held abroad or that similar orders as can be made under the 1996 Act cannot be made by virtue of the court's jurisdiction over property held under an English trust.'

h 19. Jacob J accordingly held in favour of the trustee on the second issue, and dismissed Mr and Mrs Pollard's appeal.

The arguments on this appeal

20. In support of the appeal, Mr Prentis of counsel (for Mr and Mrs Pollard), in j an admirably clear and succinct argument, submits that the question whether a particular right is a right in rem or a right in personam has to be answered by reference to European law, and that it does not follow from the fact that English law categorises a particular type of ownership interest as an equitable interest that such an interest cannot give rise to rights in rem. He referred us in this connection to the discussion about rights in rem contained in the report by Professor Peter Schlosser (OJ 1979 C59 p 71) pp 120–121 (paras 163–168) and to

the decision of the Court of Justice in *Reichert v Dresdner Bank* Case C-115/88 [1990] ECR I-27.

21. Mr Prentis submits that in deciding whether art 16 applies to these proceedings the court must look at the substance of the dispute, rather than the form of the relief sought or of the order made. He submits that in substance the proceedings concern the ownership of immovable property in another contracting state, and are accordingly 'proceedings which have as their object rights in rem in immovable property' for the purposes of art 16(1). In support of this submission, Mr Prentis relies strongly on *Re Hayward (decd)* [1997] 1 All ER 32, [1997] Ch 45, where Rattee J held that proceedings brought by a trustee in bankruptcy seeking a declaration that the bankrupt's interest in foreign land formed part of his estate for bankruptcy purposes were not within the 'bankruptcy' exception and were caught by art 16(1).

22. Mr Prentis submits that the instant case is on all fours with *Re Hayward*. He submits that the relief sought by the trustee in the instant case is in substance the same as that which was sought by the trustee in *Re Hayward*, and that the fact that in the instant case it may be possible to frame the relief in terms of an order in personam against Mr and Mrs Pollard that they take certain steps, the effect of which will be to alter the ownership of the property in question, should not disguise the fact that what are at stake in the proceedings are rights of ownership: rights in rem.

23. Mr Prentis seeks to distinguish the decision of the Court of Justice in *Webb v Webb* Case C-294/92 [1994] 3 All ER 911, [1994] ECR I-1717 on the footing that in that case the claimant was seeking to establish a beneficial interest under a resulting trust, whereas in the instant case the trustee's beneficial interest in Mr Pollard's share in the Portuguese property is not in issue. He submits that, in contrast to *Webb v Webb*, what is in issue in the instant case is the exercise of an established right of ownership.

24. Mr Prentis does not repeat in this court the submission which he made to Jacob J to the effect that the English court has no jurisdiction to make orders in relation to trust property held abroad: he accepts that such jurisdiction exists, independently of the 1996 Act. He submits, however, that it is a jurisdiction which the court will rarely exercise in practice, and that it should not be exercised in the instant case.

25. As to the 'bankruptcy' exception in art 1 of the convention, Mr Prentis submits that Jacob J reached the right conclusion for the reasons he gave. In support of this submission Mr Prentis relies once again on *Re Hayward*.

26. In opposition to the appeal, Mr David Marks of counsel (for the trustee) submits that the proceedings do not in any way concern title to land, and that the judge correctly recognised that they concerned the declaration and enforcement of the trustee's rights as against Mr and Mrs Pollard, albeit in respect of foreign land.

27. In support of the respondent's notice, Mr Marks submits that in any event the proceedings fall within the 'bankruptcy' exception in art 1, with the result that art 16 does not apply to them. He submits that Rattee J in *Re Hayward* gave too restrictive an interpretation to the word 'bankruptcy' in this context. He submits that on its true construction the exception extends not merely to the proceedings which led to the making of the bankruptcy order itself but to subsequent proceedings in the bankruptcy.

a *Conclusions*

28. I turn first to the 'bankruptcy' exception, since if the proceedings are within that exception the question whether art 16(1) applies does not arise.

29. In *Re Hayward* Rattee J concluded, as noted earlier, that proceedings by a trustee in bankruptcy seeking a declaration as to the ownership of foreign land did not fall within the exception. He expressed his conclusion in the following b passage from his judgment:

> 'So far as the reference in art 1 of the convention to bankruptcy is concerned, [counsel for the trustee] forcefully and attractively argued that the claim made by the originating application is a matter of bankruptcy, because that claim depends essentially on the bankruptcy of the late Mr Hayward. c Only by virtue of that bankruptcy does the trustee have the claim which he seeks to assert in the proceedings ... However, the nature of the claim made by the trustee in the proceedings, in my judgment, is not a matter of bankruptcy in the sense that any question of bankruptcy is the principal subject matter of the proceedings. The claim made in the proceedings is d essentially a claim by the trustee to recover from a third party ... assets said to belong to the bankrupt's estate and, therefore, to be vested in the trustee.' (See [1997] 1 All ER 32 at 41, [1997] Ch 45 at 54.)

30. In my judgment Rattee J applied the correct test for determining whether proceedings fall within the 'bankruptcy' exception, viz: is bankruptcy the principal e subject matter of the proceedings? The mere fact that the claimant happens to be a trustee in bankruptcy cannot be sufficient, in my judgment, to bring the proceedings within the exception.

31. Applying that test to the instant case, the conclusion follows, in my judgment, that the proceedings are not within the exception. Accordingly the judge was right to conclude that the convention applies.

f 32. I turn, then, to the question whether the proceedings fall within art 16(1) as being 'proceedings which have as their object rights in rem in immovable property'.

33. The concept of proceedings which have as their 'object' a particular category of right is not a concept which I find entirely easy to grasp. Proceedings g may involve a dispute as to the existence of a right; they may seek relief by way of exercise of a right. Indeed, in one sense it can be said that all proceedings involve legal rights of some kind. So in answering the question whether a particular category of right is the 'object' of the proceedings for the purposes of art 16(1) an element of judicial interpretation of the article is required. Fortunately, this has h been provided in a number of decisions of the Court of Justice and in various authoritative texts, to which I now turn.

34. In the first place, it appears clearly from the decisions of the Court of Justice in *Gourdain v Nadler* Case 133/78 [1977] ECR 733 and *Reichert v Dresdner Bank* Case C-115/88 [1990] ECR I-27 that the question whether the proceedings are 'proceedings which have as their object rights in rem in immovable property' for j the purposes of art 16(1) has to be considered in the light of Community law and in a pan-European context. Thus in *Reichert*'s case the court said:

> 'First of all, it is evident that in order to ensure that the rights and obligations arising out of the Convention for the Contracting States and for individuals concerned are as equal and uniform as possible, an independent definition must be given in Community law to the phrase "in proceedings

which have as their object rights *in rem* in immovable property", as has been done by the Court, with regard to other grounds of exclusive jurisdiction laid down in Article 16, in its judgment ... in Case 73/77 *Sanders v Van der Putte* [1977] ECR 2383—concept of "tenancies of immovable property" ... —and ... in Case 288/82 *Duijnstee v Goderbauer* [1983] ECR 3663—concept of "proceedings concerned with the registration or validity of patents" ... Secondly, as the Court has already held, Article 16 must not be given a wider interpretation than is required by its objective, since it results in depriving the parties of the choice of forum which would otherwise be theirs and, in certain cases, results in their being brought before a court which is not that of any of them (... *Sanders v Van der Putte*, cited above) ... In those circumstances, Article 16(1) must be interpreted as meaning that the exclusive jurisdiction of the Contracting State in which the property is situated does not encompass all actions concerning rights *in rem* in immovable property *but only those which both come within the scope of the Brussels Convention and are actions which seek to determine the extent, content, ownership or possession of immovable property or the existence of other rights in rem therein* and to provide the holders of those rights with the protection of the powers which attach to their interest.' (See [1990] ECR I-27 at 41–42 (paras 8, 9, 11); my emphasis.)

35. In his report (OJ 1979 C59 p 71), Professor Schlosser points out (at p 120, para 166) that the concept of a right in rem, as distinct from a right in personam 'is common to the legal systems of the original Member States ... even though the distinction does not appear everywhere with the same clarity'.

36. Professor Schlosser continues:

'A right *in personam* can only be claimed against a particular person; thus only the purchaser is obliged to pay the purchase price and only the lessor of an article is obliged to permit its use. A right *in rem*, on the other hand, is available against the whole world. The most important legal consequence flowing from the nature of a right *in rem* is that its owner is entitled to demand that the thing in which it exists be given up by anyone not enjoying a prior right.'

37. The rationale underlying art 16 was identified by the Court of Justice in *Sanders v Van der Putte* Case 73/77 [1977] ECR 2383 at 2390–2391 (para 13), where the court stated:

'... actions concerning rights *in rem* in immovable property are to be judged according to the rules of the State in which the immovable property is situated *since the disputes which arise result frequently in checks, inquiries and expert assessments which must be carried out on the spot, with the result that the assignment of exclusive jurisdiction satisfies the need for the proper administration of justice.*' (My emphasis.)

38. In *Webb v Webb* Case C-294/92 [1994] 3 All ER 911, [1994] ECR I-1717, a father provided the funds to purchase a flat in the South of France. The flat was transferred into the sole name of his son. Subsequently, the father brought proceedings in England for a declaration that the son held the flat as trustee and for an order requiring the son to execute the documents necessary to vest legal title in the father. The son challenged the jurisdiction of the English court on the ground that art 16(1) applied, so that the French courts had exclusive jurisdiction. The judge at first instance held that the action was not an action in rem, within

a the meaning of art 16(1). On appeal by the son, this court referred to the Court of Justice for a preliminary ruling on the question whether art 16(1) applied. The Court of Justice held that for art 16(1) to apply, it was not sufficient merely that a right in rem in immovable property was involved in the action or that the action had a link with immovable property, but that the action had to be based on a right in rem and not on a right in personam; and that the father was seeking only b to assert rights against the son. Accordingly the court ruled that art 16(1) did not apply to the father's action.

39. In his opinion in *Webb v Webb*, Advocate General Darmon identified the question on which a ruling was required in the following terms:

> '... does an action brought by a person against another person for a c declaration that the other person holds immovable property as trustee and for an order requiring the latter to execute such documents as should be required to vest the legal ownership in the plaintiff constitute an action in rem within the meaning of art 16(1) of the convention?' (See [1994] 3 All ER 911 at 920, [1994] ECR I-1717 at 1720 (para 8).)

d 40. In para 11 of his opinion, the Advocate General said:

> 'Where art 16 is concerned, it should be borne in mind that this provision ... determines which courts are to have jurisdiction where the *principal subject matter* of the claim relates to a matter mentioned therein.' (See [1994] 3 All ER 911 at 920, [1994] ECR I-1717 at 1721.)

e

41. Thus the Advocate General equated proceedings which have 'as their object' rights in rem (see art 16(1)) with proceedings where the 'principal subject matter' of the claim relates to rights in rem.

42. Later in his opinion, after citing *Reichert v Dresdner Bank* Case C-115/88 f [1990] ECR I-27, and after summarising the opposing arguments, the Advocate General said:

> 'The question is not an easy one and I have pondered on the correct approach to take, for the claim of ownership undeniably underlies the claim for the recognition of [a trust in favour of the father] ... However, the g approach which looks at the actual *aim* pursued by the [father] is not supported by the relevant provision, by prevailing academic opinion or by the case law of the court. The jurisdiction ratione materiae of a court must necessarily be assessed in the light of the *subject matter* of the claim, as defined in the originating application, without looking at purpose ...' (See [1994] 3 All ER 911 at 923, [1994] ECR I-1717 at 1724 (paras 27–28).)

h

43. In para 32 of his opinion ([1994] 3 All ER 911 at 924, [1994] ECR I-1717 at 1725), the Advocate General noted the requirement of European case law for a restrictive interpretation of art 16. In para 34 he quoted from Professor Schlosser's report (a passage quoted earlier in this judgment). He then turned to consider the j nature of the father's claim, concluding that by his claim the father was seeking to establish a right of ownership as against the son, as opposed to asserting an existing right of ownership, and that on that analysis the claim was based on a purely personal relationship ([1994] 3 All ER 911 at 925, [1994] ECR I-1717 at 1726 (para 38)).

44. In para 46 of his opinion ([1994] 3 All ER 911 at 926, [1994] ECR I-1717 at 1728) the Advocate General, in a further reference to Professor Schlosser's report,

expressed the view that 'only actions bearing *directly* upon "the extent, content or ownership of immovable property" fall within the scope of art 16(1)'. *a*

45. In para 48 of his opinion the Advocate General stated as follows:

> 'The dividing line [between proceedings which fall within art 16(1) and those which do not] therefore appears to lie between actions whose principal subject matter is a dispute over ownership between persons who do not claim inter se any fiduciary relationship and actions concerning a breach of fiduciary duty which, if found to have been committed, will have effects in rem. In such a case, the personal nature of the relations is, in my view, the overriding factor.' (See [1994] 3 All ER 911 at 926, [1994] ECR I-1717 at 1728.) *b*

46. As I read that passage, the Advocate General is drawing a distinction between on the one hand an action in which an existing right of ownership is asserted against a stranger, and on the other hand an action in which one party seeks to establish a right of ownership against the other party as having arisen out of some personal relationship between them. In each case the action concerns a right of ownership, but whereas in the former case the 'principal subject matter' of the action (to use the Advocate General's expression) is the assertion of an established right, in the latter case the principal subject matter of the action is the personal relationship which is said to give rise to the right. *c* *d*

47. In para 62 of his opinion, the Advocate General refers to the rationale of art 16, saying:

> 'Finally, I would observe that the essential reason for conferring sole jurisdiction under art 16(1), as recognised by the court in *Reichert*'s case, namely that the courts of the locus rei sitae are better placed to ascertain the facts satisfactorily and to apply the rules and practices of that locus, is irrelevant where, as in this case, the principal subject matter of the dispute is the possible existence of a fiduciary relationship between the parties.' (See [1994] 3 All ER 911 at 928–929, [1994] ECR I-1717 at 1731.) *e* *f*

48. In saying that the rationale of art 16 was 'irrelevant' on the facts of that case, the Advocate General was (as I understand him) simply making the point that the rationale did not apply in that case since the French courts were not in as good a position as the English courts to ascertain the relevant facts as to the existence or otherwise of a fiduciary relationship between father and son, nor did any question of French law and practice arise in relation to the determination of that issue. It is plainly implicit in this paragraph, as I read it, that he regarded the fact that the issue in the case fell outside the rationale underlying art 16 as a further ground for concluding that art 16 did not apply. *g* *h*

49. The Advocate General concluded his opinion by proposing that the court should rule that an action brought by a person against another person for a declaration that the latter holds immovable property as trustee and for an order requiring the latter to execute such documents as should be required to vest the legal ownership in the plaintiff does not constitute an action in rem within the meaning of art 16(1). *j*

50. In its judgment, the court accepted the reasons and conclusion of the Advocate General. The court said:

> 'Article 16 confers exclusive jurisdiction in the matter of rights in rem in immovable property on the courts of the contracting state in which the property is situated. In the light of the court's judgment in *Reichert v Dresdner*

a *Bank* Case C-115/88 [1990] ECR I-27, where the court had to rule on the question whether the exclusive jurisdiction prescribed by that article applied in respect of an action by a creditor to have a disposition of immovable property declared ineffective as against him on the ground that it was made in fraud of his rights by his debtor, it follows that it is not sufficient, for art 16(1) to apply, that a right in rem in immovable property be involved in the action or b that the action have a link with immovable property: the action must be based on a right in rem and not on a right in personam, save in the case of the exception concerning tenancies of immovable property … The aim of the proceedings before the national court is to obtain a declaration that the son holds the flat for the exclusive benefit of the father and that in that capacity he is under a duty to execute the documents necessary to convey ownership of c the flat to the father. The father does not claim that he already enjoys rights directly relating to the property which are enforceable against the whole world, but seeks only to assert rights as against the son. Consequently, his action is not an action in rem within the meaning of art 16(1) of the convention but an action in personam … Nor are considerations relating to d the proper administration of justice underlying art 16(1) of the convention applicable in this case.' (See [1994] 3 All ER 911 at 930, [1994] ECR I-1717 at 1738 (paras 14–16).)

51. The court accordingly held that the action was not an action in rem, within the meaning of art 16(1).

e 52. As noted earlier, Mr Prentis seeks to distinguish *Webb v Webb*, on the basis that in the instant case (and in contrast to the father in *Webb v Webb*) the trustee 'already enjoys rights directly relating to the property which are enforceable against the whole world' in that he has an indisputable beneficial interest in the property by virtue of the operation of the 1986 Act. In my judgment, however, the distinction f which Mr Prentis seeks to draw is a false one. Reading the judgment of the court in *Webb v Webb* in context, I take the reference to a claim based on existing rights to be a reference to proceedings in which the claimant seeks to assert a property right which is by its nature a right enforceable against third parties, in contrast to proceedings based on a personal relationship between claimant and defendant.

g 53. In my judgment, the following factors appear from the authorities to which I have referred as being relevant to the question whether art 16(1) applies in the instant case: (1) Given that its effect is to override the parties' choice of forum, art 16 is to be given a restrictive interpretation (see *Reichert v Dresdner Bank* Case C-115/88 [1990] ECR I-27). (2) The rationale underlying art 16 is 'the proper administration of justice', on the footing that the courts of the contracting state h in which the property is situated will be best placed to conduct any factual investigation which may be required, and to apply local law and practice (see *Sanders v Van der Putte* Case 73/77 [1977] ECR 2383 and para 62 of the Advocate General's opinion in *Webb v Webb* Case C-294/92 [1994] 3 All ER 911 at 928–929, [1994] ECR I-1717 at 1731). (3) In considering whether art 16(1) applies in any j particular case, it is material to have regard to whether that rationale applies: that is to say, whether the proceedings involve a factual investigation which is best carried out by the courts of the state in which the property is situated, and/or questions of local law and practice are raised (see para 16 of the court's judgment in *Webb v Webb* Case C-294/92 [1994] 3 All ER 911 at 930, [1994] ECR I-1717 at 1738). (4) The expression 'which have as their object' in art 16(1) is synonymous with 'which have as their principal subject matter' (see para 11 of the Advocate General's opinion in *Webb v Webb* Case C-294/92 [1994] 3 All ER 911 at 920, [1994] ECR I-1717 at 1721). (5) 'Subject matter' in this context is not to be confused with 'aim' or 'purpose' (see para 28 of the Advocate General's opinion in *Webb v Webb* Case C-294/92 [1994] 3 All ER 911 at 923, [1994] ECR I-1717 at 1724). a

54. Returning to the instant case, it seems plain in the first place that in so far as the court is minded to make orders in personam along the lines suggested by the judge, the rationale underlying art 16(1) can have no application, since no issue arises as to the factual situation in Portugal, nor do the proceedings involve any question of Portuguese law or practice. Prima facie, therefore, there is no reason why art 16(1) should apply. b

55. In the second place, the proceedings do not seek to assert any property right against third parties/strangers: rather, they raise personal issues as between the trustee on the one hand and Mr and Mrs Pollard on the other. On that footing they are, in my judgment, on all fours with the proceedings in *Webb v Webb*. c

56. The fact that, as Mr Prentis submitted, the trustee's ultimate aim or purpose in prosecuting the proceedings is to effect a change in the ownership of the property by achieving its sale is not material. What has to be looked at is the subject matter of the proceedings. In the light of *Webb v Webb*, the fact that the resolution of a dispute as to personal rights (rights in personam) may impact upon property rights enforceable against third parties/strangers (rights in rem) does not in my judgment lead to the conclusion that the subject matter of the proceedings for the purposes of art 16(1) is rights in rem. d

57. I turn next to *Re Hayward (decd)* [1997] 1 All ER 32, [1997] Ch 45, on which Mr Prentis places so much reliance. e

58. In *Re Hayward*, a villa in Minorca was purchased by two individuals who contributed equally to the purchase price. They were registered in the Minorcan property register as owners of the property 'in indivisible halves'. One of the joint owners was subsequently made bankrupt. On his death intestate, his widow purported to transfer his interest in the villa to the other registered owner in satisfaction of a debt she owed him for money which he had spent on the villa. The trustee in bankruptcy of the deceased bankrupt applied in the county court for a declaration that the bankrupt's interest in the villa formed part of his estate for bankruptcy purposes. The trustee also sought an order that the bankrupt's widow and the remaining registered owner take steps to rectify the Minorcan property register so as to show the trustee as owner of the deceased bankrupt's share, together with an order for sale of the villa and the division of the net proceeds of sale equally between the trustee and the other registered owner. The county court judge struck out the proceedings on the grounds (a) that they did not fall within the 'bankruptcy' exception in art 1 of the convention, and (b) that they were 'proceedings which have as their object rights in rem in immovable property' for the purposes of art 16(1), so that the Spanish courts had exclusive jurisdiction. As noted earlier, in dismissing the trustee's appeal Rattee J agreed with the county court judge that the proceedings fell within art 16(1). He also held that the claim for rectification of the Minorcan property register fell within art 16(3) (proceedings which have as their object the validity of entries in public registers). f g h j

59. In my judgment, *Re Hayward* is distinguishable from the instant case in that the principal subject matter of the proceedings in *Re Hayward* was the ownership of the Minorcan property. As Rattee J said:

a 'The essence of the present proceedings ... was an attempt by the trustee to establish and protect, and indeed perfect, what he alleged was his entitlement as trustee in the bankruptcy of Mr Hayward to what had been Mr Hayward's half-share in the villa.' (See [1997] 1 All ER 32 at 35, [1997] Ch 45 at 48.)

60. On that basis, Rattee J was correct, in my judgment, to conclude that art 16(1) applied. By contrast, the proceedings in the instant case do not raise any b issue as to title to land. The trustee in the instant case is not seeking to establish or protect, let alone perfect, his title to Mr Pollard's interest in the Portuguese property. I therefore conclude that Mr Prentis cannot gain any assistance from *Re Hayward* in the instant case.

61. Accordingly, for the reasons I have given I conclude that the proceedings c in the instant case do not fall within art 16(1).

62. I turn, lastly, to Mr Prentis' alternative submission that the English court will rarely exercise its jurisdiction (the existence of which is now accepted) to make orders relating to trust property abroad, and that it should not exercise that jurisdiction in the instant case. In oral argument, Mr Prentis did not elaborate on this submission, which should in my judgment be rejected. Whether the English d court in any particular case will consider it appropriate to make an order relating to trust property abroad will depend on the nature of the order sought and on the facts of the case. In the instant case, the orders which the court is minded to make require steps to be taken within the jurisdiction by a trustee who is himself within the jurisdiction. That being so, I can see no jurisdictional or other objection to the e making of those orders.

63. I accordingly conclude that the Portuguese courts do not have exclusive jurisdiction in relation to the proceedings in the instant case.

64. For those reasons, I would dismiss this appeal.

POTTER LJ.

f 65. I agree.

KENNEDY LJ.

66. I also agree.

Appeal dismissed. Permission to appeal refused.

Dilys Tausz Barrister.

Amber v Stacey

COURT OF APPEAL, CIVIL DIVISION

SIMON BROWN LJ AND SIR ANTHONY EVANS

11 OCTOBER, 15 NOVEMBER 2000

Costs – Order for costs – Discretion – Payment into court – Claimant rejecting defendant's written offer to pay £4,000 in settlement of action – Defendant paying £3,000 into court several months after claimant's rejection of offer – Claimant failing to beat payment in – Recorder ordering claimant to pay defendant's costs from date of written offer – Whether recorder in error in treating written offer in same way as payment in – CPR 44.3.

In August 1997 the claimant carried out works to the defendant's shop and supplied equipment for it. No price was agreed, and so a reasonable sum became due. In September 1997 the claimant rendered an invoice in the sum of £7,579·86. On 23 September the claimant's solicitors wrote a letter before action to the defendant's solicitors and on the following day a county court summons was issued. On 1 October the defendant's solicitors wrote to the claimant's solicitors, offering a settlement of £4,000 plus costs, and stating that they would advise the defendant to pay that sum into court if the offer was not accepted. The claimant's solicitors replied on 10 October, stating that the sum offered would not be accepted, whether paid into court or otherwise. However, it was not until 7 August 1998 that the defendant paid any money into court, and then only in the sum of £2,000. A further payment in of £1,000 was made on 20 January 1999. When the case came to trial in April 1999, the recorder dismissed the defendant's counterclaim and gave judgment for the claimant in the sum of £2,321. He concluded, however, that the claimant had acted unreasonably in commencing the proceedings and in refusing the defendant's written offer of settlement. Thus, in the exercise of his discretion under CPR 44.3[a], the recorder ordered the claimant to pay the defendant's costs not merely from the date of the second payment in, but for the whole period from 1 October 1997, the date of the written offer. The claimant appealed against the costs order in respect of the period before the second payment in, contending that the judge had erred in treating the defendant's written offer as if it were a payment into court made on the date it was written.

Held – Although there had been ample justification for the recorder to deprive the claimant of his costs from 1 October 1997 until 20 January 1999, he had erred in law in making the same costs order as he would have done if the defendant had made the payment in at the start of that period and succeeded on all issues at trial. The claimant's intemperate response to the written offer had not prevented the defendant from making the payment in, and if he had done so he would have been securely protected in respect of costs. When the first payment in was made, it was for a lesser amount. Moreover, the defendant's counterclaim remained in issue at the trial, and on that issue the claimant had succeeded. In those circumstances, the recorder had made an error of principle which was outside the wide discretion given to the court by CPR 44.3. However, the recorder had

a Rule 44.3 is set out at p 93 *g* to p 94 *a*, post

a understandably felt that the claimant's approach was unreasonable throughout, and that a more ameliorative response to the letter would have resulted in a generous settlement and would have made further proceedings unnecessary. Thus even in that respect, the order was not wholly wrong. To give effect to the recorder's views on the relevant matters affecting the court's discretion, the claimant would be ordered to pay half of the defendant's costs for the period from b 1 October 1997 to 20 January 1999. Accordingly, the appeal would be allowed in part (see p 95 *d* to *f* and *h* to p 96 *c*, post); *Ford v GKR Construction Ltd* [2000] 1 All ER 802 considered.

Per Simon Brown LJ. There are compelling reasons of principle and policy why those prepared to make genuine offers of monetary settlement should do so by way of payments into court. That way lies clarity and certainty, or at least c greater clarity and certainty than in the case of written offers. Payments into court answer all questions as to genuineness, the offeror's ability to pay, whether the offer is open or without prejudice and the terms on which the dispute can be settled. They are clearly to be encouraged, and written offers, although obviously relevant, should not be treated as precise equivalents (see p 96 *d* to *g*, post).

d

Notes

For the exercise of the court's discretion to award costs, see 37 *Halsbury's Laws* (4th edn) para 714.

e

Cases referred to in judgments

Elgindata Ltd, Re (No 2) [1993] 1 All ER 232, [1992] 1 WLR 1207, CA.

Ford v GKR Construction Ltd [2000] 1 All ER 802, [2000] 1 WLR 1397, CA.

f *Gwembe Valley Development Co Ltd (in receivership) v Koshy (No 2)* (2000) Times, 30 March, Ch D.

Cases also cited or referred to in skeleton arguments

Chocoladefabriken Lindt & Sprungli AG v Nestlé Co Ltd [1978] RPC 287.

g *Chrulew v Borm-Reid & Co (a firm)* [1992] 1 All ER 953, [1992] 1 WLR 176.

Cutts v Head [1984] 1 All ER 597, [1984] Ch 290, CA.

Gupta v Klito (1989) Times, 23 November, [1989] CA Transcript 1063.

Norwich Union Life Insurance Society v Tony Waller Ltd (1984) 270 EG 42.

h *Singh v Parkfield Group plc* (1994) Times, 27 May, QBD.

Walker v Wilsher (1889) 23 QBD 335, CA.

Appeal

j The claimant, Robert Amber, appealed with permission of Sir Anthony McCowan granted on 12 November 1999 from the order of Mr Recorder Clarkson QC made at the Yeovil County Court on 30 April 1999 requiring the claimant to pay the costs of the defendant, Bernard Hugh Stacey, from 1 October 1997, the date of a written offer of settlement made by the defendant, rather than 20 January 1999, the date of a payment into court which the claimant had failed to beat. The facts are set out in the judgment of Sir Anthony Evans.

Jonathan Sharp (instructed by *Battens,* agents for *Poole & Co*, Yeovil) for the claimant. a
Richard Hickmet (instructed by *Alan R Walton & Co*, Somerton) for the defendant.

Cur adv vult

15 November 2000. The following judgments were delivered. b

SIR ANTHONY EVANS (giving the first judgment at the invitation of Simon Brown LJ).

1. This appeal is against a costs order made by Mr Recorder Clarkson QC in the Yeovil County Court on 30 April 1999. c

2. He had previously given judgment for the claimant for a total sum of £2,321·16 including interest after a three-day hearing. The claim was for £7,579·86. Both sums include VAT. He also dismissed the counterclaim.

3. The outline facts can be shortly stated. The claimant is a contractor and supplier of new and second-hand equipment to the catering trade. The defendant is a butcher at premises in High Street, Somerton, Somerset. In August 1997 the d claimant carried out works to refurbish the meat preparation area in a separate building at the rear of the defendant's shop, and to supply equipment for it.

4. No price was agreed and so a reasonable sum became due. The claimant rendered his invoice dated 2 September 1997:

> 'Clad out Room Rear of Shop sort out Electric and Plumbing Fit Sliding e Door Clad [1¼] Walls in Small Room Leave Clean & Tidy
>
> | | |
> |---|---|
> | PRICE | £6,450·95 |
> | VAT 17½% | £1,128·91 |
> | | £7,579·86 …' |

5. The county court summons was issued on 24 September 1997. The recorder f described the claimant as 'unnecessarily precipitate'. The defendant challenged the amounts claimed for different items of work and goods supplied, with a major degree of success. The recorder found that the reasonable sum due was no more than £1,751·94 plus VAT, a total of £2,058·52. That sum together with interest produced the figure of £2,321·16 for which judgment was given. g

6. The defendant paid £2,000 into court on 7 August 1998 and a further £1,000 making a total of £3,000 on 20 January 1999. It was not disputed that the claimant was rightly ordered to pay the defendant's costs from the date of the second payment in, notwithstanding that the claim succeeded to the extent that it did.

7. The appeal arises because the recorder also ordered the claimant to pay the h defendant's costs for an earlier period, from 1 October 1997. On that date the defendant's solicitors wrote to the claimant's solicitors in reply to their letter dated 23 September, which was effectively their letter before action although the summons was issued on the following day. In the course of a two-page letter and a detailed reply, the defendant's solicitors said: j

> 'Before we launch into a Defence and the Request for Further and Better Particulars of the Claim, we are instructed to put forward a proposal that our Client will settle the Claim at £4,000 plus VAT plus the Court fee and Solicitors costs on Summons to see an end to the matter. If your Client is not prepared to agree then we will advise our Client to pay this sum into Court and to bring in his Quantity Surveyor and the matter will be litigated most vehemently.'

a 8. On 10 October, the day the defence and counterclaim was filed, the claimant's solicitors responded to this letter, and they concluded:

> 'In summary, our client does not accept your contentions and is not going to accept the sum of £4,000·00 plus VAT etc whether paid into Court or otherwise.'

b 9. No payment into court was made then nor at any time until 7 August 1998 when as stated above the sum was £2,000 only.

The counterclaim

10. By his counterclaim, which the recorder dismissed, the defendant c counterclaimed £675 for the cost of dismantling part of the work and further contended that the value of the works was no more than £1,500.

11. The recorder dismissed the counterclaim and expressly rejected any contention that the work done was worthless.

The costs order

d 12. Having heard submissions from counsel, the recorder made the following costs order: 'The claimant to pay the defendant's costs from 11 February 1999 and from the date of the defendant's letter of 1 October 1997.'

He gave the following reasons, referring to the letter:

> e 'I consider that the plaintiff was given a very good offer then. I consider that it is quite clear from the way he conducted himself that he was precipitate in bringing this action, the defendant was conciliatory … I consider that it was a genuine offer. It was a generous offer. If it had been sensibly accepted on 1 October 1997, Mr Stacey and indeed Mr Amber would have f been put to much less costs and much less concern. The opportunity should have been taken then, grasped and the matter finalised. I consider this litigation was ill-advised to proceed on the basis it did …'

The appeal

13. Mr Sharp for the claimant submits that the recorder erred in treating the g offer made by the letter as if it was, in effect, a payment into court on the date it was written. No such payment was made. Moreover, the defendant's solicitors stated expressly that one would be made, if the offer was refused, and it was not. The recorder, he submitted, was not entitled to deprive the successful claimant of his costs, or to order him to pay the defendant's costs, before the effective h payment into court on 11 February 1999, whether under the Civil Procedure Rules (CPR) or under the old Rules of the Supreme Court.

14. Mr Hickmet responded that the recorder was entitled to deprive the claimant of his costs, and to order him to pay the defendant's costs from 1 October—effectively, the whole costs of the action—both under the old rules and under the j new.

'Without prejudice'

15. Mr Sharp raised a further submission, that the relevant paragraphs of the 1 October 1997 letter were written 'without prejudice' and therefore were privileged and should have been ignored by the recorder. The fact that the letter could have been headed, but was not, either 'without prejudice' or 'without prejudice as to

costs', is not of course fatal to this objection. Nor is the fact the whole letter was included in the agreed bundle without objection from either party. We were told a certain amount about references made by both counsel to the status of the letter in the course of the trial, but no transcript of that part of the proceedings was available. It was never suggested, it seems, that the £4,000 plus VAT (total £4,700) offer should be regarded as an admission of liability by the defendant, by whom it was made. In the result, the letter was treated as if it was expressly marked 'without prejudice as to costs'.

16. Although Mr Sharp did not formally abandon this submission, he accepted that it was not raised at the trial and that for that reason no evidence was directed towards it. We consider that it ought not to be raised on this appeal and that in any event it appears to be ill-founded, on the material available to us, for the reasons indicated above.

New or old rules?

17. The CPR became effective on 26 April 1999, only four days before the recorder's judgment in this case. The 'old' CCR were in force throughout the relevant period from 24 September 1997 when the summons was issued until 11 February 1999 when a sum exceeding the amount of the judgment was paid into court.

18. Both parties' counsel accepted before us that the recorder was entitled and bound to apply the 'new' CPR when the costs order was made on 30 April 1999, but they also agreed, as we understand it, that the recorder was correct to approach the exercise of discretion under the CPR, as he felicitously put it in the course of argument:

> '... as part of the discretion it will only be appropriate to look at the conduct at the time under the old rules. I think that is the fair way of looking at it.'

19. CCR Ord 11, r 10 was in the following terms:

> '(1) A party to proceedings may at any time make a written offer to any other party to those proceedings which is expressed to be "without prejudice save as to costs" and which relates to any issue in the proceedings.
>
> (2) ... the court shall, in exercising its discretion as to costs, take into account any offer which has been brought to its attention: Provided that ... the court shall not take such an offer into account if, at the time it is made, the party making it could have protected his position as to costs by means of a payment into court.'

20. RSC Ord 22, r 14 was to the same effect.

21. Also under the old rules, the judgment of this court in *Re Elgindata Ltd (No 2)* [1993] 1 All ER 232, [1992] 1 WLR 1207 recognised that as a matter of general principle and in the exercise of the court's discretion there were circumstances in which a successful party might be deprived of his own costs and even might be ordered to pay the costs of an unsuccessful party. That was a case where the party which succeeded in the litigation overall had raised other allegations on which he had failed. He had raised them unreasonably and improperly, and the length and costs of the proceedings had expanded accordingly. In the present case, it could not be said that superfluous issues were raised or contested by the plaintiff, but if the old rules had applied, it would have been necessary to consider whether the recorder's findings, that the whole litigation was precipitate and unnecessary,

a entitled the court to apply the same principle and to deprive the plaintiff of his costs, even order him to pay the defendant's costs.

22. The principles of *Re Elgindata Ltd (No 2)* have been held to apply under the 'new' CPR (see *Gwembe Valley Development Co Ltd (in receivership) v Koshy (No 2)* (2000) Times, 30 March, to which Mr Sharp helpfully referred us). Our starting point under the new rules, however, must be the relevant express rules, which b are found in Pts 36 and 44.

23. Part 36.3(1) may be regarded as equivalent to the former CCR Ord 11, r 10 and RSC Ord 22, r 14:

> '36.3(1) Subject to rules 36.5(5) and 36.23 [neither of which applies in the present case], an offer by a defendant to settle a money claim will not have c the consequences set out in this Part unless it is made by way of a Part 36 payment.'

24. A Pt 36 payment is a payment into court (Pt 36.2(1)(a)). Part 36 begins with the following introductory rule, headed 'Scope of this Part':

> d '36.1(1) This Part contains rules about—(a) offers to settle and payments into court; and (b) the consequences where an offer to settle or payment into court is made in accordance with this Part.
>
> (2) Nothing in this Part prevents a party making an offer to settle in whatever way he chooses, but if that offer is not made in accordance with this Part, it will only have the consequences specified in this Part if the court e so orders.'

25. The cost consequences of a Pt 36 payment which the claimant fails to beat are set out in r 36.20(2):

> '(2) Unless it considers it unjust to do so, the court will order the claimant f to pay any costs incurred by the defendant after the latest date on which the payment or offer could have been accepted …'

26. This consequence does not follow the claimant's refusal of the offer made in the 1 October letter, however, because no Pt 36 payment was made in respect of that offer of £4,000 plus VAT: CPR 36.3(1) so provides.

g 27. The general rules about costs are found in Pt 44. Rule 44.3 reads:

> '(1) The court has a discretion as to—(a) whether costs are payable by one party to another; (b) the amount of those costs …
>
> (2) If the court decides to make an order about costs—(a) the general rule is that the unsuccessful party will be ordered to pay the costs of the successful h party; but (b) the court may make a different order.
>
> (3) …
>
> (4) In deciding what order (if any) to make about costs, the court must have regard to all the circumstances, including—(a) the conduct of all the parties; (b) whether a party has succeeded on part of his case, even if the has j not been wholly successful; and (c) any payment into court or admissible offer to settle made by a party which is drawn to the court's attention (whether or not made in accordance with Part 36) [followed by express reference to further costs provisions in Pt 36].
>
> (5) The conduct of the parties includes—(a) conduct before, as well as during the proceedings … (b) whether it was reasonable for a party to raise, pursue or contest a particular allegation or issue; (c) the manner in which a

party has pursued or defended his case or a particular allegation or issue; (d) whether a claimant who has succeeded in his claim, in whole or in part, exaggerated his claim.'

a

28. The interrelationship between the payment into court provisions in Pt 36 and the general rules stated in Pt 44 was considered by this court, sitting in Cardiff, in *Ford v GKR Construction Ltd* [2000] 1 All ER 802, [2000] 1 WLR 1397. That was the converse of the present case. The claimant recovered less damages than the amount of the payment into court (judgment was given before the CPR came into force). The defendants nevertheless were ordered to pay the whole of the claimant's costs, including those incurred after the date of the payment in. The initial reaction of Judge LJ, who gave the leading judgment, was that the judge was wrong to make that order (see [2000] 1 All ER 802 at 807, [2000] 1 WLR 1397 at 1400). However, he considered that 'the judge reaching his decision about costs is required to take into account all relevant aspects of the litigation', and the court held that the order was justified in the circumstances of that case, in particular because of the late introduction of evidence by the defendants which had the effect of reducing the amount of the judgment below that of the payment in. Judge LJ concluded:

b

c

d

'Indeed [the judge's] judgment has served to underline [not "undermine"] the importance, rightly and increasingly, to be attached to civil litigation being conducted openly between the parties with the real issues between them efficiently and quickly identified and investigated, without, as it now seems to me, any unfairness to these defendants in this case.' (See [2000] 1 All ER 802 at 808, [2000] 1 WLR 1397 at 1402.)

e

29. Lord Woolf MR added this, after referring to CPR Pt 36:

'I also draw attention to the fact that the rules refer to the power of the court to make other orders and make it clear that the normal cost consequence of failing to beat the sum paid in does not apply when it is unjust that it should do so. If a party has not enabled another party to properly assess whether or not to make an or offer, or whether or not to accept an offer which is made, because of non-disclosure to the other party of material matters, or if a party comes to a decision which is different from that which would have been reached if there had been proper disclosure, that is a material matter for a court to take into account in considering what orders it should make.' (See [2000] 1 All ER 802 at 810, [2000] 1 WLR 1397 at 1403.)

f

g

30. The circumstances of the present case of course are wholly different. But the recorder had the wide discretion permitted by CPR 44.3, and Lord Woolf's statement of principle is relevant also.

h

31. The background to the recorder's conclusion, quoted above, that the offer made on 1 October was a genuine and generous offer was his finding that the claimant grossly exaggerated almost all the individual items of his claim. Overall, he found that the claimant undertook to produce a professional job but the product rated no more than 80% on a DIY scale and 25% on a professional basis. For cladding, the claim was £1,875·50, later reduced to £1,800. This involved a 'ridiculous' mark-up of 74%. £493·79 was allowed. The cold store door was invoiced at £1,000. It was second-hand and acquired by the claimant for £20. The door had 'some short-term value' and the judge allowed £200. A sink that was

j

a provided was scrap and had no value. The claim for labour was 134 hours at £22·50p per hour, a total of £3,015. The judge allowed 50 hours at £12·50, total £625. He found the defendant's expert, Mr Carruthers, a persuasive and helpful witness, and it appears from the judgment that the plaintiff's expert 'declared himself unable to challenge Mr Carruthers' opinion as to installation, fixing and sealing'.

32. On the other hand, the judge rejected the defendant's contention that the b work done was worthless and his claim for £675 removal costs. He also found that the reasonable sum due was rather more than the valuation of £1,500 which the defendant also put forward.

33. The judge's reference to the claimant having been 'precipitate' in bringing the action is supported by the evidence we have seen regarding the circumstances in which the summons was issued. The claimant's original brief invoice, quoted c above, was followed by a meeting at the defendant's home, at which some details were given. The defendant wrote a reasoned and, in the light of the judge's findings, reasonable letter dated 23 September, which his solicitors referred to in theirs of 1 October which contained the £4,000 plus VAT offer. The claimant's response, however, had been to instruct his solicitors to issue the summons on 24 September, d and it was served between then and 1 October.

Conclusion

34. In my judgment, there was ample justification for the judge's order depriving the claimant of his costs from 1 October 1997 until 20 January 1999, notwithstanding that no payment in which exceeded the amount of the judgment e was made until the later date. The judge took account not only of the refusal of the much higher offer made in immediate response to the issue of the summons, but also of the whole of the claimant's 'precipitate' conduct in commencing the proceedings when he did. He found in effect that this conduct was unreasonable and that, if the claimant had acted reasonably, the proceedings were unnecessary f and would never have taken place. To this extent, in my judgment, he was entitled to make the order that he did. I add that I would have reached the same conclusion in accordance with *Re Elgindata (No 2)* principles, even if the 'old' rules still applied. Under the CPR, the position is clear.

35. More difficult is whether the judge was entitled to order the claimant to pay the defendant's costs during the same period. This order means that the g defendant is put in the same position as regards costs as if a Pt 36 payment was made on 1 October 1997 (actually rather better, because the claimant would have had a short period within which to accept or refuse the payment in). Yet the defendant did not make the payment in, although his solicitors said that he would do so. The claimant's intemperate response did not prevent him from making h the payment, and if he had done so he would have been securely protected in respect of costs and partly at least in respect of loss of interest. When the first payment in was made, it was for a lesser amount. Moreover, the defendant's counterclaim remained in issue at the trial, and on that issue the claimant succeeded.

j 36. I am persuaded in these circumstances that the recorder erred in law when he made the same costs order as he would have done if the defendant had made the payment in and had succeeded on all issues at the trial. This seems to me to be an error of principle which is outside the wide discretion given to the court by CPR 44.3. I also consider that this part of the order was not consistent with the 'old' CCR and RSC and the principles stated in *Re Elgindata (No 2)*. It may well be that, if the old rules remained in force, it would be necessary to hold that the claimant could not be ordered to pay any part of the defendant's costs during the period in question. a

37. However, the CPR do apply and they permit the court a wide discretion. The recorder understandably felt that the claimant's approach was unreasonable throughout and that a more ameliorative response to the letter would have resulted in a generous settlement for him and would have made further proceedings unnecessary. I would hold that even in this respect the order was not wholly wrong, b and that to give effect to the recorder's views on relevant matters affecting the court's discretion, the claimant should be ordered to pay a proportion, namely, one half of the defendant's costs for the period from 1 October 1997 to 20 January 1999.

38. To that extent in my judgment the appeal succeeds.

c

SIMON BROWN LJ.

39. I agree. Clear though it is that the claimant behaved thoroughly unreasonably from first to last, and tempting though it is therefore to uphold the recorder's order in full measure, I share my Lord's view that it was wrong to treat the letter of 1 October 1997 for all the world as though it constituted a payment d into court. There are to my mind compelling reasons of principle and policy why those prepared to make genuine offers of monetary settlement should do so by way of Pt 36 payments. That way lies clarity and certainty, or at any rate greater clarity and certainty than in the case of written offers.

40. Of course payments into court are not themselves necessarily decisive: *Ford v* e *GKR Construction Ltd* [2000] 1 All ER 802, [2000] 1 WLR 1397 is a good illustration of that. Defendants who pay in too little or too late, just as claimants who fail to take out what ultimately proves to be enough (Mrs Ford being one such), may nevertheless be able to establish that it was their opponent's unreasonable conduct which prevented them from making a properly informed decision about their prospects in the litigation, and thus avoid what in a Pt 36 case would be the usual f costs order. But that was not the basis of the defendant's argument on costs here; nor, indeed, could it have been consistently with his being prepared to make the £4,000 offer in the first place and his eventual payments in, first of £2,000 and then of a further £1,000.

41. Payments into court have advantages. They at least answer all questions g as to (a) genuineness, (b) the offeror's ability to pay, (c) whether the offer is open or without prejudice, and (d) the terms on which the dispute can be settled. They are clearly to be encouraged, and written offers, although obviously relevant, should not be treated as precise equivalents.

Appeal allowed in part.

Dilys Tausz Barrister.

a

Brown v Stott (Procurator Fiscal, Dunfermline) and another

PRIVY COUNCIL

b LORD BINGHAM OF CORNHILL, LORD STEYN, LORD HOPE OF CRAIGHEAD, LORD CLYDE AND THE RT HON IAN KIRKWOOD

6–9 NOVEMBER, 5 DECEMBER 2000

Criminal evidence – Admissions and confessions – Statutory power – Power to require information – Incriminating answer to question put under statutory power to require c *information – Statutory provision requiring defendant to identify driver of car – Defendant admitting that she was driver and being charged with driving car after consuming excessive alcohol – Whether use of admission in evidence by prosecution infringing defendant's right to fair hearing – Road Traffic Act 1988, s 172(2)(a) – Human Rights Act 1998, Sch 1, Pt I, art 6(1).*

d

Human Rights – Right to a fair hearing – Right against self-incrimination – Whether right against self-incrimination absolute – Human Rights Act 1998, Sch 1, Pt I, art 6(1).

Road Traffic – Offence – Self-incrimination – Driver of vehicle – Statutory provision requiring defendant to identify driver of car – Defendant admitting that she was driver e *and being charged with driving car after consuming excessive alcohol – Whether use of admission in evidence by prosecution infringing defendant's right to fair hearing – Road Traffic Act 1988, s 172(2)(a) – Human Rights Act 1998, Sch 1, Pt I, art 6(1).*

The police were called to a superstore where the defendant, B, was suspected of f having stolen a bottle of gin. They judged her to be the worse for drink, and asked her how she had come to the store. B replied that she had travelled by car, and pointed to a car in the store car park which she said was hers. In the exercise of their powers under s 172(2)(a)[a] of the Road Traffic Act 1988, which applied only where the driver of a vehicle was alleged to have committed certain specified offences, the police required B to say who had been driving her car at the time it would g have been driven to the store car park. Failure to comply with such a requirement was a criminal offence, punishable by a fine of not more than £1,000, mandatory endorsement of the offender's licence and, at the court's discretion, disqualification from driving. In compliance with s 172(2)(a), B stated that she had been the driver of the car at the relevant time. The police then administered h a breath test which proved positive. B was charged with one of the offences to which s 172 applied, namely driving a car after consuming excessive alcohol contrary to s 5(1)(a) of the 1988 Act. The procurator fiscal intended to rely at trial on the admission obtained from B under s 172(2)(a). However, she contended that the use in evidence of that admission would infringe her right to a fair j hearing under art 6(1)[b] of the European Convention for the Protection of Human Rights and Fundamental Freedoms 1950 (as set out in Sch 1 to the Human Rights Act 1998). That contention was accepted by the High Court of Justiciary of Scotland which held that the use of the admission by the prosecution would

a Section 172, so far as material, is set out at p 103 *a* to *e*, post

b Article 6 is set out at p 104 *e* to *h*, post

infringe B's right not to incriminate herself, a right implicit within art 6(1) of the convention. The procurator fiscal appealed that decision to the Privy Council as a devolution issue under the Scotland Act 1998. a

Held – The leading of evidence by the prosecution of an admission obtained under s 172(2)(a) of the 1988 Act did not infringe a defendant's right to a fair hearing under art 6 of the convention. Although the overall fairness of a criminal trial could not be compromised, the constituent rights comprised within art 6, whether expressly or implicitly, were not themselves absolute. Limited qualification of those rights, including the right against self-incrimination, was acceptable if it was reasonably directed by national authorities towards a clear and proper public objective and represented no greater qualification than what was called for by the situation. There was a clear public interest in enforcement of road traffic legislation, and s 172, properly applied, did not represent a disproportionate response to the high incidence of death and injury on the roads caused by misuse of motor vehicles. It provided for the putting of a single, simple question, and the answer could not in itself incriminate the suspect, since it was not without more an offence to drive a car. Section 172 did not sanction prolonged questioning about facts alleged to give rise to criminal offences, and the penalty for declining to answer was moderate and non-custodial. There was no suggestion of improper coercion or oppression such as might give rise to unreliable admissions and so contribute to a miscarriage of justice. If there were evidence of such conduct, the trial judge would have ample power to exclude the admission. Furthermore, all who owned and drove motor vehicles knew that by doing so they subjected themselves to a regulatory regime which was imposed because the use of cars was recognised to have the potential to cause grave injury. It followed, in the instant case, that the prosecution was entitled to lead evidence of B's answer given under s 172. Accordingly, the appeal would be allowed (see p 101 *j*, p 115 *c f h* to p 116 *a e* to *h*, p 117 *a b*, p 119 *f* to *j*, p 120 *e j* to p 121 *b h j* p 122 *j* to p 123 *b d*, p 130 *a* to *c*, p 131 *g h*, p 132 *b* to *d f* to *h*, p 133 *c d*, p 134 *h*, p 137 *a d e* to p 138 *a*, p 139 *d* to *f*, p 140 *a* to *j*, p 141 *c d* and p 142 *a* to *d*, post). b c d e f

Saunders v UK (1997) 2 BHRC 358 distinguished.

Notes

For the right to a fair trial and for the duty to give information as to the identity of a driver, see respectively 8(2) *Halsbury's Laws* (4th edn reissue) paras 134–137 and 40(2) *Halsbury's Laws* (4th edn reissue) para 726. g

For the Road Traffic Act 1988, s 172, see 38 *Halsbury's Statutes* (4th edn) (1995 reissue) 1011.

For the Human Rights Act 1998, Sch 1, Pt I, art 6, see 7 *Halsbury's Statutes* (4th edn) (1999 reissue) 523. h

Cases referred to in judgments

A-G of Hong Kong v Lee Kwong-kut, A-G of Hong Kong v Lo Chak-man [1993] 3 All ER 939, [1993] AC 951, [1993] 3 WLR 329, PC.

Airey v Ireland (1979) 2 EHRR 305, ECt HR. j

Arrows Ltd (No 4), Re, Hamilton v Naviede [1994] 3 All ER 814, [1995] 2 AC 75, [1994] 3 WLR 656, CA.

Ashingdane v UK (1985) 7 EHRR 528, ECt HR.

Bates v UK [1996] EHRLR 312, E Com HR.

Brandstetter v Austria (1991) 15 EHRR 378, ECt HR.

British Broadcasting Corp, Petitioners (No 2) 2000 SLT 860, HC of Just.
Brown v HM Advocate 1966 SLT 105, HC of Just.
California v Byers (1971) 402 US 424, US SC.
Campbell and Fell v UK (1984) 7 EHRR 165, ECt HR.
Chalmers v HM Advocate 1954 JC 66, HC of Just.
Codona v HM Advocate 1996 SLT 1100, HC of Just.
Condron v UK (2000) 8 BHRC 290, ECt HR.
DN v Netherlands App No 6170/73 (26 May 1975, unreported), E Com HR.
Doorson v Netherlands (1996) 22 EHRR 330, ECt HR.
Edwards v A-G for Canada [1930] AC 124, PC.
Edwards v UK (1992) 15 EHRR 417, ECt HR.
Fayed v UK (1994) 18 EHRR 393, ECt HR.
Fitt v UK (2000) 30 EHRR 480, ECt HR.
Foster v Farrell 1963 JC 46, HC of Just.
Funke v France (1993) 16 EHRR 297, ECt HR.
Golder v UK (1975) 1 EHRR 524, ECt HR.
HM Advocate v Hepper 1958 JC 39.
H v UK App No 15023/89 (4 April 1990, unreported), E Com HR.
H v UK (1985) 45 DR 281, E Com HR.
Hoekstra v HM Advocate [2000] 1 AC 216, PC.
Hoffman v United States (1951) 341 US 479, US SC.
Jersild v Denmark (1995) 19 EHRR 1, ECt HR.
JP, KR and GH v Austria (1989) DR 62, E Com HR.
Khan v UK (2000) 8 BHRC 310, ECt HR.
Kostovski v Netherlands (1989) 12 EHRR 434, ECt HR.
Lam Chi-ming v R [1991] 3 All ER 172, [1991] 2 AC 212, [1991] 2 WLR 1082, PC.
Lawrie v Muir 1950 JC 19, HC of Just.
Lingens v Austria (1981) 4 EHRR 373, E Com HR.
Lithgow v UK (1986) 8 EHRR 329, ECt HR.
M v UK (1987) 52 DR 269, E Com HR.
Montgomery v HM Advocate, Coulter v HM Advocate [2001] 2 WLR 779, PC.
Murray v UK (1996) 22 EHRR 29, ECt HR.
National & Provincial Building Society v UK (1997) 25 EHRR 127, ECt HR.
Osman v UK (1998) 5 BHRC 293, ECt HR.
People (Attorney General) v Gilbert (No 14 of 1972) [1973] IR 383.
Pullar v UK (1996) 22 EHRR 391, ECt HR.
R v Chauhan (13 July 2000, unreported), Crown Ct at Birmingham.
R v DPP, ex p Kebilene [1999] 4 All ER 801, [2000] 2 AC 326, [1999] 3 WLR 972, HL.
R v Jones [1994] 2 SCR 229, Can SC.
R v White (1999) 7 BHRC 120, Can SC.
Robb v HM Advocate 2000 JC 127, HC of Just.
Salabiaku v France (1988) 13 EHRR 379, ECt HR.
Saunders v UK (1997) 2 BHRC 358, ECt HR.
Schenk v Switzerland (1988) 13 EHRR 242, ECt HR.
Sheffield v UK (1998) 5 BHRC 83, ECt HR.
Smith v Director of Serious Fraud Office [1992] 3 All ER 456, [1993] AC 1, [1992] 3 WLR 66, HL.
Soering v UK (1989) 11 EHRR 439, ECt HR.
Sporrong v Sweden (1982) 5 EHRR 35, ECt HR.
Tinnelly & Sons Ltd v UK (1998) 4 BHRC 393, ECt HR.
Tora Tolmos v Spain (1995) 81 DR 82, E Com HR.

van Mechelen v Netherlands (1997) 2 BHRC 486, ECt HR.
Waite v Germany (1999) 6 BHRC 499, ECt HR.
X v UK (1972) 42 CD 135, E Com HR.
X v UK (1993) 15 EHRR CD 113, E Com HR.

a

Appeal

Richard G Stott, the procurator fiscal, Dunfermline, appealed with leave from the decision of the High Court of Justiciary of Scotland (Lord Justice General (Lord Rodger of Earlsferry), Lord Marnoch and Lord Allanbridge) on 4 February 2000 (2000 JC 328) allowing an appeal by the respondent, Margaret Anderson Brown, from the decision of Sheriff Forbes at the Sheriff Court, Dunfermline on 23 July 1999 refusing her notice of minute that she intended to raise a devolution issue within the meaning of Sch 6 of the Scotland Act 1998 on the ground that she had been compelled to incriminate herself by making an admission, under s 172(2)(a) of the Road Traffic Act 1988, whilst the police were investigating a charge of driving a car after consuming excessive alcohol contrary to s 5(1)(a) of the Road Traffic Act 1988, and that the use in evidence of the admission would breach her right to a fair hearing under art 6(1) of the European Convention for the Protection of Human Rights and Fundamental Freedoms 1950. The Advocate General for Scotland intervened in the proceedings before the High Court and was second appellant in the appeal to the Privy Council. The facts are set out in the judgment of Lord Bingham of Cornhill.

b

c

d

The Solicitor General for Scotland (*Neil Davidson QC*) and *Robert McCreadie* (of the Scottish Bar) (instructed by the *Crown Office*, Edinburgh) for the procurator fiscal.

e

The Advocate General for Scotland (*Dr Lynda Clark QC*) and *Philip Sales* (instructed by the *Office of the Solicitor to the Advocate General for Scotland*) for the Advocate General.

Ian Duguid QC, *Simon di Rollo* and *Lorenzo Alonzi* (all of the Scottish Bar) (instructed by *Balfour & Manson*, Edinburgh) for the respondent.

f

Their Lordships took time for consideration.

5 December 2000. The following judgments were delivered.

g

LORD BINGHAM OF CORNHILL. In the early hours of 3 June 1999 the police were called to a 24-hour superstore in Dunfermline where the respondent, Miss Brown, was suspected of having stolen a bottle of gin. The officers who attended judged her to be the worse for drink. Asked how she had come to the store, she said she had travelled by car. It seems that she made some reference to a kitten which was in the car. She was charged with theft and taken to the police station, but before leaving the store she pointed to a car in the store car park which she said was hers. At the police station the police found the keys of the car in her handbag. Exercising what they took to be their powers under s 172(2)(a) of the Road Traffic Act 1988, the police required her to say who had been driving her car at about 2.30 a m when she would have travelled in it to the store car park. She replied 'It was me'. A breath test was then administered to her, which proved positive.

h

j

The respondent was prosecuted for two offences: theft; and driving a car after consuming excessive alcohol, contrary to s 5(1)(a) of the 1988 Act. She indicated her intention to plead not guilty to both charges.

a On 1 July 1999 the respondent gave written notice of her intention to raise a devolution issue under s 98 of and Sch 6 to the Scotland Act 1998. The issue was whether, compatibly with the respondent's rights under art 6 of the European Convention for the Protection of Human Rights and Fundamental Freedoms (Rome, 4 November 1950; TS 71 (1953); Cmd 8969) (the convention), the procurator fiscal at Dunfermline, as prosecutor, could rely at trial on the b respondent's admission compulsorily obtained under s 172(2)(a) of the 1988 Act.

The Sheriff Court at Dunfermline heard argument whether a devolution issue had been raised. In the course of this argument it was accepted (as it still is) that the procurator fiscal acted on behalf of the Lord Advocate, a member of the Scottish Executive, and that the procurator fiscal intended at the forthcoming trial of the respondent to lead evidence of her admission made under s 172(2)(a) c of the 1988 Act. Evidence of this admission was treated as necessary to prove the identity of the driver. The sheriff ruled, in a reserved judgment, that no devolution issue had been raised, but he gave leave to appeal against his decision and the respondent appealed to the High Court of Justiciary. At that stage the Advocate General for Scotland exercised her right to intervene.

d The appeal was heard in the High Court of Justiciary on 5 November 1999 and 6 and 7 January 2000 before the Lord Justice General (Lord Rodger of Earlsferry), Lord Marnoch and Lord Allanbridge. For reasons given in a reserved judgment delivered on 4 February 2000 (2000 JC 328), the respondent's appeal was allowed and it was declared that the procurator fiscal had no power to lead and rely on evidence of the admission which she had been compelled to make under s 172(2)(a) e of the 1988 Act. Leave to appeal to the Judicial Committee of the Privy Council was given on 8 February 2000.

On the facts summarised above (which the respondent reserves the right to challenge hereafter), three broad issues have been argued before the Board. The first is whether the respondent has in truth raised a devolution issue as defined by f the Scotland Act. This was not an issue argued before the High Court. It was raised before the Board by the Solicitor General for Scotland on behalf of the procurator fiscal, prompted by the decision of the Board in *Montgomery v HM Advocate, Coulter v HM Advocate* [2001] 2 WLR 779. Both the Advocate General and the respondent submitted to the Board that the respondent had raised a devolution issue. The second issue is whether, compatibly with the respondent's g rights under art 6 of the convention, the procurator fiscal may lead evidence of the admission which she was compelled to make under s 172(2)(a) of the 1988 Act at her trial for the offence charged under s 5 of that Act. On this issue the Solicitor General and the Advocate General united to challenge the decision of the High Court. The third issue only arises for decision if the second issue is resolved in h the respondent's favour, and it turns on the peculiar circumstance that, when these events occurred, the Human Rights Act 1998 had not been brought fully into force in Scotland. The issue is whether, even if the leading of such evidence would be incompatible with the respondent's rights under art 6, the Procurator Fiscal may none the less lawfully lead such evidence.

j On the first of these three issues I agree with the conclusion reached by my noble and learned friend Lord Hope of Craighead that a devolution issue has been raised. I also agree with his reasons for reaching that conclusion. There is nothing I can usefully add.

For reasons given in the body of this opinion, I (in common with all of their Lordships) would resolve the second issue in favour of the procurator fiscal and the Advocate General and adversely to the respondent. This makes it unnecessary to resolve the third issue, and I think it undesirable to offer unauthorative observations on an issue which is by no means straightforward and which seems likely to call for decision before long.

This opinion accordingly deals with only the second issue defined above. In addressing this issue, I would wish to acknowledge the help which the Board has received from a written submission made, by leave of the Board, by JUSTICE.

The judgment of the High Court of Justiciary

The High Court concluded that the leading by the Procurator Fiscal of evidence of the respondent's admission made under s 172 of the 1988 Act, at her trial for an offence against s 5, would infringe her right to a fair trial guaranteed by art 6 of the convention. Its reasons for that conclusion were given by the Lord Justice General, in a judgment with which Lord Marnoch and Lord Allanbridge concurred. The court reached its conclusion by the following important steps.

(1) The European Court of Human Rights has recognised a right to silence and a right against self-incrimination at trial, both derived from art 6(1) of the convention. There is no difference in principle between a requirement to admit the driving of a car made out of court before trial and a similar requirement to testify at trial. To be effective, the right to silence and the right not to incriminate oneself at trial imply the recognition of similar rights at the stage when the potential accused is a suspect being questioned in the course of a criminal investigation (see 2000 JC 328 at 335–339).

(2) To assess whether a person has incriminated himself or herself, the essential consideration is the use to which evidence obtained under compulsion will be put. The concept is not confined to admissions of wrongdoing or to remarks which are directly incriminating. As the respondent's reply would contribute to the proof that she had driven her car on the occasion in question, and thus provide one of the essential links in the chain of testimony against her, it would be self-incriminating for the purposes of art 6(1) of the convention (see 343).

(3) The right not to incriminate oneself is a 'testimonial immunity', protecting a person against being forced to speak. This distinguishes an obligation to answer a question from the taking of samples and the obtaining of documents, since neither of these require the person to speak and the evidence obtained is already in existence (see 344–345).

(4) There is nothing exceptional, either in the nature of the road traffic offence which the respondent had allegedly committed, or in the difficulty of proving the offence without obtaining her admission under s 172 of the 1988 Act, which would justify any infringement of her right not to incriminate herself guaranteed by art 6 of the convention (see 346).

(5) Section 172 applies only where the driver of a vehicle is alleged to have committed a relevant offence. Unlike the provisions considered in other cases reviewed by the court, s 172 has no wider regulatory, non-criminal purpose but exists only to assist the police to identify the driver of a vehicle at the time of an alleged offence (see 349). Both the Lord Justice General and Lord Marnoch in his additional observations paid close attention to, and were strongly influenced by, the decision of the European Court in *Saunders v UK* (1997) 2 BHRC 358.

The decision of the High Court has been followed in England in *R v Chauhan* (13 July 2000, unreported), admissions made under s 172 of the 1988 Act by two drivers on whom notice of intended prosecution had been served were excluded by the trial judge.

a *Section 172 of the Road Traffic Act 1988*

So far as material, s 172 of the 1988 Act at the relevant time provided:

> '(1) This section applies—(a) to any offence under the preceding provisions of this Act except—(i) an offence under Part V, or (ii) an offence under section 13, 16, 51(2), 61(4), 67(9), 68(4), 96 or 120, and to an offence under section 178 of this Act, (b) to any offence under sections 25, 26 or 27 of the Road Traffic b Offenders Act 1988, (c) to any offence against any other enactment relating to the use of vehicles on roads, except an offence under paragraph 8 of Schedule 1 to the Road Traffic (Driver Licensing and Information Systems) Act 1989, and (d) to manslaughter, or in Scotland culpable homicide, by the driver of a motor vehicle.
>
> c (2) Where the driver of a vehicle is alleged to be guilty of an offence to which this section applies—(a) the person keeping the vehicle shall give such information as to the identity of the driver as he may be required to give by or on behalf of a chief officer of police, and (b) any other person shall if required as stated above give any information which it is in his power to give and may lead to identification of the driver.
>
> d (3) Subject to the following provisions, a person who fails to comply with a requirement under subsection (2) above shall be guilty of an offence.
>
> (4) A person shall not be guilty of an offence by virtue of paragraph (a) of subsection (2) above if he shows that he did not know and could not with reasonable diligence have ascertained who the driver of the vehicle was …
>
> e (7) A requirement under subsection (2) may be made by written notice served by post; and where it is so made—(a) it shall have effect as a requirement to give the information within the period of 28 days beginning with the day on which the notice is served, and (b) the person on whom the notice is served shall not be guilty of an offence under this section if he shows either that he gave the information as soon as reasonably practicable after the end of that f period or that it has not been reasonably practicable for him to give it.'

It is evident that the power of the police to require information to be given as to the identity of the driver of a vehicle only arises where the driver is alleged to be guilty of an offence to which the section applies. Those offences include the most serious of driving offences, such as manslaughter or culpable homicide, causing g death by dangerous driving, dangerous and careless driving, causing death by careless driving when under the influence of drugs or drink, and driving a vehicle after consuming alcohol above the prescribed limit. They also include the offence, in Scotland, of taking and driving away a vehicle without consent or lawful authority. The offences excluded are of a less serious and more regulatory nature. h They include offences in relation to driving instruction, the holding of motoring events on public ways, the wearing of protective headgear, driving with uncorrected defective eyesight and offences pertaining to the testing, design, inspection and licensing of vehicles. The penalty for failing to comply with a requirement under sub-s (2) is a fine of (currently) not more than £1,000: in the case of an individual, j disqualification from driving is discretionary but endorsement of the licence is mandatory. The requirement to supply information under sub-s (2) may be made of 'the person keeping the vehicle' or 'any other person', irrespective of whether either of them is suspected of being the driver alleged to have committed the relevant offence. In this case, it is clear that the respondent, when required to give information, was suspected of committing the offence for which she was later prosecuted.

It has been held in Scotland that an oral admission made in response to a requirement under the section which preceded s 172 of the 1988 Act is admissible in evidence (see *Foster v Farrell* 1963 JC 46). This has never to my knowledge been doubted in England and Wales. Where notice of the requirement under s 172(2) is given by post and an admission of driving is made in writing, s 12 of the Road Traffic Offenders Act 1988 presumes the admission to be made by the person to whom the notice was sent both in England and Wales and (by amendment, although to a more limited extent: para 85 of Sch 4 to the Road Traffic Act 1991) in Scotland.

Section 172 is by no means the only provision in United Kingdom road traffic legislation which requires information to be given even though the giving of the information may contribute to proof of an offence against the giver. The duty to report an accident under s 170 of the 1988 Act, the duty to give information concerning insurance cover under s 171 of that Act and the duties imposed by s 112 of the Road Traffic Regulation Act 1984 and s 46 of the Vehicle Excise and Registration Act 1994, if complied with, may all have the incidental effect of facilitating proof of a criminal offence committed by the giver of the information.

Article 6 of the convention

Attention has often, and rightly, been drawn to contrasts between different articles of the convention. Some (such as arts 3 and 4) permit no restriction by national authorities. Others (such as arts 8, 9, 10 and 11) permit a measure of restriction if certain stringent and closely prescribed conditions are satisfied. Article 6 is in these terms:

> '**Right to a fair trial**
>
> 1. In the determination of his civil rights and obligations or of any criminal charge against him, everyone is entitled to a fair and public hearing within a reasonable time by an independent and impartial tribunal established by law. Judgment shall be pronounced publicly but the press and public may be excluded from all or part of the trial in the interest of morals, public order or national security in a democratic society, where the interests of juveniles or the protection of the private life of the parties so require, or to the extent strictly necessary in the opinion of the court in special circumstances where publicity would prejudice the interests of justice.
>
> 2. Everyone charged with a criminal offence shall be presumed innocent until proved guilty according to law.
>
> 3. Everyone charged with a criminal offence has the following minimum rights: (a) to be informed promptly, in a language which he understands and in detail, of the nature and cause of the accusation against him; (b) to have adequate time and facilities for the preparation of his defence; (c) to defend himself in person or through legal assistance of his own choosing or, if he has not sufficient means to pay for legal assistance, to be given it free when the interests of justice so require; (d) to examine or have examined witnesses against him and to obtain the attendance and examination of witnesses on his behalf under the same conditions as witnesses against him; (e) to have the free assistance of an interpreter if he cannot understand or speak the language used in court.'

This article has more in common with the first group of articles mentioned above than the second. The only express qualification relates to the requirement of a 'public hearing'. But there is nothing to suggest that the fairness of the trial a itself may be qualified, compromised or restricted in any way, whatever the circumstances and whatever the public interest in convicting the offender. If the trial as a whole is judged to be unfair, a conviction cannot stand.

What a fair trial requires cannot, however, be the subject of a single, unvarying rule or collection of rules. It is proper to take account of the facts and circumstances of particular cases, as the European Court has consistently done. Before considering b the right not to incriminate oneself with which this appeal is specifically concerned, it is helpful to review the way in which the European Court has treated other rights held to be comprised within art 6.

The presumption of innocence

The right to be presumed innocent of a criminal offence until proved guilty c according to law is expressed in art 6(2) of the convention. This appears on its face to be an absolute requirement. But it has been held that it does not prohibit rules which transfer the burden to the accused to establish a defence, provided the overall burden of proof remains on the prosecution, nor does it necessarily prohibit presumptions of law or fact provided these are within reasonable limits. d In *Salabiaku v France* (1988) 13 EHRR 379 at 388 (para 28) the court held:

> 'Presumptions of fact or of law operate in every legal system. Clearly, the Convention does not prohibit such presumptions in principle. It does, however, require the Contracting States to remain within certain limits in this respect as regards criminal law … Article 6(2) does not therefore regard e presumptions of fact or of law provided for in the criminal law with indifference. It requires States to confine them within reasonable limits which take into account the importance of what is at stake and maintain the rights of the defence. The Court proposes to consider whether such limits were exceeded to the detriment of Mr. Salabiaku.'

f As Clayton and Tomlinson point out in *The Law of Human Rights* (2000) vol 1, p 662 (para 11.238), the following have been held not to violate art 6(2) of the convention: the requirement that a person charged with criminal libel prove the truth of the statement (*Lingens v Austria* (1981) 4 EHRR 373); the presumption that a person, having come through customs in possession of prohibited goods, had smuggled them (*Salabiaku v France*); the presumption that a man living with g a prostitute was knowingly living off immoral earnings (*X v UK* (1972) 42 CD 135); a presumption that a dog was a member of a specified breed (*Bates v UK* [1996] EHRLR 312); the burden on the accused to establish the defence of insanity (*H v UK* App No 15023/89 (4 April 1990, unreported)). In *R v DPP, ex p Kebilene* [1999] 4 All ER 801 at 847, [2000] 2 AC 326 at 385 my noble and learned friend Lord Hope h said:

> 'The cases show that, although art 6(2) is in absolute terms, it is not regarded as imposing an absolute prohibition on reverse onus clauses, whether they be evidential (presumptions of fact) or persuasive (presumptions of law). In each case the question will be whether the presumption is within reasonable limits.'

j

The right of access to a court

Article 6 contains no express right of access to a court, but in *Golder v UK* (1975) 1 EHRR 524 at 535–536 (para 35) the European Court held that it would be 'inconceivable' that art 6 should describe in detail the procedural guarantees afforded to parties in a pending law suit and should not first protect that which alone makes it possible to benefit from such guarantees, namely access to a court. In para 38 of its judgment (at 537) the court added: a

> 'The Court considers, accepting the views of the Commission and the alternative submission of the Government, that the right of access to the courts is not absolute. As this is a right which the Convention sets forth without, in the narrower sense of the term, defining, there is room, apart from the bounds delimiting the very content of any right, for limitations permitted by implication.' b

This expression of view was repeated in *Ashingdane v UK* (1985) 7 EHRR 528 at 546 (para 57), where the court ruled:

> 'Certainly, the right of access to the courts is not absolute but may be subject to limitations; these are permitted by implication since the right of access, "by its very nature calls for regulation by the State, regulation which may vary in time and place according to the needs and resources of the community and of individuals". In laying down such regulation, the Contracting States enjoy a certain margin of appreciation. Whilst the final decision as to observance of the Convention's requirements rests with the Court, it is no part of the Court's function to substitute for the assessment of the national authorities any other assessment of what might be the best policy in this field.' c d

These principles were repeated in *Fayed v UK* (1994) 18 EHRR 393 at 429 (para 65); and in *Tinnelly & Sons Ltd v UK* (1998) 4 BHRC 393 at 415 (para 72) the court said that while the right of access to a court might be subject to limitations— e

> 'the final decision as to the observance of the convention's requirements rests with the court. It must be satisfied that the limitations applied do not restrict or reduce the access left to the individual in such a way or to such an extent that the very essence of the right is impaired. Furthermore, a limitation will not be compatible with art 6(1) if it does not pursue a legitimate aim and if there is not a reasonable relationship of proportionality between the means employed and the aim sought to be achieved ...' f

The European Court's judgment in *National & Provincial Building Society v UK* (1997) 25 EHRR 127 at 178–179 (para 105), was to the same effect. Restrictions on the access to court of other potential litigants have also been recognised in the cases of minors (*Golder v UK* (1975) 1 EHRR 524 at 537 (para 39)), vexatious litigants (*H v UK* (1985) 45 DR 281), prisoners (*Campbell and Fell v UK* (1984) 7 EHRR 165) and bankrupts (*M v UK* (1987) 52 DR 269): see Clayton and Tomlinson, pp 640–641 (para 11.191). g h

Equality of arms

Equality of arms between the prosecutor and defendant has been recognised by the court as lying at the heart of the right to a fair trial. The scope and implications of this principle have been considered in many cases, and recently in *Fitt v UK* (2000) 30 EHRR 480 at 510–511 where the court said: j

> '44. It is a fundamental aspect of the right to a fair trial that criminal proceedings, including the elements of such proceedings which relate to procedure, should be adversarial and that there should be equality of arms between the prosecution and defence. The right to an adversarial trial

a means, in a criminal case, that both prosecution and defence must be given the opportunity to have knowledge of and comment on the observations filed and the evidence adduced by the other party (see *Brandstetter v Austria* (1991) 15 EHRR 378 at 413–414 (paras 66–67)). In addition Article 6(1) requires, as indeed does English law (see para. 18 above), that the prosecution authorities should disclose to the defence all material evidence in their b possession for or against the accused (see *Edwards v UK* (1992) 15 EHRR 417 at 431–432 (para 36)). 45. However, as the applicant recognised (see para. 38 above), the entitlement to disclosure of relevant evidence is not an absolute right. In any criminal proceedings there may be competing interests, such as national security or the need to protect witnesses at risk of reprisals or keep secret police methods of investigation of crime, which must be weighed c against the rights of the accused (see, for example, *Doorson v Netherlands* (1996) 22 EHRR 330 at 358 (para 70)). In some cases it may be necessary to withhold certain evidence from the defence so as to preserve the fundamental rights of another individual or to safeguard an important public interest. However, only such measures restricting the rights of the defence d which are strictly necessary are permissible under Article 6(1) (see *van Mechelen v Netherlands* (1997) 2 BHRC 486 at 503 (para 58)). Moreover, in order to ensure that the accused receives a fair trial, any difficulties caused to the defence by a limitation on its rights must be sufficiently counterbalanced by the procedures followed by the judicial authorities (see … *Doorson v Netherlands* (1996) 22 EHRR 330 at 358 (para 72), and … *van Mechelen v Netherlands* e (1997) 2 BHRC 486 at 503 (para 54)).'

Article 6(3)(d) of the convention

A similar approach has been taken to the application of art 6(3)(d): measures to f withhold the identity of witnesses may be justified if subject to appropriate judicial safeguards (*X v UK* (1993) 15 EHRR CD 113), but not where the procedure adopted is such as to deny the defendant his basic right to a fair trial. Such was held to be the case in *Kostovski v Netherlands* (1989) 12 EHRR 434 at 449 (para 44), where the European Court said:

g 'As on previous occasions the Court does not underestimate the importance of the struggle against organised crime. Yet the Government's line of argument, whilst not without force, is not decisive. Although the growth in organised crime doubtless demands the introduction of appropriate measures, the Government's submissions appear to the Court to h lay insufficient weight on what the applicant's counsel described as "the interest of everybody in a civilised society in a controllable and fair judicial procedure." The right to a fair administration of justice holds so prominent a place in a democratic society that it cannot be sacrificed to expediency.'

j *The admission of unlawfully obtained evidence*

The admissibility of evidence has been recognised as, generally speaking, a matter for national legal systems to regulate. *Schenk v Switzerland* (1988) 13 EHRR 242 concerned the admissibility of evidence obtained unlawfully and in breach of the defendant's rights under art 8 of the convention. In para 46 of its judgment (at 265–266) the court said:

'While Article 6 of the Convention guarantees the right to a fair trial, it does not lay down any rules on the admissibility of evidence as such, which is therefore primarily a matter for regulation under national law. The Court therefore cannot exclude as a matter of principle and in the abstract that unlawfully obtained evidence of the present kind may be admissible. It has only to ascertain whether Mr. Schenk's trial as a whole was fair.'

In that case the European Court attached weight to the fact that the case against the defendant did not rest solely on the recording of the telephone conversation which had been unlawfully made and which the defendant sought to exclude. Less weight was attached to this last feature in *Khan v UK* (2000) 8 BHRC 310, which closely resembled the case of *Schenk v Switzerland* on its facts. Here the court said (at 320):

'37. The court next notes that the contested material in the present case was in effect the only evidence against the applicant and that the applicant's plea of guilty was tendered only on the basis of the judge's ruling that the evidence should be admitted. However, the relevance of the existence of evidence other than the contested matter depends on the circumstances of the case. In the present circumstances, where the tape recording was acknowledged to be very strong evidence, and where there was no risk of it being unreliable, the need for supporting evidence is correspondingly weaker. It is true that, in the case of *Schenk v Switzerland* ((1988) 13 EHRR 242), weight was attached by the court to the fact that the tape recording at issue in that case was not the only evidence against the applicant. However, the court notes in this regard that the recording in *Schenk v Switzerland*, although not the only evidence, was described by the Criminal Cassation Division of the Vaud Cantonal Court as having "a perhaps decisive influence, or at the least a not inconsiderable one, on the outcome of the criminal proceedings" (see *Schenk v Switzerland* (at 255–259 (para 28)). Moreover, this element was not the determinative factor in the court's conclusion. 38. The central question in the present case is whether the proceedings as a whole were fair. With specific reference to the admission of the contested tape recording, the court notes that, as in *Schenk v Switzerland*, the applicant had ample opportunity to challenge both the authenticity and the use of the recording. He did not challenge its authenticity, but challenged its use at the voire dire and again before the Court of Appeal and the House of Lords. The court notes that at each level of jurisdiction the domestic courts assessed the effect of admission of the evidence on the fairness of the trial by reference to s 78 of PACE, and the courts discussed, amongst other matters, the non-statutory basis for the surveillance. The fact that the applicant was at each step unsuccessful makes no difference (see *Schenk v Switzerland* (at 266 (para 47))). 39. The court would add that it is clear that, had the domestic courts been of the view that the admission of the evidence would have given rise to substantive unfairness, they would have had a discretion to exclude it under s 78 of PACE.'

The right not to incriminate oneself

The right not to incriminate oneself and the right to silence, although distinct rights, are closely related, as acknowledged by the House of Lords in *Smith v Director of Serious Fraud Office* [1992] 3 All ER 456 at 471–472, [1993] AC 1 at 40 where Lord Mustill said:

> 'That there is strong presumption against interpreting a statute as taking away the right of silence, at least in some of its forms, cannot in my view be doubted. Recently, Lord Griffiths (delivering the opinion in the Privy Council in *Lam Chi-ming v R* ([1991] 3 All ER 172 at 179, [1991] 2 AC 212 at 222)) described the privilege against self-incrimination as "deep rooted in English law", and I would not wish to minimise its importance in any way.'

It is convenient for present purposes to consider these two rights together.

Murray v UK (1996) 22 EHRR 29 concerned the compatibility with art 6 of the convention of a rule permitting a trial court to draw adverse inferences from a failure of a defendant to answer police questions before the trial and give evidence at the trial. The court held (at 60–61):

> '45. Although not specifically mentioned in Article 6 of the Convention, there can be no doubt that the right to remain silent under police questioning and the privilege against self-incrimination are generally recognised international standards which lie at the heart of the notion of a fair procedure under Article 6. By providing the accused with protection against improper compulsion by the authorities these immunities contribute to avoiding miscarriages of justice and to securing the aim of Article 6. 46. The Court does not consider that it is called upon to give an abstract analysis of the scope of these immunities and, in particular, of what constitutes in this context "improper compulsion". What is at stake in the present case is whether these immunities are absolute in the sense that the exercise by an accused of the right to silence cannot under any circumstances be used against him at trial or, alternatively, whether informing him in advance that, under certain conditions, his silence may be used, is always to be regarded as "improper compulsion". 47. On the one hand, it is self-evident that [it] is incompatible with the immunities under consideration to base a conviction solely or mainly on the accused's silence or on a refusal to answer questions or to give evidence himself. On the other hand, the Court deems it equally obvious that these immunities cannot and should not prevent that the accused's silence, in situations which clearly call for an explanation from him, be taken into account in assessing the persuasiveness of the evidence adduced by the prosecution. Wherever the line between these two extremes is to be drawn, it follows from this understanding of "the right to silence" that the question whether the right is absolute must be answered in the negative. It cannot be said therefore that an accused's decision to remain silent throughout criminal proceedings should necessarily have no implications when the trial court seeks to evaluate the evidence against him. In particular, as the Government has pointed out, established international standards in this area, while providing for the right to silence and the privilege against self-incrimination, are silent on this point. Whether the drawing of adverse inferences from an accused's silence infringes Article 6 is a matter to be determined in the light of all the circumstances of the case, having particular regard to the situations where inferences may be drawn, the weight attached to them by the national courts in their assessment of the evidence and the degree of compulsion inherent in the situation.'

This decision was shortly followed by that in *Saunders v UK* (1997) 2 BHRC 358, an authority on which the respondent particularly relied before the High Court and the Board. Suspicion of an unlawful share support operation in the shares of

Guinness plc had led to the appointment of inspectors, who had found evidence of criminal conduct and had thereafter interviewed Mr Saunders, formerly a director and the chief executive of Guinness, on nine occasions. He was charged with numerous offences, and the prosecution sought to rely on the transcript of his interviews by the inspectors. The admissibility of such transcripts was challenged, but the judge ruled that under the relevant statute the inspectors were entitled to ask witnesses questions that tended to incriminate them, that the witnesses were under a duty to answer such questions and that the answers were admissible in criminal proceedings. The judge did however exclude the transcripts of the last two interviews, conducted after Mr Saunders had been charged, applying s 78 of the Police and Criminal Evidence Act 1984. The issue before the European Court did not concern the propriety of compelling answers to the inspectors' questions at the investigatory stage but the propriety of admitting the evidence of those answers, compulsorily obtained, in the criminal proceedings. The court ruled in Mr Saunders' favour (at 373–376):

> '68. The Court recalls that, although not specifically mentioned in art 6 of the convention, the right to silence and the right not to incriminate oneself are generally recognised international standards which lie at the heart of the notion of a fair procedure under art 6. Their rationale lies, inter alia, in the protection of the accused against improper compulsion by the authorities thereby contributing to the avoidance of miscarriages of justice and to the fulfilment of the aims of art 6 (see *Murray v UK* ((1996) 22 EHRR 29) and *Funke v France* ((1993) 16 EHRR 297)). The right not to incriminate oneself, in particular, presupposes that the prosecution in a criminal case seek to prove their case against the accused without resort to evidence obtained through methods of coercion or oppression in defiance of the will of the accused. In this sense the right is closely linked to the presumption of innocence contained in art 6(2) of the convention. 69. The right not to incriminate oneself is primarily concerned, however, with respecting the will of an accused person to remain silent. As commonly understood in the legal systems of the contracting parties to the convention and elsewhere, it does not extend to the use in criminal proceedings of material which may be obtained from the accused through the use of compulsory powers but which has an existence independent of the will of the suspect such as, inter alia, documents acquired pursuant to a warrant, breath, blood and urine samples and bodily tissue for the purpose of DNA testing. In the present case the Court is only called upon to decide whether the use made by the prosecution of the statements obtained from the applicant by the inspectors amounted to an unjustifiable infringement of the right. This question must be examined by the Court in the light of all the circumstances of the case. In particular, it must be determined whether the applicant has been subject to compulsion to give evidence and whether the use made of the resulting testimony at his trial offended the basic principles of a fair procedure inherent in art 6(1) of which the right not to incriminate oneself is a constituent element. 70. It has not been disputed by the government that the applicant was subject to legal compulsion to give evidence to the inspectors. He was obliged under ss 434 and 436 of the Companies Act 1985 … to answer the questions put to him by the inspectors in the course of nine lengthy interviews of which seven were admissible as evidence at his trial. A refusal by the applicant to answer the questions put to him could have led to a finding of contempt of court and the

a imposition of a fine or committal to prison for up to two years ... and it was no defence to such refusal that the questions were of an incriminating nature ... However, the government have emphasised, before the Court, that nothing said by the applicant in the course of the interviews was self-incriminating and that he had merely given exculpatory answers or answers which, if true, would serve to confirm his defence. In their submission only statements which are b self-incriminating could fall within the privilege against self-incrimination. 71. The Court does not accept the government's premise on this point since some of the applicant's answers were in fact of an incriminating nature in the sense that they contained admissions to knowledge of information which tended to incriminate him ... In any event, bearing in mind the concept of c fairness in art 6, the right not to incriminate oneself cannot reasonably be confined to statements of admission of wrongdoing or to remarks which are directly incriminating. Testimony obtained under compulsion which appears on its face to be of a non-incriminating nature—such as exculpatory remarks or mere information on questions of fact—may later be deployed in criminal proceedings in support of the prosecution case, for example to contradict or d cast doubt upon other statements of the accused or evidence given by him during the trial or to otherwise undermine his credibility. Where the credibility of an accused must be assessed by a jury the use of such testimony may be especially harmful. It follows that what is of the essence in this context is the use to which evidence obtained under compulsion is made in e the course of the criminal trial ... 74. Nor does the Court find it necessary, having regard to the above assessment as to the use of the interviews during the trial, to decide whether the right not to incriminate oneself is absolute or whether infringements of it may be justified in particular circumstances. It does not accept the government's argument that the complexity of f corporate fraud and the vital public interest in the investigation of such fraud and the punishment of those responsible could justify such a marked departure as that which occurred in the present case from one of the basic principles of a fair procedure. Like the Commission, it considers that the general requirements of fairness contained in art 6, including the right not to incriminate oneself, apply to criminal proceedings in respect of all types of g criminal offences without distinction from the most simple to the most complex. The public interest cannot be invoked to justify the use of answers compulsorily obtained in a non-judicial investigation to incriminate the accused during the trial proceedings. It is noteworthy in this respect that under the relevant legislation statements obtained under compulsory h powers by the Serious Fraud Office cannot, as a general rule, be adduced in evidence at the subsequent trial of the person concerned. Moreover the fact that statements were made by the applicant prior to his being charged does not prevent their later use in criminal proceedings from constituting an infringement of the right.'

j

Condron v UK (2000) 8 BHRC 290 again concerned the drawing of inferences adverse to a defendant from his failure to mention matters on which he relied at trial to the police when questioned before the trial. The applicants in this case did not seek to argue that the right to silence was absolute in the context of a jury trial, accepting the decision in *Murray v UK* as the appropriate starting point for examining the issue. In this case, however, unlike *Murray v UK*, the applicants' complaint was upheld, on the ground that the trial judge had not in the court's opinion given the jury a sufficiently restrictive direction. a

The High Court in the present case (2000 JC 328 at 340–341) derived no assistance from three decisions of the European Commission of Human Rights (the commission) to which the attention of the Board has also been drawn. In *DN v Netherlands* App No 6170/73 (26 May 1975, unreported) the applicant complained that he had been fined for two parking offences which he had not himself b committed. He had refused to identify the offender to the authorities, and under the relevant legislation he, as the owner of the vehicle, was responsible for the unlawful parking of the car unless he proved that it had been used against his will and that he could not reasonably have prevented such use. The suggestion that it was a breach of art 6(1) of the convention to punish a person who had not directly committed the punishable act was described as 'misconceived'. The c presumption of innocence, it was held, was not engaged since under Netherlands law the applicant was guilty if the car was wrongly parked without his being able or willing either to name the driver or to establish that the car had been used against his will.

Under an Austrian law, considered in *JP, KR and GH v Austria* (1989) DR 62, the d registered owner of a car was obliged to inform the authorities at their request who had last driven or parked the car. The applicants were penalised for not doing so and complained that the proceedings infringed their rights under art 6 of the convention. The commission, although prepared to assume that art 6 applied to the proceedings, were not persuaded. Referring to their earlier decision in *DN v Netherlands* the commission ruled: e

> 'The regulation here in question is based on a similar principle, in that it obliges a car owner, or other person named by the owner as the driver of the car, to assume the responsibility for the use or to name the actual driver. Thereby the person concerned is not under all circumstances obliged to incriminate himself/herself or a close relative, but may, according to the circumstances, also f show that he/she is not connected with the offence committed by the driver. For example, a car may have been used by other known or unknown persons with or without the consent of the owner of the car.'

The applicant in *Tora Tolmos v Spain* (1995) 81 DR 82 was driving his car when a police radar detected that it was breaking the speed limit. A prosecution was g begun against the driver, and the applicant was served with a notice requiring him to disclose the name and address of the driver on the occasion in question on penalty of committing a serious summary offence if he failed to answer. He answered, falsely, that he could not identify the driver, and was fined for refusing to do so. He unsuccessfully challenged the constitutionality of the relevant h provision, and complained to the commission under art 6 of the convention that the imposition of the fine breached his right not to be obliged to confess. The commission considered that the Spanish provision in question did not disclose any appearance of violating art 6.

It is certainly clear, as the High Court of Judiciary pointed out, that none of j these three applications concerned the reliance at trial on incriminating answers compulsorily obtained at an earlier stage; but the decisions are not in my view irrelevant, since it is also clear that had the applicants identified themselves as the persons responsible for committing the road traffic offence in question in each case, they would have been prosecuted for those offences. Thus, like the respondent in this case, the choice that effectively faced them was to answer the question and a be prosecuted for the substantive offence, or refuse to answer it and be penalised for that refusal.

The parties' submissions

In challenging the decision of the High Court, the Solicitor General for Scotland (representing the procurator fiscal) and the Advocate General for b Scotland made common cause. While accepting that the right of an accused person to a fair trial was absolute and could not be qualified, they relied on the case law of the European Court as showing that the constituent rights comprised within art 6 were not themselves absolute. Provided the overall fairness of the trial was not compromised, some deference should be shown towards the administrative judgment of member states on the social problems which they sought to address. c Different member states had responded to road traffic problems in different ways, but the need to minimise the incidence of death and injury on the roads, and to identify and penalise drivers who offended against laws enacted to protect the public, was obvious and the United Kingdom's response, embodied in s 172 of the 1988 Act, was proportionate and not such as to compromise a fair trial. The right d not to incriminate oneself is an important right, but not an absolute right, and it is directed (as suggested by the European Court in *Saunders v UK*) to improper compulsion, coercion and oppression likely to result in forced confessions and miscarriages of justice. In the absence of any evidence of compulsion, coercion or oppression, mere invocation of s 172 does not infringe a suspect's right to a fair trial even where it leads to an admission relied on at a later trial: the admission e here was made in response to a single unthreatening question, and although providing the prosecutor with proof of a fact necessary to convict did not of itself involve any admission of criminal conduct.

The written submission of JUSTICE was broadly to the same effect. It was submitted that the public interest could justify a more restrictive interpretation of the f right against self-incrimination in the context of road traffic prosecutions than would be permitted in relation to other offences, so long as there was no erosion of a suspect's protection against improper compulsion and unfair use of compulsorily obtained evidence.

In a cogently argued submission on behalf of the respondent, counsel supported the decision of the High Court and the reasoning on which it was based. It was g unnecessary to contend that the right not to incriminate oneself was absolute. The European Court's reasoning in *Saunders v UK* prohibited reliance on an answer compulsorily obtained before a trial to convict a defendant at trial. In the present case, the respondent had been compulsorily required to admit to her driving of the car. The procurator fiscal was now seeking to rely on that admission h to convict her of a criminal offence. Without proof of her identity as the driver she could not be convicted. There was thus a clear infringement of the respondent's right not to incriminate herself, a right recognised by the common law of Scotland well before incorporation of the convention into the law of the United Kingdom. Considerations of expediency could not be relied on to justify that infringement.

j

Conclusions

The convention is an international treaty by which the contracting states mutually undertake to secure to all within their respective jurisdictions certain rights and freedoms. The fundamental nature of these rights and freedoms is clear, not only from the full title and the content of the convention but from its preamble in which the signatory governments declared:

> '… their profound belief in those fundamental freedoms which are the foundation of justice and peace in the world and are best maintained on the one hand by an effective political democracy and on the other by a common understanding and observance of the human rights upon which they depend …'

Judicial recognition and assertion of the human rights defined in the convention is not a substitute for the processes of democratic government but a complement to them. While a national court does not accord the margin of appreciation recognised by the European Court as a supra-national court, it will give weight to the decisions of a representative legislature and a democratic government within the discretionary area of judgment accorded to those bodies (see Lester and Pannick *Human Rights Law and Practice* (1999) pp 73–76 (paras 3.20–3.26). The convention is concerned with rights and freedoms which are of real importance in a modern democracy governed by the rule of law. It does not, as is sometimes mistakenly thought, offer relief from 'The heart-ache and the thousand natural shocks That flesh is heir to'.

In interpreting the convention, as any other treaty, it is generally to be assumed that the parties have included the terms which they wished to include and on which they were able to agree, omitting other terms which they did not wish to include or on which they were not able to agree. Thus particular regard must be had and reliance placed on the express terms of the convention, which define the rights and freedoms which the contracting parties have undertaken to secure. This does not mean that nothing can be implied into the convention. The language of the convention is for the most part so general that some implication of terms is necessary, and the case law of the European Court shows that the court has been willing to imply terms into the convention when it was judged necessary or plainly right to do so. But the process of implication is one to be carried out with caution, if the risk is to be averted that the contracting parties may, by judicial interpretation, become bound by obligations which they did not expressly accept and might not have been willing to accept. As an important constitutional instrument the convention is to be seen as a 'living tree capable of growth and expansion within its natural limits' (*Edwards v A-G for Canada* [1930] AC 124 at 136 per Lord Sankey LC), but those limits will often call for very careful consideration.

Effect has been given to the right not to incriminate oneself in a variety of different ways. The Fifth Amendment to the Constitution of the United States provides that no person shall be compelled in any criminal case to be a witness against himself. The Indian Constitution (art 20(3)) provides that no person accused of any offence shall be compelled to be a witness against himself. The International Covenant on Civil and Political Rights (New York, 16 December 1966; TS 6 (1977); Cmnd 6702) provides in art 14(3)(g) that in determination of any criminal charge everyone shall be entitled to certain minimum guarantees, including a right not to be compelled to testify against himself or to confess guilt. The Canadian Charter of Rights and Freedoms confers on a person charged with an offence the right not to be compelled to be a witness in proceedings against himself in respect of that offence (s 11(c)). The New Zealand Bill of Rights Act 1990, in s 25(d), grants to everyone who is charged with an offence, in relation to the determination of the charge, certain minimum rights which include the right not to be compelled to be a witness or to confess guilt. The recently adopted constitution of South Africa grants rights to a suspect on arrest to remain silent and not to be compelled to make any confession or admission that could be used a in evidence against him (s 35(1)(a) and (c) of the constitution) and also a right to a fair trial, which includes rights to remain silent and not to testify during the proceedings and not to be compelled to give self-incriminating evidence (s 35(3)(h) and (j)). In contrast, the Universal Declaration of Human Rights (Paris, 10 December 1948; UN TS 2 (1949); Cmd 7226), in arts 10 and 11(1), grants a right to a fair trial in terms similar to the convention, but, like the convention, contains no express b guarantee of a privilege against self-incrimination. Thus the right we have to consider in this case is an implied right. While it cannot be doubted that such a right must be implied, there is no treaty provision which expressly governs the effect or extent of what is to be implied.

The jurisprudence of the European Court very clearly establishes that while the overall fairness of a criminal trial cannot be compromised, the constituent c rights comprised, whether expressly or implicitly, within art 6 are not themselves absolute. Limited qualification of these rights is acceptable if reasonably directed by national authorities towards a clear and proper public objective and if representing no greater qualification than the situation calls for. The general language of the convention could have led to the formulation of hard-edged and d inflexible statements of principle from which no departure could be sanctioned whatever the background or the circumstances. But this approach has been consistently eschewed by the court throughout its history. The case law shows that the court has paid very close attention to the facts of particular cases coming before it, giving effect to factual differences and recognising differences of degree. Ex facto oritur jus. The court has also recognised the need for a fair balance e between the general interest of the community and the personal rights of the individual, the search for which balance has been described as inherent in the whole of the convention (see *Sporrong v Sweden* (1982) 5 EHRR 35 at 52–53 (para 69), *Sheffield v UK* (1998) 5 BHRC 83 at 94 (para 52)).

The high incidence of death and injury on the roads caused by the misuse of f motor vehicles is a very serious problem common to almost all developed societies. The need to address it in an effective way, for the benefit of the public, cannot be doubted. Among other ways in which democratic governments have sought to address it is by subjecting the use of motor vehicles to a regime of regulation and making provision for enforcement by identifying, prosecuting and punishing offending drivers. Materials laid before the Board, incomplete though g they are, reveal different responses to the problem of enforcement. Under some legal systems (Spain, Belgium and France are examples) the registered owner of a vehicle is assumed to be the driver guilty of minor traffic infractions unless he shows that some other person was driving at the relevant time or establishes some other ground of exoneration. There being a clear public interest in h enforcement of road traffic legislation the crucial question in the present case is whether s 172 of the 1988 Act represents a disproportionate response, or one that undermines a defendant's right to a fair trial, if an admission of being the driver is relied on at trial.

I do not for my part consider that s 172, properly applied, does represent a j disproportionate response to this serious social problem, nor do I think that reliance on the respondent's admission, in the present case, would undermine her right to a fair trial. I reach that conclusion for a number of reasons.

(1) Section 172 of the 1988 Act provides for the putting of a single, simple question. The answer cannot of itself incriminate the suspect, since it is not without more an offence to drive a car. An admission of driving may, of course, as here, provide proof of a fact necessary to convict, but the section does not

sanction prolonged questioning about the facts alleged to give rise to criminal offences such as was understandably held to be objectionable in *Saunders v UK*, and the penalty for declining to answer under the section is moderate and non-custodial. There is in the present case no suggestion of improper coercion or oppression such as might give rise to unreliable admissions and so contribute to a miscarriage of justice, and if there were evidence of such conduct the trial judge would have ample power to exclude evidence of the admission.

(2) While the High Court was entitled to distinguish, as it did (2000 JC 328 at 344–345) between the giving of an answer under s 172 and the provision of physical samples, and had the authority of the European Court in *Saunders v UK* (1997) 2 BHRC 358 at 374 (para 69) for doing so, this distinction should not in my opinion be pushed too far. It is true that the respondent's answer, whether given orally or in writing, would create new evidence which did not exist until she spoke or wrote. In contrast, it may be acknowledged, the percentage of alcohol in her breath was a fact, existing before she blew into the breathalyser machine. But the whole purpose of requiring her to blow into the machine (on pain of a criminal penalty if she refused) was to obtain evidence not available until she did so and the reading so obtained could, in all save exceptional circumstances, be enough to convict a driver of an offence. If one applies the language of *Wigmore on Evidence* (McNaughton revision 1961) vol 8, p 318, quoted by the High Court that an individual should 'not be conscripted by his opponent to defeat himself' it is not easy to see why a requirement to answer a question is objectionable and a requirement to undergo a breath test is not. Yet no criticism is made of the requirement that the respondent undergo a breath test.

(3) All who own or drive motor cars know that by doing so they subject themselves to a regulatory regime which does not apply to members of the public who do neither. Section 172 of the 1988 Act forms part of that regulatory regime. This regime is imposed not because owning or driving cars is a privilege or indulgence granted by the state but because the possession and use of cars (like, for example, shotguns, the possession of which is very closely regulated) are recognised to have the potential to cause grave injury. It is true that s 172(2)(b) permits a question to be asked of 'any other person' who, if not the owner or driver, might not be said to have impliedly accepted the regulatory regime, but someone who was not the owner or the driver would not incriminate himself whatever answer he gave. If, viewing this situation in the round, one asks whether s 172 represents a disproportionate legislative response to the problem of maintaining road safety, whether the balance between the interests of the community at large and the interests of the individual is struck in a manner unduly prejudicial to the individual, whether (in short) the leading of this evidence would infringe a basic human right of the respondent, I would feel bound to give negative answers. If the present argument is a good one it has been available to British citizens since 1966, but no one in this country has to my knowledge, criticised the legislation as unfair at any time up to now.

With much of the High Court judgment I am in respectful agreement. The United States Supreme Court decisions in *Hoffman v United States* (1951) 341 US 479 and *California v Byers* (1971) 402 US 424 and the decisions of the Supreme Court of Canada in *R v Jones* [1994] 2 SCR 229 and *R v White* (1999) 7 BHRC 120 undoubtedly support the conclusion reached. Those courts were, however, considering different constitutional provisions. In the present case the High Court (2000 JC 328 at 346) came very close to treating the right not to incriminate oneself as absolute, describing it as a 'central right' which permitted no gradations of fairness a depending on the seriousness of the charge or the circumstances of the case. The High Court interpreted the decision in *Saunders v UK* as laying down more absolute a standard than I think the European Court intended, and nowhere in the High Court judgments does one find any recognition of the need to balance the general interests of the community against the interests of the individual or to ask whether s 172 represents a proportionate response to what is undoubtedly b a serious social problem.

In my opinion the procurator fiscal is entitled at the respondent's forthcoming trial to lead evidence of her answer given under s 172. I would allow the appeal and quash the declaration made by the High Court.

c **LORD STEYN.**

I. *The central question*

On 3 June 1999 a vehicle belonging to Miss Brown was parked in a car park of a supermarket in Dunfermline. In reliance on s 172(2) of the Road Traffic Act 1988 a police officer asked Miss Brown who had been the driver of her vehicle d when it entered the car park. She answered 'It was me'. The police asked her for a specimen of breath. She gave a specimen. The breath test was positive. A prosecution ensued. The issue arose whether the procurator fiscal could lead evidence of the admission which Miss Brown had been compelled by law to make under s 172(2). The High Court of Justiciary (2000 JC 328) held that s 172(2) is e incompatible with the implied right against self incrimination under art 6 of the European Convention for the Protection of Human Rights and Fundamental Freedoms (Rome, 4 November 1950; TS 71 (1953); Cmd 8969) (the convention) and is therefore unlawful. In coming to this conclusion the High Court of Justiciary relied strongly on observations by the European Court of Human Rights in f *Saunders v UK* (1997) 2 BHRC 358 at 373–374 (paras 68–69). In the leading judgment of the Lord Justice General (Lord Rodger of Earlsferry), given with the approval of Lord Marnoch and Lord Allanbridge, the essential reasoning was as follows (at 346):

> 'In fact the Solicitor General's argument is incompatible with the actual g approach of the court in (*Saunders v UK* (1997) 2 BHRC 358). The Court held that the general requirements of fairness contained in art 6, including the right not to incriminate oneself, apply to criminal proceedings in respect of *all* types of criminal offences without distinction, from the most simple to the most complex. The Court's conclusion on this point can be derived simply h from the generality of the wording of art 6 which applies to the determination of "*any* criminal charge". If the right not to incriminate oneself is inherent in the right to a fair hearing under art 6, then it must apply to all criminal trials covered by the article. More importantly, however, the Court's conclusion is justified by the very nature of the right. If, as the Court held, it lies at the j heart of the notion of a fair procedure, then it must be a central right which applies to any criminal trial. Moreover, it is hard to see how there could be gradations of fairness depending on the seriousness of the charges in any given case. In any event, any central right would necessarily apply to the trial of an offence, such as a contravention of sec 5(1) of the 1988 Act, which carries a possible penalty of imprisonment. In my view therefore there is nothing in the circumstances of the present case which would justify a restrictive

interpretation or application of the right conferred by art 6(1).' (Lord Justice General's emphasis.)

This comes very close to saying that the privilege against self-incrimination is an absolute convention right and that no interference with it could ever be justified. Indeed it is far from clear what space, if any, is left for treating the privilege against self incrimination as not absolute.

II. *The objectives of the convention*

In the first real test of the Human Rights Act 1998 it is opportune to stand back and consider what the basic aims of the convention are. One finds the explanation in the very words of the preambles of the convention. There were two principal objectives. The first was to maintain and further realise human rights and fundamental freedoms. The framers of the convention recognised that it was not only morally right to promote the observance of human rights but that it was also the best way of achieving pluralistic and just societies in which all can peaceably go about their lives. The second aim was to foster effective political democracy. This aim necessarily involves the creation of conditions of stability and order under the rule of law, not for its own sake, but as the best way to ensuring the well being of the inhabitants of the European countries. After all, democratic government has only one raison d'être, namely to serve the interests of all the people. The inspirers of the convention, among whom Winston Churchill played an important role, and the framers of the convention, ably assisted by English draftsmen, realised that from time-to-time the fundamental right of one individual may conflict with the human right of another. Thus the principles of free speech and privacy may collide. They also realised only too well that a single-minded concentration on the pursuit of fundamental rights of individuals to the exclusion of the interests of the wider public might be subversive of the ideal of tolerant European liberal democracies. The fundamental rights of individuals are of supreme importance but those rights are not unlimited: we live in communities of individuals who also have rights. The direct lineage of this ancient idea is clear: the convention is the descendant of the Universal Declaration of Human Rights (Paris, 10 December 1948; UN TS 2 (1949); Cmd 7226) which in art 29 expressly recognised the duties of everyone to the community and the limitation on rights in order to secure and protect respect for the rights of others. It is also noteworthy that art 17 of the convention prohibits, among others, individuals from abusing their rights to the detriment of others. Thus, notwithstanding the danger of intolerance towards ideas, the convention system draws a line which does not accord the protection of free speech to those who propagate racial hatred against minorities: art 10; *Jersild v Denmark* (1995) 19 EHRR 1 at 25–26 (para 31). This is to be contrasted with the categorical language of the First Amendment to the United States Constitution which provides that 'Congress shall make no law … abridging the freedom of speech'. The convention requires that where difficult questions arise a balance must be struck. Subject to a limited number of absolute guarantees, the scheme and structure of the convention reflects this balanced approach. It differs in material respects from other constitutional systems but as a European nation it represents our Bill of Rights. We must be guided by it. And it is a basic premise of the convention system that only an entirely neutral, impartial, and independent judiciary can carry out the primary task of securing and enforcing convention rights. This contextual scene is not only directly a relevant to the issues arising on the present appeal but may be a matrix in which many challenges under the Human Rights Act should be considered.

III. *Article 6 of the convention*

The present case is concerned with art 6 of the convention which guarantees to every individual a fair trial in civil and criminal cases. The centrality of this b principle in the convention system has repeatedly been emphasised by the European Court. But even in respect of this basic guarantee, there is a balance to be observed. First, it is well settled that the public interest may be taken into account in deciding what the right to a fair trial requires in a particular context. Thus in *Doorson v Netherlands* (1996) 22 EHRR 330 at 358 (para 70) it was held that c 'principles of fair trial also require that in appropriate cases the interests of the defence are balanced against those of witnesses or victims called upon to testify'. Only one specific illustration of this balanced approach is necessary. Provided they are kept 'within reasonable limits' rebuttable presumptions of fact are permitted in criminal legislation (*Salabiaku v France* (1988) 13 EHRR 379). Secondly, once it has been determined that the guarantee of a fair trial has been d breached, it is never possible to justify such breach by reference to the public interest or on any other ground. This is to be contrasted with cases where a trial has been affected by irregularities not amounting to denial of a fair trial. In such cases it is fair that a court of appeal should have the power, even when faced by the fact of irregularities in the trial procedure, to dismiss the appeal if in the view e of the court of appeal the defendant's guilt is plain and beyond any doubt. However, it is a grave conclusion that a defendant has not had the substance of a fair trial. It means that the administration of justice has entirely failed. Subject to the possible exercise of a power to order a retrial where appropriate such a conviction can never be allowed to stand.

f IV. *The privilege against self-incrimination*

It is well settled, although not expressed in the convention, that there is an implied privilege against self incrimination under art 6. Moreover, s 172(2) of the 1988 Act undoubtedly makes an inroad on this privilege. On the other hand, it is also clear that the privilege against self incrimination is not an absolute right. g While there is no decision of the European Court directly in point, it is noteworthy that closely related rights have been held not to be absolute. It is significant that the basic right of access to the courts has been held to be not absolute (*Golder v UK* (1975) 1 EHRR 524). The principle that everyone charged with a criminal offence shall be presumed innocent until proved guilty according h to law is connected with the privilege against self incrimination. Yet the former has been held not to be absolute (*Salabiaku v France*). The European Court has also had occasion to emphasise the close link between the right of silence and the privilege against self incrimination: *Murray v UK* (1996) 22 EHRR 29. In *Murray v UK* the European Court held that the right of silence is not absolute.

j In these circumstances it would be strange if a right not expressed in the convention or any of its protocols, but implied into art 6 of the convention, had an absolute character. In my view the right in question is plainly not absolute. From this premise it follows that an interference with the right may be justified if the particular legislative provision was enacted in pursuance of a legitimate aim and if the scope of the legislative provision is necessary and proportionate to the achievement of the aim.

V. *Section 172(2) of the Road Traffic Act 1988*

In considering whether an inroad on the privilege against self incrimination can be justified, it is necessary to concentrate on the particular context. An intense focus on s 172(2) of the 1988 Act is required. It reads as follows:

> 'Where the driver of a vehicle is alleged to be guilty of an offence to which this section applies—(a) the person keeping the vehicle shall give such information as to the identity of the driver as he may be required to give by or on behalf of a chief officer of police, and (b) any other person shall if required as stated above give any information which it is in his power to give and may lead to identification of the driver.'

The penalty for failing to comply with s 172(2) is a fine of not more than £1,000. In addition an individual may be disqualified from driving and endorsement of the driver's licence is mandatory. It is well established that an oral admission made by a driver under s 172(2) is admissible in evidence (*Foster v Farrell* 1963 JC 46).

The subject of s 172(2) is the driving of vehicles. It is a notorious fact that vehicles are potentially instruments of death and injury. The statistics placed before the Board show a high rate of fatal and other serious accidents involving vehicles in Great Britain. The relevant statistics are as follows:

	1996	1997	1998
Fatal and serious accidents	40,601	39,628	37,770

The effective prosecution of drivers causing serious offences is a matter of public interest. But such prosecutions are often hampered by the difficulty of identifying the drivers of the vehicles at the time of, say, an accident causing loss of life or serious injury or potential danger to others. The tackling of this social problem seems in principle a legitimate aim for a legislature to pursue.

The real question is whether the legislative remedy in fact adopted is necessary and proportionate to the aim sought to be achieved. There were legislative choices to be made. The legislature could have decided to do no more than to exhort the police and prosecuting authorities to redouble their efforts. It may, however, be that such a policy would have been regarded as inadequate. Secondly, the legislature could have introduced a reverse burden of proof clause which placed the burden on the registered owner to prove that he was not the driver of the vehicle at a given time when it is alleged that an offence was committed. Thirdly, and this was the course actually adopted, there was the possibility of requiring information about the identity of the driver to be revealed by the registered owner and others. As between the second and third techniques it may be said that the latter involves the securing of an admission of a constituent element of the offence. On the other hand, such an admission, if wrongly made, is not conclusive. And it must be measured against the alternative of a reverse burden clause which could without further investigation of the identity of the driver lead to a prosecution. In their impact on the citizen the two techniques are not widely different. And it is rightly conceded that a properly drafted reverse burden of proof provision would have been lawful.

It is also important to keep in mind the narrowness of the interference. Section 172(2) is directed at obtaining information in one category, namely the identity of the driver at the time when an offence was allegedly committed. The most important part of s 172(2) is para (a) since the relevant information is usually peculiarly within the knowledge of the owner. But there may be scope for using para (b) in a limited category of cases, e g when only the identity of a passenger in a the car is known. Section 172(2) does not authorise general questioning by the police to secure a confession of an offence. On the other hand, s 172(2) does, depending on the circumstances, in effect authorise the police officer to invite the owner to make an admission of one element in a driving offence. It would, however, be an abuse of the power under s 172(2) for the police officer to employ improper or overbearing methods of obtaining the information. He may go no b further than to ask who the driver was at the given time. If the police officer strays beyond his power under s 172(2) a judge will have ample power at trial to exclude the evidence. It is therefore a relatively narrow interference with the privilege in one area which poses widespread and serious law enforcement problems.

c VI. *What deference may be accorded to the legislature?*

Under the convention system the primary duty is placed on domestic courts to secure and protect convention rights. The function of the European Court is essential but supervisory. In that capacity it accords to domestic courts a margin of appreciation, which recognises that national institutions are in principle better d placed than an international court to evaluate local needs and conditions. That principle is logically not applicable to domestic courts. On the other hand, national courts may accord to the decisions of national legislatures some deference *where the context justifies* it (see *R v DPP, ex p Kebilene* [1999] 4 All ER 801 at 844, [2000] 2 AC 326 at 381 per Lord Hope of Craighead; see also Singh, Hunt and Demetriou 'Is there a role for the "Margin of Appreciation" in National Law e after the Human Rights Act?' (1999) EHRLR pp 15–22. This point is well explained in Lester and Pannick *Human Rights Law and Practice* (1999) p 74 (para 3.21):

> 'Just as there are circumstances in which an international court will recognise that national institutions are better placed to assess the needs of f society, and to make difficult choices between competing considerations, so national courts will accept that there are some circumstances in which the legislature and the executive are better placed to perform those functions.'

In my view this factor is of some relevance in the present case. Here s 172(2) g addresses a pressing social problem, namely the difficulty of law enforcement in the face of statistics revealing a high accident rate resulting in death and serious injuries. The legislature was entitled to regard the figures of serious accidents as unacceptably high. It would also have been entitled to take into account that it was necessary to protect other convention rights, viz the right to life of members of the public exposed to the danger of accidents (see art 2(1)). On this aspect the h legislature was in as good a position as a court to assess the gravity of the problem and the public interest in addressing it. It really then boils down to the question whether in adopting the procedure enshrined in s 172(2), rather than a reverse burden technique, it took more drastic action than was justified. While this is ultimately a question for the court, it is not unreasonable to regard both j techniques as permissible in the field of the driving of vehicles. After all, the subject invites special regulation; objectively the interference is narrowly circumscribed; and it is qualitatively not very different from requiring, for example, a breath specimen from a driver. Moreover, it is less invasive than an essential modern tool of crime detection such as the taking of samples from a suspect for DNA profiling. If the matter was not covered by authority, I would have concluded that s 172(2) is compatible with art 6.

VII. *Saunders v UK*

The decision of the European Court in *Saunders v UK* (1997) 2 BHRC 358 gave some support to the view of the High Court of Justiciary. With due respect I have to say that the reasoning in *Saunders v UK* is unsatisfactory and less than clear: see the critique in Andrews 'Hiding Behind the Veil; Financial Delinquency and the Law' (1997) 22 ELRev 369; Eriksen and Thorkildsen 'Self Incrimination, The Ban on Self Incrimination after the Saunders Judgment' (1997) 5(2) *J Financial Crime* 182; Davies 'Do Polluters have the right not to incriminate themselves' (1999) 143 SJ 924. The European Court (at 375–376 (para 74)) did not rule that the privilege against self incrimination is absolute. Surprisingly in view of its decision in *Murray v UK* that the linked right of silence is not absolute it left the point open in respect of the privilege against self-incrimination. On the other hand, the substance of its reasoning treats both privileges as not absolute. The court observed (at 373–374 (para 68)):

> 'The Court recalls that, although not specifically mentioned in art 6 of the convention, the right to silence and the right not to incriminate oneself are generally recognised international standards which lie at the heart of the notion of a fair procedure under art 6. Their rationale lies, inter alia, in the protection of the accused from improper compulsion by the authorities thereby contributing to the avoidance of miscarriages of justice and to the fulfilment of the aims of art 6 …'

The court emphasised the rationale of improper compulsion. It does not hold that *anything* said under compulsion of law is inadmissible. Admittedly, the court also observed:

> 'The right not to incriminate oneself, in particular, presupposes that the prosecution in a criminal case seek to prove their case against the accused without resort to evidence obtained through methods of coercion or oppression in defiance of the will of the accused. In this sense the right is closely linked to the presumption of innocence contained in art 6(2) of the convention.'

Again one finds the link with the non-absolute right of silence. In any event 'methods of coercion or oppression in defiance of the will of the accused' is probably another way of referring to improper compulsion. This is consistent with the following passage (at 374 (para 69)):

> 'In the present case the Court is only called upon to decide whether the use made by the prosecution of the statements obtained from the applicant by the inspectors amounted to an unjustifiable infringement of the right. This question must be examined by the Court in the light of all the circumstances of the case. In particular, it must be determined whether the applicant has been subject to compulsion to give evidence and whether the use made of the resulting testimony at his trial offended the basic principles of a fair procedure inherent in art 6(1) of which the right not to incriminate oneself is a constituent element.'

The expression 'unjustifiable infringement of the right' implies that some infringements may be justified. In my view the observations in *Saunders v UK* do not support an absolutist view of the privilege against self incrimination. It may be that the observations in *Saunders v UK* will have to be clarified in a further case by the European Court. As things stand, however, I consider that the High Court a of Justiciary put too great weight on these observations. In my view they were never intended to apply to a case such as the present.

VIII. *Conclusion on art 6*

That brings me back to the decision of the High Court of Justiciary. It treated the privilege against self incrimination as virtually absolute. That conclusion fits b uneasily into the balanced convention system, and cannot be reconciled with art 6 of the convention in all its constituent parts and the spectrum of jurisprudence of the European Court on the various facets of art 6.

I would hold that the decision of the High Court of Justiciary on the merits was wrong. The procurator fiscal is entitled to lead the evidence of Miss Brown's admission under s 172(2) of the 1988 Act.

c

IX. *The remaining issues*

I am in complete agreement with Lord Hope of Craighead that a devolution issue has been raised and I would respectfully endorse his reasons. I too would prefer not to express a view on the third issue.

d

X. *Disposal*

For these reasons, as well as the reasons given by Lord Bingham of Cornhill, I would allow the appeal and quash the declaration made by the High Court.

e **LORD HOPE OF CRAIGHEAD.** This is an appeal under para 13(a) of Sch 6 to the Scotland Act 1998, with leave of the High Court of Justiciary, against a determination of a devolution issue by that court. Its determination took the form of a declarator that, in the circumstances of this case, the procurator fiscal had no power when he was prosecuting the respondent on a charge of driving after consuming an excess of alcohol under s 5(1) of the Road Traffic Act 1988 to f lead and rely on evidence of an admission which the respondent was compelled to make under s 172(2)(a) of that Act that she had been the driver of a motor vehicle at or about 2.30 a m on 3 June 1999 which was parked in the car park of the Asda Superstore at the Halbeath Retail Park in Dunfermline.

g *Is the issue raised a 'devolution issue'?*

It is necessary to consider first whether the issue in this case raises a devolution issue within the meaning of para 1 of Sch 6 to the Scotland Act. This is because the jurisdiction which has been conferred upon the Judicial Committee under Sch 6 of that Act is limited to the determination of devolution issues as defined in that paragraph (see paras 10–13 of the Schedule). There was a difference of view h in the courts below on this point. The sheriff refused to hold that the minute lodged by the respondent's agent had raised a devolution issue. But in the High Court the Solicitor General did not seek to support the sheriff's reasoning. The Lord Justice General (Lord Rodger of Earlsferry) described that reasoning as manifestly untenable. He expressed his own conclusion on the point in these j words (2000 JC 328 at 331): 'I need therefore say no more about it except to confirm that the minute discloses a sharp devolution issue in terms of para 1(d) of Schedule 6 to the Scotland Act 1998.'

Doubts as to the soundness of that view and of observations to the like effect in other cases in the High Court of Justiciary were raised by their Lordships in the course of the hearing by the Judicial Committee of the appeals in *Montgomery v HM Advocate, Coulter v HM Advocate* [2001] 2 WLR 779, the reasons for decision in which were delivered on 19 October 2000. In the event, the Board were able to dispose of those appeals without coming to a concluded view on the point. As Lord Slynn of Hadley observed (at 782), all parties were prepared to argue the case on the assumption that it was a devolution issue and, indeed, all parties argued that it was. But it is unsatisfactory that this important issue should be left unresolved. In the present case their Lordships have had the advantage of detailed submissions from, on the one hand, the Solicitor General who has contended that no devolution issue has been raised and, on the other, the Advocate General who has contended the contrary. Mr Duguid QC for the respondent adopted the submissions that were advanced by the Advocate General. So I believe that it is now possible for the Board, having heard argument on both sides, to reach a decision on the matter. It is important, in the interests of certainty, that it should now do so.

The two competing arguments may be summarised as follows. On the one hand there is the argument which the Solicitor General advanced with reference to the wording of art 6(1) of the European Convention for the Protection of Human Rights and Fundamental Freedoms (Rome, 4 November 1950; TS 71 (1953); Cmd 8969) (the convention) and the observations in *Montgomery v HM Advocate* of Lord Hoffmann. On the other there is the argument advanced by the Advocate General with reference to the wording of the Scotland Act and my own observations in that case. The essential point of difference between these two arguments is whether the solution to the problem lies simply in the opening words of art 6(1) of the convention which describe the convention right to a fair trial, or whether it lies in the provisions of the Scotland Act which describe the functions of the Lord Advocate as a member of the Scottish Executive and provide a system for the determination of questions which arise in proceedings before a court or tribunal whether he has purported to act or proposes to act outside his powers under that Act.

The position which was contended for by the Solicitor General was that the act of leading and relying upon the evidence of the admission could not of itself cause any unfair determination of the charge within the meaning of art 6(1). The prosecutor's act was not incompatible with the respondent's right to a fair hearing. It was for the court to determine whether or not the evidence should be admitted, so it was only at the stage of the determination of the matter by the court that the question of fairness would arise. If the evidence was admitted the respondent would be entitled then to argue that the court, as a public authority within the meaning of s 6(1) of the Human Rights Act 1998, had acted in a way that was incompatible with her convention right. She would be entitled to seek a remedy under that Act by appealing against her conviction on the basis of that evidence. But that would not raise a devolution issue within the meaning of para 1(d) of Sch 6 to the Scotland Act, for the obvious reason that the court is not a member of the Scottish Executive.

The position which was contended for by the Advocate General was that the act of the prosecutor in maintaining the prosecution and inviting the court to rely upon the evidence was outwith the powers of the Lord Advocate as a member of the Scottish Executive because it was incompatible, within the meaning of s 57(2) of the Scotland Act, with the respondent's convention rights. While the court had the primary responsibility to ensure that the respondent had a fair trial, the effect of the Scotland Act was that this was also a responsibility of the prosecutor. The importance of this division of responsibility was underlined by the fact that, prior to the coming into force of the Human Rights Act on 2 October 2000, SI 2000/1851, a the only way of safeguarding a person's convention right to a fair trial under the devolution settlement was by challenging the acts of the prosecutor. Parliament had chosen to give effect to the international obligations of the state under the convention when it enacted the Scotland Act by imposing corresponding limits on the competence of the Scottish Parliament and the powers of the Scottish Executive. The system for the determination of devolution issues which was laid b down in that Act was designed to ensure that a remedy was available in domestic law for any infringement of a person's convention rights as soon as the relevant provisions of the Scotland Act were brought into force on 6 May 1999, SI 1998/3178.

For the reasons which I expressed more fully in my judgment in *Montgomery v HM Advocate* I consider that the solution to the problem is to be found in the c provisions of the Scotland Act. The approach which that Act has taken to the question as to how best to ensure that effect is given under the devolved system to the convention rights is that the right of the accused to receive a fair trial is a responsibility of the Lord Advocate in the prosecution of offences as well as of the court. I base this view on an analysis of the provisions of that Act. It is of cardinal d importance to a proper understanding of the point to appreciate the overall context in which the relevant provisions were enacted. At the heart of the whole question lies the scheme which Parliament has constructed for the devolution of legislative and executive competence to Scotland from Westminster.

Article 13 of the convention provides that everyone whose rights and freedoms as set forth in the convention are violated shall have an effective remedy before a e national authority. This article is not one of the convention rights to which effect is given by the Human Rights Act, but it has not been overlooked. The reason which was given for its omission from the articles set out in Sch 1 to that Act was that ss 7 to 9 of the Human Rights Act were intended to lay down an appropriate remedial structure for giving effect to the convention rights as defined by s 1(1) f of that Act. The state's obligation to provide an effective remedy before a national tribunal in the event of a violation of the convention rights also forms an important part of the background to the devolution legislation. The structure of the devolved system of government which is set out in the Scotland Act takes account of the state's obligations under the convention in the same way as it takes account of its obligations in Community law. In both respects Parliament has g chosen to legislate in a way which ensures that those obligations are respected both by the Scottish Parliament and the Scottish Executive by limiting their competence. It has also chosen to ensure that questions which arise as to whether the Parliament or the Executive have acted or are proposing to act in a way that is incompatible with any of the convention rights or with Community h law may be resolved, as devolution issues, under the system laid down in Sch 6 to the Scotland Act. The same system has been adopted for the determination of devolution issues under the Government of Wales Act 1998 and the Northern Ireland Act 1998. These systems seek to achieve uniformity in the determination of these issues throughout all parts of the United Kingdom by reserving to the j Judicial Committee of the Privy Council the power of final decision in all these matters.

One of the matters which was devolved to the Scottish Parliament and to the Scottish Executive was the system of criminal prosecution for which the Lord Advocate is responsible. The Scotland Act provides that the Lord Advocate is a member of the Scottish Executive (s 44(1)(c) of that Act). It contains provisions which are designed to ensure his independence as public prosecutor. Section 29(2)(e) of the

Scotland Act restricts the legislative competence of the Parliament in regard to any provision in any Act which would remove him from his position as head of that system. Section 48(5) of that Act provides that any decision by him in that capacity is to be taken by him independently of any other person. Section 52(6) of the Scotland Act ensures that the functions which were exercised by him immediately before he ceased to be a Minister of the Crown on the coming into force of the Scotland Act are exercisable only by the Lord Advocate. It is in the light of these provisions that s 57(3) falls to be read. It qualifies the position of the Lord Advocate in regard to the general restraint on his competence in s 57(2), which provides that a member of the Scottish Executive has no power to do any act which is incompatible with any of the convention rights or with Community law. Section 57(3)(a) provides that that subsection does not apply to an act of the Lord Advocate 'in prosecuting any offence' which, because of s 6(2) of the Human Rights Act, is not unlawful under sub-s (1) of that section.

Alongside these provisions are the powers which are given to the Advocate General for Scotland, for whose appointment provision was made by s 87 of the Scotland Act. The Advocate General for Scotland is a Minister of the Crown. As such she is a member of the United Kingdom government. Her functions include that of safeguarding the interests of the United Kingdom in the operation of the devolution settlement. Those interests include that of seeing to the fulfilment of the state's international obligations, in particular those which it owes as a contracting state under art 13 of the convention. That is the purpose of the powers that she has been given by paras 4 and 33 of Sch 6 to the Scotland Act to institute proceedings for the determination of a devolution issue and to require a court or tribunal to refer a devolution issue to the Judicial Committee. In the exercise of these powers she is entitled to exercise her own judgment independently of, and even contrary to, the views of the Lord Advocate.

It seems to me to be clear from these provisions that it was the intention of Parliament that acts of the Lord Advocate in prosecuting offences should be subject to judicial control under the devolved system. In his case, as in the case of any other member of the Scottish Executive, the question whether or not an act or proposed act of his or of any prosecutor for whose acts he is responsible is within his competence depends upon the application to that act of the concept of compatibility. If the act or proposed act is 'incompatible' with any of the convention rights it is outside his competence.

The opening words of art 6(1) of the convention provide: 'In the determination ... of any criminal charge against him, everyone is entitled to a fair and public hearing.' But the relevant question, for the purposes of the system of devolution which has been constructed under United Kingdom domestic law, is not whether these words impose a correlative obligation on the Lord Advocate in his capacity as public prosecutor. If that were the sole question, there would be much force in the argument advanced by the Solicitor General that, as the determination during a criminal trial of the criminal charge in all its aspects is a matter for the court and not the prosecutor, the acts of the Lord Advocate in that capacity lie outside the scope of the article. But the test which s 57(2) of the Scotland Act applies to his acts is not expressed in the language of obligation. It takes a broader and more inclusive form, as it requires that his acts must be compatible with any of the convention rights. It is sufficient for this restraint on his powers to operate that his purported or proposed act is inconsistent with the obligations which the state has assumed under the convention. The acts which he performs in the a course of the trial when he is leading and founding upon evidence are brought by this means within the scope of the article.

It is sufficient to satisfy the test laid down in Sch 6 to the Scotland Act that a devolution issue has 'arisen' for there to be a question as to whether or not a purported or proposed exercise of a function by a member of the Scottish executive is incompatible with a convention right. There is no need at this stage b to inquire as to whether some other person or some other public authority, such as the court, also has responsibility for giving effect to the same convention right. The fact that that other person or other public authority has the last word or has the power to intervene in such a way as to preserve or give effect to the convention rights may enable the question as to incompatibility to be answered c in the negative. It may be possible to reach that answer as a matter of relevancy or, without further inquiry, on agreed facts. But that is not to say that a devolution issue has not arisen. On the contrary, it is to answer the question that has been raised.

It is, of course, important to appreciate that the mere raising of a question will d not be enough to satisfy the definition in para 1 of Sch 6 to the Scotland Act. Paragraph 2 of the Schedule provides that a devolution issue shall not be taken to have arisen merely because of any contention of a party that appears to the court or tribunal to be frivolous or vexatious. Moreover, as the High Court of Justiciary has already held, it is not enough merely to assert that a devolution issue has arisen (see *British Broadcasting Corp, Petitioners (No 2)* 2000 SLT 860 at 866 per Lord e Kirkwood). Sufficient detail must be given in support of that proposition to show that there is a point of substance that needs to be addressed. It may be clear from the detail that has been provided that the raising of the issue is premature, or it may be clear that the question which has been raised is not a devolution issue at all within the meaning of the paragraph. In the latter case it will be proper for the f court or tribunal to say that, in the circumstances described, a devolution issue has not arisen without having to go so far as to describe the contention as frivolous or vexatious in terms of para 2 of the Schedule. That was what the Board did in *Hoekstra v HM Advocate* [2000] 1 AC 216 when it refused the petitioners' application for special leave to appeal.

g But that is not the situation in this case. The Lord Justice General (Lord Rodger of Earlsferry) dealt with this point when he said (2000 JC 328 at 332) that, as the Solicitor General had indicated in deliberately unequivocal terms that it was the procurator fiscal's intention to lead the evidence of the respondent's reply under s 172 of the Scptland Act and to rely on it in seeking a conviction, the evidence of h her admission would constitute a significant element of the evidence showing that she had driven the car on the occasion in question. He said that for this reason it was convenient, in this particular case, to decide the devolution issue relating to this evidence before the trial. In my opinion this approach, with which I agree, serves to reinforce the point that a devolution issue has indeed been raised in this case which the Judicial Committee has power to determine under j the jurisdiction that has been given to it by para 13(a) of Sch 6 to the Scotland Act.

I would hold therefore that the respondent's minute discloses a devolution issue which the Judicial Committee has power to determine, as it raises a question in terms of para 1(d) of Sch 6 to that Act which it was proper for the court to determine as a preliminary issue in these proceedings under Ch 40 of the Act of Adjournal (Criminal Procedure Rules) 1996, SI 1996/513.

The scheme of art 6(1) of the convention

As the Lord Justice General observed (at 336), the right of silence and the right against self-incrimination are not lately minted. They have been recognised as general principles of the law of Scotland at least since the beginning of nineteenth century. In neither case was the right regarded as absolute, but the judges saw it as their function to see that they were jealously safeguarded. It was appreciated from an early stage that the accused's right to silence at trial would be worthless if his right of silence and his right against self-incrimination were not available to him from the outset of the criminal investigation. So rules were developed by the judges to ensure that these rights were respected by the court and the police.

In *Chalmers v HM Advocate* 1954 JC 66 at 79, Lord Justice General Cooper said that the principles which regulate the duties of the police when questioning suspects had been stated and restated in over a score of decisions in the past 80 or 90 years. As the jurisprudence on this subject developed the ultimate test was said to have been founded upon the principle of fairness. In *Brown v HM Advocate* 1966 SLT 105 at 107, Lord Justice General Clyde observed that the test applied in all such cases was a simple and intelligible test which had worked well in practice—has what has taken place been fair or not? Other dicta to the same effect were referred to in *Codona v HM Advocate* 1996 SLT 1100 at 1105, where it was emphasised that that simple test must never be permitted to become a formality. The statutory rules relating to the questioning of persons detained at a police station and to judicial examination as a part of petition procedure, which are now to be found in ss 13 to 15 and 35 to 38 of the Criminal Procedure (Scotland) Act 1995, have been framed in such a way as to provide appropriate checks and balances in the interests of fairness to the accused.

As these provisions show, and as the judges have repeatedly emphasised in the common law context, the common law principle of fairness has always to be reconciled with the interests of society in the detection and punishment of crime (*Lawrie v Muir* 1950 JC 19 at 26 per Lord Justice General Cooper; *HM Advocate v Hepper* 1958 JC 39 at 40 per Lord Guthrie). The rule of law requires that every person be protected from invasion by the authorities of his rights and liberties. But the preservation of law and order, on which the rule of law also depends, requires that those protections should not be framed in such a way as to make it impractical to bring those who are accused of crime to justice. The benefits of the rule of law must be extended to the public at large and to victims of crime also.

Now that the common law rights of the accused have been reinforced by the right under art 6(1) of the convention to a fair trial it is necessary to re-examine and revise these principles. The scheme of the article involves the application of different tests at each stage of the inquiry from those applied by the common law. It requires that a more structured approach be taken when the overriding test of fairness is applied to the facts. But it is important to recognise nevertheless that the rule of law lies at the heart of the convention.

The final indent of the preamble to the convention refers to the common heritage of the European countries whose governments were signatory thereto of 'political traditions, ideals, freedom and the rule of law'. In *Salabiaku v France* (1988) 13 EHRR 379 at 388 (para 28) the European Court of Human Rights said that art 6, by protecting the right to a fair trial, was intended to enshrine 'the fundamental principle of the rule of law'. In *Golder v UK* (1975) 1 EHRR 524 at 535–536 (para 35) the court said that in civil matters one could scarcely conceive of the rule of law without there being a possibility of access to the courts. These statements assert the right of the individual to the protection of the rule of law a against the state. But the other side of the balance, which respects the public interest in the rule of law and the general interest of the community, was also recognised by the court in *Salabiaku v France*. It said in that case that the convention did not prohibit presumptions of fact or of law in principle, and that they were not incompatible with art 6(2) of the convention so long as they were confined within reasonable limits which take account of what is at stake and b maintain the rights of the defence. In *Pullar v UK* (1996) 22 EHRR 391 at 403 (para 32), the court said that the principle that a tribunal is to be presumed to be free of personal prejudice or partiality unless there is evidence to the contrary reflects 'an important element of the rule of law', which is that verdicts of a tribunal should be final and binding unless set aside by a superior court on the basis of irregularity or unfairness. A similar approach to the function of the rule c of law can be seen in the fact that the court has consistently recognised that, while the right to a fair trial is absolute in its terms and the public interest can never be invoked to deny that right to anybody under any circumstances, the rights which it has read into art 6 are neither absolute nor inflexible.

It is important therefore to distinguish between those convention rights which d are to be regarded as absolute and those which are not. The scheme of art 6, as Keir Starmer in *European Human Rights Law* (1999) pp 118–119 (para 3.88), has explained, is that the rights listed in arts 6(2) and 6(3) which are supplementary to art 6(1) are not intended to be an exhaustive list of the requirements of fairness in criminal proceedings. Those which are listed in art 6(3) are described as minimum rights. Once the meaning of those rights has been determined, there e is no room in their case for any implied modifications or restrictions. But the European Court and the European Commission of Human Rights (the commission) have interpreted the article broadly by reading into it a variety of other rights to which the accused person is entitled in the criminal context. Their purpose is to give effect, in a practical way, to the fundamental and absolute right to a fair trial. f They include the right to silence and the right against self incrimination with which this case is concerned. As these other rights are not set out in absolute terms in the article they are open, in principle, to modification or restriction so long as this is not incompatible with the absolute right to a fair trial. As Keir Starmer, p 182 (para 4.75) has observed, where express restrictions are provided for by the convention there is no room for implied restrictions. But where the g European Court has read implied rights into the convention, it has also read in implied restrictions on those rights.

The test of compatibility with art 6(1) of the convention which is to be applied where it is contended that those rights which are not absolute should be restricted or modified will not be satisfied if the modification or limitation 'does not pursue a h legitimate aim and if there is not a reasonable relationship of proportionality between the means employed and the aim sought to be achieved' (see *Ashingdane v UK* (1985) 7 EHRR 528 at 546–547 (para 57)). In *Sporrong v Sweden* (1982) 5 EHRR 35 at 52–53 (para 69) the court referred to the striking of a fair balance 'between the demands of the general interest of the community and the requirements of the protection of the j individual's fundamental rights'. As that case and *Salabiaku v France* (1988) 13 EHRR 379 both demonstrate, that approach has been used to support the view that, although the presumption of innocence in art 6(2) is stated in absolute terms, it is not to be regarded as prohibiting the use of reverse onus clauses so long as they are confined within reasonable limits which strike a fair balance between these competing demands and requirements. The relevant principles described in *Ashingdane v UK* were restated by the court in *Lithgow v UK* (1986) 8 EHRR 329 at

393–394 (para 194) and again in *Fayed v UK* (1994) 18 EHRR 393 at 429–430 (para 65).

I would hold therefore that the jurisprudence of the European Court tells us that the questions that should be addressed when issues are raised about an alleged incompatibility with a right under art 6 of the convention are the following. (1) Is the right which is in question an absolute right, or is it a right which is open to modification or restriction because it is not absolute? (2) If it is not absolute, does the modification or restriction which is contended for have a legitimate aim in the public interest? (3) If so, is there a reasonable relationship of proportionality between the means employed and the aim sought to be realised? The answer to the question whether the right is or is not absolute is to be found by examining the terms of the article in the light of the judgments of the court. The question whether a legitimate aim is being pursued enables account to be taken of the public interest in the rule of law. The principle of proportionality directs attention to the question whether a fair balance has been struck between the general interest of the community in the realisation of that aim and the protection of the fundamental rights of the individual.

Saunders v UK

It is plain from the opinion of the Lord Justice General, for reasons which I can well understand in view of the novelty of the question with which it was presented in this case, that the High Court found itself in some difficulty in obtaining clear guidance from the judgments of the European Court as to the scope of the right to silence and the right not to incriminate oneself (2000 JC 328 at 335). They had been recognised by the European Court as rights which, although not specifically mentioned in art 6, ought to be read into that article to secure the right to a fair trial (*Funke v France* (1993) 16 EHRR 297 at 326 (para 44); see also *Murray v UK* (1996) 22 EHRR 29 at 60 (para 45)). But the fullest description of those rights is to be found in *Saunders v UK* (1997) 2 BHRC 358 at 373–374 (paras 68–69). So it was to be expected that the High Court would rely primarily on what was said in that case for guidance. Although this guidance was supplemented by the Lord Justice General, in his carefully researched opinion, by reference to generally recognised international standards such as those expressed in judgments of the Supreme Court of Canada and the Constitutional Court of South Africa, it was the approach of the European Court in *Saunders v UK* which was his principal source. In the result it is not surprising that defects in the reasoning which are apparent on a close reading of *Saunders v UK* are to be found in the judgment of the High Court also.

The main weakness in the reasoning of the court in *Saunders v UK* lies in its failure to examine the issue, which is highlighted in the dissenting opinions of Judge Valticos and Judge Gölcüklü, as to whether the right to silence and the right not to incriminate oneself are or are not absolute rights the modification or restriction of which could in no circumstances ever be justified. The basis upon which the court proceeded, as it explained in the opening sentence of para 68 (at 373–374), was that these rights 'lie at the heart of the notion of a fair procedure under art 6'. In the discussion which follows the rights are treated as if they were rights conferred by art 6 which were not open to modification or restriction. The essence of the argument which the court accepted related to the use which was made of the evidence obtained under compulsion in the course of the criminal trial (see 375 (para 71)). That was enough to persuade the court that the rights had been breached. It is true that in para 74 of its judgment (at 375–376) the court *a* said that it did not find it necessary to examine the issue as to whether or not the rights were absolute in the light of its assessment of the use which was made at the trial of the interviews. But the reasoning upon which this observation seems to have been based appears to me, with respect, to be unconvincing. It was simply that the answers to questions put in the course of those interviews, whether directly self-incriminating or not, were used in the course of the *b* proceedings in a manner which sought to incriminate the applicant (see 375 (para 72)). Questions as to whether the procedure which was followed was designed to pursue a legitimate aim and as to whether the means employed were proportionate were not addressed.

Although the European Court was careful to confine its observations in *Saunders v UK* to the facts of that case only, the general approach which is revealed *c* by the judgment appears to be out of keeping with the mainstream of the jurisprudence which the court itself has developed as to the nature and application of the rights which it has read into art 6(1). Although it is possible as Lord Steyn has demonstrated to find indications in the judgment that the court did not regard the right of silence and the right against self incrimination as absolute, it is not easy *d* to find any clear guidance to that effect. So when the Lord Justice General came, towards the end of his judgment (2000 JC 328 at 353–354) to consider the circumstances of this case in accordance with the approach which in his view had been laid down by the court in *Saunders v UK*, he appears to have regarded the right to silence and the right not to incriminate oneself as rights of a fundamental character which fell to be treated as if they were absolute rights. He said (at 353) *e* that the respondent's right not to incriminate herself was a constituent element of the basic principles of fair procedure inherent in art 6(1) of the convention. He had already rejected arguments based on the recognition by the court in *Murray v UK* (1996) 22 EHRR 29 at 60–61 (para 47) that the right to silence was not absolute (see also *Condron v UK* (2000) 8 BHRC 290 at 303–304 (para 56)). He said that he *f* could find nothing in the circumstances of this case which would justify a restrictive interpretation or application of 'the right conferred by art 6(1)'. Consequently he did not address the question as to the legitimacy of the aim pursued by the regulatory scheme of which s 172 of the 1988 Act forms part. Nor did he examine the question of proportionality. Lord Marnoch's opinion is open to the same criticism.

g As the rights which are in question in this case are rights which are not specifically mentioned in art 6 but are rights which have been read into that article by the court, they plainly do not have the status of rights which are expressed in the convention as absolute rights. They are therefore open to modification or restriction so long as the relevant principles which apply to that *h* exercise are satisfied. The crucial questions are the two questions which the decision of the High Court has left unanswered. It is to these two questions that I now turn.

Legitimate aim and proportionality

j On the one hand there is the nature of the road traffic legislation of which s 172 of the 1988 Act forms part and the aims which it is designed to satisfy. Public safety is at the heart of the matter. Ever since use began to be made on our roads of fast-moving motor vehicles it has been appreciated that the use of this means of transport has to be regulated. The risk of injury to the drivers of these vehicles, to passengers, to people in other vehicles on the same road and to members of the public generally led to the introduction of legislation to control the construction and use of motor vehicles and the manner in which they could be driven when they were on the highway and other places to which the public has access. This was combined with a system of registration which served a fiscal purpose but had the added benefit that it enabled both the vehicles and their keepers to be identified. Although there are differences in detail, all countries which are members of the Council of Europe employ similar systems to regulate the construction and use of motor vehicles in the interests of public safety.

I do not think that it can be doubted, against this background, that the system of regulation and the provisions which the legislation contains for the detection and prosecution of road traffic offences serve a legitimate aim. As for s 172 of the 1988 Act in particular, its purpose is to enable the driver of a vehicle alleged to be guilty of an offence to which that section applies to be identified. The offences to which the section applies are the result of a process of selection which has eliminated various minor offences and reserved its application to offences which can properly be regarded as serious. The system which the legislation has laid down for the prosecution of these offences requires the prosecution to prove that the accused was driving the vehicle at the time when the offence was committed. The purpose which these offences are designed to serve would be at risk of being defeated if no means were available to enable the police to trace the driver of a vehicle who, as so often happens, had departed from the place where the offence was committed before he or she could be identified. Here too, it seems to me that a legitimate aim is being pursued.

On the other hand there is the question whether the means which it employs are proportionate to that aim and are compatible with the right of the accused to a fair trial. Has a fair balance been achieved? In order to answer this question it is necessary to examine the provision in question more closely. It has several very important characteristics.

First there are the qualifications which are written into s 172(2)(a) of the 1988 Act itself. The provision may be operated only when it is alleged that an offence has been committed of the kind to which the section applies (s 172(1)). Then there is the fact that the requirement in s 172(2)(a) to give information as to the identity of the driver may be addressed only to the person keeping the vehicle. The expression 'keeping the vehicle' is not defined, but I take this to be a reference to the person in whose name the vehicle is registered under the Vehicle Excise and Registration Act 1994 (see s 172(7) and (9) and the definition of the expression 'registered keeper' in s 172(10)). A person who submits to registration as the keeper of a motor vehicle must be taken to have accepted responsibility for its use and the corresponding obligation to provide the information when required to do so. Furthermore the requirement for which provision is made is directed to one issue only, the identity of the driver of the vehicle. It is proper to recognise that the identity of the driver is likely to be an important and indeed crucial issue at any trial. But the provision does not permit open-ended questioning of the person keeping the vehicle in order to secure an admission of guilt as to the offence. It seems to me that, bearing in mind the difficulties that may arise in tracing the driver of a vehicle after the event, this limited incursion into the right of silence and the right of the driver who is alleged to have committed an offence not to incriminate himself is proportionate.

Then there is the use which may be made of the response to the requirement in the event that the person keeping the vehicle admits that he or she was the driver of it. This is not the subject of any express provision in s 172 or of any other provision in the 1988 Act. But the approach which has been taken to provisions a of this kind is that, unless the legislation provides otherwise, answers which a person is compelled to give in response to a statutory requirement can be used against that person in criminal proceedings. It was on that basis that Lord Justice Clerk Grant proceeded when he said in *Foster v Farrell* 1963 JC 46 at 53–54 that a statement obtained from the keeper as to the identity of the driver was admissible in evidence against him. The answer to the question whether the use of the b driver's self-incriminating statement at a trial for the offence with regard to which the requirement was made is proportionate to the legitimate aim is to be found partly in the characteristics of s 172(2)(a) which I have already identified and partly in the other respects in which the legislation preserves the accused's right to a fair trial. Under Scots law the driver's admission must be corroborated, and there must be other evidence to show beyond reasonable doubt that the driver c committed the offence with which he is charged. All the usual protections against unreliable evidence and evidence obtained by oppression or other improper means remain in place.

I think therefore that it is reasonable to conclude that the limited modification which s 172(2)(a) makes, in pursuance of a legitimate aim in the public interest, d to the right to silence and the right not to incriminate oneself is compatible with the right of the accused to a fair trial. I would hold that a fair balance has been achieved between these competing interests.

Comparative material

e I would add only two further points by way of a footnote. First, the Lord Justice General derived support (at 2000 JC 328 at 352) for the view that he formed that the limited terms of the reply required by s 172(2)(a) of the 1988 Act did not enable it to be characterised as part of a system of traffic regulation, and was therefore in conflict with the right against self incrimination, from the Canadian case of *R v White* (1999) 7 BHRC 120. Reference to Canadian cases was understandable f in view of the reference in *Saunders v UK* (1997) 2 BHRC 358 at 374 (para 68) to generally recognised international standards. As Lord Woolf said in the context of the Hong Kong Bill of Rights in *A-G of Hong Kong v Lee Kwong-kut, A-G of Hong Kong v Lo Chak-man* [1993] 3 All ER 939 at 952–953, [1993] AC 951 at 972–973, in cases which are close to the borderline regard can be had to the approach g developed by the Canadian courts.

But care needs to be taken in the context of the convention to ensure that the analysis by the Canadian courts proceeds upon the same principles as those which have been developed by the commission and the European Court. It is clear from the observations by Iacobucci J in *R v White* (1999) 7 BHRC 120 at 137 (para 70) h that, even if the Crown had confined itself to the leading of the driver's admission that she was the driver at the relevant place and time, the Supreme Court of Canada would have held that her right against self-incrimination had been violated. The principle against self-incrimination is held in Canadian law, by implication, to be a principle of fundamental justice under s 7 of the charter. In para 45 of the j judgment (at 131) Iacobucci J said that the fact that it had the status of an overarching principle did not imply that it provided an absolute protection and that it was contextually sensitive. There are signs here of an approach which is not dissimilar to that which the European Court takes when it is examining issues as to legitimate aim and proportionality. But the questions which the Supreme Court of Canada was asking itself were not the same and there are some important differences of detail. So I do not think that the balancing of the relevant principles which was undertaken in that case can be regarded as a reliable guide as to how the balance ought to be struck in the European context.

The second point relates to the use of materials from other signatory countries to the convention. References in the preamble to the convention to these countries' common heritage of political traditions, ideals, freedom and the rule of law and by the European Court to the fact that generally recognised international standards lie at the heart of the notion of a fair procedure under art 6 (eg *Saunders v UK* (1996) 23 EHRR 313 at 373–374 (para 68)) encourage resort, as a check, to a comparative exercise based on the use of such materials.

The Lord Justice General pointed out (2000 JC 328 at 341) that none of the commission cases to which the High Court was referred (*Tora Tolmos v Spain* (1995) 81 DR 82, *DN v Netherlands* App No 6170/73 (26 May 1975, unreported) and *JP, KR and GH v Austria* (1989) DR 62) concerned the use of any reply as evidence in a trial. But I agree with Lord Bingham of Cornhill for the reasons he has given that these cases, in which it was held that the requirement to name the driver did not violate the presumption of innocence, are not irrelevant. Reference was also made in the course of the hearing before the Board to other comparative material. There was no consistent pattern, as in some countries such as Ireland a statement by the owner of a vehicle when asked to say who was driving it cannot be used against him in evidence (*People (Attorney General) v Gilbert (No 14 of 1972)* [1973] IR 383). But some of this material was to the same effect as that in the three commission cases. For example, in Belgium s 67 bis of an Act of 4 August 1996 which forms part of a chapter entitled 'identification of the offender' contains a presumption that the owner of the vehicle has committed the offence unless he proves the contrary. In France arts L21–1 and L21–2 of the Code de la route contain a similar presumption, as they require the owner of the vehicle to pay the fine incurred for offences relating to parking, speed limits and traffic lights unless he can prove all the elements required in law to establish that he is not the offender.

These examples show that the social problems associated with the use on public roads of motor vehicles have been addressed by these countries in a manner which restricts to some extent the presumption of innocence. But the restriction is regarded as having a legitimate aim and as striking the right balance between the general interest of the community and the fundamental rights of the individual. The solution which s 172 of the 1988 Act has adopted is not the same, but it stands up to comparison with that which has been adopted in other countries.

Conclusion

For these reasons I too would allow the appeal and quash the declaration which was made by the High Court.

LORD CLYDE. I am in entire agreement with my noble and learned friend Lord Hope of Craighead that in this case a devolution issue has arisen and accordingly that the Board has the jurisdiction to hear the appeal. Having also made some observations on this point in the case of *Montgomery v HM Advocate, Coulter v HM Advocate* [2001] 2 WLR 779 I shall briefly set out my own reasoning, but I believe that this in no way differs from the reasons given by Lord Hope.

Whether there is or is not a devolution issue is a matter to be determined solely by reference to Pt I of Sch 6 of the Scotland Act 1998. The definition in para 1 of that Schedule includes, in sub-para (d): 'a question whether a purported or proposed a exercise of a function by a member of the Scottish Executive is, or would be, incompatible with any of the Convention rights …'

In the present case the Lord Advocate through a procurator fiscal is proposing to lead and found upon the evidence of the answer given by the respondent in reply to a question by a police officer asked under s 172 of the Road Traffic Act 1988 regarding the identity of the driver of a car. The Lord Advocate is a member b of the Scottish Executive. In leading the evidence he is proposing to exercise one of his functions. The word 'functions' includes powers and duties (s 126(1) of the Scotland Act). The challenge has been made that the exercise of that function by him would be incompatible with the respondent's right to a fair trial under art 6(1) of the European Convention for the Protection of Human Rights and Fundamental Freedoms (Rome, 4 November 1950; TS 71 (1953); Cmd 8969) (the c convention). The question does not seem to me to be frivolous or vexatious so as to be excluded under para 2 of the Schedule. For the purposes of the Scotland Act and more particularly for the purposes of the jurisdiction of the Privy Council it seems to me that a 'devolution issue', whether meritorious or not, has arisen.

It is important to note that each of the categories of devolution issue which are d set out in para 1 of Sch 6 describes and identifies a 'question'. Apart from the extreme case for which provision is made in para 2 the merits of the question in fact or in law do not disqualify the question from being a devolution issue. The question must of course satisfy one or other of the descriptions set out in para 1. The person seeking to raise a devolution issue must plead himself into one or other of the paragraphs. As Lord Kirkwood has pointed out (*British Broadcasting* e *Corp, Petitioners (No 2)* 2000 SLT 860 at 866) it is not enough simply to assert that a devolution issue has arisen. If the person fails to plead himself into any of the paragraphs then it will be evident that there is no devolution issue at stake. But provided that the question can be seen to fall within one of the paragraphs it will not be disentitled from qualifying as a devolution issue simply because the f contentions which are advanced are found to be defective in point of law. Only if the defect is of such an extreme kind as to make the contention frivolous or vexatious will the matter fail to be a devolution issue.

That a question is raised prematurely should not prevent it qualifying as a devolution issue. How the court may deal with the question is a distinct matter from the identification of the question as a devolution issue. There may well be g cases where the court may consider that the issue has been raised prematurely and may refuse to deal with the merits at least at that stage. In the context of the admissibility of evidence in a criminal trial it may often be the case that an issue of fairness should be left to be determined in the first instance by the trial judge. *Robb v HM Advocate* 2000 JC 127 may serve as an example. Conversely there may h be cases where it is practical and useful to determine such a matter in advance of trial. Such a case might be where some piece of evidence was critical for the prosecution and it could be determined in advance of the trial that its admission would be necessarily unfair.

As I understood the argument presented by the Solicitor General, he was not j contending that there was no devolution issue in the sense which I have described. The question which he argued was that the leading of this evidence was not something which fell within the scope of art 6(1) of the convention, for the reason that the fairness of the trial was matter for the court to resolve and not matter for the prosecution. He based his argument essentially upon the opening words of the article, 'In the determination of … any criminal charge against him'. He argued that the actings of the Lord Advocate in leading and founding upon the evidence did not fall within the determination of the trial. This is a question of the interpretation of art 6. *a*

In my view the argument involves too narrow and exact a construction of the article. I do not consider that the scope of the article is limited to the decision-making process or to the obligations of those vested with the task of making the determination of the issues in the case. It is concerned with proceedings which are determinative of civil rights or obligations or of criminal charges, but it does *b* not seem to me that it excludes activities occurring during the criminal trial which bear upon the fairness of the proceedings. The fairness of the leading of particular evidence by the prosecution seems to me to be something which can fall within the scope of art 6 and the present is a case where it can usefully be determined whether the leading of the particular admission by the respondent *c* would or would not be compatible with the obligation imposed on the Lord Advocate under that article.

The principal issue in the appeal is whether the response to the question put by the police officer to the respondent under s 172 of the 1988 Act may properly be led as evidence against her at her trial when she has been charged with a contravention of s 5(1)(a) of that Act. The view taken by the High Court of *d* Justiciary is that the leading of such evidence would be contrary to her right to a fair trial under art 6.

The right not to incriminate oneself has for a long time been recognised as a basic ingredient in the concept of a fair trial in Scotland. There is no difficulty in holding it to be implied in art 6 and no difficulty in recognising that right as *e* wholly consonant with the tradition of Scottish criminal law and practice. In England it has been described as one of the basic freedoms secured by English law (*Re Arrows Ltd (No 4)*, *Hamilton v Naviede* [1994] 3 All ER 814 at 820, [1995] 2 AC 75 at 95 per Lord Browne-Wilkinson). At common law it may well be that the admission by the respondent would be held inadmissible. The respondent was at *f* the particular stage when the question was asked of her a suspect. Indeed from the facts which the police already knew it may have been fairly obvious that she was almost certainly the driver. In general, statements by a suspect to the police will be inadmissible unless they have been fairly obtained (*Renton and Brown's Criminal Procedure* (6th edn looseleaf (1996) paras 24–39). Without any caution being given it can be strongly argued that the statement would be excluded as *g* unfair. But Parliament has provided in s 172 of the 1988 Act for an obligation to answer a question on the identity of the driver. The question then is whether that provision, at least in the context of the question being asked of the driver, is compatible with art 6(1) of the convention.

The convention is plainly a living instrument. The convention rights may be *h* open to new applications as society develops and changes and the applications may differ between different member states of the convention. But it is also to be remembered that it is dealing with the realities of life and it is not to be applied in ways which run counter to reason and common sense. The convention is intended to guarantee 'not rights that are theoretical or illusory but rights that are *j* practical and effective' (*Airey v Ireland* (1979) 2 EHRR 305 at 314–315 (para 24)). If the convention was to be applied by the courts in ways which would seem absurd to ordinary people then the courts would be doing disservice to the aims and purposes of the convention and the result would simply be to prejudice public respect for an international treaty which seeks to express the basic rights and freedoms of a democratic society.

a The single theme which runs through the whole of art 6 is the right of a litigant or an accused to have a fair trial. That theme is of course nothing new in the history of civil or criminal proceedings in the United Kingdom. But while there can be no doubt that the right to a fair trial is an absolute right, precisely what is comprised in the concept of fairness may be open to a varied analysis. It is not to be supposed that the content of the right is necessarily composed of rigid rules b which provide an absolute protection for an accused person under every circumstance. The right presently under discussion is not expressly set out in art 6 but is to be implied as an element in a fair trial. The jurisprudence of the European Court of Human Rights demonstrates that several of the particular rights which similarly by implication fall within the scope of art 6 are not absolute rights. For example it was held in *Murray v UK* (1996) 22 EHRR 29 at 60 (para 47) that even c the right to silence may be qualified where the silence may call for an explanation. Other examples can be found in the obligation to disclose evidence (*Fitt v UK* (2000) 30 EHRR 480 at 510–511 (para 45)), and the right of access to a court (*Tinnelly & Sons Ltd v UK* (1998) 4 BHRC 393 at 415 (para 72)). It seems to me that the right in issue in the present case, the right not to incriminate oneself, which is a right d implied but not expressed in the article, and is a right not far removed from the right to silence, is also not absolute but may be open to exception. It would have been helpful if the judgment in *Saunders v UK* (1997) 2 BHRC 358 had provided clearer guidance on this point and the absence of that guidance may have helped to distract the judges of the High Court from a more detailed exploration of the e point.

The only question then is whether the statutory exception here in issue can be justified and I have little difficulty in giving an affirmative answer to that question. Section 172 of the 1988 Act provides a means for the police to ascertain the identity of a driver where the driver is alleged to be guilty of an offence to f which the section relates. The purpose of the provision is plainly a legitimate one in the context of the importance in the public interest in securing the prosecution of offenders such as drunk drivers and enabling the identification of drivers to be discovered where it can be often difficult to do so. The importance of securing safety on the roads and of minimising the risks of accidents and injuries caused by motor vehicles is too obvious to require elaboration. While the statutory power g to require an answer is fortified by a criminal sanction, the penalty is relatively light, not involving imprisonment except in the failure to pay the fine which may be imposed. I consider that the Solicitor General was correct in submitting that compulsion by itself is not necessarily fatal to the admission of a self-incriminatory admission, but that improper compulsion would be. There is no suggestion in h the present case of any improper compulsion. Indeed in the present case it does not appear that any mention was made of the sanction which could be invoked on a failure to provide the information. Furthermore, the power can only be exercised by or on behalf of a chief officer of police. Moreover the power is limited to the single point of the identity of the driver. That is of course a critical j and essential ingredient of the offence but it is not the whole of it. Nor is the admission necessarily final and conclusive. The case is distinct from that of *Saunders v UK* where use was made of various answers made in the course of an inquiry by the Department of Trade and Industry and from that of *R v White* (1999) 7 BHRC 120 where use was sought to be made of three conversations with the police following a road accident. It seems to me that the power to obtain and use the single admission of the identity of the driver is a proportionate measure which sufficiently balances the interests of an accused person and the interests of the public in the particular context of particular offences under the 1988 Act. a

On the whole matter I agree that the appeal should be allowed. It cannot be affirmed that the leading of the admission would necessarily breach the respondent's right to a fair trial.

THE RT HON IAN KIRKWOOD. On the preliminary issue I agree with Lord Hope of Craighead, for the reasons given by him, that the respondent's minute discloses a devolution issue which the Judicial Committee has power to determine. I also agree with your Lordships that it is not necessary in the present proceedings for us to resolve the third issue. b

The principal matter argued before us was whether, compatibly with the respondent's rights under art 6 of the European Convention for the Protection of Human Rights and Fundamental Freedoms (Rome, 4 November 1950; TS 71 (1953); Cmd 8969) (the convention), the procurator fiscal would be entitled at the respondent's trial to lead and seek to rely on the admission which was competently obtained from her under s 172(2)(a) of the Road Traffic Act 1988. c

Counsel for the respondent made it clear that no objection was being taken to the fact that the respondent, who was the registered keeper of the vehicle, had been required in terms of s 172(2)(a) to give information as to the identity of the driver at the time the alleged offence was committed. Counsel's submission was that the procurator fiscal's proposal to lead evidence at her forthcoming trial of her admission that she had been the driver contravened her implied right under art 6 of the convention not to incriminate herself. d e

The right to silence and the right not to incriminate oneself, which are separate but related rights, have been part of Scots common law for at least 200 years (*Hume's Commentaries on the Law of Scotland* (4th edn, 1844) vol 2, pp 336–337, and *Alison's Practice of the Criminal Law of Scotland* (1833), pp 586–587). In the present case it is common ground that the respondent was a suspect when she was required to provide information as to the identity of the driver under s 172 and there is no doubt that at common law she could not have been compelled to admit to a police officer that she had been the driver of the car at the time the alleged offence was committed. However, in *Foster v Farrell* 1963 JC 46 an accused person had been required by a police officer acting in pursuance of s 232(2) of the Road Traffic Act 1960 (which was in similar terms to s 172(2) of the 1988 Act) to say who was the driver of a motor car at the time an alleged offence had been committed by the driver of the car. The accused was not the owner of the car, which was registered in the name of a company of which he was the managing director, but he admitted that he had been driving the car at the material time. In the particular circumstances of that case it was held that the accused's statement was inadmissible at his trial because it had not been proved that the statement had been elicited by a police officer who had been authorised, either generally or specially, by a chief officer of police to require the giving of such information. However, the court went on to consider whether an admission which had lawfully been obtained under s 232 of the 1960 Act was not only available to the police for the purpose of assisting in their investigations but was also available in evidence at the trial of the individual who had made the admission. The Crown conceded that the statement would not have been admissible at common law but contended that the statement was admissible by reason of the provisions of s 232 of the 1960 Act. The Lord Justice Clerk (Grant) referred (at 52) to 'the general common law principle that a man cannot be compelled to give information f g h j a which may incriminate him' but held that the common law had no relevance in relation to a statement lawfully and properly obtained under express statutory authority. He stated (at 53) that there was no limitation set by s 232, either expressly or impliedly, to the use which could be made of such a statement. In particular, there was no provision to the effect that a statement made in answer to a request under s 232 should not be admissible in evidence against the maker b of the statement. It was also observed by the Lord Justice Clerk (at 54) that in England and Wales a statement made under s 232 was admissible in evidence. It was held by the court that a statement made by a person under s 232 was 'clearly admissible in evidence against him in Scotland as in England'. So far as I am aware, the authority of the decision in *Foster v Farrell* has not hitherto been called into question.

c In the present case it was submitted by counsel for the respondent: (1) that the right to a fair trial is an absolute right; (2) that the right to silence and the right not to incriminate oneself are rights implied in art 6 of the convention; and (3) that the procurator fiscal's proposal to lead evidence of the respondent's admission under s 172 of the 1988 Act that she was the driver of the car at the time the d alleged offence was committed would contravene her convention right not to incriminate herself and she would not be able to receive a fair trial. I agree that the right to a fair trial is an absolute right, although what is a fair trial must depend on the circumstances of each individual case, and it was common ground that the right to silence and the right not to incriminate oneself are implied in art 6. However, I agree with your Lordships that the implied right not to incriminate e oneself cannot properly be regarded as an absolute right. In my opinion it is not a right of such a special character as to lead to the conclusion that, in the interests of justice, it is not capable of limitation to any extent in any circumstances. It is a right which is capable of being limited by law to some extent, always provided that the limitation is shown to be necessary to protect the legitimate interests of f the community, and it is significant that a number of other rights implied in art 6 have been held not to be absolute rights.

In *Soering v UK* (1989) 11 EHRR 439 at 468 (para 89) the European Court of Human Rights observed as follows:

> g 'Furthermore, inherent in the whole of the Convention is a search for a fair balance between the demands of the general interest of the community and the requirements of the protection of the individual's fundamental rights.'

In *R v DPP, ex p Kebilene* [1999] 4 All ER 801 at 847, [2000] 2 AC 326 at 384 Lord Hope of Craighead stated:

> h 'There is also the question of balance, as to the interests of the individual as against those of society. The convention jurisprudence and that which is to be found from cases decided in other jurisdictions suggests that account may legitimately be taken, in striking the right balance, of the problems which the legislation was designed to address ... As a matter of general j principle therefore a fair balance must be struck between the demands of the general interest of the community and the protection of the fundamental rights of the individual: see also *Sporrong v Sweden* ((1982) 5 EHRR 35 at 52 (para 69)).'

So, in order to justify a limitation of an implied convention right there must be pursuance of a legitimate aim and the proposed limitation must be proportionate to the aim which is sought to be achieved (*Osman v UK* (1998) 5 BHRC 293 and *Waite v Germany* (1999) 6 BHRC 499).

Counsel for the respondent conceded that the proposed limitation of the right not to incriminate oneself, by permitting evidence to be led at the trial of an accused of an admission made under s 172 of the 1988 Act, did have a legitimate aim and, indeed, it is difficult to see how that concession could have been withheld. The driving of a motor vehicle is a lawful activity which is engaged in by a large proportion of the adult population, but at the same time it is a potentially dangerous activity. That this is so is illustrated by the recent road accident death and injury statistics applicable to the United Kingdom which were laid before us. Accordingly, it is natural for the state to seek to regulate that activity and it is inevitable that that regulation will result in limitations being imposed on the rights of individuals. Regulation is required in the interests of the safety of the population in general and owners and drivers of motor vehicles accept that there are rules which have to be observed. In that connection one consideration is that it is in the public interest that those who commit motoring offences are detected and brought to justice. And it must be recognised that it can be difficult for the police to identify drivers of vehicles alleged to have committed moving traffic offences.

The contention advanced by counsel for the respondent was that, while a legitimate aim was sought to be achieved, permitting the procurator fiscal to lead evidence of her admission at her trial was not proportionate. So far as the issue of proportionality is concerned, it is, in my opinion, important to recognise the very limited scope of the information which the respondent was required to provide in terms of s 172. What she was required to do was to give such information as she had as to the identity of the driver at the time the alleged offence was committed, and the keeper of a motor vehicle may be expected to be in the best position to know who was driving the vehicle at any particular time. The reply given by the registered keeper of a vehicle, or 'any other person' who may be required to provide the necessary information, will not necessarily be self-incriminating as the person to whom the question is addressed may be able to state that some other person was the driver or may genuinely not be in a position to say who was driving. However, even if the person to whom the question was addressed was the driver at the material time, and was under a legal obligation to admit that fact, no questions can be asked about the speed at which, or the manner in which, the car was being driven or any other circumstances relating to the alleged offence. While it must be recognised that the respondent's admission that she was the driver will be an important adminicle of evidence in the Crown case at the trial, the Crown will still require to satisfy the court that the admission was reliable, provide corroboration of the admission and prove beyond reasonable doubt that the driver of the vehicle was guilty of committing an offence to which s 172 applied. The respondent was not, and could not be, asked to admit her guilt of the alleged offence nor was there any question of her being required to go into the witness box and be subjected to cross-examination. Further, while she was compelled to provide the information required of her under s 172(2)(a) of the 1988 Act, and her failure to comply with that requirement would have meant that she would be guilty of an offence under s 172(3), it has to be borne in mind that the offence is a summary one and that the maximum sentence is a level three fine (at present £1,000), disqualification being discretionary and endorsement obligatory. A custodial sentence cannot be imposed.

a It was submitted by counsel for the respondent at one stage that a more proportionate measure would have been to create a statutory presumption that the registered keeper had been driving the vehicle at the time of the alleged offence. But it does not seem to me that that could be regarded as a more proportionate measure as, if the keeper wished to challenge the presumption, he or she would require to go into the witness box and would be open to b cross-examination not only as to whether he or she was the driver but also in relation to the circumstances in which the offence was committed. In a case where a person admits under s 172 to having been the driver of the car at the material time, and evidence of that admission is led at the trial, it will still be for the court to decide (except in a case where s 12(4) of the Road Traffic Offenders Act 1988 applies) whether or not to accept that evidence and what weight should c be placed on it. It would, for example, be open to an accused person to give evidence that the alleged admission was never made or that, while an admission of being the driver had been made, the admission had been made in error. If there was evidence of coercion, oppression, unfair inducement or other improper compulsion having been used, the evidence of the admission would be rejected. d In my opinion the provisions of s 172, taken along with the right of the prosecutor to seek to rely on an admission made by an accused under that section, is a proportionate response when balanced against considerations of public safety and the interests of the community. Further, the limitation on the respondent's right not to incriminate herself will not, in my view, be incompatible with her right to a fair trial.

e In reaching their decision the High Court relied heavily on observations made by the European Court in *Saunders v UK* (1997) 2 BHRC 358, a case in which the facts were very different from the facts in the present case. In para 68 (at 373–374) the court made the following observations:

> f 'The Court recalls that, although not specifically mentioned in art 6 of the convention, the right to silence and the right not to incriminate oneself are generally recognised international standards which lie at the heart of the notion of a fair procedure under art 6. Their rationale lies, inter alia, in the protection of the accused against improper compulsion by the authorities thereby contributing to the avoidance of miscarriages of justice and to the g fulfilment of the aims of art 6 (see *Murray v UK* (1996) 22 EHRR 29 and *Funke v France* (1993) 16 EHRR 297). The right not to incriminate oneself, in particular, presupposes that the prosecution in a criminal case seek to prove their case against the accused without resort to evidence obtained through methods of coercion or oppression in defiance of the will of the accused. In h this sense the right is closely linked to the presumption of innocence contained in art 6(2) of the convention.'

The court went on to state (at 375–376 (para 74)): 'The public interest cannot be invoked to justify the use of answers compulsorily obtained in a non-judicial investigation to incriminate the accused during the trial proceedings.'

j However, in spite of those observations, the court did not find it necessary to decide whether the right not to incriminate oneself is absolute or whether infringements of it may be justified in particular circumstances, so that that issue has been left open. In *Murray v UK* (1996) 22 EHRR 29 at 60 (para 45) and in *Saunders v UK* (1997) 2 BHRC 358 at 373–374 (para 68) the court stated that an accused had to be protected against 'improper compulsion' by the authorities, examples of improper compulsion being coercion and oppression, in order to contribute to avoiding miscarriages of justice and to securing the aims of art 6 of the convention. In the present case there was no suggestion of coercion or oppression and I do not consider that, in the context of the regulatory system which has been brought into operation in the United Kingdom in relation to road traffic and the public interest involved, the use in evidence of a very limited admission lawfully obtained under statutory authority can be regarded as improper compulsion. In the circumstances I consider that the High Court, which did not have the benefit of submissions on the issues of balance and proportionality, placed too much weight on the observations in *Saunders v UK*, a case in which the European Court appears to have laid down a more absolute standard than the other jurisprudence of the court indicates.

On the whole matter I have reached the conclusion, having regard to the very limited nature of the information which the respondent was required to provide under s 172(2)(a) of the 1988 Act, balanced against the legitimate aim sought to be achieved in the general interests of the community, that the test of proportionality has been passed and that evidence of the respondent's admission can be led in evidence at her forthcoming trial without infringing any of her convention rights under art 6. For the reasons which I have endeavoured to give, and the reasons more fully set out by your Lordships, with which I respectfully agree, I too would allow the appeal and quash the declaration made by the High Court.

Appeal allowed.

Dilys Tausz Barrister.

a

Card Protection Plan Ltd v Customs and Excise Commissioners

[2001] UKHL/4

b HOUSE OF LORDS

LORD SLYNN OF HADLEY, LORD JAUNCEY OF TULLICHETTLE, LORD NOLAN, LORD STEYN AND LORD HOFFMANN

28 JUNE 2000, 31 JANUARY 2001

c *Insurance – Indemnity insurance – Credit card protection plan offering cardholders indemnification and other forms of assistance on loss or theft of card – Plan operator instructing insurance broker to arrange insurance for cardholders under block policy – Whether plan constituting one whole supply or several individual supplies of services – Value Added Tax Act 1983, s 17, Sch 6, Group 2 – Council Directive (EEC) 77/388, art 13(B).*

d

The appellant company, CPP, offered credit card holders a card protection plan comprising, inter alia, indemnification against financial loss arising from unauthorised use of credit cards and the execution of the necessary notification formalities in the case of loss or theft. CPP did not provide the insurance itself, e but instead instructed an insurance broker to arrange a block insurance policy covering its customers' claims. As part of the plan, CPP kept a confidential register of all credit cards, ordered replacement cards, operated a change of address service, and supplied lost key location tags and luggage stickers to ensure the quick return of lost keys and luggage. The Customs and Excise Commissioners decided that the fee for the services supplied under the plan was fully taxable at f the standard rate of value added tax (VAT). CPP appealed, contending that the supply fell within an exemption provided by s 17[a] of, and Group 2[b] of Sch 6 to, the Value Added Tax Act 1983 (which implemented art 13(B)[c] of Council Directive (EEC) 77/388), namely the making of arrangements for the carrying on of insurance business. That contention was rejected by the appeal tribunal which g held that the fee paid was wholly liable. On CPP's appeal to the High Court, the judge held the protection plan included services which did fall within the exemption, but that the 'convenience' services constituted a separate non-exempt supply. The Court of Appeal agreed with the tribunal, and CPP appealed to the House of Lords which referred a number of questions to the Court of Justice of the European Communities, including (i) whether a service of the kind provided h by CPP constituted 'insurance … transactions' for the purposes of art 13(B)(a) of the directive and (ii) what test was to be applied in deciding whether a transaction consisted for VAT purposes of a single composite supply or two or more distinct supplies. The Court of Justice held that the expression 'insurance transactions' included the provision of insurance cover by a taxable person who, though not j himself an insurer, procured, in the context of a block policy, insurance cover for his customers by making use of the supplies of an insurer who assumed the risk insured. The court further held that there was a single supply where one or more

a Section 17, so far as material, is set out at [7], post

b Group 2 is set out at [7], post

c Article 13(B), so far as material, is set out at [6], post

elements were to be regarded as constituting the principal service, while one or more elements were to be regarded as an ancillary service, ie a service which did not constitute for customers an aim in itself, but a means of better enjoying the principal service supplied. Accordingly, it fell to be determined by their Lordships whether the arrangements made by CPP constituted a single supply with some ancillary services or whether there were two independent supplies, namely an exempt insurance supply and a non-exempt card registration service.

Held – It was clear from the Court of Justice's judgment that the task of the national court was to have regard to the 'essential features of the transaction' to see whether it was 'several distinct principal services' or a single service and to ensure that what, from an economic point of view, was in reality a single service should not be 'artificially split'. An overall view was to be taken and over-zealous dissecting and analysis of particular clauses should be avoided. In the instant case, the essential feature or dominant purpose of the scheme was to obtain the provision of insurance cover against loss arising from the misuse of credit cards or other documents. In so far as there were services which were not independently to be categorised as insurance, they were ancillary and in some cases minor features of the plan. They were preconditions to the client making a claim for cash indemnity or assistance or a precondition of the furnishing of insurance cover. To regard the provision of insurance as ancillary or subsidiary to the registration of credit card numbers was unreal and the consequences for the client of being able to take protective action with CPP with whom the cards were registered was closely linked to the insurance service. It was not possible to say that some elements of the transaction were 'economically dissociable' from the others. Accordingly, the transaction performed by CPP was to be regarded for VAT purposes as comprising a principal exempt insurance supply, and the other supplies in the transaction were ancillary so that they were to be treated as exempt for VAT purposes. The appeal would therefore be allowed (see [22] and [25]–[33], post).

Notes

For insurance as an exempt supply, see 49(1) *Halsbury's Laws* (4th edn reissue) para 146.

The Value Added Tax Act 1983, s 17, Sch 6, Group 2, has been replaced by the Value Added Tax Act 1994, s 31, Sch 9, Group 2, for which see 50 *Halsbury's Statutes* (4th edn) (2000 reissue) 78, 243.

Cases referred to in opinions

Customs and Excise Comrs v Madgett; Madgett v Customs and Excise Comrs Joined cases C-308/96 and C-94/97 [1998] ECR I-6229, [1998] STC 1189, ECJ.

EC Commission v UK Case 353/85 [1988] 2 All ER 557, [1988] ECR 817, ECJ.

Appeal

The appellant taxpayer, Card Protection Plan Ltd (CPP), appealed with leave of the Appeal Committee of the House of Lords given on 27 June 1994 from the decision of the Court of Appeal (Balcombe, Butler-Sloss LJJ and Sir John Megaw) on 23 November 1993 ([1994] STC 199) dismissing its appeal and allowing a cross-appeal by the respondent, the Commissioners of Customs and Excise, from the decision of Popplewell J on 1 July 1992 ([1992] STC 797) allowing in part CPP's appeal from the decision of the Value Added Tax Tribunal (Judge Medd QC) a on 14 December 1990 ([1991] STI 79) dismissing its appeal from a decision of the commissioners given in a letter dated 23 February 1990 that value added tax was payable at the standard rate on the fee paid by customers for the services provided under CPP's Card Protection Plan. By order of 15 October 1996, the House of Lords referred to the Court of Justice of the European Communities for a preliminary ruling four questions on the interpretation of Council Directive b (EEC) 77/338 (on the harmonisation of the laws of the member states relating to turnover taxes—Common system of value added tax: uniform basis of assessment). The Court of Justice gave its answers in a judgment delivered on 25 February 1999 ([1999] All ER (EC) 339, [1999] 2 AC 601). The facts are set out in the opinion of Lord Slynn of Hadley.

c *Roderick Cordara QC* and *Perdita Cargill-Thompson* (instructed by *Hutchinson Mainprice & Co*) for CPP.

Nicholas Paines QC and *Peter Mantle* (instructed by the *Solicitor for the Customs and Excise*) for the commissioners.

d Their Lordships took time for consideration.

31 January 2001. The following opinions were delivered.

LORD SLYNN OF HADLEY. My Lords,

e [1] Dr PR Howell paid to the appellants (CPP) a fee of £16 for services to be provided to him. The question on this appeal (which affects a large number of CPP's clients) is whether that payment is wholly liable to value added tax (as the commissioners contend and as the London Value Added Tax Tribunal ([1991] STI 79) and the Court of Appeal ([1994] STC 199) held) or exempt as constituting f the making of insurance arrangements for the carrying on of insurance business (as CPP contends), or partly liable since some of the services are and some are not exempt (as Popplewell J held ([1992] STC 797)). The question has to be decided in the light of answers given by the Court of Justice of the European Communities to questions referred by your Lordships' House pursuant to art 177 g (now art 234 EC) of the EC Treaty.

[2] The parties are agreed that the Card Protection Plan operated by CPP is, as found by the tribunal—

> 'intended to ensure that a person who has paid the appropriate fee ... suffer[s] as little financial loss or inconvenience as possible if credit cards or h certain other types of property (eg car keys, passports, share certificates, insurance policies) belonging to him are stolen or lost.'

When a person applies to join the scheme and his application is accepted, he receives a 'policy pack' with a registration form, a change of address form, j property and telephone stickers, medical emergency warning cards and card change forms, property tags and luggage labels. His name and address and the serial number of credit cards and other property are recorded. He is given a number to ring if he loses any of these documents and CPP passes on any reported loss to the insurer so that steps can be taken to prevent or limit use of the card. The documents he is sent include a statement of '15 Important reasons why you should join Card Protection Plan'. This statement has been treated as constituting the key document in the case and in view of the question which arises it is necessary to set it out in full. *a*

'1. *Confidential Registration of all Cards*—accurate computer records will be kept of all your valuable cards.

2. *£750 Insurance Cover*—against fraudulent use on any one claim, provided loss notification is received within 24 hours of discovery of loss. *b*

3. *Unlimited Protection*—you have £750 cover up to the moment of your call to CPP. After that your protection against fraudulent use is unlimited.

4. *Immediate Loss Notification*—free 24 hour ACTIONLINE to receive your loss reports and act immediately to protect you. ACTIONLINE stickers provided for your phone, diary or wallet, so our vital ACTIONLINE number is always at hand. *c*

5. *Replacement cards*—can be ordered when losses are notified, thus minimising your inconvenience.

6. *Change of Address Service*—all card insurers can be notified before you move to ensure your cards don't get into the wrong hands.

7. *Lost key Location*—key tags with your unique policy number and our FREEPOST address help ensure keys can quickly be returned to you in confidence, when found. *d*

8. *Valuable Property & Document Protection*—register serial numbers of your property and details of policies, shares, passports, etc for your own security and to assist in notifying police or making insurance claims in the event of loss or theft. Through our insurance cover you can claim up to £25 on communications costs when assisting police or claiming against personal insurance in respect of items registered with CPP. Includes phone calls, correspondence, postage, etc but not travel costs. *e*

9. *£500 Emergency Cash*—rushed anywhere in the world upon approval if you are stranded and have lost your cards. An interest free advance repayment within 14 days. *f*

10. *Lost Luggage Recovery*—with CPP stickers lost luggage and other personal property such as briefcase or handbag can be quickly identified and owners advised of its location. Our special insurance cover entitles you to claim up to £25 on communications costs incurred arranging recovery of keys or luggage protected by CPP tags and stickers. This includes phone calls, correspondence, postage, etc, but not travel costs. *g*

11. *Emergency Medical Cover Worldwide*—in the event of illness or an accident abroad you need professional help, fast. We provide 24 hour emergency cover and one phone call secures medical advice and assistance in English and other languages, anywhere in the world. If necessary, at your expense, a full consultation, and even medical repatriation by air—with all necessary specialist personnel—can be arranged for you. *h*

12. *Emergency Airline Ticket*—if your credit cards and cash are lost or stolen and you're stranded overseas, CPP's travel cover means arrangements can be made, upon approval, to issue an air ticket to get you home. Cost repayable within 14 days. *j*

13. *Computer Update Services*—confidential printout of your card details for you to check, annually.

14. *Medical Emergency/Warning Card*—dual purpose—to warn that all your cards are protected, and also to provide medical information that can save vital seconds in an emergency. Carry with you at all times.

a 15. *Car Hire Discounts*—you can claim valuable discounts on car rental from Hertz, Avis and Europcar worldwide.'

To cover claims made by its clients CPP instructed an insurance broker to arrange a policy of insurance. Such a policy was taken out for periods of a year and at the relevant time was with the Continental Insurance Co of London plc (Continental) and covered the period from 1 September 1989 to 31 August 1990. b The insurers guaranteed to indemnify the insured against loss as more fully set out in the policy detailed in the schedule to the policy. The schedule provided that the assured were 'various individual members of Card Protection Plan as per schedule'. Sections A to F of the interest specified in the policy covered liability of the cardholder in respect of direct financial loss arising from the wrongful use c of any lost or stolen cards, the costs of reuniting CPP's clients with their luggage, the costs of assisting the police and/or making insurance claims against individual members' insurances and the costs of providing medical assistance and emergency cash and airline tickets. It is to be seen that these cover the heads of claim to which the client was entitled under the 15 reasons.

[3] By letter dated 28 October 1983 the commissioners accepted that the d benefits supplied by CPP to its customers was an exempt supply, but by letter dated 23 February 1990 the commissioners decided that the supply to Dr Howell of the services provided in the agreement was fully taxable at the standard rate of VAT firstly because the package of services was essentially to maintain a register of card numbers, to provide a notification loss service and to prevent liability e from unauthorised use and secondly because there was no supply of insurance by Continental to the client and no privity of contract between Continental and the client.

The relevant legislation

[4] The Value Added Tax Act 1983 was enacted to give effect to Council f Directive (EEC) 77/388 (OJ 1977 L145 p 1) (the Sixth Directive).

[5] VAT is payable on the supply of services made in the United Kingdom where it is 'a taxable supply made by a taxable person in the course or furtherance of any business carried on by him', other than an exempt supply (see s 2(1) and (2) of the 1983 Act).

g [6] Article 13(B) of the Sixth Directive provides that:

> 'Without prejudice to other Community provisions, Member States shall exempt the following under conditions which they shall lay down for the purpose of ensuring the correct and straightforward application of the exemptions and of preventing any possible evasion, avoidance or abuse:
> h (a) insurance and reinsurance transactions, including related services performed by insurance brokers and insurance agents ...'

[7] Pursuant to that obligation s 17(1) of the 1983 Act provided that: 'A supply of goods or services is an exempt supply if it is of a description for the time being specified in Schedule 6 to this Act.' At the time of the commissioners' decision j (23 February 1990) Sch 6 included:

> 'Group 2—Insurance
> Item No.
> 1. The provision of insurance and reinsurance by persons permitted, in accordance with section 2 of the Insurance Companies Act 1982, to carry on insurance business ...

> 3. The making of arrangements for the provision of any insurance or reinsurance in items 1 and 2.
>
> 4. The handling of insurance claims by insurance brokers, insurance agents and persons permitted to carry on insurance business as described in item 1.'

With effect from 1 December 1990 item 1 was amended (by art 2 of the Value Added Tax (Insurance) Order 1990, SI 1990/2037) but not in a way relevant to the present appeal.

[**8**] The First Council Directive on the co-ordination of laws relating to the business of direct insurance other than life insurance (Council Directive (EEC) 73/239 (OJ 1973 L228 p 3), as amended by Council Directive (EEC) 84/641 (OJ 1984 L339 p 21), defines the classes of business to which the directive applies. It included (point A(18) of the Annex to the directive):

> '18. *Assistance*
>
> Assistance for persons who get into difficulties while travelling, while away from home or while away from their permanent residence.'

The litigation so far

[**9**] On CPP's challenge to the commissioners' decision, the tribunal, in reasons given by Judge Medd QC, concluded from a review of the 15 reasons that CPP undertook—

> 'first and foremost, to register on its computer the number, and type of all his credit cards and also the serial numbers of his other valuable property and documents such as passports, insurance policies, share certificates etc.'

That was the 'fundamental service that enabled the company to provide all these services'. The insurance cover negotiated by CPP with Continental ensured that CPP could carry out its undertakings given to its clients which might involve having to pay the clients who suffered a loss. Such undertakings were to be found in items 2, 3, 8, 9, 10 and 12 of the 15 reasons. The supply made to Dr Howell was—

> 'a single supply of a service that can conveniently be called a card registration service, by which [CPP] undertook to register his various cards etc and, having done that, to take such action or pay such sum as they undertook to take or pay'

if any of the relevant contingencies occurred.

[**10**] As the judge held, if Continental was not providing insurance for the clients of CPP, then CPP 'cannot have been making arrangements for the provision of insurance for the customers'.

[**11**] Popplewell J ([1992] STC 797 at 803–804) after a detailed analysis of the insurance policy issued by Continental held that section A indemnified the cardholder against unlimited loss (subject to a limit during the first 24 hours):

> '... that indemnity is an indemnity covering the cardholder. It is not an indemnity given to the company against a claim by the cardholder ... there is scarcely any part of the policy which gives [CPP] any right against the insurance company.'

He rejected the argument that there was no privity of contract between the cardholder and Continental so there could be no exemption. Arrangements for a the provision of insurance enforceable by the cardholder could still be made by CPP.

[12] The judge concluded (at 807) that there was in the protection plan the making of arrangements for the provision of insurance within Sch 6 to the 1983 Act. The 'convenience' services were however 'a separate part of the plan unrelated to the insurance'. There were thus two supplies and it was necessary b to decide which was the major supply.

[13] The Court of Appeal ([1994] STC 199) dismissed CPP's appeal contending that there was a single supply of insurance. On the contrary the court found that there was a single supply of a card registration service to which the supply of insurance was incidental so that the commissioners' cross-appeal to that effect was allowed.

c

[14] Balcombe LJ, with whom Butler-Sloss LJ agreed, thought (at 207) that practical difficulties indicated that in a comparatively simple transaction, as here, the court should not seek to find two supplies. On the basis that the relevant terms of the contract were to be found in the 15 reasons, he held (at 207–208) that points 4 to 7 and 13 to 15 were services of convenience and could not be seen as d insurance. Points 8 to 11 had an insurance element but it was subsidiary to the registration or convenience service. Points 2 and 3 were pure insurance. Point 12 had equal elements of convenience and insurance. If on the other hand he had concluded that the insurance element had been predominant there would have been the arranging for the provision of insurance.

e [15] Sir John Megaw accepted that the cardholders could claim directly against insurers under the policy with Continental. This had been arranged by CPP which was not and could not lawfully under the Insurance Companies Act 1982 issue a policy of insurance itself. He rejected CPP's claim that the 'package of services' was an arrangement for the provision of insurance services, or that it was right to divide it up into two parts, one of insurance and therefore exempt, f the other of non-exempt services.

[16] When the appeal first came before the House, your Lordships' House referred to the Court of Justice the following questions:

> '(1) Having regard to the provisions of the sixth directive and in particular to art 2(1) thereof, what is the proper test to be applied in deciding whether g a transaction consists for VAT purposes of a single composite supply or of two or more independent supplies?
>
> (2) Does the supply by an undertaking of a service or services of the kind provided by CPP through the card protection plan operated by them constitute for VAT purposes a single composite supply or two or more h independent supplies? Are there any particular features of the present case, such as the payment of a single price by the customer or the involvement of Continental as well as CPP, that affect the answer to that question?
>
> (3) Do such supply or supplies constitute or include "insurance … transactions, including related services performed by insurance … agents" j within the meaning of art 13(B)(a) of the sixth directive? In particular, for the purpose of answering that question: (a) does "insurance" within the meaning of art 13(B)(a) of the sixth directive include the classes of activity, in particular "Assistance" activity, listed in the Annex to Directive 73/239, as amended by Directive 84/641? (b) Do the "related services [of] … insurance agents" in art 13(B)(a) of the sixth directive constitute or include the activities referred to in art 2 of Council Directive (EEC) 77/92 (OJ 1977 L26 p 14)?

(4) Is it compatible with art 13(B)(a) of the sixth directive for a member state to restrict the scope of the exemption for "insurance ... transactions" to supplies made by persons permitted to carry on insurance business under the law of that member state?'

The court in its judgment (Case C-349/96 [1999] All ER (EC) 339 at 358 et seq, [1999] 2 AC 601 at 621 et seq) noted that 'insurance transactions' and the concept of insurance are not defined either in the sixth directive or in Directive 73/239 but said:

'17 ... the essentials of an insurance transaction are, as generally understood, that the insurer undertakes, in return for prior payment of a premium, to provide the insured, in the event of materialisation of the risk covered, with the service agreed when the contract was concluded.

18. It is not essential that the service the insurer has undertaken to provide in the event of loss consists in the payment of a sum of money, as that service may also take the form of the provision of assistance in cash or in kind of the types listed in the annex to Directive 73/239 as amended by Directive 84/641. There is no reason for the interpretation of the term "insurance" to differ according to whether it appears in the directive on insurance or in the sixth directive.' (See [1999] All ER (EC) 339 at 362, [1999] 2 AC 601 at 625.)

CPP did not itself undertake to provide insurance cover. It held a block insurance policy under which its customers were the insured.

'21 ... It procures for those customers, for payment, in its own name and on its own account, to the extent of the services mentioned in the Continental policy, insurance cover by having recourse to an insurer. Consequently, for the purposes of VAT, there is a supply of services between Continental and CPP on the one hand, and between CPP and its customers on the other, and the fact that Continental under the terms of its contract with CPP provides insurance cover directly to CPP's customers is not material in this respect.

22 ... the expression "insurance transactions" is broad enough in principle to include the provision of insurance cover by a taxable person who is not himself an insurer but, in the context of a block policy, procures such cover for his customers by making use of the supplies of an insurer who assumes the risk insured.' (See [1999] All ER (EC) 339 at 362, [1999] 2 AC 601 at 625–626.)

[**17**] What is done here by CPP thus constitutes an insurance transaction for the purposes of art 13(B)(a) of the sixth directive.

[**18**] The court further held that in deciding whether a transaction which comprises several elements is to be regarded as a single supply or as two or more distinct supplies to be assessed separately, regard must first be had to all the circumstances in which that transaction takes place, taking into account:

'29 ... first, that it follows from art 2(1) of the sixth directive that every supply of a service must normally be regarded as distinct and independent and, second, that a supply which comprises a single service from an economic point of view should not be artificially split, so as not to distort the functioning of the VAT system, the essential features of the transaction must be ascertained in order to determine whether the taxable person is supplying a the customer, being a typical consumer, with several distinct principal services or with a single service.

30. There is a single supply in particular in cases where one or more elements are to be regarded as constituting the principal service, whilst one or more elements are to be regarded, by contrast, as ancillary services which share the tax treatment of the principal service. A service must be regarded b as ancillary to a principal service if it does not constitute for customers an aim in itself, but a means of better enjoying the principal service supplied (see the judgment in *Customs and Excise Comrs v Madgett* (Joined cases C-308/96 and C-94/97 [1998] ECR I-6229 at 6259, [1998] STC 1189 at 1206, para 24).' (See [1999] All ER (EC) 339 at 363, [1999] 2 AC 601 at 627.)

c Even if a single price is charged for the arrangements, which may indicate a single supply, it must still be considered whether the arrangements in the present case indicated that:

'31 ... the customers intended to purchase two distinct services, namely an insurance supply and a card registration service, then it would be necessary d to identify the part of the single price which related to the insurance supply, which would remain exempt in any event. The simplest possible method of calculation or assessment should be used ...' (See [1999] All ER (EC) 339 at 363–364, [1999] 2 AC 601 at 627.)

e Accordingly it is for the national court:

'32 ... to determine, in the light of the above criteria, whether transactions such as those performed by CPP are to be regarded for VAT purposes as comprising two independent supplies, namely an exempt insurance supply and a taxable card registration service, or whether one of those two supplies f is the principal supply to which the other is ancillary, so that it receives the same tax treatment as the principal supply.' (See [1999] All ER (EC) 339 at 364, [1999] 2 AC 601 at 627.)

Finally, if the transaction is an insurance transaction, it is exempt whether or not it is authorised by national law, ie by the 1982 Act which transposed Directive g 73/239 into United Kingdom law but on the basis of the introductory sentence of art 13(B) of the sixth directive, defined those authorised to provide insurance in s 2. CPP is not so authorised under that section although any contract of insurance underwritten by it would be enforceable against it by virtue of s 132 of the Financial Services Act 1986.

h **[19]** It is thus plain from the Court of Justice's judgment that some at any rate of what CPP provides for its clients constitutes the provision of an insurance transaction and therefore of insurance services within the meaning of Group 2 of Sch 6 to the 1983 Act.

[20] In the circumstances on the appeal there is only one question for your j Lordships to decide. Do the arrangements made constitute a single supply with some ancillary services or are there two independent supplies, an exempt insurance supply and a non-exempt card registration service?

[21] Although the tribunal heard oral evidence of the way the plan works it is plain that everything turns on the interpretation of the written arrangements in particular as set out in the 15 reasons. Thus although the tribunal came to one conclusion on this question, and was supported by the Court of Appeal, its seems to me that it is open as a matter of law for your Lordships to review afresh the scheme although in doing so I pay full regard to the views of the courts below. a

[22] It is clear from the Court of Justice's judgment that the national court's task is to have regard to the 'essential features of the transaction' to see whether it is 'several distinct principal services' or a single service and that what from an economic point of view is in reality a single service should not be 'artificially split'. It seems that an overall view should be taken and over-zealous dissecting and analysis of particular clauses should be avoided. b

[23] I accept that it is possible, as Mr Paines QC has contended, to find that some of the 15 points if separated out and seen in isolation do not on the face of it provide for insurance as commonly understood. For example, point 1 provides only for an accurate computer record; point 6 provides for a change of address service; point 13 provides for a computer update service. c

[24] But there are points which indisputably provide for insurance of the most obvious kind. Thus point 2 provides for £750 cover for fraudulent use on any one claim; point 3 provides for £750 cover up to the moment of the call to notify CPP—'After that your protection against fraudulent use is unlimited.' These points reflect the insurance provided in section A of the policy issued by Continental to CPP for which clients are assured. Others it seems to me fall within class 18 ('Assistance') in point A of the Annex to Directive 73/239 as amended by Directive 84/641, eg points 4, 9, 10, 11 and 12, since it is clear that the service may consist of cash or acts in kind for the purposes of the sixth directive. d

e

[25] If one asks what is the essential feature of the scheme or its dominant purpose, perhaps why objectively people are likely to want to join it, I have no doubt it is to obtain a provision of insurance cover against loss arising from the misuse of credit cards or other documents. That is why CPP is obliged to, and does, arrange, through brokers, with an insurance company like Continental for that cover to be available. f

[26] For the loss to be kept to the minimum it is valuable that the client should be able to notify CPP of the loss of a card and that CPP should be able to notify the company issuing the credit card. It is particularly useful if the client is abroad. For this purpose CPP needs an up-to-date record of cards with the necessary details and the client needs a replacement card if cards are stolen or lost. To assist in the administration of the scheme, luggage tags and a medical warning card are useful. Yet all of these are ancillary or incidental to the main objective of the scheme ie financial protection against loss. The fact that the emergency cash advance and the cost of an emergency air ticket have to be reimbursed does not prevent those services from falling within 'Assistance' in class 18 of Directive 73/239. They clearly fall within the Court of Justice's definition of insurance. g h

[27] The dominant purpose in my view is thus plainly one of insurance principally as to the provision of £750 and then of unlimited protection under reasons 2 and 3 but also in the other financial provisions such as those for dealing with seeking police help and pursuing claims in reason 8.

[28] In so far as there are services which are not independently to be categorised as insurance they are in my view ancillary and in some cases minor features of the plan. They were, as CPP contends, preconditions to the client making a claim for cash indemnity or assistance or a precondition of the furnishing of insurance cover. I doubt whether they can in any event be regarded as sufficiently coherent as to be treated as one separate supply but even if they can it is ancillary to the provision of insurance. To regard the provision of insurance j

a as ancillary or subsidiary to the registration of credit card numbers is unreal and the consequences for the client of being able to take protective action with CPP with whom the cards are registered is closely linked to the insurance service. It is not possible to say that some elements of the transaction are 'economically dissociable' from the others (see *EC Commission v UK* Case 353/85 [1988] 2 All ER 557, [1988] ECR 817).

b **[29]** I would therefore hold in response to para 32 of the Court of Justice's judgment (see [1999] All ER (EC) 339 at 364, [1999] 2 AC 601 at 627) that the transaction performed by CPP for Dr Howell is to be regarded for VAT purposes as comprising a principal exempt insurance supply and the other supplies in the transaction are ancillary so that they are to be treated as exempt for VAT purposes. CPP is entitled to its costs before your Lordships' House and below c against the commissioners.

LORD JAUNCEY OF TULLICHETTLE. My Lords,

[30] I have had the advantage of reading in draft the speech of my noble and learned friend Lord Slynn of Hadley. For the reasons he gives I would also make d the order which he proposes.

LORD NOLAN. My Lords,

[31] I have had the advantage of reading in draft the speech of my noble and learned friend Lord Slynn of Hadley. For the reasons he gives I would also make the order which he proposes.

e

LORD STEYN. My Lords,

[32] I have had the advantage of reading in draft the speech of my noble and learned friend Lord Slynn of Hadley. For the reasons he gives I would also make the order which he proposes.

f

LORD HOFFMANN. My Lords,

[33] I have had the advantage of reading in draft the speech of my noble and learned friend Lord Slynn of Hadley. For the reasons he gives I would also make the order which he proposes.

Appeal allowed.

Dilys Tausz Barrister.

R v Offen and other cases

a

COURT OF APPEAL, CRIMINAL DIVISION

LORD WOOLF CJ, STEEL AND RICHARDS JJ

17 OCTOBER, 9 NOVEMBER 2000

b

Sentencing – Life imprisonment – Life imprisonment for second serious offence – Whether imposition of automatic life sentence for second serious offence compatible with provisions of human rights convention – Crime (Sentences) Act 1997, s 2 – Human Rights Act 1998, s 3, Sch 1, Pt I, arts 3, 5, 7.

c

In five cases heard together by the Court of Appeal, common issues arose on the interpretation of s 2[a] of the Crime (Sentences) Act 1997 (now s 109 of the Powers of Criminal Courts (Sentencing) Act 2000). Under s 2, the court was required to impose an automatic life sentence on a person convicted of a serious offence, committed after the commencement of that provision and when he was 18 or over, who had previously been convicted of another serious offence, unless it was of the opinion that there were exceptional circumstances relating to either of the offences or to the offender which justified its not doing so. In previous cases, the Court of Appeal had held that the rationale of s 2, namely that those who had been convicted of two qualifying serious offences presented a serious and continuing danger to the safety of the public, was relevant in determining whether the exceptional circumstances justified the court in not imposing a life sentence, but was not relevant to the question whether such circumstances existed in the first place. In each of the cases before the court, the defendant had pleaded guilty to, or been convicted of, a serious offence within the meaning of s 2, and had also been convicted of such an offence before the implementation of the 1997 Act. In four of those cases, the trial judges had concluded that there were no special circumstances, and the defendants appealed from the imposition of life sentences under s 2. In the fifth case, that of S, the Attorney General challenged the trial judge's decision not to impose such a sentence on the grounds of exceptional circumstances. In each case, it was contended either that the interpretation of s 2 was affected by s 3[b] of the Human Rights Act 1998 (which required the court, so far as possible, to read and give effect to primary legislation in a way which was compatible with rights under the European Convention for the Protection of Human Rights and Fundamental Freedoms 1950), or that s 2 was incompatible with convention rights (as set out in Sch 1 to the 1998 Act). The defendants relied in particular on the prohibition against inhuman or degrading treatment or punishment in art 3[c] and the right to liberty under art 5[d]. They also relied on art 7(1)[e] of the convention which prohibited, inter alia, the imposition of a penalty heavier than one that was applicable when the criminal offence had been committed.

d e f g h j

a Section 2, so far as material, is set out at p 159 *h* to p 160 *d*, post
b Section 3, so far as material, is set out at p 159 *g*, post
c Article 3 is set out at p 174 *a*, post
d Article 5, so far as material, is set out at p 174 *b c*, post
e Article 7(1) is set out at p 172 *e f*, post

a **Held** – Section 2 of the 1997 Act would not contravene the rights under arts 3 and 5 of the convention if it were applied so that it did not result in offenders being sentenced to life imprisonment when they did not constitute a significant risk to the public. If the offender did pose such a risk, the court could impose a life sentence under s 2 without contravening the convention. Such a construction was in accordance with the duty imposed on the court by s 3 of the 1998 Act. It b also took account of the rationale of s 2 of the 1997 Act which was highly relevant not only when the court had already decided that there were exceptional circumstances, but also when considering whether or not such circumstances existed. The policy and intention of Parliament in enacting s 2 was to protect the public against a person who had committed two serious offences. It was not therefore intended to apply to someone in relation to whom it was established c that there would be no need for protection in the future. The time that had elapsed between the two serious offences could, but would not necessarily, reflect on whether there was any danger against which the public needed protection. The same was true of two differing offences, and the age of the offender. Those were all circumstances which could give rise to the conclusion d that what could be normal and not exceptional in one context was exceptional in another context. If that approach were not adopted, the approach to exceptional circumstances could be unduly restrictive. As regards art 7(1) of the convention, the automatic life sentence under s 2 was being imposed for the second serious offence committed by the offender, not in relation to the earlier offence. It followed that the imposition of an automatic life sentence under s 2 would not e contravene art 7(1) of the convention. In two of the instant cases, the defendants did not present a significant risk to the public and their appeals against sentence would therefore be allowed. In the remaining cases, however, the defendants did present such a risk. Accordingly, their appeals against sentence would be dismissed, while in S's case a life sentence would be imposed under s 2 (see p 159 f *d* to *f*, p 169 *j* to p 171 *a c* to *g*, p 173 *b c h j*, p 175 *g* to p 176 *a g h* to p 177 *d j* and p 178 *b c*, post).

R v Taylor [1996] 2 Cr App R 64 applied.

R v Kelly, A-G's Reference (No 53 of 1998) [1999] 2 All ER 13 and *R v Buckland* [2000] 1 All ER 907 considered.

g **Notes**

For the prohibition on inhuman and degrading treatment or punishment, the right to liberty and the prohibition on retrospective laws, see 8(2) *Halsbury's Laws* (4th edn reissue) paras 124, 127, 148, and for automatic life sentences for a second serious offence, see Supp to 11(2) *Halsbury's Laws* (4th edn reissue) para 1202B.1.

h For the Human Rights Act 1998, s 3, Sch 1, Pt I, arts 3, 5, 7, see 7 *Halsbury's Statutes* (4th edn) (1999 reissue) 502, 522, 523.

Cases referred to in judgment

A-G's Reference (No 30 of 1993) (1995) 16 Cr App R (S) 318, CA.

j *McIntosh v HM Advocate* 2000 SCCR 1017, HC of Just.

Quinn v France (1995) 21 EHRR 529, ECt HR.

R v Buckland [2000] 1 All ER 907, [2000] 1 WLR 1262, CA.

R v Governor of Brockhill Prison, ex p Evans (No 2) [2000] 4 All ER 15, [2000] 3 WLR 843, HL.

R v Kelly, A-G's Reference (No 53 of 1998) [1999] 2 All ER 13, [2000] QB 198, [1999] 2 WLR 1100, CA.

R v Offen [2000] Crim LR 306, CA.
R v Taylor [1996] 2 Cr App R 64, CA.
R v Turner [2000] 1 Cr App R (S) 472, CA.
R v Williams [2000] Crim LR 597, CA.
Taylor v UK [1998] EHRLR 90, E Com HR.
Weeks v UK (1987) 10 EHRR 293, ECt HR.
Welch v UK (1995) 20 EHRR 247, ECt HR.

Cases also cited or referred to in skeleton arguments
Adamson v UK App No 42293/98 (26 January 1999, unreported), E Com HR.
A-G of Hong Kong v Lee Kwong-kut [1993] 3 All ER 939, [1993] AC 951, PC.
A-G of the Gambia v Momodou Jobe [1984] AC 689, [1984] 3 WLR 174, PC.
A-G's Reference (No 23 of 1997) [1998] 1 Cr App R (S) 378, CA.
A-G's Reference (No 4 of 1998) [1998] 2 Cr App R (S) 388, CA.
A-G's Reference (No 27 of 1999) [2000] 1 Cr App R (S) 237, CA.
A-G's Reference (No 71 of 1999) [1999] 2 Cr App R (S) 369, CA.
Albert v Belgium (1983) 5 EHRR 533, ECt HR.
Belgium Linguistic Case (No 2) (1968) 1 EHRR 252, ECt HR.
Botta v Italy (1998) 4 BHRC 81, ECt HR.
Brown v Stott (Procurator Fiscal, Dunfermline) 2000 JC 328, HC of Just.
C v Federal Republic of Germany (1986) 46 DR 176, E Com HR.
Caballero v UK (2000) 30 EHRR 643, ECt HR.
CC v UK [1999] Crim LR 228, ECt HR.
Costello-Roberts v UK (1993) 19 EHRR 112, ECt HR.
Darmalingum v The State (1999) 8 BHRC 662, [2000] 1 WLR 2303, PC.
De Freitas v Permanent Secretary of Ministry of Agriculture, Fisheries, Lands and Housing [1999] 1 AC 69, [1998] 3 WLR 675, PC.
Doody v Secretary of State for the Home Dept [1993] 3 All ER 92, sub nom *R v Secretary of State for the Home Dept, ex p Doody* [1994] 1 AC 531, HL.
Herczegfalvy v Austria (1992) 15 EHRR 437, ECt HR.
Hussain v UK (1996) 22 EHRR 1, ECt HR.
Ibbotson v UK [1999] EHRLR 218, E Com HR.
Ireland v UK (1978) 2 EHRR 25, ECt HR.
Kokkinakis v Greece (1993) 17 EHRR 397, ECt HR.
Litster v Forth Dry Dock and Engineerring Co Ltd [1989] 1 All ER 1134, [1990] 1 AC 546, HL.
Marleasing SA v La Comercial International de Alimentación SA Case C-106/89 [1990] ECR I-4135.
Minister of Home Affairs v Fisher [1979] 3 All ER 21, [1980] AC 319, PC.
Niemietz v Germany (1992) 16 EHRR 97, ECt HR.
Nottingham City Council v Amin [2000] 2 All ER 946, [2000] 1 WLR 1071, DC.
Osman v UK (1998) 5 BHRC 293, ECt HR.
Pickstone v Freemans plc [1988] 2 All ER 803, [1989] AC 66, HL.
Porter Harris v UK App No 1882/91 (1 July 1992, unreported), E Com HR.
R v Broadcasting Standards Commission, ex p British Broadcasting Corp (Liberty intervening) [2000] 3 All ER 989, [2000] 3 WLR 1327, CA.
R v Chapman [2000] 1 Cr App R (S) 377, CA.
R v Crow, R v Pennington (1994) 16 Cr App R (S) 409, CA.
R v Dalton [1995] 2 All ER 349, [1995] QB 243, CA.
R v DPP, ex p Kebilene [1999] 4 All ER 801, [2000] 2 AC 326, HL.
R v Gabbidon, R v Bramble [1997] 2 Cr App R (S) 19, CA.

a b c d e f g h j

a *R v Hercules* (1980) 2 Cr App R (S) 156, CA.
R v Hodgson (1967) 52 Cr App R 113, CA.
R v King, R v Simpkins (1973) 57 Cr App R 696, CA.
R v Mansell (1994) 15 Cr App R (S) 771, CA.
R v Oakes (1986) 26 DLR (4th) 200, Can SC.
R v Parole Board, ex p Bradley [1990] 3 All ER 828, [1991] 1 WLR 134, DC.
b *R v Parole Board, ex p Lodomez* (1994) 26 BMLR 162, DC.
R v Parole Board, ex p Watson [1996] 2 All ER 641, [1996] 1 WLR 906, CA.
R v Queen (1981) 3 Cr App R (S) 245, CA.
R v Secretary of State for the Home Dept, ex p Stafford [1998] 4 All ER 7, [1999] 2 AC 38, HL.
R v Thomas [1996] 1 Cr App R (S) 208, CA.
R v Wood [2000] 3 All ER 561, [2000] 1 WLR 1687, CA.
c *Selmouni v France* (1999) 7 BHRC 1, ECt HR.
Smith v The Queen (1987) 40 DLR (4th) 435, Can SC.
Soering v UK (1989) 11 EHRR 439, ECt HR.
SP v UK (Application No 43478/1998) 18 January 2000, E Com HR.
S v Tcoeib (1996) 7 BCLR 996, Nm SC.
d *S v Vries* (1996) 12 BCLR 1666, Nm HC.
Stubbings v UK (1996) 1 BHRC 316, ECt HR.
SW v UK, CR v UK (1995) 21 EHRR 363, ECt HR.
Teixera de Castro v Portugal (1998) 4 BHRC 533, ECt HR.
Three Rivers DC v Bank of England (No 2) [1996] 2 All ER 363.
Thynne v UK (1990) 13 EHRR 666, ECt HR.
e *Treholt v Norway* (1991) 71 DR 168, E Com HR.
Tyrer v UK (1978) 2 EHRR 1, ECt HR.
V v UK (1999) 30 EHRR 121, ECt HR.
Van Droogenbroeck v Belgium (1982) 4 EHRR 443, ECt HR.
Vasquez v R [1994] 3 All ER 674, [1994] 1 WLR 1304, PC.
f *Veen v The Queen (No 2)* (1988) 164 CLR 465, Aust HC.
Webb v Emo Air Cargo (UK) Ltd (No 2) [1995] 4 All ER 577, [1995] 1 WLR 1454, HL.
Winterwerp v Netherlands (1979) 2 EHRR 387, ECt HR.
Wynne v UK (1994) 19 EHRR 333, ECt HR.
X v Federal Republic of Germany (1976) 6 DR 127, E Com HR.
X v UK (1981) 4 EHRR 188, ECt HR.

g

Appeals against sentence, applications for leave to appeal against sentence, application for leave to appeal against conviction and application for leave to refer sentence

h *R v Offen*

The defendant, Matthew Barry James Offen, appealed against the sentence of life imprisonment imposed on him, under s 2 of the Crime (Sentences) Act 1997, by Judge Hayward in the Crown Court at Lewes on 28 May 1999 following his plea of guilty to robbery. The Court of Appeal had dismissed a previous appeal, but j the case was referred back to it by the Criminal Cases Review Commission on 13 October 2000. The facts are set out in the judgment of the court.

R v McKeown

The defendant, Darren McKeown, appealed with leave of the single judge against the sentence of life imprisonment imposed on him, under s 2 of the Crime (Sentences) Act 1997, following his conviction before Judge Spittle and a jury in the Crown Court at Durham on 11 May 2000 for causing grievous bodily harm with intent. The facts are set out in the judgment of the court. *a*

R v McGilliard

The defendant, Peter Wilson McGilliard, applied for leave to appeal against the sentence of life imprisonment imposed on him, under s 2 of the Crime (Sentences) Act 1997, by Judge Appleby QC in the Crown Court at Derby on *b* 28 May 1999 following his plea of guilty to wounding with intent to cause grievous bodily harm. The facts are set out in the judgment of the court.

R v Okwuegbunam

The defendant, Kristova Okwuegbunam, applied for leave to appeal against the *c* sentence of life imprisonment imposed on him, under s 2 of the Crime (Sentences) Act 1997, by Judge Stokes QC in the Central Criminal Court on 25 July 2000 following his plea of guilty to manslaughter. The facts are set out in the judgment of the court.

d

R v S

The defendant, Stephen S, applied (i) for leave to appeal against his conviction on 2 March 2000 at the Central Criminal Court before Judge Capstick QC and a jury of five counts of indecent assault, five counts of attempted rape, five counts of rape, one count of buggery and one count of assault occasioning actual bodily harm, and (ii) for leave to appeal against the sentence of 12 years imprisonment imposed on *e* him for those offences. The Attorney General applied for leave under s 36 of the Criminal Justice Act 1988 to refer the sentence to the court as unduly lenient on the ground that the judge should have imposed a sentence of life imprisonment under s 2 of the Crime (Sentences) Act 1997. The facts are set out in the judgment of the court.

f

Edward Fitzgerald QC and *Phillippa Kaufmann* (assigned by the *Registrar of Criminal Appeals*) for Offen.

Christopher John Knox (assigned by the *Registrar of Criminal Appeals*) for McKeown.

Joel Bennathan (assigned by the *Registrar of Criminal Appeals*) for McGilliard.

Edward Fitzgerald QC and *Daniel Friedman* (assigned by the *Registrar of Criminal* *g* *Appeals*) for Okwuegbunam.

Alastair Edie (assigned by the *Registrar of Criminal Appeals*) for S.

David Perry (instructed by the *Crown Prosecution Service*) for the Crown and (instructed by the *Treasury Solicitor*) for the Attorney General.

h

Cur adv vult

9 November 2000. The following judgment of the court was delivered.

LORD WOOLF CJ.

j

1. This judgment relates to five appeals. In each case where leave is required to appeal against sentence, we give leave. The five appeals all involve s 2 of the Crime (Sentences) Act 1997. (This is now s 109 of the Powers of the Criminal Courts (Sentencing) Act 2000. In this judgment we will refer to s 2 in the 1997 Act.) The application of s 2 has already given rise to a number of decisions by this court. They illustrate the problems which can arise in practice in applying

a statutory provisions which require the courts to impose an automatic life sentence on certain offenders.

2. The policy of Parliament for establishing the automatic life sentences emerges clearly from the then government's White Paper *Protecting the Public: the Government's Strategy on Crime in England and Wales* (1996) (Cm 3190). In para 10.11 the White Paper states:

b

> 'Too often in the past, those who had shown a propensity to commit serious violent or sex offences have served their sentences and been released only to offend again. In many such cases, the danger of releasing the offender has been plain for all to see—but nothing could be done, because once the offender has completed the sentence imposed, he or she has to be released. c Too often, victims have paid the price when the offender has repeated the same offences. The Government is determined that the public should receive proper protection from persistent violent or sex offenders. That means requiring the courts to impose an automatic indeterminate sentence, and releasing the offender if and only if it is safe to do so.'

d 3. In *R v Buckland* [2000] 1 All ER 907 at 912–913, [2000] 1 WLR 1262 at 1268 Lord Bingham of Cornhill CJ described the rationale of s 2 in these terms:

> 'The section is founded on an assumption that those who have been convicted of two qualifying serious offences present such a serious and continuing danger to the safety of the public that they should be liable to indefinite e incarceration and, if released, should be liable indefinitely to recall to prison. In any case where, on all the evidence, it appears that such a danger does or may exist, it is hard to see how the court can consider itself justified in not imposing the statutory penalty, even if exceptional circumstances are found to exist. But if exceptional circumstances are found, and the evidence f suggests that an offender does not present a serious and continuing danger to the safety of the public, the court may be justified in imposing a lesser penalty.'

4. The reason why we have heard these appeals together is because in each case it is contended that either the interpretation of s 2 of the 1997 Act is affected g by s 3 of the Human Rights Act 1998, or that s 2 is incompatible with a convention right so that the defendants are entitled to a declaration of incompatibility. The impact of the 1998 Act on the interpretation of legislation arises under s 3 of that Act, which provides: '(1) So far as it is possible to do so, primary legislation and subordinate legislation must be read and given effect in a way which is compatible with the Convention rights.'

h

THE LEGISLATION

5. Section 2 of the 1997 Act, so far as relevant, is in the following terms:

> '(1) This section applies where—(a) a person is convicted of a serious j offence committed after the commencement of this section; and (b) at the time when that offence was committed, he was 18 or over and had been convicted in any part of the United Kingdom of another serious offence.
>
> (2) The court shall impose a life sentence, that is to say—(a) where the person is 21 or over, a sentence of imprisonment for life; (b) where he is under 21, a sentence of custody for life under section 8(2) of the Criminal Justice Act 1982 ("the 1982 Act"), unless the court is of the opinion that there

are *exceptional circumstances relating to either of the offences or to the offender which justify its not doing so*.

(3) Where the court does not impose a life sentence, it shall state in open court that it is of that opinion and what the exceptional circumstances are.

(4) An offence the sentence for which is imposed under subsection (2) above shall not be regarded as an offence the sentence for which is fixed by law.

(5) An offence committed in England and Wales is a serious offence for the purposes of this section if it is any of the following, namely—(a) an attempt to commit murder, a conspiracy to commit murder or an incitement to murder; (b) an offence under section 4 of the Offences Against the Person Act 1861 (soliciting murder); (c) manslaughter; (d) an offence under section 18 of the Offences Against the Person Act 1861 (wounding, or causing grievous bodily harm, with intent); (e) rape or an attempt to commit rape; (f) an offence under section 5 of the Sexual Offences Act 1956 (intercourse with a girl under 13); (g) an offence under section 16 (possession of a firearm with intent to injure), section 17 (use of a firearm to resist arrest) or section 18 (carrying a firearm with criminal intent) of the Firearms Act 1968; and (h) robbery where, at some time during the commission of the offence, the offender had in his possession a firearm or imitation firearm within the meaning of that Act.' (My emphasis.)

6. The following features of the section will be noted. (i) It refers to two offences having been committed by the offender. (ii) It is only the second offence ('the trigger offence') which has to have been committed after the commencement of the section. The earlier offence may have been committed at any time. (iii) When the second offence is committed the offender is required to be over 18 but there is no age requirement in relation to the first offence. (iv) The proviso of 'exceptional circumstances' applies to both offences. The 'exceptional circumstances' can relate either to the offences or to the offender but what constitutes exceptional circumstances is not otherwise defined by the section. (v) All offences identified as serious offences are offences for which life imprisonment could be imposed quite apart from s 2.

THE FACTS OF THE DIFFERENT APPEALS

7. The relevant circumstances of each appeal can be shortly summarised as follows.

Matthew Barry James Offen

8. On 28 May 1999 the defendant Matthew Offen, now 35 years of age, pleaded guilty at Lewes Crown Court to an offence of robbery involving the use of an imitation firearm, committed on 26 January 1999. On 19 January 1990 he had been convicted of an offence of robbery committed in September 1989 and of an offence of going equipped for theft for which he was sentenced to thirty months imprisonment.

9. Matthew Offen's case was therefore one to which s 2 of the 1997 Act applied. Finding there were no exceptional circumstances which justified his not doing so, the judge imposed a term of life imprisonment under s 2. A period of 14 months was specified under s 28 of the 1997 Act. The judge indicated that had he not been required to pass a life sentence he would have imposed a determinate sentence of three years imprisonment and that he had taken into account the time spent in custody before sentence was passed. On 28 October 1999, in the Court

a of Appeal Criminal Division, Matthew Offen's appeal against his life sentence was dismissed ([2000] Crim LR 306). The court found that there were no exceptional circumstances in relation to the offence or the offender which would justify the court in not imposing a sentence of life imprisonment.

10. The defendant's case has now been referred back to the Court of Appeal under s 9(1)(b) of the Criminal Appeal Act 1995.

b 11. The facts of the robbery in 1999 are that the defendant, carrying a sports bag, entered a building society in Hove in the early afternoon of 26 January 1999. His appearance was unkempt, and one of the employees formed the impression that he was homeless. He approached the counter, put the sports bag on top of it and took out a plastic bag containing a toy gun. Two cashiers were sitting at the counter and the defendant pointed the gun at one of them who believed it to c be a real gun. The defendant told the cashier, 'Give me your money, put it in the bag'. The cashier asked if he was joking to which the defendant said, 'No, put the money in the bag'. To one employee he appeared to be nervous. When it became clear that he was serious the cashier removed from the till a wad of notes, later found to be £960, and placed it in the sports bag. The cashier told the defendant d this was all they had. The defendant then said, 'I'm sorry I have to do this' or words to that effect. He put the plastic bag containing the toy gun into his holdall and left.

12. A customer who witnessed the robbery told the staff to sound the alarm and a security camera was activated. Two employees stated that they were fearful for their safety. The senior branch assistant stated that she was extremely e scared both for herself and other members of staff. The customer was heard to shout, 'I'm not letting you lot get into trouble' as she left the building society. She followed the defendant and grabbed the holdall from his right hand, and returned it. The defendant continued to walk away.

13. At about 3 pm the same afternoon the defendant spoke to some friends f who ran a local store and said that he had robbed a bank. It was noted that he was wearing slippers. When he was told he would have to tell the police, the defendant denied the truth of what he had said, saying he had made it up. The next day his friends telephoned the police and the defendant was arrested. He was interviewed and admitted the offence, and said that a voice in his head had made him do it. He had not taken his medication and had been hearing voices all g day.

14. He told the police that he had bought two toy guns from a toy shop a couple of months before. The second, a water pistol, being a back-up in case the first gun did not work. He said he bought the guns in order to hold up building societies. He also explained that he was wearing his slippers at the time of the h robbery because his feet were wet. He apologised for his actions and said he would not commit another robbery and that he needed help not prison. In a second interview he told the police he had no need of the money and said he had worn a hat at the time of the robbery to disguise his face and had wrapped the toy gun up in a plastic bag so that the staff would not realise it was a fake. He had j hoped to get about £2,000 from the robbery and had intended to spend the money on prostitutes.

15. The facts of the offence of robbery for which the defendant was sentenced in January 1990 were similar. The defendant purchased a toy gun then used it, in its plastic bag, to threaten the staff of a building society next door to the toy shop. He asked for 'the money' and was given about £3,000. According to the defendant, he spent only a small amount of the money before giving himself up to the police.

He was found to be in possession of a knife which he said he had intended to use to commit an earlier robbery but had changed his mind as he did not like the idea of waving a knife around.

16. The judge had before him two medical reports and a pre-sentence report. The pre-sentence report referred to a diagnosis of schizophrenia and described the defendant as presenting a medium risk of reoffending and a low risk of harm to the public.

17. On 28 January 1999, the defendant was assessed by Dr Blackwood who noted that since his imprisonment in 1990, the defendant had been involved with out-patient psychiatric services, attended a day centre each day, and was currently on medication. It was noted that the offence was motivated by 'voices' telling him to rob. These were said to be pseudo-hallucinations, not truly psychotic experiences.

18. On 19 May 1999, Dr T Buck, clinical assistant to Dr Allison, consultant psychiatrist at the Mill View Hospital, reported that the defendant suffered mild to moderate depressive illness and at times has pseudo-psychiatric voices in his head. His current mental state was fairly stable with no sign of depression or other major mental illness. On the question of risk and disposal, Dr Buck stated his opinion that 'Mr Offen is not a danger to society'.

19. In a report dated 15 April, Dr Buck stated that the defendant had told the police that on the day of the robbery he had not taken his medication and Dr Buck had concluded this may have led to an increase in the intensity of his symptoms. No medical disposal was appropriate.

20. The judge referred to the defendant's mental problems and the fact that he had not taken his medication on the day of the incident. He did not consider whether the defendant's lack of 'dangerousness' amounted to an exceptional circumstance. He considered the defendant's history of mental problems and the diagnosis that he was not suffering from any major mental illness. He also considered the circumstances of the robbery and concluded that there were no exceptional circumstances relating to either the offence or the offender. The judge expressed the view that he thought it unlikely that Parliament had this sort of case in mind when it passed these provisions.

21. The defendant has now served the specified period under s 28 of the 1997 Act. A psychiatric report dated 6 September 2000 prepared by Dr Sameer P Sarker, specialist registrar in forensic psychiatry at the Institute of Psychiatry at Maudsley, for consideration by the Parole Board 'echoes the opinion expressed by Dr Hadyn Smith five years ago that Mr Offen is not a person who is dangerous to anybody including himself'. He suggested, inter alia, regular supervision, support and monitoring. There is nothing before the court which sets out any contrary medical or other opinion.

Darren McKeown

22. On 11 May 2000, in the Crown Court at Durham, the defendant Darren McKeown, who is aged 27 years, was convicted of an offence of causing grievous bodily harm with intent. On 3 May 1990 the defendant had been sentenced to a period of two years detention in a young offenders institution for an offence of wounding with intent. On 11 May 2000, he was sentenced to life imprisonment pursuant to s 2 of the 1997 Act.

23. Under s 28 of that Act, the judge specified that 18 months imprisonment was the appropriate term and that the determinate term would have been three years imprisonment.

24. The defendant appeals against his sentence by leave of the single judge.

25. The facts of the offence arise out of an incident which took place at about midnight on 9/10 July 1999. Mr Seymour (aged 42 years), the complainant, and the defendant were acquainted because some weeks earlier there had been a confrontation between them over the purchase of a ring.

26. On 9 July, Mr Seymour was walking down a street in Consett. He had been drinking. The defendant approached him and demanded an apology. Mr Seymour refused to give one, whereupon the defendant punched him to the ground then kicked him in the face and head.

27. Mr Seymour sustained fractures of the nose, cheekbone and jawbone. Plating and wiring were required. He also had two black eyes, double vision and headaches.

28. When arrested and interviewed, the defendant said he pushed Mr Seymour in self-defence.

29. The facts of the earlier offence are not fully before the court save that when the defendant was 16 years old he committed the offence during New Year 1989/1990. He was just 17 years old when sentenced.

30. The judge had the defendant's antecedent record which disclosed offending which ceased in 1995. There were no offences recorded between 1991 and 1995. There was also a pre-sentence report dated 30 December 1999 which assessed the defendant as presenting a medium risk of reoffending and concluded that his risk to the public was low.

31. In sentencing the defendant to life imprisonment, the judge who had conducted the trial referred to the life sentence as the only sentence he was allowed to impose by law. He indicated that he was satisfied, on the evidence that he had heard, that the defendant did not go out with violence on his mind or with any intent that violence would be occasioned by him. He described a single kick, clearly to be seen on 'the video' and said that there was no prolonged attack and that the defendant removed himself from the scene, he was not removed.

32. The judge, having fixed the determinate sentence of three years, went on to say that had the circumstances been different, then no doubt the sentence would have been different also.

33. The judge took into account that the defendant had accepted responsibility for his actions by pleading guilty to unlawfully causing grievous bodily harm and that the trial had been on the issue of intent.

Peter Wilson McGilliard

34. On 28 May 1999, at the Crown Court at Derby, the defendant Peter McGilliard, who is aged 37 years, having earlier pleaded guilty to an offence of wounding with intent to do grievous bodily harm, was sentenced to life imprisonment pursuant to s 2 of the 1997 Act. On 24 July 1984, he had been sentenced for an offence of culpable homicide to a term of six years imprisonment.

35. It was conceded by counsel and concluded by the judge that there were no exceptional circumstances which would allow any other sentence to be passed.

36. The judge specified that the period to be served before the defendant could be considered for parole be three and a half years, less four months and three weeks already served on remand. The notional determinate sentence was fixed at seven years imprisonment.

37. McGilliard was refused permission to appeal by the single judge.

38. The facts of the current offence concern an incident on 4 December 1998. The defendant visited a public house in Linton, Derbyshire. He became drunk and abusive, several customers describe him as a nuisance and shouting at people.

Shaun Taylor, the complainant, remonstrated with the defendant who swore at him, then he punched the defendant to the floor and kicked him. The defendant left the public house bleeding and making threats that he would return to shoot Mr Taylor. The defendant's injuries were such as to require hospital treatment the next day. Shortly afterwards, the defendant returned and called on Mr Taylor to come outside and fight. He began to throw beer glasses around the bar, someone tried to push him out and Mr Taylor followed him. The defendant then produced a knife (described as a kitchen knife with an eight-inch blade) and lunged forward and stabbed Mr Taylor in the abdomen. The knife was further described by the judge in sentencing as a fearsome long-bladed kitchen knife of the butchering type.

39. The wound penetrated the full thickness of the abdominal wall, the underlying bowel was damaged and surgery was required to close the wounds. He remained in hospital for nine days, but by late January 1999 was considered to have made a full recovery.

40. The defendant was arrested and the knife fell from his jeans. In interview, he denied stabbing anyone but said he tried to protect himself against blows from the complainant and had taken a knife off him.

41. The facts of the culpable homicide offence for which he was sentenced in 1984 are not before the court. The defendant maintained to Dr Earp, consultant psychiatrist who examined him and reported on 21 March 1999, that he denied that offence. He was aged 17 years and pleaded guilty on the advice of his counsel, which he now believes was a mistake.

42. The psychiatric report indicated that no medical disposal was appropriate for the current offence. The defendant denied responsibility for the complainant's wound. Dr Earp described a serious alcoholic dependency syndrome. On the day of the offence Dr Earp was told the defendant had consumed alcohol throughout the day and injected himself with heroin.

43. In addition to Dr Earp's report, the judge had a pre-sentence report dated 16 April 1999, prepared by Mr Nick Hyde, and the court had the defendant's antecedent record.

44. The antecedent record disclosed repeated offences of violence and assaults, as well as offences of dishonesty, criminal damage, drunkenness and involvement with controlled drugs. He has served nine custodial sentences, has been fined and his response to probation and community service was assessed as poor.

45. The pre-sentence report specifically addressed the risk of reoffending which was described as high. The risk being of personal injury which could be serious or fatal. Both Dr Earp and Mr Hyde refer to lack of motivation to achieve change or give up drink.

Kristova Okwuegbunam

46. On 25 July 2000, in the Central Criminal Court, the defendant Kristova Okwuegbunam, who is 33 years of age, was sentenced to life imprisonment pursuant to s 2 of the 1997 Act for an offence of manslaughter to which he had previously pleaded guilty on change of plea. The period specified pursuant to s 28 of that Act as the minimum period to be served by the defendant was two and a half years. An application for leave to appeal against sentence has been referred to the full court by the registrar.

47. The deceased was the mother of the defendant's children. Although he did not live with her, he was a frequent visitor to her flat. She was found dead at the flat on 17 January 2000. The basis of the defendant's plea was, first, that he had

a struck her twice to the head on the evening of 16 January during the course of an argument precipitated by her chastisement of their son. The blows were not of sufficient force to indicate an intention to cause really serious injury. The injuries inflicted were a black eye, a cut below the eyebrow, a fractured nose and associated bruising. In addition, the blows caused a subdural haemorrhage which was the cause of death the following day. On the following morning, the b defendant insisted that the deceased take a cold bath. He said in interview that this was because she had been neglecting herself as a result of her depressive condition and her body odour was annoying him. The subdural haemorrhage was activated while the deceased was in the bathroom and led to death. In interview, the defendant said that the deceased had been reluctant to get into the bath and he had pushed her down, but not so that her head was under water. She c then slipped two or three times when trying to get out of the bath. He realised that something was wrong and pulled her out. Although the prosecution opened the case on the basis that they did not accept the defendant's account of what happened in the bathroom, the prosecution did accept that there was no evidence that he struck the deceased at that stage.

d 48. In sentencing the defendant on the basis upon which he had pleaded guilty, the judge observed that this was none the less a serious case in which a human life had been lost as a result of violent conduct by the defendant against a slightly built woman in her own home, that violence being followed by his forcing her to take a cold bath, whereupon she died. There was a strong element of bullying and humiliation in what the defendant did. It was not the kind of case e where a blow struck during a wholly unexpected confrontation with a stranger had had unforeseen and tragic consequences. It had also to be seen against the background of the defendant's previous offending.

49. The defendant had a conviction for rape in 1990 for which he received a sentence of five years' imprisonment following a plea of guilty. It was that offence f which made the case subject to s 2 of the 1997 Act. The prosecution case was that the defendant had on that occasion abducted a 13 year old girl by threatening to harm her with a large piece of broken glass. He had taken her to his home and raped her there. The defendant has always maintained, and it was advanced on his behalf in mitigation at the time, that he knew the victim and that neither glass nor any other weapon was used. In addition to the sentence for rape, the g defendant received on that occasion a consecutive sentence of two years for assault occasioning actual bodily harm. That assault was committed on the deceased, the defendant striking her in the face and causing her injury. Although dealt with at the same time as the rape, it was an unrelated incident.

50. Prior to 1990, the defendant had convictions for three offences of dishonesty, h one of threatening behaviour and one of common assault. Since the offences for which he was dealt with in 1990, he has been convicted of one offence of criminal damage in 1996, for which he was given a conditional discharge, and two offences of dishonesty in 1998 and 1999, for which he was fined.

51. There was no report of any significance before the sentencing judge, the j defendant having made clear to the probation service that he did not wish to participate in the preparation of a pre-sentence report.

52. Detailed submissions were made to the sentencing judge as to the approach to be adopted under s 2 of the 1997 Act, including questions of compatibility with the convention. The judge gave a detailed ruling, in which he came to the conclusion that there were no exceptional circumstances in the case and it was therefore unnecessary for him to go on to consider the question of danger. A life

sentence had to be imposed under s 2. Had the judge been imposing a determinate sentence, it would have been one of six years. The specified period of two and a half years made allowance for the time spent by the defendant in custody. In reaching his view on the notional determinate sentence, the judge took into account, as is apparent from earlier passages in his sentencing remarks, the plea of guilty, the fact that it had been very difficult for the defendant to accept that he had caused the death of the deceased (a subdural haemorrhage leading to death in this way being extremely rare), the fact that the defendant had given himself up to the police on the day of the death, and the apparently frail mental health of the deceased.

53. The application for leave to appeal against sentence is based not on any challenge to the appropriateness of the six year notional determinate sentence, but on the submission that if s 2 is read in such a way as to comply with the convention, this case should be regarded as one where exceptional circumstances apply and a life sentence is neither necessary nor appropriate.

Stephen S

54. The defendant Stephen S, who is 41 years of age, was convicted in the Central Criminal Court on 2 March 2000 on five counts of indecent assault on a female (counts 1, 3, 5, 7 and 8 on the indictment), five of attempted rape (counts 2, 4, 9, 10 and 11), five of rape (counts 6, and 12 to 15), one of buggery (count 16) and one of assault occasioning actual bodily harm (count 17). The verdicts on counts 1 to 7 and 12 to 17 were unanimous; those on counts 8 to 11 were by a majority. He was sentenced to a total term of 12 years imprisonment, the sentences on the individual counts being concurrent and ranging from 12 months imprisonment on count 17 to 12 years imprisonment on counts 6, 14, 15 and 16.

55. The court has before it a renewed application by Stephen S for leave to appeal against conviction following refusal by the single judge, an application by him for leave to appeal against sentence which has been referred to the full court by the single judge, and an application by the Attorney General under s 36 of the Criminal Justice Act 1988 for leave to refer the sentence to the court as an unduly lenient sentence.

56. The victims of the offences were the offender's daughters, C (born on 28 August 1984 to his then wife TS) and L (born 15 December 1988 to his then wife KS). Counts 1 to 7 and 17 related to L and counts 8 to 16 to C. The matters came to light following a physical assault against L on 26 January 1999 which was the subject of count 17. On that occasion, the offender became angry with L when he found that an alarm clock he had recently bought her had been broken. He pulled her off her bed, threw her against a wardrobe, punched her in the stomach and hit her head against the bed. A little later, during breakfast, he punched her in the eye, pushed her against the wall and struck her back. The violence was witnessed in part by her mother who then sought protection for herself and L and subsequently moved into a refuge. When arrested in relation to the physical assault, the offender denied any violence towards L. While L was at the refuge, however, she revealed a history of sexual abuse by the offender which resulted in his re-arrest. Shortly afterwards, C revealed that he had abused her too from an early age.

57. The offender married T in 1983. After the birth of C, he began a relationship with K. They married in March 1989 after L had been born and the offender and T had divorced. The offender was granted custody of C. Three further children

a were born to the offender and K in 1993, 1995 and 1997. The family lived first at Brentford, then in Carshalton and latterly in Hamworth.

58. The substance of the allegations made by the daughters was as follows. The offences against C began with indecent assaults when she was aged five or six, and moved to attempted rape and rape when she was aged between about 8 and 12. Sexual contact was very frequent and involved digital penetration, oral b sex against her and by her, and full sexual intercourse without contraception. On one occasion, he persuaded L to commit an indecent assault on C. C was very frightened of him and witnessed violence from him against her step-mother, as well as being frequently on the receiving end herself. He said that if she told anyone he would shoot her, all the family and then himself. He also said that the conduct was normal and an acceptable family practice. She knew that it was not c normal but was too frightened of him to say anything. He said he would continue doing it even after she had a boyfriend and was married. In the months before his arrest, he had begun inserting his finger in her anus, and on at least one occasion he inserted his penis about half way, saying that when she was older he could insert it all the way. Medical examination of C confirmed the existence of d two hymenal tears indicative of penetration of her vagina by an object, but not capable of showing what that object was or when penetration occurred. It was not established that full penile penetration had taken place. There were no injuries indicative of anal penetration, but it was possible for such penetration to have occurred without leaving signs of injury.

59. The offences against L started when she was five years old. The offender e came to her during the night naked and took her pyjamas off, saying he wanted a cuddle. He touched her private parts and put her hand on his penis. This first happened when her mother was in hospital giving birth to one of her brothers in August 1995. Thereafter there were numerous assaults when her mother was out of the house at work. The offender would lie on top of her, both of them naked, f trying to penetrate her vagina. He said that until her 'hole' was a bit bigger it would carry on like that and that she was better at sex than her mother. When she was nine years old the abuse progressed to rape as well as indecent assault. It continued until just before she and her mother left home in January 1999. She had also seen the offender commit offences with C when she had been looking into the room, and there had been one occasion when he had got her to touch C's g vagina. The offender made various threats as to what would happen to her if she told anyone about his conduct. He would generally be nice to her when he had sex with her, but would beat her and other members of the family at other times.

60. At trial, evidence for the prosecution was given by both daughters and their mothers. There was also medical evidence. The defendant gave evidence h in his own defence, denying the offences and saying that the girls and one or both of their mothers had conspired to make false charges against him.

61. The offender has a large number of previous convictions, mainly for driving offences but also including offences of dishonesty, the supply of drugs, criminal damage, threatening behaviour, possession of an offensive weapon and j violence. The offences of violence include common assault, assault on the police, assault occasioning actual bodily harm, causing grievous bodily harm and causing grievous bodily harm with intent. Most important is an offence of causing grievous bodily harm with intent, for which he was sentenced in November 1993 initially to 240 hours of community service. On an Attorney General's reference, a sentence of 18 months imprisonment was substituted. That offence involved an unprovoked attack with a pool cue in a public house, which left the victim

with a permanent scar to his forehead. The Court of Appeal indicated that a sentence of the order of three years would have been appropriate at first instance. a

62. The grounds of appeal against conviction have been settled by the offender himself. The original grounds have been supplemented by additional material supplied to this court after refusal of leave by the single judge. In summary, it is contended that the convictions are unsafe because offences are alleged to have been committed on dates or at times or at places when or where b they could not have been committed. There are inconsistencies between the verdicts on the various counts, or between the judge's directions on various counts. The convictions are also said to have been unsafe because the jury was told that he had been in prison before. Matters are raised as to the credibility of witnesses, as to the unsatisfactory nature of the medical evidence and as to other aspects of the evidence at trial. It is said that the summing-up was confused and c unclear. Complaints are made about the conduct of the offender's legal team, both in relation to witnesses called and questions asked and as regards other matters. In view of those complaints, the comments of the offender's counsel were obtained after a waiver of privilege. We have taken those comments into account in reaching our decision.

d

63. After careful consideration of all the matters raised by the offender, we have reached the clear conclusion that there is no arguable case as regards appeal against conviction. We adopt the reasons given by the single judge in refusing leave:

> 'The grounds relating to dates and allegedly inconsistent verdicts are not e made out; inevitably after such a lapse of time dates would be uncertain and the jury was entitled to convict as they did. The learned judge dealt properly with the evidence of bad character that had been introduced. The verdicts were not inconsistent with the medical evidence, which was placed before the jury in a form as favourable to you as could have been arranged. There is nothing in the point you make about the cross-examination or alleged f failure to cross-examine. As to the summing up, that was at times lacking in clarity, but the agreed summary placed before the jury at the end sufficiently remedied any deficiencies. The convictions are not unsafe.'

64. Nothing in the additional material supplied to the court by the offender since the refusal of leave by the single judge affects the validity of those reasons g or raises new points of substance. Accordingly, the renewed application for leave to appeal against conviction is refused.

65. We turn to consider issues that arise in relation to sentence. In passing sentence, the judge referred to the fact that there had been no plea of guilty and the girls had had to give evidence and re-live what had happened to them. There h had been a gross breach of trust. The offences occurred over a long period and the offender had set out to corrupt the girls. The offences and their effect on the girls had grown more serious as the girls grew older. The offender did not have a good character. It was in those circumstances that the judge was passing an overall sentence of 12 years.

j

66. After the judge had passed sentence, his attention was drawn by counsel to s 2 of the 1997 Act and to the existence of the s 18 offence in 1993 which, in conjunction with the recent offences, engaged the provisions of that section. The judge ruled that an automatic life sentence need not be passed because there were exceptional circumstances, namely that the offender had been found guilty on this occasion of offences falling into a totally different category from the offence

a in 1993. Had the sexual offences been a repetition of earlier sexual offences, then a life sentence would have followed. Because they were entirely different from the earlier offence, it was not necessary to pass a life sentence.

67. In his reference to this court, for which we have given leave, the Attorney General submits that the sentence passed was unduly lenient, in that the judge ought to have imposed a life sentence under s 2 of the 1997 Act. The judge erred b in principle in forming the opinion that the difference in type between the relevant serious offences amounted to exceptional circumstances within the meaning of s 2(2) of the 1997 Act (see *R v Kelly, A-G's Reference (No 53 of 1998)* [1999] 2 All ER 13 at 21, [2000] QB 198 at 209).

68. Mr Edie, for the offender, resists the submissions made on behalf of the Attorney General, contending that the judge was entitled to pass a determinate c sentence in the circumstances of this case. He contends further that the sentence of 12 years imprisonment was itself manifestly excessive.

THE LAW

69. The leading authority as to the interpretation of s 2 of the 1997 Act prior d to the coming into force of the 1998 Act is the decision of this court in *R v Kelly, A-G's Reference (No 53 of 1998)* [1999] 2 All ER 13, [2000] QB 198. In that case the then Chief Justice, Lord Bingham of Cornhill, gave a construction of 'exceptional' which has been followed in later cases. He said:

> 'We must construe "exceptional" as an ordinary, familiar English adjective, e and not as a term of art. It describes a circumstance which is such as to form an exception, which is out of the ordinary course, or unusual, or special, or uncommon. To be exceptional, a circumstance need not be unique, or unprecedented, or very rare; but it cannot be one that is regularly, or routinely, or normally encountered.' (See [1999] 2 All ER 13 at 20, [2000] QB 198 at 208.)

f

70. No criticism of 'exceptional' was made by any of the counsel appearing in the appeals, and we consider that the issues which arise on the appeals do not cast any reflection upon its appropriateness now that the European Convention for the Protection of Human Rights and Fundamental Freedoms (Rome, 4 November 1950; TS 71 (1953); Cmd 8969) (the convention) is part of our law. We therefore g gratefully adopt it.

71. Lord Bingham CJ then went on to explain that:

> 'To relieve the court of its duty to impose a life sentence under s 2(2), however, circumstances must not only be exceptional but such as, in the h opinion of the court, justify it in not imposing a life sentence, and in forming that opinion the court must have regard to the purpose of Parliament in enacting the section as derived from the Act itself and the White Paper …' (See [1999] 2 All ER 13 at 20, [2000] QB 198 at 208.)

72. Lord Bingham CJ did not apply his reasoning, that it is necessary to have j regard to the purposes of Parliament when considering whether there are exceptional circumstances. He applied it to the subsequent question of whether, assuming there are exceptional circumstances, they justify not imposing a life sentence. This has in some of the cases where s 2 has been applied accentuated the difficulties created by the section. We draw attention to this, since when deciding whether a situation is exceptional, we regard it as being of the greatest importance to have in mind the policy already identified which reflects the

intention of Parliament. That is the rationale spelt out by Lord Bingham CJ in the case of *R v Buckland* [2000] 1 All ER 907, [2000] 1 WLR 1262. a

73. In *R v Kelly*, Lord Bingham CJ, having identified the approach to s 2, went on to consider features contended in that case to establish exceptional circumstances. The first was the youth of the appellant when committing the first 'serious offence'. That was not regarded as being unusual in that case, because the offender was then already very experienced and, as Lord Bingham CJ said, 'the unhappy fact is that b many very serious crimes are committed by very youthful offenders' ([1999] 2 All ER 13 at 20, [2000] QB 198 at 209). It was also stated that the time which intervened between the offences could also not be regarded as exceptional. Attention was drawn to the fact that Parliament had not required the two qualifying offences to be committed within a specified period. Again, it was suggested that the fact that the 'serious offences' were of different kinds was not c exceptional because—

> 'the section lumps all these offences together and there is nothing to suggest that the imposition of a life sentence should depend on whether the offender has repeated the same "serious offence" or committed another. It is scarcely unusual for a defendant convicted of robbery involving the use of d firearms on one occasion to be convicted of causing grievous bodily harm with intent on another.' (See [1999] 2 All ER 13 at 21, [2000] QB 198 at 209.)

74. Finally, Lord Bingham CJ stated that the court could not 'regard the appellant as a man who, on the evidence available when he was sentenced, presented no continuing threat or danger to the public'. This last statement of e Lord Bingham CJ is important, because, it seems to us for reasons we will explain later, to go to the heart of the issue with which the court in that case was faced.

75. Later in his judgment, Lord Bingham CJ made two further points to which we should draw attention. First of all, he made it clear that that was a case which apart from s 2 of the 1997 Act would not have resulted in a life sentence. The f other point was in relation to the argument which was advanced relying on arts 3 and 5 of the convention. Lord Bingham CJ declined to address that argument because at that time the convention could only be used as an aid to construction when an ambiguity existed and the court thought there was no ambiguity as to the interpretation of s 2 of the 1997 Act. However, Lord Bingham CJ added ([1999] 2 All ER 13 at 22, [2000] QB 198 at 210): '… in any event, as already pointed out, g we do not find it possible to regard the appellant as a man who is shown not to represent a continuing danger to the public.'

76. The approach adopted as to the application of s 2 in *R v Kelly* has naturally been followed in the subsequent cases. It has, however, been subject to academic criticism as an unduly narrow approach to 'exceptional circumstances'. In view h of that criticism, it is convenient to refer next to the decision of *R v Buckland*, from which we have already made a citation. The facts of *R v Buckland* were very similar to the facts in the appeal of Offen which is before us. Lord Bingham CJ ([2000] 1 All ER 907 at 910, [2000] 1 WLR 1262 at 1265) described it as 'an almost farcical caricature of a professional bank hold-up. Although obviously distressing to j the staff of the bank …' In deciding whether or not the court was required to impose a life sentence, the court, as Lord Bingham CJ made clear, had looked at various reports and then come to a judgment that: (i) these were exceptional circumstances; and (ii) these circumstances justified not imposing a life sentence.

77. Lord Bingham CJ stated that 'on all the evidence, it is safe to conclude that the appellant does not present a serious and continuing danger to the public such

a as could justify the imposition of a life sentence' ([2000] 1 All ER 907 at 913, [2000] 1 WLR 1262 at 1269).

78. *R v Buckland* was regarded by Mr Perry, who appeared on behalf of the Crown and for whose help we are most grateful, as representing a more flexible approach than had been adopted in the earlier authorities, and he accepted that it reflected the approach that should be adopted in the future if his submissions b were accepted by this court. He also conceded that if the decision in *R v Buckland* had been available when Offen came before the Court of Appeal on the original appeal against sentence, the Court of Appeal would probably have taken a different view from that which they did.

79. Before leaving *R v Buckland*, and turning to the decision in *R v Offen* [2000] c Crim LR 306, we should point out that we regard it as a striking feature of the reasoning in *R v Buckland*, as in the case of *R v Kelly*, that the court regarded the rationale of the section as being relevant when the court had already come to its conclusion that there are exceptional circumstances and not as to whether the exceptional circumstances exist. We would suggest that quite apart from the impact of the 1998 Act, the rationale of the section should be highly relevant in d deciding whether or not exceptional circumstances exist. The question of whether circumstances are appropriately regarded as exceptional must surely be influenced by the context in which the question is being asked. The policy and intention of Parliament was to protect the public against a person who had committed two serious offences. It therefore can be assumed the section was not intended to e apply to someone in relation to whom it was established there would be no need for protection in the future. In other words, if the facts showed the statutory assumption was misplaced, then this, in the statutory context was not the normal situation and in consequence, for the purposes of the section, the position was exceptional. The time that elapsed between the two serious offences could, but would not necessarily reflect, on whether, after the second serious offence was f committed, there was any danger against which the public would need protection. The same is true of two differing offences, and the age of the offender. These are all circumstances which could give rise to the conclusion that what could be normal and not exceptional in a different context was exceptional in this context. If this approach is not adopted, then in the case of the serious offences g listed in the section, the gravity of which can vary very greatly, the approach to exceptional circumstances could be unduly restrictive. This is illustrated by the extensive range of situations which can constitute the offence of manslaughter.

80. Turning to the decision of this court on the initial appeal by Offen, we find this very point being made by the court as a justification for saying that there are h no exceptional circumstances. Jowitt J, when giving the judgment of the court, indicated that robberies vary greatly in their seriousness. He then went on to say that it is clear that a robbery cannot be regarded as exceptional merely because it is at the lower end of the scale of gravity. He then turned to Offen himself and considered his characteristics without considering whether Offen would give rise j to any danger in the future. We suggest that, if the policy behind the section had been taken into account, the approach would have been different.

81. In a case which again has a resemblance to *R v Offen*, *R v Williams* [2000] Crim LR 597, the court were prepared in the light of *R v Buckland* to regard the circumstances of the offence as being exceptional, however, having considered the pre-sentence report and the 47 previous convictions of the appellant, the court decided that the appellant did represent a serious danger to the safety of the

public and in those circumstances a life sentence under s 2 of the 1997 Act was justified. *a*

82. The other case to which it is necessary to refer before turning to the 1998 Act, is *R v Turner* [2000] Cr App R (S) 472. That was a case where the appellant was convicted of an offence under s 18 of the Offences Against the Person Act 1861 as a consequence of his being involved in a brawl during the course of which he lost his temper and continued to strike the victim after he was on the ground. This *b* was a serious offence for the purposes of s 2 of the 1997 Act. Unfortunately, 22 years before, the offender had also been convicted of manslaughter and sentenced to three years imprisonment. During the intervening period, he had only been convicted of one motoring offence. This court came to the conclusion that s 2 has the consequence that a judge can be compelled to pass a sentence of life imprisonment notwithstanding the fact that it offends his sense of justice. The *c* court therefore loyally gave effect to the earlier authorities and decided that they had no alternative but to uphold the sentence of life imprisonment under s 2. This decision underlines why, notwithstanding the more flexible approach of this court in *R v Buckland* endorsed by Mr Perry, each of the defendants strongly relies upon the 1998 Act. *d*

THE HUMAN RIGHTS ACT 1998

83. The defendants contend that as previously applied, s 2 of the 1997 Act is incompatible with arts 3, 5, 7 and 8 of the convention.

ARTICLE 7 *e*

84. As the argument as to art 7 of the convention is discrete, it is convenient to start with that article. It is art 7(1) which is relevant. It provides:

> 'No one shall be held guilty of any criminal offence on account of any act or omission which did not constitute a criminal offence under national or international law at the time when it was committed. Nor shall a heavier *f* penalty be imposed than the one that was applicable at the time the criminal offence was committed.'

85. The arguments advanced by Mr Fitzgerald QC on behalf of Offen and Okwuegbunam and advanced by Mr Bennathan on behalf of McGilliard differed. The difference, however, is as to whether it is possible to remedy the breach of *g* art 7 which they allege s 2 of the 1997 Act involves by a process of interpretation relying on s 3 of the 1998 Act, or whether it is necessary for the court to make a declaration of incompatibility under s 4 of the 1998 Act. Fortunately, it is not necessary to resolve this issue, because we do not consider that s 2 involves a contravention of art 7. *h*

86. Mr Fitzgerald advances the argument, which is adopted by all defendants, that there is a contravention. He submits that the argument has two aspects. Both involve changing the consequences of a conviction of the first serious offence after the date of the offence and after the sentence for which it was imposed. It is submitted that after a punishment for the first serious offence had *j* been imposed, the subsequent coming into force of s 2 of the 1997 Act increased the penalty for the initial offence since the offender then became liable, if he committed a further serious offence, to be automatically sentenced to life imprisonment. It is also submitted that s 2 itself increased the penalty for the first serious offence since on conviction of the second serious offence a life sentence would be imposed, in reality, in respect of both offences.

a 87. Mr Fitzgerald's argument was well illustrated by the practice in association football of sending off a player who is shown two yellow cards. If the rule which brings this about was to be imposed after one yellow card had been shown this would give greater significance to the first yellow card than was the case when it was shown. It could adversely effect a player since if a player knew he would be sent off if he had two yellow cards, he would make greater efforts to avoid being b shown even the first yellow card.

88. This attractive argument depends upon treating the life sentence as being imposed at least in part for both offences. This is not, however, the manner in which, in our judgment, s 2 of the 1997 Act works. Section 2 imposes the penalty of the automatic life sentence for the second offence above. The imposition of c the automatic life sentence is, however, subject to certain conditions. Those are that the offender was 18 or over and that he had been previously convicted of another serious offence. The language of s 2(1) makes this clear. The sentence is not being imposed in relation to the earlier offence. The position is similar to that considered by this court in *R v Taylor* [1996] 2 Cr App R 64 and by the European Commission of Human Rights (the commission) in *Taylor v UK* [1998] EHRLR 90 d which arose out of the changes in making confiscation orders introduced by the Drug Trafficking Offences Act 1986.

89. Although the 1986 Act allowed the court to make a confiscation order in respect of 'benefits' which accrued before the 1986 Act came into force, the offence which triggered the confiscation order was committed after the 1986 Act e came into force. That decision is not inconsistent with *Welch v UK* (1995) 20 EHRR 247 at 262 (para 28). The distinction between *Taylor* and *Welch v UK* is that in *Welch v UK* the confiscation order had been made in relation to a criminal offence committed before the relevant legislation, the 1986 Act, came into force. In *Taylor* the triggering offence was committed after that Act came into force. f Accordingly in *Taylor* it was in order, as a matter of domestic law, to make a confiscation order to recover benefits from drug trafficking which accrued to Taylor before the 1986 Act came into force. It was the date of the offence which was critical. It was when and because he committed the trigger offence that he became liable to have his earlier benefits from drug trafficking confiscated. Although *Taylor* was decided by this court under domestic law, art 7 of the g convention was examined and the reasoning was endorsed by the commission, which found Taylor's application manifestly ill-founded. Mr Bennathan, on behalf of Mr McGilliard, and Mr Edie, in his submissions on behalf of S, contend that *Taylor* is distinguishable from the position here. Clearly, the statutory provisions differ but the reasoning is the same. Mr Edie also refers to the recent decision of h the Inner House in Scotland in *McIntosh v HM Advocate* 2000 SCCR 1017. However, the issue in that case turned on art 6(2) and not art 7 and we do not find it assists here.

90. The serious offences are, as we have already pointed out, all sentences in relation to which the court can pass a life sentence quite apart from s 2. Before j imposing a *discretionary* life sentence, the court would pay the greatest regard to the previous record of the offender. The fact that the previous record influenced the court into imposing a life sentence would not mean that the offender was being sentenced or having his sentence increased for the earlier offences. Here, the first offence and the penalty imposed for it remain the same after the coming into force of s 2 of the 1997 Act; it is the penalty for the trigger offence which s 2 changes.

ARTICLES 3 AND 5

91. The relevant provisions of art 3 and art 5 of the convention are as follows: a

'*Article 3: Prohibition of torture*

No one shall be subjected to torture or to inhuman or degrading treatment or punishment ...

Article 5: Right to Liberty and Security b

1. Everyone has the right to liberty and security of person. No one shall be deprived of his liberty save in the following cases and in accordance with a procedure prescribed by law—(a) the lawful detention of a person after conviction by a competent court ...

4. Everyone who is deprived of his liberty by arrest or detention shall be entitled to take proceedings by which the lawfulness of his detention shall be c decided speedily by a court and his release ordered if the detention is not lawful.'

92. In approaching these articles, it is important to recognise that the 1998 Act is a constitutional instrument introducing into domestic law the relevant articles of the convention. The consequence of s 3 of the 1998 Act is that legislation which d affects human rights is required to be construed in a manner which conforms with the convention wherever this is possible. In support of his contention that there is no need for a change in the construction of s 2 of the 1997 Act, Mr Perry relies upon the more flexible approach adopted to s 2 in the more recent authorities, and in *R v Buckland* in particular. In addition, he refers to the e consequences of the imposition of an automatic life sentence. He reminds the court of the present practice as to the setting of a tariff and the independent review by the parole board which follows the expiry of the tariff. If the parole board are of the view that a prisoner should be released, the Home Secretary must release him. Although this may not have been the position in the past, the present arrangements for the review of those subject to an automatic or f discretionary life sentence, he submits, are now convention compliant. The aim of s 2 of the 1997 Act is not to increase the time offenders spend in prison as a punishment for the offence they have committed, but to provide for an assessment to be made to see whether the offender poses a real risk to the public, in which event his release is deferred. He argues that this regime is not one which g contravenes either art 3 or art 5. He submits that there is no question of the automatic life sentence amounting to torture or inhuman or degrading treatment or punishment which would contravene art 3.

93. As to art 5, Mr Perry accepts that the overall purpose of the article is to ensure that no one is deprived of his liberty in an 'arbitrary fashion' (see *Quinn v France* (1995) 21 EHRR 529 at 548–549 (para 42)). He relies in particular on *Weeks v* h *UK* (1987) 10 EHRR 293. The significance of that decision was that the court considered the appellant's renewed detention after being released on licence was lawful and that the rehabilitation of offenders was a legitimate aim. (This country fell foul of art 5(4) because of the absence at that time of any procedure by which the lawfulness of the offender's detention could be determined by a properly j constituted independent board. That defect has since been remedied.)

94. Not surprisingly, Mr Fitzgerald takes a very different view of the relationship between s 2 of the 1997 Act and arts 3 and 5. He stresses that life imprisonment is the most serious punishment that the courts in this jurisdiction can impose. It means that although a prisoner may be released, he still remains liable to be recalled. That liability is a permanent one. In addition, he contrasts

a the position of a life sentence prisoner with that of a prisoner sentenced to a determinate sentence. When a determinate sentence has been served, release is automatic. In the case of a life sentence prisoner, he will not be released after the end of the tariff period unless the parole board can be satisfied that he does not constitute a risk to the public for the future. This is the very object s 2 was designed to achieve in relation to those who would not be sentenced to life b imprisonment before that section came into force. It is clear that as a result of s 2, offenders are now being sentenced to life imprisonment when there is no objective justification for that sentence. Such a result can be categorised as being arbitrary and not proportionate.

95. In his speech in *R v Governor of Brockhill Prison, ex p Evans (No 2)* [2000] 4 All ER 15 at 29–30, [2000] 3 WLR 843 at 858, Lord Hope of Craighead considered the c relationship between art 5 of the convention and our domestic law. In the course of doing so, he recognised that the question would arise as to whether, 'assuming that the detention is lawful under domestic law', it is nevertheless open to criticism on the ground that it is arbitrary because, for example, it was resorted to in bad faith or was not proportionate'. Here no question of bad faith arises. In d addition, we recognise that there have been, and will be, cases where s 2 of the 1997 Act has, and will, operate in a proportionate manner. However, as the section has hitherto been interpreted, it can clearly operate in a disproportionate manner. It is easy to find examples of situations where two offences could be committed which were categorised as serious by the section but where it would be wholly disproportionate to impose a life sentence to protect the public. e Whenever a person is convicted of an offence, there is always some risk that he or she may offend again. Equally, there are a significant number of cases in which two serious offences will have been committed where the risk is not of a degree which can justify a life sentence. We refer again to the very wide span of manslaughter, which is a serious offence within the 1997 Act. An unjustified push f can result in someone falling, hitting his head and suffering fatal injuries. The offence is manslaughter. The offender may have committed another serious offence when a young man. A life sentence in such circumstances may well be arbitrary and disproportionate and contravene art 5. It could also be a punishment which contravenes art 3.

96. The problem arises because of the restrictive approach which has so far been g adopted to the interpretation of exceptional circumstances in s 2. If exceptional circumstances are construed in a manner which accords with the policy of Parliament in passing s 2, the problem disappears.

97. Section 2 of the 1997 Act establishes a norm. The norm is that those who commit two serious offences are a danger or risk to the public. If in fact, taking h into account all the circumstances relating to a particular offender, he does not create an unacceptable risk to the public, he is an exception to this norm. If the offences are of a different kind, or if there is a long period which elapses between the offences during which the offender has not committed other offences, that may be a very relevant indicator as to the degree of risk to the public that he j constitutes. Construing s 2 in accordance with the duty imposed upon us by s 3 of the 1998 Act, and taking into account the rationale of the section as identified by Lord Bingham CJ gives content to exceptional circumstances. In our judgment, s 2 will not contravene convention rights if courts apply the section so that it does not result in offenders being sentenced to life imprisonment when they do not constitute a significant risk to the public. Whether there is significant risk will depend on the evidence which is before the court. If the offender is a significant

risk, the court can impose a life sentence under s 2 without contravening the convention. Either there will be no exceptional circumstances, or despite the exceptional circumstances the facts will justify imposing a life sentence.

98. Under s 2 it will be part of the responsibility of judges to assess the risk to the public that offenders constitute. In many cases the degree of risk that an offender constitutes will be established by his record, with or without the assistance of assessments made in reports which are available to the court. If a court needs further assistance, they can call for it. The courts have traditionally had to make a similar assessment when deciding whether a discretionary life sentence should be imposed. There should be no undue difficulty in making a similar assessment when considering whether the court is required to impose an automatic life sentence, although the task will not be straightforward, because of the lack of information as to the first serious offence which will sometimes exist because of the passage of time.

99. This does not mean that we are approaching the passing of an automatic life sentence as though it is no different from the imposition of a discretionary life sentence. Notwithstanding the interpretation resulting from the application of s 3(1) of the 1998 Act suggested, s 2 of the 1997 Act will still give effect to the intention of Parliament. It will do so, however, in a more just, less arbitrary and more proportionate manner. Section 2 will still mean that a judge is obliged to pass a life sentence in accordance with its terms unless, in all the circumstances, the offender poses no significant risk to the public. There is no such obligation in cases where s 2 does not apply. In addition, if the judge decides not to impose a life sentence under s 2, he will have to give reasons as required by s 2(3). Furthermore, the issue of dangerousness will have to be addressed in every case and a decision made as to whether or not to impose a life sentence.

100. The objective of the legislature, identified by Lord Bingham CJ, will be achieved, because it will be mandatory to impose a life sentence in situations where the offender constitutes a significant risk to the public. Section 2 of the 1997 Act therefore provides a good example of how the 1998 Act can have a beneficial effect on the administration of justice, without defeating the policy which Parliament was seeking to implement.

101. In view of our conclusions as to the impact of arts 3 and 5 of the convention, it is not necessary to consider art 8.

102. We now turn to consider the consequences of our conclusions as to the law on the individual cases which are before us.

CONCLUSIONS

Offen

103. In order to decide whether this is a case where exceptional circumstances apply for the purpose of s 2 of the 1997 Act, we have considered whether the material supports the existence of a finding of significant risk to the public. Apart from the two relevant convictions, the defendant has two convictions of theft recorded against him in 1990. The pre-sentence report and the medical reports do not support such a finding. We conclude that the defendant is not to be regarded as presenting a significant risk to the public. This is a case where, in our judgement, exceptional circumstances do exist and a life sentence is inappropriate. We therefore allow this appeal, set aside the life sentence and substitute for it a determinate sentence of three years imprisonment.

McKeown

104. In our judgment and, taking into account the findings of the judge, the circumstances of this offence, although a serious offence, are not such as to warrant a substantial prison sentence. The determinate sentence fixed by the judge was appropriate. Further there is here no material from which it could be concluded that the defendant presents a significant risk to the public. In this case, therefore, we conclude that exceptional circumstances exist and that the case does not fall within the rationale of s 2. We allow the appeal, set aside the life sentence and substitute a sentence of three years imprisonment.

McGilliard

105. In our judgment, the matters set out properly lead us to conclude: (i) that on 4 December 1998 the defendant committed a grave offence sufficient to warrant a substantial prison sentence; and (ii) that the defendant presents a serious and continuing danger to the public.

106. The defendant's antecedent record for unlawful violence and the circumstances of the present offence, the pre-sentence reports and the medical reports clearly indicate that there are here no exceptional circumstances which would permit a court not to pass a life sentence under s 2 of the 1997 Act. We confirm the notional determinate sentence of seven years as entirely appropriate for the offence which the defendant admitted and dismiss the appeal.

Okwuegbunam

107. No finding as to dangerousness was made by the sentencing judge. We have considered the question for ourselves, in order to decide whether exceptional circumstances exist in this case. Our assessment has been made on the basis of the antecedents and the circumstances of the offences themselves, to the extent that they are known. There is no pre-sentence or medical report to assist us.

108. As regards the trigger offence of manslaughter, we take account of the fact that death resulted unexpectedly from two blows inflicted without an intention to cause serious harm. On the other hand, for the reasons given by the judge in his sentencing remarks, this was an offence of some gravity. In our view, the notional determinate sentence of six years was generous to the defendant and the figure could have been higher. The defendant had received a substantial custodial sentence in 1990 for an offence of violence on the same victim, though account must of course be taken of the lapse of time and the absence of any further offences of violence during the intervening period. As to the offence of rape for which he received a sentence of five years imprisonment in 1990, we bear in mind what the defendant says about the circumstances of the offence, as communicated to us in oral and written submissions on his behalf. We give him the benefit of the doubt on those matters, since the material now available does not disclose whether his account was accepted at the time or not. The fact remains that it was a very serious offence committed against a young girl.

109. We have not found this an easy case to decide. It is close to the borderline. Taking everything into account, however, we have come to the conclusion that the defendant constitutes a significant risk to the public. The case therefore falls within the rationale of s 2, exceptional circumstances do not exist, and a life sentence was rightly imposed. Accordingly, we dismiss the appeal itself.

Stephen S

110. The judge was, in our view, wrong to treat the difference in type between the earlier s 18 offence and the new sexual offences as amounting to exceptional circumstances. That difference is a relevant consideration but is not sufficient to justify such a conclusion. We have considered whether exceptional circumstances exist in this case in the light of the principles laid down in this judgment. There was no finding by the judge on the question of dangerousness. The matter was not covered by any reports before the court. In our judgment, however, the long history of offending, including numerous offences of violence, together with the detailed circumstances of the sexual offences and violence towards the offender's own daughters (in relation to whom he showed no remorse in his stance at trial), warrants the conclusion that he does pose a significant risk to the public. This case falls within the rationale of s 2 of the 1997 Act. We hold that there are no exceptional circumstances. The Attorney General's reference succeeds and a life sentence under s 2 will be substituted for the determinate sentence of 12 years. It follows that the renewed application to appeal against sentence fails, though the points of substance raised in it are considered below in the context of tariff.

111. We must also specify a period for the purposes of s 28 of the 1997 Act. We take as our starting point a notional determinate sentence of 12 years, corresponding to the sentence passed by the judge below. Mr Edie submitted that 12 years was manifestly excessive and drew our attention to a number of authorities in support of that submission. We are satisfied, however, that 12 years was an entirely appropriate sentence for these terrible offences against the offender's own daughters. In specifying the period under s 28, we make an appropriate deduction from that notional determinate sentence and a further reduction to take account of the fact that the offender spent 11 months and 11 days on remand in custody before sentence was passed. Taking everything into account, we specify a period of five and a half years to commence from the date the judge passed sentence.

Offen's and McKeown's appeals allowed. McGilliard's and Okwuegbunam's applications for leave to appeal granted, but appeals dismissed. S's applications for leave to appeal against conviction and sentence refused. Attorney General's application for leave to refer S's sentence granted, and reference allowed. Leave to appeal refused.

Kate O'Hanlon Barrister.

30 January 2001. The Appeal Committee of the House of Lords refused leave to appeal.

Hyams v Plender

COURT OF APPEAL, CIVIL DIVISION

PETER GIBSON AND BROOKE LJJ

31 AUGUST, 1 SEPTEMBER 2000

Practice – Appeal – New provisions relating to appeals in civil proceedings – Dismissal on paper of applications for permission to appeal – Provision of transcripts at public expense to unrepresented appellants – Guidance – CPR Pt 52, Practice Direction.

(1) Where a High Court judge has refused, on a consideration of the papers, an application for permission to appeal on the grounds of non-compliance with the Practice Direction to CPR Pt 52, but the applicant disputes such non-compliance, there is no proper basis for the High Court's practice of refusing to allow a hearing for reconsideration of that decision. Nor is there any basis in law for any practice of construing as an undertaking—whose breach will lead to dismissal of the appeal—a statement by a litigant in person, in his appellant's notice, that a skeleton argument will be lodged within 14 days. Moreover, although a judge may properly be brief in explaining his conclusion on an application for permission to appeal, it is not sufficient for him merely to say that there has been non-compliance with the Pt 52 Practice Direction. Rather, that non-compliance should be identified (see p 181 *h j*, p 182 *g h j* to p 183 *a c*, post).

(2) All would-be appellants need to realise that the filing of a notice of appeal does not automatically stay the effect of the judgment appealed against, and that an appeal court is unlikely to be able to grant them any relief at all, whether by way of a stay of the order appealed against or otherwise, unless it is able to consider the reasons given by the judge in the court below for making the order under challenge. Under para 5.17[a] of the Practice Direction to CPR Pt 52, the court may certify that the cost of obtaining an official transcript should be borne at public expense where the lower court or appeal court is satisfied that an unrepresented appellant is in such poor financial circumstances that the cost of a transcript would be an excessive burden. In respect of a request for an official transcript of evidence or proceedings, para 5.18[b] requires that the court must also be satisfied that there are reasonable grounds of appeal. Paragraph 5.18 further provides that, wherever possible, a request for a transcript at public expense should be made to the lower court. If that direction is observed, many of the delays which have disfigured the conduct of county court appeals in the past will probably be avoided. If the lower court makes an order for the provision of a transcript at public expense, it is essential that it is put into effect by the court's staff forthwith, so that there will then be no avoidable delay in the conduct of the appeal. It is also essential that arrangements are made by which the appeal court may give necessary directions under paras 5.17 and 5.18 (see p 183 *b g*, p 184 *a* to *d* and *f* to *h*, post).

Case referred to in judgments

Tanfern Ltd v Cameron-MacDonald [2000] 2 All ER 801, [2000] 1 WLR 1311, CA.

a Paragraph 5.17 is set out at p 184 *a*, post

b Paragraph 5.18 is set out at p 184 *b*, post

Case also cited or referred to in skeleton argument
Biguzzi v Rank Leisure plc [1999] 4 All ER 934, [1999] 1 WLR 1926, CA.

a

Application for permission to appeal
The defendant, Donald Plender, applied for permission to appeal from the order of Evans-Lombe J on 12 June 2000 dismissing his application for permission to appeal to the High Court from the order of Judge Collins at Wandsworth County Court on 27 April 2000 requiring Mr Plender to give the claimant, John Kennerley Hyams, possession of 8 Albert Studios, Albert Bridge Road, London SW11 by 27 July 2000 and to pay Mr Hyams £12,000 in respect of arrears and mesne profits. Mr Plender further applied for a stay of that order. The facts are set out in the judgment of Peter Gibson LJ.

b

c

Francis Moraes (instructed by *Bar Pro Bono Unit*) for Mr Plender.

PETER GIBSON LJ.

1. The defendant Donald Plender applies for permission to appeal against the order made by Evans-Lombe J on 12 June 2000 dismissing Mr Plender's application for permission to appeal to the High Court from the order of Judge Collins in the Wandsworth County Court on 27 April 2000. By Judge Collins' order possession of 8 Albert Studios, Albert Bridge Road, London SW11 was granted to the claimant, John Hyams, and Mr Plender was ordered to pay Mr Hyams a net sum of £12,000 in respect of arrears and mesne profits at a daily rate of £10·86 until possession is given. The possession order required Mr Plender to give possession by 27 July 2000. Mr Plender seeks a stay of that order which has not yet been enforced.

d

e

2. Mr Plender decided to appeal against Judge Collins' order. He thought that he had to appeal to this court and that he had 28 days within which to lodge his appellant's notice. But the appellant's notice, which included an application for permission, was not lodged until after 2 May and so the provisions of the RSC, which until that date permitted an appellant 28 days for appealing to this court, ceased to apply (*Tanfern Ltd v Cameron-MacDonald* [2000] 2 All ER 801, [2000] 1 WLR 1311). Instead CPR Pt 52 governs the appeal, including any application for permission to appeal, which lies to the High Court. The stricter time limits of CPR 52.4(2)(b) apply: no direction having been given by Judge Collins as to the period for filing the appellant's notice, Mr Plender had only 14 days within which to file that notice in the High Court.

f

g

3. Mr Plender had had counsel acting for him before Judge Collins, but thereafter until the hearing before this court he acted in person, obtaining the assistance of the Citizens' Advice Bureau (the CAB) in the law courts and completing the appellant's notice on 25 May. That was considered on paper by Evans-Lombe J who on 12 June 2000 refused the application for permission to appeal, the ground stated for that refusal being 'For non-compliance with Practice Direction (Part 52)'. No further details of that non-compliance are given.

h

4. Even before Evans-Lombe J had given his decision, on 7 June 2000 the CAB wrote on behalf of Mr Plender to Neuberger J indicating that they had not been able to prepare Mr Plender's skeleton argument because they had not obtained a copy of the transcript of judgment. They asked for an extension of time for lodging that skeleton argument. They also on the same day wrote to Judge Collins, asking for an order that a transcript of the judgment of 27 April 2000 be provided to Mr Plender at public expense. On 12 June Judge Collins made that order. The judgment of Judge Collins was subsequently supplied to Mr Plender and lodged

j

a with the Civil Appeals Office on 13 July. On 9 August the CAB was informed by an officer in the office of the clerk of the lists that the High Court would not reconsider an application for leave to appeal at an oral hearing if the application has been dismissed, following consideration by the judge of the papers, on the ground of non-compliance with the Pt 52 Practice Direction. On 14 June Neuberger J extended time for filing a skeleton argument until 27 June. On 26 June Mr Plender b filed a skeleton argument.

5. Mr Plender was unhappy with the decision of Evans-Lombe J. But instead of requesting that the decision be reconsidered at a rehearing pursuant to r 52.3(4), he filed an appellant's notice on 26 June, seeking to appeal to this court from that decision.

6. Although Mr Moraes for Mr Plender sought to argue that in the c circumstances this court has jurisdiction to entertain the proposed appeal from the refusal by Evans-Lombe J of permission to appeal from Judge Collins' order, in my judgment it is plain that this court lacks that jurisdiction. By s 54(4) of the Access to Justice Act 1999: 'No appeal may be made against a decision of a court under the section to give or refuse permission …'

d 7. Evans-Lombe J's decision was under s 54 of the Act in that Pt 52 was made pursuant to s 54. If Mr Plender's proposed appeal from Judge Collins' order is to proceed, Mr Plender must apply out of time for a rehearing of his application in the High Court.

8. However, this application has been listed before this court to provide guidance in such cases, and, in the hope that it may provide assistance, I shall e comment on the facts of the application.

9. I have already drawn attention to the absence of particulars of what requirement of the Pt 52 Practice Direction had in Evans-Lombe J's view not been complied with. Mr Plender has assumed that the judge was referring to the fact that he had provided neither a skeleton argument nor a transcript of the judgment.

f 10. In his appellant's notice Mr Plender refers to the extension of time granted by Neuberger J and submits that as a litigant in person he is not obliged to file a skeleton argument. That is correct: para 5.9(3) of the Pt 52 Practice Direction states: 'An appellant who is not represented need not lodge a skeleton argument but is encouraged to do so since this will be helpful to the court.'

11. It is therefore doubtful if this is what Evans-Lombe J had in mind.

g 12. It may be that the point taken by Evans-Lombe J referred to the fact that in the appellant's notice, which was put before the judge, next to the tick box against 'Your skeleton argument (if separate)' Mr Plender had written 'to be prepared within 14 days', and there was no skeleton argument provided for the judge. As appears from a letter written on 19 June by the CAB to the office of h the clerk of the lists, Mr Plender was advised by that office of what was said to be the practice in the High Court, if an appellant indicates in the appellant's notice that a skeleton argument will be lodged within 14 days, to construe that as an undertaking, non-compliance with which would lead to the dismissal of the appeal. If that is the practice, it appears to have no basis in law. It is plain that j the litigant in person has given no undertaking, in the sense known to lawyers. The absence of a skeleton provided no justification for the refusal of permission in the circumstances of this case.

13. Paragraph 5.6(7)(b) of the Pt 52 Practice Direction requires the provision of 'a suitable record of the reasons for judgment of the lower court', and when the judgment has been officially recorded an approved transcript of that record should be provided (para 5.12). When an appellant has not been able to obtain an official

transcript or other suitable record of the decision within the time for filing the appellant's notice, the appellant must complete the appellant's notice to the best of his ability on the basis of the documents available (para 5.13). Next to the tick box in the appellant's notice against 'a suitable record of the reasons for the judgment of the lower court', Mr Plender wrote: 'This I am applying to be provided at public expense.' Thereby he complied with para 5.7 which directed him to give the reasons why a required document was not currently available. Again it is doubtful if the absence of a judgment provided Evans-Lombe J with a reason for refusing permission.

14. Another requirement of the Practice Direction is that an application for permission to appeal should be made orally at the hearing at which the decision to be appealed against is made (para 4.6). But para 4.7 provides that where no such application is made, an application may be to the appeal court, and in this case such an application was made to the High Court, which constitutes the appeal court for that purpose.

15. A point taken by Mr Hyams' solicitors is that Mr Plender did not lodge his application for leave within the time limits laid down. But the time limits are laid down not in the Practice Direction but in CPR 52.4. However, para 5.2 of the Practice Direction provides that where an appellant requires an extension of time for filing his appellant's notice, the notice should state the reason for the delay and the steps taken prior to the application being made. Mr Plender merely states that: 'It would be just and equitable for my appeal, which has merit, to be heard by the Court of Appeal.' He also refers to evidence on which he wished to rely as including the fact that he was not informed of the change in the rules on 2 May 2000 and the fact that with his solicitor he discussed lodging an application but that he ascertained that his solicitor could not do this for him. Whilst the requirement of para 5.2 may be what Evans-Lombe J had in mind, I for my part would not regard this as a proper ground for refusing permission in the light of the knowledge which we now have of Mr Plender's active attempts to launch an appeal. In this context it is appropriate to recognise that some uncertainty surrounded the introduction of Pt 52, which, it is to be hoped, has been dispelled by the judgment in the *Tanfern* case. It is also right to take note of the fact that Mr Plender, although a litigant in person, properly sought help for his proposed appeal and that prior to Evans-Lombe J's decision steps had been taken to remedy gaps in the documentation to be provided. It may well be that the judge was not aware of the correspondence with Neuberger J and Judge Collins.

16. I must also comment on the practice, referred to in para 4 above, that the High Court will not allow a hearing for the reconsideration of a decision to refuse permission to appeal on the ground of non-compliance with the Pt 52 Practice Direction. I can see no proper basis for that practice in circumstances where the non-compliance is challenged, as it is in the present case. There may well be other circumstances where a hearing ought to be permitted, for example once there has been compliance with the Practice Direction after the refusal of permission on paper.

17. There is one other point to which I would draw attention. This arises from a complaint by Mr Plender that the decision of Evans-Lombe J breached art 6 of the European Convention for the Protection of Human Rights and Fundamental Freedoms (Rome, 4 November 1950; TS 71 (1953); Cmd 8969). The Human Rights Act 1998 comes into force on 2 October 2000. A litigant will have a right to a reasoned decision under art 6. On an application for leave the judge dealing with the application can, in my view, properly be brief in explaining his conclusion.

a But, as will be apparent from this judgment, merely to say that the Pt 52 Practice Direction has not been complied with may give rise to a real difficulty in knowing what requirement of that Practice Direction has, in the judge's view, not been met. In my judgment the judge should have identified how the Practice Direction was not complied with. I emphasise that this can be done briefly. But it should not be left to the conjecture of the litigant.

b 18. I have had the opportunity of seeing the judgment which Brooke LJ is about to give. I agree with it.

19. For the reasons which I have given this application for permission and the ancillary application for a stay must be dismissed.

c **BROOKE LJ.**

20. I agree.

21. Much of the difficulty that has arisen in this case stemmed from the fact that the papers appear to have been placed before Evans-Lombe J by the staff in the clerk of the lists appeal office in ignorance of the fact that the Citizen's Advice d Bureau (the CAB) was engaged in correspondence with Neuberger J, through his clerk, seeking an extension of time for lodging a skeleton argument. We do not know exactly how this came to happen—Mr Plender believed that he had been told by someone in that office that Neuberger J was considering his appeal—but it is a vivid example of the way in which serious difficulties may arise if correspondence is not channelled to judges through the relevant court administrative e office.

22. A further substantial difficulty arose from the fact that although Judge Collins gave an oral reasoned judgment in court on 27 April 2000, no note or transcript of his judgment had been filed at the High Court by the time Evans-Lombe J made his order six weeks later. I am adding this short judgment on my own because I am very f conscious, as a former supervisory Lord Justice for county court appeals, of the delays which have occurred in the past at Court of Appeal level because litigants have not lodged a transcript or note of the judgment with the speed which the proper conduct of an appeal demands. Now that the time for appealing in a case like this has been reduced, it is of even greater importance that such documents are lodged promptly.

g 23. All would-be appellants need to realise that the filing of a notice of appeal does not automatically stay the effect of the judgment appealed against, and that an appeal court is unlikely to be able to grant them any relief at all, whether by way of a stay of the order appealed against or otherwise, unless it is able to consider the reasons given by the judge in the court below for making the order h under challenge.

24. In paras 34 and 35 of my judgment in *Tanfern Ltd v Cameron-MacDonald* [2000] 2 All ER 801 at 809, [2000] 1 WLR 1311 at 1317–1318, I described the need for a suitable record of all judgments to be made. I read into my judgment paras 5.12 and 5.13 of the new Practice Direction supplementing CPR Pt 52. Three other j paragraphs of that Practice Direction are also relevant in the present context:

'5.14 Advocates' brief (or, where appropriate, refresher) fee includes: (1) remuneration for taking a note of the judgment of the court; (2) having the note transcribed accurately; (3) attempting to agree the note with the other side if represented; (4) submitting the note to the judge for approval where appropriate; (5) revising it if so requested by the judge; (6) providing any copies required for the appeal court, instructing solicitors and lay client; and (7) providing a copy of his note to an unrepresented appellant ...

5.17 Where the lower court or the appeal court is satisfied that an unrepresented appellant is in such poor financial circumstances that the cost of a transcript would be an excessive burden the court may certify that the cost of obtaining one official transcript should be borne at public expense.

5.18 In the case of a request for an official transcript of evidence or proceedings to be paid for at public expense, the court must also be satisfied that there are reasonable grounds for appeal. Whenever possible a request for a transcript at public expense should be made to the lower court when asking for permission to appeal.'

25. This Practice Direction applies to all the appeals that are covered by CPR Pt 52. So far as paras 5.17 and 5.18 are concerned, it should be noted that an important distinction is made, by implication, between a transcript of a judgment and transcripts of evidence or proceedings. In each case the relevant court must be satisfied as to the matters set out in para 5.17. In each case it has a general discretion, which must be exercised judicially, whether or not to grant the request for the provision of a transcript at public expense. In the case of a request for transcripts of evidence or proceedings, which can be very expensive, it must also be satisfied that there are reasonable grounds for appeal. It goes without saying that any such order must be limited to the provision of such transcripts as are necessary for the fair disposal of the appeal.

26. It would probably be helpful if general guidance could be given to judges as to the way in which the discretion conferred by para 5.17 of the Practice Direction should be exercised, since we have been told by counsel that the CAB of the Royal Courts of Justice has encountered a good deal of inconsistency in this regard.

27. I also wish to emphasise the direction in para 5.18 of the Practice Direction to the effect that wherever possible a request for a transcript at public expense should be made to the lower court. This is very important, because if this direction is observed it will be likely to avoid a lot of the delays which have disfigured the conduct of county court appeals in the past. We have been told, for instance, that the CAB at the Royal Courts of Justice, which does commendable work in assisting lay litigants with their appeals, would find it very much more straightforward if it could apply to the High Court for the necessary order than have to incur the delay and often the hassle involved in seeking such an order from the lower court after the case has been disposed of at that court. If the lower court makes such an order, it is essential that it is put into effect by the court's staff forthwith, so that there will then be no avoidable delay in the conduct of the appeal.

28. It is also essential that arrangements are made by which the appeal court may give any necessary directions under paras 5.17 and 5.18. We understand that the High Court has not yet provided facilities for judges or masters to make orders of this kind, but it is necessary for appropriate arrangements to be put in place now. In the Civil Appeals Office such applications have been made in recent times to a deputy master, with a right to a review or reconsideration by one or more of the judges of the Court of Appeal (for the relevant jurisdiction see now CPR 52.16). I would not wish to be prescriptive about the form any such arrangements in the High Court might take, whether in the Royal Courts of Justice or in a district registry, but since the Practice Direction gives the appeal court the power to order a transcript at public expense, it goes without saying

a that arrangements must be made whereby judges or masters of the court are able to exercise that power when an application for such an order is made.

29. The court has been shown in connection with this appeal a number of helpful documents published this year by the Court Service for the use of would-be appellants. In addition to the clear information contained in the appellant's notice (or the respondent's notice, as the case may be) there is a leaflet entitled 'I want b to appeal' and another leaflet entitled 'Guidance Notes on completing the appellant's notice'. These leaflets, helpful as they are, do not include any emphasis on the vital importance of setting in motion the provision of the judge's reasons (whether in a note or in a transcript) as fast as possible as soon as a decision is taken to seek permission to appeal. Until those reasons are available, the appeal court is, as I have said, unlikely to be able to grant any relief at all, a consequence c which may be just as prejudicial to the would-be appellant as it certainly will be to the efficient conduct of the appeal. Most of the other documents required by the appeal court are already in existence; so all that is needed is that they be copied (*if necessary*) and filed at the appeal court. The judge's reasons, on the other hand, except in the case of a handed down written judgment, will take time to obtain.

Applications dismissed.

Gillian Crew Barrister.

Re UCT (UK) Ltd (in administration)

a

CHANCERY DIVISION (COMPANIES COURT)

ARDEN J

19 JUNE 2000

b

Company – Winding up – Preferential payments – Voluntary winding up – Whether court having power to authorise administrators of company going into voluntary liquidation to pay persons who would be preferential creditors on a compulsory liquidation sums due if company compulsorily wound up – Insolvency Act 1986, ss 14, 18(3), Sch 1, para 13.

c

The joint administrators of a company applied, under s 18[a] of the Insolvency Act 1986, for the discharge of the administration order. Section 18(3) empowered the court, on such an application, to discharge or vary the administration order and make such 'consequential provision' as it thought fit. The administrators anticipated that the company would be put into voluntary liquidation immediately following the discharge of the order. Such a winding up would have been advantageous to creditors by avoiding the costs of a compulsory winding up. However, it would have resulted in some of the creditors losing the status of preferential creditors which they would have enjoyed on a compulsory winding up. Accordingly, the administrators sought a direction that they were entitled to transfer to themselves a sum to be held on trust for the benefit of those creditors who would have been preferential if the company had gone into compulsory liquidation. The issues arose as to whether the court had jurisdiction to make such a direction as a 'consequential provision' under s 18(3) and whether the administrators could carry it out under s 14[b] of, and para 13[c] of Sch 1 to, the Act which empowered them to make any payment incidental or necessary to their functions.

d e f

Held – For the purposes of s 18(3) of the 1986 Act, a consequential provision was any provision which resulted directly or indirectly from the discharge of the administration order. Such a provision would be consequential even though it would have to take effect immediately before the discharge because it would be a direction made to the administrators and they would cease to hold office on discharge of the administration order. In the instant case, the direction sought was necessitated by the application for discharge since there would have to be a liquidation, and voluntary liquidation was the preferred route. It followed that the court had power to make the proposed direction, provided that the administrators had power to make the proposed payment to themselves on trust as a payment incidental or necessary to their functions. Those functions extended to putting the company, in a manner which was most advantageous to creditors, into a position from which it could make distributions to creditors. That would be achieved in the instant case by putting the company into a position whereby it could enter into a voluntary liquidation. The proposed payment to the administrators as trustees was a payment which would enable that process to be

g h j

a Section 18, so far as material, is set out at p 189 *e f*, post

b Section 14 is set out at p 189 *d*, post

c Paragraph 13 provides: 'Power to make any payment which is necessary or incidental to the performance of his functions.'

a achieved, and accordingly came within para 13 of Sch 1 to the Act. It was therefore within the administrators' statutory powers to make the payment and to carry out the terms of the proposed trust. Accordingly, the court would direct the administrators to transfer monies into a trust account, and order the discharge of the administration order, with the transfer to the trust account having to take effect before the discharge (see p 191 *c f* to p 192 *b*, post).

b *Re Powerstore (Trading) Ltd, Re Homepower Stores Ltd* [1998] 1 All ER 121 not followed.

Dictum of Jacob J in *Re Mark One (Oxford Street) plc* [1999] 1 All ER 608 at 611 not followed.

Notes

For the discharge of administration orders and the powers of administrators, see c 7(3) *Halsbury's Laws* (4th edn reissue) paras 2096–2097.

For the Insolvency Act 1986, ss 14, 18, Sch 1, para 13, see 4 *Halsbury's Statutes* (4th edn) (1998 reissue) 749, 752, 1095.

Cases referred to in judgment

d *Mark One (Oxford Street) plc, Re* [1999] 1 All ER 608, [1999] 1 WLR 1445.

Norditrack (UK) Ltd (in administration), Re [2000] 1 All ER 369, [2000] 1 WLR 343.

Powerstore (Trading) Ltd, Re, Re Homepower Stores Ltd [1998] 1 All ER 121, [1997] 1 WLR 1280.

WBSL Realisations 1992 Ltd, Re, Re Ward Group Ltd [1995] 2 BCLC 576.

e **Application**

By application dated 13 June 2000 Nicholas James Dargan and Ralph Stephen Preece, the joint administrators of UCT (UK) Ltd, applied for (i) the discharge of the administration order made on 6 December 1999 conditionally upon the passing of a resolution for voluntary winding up of the company, (ii) directions f that they were entitled to retain in a designated trust account sums to pay those persons who were preferential creditors on 6 December 1999 and (iii) their release as administrators under s 20 of the Insolvency Act 1986. The facts are set out in the judgment.

g *Felicity Toube* (instructed by *Berwin Leighton*) for the joint administrators.

ARDEN J. This is an application by the joint administrators of UCT (UK) Ltd for: (1) discharge of the administration order made on 6 December 1999, such discharge to take effect immediately prior to the passing of a resolution for voluntary winding up of the company; (2) directions that the joint administrators h are entitled to retain in a designated trust account sums to pay those persons who were preferential creditors as at the date of the administration order on 6 December 1999; and (3) release of the administrators under s 20 of the Insolvency Act 1986. Ms Toube, who appears for the joint administrators, is content that the joint administrators make a transfer to a designated trust account for preferential j creditors immediately prior to discharge of the administration order.

The company's business was the provision of services to the pharmaceutical industry, providing laboratory services for human medical trials. The administration order was made for three of the purposes specified in s 8(3) of the 1986 Act. The first purpose of the administration order was a more advantageous realisation of the company's assets than would be effected on a winding up. That purpose has been achieved. The second purpose of the administration order was approval of a voluntary arrangement which is not capable of achievement. The third purpose of the administration order was the survival of the whole or part of the company's business. That purpose is likewise not now capable of achievement. a

Certain steps have been taken in the administration. A funding facility was agreed. In addition new terms were agreed with the landlord of the trading premises. Ultimately the company vacated those premises on 8 March 2000 after it had ceased trading. The support of the company's courier companies was ensured. The majority of employees were made redundant to reduce labour costs and the contracts of employment with the rest of the employees were terminated on 6 March 2000. The support of the company's customers and creditors was obtained. b

However, it became clear at a certain point that it was not possible for the business to be sold. The administrators therefore continued to trade simply to complete the company's obligations. The company's contracts were all transferred by February 2000 and at that point, 90% of preadministration and 95% of post-administration debtors were collected. The original estimated outcome projected that there would be a dividend of 5% to unsecured creditors. That estimate has now been increased to 8·16% and therefore the outcome has been more successful than was originally expected. c d

At a meeting held pursuant to s 23 of the Act on 22 December 1999, all the creditors present, in person or by proxy, and voting, including UCT International Ltd, which is the sole shareholder of the company, approved the joint administrators' proposals and a creditors' committee was formed. The creditors' committee approved the remuneration of the joint administrators and a proposal that the company should be placed into voluntary liquidation. The joint administrators anticipate that a resolution will be passed by the sole shareholder immediately following the discharge of the administration order and then a meeting of creditors under s 98 of the Act will be held on about 29 June. e

Certain of the company's creditors would have been preferential if the company had gone into compulsory liquidation, but will not be preferential if it goes into voluntary liquidation. Therefore the proposed order provides that a sum should be retained in a trust account to enable those creditors to be paid. The position is that the creditors have approved, as I have explained, the entry of this company into voluntary liquidation and I am informed that there is a significant financial advantage for this company going into voluntary liquidation as opposed to compulsory liquidation because the costs involved in transferring funds into the insolvency services account will not be incurred. f g

Accordingly, the application which Ms Toube makes is for the discharge of the administration order, the release of the administrators and a direction that the administrators retain on trust sums which would be preferential if the company were to be put into compulsory liquidation. It would then be the function of the administrators, after their discharge, in pursuance of the trust, to agree the sums due to the preferential creditors, to ensure that the payments due to them are made and to account for any balance to the voluntary liquidator. h

Now as I have explained, the company is a wholly owned subsidiary of another company, UCT International Ltd. So far as discharge of the administration is concerned, I am satisfied that this is a proper case with which the court should discharge an administration order as the administrators have now collected in such of the assets as they are able to collect in and there is no further purpose to be achieved in this administration. The administration order has, in my judgment, to be discharged immediately prior to a voluntary liquidation resolution: see j a *Re Norditrack (UK) Ltd (in adminstration)* [2000] 1 All ER 369, [2000] 1 WLR 343. There is no question of a conditional resolution for voluntary liquidation in this case as was proposed in *Re Norditrack (UK) Ltd.*

I am likewise satisfied this is a proper case in which to make the release sought. There has been no claim made against the administrators and the period of 28 days which is proposed will give creditors an opportunity to make a claim if b they wish to do so. I am satisfied that this is a sufficient period. Creditors have for some considerable time known of the intention to bring the administration order to an end.

I now turn to the further matter which is whether the court should make an order which empowers and requires the administrators to transfer a sum to be held on trust for the benefit of those creditors who would have been preferential c if the company had gone into compulsory liquidation as opposed to voluntary liquidation. I have explained the reasons for this course and the effect of this order. I start by referring to the material parts of ss 14 and 18 of the Act. Section 14 provides:

> d '(1) The administrator of a company—(a) may do all such things as may be necessary for the management of the affairs, business and property of the company, and (b) without prejudice to the generality of paragraph (a), has the powers specified in Schedule 1 to this Act …
>
> (3) The administrator may apply to the court for directions in relation to any particular matter arising in connection with the carrying out of his e functions.'

Section 18 of the Act provides:

> '… (2) The administrator shall make an application under this section if—(a) it appears to him that the purpose or each of the purposes specified in f the order either has been achieved or is incapable of achievement …
>
> (3) On the hearing of an application under this section, the court may by order discharge or vary the administration order and make such consequential provision it thinks fit, or adjourn the hearing conditionally or unconditionally, or make an interim order or any other order it thinks fit.'

g These provisions have been considered on a number of occasions by the court, in particular in *Re Powerstore (Trading) Ltd, Re Homepower Stores Ltd* [1998] 1 All ER 121, [1997] 1 WLR 1280, *Re WBSL Realisations* 1992 *Ltd, Re Ward Group Ltd* [1995] 2 BCLC 576 and *Re Mark One (Oxford Street) plc* [1999] 1 All ER 608, [1999] 1 WLR 1445.

In *Re Powerstore (Trading) Ltd,* Lightman J was asked to give a direction to h administrators in similar form to the directions which I am asked to make. Lightman J held that he had no jurisdiction under s 18(3) of the Act to give any direction to liquidators and Ms Toube has not in any way sought to challenge that. He went on to hold that he had no jurisdiction to give a direction to the administrators in that case because the proposed trust was not for the purposes of the administration. He referred to para 13 of Sch 1 to the Act, which enables j administrators to make any payment which is necessary or incidental to the performance of their functions. He held:

> 'Where there are sufficient reasons for doing so, (and the reasons should be substantial since the course is less straightforward), I see no reason why the administrators should not in the exercise of this power, as the medium for distribution and payment, pay the moneys to a trustee on trust to make

such distribution of payment; and the court can give to the administrators a direction to this effect under ss 14(3) and 18(3). Neither form of order involves the giving of any directions to the future liquidators or indeed anyone other than the administrators; nor do they involve disapplying the statutory scheme on the subsequent liquidation, for the funds paid or earmarked for the "preferred" or other creditors never become free assets of the company in the subsequent liquidation available for creditors generally. The insuperable problem in this case, however, is that the purpose of the proposed payment is not the more advantageous realisation of the companies' assets but a more advantageous method of distribution of assets. The power conferred by para 13 of Sch 1 to the 1986 Act is accordingly inapplicable. The power conferred by s 14(1) of the Act is likewise inapplicable because the proposed direction is not necessary for the management of the affairs, business or property of the companies. In the circumstances with considerable regret I must hold that I do not have jurisdiction to make the second of the two alternative forms of order.' (See [1998] 1 All ER 121 at 126–127, [1997] 1 WLR 1280 at 1285–1286.)

In his judgment, Lightman J distinguished the earlier authority of *Re WBSL Realisations* 1992 *Ltd*. In that case there had been an administration order for the purposes of the more advantageous realisation of the assets of the company than would be effected on a winding up. Knox J gave the administrators power to agree and pay (1) the preferential creditors of one company, W plc, and (2) both the preferential and unsecured creditors of its solvent wholly owned subsidiary, so as to ensure that a possible surplus from a pension fund was not lost by any preferential creditor putting W plc into liquidation. In so doing, Knox J relied on para 13 of Sch 1 to the Act, that is the power given to an administrator to make any payment which is necessary or incidental to the performance of his functions. As I have said, Lightman J considered that *Re WBSL Realisations* 1992 *Ltd* was distinguishable because a direction to hold moneys on trust for the benefit of preferential creditors, made at the time of discharge, was, in his judgment, not for the purposes of a more advantageous realisation of assets but for the purposes of distribution.

This issue came before Jacob J in the later case of *Re Mark One (Oxford Street) plc*. Jacob J held that the court had inherent power over administrators as officers of the court and that the Act did not cut down on that power. In addition, Jacob J held that the court has power under s 18(3) of the Act to 'make ... any other order as it thinks fit' and that this jurisdiction is wider than simply making an order for the purposes of administration. It is a power which arises when the purposes of administration have been achieved or become incapable of achievement.

Accordingly, the position with which I am faced is that there are decisions of two judges of this division of the High Court on s 18(3) and on s 14 of the Act in relation to the very matter in respect of which I am asked to make an order. Ms Toube has taken me succinctly to the authorities. She has submitted firstly that if Lightman J held that the payment had to be for the purpose of the administration order then that ruling was only in relation to the jurisdiction of the court under s 14 and does not affect the jurisdiction of the court under s 18. Her alternative submission is that if there has to be some connection with the purposes for which the administration order was made, then in this case the proposed direction to the administrators to transfer moneys to be held on trust for the preferential creditors would be a proper exercise of a power for the purposes of the administration. One of the objects for which the administration order was a made was to enable assets to be realised more advantageously than on winding up and it would be a narrow interpretation of that power if it did not enable the court to authorise the administrators to take steps to ensure that those assets were preserved and not expended in a way which could be avoided.

Now in my judgment, there are two matters as to which the court has to be satisfied. The court has to be satisfied that it has power under s 18 of the Act to b make the direction requested and likewise that the administrators have statutory power to carry out the order. Under s 18(3) the court has power when making an order for discharge to make such other consequential provision as it thinks fit. In my judgment, those are the operative parts of the section and not the concluding words 'or make … any other order it thinks fit'. That is because in relation to discharge or variation, this wording of the section is: '… the court may c by order discharge or vary the administration order and make such consequential provision as it thinks fit.'

Thus on this small point, I differ from the judgment of Jacob J. The question is then what is the meaning of consequential provision for the purposes of s 18(3)? In my judgment it means any provision which results directly or indirectly from d the discharge of the administration order.

In this case there clearly has to be a discharge of the administration order. The purposes for which the administrators were appointed have now been achieved or become spent and the time has come when the moneys have to be distributed to creditors and the appropriate medium in this case is through a liquidation. The creditors wish to avoid the costs of a compulsory liquidation and the creditors e would be better off if the course proposed by Ms Toube is taken than if the company goes into compulsory liquidation. She submits, in my view, rightly, that if I am not able to make this direction then the company will have to go into compulsory liquidation in order to preserve the rights of preferential creditors.

In my judgment, a provision is consequential even though it will have to take f effect immediately before the discharge because it is a direction which is being made to the administrators and they of course will cease to hold office on discharge of the administration order. As I see it, this particular direction is necessitated by the application for discharge since there will have to be a liquidation and voluntary liquidation is the preferred route. Accordingly I am satisfied that the court has power to make the proposed direction, provided that the administrators have g power to make the proposed payment to themselves on trust.

In that connection I turn to s 14 of the Act and to Sch 1. Paragraph 13 empowers administrators to make the payments which are necessary or incidental to the performance of their functions. I agree with Ms Toube that part of the function of the administrators is to bring the administration to a conclusion in the manner h which seems to them to be in the best interests of the creditors. I note that under Sch 1 the administrators have the power to present a petition for the winding up of the company; in other words, their functions extend to bringing the administration to a conclusion and ensuring that the company is put into a position from which it can make distributions to creditors.

j As I see it, it is part of their function to put the company in that position in a manner which is most advantageous to creditors. In this particular case, that is achieved by first putting the company in a position whereby it can enter into voluntary liquidation. As I see it, the proposed payment to the administrators as trustees is a payment which will enable that process to be achieved and therefore comes within para 13 of Sch 1. The payment is 'necessary or incidental' to the performance by them of their functions. It is accordingly within their statutory powers to make this payment, and it follows to carry out the terms of the proposed trust.

a

Accordingly, I propose to make the following order. First there will be a direction to the administrators to transfer moneys into a trust account and that will be on terms of course that they accept the trust. There will need to be some wording to make it clear what the trust is. Then the second part of the order will be to discharge the administration order. Then thirdly, the order will provide for the release of the administrators. The transfer to the trust account has to take effect before the discharge

b

Order accordingly.

Celia Fox Barrister.

a

Borealis AB (formerly Borealis Petrokemi AB) v Stargas Ltd and another (Bergesen DY A/S, third party)

The Berge Sisar

b

[2001] UKHL/17

HOUSE OF LORDS

LORD HOFFMANN, LORD MACKAY OF CLASHFERN, LORD COOKE OF THORNDON, LORD HOPE OF CRAIGHEAD AND LORD HOBHOUSE OF WOODBOROUGH

c 17, 18 MAY 2000, 22 MARCH 2001

Shipping – Bill of lading – Transfer of rights and liabilities – Statutory provision rendering lawful holder of bill of lading liable under contract of carriage if it 'demanded delivery' of cargo – Meaning of 'demanded delivery' – Carriage of Goods by Sea Act 1992, d *ss 2, 3(1).*

In October 1993 the claimant buyers agreed to purchase a quantity of liquid propane from the first defendant, S Ltd, under a contract which allegedly contained a requirement that the cargo should not contain more than a certain degree of corrosive compounds. The cargo was shipped from Saudi Arabia to e Sweden by the second defendant, SA, under five bills of lading on a vessel chartered to S Ltd by the shipowners. During the voyage, S Ltd's agents asked the shipowners to deliver the cargo to the buyers without production of the bills of lading, and undertook to indemnify them for any consequent liability or loss. On arrival, the vessel went alongside the buyers' jetty and routine samples were f taken from its tanks. Analysis of the samples showed that the cargo had been contaminated by corrosive compounds. The buyers therefore rejected the cargo and the vessel was not allowed to discharge. On 11 November 1993 the buyers sold the cargo on, and discharge was completed at another port on 24 November. The buyers received the endorsed bills of lading from S Ltd on 19 or 20 January 1994, and forwarded them to the ultimate purchaser. Subsequently, the buyers brought an g action against S Ltd, alleging that the propane had not complied with the contract specification at the time of shipping. In response, S Ltd alleged that the contamination had occurred on board the vessel and was not their responsibility. They also brought third party proceedings against the shipowners, claiming an indemnity in respect of any liability they might be under to the buyers. The shipowners counterclaimed h against S Ltd for the cost of cleaning the vessel, and brought a similar claim against the buyers, alleging that the latter were liable, as holder of the bills of lading, for the alleged breach by SA of its obligation not to ship a dangerous cargo. In response, the buyers amended their writ to join SA which subsequently applied unsuccessfully to have service of the writ upon them set aside. On SA's appeal, the Court of Appeal j held, by a majority, that the shipowners' claim against the buyers was bad in law, and that there was therefore no justification for joining SA. Accordingly, the appeal was allowed, and the shipowners appealed to the House of Lords, contending that the buyers had become liable when they received the bills of lading. In so contending, they relied on s 3(1)[a] of the Carriage of Goods by Sea Act 1992, which provided that

a Section 3, so far as material, is set out at [29], post

where s 2(1)[b] operated in relation to any document to which the Act applied and the person in whom rights were vested by virtue of that subsection took or 'demands delivery' from the carrier of any of the goods to which the document related (para (a)); made a claim under the contract of carriage against the carrier in respect of any of those goods (para (b)); or was a person who, at the time before those rights were vested in him, took or 'demanded delivery' from the carrier of any of those goods (para (c)), that person became subject to the same liabilities under that contract as if he had been a party to it. Section 2(1) transferred to, and vested in, the lawful holder of the bill of lading all rights of suit under the contract of carriage as if it had been a party to that contract. Their Lordships were therefore required to determine what constituted a 'demand' for 'delivery' for the purposes of s 3(1) and whether the sellers had made such a demand.

Held – On the true construction of s 3(1) of the 1992 Act, the phrase 'demands delivery' referred to a formal demand made to the carrier or his agent asserting the contractual right as the endorsee of the bill of lading to have the carrier deliver the goods to him. However, a 'demand' made without any basis for making it or insisting upon compliance was not in reality a demand at all. Accordingly, it would be unlikely that para (c) would ever apply save where there had been an actual delivery of the cargo. Taking delivery in paras (a) and (c) meant the voluntary transfer of possession from one person to another. That was more than simply co-operating in the discharge of the cargo from the vessel. Such discharge was a necessary operation in the interests of the ship as well as of the cargo, and required the co-operation of others besides the shipowner. Providing that co-operation should not be confused with delivery. The 'delivery' to which s 3 referred was that which involved a full transfer of the possession of the relevant goods by the carrier to the holder of the bill of lading. The surrender of the relevant endorsed bill of lading to the carrier or his agent before or at the time of delivery would ordinarily be an incident of such delivery. Where that was not done, the carrier would ordinarily require a letter of indemnity. In the instant case, the shipowners had failed to make out even an arguable case that the buyers had demanded delivery of the cargo. The vessel had been under charter to S Ltd, and it was they who had given orders to the shipowners, and had offered and given them the letter of indemnity. The only thing done by the buyers was to direct the master to their import jetty and then, having allowed the vessel to berth there, to take routine samples from the cargo tanks before clearing her for discharge into their terminal. Those were exactly the type of co-operative acts, assisting the shipowners and charterers, which could not be treated as a demand to deliver. What occurred did not even get as far as the buyers expressing their willingness to receive the cargo into their terminal. If the facts had disclosed something more positive on the part of the buyers, it was difficult to visualise that it could have had an appropriately unequivocal character or could have amounted to a demand for the purposes of s 3(1)(c). Accordingly, the shipowners' appeal would be dismissed, their claim against the buyers would be struck out and leave to join SA would be set aside (see [1]–[4], [33], [35], [36], [38]–[40], [46], post).

Per curiam. (1) The phrase 'makes a claim under the contract of carriage' in s 3(1)(b) of the 1992 Act refers to a formal claim against the carrier asserting a legal liability of the carrier under the contract of carriage to the holder of the bill of lading (see [1]–[4], [33], post).

b Section 2, so far as material, is set out at [29], post

a (2) Where all the rights of suit under the contract of carriage have been transferred to, and become vested in, the endorsee of a bill of lading pursuant to s 2(1) of the 1992 Act, and he becomes subject to the liabilities under that contract pursuant to s 3(1), he ceases, on the true construction of the Act, to be so liable when he endorses over the bill of lading to another so as to transfer his rights of suit to that other. In those circumstances, the mutuality which is the rationale for b imposing the liability has gone. However, other factors are likely to come into play which, perhaps decisively, will affect the respective rights and liabilities of the relevant parties (see [1]–[4], [40], [45], post).

Decision of the Court of Appeal [1998] 4 All ER 821 affirmed.

Notes

c For liabilities of a person who becomes lawful holder of a transferable bill of lading, see 43(2) *Halsbury's Laws* (4th edn reissue) para 1564.

For the Carriage of Goods by Sea Act 1992, ss 2, 3, see 39 *Halsbury's Statutes* (4th edn) (1995 reissue) 504, 506.

d **Cases referred to in opinions**

Aegean Sea Traders Corp v Repsol Petroleo SA, The Aegean Sea [1998] 2 Lloyd's Rep 39.

Albazero, The [1976] 3 All ER 129, [1977] AC 774, [1976] 3 WLR 491, HL.

Allen v Coltart (1883) 11 QBD 782.

Aramis, The [1989] 1 Lloyd's Rep 213, CA.

e *Brandt & Co v Liverpool Brazil and River Plate Steam Navigation Co Ltd* [1924] 1 KB 575, [1923] All ER Rep 656, CA.

Bryans v Nix (1839) 4 M & W 775, 150 ER 1634.

Cock v Taylor (1811) 13 East 399, 104 ER 424.

Dawes v Peck (1799) 8 Term Rep 330, 101 ER 1417.

f *Dublin City Distillery Ltd v Doherty* [1914] AC 823, HL.

Effort Shipping Co Ltd v Linden Management SA, The Giannis NK [1998] 1 All ER 495, [1998] AC 605, [1998] 2 WLR 206, HL.

Enichem Anic SpA v Ampelos Shipping Co Ltd, The Delfini [1990] 1 Lloyd's Rep 252, CA.

Evans v Nichol (1841) 3 M & G 614, 133 ER 1286.

Fox v Nott (1861) 6 H & N 630, 158 ER 260.

g *Glyn, Mills, Currie & Co v East and West India Dock Co* (1880) 6 QBD 475, CA.

Kum v Wah Tat Bank [1971] 1 Lloyd's Rep 439, PC.

Leigh & Sillavan Ltd v Aliakmon Shipping Co Ltd, The Aliakmon [1986] 2 All ER 145, [1986] AC 785, [1986] 2 WLR 902, HL.

Lickbarrow v Mason (1787) 2 Term Rep 63, [1775–1802] All ER Rep 1, 100 ER 35.

h *Margarine Union GmbH v Cambay Prince Steamship Co Ltd, The Wear Breeze* [1967] 3 All ER 775, [1969] 1 QB 219, [1967] 3 WLR 1569.

Mitsui & Co Ltd v Novorossiysk Shipping Co, The Gudermes [1993] 1 Lloyd's Rep 311, CA.

Sanders Bros v Maclean & Co (1883) 11 QBD 327, CA.

Sanders v Vanzeller (1843) 4 QB 260, 114 ER 897.

j *Sewell v Burdick* (1884) 10 App Cas 74, HL.

Smurthwaite v Wilkins (1862) 11 CBNS 842, 142 ER 1026.

Stindt v Roberts (1848) 17 LJQB 166.

Thompson v Dominy (1845) 14 M & W 403, 153 ER 532.

Wait, Re [1927] 1 Ch 606, [1926] All ER Rep 433, CA.

Young v Moeller (1855) 5 E & B 755, 119 ER 662.

Appeals

The third party, Bergesen DY A/S, appealed with leave of the Appeal Committee of the House of Lords given on 21 April 1999 from the decision of the Court of Appeal (Millett and Schiemann LJJ, Sir Brian Neill dissenting) on 30 July 1998 ([1998] 4 All ER 821, [1999] QB 863) whereby it (i) allowed an appeal by the second defendant, Saudi Arabian Oil Co (Saudi Aramco), from the decision of Waller J ([1997] 1 Lloyd's Rep 642) on 19 November 1996 dismissing its application to set aside the order of Clarke J on 30 October 1995 granting leave to the plaintiff, Borealis AB, to issue and serve on Saudi Aramco outside the jurisdiction a writ claiming an indemnity in respect of any liability it might be under to Bergesen; and (ii) struck out Bergesen's claim against Borealis. A conjoined appeal by Borealis against the Court of Appeal's decision to allow Saudi Aramco's appeal was dependent on the outcome of Bergesen's appeal against the decision to strike out its claim since it was accepted that it would be proper for Borealis to be given leave to join Saudi Aramco to the proceedings if Bergesen had an arguable case against it. The first defendant, Stargas Ltd, took no part in the proceedings before the Court of Appeal or the House of Lords. The facts are set out in the opinion of Lord Hobhouse of Woodborough.

Iain Milligan QC and *Simon Kverndal* (instructed by *Middleton Potts*) for Bergesen.
Andrew Popplewell QC (instructed by *Waltons & Morse*) for Borealis.
Jonathan Gaisman QC and *Stephen Kenny* (instructed by *Richards Butler*) for Saudi Aramco.

Their Lordships took time for consideration.

22 March 2001. The following opinions were delivered.

LORD HOFFMANN. My Lords,

[1] I have had the advantage of reading in draft the speech prepared by my noble and learned friend Lord Hobhouse of Woodborough. For the reasons which he gives, I would dismiss the appeal by Bergesen, and make the other orders that he has proposed

LORD MACKAY OF CLASHFERN. My Lords,

[2] I have had the advantage of reading in draft the speech prepared by my noble and learned friend Lord Hobhouse of Woodborough. For the reasons, which he gives, I would dismiss the appeal by Bergesen, and make the other orders that he has proposed.

LORD COOKE OF THORNDON. My Lords,

[3] I have had the advantage of reading in draft the speech prepared by my noble and learned friend Lord Hobhouse of Woodborough. For the reasons given by him, I would dismiss the appeal by Bergesen and make the other orders that he has proposed.

LORD HOPE OF CRAIGHEAD. My Lords,

[4] I have had the advantage of reading in draft the speech to be given by my noble and learned friend Lord Hobhouse of Woodborough. I agree with him that on the agreed primary facts Bergesen have failed to make out an arguable case that Borealis demanded the delivery of the cargo from the vessel into the terminal

a at Stenungsund within the meaning of s 3(1)(c) of the Carriage of Goods by Sea Act 1992. For the reasons that he has given I would dismiss the appeal by Bergesen, and I make the other orders that he has proposed.

LORD HOBHOUSE OF WOODBOROUGH. My Lords

[5] On 23 October 1993, the Norwegian flag LPG tanker Berge Sisar loaded a b cargo of about 42,500 metric tons of liquid propane at the terminal of the Saudi Arabian Oil Co (Saudi Aramco) at Yanbu. The vessel sailed to Stenungsund in Sweden arriving there on 6 November. On arrival, the vessel went alongside the intended receivers' jetty and routine samples were taken from the ship's tanks and analysed. The analysis showed that the cargo had been contaminated by corrosive hydrogen sulphide compounds. The intended receivers, Borealis AB, rejected c the cargo and the vessel was not allowed to discharge the contaminated propane at Stenungsund. The terminal at Stenungsund was not able to handle the contaminated cargo. The vessel was diverted back to Terneuzen in Holland where the necessary facilities existed for dealing with a contaminated cargo. The cargo was discharged into the Dow terminal at Terneuzen between 17 and 24 November. d The vessel's tanks and lines had then to be cleaned so that subsequent cargoes would not be contaminated.

[6] The financial consequences were substantial. There were the wasted costs at Stenungsund, the costs of diverting back to Terneusen and discharging there, the delay to the vessel, the reduced value of the contaminated cargo in comparison with a sound cargo and the cost of the clean-up. These events led to e the making of claims and cross-claims by and against the various parties involved in the venture and has given rise to disputes between them. Factually, the disputes primarily relate to the time at which and the reason why the propane became contaminated. Legally, the disputes relate to the division of responsibility and risk between those parties. The relevant contracts governing the various f relationships were of two different types. Firstly, there were the contracts covering the sales and purchases of the propane. Secondly, there were the contracts covering the employment of the vessel and the carriage of the cargo.

[7] The chain of sellers and buyers started with the producers of the propane, Saudi Aramco. Part of the propane it sold direct to the first buyer, Stargas Ltd of St Helier, Jersey, and part to various intermediaries who on-sold to Stargas. These g contracts were on FOB Yanbu terms with a quality/description condition. Stargas on-sold the propane to Borealis AB of Stenungsund (then called Statoil Petrokemi AB) on CFR terms, one safe berth Stenungsund, with the liberty to the buyer to nominate a different discharging port within the range nominated by the seller (with an adjustment to the price). The date of the contract was 13 October h 1993 and there was an English law and jurisdiction clause. Title, beneficial ownership and risk were to pass at ship's manifold at the loading port. The contract also provided that, after transfer of title to the buyer, the product was to be carried by the seller as carrier on the terms of the ASBATANKVOY charterparty. It is alleged that the specification included a requirement that the cargo should not j contain corrosive compounds such as to give rise to a result worse than 1B when measured by the copper corrosion test method ASTM D-1838.

[8] Borealis were the intended receivers of the cargo. The terminal at Stenungsund was theirs and had not the contamination been discovered, the cargo would have been discharged there. On the discovery of the contamination, Borealis refused to take the contaminated cargo and sold it to Dow Europe at a much reduced price; the contract was dated 11 November at which time the vessel was lying in

the anchorage off Stenungsund, having been ordered off Borealis's jetty the previous day. The terms were CIF Terneuzen with the quality as per the analysis of the Stenungsund samples. The payment terms were essentially cash against documents (letter of indemnity acceptable) and there was an English law and jurisdiction clause.

[9] The vessel was owned by Bergesen DY A/S of Oslo. By a voyage charterparty dated London 27 September 1993 on the ASBATANKVOY form, Bergesen chartered the vessel to Stargas for a voyage from Yanbu to one or two safe ports at charterers' option, one safe berth each port, out of Le Havre–Hamburg range (including UK and Stenungsund) or other options with a cargo of fully refrigerated propane and/or butane. The charterparty included a clause paramount and a London arbitration clause. It also provided that:

> 'The master shall upon request sign bills of lading in the form [printed at the foot of the charterparty] for all cargo shipped but without prejudice to the rights of the owner and charterer under the terms of this charter.'

[10] Five bills of lading were issued at Yanbu dated 23 October 1993 signed for and on behalf of the master. They acknowledged the receipt on board in apparent good order and condition of various tonnages of A-140 liquefied petroleum gas shipped by Saudi Aramco for carriage to one or more safe ports Netherlands and delivery there. The consignees named in the bills of lading were respectively the parties who had bought the relevant quantity of propane from Saudi Aramco. Thus, two named Banque Paribas for account of Stargas or order, one Banque Indosuez for account of Dendron Ltd BVI or order, one Chevron International or order and one Trammo Gas or order. The bills of lading incorporated the terms of the charterparty, including the arbitration clause.

[11] The naming of the banks in three of the bills of lading was no doubt because they were the bankers through whom the relevant buyers were to pay Saudi Aramco. The passing of the bills of lading down the line took some time and on 27 October, in the expectation that the vessel would arrive in northern Europe before the bills of lading, the charterers' agents (that is to say Stargas's agents) telexed the shipowners' agents, referring to the charterparty and the forthcoming discharge in Stenungsund, stating that the relevant bills of lading had not yet arrived and requesting the shipowners to deliver the cargo to Borealis without production of the bills of lading. In consideration of the shipowners complying with this request, the charterers, Stargas, undertook to indemnify the shipowners for any consequent liability or loss. The charterparty gave them this option. By the letter of indemnity, the charterers also gave the usual undertaking—

> 'as soon as all the original bills of lading for the above goods shall have arrived and/or come into our possession, to produce and deliver the same to you whereupon our liability hereunder shall cease.'

The telex concluded by charterers confirming their orders that the vessel was 'to proceed to Stenungsund to discharge the entire b/l quantity for the account of receivers [Borealis]' and requesting the shipowners' agents to instruct the master accordingly. By a telex later the same day, the shipowners confirmed their receipt and acceptance of the charterers' letter of indemnity for discharge of the cargo without presentation of the original bills of lading at the declared discharge port, Stenungsund, and that they, the shipowners, had instructed the master to deliver the cargo to Borealis.

a [12] The vessel arrived at the anchorage at Marstrand fjord off Stenungsund on the evening of 5 November after darkness had fallen. She proceeded into Stenungsund the following morning arriving at 0923 hrs and finished berthing at 1020 hrs. The master's notice of readiness (tendering the vessel to Borealis as being ready to commence discharge) was timed at 1800 hrs on 5 November but was recorded as having been received at 0925 hrs on 6 November. No bills of b lading were presented at Stenungsund. The on-carriage of the cargo by the vessel to Terneuzen was arranged by Stargas apparently under the option to nominate a second discharge port given to them in the charterparty and Stargas gave the shipowners a further letter of indemnity for the vessel to deliver the cargo there to Dow Europe without production of the bills of lading. It was under the instructions of Stargas as charterers that the vessel sailed from Stenungsund to c Terneuzen and delivered the cargo there to Dow Europe. As previously stated, the discharge of the cargo at Terneuzen was completed on 24 November.

[13] The evidence about what happened to the original bills of lading was somewhat exiguous but it is agreed by the parties to this appeal (on the basis of what is said in the affidavit of the solicitor acting for Borealis) that on 18 January d 1994 Stargas forwarded the bills of lading to Borealis who received them on 19 or 20 January and that Borealis forwarded them on to Dow Europe on 20 January. They were then presumably surrendered by Dow Europe or Stargas to the shipowners or their agents in accordance with the undertaking in the charterers' letter of indemnity. The photocopies of the original bills of lading in the papers before the House show that the bills of lading were endorsed by each party in the e line to the next so that each holder of the relevant bill of lading when he received it held it as an endorsee from the preceding holder.

[14] The litigation to which this state of affairs gave rise began with an action started by Borealis against Stargas in the Commercial Court in London. This was in accordance with the jurisdiction clause in their sale contract. The cause of f action relied upon in the writ as issued was that the propane had not complied with the contract specification at the time of shipment; ie their factual case was that the contamination had occurred before loading at Yanbu. The response of Stargas was to deny that there had been any contamination of the propane before loading and to allege that it had occurred on board the vessel and was not their responsibility. They joined Bergesen (the shipowners) as third parties claiming g an indemnity from them in the event that they, Stargas, might be held liable to Borealis for post-shipment contamination. The causes of action alleged were breach of the charterparty or breach of duty as bailee.

[15] Bergesen then counterclaimed in the third party proceedings against Stargas for the cost of cleaning the vessel's tanks, pumps and lines; this was on the h basis that the cargo was already contaminated before shipment. The cause of action alleged was damages for the breach of a term of the charterparty warranting the fitness of the cargo for carriage upon the vessel. But Bergesen, by a notice served under RSC Ord 18, r 8, also made a claim for these costs from Borealis on the basis that Bergesen was entitled to recover them from Borealis as j the holder of the bills of lading liable under the Carriage of Goods by Sea Act 1992 for the breach of the shipper's, that is Saudi Aramco's, obligation under art IV, r 6 of the amended Hague Rules not to ship a dangerous cargo. The nature and extent of this obligation is discussed in the speech of Lord Lloyd of Berwick in *Effort Shipping Co Ltd v Linden Management SA, The Giannis NK* [1998] 1 All ER 495, [1998] AC 605. Bergesen have made a corresponding claim directly against Saudi Aramco and this has, at Saudi Aramco's insistence, proceeded in arbitration in London in

accordance with the arbitration clause incorporated in the bills of lading. Borealis have not sought to refer the claim against them to arbitration and have responded to it by denying that it was a party liable to Bergesen under the bills of lading. In the alternative, if it was liable to Bergesen under the bills of lading, Borealis claimed damages against Bergesen for breach of contract or duty as carriers. Borealis also further amended their writ and points of claim to join Saudi Aramco and claimed an indemnity and/or contribution under s 1 of the Civil Liability (Contribution) Act 1978 in respect of any liability which Borealis might be held to be under to Bergesen. Borealis have also added to their claim against Stargas under the sale contract a claim in respect of any sum they may be adjudged liable to pay Bergesen in respect of the clean up costs.

[16] Saudi Aramco applied to the commercial judge to set aside the service of the amended writ upon them. Waller J ([1997] 1 Lloyd's Rep 642) dismissed the application. Saudi Aramco appealed to the Court of Appeal arguing additionally that the claim of Bergesen against Borealis could not succeed and therefore there was no proper basis for the claim over of Borealis against them. Bergesen were therefore invited to address the Court of Appeal as well as Borealis and Saudi Aramco and the hearing was adjourned to enable them to do so. Bergesen put in additional evidence and further amended their notice of claim against Borealis. The issue to be decided developed into one of assessing whether Bergesen had a good arguable case against Borealis. If they had not, then the claim of Bergesen against Borealis should be struck out; but, if they did, then it was appropriate that Borealis should be allowed to join Saudi Aramco. The Court of Appeal ([1998] 4 All ER 821, [1999] QB 863) by a majority, Sir Brian Neill dissenting, allowed the appeal. The point upon which Saudi Aramco succeeded was that which they had raised for the first time in the Court of Appeal, that Bergesen's claim against Borealis was bad in law. It followed from this that the justification for joining Saudi Aramco also failed. Bergesen have appealed to your Lordships' House. The response to the appeal has been argued in the name of Borealis, it being sensibly agreed that Saudi Aramco should abide by the outcome of the appeal. The argument on this appeal has been confined to the questions of law raised and their application to the facts of this case. But again the focus of the argument has changed. Borealis has been allowed to withdraw a factual concession made in the Court of Appeal and a legal question which was not in controversy in the Court of Appeal has now come to the forefront of the case.

[17] The question raised by Borealis's joinder of Saudi Aramco is whether Bergesen has a good arguable case in contract against Borealis. The question breaks down into two subsidiary questions. First, did Borealis ever become liable to Bergesen under s 3 of the 1992 Act. It is the case of Bergesen that Borealis became liable when they received the endorsed bills of lading from Stargas on 19 or 20 January 1994. (This is the question which was covered by the concession.) If the answer to this question is in the affirmative, the second subsidiary question is whether Borealis ceased to be so liable when they endorsed the bills of lading over to Dow Europe on 20 January. Bergesen submit that, once liable, Borealis remained liable under s 3(1) of the 1992 Act notwithstanding that they had endorsed the bills of lading over to another. Borealis submitted that they did cease to be liable. It was on this last point that there was the difference of opinion in the Court of Appeal, Sir Brian Neill preferring the view that their liability continued, the majority, Millett and Schiemann LJJ, holding that it did not. Both of these subsidiary questions involve the construction of the 1992 Act. Their

a unanimous answer to the first of these questions was effectively predetermined by the concession made during the hearing there by counsel for Saudi Aramco.

The 1992 Act: its genesis

[**18**] The predecessor of the 1992 Act was the Bills of Lading Act 1855. It was a short Act consisting of only three sections, of which only the first two are of b present relevance. The preamble explained why it had been passed:

> 'Whereas by the custom of merchants a bill of lading of goods being transferable by endorsement, the property in the goods may thereby pass to the endorsee, but nevertheless all rights in respect of the contract contained in the bill of lading continue in the original shipper or owner; and it is c expedient that such rights should pass with the property …'

Endorsed bills of lading were recognised by the law merchant to be symbols of the goods by the delivery of which the goods covered by the bill of lading could likewise be delivered. This was an application of the principles of bailment and attornment (*Sanders Bros v Maclean & Co* (1883) 11 QBD 327; *Dublin City Distillery* d *Ltd v Doherty* [1914] AC 823). In the *Sanders Bros* case Bowen LJ said (at 341):

> 'The law as to the indorsement of bills of lading is as clear as in my opinion the practice of all European merchants is thoroughly understood. A cargo at sea while in the hands of the carrier is necessarily incapable of physical delivery. During this period of transit and voyage, the bill of lading by the e law merchant is universally recognised as its symbol, and the indorsement and delivery of the bill of lading operates as a symbolical delivery of the cargo. Property in the goods passes by such indorsement and delivery of the bill of lading, whenever it is the intention of the parties that the property should pass, just as under similar circumstances the property would pass by an actual delivery of the goods. And for the purpose of passing such property f in the goods and completing the title of the indorsee to full possession thereof, the bill of lading, until complete delivery of the cargo has been made on shore to some one rightfully claiming under it, remains in force as a symbol, and carries with it … the full ownership of the goods … It is a key which in the hands of a rightful owner is intended to unlock the door of the g warehouse, floating or fixed, in which the goods may chance to be.'

The bill of lading acknowledges the receipt of the goods from the shipper for carriage to a destination and delivery there to the consignee. It therefore evidences a bailment with the carrier who has issued the bill of lading as the bailee and the consignee as bailor. This analysis was already well recognised before 1855 as is h demonstrated by *Bryans v Nix* (1839) 4 M & W 775, 150 ER 1634 and *Evans v Nichol* (1841) 3 M & G 614, 133 ER 1286. But the consignee need not be named and the bill of lading may simply say 'deliver to the bearer' or to 'order' or 'to order or assigns' or similar words. The contribution of the law merchant had been to recognise the attornment as transferrable and therefore the indorsement and j delivery of the bill of lading as capable of transferring the endorser's right to the possession of the goods to the endorsee (*Lickbarrow v Mason* (1787) 2 Term Rep 63, [1775–1802] All ER Rep 1; *Kum v Wah Tat Bank* [1971] 1 Lloyd's Rep 439 at 446–449 per Lord Devlin). What effect this would have on the title to the goods depended on the circumstances and the intention of the transferor and transferee (*Sewell v Burdick* (1884) 10 App Cas 74; *Glyn, Mills, Currie & Co v East and West India Dock Co* (1880) 6 QBD 475).

[**19**] However, as the preamble stated, the law merchant had not recognised any similar transfer of the contractual rights (*Thompson v Dominy* (1845) 14 M & W 403, 153 ER 532). The bill of lading evidences a contract of carriage. The parties to that contract are the issuing carrier, usually the shipowner although it may be a charterer, and the shipper or his principal. Where there is a named consignee it may be inferred that the contracting party is the consignee not the shipper: *Dawes v Peck* (1799) 8 Term Rep 330, 101 ER 1417 and the other cases cited by Brandon J in *The Albazero* [1977] AC 774 at 786. But, where the principal was the shipper, the contract was with him and remained with him. The rights and obligations in contract became separated from the right of the endorsee to the possession, and to demand the delivery up, of the goods.

[**20**] There was a qualification of this. The bill of lading evidenced a bailment upon terms, typically conditions which qualified the obligation to deliver up the goods to the bailor, including the discharge of liens or the performance of any requirements for unloading the goods from the ship. These conditions would be stated in the bill of lading or incorporated from a charterparty. For liens which are common law liens, e g the lien for freight or for general average, unless the bill of lading contained words waiving or negativing the lien (as by stamping the bill of lading 'freight prepaid'), the bill of lading holder had no right to the possession of the goods without first discharging the liens. At the time of the passing of the 1855 Act, the recognition of the carrier's liens as a qualification of the rights of the endorsee against the shipowner was well established: *Cock v Taylor* (1811) 13 East 399, 104 ER 424, *Sanders v Vanzeller* (1843) 4 QB 260, 114 ER 897, *Stindt v Roberts* (1848) 17 LJQB 166 and *Young v Moeller* (1855) 5 E & B 755, 119 ER 662. It took a bit longer fully to work out all the contractual implications. In 1883, Cave J, following the earlier decisions, said in *Allen v Coltart* (1883) 11 QBD 782 at 785:

> '... where goods are deliverable to the holder of a bill of lading on certain conditions being complied with, the act of demanding delivery is evidence of an offer on his part to comply with those conditions, and the delivery accordingly by the master is evidence of his acceptance of that offer.'

In 1923 the Court of Appeal authoritatively expanded the inferred contract as fully encompassing the rights and obligations of the carrier on the terms of the bill of lading: *Brandt & Co v Liverpool Brazil and River Plate Steam Navigation Co Ltd* [1924] 1 KB 575, [1923] All ER Rep 656, Bankes, Scrutton and Atkin LJJ, affirming a decision of Greer J (a combination of unparalleled distinction in this field). The plaintiff was a person who was claiming damages from the shipowner for negligence in the carriage of a consignment of goods. He was not able to bring himself within the terms of the 1855 Act but he succeeded on the contract to be inferred from the presentation of the bill of lading and the delivery of the goods against it. Atkin LJ ([1924] 1 KB 575 at 598–599, [1923] All ER Rep 656 at 663–664) outlined the route by which the law had developed. He referred to the inferred undertaking by the bill of lading holder to pay the sums due in respect of the carriage of the goods and asked whether there was any corresponding obligation on the part of the shipowner in that inferred contract. He continued:

> 'It appears to me that just as plainly the assignee is bound by an implied contract, so is the shipowner, and the shipowner's obligation in the case where freight has in fact been paid by the holder of the bill of lading, is that he will deliver the goods ... Is it a contract to deliver the goods on the terms of the bill of lading? Shipowners would be surprised to hear it suggested that

> having undertaken to carry goods upon terms in their bill of lading qualifying and limiting their liability they are nevertheless under an absolute obligation to deliver the goods and not an obligation qualified by the exceptions in the bill of lading … no other contract could be properly inferred.' (See [1924] 1 KB 575 at 599–600, [1923] All ER Rep 656 at 664.)

The inferred contract is not a fiction. It is a contract which the court concludes has come into existence because that is the proper finding of fact to make on the evidence in the case. Thus there has to be the requisite element of offer and acceptance and mutuality. This has been stressed in the modern authorities such as *The Aramis* [1989] 1 Lloyd's Rep 213 and *Mitsui & Co Ltd v Novorossiysk Shipping Co, The Gudermes* [1993] 1 Lloyd's Rep 311; if the facts do not justify it, the court will decline to find that there was a contract.

[21] The common law was thus able, without the assistance of statute, to accommodate the contractual position of the consignee who was the person for whom the shipper was entrusting the goods to the carrier and the position of the holder of the bill of lading who was taking delivery from the carrier at destination against presentation of the bill of lading. The 1855 Act was primarily concerned with the position of endorsees who did not come into either category but the drafting was sufficiently wide to be all embracing. Sections 1 and 2 provided:

> 'I. Every Consignee of Goods named in a Bill of Lading, and every Endorsee of a Bill of Lading to whom the Property in the Goods therein mentioned shall pass, upon or by reason of such Consignment or Endorsement, shall have transferred to and vested in him all Rights of Suit, and be subject to the same Liabilities in respect of such Goods as if the Contract contained in the Bill of Lading had been made with himself.
>
> II. Nothing herein contained shall prejudice or affect any right of stoppage, *in transitu*, or any right to claim freight against the original shipper or owner, or any liability of the consignee or endorsee by reason or in consequence of his being such consignee or endorsee, or of his receipt of the goods by reason or in consequence of such consignment or endorsement.'

The drafting of the 1855 Act gave rise to criticisms and difficulties. Two of them are presently relevant and of importance to the understanding of the 1992 Act.

The passing of 'Property' 'upon or by Reason of' the endorsement

[22] This problem was the subject of the decision of your Lordships' House in *Sewell v Burdick* (1884) 10 App Cas 74. It has two aspects. The first is what does the word 'property' encompass. Is it limited to the general property in the goods, that is, the legal title to the goods as is transferred by a sale? Or does it include the special property which signifies the right to possession? In *Sewell*'s case it was decided that it should be limited to the passing of the general property. The primary reason for reaching that conclusion was that bills of lading are as often as not used as security documents facilitating the financing by banks of merchants' sale transactions (eg under documentary letters of credit). A bank's interest is to use the possessory right to the document and the goods it represents as security; its interest is not to enter into contractual relations with the carrier, still less, to undertake contractual obligations towards the carrier. The decision in *Sewell*'s case was that a transaction of pledge accompanied by the endorsement of the bill of lading over to the pledgee did not come within the scope of s 1 and did not

transfer to the pledgee any contractual rights nor subject the pledgee to any contractual liabilities under the bill of lading. a

[23] The other aspect was that the passing of the property had to be 'upon or by reason of [the] consignment or endorsement'. But property under a contract of sale passes when the parties to that contract intend it to pass; it passes by reason of the contract of sale, not by reason of the endorsement of the bill of lading (s 18 of the Sale of Goods Acts 1893 and 1979). Under an fob contract, the property b in the goods prima facie passes upon shipment not upon the endorsement of or other dealing with the bills of lading. A contract for the international sale of goods commonly includes an express term covering the transfer of title. Similarly, ss 18(2) and 19(2) of the Sale of Goods Acts made relevant the question whether the seller has by taking a bill of lading making the goods deliverable to his own order reserved the right of disposal. The difficulties of using the criterion in the c 1855 Act were increased by simple logistics. The goods would arrive and be discharged and delivered before the documents had completed their progress down the chain of the intermediate buyers and sellers and their banks. The endorsement of those documents ceases to have any role in relation to the possession or legal ownership of the goods (*Enichem Anic SpA v Ampelos Shipping Co Ltd, The* d *Delfini* [1990] 1 Lloyd's Rep 252). In the present case, by January 1994, the cargo of propane had probably long since been processed at Terneuzen and had ceased to exist.

[24] There were cases therefore where the 1855 Act could not be used and where the tool of inferring a *Brandt* contract became less and less useful (eg *The Aramis*). There were related problems arising from changed patterns of trade. e Cargoes were shipped in bulk. Bills of lading were issued for quantities out of undivided consignments and those quantities were then sold to different buyers and the various bills of lading endorsed over to them. Such endorsements were ineffective to pass the legal title in part of an undivided whole to a purchaser (*Re Wait* [1927] 1 Ch 606, [1926] All ER Rep 433: see now the Sale of Goods (Amendment) f Act 1995). Further, the practice of issuing delivery orders for parcels out of a bulk cargo were similarly ineffective and the intended buyers were left without remedy against the carrier (*Margarine Union GmbH v Cambay Prince Steamship Co Ltd, The Wear Breeze* [1967] 3 All ER 775, [1969] 1 QB 219; *Leigh & Sillavan Ltd v Aliakmon Shipping Co Ltd, The Aliakmon* [1986] 2 All ER 145, [1986] AC 785).

g

'Subject to the Same Liabilities'

[25] The use of this phrase in the 1855 Act gave rise to immediate difficulty. What was the position of an endorser after he had endorsed over the bill of lading to another? How did endorsement affect the liabilities of the shipper? The answer was given in *Fox v Nott* (1861) 6 H & N 630, 158 ER 260 and *Smurthwaite v Wilkins* h (1862) 11 CBNS 842, 142 ER 1026. The endorser is not liable after he has endorsed over the bill of lading to another who is; the shipper remains liable as an original party to the contract. Two considerations seem to have weighed with the courts in these and the later cases (see *Effort Shipping Co Ltd v Linden Management SA, The Giannis NK* [1998] 1 All ER 495 at 502–504, [1998] AC 605 at 615–618 per Lord j Lloyd of Berwick). The words 'subject to the same liabilities' were to be contrasted with the words 'have transferred to him'. The liability of the endorsee was to be additional to that of the original contracting party. The other was to follow the reasoning which underlay the *Allen v Coltart* line of authority. It is the use of the bill of lading to demand and take delivery of the goods which is the basis of liability. Thus Erle CJ said in *Smurthwaite*'s case:

a 'Looking at the whole statute, it seems to me that the obvious meaning is that the assignee *who receives the cargo* shall have all the rights and bear all the liabilities of a contracting party; but that, if he passes on the bill of lading by indorsement to another, he passes on all the rights and liabilities which the bill of lading carries with it.' (See (1862) 11 CBNS 842 at 848, 142 ER 1026 at 1028–1029; Erle CJ's emphasis.)

b He rejected the argument that the endorser having passed on all his rights to the endorsee should retain all his liabilities in respect of the goods, saying:

'Such a construction might be very convenient for the ship-owner but it would be clearly repugnant to one's notions of justice.' (See 11 CBNS 842 at 849, 142 ER 1026 at 1029.)

c

The judgment of Erle CJ was approved by the Earl of Selborne LC in *Sewell v Burdick* (1884) 10 App Cas 74 at 86–88 (see also 83) and he echoed his language when he referred to a person who had had the bill of lading endorsed to him while the goods were at sea and who then chooses to take advantage of his d possession of the bill of lading to 'take the position of full proprietor upon himself with its corresponding burdens if he thinks fit'; 'and that he actually does so as between himself and the ship-owner if and when he claims and takes delivery of the goods by virtue of that title'.

e *The drafting of the 1992 Act*

[**26**] By 1980 the difficulties in the 1855 Act had assumed serious proportions and the 1855 Act was failing to meet the needs of the mercantile community and the changed pattern of international trade and carriage by sea. There were other points of concern as well. In certain trades the use of paper bills of lading was becoming increasingly obsolete. Electronic documents were coming into use. f Documents other than bills of lading were being used for the purposes previously served by bills of lading. Another related question which had to be considered particularly in the drafting of any new legislation was the concept when a bill of lading became 'accomplished', i e ceased to be capable of transferring rights to an endorsee (save by estoppel). This was always a potential problem under the 1855 g Act but did not cause significant problems in practice. It was however a problem which would have to be faced by the draftsman of a replacement for the 1855 Act.

[**27**] The existing state of the law having been recognised to be unsatisfactory, the question was referred to the Law Commission and the Scottish Law Commission. Their joint report, *Rights of suit in respect of carriage of goods by sea* (Law Com No 196, Scot Law Com No 130), was published in March 1991 and appended a draft bill. h They concentrated upon the carriage of goods by sea and the adequacy of the 1855 Act and did not in that report make recommendations for the amendment of the Sale of Goods Act 1979. They reviewed in detail the various aspects to which I have referred. They made recommendations for reform. They rejected as inadequate amendments to s 1 of the 1855 Act which would simply have j removed the requirement that the holder should have become the owner of the goods 'upon or by reason of' the endorsement or which would have removed all reference to property in s 1, so that it sufficed for the purposes of both rights and liabilities that the person was the holder of the bill of lading. They preferred instead an approach which severed the link between property and right of action and transferred the rights of suit to the holder without more, but not the liabilities. They recommended that there should not be an automatic linking of

contractual rights and liabilities; pledgees would not be liable 'unless they sought to enforce their security' (para 2.31). In support of their recommendation they said (para 2.34(iv)):

> 'The statutory assignment model of the 1855 Act is familiar to international traders ... Our reform is an evolutionary one which recognises that those parts of the 1855 Act which have worked well should be retained ...'

As regards the point at which the bill of lading ceases to be a transferable document of title, they adopted the existing test of delivery of the goods to the person entitled to receive them (para 2.42). As regards the liability of the holder under the bill of lading, their recommendation was in essence that a holder who seeks to take the benefit of the contract of carriage should not be permitted to do so without the corresponding burdens (paras 3.15–3.22). I will come back later to what they said.

[**28**] The recommendations are summarised in Pt VII of the report and the appended draft bill was designed to reflect those recommendations. The bill was enacted without substantive amendment. Your Lordships are entitled to look at the report in order to identify the mischief to which the Act is directed and, in the case of ambiguity, to help in resolving any such ambiguity.

The 1992 Act

[**29**] Not the whole of the 1992 Act is relevant to the present appeal. It is not necessary to quote those provisions which extend the descriptions of documents which are to be recognised as having a similar function to bills of lading nor the sections which revise s 3 of the 1855 Act. I will confine my quotation to what is directly relevant to bills of lading and the present appeal.

> 'An Act to replace the Bills of Lading Act 1855 with new provision with respect to bills of lading and certain other shipping documents ...
>
> **1.**—(1) This Act applies to ... any bill of lading ...
>
> **2.** *Rights under Shipping Documents.*—(1) Subject to the following provisions of this section, a person who becomes—(a) the lawful holder of a bill of lading ... shall (by virtue of becoming the holder of the bill ...) have transferred to and vested in him all rights of suit under the contract of carriage as if he had been a party to that contract.
>
> (2) Where, when a person becomes the lawful holder of a bill of lading, possession of the bill no longer gives a right (as against the carrier) to possession of the goods to which the bill relates, that person shall not have any rights transferred to him by virtue of subsection (1) above unless he becomes the holder of the bill—(a) by virtue of a transaction effected in pursuance of any contractual or other arrangements made before the time when such a right to possession ceased to attach to possession of the bill; or (b) as a result of the rejection to that person by another person of goods or documents delivered to the other person in pursuance of any such arrangements ...
>
> (4) Where, in the case of any document to which this Act applies—(a) a person with any interest or right in or in relation to goods to which the document relates sustains loss or damage in consequence of a breach of the contract of carriage; but (b) subsection (1) above operates in relation to that document so that rights of suit in respect of that breach are vested in another person, the other person shall be entitled to exercise those rights for the benefit of the person who sustained the loss or damage to the same extent as

a they could have been exercised if they had been vested in the person for whose benefit they are exercised.

(5) Where rights are transferred by virtue of the operation of subsection (1) above in relation to any document, the transfer for which that subsection provides shall extinguish any entitlement to those rights which derives—(a) where that document is a bill of lading, from a person's having been an original b party to the contract of carriage; or (b) in the case of any document to which this Act applies, from the previous operation of that subsection in relation to that document …

3. *Liabilities under Shipping Documents.*—(1) Where subsection (1) of section 2 of this Act operates in relation to any document to which this Act applies and c the person in whom rights are vested by virtue of that subsection—(a) takes or demands delivery from the carrier of any of the goods to which the document relates; (b) makes a claim under the contract of carriage against the carrier in respect of any of those goods; or (c) is a person who, at a time before those rights were vested in him, took or demanded delivery from the carrier of any of those goods, that person shall (by virtue of taking or d demanding delivery or making the claim or, in a case falling within paragraph (c) above, of having the rights vested in him) become subject to the same liabilities under that contract as if he had been a party to that contract …

(3) This section, so far as it imposes liabilities under any contract on any e person, shall be without prejudice to the liabilities under the contract of any person as an original party to the contract.

5. *Interpretation etc.*—(1) In this Act … "the contract of carriage"—(a) in relation to a bill of lading … means the contract contained in or evidenced by that bill … ; … "holder", in relation to a bill of lading, shall be construed f in accordance with subsection (2) below …

(2) References in this Act to the holder of a bill of lading are references to any of the following persons, that is to say—(a) a person with possession of the bill who, by virtue of being the person identified in the bill, is the consignee of the goods to which the bill relates; (b) a person with possession of the bill as a result of the completion, by delivery of the bill, of any g indorsement of the bill or, in the case of a bearer bill, of any other transfer of the bill; (c) a person with possession of the bill as a result of any transaction by virtue of which he would have become a holder falling within paragraph (a) or (b) above had not the transaction been effected at a time when possession of the bill no longer gave a right (as against the carrier) to possession of the goods h to which the bill relates; and a person shall be regarded for the purposes of this Act as having become the lawful holder of a bill of lading wherever he has become the holder of the bill in good faith.

(3) References in this Act to a person's being identified in a document include references to his being identified by a description which allows for j the identity of the person in question to be varied, in accordance with the terms of the document, after its issue; and the reference in section 1(3)(b) of this Act to a document's identifying a person shall be construed accordingly.

(4) Without prejudice to sections 2(2) and 4 above, nothing in this Act shall preclude its operation in relation to a case where the goods to which a document relates—(a) cease to exist after the issue of the document; or (b) cannot be identified (whether because they are mixed with other goods

or for any other reason); and references in this Act to the goods to which a document relates shall be construed accordingly. a

6.— ... (2) The Bills of Lading Act 1855 is hereby repealed.'

[**30**] This Act, in accordance with the view expressed in the report, retains much of the basic structure of the 1855 Act. Much of its increased length and complexity derives from the fact that it covers other documents—way bills and b delivery orders—besides bills of lading. It makes separate provision for the rights and the liabilities of a bill of lading holder. Section 2(1) makes being the lawful holder of the bill of lading the sole criterion for the right to enforce the contract which it evidences and this transfer of the right extinguishes the right of preceding holders to do so (s 2(5)). There are two qualifications: in simplified terms, the holder can sue and recover damages on behalf of another with an interest in the c goods (s 2(4)), and the transfer of a bill of lading after it has ceased to give a right to the possession of the goods does not confer any right of suit against the carrier unless the transfer was pursuant to an earlier contract or to the revesting of that right after a rejection by a buyer (s 2(2) and s 5(2)). In the present case the provisions of s 2 do not give rise to any problem. Until, anyway, the discharge of d the propane from the vessel at Terneusen to Dow Europe in the second half of November 1993, the bills of lading remained effective to give a right to the possession to the cargo as against Bergesen. Both the contract between Stargas and Borealis and that between Borealis and Dow Europe were made before that time. Therefore, Borealis and Dow Europe were in January 1994 successively holders of the bills of lading who came within the provisions of s 2(1) and (2) and e the extended definition of 'holder' in s 5(2).

[**31**] Section 2 of the 1992 Act has adopted a different and more generous approach to the transfer of contractual rights than that adopted by s 1 of the 1855 Act in that it wholly omits the 'property' criterion. A party who takes a bill of lading as security, as a pledgee, has the contractual rights transferred to him under s 2. f He can enforce them against the carrier or not as he chooses and may, if he chooses to do so, recover from the carrier also on behalf of the person with the full legal title (s 2(4)). This leaves the question whether the pledgee or similar person should come under any liability to the carrier. Under the 1855 Act he did not because he did not come within s 1 of that Act and acquired neither rights nor liabilities. The draftsman of the 1992 Act respected the commercial reasoning g upon which *Sewell*'s case was based and did not require bankers and others taking the documents as security to have to accept any liabilities merely by reason of being the holders of the bills of lading. Section 3(1) imposes additional requirements before a holder of a bill of lading comes under any contractual liability to the carrier. The solution adopted by the draftsman was to use the principle that he h who wishes to enforce the contract against the carrier must also accept the corresponding liabilities to the carrier under that contract. This was the view expressed by the Earl of Selborne LC. It is the rationale of the cases leading up to the *Brandt* case. It is a principle of mutuality. It was spelled out in the commissions' report. j

'3.15 ... However, where the holder of the bill of lading enforces any rights conferred on him under the contract of carriage he should do so on condition that he assumes any liabilities imposed on him under that contract ...

3.18 We see in general no unfairness in making the person who either claims delivery or who takes delivery of the goods, from being subject to the a terms of the contract of carriage, since in both cases the person is enforcing or at least attempting to enforce rights under the contract of carriage …

3.22 … Furthermore, it is unfair that the carrier should be denied redress against the indorsee of the bill of lading who seeks to take the benefit of the contract of carriage without the corresponding burdens.'

b But it must be observed that all these statements in the report, like the terminology used in the 1992 Act, are expressed in terms which refer explicitly to 'the contract of carriage' and not to the right of the holder of the endorsed bill of lading to the possession of the goods as the bailor as against the bailee. It is thus categorising the delivery up of the goods in this context as the performance of a contractual obligation not a bailment obligation. This is not objectionable since c where there is a contract of carriage the contract certainly includes a contractual obligation to deliver the goods. A bill of lading invariably includes words evidencing the carrier's agreement to deliver the goods at destination to 'or order or assigns' or words to that effect; the bailment is a contractual bailment. The relationship of the original parties to the contract of carriage is a contractually d mutual relationship, each having contractual rights against the other. The important point which is demonstrated by this part of the report, and carried through into the 1992 Act is that it is the contractual rights, not the proprietary rights (be they general or special), that are to be relevant. The relevant consideration is the mutuality of the contractual relationship transferred to the endorsee and the reciprocal contractual rights and obligations which arise from that relationship.

e [32] In giving effect to this intention, s 3 of the 1992 Act postulates first that the holder in question must be a person in whom the contractual rights of suit have been vested by s 2(1). The language of s 2(1) adopts and is identical to the corresponding words in the 1855 Act, 'shall have transferred [to] and vested in him all rights of suit'. Section 3(1)(a) and (b) relate to a person who, being a f person who has those rights, chooses to exercise them either (a) by taking or demanding delivery of the goods or (b) by making a claim under the contract of carriage contained in or evidenced by the bill of lading. Both involve an enforcement by the endorsee of the contractual rights against the carrier transferred to him by s 2(1). Under (a) it is by enjoying or demanding the performance of the carrier's contractual delivery obligation. Under (b) it is by claiming a remedy for some g breach by the carrier of the contract of carriage. Each of (a) and (b) involves a choice by the endorsee to take a positive step in relation to the contract of carriage and the rights against the carrier transferred to him by s 2(1). It has the character of an election to avail himself of those contractual rights against the carrier. There are however difficulties which neither the drafting nor the report h faces up to. Whilst taking delivery is a clear enough concept—it involves a voluntary transfer of possession from one person to another—making a 'demand' or 'claim' does not have such a specific character and, what is more, may be tentative or capable of being resiled from, a point commented upon by Millett LJ in the Court of Appeal ([1998] 4 All ER 821 at 836, [1999] QB 863 at 884). Delivery j brings an end to the actual bailment of the goods and is (save in special circumstances) the final act of contractual performance on the part of the carrier. Claims or demands may on the other hand be made at any stage (although usually only made after the end of the voyage) and there may at the time still be performance obligations of the carrier yet to be performed.

[33] To 'make a claim' may be anything from expressing a view in the course of a meeting or letter as to the liability of the carrier to issuing a writ or arresting

the vessel. A 'demand' might be an invitation or request, or, perhaps, even implied from making arrangements; or it might be a more formal express communication, such as would have sufficed to support an action in detinue. From the context in the 1992 Act and the purpose underlying s 3(1), it is clear that s 3 must be understood in a way which reflects the potentially important consequences of the choice or election which the bill of lading holder is making. The liabilities, particularly when alleged dangerous goods are involved, may be disproportionate to the value of the goods; the liabilities may not be covered by insurance; the endorsee may not be fully aware of what the liabilities are. I would therefore read the phrase 'demands delivery' as referring to a formal demand made to the carrier or his agent asserting the contractual right as the endorsee of the bill of lading to have the carrier deliver the goods to him. And I would read the phrase 'makes a claim under the contract of carriage' as referring to a formal claim against the carrier asserting a legal liability of the carrier under the contract of carriage to the holder of the bill of lading.

[34] But this is not the end of this problem. The use of the word 'demand' is problematic as is the phrase 'or at least attempting to enforce rights' in para 3.18 of the report. (It seems that those who wrote para 3.18 had in mind such exceptional situations as where the cargo is destroyed while the vessel is waiting to discharge at the discharge port and after a demurrage liability recoverable under the bill of lading has arisen—an intriguing and, if I may be forgiven for saying so, a relatively unilluminating example.) If the carrier accedes to the demand and gives delivery as demanded, the demand is subsumed in the taking of delivery. If the carrier rejects the demand, a new scenario arises: is the endorsee going to make a claim against the carrier for refusing to comply with the demand? If the endorsee chooses to let the matter drop and not to make a claim, what significance of the demand remains? What principle of mutuality requires that the endorsee shall nevertheless be made subject to the liabilities of a contracting party? What if the endorsee chooses to endorse over the bill of lading to another to whom the carrier is willing to and does deliver the goods? The task of the judge, arbitrator or legal adviser attempting to construe s 3(1) is not an easy one and it is necessary to try and extract from it some self-consistent structure.

[35] So far I have been concentrating on paras (a) and (b). Paragraph (c) presents further problems. It raises the relatively common situation where the vessel and its cargo arrive at the destination before the bills of lading have completed their journey down the chain of banks and buyers. The intended receiver has not yet acquired any rights under s 2(1). He is not entitled to demand delivery of the goods from the carrier. He may or may not be the owner of the goods but he quite probably will not at that time have the right to the possession of the goods; an earlier holder of the bill of lading may be a pledgee of the goods. This situation is dealt with commercially by delivering the goods against a letter of indemnity provided by the receiver (or his bank) which will include an undertaking by the receiver to surrender the bill of lading to the carrier as soon as it is acquired and will include any other stipulations and terms which the situation calls for. It may well at that time, either expressly or by implication, give rise to a *Brandt* type of contract on the terms of the bill of lading. But again the question arises: what is the character and the role of the demand referred to in para (c)? Ex hypothesi, the intended receiver had no right to make the demand and the carrier had no obligation to accede to it unless there was some other contract between the receiver and the carrier, eg a charterparty, which gave rise to that right and obligation in which case ss 2 and 3 have no application to that transaction.

a Paragraph (c) clearly involves an anticipation that the s 2(1) rights will be transferred to the receiver. The parenthesis which follows emphasises this 'by virtue of having the rights vested in him'. This shows that it is a necessary condition of the receiver's becoming liable under s 3(1) that the rights are vested in him by the operation of s 2(1). The inclusion of the word 'demanded' remains problematical. A rightly rejected demand for delivery by one who is not entitled b to delivery is an act devoid of legal significance. What is significant is if the carrier decides (voluntarily) to accede to the demand and deliver the goods to the receiver notwithstanding the non-arrival of the bill of lading. Paragraph (c) does not include the making of a claim. The draftsman has accepted the irrelevance of a claim made by one who has no contractual standing to make it. Unless facts c occur which give a relevance to the inclusion of the word 'demanded' in para (c), in my view the scheme of ss 2 and 3 requires that any such demand be treated as irrelevant for the purposes of s 3(1) and that the 1992 Act be construed accordingly. A 'demand' made without any basis for making it or insisting upon compliance is not in reality a demand at all. It is not a request made 'as of right', which is the primary dictionary meaning of 'demand'. It is not accompanied by d any threat of legal sanction. It is a request which can voluntarily be acceded to or refused as the person to whom it is made may choose. Accordingly it will be unlikely in the extreme that para (c) will ever apply save where there has been an actual delivery of the cargo.

[**36**] Taking delivery in paras (a) and (c) means, as I have said, the voluntary e transfer of possession from one person to another. This is more than just co-operating in the discharge of the cargo from the vessel. Discharge and delivery are distinct aspects of the international carriage of goods (see generally *Scrutton on Charterparties* (20th edn, 1996) section XIII). Although the normal time for delivering cargo to the receiver may be at the time of its discharge from the vessel, that is not necessarily f so. There may be a through contract of carriage. The goods may need to be unpacked from a container. The vessel may need to discharge its cargo without delay into a terminal. The discharge of the vessel is a necessary operation in the interests of the ship as well as of the cargo and requires the cooperation of others besides the shipowner. Providing that cooperation should not be confused with demanding delivery. The unloading of one cargo is for the shipowner the necessary g preliminary to the loading of the next. Damaged or contaminated cargoes may need especial discharge because they may cause damage or pollution. Any unnecessary delays will cost the shipowner money and a loss to the charterer through incurring demurrage or forfeiting dispatch. Where the vessel is operating under a charterparty it is more likely than not that the obligation to discharge will h be that of the charterer. The charterer will be responsible for providing or arranging a berth at which the vessel can discharge. Where the cargo is a bulk cargo which has been sold by the charterer to the intended receiver, the contract of sale may require the buyer to perform the seller's charterparty obligations in relation to the discharge of the vessel. The delivery to which s 3 is referring is that j which involves a full transfer of the possession of the relevant goods by the carrier to the holder of the bill of lading. The surrender of the relevant endorsed bill of lading to the carrier or his agent before or at the time of delivery will ordinarily be an incident of such delivery. Where that is not done, the carrier will ordinarily require a letter of indemnity. The letter of indemnity will probably be the best evidence of what arrangement has been made and will probably contain appropriate express terms.

The facts: the 'demand'

a

[37] My Lords, I have earlier set out the facts covering what occurred during and before the vessel's visit to Stenungsund in early November 1993. Although Borealis had earlier disputed that what had occurred had amounted to the making of a demand for the delivery of the goods, the point did not arise before Waller J. Before the Court of Appeal, the case was argued differently. It was conceded that Borealis had made a demand for the delivery of the cargo to them at Stenungsund. The court accordingly proceeded to decide the appeal on the basis that there had been a short period on 20 January 1994 when Borealis had been the holder of the bills of lading and had accordingly become a person who then had the rights under the contracts of carriage vested in him. That was why the critical issue in the Court of Appeal became whether the endorsement on to Dow Europe altered the application of s 3(1) to Borealis. In your Lordships' House the correctness of the concession was questioned and leave to withdraw it was sought. Counsel for Bergesen very fairly accepted that, if Borealis or Saudi Aramco had argued the point in the Court of Appeal, he could not have objected nor could he submit that his clients were prejudiced by its being argued in your Lordships' House. The primary facts are not in dispute. Your Lordships have allowed the concession to be withdrawn and have heard full argument upon the question whether it is right to say that Borealis demanded delivery of the cargo from Bergesen at Stenungsund.

b

c

d

[38] It will be apparent that in my judgment what occurred fell far short of amounting to the making of any demand for delivery on the part of Borealis. The vessel was under charter to Stargas. It was Stargas (or their agents) who gave orders to Bergesen. It was Stargas who offered and then gave the letter of indemnity to Bergesen against their agreement to deliver to Borealis without production of the bills of lading. The only thing done by Borealis appears to have been to direct the master to their import jetty and then, having allowed her to berth there, to take the routine samples from the cargo tanks before clearing the vessel for discharge into their terminal. These are exactly the type of co-operative acts, assisting the shipowners and charterers, to which I have referred earlier and which cannot on any view be treated as a demand by Borealis to deliver. Further, the trade in which these parties were involved necessitates the routine sampling of the cargo before it can be decided whether the vessel can be allowed to discharge its cargo into the terminal. It is elementary that in the ordinary course the nature and quality of the cargo must be established first. As the facts of the present case illustrate, it is always possible that the cargo may unexpectedly turn out to be contaminated or have some other characteristic which makes it unfit or unsafe for discharge into the terminal. What occurred did not get even as far as the stage of Borealis expressing their willingness to receive this cargo into their terminal. It fell a long way short of amounting to any demand or request that it should be. Once Borealis knew what the true characteristics of the cargo were, they refused to accept it from the ship.

e

f

g

h

[39] It follows that, as a matter of fact, Bergesen have failed on the agreed primary facts to make out even an arguable case that Borealis demanded the delivery of this cargo. If the facts had disclosed something more positive on the part of Borealis, it is difficult to visualise that it could have had an appropriately unequivocal character or could have amounted to a demand for the purposes of para (c) of s 3(1). The considerations discussed in [35] and [36] above would apply both as a matter of the proper use of language and as a matter of the interpretation of s 3(1) in its schematic context including the guidance given by a consideration of the report.

j

The secondary question: endorsement on and s 3(1)

[**40**] The answer which I have given to the question whether there was a demand is decisive of the appeals. If there was no demand by Borealis, there cannot be any liability of Borealis under s 3(1) whatever answer is given to the secondary question which was decisive in the Court of Appeal. The secondary question is easily formulated: when an endorsee of a bill of lading who has both had transferred to and vested in him all the rights of suit under the contract of carriage pursuant to s 2(1) and become subject to the liabilities under that contract pursuant to s 3(1), does he cease to be so liable when he endorses over the bill of lading to another so as to transfer his rights of suit to that other?

[**41**] The remarkable thing is that the report does not refer to this question at all and the 1992 Act contains no express provision covering it even though there are express provisions dealing with similar matters such as s 2(5) (extinction of rights) and s 3(3) (preservation of liabilities). It clearly was not foreseen as being a live issue. One of the reasons, I believe, must have been that they did not visualise there being anything tentative about any of the triggering steps referred to in the three paragraphs of s 3(1). They were contemplating actions of the bill of lading holder or receiver which would take place after the completion of the voyage. They did not have in mind conduct which could be resiled from or circumstances which would leave open the possibility of doing so. They did not visualise that casualties and disputes might arise during the course of a voyage which could give rise to the possible operation of s 3(1) and yet, in the event, not put an end to the carriage or the subsequent onward transfer of the bills of lading. Three things follow from this. The first is that no special significance can be attached to the fact that there is no express provision which provides the answer one way or the other in the 1992 Act. The problem was not seen to be a problem and the question was not seen to require an answer. Secondly, it underlines that a relatively stringent approach should be adopted to the interpretation of s 3(1). The character of the conduct which attracts the liability imposed by s 3(1) is expected to have an element of relative finality; it is not conduct which is tentative or equivocal nor conduct which is equally consistent with the person leaving it to a later endorsee to exercise the rights transferred by s 2(1). Thirdly, the answer to the question must be found by seeking out from the drafting of the 1992 Act and the report, pursuant to which the 1992 Act was drafted, what is the scheme of the statutory provisions and what principles they reflect.

[**42**] Valuable discussions of the various countervailing arguments for one view or the other are to be found in the judgments of the Court of Appeal, particularly the dissenting judgment of Sir Brian Neill ([1998] 4 All ER 821 at 831–834, [1999] QB 863 at 878–881) who was able to draw upon his particular experience in this field of law. Similarly your Lordships have had the assistance of citation from the judgment of Thomas J in *Aegean Sea Traders Corp v Repsol Petroleo SA, The Aegean Sea* [1998] 2 Lloyd's Rep 39 which dealt with a number of other points besides this one. Your Lordships were also referred to a short article by Francis Reynolds QC in [1999] LMCLQ 161 which draws attention to the importance of the factual context in which any such question arises and notes the importance of the concession which was made in the present case in the Court of Appeal and the artificiality of the situation which resulted with liability being said to arise from a momentary passage of the bills of lading two months later through the hands of Borealis.

[**43**] I agree with the sentiment of Professor Reynolds that it is likely that the particular facts will be of importance in any subsequent case concerning the

interrelation of ss 2 and 3 of the 1992 Act. It is possible that the conduct of one or other party may give rise to estoppels as where one party has been led to exercise forbearance in reliance upon some conduct of the other. In most cases there will be other documents or agreements to take into account besides the bill of lading such as charterparties, letters of indemnity, non-separation agreements, or ad hoc agreements. With these caveats, I will shortly state my conclusion on the secondary question itself as a matter of the construction of the 1992 Act unqualified by any special factors.

[44] I consider that there are two principles which are stated in the report and reflected in the drafting of the 1992 Act which show an intention on the part of the draftsman to preserve the decision in *Smurthwaite*'s case. The first is the intention to preserve the well tried and familiar structure of the 1855 Act having removed its dependence upon concepts of the passing of property. In the report, this approach surfaces in most of the relevant discussion and recommendations: see [27] above and paras 2.22, 2.34, 2.40–2.41 and 3.9–3.24 of the report. In the 1992 Act s 2(1) and s 3(1) adopt the crucial wording of the 1855 Act which formed the basis of *Smurthwaite*'s case and similar cases 'shall have transferred to and vested in him all rights of suit under the contract of carriage as if'—'shall become subject to the same liabilities under that contract as if'. Those words having been previously construed as having a certain effect, their repetition in the 1992 Act implies that the draftsman expected them to continue to be construed in the same way. *Smurthwaite*'s case is referred to in the report and is adopted rather than criticised. There is no provision in the 1992 Act which contradicts the intention that that decision should still have force.

[45] The second principle is that of mutuality (or, if preferred, reciprocity or fairness). I have already quoted passages from the report demonstrating that this was the guiding principle in arriving at the recommendations which have led to s 3(1). Section 3(1) is drafted following this principle because it makes it fundamental that, for a person to be caught by s 3(1), he must be the person in whom the rights of suit under the contract of carriage are vested pursuant to s 2(1). The liability is dependant upon the possession of the rights. It follows that, as there is no provision to the contrary, the 1992 Act should be construed as providing that, if the person should cease to have the rights vested in him, he should no longer be subject to the liabilities. The mutuality which is the rationale for imposing the liability has gone. There is no longer the link between benefits and burdens. I have already commented upon the fact that the report refers to *Smurthwaite*'s case and adopts it without criticism. It was in that case that Erle CJ said:

> '… the contention is that the consignee or assignee shall always remain liable, like the consignor, although he has parted with all interest and property in the goods by assigning the bill of lading to a third party before the arrival of the goods. The consequences which this would lead to are so monstrous, so manifestly unjust, that I should pause before I consented to adopt this construction of the act of parliament.' (See (1862) 11 CBNS 842 at 848, 142 ER 1026 at 1028.)

I recognise, and emphasise yet again, that it is likely that individual cases will be more complicated than that here visualised by Erle CJ and other factors are likely to come into play which, maybe decisively, will affect the respective rights and liabilities of the relevant parties. But as a matter of the construction of the 1992 Act per se, what he says remains apt and reflects the same principle as that adopted by the report and is supported, not contradicted, by the 1992 Act.

Conclusion

a

[**46**] It follows that I consider, my Lords, that the appeal of Bergesen should be dismissed together with the dependent appeal involving Saudi Aramco. The result is that the order of the Court of Appeal should be upheld. The claim of Bergesen against Borealis under the contract of carriage should be struck out. The leave to join Aramco should be set aside. The costs of both of the appeals to your Lordships' House should be paid by Bergesen.

Appeals dismissed.

Celia Fox Barrister.

R v Weir

a

HOUSE OF LORDS (APPEAL COMMITTEE)

LORD BINGHAM OF CORNHILL, LORD HOFFMANN, LORD HOPE OF CRAIGHEAD, LORD CLYDE AND LORD HUTTON

b

22 JANUARY, 5 FEBRUARY 2001

House of Lords – Appeal from Court of Appeal, Criminal Division – Prosecutor's petition for leave to appeal – Whether House of Lords having power to grant extension of time to prosecutor to apply for leave to appeal – Criminal Appeal Act 1968, s 34 – Human Rights Act 1998, Sch 1, Pt I, arts 2, 3, 6, 8.

c

The defendant, W, was convicted of murder, burglary and assault occasioning actual bodily harm. His appeal against conviction was allowed by the Court of Appeal which held that a statutory provision rendered inadmissible a DNA sample which had been used in evidence against him. The Director of Public Prosecutions applied for leave to appeal to the House of Lords, but his application was rejected by the Judicial Office because it was lodged one day after the 14-day time limit established by s 34(1)[a] of the Criminal Appeal Act 1968. Under s 34(2), the House of Lords had power, on an application by the defendant, to extend the time for appealing to the House, but there was no such provision in respect of an appeal by the prosecution. Subsequent to the rejection of the Director's application, the House of Lords delivered judgments on an Attorney General's reference in another case, which had the effect of reversing the Court of Appeal's decision on the point of law raised in W's case. The day after those judgments were delivered, the Director lodged a petition seeking an extension of time in which to seek leave to appeal in W's case. He contended that, on the proper construction of the legislation, the House had power to grant such an extension, and that a conclusion to the contrary would breach art 6[b] of the European Convention for the Protection of Human Rights and Fundamental Freedoms 1950 (as set out in Sch 1 to the Human Rights Act 1998) since it would deny him effective access to a court and an opportunity which would have been open to a defendant. Article 6 provided, inter alia, that everyone was entitled to a fair hearing in the determination of his civil rights or any criminal charge against him. Alternatively, the Director relied on the general public interest which a prosecutor represented, including the interests of victims and potential victims, to contend that the denial of an extension of time would breach arts 2, 3 and 8 of the convention—the right to life, the prohibition on inhuman and degrading treatment and the right to respect for a person's physical integrity.

d

e

f

g

h

Held – The House of Lords had no power to extend time for an application by the prosecution for leave to appeal. Although Parliament had provided since 1907 for a defendant's time to be extended on his application for leave to appeal to the Court of Criminal Appeal or the Court of Appeal, and had since 1960 provided for the defendant's time to be extended on an application for leave to

j

a Section 34 is set out at [12], post

b Article 6, so far as material, is set out at [17], post

a appeal to the House of Lords, it had never at any time provided for time to be extended in favour of a prosecutor seeking to appeal to the House of Lords. Where a time limit was laid down and no power was given to extend it, the ordinary rule was that the time limit should be strictly observed. Moreover, it was not hard to infer why Parliament should have allowed a defendant, who might be in prison and have difficulty in giving instructions or obtaining legal aid, b a measure of latitude which it did not allow to a professional prosecutor. Furthermore, Parliament plainly considered that a defendant, successful in the Court of Appeal, should be entitled to know definitely, at the expiry of the specified period, whether the decision in his favour was to be challenged or not. The construction of the statute was clear, and that the House of Lords was powerless to grant a prosecutor leave to appeal unless he applied within the c 14-day period. That conclusion was not affected by the convention. As regards art 6, the civil rights of the Director were not in issue and he was not charged with a criminal offence. Indeed, nothing in the language of that provision suggested that it was directed in any way to the position of a prosecutor. The convention had been conceived in the aftermath of war as a bulwark to protect private citizens d against the abuse of power by the state and public authorities. That explained why certain important rights were guaranteed to criminal defendants. It would stand the convention on its head to interpret it as strengthening the rights of prosecutors against private citizens. Further, although a contracting state was obliged to afford adequate protection of convention rights by its laws, that principle could not be transposed to the instant case. If the Court of Appeal made an e erroneous legal decision in favour of a defendant, it could be corrected. If, however, the Director sought to correct such a decision he had to comply with the time limit, which had not been criticised as unreasonable. Accordingly, the petition would be dismissed (see [14] and [17]–[21], post).

f **Notes**

For applications for leave to appeal to the House of Lords in criminal proceedings, see 11(2) *Halsbury's Laws* (4th edn reissue) para 1438.

For the Criminal Appeal Act 1968, s 34, see 12 *Halsbury's Statutes* (4th edn) (1997 reissue) 400.

g For the Human Rights Act 1998, Sch 1, Pt I, arts 2, 3, 6, 8, see 7 *Halsbury's Statutes* (4th edn) (1999 reissue) 522, 523, 524.

Cases referred to in report

A-G's Reference (No 3 of 1999) [2001] 1 All ER 577, [2001] 2 WLR 56, HL; *rvsg* [2000] h 4 All ER 360, [2000] 3 WLR 1164, CA.

Barker v Palmer (1881) 8 QBD 9.

Costello-Roberts v UK (1993) 19 EHRR 112, ECt HR.

Golder v UK (1975) 1 EHRR 524, ECt HR.

j *Omar v France* (1998) 29 EHRR 210, ECt HR.

Osman v UK (1998) 5 BHRC 293, ECt HR.

Petch v Gurney (Inspector of Taxes) [1994] 3 All ER 731, CA.

Poitrimol v France (1993) 18 EHRR 130, ECt HR.

X v Netherlands (1985) 8 EHRR 235, ECt HR.

Petition for leave to appeal

The Director of Public Prosecutions applied for leave to appeal out of time from the decision of the Court of Appeal (Swinton Thomas LJ, Butterfield and Rafferty JJ) on 26 May 2000 allowing an appeal by the respondent, Michael Clive Joseph Weir, against his convictions on 12 July 1999 for murder, burglary and assault occasioning actual bodily harm after a trial before Scott Baker J and a jury at the Central Criminal Court. The facts are set out in the report of the Appeal Committee.

David Perry and *Duncan Penny* (instructed by the *Crown Prosecution Service*) for the Director.

Sir Derek Spencer QC and *Rufus D'Cruz* (instructed by *Traymans*) for the respondent.

Their Lordships took time for consideration.

5 February 2001. The following report was delivered.

LORD BINGHAM OF CORNHILL.

[1] The committee have met and heard counsel on the petition of the Director of Public Prosecutions for an extension of time in which to seek leave to appeal (and for leave to appeal) against a decision of the Court of Appeal, Criminal Division quashing the conviction of the respondent on counts of murder, burglary and assault. The threshold issue before the committee is whether the House has power to grant such an extension of time.

The facts

[2] On 1 August 1997 the respondent was charged with certain drug offences and a sample of saliva was taken from him for DNA profiling purposes. On 29 October 1997 these charges were dropped, proceedings were discontinued and the respondent was discharged. Section 64(1) of the Police and Criminal Evidence Act 1984 required the respondent's DNA samples to be destroyed as soon as practicable. The samples were duly destroyed, but the DNA profile obtained from the samples remained on a DNA database in searchable form.

[3] On 28 January 1998 a married couple were attacked, and as a result of the attack the husband died in June 1998. At the scene of the crime there was found a glove stained with blood, which on analysis was found to match the respondent's profile held on the DNA database. The respondent was arrested on 4 June 1998 and denied involvement in the January attack. Two samples of blood were voluntarily given by him on 5 June. Comparison of these samples with the DNA profile obtained from the bloodstained glove showed a close and rare match.

[4] The respondent was prosecuted. The case against him rested on the blood samples taken on 5 June and the match with the blood found on the glove. At a preliminary hearing at the Central Criminal Court it was submitted to the Recorder of London on behalf of the respondent that the evidence of the DNA profile obtained from the blood samples given on 5 June should not be admitted. Reliance was placed on s 64(3B) of the 1984 Act, which provided that, where samples were required to be destroyed under sub-s (1) of the section, information derived from the sample of any person entitled to its destruction should not be used in evidence against the person so entitled or for the purposes of any

a investigation of an offence. The Recorder rejected that submission and ruled that the evidence might be led. The respondent was accordingly tried at the Central Criminal Court and convicted of murder, burglary and assault occasioning actual bodily harm. He was sentenced to concurrent terms of life, four years' and two years' imprisonment.

[5] The respondent appealed to the Court of Appeal, which allowed his appeal b and quashed his conviction. The written judgment of the court was handed down on 26 May 2000. Application was then made on behalf of the Director that the court should certify a point of law of general public importance and give leave to appeal to the House of Lords. The court did not give its decision on those applications until 14 June 2000, when it certified a question but refused leave to c appeal. The question certified was:

> 'Where a sample of DNA is lawfully taken from an accused in respect of offence A, of which the accused is acquitted, and as a result of information derived from that sample following the acquittal he is investigated in respect of offence B, is evidence obtained during the course of that investigation (and d in particular a fresh sample of DNA taken from the accused in respect of offence B) admissible on behalf of the prosecution at a subsequent trial of the accused in respect of offence B, notwithstanding s 64(3B) of the Police and Criminal Evidence Act 1984.'

e [6] It so happened that the issue at the heart of the respondent's appeal was also the subject of *A-G's Reference (No 3 of 1999)* [2001] 1 All ER 577, [2001] 2 WLR 56. Argument in that case was heard in the Court of Appeal ([2000] 4 All ER 360, [2000] 3 WLR 1164) on 18 April 2000, the day before the argument in the respondent's appeal. Judgment on the reference was also given on 26 May 2000 and was (in brief) that s 64(3B) of the 1984 Act expressly forbade the use, either in evidence f or for the purposes of investigating any offence, of information derived from, or the use of, a DNA sample which should have been destroyed under s 64(1). In quashing the respondent's conviction the Court of Appeal also relied on this line of reasoning.

[7] The point of law referred to the Court of Appeal in *A-G's Reference (No 3 of 1999)* g was in terms very similar to those of the certified question in this case. Having given its decision, the Court of Appeal referred the question to the House under s 36(3) of the Criminal Justice Act 1972. The House heard argument on the reference and on 14 December 2000 judgments were delivered which in effect upheld the contentions advanced by the Attorney General and differed from the h conclusion reached by the Court of Appeal. It was held that failure to comply with s 64(1) did not render inadmissible evidence of a later DNA profile based on later samples where the taking of those later samples had been prompted by reliance on the product of an earlier investigation which should have been destroyed; the admission of such evidence was to be controlled by the trial judge in exercise of the discretion conferred or confirmed by s 78 of the 1984 Act. Had j this reasoning been applied in the respondent's case, the Court of Appeal would not have quashed the respondent's conviction on the ground relied on by that court. Taking the view of the law which it did, the Court of Appeal found it unnecessary to review the judge's decision not to exclude the DNA evidence against the respondent under s 78, and so expressed no conclusion on that point.

[**8**] Following the adverse decision of the Court of Appeal in the present case, the Director gave notice of application for leave to appeal to the House of Lords, but his application was lodged one day after the 14-day period limited by statute and the Judicial Office accordingly rejected the application. The present petition seeking leave to apply to the House for leave notwithstanding the expiry of the statutory time limit was lodged on 15 December 2000.

The legislation

[**9**] Until 1907 no avenue of appeal was open to a defendant convicted on indictment except by writ of error, and a prosecutor had no right of appeal. The Criminal Appeal Act 1907 established a Court of Criminal Appeal and conferred a right of appeal on a defendant convicted on indictment subject to the grant of leave (unless the appeal involved a question of law alone or the trial judge gave a certificate). Section 7(1) of the 1907 Act, so far as relevant, provided:

> 'Where a person convicted desires to appeal under this Act to the Court of Criminal Appeal, or to obtain the leave of that court to appeal, he shall give notice of appeal or notice of his application for leave to appeal in such manner as may be directed by rules of court within ten days of the date of conviction ... Except in the case of a conviction involving sentence of death, the time, within which notice of appeal or notice of an application for leave to appeal may be given, may be extended at any time by the Court of Criminal Appeal.'

Section 1(6) of that Act provided:

> 'If in any case the Director of Public Prosecutions or the prosecutor or defendant obtains the certificate of the Attorney General that the decision of the Court of Criminal Appeal involves a point of law of exceptional public importance, and that it is desirable in the public interest that a further appeal should be brought, he may appeal from that decision to the House of Lords, but subject thereto the determination by the Court of Criminal Appeal of any appeal or other matter which it has power to determine shall be final, and no appeal shall lie from that court to any other court.'

At that stage there was no statutory time limit restricting the period within which application might be made to the Attorney General for his certificate. Section 16(1) of the Criminal Justice Act 1925 required such application to be made within seven days. The statute conferred no power to extend that period.

[**10**] The Administration of Justice Act 1960 governed appeals to the House of Lords from the Court of Criminal Appeal and from the Queen's Bench Divisional Court in criminal cases. Section 2, so far as relevant, provided:

> '(1) Subject to the provisions of this section, an application to the court below for leave to appeal shall be made within the period of fourteen days beginning with the date of the decision of that court; and an application to the House of Lords for such leave shall be made within the period of fourteen days beginning with the date on which the application is refused by the court below ...
>
> (3) Except in a case involving sentence of death, the House of Lords or the court below may, upon application made at any time by the defendant, extend the time within which an application may be made by him to that House or that court under subsection (1) of this section.'

a [11] Rights of appeal are now governed by the Criminal Appeal Act 1968. By s 1 of that Act a person convicted on indictment may appeal to the Court of Appeal against conviction, subject to obtaining the leave of the court or a certificate of the trial judge. By s 9 a person convicted on indictment may appeal to the Court of Appeal against sentence, subject to obtaining leave. By s 18 notice of appeal or of application for leave to appeal must be given within 28 days from the date of the b conviction, verdict or finding appealed against or from the date on which sentence was passed. The time for giving notice under the section may be extended either before or after it expires by the Court of Appeal. None of these sections gives a right of appeal to the Court of Appeal to the prosecution.

[12] Section 33 of the 1968 Act provides for an appeal to the House of Lords at the instance of the defendant or the prosecutor from any decision of the Court of c Appeal. It is provided in sub-s (2) as follows:

> 'The appeal lies only with the leave of the Court of Appeal or the House of Lords; and leave shall not be granted unless it is certified by the Court of Appeal that a point of law of general public importance is involved in the decision and it appears to the Court of Appeal or the House of Lords (as the d case may be) that the point is one which ought to be considered by that House.'

Section 34 of the 1968 Act lies at the heart of this application. It provides:

> '(1) An application to the Court of Appeal for leave to appeal to the House e of Lords shall be made within the period of fourteen days beginning with the date of the decision of the Court; and an application to the House of Lords for leave shall be made within the period of fourteen days beginning with the date on which the application for leave is refused by the Court of Appeal.
>
> (2) The House of Lords or the Court of Appeal may, upon application made at any time by the defendant, extend the time within which an application may f be made by him to that House or the Court under subsection (1) above.
>
> (3) An appeal to the House of Lords shall be treated as pending until any application for leave to appeal is disposed of and, if leave to appeal is granted, until the appeal is disposed of; and for purposes of this Part of this Act an application for leave to appeal shall be treated as disposed of at the expiration g of the time within which it may be made, if it is not made within that time.'

Construction

[13] Mr Perry, representing the Director, accepted that his application to the House of Lords for leave to appeal had not been made in the period of 14 days h beginning with the date on which the application for leave had been refused by the Court of Appeal. The application was only one day late, but counsel accepted that it was out of time. But he contended that on a proper construction of the legislation that delay was not fatal, since the House had power to extend time so as to permit the application to be made.

[14] Mr Perry found it difficult to advance any coherent argument to support j this construction, and in the opinion of the committee there are several insuperable objections to it. (1) Parliament has since 1907 provided for a defendant's time to be extended on his application for leave to appeal to the Court of Criminal Appeal or the Court of Appeal, and has since 1960 provided for the defendant's time to be extended on application for leave to appeal to the House of Lords. But it has

never at any time provided for time to be extended in favour of a prosecutor seeking to appeal to the House of Lords, and no such provision is to be found in the current legislation. (2) Where a time limit is laid down and no power is given to extend it, the ordinary rule is that the time limit must be strictly observed. As Millett LJ put it in *Petch v Gurney (Inspector of Taxes)* [1994] 3 All ER 731 at 738:

> 'If the only time limit which is prescribed is not obligatory, there is no time limit at all. Doing an act late is not the equivalent of doing it in time. That is why Grove J said in *Barker v Palmer* (1881) 8 QBD 9 at 10—"provisions with respect to time are always obligatory, unless a power of extending the time is given to the court". This probably cannot be laid down as a universal rule, but in my judgment it must be the normal one. Unless the court is given a power to extend the time, or some other and final mandatory time limit can be spelled out of the statute, a time limit cannot be relaxed without being dispensed with altogether; and it cannot be dispensed with altogether …'

(3) It is not hard to infer why Parliament should have drawn a sharp distinction between the position of a defendant and that of a prosecutor. A defendant unsuccessful in the Court of Appeal may well be in prison and experience difficulty in giving instructions, obtaining legal aid and perhaps instructing different solicitors and counsel for an appeal to the House. A measure of latitude is therefore allowed to him. But none of these problems would prevent a professional prosecutor who had already appeared at the trial and in the Court of Appeal making application to the House of Lords within the period of 14 days. Reference was made by Mr Perry to private prosecutors, but the Act draws no distinction between private and public prosecutors, and Parliament may well have discounted the possibility that private prosecutors would be raising erudite problems of criminal law in the Court of Appeal and the House of Lords. Parliament plainly considered that a defendant, successful in the Court of Appeal, should be entitled to know definitely, at the expiry of the specified period, whether the decision in his favour was to be challenged or not. (4) The appellate jurisdiction of the House in criminal matters is statutory. Subject to the Human Rights Act 1998, which is considered below, the House has no right or power to modify the statute by which its powers are governed. The construction of the statute is clear and unless the prosecutor applies for leave to appeal to the House within the period of 14 days the House is powerless to grant leave to appeal.

The Human Rights Act 1998

[15] In the course of argument Mr Perry virtually accepted that his argument depended on the effect of the 1998 Act and the European Convention for the Protection of Human Rights and Fundamental Freedoms (Rome, 4 November 1950; TS 71 (1953); Cmd 8969) which it incorporated into the law of the United Kingdom. He placed particular reliance on three articles of the convention.

[16] The first was art 6, and reference was made to the right of access to a court upheld by the European Court of Human Rights in *Golder v UK* (1975) 1 EHRR 524. It was argued that to deny the Director an extension of time in which to apply to the House was to deny him effective access to a court, and deny him an opportunity which would have been open to a defendant. The committee's attention was also drawn to cases such as *Poitrimol v France* (1993) 18 EHRR 130 and *Omar v France* (1998) 29 EHRR 210.

a [17] In the opinion of the committee this argument cannot be sustained, again for several reasons. (1) Article 6(1) of the convention opens by providing:

> 'In the determination of his civil rights and obligations or of any criminal charge against him, everyone is entitled to a fair and public hearing within a reasonable time by an independent and impartial tribunal established by law …'

b and continues in art 6(2) and (3) by providing certain important guarantees for 'Everyone charged with a criminal offence'. The civil rights of the Director are not here in issue and he is not charged with a criminal offence. Nothing in the language of this provision suggests that it is directed in any way to the position of a prosecutor. (2) The convention was conceived in the aftermath of war as a c bulwark to protect private citizens against the abuse of power by state and public authorities. This explains why certain important rights are guaranteed to criminal defendants. But it would stand the convention on its head to interpret it as strengthening the rights of prosecutors against private citizens. In truth, the present situation does not engage the human rights of the Director at all. (3) In none of the cases to which the committee was referred was judgment given in favour of d a prosecutor. The facts of the cases cited were altogether different. (4) The Director could show no breach of any human right if statute gave him no right of appeal to the House of Lords, as indeed he has no right of appeal to the Court of Appeal. His position cannot be stronger because Parliament has given him a right of appeal from the Court of Appeal to the House of Lords subject to compliance e with a reasonable time limit, which his officials have unfortunately failed to observe.

[18] Alternatively, and relying on the general public interest which a prosecutor represents, including the interests of victims and potential victims, Mr Perry relied on art 2 (the right to life), art 3 (the prohibition of inhuman and degrading treatment) and art 8 (the right to respect for a person's physical integrity). f Reliance was placed in particular on *X v Netherlands* (1985) 8 EHRR 235, *Costello-Roberts v UK* (1993) 19 EHRR 112 and *Osman v UK* (1998) 5 BHRC 293. In all these cases the question was whether a state, by its defective laws, had failed to afford adequate protection to the human rights of the complainant, who claimed to have been inadequately protected. A contracting state is obliged to g afford adequate protection of convention rights by its laws. But this principle cannot be transposed to the present case. English law enables those who commit crimes, like the respondent, to be prosecuted and, if convicted, punished. If the Court of Appeal makes an erroneous legal decision in favour of a defendant it can be corrected. But if the Director seeks to correct such a decision he must comply with the time limit, which is not criticised as unreasonable. There is no legal h lacuna. There would still be adequate protection of the rights of those who have suffered or who are liable to suffer injury at the hands of violent criminals if there were no right of appeal by the prosecutor to the House of Lords, as is the case in Scotland.

[19] The committee fully appreciate the public role and responsibility of the j Director, and fully appreciate also the acute anxiety to which this case has understandably given rise. But the House has to apply the law as laid down by Parliament, and nothing in the Human Rights legislation entitles the House to depart from the clear language of the statute, which does not in any way offend against the convention.

[20] We are of the clear opinion that the Judicial Office was right to reject the petition lodged on 28 June 2000 on the ground that it was out of time; and the House has no power to extend time for applying for leave.

Recommendation

[21] The committee recommend that the petition be dismissed as inadmissible and that the costs incurred by the respondent be paid out of central funds in accordance with s 16(5)(d) of the Prosecution of Offences Act 1985.

Petition dismissed.

Kate O'Hanlon Barrister.

a

R (on the application of Structadene Ltd) v Hackney London Borough Council

QUEEN'S BENCH DIVISION (ADMINISTRATIVE COURT)

ELIAS J

b 19 OCTOBER, 10 NOVEMBER 2000

Local authority – Land – Power to sell land – Statutory provision prohibiting local authorities from disposing of land for less than best possible consideration without Secretary of State's consent – Respondent authority entering into contract for sale of c *land in breach of that provision – Applicant obtaining injunction restraining completion of sale – Authority contending that transaction valid by virtue of statutory provision protecting third parties on 'disposal' of property – Whether disposal taking place on entry into contract or on conveyance – Local Government Act 1972, ss 123, 128(2).*

d The respondent local authority let 12 light industrial units to tenants who used the premises for small businesses. The authority decided to sell the property, and its decision came to the attention of the applicant property company, S Ltd, which was informed by the authority's agent that the property was to be sold at auction. S Ltd informed the agent that it was interested in purchasing the e property and, after becoming aware that the tenants were also interested, made it plain that it was intending to bid at the auction. At 9.45 am on the day of the auction, the authority informed S Ltd that it had decided not to continue with the auction because it had agreed, subject to contract, to sell to the tenants. The latter had been given until 10 am to sign an auction contract. S Ltd discovered that the tenants had agreed to pay £400,000, and immediately put in an offer of f £450,000, subsequently increased to £500,000. Those offers were rejected by the authority, and shortly afterwards, at about midday, the authority entered into a formal contract with the tenants. S Ltd obtained an injunction to prevent completion of the sale and was granted permission to apply for judicial review. On that application, it relied, inter alia, on s 123(2)[a] of the Local Government Act g 1972 which prohibited a council from disposing of land for a consideration less than the best that could be reasonably obtained, save with the consent of the Secretary of State. The authority conceded that it had breached s 123, and had therefore acted unlawfully, but contended nevertheless that the contract was valid and could not be set aside. It relied on s 128(2) [b] of the 1974 Act which h provided that where a local authority purported to dispose of land, then, in favour of any person claiming under the authority, the 'disposal' so purporting to be made 'shall not be invalid by reason that any consent of a Minister which is required thereto has not been given'. The issue therefore arose whether the entry into the contract of sale had constituted a disposal within the meaning of s 128(2).

j

Held – For the purposes of s 128(2) of the 1972 Act, a disposal occurred on conveyance, not on the entry into the contract for sale. It followed that the protection

a Section 123, so far as material, is set out at p 228 *j* to p 229 *e*, post

b Section 128(2) is set out at p 229 *f g*, post

afforded to third parties by that provision applied only once completion had taken place. Such a construction was supported by the way the term 'disposal' was used in s 123, particularly sub-s (2B), which provided that where the authority disposed of land that it was obliged, under certain statutory provisions, to hold for the enjoyment of the public, it would be freed from any such trust 'by virtue of the disposal'. Those words suggested that it was the very act of disposal that brought the trust to an end, and it would be strange if sub-s (2B) relieved the authority of its duties on entering into a contract for sale rather than on conveyance when it was no longer in a position to control the land in question. Another such indication was to be found in s 123(6), which related to the receipt of capital money in respect of a disposal of land held for charitable purposes. That sub-section envisaged that the payment was received in respect of the disposal. It was plainly received for the land itself, and was usually paid on transfer, not for the equitable interest arising on the contract of sale. Furthermore, although the grant of an option was a disposal, that did not mean that a contract for sale had to be treated likewise. An authority did not by contract give up its rights as owner of the property. Those were retained; the equitable interest conferred on the purchaser of property was only of a limited nature. It followed that in the instant case s 128(2) did not apply since the sale to the third party tenants had not been carried into effect. Accordingly, S Ltd was entitled to have the decision to sell quashed and the contract set aside (see p 231 *e* to *h*, p232 *e*, p 233 *d h j*, p 237 *a*, post); *Mainwaring v Trustees of Henry Smith's Charity* [1996] 2 All ER 220, *Wilkins v Horrowitz* [1990] 2 EGLR 217 and *R v Pembrokeshire CC, ex p Coker* [1999] 4 All ER 1007 considered.

Per curiam. The protection given to third parties by s 128(2) of the 1972 Act applies whenever the required consent is not given, even where such consent is sought and refused (see p 229 *j* to p 230 *a*, post).

Notes

For the disposal of local authority land, see 28 *Halsbury's Laws* (4th edn) para 1222.

For the Local Government Act 1972, ss 123, 128, see 25 *Halsbury's Statutes* (4th edn) (1997 reissue) 278, 283.

Cases referred to in judgment

Associated Provincial Picture Houses Ltd v Wednesbury Corp [1947] 2 All ER 680, [1948] 1 KB 223, CA.

Bromley LBC v Greater London Council [1982] 1 All ER 129, [1983] 1 AC 768, [1982] 2 WLR 62, HL.

Mainwaring v Trustees of Henry Smith's Charity [1996] 2 All ER 220, [1998] QB 1, [1996] 3 WLR 1033, CA.

R v Falmouth and Truro Port Health Authority, ex p South West Water Ltd [2000] 3 All ER 306, [2000] 3 WLR 1464, CA.

R v Pembrokeshire CC, ex p Coker [1999] 4 All ER 1007.

Trustees of the Chippenham Golf Club v North Wiltshire DC (1991) 64 P & CR 527, CA.

Wilkins v Horrowitz [1990] 2 EGLR 217.

Application for judicial review

The applicant, Structadene Ltd, applied for judicial review of the entry by the respondent, Hackney London Borough Council, into a contract for the sale of a Units 1–12 Tilia Road, London E5 to various third parties on 7 March 2000. The facts are set out in the judgment.

Kelvin Rutledge (instructed by *Eversleys*) for the applicant.
John Hobson QC (instructed by *Naomi Passman*) for the council.

Cur adv vult

b

10 November 2000. The following judgment was delivered.

ELIAS J.

The applicant in this action, a well-established property company, seeks c judicial review of the decision of the respondent council to sell certain properties to third parties, and to have the contract whereby the sale has been agreed set aside. It also seeks an order of mandamus requiring the council to sell the property by auction. The respondent council concedes that it did indeed act unlawfully in entering into the contract in that it did not take proper steps to obtain the best value pursuant to s 123 of the Local Government Act 1972 nor, in d the alternative, did it obtain the consent of the Secretary of State for the sale. If his consent is given then a sale which is for less than best value is none the less lawful. The council, however, contends that the court cannot now quash the decision or set aside the contract. It submits that the rights of third parties are protected by s 128(2) of the Act, and cannot now be unravelled. The council e accepts that it would be open to the court to declare the decision unlawful, but says that there would at this stage be no purpose in such relief being given. The applicant contends that in the circumstances of this case the contract can be set aside and that effective relief for the admittedly wrongful act is to hand. Whether that is right depends upon the proper construction of s 128(2) and its application to the facts.

f

The background

This can be stated relatively briefly. The material facts are not in dispute and are summarised in a witness statement of Anthony Kent, the solicitor acting for the applicant. The council let 12 light industrial units to tenants, who used the g premises for small businesses. The council decided to sell the property. This came to the attention of the applicant who contacted the agent charged with selling the property. The agent informed the applicant that it was to be sold at auction. The council's advice was apparently that the market value would be £400,000. One of the applicant's directors, a Mr Watson, inspected the property and also visited the offices of the council's solicitor for the purpose of inspecting certain documents h relating to the property. Mr Watson informed the agent that the applicant was interested in the property. The property subsequently appeared on the agent's particulars for auction to be held on 7 March 2000. The applicant later became aware that the tenants were also interested but it reiterated its interest and made it plain that it was intending to bid at the auction. There was apparently some j potential difficulty with a lease, but after taking legal advice the company resolved to go ahead and seek to buy the property.

On the day of the auction, at 9.45 am, Mr Kent contacted the council's solicitors and was told that the council had resolved not to continue with the auction because they had agreed, subject to contract, to sell to the tenants. The tenants had been given until 10 am in which to sign an auction contract. It seems that the applicant discovered that the tenants had agreed to pay £400,000. In any event authority was obtained by Mr Kent immediately to put in an offer of £450,000. It is accepted that this offer was in fact made before any contract had been signed with the tenants. Later that morning Mr Watson went to the agent's office in the hope of being able to sign an agreement. He was told by the agent that his instructions were to sell the property to the tenants, and the offer was rejected. The offer was increased to £500,000, but that also was rejected. Mr Watson was told that the property was not available to the company. Shortly thereafter, at about midday, the formal contract was entered into with the tenants. The applicant successfully obtained an injunction to prevent the sale being completed and was granted leave to apply for judicial review.

The council has put in evidence a witness statement from Ms Olorun-Rinu. She is an officer of the council, being corporate property manager. Curiously she does not say why the council acted as it did. The statement suggests, but does not state in terms, that the council may have been intending to comply with one of its standing orders which gives statutory tenants the first opportunity to purchase the property which they rent in the event of a sale. But only some of the tenants fell into this category. It may be that the council wished to help small businesses, but again that would be speculation. What is plain is that the council had received advice that the market value was £400,000 and had agreed to sell the property to the tenants once their offer was raised to that price. It is also clear that before entering into the contract the council turned down an unambiguous offer which was £100,000 better than the offer it accepted.

The grounds of review

The applicant contends that the council acted unlawfully on a number of grounds. First it submits that there was a clear breach of s 123. In addition, it contends that the council was in breach of its fiduciary duties to the ratepayers; that it acted in a *Wednesbury* unreasonable manner (see *Associated Provincial Picture Houses Ltd v Wednesbury Corp* [1947] 2 All ER 680, [1948] 1 KB 223); that it frustrated the applicant's legitimate expectation that the council should hold an auction and sell to the highest bidder, or at least give the applicant a chance to make representations before changing the sale procedure; and finally, that it acted unfairly.

Mr Hobson QC for the council realistically accepted that in the circumstances the council had acted unlawfully in that it had infringed s 123. He accepted that it is required to take active steps to try to obtain the best price for the property and that it had failed to do that. He denied, however, that it had acted unlawfully in any of the other ways alleged. Whether it did or not is potentially material for reasons which I will explain below. As I have indicated, he relied upon s 128(2) as the basis for saying that the contract was none the less valid and could not be set aside by the court. The tenants have chosen not to be separately represented but I have received a written submission in which they say that they entered into the contract in good faith, and have incurred losses as a result of the injunction that the applicant obtained holding up the completion. They support the council's arguments.

The legislation

Section 123 of the 1972 Act (as amended) provides as follows:

'(1) Subject to the following provisions of this section, a principal council may dispose of land held by them in any manner they wish.

a (2) Except with the consent of the Secretary of State, a council shall not dispose of land under this section, otherwise than by way of a short tenancy, for a consideration less than the best that can reasonably be obtained.

(2A) A principal council may not dispose under subsection (1) above of any land consisting or forming part of an open space unless before disposing of the land they cause notice of their intention to do so, specifying the land

b in question, to be advertised in two consecutive weeks in a newspaper circulating in the area in which the land is situated, and consider any objections to the proposed disposal which may be made to them.

(2B) Where by virtue of subsection (2A) above a council dispose of land which is held—(a) for the purposes of section 164 of the Public Health Act 1875 (pleasure grounds); or (b) in accordance with section 10 of the Open

c Spaces Act 1906 (duty of local authority to maintain open spaces and burial grounds), the land shall by virtue of the disposal be freed from any trust arising solely by virtue of its being land held in trust for enjoyment by the public in accordance with the said section 164 or, as the case may be, the said section 10 …

d (6) Capital money received in respect of a disposal under this section of land held for charitable purposes shall be applied in accordance with any directions given under the Charities Act 1993.

(7) For the purposes of this section a disposal of land is a disposal by way of a short tenancy if it consists—(a) of the grant of a term not exceeding seven years, or (b) of the assignment of a term which at the date of the assignment

e has not more than seven years to run, and in this section "public trust land" has the meaning assigned to it by section 122(6) above.'

Section 128(2) provides:

'Where under the foregoing provisions of this Part of this Act or under any

f other enactment, whether passed before, at the same time as, or after, this Act, a local authority purport to acquire, appropriate or dispose of land, then—(a) in favour of any person claiming under the authority, the acquisition, appropriation or disposal so purporting to be made shall not be invalid by reason that any consent of a Minister which is required thereto has not been given or that any requirement as to advertisement or consideration of

g objections has not been complied with, and (b) a person dealing with the authority or a person claiming under the authority shall not be concerned to see or enquire whether any such consent has been given or whether any such requirement has been complied with.'

h The concept of land is defined in s 270 as follows: '… "land" includes any interest in land and any easement or right in, to or over land'.

It is pertinent at this stage to note a number of features about these provisions. First, the concept of disposal occurs both in ss 123 and 128. Both parties agree, correctly in my view, that it must bear the same meaning in each section. Second, the protection in s 128 arises only where there is a 'disposal' as defined. Third, the

j disposal need not be of the freehold or leasehold estate; it can be of an interest in land, (unless the concept of land in these provisions is different to its general meaning in the Act). Moreover, the concept of an interest in land is on the face of it wide enough to embrace both a legal and equitable interest. Fourth, the protection to third parties is provided whenever the required consent is not given. The subsection does not say whenever it is sought and not given, or whenever it should have been sought but was not; accordingly in my opinion the subsection could apply even where the consent was sought and refused. This construction is supported in my view by para (b) of the subsection. Finally the disposal is not protected from invalidity as against every alleged legal defect, but only where the defect consists of the failure to obtain the Secretary of State's consent. a

Of course s 128 does not operate to the benefit of the council itself. The applicant can still obtain such relief, other than rendering invalid the disposal itself, as the court is able to grant. Plainly, safeguarding the interests of third parties potentially diminishes—and may significantly diminish—the effectiveness of any relief, particularly where the applicant is a rival bidder for the property. However, it is wrong to say—as counsel for the applicant did in the course of submissions—that if s 128 applies, there is no incentive for councils to comply with the law. In an appropriate case the fact that s 128 applies would not, for example, prevent any officers or councillors at fault being subject to a surcharge for losses incurred by the council. b c

Does s 128(2) apply? d

This is the fundamental issue in this case. Mr Rutledge for the applicant submits that it does not for three reasons. First, he submits that there was not a disposal of land merely by virtue of the entering into the contract with the tenants. He says that completion would be necessary. Second, he contends that in any event the conduct of the council was unlawful for a number of reasons which were quite independent of the failure to obtain consent, and that the subsection provides no shield against those attacks. Finally, he submitted that the provision only applied in any event when the council intended to dispose of land by the route of the Secretary of State's consent and would not apply where it was intending to get the best value. He further contended that it was seeking to get the best value in this case. I shall consider each of these arguments in turn. e f

Has there been a disposal?

The first issue which arises is whether the entry into the contract constituted a 'disposal' at all within the meaning of s 128(2). There is no statutory definition of disposal in the 1972 Act. g

Mr Hobson's argument is very simple. He says that once a contract for the sale of land has been entered into, the purchaser of the land has an equitable interest; the vendor holds the property on trust for the purchaser. Accordingly, he submits that at that stage there is a disposal of the land. Whilst it is not a disposal of the whole legal estate, it is the disposal of an interest in land and that is sufficient. Mr Rutledge submits that there is no disposal until the legal estate is conveyed, and that whilst an equitable interest is created by the contract, this does not give rise to a disposal as such within the meaning of the section. h

Logically it might be argued that if the council is right, then there would be two disposals, one on exchange of contract when the equitable interest was passed, and one on completion when the legal title was passed. However, I cannot imagine that Parliament could conceivably have intended such a bizarre result, with consent technically having to be obtained on each occasion (assuming that the land was sold for below the best price) notwithstanding that the terms of the deal would not have changed between contract and conveyance. Accordingly, the question j a is which construction is to be preferred, reading the statute fairly and bearing in mind the context.

In my view there is no linguistic reason why the word 'disposal' should not be used to describe the creation of the equitable interest arising when a sale contract is entered into. Indeed, s 262 of the Housing Act 1985 expressly defines a disposal as including 'a conveyance … or contract to convey, an estate or interest not b previously in existence'. There the statute puts the matter beyond doubt. However, I start from the premise that if, in a sale of land, one has to choose between contract and conveyance as the moment when the disposal occurs, the concept would more naturally describe the transfer of the legal interest on conveyance rather than the creation of the equitable interest by the contract.

c I have been referred to other statutory provisions where the concept of disposal arises but they are of limited utility because the concept is used in different ways in different statutes. Different meanings are given in different contexts. As I have said, the definition in Pt VIII of the 1985 Act puts the issue beyond dispute for the purposes of that Part by expressly providing that there is a disposition when the contract is made. By contrast, in *Mainwaring v Trustees of* d *Henry Smith's Charity* [1996] 2 All ER 220, [1998] QB 1 the Court of Appeal had to decide whether there was a relevant disposal on the entry into the contract or on conveyance for the purposes of s 4 of the Landlord and Tenant Act 1987. The court held that the disposal took effect on conveyance. I shall consider this case further below.

e I shall consider the question of construction by analysing the statutory language construed in context, any relevant legal authorities, and the policy implications of the rival constructions.

Turning first to the statute. There are in my view some indications in s 123 itself as to how the concept is to be construed. The following features lend support to the argument that the disposal occurs on conveyance. (1) Subsection (2B) f provides that where the authority disposes of land which it is obliged to hold under certain statutory provisions for the enjoyment of the public, it will be freed from any such trust 'by virtue of the disposal'. These words suggest in my view that it is the very act of disposal that brings the trust to an end. It would be strange if this subsection meant that the authority was relieved of its duties once g a contract to sell the land was made. One would not expect it to be free of its duties until it was no longer in a position to control the land in question, and that would be on conveyance. Yet if the council is right and the contract fixes the time of disposal, the making of the contract of itself brings the trust obligations to an end. If for some reason the conveyance never took effect, such as where there was termination of the contract by mutual agreement, then it would seem that h the authority would retain control of the land but apparently unencumbered by the former trust duty. (2) Subsection (6) envisages that the payment is received in respect of the disposal. However, it is plainly received for the land itself, and is usually paid on transfer. It is not paid for the equitable interest arising on the contract of sale and nor is it measured by the value of that interest. (3) Both j sub-ss (2) and (7) refer to a disposal *by way of* a short tenancy. This suggests that it is the tenancy itself which is created by the disposal rather than any agreement to create the tenancy.

On the other hand, sub-s (2A) arguably lends support to the council's construction. This requires the authority to advertise and consider objections before land consisting of an open space can be disposed of. Plainly the purpose of this is to ensure that no commitment to sell is made before the objections are considered. This will be achieved only if the relevant steps are taken before the contract is made. By referring to the need to take these steps before disposal, the statute arguably implies that this means the contract being made. The point does not seem to me to be altogether clear, however, since the section could be implying that the steps should be taken long enough before disposal to ensure that the purpose of the provision can be achieved. That would mean that it would need to be in fact before the contract is concluded.

Mr Hobson places considerable store by the fact that an option to purchase would fall within the terms of s 123. If that is so, he says, then a fortiori an agreement to sell must do so. It would be irrational were it otherwise since the option is created prior to the contract. I see considerable force in this submission. However, an identical argument was advanced and rejected before the Lands Tribunal in *Wilkins v Horrowitz* [1990] 2 EGLR 217. That decision was in turn cited with approval and followed by the Court of Appeal in *Mainwaring*'s case, to which I have made reference, in a judgment of Sir Thomas Bingham MR, delivering the judgment of the court. Moreover, in that case also the grant of an option was expressly included in the definition of 'disposal'. Notwithstanding that, the court held that in the case of a sale of the freehold, the contract did not constitute the disposal. In *Wilkins*'s case the tribunal thought it relevant to ask whether the landlord had given up his rights qua landlord; it held that since he retained his right to the rents and profits and was responsible for subletting (albeit after consultation with the purchaser) he had not. Applying that principle here, in my view it would be wrong to say that the council had by the contract given up its rights as owner of the property. Plainly these were retained; the equitable interest conferred on the purchaser of property is only of a limited nature.

In my opinion, therefore, the balance of the argument based on the statutory provisions considered in isolation is in favour of treating the conveyance as the point at which disposal occurs.

I now turn to consider whether the authorities cast doubt on this construction. Section 128 itself appears to have been considered in only one case. It was analysed in the decision of Lightman J in *R v Pembrokeshire CC, ex p Coker* [1999] 4 All ER 1007. In that case the respondent council leased a property for 5 years but with an option to renew for 99 years. Lightman J considered that the lease and option had to be treated as one transaction. On the facts he held that there was no breach of s 123 but he went on to consider what the effect of s 128(2) would have been had there been a sale at an undervalue. He said this (at 1013–1014):

> 'The language of s 128(2) is perfectly clear and unambiguous: in favour of a person claiming under the council (and that includes CSSL as lessee under the lease), the lease is not invalid even if a higher rent or a greater consideration could have been obtained and the necessary consent of the minister was not obtained … But on no basis does s 128(2) limit the jurisdiction of the court to examine the legality of the conduct of the council in granting the lease or to grant any proper declaratory relief; what it does do is to protect the title of CSSL from exposure to risk of the invalidity of the lease by reason of the failure of the council to obtain a required consent and precludes the grant of any relief impugning the validity of, or setting aside, the lease on this ground.

It should be pointed out, however, that in *Ex p Coker* the issue was not whether the disposal took effect on contract or conveyance, but the reference to the

a protection of title in the passage I have quoted lends some support for the view that it takes effect on the latter.

The other case in which there is a brief reference to the concept of disposal, although in the context of s 123 rather than s 128, is the decision of the Court of Appeal in *Trustees of the Chippenham Golf Club v North Wiltshire DC* (1991) 64 P & CR 527. The case in fact raised the question whether the council had power to grant an b option under the Local Government Act 1933, the predecessor of the 1972 Act. The court held that it did not, but in the course of giving his judgment (with which Neill and Woolf LJJ agreed), Scott LJ (at 532) expressed the view, obiter, that:

> 'It may be noticed that section 123 by comparison with sections 164 and c 165 of the 1933 Act considerably widens the powers of local authorities. "Dispose of" is a verb of comprehensive scope. I would accept that the grant of an option to purchase or, for that matter, to take a lease of land would be authorised by section 123(1).'

Mr Hobson relies strongly on this dictum. It certainly supports his contention d that the section confers a power to enter into an option, and that the grant of the option will constitute a 'disposal' within the meaning of the section. But for reasons I have already given, I do not agree with Mr Hobson that because the grant of an option is a disposal, the contract to sell must necessarily be treated likewise.

e A further question is whether considerations of policy would tend to favour one or other particular construction. Mr Hobson submits that since the section is plainly intended to protect third parties, there is a cogent argument that it will do so more effectively if the consent of the Secretary of State is obtained prior to the contract being made at all. There is considerable force in that submission, but as f against that, it can be countered that there is nothing in the applicant's construction, which would prevent the consent being obtained then. The council is clearly at liberty to obtain the consent before contract if it so wishes. The issue in my view is whether the statutory objective is better served if the third party purchaser is protected from the moment he enters into the contract or if his g agreement may be set aside, absent the Secretary of State's consent, any time up to completion. It seems to me that there is nothing intrinsically unjust or in conflict with the statutory purpose, in so far as it can be gleaned, in adopting the latter option. It means that once the purchaser has good title, that cannot be upset by the Secretary of State's failure to give consent, but that until that time h the purchaser remains vulnerable. Giving the provision a narrower rather than a wider meaning may also be justified by the consideration that it will sometimes preclude any effective remedy for what is plainly unlawful conduct.

I have not found this an easy matter, but taking all these considerations into account, in my judgment the better view is that the protection afforded by j s 128(2) applies only once completion has taken place. It follows that it does not apply in this case since the sale to the third party tenants had not been carried into effect. The applicant is accordingly entitled to the relief it seeks of having the decision quashed and the contracts set aside.

In case I am wrong about this, I shall consider the other two arguments advanced by Mr Rutledge.

Has the council acted unlawfully in ways falling outside the subsection?

Mr Rutledge contends that s 128(2) will apply only where the sole feature of the decision which renders it unlawful is the failure to obtain consent. I have no doubt that that is correct; the provision states in terms that the invalidity is not to arise 'by reason that any consent ... has not been given'. It is important to appreciate, however, that this is not the same as saying that the purchaser should be treated as if the consent had been given. That is not what the statute says. In my opinion the purchaser can use the provision as a shield to fend off any challenge that he has failed to obtain consent, but he cannot use it to fashion a sword entitling him to claim that he has consent.

This distinction is important. It can be tested by considering the arguments in this case. The applicant contends that the decision of the council is unlawful for a number of reasons including breach of fiduciary duty, *Wednesbury* unreasonableness, and for procedural errors. If the council had in fact obtained consent, or alternatively if the purchaser could rely upon s 128 to require the court to act as if consent had been given, this would in my judgment prevent certain of these claims being pursued. These would be claims alleging such legal defects as would effectively be remedied by the grant of consent. In my view they would include any defect which arises out of the failure to obtain best value, whether it is a blatant failure or one involving a breach of fiduciary duty. It seems to me that the Secretary of State has a wide discretion to give his consent and can do so even if the council has struck a balance between non-economic or social benefits on the one hand, and financial benefits on the other, which would put it in breach of its fiduciary duty at common law. If it were otherwise, this would involve assuming that Parliament must have intended that the Secretary of State could only give consent so as to validate a sale for less than the best price in circumstances where the courts would have held the agreement to be lawful at common law. That, in my view, is an improper construction of the provision, and is inconsistent with the broad statutory language. I consider that in giving his consent, the Secretary of State can take into account a wider range of considerations than would be open to the council at common law; he can spread the cloak of legality where it would not otherwise exist. Accordingly, if the section were to involve deeming consent to have been given, this would significantly limit the potential grounds of challenge. The consent would render a potentially unlawful disposal at common law lawful.

However, the subsection in my judgment does not go that far. It only relieves the purchaser from the *failure to obtain* consent. Accordingly, in so far as the applicant is able to identify breaches of the law going beyond or operating independently of that breach, the provision will not give any protection. This therefore raises the question of whether the allegations that the council acted unlawfully for reasons other than the failure to obtain consent are available in this case.

The claims in this case

Mr Rutledge submits that there are four breaches of law by the council in accepting the tenants' offer, quite independently of the failure to get the best price under s 123. First, he says that the council acted in breach of its fiduciary duty. Second, he says that it acted *Wednesbury* unreasonably in accepting the sum it did. The third and fourth grounds in my view are interrelated; the third ground is that there was a legitimate expectation that the council would hold an auction and that it would award the property to the highest bidder. It is alleged that at least a it should have heard representations from the applicant before deciding to resile from that course. The fourth ground was that the council had acted unfairly in not holding the auction as promised. In my view this adds nothing to the legitimate expectation argument. It is the existence of a legitimate expectation, which in my view creates any duty to act fairly, and this in turn requires that the party with the expectation is consulted before the expectation is frustrated. But b if there is no such expectation then I do not see any other basis for the council being under a duty to consult before changing its decision to take the sale to auction.

As I have already indicated, the council has not provided any proper explanation why it took the decision which it did. Prima facie I consider that the applicant has made out its claim that the council acted in breach of its fiduciary duty and there c is no evidence which effectively counters that allegation. I accept that in an appropriate case it is possible for a council successfully to contend that there are social or other benefits to the local community which outweigh the loss resulting from the failure to obtain the best price. The interests of the local taxpayers are not decisive but must be taken into account (see *Bromley LBC v Greater London* d *Council* [1982] 1 All ER 129, [1983] 1 AC 768). However, in the absence of any indication of what these advantages were perceived to be, I cannot speculate whether they existed or not. In general, however, in the absence of some such benefit, it will be a breach of the fiduciary duty if the council fails to obtain the best price for the local taxpayers (see *Bromley LBC v Greater London Council* [1982] 1 All ER 129 at 165, [1983] 1 AC 768 at 829 per Lord Diplock). I therefore hold that e the council is in breach of that duty.

For essentially the same reason I am compelled to find that it acted *Wednesbury* unreasonably. A rational council would not have rejected an offer which was £100,000 more favourable than the offer which it in fact accepted, in the absence at least of cogent countervailing considerations. The evidence does not enable f me to say what the relevant factors are which could render the decision a rational one.

Mr Hobson did not strongly resist this analysis. However, he said that these particular defects did not enable the applicant to surmount the hurdle of s 128. Initially I was inclined to agree with him, but on reflection I think that this g argument involves treating s 128 as though the court must assume that consent has been granted. If this were the proper effect of the section, I would agree with Mr Hobson, but for the reasons I have given, I do not believe that it is. It follows that for this reason also I consider that s 128 is not a barrier to the applicant obtaining the relief he seeks.

The procedural challenge, if made good, falls into a different category to the h other two allegations. This is because even if I am wrong in concluding that s 128 cannot remedy those breaches, any procedural breach would fall into a different category. It would not be capable of being remedied by the consent of the Secretary of State since it is not directly related to the failure to obtain the best price. Accordingly, as Mr Hobson accepted, it remains unaffected by the failure j to obtain that consent.

Was there a procedural failure in this case? It is said that there was a legitimate expectation arising from the fact that the agents for the council sent the auction information to the applicant and that the applicant acted upon that by following up and inspecting certain documents relating to the property. The argument was advanced on the basis that there was both what is termed a substantive and a procedural legitimate expectation. The former, it was submitted, prevented the council from resiling from its undertaking to hold an auction at all, unless there was an overriding public interest to justify the reversal. It was said that no such interest had been demonstrated here. The latter argument was that in any event any decision to revoke the decision to go to auction should have been taken only after consultation had been carried out.

I reject both these submissions. I do not believe that the mere giving of information about the auction constituted the creation of a legitimate expectation that the council would not thereafter choose to sell the property in some other way. It was not in my judgment a promise given specifically to the applicant or those similarly placed; it was merely a statement of the council's then intentions. The fact that the applicant took steps pursuant to the information in anticipation of the auction would assist it in demonstrating that it had acted on any representation made, but it does not of itself go to the existence of the representation. (Such reliance is in any event only relevant where the applicant is relying on the substantive concept of legitimate expectation; it has no relevance to the purely procedural doctrine: see *R v Falmouth and Truro Port Health Authority, ex p South West Water Ltd* [2000] 3 All ER 306 at 309, [2000] 3 WLR 1464 at 1467 per Simon Brown LJ.) Nor do I accept that there was a duty on the council to consult all those whom it might have known or suspected were potentially interested in purchasing the property at auction.

In short, I do not think that it was unfair for the council to change its mind, either at all or without giving the applicant the opportunity to make representations first. The challenge based on legitimate expectations therefore fails.

Was the proposed sale of a kind caught by s 128?

The argument here was that s 123 envisages just three types of lawful sale; the short-term lease, the sale for best value, and the sale with the Secretary of State's consent. Mr Rutledge submitted that s 128 applies only to cases where the authority intended to go down the consent route but for some reason failed to obtain the requisite consent. If the authority intended to go down another route, then the section is not applicable. In this case he submits that it did intend to go down the best value route and therefore s 128 could not bite.

I reject this argument. There is in my judgment no warrant for it in the statutory language. No distinction of any kind is made between the different circumstances in which consent might have been, but has not been, obtained. The third party purchaser is simply not concerned with the council's intentions at all. He is protected from any failure to obtain relevant consent, irrespective of why or in what circumstances there was a failure to obtain it. Moreover, I do not see how the principle could be applied in practice. In this very case it seems to me impossible to say which route the council intended to go down. In particular, it seems to me impossible to say, as the applicant must if this argument is to succeed, that the council here was intending to go down the best value route. Indeed, the evidence is to the contrary. The fact is that the council deliberately chose, for whatever justification, not to obtain best value. The notion that one can identify an unlawful act and say that, had it been lawful, it would have been carried out in one particular lawful way as opposed to another, is in my view false. For these reasons, I would reject this particular argument.

Conclusion

a In my view s 128(2) does not save the contract entered into in this case. There has never been a disposal within the meaning of the subsection, and in addition the applicant has in my judgment successfully contended that the council erred in law in ways not caught by the provision. Accordingly the applicant is entitled in my opinion to have the decision to sell to the tenants quashed, and to have the b contract declared invalid. I am not, however, prepared to issue mandamus to require the council to carry out an auction. In my view it would be wrong for me to dictate the particular route by which the council must ensure compliance with the law if and when it sells this property. I do not consider that the applicant had a substantive legitimate expectation that an auction would be held, and accordingly it would be wrong to compel the council to sell in that way as though it had.

Order accordingly.

Dilys Tausz Barrister.

Markfield Investments Ltd v Evans

a

COURT OF APPEAL, CIVIL DIVISION
SIMON BROWN, MUMMERY AND LATHAM LJJ
2, 9 NOVEMBER 2000

b

Limitation of action – Land – Adverse possession – Period of adverse possession – Owner bringing action for recovery of land – Action being struck out nine years later for want of prosecution – Owner bringing fresh action for recovery of land – Whether issue of writ in first action stopping time running in trespasser's favour for purposes of second action – Limitation Act 1980, s 15.

c

The respondent, E, was in exclusive occupation of land whose paper title was held by the appellant, M Ltd. E claimed to have been in continuous and exclusive occupation of the land since 1977, but M Ltd alleged that trespassers had been removed in 1978 and that inspections in 1979 had found the land unoccupied. In 1990 M Ltd's predecessor in title had commenced an action for recovery of the land, but that action had been dismissed in January 1999 for want of prosecution. In July 1999 M Ltd brought a fresh action for recovery of the land. On the determination of a preliminary issue, M Ltd contended that the issue of the writ in the 1990 action had stopped time running in E's favour for the purposes of the 12-year limitation period in s 15[a] of the Limitation Act 1980, and that accordingly E could not rely in the second action on her occupation of the property since the issue of the writ in the first action. That contention was rejected by the judge, and M Ltd appealed.

d

e

Held – Where proceedings for the recovery of land had been dismissed for want of prosecution, but the party holding the paper title subsequently brought a fresh action for recovery of that land, the issue of the writ in the first action did not, for the purposes of the second action, prevent time running in favour of the person in adverse possession. Rather, the writ merely prevented the true owner from being time-barred under s 15 of the 1980 Act for the purposes of the action which it had commenced, providing 12 years adverse possession had not already accrued. The period in possession after the issue of the writ in the first action was not to be ignored in the second action merely because that same period would have been ignored in the first action. For the purposes of any particular action, the issue of a writ in earlier proceedings was no more relevant than a demand for possession, and such a demand did not stop time running afresh. A conclusion to the contrary would mean that all the true owner would have to do to avoid adverse possession claims was issue (and perhaps serve) a writ every 12 years without more. It followed in the instant case that the preliminary issue had been decided correctly, and accordingly the appeal would be dismissed (see p 242 *j* to p 243 *d*, post).

f

g

h

BP Properties Ltd v Buckler (1987) 55 P & CR 337 and *Mount Carmel Investments Ltd v Peter Thurlow Ltd* [1988] 3 All ER 129 considered.

j

Notes

For the limitation period for the recovery of land, see 28 *Halsbury's Laws* (4th edn reissue) para 919.

---

a Section 15, so far as material, is set out at p 240 *g*, post

a For the Limitation Act 1980, s 15, see 24 *Halsbury's Statutes* (4th edn) (1998 reissue) 716.

Cases referred to in judgments

BP Properties Ltd v Buckler (1987) 55 P & CR 337, CA.

b *Fairweather v St Marylebone Property Co Ltd* [1962] 2 All ER 288, [1963] AC 510, [1962] 2 WLR 1020, HL.

Mount Carmel Investments Ltd v Peter Thurlow Ltd [1988] 3 All ER 129, [1988] 1 WLR 1078, CA.

Cases also cited or referred to in skeleton arguments

c *Buckinghamshire CC v Moran* [1989] 2 All ER 225, [1990] 1 Ch 623, CA.

Powell v McFarlane (1979) 38 P & CR 452.

R B Policies at Lloyd's v Butler [1949] 2 All ER 226, [1950] 1 KB 76.

Appeal

d The appellants, Markfield Investments Ltd, appealed with permission of Swinton Thomas LJ granted on 11 July 2000 from the decision of Judge Samuels QC at Truro County Court on 22 May 2000 whereby, on the determination of a preliminary issue, he held that the claim by the respondent, Barbara Evans, to have acquired adverse possession of land whose paper title was held by the e appellants had not been interrupted by the issue of a writ in a previous action for the recovery of that land, brought by the appellants' predecessor in title on 7 August 1990, which had been struck out for want of prosecution on 5 January 1999. The facts are set out in the judgment of Simon Brown LJ.

Mark Treneer (instructed by *Hancock Caffin*, Truro) for the appellants.

f *Christopher Elliot* (instructed by *Follett Stock*, Truro) for the respondent.

Cur adv vult

9 November 2000. The following judgments were delivered.

g

SIMON BROWN LJ.

1. This appeal raises a short point of law in connection with adverse possession. The appellants hold the paper title to the land in question; the respondent is in exclusive occupation of it. The appeal is brought against the order of Judge h Samuels QC in the Truro County Court on 22 May 2000 made on the hearing of a preliminary issue, ruling—

> 'that the [respondent's] claim to have acquired adverse possession of the relevant premises was not interrupted by the issue and subsequent dismissal for want of prosecution of the action by Lym Ltd against the [respondent].'

j

The appellants, let me explain at once, are the successors in title to Lym Ltd (a company in liquidation) (whom I shall call Lym). The action by Lym against the respondent (the first action) was brought on 7 August 1990 and dismissed for want of prosecution on 5 January 1999. It is the appellants' contention that the mere fact of issuing (or perhaps issuing and serving) proceedings for the recovery of land stops time running in favour of the person in adverse possession.

2. Although the point arising is a pure point of law, I will briefly sketch in the factual background so as to show its practical consequences in the present circumstances.

3. The relevant property is a dwelling house and land known as 'Riverside', Weir, Restronguet, Falmouth, in Cornwall. The respondent claims to have been in continuous and exclusive occupation of the property since the summer of 1977, jointly with a Mr Hoskins until 1989 and thereafter alone. The appellants say that in 1978 Lym removed from the land a number of trespassers then occupying it, and that on each of three inspection visits subsequently made in 1979 they found the property unoccupied.

4. Early in 1990 Lym instructed contractors to carry out works of clearance in the garden. The respondent acknowledges as much but denies that these works were inconsistent with her continuing exclusive possession. She furthermore asserts that she had in any event by 1990 been in continuous adverse possession for 12 years and was accordingly entitled to the land as against Lym.

5. On 7 August 1990, as stated, Lym commenced the first action which was ultimately dismissed for want of prosecution on 5 January 1999. The present action was then brought on 22 July 1999 and it is, of course, in this second action that the preliminary issue was directed to be tried. Whatever its outcome, either side could still succeed in their claim for possession. But whereas if the appeal fails the respondent will only have to establish that Lym's clearance work in 1990 did not end her exclusive occupation of the land (as an alternative to 12 years' occupation prior to the clearance work), if it succeeds she will have to establish that she had been in continuous occupation since before August 1978 (despite Lym's evidence that the property was vacant in 1978/1979).

6. Those considerations, however, are essentially by the way. The sole issue before us is whether the first action, despite its dismissal for want of prosecution, nevertheless had the effect of preventing the respondent in the second action from praying in aid her continued occupation during the eight-and-a-half years whilst that first action remained alive as years of adverse possession.

7. Before addressing the argument it is convenient first to set out the material provisions of the Limitation Act 1980.

8. Section 15(1) provides:

> 'No action shall be brought by any person to recover any land after the expiration of twelve years from the date on which the right of action accrued to him or, if it first accrued to some person through whom he claims, to that person.'

9. Section 17 provides:

> 'Subject to ... (b) section 75 of the Land Registration Act 1925; at the expiration of the period prescribed by this Act for any person to bring an action to recover land ... the title of that person to the land shall be extinguished.'

10. Section 75 of the Land Registration Act 1925 provides that the paper owners' registered title is not extinguished by the adverse possession but is held on trust for the adverse possessor who may then apply to have himself registered with the title.

11. Schedule 1 to the 1980 Act supplements s 15 by dictating when a cause of action accrues. The relevant paragraphs are:

a '1. Where the person bringing an action to recover land, or some person through whom he claims, has been in possession of the land, and has while entitled to the land been dispossessed or discontinued his possession, the right of action shall be treated as having accrued on the date of the dispossession or discontinuance …

b 8.—(1) No right of action to recover land shall be treated as accruing unless the land is in the possession of some person in whose favour the period of limitation can run (referred to below in this paragraph as "adverse possession"); and where under the preceding provisions of this Schedule any such right of action is treated as accruing on a certain date and no person is in adverse possession on that date, the right of action shall not be treated as accruing unless and until adverse possession is taken of the land.

c (2) Where a right of action to recover land has accrued and after its accrual, before the right is barred, the land ceases to be in adverse possession, the right of action shall no longer be treated as having accrued and no fresh right of action shall be treated as accruing unless and until the land is again taken into adverse possession.'

d 12. Essentially, therefore, the true owners' cause of action accrues once his land is in adverse possession, and continues to be treated as accrued unless and until the land ceases to be in adverse possession. Adverse possession may cease (a) by the occupier vacating the premises, (b) by the occupier giving a written acknowledgment of the true owner's title (see ss 29 and 30 of the Act), (c) by the true owner's grant of a e tenancy or licence to the occupier (even a unilateral licence (see *BP Properties Ltd v Buckler* (1987) 55 P & CR 337), or (d) by the true owner physically re-entering upon the land. Once, however, the land has been in continuous adverse possession for 12 years, the owner is barred by s 15 from bringing an action to recover it and, indeed, his title to the land (assuming, as here, that it is registered) becomes held in trust for the f adverse possessor who may himself apply to have the title registered in his own name.

13. On the face of the legislation, therefore, the true owner can succeed in an action to recover land provided he brings his action within 12 years; otherwise not. Apply that approach to this case. Had the appellants pursued the first action and proved that it had been brought before the respondent had enjoyed a continuous period of 12 g years' adverse possession, they would have been held entitled to recover the land. Because, however, they did not pursue and succeed upon that first action, they must now depend upon a second action and prove that it in turn was brought before the respondent had been in continuous adverse possession for 12 years.

14. How, then, does Mr Treneer for the appellants seek to benefit from the h abortive first action? As I understand his argument, it is that adverse possession ceases not only in the four ways I have already identified, but also by the issue (or perhaps issue and service) of a claim for possession. Such a proceeding, he submits, is equivalent to re-entry onto the land: it constitutes a form of constructive possession by the true owner, sufficient at any rate to bring to an end the occupier's exclusive possession of the land.

j 15. In support of this argument Mr Treneer relies upon a passage in Cheshire and Burn's *Modern Law of Real Property* (16th edn, 2000) p 987 reading:

'THE METHODS BY WHICH TIME MAY BE PREVENTED FROM RUNNING

Time which has begun to run under the Act is stopped, either when the owner asserts his right or when his right is admitted by the adverse possessor.

A. ASSERTION OF OWNER'S RIGHT

Assertion of right occurs when the owner takes legal proceedings or makes an effective entry onto the land.' a

16. No authority is cited for that proposition but I have no doubt that it is intended to reflect the views of this court expressed by Dillon LJ in *Buckler's* case:

> 'If proceedings to recover land are begun before there has been 12 years' b adverse possession—e.g. if they are begun in the eleventh year—then the right of action is, on the wording of ... section 15 of the 1980 Act, unaffected by the subsequent expiration of the 12-years period while the proceedings are pending. If that is so, it could not, in my judgment, be a correct reading of [s 17 of the 1980 Act], to hold that the title of the plaintiff to the land is c extinguished while an action for the recovery of the land, launched in due time, is still pending. On Lord Radcliffe's approach [in *Fairweather v St Marylebone Property Co Ltd* [1962] 2 All ER 288 at 291, [1963] AC 510 at 535] the title can only then be extinguished if or in so far as it cannot be established and vindicated by *the action* which has been brought in due time. So again, if an action to recover land is brought within the 12 years and judgment for d possession is given *in that action,* albeit after the expiration of the 12 years, it would be idle to suppose that the judgment for possession could, because of the expiration of the 12 years, never be enforced. The judgment must be enforceable if *the action* was started in due time.' (See (1987) 55 P & CR 337 at 344; my emphasis.)

e

17. In short, both Cheshire and Burn, and Dillon LJ, are making the point that, once proceedings are brought in time, the occupier cannot then seek to rely on the subsequent passage of time to establish within those proceedings a defence by way of adverse possession.

18. Nor is any support for the appellants' argument to be found in Nicholls LJ's f judgment in *Mount Carmel Investments Ltd v Peter Thurlow Ltd* [1988] 3 All ER 129 at 135, [1988] 1 WLR 1078 at 1085:

> '... no one, either lawyer or non-lawyer, would think that a householder ceases to be in possession of his house simply by reason of receiving a demand that he should quit ... On [the owner's] argument, time starts to run g afresh by making a demand for possession. That is in flat contradiction to the long-recognised position and the statutory scheme where a squatter is in possession of another's land. Unless the squatter vacates or gives a written acknowledgment to the owner, the owner has to issue his writ within the prescribed time limit. Otherwise he is barred, because by s 15(1) he is barred h from bringing any action to recover the land after the expiration of the 12-year period.'

19. None of these writings address the situation arising on the instant appeal where the owner fails in his action but nevertheless seeks to rely upon the mere fact of having brought it to make good a second action. j

20. That seems to me impossible on the plain wording of the statute. With regard to any particular action the relevant time, and the only relevant time, for consideration of adverse possession is that which has expired before such action is brought. That is the language of s 15 and, as Dillon LJ explained, that is the effect of the legislation. The fallacy in Mr Treneer's argument is in supposing that because one ignores in the first action any adverse possession which follows the

a writ, so too that same adverse possession falls to be ignored in the second action. That is just not so and there is nothing in the statute or authorities to suggest that it is. For the purposes of any particular action, the issue of a writ in earlier proceedings is no more relevant than a demand for possession. In the *Mount Carmel Investments* case such a demand was held not to start time running afresh; no more would the service (still less the mere issue) of some earlier writ. Were b it otherwise, as the respondent points out, all the true owner would have to do to avoid adverse possession claims is issue (and perhaps serve) a writ every 12 years without more.

21. In summary, there is no question of the issue of a writ 'stopping time from running' (itself a non-statutory concept and perhaps a misleading rather than helpful expression). The issue of a writ, for the purposes of the action which it c begins, prevents the true owner from being time barred under s 15 providing 12 years' adverse possession have not already accrued. It serves no other purpose.

22. It follows that I would reject Mr Treneer's argument, hold that the judge below correctly decided the preliminary issue (although it was perhaps not formulated in the most helpful terms), and dismiss this appeal.

d

MUMMERY.

23. I agree.

LATHAM.

24. I also agree.

Appeal dismissed.

Dilys Tausz Barrister.

R v Central Criminal Court, ex parte Bright
R v Central Criminal Court, ex parte Alton
R v Central Criminal Court, ex parte Rusbridger

QUEEN'S BENCH DIVISION, DIVISIONAL COURT

JUDGE LJ, MAURICE KAY AND GIBBS JJ

3, 4, 21 JULY 2000

Criminal evidence – Special procedure material – Application for production of special procedure material – Access conditions – Whether judge having to be satisfied personally that access conditions fulfilled – Whether privilege against self-incrimination precluding making of production order – Police and Criminal Evidence Act 1984, s 9, Sch 1, paras 1, 2, 4.

S, a former employee of the Security Service, was under investigation for alleged breaches of the Official Secrets Act 1989. He had alleged that the British security services had been involved in an unsuccessful plot to assassinate a foreign head of state, which had resulted in the deaths of innocent bystanders. That allegation was denied by the Foreign Secretary in a radio interview. The following day, the Guardian newspaper printed an article analysing the Foreign Secretary's remarks and identifying a number of issues arising from S's assertions. Two days later, a letter attributed to S, responding to the article, was published in the Guardian's correspondence column (S's letter). That letter was sent by an e-mail which was deleted on the day of the publication in accordance with the newspaper's usual practice. The following Sunday, the Observer newspaper published an article, written by B, which referred to a letter sent by S to the Home Secretary, setting out full details of the alleged plot (the Home Secretary's letter), and made it clear that S had disclosed to B the names of two serving intelligence officers allegedly involved in the plot. A few days later, S made a statement on his website, describing a meeting between him and B, criticising the latter's article, complaining of the inability of journalists to 'copy accurately out of the documents I give them', and asserting that he had sent a copy of the Home Secretary's letter to the Observer. Subsequently, the police applied under s 9[a] of and para 4 of Sch 1 to the Police and Criminal Evidence Act 1984 for a production order in respect of special procedure material, seeking from the editor of the Guardian, R, all files, documents and records relating to S's letter in an attempt to discover the latter's e-mail address. They also applied for similar orders against B and the editor of the Observer, A, in respect of all files, documents, accounts and other records relating to B's article. Paragraph 4 of Sch 1 provided that an order under that paragraph was an order that the person who appeared to the circuit judge to be in possession of the material to which the application related 'shall—(a) produce it to a constable for him to take away; or (b) give a constable access to it'. By virtue of para 1[b], such an order, which was enforceable by penal

a Section 9, so far as material, provides: '(1) A constable may obtain access to excluded material or special procedure material for the purposes of a criminal investigation by making an application under Schedule 1 below and in accordance with that Schedule ... '

b Paragraph 1 is set out at p 258 *d*, post

sanction, could only be made if a circuit judge was satisfied that the access conditions in para 2[c] or para 3 were fulfilled. The access conditions in para 2 included requirements that there were reasonable grounds for believing that a serious arrestable offence had been committed (para 2(a)(i)), that the material was on premises specified in the application (para 2(a)(ii)) and that it was likely to be relevant evidence (para 2(a)(iv)). They also included a requirement that it was in the public interest that the material should be produced or that access to it should be given, having regard to the benefit likely to accrue to the investigation if the material was obtained, and the circumstances under which the person in possession of the material held it (para 2(c)). In support of the applications, evidence was given by a police officer, F, who, though having virtually no personal knowledge of the case, asserted that the Observer appeared to be in possession of material covered by the 1989 Act, that the disclosure of that material in B's article might constitute a breach of the Act, that he had reasonable grounds to believe that B had committed such a breach and the inquiry was hampered by lack of information in respect of S's letter. Another officer, who had much greater knowledge of the facts, was present throughout the hearing, but his presence was not disclosed. A witness for the Guardian gave uncontested evidence that it was extremely unlikely that a copy of S's e-mail would still exist on a backup tape. The judge nevertheless concluded that such material might be recoverable by persons of appropriate expertise, held that the para 2 access conditions were fulfilled in each application and proceeded to make the orders sought against the editors, R and A, and B. On their applications for judicial review, the court considered whether the police evidence had been adequately prepared, whether a judge could rely on the reasonable opinion of a police officer in determining whether the access conditions had been satisfied, whether the public interest considerations in para 2(c) were open-ended or confined to those set out in that provision and whether the privilege against self-incrimination precluded the making of an order under Sch 1 in a case where that privilege could be invoked.

Held – (1) While acknowledging the sensitivities which could arise in cases involving national security, a judge could not, generally speaking, proceed on the basis of a bare assertion by a police officer on an application under s 9 of the 1984 Act. If, in the instant case, public disclosure of details of S's offence would itself have prejudiced national security, a properly drafted, careful summary of the relevant factors would probably have sufficed. If the national interest would have been prejudiced by any publication at all, arrangements could have been made to provide the judge with necessary evidence by adopting a procedure similar to that used in public interest immunity applications. It was not satisfactory for the officer giving evidence to the court and attending for the purposes of being cross-examined to know as little about the case as F. It was equally unsatisfactory that the presence of an officer who knew rather more than F did was not disclosed. The application demanded full and proper disclosure. All those matters would have been relevant to the exercise of the judge's discretion, and were also directly relevant to the question whether the access conditions had been established (see p 255 *d* to *g*, p 269 *j* to p 270 *c* and p 276 *j*, post).

(2) Having regard to the wording of para 1 of Sch 1 to the 1984 Act, it was clear that the judge had to be satisfied personally that the statutory requirements had been established when determining whether to make an order under that

c Paragraph 2 is set out at p 258 *e* to *g*, post

Schedule. Thus he could not simply ask himself whether the decision of the police officer making the application was reasonable, nor whether it would be susceptible to judicial review on *Wednesbury* grounds. The purpose of para 1 was to interpose between the opinion of the police officer seeking the order and the consequences to the individual or organisation to whom the order was addressed the safeguard of a judgment and decision of a circuit judge. It was equally clear that the constable making the application had to satisfy the judge that the relevant set of conditions in para 2 was established. That appeared to follow as an elementary result of the fact that an order would force or oblige the individual against whom it was made to act under compulsion when, without the order, he would be free to do otherwise. Moreover, grounds for belief and not merely grounds for suspicion were required and the material to be produced or disclosed was not merely general information which might be helpful to police inquiries but evidence in the sense in which that term was applied in the Crown Court, ie relevant and admissible at trial (see p 259 *f* to p 260 *a*, p 269 *j* to p 270 *c* and p 276 *j*, post); *IRC v Rossminster Ltd* [1980] 1 All ER 80 considered.

(3) On its true construction, para 2(c) of Sch 1 to the 1984 Act was not an open-ended public interest condition, and was instead restricted to matters referred to in that provision. Such matters as freedom of expression and (Gibbs J dissenting) the privilege against self-incrimination fell to be considered only in the context of the statutorily conferred judicial discretion once the judge was satisfied that the specific access conditions had been satisfied. In exercising that discretion, the judge might also consider, for example, the effect of the order on third parties, the antiquity of the matters under investigation and an apparent disproportion between what might possibly be gained by the production of journalistic material and the offence to which it was said to relate, to the potential stifling of public debate. Premises were not to be entered by the forces of authority or the state to deter or diminish, inhibit or stifle the exercise of an individual's right to free speech or the press of its freedom to investigate and inform. However, while he had to be alert to the need to safeguard basic freedoms, the judge had to acknowledge simultaneously the public interest which underpinned the legislation, namely that crime should be discouraged and those responsible for crime should be detected and brought to justice (see p 260 *f* to p 261 *c*, p 263 *g*, p 272 *g* and p 278 *c* to *f*, post); *Entick v Carrington* [1558–1774] All ER Rep 41 considered.

(4) Although the risk of self-incrimination was to be taken into account in the exercise of the judge's discretion under para 1 of Sch 1 to the 1984 Act, an order could be made under that Schedule (Judge LJ dissenting) even though it would or might oblige the person against whom the order was directed to incriminate himself. Parliament had laid down a detailed code for controlling the circumstances in which a production order might be made in relation to journalistic material. It did not include an exception for material which might incriminate the journalist (see p 266 *h*, p 275 *d e* and p 277 *j* to p 278 *a*, post); *R v Hertfordshire CC, ex p Green Environmental Industries Ltd* [2000] 1 All ER 773 considered.

(5) In the instant case, the application by R would be allowed, and the order against him quashed, since the para 2 access conditions had not been fulfilled. As regards to the orders made against B and A, the para 2 access conditions had been satisfied only in respect of the Home Secretary's letter. The risk of self-incrimination was non-existent in respect of that letter and there was no realistic possibility that a production order would stultify the proper functioning of the press. Moreover, the public interest would be properly served by an order limited (Maurice Kay J

a dissenting) to that single document. Accordingly, save in that respect, the applications by B and A would also be allowed (see p 268 *b*, p 269 c to *e*, p 275 *h* to p 276 *h* and p 278 *g h*, post).

Per Judge LJ and Gibbs J. The distinction between the requirement to produce documents under para 4(a) of Sch 1 to the 1984 Act and the requirement to give access to them under para 4(b) does not diminish the coercive quality of the b procedure. Thus an order requiring a journalist only to give 'access' to material in his possession does not eliminate the potential for self-incrimination (see p 266 *f* to *h* and p 277 *g*, post).

Notes

For orders for the production of special procedure material, see 11(1) *Halsbury's* c *Laws* (4th edn reissue) para 677.

For the Police and Criminal Evidence Act 1984, s 9, Sch 1, paras 1, 2, 4, see 12 *Halsbury's Statutes* (4th edn) (1997 reissue) 813, 882, 883.

Cases referred to in judgments

d *A-G v Guardian Newspapers Ltd* (No 2) [1988] 3 All ER 545, [1990] 1 AC 109, [1988] 3 WLR 776, HL.

Allenet de Ribemont v France (1995) 20 EHRR 557, ECt HR.

Associated Provincial Picture Houses Ltd v Wednesbury Corp [1947] 2 All ER 680, [1948] 1 KB 223, CA.

Derbyshire CC v Times Newspapers Ltd [1993] 1 All ER 1011, [1993] AC 534, [1993] e 2 WLR 449, HL.

Entick v Carrington (1765) 19 State Tr 1029, [1558–1774] All ER Rep 41.

Fayed v UK (1994) 18 EHRR 393, ECt HR.

Funke v France (1993) 16 EHRR 297, ECt HR.

IRC v Rossminster Ltd [1980] 1 All ER 80, [1980] AC 952, [1980] 2 WLR 1, HL.

f *R v Bristol Crown Court, ex p Bristol Press and Picture Agency Ltd* (1986) 85 Cr App Rep 190, DC.

R v Crown Court at Lewes, ex p Hill (1990) 93 Cr App Rep 60, DC.

R v Crown Court at Northampton, ex p DPP (1991) 93 Cr App Rep 376, DC.

R v Director of Serious Fraud Office, ex p Smith [1992] 3 All ER 456, [1993] AC 1, [1992] 3 WLR 66, HL.

g *R v Hertfordshire CC, ex p Green Environmental Industries Ltd* [2000] 1 All ER 773, [2000] 2 WLR 373, HL.

R v Norwich Crown Court, ex p Chethams [1991] COD 271, DC.

R v Secretary of State for the Home Dept, ex p Simms [1999] 3 All ER 400, [1999] 3 WLR 328, HL.

h *Reynolds v Times Newspapers Ltd* [1999] 4 All ER 609, [1999] 3 WLR 1010, HL.

Saunders v UK (1997) 23 EHRR 313, ECt HR.

Serves v France (1999) 28 EHRR 265, ECt HR.

Verrall v Great Yarmouth BC [1981] QB 202, [1980] 3 WLR 258, *affd* [1980] 1 All ER 839 [1981] QB 202, [1980] 3 WLR 258, CA.

j

Applications for judicial review

R v Central Criminal Court, ex p Bright; R v Central Criminal Court, ex p Alton

Martin Bright, a correspondent of the Observer newspaper, and Roger Alton, the newspaper's editor, applied for judicial review of orders made by Judge Stephens QC at the Central Criminal Court on 17 March 2000 under s 9 of and Sch 1 to the

Police and Criminal Evidence Act 1984 requiring them to produce to the police all files, documents and accounts and other records in relation to an article entitled 'Two spies named in Libya plot', published in the Observer on 27 February 2000. The facts are set out in the judgment of Judge LJ.

R v Central Criminal Court, ex p Rusbridger

Alan Rusbridger, the editor of the Guardian newspaper, applied for judicial review of an order made by Judge Stephens QC at the Central Criminal Court on 17 March 2000 under s 9 of and Sch 1 to the Police and Criminal Evidence Act 1984 requiring him to produce to the police all files, documents and other records concerning a letter published in the newspaper's correspondence column on 17 February 2000. The facts are set out in the judgment of Judge LJ.

Michael Tugendhat QC (instructed by *Jan Johannes*) for Alan Rusbridger and Roger Alton.

Ben Emmerson QC (instructed by *Birnberg Peirce & Partners*) for Martin Bright.

Clare Montgomery QC and Ian Leist (instructed by the *Crown Prosecution Service*) for the Crown.

JUDGE LJ.

1. These are separate but linked applications for judicial review of the orders made on 17 March 2000 at the Central Criminal Court by His Honour Judge Martin Stephens QC under s 9 of and para 2 of Sch 1 to the Police and Criminal Evidence Act 1984.

2. In the course of careful and wide-ranging submissions by Mr Michael Tugendhat QC and Mr Ben Emmerson QC it was suggested that the applications raised important issues about the freedom of the press in this country. So, without providing a detailed or comprehensive summary of all the events which led up to the applications, I must sketch in some of the background.

3. It is fairly well known that from about 1997 a former employee of the Security Service, David Shayler, has been under investigation for alleged breaches of the Official Secrets Act 1989, and, to use colloquial language, that he is wanted by the police in this country. He is believed to be resident in France and earlier extradition proceedings against him in the courts of that country were unsuccessful.

4. Mr Shayler's activities have given rise to considerable public debate. Perhaps the most alarming feature is his allegation that in 1996 British Security Services were involved in a failed bomb plot to assassinate Colonel Gaddafi, the head of state of Libya, which nevertheless resulted in the deaths of innocent bystanders. This allegation was dismissed by the Foreign Secretary in 1998 as pure fantasy. If true it is difficult to overestimate its enormity: a conspiracy to murder the head of another state, resulting not in his death, but in the deaths of innocent people who were not its intended targets. Again, if true, the circumstances in which such a plan was conceived and developed, and the identity of those who were informed about and approved it, or turned a blind eye to it, and equally, those who were deliberately kept in ignorance, raise critical public issues about the activities of the Security Services and those responsible for them.

5. If false, the fact that the allegations were made at all is itself inevitably damaging to the Security Services.

6. There are those who would instinctively believe the worst of the Security Services and, whatever the evidence, would remain invincibly confident that Mr Shayler had lifted a veil over an obscure and dark corner of public life. In their

a minds, at any rate, something of the smear would stick. No doubt, too, even false allegations of this kind can be used, and would continue to be used, to attack the Security Services, and to undermine public confidence in their activities. Nevertheless, in its own way, the refutation of this allegation is also a matter of public importance. The story of the Gaddafi bomb plot is either true or it is false, and unless there are compelling reasons of national security, the public is entitled b to know the facts, and as the eyes and ears of the public, journalists are entitled to investigate and report the facts, as I hope they would, dispassionately and fairly, without pre-judgment or selectivity.

7. Mr Shayler is a regular newspaper correspondent. The first article drawn to our attention is a letter dated 28 September 1997 published in the Mail on Sunday in the form of a letter to the Prime Minister. Subsequent letters or articles by or c about him have appeared in The Times, the Independent, the Evening Standard, the Sunday Times, and the Daily Telegraph (an interview). He has been the subject of a Panorama programme. Throughout 1999 he wrote articles for Punch magazine. He has a website (www.shayler.com) to which he makes written contributions on a regular basis and which therefore are generally accessible.

d 8. In 1999, 'MI5 and the Shayler affair' was the subject of a new book entitled *Defending the Realm: MI5 and the Shayler Affair* by Mark Hollingsworth and Nick Fielding. In view of the material which was to emerge later one passage in Ch 6, 'Bombings, Assassination and the Bugging of a Journalist' requires quotation:

> 'Shayler later said, I briefed my boss at MI5 during the course of the e operation on planning and funding. One other officer in MI5 was fully briefed on the operation. The three MI6 officers were called PT16, PT16 Ops B, and the man meeting and running Tunworth, PT16B. As Shayler told … "PT16B, who was my opposite number in SIS [Secret Intelligence Service] (MI6), started to talk about how this guy was involved in trying to plan an assassination attempt on Gaddafi, using a Libyan Islamic extremist group".'

f

9. On Sunday 13 February 2000 the debate was revived. An article from the Press Association purporting to link MI6 with an attempt to assassinate the Libyan leader Muammar Gaddafi was posted on the Internet. It ran under the headline 'MPs demand enquiry into Gaddafi assassination plot'. The article went on to refer to the first emergence of such claims—

g

> 'when former MI5 officer David Shayler began alleging that the security services were out of control. He claimed in a BBC Panorama programme that his opposite number in MI6, code named PT16B, had told him Britain paid about £100,000 to back the plot … Paris-based Mr Shayler, who fought h off a British extradition attempt, claimed that the British Government had colluded in the details of deaths of innocent civilians.'

10. The report went on to record the Foreign Secretary's dismissal of the allegations, and the demand for an inquiry 'into the affair' by the Shadow Foreign Secretary and the Liberal Democrat foreign affairs and defence spokesman.

j 11. Mr Wadham, director of Liberty, was said to have called for a Parliamentary Committee 'with real teeth' to oversee the work of the Security Services.

12. A very long article, entitled 'Cook misled public over Libya plot', appeared in the Sunday Times for the same date. In this article references were again made to the claims by Shayler and the circumstances in which he was told, and by whom (PT16B), of the plot. The vigorous denial by the Foreign Office of these claims was recorded. The article ended by noting that the Sunday Times had

complied with a request by the Secretary of the Government's Defence, Press and Broadcast Advisory Committee 'not to print the address of the website' on which the report was published.

a

13. On the following morning both the Birmingham Post and the Scotsman published articles to similar effect.

14. Perhaps inevitably, given the importance of the issues, on the same day the Foreign Secretary, Mr Robin Cook, made himself available for interview on the BBC Today programme. In the course of the interview he is recorded as saying that he was 'absolutely satisfied that the previous Foreign Secretary did not authorise an assassination attempt' adding:

b

> '... the Secret Intelligence Service had never put forward such a proposal for an assassination attempt, and in my time in office I have never seen any evidence that SIS is interested in such an escapade.'

c

15. On the following day, 15 February, the Guardian newspaper printed an article by Richard Norton-Taylor, 'Words of a Weasel', analysing the Foreign Secretary's remarks and identifying a number of issues arising from David Shayler's assertions. He said that—

d

> 'you do not need to take all of Shayler's claims at face value to suggest that the episode raises serious questions about MI6's lack of accountability. Shayler, exiled in Paris, will be delighted to know that the cross party parliamentary intelligence committee—which in the past has dismissed his allegations as nothing more than disaffected rantings—will raise the matter at a meeting today.'

e

16. On 17 February, a letter attributed to David Shayler, giving the address, 'Paris, France', was printed in the correspondence column of the Guardian newspaper. The letters column contains this written assurance:

f

> 'We do not publish letters where only an email address is supplied; please include a full postal address and a reference to the relevant article. If you do not want your email address published, please say so. We may edit letters.'

17. Under the heading 'MI6 and Gadaffi', the letter reads:

g

> '"Shayler's apparent exaggeration gave Cook an easy way out", asserts Richard Norton Taylor (Words of a weasel, February 15th) about the MI6 report which has appeared on the internet. I would like to confirm that the report is genuine and that its source was Tunworth, who passed his information to PT16/B (an MI6 officer). PT16/B explained to me that MI6 put it out to Whitehall that MI6's customers would be informed of the planned coup but would not be alerted to MI6's involvement. I would like to make it clear that I have exaggerated nothing. I have never claimed the CX report in question confirmed that MI6 funded the plot. The coup plan it discusses does though match exactly the account I gave of the Gaddafi plot in Secrets and Lies, a document I prepared to defend myself in June 1999. I have pointed out that Robin Cook told the Frost programme of August 9 1998: "There was no Government inspired plan to assassinate Colonel Gadaffi. There was no (MI6) proposal to do it and I am fairly clear that there has never been any (MI6) involvement". The CX report demonstrates that an MI6 agent was involved in a plot to assassinate Colonel Gaddafi. All MI6 agents are run by at least one officer so, by extension, an MI6 officer was involved.'

h

j

a 18. There is nothing to suggest that the Guardian solicited or invited the letter. It simply received a letter from one of its readers and the editor (Mr Alan Rusbridger) decided that it should be published. In view of the comments directed at Mr Shayler personally, two days earlier, it was perfectly reasonable to publish his response. Simultaneously, however, it was decided to omit from the published letter a number of matters considered to be 'political rantings' which b failed to advance the public debate. So the letter was edited accordingly.

19. Mr Shayler did not seek confidentiality, and, as far as the evidence goes, he did not expressly accept the invitation at the head of the letters column to indicate that he did not want his e-mail address published.

20. The Metropolitan Police Special Branch, responsible for the investigation into the activities of Shayler, contacted the legal representative of the Guardian c newspaper on 18 February, informing her of the investigation. By letter dated 19 February (apparently sent on the 18th itself) her assistance was sought:

> '... with this investigation ... [we] request from you any and all information relating to the publication of this letter which may be in your possession or control, that may assist the enquiry.'

d

21. By letter dated 21 February the legal department of the Guardian and the Observer responded that: '1. The Guardian does not possess the original letter. 2. We were not sent any additional documents ...'

22. It concludes:

e

> 'As the letter from David Shayler was published in any event, it is unlikely that a copy of the original would add anything to your investigation. In any event, the Guardian does not have the original letter.'

23. On Saturday 26 February, before the Observer for the following day was published, the Treasury Solicitor and MI5 made a number of telephone calls to f the Observer which, according to a statement by Shayler on his website, followed a contact he had made with MI5. According to a subsequent letter from the legal adviser of the Observer, MI5 saw the following day's newspaper in draft. No effort was made to prevent publication. So, on 27 February, an article was published on the front page of the Observer newspaper under the headline 'Two spies named in Libya plot', and written by Martin Bright, the Observer's home g affairs correspondent.

24. The lengthy article describes Shayler as the 'renegade MI5 agent' and suggests that he had—

h

> 'dramatically escalated his battle with the Government when he named two serving intelligence officers ... involved in a covert operation to assassinate Libyan dictator Colonel Muammar Gaddafi.'

The article claims that the names of the agents involved in the plot—

j

> 'have been disclosed to the Observer, but for legal reasons we are prevented from publishing them. News that Shayler is revealing the identities of agents will send shockwaves through the Intelligence Services ... It will also intensify the Government's determination to pursue the errant agent, currently in exile in Paris, through the courts.'

25. The article then refers to a letter, for reasons which will appear crucial in these applications, sent by Shayler to the Home Secretary, Jack Straw, with 'full details of the alleged plot on 24th November last year', speaks of a 'weekend of

high drama', and purports to include a quotation directly from Shayler himself in Paris, adding that he claimed that he had 'attended several high-level meetings between MI5 and MI6 throughout the autumn of 1997 at which the plot was discussed openly'. *a*

26. The article concludes:

> 'In the past month Shayler has increased the intensity of his campaign for an amnesty to allow him to return to Britain. He is also poised to release more details about MI5 reports into the bombing of the Israeli Embassy in 1994.' *b*

27. On 29 February Mr Shayler made a long statement on his website, purporting to be a narrative account of events following a meeting at an unspecified location which had taken place with Mr Bright on 24 February, 'to brief him on the issues around my case'. He was plainly extremely dissatisfied with the article in the Observer and ended by recording that he would not be— *c*

> 'working with the Observer again, partly because of its representation of my story and partly because of the basic inaccuracies in the front page piece. Journalists these days, it seems, cannot even copy accurately out of the documents I give them. I fail to understand why a newspaper like the Observer feels the need to attack a whistle blower who has stood up against the Intelligence Services ... No wonder the Observer's circulation has plummeted so rapidly in recent years.' *d*

28. The article includes assertions by Shayler that on 25 February he sent a copy of the submission he made to the government to the Observer, and that Bright had telephoned him to say that the Observer was to publish the name of PT16/B and that the Observer had asked him 'to put PT16/Bs identity on the Internet so the paper could publish it without breaking the injunction'. Shayler says that he refused to do so and that accordingly the Observer decided not to use the name in the first edition. *e*

29. On 1 March 2000 two separate letters were sent to the legal department of the Guardian Newspapers, the first relating to the letter published in the Guardian. The Metropolitan Police asserted: *f*

> 'The letter published by the Guardian on 17 February must have been received in some form at the newspaper. I wish to know in what form the material was received by the Guardian and who is now in possession of the original material/letter.' *g*

30. The notice of application directed to the editor of the Guardian, Alan Rusbridger, sought:

> 'All files, documents and other records, whether those records are in written form, are kept on microfilm, magnetic tape or any other form of mechanical or electronic data retrieval mechanism, or correspondence concerning ... The letter which appeared ... On Thursday 17 February 2000.' *h*

31. The second letter dated 1 March concerned the article in the Observer. It asserted: *j*

> 'A criminal investigation has been initiated into alleged breaches of the Official Secrets Act ... It is proposed to make application for Production Orders ... for material held by you in relation to the article which appeared on page one of the Observer on Sunday 27th of February 2000 ... The material sought is any and all files, documents, audio, or any other records held, controlled or

otherwise in your possession, whether directly or indirectly in relation to the article published in the Observer on Sunday 27 February 2000, whether those records are in written form or kept on microfilm, magnetic tape or other form of mechanical or electronic data retrieval mechanism.'

32. The notices of application to the author of the article, Martin Bright, and the editor of the Observer, Roger Alton, were directed to—

> 'all files, documents and accounts and other records, whether those records are in written form, kept on micro film, magnetic tape or any other form of mechanical or electronic data retrieval mechanism in relation to the article published in The Observer on Sunday 27 February 2000 entitled Two Spies named in Libya Plot.'

33. On 3 March, by fax, the legal department for the Guardian replied:

> 'You have not provided any reason why you would need to see the original letter, and it is difficult to see how it would be of any value to your investigation.'

34. The same writer, writing from the legal department for the Observer, responded to the relevant notice of application:

> 'Your letter is not specific about which offences you are investigating, but you refer to the Official Secrets Act 1911–1989. I have made enquiries and I am satisfied that the Observer is not in possession of any relevant material.'

35. On 10 March the legal department of the Guardian confirmed:

> 'The letter from David Shayler was sent to the Guardian by email, and this email was deleted on the day of publication. The Guardian does not have any other material, unless there is data which we have not yet been able to trace on our database. This data will be in a form which can be recovered only by specialists in information technology, with sufficient expertise to find and recover this material. The Guardian has a policy of not storing information sent to the Letters Page, as it is aware of its responsibilities to protect personal data under the Data Protection Act. The contents of letters may be intended for publication, but writers do not expect these documents to be stored indefinitely …'

36. On 14 March, that is on the first day of the hearing of the application, the legal department of the Observer wrote on behalf of the editor:

> 'You should know that it is normal procedure for journalists to dispose of records of information given to them in confidence by their sources. I have made enquiries about the email system at the Observer. The IT department have informed me that the backup tapes for 25 to 27 February were used during that week, so that no material deleted on or before those dates survives in the system. In any event, the Observer email system is password protected and private. Each person has a personal address and no-one else has access to that persons emails … The editor does not have the authority to access journalists emails without permission, and it is right that this would be a breach of the journalists privacy. Journalists value their independence and it is the Observer's policy to respect their rights. I am also writing to find out whether you are aware of the telephone calls between Government Departments and the Observer on Saturday, 26 February 2000? The Treasury Solicitor called, as did MI5. No application was made for any injunction that

night, and MI5 said that they had seen the paper and were no longer worried.' a

37. The information in support of the present application by DS Flynn asserts that:

> 'The Observer newspaper appears to be in possession of material covered by the Official Secrets Act. The disclosure of this information in the article of 27 February may constitute a breach of Sec 5 OSA 1989. Parts of this b submission may contain material which is extremely sensitive and its disclosure to any unauthorised person is likely to lead to serious harm to the security of the State by purporting to detail methods and investigative techniques of the intelligence and security services.'

38. The reference to s 5 of the 1989 Act was a significant development: c attention was no longer exclusively directed at Shayler.

39. In the information DS Flynn referred to a damage assessment conducted by the Security Services. He said that their assessment was that the 'disclosure of details contained in The Observer article "Two spies named in Libya plot" of 27 February is extremely damaging.' d

40. The precise nature of the damage is unspecific, but significantly no similar references were made to any damage assessment alleged to arise from the Shayler letter to the Guardian.

41. The information in support of the application against the Guardian includes DS Flynn's assessment that: e

> 'The enquiry is hampered by the lack of the information which may be held in respect of the letter by David Shayler, the substantive part of which was published on 17 February 2000 in the Guardian newspaper and the article entitled "Two Spies named in Libya plot" published on 27 February 2000 in the Observer newspaper.' f

42. In context, the reference to 'the enquiry' appears to be the inquiry into the material in the possession of the Observer.

43. EVIDENCE AT THE HEARING

44. *Generally* g

45. Three important preliminary points arise. Throughout the hearing, everyone, including the judge himself, proceeded on the assumption that an offence against the 1989 Act amounted to a 'serious arrestable offence' for the purposes of the 1984 Act. Unfortunately, although referred to in the application, in the course of the argument no one drew the attention of the judge to s 116 of h the Act. I shall return later to the significance of this error.

46. DS Flynn gave evidence. In reality he knew nothing, or virtually nothing, about the case. He was 'tasked' to apply for the orders and they represented his first involvement in the Shayler investigation. He was entrusted with that responsibility because police policy required that an officer making such an j application should be a 'qualified financial investigator, having completed the appropriate courses'.

47. At the hearing before us we were told that another officer, Insp Lerner, who had much greater knowledge of the facts, was present throughout the hearing. Mr Tugendhat told us that this was the first he knew of the presence and availability of any police officer with more information of the facts than DS Flynn.

a It is not insignificant that at one stage in his submission to Judge Stephens, Mr Tugendhat complained:

> 'It is entirely unsatisfactory that the information should be based, as it clearly is, on hearsay. And insofar as it is not based on hearsay, on the facts of this case it is even more unsatisfactory because this officer has not, hitherto, been responsible for this investigation. So he does not know the b background. He is starting from scratch. He is in no position to give any informed assistance to the court as to what is or what is not to be of likely value in this investigation. And insofar as it is hearsay from another officer, Mr Lerner, it is unsatisfactory because it is impossible to ask any questions.'

48. The judge intervened and asked Mr Tugendhat whether he would have c sought to question Insp Lerner if he had known of his existence. Mr Tugendhat replied that he would. He ended this part of his submission by commenting that DS Flynn lacked any sufficient authority to provide appropriate information, saying: 'Mr Lerner is not either but at least I could have found out from Mr Lerner who is.'

d 49. It is unfortunate that these observations did not lead to the obvious response that Mr Lerner was indeed present and available at court.

50. Moreover, in my judgment the evidence should have been rather more carefully prepared. While acknowledging the sensitivities which can arise in cases involving national security, generally speaking the judge cannot proceed on the basis of bare assertion by a police officer. If public disclosure of the details of e Shayler's offences would itself have prejudiced national security a properly drafted, careful summary of the relevant factors would probably have sufficed. Ultimately if the national interest would have been prejudiced by any publication at all, arrangements could have been made to provide the judge with necessary evidence by adopting a procedure similar to that used in PII applications (that is f public interest immunity). It is not satisfactory for the officer giving evidence to the court, and attending for the purposes of being cross-examined by the persons against whom the information is directed, to know as little about the case as DS Flynn, and for different reasons, equally unsatisfactory that the presence of an officer who knew rather more than he did was not disclosed. This application demanded full and proper disclosure. All these matters would be relevant to the g exercise of the judge's discretion, but more important, they are also directly relevant to the question whether the access conditions were established.

51. We must focus on the evidence actually produced by the Crown in support of the application. We inquired of Miss Claire Montgomery QC whether she wished to call or introduce any further evidence. She courteously declined.

h 52. The third point for emphasis is that, apart from any other distinctions between the position of the Guardian and the Observer and Mr Bright, it is clear that whereas the Guardian came into possession of a letter from Mr Shayler, with one exception there is no evidence that either Mr Bright or the Observer ever did so. The published article and Shayler's website entry referred in some detail to j conversations, but the only document to which any specific reference is made is a submission or letter sent to the government by Shayler in November 1999.

53. *The Guardian*

54. Stripped to essentials, what DS Flynn was after was 'Shayler's email address'.

55. He required the letter because there may be material that may contain evidence in relation to the offences that are being investigated, i e disclosures by

David Shayler 'and that the email "would reveal Mr Shayler's email address which may further open new lines of enquiry"'. That, he said, would add to the evidence. When he was asked whether the code name PT16B had been mentioned to him before or whether he had material which disclosed that name his response was not entirely clear, but he said that he had 'never seen any original documents relating to PT16'.

56. He was cross-examined whether there were reasonable grounds for believing that there was any relevant material on the Guardian's premises. DS Flynn replied that he was 'not a computer expert', but he added that material which had 'been received by computers can be obtained when one has thought deleted … if there is material on the computer there may be experts that can find it'. Later he was to say that the investigation might recover evidence which would benefit Mr Shayler. He did not face up to the question whether Shayler's e-mail address was already known to the investigating authorities, or the Home Office, with whom Shayler claimed on his website that he had communicated. Finally, DS Flynn did not attempt to refute or question Mr Elliott's evidence on behalf of the Guardian.

57. The unchallenged evidence of Mr Chris Elliott, executive editor for the Guardian, dealt with the receipt of the letter. It was—

> 'sent by email to our letters page address, which is letters@guardian.co.uk. Liz McGregor is the letters editor and she has given me details of what happened. The letter was edited to make it shorter and more readable. The part of the letter that was not published was what she described as "political rant" and was edited out because it was not of interest to readers. The email was deleted on 17 or 18 February. The Guardian's policy is not to keep the personal data of letter writers as it is aware that it may have obligations under the Data Protection Act. This is particularly so when letter-writers have indicated that their details are confidential. Members of the public who write to the letters page do not expect their letters or personal details to be kept indefinitely, and do not give their permission for these details to be stored. We delete letters and email addresses so that letter writers can be sure that we will not disclose their personal details and this data will not be used for any collateral purpose, such as marketing. The information technology (IT) department has confirmed that the email from David Shayler was deleted on 17 or 18 February. It is extremely unlikely that a copy of the email is still on our backup tape … We recycle tapes by copying over them.'

58. *The Observer and Mr Bright*

59. The assertions made in the Observer article were briefly examined with DS Flynn, when the investigation was said to include 'offences that may have been committed by Mr Shayler or, indeed, any person connected with this affair'. He went on to say that it was 'possible' that Mr Alton and Mr Bright would be subject of a criminal investigation, but he added that he only referred to Mr Bright in the context of Shayler's website because Shayler claimed that he had met Mr Bright and had discussions with him. He was of course under a duty to investigate any 'collateral offences' which might be disclosed by the investigation.

60. When he was cross-examined DS Flynn agreed that he was inviting the judge 'to consider that there are reasonable grounds to believe that Mr Bright may have committed an offence contrary to s 5 (of the Official Secrets Act)'. He

a went on to agree that Mr Bright was 'under investigation for such an offence'. Finally the judge asked a direct question:

> 'Is your evidence that you have reasonable grounds to believe that Mr Bright has contravened the section? *A* It is, my Lord.'

61. Neither Mr Bright nor Mr Alton (the editor of the Observer) gave evidence. b They would have been entitled to do so, and while so entitled, to refuse to answer questions which might incriminate them. I cannot help pondering about the likely disinhibiting effect of the belief expressed by DS Flynn, certainly in the case of Mr Bright, that although he knew virtually nothing about the case personally, he had reasonable grounds for believing that Mr Bright had contravened the 1989 Act. The Crown was not prepared to give an undertaking to the effect that c evidence obtained as a result of the production order would not be used in criminal proceedings against Mr Bright or Mr Alton. Instead, and much more generally, and without providing any binding commitment, the risk of prosecution was said to be minimal. Understandably, that provided little comfort. Unlike DS Flynn, but like Judge Stephens, I have considerable reservations whether d there is any evidence at all that Mr Bright can be said to have 'disclosed' anything to anyone for the purposes of s 5 of the 1989 Act, which was not already included in the published article. That said, if the entry on Shayler's website were accurate—and it seems to have represented a significant factor in DS Flynn's analysis—then Mr Bright was actively inciting Shayler to commit offences under s 1 of the 1989 Act.

e 62. After that lengthy recitation of the evidence before Judge Stephens, I can turn to the relevant legislative framework.

63. THE LEGISLATION

64. Part II of the 1984 Act contains detailed statutory provisions governing the f powers of the police to enter and search premises and to seize property from them.

65. Section 8 empowers a justice of the peace who is satisfied that there are reasonable grounds for believing a number of specific matters, including that a serious arrestable offence has been committed, to issue a warrant authorising a constable to enter and search premises. No express reference is made to the g public interest, but a special provision was made in relation to items subject to legal professional privilege, of some significance for present purposes. By s 10(2) where the items in question are held for the purposes of crime, they fall outside the ambit of legal professional privilege. Once authorised, if necessary, reasonable force may be used to effect entry (see s 117). However, these powers do not h extend to 'excluded material or special procedure material'.

66. Section 11 explains the meaning of excluded material, and by s 11(2) provides:

> 'A person holds material other than journalistic material in confidence for the purposes of this section if he holds it subject—(a) to an express or implied undertaking to hold it in confidence; or (b) to a restriction on disclosure or j an obligation of secrecy contained in any enactment, including an enactment contained in an Act passed after this Act.'

67. Section 11(3) provides:

> 'A person holds journalistic material in confidence for the purposes of this section if—(a) he holds it subject to such an undertaking, restriction or obligation; and (b) it has been continuously held (by one or more persons)

subject to such an undertaking, restriction or obligation since it was first acquired or created for the purposes of journalism.' a

68. In brief therefore s 11(3) is linked to both paras (a) and (b) of s 11(2).

69. Journalistic material is defined by s 13 as 'material acquired or created for the purposes of journalism', provided 'it is in the possession of a person who acquired or created it for the purposes of journalism' (see s 13(2)). Finally s 13(3) explains that: b

'A person who receives material from someone who intends that the recipient shall use it for the purposes of journalism is to be taken to have acquired it for those purposes.'

70. Section 14(1) explains the meaning of 'special procedure material' as '(a) material to which subsection (2) below applies; and (b) journalistic material, other than excluded material.' c

71. I can now turn to the special procedure provisions found in Sch 1 to the Act.

72. This provides:

'1. If on an application made by a constable a circuit judge is satisfied that one or other of the sets of access conditions is fulfilled, he may make an order under paragraph 4 below.' d

73. That order is for the production of material to a constable or the provision of access to it.

e

'2. The first set of access conditions is fulfilled if—(a) there are reasonable grounds for believing—(i) that a serious arrestable offence has been committed; (ii) that there is material which consists of special procedure material or includes special procedure material and does not also include excluded material on premises specified in the application; (iii) that the material is likely to be of substantial value (whether by itself or together with other material) to the investigation in connection with which the application is made; and (iv) that the material is likely to be relevant evidence; [which by the application of s 8(4) means anything that would be admissible in evidence at a trial for the offence] (b) other methods of obtaining the material—(i) have been tried without success; or (ii) have not been tried because it appeared that they were bound to fail; and (c) it is in the public interest, having regard—(i) to the benefit likely to accrue to the investigation if the material is obtained; and (ii) to the circumstances under which the person in possession of the material holds it, that the material should be produced or that access to it should be given.' f g

h

74. In these applications access condition 2(b) was established, and needs no further mention.

75. By contrast with the situation before Judge Stephens, it was appreciated before us that some, but not all, arrestable offences are serious. The 1989 Act is not included in either Pts I or II of Sch 5 to the 1984 Act. Therefore an offence contrary to any provisions of the 1989 Act is only a 'serious' arrestable offence if it has or is intended or likely to lead to any of the consequences specified in s 116(6) of the Act. These include not harm, but 'serious' harm to the security of the state, or death or serious injury. j

76. In truth, in the case of the Guardian, there is very little evidence to this effect. So far as the Observer is concerned, nothing has been produced to

a contradict the assertion that the draft 'offending' article was seen by MI5 before it was published without any subsequent effort by MI5 to discourage publication. Judge Stephens concluded that the article itself provided the main source of material from which to conclude that an offence contrary to s 1 of the 1989 Act had been committed. He proceeded on the basis that the only relevant arrestable offence or offences were committed by Shayler: so he ignored DS Flynn's b evidence in so far as it related to Mr Bright and the Observer. For the reasons already given he did not specifically ask himself whether Shayler's offence was 'serious' but the internal language of the article itself, suggesting that Shayler had identified two agents involved in the bomb plot to Mr Bright and that this had sent 'shockwaves' through the intelligence system, would have provided him with sufficient grounds for believing that a serious arrestable offence had indeed c been committed by Shayler.

77. A successful application results in an order by the judge which is directed to the person who appears to be in possession of the relevant material. Entry to his premises is not immediately authorised. The order imposes a personal obligation on the individual to whom it is addressed. Very precise statutory provisions deal d with practical problems (for example, where it is impracticable to communicate with the person entitled to grant entry to the relevant premises). For present purposes, however, the significant feature is that failure to comply with the order exposes the person to whom it is addressed to process, and penalty, 'as if he had committed a contempt of court' (see para 15 of Sch 1). Similar provisions are found in s 20(2) of the Juries Act 1974 and s 6(5) of the Bail Act 1976. Therefore, no doubt e as it should be, non-compliance with the order of the circuit judge is regarded as a very serious matter, which may have major consequences, including an order of imprisonment. On this basis alone it therefore behoves a judge to act with great circumspection before making an order.

78. In my judgment, and contrary to Miss Montgomery's submission, it is clear f that the judge personally must be satisfied that the statutory requirements have been established. He is not simply asking himself whether the decision of the constable making the application was reasonable, nor whether it would be susceptible to judicial review on *Wednesbury* grounds (see *Associated Provincial Picture Houses Ltd v Wednesbury Corp* [1947] 2 All ER 680, [1948] 1 KB 223). This follows from the express wording of the statute, 'if … a circuit judge is satisfied g that one … of the sets of access conditions is fulfilled'. The purpose of this provision is to interpose between the opinion of the police officer seeking the order and the consequences to the individual or organisation to whom the order is addressed the safeguard of a judgment and decision of a circuit judge. This conclusion is consistent with the approach suggested in *IRC v Rossminster Ltd* [1980] h 1 All ER 80, [1980] AC 952, as well as a series of decisions in the Divisional Court of which *R v Crown Court at Lewes, ex p Hill* (1990) 93 Cr App Rep 60 represents a valuable example.

79. In my judgment it is equally clear that the constable making the application must satisfy the judge that the relevant set of conditions is established. This j appears to follow as an elementary result of the fact that an order will force or oblige the individual against whom it is made to act under compulsion when, without the order, he would be free to do otherwise. Again, if authority is required, I refer to the reasoning of Lord Diplock in *IRC v Rossminster Ltd* [1980] 1 All ER 80 at 93, [1980] AC 952 at 1011 where he said 'the onus would be on the officer to satisfy the court that there did in fact exist reasonable grounds …' And I should emphasise, under the rules currently under consideration, grounds for

belief, not merely grounds for suspicion, are required, and the material to be produced or disclosed is not merely general information which might be helpful to police inquiries, but evidence in the sense in which that term is applied in the Crown Court, 'relevant and admissible' at a trial.

80. Another feature of the rules arises from the clear language that if the relevant set of access conditions is fulfilled then the judge is empowered, but not bound, to make the order. Assuming that access conditions are established to his satisfaction, he has a discretion or power to refuse the application. Given the detailed pre-requirements of the order which mean, among other things, that the judge has no power to make the order unless he is satisfied in the public interest that he should do so, this is a little surprising. If he is so satisfied, how, putting the matter rhetorically, can he refuse the order?

81. Miss Montgomery suggested that the answer was that he could not, and she relied on the decision in *R v Crown Court at Northampton, ex p DPP* (1991) 93 Cr App Rep 376. I do not so read this decision. The circuit judge purported to exercise his discretion on the basis that the application was '"a sledgehammer to crack a nut"', and therefore that it was not in the public interest to make the order. Given that he had already decided that a serious arrestable offence had been committed—

> 'it was hardly consistent for him to reach the conclusion that this was anything other than a serious matter and one which the public had an interest in seeing was brought to justice.' (See (1991) 93 Cr App Rep 376 at 381.)

So the exercise of his discretion was wrong.

82. I agree with that conclusion, but I do not accept that it has the consequence for which Miss Montgomery contended. That would have required para 1 to read 'if … a circuit judge is satisfied … he ["shall"] make an order'. That is not what it says.

83. The answer appears to arise from the somewhat limited conditions which are said expressly to be relevant to the 'public interest'. They are restricted to the potential benefit to the investigation and the circumstances in which the person against whom the order is sought 'holds' the material. So, for example, nothing is said about open discussion in the media of questions of public importance or the consequences to which the person against whom the order is made may be exposed. Mr Emmerson's first position was that para (c)(ii) in particular, was to be given very wide effect, in practice covering anything which might in a general way be said to be a matter of 'public interest', including the privilege against self-incrimination. If he is wrong, however, and for the reasons which lead me later in this judgment to the conclusion that special procedure orders do not exclude the privilege against self-incrimination I believe that he is, his fall-back position would be that the matters which could not otherwise be considered as matters of public interest as defined in para (c) fall to be considered when the judge decides whether to exercise his discretion.

84. This provision, as it seems to me, is the final safeguard against an oppressive order and, in an appropriate case, provides the judge with the opportunity to reflect on and take account of matters which are not expressly referred to in the set of relevant access conditions and, where they arise, to reflect on all the circumstances, including, where appropriate, what can, without exaggeration, be described as fundamental principles. This approach was endorsed in *R v Bristol Crown Court, ex p Bristol Press and Picture Agency Ltd* (1986) 85 Cr App Rep 190 where Glidewell LJ (at 196) noted with approval that

a the judge at the Crown Court had rightly taken into account both 'the importance of the impartiality and independence of the press', and 'the importance of ensuring that members of the press can photograph and report what is going on without fear of their personal safety'. Neither of these considerations is included in the public interest considerations specifically identified in para 2(c).

b 85. Without attempting any comprehensive list of such matters, they might include, for example, the effect of the order on third parties, and any consequent damage to them, or the antiquity of the matters under investigation, or an unexplained re-investigation of matters formally investigated many years earlier, or that, notwithstanding that the offence under consideration is serious, the result of the prosecution would inevitably be a nominal sentence because of circumstances c personal and particular to the potential defendant. Again, in my judgment, the judge may take account of an apparent disproportion between what might possibly be gained by the production of the material and the offence to which it is said to relate, and, for the reasons set out in detail below, in the case of journalistic material, to the potential stifling of public debate, and, in cases arising d under s 9 and Sch 1 to the risk of imposing an obligation requiring the individual to whom the order is directed to incriminate himself.

86. I must reflect on these last two considerations in greater detail.

87. It seems improbable that the European Convention for the Protection of Human Rights and Fundamental Freedoms (Rome, 4 November 1950; TS 71 (1953); Cmd 8969) (the convention) was foremost in the mind of Parliament e when this special procedure was enacted. Our attention was drawn to a number of decisions of the European Court of Human Rights. I have considered them with care. That said, by now, we surely fully appreciate that the principles to be found in arts 6 and 10 of the convention are bred in the bone of the common law and indeed, in some instances at any rate, the folk understanding of the f community as a whole. I do not intend to imply any criticism of the submissions made by any of the counsel in these applications, each of whom advanced submissions of great clarity and appropriate economy, when I say that generally, the vast and increasingly lengthy number of citations in numerous skeleton and oral arguments of the decisions of the European Court, simply repeating in different language long-standing and well-understood principles of the common g law, suggests that perhaps we do not.

88. For this reason, but in the context of this particular schedule only I shall illustrate what I am driving at by focusing on proceedings which may culminate in entry by the police into the premises of the Guardian and the Observer newspapers, reminding myself that in his *Introduction to the Study of the Law of the* h *Constitution* (6th edn, 1902) p 203, Dicey, in a memorable observation, explained that as a matter of general principle, 'with us individual rights are the basis not the result of the law of the constitution'.

89. The common law principle was expressed nearly 250 years ago in the famous case of *Entick v Carrington* (1765) 19 State Tr 1029, [1558–1774] All ER j Rep 41.

90. Entick was a clerk whose home in Stepney was broken into by Carrington and three other 'Messengers in Ordinary to the King'. Their defence was that they were acting under the authority of a warrant issued by the Earl of Halifax, a member of the Privy Council, and one of the principal Secretaries of State, which authorised and requested them to make strict and diligent search for the plaintiff and to bring him with his books and papers in safe custody to be examined.

91. The issue was whether the Secretary of State had jurisdiction to seize the papers. The report, clearly mistakenly, refers ((1765) 19 State Tr 1029 at 1063, [1558–1774] All ER Rep 41) to 'the defendants' papers':

> '... if this point should be determined in favour of the jurisdiction, the secret cabinets and bureaus of every subject in this Kingdom will be thrown open to the search and inspection of a messenger, whenever the secretary of state shall think fit to charge, or even to suspect, a person to be the author, printer, or publisher of a seditious libel ... This power, so claimed by the secretary of state, is not supported by one single citation from any law book extant.' (See (1765) 19 State Tr 1029 at 1063–1064, [1558–1774] All ER Rep 41.)

92. The judgment of Lord Camden CJ includes statements of fundamental principle:

> 'No man can set his foot upon my ground without my licence, but he is liable to an action, though the damage be nothing ... If he admits the fact, he is bound to shew by way of justification, that some positive law has empowered or excused him. The justification is submitted to the judges, who are to look into the books; and if such a justification can be maintained by the text of the statute law, or by the principles of common law. If no such excuse can be found or produced, the silence of the books is an authority against the defendant ...' (See (1765) 19 State Tr 1029 at 1066, [1558–1774] All ER Rep 41.)

93. He continued:

> 'Papers are the owner's goods and chattels ... and are so far from enduring a seizure ... they will hardly bear an inspection; and though the eye cannot by the laws of England be guilty of trespass, yet where private papers are removed and carried away, the secret nature of those goods will be an aggravation of the trespass, and demand more considerable damages in that respect. Where is the written law that gives any magistrate such a power? I can safely answer, there is none; and therefore it is too much for us without such authority to pronounce a practice legal, which would be subversive of all the comforts of society.' (See (1765) 19 State Tr 1029 at 1066, [1558–1774] All ER Rep 41.)

94. At much the same time William Pitt, Earl of Chatham (1708–1778), with greater rhetorical flourish was expounding the same principle, when he said:

> 'The poorest man may in his cottage bid defiance to all the forces of the Crown. It may be frail—its roof may shake—the wind may blow through it—the storm may enter—the rain may enter—but the King of England cannot enter—all his force dares not cross the threshold of the ruined tenement.'

95. The measured language of the judge and the emotion of the orator are encapsulated in the simple phrase that an Englishman's home is his castle. These principles were clearly understood in this country while an absolute monarch still reigned in France. If the Bourbon monarch, Louis XV, had heard of such language used by a prominent politician, and former First Minister, the speaker's best hope would have been for the king to have assumed that he was joking. But even that would not have prevented some fawning minion from despatching a

a *lettre de cachet* to ensure that he was locked up, indefinitely, and without trial. It is, hardly surprising therefore, that Voltaire, having twice been imprisoned in the Bastille, and eventually forced to live in exile, and notwithstanding what we can now appreciate were its great defects then, so greatly admired our constitution.

96. Linked with this by now ancient understanding of the autonomy of each individual's premises was the 'much-prized and indispensable freedom' spoken of b by Watkins J, in *Verrall v Great Yarmouth BC* [1981] QB 202 at 205, [1980] 3 WLR 258 at 261, and encapsulating the historical truth that:

> 'I am concerned with a fundamental freedom which this country has prided itself on maintaining, and for which much blood has been spilt over the centuries, namely freedom of speech.'

c 97. These principles are interlinked. Premises are not to be entered by the forces of authority or the state to deter or diminish, inhibit or stifle the exercise of an individual's right to free speech or the press of its freedom to investigate and inform, and orders should not be made which might have that effect unless a circuit judge is personally satisfied that the statutory preconditions to the making d of an order are established, and, as the final safeguard of basic freedoms, that in the particular circumstances it is indeed appropriate for an order to be made.

98. Inconvenient or embarrassing revelations, whether for the Security Services, or for public authorities, should not be suppressed. Legal proceedings directed towards the seizure of the working papers of an individual journalist, or the premises of the newspaper or television programme publishing his or her e reports, or the threat of such proceedings, tend to inhibit discussion. When a genuine investigation into possible corrupt or reprehensible activities by a public authority is being investigated by the media, compelling evidence is normally needed to demonstrate that the public interest would be served by such proceedings. Otherwise, to the public disadvantage, legitimate inquiry and f discussion, and 'the safety valve of effective investigative journalism', the phrase used in a different context by Lord Steyn in *R v Secretary of State for the Home Dept, ex p Simms* [1999] 3 All ER 400 at 412, [1999] 3 WLR 328 at 341, would be discouraged, perhaps stifled.

99. What does not follow from the initiation of proceedings is that a stifling exercise is on foot. The judge, alert to the need to safeguard basic freedoms, must g simultaneously acknowledge the public interest which underpins the relevant legislation, and s 9 and Sch 1 in particular, that crime should be discouraged and those responsible for crime should be detected and brought to justice. Balancing these interests where they appear to be in conflict is a decision to be made in each individual case where apparent conflict arises.

h 100. These principles, which I derive from the common law, are interlinked. They are encapsulated and reflected in the convention. (See *A-G v Guardian Newspapers Ltd* (No 2) [1988] 3 All ER 545, [1990] 1 AC 109 and *Derbyshire CC v Times Newspapers Ltd* [1993] 1 All ER 1011, [1993] AC 534.) While account must be taken of reported decisions of the European Court which serve to supplement or clarify these j principles, I do not find it necessary to refer to any of these decisions to discover the principles which apply to this one, and should not have done so if this judgment were delivered on 3 October 2000, immediately after the Human Rights Act 1998 comes into force.

101. The next matter for consideration is Mr Emmerson's contention that a successful application against Mr Bright would infringe his privilege against self-incrimination.

102. Mr Tugendhat adopted these submissions in relation to the Observer. In the course of the written and oral argument attention was drawn to the decisions of the European Court of Human Rights in *Saunders v UK* (1997) 23 EHRR 313, and *Serves v France* (1999) 28 EHRR 265. a

103. Perhaps Mr Emmerson will forgive me for failing to avoid the temptation to return to the observations of Lord Camden towards the end of his judgment in *Entick v Carrington* (1765) 19 State Tr 1029 at 1073, [1558–1774] All ER Rep 41: b

> 'It is very certain, that the law obligeth no man to accuse himself; because the necessary means of compelling self-accusation, falling upon the innocent as well as the guilty, would be both cruel and unjust; and it should seem, that search for evidence is disallowed upon the same principle. There too the innocent would be confounded with the guilty.' c

104. Differing reasons for the rule against self-incrimination have emerged over the years, and the entire subject was recently illuminated by Lord Mustill in *R v Director of Serious Fraud Office, ex p Smith* [1992] 3 All ER 456, [1993] AC 1.

105. In *R v Hertfordshire CC, ex p Green Environmental Industries Ltd* [2000] 1 All ER 773, [2000] 2 WLR 373, the impact of art 6(1) and (2) of the convention, and the relevant decisions of the European Court on these provisions, were analysed by Lord Hoffmann in the context of domestic legislation, the Environmental Protection Act 1990. Without implying any disrespect for the decisions of the European Court, sitting in the Divisional Court in England, where such a decision, or group of decisions has been examined by the House of Lords or Court of Appeal, this court is bound by the reasoning of the superior courts in our jurisdiction. We are not permitted to re-examine decisions of the European Court in order to ascertain whether the conclusion of the House of Lords or Court of Appeal may be inconsistent with those decisions, or susceptible to a continuing gloss. The principle of stare decisis cannot be circumvented or disapplied in this way, and if it were, the result would be chaos. In my judgment, in this court it is appropriate to consider and apply the principles against self-incrimination as explained in *Ex p Green Environmental Industries Ltd* but we should not now attempt to revisit the decisions in *Saunders v UK, Funke v France*, and *Serves v France*, and attempt to reconcile their apparent contradictions. So far as we are concerned the impact of this group of decisions has been authoritatively decided. We have been told how they should be taken into account. d e f g

106. I respectfully venture to suggest that when the 1998 Act comes into force the possible relevance of the decisions of the European Court for the purposes of s 2(1) should be examined in the light of any available analysis by the House of Lords and the Court of Appeal, and in that way properly but sufficiently taken into account. It would therefore be unnecessary to recite massive passages from the judgments, and inappropriate to seek to undermine the decisions of our superior courts about their true ambit. h

107, 108. The question which therefore arises from the statutory provisions relating to special procedures is whether Mr Bright was entitled to rely on the privilege against self-incrimination as a ground on which the judge should have decided to refuse the application made against him, or, at the very least, as a significant factor bearing on the exercise of his discretion. j

109. In *R v Hertfordshire CC, ex p Green Environmental Industries Ltd* [2000] 1 All ER 773 at 778, [2000] 2 WLR 373 at 378, Lord Hoffmann explained that:

a 'The question of whether a statute which confers a power to ask questions or obtain documents or information excludes the privilege against self-incrimination in one or other of its forms is therefore one of construction.'

110. Section 71(2) of the 1990 Act provided:

'For the purpose of the discharge of their respective functions … (b) a b waste regulation or authority, may, by notice in writing served on him, require any person to furnish such information specified in the notice as the … authority … reasonably considers … it needs …'

111. Non-compliance, without reasonable excuse, amounted to an offence.

112. Lord Hoffmann went on to explain that the powers were created—

c 'not merely for the purpose of enabling the authorities to obtain evidence against offenders but for the broad public purpose of protecting the public health and the environment. Such information is often required urgently and the policy of the statute would be frustrated if the persons who knew most about the extent of the health or environmental hazard were entitled d to refuse to provide any information on the grounds that their answers might tend to incriminate them … the request under s 71(2) does not in itself form a part, even a preliminary part, of any criminal proceedings. It does not therefore touch the principle which prohibits interrogation of a person charged or accused …' (See [2000] 1 All ER 773 at 779–780, [2000] 2 WLR 373 e at 379.)

113. With these principles in mind I turn to ss 8 and 9 of the 1984 Act which are directed to the proper investigation of a serious crime, after its commission, or, more accurately, when there are reasonable grounds for believing that it has been committed, and involve the search for likely relevant and admissible f evidence. These sections are directly concerned with the criminal process and the search for incriminating material in serious arrestable offences. That indeed is their exclusive purpose. Neither has anything to do with public administration.

114. Under s 8 a warrant to enter premises owned or occupied either by a suspect or someone against whom no hint of suspicion arises may be granted. If necessary force may be deployed. During the course of the search incriminating g material may be seized, and if so, used at a subsequent trial. The privilege against self-incrimination is untouched. Of itself the warrant does not permit a suspect to be questioned, and apart from permitting the entry and search, the individual in the premises, whether a suspect or not, is not required personally to assist or indeed do anything at all. He is entitled to remain entirely passive.

h 115. By contrast, an order under s 9 imposes a specific obligation, enforceable by a penal sanction, to produce or grant access to material which is likely to be relevant and admissible at a subsequent trial. It would be an odd and surprising development if the special procedure rules excluded the privilege against self-incrimination, when the same privilege is maintained in s 8. At the risk of j repetition, this permits the search of the premises, but does not require a suspect to produce incriminating material to the police, or to give them access to it, although the police themselves may open doors and drawers as part of a legitimate search. Any admissible evidence is discovered by the searching officers, not handed over or made available to them under compulsion.

116. It is improbable that Parliament anticipated that an order under s 9 and Sch 1, but not s 8, would be made against a suspect, obliging him to elect between

handing over or providing access to self-incriminating material and rendering himself liable to imprisonment for failing to do so, or that, so far as a 'suspect' is concerned, his position under s 9 should in any way differ from the position of a suspect in s 8 proceedings. No express provision to this effect is made.

117. Although this point was not closely addressed in argument, I shall return to the way in which journalistic material is defined in s 13. The journalist must acquire or create the material for the purposes not of crime, but journalism. Section 13(3) is directed to the intention of the conveyor of the materials. If he intends that it should be used for journalism there is a rebuttable presumption that it was acquired by the recipient for that purpose. But if not, if, for example, the recipient's purpose was to conceal evidence of a crime, the material is not journalistic material. In summary, if a journalist acquires material for the purposes of crime, or receives it other than for the purposes of journalism, it falls outside the ambit of s 13(1). The objective of s 9 is to enable the police to obtain journalistic material in the possession of a journalist, which is relevant to the criminal activities of others, including the individual who provided him with the material.

118. Focusing exclusively on para 4(b) of Sch 1, it is suggested that an order which simply provides that a journalist should give the police 'access' to material in his possession cannot give rise to any potential for self-incrimination. I respectfully disagree. In my view the requirements in para 4(a) and (b) should be read together. Read in this way they represent the process by which access may be gained by the police to journalistic material. It may be impossible, or highly inconvenient, for material to be physically produced by the journalist to the investigating officers. He may need a critical document: he may have put the material sent to him into a computer which he needs to use, or into electronic form, or on microfile or magnetic tape. So, as an alternative to handing the material over to the police officer he must provide access to it. In my view all this forms part of the same process. Neither this procedure, nor the procedures under s 8 are intended to result in self-incrimination, and if either had been, express language would have been used.

119. In any event, even if it were right to treat the obligation under para 4(b) as a distinct provision, the question of self-incrimination would still arise. In short, the contrary view proceeds on the basis that no question of self–incrimination can arise where a police officer says to a 'suspect' journalist, in possession of material acquired or created in the course of his profession, 'I demand that you give access to your notebooks' or, in the language of the current application, your 'files … or microfilm, magnetic tape or any form of mechanical or electronic data retrieval mechanism'. In my view, in such circumstances, if the suspect journalist were obliged to take any positive step to comply with the demand, he would be providing or helping to provide material which could be used at his trial. Passive giving of access in such circumstances is improbable: unlike 'allow' or 'permit', 'give' implies more than mere passivity.

120. The present applications have proceeded on the basis that save for the purposes of comparison s 8 did not arise for consideration. Therefore no argument was addressed to the question whether an application could be made against a 'suspect' journalist or newspaper under s 8, and I expressly decline to say anything about the possibility. Assuming, however, that it could not be so deployed in circumstances like the present, I remain of the view that s 9 and Sch 1 do not provide sufficient authority for the proposition that Mr Bright, and the Observer, must produce documents or give access to material which may incriminate them.

a 121. Finally, I must add, that as a matter of fundamental principle, and for the reasons analysed earlier in this judgment, if I am wrong, I have no doubt that in exercising his discretion, the judge should take account of the fact that a possible consequence of his order would be the danger of self-incrimination. This factor does not, in my judgment, become irrelevant because of the undoubted discretion provided in s 78 of the Act for the trial judge to exclude evidence.

b

122. CONCLUSIONS

123. I can now turn to my conclusions.

124. *The Guardian*

125. The information against the Guardian was unspecific. Without repeating c all the matters set out in the information it was said that parts of the submission 'may' contain extremely sensitive material. No damage assessment was referred to in the information. In the application concerning the Guardian, I have considerable doubts whether there is any sufficient evidence to justify the conclusion that there were reasonable grounds for believing that a serious arrestable offence had been d committed.

126. Judge Stephens decided that condition (a)(ii) was fulfilled, notwithstanding the unchallenged evidence of Mr Elliott that it was 'extremely unlikely that a copy of the e-mail is still on our backup tapes'. From the judge's comments that 'such material may be recoverable by persons of appropriate expertise', he proceeded to the conclusion that there 'is' special procedure material at the e Guardian's premises. I respectfully disagree: on the evidence, at most, there was the possibility that such material might be available.

127. Miss Montgomery persuasively sought to explain how material in electronic form could be recovered. But the evidence of DS Flynn was less convincing than Miss Montgomery's submission, not because he was dissembling f or untruthful, but no doubt because he had very little personal knowledge of the process and the likelihood of success.

128. I further doubt whether the evidence being sought, that is, Shayler's e-mail address, would provide relevant and admissible evidence against him. Although he wrote a letter to a newspaper when interest in his activities, and his allegations, was heightened, and did so without claiming confidentiality, it has g not been demonstrated that anything in that letter as printed would do more than help with the general police inquiry. That would not make it relevant and admissible as evidence at Shayler's trial and there was no evidence to explain why his e-mail address would, or should, of itself be so treated. Given the scarcity of information about Shayler's alleged offences it is also difficult to examine h whether the material sought by DS Flynn was likely to be of 'substantial' value to the investigation. In all the circumstances I am not impressed with the proposition that the ability of the Crown unequivocally to prove that Shayler actually wrote the letter published under his name in the Guardian is of substantial importance. And if it were, the point could be proved by calling a j witness from the Guardian to explain that the original was no longer available.

129. I must deal with the suggestion, implicit in Mr Tugendhat's argument, that prior and extensive publicity of material falling within the 1989 Act should lead to the conclusion that it may be repeated with impunity. Constant repetition may be a relevant consideration in civil proceedings for an injunction, but every repetition may constitute another serious offence. Nevertheless, when the judge's final exercise of discretion comes to be made, he should balance precisely

what national interest, or which individual's safety was being endangered, by repetition of material already in the public domain. In short, although Shayler would not avoid conviction for criminal disclosure merely because he had constantly repeated his disclosures, repetition might make it disproportionate for the special procedure to be deployed against a newspaper which printed a letter from him in response to its own earlier publication of an article critical of him, particularly when the letter contained nothing of any fresh significance.

130. In my judgment the necessary access conditions were not established. No question of the exercise of the judge's discretion arose. The order should not have been made. The application should be allowed.

131. *The Observer and Mr Bright*

132. This case is more difficult.

133. Judge Stephens proceeded on the basis that the only relevant available offence or offences were committed by Shayler: so he ignored DS Flynn's evidence in so far as it related to possible criminal proceedings against Mr Bright and the Observer. As far as he was concerned, the application related to Shayler's activities alone. Nevertheless the question of incitement by Mr Bright remains open. The risk of self-incrimination leads me to exclude from a production order under s 9 any record of Mr Bright's words to Shayler.

134. Mr Bright's article purported to report details of his conversation with Shayler. There is a clear distinction between material which is likely to be of 'substantial value' to the investigation (see para 2(a)(iii)) and material likely to provide 'benefit' to the investigation (see para 2(c)(i)) and the presence on the Observer's premises of evidence likely to be relevant and admissible at Shayler's trial (see para 2(a)(iv)). What Shayler said to Mr Bright would be admissible against Shayler, but Mr Bright's notebooks and records of what Shayler said to him would prove nothing against Shayler. Although the information given to Mr Bright from Shayler might be extremely interesting, probably of value to the overall investigation, apart possibly from ss 23 and 24 of the Criminal Justice Act 1988, any admissible evidence against Shayler arising from his discussions with Mr Bright is to be found either in Shayler's comments on his own website or in oral testimony from Mr Bright. In this context therefore he would be a potential witness against Shayler and apart from refreshing his memory from any contemporaneous notes, it is difficult to see how his records of the conversations would fall within para 2(a)(iv).

135. So what is left? Shayler's website entry suggests that on 25 February he sent the Observer a copy of the submission he had made to the government in the previous November. Mr Bright's article purports to refer to the submission or letter, apparently sent to Mr Straw, the Home Secretary. From the details given in the article it is reasonable to infer that Mr Bright was either in possession of the letter, or at the very least of his own note taken directly from it, when the article was written. Shayler was scathing of the article, complaining, but only in a general sense, that journalists 'cannot even copy accurately out of the documents I give them'. Therefore, notwithstanding those words, I am unable from the material as a whole to draw the further conclusion that there are reasonable grounds for believing that Shayler disclosed or sent any other document to Mr Bright or the Observer.

136. The slow development of the Observer's claim that 'relevant' records would 'normally' be destroyed, and the absence of any evidence from Mr Alton or Mr Bright to the effect that he had never been or was not still in possession of the

November 1999 letter, or that he had indeed destroyed all his records, entitled the judge to approach the case on the basis that there were reasonable grounds for believing that Mr Bright or Mr Alton were still in possession of this letter.

137. The proper analysis of the information about the letter has forced me to pause and reflect. There is no evidence from any police officer about the possible significance of the document, nor that the original was indeed sent to the Home Secretary by Shayler, nor any explanation of why Shayler's original letter cannot be produced to the police. However, the document must be put into context, and examined as part of the overall concern about Shayler's criminality, and for the purposes of the access conditions, not simply ring-fenced and isolated from the rest of the case. Therefore, for different reasons to those which attracted Judge Stephens, I have concluded that there are reasonable grounds for believing that the access conditions in para 2(a) are fulfilled in relation to this single document, but not in relation to any other material included in the application.

138. For present purposes I doubt whether the Crown would regard Shayler as a witness of truth. He is, in any event, unlikely to return willingly to the jurisdiction to be called to give evidence against Mr Bright. The prospect of criminal proceedings against Mr Bright or the Observer arising from Shayler's decision to disclose to the Observer a copy of the letter he had sent to the government in November 1999 is theoretical and the risk of self-incrimination is non-existent. Finally, there is no realistic possibility that a warrant issued under s 9 in relation to this document could possibly serve to stultify the proper functioning of the press. Shayler disclosed that he had sent the letter. It was a copy of a letter he had already sent to the Secretary of State. He invoked no journalistic confidence for it, and, save on an imaginary basis, none could be implied. I have considered the particular public interest conditions identified in para 2(c). In my view the public interest is properly served by an order limited to this single document. In effect therefore, this application, too, is allowed.

139. If I were wrong about the very limited ambit of the order which should follow in this case, I add, by way of footnote, that, in addition to the considerations in para 2(c), and assuming that I am wrong about the proper construction of s 9 in relation to self-incrimination, for the purposes of exercising discretion I should have much more closely analysed the dangers of prosecution against Mr Bright for incitement, and second, and even more important in this particular case, I should have attached considerable weight to the potential danger that would have followed an order.

140. In the wide terms sought in the original application, I believe that it would have had a devastating and stifling effect on the proper investigation of the Shayler story. Virtually any journalist who made contact with him, and any newspaper publishing an article based on discussions with Shayler, would be at risk of a similar application to the present. To my mind that would be an unhealthy development, quite disproportionate to any practical advantages to the prosecution process.

141. Finally, I should add that this judgment is concerned only with the deployment of warrants under s 9 and Sch 1. Nothing said in it is intended or should be regarded as having any bearing on civil proceedings for an injunction.

142. **MAURICE KAY J.** I agree that the application on behalf of Mr Rusbridger and the Guardian should be granted. I have reached this conclusion for reasons which can be stated more laconically than those given by Judge LJ. Quite simply, I consider that, on the material before him, His Honour Judge Martin Stephens QC

ought not to have been satisfied that there were reasonable grounds for believing that there was material consisting of or including special procedure material on the premises specified in the application. Accordingly, he ought not to have found access condition 2(a)(ii) in Sch 1 to the Police and Criminal Evidence Act 1984 to have been fulfilled. It may be that other access conditions were not fulfilled either but I do not intend to address that further. I entirely agree with what Judge LJ has said about the requirement for the circuit judge to be *satisfied* that the access conditions are fulfilled. I also agree with his analysis of the evidence relating to condition 2(a)(ii) in respect of the Guardian and attach particular significance to the unchallenged evidence of Mr Elliott who was made available for but was not the subject of cross-examination. In my judgment, the evidence relating to condition 2(a)(ii), taken at its highest, amounted to no more than a speculative possibility that the material was on the premises at the material time. As that in itself entitles the Guardian to succeed in their application, I consider it unnecessary to address the other points advanced on its behalf. Perhaps I should add that, in my view, the application on behalf of the Guardian raises no great principle of press freedom.

143. The application on behalf of Mr Bright, Mr Alton and the Observer does not admit of such a simple solution. Taking Mr Bright's article at face value, it seems clear that Shayler has disclosed to him names of two serving intelligence officers whom Shayler alleges were involved in a plot to assassinate the Libyan head of state. An editorial decision has been taken not to publish the names. It is necessary to stand back and consider the circumstances in which the application to the judge was made. For some time the police have been investigating Shayler. As I understand it he is suspected of having committed offences under the Official Secrets Act 1989. That is the basis upon which his extradition was sought, albeit unsuccessfully. His disclosures may be true or false. In either case, he may have committed offences because s 1(2) of the 1989 Act extends to a statement 'which *purports* to be a disclosure of … information' (my emphasis). A journalist to whom Shayler has disclosed any relevant 'information, document or article' does not commit an offence under s 5 merely by receiving or retaining such things. The offence under s 5(2)—or, for that matter, s 5(6)—is committed when the recipient discloses them without lawful authority.

144. In order to obtain a production order, the police first had to satisfy the judge that the access conditions were fulfilled by satisfying him that there were reasonable grounds for believing the specified matters. Our task is to consider whether the satisfaction of the judge was lawful. I shall deal with the conditions in their statutory sequence.

145. *Access condition (a)(i): 'that a serious arrestable offence has been committed'*

146. Whilst it is unfortunate that the judge was not referred to s 116 of the 1984 Act on the meaning of 'serious arrestable offence', it seems to me to be incontrovertible that the disclosure by Shayler of the names of two serving intelligence officers—whether the accompanying allegations are true or false—is likely to lead to 'serious harm to the security of the State'.

147. 'Likely' in this context should be given the same meaning as in para 2(a) of the access conditions, namely 'such as well might happen' rather than the higher hurdle of 'more probable than not' (see *R v Norwich Crown Court, ex p Chethams* [1991] COD 271). In my judgment, to disclose the names in question to the media in the context of the grave allegation of the assassination plot—true or false—is such that serious harm to the security of the state (including its security

a officers) might well ensue. If the judge had been referred to the correct test, I do not doubt that he would have found it fulfilled. On the other hand, I do not consider that any offence which Mr Bright may have committed under s 5 could be characterised as a *serious* arrestable offence. He did not publish the names of the intelligence officers and what he did publish does not seem to have included anything significant that was not already in the public domain.

b

148. *Access condition (a)(ii): 'that there is material which consists of special procedure material or includes special procedure material and does not also include excluded material on the premises specified in the application'*

149. So far as this condition is concerned, the evidence is much stronger in c relation to the Observer than in relation to the Guardian. Miss Montgomery QC submitted that there was no evidence of actual destruction or deletion and the timescale was short. Shayler's website stated that the material went into the possession of its recipient at the Observer on 25 February. The article was published on 27 February and the notice of application for a production order d was served on 1 March. The material was seen and considered by editorial and legal staff. There was contact with the security services. As Judge LJ has observed, neither Mr Bright nor Mr Alton gave evidence before the judge. It has never been suggested that Shayler sought to impose confidentiality in relation to the material and the evidence does not point to an implied obligation of confidentiality. In my judgment there was ample evidence from which the judge could properly infer e that there was special procedure material (not including excluded material) on the specified premises. I shall come back to the extent of such material later.

150. Although Mr Emmerson QC sought to attach importance to the language of the judge—'may still exist and be recoverable'—as being evidentially insufficient, I am confident that the judge was satisfied, and properly satisfied, f that there were reasonable grounds for believing that there was, at the date of the hearing, material on the premises. When I come to consider access condition (a)(iv) I shall address the question of whether it is 'likely to be relevant evidence' against Shayler.

g 151. *Access condition (a)(iii): 'that the material is likely to be of substantial value (whether by itself or together with other material) to the investigation in connection with which the application is made'*

So far as 'the investigation in connection with which the application is made' is concerned, the documents in support of the application to the judge referred to h ss 1 and 5 of the 1989 Act. Any offence under s 1 could only have been committed by Shayler, whereas any offence under s 5 could, in the circumstances of this case, only be committed by a recipient of the material at the Observer who went on to disclose it. So far as Shayler is concerned, the investigation is legitimately concerned with whatever he has disclosed to the newspaper, whether or not it j has subsequently been published. Moreover, to prove a case against Shayler, the prosecution would need to prove the material that he is alleged to have disclosed to the Observer. Mere proof of the article in the edition of 27 February would prove nothing as against Shayler. The judge was clearly entitled to be satisfied as to condition (a)(iii), quite apart from any question of a prosecution of Mr Bright. The fact that such a prosecution remains a possibility is an additional but unnecessary factor so far as condition (a)(iii) is concerned.

152. *Access condition (a)(iv): 'that the material is likely to be relevant evidence'*

153. This condition is more difficult. Any material that was created by Mr Bright would be relevant and admissible against him—for example, notes of conversations or drafts of articles. However, as I have said, he cannot be said, on the material before us, to have committed a *serious* arrestable offence under s 5. Nor would such material be admissible against Shayler if he were to stand trial for a serious arrestable offence under s 5. It seems to me that, for this access condition to be met, the judge had to be satisfied that there were reasonable grounds for believing that there was journalistic material on the premises which was likely to be relevant evidence *against Shayler*. In my judgment, there was a basis for the judge to have been so satisfied. The Shayler website for 29 February contains his account of his dealings with Mr Bright and the Observer over the previous few days. Ignoring the more self-serving parts of it, it says of Mr Bright's article: 'Journalists these days, it seems, cannot even copy accurately out of *the documents I give them*' (my emphasis).

154. Moreover, parts of the text of Mr Bright's article seem to me to be consistent with having been compiled from documentary material provided by Shayler, including a copy of a letter which Shayler claimed to have sent to the Home Secretary and which included, 'full details of the alleged plot … including the name of a MI6 officer who ran the operation and, according to Shayler, paid for the assassination attempt.' Any such material would be relevant and admissible against Shayler in relation to a charge upon the serious arrestable offence of disclosing such material to Mr Bright.

155. *Access condition (b)(i): 'other methods of obtaining the material … have been tried without success'*

156. The application was only made after attempts to procure voluntary production had been unsuccessful. The fulfilment of this condition was therefore self-evident. In the circumstances, consideration of the alternative condition (b)(ii)—methods not tried because bound to fail—did not arise.

157–159. *Access condition (c): 'it is in the public interest, having regard—(i) to the benefit likely to accrue to the investigation if the material is obtained; and (ii) to the circumstances under which the person in possession of the material holds it, that the material should be produced or that access to it should be given'*

160, 161. I agree with Judge LJ that this is not an open-ended public interest condition and that, for example, the important submissions made by Mr Emmerson about self-incrimination and freedom of expression fall to be considered in the context of the statutorily conferred judicial discretion once the judge is satisfied that the specific access conditions have been fulfilled. Having arrived at this position it is a short step to satisfaction as to condition (c) in the circumstances of this case. The benefit likely to accrue to the investigation if the material is obtained is that, if and when Shayler becomes available to the jurisdiction, the investigating officers will be in a much stronger position to charge him with and prove against him a serious arrestable offence than they would be if the material was not obtained. On the facts of this case, there is a substantial public interest in that. It does not need *R v Crown Court at Northampton, ex p DPP* (1991) 93 Cr App Rep 376 to lead me to that conclusion, and I do not find it necessary to analyse that authority. Moreover, the circumstances in which one or more people at the Observer are holding the material do not, in my judgment, give rise to any great countervailing public interest. The material is not being held in circumstances of a confidentiality. Inferentially, it was provided by Shayler with a view to its dissemination. Part of it has been published. I do not find any error of law in the judge's perception of the balancing of the public interest in light of the competing facts which were relevant at this stage of the exercise.

162. It follows from what I have said that, in my judgment, Judge Stephens was entitled to be satisfied that the access conditions were fulfilled in relation to b Mr Bright, Mr Alton and the Observer. That brings me to one of the more difficult parts of this case, and the part which makes it a case of importance beyond its own parameters. I do not doubt that, when exercising the overarching discretion to grant or to refuse a production order, a judge must have due regard to the human rights and fundamental freedoms of the persons against whom the order is sought.

c 163. In my judgment, if human rights and fundamental freedoms have a crucial role in this case, it is only likely to be by reference to the protection against self-incrimination, to which I shall shortly return. However, Mr Emmerson sought to rely also on freedom of expression. There is certainly high authority for the proposition that, even before the coming into force of the Human Rights d Act 1998, the common law right to freedom of expression is to be treated as co-extensive with art 10 of the European Convention for the Protection of Human Rights and Fundamental Freedoms (Rome, 4 November 1950; TS 71 (1953); Cmd 8969) (the convention) (see *A-G v Guardian Newspapers Ltd* (No 2) [1988] 3 All ER 545 at 660, [1990] 1 AC 109 at 283–284 per Lord Goff of Chieveley, and *Reynolds v Times Newspapers Ltd* [1999] 4 All ER 609 at 628, [1999] 3 WLR 1010 e at 1029 per Lord Steyn). However, notwithstanding Mr Emmerson's powerful submissions and those of Mr Tugendhat QC, I am not persuaded that this case is concerned with freedom of expression. The Observer has already published that part of the material which it wished to publish. It is under no duty of confidentiality to Shayler in relation to the remaining material. In any event, it f would not be the granting of a production order that would inhibit further publication, but the risk of criminal liability under s 5 of the 1989 Act. I am not impressed by the argument that to grant a production order in relation to special procedure material which is not the subject of an obligation of confidentiality to the source of the material would stand as a disincentive to future whistle-blowers or other suppliers of information to the media to act in the public interest by g disclosing important material. It is usually open to them to demand confidentiality as to their identity as the price of their disclosure.

164. It seems to me that the real issue in relation to the Observer is not freedom of expression or respect for correspondence (which crept into the submissions but, almost unnoticed, crept out again) but the privilege against h self-incrimination. It is clear from the evidence before the judge that the investigation in respect of which the application was being made included an investigation into an offence under s 5, as to which the only suspects could be employees of the Observer, especially Mr Bright. To that extent, the investigating officers assert that there are reasonable grounds to believe that he has committed such an j offence and, whereas it is suggested that it is unlikely that he will be prosecuted, an undertaking not to prosecute has not been forthcoming. We must therefore assume that he is at risk of prosecution. It is inherent in the application for the production order that, if granted, it would require him to produce 'relevant evidence' and that the material produced would be 'likely to be of substantial value … to the investigation', which includes investigation into an alleged offence committed by Mr Bright himself. Against this background, Mr Emmerson submitted

that the privilege against self-incrimination has an important place in the protections developed by both domestic law and pursuant to art 6 of the convention. It was incumbent upon the judge to have proper regard to it when exercising his discretion whether or not to grant the production order. In effect, the submission was that the discretion ought to have been exercised in a way which was consistent with the privilege or right as recognised by the common law and the convention and not in a way which would conflict with such an important protection.

165. The privilege or right is not an absolute one and there are numerous examples of legislation interfering with it. Indeed, Lord Mustill said in *R v Director of Serious Fraud Office, ex p Smith* [1992] 3 All ER 456 at 472, [1993] AC 1 at 40: 'statutory interference with the right is almost as old as the right itself' but that the court should be 'more than ever cautious before concluding that Parliament really intended to exclude it'. In the circumstances of the present case, Parliament has not excluded it, but has created a judicial discretion where its implications have to be considered.

166. The Strasbourg jurisprudence in this area is extensive. We have been taken to the leading cases including *Fayed v UK* (1994) 18 EHRR 393; *Saunders v UK* (1997) 23 EHRR 313; *Funke v France* (1993) 16 EHRR 297 and *Serves v France* (1999) 28 EHRR 265. I agree with Judge LJ that since this Strasbourg jurisprudence has recently been considered by the House of Lords in *R v Hertfordshire CC, ex p Green Environmental Industries Ltd* [2000] 1 All ER 773, [2000] 2 WLR 373, this court ought to be guided by what the House of Lords said (although the matter would not be quite so simple if we were considering this case after 2 October 2000 because of s 2(1)(a) of the 1998 Act). However, there are other parts of the speech of Lord Hoffmann to which I feel obliged to refer.

167. The principle which Lord Hoffmann extracted from *Saunders'* case was expressed by him in the following terms:

> '... the European jurisprudence under art 6(1) is firmly anchored to the fairness of the trial and is not concerned with extra-judicial inquiries. Such impact as art 6(1) may have is upon the use of such evidence at a criminal trial.' (See [2000] 1 All ER 773 at 781, [2000] 2 WLR 373 at 381.)

168. *Serves'* case on the other hand—

> 'turns on the fact that Captain Serves was at risk of being required to incriminate himself in the very proceedings in which he was ... charged with murder. The questions were to be put to him as part of the judicial process. The case is therefore not relevant to extra-judicial inquiries.' (See [2000] 1 All ER 773 at 782, [2000] 2 WLR 373 at 382.)

169. As to *Funke*'s case, upon which Mr Emmerson placed most reliance, Lord Hoffmann ([2000] 1 All ER 773 at 782, [2000] 2 WLR 373 at 382) considered that it contains 'obscurities in reasoning' adding:

> 'It is however clear that the court in the *Saunders'* case did not regard this case as casting doubt upon the clear distinction which it drew between extrajudicial inquiries and the use of the material thereby obtained in a subsequent criminal prosecution.' (See [2000] 1 All ER 773 at 783, [2000] 2 WLR 373 at 383.)

170. Accepting these statements of principle, the next question is how they apply to the facts of the present case. Mr Emmerson submitted that art 6 applies to a person who is under investigation but has not yet been charged and that

a 'charge' has a special meaning in the convention law in the sense that art 6 applies as soon as an individual is 'substantially affected' by the actions of the investigating or prosecuting authorities. He referred to a number of authorities, the most recent of which is *Allenet de Ribemont v France* (1995) 20 EHRR 557. To operate on the level which Mr Emmerson seemed to be suggesting, such a principle would not live easily with *Saunders'* case. However, it is apparent from the judgment in b *Allenet de Ribemont v France* (1995) 20 EHRR 557 at 575 that the case turned on the fact that, at the material time, a judicial investigation had already begun and it was that that made the suspect a person 'charged with a criminal offence' within the meaning of art 6(2). Indeed he was already under arrest and in police custody as part of the judicial investigation.

171. Miss Montgomery submitted that, in the light of *Saunders'* case and *Ex p* c *Green Environmental Industries Ltd*, the present case does not give rise to a breach of art 6. In the event that Mr Bright is prosecuted, the trial judge will be able to decide whether any material obtained by reason of the production order is to go before the jury. At that stage, s 78 of the 1984 Act and art 6 can both be properly considered.

d 172. In my judgment, Miss Montgomery is right. At the point when the judge in the Central Criminal Court was considering this, and more, there was no question of the making of a production order contravening art 6(1). Moreover, the making of an order does not fly in the face of the privilege against self-incrimination. Parliament has laid down a detailed code for controlling the circumstances in which a production order may be made in relation to e journalistic material. It does not include an exception for material which may incriminate the journalist. Journalistic material is either special procedure material or excluded material and, in either case, is beyond the reach of the police under the general provision relating to warrants to search and enter premises (see s 8). Production orders are more tightly controlled by the access conditions and f by the exercise of judicial discretion at the higher level. Their execution, initially at least, is less coercive and invasive although it is true that non-compliance may lead to a warrant and/or contempt proceedings (see paras 12 and 15 of Sch 1). To the extent that Judge LJ attaches importance to the notion that, under s 9, there is an obligation upon the journalist actually to *produce* the material which may incriminate him, I respectfully disagree with his analysis. The journalist, out of g deference to his profession, is given the option *either* to produce it to a constable for him to take away *or* to give a constable access to it. He is not obliged physically to hand it over and, if he chooses not to do so, his position under the alternative of giving access is not very different from the s 8 warrant procedure.

173. Where does all this lead? In my judgment, the making of this production h order did not contravene art 6 or any other provision of the convention and nor did it offend the privilege against self-incrimination in domestic law. If I am wrong in my conclusion about art 6 and the common law of self-incrimination, I am still not persuaded that the making of a production order in the case of the Observer was legally erroneous. In respect of what alleged offence may Mr j Bright be at risk of incriminating himself? On the material before the court, the answer must be an offence of disclosure under s 5 in relation to the article of 27 February. The application for the production order referred only to s 5 in the case of Mr Bright (and s 1 in the case of Shayler). As I understand it, Mr Bright does not dispute that he was the author of the article which bears his name or that its contents came, at least in part, from Shayler. There is no suggestion that he has made any other disclosures which may amount to offences under s 5. In these

circumstances, it does not seem to me that he would be placed in any greater jeopardy than already exists if the production order stands. Whilst that is not a point that was advanced to the judge at the Central Criminal Court or to us, it disposes me to the view that, in the context of the ultimate judicial discretion, it is a matter which would militate against the total refusal of a production order.

174. Nevertheless, it was entirely appropriate for the judge to consider the implications for Mr Bright as a suspect when considering whether or not, in his ultimate discretion, to make the order. That is what he did, albeit by reference to a wider construction of access condition 2(c), rather than in relation to the general discretion under para 1. He considered the Strasbourg jurisprudence and the common law. Since I am satisfied that the judge was entitled to find that the access conditions were fulfilled, all that remains to consider is whether the exercise of his ultimate discretion was legally erroneous and amenable to challenge and, if the production order is to stand, what its scope should be. In my judgment, he exercised discretion generally in a way that is not susceptible to judicial review.

175, 176. I agree, however, with Judge LJ, that where it is apparent that the access conditions are not satisfied in relation to a particular category of material, that category must be excluded from the production order. In the circumstances of this case, that applies to any document created by Mr Bright. However, where the access conditions *are* satisfied in relation to one or more items of journalistic material, I would uphold the production order in relation to not only the one or more items that have been specifically identified, but also to any other material of the same category. Thus, in the present case, I would extend it to *any* material which Mr Bright obtained from Shayler. In other words, I do not think that it is necessary for the police to satisfy the judge as to each and every document. If they had satisfied him as to an item of a category or type of material, everything falling within that category or type should be produced. If a judge was satisfied that X was in possession of special procedure material in the form of a letter from Y and was minded to make a production order in respect of it, it would be most unfortunate if the production order did not extend to any other letters to X from Y which were of similar significance. It would be absurd if the production order were limited to a specific letter that was identified and, upon that letter being produced, it referred to an earlier letter and a fresh application had to be made for the production of that earlier letter. As one document led to another, there might have to be a wholly undesirable series of applications with the possible loss or destruction of important material between applications.

177. Accordingly, in relation to Mr Bright and the Observer, I conclude that there was material upon which a production order might properly have been made but that, in my judgment, the scope of it ought to have been more limited. So far as that limitation is concerned, I would limit it to the letter to which I have referred, together with any other documentation which was provided to Mr Bright by Shayler.

178, 179. **GIBBS J**. I agree that the application on behalf of Mr Rusbridger and the Guardian should be allowed. For the reasons given by Judge LJ, the access conditions in para 2 of Sch 1 to the Police and Criminal Evidence Act 1984 were not fulfilled. I do not find it either necessary or helpful to add anything further on the subject of these applications.

180. I agree also that the applications on behalf of Mr Alton, the Observer and Mr Bright raise altogether more difficult questions.

a 181. A question of considerable importance is whether the powers of the police under s 9 of the 1984 Act may be invoked when the effect would or may be to oblige a person at whom an application under that section is directed to incriminate himself. On that question I respectfully agree with the opinion of Maurice Kay J, and (save where indicated hereafter) the reasons which he gave for that opinion in his judgment. I would wish to add only a few observations of b my own.

182. The potential for self-incrimination could arise in several different ways. It could arise where the serious arrestable offence referred to in para 2(a)(i) of Sch 1 was believed to have been committed by the very person against whom the application is directed. It could arise where the principal target of the investigation was a person other than the recipient of the application, but where c at the same time there were grounds for believing that the latter may also incriminate himself by complying with an order. It could arise also where there was nothing known to the applicant which would suggest that compliance with the order would incriminate the person in possession of the material, yet where the latter believed that such material was likely to incriminate him. In the present d case (taking the informations at face value) an order would not require Mr Shayler, who is the principal target of the investigation, to incriminate himself; yet it would potentially have that effect on Mr Bright. These examples demonstrate that there are a number of different ways in which the right against self-incrimination may arise in connection with applications under s 9; and show further, that the degree of weight to be attached to that right in individual factual e situations may vary infinitely. This is in my judgment important when one comes to consider the question of access conditions (c)(i) and (ii), and/or the exercise of discretion under para 1 of the Schedule.

183. It may also be useful to note that the warrant procedure may be adopted in situations which might otherwise call for a production order if 'service of f notice of an application for an order under paragraph 4 above may seriously prejudice an investigation' (see sub-para 14(d)). This appears to contemplate a situation in which a person to whom an order is directed is so closely connected with the matters being investigated that notice to such a person may in itself have a serious adverse effect upon the investigation. The most obvious reason for such a situation to arise is fear by the recipient of the order that production of the g material may incriminate him.

184. I respectfully differ from the reasoning of Maurice Kay J on this topic in two particular respects; first, on the distinction made between the requirements under para 4(a) to produce the documents and para 4(b) to give access to them. I respectfully agree with Judge LJ that this distinction does not diminish the h coercive quality of the procedure. Secondly, I attribute greater importance to the distinction drawn by Mr Emmerson QC between a requirement to produce incriminating documents or answer questions in the context of regulatory as opposed to purely criminal investigations. This is the distinction based upon the contrast between (for example) *Saunders v UK* (1997) 23 EHRR 313 and *Funke v* j *France* (1993) 16 EHRR 297.

185. I nevertheless conclude that s 9 by necessary implication includes the power for the Crown Court to make production orders which actually or potentially infringe a person's right against self-incrimination. This right whilst of considerable importance at common law has never been considered absolute. Whilst recognised in much more recent times in the European human rights jurisprudence, it is not, in fact, *expressly* guaranteed by art 6 of the convention. However, it is, in my

judgment, vital to couple with my conclusion on s 9 the recognition that in it Parliament has created safeguards in the form of a series of access conditions fulfilment of which have to be proved to a court; and further a judicial discretion which can and must be exercised before a production order can be made. As will appear, the extent to which any order made may infringe the right against self-incrimination is in my view an important consideration in this process.

186. I turn now to the specific access conditions. For the reasons given by Judge LJ I consider that access condition (a) is only fulfilled as to the copy letter to the Home Office and not otherwise.

187. I agree with the opinion of Judge LJ on the extent to which access condition (b) is fulfilled.

188. I turn now to access condition (c). I accept that (c)(i) and (ii) set boundaries or limitations on the extent to which the court is entitled to explore the wide and potentially problematic territory of 'public interest'. I do not, however, agree that it places off limits such issues as self-incrimination. On the contrary, the words of (c)(ii) appear to me to be apt to cover as 'circumstances under which a person in possession holds it' the fact that the journalistic material in question is held pursuant to a genuine press story on a matter of important public debate. It is also apt to cover the circumstance that possession of the material may incriminate that person. I cannot think that the wording of (c)(ii) was intended to be confined to matters as narrow as, for example, whether the material was held on disk, in a filing cabinet or a carrier bag. It seems to me that Parliament contemplated a balancing exercise to be conducted by weighing factors such as the two I have just mentioned against the fact and degree of any benefit shown to be likely to accrue to the investigation pursuant to (c)(i). I am reinforced in that view by the important point made by Mr Emmerson, to which I have already referred, namely that the powers under s 9 arise solely in the context of a criminal investigation, one of whose targets is or may be Mr Bright. It is not sufficient therefore to say that his position can be safeguarded at trial by invoking s 78. The court must direct itself to consider the position of Mr Bright and others at the Observer and their rights in a criminal context, so far as is permitted by the scope of Sch 1, at this stage.

189. That process of consideration is no more than a modern expression of Lord Camden CJ's statement of principle in *Entick v Carrington* (1775) 19 State Tr 1029, [1558–1774] All ER Rep 41 already quoted by Judge LJ. This emphasises the need for careful judicial scrutiny to justify any claimed power of the state to encroach on a person's right of property.

190. For the reasons given by Judge LJ, I find that in relation only to the copy letter which he defined, the balance weighs heavily in favour of disclosure. In relation to that letter, there is effectively no risk of self-incrimination by Mr Bright or anyone else at the Observer in the disclosure of that document alone. The sending of such a document to the Observer was a serious arrestable offence on the part of Mr Shayler (or there are good grounds to believe that it was); and the document itself is likely to be of central benefit to the investigation of that offence.

191. Subject to that single exception, I would disallow the terms of the production order as to any wider definition of material. The principal reason for this is the non-fulfilment of access condition (a). However, even assuming that the Crown had overcome that hurdle so as to justify the production of some further category or categories of document, I would hold that access condition (c) was not fulfilled.

a 192. I would make that finding upon the exercise of a judgment on the factors set out in (c)(i) and (ii) based upon the evidence in this case. Our attention was drawn to remarks in the Divisional Court in *R v Crown Court at Northampton, ex p DPP* (1991) 93 Cr App Rep 376. These were to the effect that once a judge had concluded under para 2(a)(i) of the Schedule that a serious arrestable offence had been committed, it will normally be inconsistent with that finding to refuse an b application for access to materials by finding under para 2(c) that it is not in the public interest that access should be given. As a statistical prediction that may well be accurate. It was a justifiable comment on the facts of that particular case. In my judgment, however, it cannot and should not be taken as a matter of law to fetter the exercise of the court's independent judgment to consider as a separate matter in every case whether access condition (c) has been fulfilled. c Briefly the reasons why I would hold (save in relation to the one document) that access condition (c) is not fulfilled are these: on the face of it, there is no significant reason to think that Mr Bright was doing other than pursuing a genuine journalistic story on a matter of public interest and legitimate public debate.

193. Further, Mr Emmerson is justified in contending on Mr Bright's behalf d that there is a real danger or likelihood of self-incrimination. It is true that it may be difficult on the basis of the evidence available to the court to rationalise the source of that likelihood. Four points, however, need to be borne in mind.

194. (1) The informations seeking the orders actually specify offences under s 5 of the Official Secrets Act 1989 as well as s 1. Such offences can only have been committed by Mr Bright as opposed to Shayler.

e 195. (2) DS Flynn in evidence said that he had reasonable grounds to believe that an offence under s 5 had been committed by Mr Bright.

196. (3) There have been repeated and considered refusals to give undertakings not to prosecute Mr Bright.

197. (4) The evidence about the extent of damage caused by publication of the f article to the security of the state was in the form of an assertion by DS Flynn. The limitations upon the value of that evidence and the unfortunate non-disclosure of the presence in court of Mr Lerner have already been analysed by Judge LJ. I agree with his analysis.

198. The significance of the fourth point in this context is that the court was not given the necessary material to assess the basis of DS Flynn's assertion and g thus the likelihood or otherwise of self-incrimination. At its face value his assertion gave serious grounds for believing that Mr Bright would be prosecuted. Was it no more than mere assertion? Or was there some other undisclosed ground for believing that a prosecution of Mr Bright would be justified?

199. The plain fact is that the extent and quality of the evidence before the h court were inadequate to permit a sensible judgment to be made. For that reason it would not be right to reach any conclusion other than that Mr Flynn's opinion may have been correct about the commission of an offence by Mr Bright.

200. All these matters in my judgment underline the correctness of Judge LJ's views about the need to provide the court with the necessary evidence to make a j proper assessment of the access conditions. I agree with his observations about the adoption if necessary where the evidence includes confidential information of a procedure similar to that used in public interest immunity applications. Such a procedure may not infrequently be necessary to enable the court to exercise an informed judgment. The deficiencies in the evidence here give rise to a situation in which the court is faced with a bald assertion of the belief that Mr Bright has committed serious offences or a serious offence, but is left to speculate as to the

grounds for that belief. That situation in my view would make it unsafe and wrong to find that access condition (c) is fulfilled save in respect of the one document already mentioned.

201. Alternatively, if my interpretation of (c)(ii) is wrong, I would for similar reasons exercise my discretion against granting an order except to the limited extent mentioned.

202. I recognise the logic of Maurice Kay J's reasoning which justifies the extension of the material to be disclosed to a wider class of documents than simply the letter. Had the evidence available to the court been more satisfactory I may have adopted that reasoning. But given the current state of the evidence I am disinclined to uphold any order which carries with it any real possibility of infringing Mr Bright's right against self-incrimination. I acknowledge that if there were to be sustainable grounds for believing that further disclosable procedure material is in possession of the Observer, or such grounds were to emerge, a further application might (and I emphasise 'might') be justified.

203. I acknowledge Maurice Kay J's reservations about unnecessarily prolonging the proceedings; but I nevertheless consider on the evidence here that a cautious approach is justified.

204. As to the width of the terms of the original application, I respectfully associate myself fully with the remarks of Judge LJ as to their potentially stifling effect on any or any useful reporting of the Shayler story.

205. I am compelled, it follows, to disagree with the views of the judge at the Central Criminal Court as to access conditions (a) and (c) and also as to the exercise of discretion, but in so deciding I recognise the difficulty of the task with which he was confronted and have no wish in this judgment to appear unduly critical.

206. In the result, I respectfully agree with the conclusions reached by Judge LJ and with the one exception specified by him. The application to this court should be allowed.

Order accordingly.

Dilys Tausz Barrister.

a

Hewlings v McLean Homes East Anglia Ltd

QUEEN'S BENCH DIVISION, DIVISIONAL COURT

ROSE LJ AND RAFFERTY J

25 JULY 2000

b

Nuisance – Statutory nuisance – Complaint to justices – Proceedings against company – Service of statutory notice prior to commencement of proceedings – Complainant sending notice to company but not to its registered office – Whether notice properly served – Environmental Protection Act 1990, ss 82, 160.

c

The respondent company was carrying out works on a site adjacent to the complainant's home. He wrote to H, the company's director and general manager, at an address known as Tartan House, complaining of a nuisance caused to his property by the company's work. H replied by a letter bearing the company's name and two addresses: Tartan House at the top of the page and the d address of the company's registered office at the bottom of the page. Thereafter the complainant's solicitors wrote to H as director and general manager of the company at Tartan House, giving notice pursuant to s 82[a] of the Environmental Protection Act 1990 that the complainant intended to bring proceedings requiring the company to abate the alleged nuisance and warning that, if the e alleged nuisance was not abated within three days, proceedings might be brought. H acknowledged receipt in a letter sent from Tartan House, but which also showed the address of the registered office. Subsequently, a summons was issued and served upon the company. At the hearing, the company contended that the s 82 notice had not been served on its registered office in accordance with the requirements of s 160[b] of the 1990 Act. Section 160 provided that the notice f 'may' be served by leaving it at, or posting it to, the relevant person's proper address (sub-s (2)); that in the case of a body corporate, the notice 'may' be served on, or given to, the secretary or clerk of that body (sub-s (3)); and that in the case of such a body or their secretary or clerk, the proper address 'shall' be the registered or principal office of that company (sub-s (4)). The magistrates held that the g requirements as to service under s 160 were mandatory; that a failure to serve in accordance with that section could not be corrected; that a s 82 notice had to be served upon the company or its secretary at its registered office; that as the company was registered in England and Wales, it had, in compliance with the Companies Act 1985, a secretary and a registered office; and that, as a matter of law, the company could not have a principal office and H could not be its h secretary or clerk. They therefore held that the notice had not been properly served and dismissed the complaint. The complainant appealed by way of case stated.

Held – The requirements as to service contained in s 160 of the 1990 Act were j permissive, not mandatory. That could be seen from the explicit use of the word 'may' as opposed to the word 'must' which was used in other parts of the statute. Thus other means of service were sufficient and a failure to comply was amenable to correction. Moreover, for the purposes of s 160, a limited company

a Section 82, so far as material, is set out at p 283 *h* to p 284 *b*, post

b Section 160, so far as material, is set out at p 284 *e* to *g*, post registered in England and Wales could have a principal office and clerk as well as a company secretary. It followed that service could be effected upon the company or its secretary at its registered office, or upon its secretary or clerk at its principal office. Such a construction was consistent with the purpose of s 82 of the 1990 Act, namely the provision of a summary procedure for lay people to gain relief from nuisances. The statute contemplated less rigidity than company legislation, and its purpose was not to be frustrated by the introduction of any technical obstacle. In the instant case, the magistrates should have found that Tartan House was the company's principal office, and there had been ample material before them demonstrating that the company knew full well what was being alleged against it. No prejudice could possibly have been caused by sending the notice to one address rather than another in circumstances where H, a woman in a position of authority, and someone prepared to acknowledge that authority to the complainant, was in receipt of the notice and had acted upon it. Accordingly, the s 82 notice had been properly served, and the appeal would therefore be allowed (see p 285 *e* to *j*, p 286 *a j* to p 288 *f*, post).

Leeds v London Borough of Islington [1998] Env LR 655, *Pearshouse v Birmingham City Council* [1999] LGR 169 and *Hall v Kingston upon Hull City Council, Ireland v Birmingham City Council, Baker v Birmingham City Council* [1999] 2 All ER 609 considered.

Notes

For summary proceedings for abatement of a statutory nuisance, see 34 *Halsbury's Laws* (4th edn reissue) para 87.

For the Environmental Protection Act 1990, ss 82, 160, see 35 *Halsbury's Statutes* (4th edn) (1998 reissue) 862, 907.

Cases referred to in judgments

Hall v Kingston upon Hull City Council, Ireland v Birmingham City Council, Baker v Birmingham City Council [1999] 2 All ER 609, DC.
Leeds v London Borough of Islington [1998] Env LR 655, DC.
Pearshouse v Birmingham City Council [1999] LGR 169, DC.

Cases cited or referred to in skeleton arguments

Halki Shipping Corp v Sopex Oils Ltd [1998] 2 All ER 23, [1998] 1 WLR 726, CA.
R v Crown Court at Liverpool, ex p Cooke [1996] 4 All ER 589, [1997] 1 WLR 700, DC.
R v Dudley Magistrates' Court, ex p Hollis, Hollis v Dudley Metropolitan BC, Probert v Dudley Metropolitan BC [1998] 1 All ER 759, [1999] 1 WLR 642, DC.
Sharpley and Manby's Arbritation, Re [1942] 1 All ER 66, sub nom *Sharpley v Manby* [1942] 1 KB 217, CA.
Singh v Atombrook Ltd [1989] 1 All ER 385, [1989] 1 WLR 810, CA.
Stylo Shoes Ltd v Prices Tailors Ltd [1959] 3 All ER 901, [1960] Ch 396.
Vignes v Stephen Smith & Co Ltd (1909) 53 Sol Jo 716.

Case stated

The appellant, Richard Hewlings, appealed by way of case stated from the decision of justices sitting at Cambridge on 20 July 1998 dismissing his proceedings for statutory nuisance against the respondent, McLean Homes East Anglia Ltd, on the grounds that a notice served by him on the respondent under s 82 of the Environmental Protection Act 1990 failed to comply with the requirements for service in s 160 of that Act. The questions for the opinion of a the High Court are set out at p 286 *j* to p 287 *a*, post. The facts are set out in the judgment of Rafferty J.

Robert McCracken (instructed by *Richard Buxton*, Cambridge) for the appellant.
Timothy Jones (instructed by *Gateley Wareing*, Birmingham) for the company.

b **RAFFERTY J.**

1. The respondent company was working on a site adjacent to the appellant's private home, a listed building, when, in June 1998, he wrote to Mrs Frances Hill, accepted as being the director and general manager of the respondent company, at Tartan House, Etna Road, Bury St Edmunds, Suffolk. In his letter he complained c of the nuisance caused to him by work that created noise, dust and damage to the drains of his house and the foundations of his wall. He made plain that he was worried about vibrations from the work which might damage his grade 2 listed house.

2. By 1 July 1998 Mrs Hill was responding by letter, telling the appellant that the works and their progress were essential. That letter bore in its heading the d name of the respondent, and not only the address to which it had been sent, to which I shall for shorthand purposes refer now as Tartan House, but also 'Registered Office, Crestwood House, Birches Rise, Willenhall, West Midlands', an address to be found at the bottom of the page. Mrs Frances Hill signed that letter in her capacity as director and general manager of the company.

e 3. On 7 July 1998 the appellant's solicitors wrote to her, in her capacity as director and general manager, sending the letter to Tartan House, and giving her notice, under s 82 of the Environmental Protection Act 1990, that he intended to bring proceedings requiring abatement of nuisance and warning that were there not abatement within three days proceedings might be brought.

f 4. It is agreed that Mrs Hill received that letter the next day, 8 July 1998, acknowledging it by her letter of 9 July, sending her acknowledgment from Tartan House and remarking, importantly, as follows: 'As a reputable company we take these matters seriously and I will get back to you once I have concluded my investigations.'

5. That letter showed the Crestwood House address.

g 6. By the 15th, a summons was issued. Parties assembled in due course at Cambridge Magistrates' Court where this matter proceeded to trial on 20 July 1998. The respondent company for these purposes is categorised as McLean Homes East Anglia Ltd and is wholly owned by George Wimpey plc. The Crestwood House address is that of its registered office.

h 7. Before the magistrates the respondent took the preliminary point that notice had not been properly served under s 82(7). I turn to the relevant provisions.

8. In its applicable parts s 82 reads as follows:

> '(1) A magistrates' court may act under this section on a complaint made j by any person on the ground that he is aggrieved by the existence of a statutory nuisance.
>
> (2) If the magistrates' court is satisfied that the alleged nuisance exists, or that although abated it is likely to recur on the same premises, the court shall make an order for either or both of the following purposes—(a) requiring the defendant to abate the nuisance, within a time specified in the order, and to execute any works necessary for that purpose; (b) prohibiting a recurrence of

the nuisance, and requiring the defendant, within a time specified in the order, to execute any works necessary to prevent the recurrence ...

(6) Before instituting proceedings for an order under subsection (2) above against any person, the person aggrieved by the nuisance shall give to that person such notice in writing of his intention to bring the proceedings as is applicable to proceedings in respect of a nuisance of that description and the notice shall specify the matter complained of.

(7) The notice of the bringing of proceedings in respect of a statutory nuisance required by subsection (6) above which is applicable is—(a) in the case of a nuisance falling within paragraph (g) of section 79(1) above, not less than three days' notice ...'

A noise emitted from premises so as to be prejudicial to health or a nuisance, constitutes a statutory nuisance under s 79(1)(g) of the Act. Persons other than a district council may lodge a complaint to a magistrates' court if they are aggrieved by the existence of the statutory nuisance established under s 82(1). Before doing so they must give no less than three days' notice to the prospective defendant.

9. As a matter of fact in this case that was done.

10. The potential consequences of non-compliance with the notice label proceedings as either criminal or at the very least quasi-criminal in nature. Section 160 of the Act applies to any notice required or authorised.

11. The material words in s 160 are as follows:

'(2) Any such notice [that being a s 82 notice] required or authorised to be served on or given to a person ... may be served or given by delivering it to him, or by leaving it at his proper address, or by sending it by post to him at that address.

(3) Any such notice—(a) in the case of a body corporate, may be served on or given to the secretary or clerk of that body ...

(4) For the purposes of this section and section 7 of the Interpretation Act 1978 ... the proper address of any person on or to whom any such notice is to be served or given should be his last known address, except that—(a) in the case of a body corporate or their secretary or clerk, it shall be the registered or principal office of that body ... and for the purposes of this subsection the principal office of a company registered outside the United Kingdom ... shall be their principal office within the United Kingdom.'

12. I turn now to the rival contentions of the parties, the respondent averring that sub-s (4) deals only with companies registered outside the United Kingdom and cannot catch this respondent company. I find nothing on the language of the statute to make that contention valid. Whether or not company law legislation is designed specifically for the protection of the environment it nevertheless, as we shall see, contemplates a lay person enjoying its protection. All this subsection seems to me to achieve, if a company should be registered outside the United Kingdom, is provision as to its principal office.

13. Section 160(5) allows recipients of a notice to specify a further address for service. The abatement notice sent on 7 July 1998 was served, says the appellant, on the respondent at its proper address, that being its principal office. Alternatively, upon Mrs Hill as secretary or clerk of that body corporate at its proper address. Alternatively, that her July acknowledgment of receipt of the notice showed that in whatever capacity and at whatever address she had had

a service. Alternatively, were notice not properly served, such failure can be corrected, since the provisions of s 160 of the Act were permissive and therefore do not exclude alternative methods of service.

14. Mrs Hill must have been, for the purposes of s 160(3), on notice, and prejudice to the respondent company is not made out.

15. The court was entitled to find that Tartan House was the principal office b of the company on the basis of Mrs Hill's letter. The Wimpey Directory lists: 'McLean Homes East Anglia, Director and General Manager: Frances Hill, Tartan House, Etna Road, Bury St Edmunds, Suffolk'.

16. The respondent, however, contends that before s 79 proceedings can be instituted there must be (under s 82) notice in writing of the intention to bring proceedings within three days. Section 160, it contends, specifies the means of c service in the case of a company as follows: service on the company's secretary or delivery of notice to him; service on the company or its secretary at its proper address; or service on the company, or its secretary, by postal delivery at the proper address or to him.

17. The magistrates reached these conclusions: that the proceedings were of a d criminal nature; the requirements as to service of notice under s 160 were mandatory; failure to serve in accordance with that section was not amenable to correction; such notice had to be served upon the company or its secretary by leaving the notice at the registered office, or serving it by post to the registered office. As the company was registered in England and Wales, it had, in compliance with the Companies Act 1985 a secretary and a registered office. As e a matter of law it could not have a principal office, and Mrs Hill could not be its secretary or clerk. Therefore the notice had been improperly served.

18. The notice requirements under s 82 of the 1990 Act need to be construed in accordance with their purpose within the legislation. That, in my judgment, is to provide a summary procedure for lay people to gain relief from nuisances.

f 19. I reject the respondent's contention that this court should consider whether the legislation is navigable by solicitors. This is not company legislation, but a statute specifically directed to the protection of the environment and contemplating action taken by the aggrieved layman, just as in this case.

20. The court considered the proper approach to the notice requirements under s 82 in the well-rehearsed authority of *Hall v Kingston upon Hull City Council,* g *Ireland v Birmingham City Council, Baker v Birmingham City Council* [1999] 2 All ER 609, where giving the judgment of the court, Mitchell J remarked (at 624):

> 'This aspect [that is s 82] of the 1990 Act is intended to provide ordinary people, numbered amongst whom are those who are disadvantaged … with h a speedy and effective remedy … Parliament's intention, in the absence of compelling statutory language, should not in our view be frustrated by introducing into this straightforward and swift statutory remedy any technical obstacle of which the ordinary citizen will almost certainly be unaware.'

j 21. It is a fact that the respondent company's manager and director, Mrs Hill, had knowledge of this notice and, in my view, was authorised to deal with it. If it matters, directors have extensive powers, as is well established. But s 160 is in any event permissive not mandatory.

22. It is worth considering the decision of this court in the case of *Leeds v London Borough of Islington* [1998] Env LR 655, where Schiemann LJ, giving the judgment of the court, said (at 658):

'... so far as bodies corporate are concerned, section 160(3) identifies the person on whom the notice is to be served. Section 160(4) identifies the address for service. Section 160(5) provides that in the specified circumstances an address alternative to that in section 160(4) can be used.'

23. Pausing there, for a moment, that seems to me to fortify the conclusion that I have already reached, which is that this Act contemplates less rigidity than company legislation.

24. Returning to *Leeds'* case, there the notice in question was addressed to the senior estate manager, not to the clerk of the relevant local authority. His Lordship continues (at 658):

'The use of the word "may" in this context is not one which indicates that the persons specified in section 160(3) is one of a number of persons who may be served when it is sought to apprise a corporate body of the existence of a notice. If that was so, the subsection would be redundant.'

25. He goes on later to say this (at 661):

'It is clear from the case law ... that the requirements as to what can constitute the giving of notices have been liberally interpreted ... The reasoning behind such liberal interpretation has no application to cases under the [1990 Act] which involve possible criminal penalties.'

26. The respondent accepts that those comments were inevitably obiter, coming as they did after a reserved judgment.

27. Turning to the authority of *Hall's* case [1999] 2 All ER 609 the judgment reads (at 619): 'We do not overlook Schiemann LJ's observation in *Leeds v Islington London BC*.' It continues (at 619–620):

'The point Schiemann LJ was there considering was taken by the court after reserving judgment and appears in any event to have been obiter. The case at the hearing had turned upon whether an alternative address for service of a s 82(6) notice had been specified within the meaning of s 160(5). As we have already stated, the court held that no alternative address for the purpose of serving s 82(6) notices was specified on the rent-card. Had the court reached a different conclusion, before it could have concluded that there had been service of the s 82(6) notice for the purposes of s 160(5), it would also have been necessary to consider whether "the person to be served with or given any such notice" was the person who had specified the alternative address.'

28. The appellant suggests further or alternatively that if the procedure under s 160(2) is not, as he contends, permissive but mandatory, then the warning notice was delivered to the respondent company, as established by its acknowledgment on 8 July. Therefore, the provisions of s 160(2) were met, as the first of those three alternatives I have already considered, that is delivery. If he is wrong about that, he argues then as one of the proper addresses of the respondent company is its principal office, another is its registered office, and as Mrs Hill answered on notepaper reciting, both, service is in terms contemplated by the statute.

29. The questions for the opinion of this court are posed as follows, and they provide a useful framework for drawing together the arguments put to us today. First:

a 'Whether, in the case of these proceedings the requirements as to service contained in s 160 of the 1990 Act are mandatory, that no other means of service of the notice is sufficient, and whether failure to comply with those provisions is a defect capable of correction.'

30. I would answer that first question, no. The provisions contained within s 160 of the Act seem to me to be clearly on their face permissive as is demonstrated b by the explicit use of the word used 'may' in contrast to the selected word 'must' in other parts of the statute.

31. 'No other means of service of the notice is sufficient, and whether failure to comply with those provisions is a defect capable of correction.' In my view other means of service are sufficient and failure to comply is amenable to correction.

c 32, 33. Second:

'Whether in the case of a limited company registered in England and Wales there can only be a company secretary and a registered office, and not a principal office and clerk …'

d I would answer 'no'.

'Whether in the case of a limited company service must be effected upon the company or its secretary at its registered office or whether it can be effected upon it or its secretary or clerk at its principal office.'

I would answer 'yes'. Third:

e 'If in the case of a limited company registered in England and Wales under the Companies Act 1985 there can be a "principal office", we [the magistrates] (i) could or (ii) should have found on the basis of the documents specified in paragraph 3(e) above [the statement of case] that Tartan House was the principal office of the respondent company.'

f 34. This seems to me to distil one of the two crucial questions. I would answer 'yes' to both: the court could and should have found, on the basis of documents before it, that Tartan House was the principal office of the respondent company.

35. The reason that that seems to me clear is to be found, first of all, in the judgment of the Lord Bingham of Cornhill CJ in *Pearshouse v Birmingham City* g *Council* [1999] LGR 169 at 182–183 where he remarked:

'Section 82 is intended to provide a simple procedure for a private citizen to obtain redress when he or she suffers a statutory nuisance of any one of the various kinds itemised in section 79(1), which may relate to the state of h the premises or the emission of smoke or the emission of fumes or gases, or dust, steam, smell or other effluvia arising on premises, or the accumulation or deposit, or the keeping of an animal, or noise, or anything else declared by statute to be a statutory nuisance. It would frustrate the clear intention of Parliament if the procedure provided by section 82 were to become bogged down in unnecessary technicality or undue literalism. It is important that the j system should be operable by people who may be neither very sophisticated nor very articulate, and who may not in some cases, unlike this [appellant], have the benefit of specialised and high quality advice.'

36. Those sentiments were echoed in *Hall*'s case to which I have referred. Mitchell J in *Hall*'s case, dealing with the titles secretary, clerk, or equivalent, describes these nouns as—

> 'simply vehicles by which the "person to be served" may be served. In our judgment the Act does not identify the class of persons who can, on behalf of a body corporate, "specify" for the purposes of s 160(5).' (See [1999] 2 All ER 609 at 620.)

37. Further (at 621): 'In our judgment what matters in the circumstances currently under review is the reality of the situation.'

38. That seems to me perfectly to sum up the genesis of this legislation, and helpfully to distil this court's proper approach to interpretation of its sections.

39. I return to the final question posed for this court, number 4:

> 'Whether there was material before us [the magistrates] upon which we (i) could or (ii) should have found that notice pursuant to s 82 of the Act had been given to the respondent company.'

40. This seems to me the second of two issues I have described as crucial. Accepting the label given to penalties in this case as either criminal or quasi-criminal, there was ample material before the magistrates to demonstrate that the respondent company knew full well what was being alleged against it. I cannot identify any prejudice that could possibly be caused by the sending of the notice to one address or another address, when it is a fact that Mrs Frances Hill, a woman in a position of authority, and someone prepared to acknowledge that authority to the appellant, was in receipt of the notice and acted upon it.

41. *Hall*'s case epitomises the proper approach to Parliament's intention, that is to provide a straightforward remedy to ordinary folk; it should not be frustrated by the introduction of any technical obstacle. I would respectfully adopt these sentiments echoing as they do the resonating words of Lord Bingham in *Pearshouse*'s case, and I would answer, for the reasons I have given, the questions in the way I have set out.

ROSE LJ.

42. I agree.

43. Accordingly the appeal will be allowed. Subject to any submission to the contrary, the case will be remitted to the Cambridge justices for them to hear and determine the complaint of 15 July 1998.

Appeal allowed.

Dilys Tausz Barrister.

a

Douglas and others v Hello! Ltd

COURT OF APPEAL, CIVIL DIVISION

BROOKE, SEDLEY AND KEENE LJJ

22, 23 NOVEMBER, 21 DECEMBER 2000

b

Equity – Breach of confidence – Injunction – Celebrity couple giving magazine exclusive rights to publish photographs of their wedding – Rival magazine planning to publish unauthorised photographs of wedding – Judge granting injunction restraining rival magazine from publishing photographs – Whether injunction should be discharged – c *Whether law protecting person's privacy in absence of obligation of confidence – Human Rights Act 1998, s 12, Sch 1, Pt I, arts 8, 10 – Press Complaints Commission Code of Practice* (1997), *cl 3.*

The first and second claimants, D and Z, two internationally-famous film stars, d were engaged to be married. They entered into an agreement with the third claimant, N plc, the publisher of a weekly celebrity magazine, giving it exclusive rights to publish colour photographs of their wedding. Under the agreement, D and Z retained rights of approval over anything that was to be published, and undertook to use their best efforts to ensure that no other media were permitted access to the wedding and that no guests or anyone else present would be allowed e to take photographs. To that end, all service companies involved in the wedding were required to enter confidentiality agreements, prohibiting them and their employees from keeping, disclosing, using or selling any photograph, film or videotape obtained at the wedding reception. In addition, the wedding invitations stated that the couple 'would appreciate' no photography or video devices at the f ceremony or reception, and guests were only given access to the wedding after being checked by a professional security service for cameras, videotape machines and other recording devices. Two days after the wedding, Z warned N plc that another magazine was about to publish unauthorised photographs of the wedding. Later that evening, a judge granted an interim injunction restraining H Ltd, the publisher of a rival celebrity magazine, from publishing the disputed photographs. g At a hearing the next day, another judge continued the injunction until trial or further order. On H Ltd's appeal, the court considered the interrelationship between the right to respect for private life in art 8[a] of the European Convention for the Protection of Human Rights and Fundamental Freedoms 1950 (as set out in Sch 1 to the Human Rights Act 1998); the right to freedom of expression in h art 10(1)[b] of the convention; the qualification to that right in art 10(2) (such restrictions as were prescribed by law and were necessary in a democratic society for, inter alia, the protection of the reputation or rights of others and preventing the disclosure of information received in confidence); and the provisions of s 12[c] of the 1998 Act, which applied if a court was considering granting any relief which, if granted, might affect the convention right to freedom of expression. j Under s 12(3), no such relief was to be granted so as to restrain publication before trial unless the court was satisfied that the applicant was likely to establish that the publication should not be allowed. Section 12(4) required the court to have

a Article 8 is set out at p 322 *g h*, post

b Article 10 is set out at p 322 *c*, post

c Section 12 is set out at p 321 g to p 322 *a*, post

particular regard to the importance of the convention right to freedom of expression and, where the proceedings related to journalistic, literary or artistic material, to, inter alia, any relevant privacy code. In that context, D and Z relied on cl 3[d] of the Press Complaints Commission's Code of Practice (the press code) which provided, inter alia, that everyone was entitled to respect for his private and family life. Issues arose as to whether s 12(3) gave art 10 priority over art 8; if so, whether that subsection was compatible with the convention; and whether English law protected a person from unwanted intrusions into a person's privacy in the absence of an obligation of confidence.

Held – On its true construction, s 12(3) of the 1998 Act did not seek to give priority to one convention right over another. It simply dealt with the interlocutory stage of proceedings and with how the court was to approach matters at that stage in advance of any ultimate balance being struck between rights which might be in potential conflict. It required the court to look at the merits of the case and not merely to consider whether there was a serious issue to be tried. Thus the court had to look ahead to the ultimate stage and to be satisfied that the scales were likely to come down in the applicant's favour. That did not conflict with the convention since it merely required the court to apply its mind to how one right was to be balanced, on the merits, against another right, without building in additional weight on one side. Section 12(3) certainly made prior restraint (ie before trial) more difficult in cases where the right to freedom of expression was engaged than where it was not. However, s 12 did not give the art 10(1) right to freedom of expression a presumptive priority over other rights. Rather, it required the court to consider art 10(2) along with art 10(1), and by doing so to bring into the frame the conflicting right to respect for privacy. Indeed, the statutory provisions, coupled with the current wording of the press code, meant that in any case where the court was concerned with issues of freedom of expression in a journalistic, literary or artistic context, it was bound to pay particular regard to any breach of the rules set out in cl 3 of the code, especially where none of the public interest claims set out in the preamble to the code was asserted. A newspaper which flouted cl 3 was likely in those circumstances to have its claim to entitlement to freedom of expression trumped by art 10(2) considerations of privacy. In the instant case, D and Z were likely to establish that publication should not be allowed on confidentiality grounds, or were likely to succeed at trial in establishing a breach of their privacy in which H Ltd might be actionably implicated. However, the balance of convenience was in favour of H Ltd. The dominant feature of the case was that by far the greater part of D and Z's privacy had been traded and fell to be protected, if at all, as a commodity in the hands of N plc. That could be done without an injunction since any damage to the claimants could be adequately dealt with in monetary terms. In contrast, it would be difficult to compute H Ltd's losses in money terms if it were prevented from publishing the issue containing the disputed photographs. Accordingly, the appeal would be allowed and the injunction discharged (see p 303 *e f*, p 313 j to p 314 *a g*, p 315 *c d g*, p 315 *j*, p 316 *b*, p 323 *e f*, p 324 *a* to *c*, p 325 *e* to *g*, p 326 *g* to *j* to p 327 *a e f* and p 337 *d e*, post); *Kaye v Robertson* [1991] FSR 62 doubted.

Per Sedley LJ. The law recognises and will appropriately protect a right of privacy. That statement says little, save by way of a label, that the courts have not said already over the years. Among other things, it says that the right,

d Clause 3 is set out at p 313 *j*, post

a grounded as it is in the equitable doctrine of confidence, is not unqualified. However, a concept of privacy accords recognition to the fact that the law has to protect not only those people whose trust has been abused, but also those who simply find themselves subjected to an unwanted intrusion into their personal lives. The law no longer needs to construct an artificial relationship of confidentiality between intruder and victim: it can recognise privacy itself as a legal b principle drawn from the fundamental value of personal autonomy (see p 316 *h* and p 320 *c* to *e*, post).

Notes

For interlocutory injunctions restraining breach of confidence, see 8(1) *Halsbury's Laws* (4th edn reissue) para 491, and for the rights to respect for privacy and c freedom of expression, see 8(2) *Halsbury's Laws* (4th edn reissue) paras 149–150, 158–159.

For the Human Rights Act 1998, s 12, Sch 1, Pt I, arts 8, 10, see 7 *Halsbury's Statutes* (4th edn) (1999 reissue) 510, 524.

d **Cases referred to in judgments**

A v UK (1998) 5 BHRC 137, ECt HR.

A-G v Guardian Newspapers Ltd (No 2) [1988] 3 All ER 545, [1990] 1 AC 109, [1988] 3 WLR 776, HL.

Airey v Ireland (1979) 2 EHRR 305, ECt HR.

Albert (Prince) v Strange (1849) 1 Mac & G 25, 41 ER 1171, LC.

e *American Cyanamid Co v Ethicon Ltd* [1975] 1 All ER 504, [1975] AC 396, [1975] 2 WLR 316, HL.

Argyll (Margaret), Duchess of v Duke of Argyll [1965] 1 All ER 611, [1967] Ch 302, [1965] 2 WLR 790.

Balfour v Balfour [1919] 2 KB 571, [1918–19] All ER Rep 860, CA.

f *Barrymore v News Group Newspapers Ltd* [1997] FSR 600.

Bernstein (Lord) of Leigh v Skyviews and General Ltd [1977] 2 All ER 902, [1978] QB 479, [1977] 3 WLR 136.

Botta v Italy (1998) 4 BHRC 81, ECt HR.

Cambridge Nutrition Ltd v British Broadcasting Corp [1990] 3 All ER 523, CA.

Carson v Here's Johnny Portable Toilets Inc (1983) 698 F 2d 831, US Ct of Apps, 6th Cir.

g *Coco v AN Clark (Engineers) Ltd* (1969) 86 RPC 41.

Creation Records Ltd v News Group Newspapers Ltd [1997] EMLR 444.

Donoghue (or M' Alister) v Stevenson [1932] AC 562, [1932] All ER Rep 1, HL.

Dudgeon v UK (1981) 4 EHRR 149, ECt HR.

Express Newspapers plc v News (UK) Ltd [1990] 3 All ER 376, [1990] 1 WLR 1320.

h *Flannery v Halifax Estate Agencies Ltd* [2000] 1 All ER 373, [2000] 1 WLR 377, CA.

Fraser v Evans [1969] 1 All ER 8, [1969] 1 QB 349, [1968] 3 WLR 1172, CA.

Haseldine v CA Daw & Son Ltd [1941] 3 All ER 156, [1941] 2 KB 343, CA.

Hellewell v Chief Constable of Derbyshire [1995] 4 All ER 473, [1995] 1 WLR 804.

Hubbard v Vosper [1972] 1 All ER 1023, [1972] 2 QB 84, [1972] 2 WLR 389, CA.

j *Kaye v Robertson* [1991] FSR 62, CA.

Les Éditions Vice-Versa Inc v Aubry (1998) 5 BHRC 437, Can SC.

Lopez Ostra v Spain (1994) 20 EHRR 277, ECt HR.

Malone v Comr of Police of the Metropolis (No 2) [1979] 2 All ER 620, [1979] Ch 344, [1979] 2 WLR 700.

Merkur Island Shipping Corp v Laughton [1983] 2 All ER 189, [1983] 2 AC 570, [1993] 2 WLR 778, HL.

Morris v Beardmore [1980] 2 All ER 753, [1981] AC 446, [1980] 3 WLR 283, HL.
NWL Ltd v Woods [1979] 3 All ER 614, [1979] 1 WLR 1294, HL.
Observer v UK (1991) 14 EHRR 153, ECt HR.
Pollard v Photographic Co (1888) 40 Ch D 345.
R v Advertising Standards Authority Ltd, ex p Vernons Organisation Ltd [1993] 2 All ER 202, [1992] 1 WLR 1289.
R v Central Independent Television plc [1994] 3 All ER 641, [1994] Fam 192, [1994] 3 WLR 20, CA.
R v Khan (Sultan) [1996] 3 All ER 289, [1997] AC 558, [1996] 3 WLR 162, HL.
Schering Chemicals Ltd v Falkman Ltd [1981] 2 All ER 321, [1982] QB 1, [1981] 2 WLR 848, CA.
Shelley Films Ltd v Rex Features Ltd [1994] EMLR 134.
Spencer (Earl) v UK (1998) 25 EHRR CD 105, E Comm HR.
Stephens v Avery [1988] 2 All ER 477, [1988] Ch 449, [1988] 2 WLR 1280.
Stjerna v Finland (1994) 24 EHRR 194, ECt HR.
Tuck & Sons v Priester (1887) 19 QBD 629, CA.
Tucker v News Media Ownership Ltd [1986] 2 NZLR 716.
Woodward v Hutchins [1977] 2 All ER 751, [1977] 1 WLR 760, CA.
X v Netherlands (1985) 8 EHRR 235, ECt HR.

Cases also cited or referred to in skeleton arguments

A-G v Barker [1990] 3 All ER 257, CA.
A-G v Blake (Johnathan Cape Ltd, third party) [1998] 1 All ER 833, [1998] Ch 439, CA; *affd* [2000] 4 All ER 385, [2001] 1 AC 268, HL.
Bolkiah (Prince Jefri) v KPMG (a firm) [1999] 1 All ER 517, [1999] 2 WLR 215, HL.
Boulting v Association of Cinematograph, Television and Allied Technicians [1963] 1 All ER 716, [1963] 2 QB 606, CA.
Colombia Picture Industries Inc v Robinson [1986] FSR 367.
Esso Petroleum Co Ltd v Kingswood Motors (Addlestone) Ltd [1973] 3 All ER 1057, [1974] QB 142.
F v Wirral Metropolitan BC [1991] 2 All ER 648, [1991] Fam 69, CA.
Faccenda Chicken Ltd v Fowler [1986] 1 All ER 617, [1987] Ch 117, CA.
Francome v Mirror Group Newspapers Ltd [1984] 2 All ER 408, [1984] 1 WLR 892, CA.
Home Office v Harman [1982] 1 All ER 532, [1983] 1 AC 280, HL.
H-S (minors: protection of identity), Re [1994] 3 All ER 390, [1994] 1 WLR 1141, CA.
Indata Equipment Supplies Ltd (t/a Autofleet) v ACL Ltd [1998] 1 BCLC 412, CA.
Kelly v British Broadcasting Corp [2001] 1 All ER 323, [2001] Fam 59.
Law Debenture Trust Corp plc v Ural Caspian Oil Corp Ltd [1995] 1 All ER 157, CA.
Lumley v Gye (1853) 2 E & B 216, [1843–60] All ER Rep 208.
Missing Link Software v Magee [1989] 1 FSR 361.
Ocular Sciences Ltd v Aspect Vision Care Ltd, Galley v Ocular Services Ltd [1997] RPC 289.
R v Broadcasting Complaints Commission, ex p Granada Television Ltd [1995] EMLR 163, CA.
R v Broadcasting Standards Commission, ex p British Broadcasting Corp (Liberty intervening) [2000] 3 All ER 989, [2000] 3 WLR 1327, CA.
R v Secretary of State for the Home Dept, ex p McQuillan [1995] 4 All ER 400.
Rantzen v Mirror Group Newspapers (1986) Ltd [1993] 4 All ER 975, [1994] QB 670, CA.
Reynolds v Times Newspapers Ltd [1999] 4 All ER 909, [1999] QB 670, HL.
Satnam Investments Ltd v Dunlop Heywood & Co Ltd [1999] 3 All ER 652, CA.
Seager v Copydex Ltd [1967] 2 All ER 415, [1967] 1 WLR 923, CA.
Secetary of State for the Home Dept v Central Broadcasting Ltd [1993] EMLR 253, CA.

a *Service Corp International plc v Channel Four Television Corp* [1999] EMLR 83.
Times Newspapers Ltd v MGN Ltd [1993] EMLR 443, CA.
Tolley v J S Fry & Sons Ltd [1931] AC 333, [1931] All ER Rep 131, HL.
United Pan-Europe Communications NV v Deutsche Bank AG [2000] 2 BCLC 461, CA.
Wyatt v Wilson (1820), unreported.
X v Y [1988] 2 All ER 648.
b *Z (a minor) (freedom of publication), Re* [1995] 4 All ER 961, [1997] Fam 1, CA.
Zockoll Group Ltd v Mercury Communications Ltd [1998] FSR 354, CA.

Appeal

The defendant, Hello! Ltd, publisher of Hello! magazine, appealed from the order of Hunt J on 21 November 2000 continuing an injunction granted by Buckley J on c 20 November 2000 restraining it from publishing issue 639 of that magazine which contained photographs of the wedding of the first and second claimants, Michael Douglas and Catherine Zeta-Jones, who had granted the third claimant, Northern & Shell plc, publisher of OK! magazine, exclusive rights to publish photographs of their wedding. The facts are set out in the judgment of Brooke LJ.

d

Henry Carr QC and *Giles Fernando* (instructed by *Charles Russell*) for Hello!.
Michael Tugendhat QC and *David Sherborne* (instructed by *Theodore Goddard*) for the claimants.

e 23 November 2000. The appeal was allowed for reasons to be given later.

21 December 2000. The following judgments were delivered.

BROOKE LJ.

1. On 22 and 23 November 2000 we heard an appeal by the defendants f Hello! Ltd against an injunction granted by Hunt J on 21 November restraining them until trial or further order from publishing or further publishing photographs of the first and second claimants Michael Douglas and Catherine Zeta-Jones taken at their wedding at the Plaza Hotel New York on 18–19 November 2000. The judge's order also granted the claimants other relief, the precise details of g which are immaterial for the purposes of this judgment.

2. We discharged the injunction at the end of the hearing of the appeal and said that we would give our reasons for allowing the appeal in due course.

3. The defendants are the proprietors of Hello! magazine. The third claimants Northern & Shell plc are the proprietors of OK! magazine. These two magazines h are rivals in the same market. At the time we heard the appeal the most recent circulation figures from the Audit Bureau of Circulation (ABC) showed that they were neck and neck, with Hello! showing an average weekly circulation of 458,663, and OK! lagging slightly behind at 455,162. Mr Ashford, who is the editorial director of OK!, has told the court that the ABC rating at the end of the ABC year has an enormous effect on the rates which magazines can charge advertisers j over the next six months, so that the magazine which has the highest rating has a significant advantage over its rival(s). Mr Ashford added that the Douglas wedding, for which OK! had secured exclusive rights, was the last important feature before the end of the ABC year.

4. Three matters need to be made clear at the outset of this judgment. The first is that this is not the trial of the action. The court is not concerned to decide whether, as the claimants contend, Hello! has acted unlawfully. If at the trial it is

held that Hello! has acted unlawfully, it is likely that it will have to pay the claimants very substantial sums of money, whether as damages or as a consequence of any account they may be ordered to make in relation to all the profits it has received as a result of its unlawful acts. Since it decided to proceed with the publication of issue 639 of its magazine after we discharged the injunction, and after it had had the opportunity of reading all the evidence which the claimants placed before the court, it could have no possible excuse for its behaviour if it were held that it has acted unlawfully.

5. We are not concerned with matters of this kind. Our sole concern is to decide whether in accordance with well-established principles an injunction restraining this publication should be continued in force until trial, thereby in effect 'killing' this weekly issue of Hello!.

6. Secondly, this judgment is given in the context of litigation conducted at great speed. Mr Maninder Gill, who is the third claimants' head of legal affairs, first heard at 7.30 pm on the evening of Monday 20 November that Hello! were likely to publish the disputed photographs the following morning. Leading counsel obtained injunctive relief from Buckley J over the telephone later that evening. The hearing before Hunt J took place the following day, when three witness statements on behalf of the claimants (Martin Kramer, Maninder Gill and Martin Ellice) and two witness statements on behalf of the defendants (Sally Amanda Cartwright and Timothy Moore) were placed before the court. The defendants immediately appealed to a two judge division of this court (which was unable to agree) and when we started to hear the appeal the following day we decided that it would be fair to allow both sides to adduce further evidence on the clear understanding that we realised that the other side had had no opportunity, or no sufficient opportunity, to rebut any of this new evidence if it had wished to do so. We therefore admitted four more witness statements on behalf of the claimants (Stanley Sydney Myerson, Paul Anderson, Paul Ashford and Martin Smith) and three more witness statements on behalf of the defendants (Sally Amanda Cartwright 2nd, Christopher Hutchings and Maria-José Doughty).

7. The third preliminary matter is that even if we had not decided to admit all this new evidence, we would have had to exercise our discretion afresh on the hearing of this appeal because we have virtually no idea what matters the judge took into account and what he did not take into account when he exercised his discretion to continue the injunction. After a long hearing we were told that he simply said that he had no doubt that these images were confidential and that the defendants were in breach of confidence, and probably contract and malicious falsehood as well, and that he would continue Buckley J's order. The defendants appealed against his order on nine separate grounds, all of which appear to me well founded. The essence of their complaint is set out in the first ground of appeal: 'The learned Judge failed to give any or sufficient reasons in support of his decision to continue the injunction granted without notice by Mr Justice Buckley on Monday 20 November.'

8. This court has said repeatedly in recent years that the giving of reasons forms an important part of the judicial function. See, in particular, *Flannery v Halifax Estate Agencies Ltd* [2000] 1 All ER 373 at 377–378, [2000] 1 WLR 377 at 381–382. Like the defendants, we do not know why the judge decided that the nine photographs of which the claimants make complaint were without doubt published in breach of confidence. We do not know why he concluded that the photographs contained information possessing the necessary quality of confidence. We do not know what he identified as the necessary elements of malicious falsehood

a or the tort of interference with contractual relations, or why he concluded that those elements would in each case probably be proved by the claimants at trial.

9. There is no indication that he weighed the injustice likely to be caused to the defendants in continuing the injunction against the injustice likely to be caused to the claimants if he refused to continue it. Nor did he say whether he gave any or any proper weight to the fact that the continuation of the injunction b was to cause the defendants to be unable to distribute almost the entirety of one of its weekly issues. Because he failed in all these respects, this court, as I have said, has had to exercise its own discretion in deciding whether or not to continue the interim injunction granted by Buckley J. I wish to stress that a judge does not have to give long reasons. The error made by Hunt J was that for all practical purposes he did not give any reasons at all, with the result that neither an c appellate court nor the parties are able to understand precisely why he exercised his discretion in the way he did.

10. I turn now to the evidence. It is common ground that Hello! is published in the London area on Tuesday of each week and in other parts of the country on Wednesdays. OK! follows in each respect three days later. While OK! complain d that Hello! behaved improperly on the occasion which is at the centre of this appeal, Hello! adduced evidence which purported to show that this was merely a case of the pot calling the kettle black, and that OK! had been no stranger to similar spoiling tactics in the past. The evidence on these matters must be approached with care, prepared as it was on each side with great speed and not tested in cross-examination. None of it was before the judge. It ran along the e following lines.

11. In September 1998 Hello! paid a very substantial sum for the right to publish an exclusive feature about the wedding of Gloria Hunniford, the television personality. Its agreement with Miss Hunniford contained a confidentiality clause which had the purpose of achieving full exclusive coverage for Hello!.

f 12. On that occasion OK! published its issue 128 a few days before Hello! published its wedding photographs. OK! magazine that week bore the banners 'OK! ALWAYS FIRST FOR WEDDINGS' and 'GLORIA HUNNIFORD'S EXCLUSIVE WEDDING DAY' on its cover, which also boasted 'COMPLETE COVERAGE & BEAUTIFUL PICTURES INSIDE'. Six pages of wedding photographs appeared on pp 42–47. g Hello! complain that these pictures were obviously not authorised by Hello! or by the married couple, and that they must have been obtained in similar circumstances (ie surreptitiously) to those of which OK! make complaint in this action.

13. In its response OK! does not suggest that it did not know that Hello! had exclusive rights to the Hunniford wedding coverage. It contents itself with saying h that there had been no international publicity identifying the possessor of the exclusive media rights in advance of the Hunniford wedding. There was no security operation equivalent to that conducted at the Douglas wedding. The guests at the Hunniford wedding were issued with disposable cameras and encouraged to take photographs by the bride and groom, who had agreed to pose for pictures on j public ground in their wedding attire. OK! also says that it understands that the sums paid for the right of coverage for the Hunniford wedding were far smaller. It adds that neither the bride nor groom, nor to the best of its recollection, Hello!, ever complained, and that it has had subsequent business relationships with both bride and groom.

14. After giving three other examples of spoiling tactics by OK! (which OK! confesses and avoids, largely on the basis that it did nothing unlawful), Hello!

makes two other substantive complaints about the conduct of OK! in relation to wedding photographs. The first relates to the wedding of Santa Palmer-Tomkinson in November 1998. OK! claimed it had an exclusive interview and pictures inside the synagogue, thereby giving the impression that it was covering the wedding exclusively, shortly before Hello! provided its own extensive coverage, whereas all that OK! had secured had been an exclusive interview with the rabbi who had conducted the wedding.

15. The other complaint made by Hello! related to the wedding of Brad Pitt and Jennifer Aniston in August 2000. An official wedding photograph appeared on the cover of OK! issue 225, accompanied by a big banner proclaiming 'INSIDE THE MOST UNIQUE WEDDING EVER. WORLD EXCLUSIVE INTERVIEW AND PICTURES. ONLY IN THE UK!' In fact the article in OK! about that wedding merely showed pictures that were available to every publication in the open market, whereas the 'World Exclusive' referred to a different wedding, a small photograph of which appeared in the top right hand corner of the cover. OK!, in its response, maintained, unconvincingly to my mind, that there ought not to have been any confusion.

16. None of this evidence was before the judge. At the very least, it is hard to see how OK! could have sanctioned a claim for damages against Hello! for malicious falsehood, based on the two words 'Exclusive Photographs' on the cover when this evidence tends to show that OK! itself was willing to give a very elastic meaning to the word 'Exclusive' when it was indulging in its own spoiling tactics.

17. OK! bases its claim in the present action on the rights it secured under an agreement it made with Mr Douglas and Ms Zeta-Jones on 10 November 2000, eight days before the wedding. It undertook to pay a very large sum of money to each of them in respect of these rights, payable not later than one week before the wedding. OK! asserted that Hello! offered three times the eventual contract sum for rights to exclusive coverage, but that the couple trusted OK! to project only the images they wanted projected to the public. Hello! does not dispute that it tendered for the rights, although we were told that it did dispute that it had offered three times as much as OK!. At all events, this evidence shows that Hello! knew that exclusive rights were to be granted for coverage of the wedding, and that it did not secure them themselves.

18. The 10 November agreement, in summary, provided that the third claimants were granted exclusive rights for a nine-month period to publish colour photographs of the wedding taken by a photographer hired by Mr Douglas and Ms Zeta-Jones, and to publish an article, including a story and photographs, about the wedding. It was also granted similar rights for a similar period in respect of the consent to use Mr Douglas' and Ms Zeta-Jones' name, voice, signature, photograph or likeness in connection with the wedding. The couple retained wide rights of approval in relation to anything that was to be published and the identity of any other publications in which published material might appear. Mr Douglas and Ms Zeta-Jones undertook to use their best efforts to ensure that:

> '… no other media (including but not limited to photographers, television crews or journalists) shall be permitted access to the Wedding, and that no guests or anyone else present at the Wedding (including staff at the venues) shall be allowed to take photographs.'

19. If any infringing material was used by a third party, OK! undertook to pursue all necessary legal action to cause such infringement to cease, if requested to do so.

a The obligation to provide security rested with Mr Douglas and Ms Zeta-Jones. There was also a profit-sharing agreement in relation to the exploitation of the rights once OK! had recouped its original investment.

20. OK! adduced evidence to the effect that it had been widely reported in the international media before the event that there would be security at the wedding, and that no one would be allowed to photograph or videotape anything at the b wedding or the wedding reception. It was also made clear in the media coverage that the news media (including the paparazzi tabloids) would not be permitted to gain access to the wedding or reception so that they could not take any photographs of the couple, or any of the members of their family, or the other wedding guests. Mr Ashford described a sophisticated large-scale operation, planned with military precision, to try to ensure that no other media reporting c took place.

21. Mr Kramer, the claimants' solicitor, has exhibited to his witness statement a memorandum dated 20 November 2000 prepared by Los Angeles attorneys for Mr Douglas and Ms Zeta-Jones. This four-page document, headed 'Facts supporting claim for injunction', professes to set out some of the facts 'which would, d hopefully, support a claim for preliminary and permanent injunctions under UK law'. Attached to this memorandum is a confidentiality agreement. This is to be signed by an 'EMPLOYEE' and its preamble states that the undertakings as to confidentiality (which include an undertaking not to take photographs) are given 'in consideration for my employment to provide services to the Douglas/Zeta-Jones family, and as a term and condition of such employment'.

e

22. In the memorandum it was explained that the confidentiality agreements prohibited each service company and each vendor which signed them (including each of their respective employees) from keeping, disclosing, using or selling any 'photograph, film, videotape, etc' which were obtained at the wedding reception. The agreements also specifically provided that any such disclosure would f constitute a material breach of them, and might also constitute a breach of trust, breach of fiduciary duty and an invasion of privacy, which would cause irreparable harm to Michael and Catherine and that, therefore, they would have the right to seek and obtain an injunction to prevent any such disclosure. The attorneys therefore suggested that if any person hired to render services in connection with g the wedding or the reception and any person employed by one of the vendors, was the person who took the unauthorised photographs and/or took the videotape from which the unauthorised images were taken, their actions in (a) smuggling a camera or videotape machine into the reception, (b) covertly and secretly taking photographs, or making a videotape during the reception, (c) then making copies of them, (d) disclosing them to others, and (e) selling and attempting to sell those h images to the media, would constitute material breaches of the express provisions of the confidentiality agreement.

23. They also said that all the guests who were invited to the wedding or the reception received with their invitation a separate written notice which stated: 'We would appreciate no photography or video devices at the ceremony or reception.' j Moreover, in order for a guest to gain access to both the wedding ceremony and the wedding reception, he or she had to go through a secure entrance or a checkpoint which was maintained by a professional security service, and by others. There was said to be a notice posted at the entrance which announced a similar message 'no photography or video devices at the ceremony or reception'. Each guest who went into the wedding ceremony and into the ballroom at the Plaza Hotel where the wedding reception was held, was visually checked to make certain that he or she

did not have any cameras, videotape machines or any other audio or video or recording devices and, where there was any suspicious circumstance, security personnel used high-tech equipment to make certain that no camera or videotape devices were smuggled into the wedding reception. Any guest who had, mistakenly, brought a camera or videotape machine with them had to turn it in or check it before entering, in order to be permitted to attend the wedding and/or the reception.

24. The attorneys added that if anyone rendering services, or working with a vendor, at the reception, had any need, in connection with their employment, to enter the room where the reception was being held, or any related private areas, they were checked to make certain that they did not have any camera, videotape machine or other audio or video recording or transmitting device, in non-compliance with the confidentiality agreement signed by their employer.

25. They also said that during the wedding reception, the security personnel looked for anyone who appeared to have, or might have, a camera or videotape machine. Security personnel saw someone with a camera on about six occasions during the reception. They immediately confiscated the camera and took the film out of it, thereby exposing the film and destroying any photographs that might have been taken. They then either escorted the person out of the reception, or if a wedding guest was involved, detained the camera until the guest was ready to leave the reception. Although a large number of security staff were monitoring the reception for this purpose, none of them reported having seen anyone else taking photographs or doing any videotaping at the reception.

26. It was also said that there was no way of gaining access to the ballroom of the Plaza Hotel without going through the security checkpoint. As a further security measure to try to keep uninvited people from crashing the wedding or reception, security passes were issued to the invited guests within 24 hours before the ceremony and each invited guest was given a specially made gold pin to wear. No one was allowed to enter the ballroom unless he or she was an invited guest or someone working at the wedding reception, and no one could see into the ballroom from outside, or take photographs or make a videotape from outside the ballroom, since there was no visual access.

27. The attorneys ended their memorandum by saying that in these circumstances it was obvious that everyone in all the categories they had mentioned was made fully aware of the prohibition against photographic equipment and agreed not to take cameras, videotape machines or other visual or audio recording devices into the wedding or the wedding reception. They suggested that it necessarily followed that every worker and every guest agreed not to take any photographs or videotape during the wedding or reception and also agreed that they would not disclose, sell, or otherwise try to commercially exploit any photographs, videotapes, or any other unauthorised recording.

28. The wedding celebrations began at 7.30 pm New York time (12.30 am GMT) on the evening of Saturday 18 November. At 7.30 pm on Monday evening, 20 November, Ms Zeta-Jones telephoned the third claimants' head of legal affairs in London. She sounded upset and told him that a magazine was about to publish unauthorised photographs taken at their wedding. An interim injunction was obtained from Buckley J, as I have said, on the telephone later that evening. Although we have not been furnished with the reasons he gave for granting the injunction, it appears that he was told that OK! had received information earlier that day from more than one source that photos were being offered for sale; that nine low-resolution photos of the wedding had been faxed to OK! from Holland;

that OK! had been told that the photos were by Phil Ramey, a well-known Californian paparazzo; that copies of Hello! were already in the United Kingdom with a photo of the wedding on the front and would be distributed very shortly; that a distributor had told Mr Martin Townsend (of OK!) that copies were coming in through Stansted for delivery to a warehouse at Borehamwood; and that efforts, which were continuing, had been made to contact the editor of Hello! after a security guard who answered the phone at their premises had been unable to help.

29. In addition to adducing copies of the memorandum and the agreements to which I have referred, OK! placed before Hunt J the following day witness statements by Mr Maninder Gill and its managing director (Mr Ellice).

30. Mr Maninder Gill said that he believed from his conversation with Ms Zeta-Jones, and from his experience as a media lawyer, that she and her husband were upset at the possible publication of the unauthorised photographs by Hello!. He said that this was because the portrayal of their image in the film and entertainment industry generally was of 'incredible importance', as it was to most celebrities. This was because of the inevitable spill-over of their persona and public image into their livelihoods. He explained that the demand by producers and directors for the service of actors and actresses was dictated to a large extent by what is commonly termed the 'pulling power' of the actor and actresses. Thus in these circumstances, he suggested, Catherine Zeta Jones and Michael Douglas would not only feel violated by an intruder, perhaps motivated by having secured a lucrative contract beforehand, taking surreptitious photographs using what must have been, in light of the highly publicised tight security, a hidden camera, but also by the fact that any unauthorised photographs published would not have been carefully selected from a large number of proof copies as suitable for publication, after careful retouching.

31. Because Ms Zeta-Jones and Mr Douglas trusted OK! to project only the images they wanted to be projected to the public, it was a condition in their agreement with OK! that they would vet the photographs of the wedding to be published by OK! before they were published. Mr Gill explained that the condition that photographs published by magazines such as OK! be carefully selected and approved and retouched before publication, was commonly demanded by celebrities because they were inevitably very anxious about controlling the images of them released to the public. Neither of them would wish to see unflattering, fuzzy photographs of them at their wedding made public. He asserted that the publication of these photographs had caused irreparable harm to them.

32. He added that his company had concluded about £750,000 worth of syndicate deals for the exclusive photographs, and that they had received numerous telephone calls and e-mails from licensees threatening to terminate the licence as a result of these unauthorised photos being published.

33. Mr Ellice for his part gave his reasons for believing that Hello! must have known and expected that it would receive photographs from the wedding, and for strongly suspecting that Hello! must have procured the photographer to act in breach of confidence and take the relevant photographs. His suspicions were based on his intimate involvement in every stage of the print and production process of OK! magazine. The final deadline for sending material to the printers would normally be 4 pm on a Tuesday prior to OK! going on sale on a Friday. If OK! sent a late feature early on Wednesday morning for delivery to the wholesalers on a Thursday night, this would present a logistical nightmare, involving an enormous amount of organisation and meticulous pre-planning. This is why he believed

that Hello! must have made prior arrangements to organise print machines, transmission, staffing and transportation including, unusually, the use of aircraft to transport the copies from their printer in Spain to the United Kingdom. a

34. Instead of reciting the effect of the other evidence before the judge before I describe the further evidence which we decided to admit, it will be much more convenient to set out now the general effect of all the other evidence we received.

35. It appears from the evidence adduced by Hello! that a company called Neneta Overseas Ltd, with an address in the British Virgin Islands, sold the exclusive United Kingdom rights in the nine photographs to which the claimants took exception to Hola SA for use in Hello! magazine, pursuant to an agreement it concluded with Mr Sanchez, the proprietor of Hello!, on Sunday 19 November. Mr Sanchez, for his part, has said that he did not commission these photos or finance them or agree a price for them in advance. One of his employees had agreed a price for them on the Sunday as soon as they had been delivered to him that day. He maintained that he merely owned the exclusive rights for publication in the United Kingdom, Spain and France and he denied that he had any agents representing him in the United States. Ms Cartwright, for her part, said that Hello! had no previous knowledge that these pictures were going to be taken until they were offered on the open market around the world on the Sunday. She explained that Hello! was then able to fit them in the magazine which was by then substantially ready. b c d

36. Mr Moore, who is the circulation director of Hello!, said that the print order had been confirmed to the printers in Spain on the Friday, and that the first copies of the magazine traditionally arrived in this country at 7 am on the Monday. This issue had been running later than usual. To the best of his knowledge the print run had started on the Sunday, and about a third of the total order had arrived at Stansted on a cargo plane at 4.50 pm on the Monday. e

37. OK! on the other hand adduced evidence from Mr Paul Anderson, its photos editor, who said that he had spoken on the telephone on the Monday with Phil Ramey (see para 28 above) who had told him that it was Mr Sanchez who owned the photos, and that he was acting as Mr Sanchez's agent in the United States. Mr Anderson said that later that evening Mr Ramey told him that he was 'pulling' the photos from all the United States magazines to which he had distributed them, because it was clear that it was now not worth his while to distribute them in the United States. f g

38. Mr Anderson said that he believed the disputed photos had been taken by a small camera which was either a digital or an ordinary camera or video camera. Their appearance suggested that the photographer was trying to take the photographs covertly, and they may have been taken with two different types of equipment, either by an amateur photographer or by a professional photographer operating under difficult conditions. h

39. The remainder of the evidence related to the damage which each side claimed that it would suffer if the injunction was, alternatively was not, continued. So far as Mr Douglas and Ms Zeta-Jones are concerned, this evidence was largely based on what Mr Maninder Gill told the court in his witness statement (see paras 30 and 31 above). We were also shown a confidential statement of the reasons why the publication of each of these photographs was said to have caused them such damage. j

40. OK!, for its part, relied on the evidence about the importance of the ABC rating which I have set out in para 3 of this judgment. This, Mr Ashford said, was even more important than usual because OK! was planning to float on the stock

a market next year, and the rating would be pivotal in attracting investors. He had anticipated that the circulation of the edition of OK! containing the wedding photographs would be double the usual circulation of the magazine. He believed that this would be no longer possible if Hello! was allowed to publish, because the appetites of non-regular readers would have been sated by seeing these photos. In addition, because of Hello!'s action OK! had been forced to publish an b incomplete set of pictures a week earlier than they had planned. OK! was also concerned about the potential loss of the value of the syndication agreements they had secured.

41. Hello!, for its part, described its potential losses, if in effect it 'lost' the whole of this issue (as would be inevitable for a weekly magazine if the injunction was continued) under three main headings: the loss of advertising revenue, the c loss of readership income, and the damage to its relationship with the news trade.

42. As to the first, Ms Cartwright said that Hello! would have to refund to advertisers the costs they had paid for space in this issue. Two very important advertisers had placed time-sensitive advertisements in this issue, and in a fiercely competitive market she feared that if they let down any of their advertisers it was d probable that they would decline to advertise for some time to come. OK! had been trying for some time to make inroads into Hello!'s advertisement sales, and if issue 639 could not be put on sale, she feared that some advertisers might be so annoyed they would switch to OK! on a long-term basis.

43. She was also very concerned about the potential loss of readership if Hello! e did not appear that week. It was bought by about 456,000 people every week, a large proportion of whom were regular buyers, and it had a readership of 2·2m readers every week. She said that any interruption in the publishing schedule could be extremely damaging to reader loyalty, and it could take a considerable time to regain lost readers, as they might feel let down and cheated by the non-appearance of issue 639. Since Hello! had published regular features about f the forthcoming wedding in earlier issues, readers would have been led to expect that the wedding itself would be covered in some way in the week after it took place.

44. So far as relationships with the news trade were concerned, she said that for 12 years Hello! had always been on sale in London on a Tuesday and in the rest of g the country on a Wednesday, and the magazine had long-established relationships with 90 wholesale houses and 55,000 retailers. It occupied a premium position on the shelves because it had always been seen to be reliable and profitable, and Ms Cartwright feared that this position would be damaged (to the advantage of OK!) if it was perceived to be unreliable. She feared that if issue 639 failed to appear, h Hello! would suffer a damaging loss of confidence in the eyes of its partners in the news trade.

45. All this evidence was before the judge, but as I have already observed he failed to refer to it at all and we do not know how much weight he attributed to it. It was answered in this court by Mr Myerson, who is joint managing director j of OK!. He has been involved in the newspaper and magazine publishing business for 22 years, with particular experience in advertising and sales.

46. Mr Myerson was concerned to discount Ms Cartwright's concerns. He said that Hello! was an important publication in its sector of the market, and represented a major vehicle for advertisers which they would be very reluctant to abandon. He did not believe that they would decide not to advertise in Hello! in future if there was a legal problem which prevented the publication of the issue.

He thought that the next issues could be enlarged and that some of the advertising booked into issue 639 could be moved into a subsequent issue. *a*

47. So far as the feared loss of readers was concerned, he considered it wholly unrealistic of Ms Cartwright to suggest that a loyal reader of Hello! would stop reading the magazine because one issue did not appear. It was the content of a magazine which determined whether or not it attracted readers. Hello! was a strong product with a high profile, and there was in Mr Myerson's view no reason to *b* suppose it would not continue to maintain its current levels of readership simply because it had lost one issue.

48. He adopted a similar attitude towards Ms Cartwright's concerns about Hello!'s relationship with the news trade. He said that from the point of view of the trade Hello! was a high priced premium product with a large volume of sales. It was extremely profitable, and provided that quality was maintained it was *c* wholly unrealistic to suggest that the loss of one issue would irreparably damage its relationships with the news trade.

49. So much for the evidence. I now turn to the question we had to decide, in the exercise of our own discretion (given that we do not know how the judge decided to exercise the discretion vested in him: see paras 7–9 above). If this *d* matter goes forward and the claimants' case succeeds at trial, the bill which Hello! will have to pay is likely to be enormous, but this is a risk it decided to take, with its eyes open, after we discharged the injunction. We had to decide a very different matter, that is to say whether the court should continue the injunction which would prevent over half a million copies of issue 639 from reaching its readers at all. It goes without saying that this is a case concerned with freedom *e* of expression. Although the right to freedom of expression is not in every case the ace of trumps, it is a powerful card to which the courts of this country must always pay appropriate respect.

50. What, then, are the principles which should govern the exercise of our discretion? The House of Lords has laid down a general rule which governs most *f* cases in which a court is invited to grant an interim injunction restraining the defendant until the trial of the action from doing the things of which the claimant makes complaint. (See *American Cyanamid Co v Ethicon Ltd* [1975] 1 All ER 504, [1975] AC 396.) Once a judge has decided that there is a serious issue to be tried, he is required to weigh the respective risks that injustice may result from his deciding one way or the other on necessarily incomplete and untested evidence. *g* On the one hand there is the risk that if the injunction is refused but the claimant succeeds in establishing at the trial his legal right, for the protection of which the injunction had been sought, he may in the meantime have suffered harm and inconvenience for which an award of money can provide no adequate recompense. On the other hand there is the risk that if the injunction is granted *h* but the claimant fails at the trial, the defendant in the meantime may have suffered harm and inconvenience which is similarly irrecompensable. This is what is sometimes described as the balance of convenience.

51. There has always been a category of case in which a more stringent threshold is required. In *NWL Ltd v Woods* [1979] 3 All ER 614 at 626, [1979] 1 WLR *j* 1294 at 1307 Lord Diplock identified that type of case in these terms:

> 'Where … the grant or refusal of the interlocutory injunction will have the practical effect of putting an end to the action because the harm that will have been already caused to the losing party by its grant or its refusal is complete and of a kind for which money cannot constitute any worthwhile recompense, the degree of likelihood that the plaintiff would have succeeded

a in establishing his right to an injunction if the action had gone to trial is a factor to be brought into the balance by the judge in weighing the risks that injustice may result from his deciding the application one way rather than the other.'

52. Occasionally Parliament intervenes to make clear its wishes in particular contexts. For instance, in the context of trade disputes, s 17(2) of the Trade Union b and Labour Relations Act 1974 provided that if a defendant claimed that he acted in contemplation of furtherance of a trade dispute—

> 'the court shall, in exercising its discretion whether or not to grant the injunction, have regard to the likelihood of that party's succeeding at the trial of the action in establishing the matter or matters which would ... afford a c defence to the action.'

53. In the *NWL* case Lord Diplock and Lord Fraser of Tullybelton, who formed the majority of the three judge Appellate Committee of the House of Lords, rejected a contention that this meant that the court had to have regard to this matter to the exclusion of other matters, or that it was to be treated as of overriding d or paramount importance, or given any other special legal status. The likelihood (and the degree of likelihood) of the defendant succeeding in setting up his defence was a factor to which the court had to have regard when determining where the balance of convenience lay. Lord Fraser observed ([1979] 3 All ER 614 at 628, [1979] 1 WLR 1294 at 1309) that if the court considered that the defendant e was virtually certain to establish the defence it would naturally give more weight to this factor than if it considered that the prospect of successfully establishing the defence was doubtful.

54. Parliament resorted to a different drafting technique in s 12(3) of the Human Rights Act 1998. This subsection reads:

> f 'No [relief which, if granted, might affect the exercise of the convention right to freedom of expression] is to be granted so as to restrain publication before trial unless the court is satisfied that the applicant is likely to establish that publication should not be allowed.'

I agree with what Keene LJ says about the effect of this statutory provision in g paras 150–154 of his judgment, to which I have nothing to add.

55. Needless to say, following Lord Fraser's speech in the *NWL* case, if there is a very strong likelihood that the claimant will establish that an art 10(2) justification will succeed at trial (see art 10(2) of the European Convention for the Protection of Human Rights and Fundamental Freedoms (Rome, 4 November h 1950; TS 71 (1953); Cmnd 8969) (the convention)), this will represent a powerful reason why the court should exercise its discretion to grant an interim injunction to restrain publication. In the present case Hello! wished to publish in this country over half a million copies of its issue 639 which it had imported from its printers in Spain. In another case, however, a newspaper might wish to publish a photograph, taken on a private occasion, which it possessed in this country in j digital form. In such a case it might run into serious difficulties.

56. These difficulties would arise out of the provisions of the Data Protection Act 1998. This statute was enacted, in part, to implement Council Directive (EC) 95/46 on the protection of individuals with regard to the processing of personal data and on the movement of such data (OJ 1995 L281 p 31) which was self-avowedly concerned with the protection of an individual's convention rights to privacy (see paras (2), (10), (11) and (17) of the preamble to the directive and

art 9 of the directive itself). It follows that unless the newspaper asserted a s 32(1)(b) justification (viz that it reasonably believed that, having regard in particular to the special importance of the public interest in freedom of expression, publication would be in the public interest), a claimant who could show that the photograph had been taken of him on some private occasion without his consent would be able to satisfy a court that it was highly probable that an art 10(2) justification would succeed at trial (see the Data Protection Act 1998, s 4 and Sch 1, Pt I, para 1(a) and Sch 2). Section 13 of this Act, incidentally, grants an individual a statutory right to compensation for damage (including distress, in certain specified circumstances) against a 'data controller' who contravenes any of the requirements of the Act. This entitlement is subject to any of the defences the Act may provide.

57. On the facts of the present case, using the *American Cyanamid* test, there is clearly a serious issue to be tried in relation to the claims made by all three claimants. Although the evidence they adduced is often rather impersonal, and one might reasonably be sceptical about the efficiency of some of the security measures, given that no less than six different cameras were later found in the possession of people who had passed through the security checks, it appears that a real effort was made to inform everyone who entered the relevant parts of the hotel that the occasion had characteristics of confidentiality. In other words, people were being trusted to participate in this private occasion, in whatever role, on the strict understanding that they might not take photographic images of what they saw. There was also evidence to the effect that the images could not have been taken by someone from outside who was not bound by these obligations of confidence.

58. In those circumstances it would certainly be arguable, if the appropriate facts were established at trial, that 'unauthorised' images were taken on this private occasion by someone in breach of his or her duty of confidence, and that they therefore constituted 'confidential information' as to what was going on at the wedding and the wedding reception. In so far as Mr Douglas and Ms Zeta-Jones have not vested in OK! the right to bring this action to protect the subject matter of their agreement, they have retained the relevant rights themselves. The claimants have also adduced evidence to the effect that Hello! was on notice that this 'information' was confidential, in the sense that the principle of notice was explained by Lord Goff of Chieveley in *A-G v Guardian Newspapers Ltd (No 2)* [1988] 3 All ER 545 at 658, [1990] 1 AC 109 at 281.

59. I cannot, however, exclude the possibility that the trial judge might find, as Sedley LJ has suggested in para 112 of his judgment, that the photographer was an intruder with whom no relationship of trust or confidence had been established. In that event the court would have to explore the law relating to privacy when it is not bolstered by considerations of confidence.

60. In this context art 10(2) of the convention provides a potential justification for denying the right to freedom of expression not only by restrictions that are necessary 'for preventing the disclosure of information received in confidence', but also those that are necessary 'for the protection of the reputation or rights of others'. On the hypothesis I have suggested in para 59 above, the question would arise whether Mr Douglas and Ms Zeta-Jones had a right to privacy which English law would recognise.

61. It is well known that this court in *Kaye v Robertson* [1991] FSR 62 said in uncompromising terms that there was no tort of privacy known to English law. In contrast, both academic commentary and extra-judicial commentary by judges

a over the last ten years have suggested from time to time that a development of the present frontiers of a breach of confidence action could fill the gap in English law which is filled by privacy law in other developed countries. This commentary was given a boost recently by the decision of the European Commission of Human Rights in *Earl Spencer v UK* (1998) 25 EHRR CD 105, and by the coming into force of the Human Rights Act 1998.

b 62. I must make it clear that the hearing in our court took place in less than ideal circumstances. This litigation was conducted at such speed that Mr Carr QC was instructed for the defendants for the first time shortly before the hearing before this three-judge court, after Mr Silverleaf QC had represented them at the two hearings the previous day. Neither of them had any opportunity to prepare a written skeleton argument before these hearings, or to consider at leisure the c torrent of authority produced by Mr Tugendhat QC. He for his part had had the advantage, for a hearing in this court which started on Wednesday afternoon, of being instructed late on Monday night, but he was the first to admit to us that his skeleton arguments, which referred to nearly 40 decided cases and a plethora of statutory authority and academic and extra-judicial writings, were derived d from databases prepared on some earlier, more relaxed occasion.

63. It follows that we were deprived of the full argument to which we would have been treated if this litigation had not been conducted at such speed. Notwithstanding this handicap, it appears to me that we need to consider counsel's arguments on this point, if only to explore the strength of the claimants' privacy-based case, so far as it adds anything to their confidentiality-based case.

e 64. English law, as is well known, has been historically based on freedoms, not rights. The difference between freedom-based law and rights-based law was memorably expressed by Lord Goff of Chieveley in the course of his speech in the *Guardian Newspapers* case when he said he could see no inconsistency between English law on freedom of speech and art 10 of the convention. He said:

f

> 'The only difference is that, whereas art 10 of the convention, in accordance with its avowed purpose, proceeds to state a fundamental right and then to qualify it, we in this country (where everybody is free to do anything, subject only to the provisions of the law) proceed rather upon an assumption of freedom of speech, and turn to our law to discover the established exceptions g to it.' (See [1988] 3 All ER 545 at 660, [1990] 1 AC 109 at 283.)

65. It is against this background of freedom-based law that the law of confidentiality has been developed. For a very long time the judges of the Court of Chancery exercised an equitable jurisdiction to restrain freedom of speech in circumstances in which it would be unconscionable to publish private material. h If information is accepted on the basis that it will be kept secret, the recipient's conscience is bound by that confidence, and it will be unconscionable for him to break his duty of confidence by publishing the information to others (see *Stephens v Avery* [1988] 2 All ER 477 at 482, [1988] Ch 449 at 456). Of course, 'there is no confidence as to the disclosure of inequity', and the cases show how, on occasion, j the courts were willing to permit publication on that, or other grounds, even though the information to be published was originally given in confidence (see, for example, *Fraser v Evans* [1969] 1 All ER 8 at 11, [1969] 1 QB 349 at 362, *Hubbard v Vosper* [1972] 1 All ER 1023 at 1029, 1033, [1972] 2 QB 84 at 95, 101).

66. This is the origin of the jurisdiction which has been exercised from time to time, when the claimant founded his action on confidence, to restrain the publication of photographs or etchings which contain images of people. In the

famous case of Prince Albert's etchings, Lord Cottenham LC said (*Prince Albert v Strange* (1849) 1 Mac & G 25 at 44–45, 41 ER 1171 at 1178–1179) that the plaintiff's affidavits:

> '... state distinctly the belief of the Plaintiff, that the catalogue and the descriptive and other remarks therein contained, could not have been compiled or made, except by means of the possession of the several impressions of the said etchings surreptitiously and improperly obtained. To this case no answer is made ... If, then, these compositions were kept private, except as to some ... sent to [B] for the purpose of having certain impressions taken, the possession of the Defendant ... must have originated in a breach of trust, confidence, or contract, in [B] or some person in his employ taking more impressions than were ordered, and retaining the extra number ...'

67. In the same way North J gave relief (on the basis of 'a gross breach of faith') in *Pollard v Photographic Co* (1888) 40 Ch D 345 to a lady who commissioned a photographer to take photographs of her for her private use and found to her surprise that the photographer was incorporating her photographic image in Christmas cards for general sale. Again, when the Duchess of Argyll obtained an injunction against her former husband from publishing information about her in breach of the duty of confidence one partner to a marriage (or other intimate relationship) owes to another, Ungoed-Thomas J said of these private relationships in *Margaret, Duchess of Argyll v Duke of Argyll* [1965] 1 All ER 611 at 624–625, [1967] Ch 302 at 329–330:

> 'It ... seems to me that the policy of the law, so far from indicating that communications between husband and wife should be excluded from protection against breaches of confidence given by the court in accordance with *Prince Albert v. Strange* ((1849) 1 Mac & G 25, 41 ER 1171), strongly favours their inclusion, and in view of that policy it can hardly be an objection that such communications are not limited to business matters. Of course, the relationship between husband and wife is a delicate relationship. As ATKIN, L.J., said in the famous passage in *Balfour v. Balfour* ([1919] 2 KB 571 at 579, [1918–19] All ER Rep 860 at 865), at common law in respect of promises between husband and wife "... each house is a domain into which the King's writ does not seek to run, and to which his officers do not seek to be admitted." The protection of confidential communications between husband and wife is not, however, designed to intrude into this domain but to protect it, not to break their confidential relationship but to encourage and preserve it.'

In *Barrymore v News Group Newspapers Ltd* [1997] FSR 600 Jacob J followed these principles in a case in which a newspaper sought to publish information about features of an intimate homosexual relationship.

68. More recently, outside the domain of private domestic life, Chancery judges have granted claimants injunctions to restrain the publication of photographs taken surreptitiously in circumstances in which the photographer would be taken to have known that the occasion was a private one and the taking of photographs by outsiders was not permitted. In *Creation Records Ltd v News Group Newspapers Ltd* [1997] EMLR 444 at 453 Lloyd J said:

> 'On the plaintiff's evidence ... once the shoot was ready to begin efforts were made to prevent photography both within the roped off area and outside it. [Counsel for the plaintiffs] says on this evidence [S] must have

a been aware of the efforts to prevent people taking photographs of the shoot and can only have succeeded in doing so by being surreptitious and far from being as open as he himself deposes. If so it is a clear inference that he acted in this way because he knew otherwise he would be stopped and that, accordingly, he realised that he was not permitted to take photographs of the scene. He must have known, it is said, that the scene was intended to remain b unpublished, albeit not entirely secret, and that it was therefore confidential. By evading the security efforts by luck or guile he nevertheless acted in breach of the confidentiality to which the scene was subject. To echo the words of Megarry J, as he then was, in *Coco v A N Clark Engineers Ltd* ((1969) 86 RPC 41), the circumstances were such, he says, that any reasonable man in the shoes of [S] would have realised that on reasonable grounds he was c obtaining the information, that is to say the view of the scene, in confidence, at least to the extent that he was obliged by that confidentiality not to photograph the scene. In principle that seems to me to be an arguable case, though it clearly depends on how the facts turn out.'

69. Lloyd J observed that the facts of the earlier case, *Shelley Films Ltd v Rex* d *Features Ltd* [1994] EMLR 134, were clearer, because in that case there were signs banning photography (although the anonymous photographer was reported as having said that he did not see them), and he was also arguably not lawfully present. He added:

'Here, while admittedly [S] was lawfully at the hotel and with others was e able to gain access to the restricted area and his presence there was tolerated and even the taking of photographs was tolerated before the shoot as such began, the plaintiffs' evidence, if accepted, shows that thereafter a tighter regime of security was imposed as regards preventing photography, the tight ring of security men and minders of which the *Sun's* first article spoke. It would f of course have been clearer if each of the strangers to the shoot who were allowed to stay in the restricted area had been told that they may not take photographs thereafter. But what the plaintiffs' witnesses depose to amounts to much the same as that, although in a more general and less explicit form. I accept also that they were of course allowed to observe the scene and could therefore have gone away and told the world the ingredients of the picture, g or even made a sketch of it from memory. But being lawfully there does not mean that they were free to take photographs, and it seems to me that to be able to record it as a photographic image is different in kind, not merely in degree, from being able to relate it verbally or even by way of a sketch. That is above all because it was in photographic form that it was intended to be h preserved for the group. It is the photographic record of the scene, the result of the shoot in fact, that was to be confidential.' (See [1997] EMLR 444 at 455.)

70. In each of these two cases the judge considered that the balance of convenience favoured the granting of an injunction, and there were no other factors to dissuade him, in the exercise of a jurisdiction created by equity, from j taking that course.

71. It is well settled, then, that equity may intervene to prevent the publication of photographic images taken in breach of an obligation of confidence. In other words, if on some private occasion the prospective claimants make it clear, expressly or impliedly, that no photographic images are to be taken of them, then all those who are present will be bound by the obligations of confidence created by their knowledge (or imputed knowledge) of this restriction. English law,

however, has not yet been willing to recognise that an obligation of confidence may be relied on to preclude such unwanted intrusion into people's privacy when those conditions do not exist.

72. That was the problem at the heart of *Kaye v Robertson* [1991] FSR 62. A television celebrity was recovering from catastrophic injuries in a private room which formed part of a ward at a NHS hospital. There were notices at the entrance to the ward, and also on the door of the private room, asking visitors to see a member of staff before they visited Mr Kaye, and a list of the people who might be allowed to visit him was pinned up outside his room. Journalists from the first defendant's newspaper ignored all these notices. They claimed that Mr Kaye had consented to being interviewed (although the evidence showed that he was in no fit state to give any kind of informed consent), and they sought to publish this interview, together with a number of photographs they took during their unwelcome intrusion into his rooms. Among these photographs were some which showed substantial scars to Mr Kaye's head at the site where his severe head and brain injuries had been caused.

73. The action was not brought in confidence, and no cases derived from the law of confidence were cited to the court during the one-day hearing. In the course of his short judgment Bingham LJ said (at 70) that the case highlighted, yet again, the failure of both the common law of England and statute to protect the personal privacy of individual citizens in an effective way. He cited in this context a recent comment by Professor Basil Markinensis *The German Law of Torts: A Comparative Introduction* (2nd edn, 1990) p 318:

> 'English law, on the whole, compares unfavourably with German law. True, many aspects of the human personality and privacy are protected by a multitude of existing torts, but this means fitting the facts of each case in the pigeon-hole of an existing tort and this process may not only involve strained constructions; often it may also leave a deserving plaintiff without a remedy.'

74. In his equally short judgment Leggatt LJ referred (at 71) to the way in which the common law had developed in the United States to meet the need which the court on the present occasion was unable to fulfil satisfactorily. He described how over the last 100 years the right to privacy, or 'the right to be let alone', has gained acceptance in most jurisdictions in the United States. In particular he referred to the way in which a so-called 'right of publicity' has developed to protect the commercial interest of celebrities in their identities, citing *Carson v Here's Johnny Portable Toilets Inc* (1983) 698 F 2d 831 at 835:

> 'The theory of the right is that a celebrity's identity can be valuable in the promotion of products, and the celebrity has an interest that may be protected from the unauthorised commercial exploitation of that identity … "The famous have an exclusive legal right during life to control and profit from the commercial use of their name and personality."'

He might also have referred to the judgment of McGeehan J in *Tucker v News Media Ownership Ltd* [1986] 2 NZLR 716 as a recent example of a judge in a different common law jurisdiction seeking to do justice in a case where the plaintiff's privacy had been hurtfully invaded.

75. How different the law of England and Wales is from the law in many jurisdictions in the United States and in Canada became apparent when we were shown a recent decision of the Supreme Court of Canada in *Les Éditions Vice-Versa Inc v Aubry* (1998) 5 BHRC 437. The claimant, then aged 17, had been

a photographed in a public place, sitting on the steps of a building. She sought damages because the photograph was taken without her consent and published without her consent. She was awarded $Can 2,000 compensation, an award which was upheld, by a majority, in both the higher courts to which the defendants appealed.

76. This case vividly illustrates the rule that the courts in this country should b be very cautious, now that the Human Rights Act is in force, when seeking to derive assistance from judgments in other jurisdictions founded on some different rights-based charter.

77. The relevant provisions of what was called the Quebec Charter of Human Rights and Freedoms 1975 were in these terms:

c '**3.** Every person is the possessor of the fundamental freedoms, including freedom of conscience, freedom of religion, freedom of opinion, freedom of expression, freedom of peaceful assembly and freedom of association.

4. Every person has a right to the safeguard of his dignity, honour and reputation.

d **5.** Every person has a right to respect for his private life …

9.1. In exercising his fundamental freedoms and rights, a person shall maintain a proper regard for democratic values, public order and the general well-being of the citizens of Québec. In this respect, the scope of the freedoms and rights, and limits to their exercise, may be fixed by law …

49. Any unlawful interference with any right or freedom recognized by e this Charter entitles the victim to obtain the cessation of such interference and compensation for the moral or material prejudice resulting therefrom.'

78. The effect of the judgments of the Supreme Court (which was only divided on the question of compensation) was that the right accorded by s 5 of the Quebec Charter extended to the right of an individual to the protection of his or f her image, and that that right is violated if such an image is taken and published without its owner's consent (unless it is a merely incidental feature of a photograph of a public place). L'Heureux Dubé and Bastarache JJ said, after considering some possible defences:

g 'None of the exceptions mentioned earlier based on the public's right to information is applicable here. Accordingly, there appears to be no justification for giving precedence to the appellants other than their submission that it would be very difficult in practice for a photographer to obtain the consent of all those he or she photographs in public places before publishing their photographs. To accept such an exception would, in fact, h amount to accepting that the photographer's right is unlimited, provided that the photograph is taken in a public place, thereby extending the photographer's freedom at the expense of that of others. We reject this point of view. In the case at bar, the respondent's right to protection of her image is more important than the appellant's right to publish the photograph of the j respondent without first obtaining her permission.' (See (1998) 5 BHRC 437 at 452 (para 28).)

79. The right to respect for private and family life which is created by art 8(1) of the convention appears at first sight similar to the right to respect for private life created by s 5 of the Quebec Charter. They both owe their origin to art 12 of the Universal Declaration of Human Rights (Paris, 10 December 1948; UN TS 2 (1949); Cmd 7226), which provides that:

'No one shall be subjected to arbitrary interference with his privacy, family, home and correspondence, nor to attacks upon his honour and reputation. Everyone has the right to the protection of law against such interference or attacks.'

a

80. They are, however, different in one obvious respect. The combination of s 9.1 and 49 of the Quebec Charter makes it clear that that charter has what is called 'horizontal effect', in the sense that one private individual or entity can seek redress from another in relation to a breach of a right accorded by the Quebec Charter, as indeed occurred in the *Vice-Versa* case. Article 8(1) of the convention appears, read literally, to create an equally free-standing right, and its language reflects the intention set out in the preamble to the convention, namely that one of the methods identified by the Council of Europe for achieving greater unity between its members was the maintenance and further realisation of human rights and fundamental freedoms. The preamble goes on to state that the Council of Europe had resolved (through the machinery of the convention) to take the first steps for the collective enforcement of certain of the rights stated in the Universal Declaration of Human Rights. To this end art 1 declares that: 'The High Contracting Parties shall secure to everyone within their jurisdiction the rights and freedoms defined in Section 1 of the Convention.'

b

c

d

81. When it is read more closely, however, the convention (unlike the Quebec Charter) seems to be primarily concerned with giving individuals rights against the state (to be equated with public authorities in the language of art 8(2)). Thus art 8(2) is concerned only with the circumstances in which a public authority may legitimately interfere with the exercise by an individual of his right to private and family life, and s 8 of the Human Rights Act is concerned only with the power of a court to award compensation against acts of public authorities for unlawful acts which are incompatible with a convention right. The Human Rights Act gives the court no such statutory power to order one private entity to pay compensation to another in respect of a breach of convention rights.

e

f

82. An English judge interpreting the Human Rights Act and the convention is therefore confronted with something of a dilemma. On the one hand, art 8(1) of the convention appears to create a right, exercisable against all the world, to respect for private and family life. On the other hand, art 8(2) of the convention, s 8 of the Human Rights Act, and the general philosophy of both the convention and the Act (namely that these rights are enforceable only against public authorities), all appear to water down the value of the right created by art 8(1).

g

83. In a series of decisions the European Court of Human Rights has addressed this dilemma by relying on the positive duty imposed on the member states by art 1 of the convention (see para 80 above). A vivid example of this technique at work can be seen in the judgment of the court in *A v UK* (1998) 5 BHRC 137 when it was concerned with a complaint under art 3 by a boy who had been hit by his stepfather with a garden cane. The court said:

h

'The court considers that treatment of this kind reaches the level of severity prohibited by art 3 … It remains to be determined whether the state should be held responsible, under art 3, for the beating of the applicant by his stepfather … The court considers that the obligation on the high contracting parties under art 1 of the convention to secure to everyone within their jurisdiction the rights and freedoms defined in the convention, taken together with art 3, requires states to take measures designed to ensure that individuals within their jurisdiction are not subjected to torture or inhuman or

j

a degrading treatment or punishment, including such ill-treatment administered by private individuals …' (See (1998) 5 BHRC 137 at 141 (paras 21–22).)

84. In other words, the court was saying that the boy had the right under art 3 of the convention not to be subjected to inhuman or degrading treatment or punishment, and although it was his stepfather who had administered the treatment which breached that right, he was entitled to make a complaint against b the state for its failure, in breach of art 1, to secure his art 3 right.

85. From time to time the court at Strasbourg has adopted a similar approach when applicants have complained to it that their art 8(1) right to respect for their private and family life has been violated. Examples can be seen in *Airey v Ireland* (1979) 2 EHRR 305 at 314 (paras 22–23), *X v Netherlands* (1985) 8 EHRR 235 at 239–240, 241 c (paras 23 and 27), *Stjerna v Finland* (1994) 24 EHRR 194 at 214 (para 38), *Lopez Ostra v Spain* (1994) 20 EHRR 277 at 295, 296 (paras 51 and 55), and *Botta v Italy* (1998) 4 BHRC 81 at 88–89 (paras 33–34). In *X v Netherlands* the court said (at 239–240 (para 23)):

'The Court recalls that although the object of Article 8 is essentially that of d protecting the individual against arbitrary interference by the public authorities, it does not merely compel the State to abstain from such interference: in addition to this primarily negative obligation, there may be positive obligations inherent in an effective respect for private or family life. These obligations may involve the adoption of measures designed to secure respect e for private life even in the sphere of the relations of individuals between themselves.'

86. In *A v UK* it was the deficiencies of the common law, in relation to the physical chastisement of children, which led the court to conclude that the United Kingdom had violated the convention. This country narrowly escaped a similar finding by f the European Commission of Human Rights in *Earl Spencer*'s case. A photograph of Lady Spencer had been taken with a telephoto lens while she was walking in the grounds of a private clinic at which she was receiving treatment. This photograph was published under the caption: 'SO THIN: Victoria walks in the clinic grounds this week.' Relying on the decision of this court in *Kaye v Robertson*, she did not pursue a claim in the English courts, but the commission held that she g should have pursued her remedies in these courts first. It appears that the eloquence of the advocate for the United Kingdom government persuaded the commission that English law provided her with a potentially satisfactory remedy in an action for breach of confidence.

87. In this respect the commission relied heavily on the strong and detailed h case of the applicants in the domestic proceedings which pointed to their former friends as the direct source of the essential confidential information that had been published. Its determination ended in these terms:

'Accordingly, the Commission considers that the parties' submissions indicate that the remedy of breach of confidence (against the newspapers and j their sources) was available to the applicants and that the applicants have not demonstrated that it was insufficient or ineffective in the circumstances of their cases. It considers that, in so far as relevant doubts remain concerning the financial awards to be made following a finding of a breach of confidence, they are not such as to warrant a conclusion that the breach of confidence action is ineffective or insufficient but rather a conclusion that the matter should be put to the domestic courts for consideration in order to allow those courts,

> through the common law system in the United Kingdom, the opportunity to develop existing rights by way of interpretation.' (See (1998) 25 EHRR CD 105 at 117–118.)

88. The commission appears to be saying that since the authorities in this country have been content to leave it to the judges to develop the law in this sensitive field, it is the judges who must develop the law so that it gives appropriate recognition to art 8(1) rights. Whether they do so in future by an extension of the existing frontiers of the law of confidence, or by recognising the existence of new relationships which give rise to enforceable legal rights (as has happened in relation to the law of negligence ever since the 3–2 decision of the House of Lords in *Donoghue (or M' Alister) v Stevenson* [1932] AC 562, [1932] All ER Rep 1) is not for this court, on this occasion, to predict. The versatility of the common law to adapt to new situations was well described by Scott LJ in *Haseldine v CA Daw & Son Ltd* [1941] 3 All ER 156 at 174, [1941] 2 KB 343 at 362–363:

> 'The common law of England has throughout its long history developed as an organic growth, at first slowly under the hampering restrictions of legal forms of process, more quickly in the time of Lord Mansfield, and in the last 100 years at an ever-increasing rate of progress, as new cases, arising under new conditions of society, of applied science, and of public opinion, have presented themselves for solution by the courts.'

89. Recent annual reports of the Law Commission show how successive governments have been content to leave the development of the law in these fields to the judges. As long ago as 1981 the Law Commission recommended to Parliament that the law of confidence should be reformed and codified (see its *Report on Breach of Confidence* Law Com No 110 (1981)), but although this recommendation was accepted by a former government it was never implemented. The Commission's *Thirty-third Annual Report 1998* (Law Com No 258, p 5) describes how in 1998, following the *Earl Spencer* decision, a new government rejected that report 'because developing case law since its publication had clarified the scope and extent of the breach of confidence action, as confirmed by the European Commission on Human Rights'.

90. In its *Twenty-eighth Annual Report 1993* (Law Com No 223, p 25) the Law Commission described how one of the commissioners had recently assisted in the preparation of a government consultation paper on the infringement of privacy (which did not lead to the enactment of legislation). The Commission's anxieties, if the law of privacy was put on a statutory basis but not the law of confidence, were clearly articulated in para 2.25 of that report. In the event, the executive and the legislature took the line of least resistance and left the development of both these fields of law to the judiciary, and that is how matters now stand. That members of the Appellate Committee of the House of Lords are uneasy about the present condition of our law is evident from the observations of Lord Browne-Wilkinson and Lord Nicholls in *R v Khan (Sultan)* [1996] 3 All ER 289 at 291, 302, [1997] AC 558 at 571, 582–583. On other occasions during the last 20 years some of our most senior judges have underlined the importance of the right to privacy: see Lord Scarman in *Morris v Beardmore* [1980] 2 All ER 753 at 763, [1981] AC 446 at 464 ('fundamental'), Lord Denning MR in *Schering Chemicals Ltd v Falkman Ltd* [1981] 2 All ER 321 at 333, [1982] QB 1 at 21 ('fundamental') and Lord Keith of Kinkel in *A-G v Guardian Newspapers Ltd (No 2)* [1988] 3 All ER 545 at 639, [1990] 1 AC 109 at 255 ('clearly one which the law should in this field seek to protect').

a 91. One difficulty which will confront the courts when they have to tackle this problematic issue head-on is that art 1 of the convention, on which a state's positive duty is founded when it is brought before the international court which has the duty of enforcing member states' duties under the convention, does not find its way into the Schedule to the Human Rights Act which sets out the 'Convention rights' referred to in ss 2, 3, 4, 6 and 7 of the Act. On the other hand, b when a court determines a question which has arisen in connection with a convention right, it must take into account any relevant judgment of the European Court of Human Rights (s 2(1)(a) of the Human Rights Act), and those judgments have made it clear that the law-making body of the member states has the positive duty identified in the judgments to which I have referred. Where Parliament in this country has been so obviously content to leave the development of c the law to the judges, it might seem strange if the absence of art 1 from our national statute relieved the judges from taking into account the positive duties identified by the court at Strasbourg when they develop the common law. In this judgment, however, I have the luxury of identifying difficult issues: I am not obliged to solve them.

d 92. One matter, however, is clear, and this makes the task of the court that much easier on the present occasion. One of the Law Commission's anxieties in 1993 was that the law might develop in such a way that breaches of privacy, but not breaches of confidence, would be subject to statutory defences which the common law had not yet clearly recognised. In this respect, at least, Parliament has now intervened to provide that where proceedings relate to material which e the respondent claims, or which appears to the court, to be journalistic, literary or artistic material, the court must have regard, among other things, to any relevant privacy code (s 12(4) of the Human Rights Act). In this context we were shown by Mr Tugendhat the Code of Practice ratified by the Press Complaints Commission in November 1997, which states that all members of the press have f a duty to maintain the highest professional and ethical standards, and that the code sets the benchmarks for those standards: 'It both protects the rights of the individual and upholds the public's right to know'.

93. The code covers 16 discrete topics, the third of which is 'Privacy'. This is one of the topics where the code makes clear that there may be exceptions to the rules set out in the code where they can be demonstrated to be in the public g interest. This phrase is said to include: (i) detecting or exposing crime or a serious misdemeanour; (ii) protecting public health and safety; and (iii) preventing the public from being misled by some statement or action of an individual or organisation. The rules on privacy are disarmingly simple:

h '3. **Privacy**

(i) Everyone is entitled to respect for his or her private and family life, home, health and correspondence. A publication will be expected to justify intrusions into any individual's private life without consent; (ii) The use of long lens photography to take pictures of people in private places without j their consent is unacceptable. Note—Private places are public or private property where there is a reasonable expectation of privacy.'

94. It appears to me that the existence of these statutory provisions, coupled with the current wording of the relevant privacy code, mean that in any case where the court is concerned with issues of freedom of expression in a journalistic, literary or artistic context, it is bound to pay particular regard to any breach of the rules set out in cl 3 of the code, especially where none of the public

interest claims set out in the preamble to the code is asserted. A newspaper which flouts cl 3 of the code is likely in those circumstances to have its claim to an entitlement to freedom of expression trumped by art 10(2) considerations of privacy. Unlike the court in *Kaye v Robertson* [1991] FSR 62, Parliament recognised that it had to acknowledge the importance of the art 8(1) respect for private life, and it was able to do so untrammelled by any concerns that the law of confidence might not stretch to protect every aspect of private life.

95. It follows that on the present occasion it is not necessary to go beyond s 12 of the Human Rights Act and cl 3 of the code to find the ground rules by which we should weigh the competing considerations of freedom of expression on the one hand and privacy on the other. So far as privacy is concerned, the case of the first and second claimants is not a particularly strong one. They did not choose to have a private wedding, attended by a few members of their family and a few friends, in the normal sense of the words 'private wedding'. There is nothing in the court's papers to belie the suggestion at p 88 of the disputed issue 639 of Hello! that they invited 250 guests, and the trappings of privacy in this context are identical with the trappings of confidentiality to which I have alluded earlier in this judgment. Although by cl 6 of their agreement with OK! they undertook to use their best efforts to ensure that their guests 'shall not publish and/or broadcast ... or write any article about, or give any extended comment, report or interview to any media concerning the Wedding', there is no evidence before the court which shows that they took any steps to enforce that undertaking, so far as their guests were concerned.

96. Mr Carr did not seek to have recourse to any public interest defence, and I did not obtain any assistance from his citation of the very general principles stated by members of this court in *Woodward v Hutchins* [1977] 2 All ER 751, [1977] 1 WLR 760, a case which preceded modern developments in practice (at any rate in the Queen's Bench Division) in relation to breach of confidence claims and which was concerned with the appropriateness of an injunction framed in astonishingly wide terms. Either the claimants will establish at trial that this particular occasion successfully retained the necessary indicia of confidentiality, so far as the taking of photographic images is concerned, or they will not. I do not consider that their privacy-based case, as distinct from their confidentiality-based case, adds very much. I am satisfied, however, that on the present untested evidence the claimants are 'likely to establish that publication should not be allowed' on confidentiality grounds. This is not, however, the end of the matter, as I must turn to other factors affecting the balance of convenience and the manner in which the court should exercise its equitable jurisdiction.

97. So far as Hello!'s case is concerned, it appears to me on the evidence that there is a substantial risk that if an injunction 'killing' this weekly edition of Hello! were to turn out to have been wrongly granted, Hello! would suffer damages which it would be extremely difficult to quantify in money terms. Although I take into account Mr Myerson's emollient evidence in answer, there appears on first impression to be a good deal of force in Ms Cartwright's evidence to the effect that Hello! would be likely to suffer losses over and above the financial loss associated with killing this edition which it would be very difficult to compute in money terms.

98. So far as OK! is concerned, if it wins at the trial, it will be able to have recourse to the very powerful weapon, fashioned by equity, of requiring Hello! to account to it for all the profits it has made from the publication of issue 639. Even if it prefers to pursue its remedy in damages, I cannot see anything in its

a evidence which would make it particularly difficult for experienced accountants to compute its financial losses. Before deciding to pay Mr Douglas and Ms Zeta-Jones sums of the magnitude set out in its agreement with them, OK! must have had a pretty good idea of the income stream it hoped to generate from the exploitation of the rights it was acquiring. Since Hello! did not publish issue 639 until after it had seen OK!'s evidence in this court, it could not realistically maintain b that the losses claimed by OK! were too remote or were otherwise unforeseeable. I have not overlooked Mr Ashford's evidence about the possible adverse effect of this incident on the success, or otherwise, of next year's planned float on the stock market, but Mr Ashford did not spell out in any way the possible impact this might have on OK! itself, as opposed to its owners.

c 99. It therefore appears to me that the balance of convenience, as between OK! and Hello!, therefore favours Hello! because it might be very difficult for Hello! to compute its losses in money terms if issue 639 was killed, whereas OK! did not appear to face the same difficulties if publication was allowed. There was no suggestion in the evidence that Hello! might be unable to pay the huge sums d it might be held liable to pay (whether as damages or by way of an account of profits) if this action succeeded at trial.

100. As between these two parties, therefore, the balance of convenience appeared to favour leaving OK! to assert its legal rights at the trial of what is essentially a commercial dispute between two magazine enterprises which are not averse to exercising spoiling tactics against each other. I am not sorry to reach e this conclusion because although it would have been wrong to withhold relief on equitable grounds alone, features of OK!'s past conduct, even making allowance for the fact that it did not have much time to defend itself against Hello!'s charges, appear to have made it an unattractive suitor for the bounty of a court of equity. The case of *Express Newspapers plc v News (UK) Ltd* [1990] 3 All ER 376, [1990] 1 WLR f 1320, which Mr Carr showed to us, is not directly applicable, because Browne-Wilkinson V-C was concerned in that case with 'tit for tat' behaviour by competing newspapers within the context of a single legal action, but it is illustrative of the reasons why courts are not likely to lean over backwards to grant equitable relief to magazines which behave in the manner attributed to OK!, g which is described in paras 11–16 of this judgment.

101. The matter which gave me greater cause for hesitation was whether having decided that the balance of convenience favoured the withholding of injunctive relief so far as OK! was concerned, Mr Douglas and Ms Zeta-Jones were nevertheless entitled to the protection of an injunction. In the end I came h to agree with the views expressed on this issue by Sedley LJ, to which I have nothing to add.

102. I would add that I have read the judgment of Keene LJ, and agree, for the reasons he gives, that if we are not willing to continue the injunction on confidence grounds, there is certainly no reason to continue it on the basis of the j complaints of malicious falsehood or unlawful interference with contractual relations. Counsel for the claimants may wish to consider in these circumstances whether it would be better for this action to be transferred at this stage to the Chancery Division, on the grounds that the malicious falsehood claim appears to be hopeless and the Chancery Division has greater expertise in taking accounts.

103. It was for these reasons that I decided that the injunction should be discharged.

SEDLEY LJ.

a

104. We have taken time to set out our reasons for discharging the injunction prohibiting Hello! from publishing illicitly-taken photographs of the wedding of the two first-named claimants because the case trenches upon an important and developing area of our law. The relevant history is set out in the judgment of Brooke LJ.

105. Let me first set out my conclusions. (a) The case in malicious falsehood is misconceived. (b) The case for an unlawful interference with contractual relations is not yet made out. (c) If there is a breach of copyright, it can be adequately compensated for in damages. (d) The two first-named claimants have a legal right to respect for their privacy, which has been infringed. (e) The circumstances of the infringement are such that the claimants should be left to their remedy in damages. The first three of these can be very shortly explained.

b

c

106. Hello! is entitled to claim that the pictures it is publishing are exclusive to it because they are. The magazine is not claiming to have the exclusive rights to the wedding photographs. There is therefore no falsehood in the words 'Exclusive photographs' on the cover of the disputed issue.

107. It may well turn out that the claimants can establish at trial a sufficient probability that Hello!'s photographs were obtained by means which were unlawful in the State of New York, and that Hello!, by reason of what it knew when it bought the rights, is sufficiently implicated in the illegality to establish an unlawful interference with the claimants' contract. But we lack any evidence of New York State law—for example, in what circumstances an unauthorised entry becomes a crime there, or whether a prohibited act by a lawful visitor renders their presence a trespass ab initio. The factual evidence we have does not enable us to form more than a provisional view of how the contested photographs were obtained.

d

e

108. Mr Tugendhat QC has understandably not pressed the copyright issue, and it requires no further comment. I turn therefore to the main issues.

f

Is there today a right of privacy in English law?

109. The common law, and equity with it, grows by slow and uneven degrees. It develops reactively, both in the immediate sense that it is only ever expounded in response to events and in the longer-term sense that it may be consciously shaped by the perceived needs of legal policy. The modern law of negligence exemplifies both senses.

g

110. The history of the law of confidence, however, while it displays many instances of the first kind of reactivity, has shown little of the second. The courts have done what they can, using such legal tools as were to hand, to stop the more outrageous invasions of individuals' privacy; but they have felt unable to articulate their measures as a discrete principle of law. Nevertheless, we have reached a point at which it can be said with confidence that the law recognises and will appropriately protect a right of personal privacy.

h

111. The reasons are twofold. First, equity and the common law are today in a position to respond to an increasingly invasive social environment by affirming that everybody has a right to some private space. Secondly, and in any event, the Human Rights Act 1998 requires the courts of this country to give appropriate effect to the right to respect for private and family life set out in art 8 of the European Convention for the Protection of Human Rights and Fundamental Freedoms (Rome, 4 November 1950; TS 71 (1953); Cmd 8969) (the convention). The difficulty with the first proposition resides in the common law's perennial

j

a need (for the best of reasons, that of legal certainty) to appear not to be doing anything for the first time. The difficulty with the second lies in the word 'appropriate'. But the two sources of law now run in a single channel because, by virtue of ss 2 and 6 of the Human Rights Act, the courts of this country must not only take into account jurisprudence of both the European Commission of Human Rights and the European Court of Human Rights which points to a b positive institutional obligation to respect privacy; they must themselves act compatibly with that and the other convention rights. This, for reasons I now turn to, arguably gives the final impetus to the recognition of a right of privacy in English law.

112. The reason why it is material to this case is that on the present evidence it is possible that the photographer was an intruder with whom no relationship c of trust had been established. If it was a guest or an employee, the received law of confidence is probably all that the claimants need.

Common law and equity

113. Lawyers in this country have learned to accept that English law d recognises no right of privacy. It was for this express reason that counsel for the actor Gordon Kaye instead put his case against the Sunday Sport, whose reporter and photographer had shamefully invaded the hospital room where Mr Kaye was recovering from serious head injuries, not as a breach of privacy, which it plainly was, but as a case of libel, malicious falsehood, trespass to the person and passing off. He managed only to hold an injunction to stop the paper claiming, by way e of malicious falsehood, that Mr Kaye had voluntarily given an interview. But this court in *Kaye v Robertson* [1991] FSR 62 did not affirmatively consider and decide whether there is a right of privacy in English law. The court adopted—for it plainly shared—counsel's assumption that there was none. Thus Glidewell LJ (at 66), giving the leading judgment, introduced his reasons in this way:

f

> 'It is well-known that in English law there is no right to privacy, and accordingly there is no right of action for breach of a person's privacy. The facts of the present case are a graphic illustration of the desirability of Parliament considering whether and in what circumstances statutory provision can be made to protect the privacy of individuals.'

g

114. Bingham LJ, agreeing, said (at 70): 'This case nonetheless highlights, yet again, the failure of both the common law of England and statute to protect in an effective way the personal privacy of individual citizens.'

115. Leggatt LJ, also agreeing, spoke of the way in which United States law had responded to 'the need which in the present case we are unable to fulfil h satisfactorily'. Recognising that this meant an enforceable right to privacy he said (at 71): 'This right has been so long disregarded here that it can be recognised only by the legislature.'

116. Nobody supposes that the members of the court which expressed this view were unfamiliar with the body of cases of which the best-known is *Prince Albert v* j *Strange* (1849) 1 Mac & G 25, 41 ER 1171 or therefore that their assent to counsel's concession was per incuriam. But it is unhelpful now to speculate whether they would have maintained their view had the point been argued before them. The legal landscape has altered.

117. The argument would not have been that a right of privacy had been spelt out by the courts: plainly it had not. It would have been, as it has been in Mr Tugendhat's condensed but convincing submission, that the tort of breach of

confidence contains all that is necessary for the fair protection of personal privacy, and that it is now a relatively small step to articulate it in that way—as was done four years after *Kaye v Robertson* by Laws J in *Hellewell v Chief Constable of Derbyshire* [1995] 4 All ER 473 at 476, [1995] 1 WLR 804 at 807:

> 'I entertain no doubt that disclosure of a photograph may, in some circumstances, be actionable as a breach of confidence ... If someone with a telephoto lens were to take from a distance and with no authority a picture of another engaged in some private act, his subsequent disclosure of the photograph would, in my judgment, as surely amount to a breach of confidence as if he had found or stolen a letter or diary in which the act was recounted and proceeded to publish it. In such a case, the law would protect what might reasonably be called a right of privacy, although the name accorded to the cause of action would be breach of confidence.'

118. This was of course obiter, but it has been understandably influential in the thinking of lawyers and commentators since it was said. The examples given by Laws J of invasions of privacy in the absence of some extant confidential relationship are taken from the speech of Lord Goff of Chieveley in *A-G v Guardian Newspapers Ltd (No 2)* [1988] 3 All ER 545 at 658–659, [1990] 1 AC 109 at 281:

> 'I realise that, in the vast majority of cases, in particular those concerned with trade secrets, the duty of confidence will arise from a transaction or relationship between the parties, often a contract, in which event the duty may arise by reason of either an express or an implied term of that contract. It is in such cases as these that the expressions "confider" and "confidant" are perhaps most aptly employed. But it is well-settled that a duty of confidence may arise in equity independently of such cases; and I have expressed the circumstances in which the duty arises in broad terms, not merely to embrace those cases where a third party receives information from a person who is under a duty of confidence in respect of it, knowing that it has been disclosed by that person to him in breach of his duty of confidence, but also to include certain situations, beloved of law teachers, where an obviously confidential document is wafted by an electric fan out of a window into a crowded street, or where an obviously confidential document, such as a private diary, is dropped in a public place, and is then picked up by a passer-by. I also have in mind the situations where secrets of importance to national security come into the possession of members of the public ...'

119. This passage, it seems to me, dulls the edge of the decision of Griffiths J in *Lord Bernstein of Leigh v Skyviews and General Ltd* [1977] 2 All ER 902, [1978] QB 479, a decision which in any event assumed that there was no legal right to privacy and focused instead on whether the law of trespass could fill the gap (see in particular [1977] 2 All ER 902 at 907–908, [1978] QB 479 at 488).

120. I do not propose to go through the body of recent extra-judicial writings by judges on the subject, which Mr Tugendhat has put before us. While these are valuable indicators to those who read them of changes in the legal climate, their authors would be the first to stress that they are not a source of law. It would be less than candid, however, not to acknowledge a debt to two particular essays. One is the survey of the field as it lies at present in Sir Brian Neill's essay 'Privacy: a challenge for the next century' in *Protecting Privacy*, ed Basil Markesinis (1999). The other is the celebrated essay by Samuel D Warren and Louis D Brandeis

a (at that time partners in a Boston legal practice; the latter to become an associate justice of the Supreme Court), 'The right to privacy' (1890) 4 Harv LR 193, deriving from chiefly English case-law what they memorably named 'the right of the individual to be let alone' as a free-standing right independent of property rights. As all these authors recognise, law emerges case by case from issues which have been argued out.

b 121. The cases in which the entitlement to the protection of confidences has been argued out are, in fact, numerous. In the leading case of *Margaret, Duchess of Argyll v Duke of Argyll* [1965] 1 All ER 611 at 616–619, [1967] Ch 302 at 318–322, Ungoed-Thomas J considered in detail *Prince Albert*'s case, itself reliant on earlier authority, and such intervening cases as *Tuck & Sons v Priester* (1887) 19 QBD 629. He concluded that a duty of confidence, which may be implied as well as express, c may be broken independently of any property or contract rights, and that such a breach can be restrained in equity. He cited some important passages from the judgment of Lord Cottenham LC in *Prince Albert*'s case, including one in which Lord Cottenham LC rejected the argument that he should follow those cases which held that a title at law must first be established. Of these he said:

d

> '... [they] have no application to cases in which the Court exercises an original and independent jurisdiction, not for the protection of a merely legal right, but to prevent what this Court considers and treats as a wrong, whether arising from violation of unquestioned right, or from breach of confidence or contract, as in the present case ...' (See (1849) 1 Mac & G 25 e at 46–47, 41 ER 1171 at 1179.)

And he described the case as one 'where the privacy is the right invaded' (the first 'the' may be a printer's interpolation).

122. Whether or not the fusion of law and equity would by itself have been sufficient to introduce an entitlement to damages for the violation of this right, in f the *Guardian Newspapers* case, Lord Goff said:

> 'The remedy of an account is alternative to the remedy of damages, which in cases of breach of confidence is now available, despite the equitable nature of the wrong, through a beneficent interpretation of the Chancery Amendment Act 1858 (Lord Cairns' Act) ...' (See [1988] 3 All ER 545 at 662, g [1990] 1 AC 109 at 286.)

123. This passage was cited, along with much other relevant English law, by the commission in *Earl Spencer v UK* (1998) 25 EHRR CD 105. By its decision the commission declared inadmissible the complaint of the Earl and Countess that English law failed to protect their privacy against what on any view had been h hurtful and invasive publicity. The reason was that the United Kingdom government had submitted successfully that, although 'there is no law of privacy, as such, in England and Wales' (see *Kaye v Robertson*), the tort of breach of confidence was now well established; that its scope and extent, in particular as to damages (see *Malone v Comr of Police of the Metropolis (No 2)* [1979] 2 All ER 620, [1979] Ch 344 j per Megarry V-C) were still in issue; but that the remedy 'was available to the applicants and the applicants have not demonstrated that it was insufficient or ineffective in the circumstances of their cases'.

124. Of course neither Her Majesty's government, which has the conduct of the United Kingdom's cases in Strasbourg, nor the commission (during its lifetime), had power to determine what the law of England and Wales is; but the fact that this unanimous conclusion could emerge from a detailed consideration,

after written and oral argument, of the state of the extant English authorities by a body of distinguished European jurists is of real persuasive force. It would not be a happy thing if the national courts were to go back without cogent reason on the United Kingdom's successful exegesis of its own law. It was while *Earl Spencer*'s case was pending in the commission that the House of Lords heard and decided *R v Khan (Sultan)* [1996] 3 All ER 289, [1997] AC 558. There Lord Nicholls of Birkenhead said:

> 'I prefer to leave open for another occasion the important question whether the present, piecemeal protection of privacy has now developed to the extent that a more comprehensive principle can be seen to exist.' (See [1996] 3 All ER 289 at 302, [1997] AC 558 at 582–583.)

125. I would conclude, at lowest, that Mr Tugendhat has a powerfully arguable case to advance at trial that his two first-named clients have a right of privacy which English law will today recognise and, where appropriate, protect. To say this is in my belief to say little, save by way of a label, that our courts have not said already over the years. It is to say, among other things, that the right, grounded as it is in the equitable doctrine of breach of confidence, is not unqualified. As Laws J said in *Hellewell v Chief Constable of Derbyshire* [1995] 4 All ER 473 at 476, [1995] 1 WLR 804 at 807: 'It is, of course, elementary that, in all such cases, a defence based on the public interest would be available.'

126. What a concept of privacy does, however, is accord recognition to the fact that the law has to protect not only those people whose trust has been abused but those who simply find themselves subjected to an unwanted intrusion into their personal lives. The law no longer needs to construct an artificial relationship of confidentiality between intruder and victim: it can recognise privacy itself as a legal principle drawn from the fundamental value of personal autonomy.

127. It is relevant, finally, to note that no Strasbourg jurisprudence contra-indicates, much less countermands, the establishment in national legal systems of a qualified right of privacy; and that the courts of France and Germany, to take two other signatories of the convention, have both in recent years developed long-gestated laws for the qualified protection of privacy against both state and non-state invasion (see Etienne Picard, 'The right to privacy in French law' in *Protecting Privacy*, ed Basil Markesinis (1999); Basil Markesinis *The German Law of Torts: A Comparative Introduction* (3rd edn, 1994) pp 63–66).

The Human Rights Act 1998

128. The Human Rights Act was brought into force on 2 October 2000. It requires every public authority, including the courts, to act consistently with the convention. What this means is a subject of sharp division and debate among both practising and academic lawyers: does it simply require the courts' procedures to be convention-compliant, or does it require the law applied by the courts, save where primary legislation plainly says otherwise, to give effect to the convention principles? This is not the place, at least without much fuller argument, in which to resolve such a large question. But some attitude has to be taken to Mr Tugendhat's submission that, whatever the current state of common law and equity, we are obliged now to give some effect to art 8, among other provisions, of the convention.

129. It is helpful, first of all, to see how much change he is soliciting. If he is right in his primary submission then the law is today adequately configured to respect the convention. If it is not—for example if the step from confidentiality

a to privacy is not simply a modern restatement of the scope of a known protection but a legal innovation—then I would accept his submission (for which there is widespread support among commentators on the Human Rights Act: see in particular Murray Hunt 'The "Horizontal Effect" of the Human Rights Act' [1998] PL 423) that this is precisely the kind of incremental change for which the Human Rights Act is designed: one which without undermining the measure of b certainty which is necessary to all law gives substance and effect to s 6 of that Act:

> '*Acts of public authorities.*—(1) It is unlawful for a public authority to act in a way which is incompatible with a Convention right.
>
> (2) Subsection (1) does not apply to an act if—(a) as the result of one or more provisions of primary legislation, the authority could not have acted c differently; or (b) in the case of one or more provisions of, or made under, primary legislation which cannot be read or given effect in a way which is compatible with the Convention rights, the authority was acting so as to give effect to or enforce those provisions.
>
> (3) In this section "public authority" includes—(a) a court or tribunal …
>
> d (6) "An act" includes a failure to act …'

130. Such a process would be consonant with the jurisprudence of the European Court of Human Rights, which s 2 of the Human Rights Act requires us to take into account and which has pinpointed art 8 of the convention as a locus of the doctrine of positive obligation. Thus in *X v Netherlands* (1985) 8 EHRR 235 at e 239–240 (para 23), the court said:

> 'The Court recalls that although the object of Article 8 is essentially that of protecting the individual against arbitrary interference by the public authorities, it does not merely compel the State to abstain from such interference: in addition to this primarily negative obligation, there may be f positive obligations inherent in an effective respect for private or family life. These obligations may involve the adoption of measures designed to secure respect for private life even in the sphere of the relations of individuals between themselves.'

131. More immediately to the present point is s 12 of the Human Rights Act. g This provides:

> '*Freedom of expression.*—(1) This section applies if a court is considering whether to grant any relief which, if granted, might affect the exercise of the Convention right to freedom of expression.
>
> h (2) If the person against whom the application for relief is made ("the respondent") is neither present nor represented, no such relief is to be granted unless the court is satisfied—(a) that the applicant has taken all practicable steps to notify the respondent; or (b) that there are compelling reasons why the respondent should not be notified.
>
> (3) No such relief is to be granted so as to restrain publication before trial j unless the court is satisfied that the applicant is likely to establish that publication should not be allowed.
>
> (4) The court must have particular regard to the importance of the Convention right to freedom of expression and, where the proceedings relate to material which the respondent claims, or which appears to the court, to be journalistic, literary or artistic material (or to conduct connected with such material), to—(a) the extent to which—(i) the material has, or is

about to, become available to the public; or (ii) it is, or would be, in the public interest for the material to be published; (b) any relevant privacy code. *a*
(5) In this section—"court" includes a tribunal; and "relief" includes any remedy or order (other than in criminal proceedings).'

132. There is no need to look at the parliamentary genesis of this section in order to see that it, with s 13 of the Human Rights Act, is of a different kind from the rest of the Act. It descends from the general to the particular, singling out one *b* convention right and making procedural and substantive provision for litigation in which the right is directly or indirectly implicated. The convention right in question is the right to freedom of expression contained in art 10:

'1. Everyone has the right to freedom of expression. This right shall include freedom to hold opinions and to receive and impart information and *c* ideas without interference by public authority and regardless of frontiers ...
2. The exercise of these freedoms, since it carries with it duties and responsibilities, may be subject to such formalities, conditions, restrictions or penalties as are prescribed by law and are necessary in a democratic society ... for the protection of the reputation or rights of others, for preventing the *d* disclosure of information received in confidence, or for maintaining the authority and impartiality of the judiciary.'

133. Two initial points need to be made about s 12 of the Human Rights Act. First, by sub-s (4) it puts beyond question the direct applicability of at least one article of the convention as between one private party to litigation and *e* another—in the jargon, its horizontal effect. Whether this is an illustration of the intended mechanism of the entire Act, or whether it is a special case (and if so, why), need not detain us here. The other point, well made by Mr Tugendhat, is that it is 'the Convention right' to freedom of expression which both triggers the section (see s 12(1)) and to which particular regard is to be had. That convention right, when one turns to it, is qualified in favour of the reputation and rights of *f* others and the protection of information received in confidence. In other words, you cannot have particular regard to art 10 without having equally particular regard at the very least to art 8:

'*Right to respect for private and family life*
1. Everyone has the right to respect for his private and family life, his *g* home and his correspondence.
2. There shall be no interference by a public authority with the exercise of this right except such as is in accordance with the law and is necessary in a democratic society in the interests of national security, public safety or the economic well-being of the country, for the prevention of disorder or crime, *h* for the protection of health or morals, or for the protection of the rights and freedoms of others.'

134. Mr Carr QC was disposed to accept this; so far as I can see he had no choice, although it is perhaps unexpected to find a claimant relying on s 12 of the 1998 Act against a publisher rather than vice versa. But he balked at what *j* Mr Tugendhat QC submitted, and I agree, was the necessary extension of the subsection's logic. A newspaper, say, intends to publish an article about an individual who learns of it and fears, on tenable grounds, that it will put his life in danger. The newspaper, also on tenable grounds, considers his fear unrealistic. First of all, it seems to me inescapable that s 12(4) makes the right to life, which is protected by art 2 of the convention and implicitly recognised by art 10(2), as

a relevant as the right of free expression to the court's decision; and in doing so it also makes art 17 (which prohibits the abuse of rights) relevant. But this in turn has an impact on s 12(3) which, though it does not replace the received test (or tests) for prior restraint, qualifies them by requiring a probability of success at trial. The gauging of this probability, by virtue of s 12(4), will have to take into account the full range of relevant convention rights.

b 135. How is the court to do this when the evidence—viz that there is and that there is not an appreciable risk to life—is no more than evenly balanced? A bland application of s 12(3) could deny the claimant the court's temporary protection, even if the potential harm to him, should the risk eventuate, was of the gravest kind and that to the newspaper and the public, should publication be restrained, minimal; and a similarly bland application of s 12(4), simply prioritising the c freedom to publish over other convention rights (save possibly freedom of religion: see s 13 of the Human Rights Act), might give the newspaper the edge even if the claimant's evidence were strong. I agree with Mr Tugendhat that this cannot have been Parliament's design. This is not only, as he submits, because of the inherent logic of the provision but because of the court's own obligation d under s 3 of the Act to construe all legislation so far as possible compatibly with the convention rights, an obligation which must include the interpretation of the Human Rights Act itself. The European Court of Human Rights has always recognised the high importance of free media of communication in a democracy, but its jurisprudence does not—and could not consistently with the convention itself—give art 10(1) of the convention the presumptive priority which is given, e for example, to the First Amendment in the jurisprudence of the United States' courts. Everything will ultimately depend on the proper balance between privacy and publicity in the situation facing the court.

136. For both reasons, and in agreement with paras 150 to 154 of the judgment of Keene LJ and para 94 of the judgment of Brooke LJ, I accept that s 12 of the f Human Rights Act is not to be interpreted and applied in the simplistic manner for which Mr Carr contends. It will be necessary for the court, in applying the test set out in s 12(3), to bear in mind that by virtue of s 12(1) and (4) the qualifications set out in art 10(2) of the convention are as relevant as the right set out in art 10(1). This means that, for example, the reputations and rights of others—not only but g not least their convention rights—are as material as the defendant's right of free expression. So is the prohibition in art 17 on the use of one party's convention rights to injure the convention rights of others. Any other approach to s 12 would in my judgment violate s 3 of the Act. Correspondingly, as Mr Tugendhat submits, 'likely' in s 12(3) cannot be read as requiring simply an evaluation of the relative strengths of the parties' evidence. If at trial, for the reasons I have given, a minor h but real risk to life, or a wholly unjustifiable invasion of privacy, is entitled to no less regard, by virtue of art 10(2), than is accorded to the right to publish by art 10(1), the consequent likelihood becomes material under s 12(3). Neither element is a trump card. They will be articulated by the principles of legality and proportionality which, as always, constitute the mechanism by which the court j reaches its conclusion on countervailing or qualified rights. It will be remembered that in the jurisprudence of the convention proportionality is tested by, among other things, the standard of what is necessary in a democratic society. It should also be borne in mind that that the much-quoted remark of Hoffmann LJ in *R v Central Independent Television plc* [1994] 3 All ER 641 at 652, [1994] Fam 192 at 203 that freedom of speech 'is a trump card which always wins' came in a passage which expressly qualified the proposition (as Lord Hoffmann has since

confirmed, albeit extra-judicially, in his 1996 Goodman Lecture) as lying 'outside the established exceptions (or any new ones which Parliament may enact in accordance with its obligations under the Convention)'. If freedom of expression is to be impeded, in other words, it must be on cogent grounds recognised by law.

137. Let me summarise. For reasons I have given, Mr Douglas and Ms Zeta-Jones have a powerful prima facie claim to redress for invasion of their privacy as a qualified right recognised and protected by English law. The case being one which affects the convention right of freedom of expression, s 12 of the Human Rights Act requires the court to have regard to art 10 of the convention (as, in its absence, would s 6 of that Act). This, however, cannot, consistently with s 3 of the Human Rights Act and art 17 of the convention, give the art 10(1) right of free expression a presumptive priority over other rights. What it does is require the court to consider art 10(2) along with art 10(1), and by doing so to bring into the frame the conflicting right to respect for privacy. This right, contained in art 8 and reflected in English law, is in turn qualified in both contexts by the right of others to free expression. The outcome, which self-evidently has to be the same under both articles, is determined principally by considerations of proportionality.

The injunction

138. In his opening argument Mr Carr, having submitted (acceptably for present purposes) that this case is a case of breach of confidence or nothing, sought to stifle that cause of action at birth by arguing that pictures such as the defendant was proposing to publish were not information at all. This had the makings of an own goal, since it might well have excluded art 10 of the convention and with it s 12 of the Human Rights Act from the defendants' own armoury. But it is plainly wrong. The offending photographs convey the simple information: 'This is what the wedding and the happy couple looked like'.

139. It is also as information, however, that the photographs invade the privacy of Mr Douglas and Ms Zeta-Jones: they tell the world things about the wedding and the couple which the claimants have not consented to. On the present evidence, whoever took the photographs probably had no right to be there; if they were lawfully there, they had no right to photograph anyone; and in either case they had no right to publicise the product of their intrusion. If it stopped there, this would have been an unanswerable case for a temporary injunction and no doubt in due course for a permanent one; perhaps the more unanswerable, not the less, for the celebrity of the two principal victims. Article 8 of the convention, whether introduced indirectly through s 12 or directly by virtue of s 6 of the Human Rights Act, will of course require the court to consider 'the rights and freedoms of others', including the art 10(1) right of Hello!. And art 10, by virtue of ss 6 and 12, will require the court, if the common law did not already do so, to have full regard to Hello!'s right to freedom of expression. But the circumstances in which the photographs must have been obtained would have robbed those rights and freedoms of substance for reasons which should by now be plain.

140. The facts, however, do not stop here. The first two claimants had sold most of the privacy they now seek to protect to the third claimant for a handsome sum. If all that had happened were that Hello! had got hold of OK!'s photographs, OK! would have proprietary rights and remedies at law, but Mr Douglas and Ms Zeta-Jones would not, I think, have any claim for breach of the privacy with which they had already parted. The present case is not so stark, because they were careful by their contract to retain a right of veto over publication of OK!'s photographs in order to maintain the kind of image which is

a professionally and no doubt also personally important to them. This element of privacy remained theirs and Hello!'s photographs violated it.

141. Article 8 of the convention, however, gives no absolute rights, any more than does the law of breach of confidence or privacy. Not only are there the qualifications under art 8(2); what para (1) requires is respect for, not inviolability of, private and family life. Taking it for the present that it is the state, represented b by the court, which must accord that respect, what amounts to respect must depend on the full set of circumstances in which the intrusion has occurred. This intrusion was by uncontrolled photography for profit of a wedding which was to be the subject of controlled photography for profit.

142. Thus the major part of the claimants' privacy rights have become the subject of a commercial transaction: bluntly, they have been sold. For reasons c more fully spelt out by Brooke LJ the frustration of such a transaction by unlawful means, if established, is in principle compensable in money, whether by way of an account of profits or damages. There is no reason in law why the cost to the wrongdoer should not be heavy enough to demonstrate that such activity is not worthwhile. The retained element of privacy, in the form of editorial control of d OK!'s pictures, while real, is itself as much a commercial as a personal reservation. While it may be harder to translate into lost money or an account of profits, it can readily be translated into general damages of a significant amount.

143. Two caveats are necessary. I do not suggest for a moment that there is a bright line between the personal and the commercial and that everything on the e commercial side, being about money, can be dealt with by an award of damages. Nor, equally, should it be thought that either art 8 or our domestic law will never protect privacy which is being turned to commercial ends. Everything will depend on the infinite variety of facts thrown up case by case.

144. In the present case, and not without misgiving, I have concluded that although the first two claimants are likely to succeed at trial in establishing a f breach of their privacy in which Hello! may be actionably implicated, the dominant feature of the case is that by far the greater part of that privacy has already been traded and falls to be protected, if at all, as a commodity in the hands of the third claimant. This can be done without the need of an injunction, particularly since there may not be adequate countervailing redress for the g defendants if at trial they stave off the claim for interference with contractual relations. The retained element of the first two claimants' privacy is not in my judgment—though I confess it is a close thing—sufficient to tilt the balance of justice and convenience against such liberty as the defendants may establish, at law and under art 10 of the convention, to publish the illicitly taken photographs.

h **KEENE LJ.**

The approach at this stage

145. This appeal concerns an interlocutory injunction which has been granted in the High Court in advance of any trial of the issues in the case. That is a j statement of the obvious, but it is none the less important, because it affects the approach to be adopted by a court. In most situations where such an injunction is sought, the court would be concerned merely with whether there was a serious issue to be tried and, if so, with the balance of convenience (see *American Cyanamid Co v Ethicon Ltd* [1975] 1 All ER 504, [1975] AC 396). However, in the present case that cannot be the appropriate approach, and neither party seeks to maintain that it is.

146. First, this is a case which falls within the principles established by this court in *Cambridge Nutrition Ltd v British Broadcasting Corp* [1990] 3 All ER 523. In the words of Kerr LJ in that case (at 535):

> 'The subject matter concerns the right to publish an article, or to transmit a broadcast, whose importance may be transitory but whose impact depends on timing, news value and topicality.'

147. In such cases, the parties are principally interested in the grant or refusal of the interlocutory injunction, even though the damages claim may well remain as a secondary objective. In such circumstances, the court must look beyond conventional *American Cyanamid* principle and seek to discern where the balance of justice lies. The present proceedings, where both OK! magazine and Hello! magazine are published weekly, are undoubtedly concerned with material whose topicality is of the essence.

148. Secondly, this court is required by s 12(1) of the Human Rights Act 1998 to apply s 12(3) thereof. Section 12(1) states: 'This section applies if a court is considering whether to grant any relief which, if granted, might affect the exercise of the Convention right to freedom of expression.' It is then provided by s 12(3): 'No such relief is to be granted so as to restrain publication before trial unless the court is satisfied that the applicant is likely to establish that publication should not be allowed.'

149. It is not in dispute that s 12(3) is applicable in this case. Mr Tugendhat QC's submission is that the phrase 'likely to establish' does not mean 'more probable than not', because that interpretation in certain circumstances could bring it into conflict with the European Convention for the Protection of Human Rights and Fundamental Freedoms (Rome, 4 November 1950; TS 71 (1953); Cmd 8969) (the convention) itself by giving priority to art 10, the right to freedom of expression, over art 8, the right to respect for private and family life. Such an automatic priority, it is said, would not be in conformity with the convention. Since s 3(1) of the Human Rights Act requires the court to construe legislation in a way which is compatible with the convention rights 'so far as it is possible to do so', s 12(3) itself must be read in a way which avoids giving precedence to art 10 rights. It is argued on behalf of the claimants that the words 'likely to establish' in that subsection should be taken to mean 'not fanciful' or 'on the cards'.

150. For my part, I do not accept that there is any need for conflict between the normal meaning to be attached to the words in s 12(3) and the convention. The subsection does not seek to give a priority to one convention right over another. It is simply dealing with the interlocutory stage of proceedings and with how the court is to approach matters at that stage in advance of any ultimate balance being struck between rights which may be in potential conflict. It requires the court to look at the merits of the case and not merely to apply the *American Cyanamid* test. Thus the court has to look ahead to the ultimate stage and to be satisfied that the scales are likely to come down in the applicant's favour. That does not conflict with the convention, since it is merely requiring the court to apply its mind to how one right is to be balanced, on the merits against another right, without building in additional weight on one side. In a situation such as the one postulated by Mr Tugendhat, where the non-art 10 right is of fundamental importance to the individual, such as the art 2 right to life, the merits will include not merely the evidence about how great is the risk of that right being breached, but also a consideration of the gravity of the consequences for an applicant if the risk materialises. The nature of the risk is part of the merits, just as it would be at

a trial when the balance had to be struck. That is as relevant at the interlocutory stage as it would be at trial. But that does not require any strained interpretation of s 12(3).

151. Certainly s 12(3) is making prior restraint (i e before trial) more difficult in cases where the right to freedom of expression is engaged than where it is not. That is not a novel concept in English law. As was said by Laws J in *R v Advertising* b *Standards Authority Ltd, ex p Vernons Organisation Ltd* [1993] 2 All ER 202 at 205, [1992] 1 WLR 1289 at 1293:

> '… there is a general principle in our law that the expression of opinion and the conveyance of information will not be restrained by the courts save on pressing grounds. Freedom of expression is as much a sinew of the common c law as it is of the European Convention on Human Rights …'

152. Perhaps more to the point, the jurisprudence of the European Court of Human Rights is generally hostile to prior restraint by the courts. Prior restraints on publication are not prohibited by the convention, as the European Court of Human Rights made clear in *Observer v UK* (1991) 14 EHRR 153, the 'Spycatcher' d case, but in that same case it went on to say (at 191 (para 60)):

> 'On the other hand, the dangers inherent in prior restraints are such that they call for the most careful scrutiny on the part of the Court. This is especially so as far as the press is concerned, for news is a perishable commodity and to delay its publication, even for a short period, may well e deprive it of all its value and interest.'

153. It is impossible to accept that a statutory provision requiring a court to consider the merits of the case and to be satisfied that the balance is likely to be struck in favour of the applicant before prior restraint is to be granted is incompatible with the convention. It follows that no strained reading of the language f of s 12(3) is needed to render it compatible with convention rights. The wording can be given its normal meaning. Consequently the test to be applied at this stage is whether this court is satisfied that the applicant is likely to establish at trial that publication should not be allowed. Even then, there remains a discretion in the court.

g

The causes of action

154. In these proceedings four causes of action are set out in the particulars of claim, but one of those, infringement of copyright, is not relied upon for the purposes of the claim for an interlocutory injunction. The remaining ones are malicious falsehood, interference with contractual relations and breach of confidence. It is h convenient to consider those claims in that order.

Malicious falsehood

155. The ingredients of this tort are well-established. It must be shown that the defendant published words which are false and that this was done maliciously, j that is to say with the intention to injure the claimant without lawful excuse: *Kaye v Robertson* [1991] FSR 62 at 67. Special damage must also be proved. But the starting point is the publication of words which are false.

156. The claimants here rely on the combination of the words 'Exclusive Photographs' on the front cover of this edition of Hello! magazine and the publication of the photographs themselves. In addition, it is said that the text of the article, by describing the security procedures in force at the event, implied

that the photographs were taken with consent. For the defendants, it is argued that the reference to 'Exclusive photographs' was not false, because those photographs were exclusive to Hello! magazine. Nor is there any evidence that anyone understood the magazine to be saying that the first two claimants had consented to an exclusive interview or to the photographs being taken.

157. At this stage in the proceedings a court has to ask itself whether a jury would find that the words in question were false, either expressly or by implication. One would think that a jury would be inclined, given the frequency with which claims to exclusivity are made by newspapers and magazines, to attach only a limited significance to the words 'Exclusive photographs'. Certainly I am unpersuaded that a jury would conclude that those words meant that Hello! magazine was in a position to publish the only photographs of the wedding. They would be more likely to take the view that the meaning was that these particular photographs were exclusive to Hello! magazine, at least within the United Kingdom. As for the alleged implication that the first two claimants had consented to the taking of these photographs, that is far from being clearly established. It is true that there are two references in the text to security at the wedding, one being to 'security so tight' that the ceremony was slightly delayed and the other being to 'elaborate security procedures'. Neither of those passages nor anything else in the text referred to any restrictions on cameras or photography. A jury would be likely to regard those references to security as being to the normal steps taken at events involving well-known people, such as the exclusion of gatecrashers. They would be unlikely to read them as meaning that the first two claimants had consented to the taking of the photographs in question.

158. That being so, the claimants fail to discharge the burden resting on them of demonstrating that a jury would be likely to regard these statements as false. In those circumstances, it would be quite wrong for an interlocutory injunction to issue to restrain publication on the basis of malicious falsehood.

Interference with contractual relations

159. It has not been denied in any of the witness statements filed on behalf of the defendants that they were aware of the existence of a contract between the first two claimants and OK! magazine. That by itself is not enough to establish that the defendants are liable in tort under this heading. The ways in which the case is put on behalf of the claimants are, first, that Hello! magazine must have instigated or been involved in the taking of the illicit photographs, and secondly that in any event they must have known when they purchased the photographs that they had been obtained by unlawful means.

160. The evidence as it stands at this stage does not establish that the claimants are likely to make out the first of those propositions. Ms Cartwright, publishing director of Hello! magazine, states that the defendants had no previous knowledge that these pictures were to be taken and she describes how they came into their possession. How that evidence would stand up at any trial is difficult to predict, but there is no direct evidence of prior knowledge on the part of the defendants, and any inference to that effect can only be uncertain at this stage.

161. The second way in which this claim is put may have more prospect of success. It would turn on whether the defendants can be shown to have used unlawful means to interfere with the existing contractual relationships: see *Merkur Island Shipping Corp v Laughton* [1983] 2 All ER 189 at 196, [1983] 2 AC 570 at 609 per Lord Diplock. Mr Tugendhat submits that, even if the defendants did

a not themselves or by their agents use unlawful means, they must have received the photographs in circumstances in which they must have been aware that those photographs had been taken illicitly. If taken by an employee of a service company engaged for the wedding, that person would have broken his or her contract by so acting. Even if taken by a guest, there could be a breach of confidence because of the request accompanying the invitation not to take b photographs and the notice to like effect at the entrance. Such a person might have become a trespasser by entering without complying with that request and the notice.

162. As Mr Tugendhat acknowledges, this is a difficult area of law, where the precise scope of the concept of 'unlawful means' remains to be settled. In the present case, it is impossible to arrive at a judgment at this stage as to whether the c controversial photographs were taken by a guest or by an employee of a contractor or indeed by more than one person. There is evidence that some guests were seen by security staff to have cameras even during the course of the reception itself. The legal position in which a guest found himself is far from clear. It is conceded by the claimants that there was no contractual relationship d between a guest and any of the claimants, and that must be so, if only because of the almost certain absence of any intent to create such a relationship. It might be that a guest who took a photograph would be held under the applicable law of New York State to be acting tortiously or in breach of confidence in the circumstances of this case, but we have no evidence to that effect. There is then the further problem of the extent to which the recipient of photographs so taken e is to be treated as liable in this tort if he was not himself involved in the 'unlawful' taking of the photographs or the instigation of it.

163. I can only conclude that the prospect of the claimants eventually establishing liability of the defendants on this basis is too uncertain to warrant the issuing of an interlocutory injunction in advance of publication.

f

Breach of confidence

164. It is this which has formed the main plank of the claimants' case. The claim is put in terms of breach of confidence in the particulars of claim, but it was said in argument by Mr Tugendhat that the case has more to do with privacy that g with confidentiality.

165. It is clear that there is no watertight division between the two concepts. *Margaret, Duchess of Argyll v Duke of Argyll* [1965] 1 All ER 611, [1967] Ch 302 was a classic case where the concept of confidentiality was applied so as, in effect, to protect the privacy of communications between a husband and wife. Moreover, h breach of confidence is a developing area of the law, the boundaries of which are not immutable but may change to reflect changes in society, technology and business practice. I reject without hesitation the submission by Mr Carr QC for the defendants that it cannot encompass photographs of an event. It is said that those photographs in the present case did not convey any information which had the quality of confidence, because the guests were not prevented from imparting the j same information subsequently, whether in words, by drawings based on recollection or any other means. This argument is unsustainable. The photographs conveyed to the public information not otherwise truly obtainable, that is to say, what the event and its participants looked like. It is said that a picture is worth a thousand words. Were that not so, there would not be a market for magazines like Hello! and OK! The same result is not obtainable through the medium of words alone, nor by recollected drawings with their inevitable inaccuracy. There is

no reason why these photographs inherently could not be the subject of a breach of confidence. a

166. Since the coming into force of the Human Rights Act, the courts as a public authority cannot act in a way which is incompatible with a convention right: s 6(1). That arguably includes their activity in interpreting and developing the common law, even where no public authority is a party to the litigation. Whether this extends to creating a new cause of action between private persons b and bodies is more controversial, since to do so would appear to circumvent the restrictions on proceedings contained in s 7(1) of the Act and on remedies in s 8(1). But it is unnecessary to determine that issue in these proceedings, where reliance is placed on breach of confidence, an established cause of action, the scope of which may now need to be approached in the light of the obligation on this court arising under s 6(1) of the Act. Already before the coming into force of c the Act there have been persuasive dicta in *Hellewell v Chief Constable of Derbyshire* [1995] 4 All ER 473, [1995] 1 WLR 804 and *A-G v Guardian Newspapers Ltd (No 2)* [1988] 3 All ER 545, [1990] 1 AC 109, cited by Sedley LJ in his judgment in these proceedings, to the effect that a pre-existing confidential relationship between the parties is not required for a breach of confidence suit. The nature of the subject d matter or the circumstances of the defendant's activities may suffice in some instances to give rise to liability for breach of confidence. That approach must now be informed by the jurisprudence of the convention in respect of art 8. Whether the resulting liability is described as being for breach of confidence or for breach of a right to privacy may be little more than deciding what label is to be attached to the cause of action, but there would seem to be merit in e recognising that the original concept of breach of confidence has in this particular category of cases now developed into something different from the commercial and employment relationships with which confidentiality is mainly concerned.

167. Because of these developments in the common law relating to confidence and the apparent obligation on English courts now to take account of the right to f respect for private and family life under art 8 when interpreting the common law, it seems unlikely that *Kaye v Robertson* [1991] FSR 62, which held that there was no actionable right of privacy in English law, would be decided the same way on that aspect today. It is noteworthy that no claim for breach of confidence was mounted in that case, and that the *Duchess of Argyll*'s case and the *Guardian* g *Newspapers* case do not seem to have been cited to the court. In the latter decision the House of Lords had made it clear that a duty of confidence could arise from the circumstances in which the information was obtained, so that the recipient was to be precluded from disclosing it to others. Consequently if the present case concerned a truly private occasion, where the persons involved made it clear that they intended it to remain private and undisclosed to the world, then I might well h have concluded that in the current state of English law the claimants were likely to succeed at any eventual trial.

168. But any consideration of art 8 rights must reflect the convention jurisprudence which acknowledges different degrees of privacy. The European Court of the Human Rights ruled in *Dudgeon v UK* (1981) 4 EHRR 149 at 165 j (para 152) that the more intimate the aspect of private life which is being interfered with, the more serious must be the reasons for interference before the latter can be legitimate. Personal sexuality, as in that case, is an extremely intimate aspect of a person's private life. A purely private wedding will have a lesser but still significant degree of privacy warranting protection, though subject to the considerations set out in art 8(2) of the convention. But if persons choose to lessen the degree of

a privacy attaching to an otherwise private occasion, then the balance to be struck between their rights and other considerations is likely to be affected.

169. In the present case, it is of considerable relevance that very widespread publicity was to be given in any event to the wedding very soon afterwards by way of photographs in OK! magazine. The occasion thereby lost much of its private nature. The claimants were by their security measures and by their b agreements with the service companies seeking not so much to protect the privacy of the first two claimants but rather to control the form of publicity which ensued. This is apparent from the witness statement of Paul Ashford, editorial director of OK! magazine, who says: 'all guests were informed they should not bring cameras *because of the exclusive deal that had been entered with OK!*' (My emphasis.)

c 170. One does not need to assume that that was the sole purpose of the various security measures. It is enough that it was clearly a very important purpose. Indeed, it was made clear by Mr Tugendhat in his submissions that what was complained of here was the loss of control over the photographs to be published, leading to damage to the image of the first and second claimants d because of unflattering photographs.

171. It may be that a limited degree of privacy remains in such a situation and it could be that at trial the claimants would succeed in obtaining a permanent injunction. There must still be some doubt about that. But even if the claimants had passed that threshold of showing that it is likely that they would obtain an injunction at trial, this court in exercising its discretion at this interlocutory stage e must still take account of the widespread publicity arranged by the claimant for this occasion. When that organised publicity is balanced against the impact on the defendants of an injunction restraining publication, I have no doubt that the scales come down in this case against prior restraint. This is a matter where any damage to the claimants can adequately be dealt with in monetary terms. In those circumstances I would allow this appeal and discharge the injunction.

Appeal allowed.

Gillian Crew Barrister.

Collings v Lee and another

a

COURT OF APPEAL, CIVIL DIVISION
NOURSE, MUMMERY AND RIX LJJ
10, 11 JULY, 19 OCTOBER 2000

b

Land registration – Overriding interest – Rights of person in actual occupation of land – Transferee agreeing to act as agent for transferors in finding purchaser for property – Transferee representing that transfer being made to named third party – Third party non-existent and transferee using that name as alias – Transferors transferring property into third party's name and transferee registering himself as proprietor under that name – Transferee granting legal charge over property to building society but transferors remaining in actual occupation – Whether transferors having overriding interest in property – Land Registration Act 1925, s 70(1)(g).

c

The claimant, Mrs C, and her late husband lived in a freehold property which was registered in their joint names and which they held as beneficial joint tenants. They wished to sell their property and were introduced to L, who claimed to be in the business of buying and selling properties. He agreed to find a purchaser for their property and to assist them in a finding a new house. To that end, he was paid a fee of £6,500. After representing to Mr and Mrs C that he had managed to effect a sale of the property to one S at a price of £250,000, L obtained the title deeds to the property from them in connection with the alleged sale, and procured the execution of a transfer of the property to S. The representation was fraudulent in that S's name was an alias used by L himself, who had not effected and had no intention of effecting a sale to a third party. Mr and Mrs C never received any part of the alleged sale price, and L was registered, under the name of S, as proprietor of the property. He later executed a legal charge of the property in favour of the defendant building society which was registered as proprietor of the charge. Mr and Mrs C remained in occupation of the property throughout, and no inquiry was made of them by the building society. L's fraud came to light as a result of inquiries made by the police, and Mrs C brought proceedings for rectification of the register against both L and the building society on the ground that the transfer to L had been fraudulent. On the summary determination of a point of law, the judge ordered rectification of the register, holding that Mrs C had an overriding interest in the property under s 70(1)(g)[a] of the Land Registration Act 1925, ie a right in actual occupation. The building society appealed, contending that the transfer of the property to L was voidable rather than void, that unless and until it was avoided by Mr and Mrs C they had no subsisting equitable interest in the property since their right to avoid the transfer was a 'mere equity', and that such a right did not fall within s 70(1)(g).

d

e

f

g

h

Held – Where a transfer of property to an agent of the transferor was obtained by fraudulent misrepresentation, and the transferor never intended that the whole legal and beneficial ownership in the property should pass to the transferee, the transferor retained an equitable interest in the property which constituted an overriding interest under s 70(1)(g) of the 1925 Act. Such a case differed from those in which the transfer was made pursuant to a contract since,

j

a Section 70, so far as material, is set out at p 334 *g h*, post

a in those cases, the transferor had intended that such ownership should pass to the transferee notwithstanding that the transfer had been obtained by fraudulent misrepresentation. In the instant case, Mr and Mrs C had not intended to transfer the property to L or to transfer it for no consideration. L had acted as their agent, and had owed them general fiduciary duties. In causing the property to be transferred to himself for no consideration and in procuring his own registration b as the proprietor, he had acted in breach of his authority as agent and his fiduciary duty, and in contravention of Mr and Mrs C's expressed intention that the property should be transferred to a third party called S for a price of £250,000. Although L's registration as proprietor was effective to vest the legal estate in him, neither the transfer nor the registration was effectual to divest Mr and Mrs C of their beneficial interest in the property. L therefore held the property on trust c for them, and whether that trust should characterised as implied, resulting or constructive was a matter of no importance. Accordingly, Mrs C had an overriding interest in the property under s 70(1)(g), and the appeal would therefore be dismissed (see p 336 *f* to *j*, p 337 *f g* and p 338 *g h*, post).

d **Notes**

For the distinction between void and voidable contracts and for overriding interests in registered land, see respectively 9(1) *Halsbury's Laws* (4th edn reissue) para 607 and 26 *Halsbury's Laws* (4th edn reissue) paras 782–784.

For the Land Registration Act 1925, s 70, see 37 *Halsbury's Statutes* (4th edn) (1998 reissue) 480.

e

Cases referred to in judgments

Agip (Africa) Ltd v Jackson [1992] 4 All ER 385, [1990] Ch 265, [1989] 3 WLR 1367; *affd* [1992] 4 All ER 451, [1991] Ch 547, [1991] 3 WLR 116, CA.

Daly v Sidney Stock Exchange Ltd (1986) 160 CLR 371, Aust HC.

f *Heinl v Jyske Bank (Gibraltar) Ltd* [1999] Lloyd's Rep Bank 511, CA.

Lonrho plc v Fayed (No 2) [1991] 4 All ER 961, [1992] 1 WLR 1.

Rolled Steel Products (Holdings) Ltd v British Steel Corp [1985] 3 All ER 52, [1986] Ch 246, [1985] 2 WLR 908, CA.

Twinsectra Ltd v Yardley [1999] Lloyd's Rep Bank 438, CA.

g

Cases also cited or referred to in skeleton arguments

Allied Irish Banks Ltd v Glynn [1973] IR 188, Ir HC.

Bainbrigge v Browne (1881) 18 Ch D 188.

Barclays Bank plc v Boulter [1997] 2 All ER 1002, [1998] 1 WLR 1, CA; *affd* [1999] 4 All ER 513, [1999] 1 WLR 1919, HL.

h

Barclays Bank plc v O'Brien [1993] 4 All ER 417, [1994] 1 AC 180, HL.

Blacklocks v J B Developments (Godalming) Ltd [1981] 3 All ER 392, [1982] Ch 183.

CIBC Mortgages plc v Pitt [1993] 4 All ER 433, [1994] 1 AC 200, HL.

City of London Building Society v Flegg [1987] 3 All ER 435, [1988] AC 54, HL

j *Hodgson v Marks* [1971] 2 All ER 684, [1971] Ch 892, CA.

Hunt v Luck [1902] 1 Ch 428, [1900–3] All ER Rep 295, CA.

Kling v Keston Properties Ltd (1983) 49 P & CR 212.

Latec Investments Ltd v Hotel Terrigal Pty Ltd (in liquidation) (1965) 113 CLR 265, Aust HC.

Lloyds Bank plc v Rosset [1988] 3 All ER 915, [1989] Ch 350, CA.

London and Cheshire Insurance Co Ltd v Laplagrene Property Co Ltd [1971] 1 All ER 766, [1971] Ch 499.

National Provincial Bank Ltd v Ainsworth [1965] 2 All ER 472, [1965] AC 1175, HL; *rvsg* sub nom *National Provincial Bank Ltd v Hastings Car Mart Ltd* [1964] 1 All ER 688, [1964] Ch 665, CA. a
Norwich and Peterborough Building Society v Steed (No 2) [1993] 1 All ER 330, [1993] Ch 116, CA.
Nurdin & Peacock plc v DB Ramsden & Co Ltd [1999] 1 All ER 941, [1999] 1 WLR 1249. b
Sherman (decd), Re, Trevenen v Pearce [1954] 1 All ER 893, [1954] Ch 653.
Shiloh Spinners Ltd v Harding [1973] 1 All ER 90, [1973] AC 691, HL.
Stump v Gaby (1852) 2 De GM & G 623, 42 ER 1015.
UCB Bank v Beasley [1995] CA Transcript 965.
Wallcite Ltd v Ferrishurst Ltd [1999] 1 All ER 977, [1999] Ch 355, CA. c
Webb v Pollmount Ltd [1966] 1 All ER 481, [1966] Ch 584.
Williams & Glyn's Bank Ltd v Boland [1980] 2 All ER 408, [1981] AC 487, HL.

Appeal

The second defendant, Halifax plc, the registered proprietor of a legal charge over a property known as 6 Strawberry Hill Road, Twickenham, Middlesex, d appealed with leave of Judge Boggis QC from his decision, sitting as a judge of the High Court, on 3 March 1999 whereby, on the summary determination of a point of law under RSC Ord 14A, he held that the claimant, Sheila Edna Collings, had an overriding interest in the property under s 70(1)(g) of the Land Registration Act 1925, and ordered rectification of the register against the Halifax and the first e defendant, Mark William Lee. The facts are set out in the judgment of Nourse LJ.

Edward Nugee QC and *Colin Braham* (instructed by *Dibb Lupton Alsop*, Leeds) for the Halifax.
James Behrens (instructed by *Teresa Evans*, Epsom) for Mrs Collings.

f

Cur adv vult

19 October 2000. The following judgments were delivered.

NOURSE LJ. This appeal raises a question under s 70 of the Land Registration Act 1925, to which the marginal note is 'Liability of registered land to overriding g interests'. So far as material, the section provides:

> '(1) All registered land shall ... be deemed to be subject to such of the following overriding interests as may be for the time being subsisting in reference thereto ... (g) The rights of every person in actual occupation of h the land or in receipt of the rents and profits thereof, save where enquiry is made of such person and the rights are not disclosed ...'

Here it is agreed both that the person who claims the interest or right was in actual occupation of the land at the material time and that no inquiry was made of her. The question is whether her interest or right is one which falls within j s 70(1)(g) of the Act.

The question arises on an appeal from a decision of Judge Boggis QC, sitting as a judge of the Chancery Division, on an application under RSC Ord 14A. There having been no trial, the facts must be taken from the pleadings, the affidavit in support of the application and the exhibits thereto. Since they are undisputed, they can be stated without reference to their source.

a In 1991 the claimant in the action, Sheila Edna Collings, was living with her late husband, Frank Herbert Collings, at 6 Strawberry Hill Road, Twickenham, Middlesex, a freehold property registered at the Land Registry. The property was registered in their joint names and was held by them as beneficial joint tenants. In or about June of that year Mr and Mrs Collings, being anxious to sell the property and move out of London, were introduced to the first defendant, Mark b William Lee, who claimed to be in the business of buying and selling properties. He agreed to find a purchaser for the property and to assist Mr and Mrs Collings in finding a new house for their occupation.

Between the beginning of July and the end of August 1991 the first defendant: (1) obtained payment of a sum of £6,500 from Mr and Mrs Collings, professedly in respect of his fees for assisting them in finding a suitable buyer for the property c and a new house for them to occupy; (2) represented to Mr and Mrs Collings that he had managed to effect a sale of the property to one Martin Nathen Styles at a price of £250,000; (3) obtained from Mr and Mrs Collings in connection with the alleged sale the title deeds to the property (principally, it may be assumed, the land certificate); (4) procured their execution of a transfer of the property d expressed to be in favour of Martin Nathen Styles; and (5) obtained payment of a further sum of £26,000 from Mr and Mrs Collings, professedly to be used as a deposit in respect of a new house for their occupation.

The first defendant's representation, that he had managed to effect a sale of the property to Martin Nathen Styles, was fraudulent in that that name was an alias for the first defendant himself, who had not effected and had no intention of e effecting a sale to a third party. Mr and Mrs Collings never received any part of the alleged sale price of £250,000, nor were the sums of £6,500 and £26,000 or any part of them repaid. In September 1992, at Isleworth Crown Court, the first defendant pleaded guilty to various offences of obtaining properties by deception, including 6 Strawberry Hill Road, and was sentenced to a total of five years' f imprisonment.

Accordingly, the reality of the transaction was that the property was transferred not to a third party called Martin Nathen Styles at a price of £250,000 but to the first defendant himself for no consideration. The transfer was executed by Mr and Mrs Collings on 27 August 1991. On 28 October 1991 the first defendant, under the name of Martin Nathen Styles, was registered as the proprietor of the g property at the Land Registry. On or about 10 January 1992, under the same name, he executed a legal charge of the property in favour of Leeds Permanent Building Society, now the second defendant, Halifax plc (the Halifax), to secure repayment of an advance to him of £125,030. On 16 January 1992 the Halifax was registered at the Land Registry as the proprietor of the charge. At all material h times prior to 31 January 1992 Mr and Mrs Collings were in actual occupation of the property. It appears likely that, if inquiry had been made of them during that period, the first defendant's fraud would have been exposed. But no such inquiry was made by or on behalf of the Halifax. On Mr Collings' death the whole of the beneficial interest in the property vested in Mrs Collings by survivorship, subject j to the legal charge, if effective.

The first defendant's fraudulent conduct towards both Mr and Mrs Collings and the Halifax became apparent in May 1992 as a result of inquiries made by the police. On 12 October 1992 solicitors acting for Mr and Mrs Collings wrote to the first defendant in prison, stating that they were instructed to apply for rectification of the register on the ground that the transfer to him had been fraudulent. There was then an unexplained delay of nearly five years before the writ in the action claiming rectification of the register against both the first defendant and the Halifax was issued on 5 August 1997. *a*

The first defendant has taken no part in the proceedings. The Halifax, while conceding that Mrs Collings has at all times had a right to set aside the transfer of the property as against the first defendant, denies that her right is an overriding interest within s 70(1)(g) of the Act. On 3 March 1999 Judge Boggis determined that Mrs Collings' right was an overriding interest and that, as such, it was binding on the Halifax. He ordered rectification of the register accordingly. Having granted the Halifax permission to appeal, he stayed the order for rectification pending the conclusion of the appeal. *b*

Before the judge and during the greater part of the hearing in this court the case was argued on a common assumption that as at 16 January 1992, when the Halifax was registered as the proprietor of the legal charge, Mr and Mrs Collings had no more than a right to set aside the transfer dated 27 August 1991 as against the first defendant. In other words, it was assumed that they did not have an equitable interest in the property. In my judgment that assumption was incorrect. On the facts of the case as I have stated them, and granted that the registration of the first defendant as the proprietor of the property was effective to vest the legal estate in him, it is clear that he at all times held it on trust for Mr and Mrs Collings. If that is the correct view, it necessarily follows that on 16 January 1992 they had an equitable interest in the property, unquestionably an overriding interest within s 70(1)(g). *c* *d*

In the first instance it is convenient to consider the question as one of principle and without reference to authority. The first and foremost consideration is that Mr and Mrs Collings constituted the first defendant their agent for the purpose of finding a buyer for the property and, subsequently, of transferring it to a third party called Martin Nathen Styles at a price of £250,000. Accordingly, at any rate from the time that he obtained payment of the sum of £6,500, the first defendant owed general fiduciary duties to Mr and Mrs Collings and, from the time that he obtained the title deeds, a particular fiduciary duty to procure its transfer to a third party called Martin Nathen Styles at a price of £250,000. *e* *f*

The first defendant did not procure the property to be transferred to a third party called Martin Nathen Styles at a price of £250,000. Instead, he caused it to be transferred to himself for no consideration and then procured the registration of himself as the proprietor thereof at the Land Registry. In taking those steps he acted in breach of his authority as Mr and Mrs Collings' agent, in breach of his particular fiduciary duty to them and in contravention of their expressed intention that the property should be transferred to a third party called Martin Nathen Styles at a price of £250,000. *g*

It was implicit in the submissions on both sides, his fraud notwithstanding, that the effect of the material provisions of the Act was that the legal estate in the property became vested in the first defendant on his registration as the proprietor thereof. However, it is clear in principle that neither the transfer nor the registration was effectual to divest Mr and Mrs Collings of their beneficial interest in the property. The first defendant held it on trust for them. Whether the trust should be characterised as implied, resulting or constructive is a matter of no importance. The first defendant having acted as he did, the plain fact is that no court of equity could allow him to assert a beneficial interest in the property as against Mr and Mrs Collings. *h* *j*

At this stage I should point out that the foregoing view of the transaction only began to emerge in exchanges between Mummery LJ and counsel when the a second of the two days of the hearing (10 and 11 July 2000) was well advanced. Mr Nugee QC, for the Halifax, justifiably complained that the point had not been taken on behalf of Mrs Collings. However, recognising that it was a pure point of law, he very properly did not object to its being taken even at that late stage. His difficulty was that he was not fully prepared to meet it. Accordingly, on 26 and 27 July we received further written submissions from Mr Nugee and Mr Braham b on behalf of the Halifax and from Mr Behrens on behalf of Mrs Collings, both sides expressing the hope that it would not be necessary for the court to reconvene in order to hear further oral submissions.

The essence of the argument advanced by Mr Nugee and Mr Braham is that the transfer of the property to the first defendant was not void, but voidable by Mr and Mrs Collings; that unless and until they avoided it they had no subsisting c equitable interest in the property, their right to avoid it being a 'mere equity'; and that such a right does not fall within s 70(1)(g). In support of that argument they rely mainly on three authorities, which I list in date order: *Daly v Sidney Stock Exchange Ltd* (1986) 160 CLR 371 at 388–390 per Brennan J, *Lonrho plc v Fayed (No 2)* [1991] 4 All ER 961 at 971, [1992] 1 WLR 1 at 11–12 per Millett J, and *Twinsectra Ltd v* d *Yardley* [1999] Lloyd's Rep Bank 438 at 461 per Potter LJ.

In my judgment the authorities relied on by Mr Nugee and Mr Braham, so far from casting doubt on the view of the transaction above propounded, confirm it. The basis of their argument is the principle stated by Millett J in the *Lonrho plc* case:

e 'A contract obtained by fraudulent misrepresentation is voidable, not void, even in equity. The representee may elect to avoid it, but until he does so the representor is not a constructive trustee of the property transferred pursuant to the contract, and no fiduciary relationship exists between him and the representee: see *Daly v Sidney Stock Exchange Ltd* ((1986) 160 CLR 371 f at 387–390) per Brennan J.' (See [1991] 4 All ER 961 at 971, [1992] 1 WLR 1 at 11–12.)

The rationale of the principle, as it applies to a transfer of property, is that even where the transfer is obtained by fraudulent misrepresentation, the transferor nevertheless intends that the whole legal and beneficial ownership in the property g shall pass to the transferee. But that was not this case. Mr and Mrs Collings did not intend to transfer the property to the first defendant and they did not intend to transfer it for no consideration. The first defendant acquired the property without their knowledge and consent and in breach of his fiduciary duty to them. The equitable interest remained vested in Mr and Mrs Collings.

The distinction between the two situations is recognised in the two further h authorities cited. Thus in *Daly*'s case, Brennan J said:

'There is no analogy between the present case and one in which a constructive trust is imposed on money or other property which is acquired by a fiduciary in breach of his duty but not pursuant to a voidable contract. j In such a case there is no question of avoiding the contract before the constructive trust is imposed.' (See (1986) 160 CLR 371 at 389–390.)

In the *Twinsectra Ltd* case Potter LJ said:

'… the distinction of importance here is that between non-consensual transfers and transfers pursuant to contracts which are voidable for misrepresentation. In the latter case, the transferor may elect whether to avoid

> or affirm the transaction and, until he elects to avoid it, there is no constructive (resulting) trust; in the former case, the constructive trust arises upon the moment of transfer.' (See [1999] Lloyd's Rep Bank 438 at 461.)

a

Other authorities, not cited to us, are to the same effect. In *Agip (Africa) Ltd v Jackson* [1992] 4 All ER 385, [1990] Ch 265 Millett J had to deal with the case, analogous to the present, of a senior and responsible officer of a company who is entrusted with possession of the company's property and then misapplies it for his own benefit:

b

> 'There was clearly a fiduciary relationship between Mr Zdiri and the plaintiffs. Mr Zdiri was not a director or a signatory on the plaintiffs' bank account, but he was a senior and responsible officer. As such he was entrusted with possession of the signed payment orders to have them taken to the bank and implemented. He took advantage of his possession of them to divert the money and cause the separation between its legal ownership which passed to the payees and its beneficial ownership which remained in the plaintiffs. There is clear authority that there is a receipt of trust property when a company's funds are misapplied by a director and, in my judgment, this is equally the case when a company's funds are misapplied by any person whose fiduciary position gave him control of them or enabled him to misapply them.' (See [1992] 4 All ER 385 at 402–403, [1990] Ch 265 at 290.)

c

d

That passage was approved by this court in *Heinl v Jyske Bank (Gibraltar) Ltd* [1999] Lloyd's Rep Bank 511. Reference may also be made to *Rolled Steel Products (Holdings) Ltd v British Steel Corp* [1985] 3 All ER 52, [1986] Ch 246, a decision of this court based both on ordinary principles of agency and on constructive trust.

e

The position being so plain, it has not become necessary for the court to reconvene in order to hear further oral submissions. I have come to a clear conclusion, although by a different route, that the decision of Judge Boggis ought to be affirmed. It thus becomes unnecessary to examine the more general question whether a mere equity, such as a right to avoid a transfer of registered land, which, though procured by fraudulent misrepresentation, is otherwise valid and effective, does or does not fall within s 70(1)(g) of the Act. Although Mr Nugee advanced a powerful argument in support of the view that it does not, it is inappropriate that such a question should be examined in a case in which the subject matter of the inquiry has been identified as a creature of a different species.

f

g

I would dismiss this appeal.

h

MUMMERY LJ. I agree.

RIX LJ. I also agree.

Appeal dismissed.

Kate O'Hanlon Barrister.

Young v National Power plc

COURT OF APPEAL, CIVIL DIVISION
SCHIEMANN, MANCE LJJ AND SMITH J
11 OCTOBER, 8 NOVEMBER 2000

Employment – Equality of treatment of men and women – Equal pay for equal work – Equal pay for work of equal value – Statutory provision requiring equal pay claim to be lodged within six months of applicant being 'employed in the employment' – Whether claim having to be brought within six months of termination of employment or within six months of termination of work forming subject matter of claim – Equal Pay Act 1970, ss 1, 2(4).

In 1969 Y became an employee of the appellant employer, and over the years she worked in several different departments. In 1991 she was transferred to the internal audit department, where she worked as a 'value for money' (VFM) analyst until May 1995. She was dismissed as redundant on 31 October 1996 and on 24 April 1997 brought a claim against the employer under s 1[a] of the Equal Pay Act 1970. She claimed that she should have been entitled to receive the same pay as male colleagues who had also been employed in the internal audit department on the grounds that, as a VFM analyst, she was doing 'work of equal value' to theirs within the meaning of s 1. Under s 2(4) of the 1970 Act, no such claim could be referred to an employment tribunal if the applicant had not been 'employed in the employment' within the six months preceding the date of the reference. The employer contended that the claim was out of time since it had not been brought within six months of Y ceasing to work as an VFM analyst. That contention was accepted by the employment tribunal which duly struck out Y's claim. She appealed, contending that she had complied with s 2(4) by lodging her application within six months of the termination of her employment. The employer argued that the expression 'employed in the employment' in s 2(4) related to the actual job on which the claim was based, not to the overall employment relationship. The Employment Appeal Tribunal preferred Y's construction of s 2(4) and accordingly allowed her appeal. The employer appealed to the Court of Appeal.

Held – On the true construction of s 2(4) of the 1970 Act, an applicant was required to lodge an application under s 1 within six months of the termination of her employment, not within six months of the termination of the work which formed the subject matter of the claim. There was a distinction within ss 1 and 2 between the words 'employment' and 'work', with 'employment' referring to the contract of employment and 'work' referring to the actual job that the employee was doing. 'Employed in the employment' in s 2(4) therefore had to mean 'employed under a contract of service'. It followed that in the instant case Y had lodged her application in time. Accordingly, the employer's appeal would be dismissed and the case would be remitted to be heard by a differently constituted employment tribunal (see p 346 *a* to *d* and p 347 *b c*, post).

Preston v Wolverhampton Healthcare NHS Trust, Fletcher v Midland Bank plc [1998] 1 All ER 528 distinguished.

---

a Section 1, so far as material, is set out at p 341 *g*, post

Notes

For equal pay for equal work, see Supp to 16 *Halsbury's Laws* (4th edn reissue) para 767.

For the Equal Pay Act 1970, ss 1, 2, see 16 *Halsbury's Statutes* (4th edn) (2000 reissue) 35, 41.

Cases referred to in judgments

Preston v Wolverhampton Healthcare NHS Trust, Fletcher v Midland Bank plc Case 78/98 [2000] All ER (EC) 714, [2000] ECR I-3201, ECJ.

Preston v Wolverhampton Healthcare NHS Trust, Fletcher v Midland Bank plc [1998] 1 All ER 528, [1998] 1 WLR 280, HL.

Levez v T H Jennings (Harlow Pools) Ltd (No 2) [2000] ICR 58, EAT.

Levez v T H Jennings (Harlow Pools) Ltd Case C-326/96 [1999] All ER (EC) 1, [1998] ECR I-7835, ECJ.

Sorbie v Trust Houses Forte Hotels Ltd [1977] 2 All ER 155, [1977] QB 931, [1976] 3 WLR 918, EAT.

Cases also cited or referred to in skeleton arguments

Eaton Ltd v Nuttall [1977] 3 All ER 1131, [1977] 1 WLR 549, EAT.

Etherson v Strathclyde Regional Council [1992] ICR 571, EAT.

Appeal

National Power plc appealed with permission from the decision of the Employment Appeal Tribunal (Judge Byrt QC, I Ezekiel and Lord Gladwin of Clee) on 29 July 1999 ([2000] ICR 78) allowing an appeal by the respondent, Nanette Rosalind Young, from the decision of an employment tribunal sitting at Bristol promulgated on 11 May 1998 striking out her claim against National Power under s 1 of the Equal Pay Act 1970 on the grounds that it had been lodged out of time. The facts are set out in the judgment of Smith J.

Damian Brown and *Melanie Tether* (instructed by *Osborne Clarke*, Bristol) for National Power.

Dijen Basu (instructed by the *Wiltshire Law Centre*, Swindon) for Mrs Young.

Cur adv vult

8 November 2000. The following judgments were delivered.

SMITH J (giving the first judgment at the invitation of Schiemann LJ).

1. This is an appeal by National Power plc from the decision of the Employment Appeal Tribunal (EAT) ([2000] ICR 78) in which they declared that the employment tribunal (ET) had jurisdiction to determine an equal pay claim brought by Mrs Nanette Young, the respondent to this appeal. The ET, sitting in Bristol, had rejected Mrs Young's claim on the ground that she had not lodged her application within the time allowed by s 2(4) of the Equal Pay Act 1970. The facts of the matter are not in dispute. The only question raised in this appeal is which tribunal correctly construed s 2(4).

2. The ET found that Mrs Young was employed by National Power plc and its predecessors from 7 July 1969 until she was dismissed as redundant on 31 October 1996. She had qualifications in management studies and was a member of the Chartered Institute of Purchasing and Supply. Her contract of employment

a incorporated the company agreement for professional staff which at para 5.2 provided:

> 'Employees shall be appointed to a company grade on the basis of the duties and responsibilities that they are required to undertake ... Employees will be expected to undertake duties and responsibilities commensurate with
b their grade and competency.'

3. Over the years, Mrs Young worked in several different departments but in 1991 she was transferred, without change of grade, from the contracts and procurement department to the internal audit department as a 'Value for Money' (VFM) analyst in the VFM Group. Initially she was the only VFM analyst; then
c another was appointed. During the next three years she participated in several VFM studies. In November 1994, she became ill and was off work, save for three days in January 1995, until 30 May 1995. On her return she was not given any further VFM work and on 3 July she was seconded to a department known as 'Group Technology' to work on a project in which her procurement and VFM skills were required. However, she was not working as a VFM analyst. When
d that project was complete, she remained on secondment with group technology. From January until May 1996 she worked at Pembroke Power Station on procurement. She then returned to the internal audit office, which was by then being reduced in size. At about this time, the VFM group ceased to exist. Mrs Young was at risk of redundancy and on 30 May 1996, she volunteered to
e leave under a severance scheme. Thereafter she worked in the internal audit department until July although not as a VFM analyst. From August she was not given any specific duties but was allowed to use company facilities for the purpose of seeking other employment. The ET found that although the employment did not terminate until 31 October 1996, Mrs Young had not worked as a VFM analyst since 30 May 1995.
f
4. On 24 April 1997, Mrs Young presented an originating application under s 1 of the 1970 Act. According to its preamble, the 1970 Act is 'An Act to prevent discrimination as regards terms and conditions of employment between men and women'. Section 1 of that Act is entitled: 'Requirement of equal treatment for men and women in same employment'. Section 1(1), as amended by s 8(1) of the
g Sex Discrimination Act 1975, provides:

> 'If the terms of a contract under which a woman is employed at an establishment in Great Britain do not include (directly or by reference to a collective agreement or otherwise) an equality clause they shall be deemed to include one.'

h

Section 1(2) explains the effect of an equality clause. Briefly summarised, an equality clause has the effect that where a women is employed on either 'like work' or 'work rated as equivalent' or 'work of equal value' as a man in the same employment, any term of the woman's contract which is less favourable than the
j comparable term in the man's contract shall be modified so as to be no less favourable.

5. Mrs Young alleged that she should have been entitled to receive the same pay as two men in the internal audit department, named Dr Gilbert and Mr Williams, on the basis that, as a VFM analyst, she was doing work of equal value to theirs. National Power resisted the application on several grounds including reliance on s 2(4) of the 1970 Act. So far as relevant, s 2(4) provides:

'No claim in respect of the operation of an equality clause relating to a woman's employment shall be referred to an employment tribunal ... if she has not been employed in the employment within the six months preceding the date of the reference.'

6. It is common ground that the word 'reference' in that subsection includes the presentation of an originating application. The point taken by National Power under s 2(4) of the 1970 Act was that Mrs Young's claim was based on a comparison of her work as a VFM analyst with two men who had also worked in the VFM function. Mrs Young had not worked as a VFM analyst since 30 May 1995 so she was only able to make an equal pay claim based on that work if she presented her application before 30 November 1995. Her employment with National Power, which had continued until 31 October 1996 (which was within six months of the date of presentation of the application), was employment in a capacity other than as a VFM analyst. So, by 24 April 1997, she was out of time and unable to present an application based on her work as a VFM analyst.

7. The regional chairman directed that jurisdiction under s 2(4) of the 1970 Act be determined as a preliminary issue. Mrs Young disputed the facts about her employment, contending that she had been employed on VFM work throughout. On that issue she lost. She did not contend that by presenting her application within the six months after the termination of her employment with National Power she had satisfied the requirements of s 2(4). The ET accepted National Power's submissions on the facts and assumed without argument that their submissions as to the proper construction of s 2(4) were correct. They held that Mrs Young was too late to base a claim on her work as a VFM analyst. As there is no provision in the 1970 Act for time to be extended on discretionary grounds, the ET struck the claim out.

8. Mrs Young appealed and following amendment of her notice of appeal the question of the construction of s 2(4) of the 1970 Act was fully argued before the EAT ([2000] ICR 78). It was argued on her behalf that by lodging her application within six months of the termination of her employment, she had complied with s 2(4). National Power sought to argue that the expression 'employed in the employment' in s 2(4) related to the actual job on which the applicant based her claim. It did not relate to the overall employment relationship. It submitted that Mrs Young had had several different jobs during her years with National Power. The two-year period specified in s 2(4) began to run each time she was moved to different work within her overall employment. It submitted that the position of someone like Mrs Young was analogous to the applicants in the case of *Preston v Wolverhampton Healthcare NHS Trust, Fletcher v Midland Bank plc* [1998] 1 All ER 528, [1998] 1 WLR 280, in which the House of Lords had considered inter alia how s 2(4) of the 1970 Act should be applied to employees who had been employed on a number of distinct short-term contracts of employment. They had held that time ran from the end of each separate contract. The EAT rejected this argument. They noted that the ET had not found that Mrs Young had had separate contracts of employment with National Power. She had had only one. Thus, *Preston*'s case was to be distinguished. They considered that the definition provisions of s 1(6) of the 1970 Act (to which we will refer in due course) should be used as an aid to construction of s 2(4). With such aid, the meaning of s 2(4) was clear. It was sufficient if an applicant brought her claim within six months of the termination of her employment. She did not have to bring it within six months of ceasing to do the work on which she would rely in order to establish her claim.

a 9. In this appeal, both sides have repeated the submissions made in the EAT. National Power submitted that the EAT misconstrued s 2(4) of the 1970 Act. It submitted again that the word 'employment' in s 2(4) related to the particular job on which the woman bases her claim to an equality clause. On its behalf, Mr Brown argued that this approach is consistent with the scheme of the legislation which requires the tribunal to analyse the work which the woman does and to compare b it with the work done by the man to see if her work is like work or equivalent work or work of equal value to his. The whole focus of the application is on the work the woman and man have done or are doing. Thus it is logical that the limitation period should relate to the time when the woman was doing that work.

10. Second, Mr Brown submitted that the case was governed by the House of c Lords decision in *Preston*'s case. Although the 1998 decision in *Preston*'s case has been superseded on some issues following reference to the Court of Justice of the European Communities (*Preston v Wolverhampton Healthcare NHS Trust, Fletcher v Midland Bank plc* Case 78/98 [2000] All ER (EC) 714, [2000] ECR I-3201), the decision still stands on the interpretation of s 2(4) of the 1970 Act, which is a matter of d domestic law. Lord Slynn of Hadley ([1998] 1 All ER 528 at 536–537, [1998] 1 WLR 280 at 289) observed that the structure of the 1970 Act appeared to be based on the incorporation of an equality clause into a specific contract of employment and not into an 'employment relationship'. In that case the term 'employment relationship' was used to denote the whole period during which the women had been employed under a succession of discrete contracts of employment. The e House held that the word 'employment' in s 2(4) referred to a discrete contract of employment. Mr Brown argued that when Mrs Young was moved from job to job by National Power, she had in effect a new contract of employment. Her 'employment relationship' lasted from 1969 until 1996 but her contract of employment as a VFN analyst only lasted from 1991 until May 1995. Thus, by f analogy with the reasoning in *Preston*'s case, her 'employment' for the purposes of the application of s 2(4) to her claim for an equality clause based on her work as a VFN analyst meant her employment in that capacity.

11. Mr Brown's third submission was that the approach he advocated accorded with sound policy considerations and common sense. If Mrs Young's submission were right, an employer might be faced with the task of investigating an equal g pay claim where the applicant had not done the work concerned for many years. Employment tribunals and the experts instructed to carry out job evaluations would have to analyse the content of a job which neither the applicant nor possibly anyone else had done for several years. This would not be fair on employers and could not have been the intention of Parliament. As a matter of h policy, it was in the public interest that a discriminatory practice or pay scheme should be rectified as early as possible. Moreover, the public would not have confidence in a system which allowed stale claims to be brought.

12. Mr Brown recognised that at the time the 1970 Act was drafted in its present form, s 2(5) of that Act operated to prevent a woman from recovering any award by j way of arrears of remuneration in respect of a time earlier than two years before the date on which the proceedings were commenced. He accepted that s 2(4) and 2(5) read together would to some extent prevent a claim being brought after a long delay. However, he submitted that even though no claim could be brought for financial loss incurred more than two years before, it might well be that an applicant would seek a declaration that she had been entitled to an equality clause many years before. He did not accept that such a claim would be struck out as an abuse

of process. He also drew our attention to the recent decision of *Levez v T H Jennings (Harlow Pools) Ltd (No 2)* [2000] ICR 58, in which the EAT implemented the effect of a ruling of the Court of Justice (*Levez v T H Jennings (Harlow Pools) Ltd* Case C-326/96 [1999] All ER (EC) 1, [1998] ECR I-7835) that s 2(5) of the 1970 Act was not compatible with art 119 of the EC Treaty (now art 141 EC) and Council Directive (EEC) 75/117 on the approximation of laws of the member states relating to the principles of equal pay for men and women (the equal treatment directive), art 2, which requires member states to introduce into their domestic law such measures as are necessary to enable all employees who consider themselves wronged by failure to apply the principle of equal pay to pursue their claims by judicial process. In *Levez*'s case, the Court of Justice had held that a claim limited to two years' loss was not an adequate remedy but had left it to the domestic court to decide how long the period should be. The EAT held that six years was appropriate as the claim for equal pay was analogous to a claim in breach of contract. The effect is that it will be open to an applicant to claim up to six years' arrears of pay if successful. Mr Brown submitted that this underlined the policy need for there to be an appropriate restriction on the time which could elapse between when the applicant stopped doing the relevant work and the date of her application.

13. In response to these submissions, Mr Basu first drew our attention to what he described as the continuing effect of an equality clause. He submitted that where the woman shows that she has been employed on like work or equivalent work or work of equal value to a man in the same employment, the effect of s 1(1) and 1(2) of the 1970 Act is to modify the terms of the woman's contract of employment which are or have become less favourable than the terms of a similar kind in the contract of a man in the same employment. Once an equality clause has operated to modify the woman's contract of employment, it remains so modified, even if she could not later satisfy the conditions for a claim under the 1970 Act, for example because the male comparator has left or been promoted and there is no one with whom she could compare herself (see *Sorbie v Trust Houses Forte Hotels Ltd* [1977] 2 All ER 155, [1977] QB 931). Once modified, the woman's contract remains modified even if the work she does is changed. That is so unless there is agreement to the contrary. Thus, argued Mr Basu, if Mrs Young were able to establish that she had been entitled to an equality clause modifying her contract (by increasing her pay) at any time from 1991 when she started work as a VFM analyst, she would have been entitled to retain that increase in pay when she was transferred away from VFM work in May 1995. Since the change in the law relating to s 2(5) of the 1970 Act in *Levez*'s case, she would now (subject to s 2(4)) be able to claim for any shortfall in her pay in the six years before presentation of her application on 24 April 1997. It would not matter that her position or those of her comparators had changed in the meantime. When the continuing effect of an equality clause is understood, it becomes clear that it must have been the intention of Parliament to limit the time by which an application be made by reference to the end of the contract of employment rather than the end of the period in which the woman had worked in the specific job by reference to which she brings her claim.

14. Second, Mr Basu submitted that the ordinary natural meaning of the words 'employed in the employment' in s 2(4) of the 1970 were clear. They mean employed under the contract of employment. Section 1(6)(a) of the 1970 Act provides that 'employed' means employed under a contract of service or of apprenticeship or a contract personally to execute any work or labour and related

a expressions are to be construed accordingly. Although the definition provisions in s 1(6) are said to apply for the purposes of that section, they must be applicable to s 2 as well, as it was inconceivable that the words 'employed' and 'employment' should have a different meaning in s 2 from s 1. In *Preston*'s case the House of Lords had held that 'employed in the employment' in s 2(4) meant employed under a contract of employment. Here Mrs Young had only ever had one contract of b employment, lasting from 1969 until 1996. The ET had not found that she had new separate contracts of employment whenever she changed jobs. Their reference to para 5.2 of the company agreement for professional staff had stressed the continuing nature of the contract of employment. Thus, *Preston*'s case was not directly in point and was of no assistance to the appellants. On the contrary, the decision of the Court of Justice ([2000] All ER (EC) 714, [2000] ECR I-3201), c gave some support to Mrs Young's contentions. The Court of Justice had said that although a provision such as s 2(4) was not in general incompatible with European law, it was objectionable if applied as it had been in *Preston*'s case so as to prevent the women who had been employed on a succession of discrete short-term contracts from relying on any contract which had terminated more d than six months before. Where the women had been in a continuing relationship with the employer, the limitation period should run from the termination of that relationship. That, submitted Mr Basu, was of considerable assistance to him as it showed that a requirement that a woman should bring her equal pay claim within six months of the termination of her employment was incompatible with European law, if it was interpreted to prevent her from claiming in respect of e earlier contracts within the same employment relationship. By analogy, it was submitted, a continuing contract of employment must involve a continuing employment relationship, even if it embraced different jobs from time to time, and it would be incompatible with European law if a woman was required to claim in respect of any such jobs before the end of the employment relationship.

f 15. Mr Basu drew our attention to the distinction in the 1970 Act between the use of the word 'work' and the word 'employment'. This distinction was seen clearly in s 1(2) of that Act where there are set out the three different bases on which a claim may be brought. For example under s 1(2)(a), the woman may make a claim on the basis that she has been 'employed on like work with a man in the same employment'. Under sub-s (2)(b) she may claim that she has been g 'employed on work rated as equivalent with that of a man in the same employment'. Under sub-s (2)(c) she may claim that she has been 'employed on work … of equal value to that of a man in the same employment'. Section 2(4) imposes a limitation period by reference to the woman's employment, not the work she was doing. If Parliament had wished to impose a limitation period by h reference to the cessation of the work on which the woman relied, it could easily have done so.

16. Mr Basu also sought to rely on a 'common sense' argument. His interpretation of s 2(4) of the 1970 Act provides a ready and workable rule whereby an employee can know without doubt the time by which an application j must be presented. Moreover, it does not require an employee to bring an equal pay claim during the course of the employment. Many employees might be reluctant to damage their relationship with their employer by making a complaint of this kind.

17. In summary, Mr Basu submitted that the position here is clear. Mrs Young was employed under a single contract of employment. Over the years her work varied. At times, she would have been able to compare her work with that of

male colleagues and to claim that her contract had been modified by the operation of an equality clause to produce parity of terms. The terms so modified would remain in force unless validly varied. Mrs Young was entitled to present a claim to the ET at any time within six months after the termination of the contract of employment which contained the equality clause.

18. We have concluded that the EAT's interpretation of s 2(4) was correct. It appears to us that, on the ordinary natural meaning of the words, s 2(4) requires a claimant to lodge her application within six months of the termination of her employment. We think that the definitions provided in s 1(6) of the 1970 Act must be applied to s 2 as well as s 1. So 'employed in the employment' in s 2(4) must mean 'employed under a contract of service'. That accords with the House of Lords' decision in *Preston*'s case. There is a distinction within ss 1 and 2 between the words 'employment' and 'work'. In our view, the distinction intended is that 'employment' refers to the contract of employment and 'work' refers to the actual job the employee was doing. So, for example, for a claim under s 1(2)(c) the woman has to prove two distinct things: first that she was doing work of equal value to that of a man whom she names as her comparator and second that she and the male comparator were in the 'same employment'. It is clear that the man and woman may be doing different jobs while in the same employment. So 'employment' must relate to the contract of employment. Section 2(4) imposes a limitation period by reference to the termination of employment. In our view, there is jurisdiction provided that the applicant brings her claim within six months of the termination of her contract of employment.

19. On the facts of this case, there was no finding by the ET that Mrs Young had had a new contract of employment when her work changed in 1991 or 1995. Indeed such a finding would have been inconsistent with the ET's finding that cl 2(5) of the company agreement was part of her contract of employment. This effectively provided for her to be moved from one job to another suitable for her grade. It is plain that Mrs Young had one contract of employment which ran from 1969 until 1996. Accordingly we reject Mr Brown's submission that this case is covered by the House of Lords' decision in *Preston*'s case. That case is of no assistance to National Power. Indeed, we think there is more force in Mr Basu's argument that, if Mr Brown's contention were right, s 2(4) would be struck down by the Court of Justice as incompatible with the equal treatment directive. Had we thought that it was arguable that Mrs Young had had a series of discrete contracts, with a new contract beginning every time National Power moved her to new work, we would have had to consider the Court of Justice's view in *Preston*'s case ([2000] All ER (EC) 714, [2000] ECR I-3201). However, that does not arise.

20. That is sufficient to deal with this appeal. We do not think it necessary or desirable to say anything about Mr Basu's submission as to the effect of an equality clause. The point does not arise for decision in this appeal. As to the parties' respective submissions based on policy and 'common sense', we say only that we accept that Parliament could sensibly have adopted either of the opposite approaches for which the two parties before have contended. Parliament's purpose must in the circumstances be gathered from the actual words it chose to use. Certainly we see no proper policy objection to a construction allowing the bringing of an equal pay claim which related back to work done by the applicant up to two years earlier. Parliament must have intended that ss 2(4) and 2(5) of the 1970 Act would together provide an appropriate balance between the interests of the two sides. Employers were protected from stale claims and employees were

a not obliged to bring their claims during their employment. The fact that the Court of Justice has declared that the two years' limit imposed by s 2(5) is too short cannot change the meaning of s 2(4). Since *Levez*'s case, employers have reduced protection from old claims. We reject Mr Brown's suggestion that employers will be open to claims for declaratory relief going back more than six years. We would be surprised if any ET were prepared to entertain any such b claim which would, in our view, usually be struck out as an abuse of process.

21. Accordingly, this appeal is dismissed and the case will be remitted, as directed by the EAT, to be heard by a differently constituted ET.

MANCE LJ. I agree.

c **SCHIEMANN LJ.** I also agree.

Appeal dismissed.

Kate O'Hanlon Barrister.

Re Whixall Old Burial Ground

a

LICHFIELD CONSISTORY COURT

CHANCELLOR JOHN SHAND

10 MAY 2000

b

Ecclesiastical law – Faculty – Secular use of consecrated ground – Burial ground – Faculty approving agreement to transfer disused burial ground to parish council as secular local authority – Parish council seeking faculty to permit holding of village dog shows and junior football tournaments in burial ground – Whether uses inconsistent with sentence of consecration – Open Spaces Act 1906, s 11(2).

c

In 1973 an agreement was entered into under the Open Spaces Act 1906 for the improvement and laying out of a detached and disused burial ground and the transfer of its management to the parish council as secular local authority. The agreement, which was approved by faculty, provided that the churchyard could only be used as an open space in accordance with the Act for the quiet enjoyment and use of the general public, and expressly prohibited the playing of games and sports. Under the Act, public money could be spent in maintaining disused burial grounds as open spaces available for the enjoyment of the public, but the areas in question remained consecrated land. Section 11(2)[a] prohibited the playing of any games or sports in a burial ground, save that in the case of a consecrated burial ground the bishop could sanction such use by licence or faculty. In 1999 the parish council petitioned for the grant of a faculty for the occasional extension of permitted uses, including village fete dog shows, an annual five-a-side junior football competition and restricted games. The incumbent opposed the petition in so far as it related to the playing of ball games, organised games/races and the holding of dog shows, contending that such uses were inconsistent with the sentence of consecration.

d

e

f

Held – Although it was clear from the authorities that consecration precluded all 'profane and common uses', the traditionally restrictive statements of law in those authorities did not apply where the management of a burial ground had already been alienated to the secular local authority under the Act. The test to be applied was not so much whether the user was ancillary to the purpose of the original consecration, but much more whether the purpose was ancillary to appropriate use under the Act. In the instant case, it could not be envisaged that dog shows would be a problem provided that the organisers ensured that the open space was subsequently cleared. Similarly, granted that sports and games were envisaged by the Act, it was difficult to see why properly organised five-a-side tournaments were inimical to the consecrated state of the burial ground. Indeed, in an era of diminishing availability of playing fields and sports tuition in schools, there was a real public interest from the point of view of health and recreation in permitting such a user. Accordingly, the faculty would be granted (see p 351 *e f* and p 352 *b c* and *g*, post).

g

h

j

---

a Section 11(2) is set out at p 351 *b*, post

a

Notes

For the purposes for which a local authority may hold a burial ground and for the use of consecrated ground for secular purposes, see respectively 10 *Halsbury's Laws* (4th edn) para 1228 and 14 *Halsbury's Laws* (4th edn) para 1973.

For the Open Spaces Act 1906, s 11, see 32 *Halsbury's Statutes* (4th edn) (1996 reissue) 30.

b

Cases referred to in judgment

All Saints, Featherstone, Re (1999) 5 Ecc LJ 391, Con Ct.

All Saints, Harborough Magna, Re (1991) 2 Ecc LJ 375, Con Ct.

Bermondsey BC v Mortimer [1926] P 87.

c *Howells, Re* [1999] 1 All ER 50, [1999] 1 WLR 307, CA.

Morley BC v St Mary the Virgin, Woodkirk (vicar and churchwardens) [1969] 3 All ER 952, [1969] 1 WLR 1867, Ch Ct.

R v Willis [1975] 1 All ER 620, [1975] 1 WLR 292, CA.

d **Petition**

By petition dated December 1999 Whixall Parish Council applied for a faculty for the occasional extension of permitted uses of the parish's disused burial ground which it held by virtue of an agreement entered into under the Open Spaces Act 1906 on 7 September 1973, and approved by faculty on 17 October 1974. The petition was opposed by the Vicar of Whixall, the Rev David Baldwin. The facts
e
are set out in the judgment.

THE CHANCELLOR. The factual issues in this case can be stated fairly briefly; the legal analysis is more complex.

On 7 September 1973 an agreement was entered into under the Open Spaces
f Act 1906, approved by faculty on 17 October 1974, for the improvement and laying out of the detached and disused burial ground at Whixall, and the transfer of its management to the parish council as secular local authority.

Clause 3(b) of the agreement reads:

g

> 'The churchyard shall be used only as an Open Space in accordance with the provisions of the said Act for the quiet enjoyment and use thereof by the general public, and the playing of games and sports therein shall be forbidden.'

Matters came to a head in the early summer of 1999 when the new incumbent, the Reverend David Baldwin, vigorously opposed the plans of the Whixall Social
h Centre Management Committee to hold a summer fair on the open space, which was to include a dog show and a five-a-side tournament. Both sides without doubt acted in good faith but perhaps the tone of the debate was not improved by the vicar's suggestion that the committee's disappointment was self-inflicted 'through the totally ludicrous belief that a burial ground should be the
j appropriate venue for such an activity'. Perhaps the vehemence of his stance was exacerbated by his not having then read the agreement approved by faculty, and by the assumption that the approved use was limited to some sort of garden of remembrance.

With commendable constructiveness however, the Parochial Church Council resolved unanimously in June 1999 to support any petition submitted by the parish council for an appropriate redefinition of permitted uses.

Objection was made by some parishioners—Mr and Mrs Cliftlands and Mr Clark—to the initial proposal that the memorials be removed and buried and to the then intended open-ended petition to approve 'sports and similar events'. However, the parish council wisely revised its plans and no longer seeks either such disturbance of memorials or an all-purpose recreation field.

The current petition, dated December 1999, is for the occasional extension of permitted uses, all activities to be under the control of the Social Centre Management Committee. The proposed purposes are: (1) village fetes, including stalls, dog shows and annual five-a-side junior football competitions; (2) refreshments, including barbecues; (3) use by the toddler group; (4) children's parties, including organised games and races for children; (5) restricted games, for example by the youth club at the discretion of the committee; and (6) access for maintenance. They do not affect the present prohibition of vehicular or bicycle access.

The objection of the incumbent is set out in his letter of 22 November 1999 and appears to be limited to the playing of ball games, organised games/races and the holding of dog shows:

> 'My primary objection is that this burial ground remains consecrated as a final resting place for generations of Whixall families. I am also aware that it is visited annually by the American relatives of one family interred in the ground.'

He suggests that other parishioners, though not objectors, have expressed unease.

He also raises an objection which, as a matter of law, I find does not carry weight. He says that another area of land adjacent to the social centre could be acquired; and he complains that this aspect has not been properly minuted although raised at meetings with the parish council.

This is not one of those cases—as where a reordering is sought of a listed building—where the petitioners must make out a case for need. I have simply got to address whether, all things being equal, the proposed uses are appropriate within the ambit of the Act.

Mr Baldwin puts his finger on the central issue when he reminds us that, not withstanding the transfer of management control to the parish council, this is still consecrated land. That, however, simply states the issue rather than resolves it.

The starting point is to be found in Newsom *Faculty Jurisdiction of the Church of England* (2nd edn, 1993) p 169:

> 'The Open Spaces Act 1906 is a useful piece of legislation in that it allows public money to be spent in maintaining disused burial grounds as open spaces available for the enjoyment of the public. But the areas in question remain consecrated land subject in full to the jurisdiction [of the Consistory Court].'

The significance of this is twofold. Primarily it preserves the jurisdiction of this court. Also, however, it has an impact on the nature of permitted use. Thus the land 'continues to be held upon the sacred uses imposed by the Sentence of Consecration as well as becoming subject to the statutory trusts of section 10 of the Act of 1906'.

Section 10 provides that the local authority shall hold the open space or burial ground in trust 'to allow, and with a view to, the enjoyment thereof by the public as an open space ... under proper control and regulation and for no other purpose'. They shall keep it 'in a good and decent state'. They may enclose it 'with proper a railings and gates, and may drain, level and lay out, turf, plant, ornament, light, provide with seats and otherwise improve it'.

Such a description at first blush does sound like a user for quiet enjoyment and contemplation, of the kind contended for in the summer by the incumbent. However, the Act plainly is not limited to this kind of purpose, for s 11(2) provides that—

b 'The playing of any games or sports shall not be allowed in any burial ground ... except that—(a) in the case of a consecrated burial ground, the bishop by licence or faculty ... may expressly sanction any such use of the burial ground, and may specify any conditions as to the extent or nature of such use.'

In other words, sports and games are not automatically to be allowed, but the Act c does envisage that they may be allowed even in the case of consecrated land.

The effect of a sentence of consecration on the proposed secular use of a church building has been considered in many cases (see *Morley BC v St Mary the Virgin, Woodkirk (vicar and churchwardens)* [1969] 3 All ER 952, [1969] 1 WLR 1867; *Re All Saints, Harborough Magna* [1991] Ecc LJ 375); and the principles are helpfully d drawn together by Chancellor Collier in the November 1999 Wakefield Consistory Court judgment of *Re All Saints, Featherstone* (1999) 5 Ecc LJ 391 and in Chancellor Wiggs illuminating article on 'The Community use of Churches' ((2000) 5 Ecc LJ 348ff). Thus it is plain that consecration precludes all 'profane and common uses'.

However, I am not convinced that the traditionally restrictive statement of law e in such authorities applies where the management of a burial ground has already been alienated to the secular local authority under the Act. The test is not so much whether the user is ancillary to the purpose of the original consecration. That is a bridge already crossed. It is much more whether the purpose is ancillary to appropriate use under the Act. Thus in *Bermondsey BC v Mortimer* [1926] P 87 a f shed for gardener's tools was authorised as a necessary concomitant of an open space, whereas a urinal was not.

It would be tempting to fall back on the sort of test propounded by Lawton LJ in the sphere of sentence in criminal cases, and to say that consecration should prevent user offensive to 'right-thinking members of the public' (*R v Willis* [1975] 1 All ER 620 at 622, [1975] 1 WLR 292 at 294). However, what is a truth universally g recognised by one sensible person may well be self-evidently ludicrous to another. As Lord Bingham CJ has recently pointed out, such a test is not very helpful—

'since the sentencing court has no means of ascertaining the views of right-thinking members of the public and inevitably attributes to such h right-thinking members its own views ... when applying this test, the sentencing court is doing little more than reflect its own opinion ...' (See *Re Howells* [1999] 1 All ER 50 at 53, [1999] 1 WLR 307 at 311.)

Extreme cases can easily be resolved by applying such a test. Thus, a local authority would plainly fall foul of the Act if it permitted a burial ground to be j used for an immoral or illegal purposes such as drug dealing or sexual promiscuity, or if it did not secure free public access by taking steps to obtain possession against travellers encamped on the land. However, in less clear-cut cases, is a chancellor to substitute his own subjective views under the guise of those of right-thinking members of society? Thus, granted that sports and games are envisaged by s 11(2), is he to give vent to traditional snobberies by sanctioning Rugby Union but not Rugby League, or to transient political correctness by disallowing 'competitive' sports? I give these examples not out of frivolity but to highlight the problem of formulating an objective test. *a*

My difficulty in this case is that the incumbent does not spell out why he considers the proposed uses are inconsistent with the sentence of consecration, doubtless because to him, although not to others, this is self-evident.

So far as the dog show is concerned, is objection raised because it is inherently flippant or (as one of the former parties opponent suggested) is it a fear of fouling by 'defecating animals'? *b*

I have no reason to think that dogs are at present excluded from this open space or, if they are not, fouling has caused any problem. I am reminded of the irrational objection one sometimes has to the practical and historically well-established proposal that sheep or cattle be allowed to graze on a churchyard in order to keep down weeds and grass. Provided that the organisers ensure that the open space is cleared after any dog show, I do not see the problem. *c*

Similarly, granted that sports and games were envisaged by the Act as long ago as 1906, what is the objection to properly organised five-a-side tournaments? In an era of diminishing availability of playing fields and sports tuition in schools, I see a real public interest from the point of view of health and recreation in permitting such a user. I find it difficult to see why it is inimical to the consecrated state of the burial ground. *d*

I find support for these conclusions in the Archbishops' Commission Report on Rural Areas 'Faith in the Countryside' (1990) ch 11, with its emphasis that church buildings (and even more so, open spaces such as this) can properly be used for purposes beyond those conventionally approved in the past. Thus one reads (para 11:3): 'The division between the Church and the Community is necessarily blurred …' Paragraphs 11:12–11:17: *e*

> 'The church (building) … is a totem, a focus of identity … The Commission was impressed by reordering which 'reviewed the use of the church building in broader community terms … The church could be used for a number of more secular activities. The best (schemes) took into account the fact that the needs of the young, aged and handicapped are the same in social activities as well as worship … Objections may arise … from those who have a narrow view of what constitutes holiness … (but) they may fail to realise that the medieval church was indeed used for a wide range of activities … There is nothing in human life in which God is not already involved …' *f* *g*

Accordingly, in principle I grant this faculty as sought. The only problem arises from the fact that these petitioners, Whixall Parish Council, seem to have delegated control of this user to the Social Centre Management Committee. I do need to be assured that, as petitioners, they do retain ultimate responsibility and—if necessary—powers of veto. The constitution of the committee should be lodged with the Registry for my perusal within 28 days. *h*

Further to the same, to save the cost and complexity of the need for a further faculty in the event of any dispute during the settling-in period for this new regime, I give both the parish council and the incumbent leave for the next five years to refer any dispute under this faculty to me for resolution.

Faculty granted.

Celia Fox Barrister.

a

Anyanwu and another v South Bank Student Union and another (Commission for Racial Equality, interveners)

[2001] UKHL/14

b

HOUSE OF LORDS

LORD BINGHAM OF CORNHILL, LORD BROWNE-WILKINSON, LORD STEYN, LORD HOPE OF CRAIGHEAD AND LORD MILLETT

26, 27 FEBRUARY, 22 MARCH 2001

c

Race relations – Discrimination – Employment – Discrimination on racial grounds – Person who knowingly 'aids' another to do act of unlawful discrimination – Meaning of 'aids' – Race Relations Act 1976, s 33(1).

d The complainants, who were of black African origin, were students at, and members of, the respondent university. They were engaged to serve as full-time salaried officers of the university's student union for a one-year term beginning on 1 August 1995. In that capacity, they were trustees of the funds of the student union. The university raised questions about their conduct as trustees, and instituted disciplinary proceedings. After initially suspending them, the university e expelled the complainants by letters dated 29 March 1996. By those letters, the complainants were forbidden from entering any university building, including the student union. That prohibition made it impossible for the complainants to perform their duties as employees of the union, and by letters of 2 April 1996 the union treated their employment contracts as at an end. The complainants sought f to challenge their suspension and expulsion in judicial review proceedings, but were refused permission to apply. They also brought complaints of unlawful racial discrimination against the student union and the university, relying on their suspension, subsequent expulsion and the termination of their employment. At a preliminary industrial tribunal hearing, during which the complainants clarified their case, the university, relying on the earlier judicial review proceedings, g applied for the proceedings against it to be struck out on the ground of res judicata. The tribunal granted that application, but its decision was reversed by the Employment Appeal Tribunal. On the university's appeal, the Court of Appeal raised the issue whether the allegations against the university could, in any event, fall within s 33(1)[a] of the Race Relations Act 1976, which provided that h a person who knowingly 'aids' another person to do an act made unlawful by the 1976 Act was to be treated for the purposes of that Act as himself doing an unlawful act of the like description. By a majority, the court held that the word 'aids' in s 33(1) contemplated a 'primary actor', who was a 'free agent' in the matter, setting out to do an act or achieve a result, and a secondary party helping him to j do it. The court further concluded that the university was the 'prime mover', and that accordingly it had not aided the student union to dismiss the complainants, even though it might well be said that it had brought about the dismissals. Accordingly, the university's appeal was allowed, and the complainants appealed to the House of Lords.

---

a Section 33 is set out at [1], post

Held – (1) The word 'aids' in s 33(1) of the 1976 Act was a familiar word in everyday use and bore no technical or special meaning in the context of that provision. A person aided another if he helped or assisted him. He did so whether his help was substantial and productive or whether it was not, provided the help was not so insignificant as to be negligible. While any gloss on the clear statutory language was better avoided, the subsection pointed towards a relationship of co-operation or collaboration; it did not matter who instigated or initiated the relationship. It was plain that, depending on the facts, a party who aided another to do an unlawful act might also procure or induce that other to do it. However, the expressions 'procure' and 'induce' were found in other sections of the 1976 Act, not in s 33, and were differently enforced; they meant something different from 'aids' and there was no warrant for interpreting 'aids' as comprising those other expressions. It was not helpful to introduce the concepts of 'free agents' and 'prime movers', which could only distract from the essentially simple test under s 33(1). Accordingly, the Court of Appeal had erred in its construction of that provision, but it was still necessary to consider whether the claims against the university could fall within s 33(1) as correctly construed (see [5], [19], [21], [23], [33], [36], [41], [42], [48], post).

(2) It was important not to strike out discrimination claims as an abuse of process except in the most obvious cases. Such cases were generally fact-sensitive, and their proper determination was always vital in the United Kingdom's pluralistic society. In the field of discrimination, perhaps more than any other, the bias in favour of a claim being examined on the merits or demerits of its particular facts was a matter of high public interest. In the instant case, the Court of Appeal, perhaps because of its concentration on the 'prime mover' and 'free agent' issues, had not considered the complainants' case as amplified and clarified at the preliminary hearing in the industrial tribunal. Fairly considered, the complainants' allegations raised an arguable case under s 33(1) against the university, and it would be wrong to strike it out. Accordingly, the appeal would be allowed and the matter remitted to an employment tribunal (see [18], [19], [24], [34], [35], [36], [40], [46], [47], [51], post).

Decision of the Court of Appeal [2000] 1 All ER 1 reversed.

Notes

For aiding discrimination, see 13 *Halsbury's Laws* (4th edn reissue) para 434.

For the Race Relations Act 1976, s 33, see 7 *Halsbury's Statutes* (4th edn) (1999 reissue) 146.

Cases referred to in opinions

Hallam v Avery [2000] 1 WLR 966, CA.

Henderson v Henderson (1843) 3 Hare 100, [1843–1860] All ER Rep 378, 13 ER 301.

Jones v Tower Boot Co Ltd [1997] 2 All ER 406, [1997] ICR 254, CA.

Savjani v IRC [1981] 1 All ER 1121, [1981] QB 458, [1981] 2 WLR 636, CA.

Appeal

The appellants, Anozie Anyanwu and Aniere Ebuzoeme, appealed with permission from the decision of the Court of Appeal (Butler-Sloss and Laws LJJ, Pill LJ dissenting) on 26 October 1999 ([2000] 1 All ER 1, [2000] ICR 221) allowing an appeal from the decision of the Employment Appeal Tribunal (Morison J, A E R Manners and B Switzer) on 19 January 1998 allowing an appeal from the decision of an industrial tribunal at London (South) on 7 April 1997 striking out a their claims against the respondent, South Bank University, for unlawful racial discrimination contrary to the Race Relations Act 1976. The Commission for Racial Equality was granted leave to intervene in the proceedings before the Court of Appeal and the House of Lords. South Bank University Students' Union, the first respondent to the appellants' discrimination claims, took no part in the appeals before the Employment Appeal Tribunal, the Court of Appeal and the b House of Lords. The facts are set out in the opinion of Lord Bingham of Cornhill.

Laura Cox QC and *Thomas Kibling* (instructed by *Charles Russell*) for the appellants.
Robin Allen QC and *Karen Monaghan* (instructed by the *Commission for Racial Equality*) for the commission as interveners.
David Bean QC and *Thomas Linden* (instructed by *Bretherton Price Elgoods*, Cheltenham) c for the university.

Their Lordships took time for consideration.

22 March 2001. The following opinions were delivered.

d

LORD BINGHAM OF CORNHILL.

[1] My Lords, this appeal turns on the correct interpretation and application of s 33(1) of the Race Relations Act 1976. Section 33 of the Act (as amended) provides:

> '(1) A person who knowingly aids another person to do an act made e unlawful by this Act shall be treated for the purposes of this Act as himself doing an unlawful act of the like description.
>
> (2) For the purposes of subsection (1) an employee or agent for whose act the employer or principal is liable under section 32 (or would be so liable but for section 32(3)) shall be deemed to aid the doing of the act by the employer or principal.
>
> f (3) A person does not under this section knowingly aid another to do an unlawful act if—(a) he acts in reliance on a statement made to him by that other person that, by reason of any provision of this Act, the act which he aids would not be unlawful; and (b) it is reasonable for him to rely on the statement.
>
> g (4) A person who knowingly or recklessly makes a statement such as is mentioned in subsection (3)(a) which in a material respect is false or misleading commits an offence, and shall be liable on summary conviction to a fine not exceeding level 5 on the standard scale.'

[2] Section 33(1) is to be read in its context, as a provision in an Act passed to h remedy the 'very great evil' of racial discrimination (as recognised by Templeman LJ in *Savjani v IRC* [1981] 1 All ER 1121 at 1125, [1981] QB 458 at 466–467) and it must be construed purposively (see *Jones v Tower Boot Co Ltd* [1997] 2 All ER 406 at 413 per Waite LJ). Since the 1976 Act is one of a trio of Acts (with the Sex Discrimination Act 1975 and the Disability Discrimination Act 1995) which contain similar statutory j provisions although directed to different forms of discrimination, it is legitimate if necessary to consider those Acts in resolving any issue of interpretation which may arise on this Act. The framework of the 1976 Act, although familiar, is important in construing s 33(1). Part I (ss 1–3) defines what, for purposes of the Act, is meant by racial discrimination. Part II (ss 4–16) provides that certain discriminatory acts in the crucially important field of employment shall be unlawful and makes certain exceptions. Part III of the Act provides that certain

discriminatory acts shall be unlawful in a number of different fields such as education (ss 17–19); the provision of goods, facilities and services by (among other providers) hotels, banks, insurers, recreational establishments, transport officers and professions (s 20); and housing (ss 21–24).

[3] Part IV of the Act is entitled 'Other unlawful acts' and includes a series of sections which includes s 33. Section 29 applies to discriminatory advertisements. Section 30 makes it unlawful for a person with authority or influence over another to instruct that other to do, or to procure or to attempt to procure that other to do, anything which is unlawful under Pts II or III of the Act. Section 31 makes it unlawful to induce or attempt to induce any person to do any act which contravenes Pts II or III of the Act. Section 32 makes employers and principals vicariously liable for the conduct of their respective employees and agents. Section 32(3) provides a defence to an employer in proceedings brought against him under the Act in respect of an act allegedly done by his employee, if he can prove that he took such steps as were reasonably practicable to prevent the employee from doing that act or from doing in the course of his employment acts of that description. Section 33, quoted above, completes this Part.

[4] Part VIII of the Act governs the enforcement of its provisions and is of obvious importance if the Act is to have the teeth which Parliament doubtless intended it should. Section 53 makes plain that these enforcement provisions are to be read as both exclusive of any other means of enforcement and as exhaustive. Consistently with the modern practice of allocating employment disputes to specially constituted employment (formerly industrial) tribunals, s 54 provides that any complaint of a racially discriminatory act made unlawful by Pt II of the Act (the sections dealing with employment), or under ss 32 or 33 in relation to such an act, must be made to an employment tribunal. The Act permits no other procedure. If the complaint is of a racially discriminatory act made unlawful by Pt III of the Act, or under ss 32 or 33 in relation to such an act, proceedings can be brought only in a designated county court in England and Wales or a sheriff court in Scotland. Again, the Act permits no other procedure. Section 63 of the Act provides that proceedings in respect of a contravention of ss 29, 30 and 31 may be brought only by the Commission for Racial Equality, a body established by s 43 of the Act with important strategic duties which are there specified.

[5] The expression 'aids' in s 33(1) is a familiar word in everyday use and it bears no technical or special meaning in this context. A person aids another if he helps or assists him. He does so whether his help is substantial and productive or whether it is not, provided the help is not so insignificant as to be negligible. While any gloss on the clear statutory language is better avoided, the subsection points towards a relationship of co-operation or collaboration; it does not matter who instigates or initiates the relationship. It is plain that, depending on the facts, a party who aids another to do an unlawful act may also procure or induce that other to do it. But the expressions 'procure' and 'induce' are found in ss 30 and 31, not s 33, and are differently enforced; they mean something different from 'aids' and there is no warrant to interpreting 'aids' as comprising these other expressions. By s 12 of the Race Relations Act 1968, the predecessor of the 1976 Act, those who deliberately aided, induced or incited another person to do an act made unlawful by Pt I of that Act were to be treated as themselves doing that act, but they could not be subjected to proceedings at the direct suit of the injured party and the 1976 Act adopted a different legislative approach. It is plain that a party who causes another to do an unlawful act does not necessarily aid him to do it. A farmer who starves his sheepdog, with the result that the ravening dog savages

a a new-born lamb, may reasonably be said to have caused the death of the lamb, but he could not be said to have aided the dog to kill the lamb. In the present appeal no issue arises on the meaning of 'knowingly' in this context and it is unnecessary to consider what an aider must know to be liable under s 33(1).

[6] Mr Anyanwu and Mr Ebuzoeme, the appellants, were students at and members of the South Bank University. As a result of elections held in May 1995 b they were engaged to serve as full-time salaried officers of the South Bank Student Union for a fixed term of one year beginning on 1 August 1995. In that capacity they were trustees of the funds of the student union, which was treated as an educational charity. Questions were raised by the university about their conduct as trustees, and disciplinary proceedings were instituted. The university suspended both appellants as members of the university by letters dated 22 February c 1996, which also forbade them from entering any university building including the student union until given permission to do so. Following the appellants' non-appearance at the disciplinary proceedings the university expelled them from the university with immediate effect by letters dated 29 March 1996 which again forbade them from entering any university building including the student d union. It was of course impossible for the appellants to perform their duties as employees of the student union if they were unable to enter its premises and by letters dated 2 April 1996 to each appellant the student union treated the appellants' employment contracts as at an end. There is an unresolved question whether by these letters the student union dismissed the appellants, or whether the student union treated the contract of employment as frustrated by supervening e impossibility of performance. That is not an issue before the House.

[7] The appellants made complaints of unlawful racial discrimination against the student union and the university (and against other personal respondents whose joinder in these proceedings has been disallowed). In his form of application Mr Anyanwu summarised the grounds of his complaint, relying on the f suspension of 22 February 1996, the expulsion on 29 March 1996 and the termination of his employment by the student union on 2 April 1996. He expressed the belief that he had been discriminated against on racial grounds, he being of black African origin. The brief summary of his complaint in the form of application was expanded in a typed statement: in this, a large number of accusations were made g against a number of parties, and Mr Anyanwu again relied on the suspension of 22 February 1996, his expulsion on 29 March 1996 and his dismissal on 2 April 1996. Mr Ebuzoeme made a similar complaint in his form of application, relying on the same three events. He also submitted a statement in support of his claim, which also made a number of accusations of racial discrimination. He also placed reliance on the letters which suspended, expelled and dismissed him, and he h summarised his case against the university in these terms:

> '(a) Refusal to accept me as equal to that of my predecessor. (b) Misuse of administration and disciplinary rules by Professor T Watkins [the deputy vice-chancellor] as vehicle for discrimination and preferential treatments j (ref: incident of the 15th December 1995). (c) Incitement of racial hatred (ref letter of the 5th February 1996). (d) My suspension and expulsion was racial because it would have handled my case differently if I was an English student. (e) It instigated my removal by its actions and inactions.'

Both the forms of application and the statements were drafted by the appellants without the benefit of legal assistance.

[8] The appellants had earlier sought, without success, to obtain permission to apply for judicial review against the university in relation to their suspension and expulsion. Relying on this refusal of permission, the university (which is the sole respondent to this appeal) applied in the industrial tribunal that the proceedings against it should be struck out on grounds of res judicata. The tribunal considered this application at a preliminary hearing on 21 March 1997. It held that the appellants' complaints against the university should be struck out as frivolous or vexatious. In the reasons for its decision issued on 7 April 1997 the tribunal said:

> '2. So far as the issues were concerned, these were clarified and agreed by the [appellants] after some discussion as follows. Both [appellants] complain against the [student union] that they discriminated against them on the ground of race first by excluding the [appellants] from the [student union's] premises on 22 February 1996 and secondly by dismissing the [appellants] on 2 April 1996. The [student union] deny both allegations and indeed claim that the contracts of employment were frustrated and not terminated by any action of the [student union]. The issues in respect of the [university] ... were agreed as follows: "(a) that they [the university] interfered with the [appellants'] contracts of employment by excluding them from their place of employment, (b) that they made various allegations against the [appellants] in connection with union funds, (c) that they made allegations against the [appellants] in respect of other employment matters for example intimidation of union staff, (d) that there had been preferential treatment in terms of funding being granted to the [student union], (e) that they used the general manager of the union to make allegations against the [appellants].
>
> 3. It was alleged that all of these actions were designed to obtain the dismissal of the [appellants].'

[9] The tribunal accepted the university's argument that the appellants' complaints against it had been or should have been the subject of previous adjudication, and made its striking-out order on that ground.

[10] The appellants appealed against this ruling to the Employment Appeal Tribunal. On the appeal the student union played no part since it was accepted that the proceedings against it would continue in any event. For reasons given by Morison J the appeal was allowed. The Appeal Tribunal understood the appellants' complaint to be that they had been dismissed by the student union from their employment on grounds of race contrary to the 1976 Act, and that the university had knowingly aided the union to do that unlawful act.

[11] The Appeal Tribunal ruled that the proceedings against the university should not have been struck out on grounds of res judicata or under the principle in *Henderson v Henderson* (1843) 3 Hare 100 at 115, [1843–1860] All ER Rep 378 at 381–382.

[12] The university challenged that ruling in the Court of Appeal, where the argument took a different turn: the Court of Appeal drew attention to s 33(1) of the Act, quoted above, and held by a majority (Butler-Sloss and Laws LJJ, Pill LJ dissenting) that even assuming the appellants' account of the facts to be correct it could not be said that the university had knowingly aided the student union to dismiss the appellants (see [2000] 1 All ER 1). Giving the first judgment Laws LJ said (at 7):

> 'The facts alleged by the [appellants] are vigorously contested, but must be taken as true for the purposes of this appeal, since the university's argument

a amounts to an application to strike out the case against it. The question for this court, as it seems to me, is whether on those alleged facts the university can conceivably be said to have "knowingly aided" the [appellants'] dismissal by the union. In expelling the [appellants] and barring them from the union premises, the university ... brought about a state of affairs in which the employment contracts were bound to be terminated. In my judgment it is a b plain affront to the language of the Act to suggest that in such circumstances the university "aided" the dismissal of the [appellants]. The verb "aid" (to which no special definition is ascribed by the statute) means "help" or "assist". Its use contemplates a state of affairs in which one party, being a free agent in the matter, sets out to do an act or achieve a result, and another party helps him to do it. The first party is the primary actor. The other is a c secondary actor. The simplest of examples may be found in the criminal law. A breaks into a house in order to burgle it. B keeps watch outside or is ready to drive off the getaway car. Plainly B "aids" A. But here, the university is the prime mover. It did not "aid" (or "help") the union to dismiss the [appellants]. It may well be said that it *brought about* their dismissal. But that d is altogether a different thing.' (Laws LJ's emphasis.)

[13] Butler-Sloss LJ agreed with him and said (at 13):

'But, for my part, I am unable, in applying the natural meaning to the word "aids", to attribute to it a meaning which distorts it. In ordinary language a person who aids another person is one who helps, supports or assists the e prime mover to do the act. On the present facts the university took steps to expel the [appellants] for its own reasons, justified or unjustified. Those expulsions, carrying with them the prohibition against entering any part of the university buildings including the students' union, cannot in ordinary language be said to be knowingly aiding the students' union to dismiss the f [appellants] within s 33(1). In this case the prime mover of the dismissal of the [appellants] was the students' union but its acts were effectively dictated to it by the prior decision of the university to expel the [appellants]. It seems clear to me that the students' union had no alternative but to dismiss the [appellants] after the university expelled them. In ordinary language can that conceivably be said to be knowingly aiding? I would answer No.'

g [14] In his dissenting judgment Pill LJ (at 9–10) noted the university's concession that for purposes of the strike-out application the dismissals of the appellants should be treated as unlawful acts within the meaning of s 33, and recited the university's argument that it had not aided the student union to do h those unlawful acts since it had itself suspended and expelled the appellants and that had led inevitably to the termination by the student union of the appellants' contracts of employment. He did not agree that the appellants' claim against the university should be struck out. He said (at 11):

'Even taking a narrow definition of the word "aid", the acts complained of, j suspension, expulsion and dismissal, and the alleged conduct of the university and the union which preceded each of them, are so entangled upon the facts alleged that it would not be appropriate to separate them at this stage. On any view, the dismissal is intimately connected with the suspension and expulsion. An environment of racial prejudice is alleged to have been "encouraged and allowed to thrive by the university and the union" (Mr Anyanwu). The union are alleged to have been "conniving with the university to remove me"

(Mr Ebuzoeme). In further and better particulars given at the request of the university, Mr Anyanwu said that "in all cases the acts of racial discrimination were carried out collectively by the respondents" (that is the university and the union).'

a

[15] Three points in particular are important in approaching the central issue in this appeal, which is whether the Court of Appeal were right to allow the university's appeal and strike out the appellants' claim against it. First, the appellants' claim against the university is advanced under, and only under, s 33(1) of the Act. Second, the appellants' claim against the student union as their former employer is brought under Pt II of the Act, under which the claim against the university under s 33(1) must also lie. Third, the issue before the House arises on demurrer: there has been no trial, and no findings of fact have been made, so the questions for decision must be answered by reference to what the appellants have alleged and not what they have proved.

b

c

[16] The first question which must be asked is: what is the act of the student union made unlawful by Pt II of the Act which it is said that the university knowingly aided the student union to do? The answer, in each case, is that the student union dismissed the appellant on discriminatory racial grounds. This is the unlawful act to which the judgments of the Appeal Tribunal and the Court of Appeal were directed. The complaint of exclusion was not, it seems, pursued, no doubt because this appears to have been an act (whether lawful or unlawful) of the university and not of the student union.

d

[17] The second question is: what is it alleged that the university did which knowingly aided the doing of that unlawful act by the student union? The answer is in my view to be found in the issues agreed in the industrial tribunal and summarised in para 2 of the tribunal's reasons, quoted above in [**8**]. Although this summary was given and agreed in the context of an argument concerning res judicata, I can see no reason why it should not be treated as an accurate and comprehensive summary.

e

f

[18] The third question is: do those allegations (if fully established) bring the appellants' complaints against the university within s 33(1) of the Act? The House is not concerned with allegations that the appellants might have made against the university in the county court under s 17 of the Act, but only with knowing aid given by the university to the student union in dismissing the appellants. I would for my part have doubted whether the appellants' allegations were sufficient to support their claim against the university on this limited basis under s 33(1), and I would have questioned whether the appellants' general claims against the university of racial prejudice, intimidation and interference (even if established) could have been said to satisfy the subsection. A majority of your Lordships do not however share my doubts, and having read the compelling opinions of my noble and learned friends Lord Steyn and Lord Hope of Craighead my reservations are assuaged if not entirely dispelled. I am content to acquiesce in the view which commends itself to the majority.

g

h

[19] I would accordingly allow the appeal, set aside the order of the Court of Appeal and remit the matter to an employment tribunal for a hearing, long overdue, against both the student union and the university. In resolving the claim against the university, the tribunal should apply the plain terms of s 33(1) as explained by your Lordships. The subsection will apply if the university is shown to have knowingly aided (or helped or assisted) the student union to dismiss the appellants. It is not helpful to introduce 'free agents' and 'prime

j

a movers', which can only distract attention from the essentially simple test which (however complicated and controversial the facts) is the test to be applied.

[20] The parties are invited to make submissions on costs; in the House and below, in writing within 14 days.

LORD BROWNE-WILKINSON.

b **[21]** My Lords, I have had the advantage of reading in draft the speech of my noble and learned friend Lord Bingham of Cornhill. I am in complete agreement with him as to the correct construction of s 33 of the Race Relations Act 1976 but do not share his doubts as to whether this is an appropriate case to strike out. On the latter point I agree with Lord Steyn in thinking that the case cannot be c properly struck out but must continue to trial. On those grounds I would allow the appeal.

LORD STEYN.

(I) Striking out

d **[22]** My Lords, the appellants were students at the South Bank University. In 1995 they came to be employed by South Bank Student Union. In 1996 they were expelled from the university and dismissed by the student union. They submitted claims under the Race Relations Act 1976. The claims against the student union were brought under s 4 of the 1976 Act, which provides that it is unlawful for an e employer to discriminate against an employee by dismissing him or subjecting him to any other detriment. The hearing of this claim on its merits has been delayed by the vicissitudes of the secondary or derivative claim against the university which was based on s 33(1) of the 1976 Act. This provision reads:

> 'A person who knowingly aids another person to do an act made unlawful f by this Act shall be treated for the purposes of this Act as himself doing an unlawful act of the like description.'

The employment tribunal struck out this claim on the grounds that the issue was res judicata; the Employment Appeal Tribunal reversed this decision; and by a majority the Court of Appeal restored the decision of the employment tribunal g on the basis of its view of the correct interpretation of the word 'aids' in s 33(1) (see [2000] 1 All ER 1).

[23] It is my understanding that your Lordships are agreed that the interpretation of s 33(1) adopted by the Court of Appeal should not be accepted. The issue now is whether on a different interpretation of s 33(1) upon which I h understand your Lordships to be agreed, the claim against the university should be struck out or whether it should be heard on its merits by the employment tribunal.

[24] In the result this is now the fourth occasion on which the preliminary question of the legal sustainability of the appellants' claim against the university j is being considered. For my part such vagaries in discrimination jurisprudence underline the importance of not striking out such claims as an abuse of the process except in the most obvious and plainest cases. Discrimination cases are generally fact-sensitive, and their proper determination is always vital in our pluralistic society. In this field perhaps more than any other the bias in favour of a claim being examined on the merits or demerits of its particular facts is a matter of high public interest. Against this background it is necessary to explain why on the allegations made by the appellants it would be wrong to strike out their claims against the university. a

(II) A narrative

[25] The university is a corporate charity, registered with the Charity Commission. The student union is an unincorporated association, regarded by the Charity Commission as having charitable objects deriving from its relationship with the university. Under the Education Act 1994 the university exercises a degree of superintendence over the student union. b

[26] During May 1995, while they were student members of the university, the appellants were elected to the executive committee of the student union. The student union employed the two appellants full-time under contracts of employment as respectively a communications officer (in the case of the first appellant) and vice-president (in the case of the second appellant). These contracts were for a year beginning from 1 August 1995. By virtue of their contracts the appellants became trustees of the funds of the student union. c

[27] The conduct of the appellants was called into question. Disciplinary proceedings were taken by the university against them. In February 1996 they were suspended from the university. By letters dated 29 March 1996 they were expelled from the university. The letters stated that they 'must not enter any university building, including the student union'. The appellants contend that they were dismissed by letters dated 2 April 1996. The student union argue that the contracts were frustrated. This issue does not arise for consideration on the present appeal. d e

[28] Both appellants challenged their expulsion by the university in judicial review proceedings. In June 1996 a judge of the High Court (Jowitt J) declined to grant leave in relation to the claim of the second appellant that the university approached the decision against him in a biased way. Subsequently, in the same month the same judge of the High Court also refused leave in relation to the first appellant's challenge to the procedure adopted which led to his expulsion. The latter decision was upheld on appeal. f

[29] By originating applications received on 21 May 1996 the appellants brought claims of race discrimination against the student union and the university in the employment tribunal. They complained of their dismissal by the student union and their expulsion from the university, alleging discrimination on the grounds of race. In June 1996 the appellants sent to the employment tribunal statements setting out their complaints about the conduct of the student union and the university. Both appellants furnished further and better particulars of their claims. g

[30] The solicitors for the university requested a preliminary hearing for the tribunal to consider, inter alia, whether the claim against the university should be struck out as frivolous and vexatious. On 21 March 1997 the preliminary hearing took place before the chairman alone. No evidence was led. On the other hand, in accordance with the customary and sensible practice of case management of the tribunal, the chairman took the opportunity to inquire into the general nature of the case advanced by the appellants against the university. At that time the precise way in which it was alleged that the university aided the student union in dismissing the appellants was not actively under consideration. The issue was whether res judicata barred the claims. Nevertheless, the chairman's elucidation was instructive. Being a critical document I set out the relevant part of his decision letter of 7 April. It reads: h j

a

'2. So far as the issues were concerned, these were clarified and agreed by the [appellants] after some discussion as follows. Both [appellants] complain against the [student union] that they discriminated against them on the ground of race first by excluding the [appellants] from the [student union's] premises on 22 February 1996 and secondly by dismissing the [appellants] on 2 April 1996. The [student union] deny both allegations and indeed claim that the contracts of employment were frustrated and not terminated by any action of the [student union]. The issues in respect of the [university] ... were agreed as follows: (a) that they interfered with the [appellants] contracts of employment by excluding them from their place of employment, (b) that they [the university] made various allegations [to the student union] against the [appellants] in connection with union funds, (c) that they made allegations against the [appellants] in respect of other employment matters for example intimidation of union staff, (d) that there had been preferential treatment in terms of funding being granted to the [student union], (e) that they used the general manager of the union to make allegations against the [appellants].

3. It was alleged that all of these actions were designed to obtain the dismissal of the [appellants].'

On the appeal to your Lordships' House it was conceded on behalf of the university that a decision on the sustainability of the appellants' claim against the university must now take full account of this amplification and clarification of the claims, viewed against the background. But that is not how the matter came before the chairman: he was only considering a technical issue res judicata. In his decision of 7 April 1997 the chairman accepted the legal argument of the university that, by reason of the earlier judicial review proceedings, the claims against the university in the employment tribunal were barred by the doctrine of res judicata.

(III) The Appeal Tribunal

[31] The appellants appealed to the Appeal Tribunal against the striking out of their claims against the university. In a judgment dated 19 January 1998 the Appeal Tribunal (Morison P presiding) allowed the appeal. The Appeal Tribunal held that the employment tribunal had erred in ruling that the claims under consideration should have been raised in the judicial review proceedings. The Appeal Tribunal also rejected a claim that it was an abuse of process to allow the claims against the university to proceed. The Appeal Tribunal remitted the claims to the employment tribunal for a substantive hearing on the merits.

(IV) The decision of the Court of Appeal

[32] The university appealed to the Court of Appeal against the decision of the Appeal Tribunal. When the appeal came on for hearing on 21 May 1999 Laws LJ raised a new point on the applicability of s 33(1) of the 1976 Act to the alleged liability of the university. The appeal was adjourned and the grounds of appeal were amended to include a ground that the university had not aided the student union within the meaning of s 33(1). On the resumed hearing the new ground was debated. It eventually formed the basis of the judgments of the majority (see [2000] 1 All ER 1). Laws LJ gave the leading judgment. He observed (at 7):

'In expelling the applicants and barring them from the union premises, the university ... brought about a state of affairs in which the employment contracts were bound to be terminated. In my judgment it is a plain affront to the language of the Act to suggest that in such circumstances the university "aided" the dismissal of the applicants. The verb "aid" (to which no special definition is ascribed by the statute) means "help" or "assist". Its use contemplates a state of affairs in which one party, being a free agent in the matter, sets out to do an act or achieve a result, and another party helps him to do it. The first party is the primary actor. The other is a secondary actor. The simplest of examples may be found in the criminal law. A breaks into a house in order to burgle it. B keeps watch outside or is ready to drive off the getaway car. Plainly B "aids" A. But here, the university is the prime mover. It did not "aid" (or "help") the union to dismiss the applicants. It may well be said that it *brought about* their dismissal. But that is altogether a different thing.' (Laws LJ's emphasis.)

The proposition that as a matter of law a prime mover cannot be said to be under s 33(1) was at the core of the reasoning of Laws LJ. It was the basis of his decision that the university did not aid the dismissal of the appellants. Laws LJ did, however, consider an alternative argument advanced by the appellants. The passage in his judgment reads (at 9):

'Miss Monaghan [for Mr Anyanwu] and Mr Crawford [for Mr Ebuzoeme] further submitted that the facts which the applicants alleged disclosed, or at least arguably disclosed, a state of affairs in which the university and the union were, in effect, deliberately aiding each other to discriminate against the applicants. That is not the case made in either applicant's Form IT1, nor in the summary conclusions of their witness statements. Mr Bean QC for the university submitted that the court should look only at the Forms IT1 in order to ascertain what was the case being made against the university. I have some sympathy with this, although I certainly accept that, given the relative informality with which proceedings before the employment tribunal are advisedly conducted, it would be wrong to adopt an excessively technical or formalistic approach to the case. However that may be, something altogether clearer would need to be asserted by the applicants for this court to proceed on the basis that the case being made involved knowing and deliberate mutual assistance between the university and the union, each acting as an independent party … I would found my conclusion on this part of the case upon the simple proposition that the allegation suggested nowhere sufficiently appears in the documents that were placed before the tribunal.'

It will be observed that Laws LJ did not consider the amplification and clarification of the appellants' allegations which were recorded by the chairman. That explanation is now by concession before the House and relevant to the issues. Butler-Sloss LJ agreed with the judgment of Laws LJ but said (at 13) that—

'the prime mover of the dismissal of the applicants was the students' union but its acts were effectively dictated to it by the prior decision of the university to expel the applicants.'

Butler-Sloss LJ did not deal with the alternative argument of counsel for the appellants which finds support in the chairman's brief summary of the appellants' allegations against the university. Lastly, Pill LJ gave a dissenting judgment in which he adopted a broader interpretation of s 33(1) and, in any event, concluded (at 11) that—

a 'the alleged conduct of the university and the union which preceded each of them [viz the expulsion and dismissal], are so entangled upon the facts alleged that it would not be appropriate to separate them at this stage.'

(V) The proper construction of s 33(1)

[33] My noble and learned friend Lord Bingham of Cornhill set out the b scheme of the 1976 Act and has explained with great care and precision how s 33(1) ought to be construed. I am in full agreement with his interpretation of this provision. It is therefore unnecessary for me to cover all the same ground. I do, however, state the major points germane to the present appeal. The correct approach is to construe the words of s 33(1) in its contextual setting. It creates a form of derivative liability predicated on the commission of an unlawful act by c another person. For present purposes the unlawful act against which s 33(1) must be considered is the alleged dismissal of the appellants by their employers (the student union) on discriminatory racial grounds. The issue of knowledge does not need to be considered on the present appeal. Focusing on the concept of knowingly *aiding*, the word is used in its ordinary sense. While there is no exact d synonym the words help, assist, co-operate, or collaborate convey more or less the right nuance. The word 'aid' is therefore not used in either an extensive or a restrictive sense. The critical question is: Does the word 'aid' in its contextual sense cover the conduct of the secondary party? It follows that it is wrong to be diverted by any inquiries not mandated by the statute as to whether the alleged aider was or was not a prime mover or a free agent. I would therefore hold that e interpretation of s 33(1) adopted by the majority in the Court of Appeal ought not to be accepted.

(VI) The approach of the Court of Appeal to the allegations of the appellants

[34] Counsel for the university abandoned earlier technical objections to f considering the explanation of the appellants' case as recorded by the chairman. Unfortunately, due perhaps to its concentration on the 'prime mover' and 'free agent' issues, the Court of Appeal did not consider the case of the appellants as amplified and clarified at the preliminary hearing. I have already cited that amplification and explanation in full. Fairly considered it conveys, or is capable of conveying, that the appellants allege, inter alia, that the university in order to g achieve the dismissal of the appellants assisted the student union, or co-operated with it, by making allegations against the appellants to the student union to the effect that the appellants were involved in irregularities in connection with union funds and were guilty of intimidation of union staff. Taking into account the summary of the chairman, read with the statements of the appellants, I am h persuaded that there is an arguable case under s 33(1) against the university. In my view it would be wrong to strike it out.

(VII) Disposal

[35] I would allow the appeal and restore the order made by the Appeal j Tribunal on 19 January 1998.

LORD HOPE OF CRAIGHEAD.

[36] My Lords, I have had the advantage of reading in draft the speeches of my noble and learned friends Lord Bingham of Cornhill and Lord Steyn. I am in full agreement with what they say about the interpretation of s 33(1) of the Race Relations Act 1976. As for its application to this case, I agree with Lord Steyn that

the appellants have an arguable case against the university and that their claims should not be struck out. I should like however to add these observations, especially in the light of the points made by my noble and learned friend Lord Millett, whose speech I have also had the advantage of reading in draft. This is because, while we are all agreed as to the result of the appeal, there are some differences between us as to the route by which we reach that result.

[37] I should like first to say that, if I had reached the view that nothing that the university is alleged to have done could as a matter of ordinary language be said to have aided the student union to dismiss the appellants, I would not have been in favour of allowing the appeal. I would have been reluctant to strike out these claims, on the view that discrimination issues of the kind which have been raised in this case should as a general rule be decided only after hearing the evidence. The questions of law that have to be determined are often highly fact-sensitive. The risk of injustice is minimised if the answers to these questions are deferred until all the facts are out. The tribunal can then base its decision on its findings of fact rather than on assumptions as to what the claimant may be able to establish if given an opportunity to lead evidence. This was the point which Pill LJ was making in his dissenting judgment in the Court of Appeal (see [2000] 1 All ER 1) when he said (at 11), that the acts complained of and the alleged conduct of the university and the student union which preceded them are so entangled upon the facts alleged that it would not be appropriate to separate them at this stage.

[38] Then there is the fact that the point of law with which this appeal is concerned was raised for the first time in the Court of Appeal. It was the Court of Appeal itself which drew attention to the terms of s 33(1) of the 1976 Act and invited argument upon it. The appellants had appealed successfully to the Appeal Tribunal against the ruling by the industrial tribunal that their claim should be struck out as frivolous or vexatious. In the result the Court of Appeal held by a majority that the claim should be struck out on an entirely different ground, which neither the industrial tribunal nor the Employment Appeal Tribunal had considered when they were examining the appellants' allegations. The appellants may well have had a genuine sense of grievance at this turn of events.

[39] Nevertheless I would have held that the claim should be struck out if I had been persuaded that it had no reasonable prospect of succeeding at trial. The time and resources of the employment tribunals ought not to taken up by having to hear evidence in cases that are bound to fail.

[40] In my opinion, however, the appellants have an arguable case against the university under s 33(1) of the Act and their claim should be remitted to an employment tribunal so that they may have an opportunity of leading their evidence. I have based this opinion on a reading of the statements which the appellants lodged in support of their applications to the tribunal and on the plain meaning of s 33(1).

[41] The critical words in s 33(1) are contained in the phrase 'who knowingly aids another person to do an act made unlawful by this Act'. The state of mind that is referred to here is actual knowledge, in contrast to that referred to in s 33(4) which uses the phrase 'knowingly or recklessly'. The activity which is indicated by the word 'aids' is best understood by reading it together with the words 'to do an act' which appear in the same phrase. It can be contrasted with the words 'instruct' and 'induce' which are used in ss 30 and 31. The word 'instructs' in s 30 is used to describe something done by a person with authority or influence. It is used in the sense of issuing an order which the other person

a must, or can be persuaded to, obey. A person who in that sense instructs, induces or causes another person to do an act may also knowingly aid him to do that act, or he may not. This is because the word 'aids' indicates an act of a different kind from that which may have *caused* the person to do the unlawful act. It indicates the giving of some kind of assistance to the other person which *helps* him to do it. The amount or value of that help or assistance is of no importance. Nor is the b time at which it is given. It may or may not have been necessary. All that is needed is an act of some kind, done knowingly, which helps the other person to do the unlawful act.

[42] I would be cautious about selecting examples to illustrate what the word 'aids' means which relate to criminal conduct. As Judge LJ said in *Hallam v Avery* [2000] 1 WLR 966 at 972, caution is required before the principles relating to the c liability of secondary parties under the criminal law are used for the purposes of construing s 33(1). Of course, examples may be given to illustrate the difference between causing or persuading somebody to do something and aiding or helping him to do something. But one must bear in mind that the word 'aids' is being used in the context which s 33(1) has set for it. This is in the context of acts made d unlawful by the Act, which are many and various and may require inferences to be drawn from a complex variety of facts and circumstances. For this purpose I think that it is enough to say that the word 'aids' should be given its plain and ordinary meaning. It requires that the facts be examined to provide the answers to two questions: (i) what was the act done by the other person which was made unlawful by the Act? (ii) Did the act which is in question aid the other person to e do that act?

[43] As for the facts, I agree with Lord Steyn that the agreed list of issues which the chairman of the industrial tribunal set out in his decision letter of 7 April 1997 provides a helpful summary of the appellants' case. But I think that in order to obtain a complete picture of the allegations which the appellants are making f against the university it is necessary to look at the statements which the appellants lodged in support of their applications. I note in passing that the issue which was before the tribunal when the agreed list of issues was prepared was whether the claims were barred by res judicata. That was a different issue from the question which has now been raised under s 33(1) of the Act. The appellants will not be confined to the points mentioned in that agreed list when they are g presenting their evidence.

[44] The picture which the appellants are seeking to present in these statements is the building up by the university of a climate of racial prejudice against them which the elected officials of the student union were unable or unwilling to withstand. Mr Anyanwu says in his statement that the university continually h threatened and intimidated officers of the union, and that the student members of the union were dissuaded from acting against the university. Mr Ebuzoeme says in his statement that the university 'instigated' his removal by its actions and inactions. Of course, if that is all that can be proved against the university it will not be enough to show that it 'aided' the student union to dismiss the appellants on j racial grounds.

[45] But the appellants do not stop there. Mr Ebuzoeme says in his statement that the student union connived with the university to remove him. Mr Anyanwu refers to a letter which was written to him by the vice-chancellor of the university on 22 March 1996 in which he said that the board of governors had approved a new interim constitution for the student union. The effect of the interim constitution was to place the affairs of the student union out of the hands of the student

members and into the hands of trustees selected and appointed by the university. They replaced those who had been elected by the student body to act as its representatives. This action appears to have been taken under s 22 of the Education Act 1994, which requires the governing body of every educational establishment to take steps to ensure the fair, democratic and financially accountable conduct of student unions. The letters of 2 April 1996 which had the effect of terminating the appellants' employment were signed by Maggie Hammond as a trustee. It appears that she was one of the persons who had been selected to act in that capacity by the university.

[**46**] I do not think that it is possible to say one way or the other at this stage, from the narrative that has been given, whether the actions of the university which are alleged against it aided the student union to do the unlawful act of which the appellants complain. But a case to this effect seems to me to be at least arguable. As Miss Cox QC observed in the course of the argument, it was only the student union that could dismiss the appellants. All the university could do was to aid the student union in effecting the dismissal. But the actions alleged against the university were intimately connected with those of the student union, and the connection became even more intimate once the interim constitution had been approved and put in place. The university's alleged actions are said to have culminated in its decision to approve the interim constitution for the student union. It was the interim constitution which enabled the university to appoint Maggie Hammond as a trustee. Within days of her appointment she signed the letters on behalf of the student union by which, in effect, the appellants were dismissed. In my opinion the facts which led to this chain of events require to be investigated.

[**47**] I would therefore, for these reasons, allow the appeal and remit the matter to an employment tribunal for a hearing against both the student union and the university.

LORD MILLETT.

[**48**] My Lords, I have had the advantage of reading in draft the speech of my noble and learned friend, Lord Bingham of Cornhill, with which I respectfully agree.

[**49**] I share his doubts whether the acts of the university relied upon, if established at trial, are capable of sustaining a finding that the university 'aided' the student union to dismiss the appellants. The university may have encouraged, induced or incited the union to dismiss them; these concepts are closely similar and merge imperceptibly into one another. Indeed, the university may well have gone further and caused or procured the union to dismiss the appellants; concepts which are distinct from but also closely related to each other. But aiding is a very different concept from encouraging or inducing on the one hand and causing or procuring on the other. It requires a much closer involvement in the act of the principal.

[**50**] In my opinion it is, however, unhelpful to have regard to words like 'co-operate' or 'collaborate', which introduce a different concept in which both parties are principals. Such words serve only to confuse the issue, since they distract attention from the particular act of the principal which the accessory is alleged to have aided. Where two parties join together to achieve a common purpose, they may no doubt be said to aid each other in achieving that purpose. But, in the course of their co-operation, each may play his separate part unaided by the other. I take a simple example. Suppose A and B decide to let a bull loose

a from a field. A opens the gate and B drives the bull out of the field. They co-operate in letting the bull loose. A may without inaccuracy also be said to have aided B to let the bull loose. But B can hardly be said to have aided A to open the gate. This serves to demonstrate the importance of identifying with precision the act of the principal to which the accessory is alleged to have lent his aid.

[**51**] For my part, I do not think that anything which the university is alleged b to have done (at least as summarised by the chairman of the industrial tribunal), even if done deliberately and with an eye to the dismissal of the appellants from their employment by the union, and even if their dismissal was one of the university's objects and not merely an incidental consequence of its actions, can as a matter of ordinary language be said to have aided the union to dismiss them. But there may be more to the appellants' case than is comprehended within the c chairman's summary, and I agree that their claim against the university should proceed to trial so that the facts can be established.

Appeal allowed.

Kate O'Hanlon Barrister.

Ashdown v Telegraph Group Ltd

a

CHANCERY DIVISION

SIR ANDREW MORRITT V-C

13, 14 DECEMBER 2000, 11 JANUARY 2001

b

Copyright – Infringement – Defence – Right to freedom of expression – Whether right to freedom of expression under human rights convention providing defence to claim for copyright infringement over and above that provided by relevant statutory code – Copyright, Designs and Patents Act 1988, ss 30, 171(3) – Human Rights Act 1998, s 12(4), Sch 1, Pt I, art 10.

c

The claimant, A, was a Member of Parliament and the former leader of the Liberal Democrats. For many years he kept confidential diaries and other records of his experiences. In October 1997 he dictated a minute of a meeting with the Prime Minister and other politicians. In an interview two years later, A referred d to his diaries and to high-level discussions, before and after the 1997 general election, concerning the possibility of a coalition cabinet comprising members of the Labour Party and the Liberal Democrats. Shortly afterwards, the minute was disclosed to the defendant newspaper by a third party, and substantial sections of it were incorporated in articles, published in the newspaper, which purported to e reveal the true story of those discussions. As a result, A brought proceedings against the newspaper for, inter alia, infringment of copyright, and applied for summary judgment in respect of that claim. The newspaper relied on the defence of fair dealing contained in s 30[a] of the Copyright, Designs and Patents Act 1988; the rule of law, recognised and preserved by s 171(3)[b] of the 1988 Act, which prevented or restricted the enforcement of copyright on grounds of public f interest; and the right to freedom of expression in art 10(1)[c] of the European Convention for the Protection of Human Rights and Fundamental Freedoms 1950 (as set out in Sch 1 to the Human Rights Act 1998)—a right that was subject, by virtue of art 10(2), to such restrictions as were prescribed by law and were necessary in a democratic society for the protection of the rights of others. The g newspaper contended that the restrictions on the right to freedom of expression imposed by the 1988 Act went further than was necessary in a democratic society, and that ss 30 and 171(3) of the 1988 Act had to be interpreted and applied in a manner that gave effect to that right. It further relied, inter alia, on s 12(4)[d] of the 1998 Act, which provided that the court 'must have particular regard to' the h convention right to freedom of expression when considering whether to grant any relief which might affect the exercise of that right, and, in the case of journalistic material, to the extent to which that material had, or was about to, become available to the public, or its publication was, or would be, in the public interest. The newspaper contended that wording of s 12(4) indicated that the j court should place extra weight on the matters referred to in that subsection.

a Section 30, so far as material, is set out at [21], post

b Section 171(3) is set out at [31], post

c Article 10 is set out at [7], post

d Section 12, so far as material, is set out at [33], post

a **Held** – The right to freedom of expression in art 10 of the convention provided no defences to an action for infringement of copyright over and above those provided by the 1988 Act. The balance between the rights of the copyright owner and those of the public had been struck by the legislative organ of the democratic state in the legislation it had enacted. There was no room for any further defences outside the code which established the particular species of intellectual b property in question. In particular, it was not open to an infringer to defend the proceedings on the basis that, although he could not make out one or more of the statutory defences, the relief sought would nevertheless be more than was necessary in a democratic society and therefore contrary to art 10(2). The needs of such a society included the recognition and protection of private property, and the provisions of the 1988 Act could and did in themselves satisfy the requirements c of art 10(2). In the instant case, the defendant was not entitled to rely on s 30 of the 1988 Act or the principle preserved by s 171(3). Nor did s 12(4) of the 1998 Act provide any reason to withhold the relief to which A would be entitled if summary judgment was given in his favour. The phrase 'must have particular regard to' did not indicate that the court should place extra weight on the matters d referred to in the subsection; rather, it pointed to the need for the court to consider the matters to which it referred specifically and separately from other relevant considerations. On the facts, however, it did not make any difference how the phrase was interpreted. There was no defence to the copyright claim with any reasonable prospect of success and no other compelling reason why that claim should go to trial. Accordingly, the application would be granted (see [14], e [20], [31], [32], [34], [35], [38], post).

Notes

For the right to freedom of expression and for the fair dealing and public interest defences to copyright infringement, see respectively 8(2) *Halsbury's Laws* (4th edn f reissue) paras 158–159 and 9(2) *Halsbury's Laws* (4th edn reissue) paras 338–339, 400.

For the Copyright, Designs and Patents Act 1988, ss 30, 171, see 11 *Halsbury's Statutes* (4th edn) (2000 reissue) 445, 557.

For the Human Rights Act 1998, s 12, Sch 1, Pt I, art 10, see 7 *Halsbury's Statutes* (4th edn) (1999 reissue) 510, 524.

g

Cases referred to in judgment

Condé Nast Publication Ltd v MGN Ltd [1998] FSR 427.

Fraser v Evans [1969] 1 All ER 8, [1969] 1 QB 349, [1968] 3 WLR 1172, CA.

Fressoz v France (1999) 5 BHRC 654, ECt HR.

h *Goodwin v UK* (1996) 22 EHRR 123, ECt HR.

Handyside v UK (1976) 1 EHRR 737, ECt HR.

Hubbard v Vosper [1972] 1 All ER 1023, [1972] 2 QB 84, [1972] 2 WLR 389, CA.

Hyde Park Residence Ltd v Yelland [2001] Ch 143, [2000] 3 WLR 215, CA.

Jersild v Denmark (1994) 19 EHRR 1, ECt HR.

j *Lion Laboratories Ltd v Evans* [1984] 2 All ER 417, [1985] QB 526, [1984] 3 WLR 539, CA.

Lithgow v UK (1986) 8 EHRR 329, ECt HR.

News Verlags GmbH v Austria (11 January 2000, unreported), ECt HR.

Pro Sieben Media AG v Carlton UK Television Ltd [1999] 1 WLR 605, [1999] FSR 610, CA.

Tennant (Lady Anne) v Associated Newspaper Group Ltd [1979] FSR 298.

Time Warner Entertainments Co LP v Channel Four Television Corp plc [1994] EMLR 1, CA.

Cases also cited or referred to in skeleton arguments

A-G v Guardian Newspapers Ltd (No 2) [1988] 3 All ER 545, [1990] 1 AC 109, Ch D, CA and HL.

Bladet Tromsø v Norway (1999) 29 EHRR 125, ECt HR.

Cala Homes (South) Ltd v Alfred McAlpine Homes East Ltd [1995] FSR 818.

Camelot Group plc v Centaur Communications Ltd [1998] 1 All ER 251, [1999] QB 124, CA.

Castells v Spain (1992) 14 EHRR 445, ECt HR.

De Geillustreerde Pers NV v Netherlands [1978] ECC 164, E Comm HR.

De Haes v Belgium (1997) 25 EHRR 1, ECt HR.

Designers Guild Ltd v Russell Williams (Textiles) Ltd [2001] 1 All ER 700, [2000] 1 WLR 2416, HL.

Express Newspapers plc v News (UK) Ltd [1990] 3 All ER 376, [1990] 1 WLR 1320.

Guerra v Italy (1998) 26 EHRR 357, ECt HR.

Hertel v Switzerland (1998) 28 EHRR 534, ECt HR.

Lenzing AG v UK [1999] EHRLR 132, E Comm HR.

Lingens v Austria (1986) 8 EHRR 407, ECt HR.

PCR Ltd v Dow Jones Telerate Ltd [1998] FSR 170.

R v DPP, ex p Kebeline [1999] 4 All ER 801, [2000] 2 AC 326, HL.

Secretary of State for Defence v Guardian Newspapers Ltd [1984] 3 All ER 601, [1985] AC 339, HL.

Service Corp International plc v Channel Four Television Corp [1999] EMLR 83.

Sunday Times v UK (1979) 2 EHRR 245, ECt HR.

Tolstoy Miloslavsky v UK (1995) 20 EHRR 442, ECt HR.

Wingrove v UK (1996) 24 EHRR 1, ECt HR.

Application for summary judgment

By application notice dated 30 June 2000 the claimant, the Rt Hon Jeremy John Durham Ashdown MP, applied under CPR Pt 24 for summary judgment on his claim for copyright infringement against the defendant, Telegraph Group Ltd, in respect of articles published in the Sunday Telegraph on 28 November 1999 which incorporated substantial sections of a confidential minute of a meeting dictated by the claimant. The facts are set out in the judgment.

Richard Spearman QC (instructed by *Bates Wells & Braithwaite*) for the claimant.
Andrew Nicol QC and *James Mellor* (instructed by *Olswang*) for the Sunday Telegraph.

Cur adv vult

11 January 2001. The following judgment was delivered.

SIR ANDREW MORRITT V-C.

[1] The claimant is a Member of Parliament and the former leader of the Liberal Democrats. It has been his practice for many years to keep diaries and other records of his experiences. He has always regarded those diaries and other records as confidential and has made it plain to those few people to whom they have been shown that they should treat them likewise. On 21 October 1997 the claimant went to 10 Downing Street for a meeting with the Prime Minister (Mr Blair), Mr Peter Mandelson, Lord Jenkins of Hillhead and Mr Jonathan Powell. Later the same day the claimant dictated a minute of that meeting (the minute). The minute was typed by his secretary and checked by the claimant. Two copies were made, one was added to the claimant's diaries and other records in his safe

a in his constituency, the other was read by a very small number of the claimant's closest advisers and then shredded.

[2] On 16 November 1999 BBC Radio 4 broadcast an interview with the claimant recorded earlier that month. He referred to his diaries and the possibility of publishing them. He referred to high-level discussions, both before and after the general election held on 2 May 1997, concerning a coalition cabinet b comprising members of the Labour Party and of the Liberal Democrats. Shortly after the interview the minute was disclosed to Mr Murphy, the political editor for the Sunday Telegraph, by, according to him, an individual—

> 'who did not work for either Paddy Ashdown or the Liberal Democrat party ... and felt that the public had been misled, that the secret [the coalition c cabinet proposal] had been kept for too long and that the record should be "set straight".'

Mr Murphy did not doubt the authenticity of the minute; he recognised that it was a secret record.

d [3] In its issue published on 28 November 1999 the Sunday Telegraph published articles written by Mr Murphy or Mr d'Ancona on pp 1, 4 and 5 and 33 respectively under the headlines: 'Revealed: Blair's secret plan to form coalition', 'Exclusive: how Blair prepared "The Full Monty" with Ashdown' and 'Mr Blair's "Full Monty" is revealed'. The articles incorporated substantial sections of the minute both in direct quotation and in paraphrase.

e [4] On 6 December 1999 the claimant started proceedings against the proprietor of the Sunday Telegraph seeking injunctions and damages or alternatively an account of profits for breach of confidence and infringement of copyright. A defence was served on 19 May 2000. On 30 June 2000 the claimant issued the application now before me for summary judgment under CPR Pt 24 in respect of his copyright claim only. He contends, in the words of CPR r 24.2(a)(ii) and (b), that f the Sunday Telegraph has 'no real prospect of successfully defending' that part of his claim and that 'there is no other compelling reason why' that part of his claim should be disposed of only at a trial.

[5] It is not disputed on this application that the minute is a copyright work and that the claimant is the owner of the copyright. Nor is it disputed that g substantial parts of the minute were copied in the issue of the Sunday Telegraph for Sunday 28 November 1999, in particular on pp 4 and 5. In its defence the Sunday Telegraph relies on the defences of fair dealing contained in s 30 of the Copyright, Designs and Patents Act 1988 and the rule of law preventing or restricting the enforcement of copyright on grounds of public interest, recognised h and preserved by s 171(3) of the 1988 Act. In addition the Sunday Telegraph relies on the provisions relating to freedom of expression contained in art 10 of the European Convention for the Protection of Human Rights and Fundamental Freedoms (Rome, 4 November 1950; TS 71 (1953); Cmd 8969) (the convention) now incorporated into the laws of the United Kingdom by the Human Rights Act 1998. The Sunday Telegraph also relies on s 12(4) of the latter Act and on other j matters said to constitute compelling reasons why the copyright claim should be disposed of at a trial.

[6] So far as I am aware and so far as the researches of counsel could ascertain there has been no previous reported case, in either the United Kingdom or in the European Court of Human Rights, in which the interaction between the right to freedom of expression conferred by art 10 and the property right conferred on the

owner of copyright, or any other intellectual property right, by the legislation of a state signatory to the convention has been considered. Moreover it appears to me that the issues which have arisen in this case in the context of copyright are likely also to arise in the context of all other intellectual property rights. It is appropriate, therefore, to consider the human rights aspect first. a

[7] Article 10 of the convention provides:

b

> '*Freedom of expression*
>
> 1. Everyone has the right to freedom of expression. This right shall include freedom to hold opinions and to receive and impart information and ideas without interference by public authority and regardless of frontiers. This Article shall not prevent States from requiring the licensing of broadcasting, television or cinema enterprises. c
>
> 2. The exercise of these freedoms, since it carries with it duties and responsibilities, may be subject to such formalities, conditions, restrictions or penalties as are prescribed by law and are necessary in a democratic society, in the interests of national security, territorial integrity or public safety, for the prevention of disorder or crime, for the protection of health or morals, d for the protection of the reputation or rights of others, for preventing the disclosure of information received in confidence, or for maintaining the authority and impartiality of the judiciary.'

[**8**] As para 2 provides, the exercise of the freedom of expression may be e 'subject to such … restrictions … as are prescribed by law and are necessary in a democratic society … for the protection of the … rights of others'. Obviously the 'rights of others' include those of the owner of a copyright. In addition art 1 of the First Protocol provides:

> '*Protection of property* f
>
> Every natural or legal person is entitled to the peaceful enjoyment of his possessions. No one shall be deprived of his possessions except in the public interest and subject to the conditions provided for by law and by the general principles of international law. The preceding provisions shall not, however, in any way impair the right of a State to enforce such laws as it deems g necessary to control the use of property in accordance with the general interest or to secure the payment of taxes or other contributions or penalties.'

Thus, in addition to his rights to the copyright, the owner thereof also has the right to its protection in accordance with art 1 to the First Protocol. h

[**9**] Section 1(1) of the 1998 Act defines 'the Convention rights' as meaning—

> 'the rights and fundamental freedoms set out in—(a) Articles 2 to 12 and 14 of the Convention, (b) Articles 1 to 3 of the First Protocol, and (c) Articles 1 and 2 of the Sixth Protocol, as read with Articles 16 to 18 of the Convention.' j

By virtue of s 2(1) of the 1998 Act a court determining a question which has arisen in connection with a convention right must take into account, inter alia, any judgment, decision, declaration or advisory opinion of the Court of Human Rights, whenever made or given, so far as, in the opinion of the court, it is relevant to the proceedings in which the question has arisen. Section 3(1) requires that:

a 'So far as it is possible to do so, primary legislation and subordinate legislation must be read and given effect in a way which is compatible with the Convention rights.'

By s 6(1) it is unlawful for a court to act in a way which is incompatible with a convention right unless obliged so to act by primary legislation. Section 7 enables a person who claims that a public authority, which includes a court, has acted in b a way made unlawful by s 6(1) to rely on the convention right or rights concerned in any legal proceedings if he is or would be a victim of the unlawful act.

[**10**] The Sunday Telegraph contends that it has a good defence to the copyright claim under ss 30 and 171(3) of the 1988 Act. It is not seeking to rely on art 10 as part of a claim pursuant to s 7 of the 1998 Act. It relies on art 10 in order to c influence either the interpretation or the application of those provisions as required by s 3(1). It submits that it is entitled to the right to freedom of expression provided for in art 10 and that the court can and should interpret and apply the provisions of the 1988 Act to give effect to it. The effect for which it contends is that the copying of the minute by the Sunday Telegraph would not constitute an infringement of copyright because what it did amounted to fair dealing with the d work within s 30 or was excused by the rule of law referred to in s 171(3).

[**11**] It is inherent in this argument that the right to freedom of expression for which art 10 provides entitles the Sunday Telegraph to deal with a copyright work in a manner not hitherto permitted by the 1988 Act. If that were not the case there would be no need to rely on the article. The Sunday Telegraph justifies e this contention by reference to the requirement in art 10(2) that the restriction on the exercise of the right to freedom of expression must be limited to that which is necessary in a democratic society. It submits that that limitation cannot be satisfied by the provisions of the legislation which imposes the restriction, that is, the 1988 Act. It contends that in every case all the individual facts must be considered to ascertain whether the restriction on the right to freedom of f expression imposed by the 1988 Act is necessary in a democratic society notwithstanding that the facts do not bring the case within any of the statutory exceptions or defences. In that connection it relies on the decisions of the Court of Human Rights in *Jersild v Denmark* (1994) 19 EHRR 1, *Goodwin v UK* (1996) 22 EHRR 123, *Fressoz v France* (1999) 5 BHRC 654 and *News Verlags GmbH v Austria* g (11 January 2000, unreported).

[**12**] I do not accept this argument. I was initially doubtful whether claims for copyright infringement involved the right to freedom of expression, as provided for by art 10, at all. Counsel for the claimant did not contend that art 10 was irrelevant to his claim for copyright infringement and on further reflection I am h satisfied that he was right not to do so. Copyright does not protect ideas, only the material form in which they are expressed. It is therefore a restriction on the right to freedom of expression to inhibit another from copying the method of expression used by the copyright owner even though there may be open to him a host of other methods of expression of the same idea. It must follow that intellectual property rights in general and copyright in particular constitute a restriction on j the exercise of the right to freedom of expression. Thus art 10 is engaged.

[**13**] It does not follow that because art 10 is engaged the facts of each case have to be considered to determine whether the restriction imposed by the law of copyright goes further than what is necessary in a democratic society. Article 10(2) recognises that the exercise of the right to freedom of expression carries with it duties and responsibilities. Thus restrictions on the exercise of the right are

permissible if they are (1) prescribed by law, (2) for the protection of rights of others and (3) are necessary in a democratic society. The Sunday Telegraph accepts that the provisions of the 1988 Act satisfy requirements (1) and (2). But inherent in the argument for the Sunday Telegraph is the submission that the provisions of the 1988 Act are incapable by themselves and without more of satisfying requirement (3). Indeed it was submitted in terms by counsel for the Sunday Telegraph that in every case the court should examine whether on the facts of that case it was necessary in a democratic society to provide for exceptions, exemptions and defences over and above those permitted by the legislation governing that species of intellectual property, however extensive they might be. If this is right then intellectual property litigation will burgeon out of control and the rights which the legislation apparently confers will be of no practical use except to those able and willing to litigate in all cases.

[14] I do not accept the submission. In my view the provisions of the Act alone can and do satisfy the third requirement of art 10(2) as well. The needs of a democratic society include the recognition and protection of private property. This is confirmed by the provisions of art 1 to the First Protocol. Such property includes copyright. As Aldous LJ observed in *Hyde Park Residence Ltd v Yelland* [2001] Ch 143 at 163, [2000] 3 WLR 215 at 232, para 55, the 1988 Act gives effect to the United Kingdom's obligations under the Berne Conventions of 1886 and 1971 (the Berne Convention of the International Union for the Protection of Literary and Artistic Works 1886, as revised at Paris on 24 July (Paris, 24 July 1971; TS 9 (1975); Cmnd 5844)) as well as pursuant to various EC Directives. Article 9 of the Berne Convention 1971 left it to the countries of the European Union thereby established to provide by their own domestic legislation for the circumstances in which a copyright work might be reproduced by others. The terms of s 30 of the 1988 Act were evidently intended to implement the latitude afforded by the Berne Convention 1971. Likewise the United Kingdom is entitled to a margin of appreciation in giving effect to the provisions of art 10 of the convention in the field of intellectual property: *Handyside v UK* (1976) 1 EHRR 737. I can see no reason why the provisions of the 1988 Act should not be sufficient to give effect to the convention right subject only to such restrictions as are permitted by art 10(2). (See generally Lucie Guibault 'Limitations found outside Copyright Law' in *Les Frontières du droit d'auteur* published by the Association Littéraire et Artistique Internationale in connection with the ALAI Study Days at Cambridge University from 14 to 17 September 1998.)

[15] It is unnecessary to describe the provisions of the 1988 Act in any detail. It is sufficient to note that in para 20.11 of Laddie, Prescott and Vitoria *The Modern Law of Copyright and Designs* (3rd edn, 2000) the authors identify 42 circumstances in which copying does not constitute an actionable infringement. Accordingly each of the 42 recognises and confirms the right to freedom of expression notwithstanding that copyright subsists in the work being copied. It is not suggested that the provisions of the 1988 Act are any more restrictive of the right of freedom of expression than those of the copyright legislation of all or most other democratic states. I can see no reason why the court should travel outside the provisions of the 1988 Act and recognise on the facts of particular cases further or other exceptions to the restrictions on the exercise of the right to freedom of expression constituted by the 1988 Act. Nor, in my view, do any of the decisions of the Court of Human Rights on which the Sunday Telegraph relied suggest otherwise.

a [16] In *Jersild v Denmark* (1994) 19 EHRR 1 the court was concerned with the conviction of a journalist for aiding and abetting the making of insulting remarks by the persons he interviewed for a TV programme. The court considered whether the conviction was necessary. It held that it was not, so that the conviction violated art 10. The court reiterated (at 25–26) that—

b '31. … freedom of expression constitutes one of the essential foundations of a democratic society and that the safeguards to be afforded to the press are of particular importance. Whilst the press must not overstep the bounds set, *inter alia*, in the interest of "the protection of the reputation and right of others", it is nevertheless incumbent on it to impart information and ideas of public interest. Not only does the press have the task of imparting such c information and ideas: the public also has a right to receive them. Were it otherwise, the press would be unable to play its vital role of "public watchdog". Although formulated primarily with regard to the print media, these principles doubtless apply also to the audio-visual media. In considering the "duties and responsibilities" of a journalist, the potential impact of the medium concerned is an important factor and it is commonly acknowledged d that the audio-visual media have often a much more immediate and powerful effect than the print media. The audio-visual media have means of conveying through images meanings which the print media are not able to impart. At the same time, the methods of objective and balanced reporting may vary considerably, depending among other things on the media in e question. It is not for this Court, nor for the national courts for that matter, to substitute their own views for those of the press as to what technique of reporting should be adopted by journalists. In this context the Court recalls that Article 10 protects not only the substance of the ideas and information expressed, but also the form in which they are conveyed.'

f I have quoted that passage at length because of the reliance placed on it by counsel for the Sunday Telegraph. It does not, in my view, suggest that it is impermissible when considering whether the restriction on the right to freedom of expression constituted by the law of copyright goes further than is necessary in a democratic society to have regard only to the terms of that legislation.

g [17] In *Goodwin v UK* (1996) 22 EHRR 123 the court was concerned with an order on a journalist to disclose his source. Such an order was permitted by s 10 of the Contempt of Court Act 1981 if it was in the interests of justice. The courts in England concluded that it was. The Court of Human Rights decided the order was, nevertheless, not necessary in a democratic society. The court said (at 143–144):

h

'40. As a matter of general principle, the "necessity" for any restriction on freedom of expression must be convincingly established. Admittedly, it is in the first place for the national authorities to assess whether there is a "pressing social need" for the restriction and, in making their assessment, they enjoy a certain margin of appreciation. In the present context, however, j the national margin of appreciation is circumscribed by the interest of democratic society in ensuring and maintaining a free press. Similarly, that interest will weigh heavily in the balance in determining as must be done under Article 10(2), whether the restriction was proportionate to the legitimate aim pursued. In sum, limitations on the confidentiality of journalistic sources call for the most careful scrutiny by the Court. The Court's task, in exercising its supervisory function, is not to take the place of the national authorities but rather to review under Article 10 the decisions they have taken pursuant to their power of appreciation. In so doing, the Court must look at the "interference" complained of in the light of the case as a whole and determine whether the reasons adduced by the national authorities to justify it are "relevant and sufficient".'

Again the court does not suggest that it cannot be enough when deciding whether the restriction is necessary in a democratic society to consider the terms of the legislation alone, more particularly where the legislation in question sets out the terms on which and the limitations subject to which a right of property subsists.

[18] *Fressoz v France* (1999) 5 BHRC 654 concerned the publication of details contained in an individual's tax return. The publisher was convicted of an offence. The court concluded that the conviction was in the unusual circumstances of that case an unnecessary restriction on the right to freedom of expression. The case was not concerned with any copyright issue. In *News Verlags GmbH v Austria* (11 January 2000, unreported) it was considered that the injunction restraining the publication of the photograph of a criminal constituted a violation of art 10. Again there was no copyright issue. Thus these cases did not touch on the problem either.

[19] Counsel for the claimant relied on the provisions of art 1 of the First Protocol. He suggested that if the principle was as wide as the Sunday Telegraph contended then the provisions of art 10 would be used to deprive a copyright owner of his possessions without compensation. In my view deprivation without compensation would not be involved. But in any event it is not the right conferred by art 1 of the First Protocol which is in point. The right with which I am concerned is the right of a copyright owner to prevent the copying of his work in all but the circumstances prescribed by the relevant legislation.

[20] If the Sunday Telegraph makes out the defences conferred or recognised by ss 30 and 171(3) of the 1988 Act then it does not need to rely on art 10. For the reasons I have sought to explain art 10 cannot be relied on to create defences to the alleged infringement over and above those for which the 1988 Act provides. The balance between the rights of the owner of the copyright and those of the public has been struck by the legislative organ of the democratic state itself in the legislation it has enacted. There is no room for any further defences outside the code which establishes the particular species of intellectual property in question. In particular it is not open to an infringer to defend the proceedings on the basis that although he cannot make out one or more of the statutory defences nevertheless the relief sought would be more than that which is necessary in a democratic society and therefore contrary to art 10(2).

[21] I turn then to the specific defences for which the 1988 Act provides and on which the Sunday Telegraph relies. The first is fair dealing. Section 30 is, so far as material, in these terms:

> '(1) Fair dealing with a work for the purpose of criticism or review, of that or another work or of a performance of a work, does not infringe any copyright in the work …
>
> (2) Fair dealing with a work (other than a photograph) for the purpose of reporting current events does not infringe any copyright in the work …'

The words omitted deal with the need for a sufficient acknowledgement. It is not disputed that there was one.

[**22**] The Sunday Telegraph relies on both limbs. I will deal with each of them in due course; but first it is necessary to describe the articles appearing on 28 November 1999 in more detail. Their general import is adequately described in the headlines I have already quoted. They set out in some detail what happened, as recorded in the minute, at the meeting on 21 October 1997. The quotations from the minute are substantial both in quantity and quality. The points made by the writers are: (1) the minute confirmed that the Prime Minister had seriously intended to form a coalition cabinet by the inclusion of two Liberal Democrat Members of Parliament in place of two cabinet ministers who were Labour Members of Parliament notwithstanding the large majority he enjoyed as the result of the election in May 1997; (2) the disclosure contradicted the denials emanating from 10 Downing Street; (3) the co-operation between the Prime Minister and the claimant went beyond discussing a coalition cabinet and extended to assisting the Liberal Democrats to win the by-election then pending in Winchester and the Liberal Democrats toning down their criticism of the government; (4) had the members of the Labour Party known how far the Prime Minister had gone in the formation of a coalition cabinet their opposition to voting reforms in the wake of the Jenkins Report would have been a full-scale revolt.

[**23**] With regard to s 30(1) the Sunday Telegraph contends in para 19 of its defence that:

> 'Further or in the alternative, the defendant published the extracts from the minutes for the purposes of criticism and review of the ideas, doctrine, philosophy and events in the minutes and their political implications. The defendant will refer to the contents of the articles and, in particular, the ideas, doctrine, philosophy and events reflected in paras 4, 14 and 18 above.'

Paragraph 4 refers to the speculation both before and after the general election concerning closer links between the Labour Party and the Liberal Democrats. Paragraph 14 refers to the degree of co-operation between the Prime Minister and the claimant as the then leader of the Liberal Democrats. Paragraph 18 covers much the same ground as paras 4 and 14 but includes the role and accuracy of the information derived from the Prime Minister's press office.

[**24**] I accept, of course, that the expression 'criticism and review' is of wide import (cf *Pro Sieben Media AG v Carlton UK Television Ltd* [1999] 1 WLR 605 at 614 per Robert Walker LJ). Likewise I accept that it is necessary to have regard to the true purpose of the work. Is it—

> 'a genuine piece of criticism and review or is it something else, such as an attempt to dress up the infringement of another's copyright in the guise of criticism, and so profit unfairly from another's work'—

(cf *Time Warner Entertainments Co LP v Channel Four Television Corp plc* [1994] EMLR 1 at 14 per Henry LJ). But what is required is that the copying shall take place as part of and for the purpose of criticising and reviewing the work. The work is the minute. But the articles are not criticising or reviewing the minute; they are criticising or reviewing the actions of the Prime Minister and the claimant in October 1997. It was not necessary for that purpose to copy the minute at all. In my judgment the articles do not come within s 30(1) because the purpose of copying the work was not its criticism or review.

a

[25] In relation to s 30(2) the Sunday Telegraph contends that the copying of the minute was for the purpose of reporting current events. In para 18 it alleges that the current events were:

> '18.1 the continuing issue over the degree and nature of actual and planned co-operation between Labour and the Liberal Democrats, and the related matter of the ability of the Liberal Democrats to influence government;
>
> 18.2 in particular, the extent to which the Prime Minister was interested in securing co-operation from the Liberal Democrats and his willingness to contemplate the removal of two Labour cabinet ministers to make way for two Liberal Democrat appointees, notwithstanding the size of the Labour majority;
>
> 18.3 the comments issued by "Downing Street" responding directly to the detailed and specific comments made by the claimant in his interview "Resigning Issues", and the related continuing saga over the role of and accuracy of information disseminated by the Prime Minister's press office;
>
> 18.4 the meeting on 21 October 1997;
>
> 18.5 the continuing issue of the way in which Tony Blair operated, independent of his cabinet and his party, and what influenced his actions ...'

b

c

d

For the claimant counsel submitted that the matters referred to in paras 18.1, 18.2, 18.3 and 18.5 were not events at all. He also submitted that they and the event specified in para 18.4 were not current. Whilst I accept that there is force in the arguments I do not accept that the Sunday Telegraph has no reasonable prospect of establishing the contrary. But assuming that it can it must also demonstrate that its copying did, in the circumstances, amount to 'fair dealing'. In this respect the Sunday Telegraph contends in para 20 of its defence that—

e

f

> 'the defendant's dealing was fair because:
>
> 20.1 in publishing the articles, the defendant was raising matters of legitimate political controversy which in no or no appreciable way competed or will compete with any publication or publications which the claimant might issue in the future;
>
> 20.2 the claimant himself had already revealed some details of the matters covered in the articles in his interview for "Resigning Issues";
>
> 20.3 it was done to promote public knowledge and public discussion of the actions and intentions of those responsible for governing the country;
>
> 20.4 the extracts from the minutes which were included in the articles were reasonably necessary and appropriate to include in the articles for the purposes for which they were written;
>
> 20.5 publication was in the public interest, as set out above.'

g

h

[26] It is well recognised that the issue of 'fair dealing' is one of fact, degree and impression (see *Hubbard v Vosper* [1972] 1 All ER 1023, [1972] 2 QB 84). Accordingly it is contended on behalf of the Sunday Telegraph that such an issue can only be resolved at a trial. For the claimant it is submitted that the relevant facts are not in dispute and that it is clear that the Sunday Telegraph does not have a reasonable prospect of establishing the necessary element of fair dealing. Reliance is placed on para 20.16 of Laddie, Prescott and Vitoria *The Modern Law of Copyright and Designs* (3rd edn, 2000). In that paragraph the authors suggest that

j

a the success or failure of the defence depends on three factors: (1) whether the alleged fair dealing is in commercial competition with the owner's exploitation of the work, (2) whether the work has already been published or otherwise exposed to the public and (3) the amount and importance of the work which has been taken.

[27] In my view each of those factors, which I accept to be the most important b ones, points strongly to a conclusion that what the Sunday Telegraph did was not fair dealing. First, it is clear that the publication by the Sunday Telegraph competed with that which the claimant might otherwise have effected. There is clear evidence that the consideration which the claimant subsequently obtained for the exploitation of his copyright in the minute as part of his diary was substantially reduced because of the publication of the articles by the Sunday c Telegraph. No doubt there would be cross-examination of the witness from The Times on whether it was the copying of the minute or the disclosure of the information it contained which caused the reduction in the price it was prepared to pay. But that would not diminish the evident commercial competition which exists between publication in the Sunday Telegraph and in any other newspaper d the claimant might have chosen. The assertion in the last part of para 20.1 of the defence is wrong.

[28] Second, there is no doubt that the minute had not previously been published nor exposed to the public. The claimant had taken great care to limit the number of people who read it and to impose on them obligations of secrecy. e Moreover the Sunday Telegraph knew not only that the minute had not been published, indeed Mr Murphy described it as secret, but that, as the claimant revealed on the 'Resigning Issues' interview, he was thinking of doing so in the not so distant future. It is not the case that during the interview for 'Resigning Issues' the claimant had already disclosed the important matters covered in the articles. Had he done so the Sunday Telegraph could not credibly have used the f headlines it did. The assertion in para 20.2 is unsustainable.

[29] I have not seen an unredacted copy of the minute. Accordingly I am unable to ascertain the importance of the parts of the minute which were not copied by the Sunday Telegraph. But I am able to see that what was copied was a substantial proportion of the minute as a whole and it has not been submitted g on behalf of the Sunday Telegraph, whose advisers have seen the whole minute, that the unpublished part contained significant further information. The assertion made in para 20.4 appears to me to be beside the point.

[30] For the Sunday Telegraph much emphasis is put on the facts that no money was paid by them for the minute, that the individual who supplied it to h them was not improperly motivated and that the disclosure of the minute was a 'political leak' of considerable political significance. In my view none of these points, asserted in one form or another in paras 20.1 and 20.3, converts what I consider to have been unfair dealing into fair dealing. It is not suggested that the claimant was in any way responsible for the leak. It was plain to the Sunday Telegraph that the minute was secret and had come into their possession without j the knowledge or approval of the claimant. The facts that the supplier was not motivated by money, did not receive any and that such 'political leaks' are not infrequent are not in my judgment sufficient to justify the description of the Sunday Telegraph's dealing with the minute as fair.

[31] For all these reasons I conclude that the fair dealing defence has no reasonable prospect of success and is not a reason for refusing the summary

judgment the claimant seeks. My conclusion in this respect is consistent with the decision of the Court of Appeal in *Hyde Park Residence Ltd v Yelland* [2001] Ch 143, [2000] 3 WLR 215. In that case the Court of Appeal also dealt with the other defence on which the Sunday Telegraph seeks to rely in this case, namely that recognised and preserved by s 171(3) of the 1988 Act. That subsection provides that 'Nothing in this Part affects any rule of law preventing or restricting the enforcement of copyright, on grounds of public interest or otherwise.' The majority of the Court of Appeal concluded, in the words of Aldous LJ, that:

> '66. The circumstances where it is against the policy of the law to use the court's procedure to enforce copyright are, I suspect, not capable of definition. However it must be remembered that copyright is assignable and therefore the circumstances must derive from the work in question, not ownership of the copyright. In my view a court would be entitled to refuse to enforce copyright if the work is: (i) immoral, scandalous or contrary to family life; (ii) injurious to public life, public health and safety or the administration of justice; (iii) incites or encourages others to act in a way referred to in (ii).' (See [2001] Ch 143 at 168, [2000] 3 WLR 215 at 236.)

[**32**] Plainly the case for the Sunday Telegraph does not come within that principle. It submits that as the decision of the Court of Appeal was given on 10 February 2000, before the 1998 Act came into force, it is not binding on me if I come to the conclusion that the right to freedom of expression is one which comes within the rule of law preserved by s 171(3). In that connection the Sunday Telegraph relies on the statement of the responsible minister made in the House of Lords when what is now s 171(3) was first introduced. But all that the Minister, Lord Beaverbrook, said was that the purpose of s 171(3) was to continue the effect of the existing case law without attempting to codify it (see 495 HL Official Report (5th series) col 632). Such a statement is unhelpful when the question is what was that effect. The decision of the Court of Appeal concluded that the effect of the existing case law was as set out in para 66 which I have already quoted. As I have already held the 1998 Act is not a reason for interpreting the 1988 Act any differently. It follows that the decision of the Court of Appeal on the scope of s 171(3) is binding on me. Accordingly I conclude that s 171(3) does not afford any defence to the copyright claim either.

[**33**] I turn then to the other factors relied on by the Sunday Telegraph. The first is s 12 of the 1998 Act. It provides, so far as relevant:

> '(1) This section applies if a court is considering whether to grant any relief which, if granted, might affect the exercise of the Convention right to freedom of expression …
>
> (4) The court must have particular regard to the importance of the Convention right to freedom of expression and, where the proceedings relate to material which the respondent claims, or which appears to the court, to be journalistic, literary or artistic material (or to conduct connected with such material), to—(a) the extent to which—(i) the material has, or is about to, become available to the public; or (ii) it is, or would be, in the public interest for the material to be published; (b) any relevant privacy code.'

The relief sought, namely injunctions and damages or an account of profits, would affect the exercise of the convention right to freedom of expression. Similarly the proceedings relate to material, the articles of 28 November 1999, or conduct connected with it of a journalistic nature. Accordingly the whole of sub-s (4) applies.

[34] It was submitted that the phrase 'must have particular regard to' indicates that the court should place extra weight on the matters to which the subsection refers. I do not so read it. Rather it points to the need for the court to consider the matters to which the subsection refers specifically and separately from other relevant considerations. On the facts of this case I do not think that it makes any difference how the phrase is interpreted.

[35] There is no doubt that the information contained in the minute, so far as revealed in the articles, has become available to the public. It may be that its publication was in the public interest. I make no finding either way on that point lest it be thought to prejudice any subsequent trial on the breach of confidence issue. But the injunction to restrain breach of copyright will not inhibit the Sunday Telegraph from using the information. It will and should restrain the further copying of the minute. In so far as the injunction will restrain the copying of the unpublished parts of the minute I am unable to form a view as to whether that material is likely to become public knowledge nor whether it would be in the public interest that it should because the unredacted minute was not put in evidence by either party. Accordingly s 12 does not provide any reason to withhold any of the relief to which the claimant would be entitled if summary judgment were given in his favour.

[36] Another factor relied on is that the claim based on breach of confidence is to proceed to trial in the normal way. It was suggested that this was a compelling reason why the copyright claim should go to trial too. It was submitted that it might prejudice the defence of the Sunday Telegraph to the breach of confidence claim if it was already subject to judgment on the copyright claim. I do not think that this provides any reason, compelling or otherwise, to withhold summary judgment on the copyright claim. Such a judgment would prevent further copying and provide redress for that which has already taken place. Subject to the breach of confidence claim the Sunday Telegraph is entitled to use the information contained in the minute provided that it does not copy it or any substantial part of it.

[37] Finally it was submitted that it was inconvenient to give summary judgment on the copyright claim at this stage because it might give rise to increased costs and the danger of inconsistent judgments if the same person did not hear the breach of confidence claim and the inquiry directed by para 6(A)(2) of the judgment on the copyright claim now sought, namely, whether the claimant was entitled to what, if any, additional damages pursuant to s 97(2) of the 1988 Act. I was referred to *Lady Anne Tennant v Associated Newspaper Group Ltd* [1979] FSR 298 and *Condé Nast Publication Ltd v MGN Ltd* [1998] FSR 427 for statements as to the normal practice to be followed. But if the claimant is entitled to summary judgment on his copyright claim because there is no defence with any reasonable prospect of success then he should not be denied it on grounds of convenience said to arise from the practice of the court. In any event I can see no problem; there would be nothing to prevent the judge trying the breach of confidence claim hearing this inquiry as well and on the same evidence. If that is the most convenient course then directions to that effect can be given. The need to deal with the copyright inquiry in a cost and time-effective way is not a reason, compelling or otherwise, why the copyright claim should go to trial.

[38] For all these reasons, in my judgment, there is no defence to the copyright claim with any reasonable prospect of success and no other compelling reason why the copyright claim should go to trial. Subject to any argument as to the form of relief sought I will make an order in the terms of the minute submitted with this application.

Order accordingly.

Celia Fox Barrister.

a

Imutran Ltd v Uncaged Campaigns Ltd and another

CHANCERY DIVISION

SIR ANDREW MORRITT V-C

b

18 OCTOBER, 14, 18 DECEMBER 2000, 11 JANUARY 2001

Injunction – Interlocutory – Principle governing grant – Right to freedom of expression – Approach to be adopted on application for interim injunction engaging convention right to freedom of expression – Human Rights Act 1998, s 12, Sch 1, Pt I, art 10.

c

The claimant, I Ltd, was engaged in research into xenotransplantation—the replacement of human organs with those of animals, usually pigs. Such research, which necessarily involved experimental work on animals, was opposed by UCL, a body whose aim was to campaign democratically and peacefully for the d cessation of animal experimentation. UCL received, from an unknown source, copies of documents belonging to I Ltd. Although L, a director of UCL, realised that the documents were confidential, he used the information they contained, and quoted extensively from them, in writing an account of pig-to-primate organ transplants. In subsequent proceedings, I Ltd obtained interim injunctions restraining UCL and L from infringing its copyright in the documents and from using or e disclosing information contained in, or derived from, confidential documents. The supply of documents or information to the statutory regulatory authorities was exempted from that prohibition. On an application by I Ltd to have the injunctions continued until trial or further order, the court considered the proper approach to an application for an interim injunction which engaged the right to f freedom of expression in art 10[a] of the European Convention for the Protection of Human Rights and Fundamental Freedoms 1950 (as set out in Sch 1 to the Human Rights Act 1998)—a right that was subject, by virtue of art 10(2), to such restrictions as were necessary in a democratic society for, inter alia, the protection of the rights of others and preventing the disclosure of information received in confidence. That issue required the court to consider s 12[b] of the 1998 Act which g applied when the court was considering whether to grant any relief which, if granted, might affect the exercise of the convention right to freedom of expression. Under s 12(3), no such relief could be granted so as to restrain publication before trial unless the court was satisfied that the applicant was 'likely to establish' that publication should not be allowed, while s 12(4) required the court to have h 'particular regard' to the importance of the convention right to freedom of expression. The defendants contended that s 12(3) imposed a higher standard than the established threshold test for the grant of an interim injunction, namely whether there was a serious question to be tried or the applicant had a real prospect of succeeding at trial in a claim to a permanent injunction. The issue also arose as to whether s 12(4) required the court to place special and extra j weight on the convention right to freedom of expression.

Held – Although, theoretically and as a matter of language, likelihood was slightly higher in the scale of probability than a real prospect of success, the

a Article 10 is set out at [21], post

b Section 12, so far as material, is set out at [16], post

difference between the two was so small that there would not be many (if any) cases which would have succeeded under the established test but would now fail because of the terms of s 12(3) of the 1998 Act. Accordingly, in the instant case, the test of likelihood would be applied without any further consideration of how much more probable that now had to be. As regards s 12(4), it had to be borne in mind that the courts had emphasised the importance of freedom of expression or speech long before the enactment of the 1998 Act. However, neither the previous authorities nor s 12(4) required the court to treat freedom of speech as paramount. There were many reported cases in which the court had had to balance freedom of expression or speech with other aspects of the public interest. Section 12(4) was not intended to direct the court to place even greater weight on the importance of freedom of expression than it already did. The requirement to pay 'particular regard' merely contemplated specific and separate consideration being given to that factor. In the instant case, I Ltd was likely to establish at the trial of the action that publication of its confidential documents should not be allowed. Moreover, the injunction to restrain breach of confidence did not go further than was necessary in a democratic society, bearing in mind that it did not restrict the ability of the defendants to communicate the information to those specialists connected with the regulatory bodies denoted by Parliament as having responsibility in the field. The balance of convenience also favoured the grant of the injunction sought. Similarly, I Ltd was likely to establish that publication by reproduction should not be allowed, and there was no reason why injunctive or other relief should be refused in respect of the claim for infringement of copyright. Accordingly, the application would be granted (see [17]–[19], [26], [27], [33], [35], [46], post).

Ashdown v Telegraph Group Ltd [2001] 2 All ER 370 applied.

Notes

For the right to freedom of expression and for interlocutory injunctions, see respectively 8(2) *Halsbury's Laws* (4th edn reissue) paras 158–159 and 24 *Halsbury's Laws* (4th edn reissue) paras 853–856.

For the Human Rights Act 1998, s 12, Sch 1, Pt I, art 10, see 7 *Halsbury's Statutes* (4th edn) (1999 reissue) 510, 524.

Cases referred to in judgment

A-G v Guardian Newspapers Ltd (No 2) [1988] 3 All ER 545, [1990] 1 AC 109, [1988] 3 WLR 776, HL.

A-G v Shayler (4 September 1997, unreported), QBD.

American Cyanamid Co v Ethicon Ltd [1975] 1 All ER 504, [1975] AC 396, [1975] 2 WLR 316, HL.

Ashdown v Telegraph Group Ltd [2001] 2 All ER 370, [2001] 2 WLR 967.

Company's application, Re a [1989] 2 All ER 248, [1989] Ch 477, [1989] 3 WLR 265.

Douglas v Hello! Ltd [2001] 2 All ER 289, [2001] 2 WLR 992, CA.

Francome v Mirror Group Newspapers Ltd [1984] 2 All ER 408, [1984] 1 WLR 892, CA.

Hubbard v Vosper [1972] 1 All ER 1023, [1972] 2 QB 84, [1972] 2 WLR 389, CA.

Hyde Park Residence Ltd v Yelland [2000] IP & T 412, [2001] Ch 143, [2000] 3 WLR 215, CA.

Initial Services Ltd v Putterill [1967] 3 All ER 145, [1968] 1 QB 396, [1967] 3 WLR 1032, CA.

Lion Laboratories Ltd v Evans [1984] 2 All ER 417, [1985] QB 526, [1984] 3 WLR 539, CA.

Morton-Norwich Products Inc v Intercen Ltd [1981] FSR 337.

NWL Ltd v Woods [1979] 3 All ER 614, [1979] 1 WLR 1294, HL.

Cases also cited or referred to in skeleton arguments

a *A-G v Newspaper Publishing plc* [1987] 3 All ER 276, [1988] Ch 333, CA.
A-G v Times Newspapers Ltd [1991] 2 All ER 398, [1992] 1 AC 191, HL.
Cambridge Nutrition Ltd v British Broadcasting Corp [1990] 3 All ER 523, CA.
Distillers Co (Biochemicals) Ltd v Times Newspapers Ltd, Distillers Co (Biochemicals) Ltd v Phillips [1975] 1 All ER 41, [1975] QB 613.
b *Galaxia Maritime SA v Mineralimportexport, The Eleftherios* [1982] 1 All ER 796, [1982] 1 WLR 539, CA.
Kelly v BBC [2001] 1 All ER 323, [2001] 2 WLR 253.
McCartan Turkington Breen (a firm) v Times Newspapers Ltd [2000] 4 All ER 913, [2000] 3 WLR 1670, HL.
c *Microdata Information Services Ltd v Rivendale Ltd* [1991] FSR 681, CA.
Nicholls v BBC [1999] EMLR 791, CA.
Niemietz v Germany (1992) 16 EHRR 97, ECt HR.
Norwich Pharmacal Co v Customs and Excise Comrs [1973] 2 All ER 943, [1974] AC 133, HL.
PCR Ltd v Dow Jones Telerate Ltd [1998] FSR 170.
d *R v Chief Constable of the North Wales Police, ex p AB* [1998] 3 All ER 310, [1999] QB 396, CA.
R v Secretary of State for the Home Dept, ex p Simms [1999] 3 All ER 400, [2000] 2 AC 115, HL.
RCA Corp v Reddingtons Rare Records [1975] 1 All ER 38, [1974] 1 WLR 1445.
e *Service Corp International v Channel Four Television Corp* [1999] EMLR 83.
Shetland Times Ltd v Wills [1997] FSR 604.
Z Ltd v A [1982] 1 All ER 556, [1982] QB 558, CA.

Applications

f The claimant, Imutran Ltd, applied for the continuation until trial or further order of interim injunctions granted by Hart J on 26 September 2000 and modified by Ferris J on 10 October 2000 restraining the defendants, Uncaged Campaigns Ltd and Daniel Louis Lyons, from misusing confidential information of Imutran and infringing its copyright in certain documents. The Royal Society for the Prevention of Cruelty to Animals (RSPCA) applied for an order requiring g Imutran to pay the costs incurred by them in obtaining the modifications to Park J's order. The facts are set out in the judgment.

Mark Warby (instructed by *Eversheds*) for Imutran.
David Bean QC (instructed by *Simons Muirhead & Burton*) for the defendants.
h *Michael Tugendhat QC* (instructed by *Olswang*) for the RSPCA.

Cur adv vult

11 January 2001. The following judgment was delivered.

j **SIR ANDREW MORRITT V-C.**

[1] This is an application by the claimant, Imutran Ltd (Imutran), for injunctions until trial or further order restraining the defendants, Uncaged Campaigns Ltd (UCL) and Mr Lyons, from misusing confidential information of Imutran or from infringing the copyright of Imutran. An interim injunction was granted by Hart J on 26 September 2000. That injunction was continued, but in modified terms, by Ferris J on 10 October 2000. Also before me is an application

by the Royal Society for the Prevention of Cruelty to Animals (RSPCA) for an order that its costs of obtaining such modification should be paid by Imutran.

[**2**] Imutran is the wholly-owned subsidiary of Novartis Pharma AG, a Swiss-owned international pharmaceutical company. It was engaged in research into xenotransplantation, that is to say the replacement of human organs with those of animals, usually pigs. Most of such research was carried out at Huntingdon Life Sciences. On 26 September 2000 Novartis Pharma AG announced that such research would, with effect from 1 January 2001, be carried on by a joint venture company in Boston, Massachusetts, USA to which the intellectual property rights and know-how of Imutran would be transferred.

[**3**] Research into xenotransplantation necessarily involves experimental work on animals. As such it is regulated by the Animals (Scientific Procedures) Act 1986. That Act provides for the licensing of personnel (s 4), projects (s 5) and scientific establishments (s 6) without which the carrying out of prescribed procedures is unlawful (s 3). The 1986 Act also provides for the appointment by the Home Secretary of inspectors with medical or veterinary qualifications (s 18) and an advisory committee called the Animal Procedures Committee (s 19). The duties of the inspectors include advising the Home Secretary on the grant of the various licences, checking on licensed projects and scientific establishments and reporting to him on any cases where the conditions imposed on the grant of a licence have not been performed or observed (s 18(2)). The functions of the Animal Procedures Committee include advising the Home Secretary on such matters concerned with the 1986 Act as they may determine (s 20(1)). The duties imposed on the Home Secretary by the 1986 Act include the duty, when considering an application for a project licence, to weigh the likely adverse effects on the animals concerned against the benefit likely to accrue as a result of the proposed project (s 5(4)).

[**4**] In addition to the regime prescribed by the 1986 Act there is the United Kingdom Xenotransplantation Interim Regulatory Authority (UKXIRA) and the Good Laboratory Practice Monitoring Authority (GLPMA). The former was set up following the report *Animal Tissue into Humans* of the advisory group under the chairmanship of Professor Ian Kennedy on the ethics of xenotransplantation. Its terms of reference include advising the Secretary of State for Health generally and on the safety and efficacy of xenotransplantation and considerations of animal welfare involved in it in particular. GLPMA is a constituent body of the Department of Health which administers the Good Laboratory Practice Regulations. They are designed to ensure that experimental data provided by scientific establishments to regulatory bodies are reliable.

[**5**] In 1993 Mr Lyons obtained from Sheffield University an honours degree in politics and philosophy. He is currently a part-time student for a PhD in the subject area of the ethical and political theory implications of xenotransplantation. He is a director of UCL which is a company limited by guarantee the aim of which is to campaign democratically and peacefully for a cessation of animal experimentation and for an end to violence towards animals generally. In 1996 UCL launched a campaign against xenotransplantation in pursuit of which Mr Lyons has submitted papers to the Secretary of State for Health and others, has attended meetings with ministers and the various regulatory bodies I have mentioned and has organised petitions to be submitted to the Secretary of State. The honesty of Mr Lyons' belief and purpose has not been challenged in these proceedings. The evidence shows that many others share his views. Whether as a result of the defendants' activities or otherwise on 17 July 2000 the House of

a Lords set up an ad hoc select committee to inquire into the use of animals in scientific experiments.

[6] In the spring of 2000 UCL received a package and a CD-ROM containing copies of a large number of documents belonging to Imutran. Mr Lyons does not know who sent them. But, on examination, Mr Lyons quickly realised that the documents emanated from Imutran and mainly concerned its programme of b primate xenotransplantation being conducted at Huntingdon Life Sciences. Over the following months Mr Lyons studied these documents and sought to reconcile them with other documents or information already available to the public. He considered that the documents raised extremely serious questions concerning animal welfare, the regulation of research by the Home Office, the standards of good laboratory practice achieved during the research, its lack of success and the c accuracy of the information on xenotransplantation conveyed by Imutran. He also appreciated that the documents UCL had received from the unknown source were confidential.

[7] Basing himself on all these documents Mr Lyons wrote *Diaries of Despair: The Secret History of Pig-to-Primate Organ Transplants*. It consists of 157 pages using the d information contained in or quoting from Imutran's documents obtained from the unknown source. Those documents are described as 'a staggering haul of secret documents', 'confidential documents' and 'leaked internal company documents'.

[8] The documents fall into five categories. They are: (1) 39 laboratory reports, covering 3,400 pages, of scientific tests conducted by Huntingdon Life Sciences on behalf of Imutran; (2) minutes of meetings between representatives of e Imutran and Novartis at which developments were reviewed and in which are set out the names of certain employees of Imutran; (3) correspondence with Imutran's research partners; (4) correspondence with Imutran's suppliers; and (5) correspondence with the Home Office and the Ministry of Agriculture, Fisheries and Food. The five classes of document have been analysed by Imutran f as containing confidential information falling into seven specified categories. I did not understand UCL or Mr Lyons to challenge either the classes of document or the analysis of the confidential information.

[9] On 19 September 2000 a journalist with the Daily Express faxed to Imutran three specific questions concerning its programme of xenotransplantation to which Imutran replied. On 21 and 22 September articles appeared in the Daily g Express commenting adversely on Imutran's programme. They were based on the *Diaries of Despair*. On 21 September Imutran learned that the *Diaries of Despair* and most of its documents in the possession of UCL had been published by UCL on its website. That and other websites were closed down by the relevant service providers on 22 September and subsequent days.

h [10] As I have already indicated Hart J made an interim order on 26 September. He had heard counsel for Imutran and the solicitor for UCL and Mr Lyons. The injunctions over 10 October restrained UCL and Mr Lyons from infringing Imutran's copyright in its documents and from using or disclosing information contained in or derived from specified confidential documents. But the provisos attached to the injunctions excepted from the prohibitions (1) the supply of j documents or information to UKXIRA, ministers at the Home Office or personnel at the Home Office having responsibility for regulating or supervising animal experimentation, or (2) the further use or disclosure of information contained in either of the articles appearing in the Daily Express published on 21 or 22 September 2000.

[11] When the order was continued by Ferris J on 10 October 2000 the first proviso was extended to members of the Animals Procedures Committee and

GLPMA and a further proviso was added permitting reproduction, use or disclosure by the RSPCA in accordance with the terms of schedule 5 to the order. With regard to the costs of the RSPCA both the RSPCA and Imutran were given liberty to apply.

[12] The application first came before me on 18 October 2000. The night before the solicitors for UCL and Mr Lyons had indicated that their clients would be prepared to limit their future publications to *Diaries of Despair* and 56 other specified pages. On the application of Imutran I adjourned the hearing of the application and ordered the return of all the other documents by UCL to Imutran. In addition I ordered Imutran to provide to UCL and Mr Lyons details of its objections to the publication of the remainder; UCL and Mr Lyons were to respond in writing to those objections. The defendants returned the requisite documents and Imutran provided details of its objections. But the defendants considered that the objections were so extensive as to make further discussion futile. Accordingly with the exception of the names and addresses of employees the defendants seek to publish and Imutran seeks to prevent the publication of all the documents provided to the defendants from the unknown source. They include all those previously published on the internet and others.

[13] In consequence of the provisos to the various orders all the relevant documents have been provided to all interested regulatory authorities. The RSPCA has called for a report on the situation revealed by the documents of Imutran from Dr Jennings, the head of its animal research department. GLPMA received and considered a copy of *Diaries of Despair*. The Home Secretary has asked the chief inspector to examine the compliance by Imutran with the conditions imposed on the grant of the various licences needed under the 1986 Act. He expects to receive the chief inspector's findings and advice in the new year. All such reports and findings will be available to the House of Lords select committee to which I referred earlier.

[14] As I have indicated the causes of action on which Imutran relies are (1) breach of confidence, and (2) infringement of copyright. Relevant to both those issues is the question (3) what is the proper approach of the court to an application for interim injunctions such as this in which the right to freedom of expression guaranteed by art 10 of the European Convention for the Protection of Human Rights and Fundamental Freedoms (Rome, 4 November 1950; TS 71 (1953); Cmd 8969) (as set out in Sch 1 to the Human Rights Act 1998) (the convention) is material. This depends on the proper construction and application of s 12 of the 1998 Act. It is convenient to deal with this issue first.

[15] Until the decision of the House of Lords in *American Cyanamid Co v Ethicon Ltd* [1975] 1 All ER 504, [1975] AC 396 it was generally considered that an applicant for interlocutory relief had to show a strong prima facie case (cf *Hubbard v Vosper* [1972] 1 All ER 1023 at 1029, [1972] 2 QB 84 at 96). In the *American Cyanamid* case the House of Lords substituted for the strong prima facie case the concept of 'a serious question to be tried' or 'a real prospect of succeeding in his claim to a permanent injunction at the trial'. That threshold test is amplified in cases in which the grant or refusal of an interim injunction would have the practical effect of putting an end to the action. In such a case the strength or otherwise of the claimant's case (in excess of the threshold of a serious question to be tried) must be brought into the balance in weighing the risk of injustice to either party by the grant or refusal of the injunction sought (see *NWL Ltd v Woods* [1979] 3 All ER 614, [1979] 1 WLR 1294). It is against that background that s 12 of the 1998 Act must be considered.

a [16] So far as material s 12 of the 1998 Act provides:

> '(1) This section applies if a court is considering whether to grant any relief which, if granted, might affect the exercise of the Convention right to freedom of expression ...
>
> (3) No such relief is to be granted so as to restrain publication before trial unless the court is satisfied that the applicant is likely to establish that b publication should not be allowed.
>
> (4) The court must have particular regard to the importance of the Convention right to freedom of expression ...'

Two issues were raised before me. The first is whether the requirement in c sub-s (3) of s 12 that the applicant 'is likely to establish' at the trial that publication should not be allowed alters the threshold test established by the *American Cyanamid* case in relation to cases to which s 12 applies. The second is whether the provisions of sub-s (4) of s 12 require the court to place special and extra weight on the convention right to freedom of expression. I will deal with them in turn.

d [17] Counsel for the defendants submitted that the requirement of likelihood imposed a higher standard than that formulated in the *American Cyanamid* case. I did not understand this to be disputed by counsel for Imutran. He submitted that whatever the standard was his case satisfied it. Theoretically and as a matter of language likelihood is slightly higher in the scale of probability than a real e prospect of success. But the difference between the two is so small that I cannot believe that there will be many (if any) cases which would have succeeded under the *American Cyanamid* test but will now fail because of the terms of s 12(3) of the 1998 Act. Accordingly I propose to apply the test of likelihood without any further consideration of how much more probable that now has to be. See *Douglas v Hello! Ltd* [2001] 2 All ER 289 at 302, 323, 327, [2001] 2 WLR 992 at 1007, f 1028, 1033 (paras 54, 136, 153).

[18] In the case of sub-s (4) it must be borne in mind that the courts emphasised the importance of freedom of expression or speech long before the enactment of the 1998 Act. See 8(2) *Halsbury's Laws* (4th edn reissue) para 107 and cases there cited. But neither those cases nor the provisions of s 12(4) of the 1998 g Act require the court to treat freedom of speech as paramount. There are many reported cases in which the court has had to balance freedom of expression or speech with other aspects of the public interest. See also *Snell's Equity* (30th edn, 2000) para 45-75.

[19] In those circumstances I do not consider that the subsection is intended h to direct the court to place even greater weight on the importance of freedom of expression than it already does. As I said in *Ashdown v Telegraph Group Ltd* [2001] 2 All ER 370 at [34], [2001] 2 WLR 967 the requirement 'to pay particular regard' contemplates specific and separate consideration being given to this factor.

[20] I turn then to the claim for breach of confidence. I have been referred to j the well-known line of cases consisting of *Initial Services Ltd v Putterill* [1967] 3 All ER 145, [1968] 1 QB 396, *Hubbard v Vosper* [1972] 1 All ER 1023, [1972] 2 QB 84, *Francome v Mirror Group Newspapers Ltd* [1984] 2 All ER 408, [1984] 1 WLR 892, *Lion Laboratories Ltd v Evans* [1984] 2 All ER 417, [1985] QB 526, *Re a Company's application* [1989] 2 All ER 248, [1989] Ch 477 and *A-G v Guardian Newspapers Ltd (No 2)* [1988] 3 All ER 545, [1990] 1 AC 109. Each of them demonstrates that the public interest in disclosure may outweigh the right of the plaintiff to protect his confidences. They demonstrate that the court will also consider how much

disclosure the public interest requires; the fact that some disclosure may be required does not mean that disclosure to the whole world should be permitted.

[21] In addition the 1998 Act requires the court, as a public authority, to take into account the right of freedom of expression conferred by art 10 of the convention. That provides:

> '*Freedom of expression*
>
> 1. Everyone has the right to freedom of expression. This right shall include freedom to hold opinions and to receive and impart information and ideas without interference by public authority and regardless of frontiers. This Article shall not prevent States from requiring the licensing of broadcasting, television or cinema enterprises.
>
> 2. The exercise of these freedoms, since it carries with it duties and responsibilities, may be subject to such formalities, conditions, restrictions or penalties as are prescribed by law and are necessary in a democratic society, in the interests of national security, territorial integrity or public safety, for the prevention of disorder or crime, for the protection of health or morals, for the protection of the reputation or rights of others, for preventing the disclosure of information received in confidence, or for maintaining the authority and impartiality of the judiciary.'

The effect of that article for present purposes is that any injunction, which by definition is a restriction on the exercise of the right to freedom of expression, must be justified as being no more than is necessary in a democratic society.

[22] For the defendants, counsel emphasised that the activities of Imutran which they abhor have now ceased. He suggested that Imutran was concerned to protect its reputation not its confidential information. He argued that, in the light of the defendants' concerns summarised in [6] above, disclosure limited to any 'proper authority', as exemplified in Employment Rights Act 1996, ss 43A to 43L, would be insufficient. He suggested at the conclusion of his submissions that the defendants should at least be free to publish *Diaries of Despair* and the 56 other documents to which they had referred on 17 October 2000.

[23] I do not accept these submissions. First, the information contained in the documents received by the defendants from the anonymous sender are in their nature confidential. Second, there can be no doubt that the defendants knew that the information contained in those documents was confidential. Not only were many of them so marked but the defendants recognised and described them as confidential or secret in *Diaries of Despair*. Third, in the absence of any claim, or evidence to support a claim, that Imutran knew and consented to the documents being provided to the defendants I infer that the defendants well knew that Imutran had not known or consented to its documents being removed from its possession and sent to the defendants. Certainly they took no steps to check with Imutran whether or not that was the case.

[24] Fourthly, the circumstances as they existed in September 2000 and now do not justify the width of disclosure the defendants seek. On 17 July 2000 the House of Lords set up its ad hoc select committee to inquire into the very matters which concerned the defendants. Since the defendants put Imutran's documents on the internet the Home Secretary and the council of the RSPCA have called for reports from the chief inspector and Dr Jennings respectively. In so far as GLPMA and UKXIRA are concerned the documents obtained by the defendants have been available to them too. There is no impediment sought or in place such

a as to inhibit any regulatory authority from investigating all the matters of which the defendants expressed concern in *Diaries of Despair*.

[**25**] Fifthly, when considering what is necessary in a democratic society and when paying particular regard to the importance of the right to freedom of expression it is relevant to consider which is the democratically selected responsible body or bodies and who would be the informed audience. In this case b Parliament has considered the issue of animal experimentation as recently as 1986. It has laid down a licensing and inspection system and a forum for and source of continuing consideration and advice in the Animal Procedures Committee. The members of that committee are themselves bound to consider the protection of animals against avoidable suffering and unnecessary use in scientific procedures (s 20(2) of the 1986 Act). Two thirds of them must be medically qualified c (s 19(3)(a)) and their annual report to the Home Secretary must be laid before Parliament (s 20(5)). In addition there is the RSPCA, GLPMA and UKXIRA all of whom have an interest in investigating one or more of the matters which concern the defendants.

[**26**] Of course, the defendants' right to freedom of expression is an element in d their democratic right to campaign for the abolition of all animal xenotransplantation or other experimentation. But they may continue to do that whether the injunction sought by Imutran is granted or not. The issue is whether they should be free to do so with Imutran's confidential and secret documents. Many of those documents are of a specialist and technical nature suitable for consideration by specialists in the field but not by the public generally. Given the provisos to the e injunction sought there would be no restriction on the ability of the defendants to communicate the information to those specialists connected with the regulatory bodies denoted by Parliament as having responsibility in the field. I do not accept in these circumstances the defendants' assertion that the relationship between Imutran and the inspectors appointed by the Home Secretary is too f close for the latter to do their job properly. If that was ever so, and there is no evidence to that effect, it is unlikely to continue given the current interest of the House of Lords select committee and the Home Secretary's instruction of the chief inspector.

[**27**] For all these reasons I conclude that Imutran is likely to establish at the trial of the action that publication of its confidential documents should not be g allowed. I also conclude that the injunction sought does not go further than is necessary in a democratic society. Paying particular regard to the importance of the right to freedom of expression I conclude nevertheless that the balance of convenience favours the grant of the injunction sought. If no injunction is granted now victory at the trial would be no consolation; the confidence would h be destroyed and the consequential damages entirely unquantifiable even if the defendants were able to pay them. By contrast if the defendants were successful at the trial they would then be able to publish anything they liked with the added benefit of knowing the views of the regulatory bodies and their experts. There is no suggestion that the delay in establishing their right, which I have to assume for the purposes of this point, will cause them any damage at all. Accordingly I will j grant the injunction sought to restrain breach of confidence.

[**28**] I pass then to the application for an interim injunction based on infringement of copyright. This claim relates only to those of the documents relating to Imutran which the defendants received from the unknown source which were written by employees of Imutran. There are 79 of them of which 77 were published on one or more of the websites the defendants used. They have been specifically identified in the analysis Imutran prepared. Though on the pleadings there is a

formal issue in relation to copyright there is no evidence to refute the obvious conclusion to be derived from the documents themselves that each of them is a copyright work of which the owner of the copyright is Imutran as the employer of the various authors. Nor, given the wholesale reproduction of them, can it be doubted that Imutran's copyright in the 77 has been infringed or that there is a sufficient threat to infringe copyright in the remaining two.

[29] In their defence the defendants rely on the defence of fair dealing for which s 30 of the Copyright, Designs and Patents Act 1988 provides. But, as their counsel made plain in his written argument, they are content that this application should be determined on the assumption that such a defence will not succeed. Accordingly the only defence to the claim for copyright infringement is that contained in para 13 of the defence served on 13 November 2000, namely that the acts complained of did not constitute infringement because they amounted to 'the disclosure of matters in the public interest'. The defendants rely in this as well as the other contexts on art 10 of the convention and s 12(4) of the 1998 Act.

[30] The existence of a public interest defence to a claim for infringement of copyright is recognised by s 171(3) of the 1988 Act. That subsection provides: 'Nothing in this part affects any rule of law preventing or restricting the enforcement of copyright, on grounds of public interest or otherwise.' It was considered by the Court of Appeal in *Hyde Park Residence Ltd v Yelland* [2000] IP & T 412, [2001] Ch 143. Aldous LJ, with whom Stuart-Smith LJ agreed, said:

> 'The circumstances where it is against the policy of the law to use the court's procedure to enforce copyright are, I suspect, not capable of definition. However it must be remembered that copyright is assignable and therefore the circumstances must derive from the work in question, not ownership of the copyright. In my view, a court would be entitled to refuse to enforce copyright if the work is: (i) immoral, scandalous or contrary to family life; (ii) injurious to public life, public health and safety or the administration of justice; (iii) incites or encourages others to act in a way referred to in (ii).' (See [2000] IP & T 412 at 434, [2001] Ch 143 at 168.)

[31] I did not understand the defendants to claim that this case fell within any of those descriptions even though one of the contentions relied on is the assertion that xenotransplantation involves the danger of lethal viruses spreading to humans (see defence, para 13(2)(b)). Rather it was submitted that I am not bound by the decision of the Court of Appeal because the 1998 Act came into force after the *Hyde Park Residence* case was decided. It was submitted in this case as in *Ashdown*'s case, which I heard immediately before this application, that one effect of art 10 of the convention is to introduce into the law of copyright a public interest defence to a claim for infringement going much wider than the Court of Appeal held in the *Hyde Park Residence* case.

[32] I dealt with that submission at some length in my judgment in *Ashdown*'s case [2001] 2 All ER 370 at [10]–[20], [32], [2001] 2 WLR 967, which I handed down immediately before I handed down this judgment. I will not repeat them. For present purposes it is only necessary to repeat the conclusion in [32] that the decision of the Court of Appeal in the *Hyde Park Residence* case is binding on me. That decision establishes that there is no public interest defence to the copyright claim pursuant to the rule of law preserved by s 171(3) of the 1988 Act.

[33] It follows from the foregoing conclusions that the cause of action for infringement of copyright is made out to such an extent that I can say with confidence that on the evidence before me it is likely that Imutran will establish a that publication by reproduction should not be allowed (cf s 12(3) of the 1998 Act). Equally, given the interaction between the law of copyright and art 10 of the convention as I consider it to be, the importance of the convention right to freedom of expression to which s 12(4) of the 1998 Act requires me to pay particular regard does not lead to the conclusion that injunctive or other relief in respect of the copyright claim should be refused.

b [34] I should refer finally to an objection taken by the defendants to the form of relief sought. The order of Ferris J made on 10 October 2000, which Imutran seeks to have continued, contains a proviso that the injunctions should not prohibit—

> c 'the use or disclosure of information derived from the Claimant's Materials which has entered the public domain by virtue of being contained in articles in the Daily Express on 21 and 22 September 2000.'

It is contended that the proviso does not make sufficiently clear what the defendants may not do. The use of such a proviso is common. It is designed to preserve the ability to repeat what has already been sufficiently publicised. It is d right that some such proviso should be included, but it does appear to me that this one is unduly convoluted. It would, in my view, be preferable to use the simpler form contained in the order made by Hooper J in *A-G v Shayler* (4 September 1997, unreported) so that the proviso would read:

> 'PROVIDED THAT these injunctions shall not prohibit ... (3) the e repetition of information (otherwise than by copying any document described in Sch 1 to this order) disclosed in the Daily Express on 21 and 22 September 2000.'

[35] For all these reasons and subject to any further points on the form of order I will make orders in the forms sought by the application to restrain breach of confidence and infringement of copyright.

f [36] I turn then to the application of the RSPCA. This is made under the liberty to apply given by the order of Ferris J made on 10 October 2000. The order sought is that Imutran should be ordered to pay the RSPCA's costs of obtaining a variation of the order of Hart J so as to permit it to use Imutran's documents as provided for in the order of Ferris J.

g [37] The order of Hart J, made on 26 September, contained injunctions restraining the defendants from infringing copyright and from 'using or disclosing' any information contained in Imutran's documents specified in the order but subject to the provisos I have already mentioned. Those provisos did not include the RSPCA amongst the authorised recipients. Hart J also required Mr Lyons to make and serve a witness statement disclosing the names and addresses of all h those who to his knowledge had possession of any copies of documents emanating from Imutran. In his witness statement made on 27 September 2000 Mr Lyons disclosed that he had sent copies of all the relevant documents to, amongst many others, the RSPCA.

[38] On Friday 29 September Imutran wrote to the RSPCA notifying them of j the order of Hart J, of which a copy was enclosed, and continuing:

> 'We have taken this step to protect commercially sensitive scientific data and other commercially confidential information. We are advised to inform you that we will continue to take whatever steps are necessary to prevent further dissemination of our confidential information. We wish to make clear however that we do not seek to stifle public debate about xenotransplantation, or to obstruct in any way proper investigation by the appropriate authorities

of allegations which have been made about this company's activities. As you will see the Order contains exceptions, permitting the republication of information already made public through articles in the Daily Express, and the communication of documents and information to the proper authorities. We confirm that we will be pleased to continue our on-going discussion and are willing to co-operate and assist any investigation you are required or consider it appropriate to make. In that regard we ask you to note that the documents that were misappropriated are unlikely to provide a full and complete version of the events referred to within the said "Diaries of Despair".'

On the following Monday 2 October Imutran sent e-mails to over 360 persons or organisations disclosed by the witness statement of Mr Lyons to have been recipients of Imutran's documents. The RSPCA was one of those to whom the e-mail was sent. It stated:

> 'On Tuesday 26 September 2000 our lawyers obtained a Court Order preventing the publication of our confidential information and infringement of our copyright. The purpose of this letter is to notify you of that Order and to inform you that we will take whatever steps are necessary to prevent further illegitimate dissemination of our confidential information and infringement of our copyrights. You are hereby put on notice of that Court Order and further dissemination by you could be treated as contempt of Court.'

The letter of 29 September must have been received on Monday 2 October contemporaneously with the e-mail sent at 1048 hrs on that day.

[**39**] Between Wednesday 4 October and Monday 9 October correspondence ensued between Imutran and the RSPCA or their respective solicitors. On 4 October the RSPCA set out at length its concerns for animal welfare. The letter described how it had downloaded from the UCL website copies of Imutran's documents and had asked Dr Jennings for a report in time for the council meeting to be held on 11 October. The letter suggested the topics Dr Jennings would be likely to cover in her report and continued:

> 'Following receipt of Dr. Jennings' report, it would be for the Council to consider whether they needed further information and whether they should seek to make representations to Home Office officials or the Government that amendments are needed to the relevant legislation or to the procedures under the legislation. They might also consider whether to seek publicity and public support for any such proposals. The full report prepared by Dr. Jennings would be likely to be used in discussions with the Home Office or the Government and to be sent to key opinion formers such as Members of Parliament and a summary prepared for wider use. We believe that the court will be sympathetic to our desire to fulfil our charitable objects in this way, however, naturally we would prefer to be able to do so without the delay and expense of having recourse to the court. Accordingly, we would be grateful if you could confirm, by close of business today, that you have no objection to our proposed use of your material. For the avoidance of doubt, we are not proposing to infringe copyright in any of "the Claimant's Copyright Documents" or to name or reveal any other identifying information in relation to your employees, ex-employers and associates.'

The letter concluded with an offer to consider any further material Imutran might like to submit.

a [**40**] On the following day the solicitors for the RSPCA wrote again confirming a telephone call concerning the request of the RSPCA for copies of the evidence relied on by Imutran before Hart J. The letter stated that:

> 'The request was made on the basis that it is clearly your intention that our client is bound by the order. As you know, our client wishes to challenge the order either by agreement with your client or in court and they are legally b entitled to know the basis on which the injunction was made. Our client clearly needs to see your client's witness statement and exhibits.'

On 6 October the solicitors for the RSPCA wrote objecting in the 'strongest possible terms' to the failure of Imutran to supply them with the evidence sought. This letter crossed with one from the solicitors for Imutran enclosing a copy of c the witness statement of Mr Talbot made in support of the application before Hart J and asking for undertakings as to confidentiality in respect of the exhibits. They added:

> 'We have noted what you say about the RSPCA's wish to commission a report from Dr. Jennings. Whilst our clients remain willing to co-operate d with any investigation which the RSPCA considers it appropriate to make, our clients need the RSPCA's assurances that it will fully consult with our clients in relation to its investigation and that if our clients agree to the RSPCA using the documents in question the RSPCA will undertake not to publish or otherwise disseminate the documents.'

e By a letter dated Monday 9 October an acceptable undertaking was given by the RSPCA in exchange for which the exhibits were provided.

[**41**] Between the receipt by the RSPCA of the exhibits and the sitting of the court the next morning counsel for Imutran and the RSPCA had agreed a form of amendment to the order of Hart J made on 26 September. The form the f amendment took was not a simple addition of the RSPCA to the list of authorised recipients, but involved the addition of a further proviso entitling RSPCA to reproduce, use or disclose Imutran's material, as defined, in accordance with a new schedule 5. That schedule contained detailed provisions in relation to the preparation of Dr Jennings' report and what might then be done with it, including a requirement that a draft thereof be sent to Imutran. An order containing this g agreed form was made by Ferris J on 10 October.

[**42**] For the RSPCA it was submitted that Imutran should pay their costs of obtaining an order in the amended form. It was submitted that the order of Hart J was defective in that it did not except use of the Imutran material by the RSPCA notwithstanding that Imutran did not object to such use. It is suggested that, as h with the normal practice in connection with freezing orders, an innocent third party should recover its costs from the person who obtained the order if it is necessary to make an application to the court. Counsel suggested that the normal form of breach of confidence order should contain a standard proviso modelled on that contained in the form of freezing order set out on p 462 of *Civil Procedure*, j Autumn 2000, vol 1 and p 276 of the *Civil Court Practice 2000*, vol 1, whereby the applicant should undertake to the court—

> '[to] pay the reasonable costs of anyone other than the Respondent which have been incurred as a result of this Order … and if the Court later finds that this Order has caused such person loss, and decides that such person should be compensated for that loss, the Applicant will comply with any Order the Court may make.'

[43] I do not accept either submission. With regard to this case the RSPCA was in no different position to anyone else who had come into possession of the Imutran documents. It did not have any right to use them otherwise than with the consent of Imutran. The fact that Imutran was prepared to give its consent on terms does not alter the fact that its consent was required. Therefore the premise to the argument for the RSPCA that it had the right to use the documents which had been improperly interfered with by the injunction granted by Hart J on 26 September is false.

[44] But it remains the case that the RSPCA did appear in court on 10 October and the costs of that appearance are in the discretion of the court. But I see no reason for making any order in its favour. The attitude of Imutran regarding the RSPCA was entirely proper throughout. The letters from the RSPCA or its solicitors dated 4 and 5 October both suggested, wrongly, that the RSPCA had the right to publicise the contents of the Imutran documents. It was reasonable for Imutran to insist that disclosure was only on the agreed terms. And had the solicitors for the RSPCA adopted a less hustling approach I have no doubt that the matter would have been dealt with by agreement between counsel without any need for the RSPCA to appear in court at all. Given my conclusion that I should make no order for the costs of the RSPCA I need say no more about whether Imutran should be permitted to add the costs paid to the RSPCA to its claim for damages or costs against the defendants, save to draw attention to *Morton-Norwich Products Inc v Intercen Ltd* [1981] FSR 337 where it was successfully done. I dismiss the application of the RSPCA.

[45] With regard to the suggestion as to the normal form of injunction in breach of confidence claims I agree with it. Counsel referred to para 5.1 of the Practice Direction to CPR Pt 25. This requires the cross-undertaking in damages to be given in respect of 'any other party served with or notified of the order'. The Practice Direction applies to breach of confidence injunctions as well as any other. But the forms prescribed by *Practice Direction (interlocutory injunctions: forms)* [1997] 1 All ER 287, [1996] 1 WLR 1551 limited the cross-undertaking in damages to the defendant and have continued to be recommended for use by the editors of *Civil Procedure*. See note 25.1.12 in both the Spring and Autumn 2000 editions. No doubt it was for this reason that the cross-undertaking in the orders made by Hart and Ferris JJ did not extend to the RSPCA. In my view pending the production of amended forms the simple amendment contemplated by para 5.1 of the Practice Direction to CPR Pt 25 should be made to the pre-existing forms in the manner suggested by counsel for the RSPCA. But for the reasons I have already given even if the amended form of undertaking had been included in the order of Hart J I do not consider that the RSPCA should have been entitled to recover under it. Further the omission appears to me to be of no importance in this case as the jurisdiction of the court under s 51 of the Supreme Court Act 1981 and CPR 48.2 would have been more than adequate to do justice between the claimant and the RSPCA had I considered that an order in favour of the RSPCA should have been made.

[46] For all these reasons I will make the orders sought against the defendants but I will make no order for costs in favour of the RSPCA.

Order accordingly.

Celia Fox Barrister.

a

Rosen v Trustees of Camden Charities

COURT OF APPEAL, CIVIL DIVISION

OTTON, WARD LJJ AND EVANS-LOMBE J

26 OCTOBER, 30 NOVEMBER 2000

b

Landlord and tenant – Leasehold enfranchisement – House – Building lease – Whether construction of house under terms of building lease an 'improvement' to 'house and premises' for purposes of determining price payable by tenant for transfer of freehold – Leasehold Reform Act 1967, ss 2(3), 9(1A).

c

In January 1850 the trustees of a charity put up for sale by auction the site of a workhouse which they owned. The successful bidder, I, entered into an agreement with the trustees whereby he undertook to construct 29 houses on the site, on completion of which he was to be granted a 99-year lease of the site from 25 December 1849. By the time the lease was granted in October 1852, the house d which was to become No 25 was complete. In 1937 the trustees granted a lease of No 25 for 66½ years from 29 September 1936. The appellant, R, was the successor in title to the 1937 lease, and sought to have the freehold transferred to him under the Leasehold Reform Act 1967. The amount payable by R to the trustees fell to be calculated pursuant to s 9(1A)[a] of the 1967 Act. Under that e provision, the price payable for a 'house and premises' was the amount which at the relevant time it might be expected to realise, if sold in the open market by a willing seller, on various assumptions, including, at para (d), the assumption that the price 'be diminished by the extent to which the value of the house and premises has been increased by any improvement carried out by the tenant or his predecessors in title at their own expense'. Section 2(3)[b] provided that where in f relation to a house let to and occupied by a tenant reference was made to the 'house and premises', the reference to premises was to be taken as referring to any garage, outhouse, garden, yard and appurtenances which at the relevant time were let to him with the house and were occupied with and used for the purposes of the house. The price payable for No 25 was determined by the Leasehold g Valuation Tribunal, but its decision was challenged before the Lands Tribunal. On a subsequent appeal by R to the Court of Appeal, he contended that the original construction of No 25 by I before the grant of the 1852 lease was capable of constituting 'an improvement' to the 'house and premises' within the meaning of s 9(1A)(d). In so contending, he submitted that the term 'house and premises', when used in that provision, simply described the premises let, which might h originally have consisted of open land or land with buildings on it unconverted to any sort of habitation.

Held – For the purposes of s 9(1A)(d) of the 1967 Act, the building of a new house on a bare site (whether a green field site or a site on which a previous building j which was not a house had been demolished) was not an improvement of the 'house and premises' but the provision of the house. From the definition of 'house and premises' in s 2(3), it was clear that 'premises' could not exist independently of a house. Moreover, when considered in the context of the 1967 Act as a whole,

a Section 9, so far as material, is set out at p 402 *g h*, post

b Section 2, so far as material, is set out at p 401 *j* to p 402 *a*, post the words 'diminished by the extent to which the value ... has been increased by any improvement carried out by the tenant or his predecessors in title at their own expense' could not be taken to contemplate a situation where a tenant under a long lease had expended money on the relevant property but had received equivalent value from the landlord in exchange, ie a valuable lease. There could be no justification for drawing a distinction between the treatment of a tenant who had acquired his long tenancy by the payment of a premium and one who had done so by the expenditure of a similar sum in the construction of a house on his landlord's land. It followed in the instant case that the building lease which I had taken from the trustees was the original bargain between them, performance of which on I's part could not be treated as an 'improvement' within s 9(1A)(d). The purpose of para (d) was to guide a valuer so as to exclude from the open market value of the house and premises any improvement carried out by the tenant or his predecessors by which the value of the house and premises had been increased. The original construction of the house in question could not constitute an improvement within para (d). Accordingly, the appeal would be dismissed (see p 403 *g* to p 404 *b f* to p 405 *a d* to *f* and p 408 *f g*, post).

Notes

For the price payable by the tenant to the landlord, see 27(2) *Halsbury's Laws* (4th edn reissue) para 1297.

For the Leasehold Reform Act 1967, ss 2, 9, see 23 *Halsbury's Statutes* (4th edn) (1997 reissue) 210, 224.

Cases referred to in judgments

Carrington Manufacturing v Saldin (1925) 133 LT 432.
Cornish v Brook Green Laundry Ltd [1959] 1 All ER 373, [1959] 1 QB 394, [1959] 2 WLR 215, CA.
Euston Centre Properties Ltd v H & J Wilson Ltd [1982] 1 EGLR 57.
Hambros Bank Executor & Trustee Co Ltd v Superdrug Stores Ltd [1985] 1 EGLR 99.
Hasham v Zenab [1960] AC 316, [1960] 2 WLR 374, PC.
Henry Smith's Charity Trustees v Hemmings [1983] 1 EGLR 94, CA.
Michaels v Harley House (Marylebone) Ltd [1999] 1 All ER 356, [2000] Ch 104, [1999] 3 WLR 229, CA.
Sainty v Minister of Housing and Local Government (1964) 15 P&CR 432, DC.
Walsh v Lonsdale (1882) 21 Ch D 9, 46 LT 858, CA.

Appeal

Morris Rosen, the tenant of residential premises known as 25 Kensington Gate, London, appealed from the decision of the Lands Tribunal (Judge Rich QC) on appeal from the decision of the Leasehold Valuation Tribunal for London whereby it determined, in accordance with s 9(1A) of the Leasehold Reform Act 1967, the price payable by the appellant to the respondent landlord, the Trustees of Camden Charities, for the transfer to him of the freehold under the provisions of the 1967 Act. The facts are set out in the judgment of Evans-Lombe J.

Simon Berry QC and *Edwin Johnson* (instructed by *David Conway & Co*) for the appellant.
Jonathan Gaunt QC (instructed by *Lee Bolton Lee*) for the trustees.

Cur adv vult

a 30 November 2000. The following judgments were delivered.

EVANS-LOMBE J (giving the first judgment at the invitation of Otton LJ).

1. This is an appeal by way of case stated from the decision of the Lands Tribunal given on 30 July 1999 by Judge Rich QC, on appeal from a decision of the Leasehold Valuation Tribunal for London, whereby that tribunal determined b in accordance with s 9(1A) of the Leasehold Reform Act 1967 what the price payable by the appellant for a transfer to him of the freehold of 25 Kensington Gate (No 25) by the owner under the provisions of that Act should be.

2. The background facts to this appeal are these: before 1850 the Trustees of the Camden Charities (the trustees) were the owners of the site of the Kensington c Workhouse. On 15 January 1850 there took place an auction at which the trustees put that site up for sale. At the auction one Inderwick was the successful bidder. His bid resulted in an agreement between the trustees and himself whereby he undertook to construct 29 houses on the site on the completion of which he was to be granted a 99-year lease of the site from 25 December 1849. The terms of this agreement have not survived. Before the tribunal there was expert evidence d of what such an agreement would probably have consisted by comparison with other such agreements entered into at around the same time whose terms are known. Experts instructed by the parties were agreed on this point. Their conclusion was described in the tribunal's judgment in this way:

e 'The experts are agreed that a normal type of building agreement at that time "would provide for mutual obligations—the obligation on the part of the builder to build the houses to carcase and roof stage and the obligation on the part of the landlord to grant a lease or leases to the builder when that stage had been reached. It would not normally have contained a contingency clause for non-fulfilment".'

f 3. The tribunal emphasised the words 'when that stage had been reached'.

4. On 9 October 1852 the trustees granted to Mr Inderwick a 99-year lease of the whole site from 25 December 1849. It is accepted that by this date the house, which was to become No 25, was complete and not only built to 'carcase and roof' stage.

g 5. By a lease, dated 8 April 1937 (the 1937 lease), the trustees granted to a Mr Guise a lease of No 25 for 66½ years from 29 September 1936. The appellant is the successor in title to the 1937 lease. He claims to have the freehold of No 25 transferred to him by the trustees pursuant to the provisions of the 1967 Act under a notice of claim assigned to him by his predecessor on 5 July 1994.

h 6. The relevant provisions of the 1967 Act are:

'**1.**—(1) This Part of this Act shall have effect to confer on a tenant of a leasehold house, occupying the house as his residence, a right to acquire on fair terms the freehold or an extended lease of the house and premises j where—(a) his tenancy is a long tenancy at a low rent … and (b) at the relevant time (that is to say, at the time when he gives notice in accordance with this Act of his desire to have the freehold or to have an extended lease, as the case may be) he has been tenant of the house under a long tenancy at a low rent, and occupying it as his residence …

2.—(1) For purposes of this Part of this Act, "house" includes any building designed or adapted for living in and reasonably so called …

(3) Subject to the following provisions of this section, where in relation to a house let to and occupied by a tenant reference is made in this Part of this Act to the house and premises, the reference to premises is to be taken as referring to any garage, outhouse, garden, yard and appurtenances which at the relevant time are let to him with the house and are occupied with and used for the purposes of the house or any part of it by him or by another occupant …

3.— … (3) Where the tenant of any property under a long tenancy, on the coming to an end of that tenancy, becomes or has become tenant of the property or part of it under another long tenancy, then in relation to the property or that part of it this Part of this Act shall apply as if there had been a single tenancy granted for a term beginning at the same time as the term under the earlier tenancy and expiring at the same time as the term under the later tenancy.

8.—(1) Where a tenant of a house has under this Part of this Act a right to acquire the freehold, and gives to the landlord written notice of his desire to have the freehold, then except as provided by this Part of this Act the landlord shall be bound to make to the tenant, and the tenant to accept, (at the price and on the conditions so provided) a grant of the house and premises for an estate in fee simple absolute, subject to the tenancy and to tenant's incumbrances, but otherwise free of incumbrances.'

7. The amount payable by the enfranchising tenant to the landlord as consideration for the transfer of the freehold to him falls to be calculated under the provisions of s 9 of the Act. Originally the right to enfranchise extended only to houses in London of a rateable value less than £400. The method of calculation of the consideration payable by the tenant in respect of such houses is set out in s 9(1).

8. The Housing Act 1974 introduced a right to acquire the freehold or long leasehold of premises held on a long lease with a higher rateable value. The method of calculation of the consideration payable by the tenant for the transfer of the freehold of premises having such a higher rateable value is in accordance the provisions of s 9(1A). It is accepted that the consideration payable by the appellant for a transfer to him of the freehold of No 25 fell to be valued in accordance with that section. So far as material to this appeal it provides as follows:

'Notwithstanding the foregoing subsection, the price payable for a house and premises,—(i) … shall be the amount which at the relevant time the house and premises, if sold in the open market by a willing seller, might be expected to realise on the following assumptions:— … (d) on the assumption that the price be diminished by the extent to which the value of the house and premises has been increased by any improvement carried out by the tenant or his predecessors in title at their own expense …'

9. The tribunal concluded that s 3(3) operated on the facts of this case so that the 1852 and 1937 leases were to be treated as one long lease to which the appellant was successor in title. No challenge is made to that conclusion.

10. The issue on this appeal is whether the original construction of No 25 by Inderwick before the grant of the 1852 lease was an 'improvement carried out by the tenant or his predecessors in title at their own expense' within the meaning of s 9(1A)(d) of the 1967 Act, so that the price payable by the tenant is to be

a diminished to the extent to which the value of the 'house and premises' has been increased by the value of the original construction.

11. This issue subdivides into two issues. The first is whether the construction of No 25 by Inderwick was capable of constituting an 'improvement' within sub-s (1A)(d). If so the second issue is whether at the time of the construction Inderwick was the 'predecessor in title' of the appellant of the long lease of No 25 b held by him as extended by the effect of s 3(3) of the 1967 Act.

12. The parties are agreed that if such construction constitutes an improvement by a predecessor in title of the appellant within sub-s (1A)(d) the enfranchisement price is £417,000. If not it is £696,000.

13. Subsection (1A)(d) refers to 'any improvement'. It was submitted by c Mr Berry QC for the appellant that the construction of a house on land was capable of constituting an improvement of that land. Like the tribunal I accept that submission but also like the tribunal, I take the view that it is beside the point. It was common ground before the tribunal that the word 'improvement' 'imports a relativity, that is there must be some subject matter for improvement'. An improvement cannot come into existence in vacuo. It must constitute an d improvement to something. The question therefore is what is the object to which the words 'any improvement' in sub-s (1A)(d) are directed.

14. Mr Berry for the appellant submitted that the object must be the premises let, namely, the land, demised by the lease which at the date of the claim to enfranchise is constituted by the 'house and premises'. He submitted that e sub-s (1A)(d) does not restrict the scope of the improvement there spoken of nor the identity of that which is to be improved. He submitted that the Act contemplates that an application to enfranchise might be made in respect of land which, when originally let, did not have a house built on it or, if there was a building on the land, one which would not fall within the definition of a house in s 2(1). Thus 'house and premises' when used in s 9(1A) and, in particular, in f sub-s (1A)(d) is to be read as simply describing the premises let which might originally have consisted of open land or land with buildings on it unconverted to any sort of habitation. It follows, so he submitted, that the construction of a house on such land was capable of constituting an 'improvement' to that land within sub-s (1A)(d).

g 15. The tribunal dealt with the matter in this way:

> 'The question is to what must the improvement relate if it is to be a relevant improvement for the purposes of the paragraph? It appears to me that grammatically Mr Gaunt (for the respondents) must be right. Mr Berry rightly says that the matter could have been made clear if the draftsman had h added the word "thereto" to "improvement" thereby referring back directly to "house and premises". But I think that in the absence of express direction elsewhere, the reference would grammatically be taken back to the last mentioned object. This, for the reasons which I have already given and are common ground, cannot be "the value". The immediate reference back is j therefore to the last words of the antecedent phrase that is "the house and premises". Certainly there is no grammatical basis for referring to the demised property which is never mentioned in the subsections and is not the subject matter of the valuation. The "house and premises" are defined by s 2 of the Act. It is provided in sub-s (3) that "the reference to premises is to be taken as referring to … appurtenances which at the relevant time are let … with the house and are occupied with and used for the purposes of the

house". It follows that in the absence of a house there is no house, nor can there be any premises, nor any "house and premises" to improve. From this it must follow that the erection of a house, where no house was there before cannot be an improvement within the paragraph.'

16. I respectfully agree with the tribunal. Subsection (1A)(d) does not use such words as 'the demised premises' nor are they used in the Act generally. The term used is 'house *and* premises' not 'house *or* premises'. From the definition of 'house and premises' in s 2(3) it is clear that 'premises' cannot exist independently of a house. The building of a new house on a bare site (whether a green field or a site on which a previous building which was not a house has been demolished) is not the improvement of 'the house and premises' but the provision of the house.

17. In *Sainty v Minister of Housing and Local Government* (1964) 15 P&CR 432 the Divisional Court were considering a case where an appellant proposed to demolish two old cottages and to replace them with two new houses of different design, on slightly different foundations. It was submitted that this proposal fell within the words 'enlargement, improvement or other alteration' of the cottages within Class I, para 1 of the Town and Country Planning General Development Order 1963, SI 1963/709 with the result that planning permission was not required. The relevant order excluded from the requirement for planning permission 'the enlargement, improvement or other alteration of a dwelling house' so long as the enlargement did not exceed certain dimensions. The court upheld the minister's view that the words of the order 'must refer to a dwelling-house which is in existence when the operations mentioned in that Class are being carried out' (see (1964) 15 P&CR 432 at 433). I accept Mr Gaunt's submission that *Sainty*'s case is analogous to the present case and supports his contentions.

18. I accept the respondent's submission that their construction of the subsection is supported by the inclusion of the words 'diminished by the extent to which the value … has been increased by any improvement carried out by the tenant or his predecessors in title at their own expense'.

19. Contrary to the views expressed by the tribunal, in my judgment, when considered in the context of the provisions of the 1967 Act as a whole, these words cannot be taken to contemplate a situation where a tenant under a long lease has expended money on the relevant property but received equivalent value from the landlord in exchange, i e a valuable lease. The Act is concerned with the position of tenants of houses holding long tenancies at low rents (see s 1(1)). In the present case Inderwick, put forward by the appellant as his predecessor in title within sub-s (1A)(d), covenanted to build a house on the trustees' land in exchange for obtaining a 99-year lease at a low rent, a valuable interest in property which he was prepared to accept in exchange for his expenditure in erecting the house on the site of No 25 amongst the other sites covered by the agreement following on the auction. Had the circumstances been different so that the trustees had already constructed the house and were offering a long lease of it at a low rent to Inderwick, he would have had to have paid a substantial premium for the grant of such a lease. It cannot be suggested that the payment of such a premium would constitute an 'improvement' within sub-s (1A)(d). There can be no justification for drawing a distinction between the treatment of a tenant who has acquired his long tenancy by the payment of a premium and one who has done so by the expenditure of a similar sum in the construction of a house on his

a landlord's land. It follows, it seems to me, that the building lease which Inderwick took from the trustees was the original bargain, between Inderwick and the trustees, performance of which on Inderwick's part cannot be treated as an 'improvement' within sub-s (1A)(d).

20. I also accept the submission of the respondents that the clear purpose of the amendment of the 1967 Act to include s 9(1A) was to provide a different b valuation regime in respect of properties of greater value than those to which the Act had previously applied. Whereas the provisions of s 9(1), which include the assumption that the property is to be valued on the basis, resulting from the application of s 15(2) so that the tenancy to be enfranchised has been extended by a further 50 years at a ground rent, are designed to enable the tenant to acquire the freehold at site value only. By contrast, s 9(1A) appears to be intended to give c the landlord the open market value of the house and premises with the resident tenant bidding and without the assumption of an extended lease at a ground rent. There is therefore included in the valuation process a method of calculating 'marriage value' upon the merger of the leasehold with the freehold. If the appellant's contentions are correct then, in cases such as the present, where the d enfranchising tenant's predecessors in title include the original builder of the house, the valuation can only be based on the site value after all.

21. In my judgment the purpose of sub-s (1A)(d) is to guide a valuer so as to exclude from the 'open market' value of the 'house and premises' which, by the first part of s 9(1A) is to constitute the 'price payable' by the tenant seeking enfranchisement, 'any improvement carried out by the tenant or his predecessors' e by which 'the value of the house and premises has been increased'. The original construction of the house in question cannot constitute an improvement within sub-s (1A)(d). This conclusion is not, as submitted by the appellant, affected by the fact that the term of the 1852 lease was expressed to commence on 25 December 1849, before the house was built, and, indeed, before the auction, and that rent f was payable and was paid by Inderwick from that date. A lease takes effect from the time of its grant notwithstanding that it may contain provisions for the backdating of payment of rent.

22. That is sufficient to dispose of the appeal but in deference to the submissions of counsel I will deal with the remaining points if briefly.

23. Those points are directed to whether Inderwick is to be treated as a 'predecessor g in title' of the appellant at the time that No 25 was constructed within the meaning of sub-s (1A)(d). No 25 had already been built by him by the time the formal lease was actually granted to him by the trustees.

24. It was submitted by Mr Berry that Inderwick would have been able to obtain specific performance of the agreement for a lease before No 25 had been h built to carcase and roof stage. Thus, at the time of construction, Inderwick held an equitable lease under the doctrine of *Walsh v Lonsdale* (1882) 21 Ch D 9 to which the appellant's lease is extended by the operation of s 3(3). Thus Inderwick was a predecessor in title to the lease held by the appellant as so extended.

25. The tribunal relying on the authority of *Cornish v Brook Green Laundry Ltd* j [1959] 1 All ER 373, [1959] 1 QB 394, a decision of the Court of Appeal, the decision of Cantley J in *Euston Centre Properties Ltd v H & J Wilson Ltd* [1982] 1 EGLR 57, and of the Court of Appeal in *Henry Smith's Charity Trustees v Hemmings* [1983] 1 EGLR 94 concluded that because it was a condition of the agreement for a lease that the granting of the lease to Inderwick was conditional upon the construction of No 25 to carcase and roof stage, Inderwick would not have become entitled to a decree of specific performance until the construction had reached that stage. The

appellant challenged that conclusion by arguing that, for a condition precedent to preclude a decree of specific performance, the condition had to be beyond the control of the applicant for the decree to perform. The condition to construct the house was not such a condition. In support of this submission the appellant cited two authorities, *Hasham v Zenab* [1960] AC 316, [1960] 2 WLR 374 cited in *Michaels v Harley House (Marylebone) Ltd* [1999] 1 All ER 356, [2000] Ch 104.

26. The tribunal dealt with this submission at p 11 of the transcript of the tribunal's reasons. I agree with the tribunal's conclusion that *Michaels'* case is no authority for the appellant's argument. The issue in that case was whether TWD's obligations under its agreement to sell the shares in the subsidiary company, to which it was to transfer the leasehold reversion, to Frogmore, meant that the subsidiary company was no longer an 'associated company' of TWD within s 4(2)(l) of the Landlord and Tenant Act 1987. This would have been the case were Frogmore in a position to enforce against TWD the contract of sale of the shares by obtaining specific performance of that contract. The Court of Appeal concluded that Frogmore was in that position. It was in this context that Robert Walker LJ said (in a passage quoted by the tribunal):

> 'I also agree with the judge that TWD's obligations under the share sale agreement were not dependent on some outside contingency beyond its control (since it could call on TWP to transfer the registered title, and it effectively controlled the company). Had TWD not completed on 25 March 1993, it could have been sued for specific performance. Had it repudiated its obligations to Frogmore before that day, it could have been sued for specific performance even before the contractual date for completion (see *Hasham v Zenab* ([1960] AC 316, [1960] 2 WLR 374)). The conditions in cl 2.1 [the completion of the property sale by TWD] would have been no defence.' (See [1999] 1 All ER 356 at 365, [2000] Ch 104 at 116.)

27. In other words TWD could only resist specific performance if there had been a condition in the contract for the sale of the shares to be performed by TWD which was beyond TWD's ability to perform. By contrast in the present case the question is whether Inderwick could obtain specific performance of the agreement for a lease before performing the condition placed on him by the agreement, namely, the construction of the house. That condition was within his power to perform but he could not have got a decree of specific performance for the grant of the lease to him until he had performed it.

28. *Hasham*'s case is no authority for the appellant's argument either. In that case the Privy Council was considering a contract for the sale of land which provided for completion on a date in the future. Before that date the vendor repudiated the contract. The opinion of the Privy Council was delivered by Lord Tucker. He said:

> 'Their Lordships are of opinion that the fallacy of the submission consists in equating the right to sue for specific performance with a cause of action at law. In equity all that is required is to show circumstances which will justify the intervention by a court of equity. The purchaser has an equitable interest in the land and could get an injunction to prevent the vendor disposing of the property. The order for specific performance often falls into two parts. The first can be of a declaratory nature and the second contain consequential directions. The first of the forms in volume 3 of the seventh edition of Seton's Forms of Judgments and Orders, at p. 2136, is clearly suitable to a

a case where the time for performance may not have arrived even at the date of the order, but in such a case, in the event of subsequent non-performance the court would not require the issue of a fresh writ before making the consequential directions for performance. The court will not, of course, compel a party to perform his contract before the contract date arrives, and would give relief from any order in the event of an intervening circumstance b frustrating the contract.' (See [1960] AC 316 at 329–330, [1960] 2 WLR 374 at 376–377.)

29. This case shows that a purchaser may commence an action for specific performance of an agreement for the sale of land to him before the actual date for completion has arrived. He will not, however, be able to obtain a decree of specific c performance until after the date for completion. Before that date, because, by reason of the contract, he has an interest in the land to be conveyed, he will be able to ask the court to intervene by way of injunction to prevent the vendor from disposing of the property elsewhere. In the present case Inderwick would have been able to ask the court to intervene by way of injunction had the trustees, d after the auction and consequent agreement for a lease, attempted to sell the land free from his interest under the agreement to have a lease granted to him on completion of the construction of the houses.

30. I agree with the trustees' submission contrary to the appellant's alternative submission, that the case of *Carrington Manufacturing v Saldin* (1925) 133 LT 432 is of no assistance in deciding this issue. The question with which we have to deal is e what was the status of Inderwick at the time when he built the house. He was not then a tenant, either at law or in equity, notwithstanding that the lease which was subsequently granted to him extended its term backward to a time before construction started.

31. In the further alternative the appellant submitted, on the authority of the f decision of Scott J in *Hambros Bank Executor & Trustee Co Ltd v Superdrug Stores Ltd* [1985] 1 EGLR 99 that, notwithstanding that Inderwick was not to be treated as a tenant in equity at the time No 25 was constructed, he has none the less to be treated as such a tenant for the purposes of sub-s (1A)(d). That case concerned the construction of a rent review clause in a lease where there was a plain expectation that it would be unfair for a tenant to be required to pay rent referable to his own g voluntary improvements. Subsection (1A)(d) is concerned with the position of a 'predecessor in title' of the applicant for enfranchisement. Those words cannot apply to somebody who happens, subsequently to doing work to premises, to become its tenant, such as a subtenant or licensee. They do apply to a person in whom the applicant's tenancy, as extended by s 3(3), is vested at the time that any h improvements to the property in question are made. The present case concerns works which were carried out under covenant as part of the consideration for the grant of a long lease at a ground rent, the benefit of which has been enjoyed by the appellant and his predecessors in title, and whether those works constitute improvements for the purpose of a valuation process prescribed for a particular j statutory purpose in the 1967 Act. Those are entirely different issues to those under consideration by Scott J in the *Hambros Bank* case. I agree with the tribunal's conclusion that the decision in that case does not assist the appellant.

32. It is then submitted by the appellant that the statutory conditions of sale provided for by s 45(6) of the Law of Property Act 1925 are to be imported into the contract resulting from s 5(1) of the 1967 Act and imposed on the parties to an enfranchisement under that Act. Section 45(6) provides:

> 'Recitals, statements, and descriptions of facts, matters, and parties contained in deeds, instruments, Acts of Parliament, or statutory declarations, twenty years old at the date of the contract, shall, unless and except so far as they may be proved to be inaccurate, be taken to be sufficient evidence of the truth of such facts, matters, and descriptions.'

33. It follows, so it is submitted, that references in the recitals to the 1852 lease to No 25 being 'put up to be let by public auction', and similar expressions using the word 'let' or 'letting', with relation to the transaction resulting from the auction, require the trustees to accept that Inderwick was, after the auction, a tenant of No 25 and so a predecessor in title of the appellant for the purposes of sub-s (1A)(d).

34. This contention must fail. Subsection (6) is subject to the proviso 'unless and except so far as they may be proved to be inaccurate'. It has been established that there was no 'letting' in the sense of the granting of a lease as a result of the transaction following the auction by reason of the legal consequences of facts which were agreed by the parties' experts to have existed at the relevant time. Further the words 'let' and 'letting' are not unambiguous and are not inappropriate to describe an agreement for a lease to be granted in the future conditional upon the performance of certain works on the landlord's land.

35. It is finally submitted that a similar result is achieved because the trustees are estopped by deed from denying the meaning of the words 'let' and 'letting' contained in the recitals to the 1852 lease. Again it seems to me, that the point fails, again because the words 'let' and 'letting' are not unambiguous of meaning. In addition the recitals to the 1852 lease contain a recital that the auctioneer—

> 'at the said letting as agent for and with the authority [of the trustees] made and signed an agreement in writing with the said John Inderwick for a lease of the said premises on the terms hereinafter contained.'

It is an agreed fact that the agreement for a lease was subject to a condition for the construction of houses by Inderwick including No 25.

36. For these reasons I would dismiss the appeal.

WARD LJ.

I agree.

OTTON LJ.

I also agree

Appeal dismissed. Permission to appeal to the House of Lords refused.

Kate O'Hanlon Barrister.

a

Chelsea Yacht and Boat Co Ltd v Pope

COURT OF APPEAL, CIVIL DIVISION
MORRITT, WALLER AND TUCKEY LJJ
6 APRIL 2000

b

Chattel – Annexation to land – Houseboat – Claimant owning houseboat moored to pontoon and embankment wall by ropes – Defendant occupying houseboat as his home under agreement with claimant – Claimant seeking possession – Whether houseboat chattel or part of land – Housing Act 1988, s 1(1).

c

The claimant, C Ltd, was the owner of a houseboat moored stern to a pontoon by rope mooring lines. Lines from the bow went to an anchor in the river bed at the foot of an embankment wall and to rings in the wall itself. The houseboat was connected to services provided by C Ltd, but those services could be disconnected, and the ropes untied, to enable it to be towed away by a barge. It was occupied d by the defendant, P, under an agreement originally reached with C Ltd's predecessor in title. C Ltd brought proceedings against P, seeking possession of the houseboat for failure to pay rent and other breaches of the agreement. On the hearing of a preliminary issue, P contended that the agreement was subject to Pt I of the Housing Act 1988 which, by virtue of s 1(1)[a], applied to a tenancy under which a dwelling house was let. The district judge accepted that contention, and e his decision was affirmed on appeal by the judge. C Ltd appealed, contending that the houseboat was a chattel and that accordingly the agreement fell outside Pt I of the 1988 Act. On the appeal, P accepted that the 1988 Act applied only to the letting of land, that the houseboat was a chattel unless it had become part of the land and that the question whether a structure had become part of the land f depended on the degree and object of the annexation to the land. In contending that the houseboat had become part of the land, P contended, inter alia, that the purpose of the annexation was to provide a home.

Held – The houseboat had not become part of the land. The attachments could be undone, and the houseboat could be moved quite easily without injury to g itself or the land. Moreover, it was not necessary to annex the houseboat to the land to enable it to be used as a home. The attachments were to prevent the houseboat from being carried by the tide or the weather up or downstream, and to provide services to it. In those circumstances, neither the degree nor the purpose of the annexation required the recognition of the houseboat as part of h the land. Such a conclusion was supported by common sense. It was common sense that a boat on a river was not part of the land. A boat, albeit one used as a home, was not of the same genus as real property. Accordingly, the agreement in the instant case was not governed by the 1988 Act, and the appeal would therefore be allowed (see p 414 *b* to *g* and p 416 *f* to *h*, post).

j *Elitestone Ltd v Morris* [1997] 2 All ER 513 applied.

Notes

For annexation of chattels to land, see 35 *Halsbury's Laws* (4th edn reissue) para 1238.

---

a Section 1, so far as material, is set out at p 411 *j*, post

For the Housing Act 1988, s 1, see 23 *Halsbury's Statutes* (4th edn) (1997 reissue) 1056. a

Cases referred to in judgments

Cory v Bristow (1877) 2 App Cas 262, [1874–80] All ER Rep 136, HL.
Elitestone Ltd v Morris [1997] 2 All ER 513, [1997] 1 WLR 687, HL.
Forrest v Greenwich Overseers (1858) 8 E & B 890, 120 ER 332. b
Holland v Hodgson (1872) LR 7 CP 328, [1861–73] All ER Rep 237, Ex Ch.
Leigh v Taylor [1902] AC 157, [1900–3] All ER Rep 520, HL.
Makins v Elson (Inspector of Taxes) [1977] 1 All ER 572, [1977] 1 WLR 221.
R v Rent Officer of Nottinghamshire Registration Area, ex p Allen [1985] 2 EGLR 153.
Stubbs v Hartnell (1997) 74 P & CR D36, CA.
Westminster City Council v Woodbury (Valuation Officer) [1991] 2 EGLR 173, CA. c

Cases also cited or referred to in skeleton arguments

Burton v London & Quadrant Housing Trust [1999] 3 All ER 481, [2000] 1 AC 406, HL.
Curl v Angelo [1948] 2 All ER 189, CA.
Family Housing Association v Jones [1990] 1 All ER 385, [1990] 1 WLR 779, CA. d
Haskins v Lewis [1931] 2 KB 1, [1930] All ER Rep 297, CA.
Ponder v Hillman [1969] 3 All ER 694, [1969] 1 WLR 1261.
R v Guildford Area Rent Tribunal, ex p Grubery [1951] EGD 286.
Skinner v Geary [1931] 2 KB 546, [1931] All ER Rep 302, CA.
Spraggs v Prentice (1950) 100 LJ 541. e
Street v Mountford [1985] 2 All ER 289, [1985] AC 809, HL.

Appeal

By notice dated 26 April 1999 the claimants, Chelsea Yacht and Boat Co Ltd, appealed with permission of Judge Cotran from his decision at West London County Court on 31 March 1999 dismissing their appeal from the decision of f District Judge Madge on 9 September 1998 whereby, on the determination of a preliminary issue, he held that the agreement under which the defendant, Justin Pope, occupied the Dinty Moore, a houseboat owned by the claimants and moored at mooring No 21, 106 Cheyne Walk, London SW10, was governed by the Housing Act 1988. The facts are set out in the judgment of Tuckey LJ. g

John Male (instructed by *Winward Fearon*) for the claimants.
Valerie Easty (instructed by *Anthony Gold, Lerman & Muirhead*) for Mr Pope.

TUCKEY LJ (giving the first judgment at the invitation of Morritt LJ).

1. Is the letting of a houseboat, the tenancy of a dwelling house for the purpose h of Pt 1 of the Housing Act 1988?

2. This question arises on appeal from Judge Cotran in the West London County Court who decided that the agreement under which the defendant, Mr Pope, occupies a houseboat on the Thames was such a tenancy.

3. The claimants, Chelsea Yacht and Boat Co Ltd, now own the houseboat. j They also run the boatyard and own the moorings where it is moored on the north side of the river upstream of Battersea Bridge in London. The boatyard has various facilities for houseboats on the embankment and on floating barges.

4. The bed of the river is owned by the Port of London Authority who, for an annual licence fee, permit the claimants to maintain among other things mooring piles, mooring pontoons and gangways to accommodate residential craft in the

a river. The licence authorises them to grant mooring licences and charge fees for the use of the moorings. The mooring pontoons rise and fall with the tide and run in a line parallel with the embankment wall in Cheyne Walk. The houseboats are moored in a line either side of and stern or bow to the pontoons. They lie across the stream held by anchors. On the pontoons the claimants provide services for the houseboats in the shape of water, gas, electricity, telephone and vacuum drainage. b These services are easily connected to the houseboats by plug-in or snap-on connections.

5. The Dinty Moore occupied by Mr Pope is a converted wooden D-Day landing craft fitted inside a steel Thames barge built by the claimants in about 1967. It is 46 feet long and 11 feet wide and is moored stern to the pontoon and the adjoining houseboats by a number of rope mooring lines. Lines from the bow c go to an anchor in the river bed at the foot of the embankment wall and to rings in the wall itself. It is connected to the services provided by the claimants. The houseboat takes the ground at about half tide. In other words it is afloat for about six hours or so and then aground for the following six hours. The conversion involved removal of the engine and the creation of permanent living accommodation d below, the layout and detail of which do not matter.

6. In 1993 the houseboat was owned by Mrs Crafter and was moored in the position I have described (mooring 21) under the terms of a mooring licence from the claimants. Mrs Crafter let it and its contents to Mr Pope on the terms of a written agreement dated 31 August 1993 (the agreement). The agreement is in a e form largely appropriate for the letting of a dwelling house. That is not surprising since it closely follows the form in the *Encyclopaedia of Forms and Precedents* (5th edn, 1991) vol 24 which is preceded by a note which says:

> 'A houseboat is a chattel, and although the hiring of a chattel cannot strictly be termed a leasing, an agreement for the hiring of a houseboat which will f remain at the same mooring place may well follow the general form of an agreement for the tenancy of real property.'

7. The agreement describes the parties as landlord and tenant and the houseboat as a single-storey vessel. The letting was for a term of six months from 1 September 1993 at an annual rent of £3,380 pa payable monthly. Mr Pope agreed to carry out g certain repairs to the houseboat straightaway, including painting its hull, and to keep it and the mooring in good and tenantable repair. He was not to allow it to obstruct the waterway or use it other than as a single private dwelling. It was not to be removed from the mooring without Mrs Crafter's permission other than to enable Mr Pope to comply with his obligations under the agreement.

h 8. Mr Pope has made his home in the houseboat since 1993. The agreement was extended at six-monthly intervals by Mrs Crafter until about 1996 when the claimants bought the houseboat from her. They extended the agreement until 30 April 1997 but then sought possession for failure to pay the rent and other breaches of the agreement. Proceedings were started in March 1998 and the j question which gives rise to this appeal, 'was the agreement governed by the Housing Act 1988?' was decided as a preliminary issue. Both the district judge and Judge Cotran, as I have said, decided that it was.

9. So far as is relevant to this case the 1988 Act applies to 'A tenancy under which a dwelling house is let' (s 1(1)). The claimants contended firstly that the houseboat is a chattel and so is incapable of being the subject of a tenancy and secondly, that in any event a houseboat is not a dwelling house.

10. It is not clear from the judge's judgment whether he appreciated that these were separate points. He appears to have accepted that the houseboat had become part of the land by annexation. He did not think such a conclusion would create difficulties, saying: 'The houseboat has been there for many years. It was bought by the plaintiff. It can be sold to somebody else. I do not see any problem relating to the ownership of the land on which it lies.'

11. At the end of his judgment he said correctly that there was no decided case dealing with a houseboat. And added:

> 'It makes not the slightest difference, as far as I am concerned, whether a houseboat lies on the land after removal from water or is attached to the river bed and/or floats for part of the day, so long as it is permanently immobile and let as such.'

12. On the second point he appears to have agreed with the district judge who said: 'I can see no reason, why in circumstances such as these, a houseboat cannot be both a dwelling house and a boat. That is, after all, what the word "houseboat" implies.'

13. On this appeal we have only heard argument on the first point, since it is accepted on behalf of Mr Pope that if the claimants are right on this point the appeal must succeed.

14. It is common ground that the 1988 Act only applies to the letting of land and that the houseboat is a chattel unless it has become part of the land by annexure.

15. The principles by which to test whether a chattel has become part of the land have recently been considered by the House of Lords in *Elitestone Ltd v Morris* [1997] 2 All ER 513, [1997] 1 WLR 687. In that case the question was whether a chalet resting only by its own weight on concrete pillars set into the ground had become part of the land. The chalet was connected to the usual services. It could not be taken down and re-erected elsewhere; it could only be removed by demolition. The House restored the assistant recorder's conclusion that it was part of the land. The headnote says:

> '... the answer to the question whether a structure became part and parcel of the land itself depended on the degree and the object of annexation to the land; that, assessed objectively, a house built in such a way that it could not be removed except by destruction could not have been intended to remain a chattel and must have been intended to form part of the realty ...' (See [1997] 1 WLR 687.)

16. Various passages in the speeches in this case are relied on by both sides. However, the broad questions which the court has to consider are accurately summarised in the headnote.

17. In considering the degree of annexation, it is obviously of importance that the chattel can be removed without injury to itself or to the land. There must also be a degree of permanence. Purpose is also important as the illustration given by Blackburn J in *Holland v Hodgson* (1872) LR 7 CP 328 at 335, [1861–73] All ER Rep 237 at 242 cited with approval in the *Elitestone* case shows. He said:

> '... blocks of stone placed one on top of another without any mortar or cement for the purpose of forming a dry stone wall would become part of the land, though the same stones, if deposited in a builder's yard and for convenience sake stacked on the top of each other in the form of a wall,

a would remain chattels. On the other hand, an article may be very firmly fixed to the land, and yet the circumstances may be such as to shew that it was never intended to be part of the land, and then it does not become part of the land. The anchor of a large ship must be very firmly fixed in the ground in order to bear the strain of the cable, yet no one could suppose that it became part of the land, even though it should chance that the shipowner b was also the owner of the fee at the spot where the anchor was dropped. An anchor similarly fixed in the soil for the purpose of bearing the strain of the chain of a suspension bridge would be part of the land.'

18. Miss Easty in her clear and spirited submissions to us on behalf of Mr Pope referred to a number of other cases under different legislation. First, she referred c to rating cases where the court had to consider whether the occupiers of a hulk (*Cory v Bristow* (1877) 2 App Cas 262, [1874–80] All ER Rep 136), a landing stage (*Forrest v Greenwich Overseers* (1858) 8 E & B 890, 120 ER 332) and the Hispaniola (*Westminster City Council v Woodbury (Valuation Officer)* [1991] 2 EGLR 173)—all in the Thames—were in rateable occupation of land. But these cases only illustrate the circumstances in which under the intricacies of rating law a chattel becomes d rateable if it occupies land or is enjoyed with land. They shed no light on the circumstances in which a chattel becomes part of the land and therefore I do not find them of assistance in this case. The same applies to the poll tax case of *Stubbs v Hartnell* (1997) 74 P & CR D36 which concerned a houseboat in the Thames.

e 19. Miss Easty also referred us to *Makins v Elson (Inspector of Taxes)* [1977] 1 All ER 572, [1977] 1 WLR 221 where the court had to consider whether the taxpayer was liable to capital gains tax upon the disposal of his mobile caravan under the terms of s 29 of the Finance Act 1965. That Act distinguished between a dwelling house and land. The question whether the caravan became part of the land did not f therefore arise and again I do not think that this decision helps to resolve the instant case.

20. Finally, Miss Easty relied on the decision of Farquharson J in *R v Rent Officer of Nottinghamshire Registration Area, ex p Allen* [1985] 2 EGLR 153 who quashed the decision of a rent officer who had registered a fair rent for a caravan on the basis that its letting fell within the Rent Act 1977. In the course of his judgment g Farquharson J said that it was not possible to say that just because the subject matter of the letting was a caravan it would not fall within the 1977 Act. However, it is clear from the judgment that the only point the judge considered was whether the caravan was a house. That is the second point in this case upon which we have not heard argument. I do not think the decision casts any real h light on the first point which we have to decide.

21. The *Elitestone* case is binding upon us and we have to apply the principles laid down in that case. How should they be applied to the facts of this case?

22. Miss Easty firstly argued that both the district judge and the judge had found the facts against the claimants in a way which did not enable this court to j interfere.

23. I do not accept this submission. The district judge decided the case on the basis that the *Elitestone* case was of no assistance. He does not appear to have addressed the question of whether the houseboat became part of the land at all. As I have already said, it is not clear whether the judge really did so either. If he did, he appears to have based his decision on the fact that the houseboat was 'permanently immobile and let as such'. But it was not permanently immobile

and it is common ground that the terms of the agreement could not of themselves have created the necessary annexure. For these reasons I do not think we are in any way bound by the findings below. *a*

24. Turning firstly to the degree of annexure it is important to bear in mind that what is required is sufficient attachment to the land so that the chattel becomes part of the land itself. Here the houseboat rested periodically on the river bed below it and was secured by ropes, and perhaps to an extent the services, to other structures. It is difficult to see how attachments in this way to the pontoons, the anchor in the riverbed and the rings in the embankment wall could possibly make the houseboat part of the land. One is bound to ask 'which land'? There is in my judgment no satisfactory answer to this question. More importantly, however, all these attachments could simply be undone. The houseboat could be moved quite easily without injury to itself or the land. The agreement contemplates that it will be moved, and, in practical terms, required Mr Pope to dry dock it if he was to fulfil his obligation to paint the hull. The fact that it cannot move under its own power is not the point. Whilst the houseboat was obviously intended to be moored where it was for the term of the agreement at least, the fact that it could and would have to be moved greatly undermines the argument based on permanence. *b* *c* *d*

25. Turning then to the object or purpose of annexure, Miss Easty strongly submits that the attachment of the houseboat was to provide a permanent home for its occupant. I do not agree. It is not necessary to annex the houseboat to the land to enable it to be used as a home. The attachments were, like the ship's anchor referred to by Blackburn J, to prevent the houseboat from being carried by the tide or the weather up or down stream and to provide the services to it. *e*

26. For these reasons I conclude that the houseboat has not become part of the land. I support this conclusion on the grounds of common sense. It is common sense that a house built on land is part of the land (see Lord Lloyd of Berwick in the *Elitestone* case [1997] 2 All ER 513 at 518–519, [1997] 1 WLR 687 at 692). So too it is common sense that a boat on a river is not part of the land. A boat, albeit one used as a home, is not of the same genus as real property. *f*

27. For these reasons I would allow this appeal and answer No to the question, 'Was the agreement governed by the Housing Act 1988?'

28. **WALLER LJ.** I agree that, for the reasons given by Tuckey LJ and those about to be given by Morritt LJ, which I have had the advantage of reading in draft, this appeal should be allowed. *g*

29. **MORRITT LJ.** The circumstances in which this appeal arises have been fully described by Tuckey LJ. I gratefully adopt his account of them. It is common ground that the Housing Act 1988 applies to lease or tenancies of land but not of equivalent agreements in relation to chattels. It is equally plain that originally both the landing craft and the barge in which it now rests were chattels. It seems to me, therefore, that there are two questions only. (1) Has the combined barge/landing-craft become part of the land? (2) If it has, is it a dwelling-house? *h* *j*

30. We heard argument on the first point only. Accordingly the views I express are directed to that point alone even if some of them might be capable of being addressed to both of them.

31. We are, of course, bound by the decision of the House of Lords in *Elitestone Ltd v Morris* [1997] 2 All ER 513, [1997] 1 WLR 687. In that case the House of Lords pointed out that the question was whether the chattel had become part

a and parcel of the land, not whether it was a fixture (see [1997] 2 All ER 513 at 517–518, [1997] 1 WLR 687 at 691). The House of Lords also approved the test formulated by Blackburn J in *Holland v Hodgson* (1872) LR 7 CP 328, [1861–73] All ER Rep 237 that the answer to the question depends on two factors, the degree and object of annexation. Lord Lloyd of Berwick ([1997] 2 All ER 513 at 519, [1997] 1 WLR 687 at 693) pointed out that the intention of the parties was only relevant b to the extent to which it could be derived from the degree and object of annexation. Illustrative of those principles in relation to a tapestry is the decision in *Leigh v Taylor* [1902] AC 157, [1900–3] All ER Rep 520 to which we were referred.

32. In addition to these three cases we were referred to a number of other cases by way of illustration. I commend Miss Easty for her diligence, but I find c them of no assistance.

33. The three rating cases, *Cory v Bristow* (1877) 2 App Cas 262, [1874–80] All ER Rep 136, *Forrest v Greenwich Overseers* (1858) 8 E & B 890, 120 ER 332 and *Westminster City Council v Woodbury (Valuation Officer)* [1991] 2 EGLR 173 were all concerned with whether there was rateable occupation of the river bed by means d of a derrick hulk, a vessel permanently moored and the landing stage. In none of them was the court concerned with the question whether the chattel in question had itself become a part of the land.

34. In *Makins v Elson (Inspector of Taxes)* [1977] 1 All ER 572, [1977] 1 WLR 221 the court was concerned with the exemption from capital gains tax afforded to the taxpayer's residence by s 29 of the Finance Act 1965. The definition of e residence for present purposes was:

> '… (a) a dwelling-house or part of a dwelling-house which is, or has at any time in his period of ownership been, his only or main residence, or (b) land which he has for his own occupation and enjoyment with that residence as f its garden or grounds …'

35. Foster J held that the taxpayer's caravan was within para (a) of that definition. It formed no part of his conclusion that in the circumstances of the case the caravan which he had described had become a part of the land itself. In *Stubbs v Hartnell* (1997) 74 P & CR D36 the court was concerned with liability to g council tax in relation to a houseboat. But liability did not depend on whether the houseboat was part of the land or not. Accordingly, it is of no direct relevance to the question before us. In *R v Rent Officer of Nottinghamshire Registration Area, ex p Allen* [1985] 2 EGLR 153 the question was whether a fully mobile caravan was a house for the purposes of the Rent Act 1977. The question whether it was part of the land was not argued. To the like effect, there is a decision in respect of a h houseboat called the Lady Betty noted in [1949] 118 JPR 376. The question was whether it was a house within the meaning of the Furnished Houses (Rent Control) Act 1946, not whether it was part of the land.

36, 37. In agreeing with the district judge, Judge Cotran said:

> j 'The factors necessary to decide the preliminary issue … were: (a) the terms of tenancy—use and removability; (b) the degree of permanence and moveability/immoveability; and (c) the nature of the structure and its use. [The district judge] said that on the facts as he found them, and on the three factors of importance, the Dinty Moore [and] nothing else, was an assured tenancy within the meaning of the Housing Act 1988. It seems to me that to argue that no houseboat can ever be protected is wrong. Certainly it is

wrong if one considers the criteria that the case law has put forward. There has been no decision on a houseboat as such but there has been, in relation to a caravan and its mobility/immobility, and it makes not the slightest difference, as far as I am concerned, whether a houseboat lies on the land after removal from water or is attached to the river bed and/or floats for part of the day, so long as it is permanently immobile and let as such.'

38. In my view there are a number of criticisms which may be made of that passage. First the terms of the tenancy do not appear to me to have any relevance to whether there has been the requisite degree or purpose of annexation. They show the intention of the parties in regard to the contract, but, as Lord Lloyd pointed out in the *Elitestone* case [1997] 2 All ER 513 at 519, [1997] 1 WLR 687 at 693 the intention of the parties is irrelevant save in so far as it is derived from the degree and object of the annexation. Second, the judge considered that the only points of importance were whether the object was permanently immobile and let as such. On the first point he was wrong as a matter of fact: the Dinty Moore could be easily detached from its moorings and service connections and towed away by a barge. The second point was only relevant if the 1988 Act applied, and that depended on whether the Dinty Moore was part of the land; thus reliance on the second point begged the question to be determined. Third, the judge did not seek to apply the *Elitestone* case, or, as was required by that decision, the twin factors of degree and object of annexation. Indeed he said that that case did not assist the argument.

39. In the light of these criticisms I reject the submission by counsel for Mr Pope that the issue was one of fact on which both judges below had reached clear conclusions with which this court should not interfere.

40. The proper test is that laid down in *Holland v Hodgson* as approved in the *Elitestone* case. The court has to consider both the degree and object of annexation. The Dinty Moore is attached to the river wall and the river, in the manner described by Tuckey LJ, ultimately by ropes and service connections. Those ropes and services may be untied and disconnected without any undue effort to enable the Dinty Moor to be towed away by a barge. Thus the degree of annexation does not require recognition of the Dinty Moore as part of the land.

41. Counsel for Mr Pope emphasised that the purpose of the annexation was to provide a home. Certainly the object of the conversion of the landing craft and its attachment to the services was to provide a home. But there is nothing to prevent the removal of the Dinty Moore from this mooring to another. The provision of a home does not necessitate annexing the structure (be it a caravan or a boat) to the land so as to become a part of it; it is sufficient that it is fitted out for living in.

42. I agree with Tuckey LJ that the Dinty Moore cannot, in these and the other circumstances to which he refers, be regarded as a part of the land. In those circumstances the second question, whether the Dinty Moore is a dwelling house within the 1988 Act, does not arise.

43. I too would allow this appeal.

Appeal allowed.

Gillian Daly Barrister.

20 November 2000. The Appeal Committee of the House of Lords dismissed Mr Pope's petition for permission to appeal.

a

National Grid Co plc v Mayes and others

International Power plc (formerly National Power plc) v Healy and others

[2001] UKHL/20

b

HOUSE OF LORDS

LORD SLYNN OF HADLEY, LORD STEYN, LORD HOFFMANN, LORD CLYDE, LORD SCOTT OF FOSCOTE

13–15, 19 FEBRUARY, 4 APRIL 2001

c

Pension – Company pension scheme – Surplus fund – Pensions scheme requiring employers to make arrangements to deal with actuarial surplus but precluding amendment 'making any of the moneys of the Scheme payable to any of the Employers' – Employers making arrangements to treat their accrued liabilities to fund as d *discharged out of surplus funds – Whether release of debt owed to fund by employers amounting to payment to them out of fund – Whether amendment required before arrangements could be made to treat employers' accrued liabilities as discharged out of surplus funds – Pensions Act 1995, s 37.*

e In 1983, when the electricity industry was in public ownership, a new pension scheme was established for the benefit of its employees, replacing two schemes established in 1947. After privatisation in 1990, the scheme was amended to become, in effect, separate schemes for a number of 'groups' corresponding to the various companies (and their subsidiaries) which had succeeded to the assets and liabilities of the former state-owned corporations. Each scheme operated by f reference to the same instrument, and provided for fixed benefits which were defined by the rules and were not related to the value of the fund. Members contributed 6% of pensionable salary to a trust fund upon which their benefits were secured, while the employers contributed the rest. Clause 14(1) required a triennial valuation in a form which enabled the assets and liabilities of each group to be considered separately. Clause 14(5) provided that if the actuary certified g that there was a surplus in the fund, the principal employer of the group 'shall make arrangements, certified by the actuary as reasonable, to deal with the surplus'. Clause 41(2)(b) prohibited an amendment 'making any of the moneys of the Scheme payable to any of the Employers'. That clause had been included in the 1947 schemes in order to obtain Revenue approval and the ensuing fiscal h benefits. In 1992 the actuary certified surpluses for two groups, the NP and NG groups, and in 1995 he certified a surplus for the NP group. Both groups decided to use part of the surpluses to reduce the amounts which the employers paid in, by treating certain accrued liabilities to the fund as discharged. Those liabilities were not contributions which might become payable at some future date, but j actual debts payable to the fund, incurred to finance extra benefits for specific employees who had been made redundant. Some of the NG scheme members objected to such use of its 1992 surplus, and their complaint was upheld by the Pensions Ombudsman. He held, inter alia, that the release of an accrued debt from the employer to the scheme amounted to paying him an equivalent in money and was therefore precluded by cl 41(2)(b). NG appealed to the High Court, while NP issued a summons seeking a declaration that its own similar arrangements were valid. The two sets of proceedings were heard together. The judge concluded that the arrangements were valid, but his decision was reversed by the Court of Appeal which held that cl 14(5) conferred no power upon the employer to discharge his debts to the fund, and that the only way in which that could be done was by an amendment to the scheme. The court suggested, however, that the discharge of a debt was not a payment to the employer within the meaning of cl 41(2)(b), and that accordingly the employers would be able to give effect to their arrangements by means of a retrospective amendment. The employers appealed to the House of Lords, but in the meantime executed suitable deeds of amendment. On the appeal, the members contended that such an amendment was precluded by s 37[a] of the Pensions Act 1995 which applied where a power was conferred on any person to make payments to the employer out of the funds which were held for the purposes of the scheme. Section 37(2) provided that where such a power was conferred on a person other than the trustees, it could be exercised not by that person but by the trustees.

Held – On the true construction of cl 41(2)(b) of the scheme, arrangements to treat accrued liabilities of the employers as discharged out of surplus funds did not constitute a payment to the employees out of the moneys of the scheme. Such a construction was consistent with the fiscal origin of that provision. Its purpose had been to prevent the employer from resorting to assets which had enjoyed the fiscal privileges accorded to the scheme. Debts from the employer to the fund which had not yet fallen due for payment had enjoyed no fiscal privileges. That background suggested that the words 'making any of the moneys of the Scheme payable to any of the Employers' were not loose language intended to be applied to any transaction which, although not ordinarily so described, had the same economic effect. Rather, they were carefully chosen to exclude the release of debts owed by the employer. It followed that, one way or another, the employers had power to do what they had done. The arrangements did not infringe any express or implied restriction on the powers of the employer. The only question was the formalities which should have been adopted. If the amendment had been needed, it was not precluded by s 37 of the 1995 Act since that provision protected only those funds which had actually been paid into the scheme. However, the amendment had not been necessary. It was a matter of pragmatic choice for the employers as to whether the arrangements made under cl 14(5) were embodied in scheme amendments or not. Accordingly, the appeals would be allowed (see [1], [2], [18]–[26], [32], [63], [71]–[74], [78], [81], post).

British Coal Corp v British Coal Staff Superannuation Scheme Trustees Ltd [1995] 1 All ER 912 overruled.

Notes

For payments of surplus to an employer, see 44(2) *Halsbury's Laws* (4th edn reissue) para 860.

For the Pensions Act 1995, s 37, see 33 *Halsbury's Statutes* (4th edn) (1997 reissue) 898.

Cases referred to in opinions

Bank of Credit and Commerce International SA (No 8), Re [1997] 4 All ER 568, [1998] AC 214, [1997] 3 WLR 909, HL.

a Section 37 is set out at [27], post

a *British Coal Corp v British Coal Staff Superannuation Scheme Trustees Ltd* [1995] 1 All ER 912.

Imperial Group Pension Trust Ltd v Imperial Tobacco Ltd [1991] 2 All ER 597, [1991] 1 WLR 589.

Landau (a bankrupt), Re, Pointer v Landau [1997] 3 All ER 322, [1998] Ch 223, [1997] 3 WLR 225.

b *Mettoy Pension Trustees Ltd v Evans* [1991] 2 All ER 513, [1990] 1 WLR 1587.

Vauxhall Motor Pension Fund, Re, Bullard v Randall [1989] PLR 49.

Appeals

National Grid Co plc and International Power plc (formerly National Power plc) c appealed with leave from the decision of the Court of Appeal (Nourse, Schiemann and Brooke LJJ) on 10 February 1999 ([2000] ICR 174) allowing appeals by members of the National Grid and National Power groups of the Electricity Supply Pension Scheme from the decision of Robert Walker J on 10 June 1997 ([1997] PLR 157) whereby he (i) allowed an appeal by National Grid d from determinations by the Pensions Ombudsman on 7 February 1997 that arrangements to treat accrued liabilities of National Grid to the scheme fund as discharged from an actuarial surplus were invalid, and (ii) upheld the validity of similar arrangements in respect of liabilities of National Power to the scheme fund. The facts are set out in the opinion of Lord Hoffmann.

e *Christopher McCall QC, Peter Crampin QC* and *Michael Furness QC* (instructed by *Eversheds*) for National Grid.

Nigel Inglis-Jones QC and *Geoffrey Topham* (instructed by *Finers Stephen Innocent*) for the members of the National Grid group scheme.

Paul Newman (instructed by *Dibb Lupton Alsop*) for the trustees of the National f Grid group scheme.

Jonathan Sumption QC, Nicholas Warren QC and *Christopher Nugee QC* (instructed by *Linklaters & Alliance*) for International Power.

Andrew Simmonds QC (instructed by *Pinsent Curtis Biddle*) for the trustees of the National Power group scheme.

g *Alan Steinfeld QC* and *John Stephens* (instructed by *Lovells*) for the representative member of the National Power group scheme.

Their Lordships took time for consideration.

h 4 April 2001. The following opinions were delivered.

LORD SLYNN OF HADLEY. My Lords,

[**1**] For the reasons given in the speeches of my noble and learned friends Lord j Hoffmann and Lord Scott of Foscote, the text of which I have had the advantage of reading, I too would allow the appeals.

LORD STEYN. My Lords,

[**2**] I have had the advantage of reading in draft the speeches of my noble and learned friends Lord Hoffmann and Lord Scott of Foscote. For the reasons they give, I would also allow the appeals.

LORD HOFFMANN. My Lords,

The Electricity Supply Pension Scheme

[3] This appeal concerns the validity of arrangements which two companies in the electricity industry made in 1992 and 1995 to deal with actuarial surpluses which had arisen in a pension scheme established for the benefit of their employees. The scheme is called the Electricity Supply Pension Scheme and was established in 1983 when the industry was in public ownership. It replaced two schemes which had been established at the time of nationalisation in 1947 and, as we shall see, perpetuated certain ancestral features. After privatisation in 1990 the scheme was substantially amended to become, in effect, separate schemes for a number of 'groups' corresponding to the various companies (and their subsidiaries) which had succeeded to the assets and liabilities of the former state-owned corporations. Each operated by reference to the same instrument and with unitised holdings in a single trust fund, but with its own employers and members. The amended scheme contains many provisions designed to ensure that the assets and liabilities of each group are kept separate and that so far as possible they operate independently.

[4] The scheme is funded, contributory and fixed benefit. Benefits are defined by the rules and not related (as in the case of a money purchase scheme) to the value of the fund. On the contrary, it is ultimately the responsibility of the employer to ensure that the fund has enough money to pay the benefits. Members contribute 6% of pensionable salary to a trust fund upon which their benefits are secured. The employers, under various heads, contribute the rest. The provisions for the employers' contributions are, by modern standards, unusual, because they do not simply contribute whatever may be from time to time considered necessary to keep the scheme fully funded. Instead, they contribute various sums which are in theory fixed without reference to the state of the fund. At periodic intervals a valuation is made by the scheme actuary and arrangements are made to deal with any deficiency or surplus which may be disclosed. I say that in theory the employers' periodic contributions have no reference to the state of the fund but the scheme provides for voluntary contributions and in practice the actuary advises the employers as to the amount of voluntary contributions needed to avoid a deficiency at the next valuation. As we shall see, the actuary may also advise on measures to reduce a prospective surplus.

Dealing with a surplus

[5] This appeal concerns the provisions for periodic valuation followed by arrangements to deal with deficiency or surplus. Clause 14(1) requires a triennial valuation in a form which enables the assets and liabilities of each group to be considered separately. Valuations were made under this clause as at 31 March 1992 and 31 March 1995. In 1992 the actuary certified a surplus of £258m in respect of the group of which National Power plc (now called International Power plc) was the principal employer and £62·3m in respect of the group of which National Grid Co plc was the principal employer. In 1995 he certified a surplus of £73·7m in the National Power group.

[6] Clause 14(5) provides that if the actuary certifies that (on the assumptions there stated) there is a surplus in the fund, the principal employer of the group 'shall make arrangements, certified by the actuary as reasonable, to deal with the surplus'. The clause requires that notice of the arrangements be given to persons

a performing various functions under the scheme, but the only express restriction on the arrangements which can be made is that they must be certified by the actuary as reasonable. The issue in this appeal is whether the arrangements made by National Power and National Grid were within the powers conferred upon them by the scheme.

[7] There are only two ways of dealing with an actuarial surplus. You can pay b more money out of the scheme or you can reduce the amount of money coming in. Both National Power and National Grid decided to use part of the surpluses by paying out more money in the form of increased benefits for members and their dependants. They also decided to reduce the amounts which the employers paid in. There is no dispute about the payments for the benefit of members, which absorbed about a third of the surpluses. As the employers paid a standard c contribution of twice that of the members (besides various additional payments) the result was that the part of the surpluses used to improve benefits was roughly in proportion to what the members had paid in. But some of the National Grid members objected to it using any part of the 1992 surplus to reduce the employers' payments into the fund.

d

The ombudsman's decision

[8] The members complained to Dr Julian Farrand, the Pensions Ombudsman. He upheld the complaints on two grounds. First, he said that in exercising any powers under the scheme, the employers had an implied obligation to act in good faith. This obligation exists by virtue of the relationship of employer and e employee and requires that the employer should not exercise his powers for a collateral purpose or in a way which would destroy or seriously damage the relationship of trust and confidence with his employees (see *Imperial Group Pension Trust Ltd v Imperial Tobacco Ltd* [1991] 2 All ER 597, [1991] 1 WLR 589). The ombudsman considered that National Grid had been in breach of this f obligation by using a substantial part of the surplus in its own interest.

[9] Secondly, the ombudsman noted that the way National Grid proposed to reduce its contributions was by treating certain accrued liabilities to the fund as discharged. I shall have to describe the nature of these liabilities in more detail later, but for the moment it is enough to say that they were not merely contributions which might become payable at some future date, depending (for g example) on whether the employer was still in business, how many people were employed and what they were earning. They were actual debts payable to the fund, incurred to fund extra benefits for specific employees who had been made redundant. The ombudsman then drew attention to the clause dealing with amendment of the scheme. By cl 41(1) and (4), the employer had a wide power h of amendment. But cl 41(2)(b) prohibited an amendment 'making any of the moneys of the Scheme payable to any of the Employers'. The ombudsman said that the release of an accrued debt from the employer to the scheme amounted to paying him an equivalent in money. If such an amendment was prohibited, the draftsman must have assumed that no power to make such payments existed j within the scheme. Clause 14(5) could not therefore be construed as conferring such a power.

The High Court decision

[10] National Grid appealed against the ombudsman's decision to the High Court. National Power, which had made similar arrangements in respect of the 1992 and 1995 surpluses, took the opportunity to issue a summons seeking a

declaration that its own arrangements were valid. Both proceedings came before Robert Walker J ([1997] PLR 157). *a*

[11] The judge held that the ombudsman had interpreted the implied duty of good faith too strictly. The employer was not a trustee. He was entitled to act in his own interests provided that he had regard to the reasonable expectations of the members. The arrangements satisfied that requirement. On this point the members now accept that the judge was right. *b*

[12] The ombudsman's other ground remains central to the dispute. Robert Walker J said that the employer's duty under cl 14(5) to make arrangements to deal with the surplus conferred a power in the broadest terms to do whatever he thought appropriate. It was not restricted by other provisions of the scheme, such as the limits on the power of amendment. It could include the repayment of money to himself. The judge therefore did not need to decide whether the *c* discharge of an accrued liability amounted to a payment to the employer. On either view, the arrangements were valid.

The Court of Appeal decision

[13] The members appealed to the Court of Appeal (Nourse, Schiemann and *d* Brooke LJJ) ([2000] ICR 174). They differed from both the ombudsman and the judge. They said that cl 14(5) conferred no power upon the employer to discharge his debts to the fund. The only way in which this could be done was by an amendment of the scheme. As there had been no amendment, the arrangements were invalid and the appeal was allowed. But, contrary to the views of the ombudsman and the judge, the Court of Appeal were not inclined to think that *e* the discharge of a debt was a payment to the employer within the meaning of cl 41(2)(b). It followed that the employers would be able to give effect to their arrangements by an amendment, which under cl 41 could be retrospective.

The deeds of amendment *f*

[14] The employers acted upon this suggestion and executed suitable deeds of amendment. Your Lordships have given leave, by consent of all the parties, for the question of their validity to be raised for the first time in this House.

Does a release of a debt count as payment?

[15] My Lords, I think that the main question in this appeal is whether the *g* arrangements to treat accrued liabilities of the employers as discharged out of surplus funds amount to a payment to the employers out of the moneys of the scheme. Once that question has been decided, the other arguments fall into place.

[16] The question is one of construction, to be answered according to familiar *h* principles. The pension scheme background is of course very important. On the other hand, some of the matters put forward as relevant by Mr Inglis-Jones QC on behalf of the National Grid members seemed to me of marginal significance. For example, he said that the main purpose of the scheme was to provide pensions for the employees. That I would certainly accept. But then he said that *j* it would be inconsistent with such a purpose to make payments or the equivalent of payments to the employer. In relation to a surplus, this does not seem to me to follow. A surplus is (by definition) money in excess of what is needed to effect the main purpose of the scheme. Next, Mr Inglis-Jones said that it must be borne in mind that part of the surplus was funded by contributions from the employees. Indeed, the whole of the funding may be said to be either their contributions or

a payment for their services. No doubt considerations of this kind have influenced the implication of an implied term of good faith, but they cannot displace the fact that the scheme confers the power to make arrangements upon the employer and no one else. In some schemes the power is more evenly distributed but in this one it is not. Mr Inglis-Jones' submissions would lead to the conclusion that the employer cannot act in his own interests, but the implied term does not go so far. b Once it is accepted that he can act in his own interests, and that the extent to which he is doing so in this case cannot be criticised, I do not see the relevance of the way in which the surplus was funded.

[**17**] Mr Inglis-Jones then said that while it might be reasonable for the employer to suspend his future contributions, the release of accrued liabilities, or actual payment of money to himself, would imperil the security of the fund. An c actuarial surplus, he said, was notional and evanescent, here today and (with the slightest change in assumptions) gone tomorrow. That argument, as it seems to me, is really an argument against doing anything about a surplus at all. From the point of view of the adequacy of the fund, there is no difference between paying money to the employer and paying it in the form of (for example) extra benefits d to classes of employees. Both result in there being less money in the fund. Clause 14(5) in my view does not require the employer to be sceptical about the actuarial certificate. Caution is a matter for the actuary in certifying the surplus and certifying the arrangements as reasonable. The employer's duty is simply to make them.

e *The tax background*

[**18**] In my opinion the most relevant background is the fiscal origin of cl 41(2)(b). Everyone agrees that it was taken over from the 1947 predecessor schemes and that it was inserted into those schemes to obtain Inland Revenue approval under s 32 of the Finance Act 1921. Mr Inglis-Jones told your Lordships f that in his experience, dating back to before the regime was changed in 1970, the Revenue would not approve a scheme under the 1921 Act and its successor (s 379 of the Income Tax Act 1952) unless such a provision was included. It has been said on more than one occasion that many provisions in pension schemes and insurance contracts have to be construed against their fiscal backgrounds (see *Mettoy Pension Trustees Ltd v Evans* [1991] 2 All ER 513 at 537, [1990] 1 WLR 1587 g at 1610 and *Re Landau (a bankrupt), Pointer v Landau* [1997] 3 All ER 322 at 329, [1998] Ch 223 at 233). So I think it is important to consider why the Revenue insisted on provisions like cl 41(2)(b).

[**19**] Schemes approved under the provisions of the 1921 Act and its successor enjoyed great fiscal privileges. Money paid into the scheme by both employer h and employees was deductible for income tax. Income from the investments of the scheme was exempt from tax. To prevent members from obtaining tax exemption twice over, the Revenue insisted that in principle they should take their benefits in the form of taxable annuities. In these circumstances, it is hardly surprising that capital payments out of the fund to the employer were anathema j to the Revenue. They did not want the employer to be able to resort to a tax sheltered fund, either temporarily or permanently, for the purposes of his business.

[**20**] This fiscal purpose explains why the clause uses the words 'making any of the moneys of the Scheme payable to any of the Employers'. They are not the most natural way of describing the release of a debt owed by the employer to the scheme (compare *Re Bank of Credit and Commerce International SA (No 8)*

[1997] 4 All ER 568 at 578–579, [1998] AC 214 at 228–229). The release of a debt is not a payment, although it does have the same economic effect, in the sense that it reduces the assets of the fund and increases those of the employer. Of course, if it appears that the purpose of the provision is to prevent such an economic effect, ie to prevent any reduction in the assets of the fund for the benefit of the employer, then it may be reasonable to give the words a sufficiently wide meaning. The fiscal background shows however that the purpose was different. It was to prevent the employer from resorting to assets which had enjoyed the fiscal privileges accorded to the scheme. But debts from the employer to the fund which have not yet fallen due for payment have enjoyed no fiscal privileges. They are not deductible for tax until they have been paid and, at any rate until they have become payable, they cannot have earned any tax free income for the scheme.

[21] This background suggests that the words 'making any of the moneys of the Scheme payable to any of the Employers' were not loose language intended to be applied to any transaction which, although not ordinarily so described, had the same economic effect. They were carefully chosen to exclude the release of debts owed by the employer. It is true that such debts, in common with most assets of the fund, are choses in action. Money (for example, deposits with a bank) usually consists of choses in action. But deposits with a bank represent money which has been paid into the tax-sheltered scheme. Money owed by the employer has not.

[22] Confirmation of this construction may be found in cl 15 of one of the old schemes (the British Electricity Authority and Area Boards Superannuation Scheme), which corresponds to cl 14 of the 1983 scheme. It also provided for periodic valuations and the certification by the actuary of a deficiency or surplus. If there was a deficiency, the principal employer (which was then the British Electricity Authority) had to make arrangements by which it and the other employers contributed to the fund—

> 'an annual deficiency contribution of such amount, and calculated to make good the deficiency over a period not exceeding 40 years from the date of the valuation, as the Authority may determine.'

[23] A deficiency contribution was therefore an accrued debt owed to the fund and payable by annual instalments. If, however, there was a surplus at the next valuation, the authority had to make arrangements to dispose of it. Clause 15(4) of the old scheme, by contrast to the general terms of cl 14(5) of the present scheme, was specific about the arrangements which had to be made. In the first place, 'the amount or the outstanding term of any existing annual deficiency contribution shall be reduced' up to the capital value of the available surplus. The debt was to be cancelled. This does not suggest that the Revenue or anyone else thought that the cancellation of a contribution debt amounted to making the moneys of the fund payable to the employer.

[24] The language of cl 41(2)(b) was taken over by the 1983 scheme at a time when a new approval regime had been introduced by the Finance Act 1970 and the Revenue did not insist upon so absolute a prohibition on payments to the employer as it had before. But this certainly does not suggest that the language of cl 41(2)(b) was intended to have a wider meaning. I think it meant the same as it did before.

[25] I therefore agree with the tentative view of the Court of Appeal that the release of an accrued debt owed by the employer is not a payment to the

a employer out of the moneys of the fund. This is contrary to the opinion of Vinelott J in *British Coal Corp v British Coal Staff Superannuation Scheme Trustees Ltd* [1995] 1 All ER 912, a decision which was very properly followed by the ombudsman. It does not however appear from the report of that case that counsel drew the attention of the judge to the fiscal background. Instead, the judge was presented (at 922) with an 'ingeniously constructed balance sheet' designed to prove that b the release of an accrued obligation did not have the same economic effect as a payment of money. Not surprisingly, he rejected the submission.

[26] This conclusion means that whether the ombudsman was right in thinking that a prohibition on payments to the employer was a fundamental principle of the scheme or whether the Court of Appeal was right in thinking that the arrangements could be effected only by amendment, the employers had, one c way or another, power to do what they did. The arrangements did not infringe any express or implied restriction on the powers of the employer. The only question is the formalities which should have been adopted. The judge's view was that the employers did not need to do more than give directions to the trustees. The Court of Appeal's view was that they should have executed a deed d of amendment. This omission they have since remedied by the retrospective deeds executed since the hearing in the Court of Appeal.

[27] The members say, however, that they have a second string to their bow. They submit that the Court of Appeal was right in saying that an amendment was needed. And although it is accepted that an amendment could have been made at the time of the valuations, they say that it is now too late. It was prohibited by e s 37 of the Pensions Act 1995, which came into force in April 1997:

> '(1) This section applies to a trust scheme if—(a) apart from this section, power is conferred on any person (including the employer) to make payments to the employer out of funds which are held for the purposes of the scheme, (b) the scheme is one to which Schedule 22 to the Taxes Act f 1988 (reduction of pension fund surpluses in certain exempt approved schemes) applies, and (c) the scheme is not being wound up.
>
> (2) Where the power referred to in subsection (1)(a) is conferred by the scheme on a person other than the trustees, it cannot be exercised by that person but may be exercised instead by the trustees; and any restriction g imposed by the scheme on the exercise of the power shall, so far as capable of doing so, apply to its exercise by the trustees.'

[28] There follow a number of statutory restrictions on the exercise of such a power by the trustees.

[29] The respondents submit that the new amendments would purport to h confer upon the principal employer a power to 'make payments to the employer out of funds which are held for the purposes of the scheme' and, the other conditions being satisfied, bring the scheme within s 37. The consequence is that by virtue of s 37(2), the power is exercisable only by the trustees and subject to the statutory conditions.

j **[30]** It will be observed that s 37(1) of the 1995 Act uses the words 'power … to make payments to the employer out of funds which are held for the purposes of the scheme'. It uses the concept of a payment out of the funds of the scheme which is similar to that used by cl 41(2)(b) and which I have suggested was not intended to include the release of an accrued debt. The members say that the words should be given a wider meaning in s 37. Clause 41(2)(b) may have to be interpreted against a fiscal background but s 37 has nothing to do with tax. It is for the protection of the members. Therefore the concept of paying the employer out of funds which are held for the purposes of the scheme should be given a wide meaning to preserve the assets of the fund, including debts owed by the employer. a

[31] I quite accept that s 37 of the 1995 Act does not have the exclusively fiscal background of cl 41(2)(b). Nevertheless, the language seems to me to show clearly that Parliament adopted the fiscal concept of payment to an employer out of the funds of the scheme. It substantially reproduces the language of s 601(1) of the Income and Corporation Taxes Act 1988, which imposes a 40% charge to tax 'where a payment is made to an employer out of funds which are or have been held for the purposes of a scheme which is or has at any time been an exempt approved scheme'. That section is plainly not intended to tax the employer on money which has never come into the scheme. b c

[32] One may ask why this more restricted concept should have been used in a statute designed for the protection of the members of the scheme. The answer, as it seems to me, is a recognition that, in a funded scheme, there are bound to be adjustments in the rate of funding. It is to be expected that the level of contributions by the employer may be increased or reduced from time to time. And although Mr Inglis-Jones sought to persuade your Lordships that the distinction between accrued and contingent liabilities was of great importance in pension law, I think that at least for this purpose it makes little commercial sense. It involves saying that, in the context of reducing a surplus, the employer cannot be released from debts which are accrued but not yet payable but can be released from paying contributions which are contingently due but (while the scheme is a going concern) virtually certain to become payable. No businessman, in estimating his ability to meet future liabilities, would make such a distinction. In my opinion the effect of s 37 of the 1995 Act is to protect only those funds which have actually been paid into the scheme. This strikes a sensible commercial balance between flexibility of funding and the interests of the members. d e f

[33] Mr Inglis-Jones also relied upon s 40 of the 1995 Act, which treats debts due and payable by the employer to the fund as if they were loans to the employer for the purposes of regulations which prohibit such investments. This, he says, shows that debts from the employer are treated as assets of the fund. But I do not think that this casts much light upon the construction of s 37, which uses the concept of 'payments' out of the funds rather than a reduction of its assets. In any case, we are not concerned with debts which were due and payable. The liabilities discharged out of surplus were debts due but not yet payable. g

[34] My Lords, these conclusions are (subject to two subsidiary arguments to which I shall have to return) sufficient to dispose of the appeal. If an amendment was needed, it has been effected. The 1992 and 1995 arrangements have been validated. But the question of whether an amendment was needed is of great practical importance to the trustees administering the scheme. After future valuations, they will need to know whether they can, as they have in the past, act upon the instructions of the employer or whether they must insist upon an amendment. I would suggest that your Lordships should decide the question. h j

Was an amendment necessary?

[35] I agree with the judge that the language of cl 14(5) is apt to confer upon the employer the power to make the arrangements which he considers necessary to deal with a surplus. The word 'shall' in my opinion connotes not only a duty but also the power to discharge that duty. I do not think that it requires the

a employer to scratch around among the other provisions of the scheme to find specific powers. But I would not go so far as the judge in saying, as he did ([1997] PLR 157 at 175–176 (para 83)), that the employer's powers were not intended to be restricted 'either specifically by cl 41(2)(b) or by what the employer could do under other clauses of the scheme, or generally by the context and purpose of the scheme'. I find it difficult to believe that the general words of cl 14(5) were b intended to give the employer power, without amendment, to do something which would contradict the express provisions of the scheme.

[36] It may also be that, as the ombudsman thought, the power is subject to implied limitations deducible from the context and purpose of the scheme. He said that there was an implied prohibition against paying the employer money from the fund. He derived this implication from cl 41(2)(b), which he said would c make no sense if cl 14(5) conferred a wide power for the employer to pay himself out of surplus. The suggestion that cl 41(2)(b) was intended only to prevent payments otherwise than out of surplus was implausible. I think that there is considerable force in this argument, at any rate if one tries to construe the scheme as a consistent whole.

d **[37]** Of course, the fact that the scheme cannot be amended to allow something to be done does not necessarily mean that a limited power to do that thing does not already exist within the scheme (see *Re Vauxhall Motor Pension Fund, Bullard v Randall* [1989] PLR 49 at 53). But such a prohibition is rather odd if the scheme already contains a very wide power. The trouble is that this scheme may not be altogether consistent. In the old predecessor schemes, there was no e inconsistency because the equivalent of cl 14(5) restricted the powers of the employer to dealing with surplus in certain specified ways: cancelling liability to pay deficiency contributions, retaining it in the fund or reducing the employers' standard contributions. There was nothing anywhere in the old scheme which could be construed as a power to pay money to the employers. The new scheme f created the difficulty by removing all the restrictions on what the employer could do about disposing of the surplus but leaving the prohibition on any amendment which would allow payments to the employer. My Lords, I do not intend to try to solve this puzzle because on the construction which I have given to making payments to the employer out of the fund, it does not arise.

[38] The real question, as it seems to me, is whether the arrangements which g the employers made to relieve themselves of liabilities contradicted the express provisions of the scheme. For this purpose it is necessary to explain in more detail what they were.

The employers' contributions

h **[39]** The contribution liabilities of the employer are set out in cl 13(1). I quote the relevant paragraphs:

> 'The Employers shall contribute to the Fund:
>
> (a) a monthly sum equal to twice the contributions for the time being paid by all Members respectively employed by them ... and ...
>
> j (e) in respect of any Member who retires under Rule 16 or person who ceases to be a Member on leaving service consequent on reorganisation or redundancy before age 50 such amount as determined by the Principal Employer on the advice of the Actuary; and
>
> (f) any sums payable in accordance with paragraph (3) of Rule 44 or sub-paragraph (2)(b) of Rule 45; and

(g) such further contributions as may from time to time be payable pursuant to the provisions of Clause 14(4) or may otherwise be determined by each Principal Employer for itself and its Participating Subsidiaries;

Provided That the contributions (whether due and payable or prospectively payable) by an Employer under sub-paragraphs (a) to (f) of this paragraph shall be reduced or suspended (whether with retrospective effect or otherwise) to the extent of:

(i) any overpayment made by an Employer pursuant to the proviso to paragraph (3) of Rule 44 as compared with the amount subsequently determined by the Group Trustees thereunder in such a manner as shall be agreed between the Group Trustees and the Employer having regard to the advice of the Actuary unless the Group Trustees otherwise determine; and

(ii) any surplus certified by the Actuary pursuant to paragraph (2) of Rule 45 in such a manner as shall have been agreed between the Co-ordinator and the Employer having regard to the advice of the Actuary unless the Co-ordinator otherwise determines.'

[**40**] Of these various heads, (a) is self-explanatory. I have omitted (b), (c) and (d), which played no part in the argument. But (e), (f) and (g) are so dense with cross-references to the rules that each requires some further explanation. The significance of the proviso I shall leave until later.

Deficiency payments

[**41**] Clause 13(1)(e) refers to amounts to be determined in respect of members who retire under rule 16 or cease to be members on account of reorganisation or redundancy before age 50. Ordinarily, a member is not entitled to start drawing his pension until he reaches pensionable age. There are all kinds of exceptions and qualifications (such as retirement on grounds of ill-health under rule 15) but that is the general rule. Rule 16(1) entitles an employer to request that the group trustees start paying a pension to a member who, after ten years service, retires on or after the age of 55. Rule 16(2) provides for similar treatment for a member who is compulsorily retired on or after the age of 50 and rule 17A(1)(c) provides that a person who ceases to be a contributor before the age of 50 consequent on reorganisation or redundancy shall be treated as having retired when he reaches the age of 50.

[**42**] These provisions for the acceleration of benefits under the scheme naturally involve additional cost and the rules provide for a determination of the amount required to fund the extra benefits and for the allocation of that cost to the appropriate employer. The determination, as we have seen, is a matter for the principal employer of the group under cl 13(1)(e). The allocation, in the case of benefits under rules 16 and 17, is effected by rules 16(3) and 17(4), both of which provide that any additional cost, as determined by the principal employer, 'shall be borne by the Employer who last employed the Member'. Payments due from employers under cl 13(1)(e) have been called 'deficiency payments' and I shall use that expression, although it must not be confused with the contributions required to make good a valuation deficiency under cl 14(4).

Supplementary payments

[**43**] Clause 13(1)(f), so far as it refers to rule 44(3), deals with the cost of another form of increased benefit (the other reference, to rule 45(2)(b), is not presently relevant). Rule 44(1), which was added by amendment in 1988, gives

a an employer a very wide power to direct the trustees to pay additional benefits, up to Inland Revenue limits, to 'Voluntary Pensioners', a term which has meant in practice employees willing to accept early retirement and their dependants. Rule 44(3) gives the trustees power, acting on the advice of the actuary, to determine the amount to be contributed by the employer to secure the additional benefits. By rule 44(4) the employer may, subject to the approval of the trustees, b pay by instalments the equivalent in value of the amount determined. These payments have been called 'supplementary payments'.

[44] Rules 16, 17 and 44 played an important part in the programme of voluntary redundancies introduced by National Grid, National Power and other successor companies after privatisation. National Power, for example, succeeded in reducing the numbers of its employees from 16,273 in 1991 to 5,139 in 1995. A c significant inducement to employees to accept redundancy or early retirement was the offer of accelerated or enhanced benefits under rules 16, 17 or 44. The result was to create substantial liabilities to make deficiency and supplementary payments.

d *Voluntary contributions*

[45] Finally, I come to cl 13(1)(g), which is relatively straightforward. It comprises payments due under cl 14(4) to correct an earlier valuation deficiency (which do not feature in this case) and voluntary contributions made by employers on the advice of the actuary by way of addition to the standard payments due under cl 13(1)(a).

e *The arrangements*

[46] I can now explain the arrangements in more detail. National Grid decided to use £18·6m (or about 30%) of the 1992 surplus to improve benefits for members. It increased the lump sum death in service benefit to four times salary and made a 10% improvement in the future accrual rate for spouses' pensions. It f gave effect to these improvements by making amendments to the scheme.

[47] The remaining £43·7m of the surplus was used, first, to reduce a 2·6% voluntary contribution under cl 13(1)(g) to 0·1% and, secondly, to fund deficiency payments under cl 13(1)(e). The first application, which was costed at £9·5m, is uncontroversial. The validity of the second is in dispute.

[48] At some time during 1992 the board was advised by the actuary that g although the triennial valuation as at 31 March 1992 was not yet finalised, a substantial surplus would be shown. The actuary advised the board to stop making deficiency payments in respect of early retirements occurring after 1 December 1992. He considered that the company would be able to appropriate part of the expected surplus to such payments. The decision to stop paying was h confirmed by the board on 25 February 1993. At that stage the valuation as at 31 March 1992 had still not been signed off but the actuaries were predicting that it would show, as it did when it was finalised a week later, a surplus of £62·3m. The actuary certified that the proposed arrangements were reasonable. The way in which they were implemented was that National Grid determined its j contributions under cl 13(1)(e) at nil and instead notionally debited the allocated surplus with the amounts which would otherwise have been determined until the money ran out in March 1995. Thereafter National Grid resumed payments into the scheme.

[49] National Power decided to apply £86m of the £258m surplus certified in respect of the 1992 valuation to improving benefits for members. These included a 50% contribution holiday for three years to 31 March 1996, and increases in

death in service benefits, children's allowances and spouses pensions. All of these were effected by amendments to the scheme. In addition, they directed the trustees to pay a 10% increase in lump sum benefits to deferred pensioners on retirement. This was not made the subject of an amendment on the ground that it involved a single non-recurrent payment.

[50] National Power applied the remainder of the 1992 surplus to extinguishing its liabilities for deficiency and supplementary payments. In 1993 it was paying these, in respect of employees who had already left, by monthly instalments. In the case of the deficiency payments, where the amount payable was a matter for its own determination, it had on the advice of the actuary been determining since April 1991 that the amount should be paid by instalments rather than a lump sum in respect of each employee. In the case of the supplementary payments, where the amount was determined by the trustees, it had agreed instalment payments with the trustees pursuant to rule 44(4).

[51] National Power's arrangements were made by the board on 1 April 1993. They decided to cease payment of deficiency and supplementary payments in respect of members who had already left service and to carry forward a notional fund of £39m to meet deficiency and supplementary payments in respect of employees who left afterwards. The actuary certified these arrangements as reasonable. They were implemented by direction to the trustees without any amendment of the scheme. The sum appropriated to such payments was exhausted by March 1994 and National Power then resumed making payments into the scheme.

[52] The arrangements in respect of the 1995 valuation were broadly similar. This time the surplus was £73·7m. The board decided to apply about £25m to the improvement of benefits for members. These included a continuation of the 50% contribution holiday for another three years and an increase in the children's allowances. These were incorporated into the scheme by amendments. The board also, without amendment, directed a 5% increase in lump sum benefits for deferred pensioners on retirement. The rest of the surplus was appropriated, as before, to funding monthly instalments of deficiency and supplementary payments in respect of employees who had already left and carrying forward sums to fund such payments in respect of employees who retired afterwards. In addition, National Power reduced its own standard contributions to 10·5% for the three years from 1 April 1996 to 31 March 1999. All this was done by notification to the trustees without an amendment of the scheme. Again the actuary certified the arrangements as reasonable.

[53] The question therefore is whether, consistently with the provisions of the scheme, the employers were entitled to direct the trustees that they should treat their liabilities for deficiency and supplementary payments as discharged out of surplus funds. The members say that this contradicted the scheme. Clause 13(1)(e) and (f) required the payments to be made and the effect of the arrangements was that the payments were not made. The employers say that the payments were made; not, it is true, out of new money but out of surplus which the rules placed at the employers' disposal, by analogy with the case of a trust fund over which the employers had a power of appointment. On this construction, there has been no contradiction of the rules. Both constructions are conceptually possible. The correct choice depends upon the language of the scheme and the practical consequences of choosing one construction rather than the other.

a

Linguistic arguments

[54] The Court of Appeal ([2000] ICR 174), in coming to their decision that an amendment was needed, were impressed by the proviso to cl 13(1), which I quoted earlier. It provides for a suspension of contributions payable by the employer under paras (a) to (f) 'whether due and payable or prospectively payable', to the extent of any overpayments the employer may have made under rule 44(3). b The Court of Appeal said that this express provision for the extinguishment of accrued liabilities showed that the employer could not have such a power by virtue of cl 14(5).

[55] This is an argument of the expressio unius variety. I think that such arguments are often perilous, especially when applied to a patchwork document c like the pension scheme. The fact that a specific provision is made in one place may throw very little light on whether general words in another place include the power to do something similar. The proviso deals with the correction of specific overpayments, whether the fund is in surplus or not. It does not help one to decide whether the employer can appropriate a surplus to the discharge of what would otherwise have been his accrued obligations. In any case, the proviso was d introduced by amendment in 1988 and cannot have changed the meaning of cl 14(5), which has been in the scheme since its inception. I should add that neither counsel for the members supported the reasoning of the Court of Appeal on this point.

[56] If any help can be derived from the terms of cl 14(5), I think it may rather e be found in the provision that the arrangements must be certified by the actuary as reasonable. By contrast, the power of amendment does not have to be certified as reasonable. Subject to the cl 41(2) prohibitions, the employer can just go ahead and do it, whether the scheme is in surplus or not. This does suggest that cl 14(5) confers a separate power, subject to its own conditions.

f

Practical arguments

[57] More important than these linguistic points, as it seems to me, are the practical consequences of insisting that the arrangements should be made by amendment. The operation of the pension scheme should not be encumbered by unnecessary technicalities. On the other hand, if the amendment procedure g provides some important safeguards for the members or the trustees, that might be a good reason to construe the scheme as requiring the employer to adopt it.

[58] For this purpose it is necessary to examine the power of amendment in more detail. Clause 41 provides:

h

> '(1) Any provision of the Scheme (including this Clause) may be amended (whether by alteration, deletion or addition and whether prospectively or retrospectively) in accordance with and subject to the following provisions of this Clause; Provided That no amendment shall be made which would affect its Approval or prevent such further amendment of the Scheme as may j be required to maintain its Approval and Status. (2) Any amendment to the Scheme shall be void to the extent to which it would otherwise have the effect of: (a) altering the main purpose of the Scheme from that of providing Benefits for Members on Retirement; (b) save as authorised or required by enactment from time to time, making any of the moneys of the Scheme payable to any of the Employers; (c) reducing any Benefit payable to a Member or payable or prospectively payable to a Beneficiary.'

[59] There follow a number of other restrictions on the amending power designed to protect the vested rights of various classes of members or other beneficiaries.

[60] Clause 41(3) and (4) provide respectively for two kinds of amendment. The first, under cl 41(3), is an amendment of the whole scheme by all the principal employers acting together. This power is not subject to consent or approval by anyone. The only requirement is that it has to be done by deed and, under sub-cl (8), notified to each subsidiary employer, the scheme trustee and the group trustees. The second kind of amendment, under cl 41(4), is by a principal employer to amend the scheme solely in relation to its own group. This is subject to a clearance procedure to make sure that the amendment will not have any impact upon the rights and liabilities of other groups or the approved status of the scheme as a whole. The amending deed must be notified to the scheme secretary (appointed by the co-ordinator, a company which represents all the principal employers) and does not take effect until the secretary has given a clearance notice (if he considers that the amendment is within the powers of the clause and will not prejudice the scheme) or, if he is of the contrary view, a dispute procedure has resolved the matter in favour of the amendment. The dispute procedure is between the amending employer and the co-ordinator, representing the other principal employers. The members and trustees are not involved. As between employer and members, therefore, an amendment (whether under cl 41(3) or (4)) is entirely a matter for the employer, subject to the restrictions in cl 41(2). The notification and dispute machinery in cl 41(4) is only for the protection of the other groups.

[61] It follows that, so far as the members are concerned, it does not in the least matter whether an application of surplus by an employer which falls outside the prohibitions in cl 41(2) is made by amendment or not. The argument that an amendment was needed only had substance when combined with the argument that such an amendment would have been prohibited by cl 41(2)(b). Deprived of that support, as the Court of Appeal thought it was, it becomes for the members a matter of pure technicality. That is demonstrated by the fact that the employers have been able to validate the arrangements simply by the execution of a deed of amendment.

[62] The other persons interested in whether the amendment procedure is used are the trustees. They administer the fund and need clear directions on how to do so. This is essentially a practical question. If the arrangements are to endure for any length of time, an amendment is the most convenient and accessible way of recording them. That is why most of the improvements in benefits for members were embodied in amendments. On the other hand, single payments credited to a particular class of pensioners were not made the subject of an amendment. Counsel for the trustees told us that they saw no administrative difficulties in acting upon directions to make such payments. Likewise, there were no problems about the directions to debit surplus with the deficiency and supplementary payments which would otherwise have been payable by the employers.

[63] The high technicality of the argument for the members on this point is shown by the fact that Mr Inglis-Jones, with his great experience of the way pension funds are administered, said that it would be perfectly acceptable for the employers to use surplus to create a reserve out of which to pay their future contributions. No amendment would be necessary. But he said that it was quite wrong to use surplus to discharge accrued liabilities. In my view, this distinction

a is unjustified. No doubt in the wake of the decision of Vinelott J in *British Coal Corp v British Coal Staff Superannuation Scheme Trustees Ltd* [1995] 1 All ER 912 the distinction was very important, because the discharge of an accrued liability was treated as a payment out of the fund to the employer. But once that construction is abandoned, as I have suggested it should be, the distinction ceases to matter. For the reasons I have already given, it makes no business sense and b therefore should not form the basis of what can be no more than an empty technical rule. In my view, therefore, it was a matter of pragmatic choice for the employers as to whether the arrangements made under cl 14(5) were embodied in scheme amendments or not.

Payment by instalments

c **[64]** That leaves two subsidiary arguments. The first was advanced by Mr Steinfeld QC for the National Power members in relation to the cancellation of the monthly instalments of accrued deficiency payments. He said that National Power was not entitled to decide unilaterally to pay these sums by instalments. A lump sum should have been paid in respect of each redundant d employee on his retirement. Therefore, if National Power had acted properly, the money would have been safely inside the scheme and protected from repayment, either by an implied restriction on the powers of cl 14(5) or by s 37 of the 1995 Act. To allow the instalments to be cancelled would be to allow National Power to take advantage of its failure to pay the money when it fell due.

[65] Several answers to this submission were canvassed in argument but in my e opinion the shortest is that I cannot see why National Power was not entitled, on the advice of the actuary, to determine that it would pay deficiency payments by instalments. Clause 13(1)(e) says that it shall pay 'such amount as determined by the Principal Employer on the advice of the Actuary'. Clause 47(e) provides that a singular word shall include the plural and there seems no contrary context in f this case. The determination is made on actuarial considerations and from an actuarial point of view, any lump sum can be translated into an appropriate stream of periodic payments. Mr Steinfeld relied upon rule 16(3), which provides that the 'additional cost' of the rule 16 benefits should be borne by the employer who last employed the member. 'Cost', he said, means the whole cost, not a series of instalments. But rule 16(3) is concerned with the allocation of liability, g not the determination of the amount. The 'cost' is whatever amount or amounts may be determined by the principal employer under cl 13(1)(e).

[66] The judge thought that the employer could not decide to pay deficiency payments by instalments. There was no express power to do so, by contrast with the express reference to making supplementary payments by instalments which h is found in rule 44(4). The Court of Appeal ([2000] ICR 174 at 185 (para 22)) agreed that rule 44(4) was a 'decisive counter-indication' which ruled out a power under cl 13(1)(e) to pay by instalments.

[67] This is another expressio unius argument and in my view just as shaky as the last one. Like rule 44, cl 13(1)(f) was introduced by amendment in 1988, j when cl 13(1)(e) was already in the scheme. So rule 44(4) can at most show what its draftsman may have thought cl 13(1)(e) meant. It cannot have changed its meaning from what it was before. Secondly, the situations contemplated by the two provisions are quite different. Under rule 44, it is trustees who determine the amount which the employer must contribute. If this is to be translated into what rule 44(4) calls 'an amount equivalent in value, by way of instalments', then naturally the trustees must agree that it really is an equivalent in value. Under cl 13(1)(e), however, it is the employer who determines, on the advice of the actuary, what is actuarially necessary to provide for the additional cost of the rule 16 and 17 benefits. There is no reason why the need for such additional funding should not be expressed as instalments rather than a lump sum. So in my view National Power was entitled to make a determination to pay by instalments and there is no wrong of which it was seeking to take advantage.

Nil determinations

[68] The last point concerns the machinery adopted by National Grid to apply surplus to the discharge of its obligations under cl 13(1)(e). As I have explained, they determined their contribution at nil and at the same time directed the trustees to debit the amount necessary to fund the benefits against the available surplus until such time as it was exhausted. The members say that the rules do not permit a nil determination. Clause 13(1)(e) requires the actual cost of the benefits to be determined.

[69] As a general proposition, this must be true. In the absence of an actual or forecast surplus against which an equivalent amount could properly be debited, it would not be right to determine the contribution at anything other than a genuine actuarial estimate of the cost of the increased benefits. I am sure that no actuary would give any other advice. But when the additional cost is debited against available surplus, the 'nil determination' is no more than a book-keeping technicality. National Grid could just as well have 'determined' its liability at the actuary's estimate of the cost of the benefits and then, instead of paying that amount, directed the trustees to treat it as discharged out of available surplus. The result would have been precisely the same and I do not think that the form of book-keeping should affect the validity of what National Grid did.

[70] Finally it is said that, on the advice of the actuary, National Grid began this practice, as I have described, before a surplus had been officially certified. The actuary considered that it was pointless to pay money into the scheme to swell what was bound to be a surplus. I think that just as there was power to determine that deficiency payments should be paid at a series of future dates by instalments, so there was power to determine that they should be paid out of future surplus. Whether this was a sensible and prudent thing to do was a matter for the advice of the actuary. But I see no objection in principle to the steps which the actuary advised in this case.

[71] I would therefore allow the appeal and declare that all the arrangements made by National Power and National Grid were valid.

LORD CLYDE. My Lords,

[72] I am in full agreement with the speech which has been delivered by my noble and learned friend Lord Hoffmann. On a proper construction of cl 41(2)(b) of the Electricity Supply Pension Scheme the release of a debt due by an employer is not the 'making any of the moneys of the Scheme payable to any of the Employers'. Nor does such a release fall within the wording of the corresponding language of s 37(1)(a) of the Pensions Act 1995. So far as the construction of cl 14(5) is concerned, despite the apparently unrestricted language I agree that it should be construed as requiring that the arrangements should be made in accordance with the whole scheme, so that if a particular arrangement involves an alteration to the provisions of the scheme an amendment will be required, but if it does not, then it may be made without amendment. The question then is which, if any, of the particular elements of the arrangement innovate upon the scheme and in that regard I agree with the views expressed by my noble and learned friends Lord Hoffmann and Lord Scott of Foscote. I also agree that on a proper construction of cl 13(1)(e) payment by instalments in accordance with the actuary's advice is permissible. The matter of the nil determination in the National Grid case seems to me to be one of form rather than substance and subject to the actuary's advice the course taken is not objectionable.

[73] I agree that the appeals should be allowed.

LORD SCOTT OF FOSCOTE. My Lords,

[74] I have had the advantage of reading a draft of the opinion of my noble and learned friend, Lord Hoffmann. I am in respectful agreement both with his reasoning and his conclusions but, in view of the importance of this case to those concerned with the administration of pension schemes, I propose to set out, in brief, my reasons for agreeing that the appeals in these two cases should be allowed.

[75] The first, and main, issue is one of construction of cl 14(5) of the Electricity Supply Pension Scheme. Clause 14(5) says that the relevant employer 'shall make arrangements … to deal with such surplus'.

[76] There was considerable debate in the courts below and before your Lordships as to whether cl 14(5) merely imposed a duty or whether it conferred also a power to implement the arrangements that the employer desired to make. The provision confers power to 'make arrangements'. To that extent it is certainly a power-conferring provision. But it does not follow that it confers power upon the employer to amend the scheme. Clause 41 contains an express power to amend the scheme. The provisions of the scheme must be construed as a whole and, so construed, cl 14(5) cannot, in my opinion, be regarded as conferring on the employer a power of amendment free from the safeguards to which the cl 41 power of amendment is subject.

[77] In my opinion, to the extent that 'arrangements' made by the employer under cl 14(5) are inconsistent with one or other of the provisions or rules of the scheme, the implementation of those arrangements requires the amendment of the scheme pursuant to cl 41.

[78] Accordingly:

(i) Arrangements made under cl 14(5) which involve altering the contribution obligations of either the employer or the employees under cl 13(1)(a) require, in my opinion, an amendment of the scheme.

(ii) An increase of the benefits payable under the rules, whether the increase takes the form of a lump sum one-off payment or any other form, requires, in my opinion, amendment of the scheme.

(iii) But the appropriation of surplus to meet accrued obligations of the employer under cl 13(1)(e) or (f) does not, in my opinion, require any amendment of the scheme. It was argued in relation to cl 13(1)(e) that the appropriation of surplus to meet an employer's obligation to make additional contributions to meet the extra cost to the fund of early retirements would be inconsistent with the terms of rule 16(3). If so, it would, consistently, with the principle I have expressed, require an amendment. In my opinion, however, the purpose of rule 16(3) was to identify which employer would have to bear the cost of an employee's early retirement. If there were adequate surplus in the fund, and a direction certified by the actuary as reasonable had been made under cl 14(5) for surplus to be appropriated to meet the cost of early retirement, no more would be needed. There would be no inconsistency between the cl 14(5) direction and the other provisions of the scheme. However, there is, in my opinion, no reason why a cl 41 amendment of the scheme should not release, or confirm the release, of an accrued but still unpaid liability in respect of contributions. I agree with Lord Hoffmann that the cl 41(2)(b) limitation on the power of amendment does not bar an amendment which releases an employer's accrued liability to pay contributions that have not yet been paid. I, too, regard *British Coal Corp v British Coal Staff Superannuation Scheme Trustees Ltd* [1995] 1 All ER 912 as having been wrongly decided on this point.

(iv) Arrangements made by the employer under cl 14(5) could take the form of a direction to the fund trustees, first, to set aside the surplus, or part of it, as a reserve fund, and, second, to appropriate the reserve fund in or towards payment of future contributions falling due under cl 13(1)(a). Directions of this character would not, in my opinion, require any amendment of the scheme unless the result were to reduce the current monthly contribution obligation of the employer to less than twice that of the members. If that were the result, an amendment of cl 13(1)(a) would be required.

(v) Arrangements made under cl 14(5) cannot take the form of a payment out of the pension fund to the employer. Absent an amendment to the scheme, the trustees could not justify making such a payment. And an amendment authorising such a payment would be barred by cl 41(2)(b).

(vi) The 5% increase in lump sum benefits on retirement provided by National Power as part of the arrangements for dealing with the 1995 surplus ought to have been included among the benefits confirmed by National Power's deed of amendment of 11 May 1999. But since no one objects to the payment of this extra benefit, the omission perhaps does not matter.

[79] As to the propriety of a cl 13(1)(e) determination of a sum to be paid by specified instalments, instead of the determination of a single lump sum, I can see nothing at all objectionable about it. The determination would necessarily have been made on the advice of the scheme actuary, who would be as well able to calculate the requisite sum to be paid by, say, five annual instalments as to calculate the requisite sum to be paid at once as a lump sum.

[80] And as to the determination of a 'nil' amount to be paid in respect of an early leaver, provided the 'nil' determination were accompanied by, and a consequence of, an appropriation directed under cl 14(5) of a suitable amount of surplus, I can see no reasonable objection to it. The appropriation would have had the consequence that nothing more was needed in order to cover the extra cost to the fund of the early retirement.

[81] I, too, would allow the appeals.

Appeals allowed.

Kate O'Hanlon Barrister.

Grobbelaar v News Group Newspapers Ltd and another

[2001] EWCA Civ 33

COURT OF APPEAL, CIVIL DIVISION

SIMON BROWN, THORPE AND JONATHAN PARKER LJJ

4–8 DECEMBER 2000, 18 JANUARY 2001

Libel and slander – Qualified privilege – Common law privilege – Public interest – Newspaper publishing series of sensational articles accusing footballer of taking bribes to fix football matches – Whether newspaper entitled to rely on defence of qualified privilege.

Libel and slander – Justification – Jury – Newspaper accusing claimant of serious wrongdoing and relying on taped admissions – Claimant alleging that he had fabricated admissions to expose wrongdoing of person to whom they were made – Jury awarding claimant damages for libel – Whether jury's verdict to be set aside as perverse.

The claimant, G, was a well-known professional footballer. One of his associates, V, approached the defendant newspaper with allegations that G had fixed football matches for money. The newspaper paid V a substantial sum for his story, but wanted corroboration before publishing it. V therefore held a series of meetings with G in which he purported to make a corrupt proposal to G for future match-fixing and sought to elicit admissions in respect of the latter's alleged past misconduct. During the course of those meetings, which were secretly recorded, G confessed to having taken money in the past for fixing matches, and accepted a sum of money from V to fix matches in the future. Subsequently, the newspaper published a series of stories, based primarily on the taped meetings, which stated, in the most sensational, emotive and categorical terms, that G was guilty of match-fixing, and held him up to public ridicule. G denied any wrongdoing and brought an action for libel against the newspaper, but before the case was tried he was charged with two offences relating to the allegations of match-fixing. After two trials, G was acquitted of both offences—the first on the verdict of the jury, and the second on the order of the judge after the jury had failed to reach a verdict. The libel action then proceeded to trial, with G claiming that he had fabricated the admissions of past corruption in order to bring V to justice and that, to the same end, he had merely pretended to accept the bribe from V to throw matches in the future. G had made no such claims when first confronted with the allegations by the newspaper, shortly before publication. The newspaper pleaded justification, but also relied on the defence of qualified privilege. The judge held that the newspaper was not entitled to rely on qualified privilege, and the issue of justification was therefore left to the jury. It returned a verdict in G's favour and awarded him damages of £85,000. The newspaper appealed, challenging the judge's ruling on qualified privilege on the ground that it would inhibit the press from pursuing its investigatory role. It also contended that the jury's verdict should be set aside as perverse—an apparently unprecedented step.

Held – (1) Where newspapers chose to publish exposés unambiguously asserting the criminal guilt of those they had investigated, they had to do so at their own financial risk. Given the obvious commercial benefits attending that style of journalism and the substantially reduced damages recoverable under modern libel law, it was absurd to suggest that a newspaper would be discouraged from pursuing its investigatory role unless protected by qualified privilege. On the contrary, the protection of publications of that nature would give rise to the altogether greater risk that newspaper investigations would become less thorough and their exposés more sensational even than at present. It was important that newspapers should not be encouraged, when buying sensational material with a view to increasing profit, to think that they could be careless with the truth because they enjoyed a wider defence than justification. Moreover, where the published allegations were of serious criminality and likely, therefore, to be followed by the accused person's arrest and trial, it was preferable not totally to prejudge, and thereby risk prejudicing, the criminal process in advance. In the instant case, the publications, judged in the round, were not protected by qualified privilege, and the newspaper would therefore be held to account for such defamatory statements as could not be proved true (see [33]–[41], [47], [108] and [200]–[213], post); *Reynolds v Times Newspapers Ltd* [1999] 4 All ER 609 applied; *GKR Karate (UK) Ltd v Yorkshire Post (No 2)* [2000] EMLR 410 distinguished.

(2) Although the Court of Appeal would be reluctant to find a jury's verdict perverse and was anxious not to usurp its function, it had a duty to intervene where it was plain from the verdict that it was so plainly wrong that no jury, acting reasonably, could have reached it on the balance of probabilities. Thus, in the instant case, it was necessary to decide whether, on all the evidence, the verdict was one properly and reasonable open to the jury. Having regard to that evidence, G's case was simply incredible and he should not be permitted to retain an unmerited award of damages. Accordingly, the appeal would be allowed and the jury's verdict set aside (see [52], [53], [92]–[96], [116], [228]–[235] and [242], post).

Notes

For the defence of qualified privilege and for setting aside a jury's verdict as perverse, see 28 *Halsbury's Laws* (4th edn reissue) paras 108, 227.

Cases referred to in judgments

A-G v Blake (Jonathan Cape Ltd, third party) [2000] 4 All ER 385, [2000] 3 WLR 625, HL.

A-G v Unger [1998] 1 Cr App R 308, DC.

Australian Newspaper Co Ltd v Bennett [1894] AC 284, PC.

Blackshaw v Lord [1983] 2 All ER 311, [1984] QB 1, [1983] 3 WLR 283, CA.

Broome v Gosden (1845) 1 CB 728, 135 ER 728, CP.

Designers Guild Ltd v Russell Williams (Textiles) Ltd [2001] 1 All ER 700, [2000] 1 WLR 2416, HL.

Evans v Davies [1991] 2 Qd R 498, Qld Full Ct.

GKR Karate (UK) Ltd v Yorkshire Post Newspapers Ltd [2000] 2 All ER 931, [2000] 1 WLR 2571, CA.

GKR Karate (UK) Ltd v Yorkshire Post Newspapers Ltd (No 2) [2000] EMLR 410.

National Justice Cia Naviera SA v Prudential Assurance Co Ltd, The Ikarian Reefer [1995] 1 Lloyd's Rep 455, CA.

O'Brien v Marquis of Salisbury (1889) 6 TLR 137, DC.

Pamplin v Express Newspapers Ltd (No 2) (1985) [1988] 1 All ER 282, [1988] 1 WLR 116, CA.

R v Carr [1956] 3 All ER 979n, [1957] 1 WLR 165, C-MAC.

a *R v Mills* (1978) 68 Cr App R 154, CA.
R v Savundranayagan [1968] 3 All ER 439n, [1968] 1 WLR 1761, CA.
Reynolds v Times Newspapers Ltd [1998] 3 All ER 961, [1998] 3 WLR 862, CA; *affd* [1999] 4 All ER 609, [1999] 3 WLR 1010, HL.

Cases also cited or referred to in skeleton arguments

b *A-G v Guardian Newspapers Ltd (No 2)* [1988] 3 All ER 545, [1990] 1 AC 109, [1988] 3 WLR 776, HL.
Brind v Secretary of State for the Home Dept [1991] 1 All ER 720, sub nom *R v Secretary of State for the Home Dept, ex p Brind* [1991] 1 AC 696, HL.
Cassell & Co Ltd v Broome [1972] 1 All ER 801, [1972] AC 1027, HL
City of Chicago v Tribune Co (1923) 139 NE 86, Ill SC.
c *Curtis Publishing Co v Butts, Associated Press v Walker* (1967) 388 US 130, US SC.
Derbyshire CC v Times Newspapers Ltd [1993] 1 All ER 1011, [1993] AC 534, HL.
Francome v Mirror Group Newspapers Ltd [1984] 2 All ER 408, CA.
Fraser v Evans [1969] 1 All ER 8, [1969] 1 QB 349, CA.
Goodwin v UK (1996) 22 EHRR 123, ECt HR.
d *Handyside v UK* (1976) 1 EHRR 737, ECt HR.
Initial Services Ltd v Putterill [1967] 3 All ER 145, [1968] 1 QB 396, CA.
Lion Laboratories Ltd v Evans [1984] 2 All ER 417, [1985] QB 526, [1984] 3 WLR 539, CA.
New York Times Co v Sullivan (1964) 376 US 254, US SC.
Rantzen v Mirror Group Newspapers (1986) Ltd [1993] 4 All ER 975, [1994] QB 670, CA.
e *Watts v Times Newspapers Ltd (Schilling & Lom (a firm), third party)* [1996] 1 All ER 152, [1997] QB 650, CA.

Appeal

The defendants, News Group Newspapers Ltd, publishers of the Sun newspaper, and Stuart Higgins, former editor of the Sun, appealed with the permission of f Otton LJ granted on 14 October 1999 from the order of Gray J on 28 July 1999 giving effect to the verdict of a jury requiring them to pay £85,000 damages for defamation to the claimant, Bruce Grobbelaar, in respect of a series of publications in the Sun on 9, 10, 11, 14, 15, 16 and 18 November 1994, accusing him of fixing the results of football matches for money. The facts are set out in the judgment of g Simon Brown LJ.

Richard Spearman QC (instructed by *Daniel Taylor*) for the defendants.
Robert Hartley QC and *Sarah Palin* (instructed by *Cuff Roberts*, Liverpool) for Mr Grobbelaar.

h *Cur adv vult*

18 January 2001. The following judgments were delivered.

SIMON BROWN LJ.

j [1] On 28 July 1999, at the end of a 16-day trial before Gray J and a jury, the respondent, Bruce Grobbelaar, was awarded £85,000 compensatory damages for defamation. The jury's verdict was unanimous. The award was in respect of a series of publications in the Sun newspaper on 9, 10, 11, 14, 15, 16 and 18 November 1994 stating that he had fixed football matches for money. The first such publication was on the front page under the banner headline 'WORLD EXCLUSIVE—GROBBELAAR TOOK BRIBES TO FIX GAMES'. The libels could hardly have been graver nor more sensationally, widely and repeatedly proclaimed. *a*

[2] The award is now challenged on appeal by the publishers and the then editor, Mr Stuart Higgins. The appellants advance two central arguments. First they contend that the jury's verdict, notably their rejection of the defence of justification, was perverse. Secondly they submit that Gray J was wrong to have ruled in the course of the trial, on 23 July, that the defence of qualified privilege *b* was not available in respect of the publications complained of.

[3] It is convenient at this early stage of the judgment to give a brief chronological account of the central facts and events underlying these proceedings.

[4] Mr Grobbelaar was a celebrated goalkeeper who joined Liverpool in 1981. In July 1992 he was invited by a fellow Zimbabwean, Mr Christopher Vincent, to *c* invest in a safari holiday business called Mondoro and over the months that followed he paid over to Mr Vincent some £50,000.

[5] In about November 1992 Mr Grobbelaar was introduced by Mr John Fashanu (another well-known footballer, then a striker for Wimbledon) to a Mr Lim (a young Asian, sometimes known as 'the short man'). Mr Grobbelaar acknowledged *d* that between then and about the spring of 1994 he received from Mr Lim cash payments totalling some £8,000. One such payment (of £1,500) was made on 30 September 1993 at a short meeting at the Hilton Hotel near Manchester Airport, Mr Grobbelaar and Mr Vincent having driven there together from Chester. These payments, Mr Grobbelaar asserted, were initially for forecasting match results (not involving Liverpool), at the rate of £250 per successful forecast, and *e* later, because he proved an inept forecaster, for information about footballers and clubs. The appellants' contrary case was that the payments—and at least one further and larger payment of £40,000—were for match-fixing rather than match-forecasting and that the £40,000 payment was made in cash on 25 November 1993 at a house in Byron Drive, North London, John Fashanu's address at the *f* time, following Liverpool's 3–0 defeat by Newcastle on 21 November. Mr Grobbelaar denied receiving any moneys on that visit. Rather, he said, the £20,000 in cash which he admitted handing over to Mr Vincent at about this date for the Mondoro project, as well as £5,000 paid on 26 November into his testimonial fund, came from his sock drawer at home, cash accumulated over the years from a number of legitimate sources. *g*

[6] On 4 January 1994 Liverpool drew 3-all with Manchester United (a match in which Mr Grobbelaar later said he had accidentally made two blinding saves and thereby lost some £120,000). This was the second of five matches to which evidence was directed.

[7] On 5 February 1994 Liverpool drew 2-all away to Norwich. The night *h* before the match Mr Vincent had driven Mr Grobbelaar from the Norwich hotel where the Liverpool team were staying to the London Hilton where again a short meeting took place between Mr Grobbelaar and Mr Lim at which £1,500 was paid over. That trip began shortly after 9 pm once the players' rooms had been checked to ensure that they had all retired for the night, and ended when *j* Mr Vincent and Mr Grobbelaar arrived back in Norwich at about 3.30 am.

[8] On 12 August 1994, during the off-season period, Mr Grobbelaar left Liverpool and joined Southampton. At about the same time he and Mr Vincent fell out: Mondoro had collapsed and Mr Vincent was wholly unable to account for the moneys Mr Grobbelaar had invested: quite possibly he had misappropriated the larger part.

a [9] On 6 September 1994 Mr Vincent went to the Sun to sell his story. The price agreed was £33,000 although he had asked for £40,000 and later asked for more. The tale he told was noted in shorthand by a Sun journalist, Mr Troup, and subsequently transcribed. It included the allegations that Mr Grobbelaar had received £40,000 after Liverpool lost the Newcastle match and that he would have been paid £80,000 had they lost the Norwich game but that they drew it
b because he accidentally saved a shot with his foot whilst diving the wrong way.

[10] There then followed a succession of covertly video and sound-recorded meetings between Mr Grobbelaar and Mr Vincent at which the Sun sought to obtain corroboration of Mr Vincent's story. I shall have to revisit these later. In essence, however, Mr Vincent was put up to making a corrupt proposal for future match-fixing and to obtaining such admissions as he could of Mr Grobbelaar's
c past misconduct.

[11] It is not disputed that in the course of these meetings Mr Grobbelaar confessed to having taken money from Mr Lim for losing matches in the past (including £40,000 for Liverpool's 3–0 defeat by Newcastle), and to having missed out on further such payments for failing to do so, and also that he took £2,000 in
d cash from Mr Vincent pursuant to a proposal that he should fix matches in the future. The critical issue at trial, however, was whether these confessions were true or false. Was Mr Grobbelaar genuinely admitting to corrupt behaviour in the past and agreeing to a fresh corrupt proposal for the future? Or was he, as he claimed, intent rather upon bringing Mr Vincent to justice and fabricating for the purpose a false account of past corruption and a mere pretence that he could be
e bribed to throw matches in future?

[12] The meetings took place respectively on 12 September 1994 (when Mr Vincent first made his corrupt proposal but the recording proved ineffective), 6 October 1994 (in Mr Vincent's hotel bedroom after two hours of unrecorded conversation in the hotel snooker room), 25 October 1994 (also in Mr Vincent's
f hotel bedroom) and 3 November 1994 (in the sitting room of a property rented for Mr Vincent by the Sun). It was at the last of these meetings that Mr Grobbelaar was graphically recorded taking £2,000 in cash, the agreement being that he would receive that sum every fortnight until he selected a particular match to be lost for which he would be paid £100,000.

g [13] Meantime, on 24 September 1994, Southampton had beaten Coventry 3–1 (despite, according to Mr Grobbelaar's taped admission on 25 October, '2 minutes into the game push[ing] the ball into the back of the net'). On 5 November 1994, after the last of the meetings, Southampton drew 3-all with Manchester City. This was the one game which the Sun's reporters attended before publication. They watched highlights of the other four on video. They could see
h nothing untoward. That did not, however, surprise them: they thought it would be impossible to detect attempted match-fixing by a skilled goalkeeper.

[14] On 8 November 1994 Mr Grobbelaar was due to fly to Zimbabwe to represent his country in an international match. At Gatwick Airport he was confronted by a number of Sun reporters and photographers and challenged with
j 'a series of grave allegations which the paper intends publishing tomorrow'. It will be necessary later to examine these exchanges in some detail but for the moment they can be summarised by saying that Mr Grobbelaar in general denied any wrongdoing. At the reporters' suggestion he then telephoned Mr Higgins and repeated his denials to him. Although Mr Grobbelaar had hinted to the journalists that he was gathering evidence against Mr Vincent, his response to Mr Higgins was rather that he had never attempted to throw a game in his life

and that the £40,000 was from his testimonial fund. He certainly never made it plain to Mr Higgins that, so far from this being a sting upon him, he himself was perpetrating a sting on Mr Vincent. Indeed, he later said in cross-examination that 'because these are the people that helped Mr Vincent' and 'had not been truthful to me', he was not 'going to give [Mr Higgins] that satisfaction'.

[15] Nothing in these exchanges persuaded the appellants to regard the taped admissions as other than genuinely corroborative of Mr Vincent's story of corruption. On the contrary, they were more than ever convinced of Mr Grobbelaar's guilt and duly went into print the following morning with the first of the publications complained of. They did so notwithstanding a faxed letter before action from Mr Grobbelaar's solicitors at 2.15 am that morning asserting his innocence and claiming damages.

[16] It was common ground at the trial that the articles, together with the many photographs and cartoons which accompanied them, meant that Mr Grobbelaar:

> '(i) Having dishonestly taken bribes had fixed or attempted to fix the result of games of football in which he had played, and
> (ii) Had dishonestly taken bribes with a view to fixing the result of games in which he would be playing.'

[17] The statement of claim was served on 21 December 1994, the defence on 4 January 1995. More important, however, was the initial reply, served on 6 July 1995, a pleading subsequently admitted to contain three basic untruths: first, Mr Grobbelaar asserted that Mr Lim ('the short man') was 'purely a figment of [his] imagination'; second, he denied the trip to John Fashanu's house in North London on 25 November 1993; third, he denied the night-time trip from Norwich to London on 5 February 1994.

[18] Meantime, on 14 March 1995, Mr Grobbelaar had been arrested and cautioned, exercising his right to remain silent. Later, on 24 July 1995, he was charged with two offences. (1) That he and Mr Lim and Mr Fashanu—

> 'on diverse days between 1 November 1992 and 9 November 1994 conspired together with others known and unknown corruptly to give and corruptly to accept gifts of money as inducements improperly to influence or attempt to influence the outcome of football matches or as rewards for having done so.'

(2) That he—

> 'on 3 November 1994 being an agent of Southampton Football Club corruptly accepted from Christopher Vincent the sum of £2,000 as an inducement or reward for doing an act in relation to the affairs or business of his principal namely improperly influencing or attempting to influence the outcome of a football match or football matches.'

[19] He twice stood trial on those counts, respectively in January/March 1997 and in June/August 1997. At the first trial the jury disagreed on both counts. At the second trial Mr Grobbelaar was acquitted by unanimous verdict on the first count but again the jury disagreed on the second count. In the ordinary way the jury were then discharged, the prosecution offered no evidence on the second count, and the judge thereupon ordered a not guilty verdict upon it.

[20] On 17 September 1997 the Football Association (FA) withdrew their disciplinary charge of match-fixing which they had brought against Mr Grobbelaar on 14 November 1994 and substituted for it a charge of assisting in betting on

a football matches other than on authorised and registered football pools. To that revised charge Mr Grobbelaar pleaded guilty on 12 December 1997 and certain suspended penalties were imposed.

[21] Just to complete the chronology, the defence of qualified privilege was first raised by the appellants in late 1998 (after the decision of the Court of Appeal in *Reynolds v Times Newspapers Ltd* [1998] 3 All ER 961, [1998] 3 WLR 862). At about b the same time Mr Grobbelaar amended his reply to admit knowing Mr Lim and to having made the two trips which he had earlier falsely denied, admissions first made at the first of the criminal trials.

[22] As stated at the outset, the jury awarded Mr Grobbelaar £85,000. The judge in his summing up had suggested to them that, depending on what conclusion they reached as to whether any significant part of the defence of c justification had been made out (assuming always, of course, that they did not find the charge 'substantially justified', a matter on which he had earlier directed them), the bracket for damages would be between around £150,000 'at the top end' and 'a very small award indeed'.

[23] It was common ground before us that the award of £85,000 was d consistent only with the jury having rejected the defence of justification in respect of both alleged conspiracies—ie both the corrupt agreement with Mr Lim in the past, and that with Mr Vincent for the future. The fact that the award was not greater than £85,000, submitted Mr Hartley QC, reflected the jury's evident disapproval of Mr Grobbelaar's initial lies. 'The jury must have accepted Mr Grobbelaar's evidence but thought he acted disgracefully in what he put in his e Reply', I noted Mr Hartley as saying.

[24] I have thus far given only an overview of the case. It is time now to address the two central grounds of appeal, beginning, as I think most convenient, with the defence of qualified privilege.

f QUALIFIED PRIVILEGE

[25] The essence of the defendant's case on qualified privilege is that professional football is both a major sport and a major industry in this country, that corruption in the Far East has had a devastating effect on the game there (dramatically reducing attendances), and that the evidence obtained by the Sun g revealed a serious risk of the same corruption (financed by Far Eastern betting syndicates) spreading to this country and damaging the sport here too. They were accordingly under a duty to inform and warn the general public of this insidious development which they had just uncovered.

[26] The judge below had to decide the issue by reference to the Court of h Appeal decision in *Reynolds'* case, the House of Lords having by then heard but not given judgment in the case. The judge accepted the newspaper's submission 'that *Reynolds'* case has introduced a more flexible and generous approach to qualified privilege', but noted also that:

> '*Reynolds'* case does confirm that the threshold questions remain whether j it can be said in the particular circumstances of the case that the publishers were under a legal, social or moral duty to publish that which they did publish and whether the readers of the publication had a legitimate interest in receiving the published information.'

[27] In the event, having concluded that 'neither the duty criteria nor the interest criteria as laid down in *Reynolds'* case is satisfied in the present case', the

judge found it 'unnecessary ... to express a view in relation to the circumstantial test'. *a*

[28] The determinative passage in the judgment below, and that to which the appellants take particular exception, is:

> 'I do not suggest that in the post-*Reynolds* era privilege is restricted to information relating to those who are answerable to the public or who have *b* public duties and responsibilities. But I am not satisfied that allegations of corruption against a footballer fall within the category of information which a newspaper can be said to be under a duty to communicate to the world at large with the assurance that, subject to malice, they will not be liable to damages even if the allegations are proved to be false. In my judgment the appropriate mode of discharging the duty which lay on the newspaper when *c* it came into possession of the material relating to the alleged match-fixing by Mr Grobbelaar was to communicate the information to the police and the regulatory body for football for them to take whatever action was in their view merited by the information. To hold that a publication such as the publication in the Sun is protected by privilege would, in my judgment, be *d* to stretch the ambit of privilege beyond that which the public interest requires. As Fox LJ observed in *Blackshaw v Lord* ([1983] 2 All ER 311 at 339, [1984] QB 1 at 42), there is a balance to be struck. Sight must not be lost of the public interest in the preservation of the right of an individual to redress for the unjustified libel on his good name. Privilege would, subject only to malice, protect the newspaper against the publication of untrue defamatory *e* statements.'

[29] He later added: 'The position might have been different if the defendants had gone to the police and the FA with the information about Mr Grobbelaar but no action against him had followed.'

[30] It is, of course, necessary now to consider that ruling in the light of the *f* House of Lords decision in *Reynolds*' case [1999] 4 All ER 609, [1999] 3 WLR 1010 including their Lordships' disapproval of the Court of Appeal's formulation of the circumstantial test as a separate test rather than an integral part of a single inquiry into whether the overall circumstances of a particular publication are such as to attract the protection of qualified privilege. Much of what was said in each of the *g* five speeches is valuable and not least this from the leading speech of Lord Nicholls of Birkenhead:

> 'The elasticity of the common law principle enables interference with freedom of speech to be confined to what is necessary in the circumstances of the case. This elasticity enables the court to give appropriate weight, in *h* today's conditions, to the importance of freedom of expression by the media on all matters of public concern. Depending on the circumstances, the matters to be taken into account include the following. The comments are illustrative only. (1) The seriousness of the allegation. The more serious the charge, the more the public is misinformed and the individual harmed, if the *j* allegation is not true. (2) The nature of the information, and the extent to which the subject matter is a matter of public concern. (3) The source of the information. Some informants have no direct knowledge of the events. Some have their own axes to grind, or are being paid for their stories. (4) The steps taken to verify the information. (5) The status of the information. The allegation may have already been the subject of an investigation which

a commands respect. (6) The urgency of the matter. News is often a perishable commodity. (7) Whether comment was sought from the plaintiff. He may have information others do not possess or have not disclosed. An approach to the plaintiff will not always be necessary. (8) Whether the article contained the gist of the plaintiff's side of the story. (9) The tone of the article. A newspaper can raise queries or call for an investigation. It need not adopt b allegations as statements of fact. (10) The circumstances of the publication, including the timing. This list is not exhaustive. The weight to be given to these and any other relevant factors will vary from case to case. Any disputes of primary fact will be a matter for the jury, if there is one. The decision on whether, having regard to the admitted or proved facts, the publication was subject to qualified privilege is a matter for the judge. This is the established c practice and seems sound. A balancing operation is better carried out by a judge in a reasoned judgment than by a jury. Over time, a valuable corpus of case law will be built up. In general, a newspaper's unwillingness to disclose the identity of its sources should not weigh against it. Further, it should always be remembered that journalists act without the benefit of the clear light of d hindsight. Matters which are obvious in retrospect may have been far from clear in the heat of the moment. Above all, the court should have particular regard to the importance of freedom of expression. The press discharges vital functions as a bloodhound as well as a watchdog. The court should be slow to conclude that a publication was not in the public interest and, therefore, the public had no right to know, especially when the information is in the e field of political discussion. Any lingering doubts should be resolved in favour of publication.' (See [1999] 4 All ER 609 at 625–626, [1999] 3 WLR 1010 at 1027.)

[31] The approach of the judge below, submits Mr Spearman QC for the appellants, can now be seen to have been altogether too restrictive and to give f too little weight to the importance of freedom of expression. Merely to have provided the police and FA with this material would have substantially delayed its communication to the public. That would have been inappropriate: the issues were of immediate concern and deserved immediate publicity.

[32] Secondly, submits Mr Spearman, the judge's ruling, if upheld, would have a chilling effect upon freedom of speech and be inimical to the press's vital g functions as both watchdog and bloodhound. Investigative journalism is not conducted with a view to bringing miscreants to justice but rather so as to sell newspapers. Instead of the press being deterred from publishing these exposés by the need to prove justification, they should be protected by the defence of qualified privilege. Thus would the courts give life-blood to the bloodhounds and h serve the wider public interest. I hope I have accurately summarised the appellants' arguments. The media, Mr Spearman told us, is very concerned about this issue. Clearly, as he submits, it is one of some general importance.

[33] As to the ten specific considerations listed by Lord Nicholls, there is much to be said (and indeed much was said) on both sides. Many of the submissions j involved deep forays into the evidence. I think it unnecessary, however, to deal in detail with any save considerations nine and ten and for the rest content myself merely with the following brief comments.

Consideration one—seriousness

The seriousness of the allegation cannot be doubted. It was very grave and, if untrue, hugely damaging to Mr Grobbelaar's reputation.

Consideration two—public concern

Equally clearly, however, the subject matter was of very substantial public concern. It is imperative that football is not tainted by corruption and that matches are competitively played rather than their outcome determined or influenced by corrupt payments in the interests of foreign gambling syndicates.

Considerations three and four—source and verification

These I take together in order to side-step the arid debate as to whether the source was Mr Vincent and the taped admissions its verification, or whether the taped admissions themselves were realistically the source for this story.

As for Mr Vincent himself, there was every reason to doubt his reliability. Plainly he had an axe to grind: he was, he told Mr Troup, destitute and shortly to be bankrupted because Mr Grobbelaar had reneged on an agreement to fund the Mondoro project. In addition, of course, he was being paid for his story. Explaining why he was not to be called at the trial, Mr Carman QC for the defendants described him as 'a wholly unreliable witness … someone whose evidence we believe may be highly suspect and whose whole character may be deeply flawed'. That, suggested Mr Hartley, was something they should have recognised from the outset.

As against that, however, there were undoubtedly aspects of Mr Vincent's story which strikingly coincided with some of Mr Grobbelaar's subsequently recorded admissions. I have already mentioned Mr Vincent's allegation that Mr Grobbelaar was paid £40,000 in cash after Liverpool lost 3–0 to Newcastle. In addition, he told Mr Troup of the trips from Chester to Manchester and from Norwich to London to see 'the short man'. There was also reference to Mr Grobbelaar having accidentally saved a goal and thereby lost out on a substantial reward—an allegation later echoed in the taped admissions albeit not, it is right to say, with regard to the same match.

What Mr Hartley criticises above all else with regard to the verification of this story is the Sun's failure to investigate the particular matches which were mentioned on the tapes to see whether Mr Grobbelaar's confessions were indeed to be regarded as true and reliable rather than simply made up. As will later appear, Mr Grobbelaar was able at the trial to call powerful and substantially unchallenged expert evidence that these five games showed, as Mr Bob Wilson (the well-known ex-goalkeeper, coach and television presenter) said, 'absolutely no evidence whatsoever of anything other than good goalkeeping … and in some cases exceptional goalkeeping'.

Consideration five—status of information

There was of course no question here of the story having already been the subject of some independent investigation which commanded respect. In truth, it had no status whatever save as an apparently genuine admission against interest.

Consideration six—urgency

As to the urgency of the matter, given that the story was a scoop for the Sun and, as Lord Nicholls observed, 'news is often a perishable commodity', immediate publication was more or less inevitable. Equally obviously, however, there was no urgency with regard to the public's need to know.

a *Consideration seven—comment sought?*

Comment was, of course, sought from Mr Grobbelaar in the sense that he was given the opportunity to refute these allegations at Gatwick Airport, first when confronted by the Sun's journalists and secondly in his telephone call to Mr Higgins. Mr Hartley criticises the confrontation as no more than an ambush—it was, indeed, admitted by the defendants to be a 'showdown' in which 'surprise was b a key element'—and undoubtedly Mr Grobbelaar was put under very great pressure at the time. If, however, qualified privilege is ever to extend to scoops and exposés of this nature, it is difficult to see what fuller opportunity for comment could be given. As Lord Nicholls observed, moreover, 'an approach to the plaintiff will not always be necessary'.

c *Consideration eight—gist of response*

Did the articles contain the gist of Mr Grobbelaar's side of the story? Given that they were substantially based on Mr Grobbelaar's taped admissions and that his 'side of the story', as it emerged during the Gatwick confrontation and phone call, consisted largely of a bald denial of wrongdoing coupled with assertions that d he had never thrown a game in his life and that the £40,000 was part of his testimonial fund, it seems to me that the gist of this *was* conveyed. That said, these assertions attracted scant mention in the massive overall coverage of the story and in any event were reported in such a way as to indicate the Sun's profound disbelief in their veracity. A headline reading 'The Grobbeliar tapes' gives the flavour of these publications. Mr Grobbelaar's ultimate response, of e course, ie his explanation that throughout the taped meetings he had been endeavouring to entrap Mr Vincent rather than succumbing to the tempting trap set by Mr Vincent, had not at that stage been vouchsafed.

Considerations nine and ten

f I come finally to what seem to me the critical considerations. Let me repeat them as formulated by Lord Nicholls:

> '(9) The tone of the article. A newspaper can raise queries or call for an investigation. It need not adopt allegations as statements of fact. (10) The circumstances of the publication including the timing.'

g [34] Here, of course, we are concerned not with a single article but with massive and relentless coverage of the story over seven separate daily issues of the Sun, generally spread across several pages and under prominent headlines. Moreover, so far from these publications 'rais[ing] questions or call[ing] for an investigation', they asserted Mr Grobbelaar's guilt in the most unequivocal of h terms: he was, the Sun proclaimed, a self-confessed cheat, who 'must never be allowed to play again'.

[35] Certain aspects of the coverage demonstrably went beyond what Mr Grobbelaar had in fact admitted on tape; for example, by its headline reading 'I let in three goals and picked up £40,000', the Sun was plainly implying that j those goals had been deliberately let in whereas Mr Grobbelaar's actual admission was that he had selected the Newcastle match to be lost 'because I knew … there's fuck all chance of winning Newcastle. I chose the Newcastle game cos I knew I could do business there.' It was also said that he was 'bitching' about his salary.

[36] Other features of the coverage calculated to add credence to the central allegation of corrupt match-fixing were unsupported even by Mr Vincent's

evidence. These included a banner headline 'Grob the liar does a flyer' implying that Mr Grobbelaar was at Gatwick with a view to evading justice rather than to play in an international, and the claim that Mr Vincent was a 'close friend' who 'was appalled at [Mr Grobbelaar's] corruption', and had 'decided to speak out for the sake of the keeper's loyal fans', rather than a paid informant in vengeful mood against Mr Grobbelaar for having brought him to penury.

[37] These considerations apart, there was much to criticise about the publications in question and those responsible for them. The language used was in the highest degree emotive: 'The ultimate betrayal', 'He fouled the field of dreams', 'Secret code of Mr Fix-it', 'Shame will haunt Grob for the rest of his life'. These are just a sample of the many headlines used in this sustained and mocking campaign of vilification. Having paraded Mr Grobbelaar's guilt, the Sun revelled in his downfall. There was in addition a lamentable involvement of his family. Whilst he was being confronted at Gatwick, other Sun reporters repeatedly knocked on the door of the family home where his wife and children were, asking for her comments and taking photographs. Another headline read: 'Shameful secret has Deb in tears.' Furthermore, in one of the editions complained of, the Sun's published questions to Mr Grobbelaar included: 'How much of what's been happening have you told the children about? Have they been getting a hard time at school?' The articles, in short, were calculated to embarrass not only Mr Grobbelaar but also his wife and children.

[38] There can be no doubt that considered as a whole this newspaper campaign carried prejudgment of guilt to its uttermost limits. It is difficult to dispute the validity of Mr Hartley's criticism that the Sun 'took upon themselves the roles of the police, prosecuting authority, judge and jury'.

[39] Can a succession of defamatory publications of this nature attract the defence of qualified privilege? How is the balance to be struck? The ultimate question, of course, is whether the general public was entitled to receive the information contained in these publications irrespective of whether in the end it proved to be true or false. Who, in other words, is to bear the risk that allegations of this sort, convincing though no doubt they appear to the newspaper when published, may finally turn out to be false? Should the risk be borne by the publishers lest the defamed claimant goes uncompensated for his lost reputation—and, indeed, powerless to regain it unless (which is unlikely) he can prove malice? Or should it be borne by the claimant himself lest the fear of an adverse damages award discourages publishers from pursuing their investigatory role or, having pursued it, from informing the public of whatever misconduct they believe they have uncovered?

[40] To my mind there can be only one answer to these questions. If newspapers choose to publish exposés of this character, unambiguously asserting the criminal guilt of those they investigate, they must do so at their own financial risk. Given the obvious commercial benefits attending this style of journalism—the editor here ordered an increase in the Sun's print run in advance of its Grobbelaar exclusive—and the substantially reduced level of damages awards now recoverable under modern libel law, it seems to me absurd to suggest that the Sun will be discouraged from pursuing its investigatory role unless protected by qualified privilege. On the contrary, the protection of publications of this nature would in my judgment give rise to the altogether greater risk that newspaper investigations would become less thorough, and their exposés more sensational, (even) than at present. As their Lordships' speeches in *Reynolds'* case—not least

a that of Lord Hobhouse of Woodborough—made plain, there is no human right to disseminate information which is untrue, no public interest in being misinformed.

[41] There is this additional consideration too. Where, as here, the published allegations are of serious criminality and likely, therefore, to be followed by the person's arrest and trial, it is surely preferable not totally to prejudge, and thereby risk prejudicing, the criminal process in advance. Attitudes have, of course, b changed radically since Salmon LJ's oft-quoted castigation of David Frost's interview of Dr Savundra shortly before the latter's arrest in 1967, 'Trial by television is not to be tolerated in a civilised society' (see *R v Savundranayagan* [1968] 3 All ER 439n at 441, [1968] 1 WLR 1761 at 1765). Nowadays, indeed, the strict liability rule under the Contempt of Court Act 1981 applies only after arrest and even then not necessarily so as to outlaw every publication as fact of the guilt c of a named person—see, for a recent illustration, *A-G v Unger* [1998] 1 Cr App R 308, albeit the court's judgment there ended with clear words of warning to those in the business of crime reporting.

[42] It is, however, one thing to recognise that an exposé such as the Sun's of Mr Grobbelaar is almost certainly immune from contempt proceedings, quite d another to suggest that the law of libel should be developed so as to relieve the publishers even of the risk of civil liability. I for my part would not go this far.

[43] There is one further authority I should mention before leaving this part of the case—*GKR Karate (UK) Ltd v Yorkshire Post Newspapers Ltd* [2000] 2 All ER 931, [2000] 1 WLR 2571 (Court of Appeal) and *GKR Karate (UK) Ltd v Yorkshire Post* e *Newspapers Ltd (No 2)* [2000] EMLR 410 (Popplewell J). The central question there was whether qualified privilege attached to the publication by the first and third defendants (respectively the publishers and journalist of the Leeds Weekly News) of an article alleging that the claimants (unnamed in the article), who promoted and taught karate in the Leeds area—

f 'rip people off by taking money for karate club membership and then just disappearing; carry out no checks on the standard or background of their instructors; overcharge for karate lessons; teach karate through instructors who are not properly qualified; falsely claim that they have full insurance cover; and in consequence give karate teaching a bad name and should be shut down.'

g

The article was based on what the second defendant, the general administrator of the English Karate Governing Body, had told the third defendant. The Court of Appeal upheld the trial judge's interlocutory order that the issues of qualified privilege and malice should be determined as preliminary issues and ruled:

h

'It is not necessary or relevant to determine whether the publication was true or not ... The question is rather whether in all the circumstances the public was entitled to know the particular information without the publisher making further such inquiries. The reliability of the source of the information is a relevant consideration, but that, in my view, is to be judged by how j objectively it should have appeared to the defendant at the time.' (See [2000] 2 All ER 931 at 938–939, [2000] 1 WLR 2571 at 2578, per May LJ.)

[44] Popplewell J then heard the preliminary issues and despite deciding that a number of considerations, judged according to Lord Nicholls' ten factors, had to be put in the balance in the claimant's favour, he concluded 'that the criticisms to which I have referred, neither individually nor cumulatively, outweigh the

interest in the free flow of information in this case'. He accordingly ruled that qualified privilege was made out.

[45] Mr Spearman invites us to make a similar ruling here. To my mind, however, there are several important distinctions to be made between that case and this. Prominent amongst them are first, that the claimants there, unlike here, were unnamed; second, that that publication was directed towards a substantially smaller readership and, no less importantly, a readership which included people who, assuming the truth of the allegations made, needed to be warned quickly for their own protection; third, that the newspaper there published but a single article and that in altogether more restrained and moderate terms than characterised the Sun's campaign in the present case; fourth, that there was in that case a substantially smaller prospect of the claimants later facing criminal trial; and fifth, that that publication was based upon information from an apparently reliable official body.

[46] Recognising though I do that we 'should be slow to conclude that a publication was not in the public interest and, therefore, the public had no right to know, [and that] any lingering doubts should be resolved in favour of publication' (as Lord Nicholls said in the passage already cited), I reach the clear conclusion that these publications judged in the round should not be held protected by qualified privilege. I have, indeed, no 'lingering doubts' whatever.

[47] Obviously the defence would have applied had the Sun merely passed on their information to the police and the FA; Mr Hartley, indeed, accepts as much. For my part I would regard it as applying too had the Sun chosen instead to publish a restrained piece couched in the language of suspicion and allegation rather than, as here, an unqualified assertion of guilt. With regard to these publications, however, I would unhesitatingly rule that the defence is unavailable and that the newspaper can be held to account for such defamatory statements as cannot be proved true.

JUSTIFICATION

[48] I turn, therefore, to the other limb of the appeal, the Sun's contention that the jury's rejection of the defence of justification was perverse and should be set aside. This is, as will readily be apparent, a bold argument. The leading text book, *Gatley on Libel and Slander* (9th edn, 1998) pp 889–890 (para 36.19), puts the position thus:

> 'Only on very strong grounds will the court in an action for defamation interfere or set aside a verdict or grant a new trial on the ground that the verdict is unreasonable or perverse. The jury are the constitutional tribunal for the decision of libel or no libel, and only in an extreme case will their verdict be set aside as unreasonable. If the words complained of are capable of a defamatory meaning and the jury have found in fact that the words do bear that meaning, the court will not set aside the verdict. And where, though the words are capable of a defamatory meaning, the jury have found in fact that the words do not bear that meaning, the verdict will not be set aside unless it is unreasonable. In the absence of any misdirection the appellate court will only interfere with a finding of the jury if it was one which a jury, viewing the whole of the evidence reasonably, could not properly find.'

[49] Just two of the authorities footnoted to that paragraph were shown to us —*O'Brien v Marquis of Salisbury* (1889) 6 TLR 137 and *Australian Newspaper Co Ltd v Bennett* [1894] AC 284. Both, let me make it plain, were concerned with the jury's

a verdict as to the meaning of the words complained of, not (as here) the question whether a particular defamatory allegation was true or false. In *O'Brien*'s case, Field J (at 137) in the Divisional Court said:

> 'If, therefore, as I think, the jury had only relevant evidence submitted to them and were properly directed as to the use they were to make of it, the only remaining question is whether the verdict ought to be set aside as being b unreasonable. The limits within which this jurisdiction of the Court ought to be exercised in an action like this are thus laid down by Chief Justice Tindal in *Broome v Gosden* ((1845) 1 CB 728 at 731, 135 ER 728 at 729):—"Unless the jury are manifestly wrong in not finding the alleged libel to bear the meaning that the plaintiff has thought fit to put upon it by the innuendo (or now any c defamatory meaning), and unless the Court can say with certainty that there has been a miscarriage of justice, no new trial will be granted." In other words, the jury are the appointed tribunal for the decision of the question of libel or no libel, and the Court ought not to invade their province unless it can be plainly seen that the verdict is perverse or so unreasonable as to lead to the conclusion that the jury have not honestly taken the facts into their d consideration.'

[50] The judgment of the Privy Council in the *Australian Newspaper* case included these passages (at 287–290):

> 'It is not disputed that, whilst it is for the Court to determine whether the e words used are capable of the meaning alleged in the innuendo, it is for the jury to determine whether that meaning was properly attached to them. It was therefore the province of the jury in the present case to determine whether the words used were written of the plaintiff, and whether they bore the defamatory sense alleged …
>
> f The question therefore is whether in all these circumstances it can be said that a jury of reasonable men could not possibly find that the article, although it contains that which had much better not have been published, did not reflect upon the plaintiff's character, or even upon his conduct in relation to the newspaper. The jury have so found, and their Lordships are of opinion that it would be exceeding the legitimate function of the Court if g the verdict was set aside and a new trial ordered, that the Court would then in reality be taking upon itself the function which the law has committed to the jury, of looking at the alleged libelous matter as a whole, and determining whether it is published of and concerning the plaintiff, and whether it bears the innuendo which the plaintiff seeks to attach to it.'

h [51] I have set out those passages at some length to illustrate both (a) the narrowness of the jury issue there in question: whether words, already ruled (by the judge) capable of bearing the defamatory meaning complained of, in fact did so; and (b) the court's great anxiety not to usurp the jury's proper function. In neither case, I should point out, was the jury's verdict overturned.

j [52] All that said, this court has, as Mr Hartley expressly acknowledged, the jurisdiction, and therefore the duty, to consider this ground of appeal and to decide whether on all the evidence the jury's verdict was indeed one properly and reasonably open to them. Of course, as I need hardly emphasise, the court will be most reluctant to find perversity in a case like this. So far as both counsel's experience goes, it would be wholly without precedent. We must remind ourselves, too, as Gray J put it to the jury, that Mr Grobbelaar's 'credibility … is at the heart of this action', and that we, unlike the jury, did not have the advantage of seeing him in the witness box. We must also remind ourselves that the burden of proving justification lay squarely on the defendants and, as Gray J observed, these 'are serious charges and of course the more serious the charge the more you will want to consider carefully before you arrive at your conclusion'.

[53] What, therefore, this court would have to conclude before allowing the appeal on this ground is that no reasonable jury could have failed to be satisfied on the balance of probabilities (to a relatively high degree of probability) that Mr Grobbelaar had indeed been party to corrupt conspiracies. This is not, moreover, a case in which any relevant misdirection can be identified. Although various criticisms were directed at the summing up, in my judgment these were wholly unfounded save (as I shall come to explain) with regard to the judge's direction on substantial justification and this, it appears to me, can have had no impact on the jury's verdict as interpreted by all in this court.

[54] I would mention just two final authorities before embarking on the exercise of examining for ourselves whether Mr Grobbelaar's account of events might as a matter of reasonable possibility be true. The first is the very recent decision of the House of Lords in *Designers Guild Ltd v Russell Williams (Textiles) Ltd* [2001] 1 All ER 700, [2000] 1 WLR 2416, a decision in a very different field of law (copyright infringement) but in which the speeches strongly caution this court against exceeding its proper appellate functions. Mr Hartley would, I think, submit that it is even less appropriate for the Court of Appeal to make original findings of fact in a jury action than in an action tried by judge alone.

[55] The second authority, referred to us by Mr Spearman, was *National Justice Cia Naviera SA v Prudential Assurance Co Ltd, The Ikarian Reefer* [1995] 1 Lloyd's Rep 455, a scuttling case, in which this court re-examined all the evidence and overturned the central factual conclusions reached below. The Court of Appeal held that the judge's principal finding that the master was an honest witness could not be accepted so that it had to make its own findings and conclusions. In doing so, the court rejected as wholly implausible one particular theory which had required eight sequential steps, each of which was either improbable or highly improbable. Mr Spearman in effect invites us to adopt the same approach here. If on analysis the plausibility of Mr Grobbelaar's account really does depend upon accepting a whole succession of improbabilities, then this court should not shrink from its duty to say so and to substitute a rational decision for the jury's irrational one. After all, Mr Spearman might have added, there is surely a greater likelihood of a jury coming to a perverse decision than a commercial judge doing so.

[56] With these thoughts in mind, I return at last to the evidence, and first, as promised, to describe in rather greater detail (albeit still only recounting a small fraction of the 70 pages of transcript), the taped admissions and the Gatwick exchanges.

THE TAPES OF THE THREE MEETINGS BETWEEN MR GROBBELAAR AND MR VINCENT

[57] The meeting recorded on 6 October 1994 begins with a long passage in which Mr Grobbelaar talks of various sexual indiscretions. Its relevance—and it alone of several such passages was for this limited purpose admitted in evidence by an interlocutory ruling of the Court of Appeal on 9 July 1999—was to indicate the apparent degree of intimacy between the two men and the atmosphere in which the various admissions subsequently came to be made. There follows this passage (V designating Mr Vincent, G designating Mr Grobbelaar):

a

'*V:* He [Mr Vincent's brother] just came to me and says why wasn't Bruce ready [with money for the Mondoro development]

G: Because I am waiting for the cash. If the ball doesn't play, then it doesn't play. Do you know in the Man United game alone ... how much money I lost.

V: Haven't a clue.

b

G: One hundred and twenty five fucking thousand pounds in cash ... Do you know the other one? ...

V: What made you choose the Newcastle game?

G: Because I knew, you know, there's fuck all chance of winning Newcastle. I chose the Newcastle game because I knew I could do business there.

c

V: Was that when Newcastle came into the Premier league last year or what?

G: Yep, and they had big bucks. So I got that cash.

[The conversation then returned to the Liverpool/Manchester United 3-all draw.]

d

G: ... in the second half I made a fucking blind—2 blinding saves, but I was diving the wrong fucking way—and that's true, as fucking living God, I dived the wrong way and I fucking went "phwoooo"—and I fucking just, just went and it fucking hit my hand.

e

V: Fucking hell. What like the ... one hit your feet [a reference, the defendants suggest, to the Norwich match]

G: Exactly ... I know that I'm my worst enemy on that, because I know I don't like to lose ... So, I don't like to lose, so it's instinct this fucking ... [There is an echo of this at the next meeting on 25 October: "I like to fucking win. I don't like to fucking lose."]

f

V: They [these backers] are prepared to give me about two grand every two weeks or so, on the basis that you pick one game in the season.

G: Fucking two grand, what's two grand?

V: Two grand every two weeks. Until you've picked a game and then if you dipped in on that game—one hundred g's ...

g

G: How many guys are in?

V: There's only two I know and they are bloody clandestine ... I met them after the races at Chester ... The guy said to me we only back sure-fire bloody winners ... I just said, listen, I might have someone who might be interested in talking to you involved with football ... and they said, listen, go back, just say it's two grand they will through me give you two grand every two weeks ...

h

G: I'll meet. Then again, I don't want to meet them. Cos they'll all know who it is ... You'd better find out who these people are, though ... Better find out how many people know ... because I'm telling you this, because it could be the fucking end of me ... There's fucking investigators all round. I don't know that these aren't investigators. [Mr Grobbelaar then referred to Lou Macari of Swindon being banned from managing for a year] ...

j

V: Do you think they might be connected to the short man or not?

G: ... I don't know how, because the short man is from the Far East, Singapore, Kuala Lumpur ... I could go right through to the end of the season and pick the last fucking game.

V: My thinking on it was that—I didn't know until tonight that the short man was back in business with you—was that if you wanted you could pick the same game for both.

G: I would.

V: About two hundred g's you know.

G: Yeah, I could fucking retire … The short man has only got one other person, and that's JF [John Fashanu] …

[There is then a reference to the trip from Norwich to see "the short man" in London.]

G: He had a fucking Rolex on his arm, a Rolex. Cos I said, well give me because I want to wear it. It was the fucking business. Three grands' worth of watch. This is yours, next time you do the business …'

[58] At the meeting on 25 October, Mr Grobbelaar told Mr Vincent that 'the short man's back' and that 'he's telling me now you're going to lose the game. So two minutes into the game I pushed the ball into the back of the net. That was the Coventry game. And then we come and steamroller … Then we won 3–1.'

[59] There then followed discussion in which Mr Grobbelaar said that he would keep the £2,000 per week in notes in a locker 'not in a bank, because they'll fucking find it', and then take it out of the country to Zimbabwe or South Africa. At that point Mr Vincent asked:

'*V:* Well what's the biggest cut you've had from the short man so far?

G: For losing that one, forty [ie £40,000].

V: But for Manchester United you would have got?

G: One hundred and twenty.'

[60] Returning to Mr Vincent's proposal, Mr Grobbelaar said: 'I just go all the way with this guy, until the end of the season, I know which game I shall pick, Liverpool, at Liverpool.' Later he said:

'Right, I've heard enough. I've had enough now. We'll make this easy. Tell him that it's on, and I'm going to pick one game. I'll pick one game, after I've picked the game nothing must be said … It's gotta be fucking right. And the greenbacks have got to be put in the fucking locker … because I don't want this fucking cash to go missing …

V: I know. I'll try and organise a safety deposit box at fucking Selfridges or something like that.

G: No, it's too fucking dangerous, they're being looked at all the fucking time … the camera is on you all the fucking time.'

[61] I come to the third and final meeting on 3 November 1994. Having discussed the Mondoro project at considerable length, Mr Vincent said:

'*V:* Before I forget now … what do you want me to do about the other fucking two grand I'm due to pick up next Tuesday or Wednesday … Do you want me to drop it off at the airport for you?' [ie at Gatwick on 8 November, a proposal to which Mr Grobbelaar assented.]

[62] A little later Mr Grobbelaar said:

'I'm doing the short man tomorrow, on Saturday … it's going to be double what he was going to give …

V: What, eighty?

a

> *G:* … No, nearer fifty. But hopefully fifty will be ready for when I go … I think I'll just put the fifty into my fucking trunk [and take it with me to Zimbabwe].
> *V:* OK, well I'll speak to these guys tomorrow …
> *G:* Don't tell them I'm doing anything else …'

b

[**63**] It was at the end of that meeting that the video showed Mr Vincent handing the £2,000 package to Mr Grobbelaar who then put it in his jacket pocket.

[**64**] So much for the tapes themselves. Indeed, so far as admissions of past match-fixing (or attempted match-fixing) go, that is perhaps more than enough. I repeat, the critical issue was not *whether* these admissions were made, but *why*. Were they genuine or were they fabricated as part of some 'sting' on Mr Vincent?

c

[**65**] I come next to what Mr Grobbelaar said at Gatwick Airport on 8 November, first at the confrontation and then on the telephone to Mr Higgins.

[**66**] When initially the suggestion was put to him that:

d

> 'You received £40,000 … from a syndicate through a middle man called the short man for basically throwing football matches … you've also attempted on several occasions with Liverpool and Southampton to do it …'

Mr Grobbelaar replied: 'Unless you come to me and say, we've got evidence … you are going to have to actually prove it first.'

e

[**67**] When told that the Sun had evidence of his receiving money, Mr Grobbelaar said 'I haven't taken it'. Asked by the reporter 'You have not taken £2,000 from him?', Mr Grobbelaar replied 'Not at all'.

f

[**68**] When it was suggested that he had agreed to receive fortnightly payments of £2,000 with a view to forfeiting one match in the season for £100,000, that being Liverpool at Liverpool, Mr Grobbelaar replied: 'I met him, yes. And I actually said to him that would never be, never able to be done, because if I ever get caught, I would be in deep trouble.' Asked 'Why did you take the £2,000 off him then?', Mr Grobbelaar replied 'I didn't'. When it was then put to him that the video showed him putting the money in his pocket, Mr Grobbelaar replied: 'Alright, I'll put it another way … that £2,000 has been put in a safe place in case of any subsequent … because I've got evidence against that person.' A little later he said:

g

h

> 'O.K., I've taken that money, right. But that money has not been, is not anywhere—it's right here. To be given back, and as I said in my previous meetings with him, to be given back to the people if everything blows up. Because I don't want to get caught in any way, shape or form in this sort of situation.'

j

[**69**] Later in the confrontation, when asked why he had said at the last meeting with Mr Vincent 'I'm going to do a short man on Saturday', Mr Grobbelaar replied: 'You can run this story if that's what you want to do. What you'll do is you'll probably destroy myself, destroy my marriage … I'm totally denying it.' Later he explained the reference to Mr John Fashanu by saying that the two of them were seeking to introduce players to the English game from Nigeria. Then comes this:

> '*Sun:* If what you say is true, do you think it's a sensible thing for a man in your position and idolised as you are to talk about throwing games, if you haven't done it?

G: I know I talk about it ... because they are putting allegations to me, can you ever throw a game and it couldn't be possible ...

Sun: ... You took £2,000 knowing what that £2,000 was for ...

G: ... that money will be put into a box, at the end of the day that money will go back to the people ... because it can be given back. The thing is that I am looking at the evidence against him ... to actually get evidence ...'

[70] The reporter having then pointed out that with regard to the Manchester United match he had said 'I made two blinding saves by diving the wrong fucking way', Mr Grobbelaar suggested that that was 'evidence I need against Vincent ... you think I would deliberately dive the wrong way?' The confrontation ended with the reporter saying that it was up to the editor whether to run the story as planned and Mr Grobbelaar responding 'Does he want the £2,000 back because I've got it there?'

[71] On the telephone to Mr Higgins Mr Grobbelaar said:

> 'I've never attempted to throw a game in my life. The money ... which a certain person has actually said that I've ... received was actually my own testimonial money [a reference to the £40,000].'

[72] Asked 'Did you accept cash to lose matches?', Mr Grobbelaar replied:

> 'No, I've never ... a certain person said to me you would get £2,000 per two weeks where you can actually pick a game at the end of the season ... He said it was going to be a sure-fire thing. I said it had to be put in a box because at the end of the day I did not want to throw matches. And if it didn't come down that money would go back to the certain person that was actually giving it to me.'

[73] When it was put to him that he had said on tape that he had accidentally made two blinding saves and lost the opportunity of receiving something like £135,000 (a mistake—the figures in fact mentioned were £120,000 and £125,000), Mr Grobbelaar replied: 'Well, if you've got that on tape, then you've got it on tape, but I never threw that game. If you look at the evidence I made two blinding saves.' When asked 'How do you explain conversations like that?', he replied 'Because of Mr Vincent's persistence in business dealings we had in Africa'.

[74] Never during the course of that telephone call did he make it plain to Mr Higgins that the Sun had got the wrong end of the stick; it was he who was investigating Mr Vincent with a view to reporting him and that was why he had made up these stories. This omission, as already stated, he ultimately explained by saying that he was not going to give Mr Higgins that satisfaction.

[75] Let me come next to the expert evidence called on Mr Grobbelaar's behalf which formed the very cornerstone of his case. This evidence, as already indicated, was essentially to the effect that in the five matches in question Mr Grobbelaar was manifestly not trying to lose but rather was displaying great goalkeeping skills. That being so, submitted Mr Hartley, it necessarily follows that Mr Grobbelaar's taped admissions to the contrary must be fabrications and this in turn confirms the veracity of his basic story of trying to trap Mr Vincent rather than vice versa.

[76] It is certainly true that Mr Bob Wilson and Mr Alan Ball (another well-known ex-footballer and Mr Grobbelaar's manager at Southampton) gave powerful evidence in support of Mr Grobbelaar's case that he had always kept

a goal to the best of his very considerable abilities and never attempted to throw a match. Mr Wilson saw 'absolutely nothing suspicious whatever' about the three goals scored by Newcastle, and described the 'two blinding saves' which on tape Mr Grobbelaar had claimed to have made accidentally in the Manchester United match as 'truly exceptional ... those two saves are of the highest quality saves that you will see'. He dismissed the notion that Mr Grobbelaar was doing it by
b accident and said that he used the first save 'in goalkeeping schools and clinics as a classic example of how to be perfectly set'. Of one of the two Norwich goals in their 2-all draw with Liverpool, a goal which again Mr Grobbelaar had claimed to have saved accidentally, in answer to a question 'Did you see anything there that would indicate that it was a save he didn't intend to make?', Mr Wilson replied 'No, that's a great save in anybody's book'. As for the goal which Coventry
c scored against Southampton when Mr Grobbelaar claimed on tape to have 'pushed the ball into the back of the net', Mr Wilson said that—

> 'a less agile goalkeeper than Bruce Grobbelaar would not possibly have touched this ball ... the angle of the body, the position of the feet off the ground, the thrust off the ground, I just, I couldn't say to you anything other
d than in my honest opinion, he is making every attempt, every attempt, to save that ball.'

[77] Mr Wilson and Mr Ball also gave evidence to the effect that you *would* be able to detect a goalkeeper who was trying to let in goals and that if you wanted a corrupt player it would be far easier to go for an outfield player than a goalkeeper.
e [78] The Sun's final case with regard to actual match-throwing, I should observe, went no further than an assertion that there were four occasions when Mr Grobbelaar tried to let in goals; the three when he made accidental saves (two against Manchester United, one against Norwich), and the one when he tipped the ball into the net against Coventry. In other words, they relied exclusively on
f the taped admissions. Their case with regard to Liverpool's 3–0 defeat by Newcastle was simply that Mr Grobbelaar had not needed to influence this result: he had specifically selected the match because he was confident of losing it anyway. The misleading headline 'I let in three goals and picked up £40,000' was, of course, on the Sun's case literally true: the fact that he did not (as was implied) intend to let them in made the taped admission more, not less, credible: Mr Wilson's
g evidence simply did not touch on it.

[79] It is convenient at this stage to notice one particular argument before us as to the situation which would arise were the jury to accept that Mr Grobbelaar had entered into these two corrupt conspiracies but conclude that he had none the less neither intended nor sought to let in goals. Mr Hartley submitted that in
h these circumstances Mr Grobbelaar would still be entitled to an award of damages on the footing that the sting of the articles was not merely that he had dishonestly accepted bribes but also that he had thrown or tried to throw matches. It was Mr Hartley's submission that the jury could properly take the view that it is altogether less serious to accept bribes without allowing it to
j influence one's conduct—that is simply to cheat the cheats—than it is deliberately to concede goals and thereby let down one's fellow players, one's club and one's supporters.

[80] The first point to be made about this argument is that it was very much a subsidiary one: as stated, Mr Grobbelaar's main case from first to last has been that he was wholly innocent of corruption and that the evidence of his play goes to show that he was fabricating admissions in order to entrap Mr Vincent. But

the second and more important point is that, as already mentioned, the jury's verdict is accepted on all sides to be consistent only with their having found Mr Grobbelaar innocent (or rather not proved on the balance of probabilities guilty) of all corruption, guilty merely of subsequent lies. Certainly an award of £85,000 would be wholly unsustainable had the jury found corruption even assuming Mr Grobbelaar nevertheless kept goal to the best of his ability. It was for this reason that I earlier suggested (in para 53) that the criticised direction as to substantial justification is in any event irrelevant. That was to the effect that the jury could find corruption proved and yet decide there was no substantial justification for these libels if they found Mr Grobbelaar not guilty of match-fixing. Lest, however, I am wrong in regarding that direction as irrelevant, I should add that it troubles me greatly. It seems to me quite unreal to suppose that, if a player takes the field knowing that he will be paid a large sum if his team lose, he will play with quite the same commitment as someone to whom victory is everything. It is simplistic to believe that bribes have no effect. And, indeed, that approach is enshrined in our substantive law, both civil and criminal. As *Bowstead and Reynolds on Agency* (16th edn, 1996) states (pp 247–248 (para 6–084)):

> 'If the relevant elements [of a bribe] are proved, it is irrelevant to show that the agent has not in fact been influenced or departed from his duty to his principal, for the acceptance of or agreement to receive a bribe is of itself a breach of his general fiduciary duty, as giving him an interest contrary to his duty to his principal.'

[81] This principle was recently applied (albeit in very different circumstances) by the House of Lords in *A-G v Blake (Jonathan Cape Ltd, third party)* [2000] 4 All ER 385 at 393, [2000] 3 WLR 625 at 634 where Lord Nicholls said:

> 'Equity reinforces the duty of fidelity owed by a trustee or fiduciary by requiring him to account for any profits he derives from his office or position. This ensures that trustees or fiduciaries are financially disinterested in carrying out their duties. They may not put themselves in a position where their duty and interest conflict. To this end they must not make any unauthorised profit. If they do, they are accountable. Whether the beneficiaries or persons to whom the fiduciary duty is owed suffered any loss by the impugned transaction is altogether irrelevant.'

[82] The situation is similar under the criminal law. An agent who accepts or agrees to accept a bribe is at common law guilty of conspiracy and it is an offence contrary to s 1 of the Prevention of Corruption Act 1906 for an agent corruptly to accept or agree to accept any gift or consideration as an inducement or reward for doing or forbearing to do any act in relation to his principal's affairs. These, indeed, were the very criminal offences charged against Mr Grobbelaar. For the purpose of these offences the prosecution have merely to prove that the defendant received a gift as an inducement to show favour; they are not required to prove that he actually did show favour in consequence of having received the gift. As Lord Goddard CJ said in *R v Carr* [1956] 3 All ER 979n, [1957] 1 WLR 165 at 166: 'It does not matter if he did not show favour. If the person did what is called double-crossed, and did not do what he was bribed for, there is no reason why he should be acquitted of taking a bribe.'

[83] Applying that dictum in *R v Mills* (1978) 68 Cr App R 154 at 158–159, Geoffrey Lane LJ said:

a 'Realising what we say is *obiter*, nevertheless we feel it right to say that in our judgment it is enough that the recipient takes the gift knowing that it is intended as a bribe. By accepting it as a bribe and intending to keep it he enters into a bargain, despite the fact that he may make to himself a mental reservation to the effect that he is not going to carry out his side of the bargain. The bargain remains a corrupt bargain, even though he may not be b intending to carry out his intended corrupt act.'

[84] There is just one further aspect of the summing up I would mention. The judge illustrated his *Pamplin* direction on the quantum of damages (see *Pamplin v Express Newspapers Ltd (No 2)* (1985) [1988] 1 All ER 282, [1988] 1 WLR 116) by suggesting that if the jury—

c

'were to conclude that the Sun have proved the willingness of Mr Grobbelaar to enter into a corrupt agreement with Mr Vincent to fix matches for £2,000 a fortnight … but you are not satisfied on the evidence that there was any corrupt agreement with the short man.'

d That might be a reason 'for reducing perhaps … very, very significantly any amount of damages'. That, I have to say, seems to me a most unhelpful suggestion. If, indeed, Mr Grobbelaar was guilty of the second conspiracy with Mr Vincent, the entire logic of his having invented the first conspiracy (as part of his scheme to entrap Mr Vincent) is destroyed. Similarly, of course, if Mr Grobbelaar was guilty of conspiracy with Mr Lim, it is inconceivable that he e would have thought of reporting Mr Vincent to the authorities for seeking to entice him into a second conspiracy. This really was an all or nothing case.

[85] I come at last to consider the probabilities of the case and it is at this point that to my mind Mr Grobbelaar's story falls apart. He had, as it seems to me, just too much to explain away: his entire dealings with Mr Lim, his remarkable visits f to Manchester and to London, his large cash transactions at around the time of the Liverpool/Newcastle match, his confessions on tape, his acceptance of Mr Vincent's first £2,000 payment (his receipt of the second thwarted only by the Gatwick confrontation), his failure during that confrontation or the subsequent telephone conversation with Mr Higgins to offer any sensible explanation for all this, and finally his calculated and sustained deceit even of his own legal team as g reflected in his initial reply.

[86] I remind myself that for the purpose of justification we must ignore the coincidences between what Mr Vincent told the Sun (as recorded in Mr Troup's note) and what thereafter Mr Grobbelaar confessed on tape: these coincidences, although relevant to qualified privilege (which falls to be judged by the h circumstances, including the Sun's grounds for belief, at the time of publication), are inadmissible on the issue of justification since Mr Vincent was not called and the Civil Evidence Act 1995 was not in force.

[87] For my part, however, even putting the Troup note entirely aside, there are simply too many improbabilities piled one upon another inherent in j Mr Grobbelaar's case for it to begin to be credible. His whole account of his relationship and dealings with Mr Lim beggars belief at every turn. His refusal even to acknowledge Mr Lim's existence he explains by saying he suspected even match-forecasting to be (as, of course, it is) contrary to FA rules. The reason he gave for denying travelling down to London before the Norwich match was that he knew it was forbidden to leave his hotel without permission and feared that his club would have strongly disapproved. All that no doubt is true but, of course, it does nothing to explain why Mr Grobbelaar should go to such extraordinary lengths to hold a clandestine meeting and receive cash from Mr Lim in person. Nor is it credible to suggest that he was anxious to discuss with Mr Lim his prospects for playing out in the Far East, the evidence being that Mr Lim was merely a football enthusiast with no connections whatever in the professional game. And what of the taped reference to Mr Lim that night having 'a fucking Rolex on his arm' and saying 'you do the business and that's yours'?

[88] Mr Grobbelaar's account of his visit to London on 25 November 1993 to see John Fashanu in Byron Drive (also initially denied) and his explanation for having very large sums of cash at around that time seem to me equally implausible. True, his account of keeping cash in his sock drawer was corroborated by his wife. That, however, can hardly be regarded as decisive.

[89] And what of the tapes themselves? It is in this connection that Mr Spearman makes some of his most telling points. He refers first to the considerable detail and fluency of what Mr Grobbelaar said at these meetings. The relationship the tapes reveal between Mr Grobbelaar and Mr Vincent appears clearly to have been friendly and uninhibited; the discussion between them was invariably frank and free-flowing. There is secondly the fact that Mr Grobbelaar had no need to fabricate previous corruption on his part in order to elicit information from Mr Vincent. It is, indeed, difficult to imagine just what object could be served by such fabrication. It is difficult too to suppose Mr Grobbelaar capable of such spontaneous and sustained invention. Third, even if it made sense to fabricate previous corruption, it would be absurd to invent a role in it for John Fashanu. That could cause nothing but problems for both of them. And what of 'the short man'? Fourth, one finds little if anything on the tapes consistent with Mr Grobbelaar trying to discover who was behind Mr Vincent's proposal, so that they too might be brought to justice, still less any attempt to record Mr Vincent making these corrupt proposals so as to substantiate the report which Mr Grobbelaar claims he intended to make. On the contrary all the emphasis was on Mr Grobbelaar's concerns at the risks he was running and on how he proposed storing and disposing of the 'greenbacks'. Fifth, although these meetings extended over several weeks, Mr Grobbelaar never told anyone else (not even his wife) about them, least of all of a plan to trap Mr Vincent in some way with a view to reporting his corrupt proposal to the authorities. Not even when he received the £2,000 cash payment on 3 November did he go to the authorities; rather he was awaiting another such payment at Gatwick on 8 November.

[90] Perhaps more striking than any of these points, however, is the absurdity of supposing that Mr Grobbelaar would ever have gone to the authorities when such a step would inevitably have brought to light all his murky past dealings with Mr Lim which, even on his own account of the matter, must irreparably have damaged his reputation in the game.

[91] And then one comes to the exchanges at Gatwick. Is it really credible that when confronted with the threat of immediate and damning tabloid exposure as a corrupt match-fixer, someone truly innocent and intent only on bringing a briber to justice would say: 'Unless you come to me and say, we've got evidence ... you are going to have to actually prove it first'? In my judgment it is not and the fact that, as one of the Sun's journalists accepted in cross-examination, at some point during the confrontation Mr Grobbelaar 'made a stab at trying to imply that it was in fact him trying to gather evidence against Mr Vincent and not the other way round' provides no sufficient argument to the contrary. Nor is it a realistic to suppose that an innocent man would decide not to tell Mr Higgins of his fundamental mistake about the tapes—a decision which would almost inevitably lead to the story's immediate publication and his own ruination—merely because 'he was not going to give him that satisfaction'.

[92] In a hotly fought case of this kind, the evidence inevitably went into the greatest detail. It is not, of course, possible within a judgment of manageable b length to discuss all of it nor indeed deal with many of the innumerable points canvassed by both sides. I have instead sought to focus on those relatively few factual issues that seem to me ultimately determinative of the case. On this approach one is left with an inescapable core of fact and circumstance which to my mind leads inexorably to the view that Mr Grobbelaar's story is, quite simply, incredible. All logic, common sense and reason compel one to that conclusion.

c [93] It is, of course, understandable how a jury, skilfully deflected from the path of logic, could have accepted Mr Grobbelaar's story or at least been left undecided about it—a result fatal to the defendants upon whom the burden lay. Not surprisingly, all Mr Hartley's emphasis was on the expert evidence to the effect that Mr Grobbelaar never deliberately let goals in. As, however, I have d endeavoured to explain, that could never excuse his acceptance of money for matches lost nor, of course, does it disprove the genuineness of his admissions of wrongdoing. It may be that Mr Grobbelaar was careful only to select games which he thought his team would lose anyway; it may be he was intending to return the bribes if the matches selected were not in the event lost; it may be that his instinct for saving goals and his will to win in the end prevailed over his e interest in losing. There are, indeed, hints of all these possibilities in what at various times he was recorded as saying. A decision on that, however, was never necessary: this paradoxically was a case where keeping one's eye on the ball, metaphorically speaking, required one actually to take it off the ball (or at any rate not to over-emphasise what happened to the ball), literally speaking. All that had f to be decided was whether Mr Grobbelaar took corrupt payments and as to that in my judgment only one rational view was possible, namely that the defendants' allegations were proved true at least up to the standard of the balance of probabilities.

[94] In the result I would allow the Sun's appeal on this ground. I confess to doing so with some misgiving. That, however, is not because I entertain the least g doubt about Mr Grobbelaar's guilt but rather because, as I earlier observed, the court must inevitably be reluctant to find a jury's verdict perverse and anxious not to usurp their function. As I also observed, however, given that we have the jurisdiction to entertain an appeal on the ground of perversity, so too we have the duty to determine it according to the best of our ability.

h [95] Nothing would have been easier than to reject this challenge on the footing that the issue was purely one for the jury who, of course, heard all the evidence for themselves. Some, no doubt, will say that that is the decision we should have reached. I cannot agree. It is, I think, the experience of all of us that juries from time to time *do* arrive at perverse verdicts. If, of course, this occurs in j a criminal trial and the verdict is one of acquittal, that simply is that. If, however, the jury perversely convict, the court can and does examine the evidence, and if persuaded to that view (or even if left merely with a lurking doubt) it will overturn the verdict. The present case raises the different consideration: should the claimant be permitted to retain an unmerited award of libel damages?

[96] In this very case, it will be remembered, successive juries at criminal trials could not agree upon a verdict (at least with regard to the second count). It

follows logically that at the very least a total of six jurors must have been satisfied beyond all reasonable doubt of Mr Grobbelaar's guilt on the second count. Is it not surprising that against that background the jury in this libel trial should unanimously have found the case unproved against Mr Grobbelaar even to the lesser standard required in a civil action? I think it not merely surprising but unacceptable. The result clearly represented a forensic triumph for Mr Hartley. In my judgment, however, it represented also an affront to justice. I would allow the appeal, set aside the jury's verdict and enter judgment for the defendants.

THORPE LJ.

[97] I express my opinion briefly on the two issues raised by this appeal, namely qualified privilege and justification. It seems to me that the resolution of those issues depends upon the realistic analysis of the surrounding facts and circumstances. For the newspaper Mr Spearman QC submits that the work done by the Sun's staff immediately prior to publication on 9 November 1994 constituted the profoundest piece of investigative journalism that the Sun had ever undertaken. Mr Hartley QC poured scorn on that description, in my opinion with justification. In reality the Sun had been approached by Mr Vincent offering to provide evidence of Mr Grobbelaar's corruption. There was no doubt that he was an associate of Mr Grobbelaar but it would not have been difficult for the Sun to have ascertained that he was an informant of doubtful repute. After an amateur attempt at recording Mr Vincent's conversation with Mr Grobbelaar the Sun invested in more professional equipment to produce audio and video record of future conversation. After three separate recordings, during the course of the last of which Mr Grobbelaar accepted £2,000 in cash from Mr Vincent, the investigation was complete. The only other preparatory step taken prior to publication was the airport challenge on the eve.

[98] At the date of publication the Sun must have appreciated that its only defence to an action in defamation was justification. That defence rested upon Mr Grobbelaar's admissions recorded during the three meetings and the evidence of Mr Vincent. In consequence of Mr Vincent's destruction in cross-examination during the criminal trials the defence of justification at this trial rested solely on the claimant's recorded admissions. Between the date of writ and the date of trial the claimant's case had evolved to the point where he challenged nothing on the record but explained that all his apparent admissions were spontaneous inventions designed to trap Mr Vincent and establish his dishonesty. The litigation strategy adopted by each party seems reasonably transparent. The claimant made the most of the videos of the matches put in question by the claimant's admissions. He relied upon the evidence of Mr Wilson called as an expert in the art of the goalkeeper. Throughout his evidence he praised the claimant's skill in almost extravagant terms. Although the defendants only asserted that the claimant had deliberately conceded one specific goal in one specific game, Mr Hartley sought Mr Wilson's opinion on all the claimant's play through all five games in which the defendants had alleged foul play in the articles. Furthermore the terms of his instructions were extremely narrow. In answer to Mr Carman QC he said:

> '... but you must remember that I have been looking purely at five games in which I was asked to look at beyond reasonable doubt anything that was untoward in those games involving Bruce Grobbelaar and his goalkeeping and that is what I've concentrated on totally.'

a [99] When cross-examined by Mr Carman on contemporaneous comment which he was said to have given to the Sun, there was the following exchange:

> '*A*. I didn't know that Bruce Grobbelaar had admitted cheating in any games, Mr Carman.
>
> *Q*. You know now of course on the tapes that he has admitted it. *A*. I have never seen any tapes.
>
> b *Q*. It is not an issue in this court that he has made those admissions, but he said he made them up. *A*. With great respect, that's not what I'm here for. I was here to look at five games and …
>
> *Q*. I do understand that but I was simply asking you if you knew about that, and you did not know from the Sun articles that he had admitted c cheating. *A*. I have heard obviously and read in other newspapers about the accusations, and so on, but I have never seen the tapes and I have never really in any detail whatsoever followed what was said in those particular tapes.'

[100] Within the confines of those instructions Mr Wilson said of the one goal d that was the subject of specific allegation, the goal in the Southampton v Coventry game:

> 'I just say to you again the angle of the body, the position of the feet off the ground, the thrust off the ground, I just, I couldn't say to you anything other than in my honest opinion, he is making every attempt, every attempt, to save that ball.'

e

[101] During the course of his cross-examination by Mr Carman, Mr Wilson accepted that it would be feasible for a corrupted goalkeeper to make deliberate mistakes, although he maintained that misconduct would be swiftly detected by the expert eye of manager, coach and regular fans. When Mr Carman suggested f that in the case of a corrupted goalkeeper the instinct to save might prevail over the intention to concede, Mr Wilson responded that it was an interesting theory. Finally in relation to the crucial goal in the Southampton v Coventry game Mr Wilson's response to Mr Carman's suggestion that the claimant had guided the ball into the goal was: 'I think it would be a truly extraordinary feat to be able to disguise it in that way.'

g [102] In summary it seems to me that whilst Mr Wilson was fulsome in his praise of the claimant's skill and steadfast in his support for his cause, the acceptance of his evidence would not absolutely exclude the possibility that the claimant had engineered an own goal in the Coventry game. In assessing the overall value of Mr Wilson's contribution it is important to bear in mind, in my h opinion, the limited nature of his instructions.

[103] On that foundation it was argued for the claimant that his case of invention was effectively corroborated. Obviously, whatever the jury might think of the claimant, they were likely to be impressed by the evidence of Mr Wilson, a renowned expert and familiar to many from his television work. In j contrast the defendant's strategy was inevitably to emphasise the transparency and detail of the claimant's admissions. After all they had no other evidence.

[104] This strategy persisted throughout the hearing of the appeal. Mr Spearman consistently demonstrated that the plaintiff's eventual explanation for his admissions went well beyond the boundary of the implausible deep into the territory of the incredible. Mr Hartley repeatedly submitted that Mr Spearman's submissions constituted a distortion of the issues. He said that the right starting

point must be the evaluation of the claimant's performance on the pitch. From that beginning the jury's verdict was not only possible but fully justified.

a

[105] Of these two strategies the defendants' was in my opinion closer to reality. In the end the crucial decision for the jury was the acceptance or rejection of the claimant's explanation for his admissions. Of course at the date of publication the Sun proceeded without much caution or moderation. Anything that could possibly be extracted either from the claimant's admissions or from the evidence of Mr Vincent was elevated and published as incontrovertible fact. By the date of trial they had abandoned the evidence of Mr Vincent. However, a significant proportion of the material published could not be justified by the admissions alone without the supporting evidence of Mr Vincent. That presented Mr Hartley with the opportunity to emphasise the allegations that the claimant had fixed or attempted to fix five specific games. That was the sting and if the jury concluded on the evidence of the claimant, his expert and the videos of the games that not a single goal had been let in deliberately that was the end of the defendant's case. The defendants said, as they were bound to say, that the sting lay in the accusations of corruption and if those allegations were proved justification was established whatever might have happened in the five specific matches.

b

c

d

[106] Certainly these rival submissions emphasise the clear boundary between dishonesty on the pitch and dishonesty off the pitch. But dishonesty on the pitch is of a different character to dishonesty off the pitch. Any agreement to accept a bribe constitutes an actionable tort as well as a criminal offence. As Mr Spearman demonstrated in reply an agreement to receive a bribe constitutes a breach of fiduciary duty and it is no defence to prove that the recipient was not influenced to depart or did not depart from his duty. Equally in crime the burden on the prosecution is only to prove receipt of the bribe and it is no defence for the recipient to show that he did not intend to keep his side of the dishonest bargain. It seems to me particularly important that that distinction is maintained in deciding issues involving the corruption of professional games players. Any employer is entitled to complete commitment and fierce determination to win from any player put onto the field of play or held in training for play. Any player who sells his commitment and determination only appears to play for his employer. Beneath the appearance he has become, if not a player for the other team, a traitor to his uniform. The resulting feelings of guilt at the betrayal and anxiety over detection must be intense. The conscious is at war with the unconscious or instinctive reaction instilled by years of training and professional play. There must be equal conflict between the desire to maintain the flow of corrupt money and the contrary desire to maintain the esteem of team-mates, manager, sports journalists and the public. The greater the individuality and egoism of the player the greater must be his need for public adulation. These complex emotional forces would be heightened by the emotional reaction to developments during the game beyond the control of the corrupt player. Inspiration and achievement in attack that would ordinarily unite the whole team would leave the greedy and corrupt defender in turmoil. The practical resolution of these conflicts would probably lead the traitor to acts far from transparent. Transparent acts would swiftly lead to deselection which would be neither in his interests nor in the interests of the corrupter. These differences lead inevitably to the distinction that one act, the corrupt agreement, is capable of clear proof whereas the other, betrayal on the pitch, is not.

e

f

g

h

j

[107] Against that analysis of what for me are the relevant realities I turn to the issues.

a

Qualified privilege

[**108**] Mr Spearman's principal reliance is upon the importance of investigative journalism fully recognised by Lord Nicholls of Birkenhead in his speech in *Reynolds v Times Newspapers Ltd* [1999] 4 All ER 609, [1999] 3 WLR 1010. But is this a case truly an instance of investigative journalism? Here the newspaper had simply paid a substantial sum of money to an informant in the belief that the b publication of his information would earn them a considerably greater sum from the profits of enhanced circulation. Whilst I accept that the exposure would never result unless there were newspapers prepared to pay substantial sums for sensational information (for Mr Vincent would have seen no personal advantage in taking his story to either the Football Association or the police) it does seem to me important that newspapers should not, when buying sensational material c with a view to increasing profit, be encouraged to think that they can be careless with the truth since they enjoy a wider defence than justification. This does not seem to me to be a case of the investigative bloodhound fulfilling some high duty to inform. The Sun's self-interest seems to have been well to the fore. That impression is certainly strengthened by the tone of the articles. As Mr Hartley d submits the involvement of the claimant's wife and children seems superfluous to the performance of any duty to inform. The cartoons, the attempt to secure his immediate suspension and the marketing of the tapes all suggest either an endeavour to break down the threatened libel action or to pursue commercial interests. The application of the ten factors identified by Lord Nicholls to the present case in my opinion justified Mr Hartley's submission that the alternative e defence of qualified privilege was for the defendant something of an afterthought rightly rejected by Gray J.

Justification

[**109**] For reasons which I have already given the crucial categorisation of fact f was into events on and off the field of play. On the pleadings it was agreed between the parties that the articles published meant that the claimant:

(i) having dishonestly taken bribes had fixed or attempted to fix the result of games of football in which he played, and

(ii) had dishonestly taken bribes with a view to fixing the result of games in which he would be playing.

g

[**110**] Mr Hartley who was responsible for this formulation said that para (i) was intended to comprehend all allegations relating to business done with Mr Lim while para (ii) related to the claimant's dealings with Mr Vincent. With the advantage of hindsight that formulation seems to me to be unfortunate. For neither party invited a half-way house. The claimant said that all his admissions h in relation to past conduct were invented and all his agreement to future misconduct was pretended. He did not accept the possibility that he could explain away one conspiracy but not the other. Equally the defendants did not seek to draw any distinction between the conspiracy with Mr Lim and the conspiracy with Mr Vincent. Either they succeeded in relation to each or they j failed on each. Again with the advantage of hindsight I do not think that this was perhaps made sufficiently clear to the jury. The judge's principal direction in relation to what the defendants had to prove in order to justify appears on pp 60 and 61 of our core bundle. There he clearly drew out the distinction between Mr Hartley's submission that he succeeded, since no misconduct on the pitch had been proved, as against Mr Carman's submission that he succeeded once corrupt agreements had been proved. The parallel direction in relation to damages comes

at pp 123 and 124 of our core bundle. In this passage the judge sought to guide the jury in the event that they concluded that the plea of justification failed but that the defendants had nevertheless proved a significant part of their case. By way of example he took the hypothesis that the defendants proved corrupt agreement with Mr Vincent but not the corrupt agreement with Mr Lim. The judge then said that in that event damages might be reduced 'perhaps—it is a matter for you—very, very significantly' to reflect the finding that the publication was partially true.

[111] At the conclusion of the summing up Mr Carman sought a further direction that if the jury were satisfied that the corrupt agreements had been proved the defendants were entitled to the verdict. The judge tentatively rejected the submission but left the question open pending the arrival of the daily transcript.

[112] On the following day with the advantage of the transcript Mr Carman renewed his submission saying:

> 'If the jury form the view on the facts that no match fixing was made out but that the claimant was party to two conspiracies and accepted money with a view to fixing matches, the second defamatory meaning of entering into dishonest agreements with a view to fixing matches is made out. We would submit that as a matter of law your lordship should bring to their attention that that would plant the badge of dishonesty as a footballer fairly and squarely …'

[113] The judges response was that that was not a matter of law but a question for the jury. Mr Carman continued to press his point and in the course of his submissions pointed out that the judge's hypothetical instance that the jury accepted only one of the two corrupt agreements was logically impossible. Nevertheless in the end the judge rejected the invitation to further direction.

[114] Viewing these developments in the round I conclude that the judge's directions were sufficient and that Mr Spearman's attack on the summing up does not succeed. It is easy to be wise with hindsight and in a perfect world the direction would have drawn out the essential distinction between what the claimant did on the pitch and what he did off the pitch. Ideally the hypotheses upon which the judge should have concentrated were not the acceptance of one conspiracy and the rejection of the other but the true choice namely between: (a) neither conspiracy; (b) both conspiracies; and (c) both conspiracies plus treachery on the pitch.

[115] Against that background I would accept Mr Hartley's submission that in order to succeed Mr Spearman has to demonstrate that the jury's verdict for the claimant together with its award of £85,000 damages was a result to which no reasonable jury could come. Mr Hartley with all his experience submits that it is unprecedented for this court to interfere with a jury's findings on disputed facts. Cases on perverse findings are all concerned with findings as to the meaning of words. However, in my opinion the key to outcome lies in Mr Hartley's submission that it was open to the jury to find both conspiracies proved and still to enter a verdict for the claimant with an award of £85,000. I couple with that submission his concession that in the light of the judge's direction as to the reduction of damages which I have cited, the award of £85,000 demonstrates that the jury absolved the claimant of any conspiracy to corrupt. Mr Hartley submits that, since it had of course been open to the jury to bring in an award of damages up to £150,000, their decision to award £85,000 reflected the claimant's

a concession that he had lied about his relationship with Mr Lim and had sustained that lie over a period of about three years.

[116] As to the submission, in my opinion it only illustrates the distortions that flow from Mr Hartley's elevation of the issue of the claimant's conduct on the pitch to an unsustainable and quite unrealistic height. The proper recognition of corruption rather than fixing as the primary issue renders Mr Hartley's b submission almost repugnant. In reality words admittedly spoken proved corruption to the hilt unless the claimant's explanation for having uttered them was arguably credible. For all the reasons given by my Lords the explanation was quite simply incredible. It was not an explanation which any reasonable jury could have accepted. I can only speculate that the jury's conceded acceptance was probably the product of a failure to properly prioritise the significance of the c claimant's actions off the pitch from the elections made on the pitch. Unless that distinction was clearly and consistently in their minds it is easy to understand how they might have placed undue reliance on the evidence of Mr Wilson. Although I recognise and respect the unique function of a jury that heard all the evidence over the course of some 16 days of trial, nevertheless it would in my opinion be d an injustice to the defendants to allow the outcome to stand. I therefore agree with my Lords that this appeal should be allowed.

JONATHAN PARKER LJ.

[117] The Sun appeals firstly against a ruling by the trial judge, made in the course of the trial, that the publications complained of in the action were not e protected by qualified privilege; and secondly against the verdict of the jury awarding damages of £85,000 to the claimant in the action, the well-known footballer Mr Bruce Grobbelaar, and the costs orders made by the judge consequent upon that award.

[118] In the action, Mr Grobbelaar claims damages for libels contained in the f editions of the Sun published on 9, 10, 11, 14, 15, 16 and 18 November 1994 respectively (seven editions). In those editions, the Sun accused Mr Grobbelaar of taking bribes to fix football matches and of having fixed or attempted to fix matches in which he had played. The material complained of (which included articles, editorials, jokes and cartoons) was derived substantially from admissions made by Mr Grobbelaar in the course of meetings with a former friend and g business associate, a Mr Christopher Vincent—meetings which the Sun had, with the connivance and co-operation of Mr Vincent but without the knowledge of Mr Grobbelaar, covertly recorded on video and audio tape.

[119] The action was commenced promptly after the initial publication, but was in effect left on hold pending the outcome of the trial and retrial of h Mr Grobbelaar and others on criminal charges arising out of the Sun's accusations. In the criminal trials, Mr Grobbelaar faced two counts. The first count alleged a conspiracy with a Mr Richard Lim (a co-defendant, whose name features prominently in the instant case) and others to accept bribes to fix football matches; the second count alleged that on 3 November 1994 Mr Grobbelaar j corruptly accepted a bribe of £2,000 from Mr Vincent to fix football matches. The second count was based on what had occurred in the course of one of the meetings between Mr Grobbelaar and Mr Vincent which the Sun had recorded. At the first criminal trial (which began on 13 January 1997 and ended on 4 March 1997) the jury were unable to agree on any verdicts and a retrial was directed. At the retrial (which began on 10 June 1997 and ended on 7 August 1997) the jury unanimously acquitted Mr Grobbelaar on the first count but were unable to

reach a majority agreement in relation to the second count. Following the retrial, the libel action was effectively revived. *a*

[**120**] The Sun has throughout accepted, not surprisingly, that the material complained of was defamatory. Nor was there any issue between the parties on the pleadings as to the defamatory meaning or meanings of that material (although this is an aspect to which I shall have to return). Mr Grobbelaar sought both aggravated and exemplary damages. The Sun pleaded justification and qualified *b* privilege (the plea of qualified privilege having been added at a relatively late stage in the proceedings). As already indicated, however, the judge ruled in the course of the trial that a defence of qualified privilege was not open to the Sun (the ruling was made on 23 July 1999, reasons being delivered on 29 July 1999). That left the Sun with the defence of justification.

c

[**121**] The trial of the action began on 5 July 1999 and ended on 28 July 1999. The first three days of the trial were mainly taken up with an appeal by Mr Grobbelaar to this court against a ruling by the judge concerning the admissibility of certain evidence. That appeal (which was partially successful) is not material for present purposes. It is, however, material to note that the hearing of the oral evidence took the best part of nine court days; that Mr Grobbelaar was *d* himself in the witness box for more than three court days; and that Mr Carman QC's cross-examination of Mr Grobbelaar took some two court days.

[**122**] The questions put before the jury at the conclusion of the trial were: (1) whether they found for Mr Grobbelaar; (2) if so, how much they awarded him by way of damages; and (3) whether any part of their award was in respect of *e* exemplary damages. The answers which the jury gave to those questions were: (1) Yes; (2) £85,000; and (3) No. In the light of the jury's award of substantial damages, the judge ordered the Sun to pay Mr Grobbelaar's costs of the action, plus 75% of his costs of his appeal (such costs having been reserved by this court to the trial judge).

f

THE MATERIAL COMPLAINED OF

[**123**] The charges made against Mr Grobbelaar by the Sun in the material complained of were, in summary; (a) that he had been party to a conspiracy with Mr Lim (known as 'the short man'), acting on behalf of a Far Eastern betting syndicate, and pursuant to that conspiracy had accepted bribes to fix football *g* matches, (b) that he had corruptly accepted a sum of £2,000 from Mr Vincent to fix football matches, and (c) that he had deliberately let in goals.

[**124**] On 9 November 1994 the Sun gave what may be described as saturation coverage to what it plainly regarded as a substantial scoop by publishing a number of articles about Mr Grobbelaar and his alleged corrupt activities. These *h* articles took up most of the first six pages of that edition of the newspaper. On the front page there appeared the banner headline 'WORLD EXCLUSIVE GROBBELAAR TOOK BRIBES TO FIX GAMES'.

[**125**] The article which followed that headline stated as a fact that Mr Grobbelaar had taken bribes and that he had fixed or attempted to fix football matches. The following extract will, I think, give a flavour of the content and *j* tone of the articles:

> 'Soccer Star Bruce Grobbelaar is exposed by The Sun today for taking massive bribes to throw key matches. The flamboyant goalkeeper pocketed £40,000 to lose a game while playing for Liverpool. Greedy Grobbelaar was offered £175,000 to let in goals in another two Premiership fixtures.'

a On p 2 of that edition appears the headline 'GROB: I let in 3 goals and picked up £40,000'. Across pp 4 and 5 of that edition runs the headline 'IF I GET CAUGHT I'M FINISHED'. Page 6 of that edition, under the headline 'THE GROBBELIAR TAPES—Soccer bribe sensation' contained extracts from the tapes of the recorded meetings between Mr Grobbelaar and Mr Vincent.

[**126**] The other editions of the Sun in respect of which complaint is made were in b more or less the same vein. The headline on the front page of the 10 November 1994 edition read 'I SAVED GOAL BY MISTAKE AND LOST £125,000'. Across pp 2 and 3 of that edition runs the headline 'THE ULTIMATE BETRAYAL' referring to Mr Grobbelaar's alleged confessions as recorded on the tapes. Under that headline appears a sub-heading which reads 'Grob: I'll throw first match back at Anfield and pick up £134,000'. The article itself begins 'Shameless Bruce c Grobbelaar planned to rake in £134,000 by throwing a game against his old club Liverpool'.

[**127**] The 10 November 1994 edition also carries an article under the headline 'SECRET CODE OF MR FIXIT' in which further extracts from the tapes are quoted. On p 6 of that edition is a cartoon depicting Mr Grobbelaar as a goalkeeper d diving to catch not a football but a bag of cash.

[**128**] Headlines in the editions of the paper on the other days in question adopted the same tone: eg 'I'LL TAKE MONEY AND RUN', 'GROB'S MASK-ERADE' (a reference to the fact that Mr Grobbelaar was at that time wearing a mask to protect a broken cheekbone), 'SMASH N'GROB', 'SMACK IN THE GROB', 'FANS PUT GROB ON TRIAL', 'GROB IN THE NICK', and so on.

e [**129**] In the 22 November 1994 edition of the paper, under the headline 'Grobbelgate: Judge for yourself', the Sun invited its readers to telephone a given number (at premium rates) in order to hear the tapes for themselves.

It is not, I think, necessary for present purposes to make any further detailed references to the material of which complaint is made.

f

THE DEFAMATORY MEANING OF THE MATERIAL COMPLAINED OF

[**130**] I return at this point to the (admitted) defamatory meaning or meanings of the material complained of. In para 11 of his consolidated amended statement of claim, Mr Grobbelaar pleads as follows:

g

> 'The said [material] meant and [was] understood to mean that the Plaintiff:
> (a) having dishonestly taken bribes had fixed or attempted to fix the result of games of football in which he had played and
> (b) had dishonestly taken bribes with a view to fixing the result of games in which he would be playing.'

h That allegation was admitted by the Sun in para 2 of its consolidated-re-re-amended defence.

[**131**] In the course of his submissions, Mr Hartley QC (for Mr Grobbelaar) informed us that his intention in drafting para 11 of the statement of claim was to refer in sub-para (a) to the alleged conspiracy with Mr Lim (which formed the j subject matter of the first of the two counts against Mr Grobbelaar in the criminal trials), and in sub-para (b) to the allegedly corrupt acceptance of £2,000 from Mr Vincent (which formed the basis of the second of the two charges against Mr Grobbelaar in the criminal trials). However, as I read those subparagraphs, sub-para (a) is directed to *actual* match-fixing or attempted match-fixing, following the acceptance of bribes—i e to alleged improper and corrupt conduct on the pitch—whereas sub-para (b) is directed to Mr Grobbelaar's alleged

acceptance of bribes to fix matches (that is to say, acceptance of bribes both from Mr Lim and from Mr Vincent). a

[132] At all events, the dual pleaded meanings of the defamatory material appear to have contributed to what was undoubtedly a stark difference in approach between Mr Hartley and Mr Carman (for the Sun) in the presentation of their respective cases to the jury.

[133] Mr Hartley, for his part, presented Mr Grobbelaar's case to the jury on b the basis that the 'sting' of the libels lay in the assertion that Mr Grobbelaar had deliberately let in goals (the first of the two pleaded meanings). On that basis, he asserted that in order for the Sun's defence of justification to succeed, the Sun had to establish that Mr Grobbelaar had been guilty of *actual match-fixing*. Thus, in his closing speech to the jury Mr Hartley said: c

> 'Those articles in The Sun accuse Mr Grobbelaar of fixing or trying to fix those five games. There cannot be any doubt about that, and indeed they have accepted it. We say it is fatal to the defendants' case that they cannot prove those accusations to be true. They have not, they cannot ... You see, Mr Carman for The Sun may duck and dive, but he cannot escape the fact d that *the defendants have failed to prove in any shape or form that Mr Grobbelaar acted improperly, or tried to act improperly, in any game. That must be a fatal flaw in their case ...*' (My emphasis.)

[134] By contrast, Mr Carman presented the Sun's case on the footing that the sting of the libels lay in the charge that Mr Grobbelaar had corruptly accepted e bribes to fix matches (the second of the two pleaded meanings). Thus, in his closing speech to the jury Mr Carman said:

> 'We say that this claimant, Bruce Grobbelaar, is disqualified from obtaining a single penny of damages if we establish on the balance of probability that f he corruptly agreed to accept money. *It would not be necessary to establish that he did actually fix any single match.* In all justice, do you, members of the jury, want to award damages of any kind in a case where you find that the claimant has corruptly agreed to accept money and, indeed, in the case of the £2,000 has accepted money for match fixing? So we stand by that defence, *that the vice and shame of Bruce Grobbelaar is entering into a corrupt agreement* g *with the short man and a corrupt agreement with Mr Vincent, amply demonstrated on the tapes.* We shall of course await with great interest in this court to see whether my learned friend Mr Hartley is so bold on behalf of Mr Grobbelaar to ask you to award a single penny of damages on the basis that, although he may have entered into a corrupt agreement, he did not fix any matches; we h say that would be an affront to justice.' (My emphasis.)

This approach by Mr Carman was reflected in his cross-examination of Mr Grobbelaar. Mr Carman began his cross-examination of Mr Grobbelaar by asking him: j

> Q: Would you ... agree that *even if a player agreed to take money corruptly but did not, in fact, throw a goal, nevertheless that would still be a very grave matter, to accept money corruptly for that purpose?*'

When Mr Grobbelaar said he did not understand the question, Mr Carman repeated it in the following terms:

a 'Q: Can you agree that if any professional player agreed to accept money to behave corruptly, *even if he did not actually throw a goal*, nevertheless the corrupt agreement would be a very grave matter indeed?'

Mr Grobbelaar then agreed with that proposition.

[**135**] So the jury was faced on the one hand by Mr Hartley saying that unless b the Sun could prove *actual match-fixing* its defence of justification must fail, and on the other hand by Mr Carman saying that it was not necessary for the Sun to prove actual match-fixing provided it could prove that Mr Grobbelaar had accepted bribes to fix matches, since if corruption be proved then Mr Grobbelaar was not entitled to damages. Nor is it in the least surprising that there should have been this difference in approach, since each side was seeking to fight the c battle on its own chosen ground. Mr Grobbelaar's case relied strongly on expert evidence from Mr Bob Wilson, the well-known broadcaster and former goalkeeper, to the effect that Mr Grobbelaar had not been guilty of actual match-fixing as alleged; whereas the Sun's case on justification was based almost entirely (since Mr Vincent was not, in the event, called to give evidence) on d Mr Grobbelaar's taped admissions of corrupt conduct.

[**136**] The judge adopted, in effect, a third approach to the meaning of the material complained of. When he came to sum the case up to the jury, he treated the two pleaded meanings as amounting to a single composite meaning. Having stated the two pleaded meanings, the judge continued:

e 'What that means, members of the jury, is that you must be satisfied by the evidence that *the dishonest taking of bribes to fix the outcome of matches was something that Mr Grobbelaar did or at least was prepared to do or to try to do*. As I say, the defence [of justification] will not fail because you are not satisfied that the defendants have proved every alleged incident of dishonest bribery or every meeting or conversation on which they rely, provided that they f have proved to your satisfaction sufficient incidents *on or off the pitch* for you to conclude that *the charge* against Mr Grobbelaar in those articles is substantially justified.' (My emphasis.)

[**137**] To my mind, the judge's conflation of the two pleaded meanings into g the single composite meaning which I have quoted is somewhat confusing and cannot have been helpful to the jury, not least because (literally interpreted) the single composite meaning is limited to 'the dishonest taking of bribes', although the concluding words 'or at least was prepared to do or try to do' suggest that the judge intended that it should also cover actual match-fixing.

[**138**] I shall have to return to this aspect later in this judgment, when h considering the Sun's case that the jury's verdict was perverse and should be set aside. For present purposes, however, I merely draw attention to the different ways in which the case was presented to the jury, since it represents a fundamental feature of the case.

j *Section 5 of the Defamation Act 1952*

[**139**] In its defence, the Sun pleaded s 5 of the Defamation Act 1952. That section provides as follows:

'In an action for libel or slander in respect of words containing two or more distinct charges against the plaintiff, a defence of justification shall not fail by reason only that the truth of every charge is not proved if the words not proved to be true do not materially injure the plaintiff's reputation having regard to the truth of the remaining charges.' *a*

[140] In the course of the trial, however, Mr Carman abandoned reliance on the section. That being so, it is not open to Mr Spearman QC (who appears for the Sun on this appeal) to rely on the section in this court.

FACTUAL AND PROCEDURAL BACKGROUND *b*

[141] I must now set out so much of the factual and procedural background as is material to the issues which arise on this appeal.

[142] Mr Grobbelaar was born on 6 October 1957, in South Africa. A few months after he was born, his parents moved to Zimbabwe (then Southern Rhodesia). In 1978 Mr Grobbelaar came to the United Kingdom with a view to playing professional football. However, he was unable to obtain a work permit, *c* so he went to Canada for two years, returning to the United Kingdom in 1980. On 16 March 1981 he joined Liverpool Football Club as a goalkeeper. He remained with Liverpool until 1994, when he was transferred to Southampton.

[143] In or about July 1992 Mr Grobbelaar met Mr Vincent, whom he may have known in his younger days in Zimbabwe. Mr Vincent interested him in *d* various ideas for property development in Zimbabwe, and Mr Grobbelaar agreed to put up £20,000 as an investment in a project for the development of a safari park to be undertaken by a company called Mondoro Wildlife Corp. Mr Grobbelaar duly paid Mr Vincent £20,000 as an investment in this project.

[144] In about November 1992 Mr Grobbelaar was introduced to Mr Lim by *e* a mutual friend, Mr John Fashanu (another well-known footballer). Mr Lim became known to both Mr Grobbelaar and Mr Vincent as 'the short man', and they habitually referred to him by that sobriquet. According to Mr Grobbelaar, he agreed with Mr Lim to provide Mr Lim with forecasts of the result of football matches (excluding any matches in which his own club was playing) on terms that Mr Lim would pay him £250 for every correct forecast. This arrangement *f* continued, according to Mr Grobbelaar, until about February 1993, when it was changed. According to Mr Grobbelaar, his ability to give accurate forecasts proved to be so limited that it was agreed that, rather than providing forecasts, Mr Grobbelaar would thereafter provide Mr Lim with information about football teams, payment for which was to be at Mr Lim's discretion. *g* Mr Grobbelaar accepts that he received from Mr Lim, as consideration for his services, a total of around £8,000.

[145] In his original reply in the action, which was served on 6 July 1995, prior to the criminal trials, Mr Grobbelaar asserted that Mr Lim was a figment of his imagination: that is to say, that Mr Lim had never existed. That was a lie, as Mr Grobbelaar subsequently accepted. Mr Grobbelaar's explanation for that lie *h* was that he was concerned that his arrangement with Mr Lim (that is to say, initially for the provision of forecasts and from early 1993 onwards for the provision of information) was or might be contrary to the rules of the Football Association (FA).

[146] It is the Sun's case that Mr Lim was, to Mr Grobbelaar's knowledge, the *j* representative of a Far Eastern betting syndicate, and that the sums paid by Mr Lim to Mr Grobbelaar were bribes to fix or attempt to fix football matches. As indicated earlier in this judgment, the Sun's defence of justification is based almost entirely on the contents of the tapes. I shall have to refer to the tapes in more detail later in this judgment, but I point out at this stage that Mr Grobbelaar does not dispute that the tapes contain admissions of corrupt behaviour on his a part, both on and off the pitch, and in particular contain admissions that his arrangement with Mr Lim was a corrupt arrangement, pursuant to which he received payments for fixing, or attempting to fix, football matches. His explanation of these admissions is that they were false, and that he invented them on the spur of the moment in an attempt to entrap Mr Vincent (whom he suspected of having behaved dishonestly in relation to the Mondoro venture) b into revealing information about corruption on Mr Vincent's part and on the part of those on whose behalf Mr Vincent purported to act, which he could pass on to the appropriate authorities, viz the FA and the police. This is Mr Grobbelaar's *only* explanation for the admissions which are recorded on the tapes. As I have said, he does not deny that the admissions were made; nor does he deny that they are admissions of corrupt behaviour on his part, not only in relation to his c arrangement with Mr Lim but also in relation to the corrupt proposal which Mr Vincent (at the Sun's instigation) made to him at the recorded meetings. Indeed, it is fundamental to Mr Grobbelaar's explanation of the admissions that they were intended to convince Mr Vincent that he (Mr Grobbelaar) had acted corruptly in the past. It is Mr Grobbelaar's case that he made the admissions of d past corrupt conduct so as gain Mr Vincent's confidence. This is an aspect of the case to which I shall have to return later in this judgment.

[147] In early 1993 Mr Grobbelaar paid Mr Vincent two further sums of £10,000 each as an additional investment in the Mondoro venture.

[148] On 30 September 1993 Mr Grobbelaar and Mr Vincent drove together from Chester to the Hilton Hotel, at Manchester International Airport, where e Mr Grobbelaar met Mr Lim and received from him £1,000 or £1,500 (the evidence is not clear which) in cash. Mr Vincent took no part in this meeting. It is Mr Grobbelaar's case that the payment was in respect of information which he had provided. According to Mr Grobbelaar, his reason for excluding Mr Vincent from the meeting was that Mr Lim had earlier expressed interest in investing in f the Mondoro venture and was awaiting a business plan which Mr Vincent had as yet failed to provide, and that in the circumstances Mr Grobbelaar considered it more appropriate that he should apologise in Mr Vincent's absence for Mr Vincent's failure to provide the business plan. The Sun, on the other hand, asserts that the purpose of the meeting was to discuss match-fixing, and that the cash was a bribe.

g **[149]** On 21 November 1993 Liverpool lost to Newcastle 3–0. The Sun's case, based on admissions by Mr Grobbelaar on the tapes, is that Mr Lim had asked Mr Grobbelaar to fix this game and that Mr Grobbelaar was paid £40,000 by Mr Lim for his services. The Sun no longer contends, however, that Mr Grobbelaar deliberately let in any of the three goals scored by Newcastle. This is in stark h contrast to the headline in the 9 November 1994 edition of the paper, which read (it will be recalled) 'GROB: I let in 3 goals and picked up £40,000'. Mr Grobbelaar denies these allegations. His denial that he deliberately let in goals is supported by the evidence of Mr Bob Wilson, who told the jury that he could see 'absolutely nothing suspicious whatsoever' about the three goals, and in relation to the j second of the three he was 'able to say … there is no goalkeeper anywhere that would have been able to save that particular goal'.

[150] On 25 November 1993 Mr Grobbelaar, together with Mr Vincent, visited Mr Fashanu at his house in Byron Drive, in Finchley, North London. The Sun contends that on this visit Mr Grobbelaar picked up £40,000, and that this was his reward for the result of the Newcastle match. Mr Grobbelaar accepts that in November 1993 he gave Mr Vincent £20,000 in cash, £3,000 of which was to pay a bill which Mr Grobbelaar owed and the balance of which was to be used in paying a deposit on a development site in Zimbabwe called Princes Grant. Mr Grobbelaar's evidence is that this payment occurred some five days before the visit to Mr Fashanu, that is to say on or about 20 November 1993. Mr Grobbelaar further agrees that on 26 November 1993 he paid a sum of £5,000 into his testimonial fund. His case is that the source of these moneys was cash which he had accumulated over a period from a number of legitimate sources and which he kept in his sock drawer in his bedroom at home. He denies that he received £40,000, or any sum, in respect of the Newcastle match, or that he was guilty of any corrupt conduct in relation to that match.

[151] In his original reply in the action Mr Grobbelaar denied that he had made this visit to Mr Fashanu's house. In evidence in this action, he was unable to explain why he had told this lie.

[152] On 4 January 1994 Liverpool played Manchester United, and drew 3–3. The Sun alleges, based on the tapes, that had Liverpool lost that match Mr Grobbelaar would have been paid £125,000. Mr Grobbelaar denies that allegation. It is not alleged by the Sun that Mr Grobbelaar deliberately let in any goals in this match, but it is alleged (based once again on the tapes) that Mr Grobbelaar saved two goals accidentally, having dived 'the wrong way'. However, Mr Bob Wilson gave evidence that the two saves in question were 'truly exceptional … Those two saves are the highest quality saves that you will see'; and he was dismissive of the notion that Mr Grobbelaar was 'doing it by accident'. Mr Wilson said he used the first save 'in goalkeeping schools and goalkeeping clinics as a classic example of how to be perfectly set'.

[153] On 4 February 1994, the night before Liverpool were due to play Norwich City away, Mr Grobbelaar (who was staying in a hotel on the outskirts of Norwich with the rest of the Liverpool team) and Mr Vincent (who had also booked himself into the same hotel) drove to London. They left Norwich after the team had had dinner, and arrived back at the hotel in the small hours of the morning of 5 February. Mr Grobbelaar did not tell his team-mates or the Liverpool management about this journey (no doubt because it constituted a serious breach of team discipline), and he lied to his room-mate in order to provide cover for his absence. The purpose of this clandestine journey was to enable Mr Grobbelaar to meet Mr Lim. The meeting took place at the Hilton Hotel, Park Lane. Mr Vincent stayed in the car throughout. It is common ground that in the course of the meeting Mr Lim paid Mr Grobbelaar £1,500 or thereabouts in cash.

[154] It is Mr Grobbelaar's case that at that time he was concerned that his contract with Liverpool was coming to an end later in 1994 and that it might not be renewed, and that the purpose of the journey to London was to discuss with Mr Lim (who had recently returned from a trip to the Far East) the prospects of Mr Grobbelaar playing football in the Far East, and that the money which Mr Lim paid him was for information which he had provided.

[155] The Sun's case, on the other hand, is that both the meeting and the payment related to Mr Grobbelaar's corrupt agreement to fix or attempt to fix the results of football matches. The Sun bases its case on the extraordinary and clandestine nature of journey; on the fact that Mr Grobbelaar could just as easily have discussed his prospects of playing in the Far East with Mr Lim over the telephone; on the fact that (as Mr Grobbelaar acknowledged in evidence) he knew nothing about Mr Lim's occupation, and in particular whether he had any a football expertise or connections, either in the Far East or elsewhere; and on admissions made by Mr Grobbelaar on the tapes.

[**156**] On 5 February 1994 Liverpool played Norwich and drew 2–2. The Sun no longer alleges that Mr Grobbelaar deliberately let in either of the two Norwich goals, despite a photograph caption in its 10 November 1994 edition which read 'Fallen cheat … Grobbelaar lets in one of the two Norwich goals'. The Sun does b allege, however, that Mr Grobbelaar saved a goal accidentally when he dived 'the wrong way' and the ball hit his foot. This allegation is based on an admission in the tapes. However, when asked in examination-in-chief 'Did you see anything there that would indicate a save he did not intend to make?', Mr Wilson replied 'No, that's a great save in anybody's book'.

[**157**] In July 1994 Mr Grobbelaar made a trip to Selangor, in Malaysia. On the c tapes, Mr Grobbelaar says: 'It wasn't by chance that I went over there. It was set up because they wanted to see how I was … I was getting sussed out by the fucking short man's people.' The Sun relies on those statements as admissions of the corrupt nature of his arrangement with Mr Lim. I have already referred to Mr Grobbelaar's explanation of the statements which he made on the tapes.

d [**158**] On 12 August 1994 Mr Grobbelaar was transferred from Liverpool to Southampton.

[**159**] On 6 September 1994 Mr Vincent contacted the Sun. This led to a meeting between Mr Vincent and Mr John Troup, a staff reporter for the Sun. The meeting took place at Mr Vincent's flat in Chirk, near Wrexham. Mr Troup e made a contemporary note of what transpired. Since Mr Vincent was not called to give evidence, and since no application was made to admit his statements as hearsay, the statements of fact which he made to Mr Troup are not evidence of those facts. However, since it is Mr Grobbelaar's case that the admissions which he made on the tapes were invented on the spur of the moment, it is in my judgment both legitimate and material to compare those admissions with f Mr Troup's evidence of what Mr Vincent told him on 6 September 1994 (that is to say, prior to the taped meetings) concerning Mr Grobbelaar's past conduct, with particular reference to Mr Grobbelaar's arrangements with Mr Lim.

[**160**] In evidence, Mr Troup told the jury that at the meeting on 6 September 1994 Mr Vincent told him that Mr Grobbelaar had been receiving cash sums from g a Malaysian betting syndicate, and that he (Mr Vincent) had been present on a number of occasions when Mr Grobbelaar had met individuals connected to the syndicate. Mr Troup went on to tell the jury that Mr Vincent had told him that Mr Grobbelaar had been paid £40,000 in cash as a result of Newcastle beating Liverpool 3–0, and that he (Mr Vincent) had attended with Mr Grobbelaar at an address in North London when Mr Grobbelaar had picked up the £40,000. h Mr Troup went on: 'He told me that Mr Grobbelaar had emerged from the house with the sum of £40,000 in cash, and that he had been given himself, Mr Vincent, half of this cash to look after for Mr Grobbelaar.'

[**161**] Mr Troup also made a contemporary note of his meeting with Mr Vincent on 6 September 1994. Under the heading 'Bribery', the note includes j the following passages:

> 'Sept/Oct 93: He came to me he said he had been approached by some guys who had a bet, a scam thing. They were working in the far east and they would pay him to give them tips on games. I drove with him to hotel in Manchester. He met this guy for about 20 minutes. We disappeared back to Chester …

Late November: Game against Newcastle. He tells me he's in to make big money if Liverpool lose at Newcastle. While I'm with him he has numerous calls to this bloke … Short Man … Liverpool got beat 3–1 [in fact, it was 3–0].

Two weeks after: It must have been the next week or the week after he said to me come we have got to go and pick this money up now. He flew down to London picked up hire car. We then went to where this guy's offices are near Lords. They said we had a meet with another guy. We had to go to this guy's house. We then followed him to house in North London posh suburb. In garage was Ferrari and Mercedes 500 … tight security. Cameras, the whole shooting match, protection guys. He is now greeted by another well known footballer. This guy was obviously betting on little teams to beat big teams. He appears from there with £40,000 in cash in £50 notes and the packs of £2,000 are drawn on Midland Bank, Marble Arch. He wants to give me some of the money to put into the company. He works out what he needs. He left me with £20,000 …

Liverpool played Norwich City at Carrow Road. He said we have to come to NCFC [Norwich City Football Club] … have to go down to London. I checked in on Friday night, he waited until 11 pm. He said we have to see the Short Man. Guy I had seen was not the main man, he was just the runner. BG said we meet the big guys tonight. I said we drive down to London at 11 pm the night before the game. We drove down to the London Hilton. He told me he had hired a chauffeur and driver. He made me put on a hat. He met these guys for five minutes …

If Liverpool lose against NCFC he would get paid £80,000. We drove back and got to hotel at 3.30 am. The net result from that game was that they drew because the one shot was on target and he dived to the right side of the ball, the thing hit his foot. He said I was trying to give it away. He didn't get his money …'

[162] On 12 September 1994 a meeting took place between Mr Grobbelaar and Mr Vincent at the Swallow Hotel, Waltham Abbey, prior to a match the following day against Tottenham Hotspur. The Sun attempted to record this meeting on audio tape, but the attempt failed. Apparently the recording device was concealed in the pocket of Mr Vincent's coat, but the material of the coat muffled the sound to the point where speech was inaudible.

[163] On 24 September 1994 Mr Grobbelaar played for Southampton against Coventry. Southampton won 3–1. The Sun alleges that Coventry's goal was deliberately let in by Mr Grobbelaar. This allegation is based on a statement by Mr Grobbelaar on the tapes that Mr Lim 'is telling me now you're going to lose the game. So two minutes into the game I push the ball into the back of the net. That was the Coventry game.' Mr Grobbelaar denies that he deliberately let in this goal. His denial is supported once again by the evidence of Mr Wilson that 'a less agile goalkeeper than Bruce Grobbelaar would not possibly have touched this ball'. Mr Wilson went on to say:

> 'The angle of the body, the position of the feet off the ground, the thrust off the ground, I just, I couldn't say to you anything other than in my honest opinion, he's making every attempt, every attempt, to save that ball.'

[164] Moreover, Mr Alan Ball, the manager of Southampton at that time, who was present at the match, said in evidence that in his opinion there was nothing odd whatsoever in Mr Grobbelaar's play.

a [165] On 6 October 1994 the first of the recorded meetings took place, in Mr Vincent's bedroom at the De Vere Hotel, in Southampton. Immediately prior to this meeting Mr Vincent and Mr Grobbelaar had been together in the snooker room at the hotel: their conversation in the snooker room was not recorded.

[166] It is clear from the general tone and content of their recorded conversation b on this occasion (as on the other occasions when their conversations were recorded) that Mr Vincent and Mr Grobbelaar were on extremely close and friendly terms, and their conversation was relaxed and uninhibited. After some talk about other matters, Mr Vincent turned to the subject of the corrupt proposal which the Sun had arranged for him to make to Mr Grobbelaar. As appears later in the tape, the proposal (which was said to have emanated from two individuals c whom Mr Vincent had met at Chester races, known as 'Richard' and 'Guy') was that Mr Grobbelaar would be paid £2,000 a fortnight, in return for which Mr Grobbelaar would 'pick one game in a season', for which he would be paid £100,000.

[167] It is plain from the way in which Mr Vincent introduced this proposal d into the conversation that he had already mentioned it to Mr Grobbelaar on an earlier occasion ('You know those guys I talked to …'). Moreover it is significant, in my judgment, that Mr Grobbelaar's immediate reaction is not to inquire further about the proposal (as one would have expected him to do had his purpose been obtain information to give to the authorities), but to express concern that whoever was behind the proposal might learn his identity.

e [168] The conversation then turned to the Mondoro venture, and Mr Grobbelaar explained that he had not been in a position to put more cash into the venture because 'I'm waiting for the cash. If the ball doesn't play, then it doesn't play.' Mr Grobbelaar then went on to say that he had lost £125,000 when Liverpool drew 3–3 with Manchester United. In response to Mr Vincent's question: 'Why f did you choose the Newcastle game?', Mr Grobbelaar replied: 'Because I knew, you know, there's fuck all chance of winning Newcastle. I chose the Newcastle game because I knew I could do business there … they had big bucks. So I got that cash.' The conversation then reverted to the Manchester United match. Mr Grobbelaar commented that Manchester United were 3–1 up at half time, but that eventually the match was drawn 3–3. Mr Grobbelaar is heard to say, in g relation to that match, 'I could have done something'. When Mr Vincent asked him what he could have done, Mr Grobbelaar replied:

> 'Because in the second half I made two fucking blind—two blinding saves, but I was diving the wrong fucking way—and that's true … I dived the wrong fucking way and I fucking went Phwoooo—and I fucking just, just went and it hit my hand.'

h

Mr Grobbelaar goes on to say 'I am my worst enemy on that, because I know I don't like to lose … its instinct'.

[169] At that point in the conversation Mr Vincent returned to his corrupt j proposal, and explained in more detail what it involved. Mr Grobbelaar's initial reaction, once again, was that his own identity might be revealed to those behind the proposal. Thus, when Mr Vincent said that Mr Grobbelaar would meet the individuals concerned, Mr Grobbelaar replied: 'I'll meet. Then again, I don't want to meet them. Because they will know who it is.'

[170] Mr Grobbelaar went on to stress the risks that he would be running if he agreed to the proposal, saying:

'Find out how many people fucking know, because I'm telling you this; because it could be the fucking end of me. And unless—you see the two grand every week is okay, I mean, you take a gamble, you can score long, there's fucking investigators all round. I don't know that these aren't investigators.'

[171] The conversation then turned to 'the short man' (ie Mr Lim). Mr Vincent asked: 'Do you think they might be connected to the short man or not?', to which Mr Grobbelaar replied: 'I don't know. There must be a syndicate opposite, opposing. I don't know how, because the short man is from the Far East.' Later, Mr Grobbelaar said: 'But the short man's boss is, if it is the same person, he's fucking big in Malaysia. We all say, that man [gestures with his hand as if cutting his throat] that's it, finish.' They then returned to the subject of Mr Vincent's proposal. Referring to the proposal, Mr Vincent said: 'My thinking on it was, that if ... I mean, I didn't know until tonight that the short man was back in business with you, was that you could pick the same game for both.' Mr Grobbelaar replied 'Yeah. I could fucking retire.'

A little later in the conversation Mr Grobbelaar said that he would like to know who were the individuals behind Mr Vincent's proposal. Mr Vincent replied that he only knew them as 'Richard' and 'Guy'. Mr Grobbelaar is then heard to say:

'How many other fucking partners are there? And how many other people know? The short man has only got one other person, and that's JF [John Fashanu]. Right now the rest are out of the country. That's all. Because he sits on his other phone and talks to me and talks to overseas and talks to me and to overseas, that's all he does ... These are in the country. So I would say, go back to him and say "Listen, the person wants to know how many people are going to know about it". Tell him, I don't want any bullshit. I want to know how many people are in, and how many people are going to know about it ... And what they do for a living as well. Because that's another thing.'

[172] The conversation then turned to the trip which Mr Grobbelaar and Mr Vincent made from Norwich to London on 4 February 1994, when Mr Grobbelaar met Mr Lim. Mr Grobbelaar is heard to say:

'He had a fucking Rolex on his arm, a Rolex. Because I said: "Well, give me because I want to wear it." It was the fucking business. Three grand's worth of watch. "This is yours next time you do the business. Plus, what you do. Now we don't talk shit", he says. "That's yours. You do the business, and that's yours."'

[173] It is the Sun's case, based on the contents of this and the other tapes, that Mr Grobbelaar's explanation that he was inventing admissions of past corruption on the spur of the moment in order to gain Mr Vincent's confidence, and that his overall purpose was to gain information about the individuals behind Mr Vincent's corrupt proposal with a view to passing such information on to the FA and the police, is simply incredible, and that no jury could reasonably believe it.

[174] A further taped meeting took place between Mr Vincent and Mr Grobbelaar at the De Vere Hotel in Southampton on 25 October 1994. At that meeting, Mr Vincent reverted once again to his corrupt proposal involving 'Richard' and 'Guy'. Once again, Mr Grobbelaar's first reaction was that his own identity might be revealed. Thus, when Mr Vincent suggested that Mr Grobbelaar might pick a match in which Southampton were playing, Mr Grobbelaar's response a was 'as soon as you tell them that team will lose they're going to pick up who it is ... They'll pick up who it is'. Mr Grobbelaar then said 'The short man's back'. Mr Vincent then asked him 'Have you done any more?' Mr Grobbelaar replied:

> 'No, not this weekend. He said, when he told me, eh, I've been trying to get hold of you. So I rang him back, and he said, what about this one, is it a, is it a Wimbledon, or is it going to be a Leeds. Now he's using W and L he
b doesn't know ... he could have said whisky or Lima. I said, it's a Wimbledon, a Wimbledon for us. He said: No, I've already done it ... You lose, and he's telling me now you're going to lose the game. So two minutes into the game I push the ball into the back of the net. That was the Coventry game ...'

[175] Later in the conversation, Mr Grobbelaar referred once again to 'the
c short man', saying:

> 'You see, I'll tell you how they bet in the short man's. They put a bet on, and the team has to lose by a certain number of goals ... So he said, the ... Coventry one, he said, just by one, and we clean up. If it's er, what'll we say,
d if it's er what did he use for a draw? He didn't use Dublin. If it's a Dundee, right? ... If it's a Dundee ... we don't know if we'll lose our money. But sometimes with a draw ... they'll retain their American money that they have actually put on it, do you see what I mean?'

Mr Vincent then reverted once again to the corrupt proposal. Mr Grobbelaar
e said he was 'fucking wary' of the proposal, later commenting 'It's too dangerous, but I'll look at it'. They then discussed methods by which the cash payments could be made, Mr Vincent suggesting that transfers could be made through Thomas Cook. Mr Grobbelaar said he preferred to receive the payments in cash (greenbacks), which he would then take to Zimbabwe. Mr Vincent then asked him 'What is the biggest cut you have had from the short man so far?', to which
f Mr Grobbelaar replied 'For losing that one, 40'.

[176] Mr Grobbelaar goes on to say that he would have received £120,000 had Liverpool lost to Manchester United (previously, Mr Grobbelaar had said he lost £125,000 on that match).

[177] Reverting to Mr Vincent's proposal, Mr Grobbelaar referred once again
g to the risks which he would have to run, saying:

> 'There is a fucking big risk, and this is what I'm fucking worried about, you know ... That's why the money is just going to be put in a fucking box. Because, if at any time I feel that it is not on, the money will go straight back to him.'

h

[178] Later in the conversation, Mr Grobbelaar volunteered that the purpose of his visit to Malaysia earlier in the year was not only to play football. He said (in a passage to which I referred earlier): 'I was getting sussed out by the fucking short man's people ... Just, you know, see what fucking person I am and if I'm fucking genuine.' He added: 'I like to fucking win. I don't like to fucking lose.'
j Later, referring once again to Mr Vincent's proposal, Mr Grobbelaar said:

> 'So what happens if I say, right, fine, fucking Man United are playing fucking next day at Man United and I say, right, Man United are going to fucking win ... If it comes off, then you'll be looking at upwards of a million, all of a sudden you say, right, we've got another one, this time its Southampton. Then he's going to come to you and say, well, how many fucking men have you got?

> … Because then you're fucking him around, and he won't like it, and he'll tell his short man … and then you get the chop and then you better watch it. You better get a bullet proof fucking vest, then … That's how fucking big it is … This is how fucking dangerous it is … When you're playing with fucking dangerous men, its fucking dangerous.'

[179] After further discussion about Mr Vincent's proposal, Mr Grobbelaar said:

> 'Right, I've heard enough. I've had [heard?] enough now. We'll make this easy. Tell him that it's on, and I'm going to pick one game. I'll pick one game. After I've picked one game, nothing must be said … Nothing must be said anywhere … If they're happy, they must tell you that they're happy … Nothing must be said. Because then they will pick out whose team it is.'

[180] The conversation then reverted to the problem of where to put the greenbacks. Mr Vincent suggested arranging for them to be placed in a safe deposit box 'at Selfridges or somewhere like that'. Mr Grobbelaar rejected that idea, saying: 'No. It's too fucking dangerous. They're being looked at all the fucking time … The camera is on you the whole fucking time.'

[181] The third and final taped meeting took place at Mr Vincent's flat on 3 November 1994. In the course of the conversation, Mr Grobbelaar volunteered that he is 'doing the short man tomorrow'. Asked by Mr Vincent how much he would receive, Mr Grobbelaar at first said that it would be about £80,000, but then corrected himself, saying that it would be nearer £50,000. He continued:

> 'But hopefully 50 will be ready for when I go … You see, the thing is, I'm not too sure what to do. I think I'll just put the fifty into my fucking trunk, lock the trunk and keep the fifty in greenbacks. That side.'

Mr Vincent asked whether he was referring to Zimbabwe, and suggested that he take the cash to Zimbabwe. Mr Grobbelaar replied: 'Yeah. That's what I'm going to do.'

[182] At the conclusion of the meeting, Mr Vincent produced a package containing £2,000 in cash, which he represented to Mr Grobbelaar as being the first of the fortnightly payments payable under the corrupt arrangement which they had earlier discussed, and to which Mr Grobbelaar had agreed. Mr Grobbelaar took the proffered package and placed it in his overcoat pocket.

[183] Following the meeting Mr Grobbelaar, according to his evidence, placed the package containing the £2,000 in cash in the glove box of his car.

[184] On 8 November 1994 Mr Grobbelaar was ambushed by journalists from the Sun when he arrived at Gatwick Airport to catch a plane to Zimbabwe. What followed was recorded. The journalists bombarded him with questions and accusations. They began by accusing him of having received £40,000 from a syndicate via a middleman known as 'the short man', and of having deliberately let in goals. They told him that they had 'video and sound evidence of you talking about that'. Mr Grobbelaar's immediate response was as follows: 'Unless you come to me and say, we have got evidence, you know, which you are going to be proving, you are going to have to actually prove it first.'

[185] The Sun relies on this answer as being wholly incompatible with Mr Grobbelaar's (later) explanation that he was seeking to entrap Mr Vincent with a view to turning him over to the authorities. If that explanation were genuine, says the Sun, it is inconceivable that Mr Grobbelaar would not have given it at the earliest possible moment, so as to make it clear that the admissions on the tapes were untrue. Mr Grobbelaar's evidence, however, was that he did not immediately reveal his plan to entrap Mr Vincent to the Sun as he did not want to give the Sun the satisfaction of having discovered it.

[186] Mr Grobbelaar denied the journalists' allegations that he had deliberately let in any goals. He also denied that he had agreed with Mr Vincent to throw a match. When accused of having met Mr Vincent and agreed this with him, Mr Grobbelaar replied: 'I met him, yes. And I actually said to him that would never be … able to be done, because if I ever got caught, I'd be in deep trouble.' When asked why he had taken £2,000 off Mr Vincent, Mr Grobbelaar at first he denied having done so. However, he then said: 'All right, I'll put it another way. That £2,000 has been put in a safe place in case of any subsequent … because I've got evidence against that person.' A few moments later, Mr Grobbelaar said:

> 'I will say there has never been anything done with any short man. There has definitely been something done with Chris Vincent, because he came to me and said it is a sure fired thing and the way to get your money back from the Mondoro thing, he feels obligated in getting that money back. And that is why he had me come to see him to tell me about the whole situation.'

Asked 'Did you agree to that?', Mr Grobbelaar replied: 'No, I didn't agree to it … The deals on … not for me to actually take the money and take it all the time … The money has not been taken.'

[187] At that point, one of the Sun journalists put it to Mr Grobbelaar that Mr Vincent had telephoned him and arranged to meet him at the Air Zimbabwe desk with the second payment of £2,000. He also described how Mr Grobbelaar had taken the package containing £2,000 in cash at the meeting on 3 November 1994. Mr Grobbelaar then said:

> 'OK. I've taken the money, right. But that money has not been, is not anywhere—it's right here. To be given back, and as I said in my previous meetings with him, to be given back to the people if everything blows up. Because I don't want to get caught in any way, shape or form, in this sort of situation.'

[188] It is to be noted that in the passages quoted above Mr Grobbelaar falsely denies the existence of 'any' short man (a denial which, as I explained earlier, also appeared in the original version of his reply in this action). He also denies that he agreed to Mr Vincent's corrupt proposal (a denial which is wholly inconsistent with his subsequent explanation that he was seeking to entrap Mr Vincent by agreeing to the corrupt proposal). As to the £2,000, Mr Grobbelaar initially denies having taken it. He subsequently corrects this, but in so doing he makes no reference to handing the £2,000 over to the authorities; rather, what he says is that the money is 'to be given back to the people if everything blows up'. Later on, in the course of the interchanges, Mr Grobbelaar effectively repeats this, saying: '… that money will be put into a box. At the end of the day that money will go back to the people that, will go back to the people.'

[189] Mr Grobbelaar then gives his explanation that he is seeking evidence against Mr Vincent (whom he distrusted), and that his admissions of having thrown or attempted to throw matches were made in order to entrap Mr Vincent into revealing more information about his corrupt proposal.

[190] It is also to be noted that in answer to questions from the journalists Mr Grobbelaar said that the £20,000 which he paid Mr Vincent in November 1993 came out of his testimonial fund. It is common ground that this was not the case. At the trial, Mr Grobbelaar's evidence was that it came from his sock drawer.

[191] The journalists concluded the ambush at Gatwick by asking Mr Grobbelaar to telephone Mr Higgins, the editor of the Sun. Mr Grobbelaar did so. The conversation was recorded. In the course of the conversation, Mr Grobbelaar asserted once again (falsely) that the £20,000 came from his testimonial fund. Mr Higgins asked him 'Did you accept cash to lose matches?' Mr Grobbelaar replied:

> 'No … It came down that a certain person said to me you would get £2,000 per two weeks where you can actually pick a game at the end of the season blah blah blah, and I said, well. He said it was going to be a push, a sure fired thing. I said, it had to be put in a box because at the end of the day, I did not want to throw matches. And if it didn't come down that money would go back to the certain person what was actually giving it to me.'

[192] Later in the conversation, Mr Grobbelaar told Mr Higgins: '… I've got to get my own evidence against that person [meaning Mr Vincent]. And I know where that person comes from now.'

[193] When Mr Higgins asked Mr Grobbelaar about the £40,000 which Mr Grobbelaar had, on the tape, admitted receiving, Mr Grobbelaar replied: 'That is the money I told you about me receiving from my testimonial fund.' As already noted, that was not true (as Mr Grobbelaar later accepted).

[194] In contrast to the inconsistencies and untruths to which I have referred, however, Mr Grobbelaar was consistent throughout his encounter with the journalists and his telephone conversation with Mr Higgins in denying that he had ever attempted to throw a match or let in goals.

QUALIFIED PRIVILEGE

[195] I turn next to the issue of qualified privilege.

[196] In ruling that a defence of qualified privilege was not open to the Sun, the judge applied the law as stated in the decision of this court in *Reynolds v Times Newspapers Ltd* [1998] 3 All ER 961, [1998] 3 WLR 862. At the date of his ruling, an appeal to the House of Lords in *Reynolds'* case had been heard, but the decision of the House of Lords had not been published. That decision is now reported at [1999] 4 All ER 609, [1999] 3 WLR 1010. Although the House of Lords rejected the Court of Appeal's formulation of the relevant factors in determining whether a defence of qualified privilege was available, it confirmed the underlying principles expressed by the Court of Appeal. Hence it is not open to the Sun to challenge the judge's ruling on the basis the decision of the House of Lords in *Reynolds'* case effectively undermines his ruling; nor did Mr Spearman seek to do so.

[197] In his ruling, the judge began by correctly posing the overall question whether it was in the public interest that the publication of the material complained of be protected by qualified privilege. After a detailed examination of the relevant authorities, and particularly the decision of the Court of Appeal in *Reynolds'* case, the judge turned to the application of the relevant principles to the facts of the instant case. He concluded that to the extent that the Sun was under any duty to publish the information in question, its duty was to alert the proper authorities, as opposed to publishing the information to the public at large. In this connection, he said:

a 'In my judgment the appropriate mode of discharging the duty which lay on the newspaper when it came into possession of the material relating to the alleged match-fixing by Mr Grobbelaar was to communicate the information to the police or the regulatory body for football for them to take whatever action was in their view merited by the information. To hold that a publication such as the publication in the Sun is protected by privilege b would, in my judgment, be to stretch the ambit of privilege beyond that which the public interest requires.'

Later in his ruling, the judge said:

'I make no criticism of the defendants for wanting to publish their sensational and exclusive story, but in my judgment they were not under a c duty, in the proper sense of that term, to publish information about the allegedly criminal conduct of a goalkeeper. The position might have been different if the defendants had gone to the police and the FA with the information about Mr Grobbelaar but no action against him followed.'

[198] Having reached that conclusion, the judge did not consider it necessary d to investigate the circumstances of publication any further, and he accordingly ruled against the Sun.

[199] In his judgment, which I have had the benefit of reading in draft, Simon Brown LJ has quoted extensively from the speech of Lord Nicholls of Birkenhead in *Reynolds'* case. I can therefore turn straight away to the various matters which e Lord Nicholls ([1999] 4 All ER 609 at 625–628, [1999] 3 WLR 1010 at 1027) identified as being matters to be taken into account in considering whether a defence of qualified privilege is available.

The seriousness of the allegations

[200] Mr Spearman accepts, as he is bound to do, that the allegations against f Mr Grobbelaar, both on and off the pitch, are extremely serious. This aspect needs no elaboration.

The nature of the information, and the extent to which the subject matter is a matter of public concern

g **[201]** In my view, allegations of corruption against a well-known professional footballer are plainly a matter of public concern. I do not share the judge's view that the Sun's duty in relation to such allegations was limited to making them known to the appropriate authorities. Investigative journalism can be of considerable public benefit, but without the incentive of being in a position to publish an exclusive story on a sensational subject a newspaper will inevitably be less h enthusiastic about committing its time and resources to investigating the story. The prospect of the resulting 'scoop' seems to me to be part and parcel of the process of investigative journalism.

The source of the information

j **[202]** Mr Spearman submits that the 'source' of the information was Mr Grobbelaar himself, through his taped admissions. It is Mr Grobbelaar's case, on the other hand, that the source of the information was Mr Vincent. On that basis, it is contended on behalf of Mr Grobbelaar that the source of the information was thoroughly disreputable.

[203] I accept Mr Spearman's submission. Had the Sun done no more than print what Mr Vincent told Mr Troup, then plainly the source of that information could only have been Mr Vincent. But in the event the Sun took the view that it was desirable that corroboration of what Mr Vincent had told Mr Troup be obtained out of the mouth of Mr Grobbelaar himself. Hence the taped meetings. In my judgment, the effective source of the material complained of was Mr Grobbelaar himself.

The steps taken to verify the information

[**204**] The Sun took steps to verify the information provided to it by Mr Vincent by arranging for Mr Vincent to put a corrupt proposal to Mr Grobbelaar and by covertly recording the occasions when this was done. An agent provocateur is never an attractive figure, but on the other hand the task of obtaining firm evidence of corruption is never likely to be an easy one and the use of an agent provocateur may provide an effective means to that end. At the same time, the manner in which the Sun carried out its investigation appears to have been amateurish, to say the least. As I recounted earlier, its attempt to record what transpired at the meeting which took place on 12 September 1994 failed because Mr Vincent's coat was too thick; and in relation to the remaining meetings, much of the conversation was, as the transcripts show, indecipherable.

[**205**] Nor, it appears, did the Sun take any steps to verify the charges of actual match-fixing by examining recordings of the matches in question, if necessary with the assistance of an expert. Most surprisingly, it appears that assistance was not even sought in this connection from the Sun's own football journalists who had been present at the matches in question.

The status of the information

[**206**] The information in question had no authoritative 'status' in the sense in which Lord Nicholls used that word (after listing the status of the information as a matter to be taken into account, Lord Nicholls went on to say: 'The allegation may have already been the subject of an investigation which commands respect.').

The urgency of the matter

[**207**] The matter was urgent only in the sense that if the information was true it was in the public interest that the guilty parties be exposed sooner rather than later. On the other hand, the date of initial publication was fixed to suit the Sun. So far as the Sun was concerned, any urgency lay in the need for it to publish a world exclusive on a sensational subject.

Whether comment was sought from the claimant

[**208**] In my judgment, the ambush of Mr Grobbelaar at Gatwick by journalists from the Sun was a thoroughly deplorable way of confronting Mr Grobbelaar with the extremely serious allegations made against him. Not only were the journalists falling over themselves to bombard Mr Grobbelaar with accusations, but the whole occasion was orchestrated by the Sun to achieve maximum publicity and to cause Mr Grobbelaar maximum surprise, embarrassment and stress. An editorial decision had already been taken to run the story, and most of the articles had been written many days before. Moreover, two journalists from the Sun were booked on the flight to Zimbabwe to follow up the story when Mr Grobbelaar arrived there. The purpose of the ambush was not to enable Mr Grobbelaar to put his side of the story, but to put him in a

a position of maximum discomfort and at the greatest possible disadvantage, for the delectation of the Sun's readers.

[209] It is true that by the time he came to speak to Mr Higgins on the telephone Mr Grobbelaar had had a few moments to compose himself, but by then the damage was done. I agree with Mr Hartley that Mr Carman's assertion to the jury that the ambush at Heathrow and the telephone call to Mr Higgins b afforded Mr Grobbelaar an opportunity to give a 'coherent, logical and rational' explanation for the admissions on the tapes is unreal. On the other hand, as I have already commented, one would have expected Mr Grobbelaar to take the earliest opportunity to make clear (if indeed it was the case) that his taped admissions were false, and that he had made them in order to entrap Mr Vincent and those for whom Mr Vincent purported to act. I shall return to this.

c

Whether the articles contained the gist of Mr Grobbelaar's side of the story

[210] The Sun did not print the reasons which Mr Grobbelaar gave for wanting to obtain evidence that Mr Vincent was dishonest (viz Mr Vincent's conduct in relation to the Mondoro project). It printed some of the exchanges d which occurred in the course of the ambush at Gatwick and in the subsequent telephone conversation between Mr Grobbelaar and Mr Higgins, but for reasons I have already given that is not a factor of any significant weight so far as qualified privilege is concerned.

The tone of the material complained of

e [211] The general tone of the printed matter can be gained from the quotations made earlier in this judgment. Not only were allegations paraded as facts, but the accused was repeatedly held up to public ridicule. It was as if the Sun had placed Mr Grobbelaar in the stocks, to be publicly mocked, abused and derided for the amusement of the populace. Nor is that all. Particularly f distasteful is the fact that one of the articles also involved Mr Grobbelaar's wife and children.

The circumstances of the publication, including the timing

[212] I described the circumstances of publication earlier in this judgment. As to timing, the publication of the material complained of was timed to suit the Sun.

g [213] Taking the above factors into account, and looking at all the circumstances in the round, I have no hesitation in concluding that it is not in the public interest that the publication of the material complained of should be protected by qualified privilege, and that the judge was right in so ruling.

h THE JUDGE'S SUMMING UP

[214] I referred earlier in this judgment to the contrasting approaches of Mr Hartley and Mr Carman in presenting their respective cases to the jury, with Mr Hartley concentrating on actual match-fixing, and Mr Carman on the alleged corrupt agreements by Mr Grobbelaar (first with Mr Lim and subsequently with j Mr Vincent). This difference of approach was, inevitably, reflected in the way the judge summed up the case to the jury.

[215] After directing the jury generally about its function, the judge turned to the defamatory meaning of the material complained of. I quoted the relevant passage from his summing up earlier in this judgment. The judge then directed the jury that what the Sun had to do in order to succeed with its defence of justification was to establish the substantial truth of the defamatory meaning (or

meanings) of the material complained of, on the balance of probabilities. In relation to substantial justification, the judge said: a

'Let me just expand a little further on what I mean by substantial justification or substantial truth. Suppose (and it is just a hypothesis to help you) you were to conclude that Mr Grobbelaar did indeed agree to take bribes and took bribes from the short man and later on agreed to take bribes and took a bribe from Mr Vincent but that for one reason or another he did not actually do anything in any match by way of attempting to fix the result by deliberately letting in goals; just suppose that that was your conclusion on the evidence; but then you would want to stand back and ask yourselves: "Are we satisfied, having arrived at that conclusion, that what was published about Mr Grobbelaar was substantially true?" The arguments might then be this: Mr Hartley might say, and indeed has said, that if there was not match that was actually fixed, that Mr Grobbelaar did not let in any goal deliberately, then that is a fatal flaw, says Mr Hartley, in the defence of justification, and it should fail. Not so, says Mr Carman; if it is established by the defendants that there were corrupt agreements then the sting of the articles is justified and the defence of justification should not fail, says Mr Carman, because the defendants cannot point to a particular match where there was any goal deliberately let in. I hope that helps you on what is meant by "substantial truth" and of course it is your province; you are the people who decide whether the substantial truth of the article has been made out.' b c d e

[216] Later in the summing up, following his review of the evidence, the judge directed the jury in relation to damages, setting out the relevant factors to be taken into account in arriving at a proper figure for compensatory damages. The judge then continued:

'But there is one important rider that I want to add, members of the jury. It is this. Supposing you were to come to the conclusion that you were not satisfied that the articles are substantially justified in the sense that I have explained to you, so that the plea of justification does not actually succeed, but you were to conclude that the Sun have proved the willingness of Mr Grobbelaar to enter into a corrupt agreement with Mr Vincent to fix matches [for] £2,000 a fortnight, or whatever it was, but you are not satisfied on the evidence that there was any corrupt agreement with the short man. Just suppose you come to that conclusion. Well, you might think: well, here is a man who has, on our view of evidence, been shown to have entered into a corrupt conspiracy, the one with Vincent, although not the one with the short man. Now, that, too, can be reflected in your award of damages, because you might in that situation feel it appropriate to reduce any award you might otherwise make quite significantly to reflect the fact that in good part what was published was true. So, that would be a reason for reducing perhaps—it is a matter for you—very, very significantly any amount of damages. But, of course, if you decide that the articles are substantially justified then of course you do not get to damages at all, so this is just an example to help you understand the way it works.' f g h j

[217] The judge then went on to refer to general levels of damages in personal injury actions, in case the jury should find the comparison helpful in deciding what level of damages to award in the instant case. The judge gave as the highest a figure an award of £100,000 upwards for paraplegia; the lowest figure he gave was £30,000 or thereabouts for the loss of an eye. The judge then suggested a bracket within which any award of damages might fall, saying:

> 'At the top end in a case of this kind you might think that an award of £150,000, something of that order, might be justified. At the lower end—but it all depends, really, on your view of the evidence. If you were to conclude b that this is a case where a significant part of the defence of justification has been made good even if the defence does not succeed, then you might want to come up with a very small award indeed, I do not know. So the lower end of the bracket comes quite low if you feel that to a significant extent the case has been proved against Mr Grobbelaar.'

c [**218**] The judge then turned to the evidence relevant to the level of damages. Having reviewed that evidence, the judge concluded his summing up by directing the jury as to the nature of exemplary damages.

THE JURY'S VERDICT

d [**219**] Mr Hartley concedes that in awarding damages of £85,000 the jury must have been satisfied not only that no actual match-fixing had taken place (ie that Mr Grobbelaar had not deliberately let in any goals in the matches in question), but also that he had not been party to any corrupt arrangement, either with Mr Lim or with Mr Vincent: in other words, that none of the charges made against him by the Sun had been proved.

e [**220**] Mr Spearman contends, as I indicated earlier, that the jury's verdict cannot stand. He submits that on the evidence (essentially, on the evidence of the tapes) the jury, acting reasonably, were bound to find that Mr Grobbelaar was party to both of the corrupt conspiracies alleged; and that on the basis of that finding the jury must have found that the Sun's defence of justification was made f out, in that the Sun had substantially justified the charges which it had made against Mr Grobbelaar. Mr Spearman accordingly invites us to set aside the jury's verdict on the basis that it was unreasonable and/or perverse.

[**221**] It is clear on authority that this court will only set aside the verdict of a jury in a defamation case on very strong grounds. As it is put in *Gatley on Libel and Slander* (9th edn, 1998) pp 889–890 (para 36.19):

g

> 'The jury are the constitutional tribunal for the decision of libel or no libel, and only in an extreme case will their verdict be set aside as unreasonable. If the words complained of are capable of a defamatory meaning and the jury have found in fact that the words do bear that meaning, the court will not set h aside the verdict. And where, though the words are capable of a defamatory meaning, the jury have found in fact that the words do not bear that meaning, the verdict will not be set aside unless it is unreasonable. In the absence of a misdirection the appellate court will only interfere with a finding of the jury if it was one which a jury, viewing the whole of the evidence reasonably, could not properly find.'

j [**222**] On the other hand—

> 'The fact that the subject matter of the jury's deliberations in such a case is a matter involving the law of defamation and of fact finding in that area does not involve some special magic. In this as in any other area of fact a jury are capable of arriving at a conclusion which is incontrovertibly wrong and

which can be set aside on appeal.' (See *Evans v Davies* [1991] 2 Qd R 498 at 511 per Macrossan CJ.) a

[223] In *Australian Newspaper Co Ltd v Bennett* [1894] AC 284, where the issue was as to the meaning of the words complained of, the Privy Council (at 287) said:

> 'It is not disputed that, whilst it is for the Court to determine whether the words used are capable of the meaning alleged in the innuendo, it is for the jury to determine whether that meaning was properly attached to them. It was therefore the province of the jury in the present case to determine whether the words used ... bore the defamatory sense alleged. [The judge below] observed in the course of his judgment that he admitted that the Court would only be justified in reversing the finding of the jury "if their decision upon that point is such as no jury could give as reasonable men." This is a correct statement of the law. Their Lordships have not, any more than the Court below had, to determine in the present case what is the conclusion at which they would have arrived, or what is the verdict they would have found. The only point to be determined is, whether the verdict found by the jury, for whose consideration it essentially was, was such as no jury could have found as reasonable men.'

b

c

d

[224] As that passage makes clear, it is not for an appellate court to second-guess the jury; it is for the jury to find the facts. On the other hand, as Macrossan CJ said in the *Australian Newspaper* case in the passage quoted above, a verdict in a defamation case involves no 'special magic'. Where it is plain from the jury's verdict that in reaching it the jury has fundamentally misdirected itself—in other words, where the verdict is so plainly wrong that no jury, acting reasonably, could have reached it—then the appellate court has not only the power but the duty to intervene. e

[225] Nor, as the authorities show, is it necessary for the Sun to establish that the judge misdirected the jury in the course of his summing up. Where such a misdirection occurs, the task of the unsuccessful party in challenging the resulting verdict will no doubt be very much easier, but the existence of a misdirection by the judge is not be a prerequisite for such a challenge. f

[226] In the instant case, I can find no misdirection in the judge's summing up. Earlier in this judgment I criticised his conflation of the two pleaded meanings of the material complained of into a single composite meaning. Further, it would in my judgment have been preferable for the judge, when dealing with substantial justification, to have explained more fully to the jury the distinction between the charges of actual match-fixing and those of corruption by accepting bribes to fix matches, and to have emphasised the seriousness of *each* category of charge. But in my judgment these criticisms of the summing up do not warrant the conclusion that there was a misdirection. g h

[227] I accordingly address the question whether the jury's verdict (based, as Mr Hartley concedes it was, on its finding that Mr Grobbelaar was innocent of both the alleged corrupt conspiracies) was one which a jury, acting reasonably, could have reached; and I address that question on the basis that there was no misdirection by the judge. j

[228] In the first place, it was plainly open to the jury to accept the evidence of Mr Bob Wilson (supported as to the Coventry match by the evidence of Mr Alan Ball) and to conclude on the basis of that evidence that, whatever their a assessment of Mr Grobbelaar's credibility, Mr Grobbelaar had not deliberately let in goals in any of the matches in question.

[229] Secondly, and on the other hand, had the jury concluded that Mr Grobbelaar was guilty of the charge of corruptly accepting bribes to fix matches, it must in my judgment, acting reasonably, have concluded that Mr Grobbelaar's claim for damages must fail. In other words, it must in my b judgment, acting reasonably, have accepted Mr Carman's proposition that it would be an 'affront to justice' for Mr Grobbelaar's claim for damages to succeed *notwithstanding that the Sun's charges that he had corruptly accepted bribes to fix matches had been made out*. As Mr Spearman demonstrated, corrupt acceptance of bribes is, in itself, a criminal offence. By contrast, Mr Hartley's contrary proposition, c namely that if the Sun failed to prove that Mr Grobbelaar had deliberately let in goals in the matches in question then Mr Grobbelaar's claim for damages should succeed *notwithstanding that the jury might have concluded that he was guilty of the charge of having corruptly accepted bribes to fix matches,* does not seem to me to bear examination. In my judgment a finding by the jury that Mr Grobbelaar had corruptly accepted bribes to fix matches must, on any rational basis, be fatal to d Mr Grobbelaar's claim for damages.

[230] In the event, the jury must have concluded; (a) that Mr Grobbelaar had not been guilty of deliberately letting in goals in the matches in question, and (b) (as is accepted by Mr Hartley) that he had not participated in either of the two alleged conspiracies and accordingly had not corruptly accepted bribes to fix e matches. Conclusion (a) is in my judgment unimpeachable, in the light of the evidence of Mr Wilson and Mr Ball. The question, therefore, is whether conclusion (b) is one which a jury could have reached, as reasonable individuals.

[231] To answer this question, it is necessary to examine the plausibility of Mr Grobbelaar's explanation for his taped admissions of corruption in the past, f and of his willingness to participate in corruption in the future: viz that he was inventing them on the spur of the moment, with a view to eliciting information from Mr Vincent (whom he suspected of having behaved dishonestly in relation to the Mondoro venture) about his corrupt proposal which he could place before the authorities. As explained earlier, this is Mr Grobbelaar's *only* explanation for those admissions.

g [232] The jury had the benefit of seeing and hearing Mr Grobbelaar give evidence. He began his evidence in the course of the afternoon of the fourth day of the trial, and completed it during the afternoon of the seventh day: so his evidence took about three court days. Moreover, he was subjected to a lengthy and penetrating cross-examination by Mr Carman, one of the most celebrated h exponents of the art of cross-examination. Mr Carman's cross-examination of Mr Grobbelaar lasted some two court days. In the circumstances, the burden on the Sun of showing that the jury were, in effect, bound to reject Mr Grobbelaar's explanation of his taped admissions is inevitably a heavy one to discharge.

[233] At the same time, any jury acting reasonably must, in my judgment, j have recognised the glaring implausibility of Mr Grobbelaar's explanation, given; (a) the tone and content of the taped conversations (some examples of which I have quoted in the course of this judgment, but there are many more), (b) the lies which Mr Grobbelaar told in the original version of his reply, (c) Mr Grobbelaar's initial reaction to the accusations levelled at him by the journalists when they ambushed him at Gatwick, and (d) the telephone conversation between Mr Grobbelaar and Mr Higgins.

[234] In relation to Mr Grobbelaar's excuse for not having immediately revealed his (alleged) plan to entrap Mr Vincent when faced by the journalists at Gatwick, I earlier made the point that, accepting the very unsatisfactory nature of that confrontation, one would nevertheless have expected Mr Grobbelaar, if his explanation for the taped admissions was true, to have reacted by immediately disclosing that the admissions were made in order to entrap Mr Vincent. His failure to do so seems to me to be a most telling factor in considering whether his explanation is credible.

[235] A number of further factors serve to confirm to the implausibility of Mr Grobbelaar's explanation for his taped admissions. These include: (i) the fact that it was unnecessary for Mr Grobbelaar to admit to past corrupt activities with Mr Lim in order to gain Mr Vincent's confidence, since it is absolutely clear from the tapes that he already enjoyed Mr Vincent's full confidence; (ii) the fact that Mr Grobbelaar chose to involve a third party, Mr Fashanu, in his allegedly false admissions, without having first warned Mr Fashanu or obtained his consent; (iii) the fact that by 8 November 1994 Mr Grobbelaar, on his own evidence, had not told anyone about his plan to entrap Mr Vincent; (iv) the fact that Mr Grobbelaar had retained the £2,000 for some five days after it was handed to him at the meeting at Mr Vincent's flat on 3 November 1994 without making any attempt to hand it over to the authorities or even to reveal to the authorities that he had it; (v) the clandestine journey from Norwich to London to meet Mr Lim, the purpose of which was said by Mr Grobbelaar to be to enable him to discuss with Mr Lim his prospects of playing football professionally in Malaysia (when, on his own admission, he did not know whether Mr Lim was involved in professional football or whether he had any contacts in the professional game in Malaysia); and (vi) the coincidence between Mr Grobbelaar's admission that he received £40,000 in November 1993 and the fact that at about the same time he paid £20,000 to Mr Vincent.

[236] I must, however, refer to two particular factors on which Mr Hartley relies, which might be said to support Mr Grobbelaar's explanation of the taped admissions.

[237] Firstly, Mr Hartley suggests that it is inherently improbable that a well-known footballer earning as much as Mr Grobbelaar was earning at the time would have put not only his career and his family but also his personal liberty in jeopardy for the sake of sums of money as relatively paltry as those which featured in the evidence in this case.

[238] Secondly, Mr Hartley relies on the evidence of Mr Bob Wilson. He submits that the significance of Mr Wilson's evidence for present purposes is that it is relevant not only to the charges of actual match-fixing but also to the admissions which Mr Grobbelaar made on the tapes as to his one successful attempt to let in a goal (in the Coventry match) and his three unsuccessful attempts to do so. If no actual match-fixing took place, submits Mr Hartley, then it must follow that Mr Grobbelaar's 'admissions' that it did take place must have been false; a conclusion which is (to put it at its lowest) consistent with Mr Grobbelaar's case that all the admissions on the tapes were false.

[239] Further, Mr Hartley reminds us that, so far as the standard of proof is concerned, the more serious the allegation the more cogent must be the evidence which is required to prove it on the balance of probabilities. Hence, the standard of proof applicable to the Sun's defence of justification is commensurately stricter, by reference to the seriousness of the allegations which it has made against Mr Grobbelaar.

a [**240**] Notwithstanding these factors, I would have no hesitation in rejecting Mr Grobbelaar's explanation of his taped admissions relating to his corrupt arrangements with Mr Lim and Mr Vincent. That, however, is not the relevant question. The relevant question is whether the jury could, acting reasonably, have concluded on the balance of probabilities (and allowing for the fact that, given the seriousness of the allegations against Mr Grobbelaar, the Sun has to b prove its case to a higher standard) that Mr Grobbelaar's explanation of those admissions was true.

[**241**] I conclude that the answer to that question is No. Assuming that the jury concluded, based on Mr Wilson's evidence, that Mr Grobbelaar's apparent admissions on the tapes to the effect that he had deliberately let in (or attempted to let in) goals were not true, that conclusion cannot outweigh all the other c factors which point inescapably to Mr Grobbelaar's explanation of his taped admissions of corrupt arrangements with Mr Lim and Mr Vincent being untrue. In my judgment, Mr Grobbelaar's explanation of those admissions is so utterly implausible that no jury, acting reasonably, could have accepted it as true. It follows, for reasons explained earlier, that the jury's verdict cannot stand, and d must be set aside.

RESULT

[**242**] In my judgment, the jury's verdict in this case represents a miscarriage of justice which this court can and must correct. In agreement with my Lords, I would allow this appeal and set aside the jury's verdict.

Appeal allowed.

Dilys Tausz Barrister.

T Choithram International SA and others v Pagarani and others

a

PRIVY COUNCIL

LORD BROWNE-WILKINSON, LORD JAUNCEY OF TULLICHETTLE, LORD CLYDE, LORD HOBHOUSE OF WOODBOROUGH AND LORD MILLETT

b

6–9 DECEMBER 1999, 29 NOVEMBER 2000

Gift – Incomplete gift – Perfecting gift – Donor executing trust deed establishing charitable foundation – Deed naming donor as one of foundation's trustees – Donor making oral declaration of gift to foundation but not transferring assets to other trustees – Whether donor's words a declaration of trust – Whether trustee in whom trust property vested bound to give effect to trust by transferring property to other trustees.

c

P, a twice-married businessman and philanthropist, owned most of the shares in, and held deposit balances with, four companies in the British Virgin Islands. Having provided generously for his first wife and numerous children, P intended to leave much of the remainder of his wealth to charity by setting up a foundation which would receive most of his assets when he died. To that end, in February 1992 he executed a trust deed establishing the foundation. The deed was expressed to be between P, defined as the settlor, and seven individuals, including P, who were defined as the trustees. Immediately after signing the deed, which created trusts in favour of charities already established by him, P stated orally that he was giving all his wealth to the foundation. He also instructed the accountant of his companies to 'transfer all my wealth with the companies to the Trust'. However, by the time of his death in March 1992, P had not executed any share transfers. Nor had he executed a declaration of trust in respect of the assets of the companies. After P's death, his first wife and her children brought proceedings against the companies and the trustees in the British Virgin Islands, claiming that the gift to the foundation had been ineffective. At trial, the judge held that a perfect gift could only be made in one of two ways, namely (i) by a transfer of the gifted asset to the donee, accompanied by an intention in the donor to make a gift, or (ii) by the donor declaring himself to be a trustee of the gifted property for the donee. He concluded that P's gift fell outside the first category, since he had not transferred the assets so as to vest title in all the trustees, and that it also fell outside the second, since P had used words of gift to the foundation rather than declaring himself a trustee. The judge therefore held that there had been an imperfect gift which could not be enforced against P's estate. His decision was upheld by the Court of Appeal of the British Virgin Islands, and the defendants appealed to the Privy Council. On the appeal, the plaintiffs contended that even if P's words were to be construed as a declaration of trust, the court could not grant an order vesting the gifted property in the whole body of the trustees since equity would not aid a volunteer.

d

e

f

g

h

j

Held – (1) Although equity would not aid a volunteer, it would not strive officiously to defeat a gift. The facts of the instant case fell between the two common-form situations. Although the words used by P were those normally appropriate to an outright gift, they were in the context essentially words of gift on trust. The foundation had no legal existence apart from the trust declared by the trust deed. Thus the words 'I give to the foundation' could only mean 'I give to the trustees of the foundation trust deed to be held by them on the trusts of the foundation trust deed' (see p 501 *e f*, post); *Milroy v Lord* [1861–73] All ER Rep 783 distinguished.

(2) In the absence of special factors, where one out of a larger body of trustees had the trust property vested in him, he was bound by the trust and had to give effect to it by transferring the trust property into the names of all the trustees. There could be no distinction in principle between the case where the donor declared himself to be sole trustee for a donee or a purpose and the case where he declared himself to be one of the trustees for that donor or purpose. In both cases his conscience was affected and it would be unconscionable and contrary to the principles of equity to allow such a donor to resile from his gift. Accordingly, in the instant case the deposit balances and the shares in the companies were held, at P's death, on the trusts of the foundation and those assets were validly vested in the trustees. The appeal would therefore be allowed (see p 501 *j* to p 502 *b e h*, post); *Bridge v Bridge* (1852) 16 Beav 315 doubted and distinguished.

Notes

For incomplete gifts, see 20 *Halsbury's Laws* (4th edn reissue) paras 63–66.

Cases referred to in judgment

Bridge v Bridge (1852) 16 Beav 315, 51 ER 800.

Milroy v Lord (1862) 4 DeGF & J 264, [1861–73] All ER Rep 783, 45 ER 1185, LJJ.

Richards v Delbridge (1874) LR 18 Eq 11.

Rose (decd), Re, Midland Bank Executor and Trustee Co Ltd v Rose [1948] 2 All ER 971, [1949] Ch 78.

Rose, Re, Rose v IRC [1952] 1 All ER 1217, [1952] Ch 499, CA.

Strong v Bird (1874) LR 18 Eq 315, [1874–80] All ER Rep 230.

Appeal

The defendants, T Choithram International SA, Bytco International SA, Bholenath Inc, Mahadev Inc, Kishore Thakurdas Pagarani, Lekhraj Thakurdas Pagarani, Ramesh Pohumal Thanwani, Ramchand Dharmadas Rajwani and Vashdev Lalchand Pamnani, appealed with leave from the decision of the Court of Appeal of the British Virgin Islands (Byron CJ (Ag), Singh and Redhead JJA) on 8 April 1998 ((1998/99) 2 OFLR 1) dismissing their appeal from the decision of Georges J on 21 January 1997 ((1997/98) 1 OFLR 239) upholding the claim by the plaintiffs, Lalibai Thakurdas Pagarani, Hasibai known as Mora Lilaram Kewlani, Rijha known as Kanta Kishinchand Jethwani, Gopi known as Vanita Jai Motiani, Kumari Dhanwanti Thakurdas Pagarani, Saraswati known as Kanchan Satish Motiani, Rukumani Aswani and John Greenwood, that the fifth to eighth defendants held upon trust for the estate of the deceased, Thakurdas Choithram Pagarani, the latter's shareholdings in the first to fourth defendants and all sums owed to him by the first to fourth defendants at the time of his death. The facts are set out in the opinion of the Board.

Michael Briggs QC and *J Stephen Smith* (instructed by *Irvings*) for the defendants.

Alan Steinfeld QC and *Stephen Moverley Smith* (instructed by *Withers*) for the plaintiffs.

The Board took time for consideration.

a

29 November 2000. The following judgment of the Board was delivered.

LORD BROWNE-WILKINSON. This is an appeal from the judgment of the Court of Appeal of the British Virgin Islands (Byron CJ (Ag), Singh and Redhead JJA) given on 8 April 1998 ((1998/99) 2 OFLR 1) upholding the decision of Georges J ((1997/98) 1 OFLR 239) that the actions of Thakurdas Choithram Pagarani (TCP) shortly before his death were insufficient to constitute a completed gift to the Choithram International Foundation (the foundation) a philanthropic body created by TCP at the same time as the gift. The case again raises, but with a new twist, the question 'when is a gift completed'.

b

c

TCP was born in 1914 in India. He was a devout Hindu. In 1928 he married the first plaintiff, Lalibai Thakurdas Pagarani, by whom he had six daughters, the second to seventh plaintiffs.

In about 1937 TCP left India and eventually established a supermarket business in Sierra Leone. Lalibai and their children remained in India. In Sierra Leone he met and in 1944 went through a ceremony of marriage with Virginia Harding who bore him eight children including three sons. The fifth and sixth defendants are sons of that union named Kishore and Lekhraj. TCP remained in Sierra Leone until the 1980s but used to return to India to visit his Indian family and those members of his Sierra Leone family whom he had taken to India to be brought up according to Indian ways and customs.

d

e

The businesses carried on by TCP were outstandingly successful and spread widely throughout the world. They were usually named 'T Choithram and Sons' and were often known simply as 'Choithrams'. In 1989 TCP brought most of his business under the umbrella of the first four defendant companies which became, in effect, holding companies. He was not the sole owner of the shares in those companies. He owned 64% whilst the eighth defendant Mr Rajwani owned 10%, Ramesh Pohumal Thanwani 10% and his sons Kishore and Lekhraj 8% each.

f

TCP used those companies, and in particularly T Choithram International SA and Bytco International SA, as his bankers. He did not draw profits out of the companies but built up credits on accounts with those companies. He also established joint accounts in the name of himself and the name of a member of the family. In consequence, after his death the individual family members became the sole owners of their respective accounts.

g

TCP throughout his life was outstandingly generous in his charitable giving. His gifts amounted to many millions of US dollars. The judge found that—

> 'having made generous provision for his first wife and each of his children, [he] intended to leave much of the remainder of his wealth to charity, to the exclusion of his children. This he hoped to achieve by setting up a foundation to serve as an umbrella organisation for those charities which he had already established and which would in due course be the vehicle to receive most of his assets when he died. This was from all accounts, a longstanding intention of the deceased.' (See (1997/98) 1 OFLR 239 at 251.)

h

j

The draft trust deed was first prepared in 1989 by London solicitors, Macfarlanes. The draft reached a final stage in 1990 but was not executed. However, as the judge found, by the end of 1991, with his health clearly failing, TCP apparently finally decided to set up the trust. The judge accepted the evidence that TCP told his son Lekhraj that he would like to sign the trust deed in London and that he a had clearly made up his mind to put pen to paper and do everything as quickly as possible.

The draft trust deed intended to establish the foundation took the form of a pilot settlement subject to the law of Jersey in the Channel Islands. It was expressed to be made between TCP (defined as the settlor) of the one part and the settlor, Mr Rajwani, Mr Thanwani, Mr Jethwani, two of TCP's sons Kishore b and Lekhraj, and a Mr Patel (who are defined as the trustees). It was recited that TCP had transferred £1,000 to the trustees 'to the intent that they should make the irrevocable settlement hereafter contained', and that further property might be paid transferred or otherwise placed under the control of the trustees. It then provided that during a defined trust period the trustees might apply the income to or for the benefit of the beneficiaries as defined and at the expiration of the c trust period should hold the capital for the T Choithram Foundation, the Choithram Charitable Trust, T Choithram Charity Trust Ltd and Choithram Fountain of Humanitarian Services Charitable Trust in equal shares absolutely, those being four charities which TCP had established during his lifetime. The 'beneficiaries' as defined were TCP and the four charitable institutions just d mentioned. Power was given to the trustees (with the consent of the protector, who was TCP) to appoint that the beneficiaries were to include such persons as they might specify.

The foundation trust deed remained unexecuted until, at the end of 1991, TCP was diagnosed as suffering from cancer. He left his home in Dubai (where he had primarily established himself after he left Sierra Leone in the 1980s) and came to e London to stay with his son Lekhraj. As already stated, it was clear that he intended to give his property to the foundation. Preparations were made for an elaborate ceremony at which he was to establish the foundation and give it all his wealth. There were summoned to his bedside in Lekhraj's house the First Secretary of the Indian High Commission in London, a Mr Sri Nivasan. In an f upstairs bedroom in Lekhraj's house on 17 February 1992 TCP executed the foundation trust deed in the presence of Mr Nivasan, Lekhraj, Kishore, Mr Rajwani and Mr Param. Mr Rajwani was an old friend and business associate of TCP. Mr Param was the accountant to TCP's companies. Immediately after signing the foundation trust deed TCP said certain words. The witnesses varied in their recollection of the details of what was said but all were in substantial agreement. g Thus the witnesses recollect him as having said 'I now give all my wealth to the trust' or 'I have given everything to the trust' or 'I'm handing all my gift, all my wealth, all my shares, to the trust' or that he made a declaration of gift of 'his shares and wealth to the Choithram International Foundation'. TCP then said to Mr Param that he, Mr Param, knew what to do and that he should transfer all his h balances with the companies to the foundation and his shares as well. Again the exact words used are not identically remembered. Mr Param was expressly picked out by the judge as a witness who impressed him as 'reliable and thoroughly trustworthy'. According to Mr Param he was instructed by TCP to 'transfer all my wealth with the companies to the trust'. According to Lekhraj, j Mr Param was instructed to transfer to the trust all his balances with the company and his shares as well. Mr Rajwani confirmed that Mr Param was directed that 'all my wealth, all my shareholding, and whatever credit balances, should be transferred to the Choithram International Foundation'.

On that evidence the judge said that he entertained no doubt that TCP executed the foundation trust deed on 17 February as alleged and that he was equally satisfied that he made a gift of all his wealth with the companies to the foundation. He also refers to the deceased having made an oral declaration giving 'all his wealth to the foundation'.

On the same day, 17 February 1992, the other trustees present in London namely Mr Rajwani, Kishore and Lekhraj signed the trust deed. The remaining trustees of the foundation who were not in London signed the foundation trust deed shortly thereafter.

On the evening of the same day, 17 February, there were meetings of the boards of directors of the four holding companies at TCP's bedside. These were attended by TCP, Mr Rajwani, Kishore and Lekhraj. Minutes were prepared and kept: the judge found that the meetings did take place. The minutes record that TCP declined to accept the chair and Mr Rajwani was elected as chairman. TCP reported that he had executed the settlement—

> 'creating the trust, Choithram International Foundation and gifted all his wealth to it and thus necessitating the company to make the required entries in its records to evidence and exhibit the change of ownership of the assets from Mr T C Pagarani to the trustees of the Choithram International Foundation.'

The meetings passed resolutions acknowledging the declaration of gift of all TCP's wealth to the foundation and resolved—

> 'that the company hereby acknowledge and confirm that the trustees of the Choithram International Foundation are henceforth the holders of the shares and assets in the company gifted to the Choithram International Foundation by Mr T C Pagarani.'

The memorandum and articles of the companies contained pre-emption rights for the holders of the remaining 36% of the shares in the companies. Within a week all the other shareholders had executed waivers of their rights. On 24 February there was a meeting of the trustees of the foundation in London attended by TCP, Mr Rajwani, Lekhraj and Kishore. TCP was elected chairman. He reported that the foundation had been established and all his wealth had been given to the trust. Amongst the other business transacted it was resolved to go ahead with an eye hospital project in Sierra Leone as agreed with representatives of the Sight Savers Association, a project involving major expenditure of funds incapable of being met by the foundation without substantial funds having been injected. The minutes were signed by TCP on 29 February at the Wellington Hospital in London to which by that date TCP had been admitted.

TCP had some time previously instructed different London solicitors, Clifford Chance, to prepare a will for him. The draft will contained a gift of the whole of his estate (other than his estate in India) to a body called the foundation. However, at the time the will was prepared the foundation had not been constituted. Mr Lock of Clifford Chance visited TCP in Golders Green on 10 January and took instructions directly from the deceased. Mr Lock advised that until the foundation was established, it would be better for TCP's residuary estate to be bequeathed for general charitable purposes and after the death the executors could then pay over the residuary estate to the foundation once established. He was instructed to revise the will on that basis and was told that 'in the meantime he and his son would prepare the necessary assignments and transfers for assets to be transferred to' the foundation. The evidence before the judge showed that Lekhraj on more than one occasion after 17 February tried to persuade TCP to a execute a will in the form excluding his Indian property but bequeathing all his other property to the foundation established by the deed dated 17 February 1992.

Lekhraj also tried to persuade TCP after 17 February to execute documents which the judge described as 'the forms which were necessary to carry out the transfer of assets'. These documents were not, as that description would suggest, share transfers of the shares in the four companies and formal assignments of the b credit balances. There were two documents, one a declaration of trust and the other a memorandum of addition, which had first been prepared in September 1990 and of which further copies were sent by Macfarlanes to Lekhraj on 12 February 1992. The documents so sent required to be updated since they did not contain the full number of the trustees nor the proper description of the foundation trust deed. However they were amended before they were presented to TCP for his c signature. The first document was directed to the first defendant and to the trustees of the foundation. The document acknowledged and declared that TCP held 1,600 fully paid ordinary shares in the capital of the first defendant which were registered in his name 'in trust for the trustees' and undertook to transfer and deal with such shares as the trustees might from time to time direct. It d further recorded that TCP thereby deposited with the trustees the certificate for the said shares and a transfer thereof executed in blank and he thereby authorised the trustees to complete the same, such authority to be irrevocable. He further undertook to account to the trustees for any dividends and gave notice to the directors of the first defendant that he had declared the above trust. The second document directed to the first defendant and to the trustees of the foundation e acknowledged and declared that TCP held his current account with the company in trust for the trustees and undertook to deal with such account as the trustees might direct.

Neither of these documents nor (their Lordships infer) similar documents relating to the other companies in the group were signed by TCP. It was the f evidence of Lekhraj that TCP did not sign the documents because he had an aversion to signing such documents and also had been advised that it was not necessary. According to this evidence TCP repeatedly said that he had done his bit, that he had given all his wealth to the foundation and there was nothing more for him to do.

TCP's daughter, Mrs Sawlani, gave evidence (apparently accepted by the g judge) that on about 8 March 1992 (that is to say the day before TCP was admitted to the intensive care unit at the Wellington Hospital) he had said to her: 'I have given up everything and I feel very happy now. What I was wanting to do, I finally did it and now everything is for them.'

It will be remembered that at the first meeting on 17 February TCP had told h Mr Param that he, Param, knew what to do and that he should transfer all TCP's balances with the companies and shares in the companies to the trustees of the foundation. Pursuant to this direction at the end of February Mr Param altered the entries in the books of the first defendant company, deleting TCP as creditor and substituting the foundation. He was himself unable to make a similar j alteration in the books of the second defendant company but left instructions to do so for his assistant Mr Tejwani. Unhappily, Mr Tejwani did not make such alterations until after the death of TCP.

As to TCP's shares in the companies, no transfers were executed by TCP during his lifetime. On 20 June 1992, after the death of TCP, the companies registered the trustees of the foundation as shareholders, cancelled TCP's share certificates and issued new share certificates.

TCP died on 19 March 1992. On 11 August 1992 Lekhraj obtained a grant of letters of administration to his estate in Sierra Leone. On 19 August 1992 the plaintiffs, being Lalibai and her children, started these proceedings in the British Virgin Islands. On 30 September 1992 the grant in Sierra Leone was resealed in the British Virgin Islands. In August 1994 there were interlocutory hearings in the British Virgin Islands.

There are separate proceedings giving rise to a separate point of appeal to the Board. Mr Kewlani, purporting to act as attorney for the children of Lalibai, applied in Sierra Leone to revoke the grant to Lekhraj. That application was struck out first, on the grounds that Mr Kewlani was not duly authorised to bring the proceedings but also on the alternative ground that the children of Virginia Harding were legitimate and entitled to participate in TCP's estate to the extent that he was intestate. Subsequently the appellants in the present appeal applied for a stay in the British Virgin Islands of similar proceedings relating to the legitimacy of the defendants. Georges J granted the defendants a temporary stay which was not appealed against. In the present proceedings the judge felt that the plaintiffs were estopped from relitigating the legitimacy issue in the British Virgin Islands by the decision in Sierra Leone. The Court of Appeal reversed this decision. There is an appeal against that part of the Court of Appeal's judgment, but the point was not argued on the appeal the parties being agreed that that issue should stand over until the appeal on the main point had been decided.

On the main issue the defendants advanced a number of arguments with a view to demonstrating that the gift to the foundation was an immediate perfected gift by TCP of all or some of TCP's wealth. Their primary argument was that TCP, having executed the foundation trust deed under which he was one of the trustees and made a gift of all his wealth to 'the foundation', thereafter held all his assets (or at least his shares in and deposits with the British Virgin Island companies which are the first four defendants) as trustee on the trusts of the foundation trust deed. The defendants also had a number of alternative arguments. First they argued that the principle in *Strong v Bird* (1874) LR 18 Eq 315, [1874–80] All ER Rep 230 entitled them to succeed because a grant of letters of administration to the estate of TCP had been obtained by Lekhraj, one of the trustees of the foundation. Next they argued that, as to the sums deposited with the companies, those companies had attorned to the trustees of the foundation when Mr Param or Mr Tejwani made the changes to the companies' books. Next, they submitted that TCP's words and actions amounted to an equitable assignment of the deposits with the companies to the trustees of the foundation, or alternatively constituted a release by TCP to the companies in consideration of the companies' undertaking contractual obligations to pay the trustees of the foundation a similar sum. Finally, the defendants repeated their argument before the judge that the trustees were validly registered as shareholders in the company either because of certain provisions in the articles of the company or under s 30 of the International Business Companies Ordinance 1984. Their Lordships will deal first with the main argument since, in their view, that is sufficient to dispose of the appeal.

In order to have made an effective gift of his shares and deposit balances to the foundation TCP must have intended to make an immediate gift on 17 February. The judge found, and repeated his finding on a number of occasions throughout the judgment, that on that date TCP did make, or attempted to make, a present immediate and unconditional gift to the foundation which was intended to be complete. This finding, if it had stood alone, would have been fully sufficient to a establish TCP's intention to make an outright gift. However, at a later stage in his judgment the judge made a further finding. At this stage in the judgment the judge was seeking to answer the second question of fact left to him by counsel for decision (viz did TCP continue his intention of gift down to the date of death?), a question only relevant to the *Strong v Bird* argument. The judge reviewed the evidence as to the events occurring after the oral declaration of trust on 17 February b and was very impressed by two elements in the evidence: first, that despite Lekhraj's promptings TCP refused to sign the further documents put before him and, second, that by the draft will (which he never executed) TCP expressly excluded his Indian property (which had been the home of Lalibai) and also contained a gift of his estate to the foundation. He reached the conclusion that the gift was not intended by the deceased to be irrevocable.

c Their Lordships do not feel able to accept the judge's inference that TCP intended the gift to be revocable. First the judge quotes a passage from the affidavit of Mr Lock of Clifford Chance saying that TCP was intending 'to prepare the necessary assignments and transfers for the assets to be transferred to the Choithram International Foundation'. Now Mr Lock and Clifford Chance were d concerned, not with the setting up of the foundation, but only with TCP's will: the setting up of the foundation was being dealt with by different solicitors, Macfarlanes. The only evidence of the further documents which Macfarlanes envisaged were the draft documents which were sent to Lekhraj by fax from Macfarlanes on 12 February 1992. These documents were not share transfers or deeds of assignment: they were declarations of trust by TCP in favour of the e trustees of the foundation and notices of addition to the funds settled by the trust deed to be executed by the trustees. Therefore, so far as the evidence extends, it was always the intention of TCP and his relevant legal advisers that the foundation should be constituted by the following steps. First, TCP would declare the foundation trust by a trust deed, he and others being the trustees; f second, TCP would declare himself as holding his assets on the trusts of the foundation trust deed; third, the other trustees would accept the gift as an addition to the trust fund constituted by the trust deed. Thus the machinery actually adopted was the same as that proposed by Macfarlanes save that the written declaration of trust was replaced by an oral immediate gift not to a person but for an abstract purpose, i e for the purposes of the foundation. A gift for 'the g foundation' can only properly be construed as a gift to the purposes declared by the trust deed and administered by the trustees.

The judge's doubts were also raised by the fact that TCP, an experienced businessman, was acting in defiance of his lawyers' advice 'with whom he had remained in close consultation'. There is no evidence of recent direct communication h between TCP and Macfarlanes: the only evidence is the fax of 12 February which was sent not to TCP but to Lekhraj. The fact is that TCP was in his last illness as a result of which he went into intensive care on 9 March and died ten days thereafter. The judge also seemed far from clear as to the nature of the documents sent by Macfarlanes on 12 February which formed the basis of the documents the j signature of which Lekhraj was seeking from TCP. The judge refers to TCP having 'the continuing intention of transferring assets by way of instruments of transfer' and 'the transfer of shares ... [remaining] unsigned'. The judge seemed to have thought that the documents would actually have vested the legal interest in the deposits and the shares in the trustees whereas the new documents, even if executed, were to have done no more than constitute TCP as trustee for the whole body of trustees of the foundation.

Finally on this aspect of the case their Lordships do not attach such importance to the will as did the judge. It is certainly true that if the gift of all his wealth was valid TCP by executing the will would not have provided for his widow and daughters in India by leaving them the land: this is a real factor to be taken into account. But their Lordships do not, as did the judge, attach importance to the draft will containing a residuary bequest to the foundation by reference to the trust deed dated 17 February. There is no evidence that TCP had anything to do with the instructions for this will (beyond refusing to sign it) and in any event it would have been common prudence for TCP to execute a will giving to the foundation anything which the inter vivos trusts had failed to attach: their Lordships do not consider the existence of the testamentary residuary gift to the foundation as in any way inconsistent with TCP having intended to make an absolute gift in his lifetime.

For these reasons their Lordships are of the view that the judge in reaching his inference that the 'gift' to the foundation was revocable was labouring under important misapprehensions. Their Lordships consider that once it is understood that, in any event, the transaction was to be carried through by TCP declaring that he held assets already vested in him as a trustee for the foundation, there is no ground for inferring that the gift was intended by TCP to be revocable or conditional on the transfer of the specific assets. In the light of all the other evidence pointing (as the judge found) quite clearly to an intention to make an immediate, unconditional gift to the foundation, their Lordships are satisfied that that was TCP's intention. Perhaps the most telling evidence of all is the minutes of the companies' meetings on the evening of 17 February. The plaintiffs launched an attack on the genuineness of the minutes but they were upheld as genuine by the judge. They record that the directors of each of the four companies, who in each case included TCP—

> 'acknowledge and confirm that the trustees of the [foundation] are henceforth the holders of the shares and assets in the company gifted to the [foundation] by Mr T C Pagarani.'

Those minutes were signed by TCP. It is hard to imagine a clearer statement of what TCP understood to be the position, i e that he had already given outright to the foundation all his interests in the company balances and the shares.

In fairness to the judge, it does not appear that his decision that there was here no complete gift was based on the fact that in his view the gift was revocable. He founded his decision on the ground that the requirements laid down in *Milroy v Lord* (1862) 4 DeGF & J 264, [1861–73] All ER Rep 783 had not been satisfied. It may well be that an immediate declaration of trust even though expressly or impliedly made revocable is a valid complete gift. Many voluntary settlements are expressly made revocable yet no one suggests that they are incompletely constituted trusts. If and so long as the trusts remains unrevoked, the trust is enforceable against the trustees and the trust property. But it is unnecessary to decide that point.

Their Lordships then turn to the central and most important question: on the basis that TCP intended to make an immediate absolute gift 'to the foundation' but had not vested the gifted property in all the trustees of the foundation, are the trusts of the foundation trust deed enforceable against the deposits and the shares or is this (as the judge and the Court of Appeal held) a case where there has been an imperfect gift which cannot be enforced against TCP's estate whatever TCP's intentions.

a The judge and the Court of Appeal understandably took the view that a perfect gift could only be made in one of two ways, viz (a) by a transfer of the gifted asset to the donee, accompanied by an intention in the donor to make a gift; or (b) by the donor declaring himself to be a trustee of the gifted property for the donee. In case (a), the donor has to have done everything necessary to be done which is within his own power to do in order to transfer the gifted asset to the donee. If b the donor has not done so, the gift is incomplete since the donee has no equity to perfect an imperfect gift (see *Milroy v Lord*; *Richards v Delbridge* (1874) LR 18 Eq 11; *Re Rose (decd), Midland Bank Executor and Trustee Co Ltd v Rose* [1948] 2 All ER 971, [1949] Ch 78 and *Re Rose, Rose v IRC* [1952] 1 All ER 1217, [1952] Ch 499). Moreover, the court will not give a benevolent construction so as to treat ineffective words of outright gift as taking effect as if the donor had declared himself a trustee for the c donee (see *Milroy v Lord*). So, it is said, in this case TCP used words of gift to the foundation (not words declaring himself a trustee): unless he transferred the shares and deposits so as to vest title in all the trustees, he had not done all that he could in order to effect the gift. It therefore fails. Further it is said that it is not possible to treat TCP's words of gift as a declaration of trust because they make d no reference to trusts. Therefore the case does not fall within either of the possible methods by which a complete gift can be made and the gift fails.

Though it is understandable that the courts below should have reached this conclusion since the case does not fall squarely within either of the methods normally stated as being the only possible ways of making a gift, their Lordships do not agree with that conclusion. The facts of this case are novel and raise a new e point. It is necessary to make an analysis of the rules of equity as to complete gifts. Although equity will not aid a volunteer, it will not strive officiously to defeat a gift. This case falls between the two common-form situations mentioned above. Although the words used by TCP are those normally appropriate to an outright gift—'I give to X'—in the present context there is no breach of the f principle in *Milroy v Lord* if the words of TCP's gift (i e to the foundation) are given their only possible meaning in this context. The foundation has no legal existence apart from the trust declared by the foundation trust deed. Therefore the words 'I give to the foundation' can only mean 'I give to the trustees of the foundation trust deed to be held by them on the trusts of the foundation trust deed'. Although the words are apparently words of outright gift they are essentially g words of gift on trust.

But, it is said, TCP vested the properties not in *all* the trustees of the foundation but only in one, i e TCP. Since equity will not aid a volunteer, how can a court order be obtained vesting the gifted property in the whole body of trustees on the trusts of the foundation? Again, this represents an over-simplified view of the h rules of equity. Until comparatively recently the great majority of trusts were voluntary settlements under which beneficiaries were volunteers having given no value. Yet beneficiaries under a trust, although volunteers, can enforce the trust against the trustees. Once a trust relationship is established between trustee and beneficiary, the fact that a beneficiary has given no value is irrelevant. It is j for this reason that the type of perfected gift referred to in class (b) above is effective since the donor has constituted himself a trustee for the donee who can as a matter of trust law enforce that trust.

What then is the position here where the trust property is vested in one of the body of trustees, viz TCP? In their Lordships' view there should be no question. TCP has, in the most solemn circumstances, declared that he is giving (and later that he has given) property to a trust which he himself has established and of which he has appointed himself to be a trustee. All this occurs at one composite transaction taking place on 17 February. There can in principle be no distinction between the case where the donor declares himself to be sole trustee for a donee or a purpose and the case where he declares himself to be one of the trustees for that donee or purpose. In both cases his conscience is affected and it would be unconscionable and contrary to the principles of equity to allow such a donor to resile from his gift. Say, in the present case, that TCP had survived and tried to change his mind by denying the gift. In their Lordships' view it is impossible to believe that he could validly deny that he was a trustee for the purposes of the foundation in the light of all the steps that he had taken to assert that position and to assert his trusteeship. In their Lordships' judgment in the absence of special factors where one out of a larger body of trustees has the trust property vested in him he is bound by the trust and must give effect to it by transferring the trust property into the name of all the trustees.

The plaintiffs relied on the decision of Romilly MR in *Bridge v Bridge* (1852) 16 Beav 315 at 324, 51 ER 800 at 804 as showing that the vesting of the trust property in one trustee, the donor, out of many is not sufficient to constitute the trust. Their Lordships have some doubt whether that case was correctly decided on this point, the judge giving no reasons for his view. But in any event it is plainly distinguishable from the present case since the judge considered that the trust could not be fully constituted unless the legal estate in the gifted property was vested in the trustees and in that case the legal estate was vested neither in the donor nor in any of the other trustees.

Therefore in their Lordships' view the assets, if any, validly included in TCP's gift to the foundation are properly vested in the trustees and are held on the trusts of the foundation trust deed.

What then are the gifted assets? It will be recalled that TCP referred to the subject matter of the gift in a number of different ways: 'all my wealth', 'everything', 'all my wealth, all my shares, to the trust', 'all his balances ... with the company ... and his shares as well', 'all my wealth with the companies'. The judge found that TCP made a gift of all his wealth with the companies, ie the deposit balances and the shares in the four defendant companies which together constitutes his whole wealth in the British Virgin Islands and are the only assets at issue in these proceedings. It was submitted that a gift of 'all my wealth' was void for uncertainty. Their Lordships express no view on that point since there can be no question but that the deposit balances and the shares in the four companies were identified by TCP as being included in the gift and the gift of them is pro tanto valid.

Their Lordships will therefore humbly advise Her Majesty that the appeal ought to be allowed and the action dismissed on the grounds that at TCP's death the deposit balances and the shares in the companies were held on the trusts of the foundation trust deed and the same are now validly vested in the trustees of the foundation.

Appeal allowed.

Ian Murphie Barrister.

a

Tarbuck v Avon Insurance plc

QUEEN'S BENCH DIVISION (COMMERCIAL COURT)

TOULSON J

b 13, 14 NOVEMBER 2000

Insurance – Legal expenses insurance – Claimant solicitors acting for insured having policy of legal expenses insurance – Insured becoming insolvent – Claimant bringing action against insurers – Whether rights under policy transferring to claimant solicitors – Third Parties (Rights Against Insurers) Act 1930, s 1.

c

The defendant insurers, A, issued a standard office or surgery policy to N in respect of a natural health business. Section 7 of the policy provided for legal expenses indemnity up to a limit of £50,000. N became involved in litigation with her landlord, for which A agreed to provide cover under the policy. N instructed d the claimant firm, T, in the action. The judge granted A relief from forfeiture on condition that she pay arrears of rent and costs to the landlord within a specified period. She failed to comply with that order and was adjudged bankrupt on the landlord's petition. T delivered a final bill in respect of work performed in the action to N after she was adjudicated bankrupt. A sought the authority of N to e pay over to T the balance of the limit of indemnity. N declined to authorise any payment to T save for a small amount in respect of the outstanding fees of an expert. T thereupon issued a writ against N for the outstanding balance of their final bill and subsequently entered judgment in default of notice of intention to defend. T then brought an action against A for the balance remaining under the policy, arguing that, pursuant to s 1[a] of the Third Parties (Rights Against Insurers) f Act 1930, N's rights under the policy of legal expenses insurance had been transferred to T following N's bankruptcy. T further argued that having obtained judgment against N, it was entitled to claim direct against A for the balance of the sum insured. A contended that s 1 of the 1930 Act did not apply to legal expenses insurance, and that accordingly N's trustee would have to claim under the policy g on her behalf (for which, on the facts, the trustee was out of time). A submitted that legal indemnity insurance fell into a different category of insurance which was not covered by the 1930 Act. The court ordered a trial of the preliminary issue whether the policy issued by A was a liability insurance policy, with the result that N's rights under the policy were transferred to T on the bankruptcy of h N pursuant to s 1 of the 1930 Act and that T was accordingly entitled to assert those rights against A.

Held – On its true construction, s 1 of the 1930 Act did not apply to legal expenses insurance. That section applied only to liability insurance, meaning insurance for j damages imposed by operation of law (such as tort or breach of contract), rather than to pecuniary loss insurance, meaning insurance for a voluntarily incurred contract debt, as with legal expenses insurance. Accordingly, the policy issued by A was not an insurance of liability covered by the Act and T therefore had no right of claim against the insurers (see p 508 *g* and p 509 *a b*, post).

a Section 1, so far as material, is set out at p 506 *c d*, post

Per curiam. The present state of the 1930 Act is unsatisfactory for failing to provide for the transfer of the rights under a legal indemnity insurance policy to the legal advisors in the event of the insured becoming insolvent (see p 509 *c*, post).

Notes

For the application of the statutory scheme of subrogation, see 25 *Halsbury's Laws* (4th edn reissue) para 679.

For the Third Parties (Rights Against Insurers) Act 1930, s 1, see 4 *Halsbury's Statutes* (4th edn) (1998 reissue) 697.

Cases cited or referred to in skeleton arguments

Firma C-Trade SA v Newcastle Protection and Indemnity Association, The Fanti [1990] 2 All ER 705, [1991] 2 AC 1, HL.

Harrington Motor Co Ltd, Re, ex p Chaplin [1928] Ch 105, CA.

Hood's Trustees v Southern Union General Insurance Co of Australasia Ltd [1928] Ch 793, CA.

M/S Aswan Engineering Establishment Co Ltd v Iron Trades Mutual Insurance Co Ltd [1989] 1 Lloyd's Rep 289.

Post Office v Norwich Union Fire Insurance Society Ltd [1967] 1 All ER 577, [1967] 2 QB 363, CA.

Royal London Mutual Insurance Society v Barrett [1928] Ch 411.

Preliminary issue

By order of Aikens J made on 15 June 2000, the court was asked to determine a preliminary issue in proceedings brought by the claimant, Philip Luke Tarbuck, against the defendant, Avon Insurance plc (the insurers). The preliminary issue was as follows: whether the Third Parties (Rights against Insurers) Act 1930 was capable of applying to the right of a litigant, under a policy of legal expenses insurance (LEI), to payment by the insurer of costs owed by the insured litigant to her solicitor, so as to cause the insured's right to be transferred to the solicitor in the event of the insured's bankruptcy. The facts are set out in the judgment.

John Davies (instructed by *Tarbucks*) for the claimant.
Aidan Christie (instructed by *Berrymans Lace Mawer*) for the insurers.

TOULSON J. Is the Third Parties (Rights against Insurers) Act 1930 capable of applying to the right of a litigant, under a policy of legal expenses insurance (LEI), to payment by the insurer of costs owed by the insured litigant to her solicitor, so as to cause the insured's right to be transferred to the solicitor in the event of the insured's bankruptcy? That is the subject of this preliminary issue. It is a question of some general importance on which there is no direct authority.

The insured is a Miss Valerie Nicholson. She ran a Natural Health Clinic in Clerkenwell. In 1989 she entered into a policy of insurance with the defendant called an Office or Surgery Policy. Section 1 provided cover in respect of damage to office contents and other risks. Section 7 was headed 'Legal Expenses'. It provided that the insurers would pay the insured's 'legal costs' up to £50,000 in connection with various types of claim. The types of legal proceedings for which there was cover under the policy included disputes arising from contracts for the supply of goods or services, disputes in connection with employment contracts, and of direct relevance in this case:

a 'Any dispute involving (i) any negligent act or omission or nuisance by a third party which results in pecuniary or physical Damage to material property owned by or the responsibility of the insured ... (ii) the possession of freehold or leasehold real property owned, occupied and used by the insured for Business purposes provided pecuniary loss is or could be sustained if a claim or legal proceedings are not pursued or defended.'

b Legal costs were defined as including: (1) solicitors costs, that is fees, costs and disbursements reasonably incurred by the 'appointed representative'; (2) third party costs, that is other parties' costs and expenses incurred in civil proceedings in respect of which the insured should become liable in court, tribunal or arbitration proceedings or under a settlement with another party; (3) expert c witness costs; and (4) awards in the form of any basic or compensation award made against the insured under various pieces of legislation concerned with employment.

The policy contained conditions which, among others, provided that the insured might nominate an appointed representative but the insurers were d entitled to reject any particular choice of appointed representative without explanation, and that the insurers would accept a claim only when it had a reasonable chance of success.

In July 1990 Miss Nicholson began proceedings against her landlord for damages for breach of a repairing covenant in her lease. The landlord counterclaimed for possession. The insurers agreed to pay Miss Nicholson's costs e in connection with the action up to the limit of indemnity of £50,000 in accordance with the terms of the policy. The claimant was appointed her appointed representative under the policy and acted for her throughout the action.

At the trial of the action in 1993 Miss Nicholson was granted relief from f forfeiture on condition that she paid arrears of rent and costs to the landlord. This she failed to do, and on 28 October 1993 she was adjudged bankrupt on a petition presented by the landlord.

On 10 August 1993 the claimant delivered a final bill to Miss Nicholson in the sum of approximately £69,000. She wrote to the insurers protesting about the bill and informing them of her bankruptcy. On 15 November 1993 the insurers g sought her written authority to pay to the claimant the balance of the indemnity available under the policy, which then came to just over £21,000. Miss Nicholson declined to authorise any payment to the claimant except for a small amount in respect of the outstanding fees of an expert.

On 17 November 1993 the claimant issued a writ against Miss Nicholson h claiming the outstanding amount of the final bill. Judgment in default of notice of intention to default was entered on 10 December 1993. Thereupon the claimant wrote to Avon claiming direct payment of the balance of the insurance monies available under the 1930 Act.

Avon's position was an entirely honourable one. They were perfectly happy j to pay the balance of the sum insured and would have done so, with knowledge of Miss Nicholson's bankruptcy, if she had consented. But they took the view that, as matter of strict law, the 1930 Act was not available to the claimant and in this they were supported by advice given to them by the Insolvency Service. So they declined to make the payment requested by the claimant. The claimant therefore brought this action against Avon for the remaining balance available under Miss Nicholson's policy.

In their defence, the insurers pleaded that the legal expenses insurance was not an insurance of liability such that the 1930 Act conferred rights on the claimant in this case. In those circumstances an order was made by consent that there should be a trial of a preliminary issue whether Miss Nicholson's policy was an insurance of liability such that the 1930 Act conferred rights on the claimant in this case.

It is well known that the 1930 Act was prompted by concerns expressed in road accident cases where an injured person obtained judgment against a careless motorist's employer which went into liquidation before satisfying the judgment. The result under the law as it stood before the 1930 Act was that the injured person had to prove in the company's liquidation and the money paid by the insurance company to the company, in order to satisfy the judgment, went to the general body of creditors. This was widely regarded as unsatisfactory and led to the passing of the 1930 Act. The wording of the 1930 Act, however, was not confined to road traffic cases or to liabilities in negligence.

Section 1(1) of the 1930 Act provides:

> 'Where under any contract of insurance a person (hereinafter referred to as the insured) is insured against liabilities to third parties which he may incur, then—(a) in the event of the insured becoming bankrupt or making a composition or arrangement with his creditors; or (b) in the case of the insured being a company, in the event of a winding-up order being made … if, either before or after that event, any such liability as aforesaid is incurred by the insured, his rights against the insurer under the contract in respect of the liability shall, notwithstanding anything in any Act or rule of law to the contrary, be transferred to and vest in the third party to whom the liability was so incurred.'

The insurance market has developed widely since 1930 and one of its more recent developments has been LEI. The concept is not entirely new. Mance Goldrein and Merkin point out in their book *Insurance Disputes* (1999) para 21.10 that defence costs of shipowners and charterers have been underwritten by P&I clubs for a very long time. It has also been common for very many years for professional indemnity policies to provide cover, not only against damages and costs awarded to claimants up to a specified limit of indemnity, but also to provide cover, often unlimited, in respect of defence costs incurred with the insurers' consent. But the marketing of LEI has grown apace in recent years and now plays an important part in the funding of litigation.

The Law Commission is presently considering the need for amendment of the 1930 Act in the light of changes in law and practice which have occurred since it was passed. In 1998 it issued a consultative report (*Third Parties (Rights Against Insurers) Act 1930: A Joint Consultative Report* (Law Com No 152)) in which legal expenses insurance received the following mention in a footnote (at p 97):

> 'It has been suggested that the Act does not apply, in any event, to legal expenses insurance as such insurance is classed under the Insurance Companies Act 1982 as a contract of first party pecuniary loss insurance rather than as liability insurance and as the failure of the insured to pay his legal adviser is distinguishable from other breaches of contract and from other events leading to the incurring of liability. See N Stanbury "Legal Expenses Insurance: beware of insolvent insureds" [1996] 92 BILA Journal 26.'

Mr Stanbury's article is interesting. He argues that the 1930 Act was intended to deal with 'a conventional contract of liability insurance', whereas LEI 'is a essentially a contract of first party pecuniary loss insurance intended to reimburse the insured for an expense which he has necessarily incurred'.

Mr Stanbury developed the distinction in the following passage:

> 'Under LEI, the insured's obligation is to pay his appointed representative's proper fees in consideration for having the benefit of agreed professional b advice and/or representation. This is a direct and fundamental liability of the insured as a term of the contract itself and can be distinguished from the more remote and less quantifiable liability (to the solicitor or some other party) arising from some breach of the contract, or arising in tort based on the contractual relationship, or arising in tort independently of the contract. In other words, is the foreseeable and controllable obligation to make a c payment voluntarily accepted under contract to be equated with the unlooked for and potentially unavoidable liability in tort for which insured indemnity is, as a matter of public policy, to be recoverable by the plaintiff notwithstanding the defendant's insolvency? Why should the Act protect the unpaid appointed representative when it is unlikely that, mutatis d mutandis, the unpaid repairer of a damaged motor vehicle, or the unpaid supplier of a replacement for stolen property, would be able to invoke the Act, even though the person with whom they had contracted was insured against such a loss.'

Counsel's argument on each side was attractively simple and concise. e Mr Davies, for the claimant, submits that the claim falls within the natural construction of the words of the 1930 Act. Both parties, he submits, foresaw when entering into the contract of insurance that in the running of Miss Nicholson's business she might become involved in litigation, with attendant legal liabilities either to her own solicitor or to the opposing party in the proceedings, and the f object of the LEI section of the policy was to provide indemnity against such liabilities up to the limit and within the terms of the policy. She was, therefore, insured against liabilities to third parties which she might incur. The fact that such a policy might itself in 1930 have been void for maintenance is not relevant, he submits, to the transferability of the insured's right in the policy under the principle created by s 1 of the 1930 Act.

g Mr Christie, for the insurers, adopted Mr Stanbury's argument. He submitted that the 1930 Act applies only to liability insurance as conventionally understood, i e insurance covering liability for damage caused to another person by some fault of the insured and not the insured person's own pecuniary loss; so there is not a 'liability' within the meaning of the 1930 Act. He also submitted that, in so far as h this LEI provides for cover in respect of the costs of the insured's own solicitor, it does not provide cover for liability to a third party; it provides cover for the insured's own loss in her voluntarily incurring a contract debt; so there is not a 'third party' within the meaning of the 1930 Act.

Although these were advanced as separate points they are, in my view, j different ways of advancing what is essentially one point. If Mr Christie is wrong in his approach on the question whether there is a liability within the meaning of the policy, then the claimant is a third party, i e someone other than the insured. Mr Christie accepted that insofar as the LEI provides cover against an opposing party's costs or cover against an award, it falls within the ambit of the 1930 Act. But he distinguishes between those parts of the LEI and that part which provides indemnity against the costs of the insured's own appointed representative.

Mr Christie placed reliance on the categorisation of insurance business under the Insurance Companies Acts and Insurance Companies (Classes of General Business) Regulations 1977, SI 1977/1552 under which LEI is not grouped as liability insurance. I do not find that particularly helpful because those provisions have a self-contained regulatory purpose and, as I have already commented, it is common ground that other parts of this LEI do fall within the scope of the 1930 Act, albeit that for regulatory purposes they would not be classed as indemnity insurance.

However, I have found the fundamental problem posed in this case very difficult. I am troubled by the unfairness of the result and the wider implications if the insurers' argument is correct. I also have trouble with the claimant's approach as a matter of construction, and I do not see a way of construing the 1930 Act so as to produce a fair and desirable result in all cases.

If the claimant acted for Miss Nicholson in the knowledge of her LEI, it would seem only fair that the balance of the insurance money available to her should go towards the claimant's costs rather than to her general creditors (or, since apparently the trustee in bankruptcy did not make a claim under the policy within the period specified in the policy, that it should be retained by the insurers).

This case may, on its facts, seem out of the ordinary in that the insurers were happy to have paid the claimant with Miss Nicholson's consent, knowing of her bankruptcy, and they only refrained from doing so because of her objection. But if their argument is right, Mr Christie accepts and indeed submits that they would have had no business to pay the claimant, even with her consent, after she became bankrupt, because the proceeds of the policy ought to have gone to her trustee for the benefit of her general creditors. Once that is recognised, the potential seriousness of the matter for solicitors acting for clients with LEI is obvious. If they are to guard against the insolvency risk, they need to ensure that they have adequate money on account or are otherwise secured for their fees, possibly by assignment in advance of the benefits of the policy. They cannot regard the client's LEI as available to cover their fees in the event of insolvency, however honourable the intentions of the client may be and however good their relationship with the client.

So the construction contended for by the insurers produces a result with which I am frankly not happy on the facts of this case, and has implications for all concerned in this class of work which they are likely to find disturbing. But there are difficulties to my mind, both historic and substantive, in construing 'liabilities to third parties which he may incur' as including a simple contract debt voluntarily incurred. As a matter of legislative history, it is improbable that the draftsman of the 1930 Act intended such a broad meaning.

There are other forms of insurance, apart from LEI, which would be affected by such a broad construction. Take the example of medical insurance. If a patient gives details of his medical insurance cover to a hospital on admission and the hospital treats him on the basis that the costs will be covered by the insurance, there is obvious injustice if, on his intervening insolvency, the proceeds of the insurance policy cannot go to the hospital, even though the patient may wish it, but must go rather to the general creditors. If, however, nothing was said about insurance at the time when treatment was provided, it is difficult to see on what principle the hospital should have any claim over money which might happen to be available to the patient under some insurance policy which covered his costs of treatment.

a I do not think that it is possible by mere construction of s 1 of the 1930 Act to achieve what might be considered a desirable result in these different situations. I have looked at the Contracts (Rights of Third Parties) Act 1999 to see whether that now affords a solution to the problem but I do not consider that it does or, at any rate, not a complete solution.

I have to choose between construing the words 'where a person is insured b against liabilities to third parties which he may incur' as limited to insurance against liabilities which may be imposed on that person by operation of law, whether for breach of contract or in tort, or as including the underwriting of liabilities voluntarily undertaken by that person, ie the payment of contract debts. I do not believe that the words were intended to include the latter. So with regret on the facts of the present case, I would hold that the claimant has no right c of claim against the insurers under the 1930 Act.

I do not regard the result as satisfactory but, in my view, the solution lies in amendment of the 1930 Act. I hope that this matter will therefore receive the attention of the Law Commission in its final report.

LEI is now a significant feature of litigation, and affording appropriate rights to d the various affected parties presents some quite difficult problems. They include potential problems of priorities where LEI covers both the insured's own costs and liability for the costs of another party. These matters need consideration on a wider basis than I have been able to give in deciding the present case.

Order accordingly.

James Wilson Barrister (NZ).

Practice Note

a

SUPREME COURT
LORD WOOLF CJ
8 APRIL 2001

b

Practice – Citation of cases in civil courts – Restrictions and rules – Categories of judgments citeable only if purporting to establish new principle or extend present law – Requirement for advocates to indicate proposition of law demonstrated by each authority cited.

c

LORD WOOLF CJ gave the following direction at the sitting of the court.

Introduction

1. In recent years, there has been a substantial growth in the number of readily available reports of judgments in this and other jurisdictions, such reports being available either in published reports or in transcript form. Widespread d knowledge of the work and decisions of the courts is to be welcomed. At the same time, however, the current weight of available material causes problems both for advocates and for courts in properly limiting the nature and amount of material that is used in the preparation and argument of subsequent cases.

2. The latter issue is a matter of rapidly increasing importance. Recent and e continuing efforts to increase the efficiency, and thus reduce the cost, of litigation, whilst maintaining the interests of justice, will be threatened if courts are burdened with a weight of inappropriate and unnecessary authority, and if advocates are uncertain as to the extent to which it is necessary to deploy authorities in the argument of any given case.

3. With a view to limiting the citation of previous authority to cases that are f relevant and useful to the court, this Practice Direction lays down a number of rules as to what material may be cited, and the manner in which that cited material should be handled by advocates. These rules are in large part such as many courts already follow in pursuit of their general discretion in the management of litigation. However, it is now desirable to promote uniformity of practice by the g same rules being followed by all courts.

4. It will remain the duty of advocates to draw the attention of the court to any authority not cited by an opponent which is adverse to the case being advanced.

5. This Direction applies to all courts apart from criminal courts, including within the latter category the Court of Appeal (Criminal Division).

h

Categories of judgments that may only be cited if they fulfil specified requirements

6.1. A judgment falling into one of the categories referred to in para 6.2 below may not in future be cited before any court unless it clearly indicates that it purports to establish a new principle or to extend the present law. In respect of judgments delivered after the date of this Direction, that indication must take the j form of an express statement to that effect. In respect of judgments delivered before the date of this Direction that indication must be present in or clearly deducible from the language used in the judgment.

6.2. Paragraph 6.1 applies to the following categories of judgment: applications attended by one party only; applications for permission to appeal; decisions on applications that only decide that the application is arguable; county court cases, unless (a) cited in order to illustrate the conventional measure of damages in a personal injury case, or (b) cited in a county court in order to demonstrate current authority at that level on an issue in respect of which no decision at a higher level of authority is available.

6.3. These categories will be kept under review, such review to include consideration of adding to the categories.

Citation of other categories of judgment

7.1. Courts will in future pay particular attention, when it is sought to cite other categories of judgment, to any indication given by the court delivering the judgment that it was seen by that court as only applying decided law to the facts of the particular case; or otherwise as not extending or adding to the existing law.

7.2. Advocates who seek to cite a judgment that contains indications of the type referred to in para 7.1 will be required to justify their decision to cite the case.

Methods of citation

8.1. Advocates will in future be required to state, in respect of each authority that they wish to cite, the proposition of law that the authority demonstrates, and the parts of the judgment that support that proposition. If it is sought to cite more than one authority in support of a given proposition, advocates must state the reason for taking that course.

8.2. The demonstration referred to in para 8.1 will be required to be contained in any skeleton argument and in any appellant's or respondent's notice in respect of each authority referred to in that skeleton or notice.

8.3. Any bundle or list of authorities prepared for the use of any court must in future bear a certification by the advocate responsible for arguing the case that the requirements of this paragraph have been complied with in respect of each authority included.

8.4. The statements referred to in para 8.1 should not materially add to the length of submissions or of skeleton arguments, but should be sufficient to demonstrate, in the context of the advocate's argument, the relevance of the authority or authorities to that argument and that the citation is necessary for a proper presentation of that argument.

Authorities decided in other jurisdictions

9.1. Cases decided in other jurisdictions can, if properly used, be a valuable source of law in this jurisdiction. At the same time, however, such authority should not be cited without proper consideration of whether it does indeed add to the existing body of law.

9.2. In future, therefore, any advocate who seeks to cite an authority from another jurisdiction must (i) comply, in respect of that authority, with the rules set out in para 8 above; (ii) indicate in respect of each authority what that authority adds that is not to be found in authority in this jurisdiction; or, if there is said to be justification for adding to domestic authority, what that justification is; (iii) certify that there is no authority in this jurisdiction that precludes the acceptance by the court of the proposition that the foreign authority is said to establish.

9.3. For the avoidance of doubt, paras 9.1 and 9.2 do not apply to cases decided in either the Court of Justice of the European Communities or the organs of the European Convention of Human Rights. Because of the status in English law of such authority, as provided by, respectively, s 3 of the European Communities Act 1972 and s 2(1) of the Human Rights Act 1998, such cases are covered by the earlier paragraphs of this Direction. a

Kate O'Hanlon Barrister.

a

Three Rivers District Council and others v Bank of England (No 3)

[2001] UKHL/16

b

HOUSE OF LORDS

LORD STEYN, LORD HOPE OF CRAIGHEAD, LORD HUTTON, LORD HOBHOUSE OF WOODBOROUGH AND LORD MILLETT

15–18 JANUARY, 22 MARCH 2001

c

Bank – Deposit-taking business – Control by Bank of England – Bank's supervisory role over commercial banks in the United Kingdom – Depositors with licensed deposit-taker suffering loss when deposit-taker failing because of fraud – Depositors alleging loss caused by Bank of England wrongly granting licence or wrongly failing to revoke deposit-taker's licence – Depositors claiming damages for tort of misfeasance in public office – Judge concluding that claim bound to fail on basis of report into collapse of d *deposit-taker – Whether judge erring in relying on inquiry report – Whether claim having no real prospect of success.*

In 1980 the Bank of England granted a licence to BCCI to carry on business as a deposit-taking institution. In so doing, the Bank was acting in its capacity as e the supervisory authority for United Kingdom deposit-takers under the Banking Act 1979. BCCI collapsed in 1991 owing to fraud on a vast scale perpetrated by its senior staff. Shortly afterwards, a Court of Appeal judge was invited to conduct a non-statutory private inquiry into the supervision of BCCI under the Banking Acts, to consider whether the action taken by the United Kingdom authorities was timely and to make recommendations. His report (the f Bingham report) contained an account of the entire sequence of events based on oral and written evidence from a large number of witnesses, including representatives from the Bank and BCCI's auditors. It also contained numerous findings of fact and expressions of opinion relevant to the questions comprised within the inquiry's terms of reference. Subsequently, several thousand depositors g brought proceedings against the Bank, seeking to recover the sums which they had lost on BCCI's collapse. They claimed that the Bank was liable in the tort of misfeasance in public office, contending that named senior officials had acted in bad faith by licensing BCCI when they knew that was unlawful, by shutting their eyes to what was happening at BCCI after the licence was granted and by failing to take steps to close BCCI at least by the mid-1980s. On the hearing of h preliminary issues, the judge, relying heavily on the Bingham report's findings and conclusions, held that the material before him contained no arguable support for the depositors' case and that there were no reasonable grounds for supposing that further evidence relating to the Bank's state of mind would become available. Accordingly, he concluded that the claim was bound to fail and j therefore struck it out. That decision was upheld by the majority of the Court of Appeal who followed the judge's approach to the Bingham report. On the depositors' appeal to the House of Lords, their Lordships determined the proper test for misfeasance in public office, and adjourned the appeal for further argument. Subsequently, the depositors served new draft particulars on the Bank. When the matter came back before the House of Lords, the Bank submitted that the claim was plainly and obviously unsustainable, that the decision to strike out the claim should therefore be upheld and that it should be given summary judgment under CPR Pt 24. *a*

Held – (Lord Hobhouse and Lord Millett dissenting) When determining whether a claim should be struck out, a court was not entitled to treat a report of the findings of a non-statutory private inquiry as conclusive on the questions a judge had to answer in the litigation or to conclude that all the available material *b* evidence on those questions had been gathered in. Neither the report nor any of its findings or conclusions would be admissible at any trial. Accordingly, in the instant case the judge and the majority of the Court of Appeal had been wrong to rely on the findings and the conclusions of the Bingham report when determining whether the claim should be struck out. The depositors had not been represented before the inquiry, the case against the Bank had not been put by counsel and the *c* investigation had been carried out behind closed doors. It followed that it was open to their Lordships to take a fresh look at the issue of strike-out, and to reconsider the depositors' draft new particulars. When examining those particulars, it was necessary to consider some of the essential elements of the tort of misfeasance in public office. First, there had to be an unlawful act or omission *d* done or made in the exercise of power by the public officer. Secondly, as the essence of the tort was an abuse of power, the act or omission had to have been done or made with the required mental element. Thirdly, the act or omission had to have been done or made in bad faith. Where the allegation was one of untargeted malice, the required mental element was satisfied if the act or omission was done or made intentionally by the public officer in the knowledge *e* that it was beyond his powers and that it would probably cause the claimant to suffer injury, or recklessly because, although he was aware that there was a serious risk that the claimant would suffer loss due to an act or omission which he knew to be unlawful, he wilfully chose to disregard that risk. As regards that form of the tort, the fact that the act or omission was done or made without an *f* honest belief that it was lawful was sufficient to satisfy the requirement of bad faith. Bad faith would be demonstrated by knowledge of probable loss on the part of the public officer or by recklessness on his part in disregarding the risk. The facts pleaded by the depositors in their fresh pleadings were capable of meeting the requirements of the tort. There was an unequivocal plea that the Bank was acting throughout in bad faith and any question as to whether the evidence *g* pointed to negligence rather than to misfeasance in public office was a matter which had to be judged not on the pleading, but on the evidence, which was a matter for decision by the trial judge. The question whether the Bank knew that loss to the depositors was probable or was reckless in the relevant sense could not be answered satisfactorily without hearing oral evidence. It could not be said, *h* therefore, that the claim had no real prospect of success, and justice required that the depositors be given an opportunity to present their case at trial so that its merits might be assessed in the light of the evidence. Accordingly, the Bank's application for summary judgment would be rejected and the depositors' appeal would be allowed (see [1], [5], [6], [8], [42]–[46], [56], [77]–[86], [95], [106]–[111], *j* [125]–[129], [132], [133], [137]–[139] and [144]–[152], post).

Decision of the Court of Appeal [1999] 4 All ER 800n reversed in part.

Notes

For deliberate abuse of public office or authority, see 1(1) *Halsbury's Laws* (4th edn reissue) para 203.

Cases referred to in opinions

Armitage v Nurse [1997] 2 All ER 705, [1998] Ch 241, [1997] 3 WLR 1046, CA.
Ashmore v Corp of Lloyd's [1992] 2 All ER 486, [1992] 1 WLR 446, HL.
Belmont Finance Corp Ltd v Williams Furniture Ltd [1979] 1 All ER 118, [1979] Ch 250, [1978] 3 WLR 712, CA.
Bourgoin SA v Ministry of Agriculture Fisheries and Food [1985] 3 All ER 585, [1986] QB 716, [1985] 3 WLR 1027, QBD and CA.
British Airways Pension Trustees Ltd v Sir Robert McAlpine & Sons Ltd (1994) 45 Con LR 1, CA.
Bullivant v A-G for Victoria [1901] AC 196, [1900–3] All ER Rep 812, HL.
Davey v Bentinck [1893] 1 QB 185, [1891–4] All ER Rep 691, CA.
Davy v Garrett (1878) 7 Ch D 473, CA.
Dellow's Will Trusts, Re, Lloyds Bank Ltd v Institute of Cancer Research [1964] 1 All ER 771, [1964] 1 WLR 451.
Drummond-Jackson v British Medical Association [1970] 1 All ER 1094, [1970] 1 WLR 688, CA.
Dunlop v Woollahra Municipal Council [1981] 1 All ER 1202, [1982] AC 158, [1981] 2 WLR 693, PC.
H (minors) (sexual abuse: standard of proof), Re [1996] 1 All ER 1, [1996] AC 563, [1996] 2 WLR 8, HL.
Harris v Bolt Burdon [2000] CPLR 9, CA.
Jarvis v Hampshire CC [2000] 2 FCR 310, CA; *rvsd* [2000] 4 All ER 504, [2000] 3 WLR 776, HL.
Jonesco v Beard [1930] AC 298, [1930] All ER Rep 483, HL.
Manifest Shipping Co Ltd v Uni-Polaris Shipping Co Ltd [2001] UKHL/1, [2001] 1 All ER 743, [2001] 2 WLR 170, HL.
Margulies v Margulies [2000] CA Transcript 444.
McDonald's Corp v Steel [1995] 3 All ER 615, CA.
McPhilemy v Times Newspapers Ltd [1999] 3 All ER 775, CA.
Medcalf v Mardell (2001) Times, 2 January, [2000] CA Transcript 2015.
Monsanto plc v Tilly (1999) Times, 30 September, [1999] CA Transcript 1924.
Moor v Lawson (1915) 31 TLR 418, CA.
Morris v Bank of America National Trust [2000] 1 All ER 954, CA.
Northern Territory of Australia v Mengel (1995) 185 CLR 307, Aust HC.
Purdy v Cambran [1999] CPLR 843, CA.
Sinclair v Chief Constable of West Yorkshire [2000] CA Transcript 2189.
Steamship Mutual Underwriting Association Ltd v Trollope & Colls Ltd (1986) 6 Con LR 11, CA.
Swain v Hillman [2001] 1 All ER 91, CA.
Taylor v Midland Bank Trust Co Ltd [1999] CA Transcript 1200.
Wallingford v Mutual Society (1880) 5 App Cas 685, HL.
Wenlock v Moloney [1965] 2 All ER 871, [1965] 1 WLR 1238, CA.
White v White [2001] UKHL/9, [2001] 2 All ER 43, [2001] 1 WLR 481, HL.
Williams and Humbert Ltd v W & H Trade Marks (Jersey) Ltd, Rumasa SA v Multinvest (UK) Ltd [1986] 1 All ER 129, [1986] AC 368, [1986] 2 WLR 24, HL.

Appeal

The claimants, Three Rivers District Council and 6,018 other depositors with the Bank of Credit and Commerce International SA (in liquidation), appealed with leave from the decision of the Court of Appeal (Hirst and Robert Walker LJJ, Auld LJ dissenting) on 4 December 1998 ([1999] 4 All ER 800n, [2000] 2 WLR 15) dismissing their appeal from the decision of Clarke J on 1 April and 10 May 1996 ([1996] 3 All ER 558) and 30 July 1997 striking out proceedings for damages for misfeasance in public office and breach of Council Directive (EEC) 77/780 brought by them against the defendant, the Bank of England. On 18 May 2000 ([2000] 3 All ER 1, [2000] 2 WLR 1220) the House of Lords dismissed the appeal in respect of the claim under the directive, determined the requirements of the tort of misfeasance in public office and adjourned the appeal for further argument in respect of the misfeasance claim. The facts are set out in the opinion of Lord Hope of Craighead.

Lord Neill of Bladen QC, Richard Sheldon QC, Robin Dicker QC, Dominic Dowley and *Barry Isaacs* (instructed by *Lovells*) for the claimants.

Nicholas Stadlen QC, Mark Phillips QC, Bankim Thanki and *Ben Valentin* (instructed by *Freshfields Bruckhaus Deringer*) for the Bank.

Their Lordships took time for consideration.

22 March 2001. The following opinions were delivered.

LORD STEYN. My Lords,

[1] For the reasons given by my noble and learned friends, Lord Hope of Craighead and Lord Hutton, I would also allow the appeal. While it is unnecessary for me to cover the same ground, I must state in outline the principal factors that proved decisive in my approach to the case.

[2] It is right at the outset to emphasise that in substance one is dealing with a striking-out application. The Bank of England (the Bank) submitted that the claims are plainly and obviously unsustainable. In aid of this submission the Bank deployed a written case of no less than 737 pages, amplified by many pages of written aids and lengthy oral argument. It was hardly a simple and obvious case for a striking out. At the end of the argument my views were that the Bank had not succeeded in establishing that it would be right and fair to strike out the claims. Having studied with care the judgments below, as well as the draft speeches on the appeal to the House, I am reinforced in my first view by a combination of the dissenting judgment of Auld LJ in the Court of Appeal, and by the majority speeches of Lord Hope and Lord Hutton.

[3] It is necessary to test the question whether the action should be struck out against the new draft particulars of claim drafted and served after the first hearing (see [2000] 3 All ER 1 at 13, [2000] 2 WLR 1220 at 1236).

[4] The case fell into two distinct parts. The first question was whether the plaintiffs have pleaded a reasonable cause of action. In essence this was a demurrer point. With due deference to contrary views I have to say that I was unimpressed by the Bank's technical arguments under this heading. The new draft particulars of claim plead the case in misfeasance in public office in clear terms and in sufficient detail to enable the Bank to prepare a defence. The Bank does not need any further particulars. I would reject the Bank's arguments under this heading.

[5] The second question was whether the action is an abuse of the court's process in that it has no realistic prospect of success. This is the more difficult and controversial aspect of the appeal. The Court of Appeal was divided on the issue. The dissenting judgment of Auld LJ is an impressive one. The judgments of Clarke J at first instance ([1996] 3 All ER 558 and 30 July 1997 (unreported)) and of the majority (Hirst and Walker LJJ) in the Court of Appeal ([1999] 4 All ER 800n,

a [2000] 2 WLR 15) are detailed and careful. Unfortunately, however, the use made by the judge and by the majority in the Court of Appeal of the Bingham report of October 1992 (*Inquiry into the Supervision of the Bank of Credit and Commerce International* (HC Paper 198 (1992–93))) was not permissible. The report is self-evidently an outstanding one produced by an eminent judge. But in law the judge and the majority erred in relying on positive conclusions and findings, and b absence of conclusions and findings, of Bingham LJ. Not only was such use of the report ruled out by settled principles of law but on broader grounds it was also unfair to the claimants. After all, the report was the outcome of a private inquiry, the claimants were not represented before Bingham LJ and the case against the Bank was not put by counsel. And the appendices to the report, which recount the history in greater detail, were not published and have never been seen by c those representing the claimants.

[**6**] In these circumstances it is necessary for the House to consider the matter entirely afresh. Since I share the views of Lord Hope and Lord Hutton I do not propose to revisit the battleground. But I must emphasise that it is indisputably the case that the Bank knew from April 1990 onwards that BCCI was in imminent d danger of collapse with inevitable loss to depositors unless there was a real prospect of an effective rescue package. The Bank has failed to persuade me that the claimants have no realistic prospect of establishing that the Bank knew that there would be no effective and comprehensive rescue or was reckless as to whether there would be one. Moreover, I do not share the confidence of the judge and the majority in the Court of Appeal that discovery and cross-examination will e not produce significant materials assisting the claimants. It is a case that should be examined and tested with the procedural advantages of a fair and public trial.

[**7**] My conclusion is therefore strongly influenced by the events from April 1990. On the other hand, I also take the view that the earlier part of the history cannot be excised. The interests of justice require that the entire action should be f permitted to go to trial. This conclusion involves no judgment about the likely outcome of the case but merely a finding that the threshold requirement for striking out has not been satisfied.

[**8**] I would, therefore, allow the appeal, dismiss the cross-appeal and give leave to the claimants to amend their pleading in terms of the new draft particulars of claim. Like Lord Hope I regard the supplementary directions sought by the g claimants as entirely reasonable, but on balance I would also leave it to the commercial judge to give appropriate directions. I apprehend that he will wish to proceed to trial with due despatch and a minimum of technical interlocutory hearings. And in proceeding to trial it is axiomatic that the trial judge will have to approach this case in a neutral fashion and without preconceptions. He will h have to ignore expressions of opinion *on the facts* in any of the speeches.

[**9**] At the request of the Bank the issue of costs is reserved. Written submissions on costs are invited within 21 days.

LORD HOPE OF CRAIGHEAD. My Lords,

j [**10**] At the previous hearing of this appeal your Lordships were concerned only with two questions of law. The first related to the ingredients of the tort of misfeasance in public office on which the plaintiffs' first ground of action depends. The second was whether the Bank of England (the Bank) was capable of being liable to the plaintiffs in damages for violation of the requirements of the First Council Banking Co-ordination Directive, Council Directive (EEC) 77/780 of 12 December 1977, on the co-ordination of laws, regulations and administrative provisions relating to the taking up and pursuit of the business of credit institutions (OJ 1977 L322 p 30) (the directive). For the reasons given in your Lordships' judgment of 18 May 2000 ([2000] 3 All ER 1, [2000] 2 WLR 1220) the second question was answered in the negative. It is not necessary to give any further consideration to the Community law issues. They no longer form any part of the plaintiffs' case against the Bank. At the further hearing of the appeal with which this judgment deals your Lordships' task has been to consider whether the facts alleged or capable of being alleged by the plaintiffs meet the test for the tort of misfeasance in public office which were identified by your Lordships in answer to the first question. The question, in short, is whether the order of the Court of Appeal upholding the order of Clarke J that the action should be struck out should be upheld on the ground that the plaintiffs have no reasonable prospect of succeeding on the claim at trial.

[11] Your Lordships have been assisted by the oral arguments which were advanced at the further hearing by Lord Neill of Bladen QC for the plaintiffs and by Mr Stadlen QC for the Bank and by the very substantial amount of written material which has been provided by each side. The issues which have had to be resolved are far from easy. Some indication of their complexity can be gathered from the fact that the written cases for the plaintiffs (including their reply) and for the Bank (including a detailed response on the facts but excluding two appendices) run to 385 and 737 pages respectively. There are two bundles of contemporaneous documents extending to 661 pages and a supplementary bundle of documents which extends to about 300 pages. The amount of material that must be read and understood to see whether the claim should be struck out is formidable. It will be necessary for me before I address the competing arguments to set out some of the facts by way of background.

[12] There are a number of preliminary points. (1) At a procedural hearing which was held on 27 June 2000 nine issues were identified for determination at the further hearing of the appeal. But it became clear in the course of the argument that there was a considerable amount of overlap between one issue and another and that it was more likely to be helpful for them to be looked at cumulatively rather than separately. So I do not propose to examine those issues one by one in this judgment. (2) In his judgment after the first hearing of this appeal my noble and learned friend Lord Steyn said ([2000] 3 All ER 1 at 13, [2000] 2 WLR 1220 at 1236) that at the further hearing there should be available a new draft pleading by the plaintiffs reflecting the position which was recorded in your Lordships' judgments. At the procedural hearing on 27 June 2000 the plaintiffs were required to serve their new draft pleading on the Bank by 17 July 2000, and they duly did so on that date. That new draft pleading is contained in a document entitled 'New draft particulars of claim'. For reasons which I shall explain later in more detail (see section (4)) it is to that document, which I shall call 'the new draft particulars', that I shall for the most part direct my attention when I am discussing the question whether the facts pleaded meet the requirements of the tort. (3) These proceedings were issued before 29 April 1999 under the Rules of the Supreme Court (RSC), which were still in force when the case was in the Court of Appeal. On 29 April 1999 the Civil Procedure Rules 1998, SI 1998/3132 (the CPR) came into force. This case is therefore subject to the transitional arrangements set out in the Practice Direction made under CPR 51.1 (Practice Direction—Transitional Arrangements). In accordance with the general principles which are set out in that practice direction the case is to proceed in the first instance under the previous rules, but any new step taken on or after 26 April 1999

is to be taken under the CPR (see Practice Direction supplementing Pt 51, paras 3, 11).

[13] The parties are agreed that the service of the new draft particulars on the Bank was a new step, and that it follows that the question whether the claim on the ground of misfeasance in public office should be struck out must now be determined under the CPR. As the CPR require that the word 'claimant' be used rather than the word 'plaintiff', I propose to adopt the same terminology from now on throughout this judgment. Rule 3.2 provides, so far as relevant to this case, that the court may strike out a statement of case if it appears to the court (a) that it discloses no reasonable cause of action or (b) that it is an abuse of the court's process. There is no exact dividing line between these two grounds (see *Civil Procedure* (2000 edn) vol 1, para 3.4.2). Mr Stadlen did not attempt to maintain an exact separation between them and in the end, as I shall explain below (in section (5)), he invited your Lordships to give summary judgment against the claimants under CPR 24.2.

[14] I propose to deal with the various matters that require to be considered at this stage in this order: (1) introductory narrative, to include (a) outline chronology, (b) the Bingham report (*Inquiry into the Supervision of the Bank of Credit and Commerce International* (HC Paper 198 (1992–93))) and (c) history of the proceedings to date; (2) the requirements of the tort; (3) whether the facts pleaded by the claimants are capable of meeting those requirements; (4) the decision of the courts below to strike out; (5) the test for summary judgment under CPR 24.2; (6) whether, applying that test, the claim should be summarily struck out; (7) the Bank's cross-appeal; and (8) conclusion and further procedure.

[15] I should also make it clear at the outset that, although I shall be using the expression 'the Bank' throughout this judgment, the claimants' position as explained in their written case is that those who were principally responsible for the regulation and supervision of BCCI SA were the officials of the Banking Supervision Division formed by the Bank in March 1980 for the purpose of implementing the Banking Act 1979 whose names are given in Sch 1 to the particulars to the new draft particulars.

(1) INTRODUCTORY NARRATIVE

(a) *Outline chronology*

[16] The history of the rise and fall of the Bank of Credit and Commerce International SA (BCCI SA) can conveniently be divided up for the purposes of this action into four periods: (1) the period prior to the grant of a full licence under the Banking Act 1979 on 19 June 1980; (2) the period from the grant of the full licence to December 1986; (3) the period from December 1986 to April 1990; and (4) the period from April 1990 to closure in July 1991. This history was set out in great detail by Clarke J in his third judgment of 30 July 1997 (unreported), in which the history was divided up into the same four periods, and it was reviewed again in Pt III of the judgment of the majority in the Court of Appeal of 4 December 1998 ([1999] 4 All ER 800n, [2000] 2 WLR 15) (Pt III of which is also unreported). I do not propose to set out that history all over again. No significance is to be attached to the fact that I have mentioned some events in the course of this narrative and omitted others. What follows is not intended to be a complete or definitive account of what happened. But for the purposes of this judgment it is necessary to provide an outline of the chronology and to identify some of the more important details in that history.

[**17**] BCCI SA was incorporated under the laws of Luxembourg on 21 September 1972. In November it established its first office in the United Kingdom and commenced its business in this country as a deposit-taker. Two years later the structure of BCCI was altered by the incorporation on 13 December 1974 of BCCI Holdings SA (Holdings) in Luxembourg of which BCCI SA became a subsidiary. On 25 November 1975 another subsidiary of Holdings called BCCI Overseas (Overseas) was incorporated in the Cayman Islands. Overseas opened its first branch in the United Kingdom in June 1976. At this stage a substantial part of the issued share capital of Holdings was owned by the Bank of America. Although the group was trading through various branches in the United Kingdom it was not subject to any regulatory system in this country. But Holdings was subject to regulation in Luxembourg by the Luxembourg Banking Commission (LBC) which at that time was that country's regulatory authority. At the end of 1977 the Bank of America decided to withdraw from its relationship with BCCI. It sold its holding of shares in Holdings to International Credit and Investment Co Ltd (ICIC) which at that time was BCCI's largest shareholder.

[**18**] Prior to the enactment of the 1979 Act banking in the United Kingdom was not subject to any formalised system of regulation. Control was exercised in an informal way by the Bank and in an indirect manner by means of various statutory provisions which gave privileges to banks which were recognised by the Board of Trade and by the Bank. Following the publication of a White Paper in 1976 (*The Licensing and Supervision of Deposit-Taking Institutions* (Cmnd 6584)) and the directive steps were taken to establish a new statutory system of banking supervision in the United Kingdom. This was contained in the 1979 Act, which came into force on 1 October 1979. It provided for the recognition of banks under s 3(1) if they satisfied the criteria in Sch 2, Pt I, and for the licensing of deposit-taking institutions under s 3(2) if they satisfied the less stringent criteria in Sch 2, Pt II. Section 3(5) of that Act provided that, in the case of an institution whose principal place of business was in a country or territory outside the United Kingdom, the Bank might regard itself as satisfied that the criteria in Sch 2 regarding those responsible for the management of the business and the prudence with which its business was being conducted were fulfilled if the relevant supervisory authorities informed the Bank that they were satisfied with respect to them and the Bank was satisfied as to the nature and scope of the supervision exercised by those authorities.

[**19**] On 1 October 1979 BCCI SA applied to the Bank for recognition as a bank under the Act. On 19 June 1980 the Bank refused recognition as a bank but granted to BCCI SA a full licence under the 1979 Act as a deposit-taker. By that date its principal place of business was in the United Kingdom. Nevertheless the Bank decided to rely under s 3(5) of the 1979 Act on the supervision of its activities by LBC. The claimants' case is that when the Bank granted the licence; (a) it did so knowingly deliberately contrary to the statutory scheme, or (b) it was recklessly indifferent to whether it was acting in accordance with the scheme, or (c) it wilfully disregarded the risk that it was not acting in accordance with that scheme, (i) in bad faith, and (ii)(a) in the knowledge that the likely consequences were losses to depositors and potential depositors, or (b) that it wilfully disregarded the risk of the consequences, or (c) that it was recklessly indifferent to those consequences (para 31 of the new draft particulars).

[**20**] During the period from June 1980 to December 1986 the activities of the BCCI Group expanded dramatically not only in the United Kingdom but throughout the world. Officials of the Bank pointed out that it was unsatisfactory

a for it as the supervising authority of BCCI SA in the United Kingdom to rely, as it had been doing under s 3(5) of the 1979 Act, on the views of LBC as to the activities of the holding company in Luxembourg. They recognised that, as the activities of BCCI continued to expand, pressure was likely to grow for its recognition as a bank under that Act. Various possible solutions were considered including, on the one hand, a proposal for the Bank to supervise the whole institution and, on the b other, the incorporation of Holdings in the United Kingdom to improve the effectiveness of the Bank's supervision of the group's activities in this country. In September 1984 the effectiveness of the existing statutory regime was called into question by the collapse of Johnson Matthey bankers. In the light of that debacle a further White Paper was produced (*Banking Supervision* (Cmnd 9695) (1985)) and the enactment of a new statute, which was to become the Banking c Act 1987, was proposed. The system introduced by the 1979 Act was to be both strengthened and simplified. In place of the dual system of recognition and licensing a single system of authorisation was to be introduced with restrictions on the use of banking names. The Bank was to be required to establish a committee to be known as the Board of Banking Supervision which was to d include six independent members as well as three members ex officio. Various other changes were to be made to the powers and duties of the Bank as regulatory authority.

[**21**] Meantime the Bank continued to rely on the views of the Luxembourg regulatory authority. In May 1983 the responsibilities of regulatory authority in that country had passed from the LBC to L'Institute Monetaire Luxembourgeois e (IML). Further memoranda passed between officials of the Bank drawing attention yet again to the fact that the real place of business of the BCCI SA was in London and that effectively the Bank and not IML was its prime supervisor. Concern was expressed about heavy losses resulting from BCCI SA's central treasury activities which had been identified by BCCI SA's auditors but not been reported to the f Bank and BCCI's lack of candour about its decision to relocate its central treasury operation from London to Abu Dhabi.

[**22**] The claimants' case regarding this period, which follows the same pattern as that set out in para 31 of the new draft particulars which relates to the first period, is that the Bank was continuing to rely on assurances from LBC and IML and, that despite its knowledge of the illegality of this arrangement and the g likelihood of losses to depositors, it failed in bad faith to take steps to revoke BCCI SA's licence under s 7 of the 1979 Act.

[**23**] The next period was marked by a number of changes in the supervisory regime and further expressions of concern about the activities of BCCI. The 1987 Act came into force on 1 October 1987. Section 3(5) of the 1979 Act was replaced by h an equivalent provision in s 9(3) of the 1987 Act. BCCI SA was deemed to be authorised under the 1987 Act by s 107 of that Act and Sch 5, para 2. An international co-operative group, known as 'the College', was established to enable the various national supervisors of the operations of the BCCI Group to meet twice yearly to discuss its financial condition. Concern was expressed at meetings j of the College about a large concentration of exposures due to the group's lending and the effect on the group's activities of the arrest of seven of its officials in Tampa, Florida in October 1988 on charges of drug trafficking, money-laundering and conspiracy. Further consideration was given to proposals for the restructuring of the group's activities with a view to achieving effective consolidated supervision in London by the Bank. On 30 January 1990 the Bank decided to continue BCCI SA's authorisation following a decision of the Tampa prosecutor to enter into a

plea-bargain agreement, approved by the court, by which BCCI SA and Overseas pleaded guilty to all counts of money-laundering and conspiracy. Concerns were expressed to the Bank by the group's auditors, Price Waterhouse, about the probity of BCCI's senior management. *a*

[24] The claimants' case regarding this period contains three specific allegations about decisions by the Bank not to withdraw the authorisation from BCCI SA. These are said to have been taken: (1) after the Bank had learned in May 1986 that BCCI, which had been dealing on a massive scale in the financial and commodity markets through its central treasury in London, had incurred losses amounting to some $US 285m (new draft particulars, Sch 5, paras 26 and 27); (2) after a paper prepared by the Bank for the Board of Banking Supervision in November 1989 had revealed serious defects in the group's structure and the existing supervisory regime and the extent to which BCCI's activities in the United Kingdom were dependent upon what happened elsewhere in the group which was largely unsupervised (new draft particulars, Sch 6, para 19); and (3) after the officials of BCCI had pleaded guilty in Tampa, Florida in January 1990 to charges of money-laundering and conspiracy (new draft particulars, Sch 6, para 24). *b* *c*

[25] The final period from April 1990 to closure in July 1991 began with expressions of concern to the Bank by Price Waterhouse about the group's serious financial problems and reports about efforts which were being made to obtain financial support from the majority shareholders. On 18 April 1990 Price Waterhouse reported to the board of Holdings that they were unable to sign the 1989 accounts. Later that month they felt able to do so in the light of expressions of support for the group by the Abu Dhabi government. In early June 1990 IML, recognising that they were no longer in a position effectively to supervise their activities, gave notice to Holdings and to BCCI SA that they must leave Luxembourg within the next 12 to 15 months. These matters were discussed at a meeting of the College on 19 June 1990 when IML repeated its ultimatum and the Cayman supervisor said that, if BCCI SA had to leave Luxembourg, Overseas would have to leave Cayman. Further consideration was given to the need for a clear group structure, consolidated supervision of its activities, relocation of the group to Abu Dhabi and the need for a clear and substantial commitment by the Abu Dhabi government of its support for it. *d* *e* *f*

[26] In October 1990 Price Waterhouse reported to Holdings' audit committee that an urgent investigation was needed to quantify the group's liabilities and its need for financial support. On 5 October 1990 a letter was produced to the College on behalf of the majority shareholders undertaking to provide support to the level indicated by Price Waterhouse. But IML refused to extend its deadline unless certain conditions were met and the supervisors did not regard the shareholders' proposals for support as acceptable. By December 1990 a revised support package had been put together which Price Waterhouse regarded as acceptable, but later that month Price Waterhouse became aware of the extent to which BCCI's financial problems were due to fraudulent activities on the part of management. On 4 March 1991 the Bank commissioned Price Waterhouse to investigate and report to it under s 41 of the 1987 Act on malpractice within BCCI. Price Waterhouse delivered their report to the Bank on 24 June 1991. It contained a comprehensive account of widespread frauds and deceptions which had been perpetrated by BCCI. Four days later the Bank decided that the proposed reconstruction of the group could not be pursued and that to protect depositors BCCI SA had to be closed down. On 5 July 1991 the Bank presented a petition for the appointment of a provisional liquidator. *g* *h* *j* a [27] The claimants' case regarding this period, as explained by Lord Neill in oral argument, is based on general allegations that the Bank failed in bad faith to face up to its responsibilities as a supervisor to take decisions that would protect the interests of depositors and potential depositors when it was aware that there was a serious and immediate threat that unless it was rescued by the Abu Dhabi government BCCI would collapse.

b

(b) *The Bingham report*

[28] The closure of BCCI on 5 July 1991 provoked widespread concern in the financial community on the ground that this action was long overdue, yet the action that was taken was criticised by depositors, employees and shareholders as precipitate. In a prompt response to that concern Bingham LJ was invited to c conduct an inquiry into the supervision of BCCI under the Banking Acts, to consider whether the action taken by all the United Kingdom authorities was timely and to make recommendations. The establishment of the inquiry was announced on 19 July 1991. Bingham LJ submitted his report to the Chancellor of the Exchequer and the Governor of the Bank in July 1992. Among the questions d which he understood to call for consideration by his terms of reference were the following. What did the United Kingdom authorities know about BCCI at the relevant times? Should they have known more? And should they have acted differently?

[29] The report (*Inquiry into the Supervision of the Bank of Credit and Commerce International* (HC Paper 198 (1992–93)) contains a masterly and eminently e readable account of the entire sequence of events from the establishment of BCCI in the United Kingdom in 1972 to its closure in July 1991. Bingham LJ took evidence both orally and in writing from a large number of witnesses and he had access to many documents. In his covering letter he paid tribute to the very high level of co-operation which he had received from, among others, the Bank and f the United Kingdom firm of Price Waterhouse, who acted from June 1987 to July 1991 as the group's auditors. He said that in deciding what was said and done during BCCI's 19-year history he had relied heavily on contemporary notes and minutes of meetings and conversations between the Bank and Price Waterhouse. His report contains numerous findings of fact and expression of opinion relevant to the questions which he understood to have been comprised within his terms g of reference. The report was published in October 1992, but eight appendices to the report were not published.

[30] Much of the claimants' pleading has been based upon material taken from that report. This is unsurprising, in view of the fact that the claimants have not yet had the benefit of discovery of documents or the obtaining of answers to h interrogatories. The assumption can properly be made at this stage that the narrative which the report contains will in due course be capable of being established by evidence once the claimants have obtained access to the relevant documents. But there are important limitations on the use which can be made of this document. I shall have to deal with this matter in more detail later when j I come to the arguments relating to strike-out, but I should like to make the following observations at this stage.

[31] The first point that has to be borne in mind is that neither the report itself nor any of its findings or conclusions will be admissible at any trial in this case. At this stage, when the only material that is available for consideration apart from the pleadings is the report and an incomplete bundle of relevant documents, it is tempting to fill in the gaps by reference to Bingham LJ's findings and the conclusions

which he was able to draw from his review of the evidence. Nevertheless a sharp dividing line must be observed between, on the one hand, his narrative of the evidence and, on the other hand, his findings and conclusions in the light of that evidence.

[32] It can, as I have said, be assumed that if the claim is not struck out the claimants will in due course have access to the evidence which provides the source material for that narrative, and that that evidence will be capable of being led by them at the trial. But, as Bingham LJ's findings and conclusions based on that narrative are inadmissible, they must be held to be incapable either of being led in evidence at the trial or of being used by either side in any other way in support of the competing arguments. As Hirst LJ observed in the Court of Appeal ([2000] 2 WLR 15 at 91), no comparable statutory provisions to those which are to be found in s 441 of the Companies Act 1985 apply to the Bingham report. The investigation which Bingham LJ conducted was a private and not a statutory inquiry. The rigorous attention which must be paid to the distinction between what would and what would not be admissible has not always been observed in the written cases, and I had the impression that it was not always being observed during the oral argument. Nor, for reasons which I shall explain later, do I think that it was always observed either by Clarke J or by the majority in the Court of Appeal in their judgments on the issues relating to the question of strike-out. This has an important bearing on the question whether those judgments were soundly based and should be upheld or whether, because they were not soundly based, the question of strike-out is now at large for your Lordships' reconsideration.

[33] A further point that should be noted at this stage about the findings and conclusions in the Bingham report is that they were the result of an investigation that lacked the benefit of statutory powers and was conducted behind closed doors. The claimants were not present nor were they represented. In the conduct of his fact-finding exercise Bingham LJ was, as he said in his covering letter, greatly assisted by the co-operation which he received especially from the Bank and Price Waterhouse. But he had no power to compel the attendance of witnesses or to require the production of documents, and there was no counsel to the inquiry. As the appendices have not been published, the claimants have not had access to all the material which Bingham LJ had before him. None of these observations are intended to suggest that the investigation was incomplete or that the report, for the purposes for which it was prepared, is in any way open to criticism. But it is plain that it cannot be suggested that Bingham LJ was in a position to conduct a fair trial of the issues relating to the tort of misfeasance in public office which the claimants are seeking to raise against the Bank in this case. In these circumstances I agree with the views which Auld LJ expressed in the Court of Appeal (at 180) in his minority judgment when he said that it would not be right to treat the Bingham report as effectively conclusive on the questions that arise in this litigation or to conclude that all the available evidence on those questions has been gathered in.

(c) *History of proceedings to date*

[34] The claimants' writ of summons was issued on 24 May 1993. On 19 July 1995 Clarke J made an order for the following questions to be tried as preliminary issues. (1) Is the defendant capable of being liable to the plaintiffs for the tort of misfeasance in public office? (2) Were the plaintiffs' alleged losses caused in law by the acts or omissions of the defendant? (3) Are the plaintiffs entitled to recover for a the tort of misfeasance in public office as existing depositors or potential depositors?

[35] On 19 July 1995 Clarke J gave the claimants leave to amend their pleadings for the purposes of these preliminary issues. On 21 August 1995 the claimants lodged a reamended statement of claim. Following Clarke J's first and second judgments of 1 April 1996 and 10 May 1996 ([1996] 3 All ER 558 and 634) in which b he expressed his preliminary conclusions on the three preliminary issues, the claimants applied for leave to re-reamend their statement of claim and the Bank made an application for the statement of claim to be struck out. Clarke J heard argument on these applications in November and December 1996. The claimants then proposed a series of further amendments to their proposed re-reamended statement of claim, and an eighth draft was lodged on 6 January 1997.

c [36] After a further hearing in April 1997 when he considered the claim as then formulated Clarke J delivered a judgment on 30 July 1997 (unreported) in which he held that, on the basis of the evidence then available, the claim was bound to fail; that, as there was no reasonable possibility that the claimants would obtain evidence in the future which might enable them to succeed, the claim was bound d to fail in the future; that in these circumstances it would be an abuse of process or vexatious or oppressive to allow the action to proceed; that the application to re-reamend the statement of claim should be refused; and the action should be struck out.

[37] When he was expressing his conclusions in his third judgment on the present material, Clarke J said:

e

> 'I have reached the firm conclusion that on the material available at present the plaintiffs have no arguable case that the Bank dishonestly granted the licence to BCCI or dishonesty failed to revoke the licence or authorisation in circumstances when it knew, believed or suspected that BCCI would probably collapse. There is nothing in the Bingham report or in the f documents which I have seen to support such a conclusion and there is much to contradict it.'

[38] In regard to the future, he recognised that Bingham LJ was not conducting a trial but an inquiry, that he did not see a number of Bank officials, that the witnesses whom he did see were not cross-examined in an adversarial g process and that there was no right of appeal. But he then went on to say that there was in his judgment no realistic possibility that he had not correctly set out the state of mind of the Bank at each stage. He concluded:

> 'In these circumstances I accept Mr Stadlen's further submission that there h is no realistic possibility of more evidence becoming available, whether by further investigation, discovery, cross-examination or otherwise, which might throw light upon the state of mind of the Bank or any of its relevant officials during the period in which BCCI was operating.'

[39] In the Court of Appeal the majority (Hirst and Robert Walker LJJ) upheld j the order pronounced by Clarke J. They asked themselves the question whether the claimants had an arguable case that the Bank actually foresaw BCCI's imminent collapse at each relevant stage. They said that they agreed with the judge's conclusion that, on the material then available, the plaintiffs did not have an arguable case that the Bank actually foresaw BCCI's imminent collapse at each relevant stage. They also agreed with him that ([2000] 2 WLR 15 at 101), in all the circumstances, it was now for all practical purposes inconceivable that new

material would emerge of such significance as to alter that conclusion. Auld LJ dissented as to the test to be applied. He (at 166) did not consider that a claimant in an action for misfeasance in public office who could establish dishonesty in the sense of a knowing and deliberately or recklessly unlawful act by the defendant need also establish some knowledge on the officer's part of consequential damage, whether in the form of foresight or foreseeability. But he (at 175) went on to consider and give his view on the question whether the claim should be struck out on the assumption that the claimants had to establish that the Bank knew, believed or suspected that its conduct would probably cause loss. He said (at 180) that there were no exceptional circumstances to justify departing from the normal rule of leaving the matter to the trial judge.

[**40**] On 21 January 1999 the Court of Appeal gave leave to the claimants to appeal to the House of Lords on the claimants' undertaking to apply to your Lordships for a direction that the correct test for misfeasance in public office should be determined before any consideration of whether the facts alleged or capable of being alleged were capable of meeting that test. On 12 May 1999 your Lordships gave the claimants leave to appeal against the refusal of leave to re-reamend the statement of claim. On 17 July 2000, as they were directed to do at the procedural hearing on 27 June 2000 which followed the delivery of your Lordships' first judgment, the claimants served the new draft particulars on the Bank.

(2) THE REQUIREMENTS OF THE TORT

[**41**] The correct test for misfeasance in public office was established by your Lordships' judgment following the previous hearing of this appeal ([2000] 3 All ER 1, [2000] 2 WLR 1220). I do not wish to repeat or to analyse what your Lordships said in that judgment. But there are two matters with which I must deal. In the first place it is necessary for me to identify my understanding of the various elements in the light of which the question whether the facts pleaded by the claimants in the new draft particulars satisfy its requirements must be tested. In the second place I must examine Mr Stadlen's argument that the claimants' pleadings are based on a misunderstanding of those requirements.

[**42**] The following are the essential elements of the tort which are relevant to the examination of the new draft particulars. First, there must be an unlawful act or omission done or made in the exercise of power by the public officer. Second, as the essence of the tort is an abuse of power, the act or omission must have been done or made with the required mental element. Third, for the same reason, the act or omission must have been done or made in bad faith. Fourth, as to standing, the claimants must demonstrate that they have a sufficient interest to sue the defendant. Fifth, as causation is an essential element of the cause of action, the act or omission must have caused the claimants' loss.

[**43**] As to standing, the interest to sue of those who were already depositors with BCCI is not in doubt. A question has been raised about the interest to sue of potential depositors. This is because a widespread economic effect resulting from the misfeasance does not give a cause of action to the public in general. But the Bank, while reserving the right to pursue the issue at trial, accepts that it is capable of being liable for the tort to claimants who were potential depositors with BCCI at the time of any relevant act or omission of misfeasance by the Bank. As to causation, the Bank submits that it is not capable of having caused loss to depositors or potential depositors where the proximate cause of the loss was the deliberate act of a third party—in this case, fraudulent acts of individuals within

a BCCI. But questions of fact are raised by this argument which are unsuitable for summary determination at this stage.

[44] The first, second and third requirements lie at the heart of the argument. No further explanation is required as to the test which must be met to satisfy the first requirement. As to the second and third requirements, the claimants do not allege that the Bank did or made the acts or omissions intentionally with the b purpose of causing loss to them. The allegation is that this is a case of what is usually called 'untargeted malice'. Where the tort takes this form the required mental element is satisfied where the act or omission was done or made intentionally by the public officer; (a) in the knowledge that it was beyond his powers and that it would probably cause the claimant to suffer injury, or (b) recklessly because, although he was aware that there was a serious risk that the claimant would suffer loss due to c an act or omission which he knew to be unlawful, he wilfully chose to disregard that risk. In regard to this form of the tort, the fact that the act or omission is done or made without an honest belief that it is lawful is sufficient to satisfy the requirement of bad faith. In regard to alternative (a), bad faith is demonstrated by knowledge of probable loss on the part of the public officer. In regard to d alternative (b), it is demonstrated by recklessness on his part in disregarding the risk. The claimants rely on each of these two alternatives.

[45] At the first hearing Mr Stadlen argued that recklessness was not sufficient to satisfy the required mental element. Your Lordships rejected this submission, with the result that it must be assumed for the purposes of the argument at this stage that the claimants are entitled to include this alternative as part of their case. e His argument at the further hearing was that as one of the essential requirements of the tort was knowledge, belief or suspicion that the act or omission would probably cause loss to depositors or potential depositors, in order to achieve harmony between the two alternatives, knowledge, belief or suspicion of 'probable loss' was a necessary element in the case of the alternative of recklessness. f He submitted that without evidence to support this requirement there could be no liability under the second, or 'untargeted malice', limb of the tort.

[46] I would reject these submissions also. The effect of your Lordships' decision following the first hearing is that it is sufficient for the purposes of this limb of the tort to demonstrate a state of mind which amounts to subjective recklessness. g That state of mind is demonstrated where it is shown that the public officer was aware of a serious risk of loss due to an act or omission on his part which he knew to be unlawful but chose deliberately to disregard that risk. Various phrases may be used to describe this concept, such as 'probable loss', 'a serious risk of loss' and 'harm which is likely to ensue'. Although I have used the phrase 'serious risk of loss', I do not think that for present purposes it is necessary to choose between h them. Further attempts to define their meaning would raise issues of fact and degree which are best considered at trial. The absence of an honest belief in the lawfulness of the conduct that gives rise to that risk satisfies the element of bad faith or dishonesty.

j (3) WHETHER THE FACTS PLEADED ARE CAPABLE OF MEETING THE REQUIREMENTS OF THE TORT

[47] The question to which I now turn relates to the adequacy of the pleadings. This is the first of the two broad grounds on which the Bank say the claim should be struck out. The issue here is directed to the sufficiency of the particulars. It is whether, assuming the facts alleged to be true, a case has been made out in the pleadings for alleging misfeasance in public office by the Bank. If it has, then

the question whether the pleading is supported by the evidence is normally left until trial. In *McDonald's Corp v Steel* [1995] 3 All ER 615 at 621 Neill LJ said: a

> 'It is true that a pleader must not put a plea of justification (or indeed a plea of fraud) on the record lightly or without careful consideration of the evidence available or likely to become available. But, as counsel for the plaintiffs recognised in the course of the argument, there will be cases where, provided a plea of justification is properly particularised, a defendant will be entitled to seek support for his case from documents revealed in the course of discovery or from answers to interrogatories.' b

I shall deal later (in section (3)) with the question to which Mr Stadlen directed the main part of his argument. This is whether there are reasonable grounds for thinking that evidence to support the allegations is or is capable of being made available. The question with which I propose to deal at this stage is whether the grounds for the claim have been properly particularised. c

[**48**] The Bank makes much of the fact that the claimants have received numerous warnings of the need for particulars to be given of the facts relied on in support of their allegations and of the many opportunities that they have been given to amend their statement of claim. Your Lordships are invited to infer from the absence of particulars, and in the light of the available evidence, that the claimants are not able to make good their allegations and that on this ground alone Clarke J was right to order that the claim should be struck out. On the other hand the claimants say that the Bank is well aware of the case that they seek to bring and that the Bank's argument is calculated to place an insuperable obstacle in their path. d e

[**49**] In my judgment a balance must be struck between the need for fair notice to be given on the one hand and excessive demands for detail on the other. In *British Airways Pension Trustees Ltd v Sir Robert McAlpine & Sons Ltd* (1994) 45 Con LR 1 at 4–5 Saville LJ said: f

> 'The basic purpose of pleadings is to enable the opposing party to know what case is being made in sufficient detail to enable that party properly to prepare to answer it. To my mind it seems that in recent years there has been a tendency to forget this basic purpose and to seek particularisation even when it is not really required. This is not only costly in itself, but is calculated to lead to delay and to interlocutory battles in which the parties and the court pore over endless pages of pleadings to see whether or not some particular point has or has not been raised or answered, when in truth each party knows perfectly well what case is made by the other and is able properly to prepare to deal with it.' g h

[**50**] These observations were made under the old rules. But the same general approach to pleadings under the CPR was indicated by Lord Woolf MR in *McPhilemy v Times Newspapers Ltd* [1999] 3 All ER 775 at 792–793:

> 'The need for extensive pleadings including particulars should be reduced by the requirement that witness statements are now exchanged. In the majority of proceedings identification of the documents upon which a party relies, together with copies of that party's witness statements, will make the detail of the nature of the case the other side has to meet obvious. This reduces the need for particulars in order to avoid being taken by surprise. This does not mean that pleadings are now superfluous. Pleadings are still j

a required to mark out the parameters of the case that is being advanced by each party. In particular they are still critical to identify the issues and the extent of the dispute between the parties. What is important is that the pleadings should make clear the general nature of the case of the pleader. This is true both under the old rules and the new rules.'

b [51] On the other hand it is clear that as a general rule, the more serious the allegation of misconduct, the greater is the need for particulars to be given which explain the basis for the allegation. This is especially so where the allegation that is being made is of bad faith or dishonesty. The point is well established by authority in the case of fraud.

[52] In *Wallingford v Mutual Society* (1880) 5 App Cas 685 at 697 Lord Selborne LC
c said:

> 'With regard to fraud, if there be any principle which is perfectly well settled, it is that general allegations, however strong may be the words in which they are stated, are insufficient even to amount to an averment of fraud of which any Court ought to take notice.'

d
In the same case Lord Watson said (at 709):

> 'My Lords, it is a well-known and a very proper rule that a general allegation of fraud is not sufficient to infer liability on the part of those who are said to have committed it. And even if that were not the rule of the
> e Common Law, I think the terms of Order XIV. would require the parties to state a very explicit case of fraud, or rather of facts suggesting fraud, because I cannot think that a mere statement that fraud had been committed, is any compliance with the words of that rule which require the Defendant to state facts entitling him to defend. The rule must require not only a general and
> f vague allegation but some actual fact or circumstance or circumstances which taken together imply, or at least very strongly suggest, that a fraud must have been committed, those facts being assumed to be true.'

[53] The Bank says that, as an allegation of misfeasance in public office involves an allegation of dishonesty or bad faith on the part of the public officer,
g particulars must be given of the facts which, if proved, would justify the allegation. It is also said that it is not enough to aver facts which are consistent either with dishonesty or with negligence. Dishonesty or bad faith must be proved, so the facts relied on must point distinctly to dishonesty. Reference was made to *Davy v Garrett* (1878) 7 Ch D 473 at 489 where Thesiger LJ said:

h
> 'It may not be necessary in all cases to use the word "fraud"—indeed in one of the most ordinary cases it is not necessary. An allegation that the Defendant made to the Plaintiff representations on which he intended the Plaintiff to act, which representations were untrue, and known to the Defendant to be untrue, is sufficient. The word "fraud" is not used, but two expressions are
> j used pointing at the state of mind of the Defendant—that he intended the representations to be acted upon, and that he knew them to be untrue. It appears to me that a Plaintiff is bound to shew distinctly that he means to allege fraud. In the present case facts are alleged from which fraud might be inferred, but they are consistent with innocence. They were innocent acts in themselves, and it is not to be presumed that they were done with a fraudulent intention.'

[54] It seems to me that it can no longer seriously be maintained by the Bank that they do not have sufficient notice of the case which is being made against them. It is abundantly clear that what the claimants are seeking to prove is misfeasance in public office. As my noble and learned friend Lord Hutton has pointed out, the draft new particulars contain detailed allegations to the effect that the Bank acted in bad faith. It has all along been common ground that the claimants cannot base their claim against the Bank in negligence. As Hirst LJ observed in the Court of Appeal ([2000] 2 WLR 15 at 32), the immunity which the Bank enjoys under s 1(4) of the 1987 Act unless it is shown that the act or omission was in bad faith goes a long way to explaining why the claimants have undertaken the burden of seeking to prove misfeasance in public office.

[55] In my view this point alone is a sufficient answer to the criticism based on Thesiger LJ's remarks in *Davy v Garrett*. The principle to which those remarks were directed is a rule of pleading. As the Earl of Halsbury LC said in *Bullivant v A-G for Victoria* [1901] AC 196 at 202, [1900–3] All ER Rep 812 at 814, where it is intended that there be an allegation that a fraud has been committed, you must allege it and you must prove it. We are concerned at this stage with what must be alleged. A party is not entitled to a finding of fraud if the pleader does not allege fraud directly and the facts on which he relies are equivocal. So too with dishonesty. If there is no specific allegation of dishonesty, it is not open to the court to make a finding to that effect if the facts pleaded are consistent with conduct which is not dishonest such as negligence. As Millett LJ said in *Armitage v Nurse* [1997] 2 All ER 705 at 715, [1998] Ch 241 at 256, it is not necessary to use the word 'fraud' or 'dishonesty' if the facts which make the conduct fraudulent are pleaded. But this will not do if language used is equivocal (see *Belmont Finance Corp Ltd v Williams Furniture Ltd* [1979] 1 All ER 118 at 131, [1979] Ch 250 at 268 per Buckley LJ). In that case it was unclear from the pleadings whether dishonesty was being alleged. As the facts referred to might have inferred dishonesty but were consistent with innocence, it was not to be presumed that the defendant had been dishonest. Of course, the allegation of fraud, dishonesty or bad faith must be supported by particulars. The other party is entitled to notice of the particulars on which the allegation is based. If they are not capable of supporting the allegation, the allegation itself may be struck out. But it is not a proper ground for striking out the allegation that the particulars may be found, after trial, to amount not to fraud, dishonesty or bad faith but to negligence.

[56] In this case it is clear beyond a peradventure that misfeasance in public office is being alleged. There is an unequivocal plea that the Bank was acting throughout in bad faith. The Bank says that the facts relied on are, at best for the claimants, equally consistent with negligence. But the substance of that argument is directed not to the pleadings as such, which leave no doubt as to the case that is being alleged, and the basis for it in the particulars, but to the state of the evidence. The question whether the evidence points to negligence rather than to misfeasance in public office is a matter which must be judged in this case not on the pleadings but on the evidence. This is a matter for decision by the judge at trial.

[57] The Bank nevertheless submits that the facts pleaded fail to meet the requirements of the tort. Three reasons are advanced in support of this argument. The first is that the claimants have failed to allege the requisite mental element as to loss. Mr Stadlen said that it was not enough for the claimants to show that the Bank knew that depositors and potential depositors were at risk. As he put it, nothing short of a properly particularised allegation of knowledge or recklessness

of probable loss, known or suspected, would satisfy the test. The second is that the pleadings do not contain a properly particularised allegation that the Bank in the person of identified officials committed acts or omissions of misfeasance dishonestly in the sense of committing them with subjective bad faith. Mr Stadlen submitted that it was well understood that an allegation of dishonesty had to be supported by particulars from which the inference of dishonesty could be drawn. A failure to satisfy this requirement was in itself a ground for a strike-out. The third is that the pleadings do not contain a properly particularised allegation that Bank officials took conscious decisions capable of amounting to acts or omissions of misfeasance. Mr Stadlen directed this part of his argument to what he described as the revocation claim. He accepted that the initial decision to licence BCCI SA was particularised. But he said that only three instances were given of decisions not to revoke, and that in the case of only one of these instances—the Bank's decision in October 1986 not to revoke notwithstanding the scale of the central treasury losses—was there any attempt to suggest that the decision was taken dishonestly.

[**58**] I would reject the first of these three arguments on the ground that it was based on a misunderstanding of the requirements of the tort. The claimants' case on the pleadings is that at each stage in the history the Bank knew that the likely consequences were that depositors and potential depositors would suffer losses, wilfully disregarded the risk of the consequences or was recklessly indifferent to the consequences (new draft particulars, paras 31–35). Knowledge that the depositors were likely to suffer loss is averred. But the claimants are also offering in the alternative to prove reckless indifference to the risk of loss. As I have already said (in section (2)) I do not think that it is necessary for present purposes to choose between the various phrases that may be used to describe the nature or degree of the risk. This would be to raise issues of fact and degree that are best considered at trial. It was not suggested that, if there was a case to be made on knowledge of probable loss, the pleading as to recklessness should be struck out at this stage. The Bank's position, as explained in its written case, is that it will not be possible to identify with precision which allegations should be struck out until the parties have seen your Lordships' judgment and that for the time being this exercise is premature.

[**59**] Mr Stadlen said that the essential difference between the parties on this part of the case at this stage is on the question whether knowledge, belief or suspicion of probable loss has to be established where the allegation is that the act or omission was done or made recklessly. He accepted that an allegation of knowledge that loss was 'likely' was, in effect, the same as an allegation that it was 'probable'. He also accepted that the words used in the new draft particulars to describe the tort, although not precisely the same as those used in your Lordships' judgment, were formulated with sufficient accuracy. But he maintained that the material referred to in the particulars did not support an allegation of knowledge, belief or suspicion of likely or probable loss. He said that none of this material came near to meeting that test, and that there was no indication in the Bingham report that material which would do so was available. At best it supported an allegation of knowledge that there was a risk of loss. But this was not enough to satisfy the test of knowledge that loss was probable.

[**60**] As I have already said more than once, I do not think that it is appropriate at this stage to attempt to define the required state of mind more precisely. This is a matter which is so bound up with the facts that it is best left until trial. It is a question of fact and degree. The greater the risk of loss the easier it is likely

to be to say that loss was probable and the easier it will be to find that where that risk was known, believed or suspected there was recklessness. The statutory powers of supervision were conferred on the Bank for the protection of depositors and potential depositors. As the fourth recital of the directive puts it, supervision of a credit institution is needed 'in order to protect savings'. The system is based on the assumption that, where that protection is lacking, deposits are likely to be at risk. The question whether at any given point of time that risk is sufficiently serious to justify a finding of recklessness on the part of a supervisor, who knows that the statutory requirements are not fulfilled, is aware of the risk but takes no action to withdraw authorisation or otherwise limit the activities of the deposit-taker, is one of degree. I would hold that it is essentially a question of fact for the trial judge. I do not think that a view on this matter can safely be formed at this stage by a reading of the available documents.

[**61**] I should add, in order to emphasise the importance which I attach to seeing this as a question of fact and degree, that I see much force in Auld LJ's observation in his dissenting judgment about the Orwellian illogicality of sharpening the test of foresight of probable damage for the purposes of the strike-out application to one of foresight of probable (imminent) collapse of BCCI. He said:

> 'If such a test is to survive it will enable a banking regulator who deliberately and knowingly does not supervise a bank as it should do (as is conceded to be arguable here), with resulting damage to its depositors, to defeat a misfeasance claim simply by saying "because I did not make the inquiries that I should have done, I did not suspect that the plaintiff would *probably* suffer loss." In short it enables a banking regulator to rely on its own deliberate and knowing illegality as a justification for its lack of foresight that it would cause damage. If "policy" and "principle" are to be invoked, it must be against providing such an incentive to a banking regulator, or any public body exercising a supervisory function over institutions in the interest of persons for whom they provide a service, not to do their duty. And to load a plaintiff/depositor with the further burden of proving that, despite the regulator's self-imposed ignorance, it foresaw damage in the particular form in which it occurred seems to me, with respect, even more illogical and unjust in a common law remedy the purpose of which is to provide a remedy for abuse of public duty.' (See [2000] 2 WLR 15 at 177.)

[**62**] The second argument on the pleadings is that the claimants have failed to give particulars of their allegation of dishonesty and to link those allegations with particular officials of the Bank. Here again regard must be paid to the fact that the claimants rely in the alternative on the concept of recklessness. I refer to the comments which I made in the previous section about Mr Stadlen's submission that an allegation of dishonesty in the sense of subjective bad faith is an essential element. The effect of your Lordships' decision following the first hearing is to the contrary. Recklessness is demonstrated where it is shown that the public officer was aware of a serious risk of loss due to an act or omission on his part which was unlawful but chose deliberately to disregard that risk. That is sufficient to establish that he did not have an honest belief in the lawfulness of the conduct which, to his knowledge, gave rise to that risk. Recklessness about the consequences, in the sense of not caring whether the consequences happen or not, will satisfy the test. In this context there is no additional element of dishonesty or bad faith that requires to be satisfied. As for the particular officials against whom the

a allegation is made, I consider that the Bank has been given sufficient notice of the claimants' case against their officials in the particulars when read with the documents.

[63] It is alleged in para 31 of the new draft particulars that the Bank in bad faith at all times from 1979 onwards purported to rely pursuant to s 3(5) of the 1979 Act, and subsequently s 9(3) of the 1987 Act, upon assurances given by b LBC/IML concerning the management and financial soundness of BCCI SA. Particulars are then given in that paragraph of the matters about this arrangement which are said to have been known to the Bank or about which it was recklessly indifferent. These are that the principal place of business of BCCI SA was in the United Kingdom, that LBC/IML did not and could not assure the Bank that it was satisfied with the management and overall financial soundness c of BCCI SA, and that for various reasons that are specified LBC/IML had declared itself unable to carry out adequate supervision of both BCCI SA and the BCCI Group. It is also said that the Bank knew that the consequence of its unlawful reliance upon LBC/IML was that BCCI SA would be and would continue to be unlawfully licensed, and subsequently authorised, and that it was recklessly d indifferent to the risk that this presented to depositors and potential depositors. In para 37 of the new draft particulars, under reference at each stage in the history to the facts and matters set out in Schs 2 to 7 of the particulars, details are given of the respects in which the motives of the Bank for breaching its statutory duties as regulator were in bad faith. It seemed to me at first sight that these particulars give ample notice to the Bank of the case which is being made against it as to the e requirement of bad faith. But the point requires further examination in the light of further points in Mr Stadlen's argument.

[64] The claimants are taken some distance down the road they must travel by a concession which the Bank made to Clarke J which the judge recorded in his third judgment in these terms:

f

> 'With one exception I shall assume that they can establish that the Bank knew, believed or suspected at each stage that its proposed act or its omission was unlawful. With that one exception, the Bank has conceded that it cannot show that the plaintiffs' case that it knew, believed or suspected that its acts or omissions were unlawful is doomed to failure. That exception is the way g that s 3(5) of the Banking Act 1979 was applied.'

[65] In the Court of Appeal, as appears both from the majority judgment and that of Auld LJ ([2000] 2 WLR 15 at 92, 179), it was understood to be common ground that there was an arguable case that the Bank was aware of illegality in its supervision of BCCI SA. Mr Stadlen objected to these passages on the ground h that the extent of the Bank's concession was being misrepresented. He said that the Bank made one very narrow concession only, which was that for the purposes of the preliminary issue it was arguable that the Bank knew, believed or suspected that it was not entitled to rely, for the purpose of ongoing supervision of BCCI SA, on assurances given by LBC/IML because after, but not before, the licence j was granted it knew, believed or suspected that its principal place of business was not in Luxembourg. I am content to accept Mr Stadlen's assurance that the concession was limited to this point. Nevertheless it seems to me to be a significant one. It limits the areas for discussion to the granting of the licence on the one hand, as to which all issues remain in play, and to the Bank's ongoing supervision on the other hand, as to which the issue relates to the question whether the pleadings reveal an arguable case as to recklessness about the consequences.

[66] With regard to the question whether the claimants have sufficiently alleged dishonesty or bad faith when the Bank granted the licence in the first place, the majority in the Court of Appeal (at 92) agreed with Clarke J's finding in his third judgment that there was material from which it was at least arguable that the Bank must have known at that stage that LBC were not regulating BCCI SA properly and that it did not have the resources to do so in the future. I agree, and I also consider that sufficient notice of the facts on which the claimants propose to rely is given in Sch 2 to the new draft particulars. As for Mr Stadlen's argument that the documents read in the light of the Bingham report do not provide any support for these particulars, I consider that issues of fact are raised here which, subject to further arguments about abuse of process, I would not expect to be answered satisfactorily in advance of a trial. As for the later stages in the history, the issue of dishonesty or bad faith is so bound up with the broad issue of recklessness that here too, subject to further arguments about abuse of process, I would hold that the issue raises questions of fact and degree which are best left for decision by the trial judge in the light of the evidence.

[67] The third argument is that there was a failure to provide particularised allegations in regard to the revocation claim. Mr Stadlen accepted that the initial decision to licence BCCI SA was particularised. But he said that, despite Clarke J's warning that particulars had to be given of the decisions that were said to amount to misfeasance, the claimants' case was still largely based on alleged omissions. He said that only three instances could be identified in the new draft particulars where it was alleged that decisions had been taken by the Bank not to revoke. These were the decision in October 1986 not to revoke the authorisation despite its knowledge of the scale of BCCI SA's central treasury losses, the decision not to revoke in December 1989 in the light of the criticisms expressed in the paper prepared by the Banking Supervision Department for the Board of Banking Supervision in November of that year and the decision not to revoke in January 1990 following the plea bargain which led to the settlement of the Tampa indictment (new draft particulars, Sch 5, para 27 and Sch 6, paras 19 and 24). He maintained that this was a fundamental defect in the revocation claim, as a conscious decision was needed to support a case of misfeasance in public office. It was not open to the claimants to rely on a general reference to the Bank's omission to act day-by-day over the entire period, as the tort required proof of acts done by the public official intentionally.

[68] In my opinion this argument is based on a misconception of the thrust of the claimants' allegations and on a misunderstanding of the requirements of the tort. The claimants' case, as Lord Neill explained, is that the Bank deliberately ran away from its responsibility as the relevant supervisory authority throughout the history of BCCI SA's activities in this country to safeguard the interests of depositors and potential depositors. He said that a series of events could be identified in the particulars to show that the Bank deliberately failed to take steps which it might have taken to deal with the situation despite its awareness of facts or circumstances which revealed the extent of the risk to those interests. I agree that particulars are given throughout the pleadings of events which are arguably of this character. Examples of such events are given in the new draft particulars (Sch 5, paras 17 and 34–35), and there are many more.

[69] Furthermore, as Lord Neill pointed out, the tort extends to decisions not to exercise powers as well as decisions to exercise them. In the early days, when the tort was largely confined to disputes over voting rights, it was invoked to deal with the improper exercise of official power. Later, it was invoked in other areas

a of official regulation through licensing and other controls of that kind. Again the typical complaint was of the improper exercise of the power. That remains true in the majority of the more modern cases. *Bourgoin SA v Ministry of Agriculture Fisheries and Food* [1985] 3 All ER 585, [1986] QB 716 is an example, as that case was concerned with the withdrawal of a licence. But, as Brennan J said in *Northern Territory of Australia v Mengel* (1995) 185 CLR 307 at 357 in a passage which was b approved in your Lordships' previous judgment in this case, any act or omission done or made by a public official can found an action for misfeasance in public office. If it were otherwise, a banking regulator would be able to defeat a misfeasance claim simply by resorting to inaction in the face of obvious and immediate risks despite the fact that it knew, believed or suspected that its reckless and deliberate course of inaction was likely to result in damage to c depositors and potential depositors. For these reasons I would reject the argument that proof of conscious decisions to act or not to act is required. In my view the tort extends to a deliberate or wilful failure to take those decisions.

[**70**] For these reasons I would hold that the facts pleaded by the claimants in the new draft particulars are capable, if proved, of meeting the requirements of d the tort. I must now turn to the alternative ground for striking out, which was that of abuse of process.

(4) THE DECISION OF THE COURTS BELOW TO STRIKE OUT

[**71**] Clarke J said that he understood it to be common ground between the parties that in appropriate circumstances the court had power to strike an action e out under its inherent jurisdiction and under RSC Ord 18, r 19. The question which he then asked himself was whether the Bank had shown that the claimants' case was bound to fail on the material presently available and that there was no reasonable possibility of evidence becoming available to them, whether by further investigation, discovery, cross-examination or otherwise sufficiently to f support their case and to give it some prospect of success. As he put it, if the Bank were to discharge that burden, it would follow that the claim was bound to fail (third judgment). He then embarked on a detailed examination of all the material which was available to the claimants to support their claim. I agree with the majority in the Court of Appeal ([2000] 2 WLR 15 at 90) that this was a vastly difficult undertaking.

g [**72**] Clarke J's conclusion, after examining the available material over many days, was that the claimants had no arguable case on the material then available that the Bank dishonestly licensed BCCI SA or dishonestly failed to revoke the licence or authorisation in circumstances when it knew, believed or suspected that it would probably collapse without being rescued (third judgment). The Court of h Appeal ([2000] 2 WLR 15 at 88, 90) agreed with the judge that it was right, in the exceptional circumstances of this case, to conduct this exercise. After reviewing the judge's conclusion in great detail, the majority agreed (at 101) with the judge that all the evidence indicated that up to April 1990 the Bank did not actually foresee BCCI SA's imminent collapse, and thereafter that it did but properly j relied on the prospect of a rescue.

[**73**] Concurrent findings of fact are not normally open to review in your Lordships' House. For the like reasons as those on which this rule is based I would not have thought that it was appropriate for your Lordships to interfere with the concurrent findings of the judge and the majority in the Court of Appeal after conducting such a detailed and time-consuming exercise unless some flaw in their reasoning could be demonstrated. There are, however, two grounds on

which it was contended they misdirected themselves. The first relates to the requirements of the tort. The second relates to the use which they made of the Bingham report. a

[74] It is not necessary for me to deal in detail with the differences which have emerged between your Lordships and the courts below as to the requirements of the tort. For the most part Clarke J's conclusions as to the legal principles to be applied which he summarised at the end of his first judgment ([1996] 3 All ER 558 at 632–633) were approved in the judgment given by your Lordships after the first hearing of this appeal ([2000] 3 All ER 1, [2000] 2 WLR 1220). The majority in the Court of Appeal said ([2000] 2 WLR 15 at 67, 101) that they were in broad agreement with the judge's conclusions on the tort and that they had adopted the same approach as he had taken when they were considering whether the claimants' case was bound to fail. But there is one point of difference which is of obvious importance, as it lies at the heart of the argument between the parties. This relates to the state of knowledge of the public officer about the prospect of loss that has to be demonstrated where the claim is based on the concept of recklessness. b c

[75] In his formulation Clarke J said that ([1996] 3 All ER 558 at 633) for the purposes of the requirement that the officer knows that his act will probably injure the claimant, it is sufficient if he has actual knowledge that his act will probably damage the claimant or, in circumstances in which he believes or suspects that his act 'will probably' damage the plaintiff, he does not ascertain whether that is so or fails to make inquires as to 'the probability' of such damage. In the Court of Appeal ([2000] 2 WLR 15 at 101) the majority asked themselves whether the claimants had an arguable case that the Bank 'actually foresaw' BCCI's imminent collapse at each relevant stage. They went on to say (at 102) that that formulation might have been too favourable to the claimants and that, in view of the stringent requirements of the tort of misfeasance in public office, the more appropriate question might be whether the Bank 'knew' that its decision would cause loss to the claimants. I would not regard the fact that the latter observation is not supported by your Lordships' judgment as important, as the majority do not say that they based their decision on this view. But it is clear that the theme of knowledge of probable loss informed the approach which was taken throughout these judgments to the question whether the claim should be struck out. d e f g

[76] Mr Stadlen sought to support this approach. But, for the reasons which I have already given, I would hold that it is not consistent with the effect of your Lordships' judgment following the first hearing. As I have already said when I was reviewing the requirements of the tort in an earlier section of this judgment (section (2)), the state of mind which amounts to subjective recklessness is demonstrated where it is shown that the public officer was aware of a serious risk of loss due to an act or omission on his part which he knew to be unlawful but chose deliberately to disregard that risk, and the question whether at any given point of time that risk is sufficiently serious to justify a finding of recklessness is one of degree. I consider that this point alone is sufficient to justify taking a fresh look at the question whether the claimants have a seriously arguable case directed to the issue of recklessness. h j

[77] Then there is the use which was made in their judgments by Clarke J and the majority in the Court of Appeal of the findings and conclusions in the Bingham report. Clarke J said (in his third judgment) that he recognised that Bingham LJ was not conducting a trial but an inquiry, that he did not see a number

a of Bank officials, that the witnesses whom he did see were not cross-examined in an adversarial process and that there was no right of appeal. But he went on to say:

> 'On the other hand, it is plain that in addition to questioning witnesses Bingham LJ considered in detail all the relevant internal documents in the possession of the Bank, which involved a perusal of a mass of documentation. As I have already said, it is clear from the terms of Bingham LJ's covering letter b to the Chancellor of the Exchequer, and indeed from many passages in the report itself, that he was applying his mind to question what was the state of mind of the Bank at each stage. In these circumstances I accept Mr Stadlen's submission that it is inconceivable that Bingham LJ was aware of material which was materially at odds with his conclusions as to the state of mind of the Bank. There is, in my judgment, no realistic possibility that he has not c correctly set out the state of mind of the Bank at each stage.
>
> While it is, of course, true that I have seen only the report and not the appendices, the published report is a summary of an even more detailed narrative in the appendices. Since, as just stated, Bingham LJ was expressly considering the state of mind of the Bank at each stage, it is in my judgment d inconceivable that there is in the appendices material which would or might support the conclusion that the Bank had the state of mind which the plaintiffs must establish. If there was, Bingham LJ would have referred to it, even if only to dismiss it. He would certainly not have disregarded it. As I have tried to indicate, at no doubt inordinate length, there is nothing in the e material which I have seen which gives arguable support for the plaintiffs' case. I would, however, go further. There is nothing in that material which gives reasonable grounds for supposing that there might be other evidence which might in the future support the plaintiffs' case. In these circumstances I accept Mr Stadlen's further submission that there is no realistic possibility of more evidence becoming available, whether by further investigation, f discovery, cross-examination or otherwise, which might throw light upon the state of mind of the Bank or any of its relevant officials during the period in which BCCI was operating.'

[78] The Court of Appeal said that, while the judge seemed to them to be putting the matter too high in the first of the two paragraphs which I have quoted g from his judgment, they agreed with him that there was no realistic possibility that the picture which would emerge if officials of the Bank were to give evidence which was tested by cross-examination would be fundamentally different. In that respect the report was, despite its informal status, an invaluable aid to distinguishing between what was a practical possibility and what was fanciful and h inconceivable ([2000] 2 WLR 15 at 91). Auld LJ disagreed with this approach. In his view Clarke J was not entitled to treat the Bingham report effectively as conclusive on the questions that arise in this litigation or to conclude that all the available evidence about the Bank's state of knowledge had been gathered in or properly tested. He said (at 180) that there were no exceptional circumstances to j justify departing from the normal rule of leaving the matter to the trial judge.

[79] As I said in a previous section of this judgment (section (1)(b)), there are important limitations on the use which can be made of the Bingham report in these proceedings. A sharp dividing line must be observed between Bingham LJ's narrative of the evidence, which is a legitimate source to which reference can be made for the purposes of the motion to strike out, and his findings and conclusions in the light of that evidence. It is not just that those findings and conclusions would not be admissible at trial. Fairness to the claimants requires that proper weight is given to the nature of Bingham LJ's inquiry and its limitations. He was not asked to determine the issues relating to the tort of misfeasance in public office which the claimants now seek to raise. These issues were not on trial in those proceedings. There is no doubt that Bingham LJ was chosen to conduct the inquiry because of his outstanding qualities as a judge and the weight of authority which his findings and recommendations would command. But those considerations must not be allowed to affect the rigorous distinction that must be maintained between those parts of the report that are and are not relevant to the Bank's motion to strike out.

[80] As I have already said, Clarke J made it clear that he recognised these limitations (in his third judgment). Nevertheless I have formed the clear impression that his view that the claim should be struck out was materially influenced by findings and conclusions and the absence of findings and conclusions in the Bingham report, and that he did not confine himself, as I consider he should have done, strictly to the narrative. I do not leave out of account the fact that he was responding to the way in which the claimants had presented their case. It is clear that they were drawing on those aspects of the report that suited them. It is not surprising that the Bank replied by pointing out those parts of the report that did not, and that the judge in his turn was drawn into this argument. Nevertheless the claimants are, in my view, entitled to say that Bingham LJ's findings and conclusions ought not to be used against them in this way. Bingham LJ's findings and conclusions about the availability of further evidence coming to light were made in proceedings to which they were not parties, and they could not challenge them on appeal. Cogent though these findings and conclusions may appear to be, the claimants are entitled to a fair trial of the claim which they have made against the Bank.

[81] In the following passage of his third judgment Clarke J explained his general approach to the Bingham report before he embarked upon a detailed consideration of the various stages in the history:

> 'Mr Stadlen submits that there is no support anywhere in the Bingham report for the conclusion that the Bank acted dishonestly, or that it knew that it was acting unlawfully or that it suspected that its acts or omission would probably cause loss to depositors or potential depositors. For the reasons already stated I shall focus only on the last of these, but I accept the submission that there is no statement in the report which gives any support for the conclusion that at any stage the Bank suspected that depositors and potential depositors would probably suffer loss as a result of the Bank's action or inaction. Yet, as stated on page iii of the covering letter to which I have already referred, it is clear that Bingham LJ was considering the Bank's state of mind at every stage. In my judgment, if Bingham LJ had formed the view that at any stage the Bank suspected that its action or inaction would probably injure depositors or potential depositors he would have said so. Thus, if he had thought that the Bank suspected that BCCI would probably collapse so that new depositors would probably lose their money at any stage of the story from 1979 to 1991 he would have said so. Yet, not only did he not say so, but his observations on the evidence are inconsistent with any such conclusion.'

[82] Thereafter during his examination of the history he made frequent reference to findings or conclusions, or to the absence of conclusions and findings, in a the Bingham report. His purpose in doing so was to explain why he was of the opinion that there was nothing in the material he had seen which gave reasonable grounds for supposing that other evidence might become available to throw light on the state of mind of the Bank during the relevant period: see the conclusion, already quoted, which he expressed. The following passage, in which he dealt with the claimants' submission that the Bank must have known when it granted b the licence that the principal place of business of BCCI was in the United Kingdom and not in Luxembourg, illustrates this point:

> 'However, the difficulty with the plaintiffs' submission is that Bingham LJ held in para 2.23 that the Bank never addressed the question what was meant by principal place of business. It assumed wrongly that the principal place of c business was in the country of incorporation. Further Bingham LJ says in para 2.24 that the Bank never inquired where the principal place of business was, in the sense of where the mind and management of the company and its central direction resided. The Bank thus treated s 3(5) of the Act as applicable and applied it. In para 2.25 Bingham LJ says that he read nothing d sinister in that approach. Moreover, on the footing that the principal place of business was in the United Kingdom, under s 36 BCCI was not entitled to describe itself as a bank, but Bingham LJ says in para 2.33 that it was not until after the licence had been granted that the Bank recognised that fact. There is, in my judgment, no material available to the plaintiffs or to the court to lead to any different conclusion.'

e

[83] Among the other passages that might be quoted are those where the judge referred to a conclusion in para 2.66 of the report in support of the view that there was no evidence that the Bank suspected in June 1986 following the central treasury losses that BCCI would probably collapse, let alone that it would probably collapse because of an absence of remedial steps; where he referred to a f conclusion in para 2.154 of the report to the same effect as to the Bank's state of mind in December 1989; and where he referred to paras 2.333 and 2.337 of the report as to the Bank's state of mind in March 1991 when it commissioned Price Waterhouse to investigate and report on malpractice within the group under s 41 of the 1987 Act.

g **[84]** In their written submissions to the Court of Appeal (para 61) the claimants said that they did not object to the court having regard to the report. But they pointed out that its contents would not be admissible in any trial and that it was odd that the judge considered it permissible or appropriate to determine factual issues by reference to it and to strike out the action in reliance upon it. Nevertheless it is clear that the majority in that court followed Clarke J's h approach, and that to a material extent their decision to dismiss the appeal was based on the same view as that which the judge had formed in the light of the findings and conclusions that Bingham LJ expressed.

[85] That there was a fundamental difference of view in the Court of Appeal on this point is clear from Auld LJ's dissenting judgment. He noted ([2000] 2 WLR 15 j at 179) the fact that Clarke J relied heavily on the Bingham report as a justification for taking the exceptional course of striking out the claim as doomed to fail. After pointing out the different functions of that inquiry from those involved in this litigation and the disadvantages that were inherent in that procedure, he said (at 180):

> 'In the circumstances, I am of the view that Clarke J. was not entitled to treat Bingham L.J.'s report effectively as conclusive on the questions he, the

judge, had to answer in this litigation or to conclude, as he did, that all the available material evidence on those questions had been gathered in. Given the greater generality of the questions in the Bingham inquiry, the limitations of it as a fact-finding exercise when compared with litigation, his acknowledgement of a number of challenges to some of his factual conclusions and the emergence of additional material since the inquiry indicating the Bank's state of knowledge as to the Gokal unrecorded loans, I can see no basis for Clarke J.'s confidence in this extraordinary and complex case for concluding that Bingham L.J. had seen and fully tested all the material evidence available or likely to become available on the issues confronting the court in this case.'

[86] I respectfully agree with and would indorse these observations. In my judgment the extent to which the opinions expressed by both Clarke J and the majority in the Court of Appeal were dependent upon passages in the Bingham report which are irrelevant to the issue of strike-out provides a further reason for taking a fresh look at this critical issue. For the same reasons I consider that the claimants' motion for leave to re-reamend the statement of claim is open to reconsideration by your Lordships. The draft re-reamended statement of claim has now been superseded by the draft new particulars, and it is to that document that I shall direct my remarks on the question whether leave should now be given.

(5) THE TEST FOR SUMMARY JUDGMENT UNDER CPR 24.2

[87] Clarke J ordered that the action should be struck out under RSC Ord 18, r 19 on the grounds that the reamended statement of claim disclosed no reasonable cause of action and that it would be an abuse of process or vexatious or oppressive to give leave to re-reamend. The parties are agreed that if the question whether the claim should be struck out is to be reconsidered it must now be determined under the Civil Procedure Rules 1998, SI 1998/3132: see the general principle stated in the Practice Direction supplementing CPR Pt 51, para 11 (Practice Direction—Transitional Arrangements). The power which is given to the court to strike out under CPR Pt 3, which is concerned with the court's case management powers, is expressed in r 3.4(2) in these terms:

'The court may strike out a statement of case if it appears to the court—(a) that the statement of case discloses no reasonable grounds for bringing or defending the claim; (b) that the statement of case is an abuse of the court's process or is otherwise likely to obstruct the just disposal of the proceedings; or (c) that there has been a failure to comply with a rule, practice direction or court order.'

[88] The parties also agree that, if Clarke J were to be held to have applied the wrong test when he ordered the action to be struck out, the relevant rules under the CPR are not confined to the provision for striking out in CPR 3.4. In *Margulies v Margulies* [2000] CA Transcript 444 the judge's decision to strike out was given pursuant to RSC Ord 18, r 19 before the coming into effect of the CPR. Nourse LJ said (at para 63) that, if the judge wrongly applied the test, the Court of Appeal would have to determine the matter pursuant to CPR 24.2. I would not go so far as to say that your Lordships are obliged to treat the Bank's motion to strike out as an application for summary judgment under r 24.2. It would, I think, be more accurate to say that your Lordships have power to do so, and that the question is whether your Lordships should exercise that power

a (see *Taylor v Midland Bank Trust Co Ltd* [1999] CA Transcript 1200, *Civil Procedure* (2000 edn) vol 1, para 3.4.6). CPR 24 sets out various procedural requirements which do not apply to r 3.4. But the claimants do not object to the application of r 24.2 on procedural grounds. So I would accept Mr Stadlen's submission that it is appropriate for the Bank's application for the claim to be struck out to be treated as if it were an application for summary judgment.

b [**89**] CPR 24.2 provides:

> 'The court may give summary judgment against a claimant or defendant on the whole of a claim or on a particular issue if—(a) it considers that—(i) that claimant has no real prospect of succeeding on the claim or issue; or (ii) that defendant has no real prospect of successfully defending the claim or issue; c and (b) there is no other reason why the case or issue should be disposed of at a trial.'

[**90**] The test which Clarke J applied, when he was considering whether the claim should be struck out under RSC Ord 18, r 19, was whether it was bound to fail (see the third judgment). Mr Stadlen submitted that the court had a wider power d to dispose summarily of issues under CPR Pt 24 than it did under RSC Ord 18, r 19, and that critical issue was now whether, in terms of CPR 24.2(a)(i), the claimants had a real prospect of succeeding on the claim. As to what these words mean, in *Swain v Hillman* [2001] 1 All ER 91 at 92, Lord Woolf MR said:

> 'Under r 24.2, the court now has a very salutary power, both to be e exercised in a claimant's favour or, where appropriate, in a defendant's favour. It enables the court to dispose summarily of both claims or defences which have no real prospect of being successful. The words "no real prospect of being successful or succeeding" do not need any amplification, they speak for themselves. The word "real" distinguishes fanciful prospects of success f or, as Mr Bidder QC [counsel for the defendant] submits, they direct the court to the need to see whether there is a "realistic" as opposed to a "fanciful" prospect of success.'

[**91**] The difference between a test which asks the question 'is the claim bound to fail?' and one which asks 'does the claim have a real prospect of success?' is not g easy to determine. In *Swain*'s case Lord Woolf MR (at 92) explained that the reason for the contrast in language between r 3.4 and r 24.2 is that under r 3.4, unlike r 24.2, the court generally is only concerned with the statement of case which it is alleged discloses no reasonable grounds for bringing or defending the claim. In *Monsanto plc v Tilly* (1999) Times, 30 November, Stuart Smith LJ said that r 24.2 gives somewhat wider scope for dismissing an action or defence. h In *Taylor*'s case he said that, particularly in the light of the CPR, the court should look to see what will happen at the trial and that, if the case is so weak that it had no reasonable prospect of success, it should be stopped before great expense is incurred.

[**92**] The overriding objective of the CPR is to enable the court to deal with cases j justly (see r 1.1). To adopt the language of art 6.1 of the European Convention for the Protection of Human Rights and Fundamental Freedoms (Rome, 4 November 1950; TS 71 (1953); Cmd 8969) (set out in Sch 1 to the Human Rights Act 1998) with which this aim is consistent, the court must ensure that there is a fair trial. It must seek to give effect to the overriding objective when it exercises any power given to it by the rules or interprets any rule (see r 1.2). While the difference between the two tests is elusive, in many cases the practical effect will be the same.

In more difficult and complex cases such as this one, attention to the overriding objective of dealing with the case justly is likely to be more important than a search for the precise meaning of the rule. As May LJ said in *Purdy v Cambran* [1999] CPLR 843 at 854:

> 'The court has to seek to give effect to the overriding objective when it exercises any powers given to it by the rules. This applies to applications to strike out a claim. When the court is considering, in a case to be decided under the Civil Procedure Rules, whether or not it is just in accordance with the overriding objective to strike out a claim, it is not necessary or appropriate to analyse that question by reference to the rigid and overloaded structure which a large body of decision under the former rules had constructed.'

[93] In *Swain*'s case Lord Woolf MR gave this further guidance:

> 'It is important that a judge in appropriate cases should make use of the powers contained in Pt 24. In doing so he or she gives effect to the overriding objectives contained in Pt 1. It saves expense; it achieves expedition; it avoids the court's resources being used up on cases where this serves no purpose, and, I would add, generally, that it is in the interests of justice. If a claimant has a case which is bound to fail, then it is in the claimant's interests to know as soon as possible that that is the position. Likewise, if a claim is bound to succeed, a claimant should know this as soon as possible ... Useful though the power is under Pt 24, it is important that it is kept to its proper role. It is not meant to dispense with the need for a trial where there are issues which should be investigated at the trial. As Mr Bidder put it in his submissions, the proper disposal of an issue under Pt 24 does not involve the judge conducting a mini-trial, that is not the object of the provisions; it is to enable cases, where there is no real prospect of success either way, to be disposed of summarily.' (See [2001] 1 All ER 91 at 94–95.)

(6) WHETHER THE CLAIM SHOULD BE SUMMARILY STRUCK OUT

[94] For the reasons which I have just given, I think that the question is whether the claim has no real prospect of succeeding at trial and that it has to be answered having regard to the overriding objective of dealing with the case justly. But the point which is of crucial importance lies in the answer to the further question that then needs to be asked, which is—what is to be the scope of that inquiry?

[95] I would approach that further question in this way. The method by which issues of fact are tried in our courts is well settled. After the normal processes of discovery and interrogatories have been completed, the parties are allowed to lead their evidence so that the trial judge can determine where the truth lies in the light of that evidence. To that rule there are some well-recognised exceptions. For example, it may be clear as a matter of law at the outset that even if a party were to succeed in proving all the facts that he offers to prove he will not be entitled to the remedy that he seeks. In that event a trial of the facts would be a waste of time and money, and it is proper that the action should be taken out of court as soon as possible. In other cases it may be possible to say with confidence before trial that the factual basis for the claim is fanciful because it is entirely without substance. It may be clear beyond question that the statement of facts is contradicted by all the documents or other material on which it is based. The simpler the case the easier it is likely to be take that view and resort to what a is properly called summary judgment. But more complex cases are unlikely to be capable of being resolved in that way without conducting a mini-trial on the documents without discovery and without oral evidence. As Lord Woolf MR said in *Swain*'s case [2001] 1 All ER 91 at 95, that is not the object of the rule. It is designed to deal with cases that are not fit for trial at all.

[**96**] In *Wenlock v Moloney* [1965] 2 All ER 871, [1965] 1 WLR 1238 the plaintiff's b claim of damages for conspiracy was struck out after a four-day hearing on affidavits and documents. Danckwerts LJ said of the inherent power of the court to strike out:

> '... this summary jurisdiction of the court was never intended to be exercised by a minute and protracted examination of the documents and facts of the c case, in order to see whether the plaintiff really has a cause of action. To do that, is to usurp the position of the trial judge, and to produce a trial of the case in chambers, on affidavits only, without discovery and without oral evidence tested by cross-examination in the ordinary way. This seems to me to be an abuse of the inherent power of the court and not a proper exercise d of that power.' (See [1965] 2 All ER 871 at 874, [1965] 1 WLR 1238 at 1244.)

Sellers LJ said ([1965] 2 All ER 87 at 874, [1965] 1 WLR 1238 at 1243) that he had no doubt that the procedure adopted in that case had been wrong and that the plaintiff's case could not be stifled at that stage, and Diplock LJ agreed.

[**97**] In the Court of Appeal the majority said ([2000] 2 WLR 15 at 86) that e 'this somewhat rigid position' had been modified in *Williams and Humbert Ltd v W & H Trade Marks (Jersey) Ltd, Rumasa SA v Multinvest (UK)* Ltd [1986] 1 All ER 129, [1986] AC 368, where Lord Templeman said ([1986] 1 All ER 129 at 139, [1986] AC 368 at 435–436) that if an application to strike out involves a prolonged and serious argument the judge should, as a general rule, decline to proceed with the f argument unless he not only harbours doubts about the soundness of the pleading but, in addition, is satisfied that striking out will obviate the necessity for a trial or will substantially reduce the burden of preparing for the trial or the burden of the trial itself (see also [1986] 1 All ER 129 at 142–143, [1986] AC 368 at 441 per Lord Mackay of Clashfern). But they were satisfied that this case fell within the exceptional class for the same reasons as those explained in the g *Williams and Humbert* case, and that Clarke J was right to embark upon the exercise. I too would not criticise the judge for undertaking the exercise. But I would also pay careful regard to what the Court of Appeal in *Wenlock*'s case regarded as objectionable. In *Morris v Bank of America National Trust* [2000] 1 All ER 954 at 966 Morritt LJ said that *Wenlock*'s case illustrated a salutary principle. He h then said:

> 'In the *Three Rivers DC* case the Court of Appeal upheld the decision of Clarke J to strike out a complicated claim for damages for misfeasance in a public office made against the Bank of England for authorising BCCI to carry on the business of banking. In that case all the evidence then available to the j plaintiff was before the court because all the facts had been investigated by Bingham LJ as he then was ... Obviously the fact of a recent inquiry is a material distinction.'

For reasons already explained (in section (4)), I do not think that the investigation that was conducted by Bingham LJ justifies a departure from the principle. I consider that both Clarke J and the majority in the Court of Appeal were wrong to approach this case on the basis that all the facts that are relevant to the claim that is being made in this case had been investigated. a

[**98**] The present case is, as everyone concerned with it has recognised, one of a quite exceptional character. The issues of fact which the claimants seek to raise are highly complex. They relate to matters in which they were not directly involved, as they were third parties to the system of regulation which was set up to protect them. They involve meetings and discussions between many parties at b which they were not represented and they extend, through no fault of theirs, over a very long period. The issues of law are also complex, as the claim depends on an assessment of the state of mind of the Bank's officials at each of the various stages in the history. Much of what was passing through their minds can be discovered by examining the documents. But the court is normally reluctant to draw inferences of the kind that need to be drawn in this case without seeing and c hearing the witnesses. Bingham LJ had that advantage. The court, so far, has not.

[**99**] My approach to this issue can therefore be summarised against this background as follows. For the reasons which I have already given (in section (3)), I consider that the claimants' pleadings give sufficient notice to the Bank of the case which they wish to present and that the facts pleaded are capable of satisfying d the requirements of the tort. That being so, I would be inclined to hold that this highly complex case should not be decided on the documents without hearing oral evidence but should go to trial. This view is reinforced by what I have said about the Bingham report. I would leave out of account the findings and conclusions in that report which the parties are agreed would at any trial be inadmissible. It is not just that, strictly speaking, they are irrelevant to any decision that might be e made by the trial judge. I also believe, for the reasons that I have just given, that it would be contrary to the overriding requirement of fairness for them to be taken into account in reaching a decision as to whether this case can be decided without hearing oral evidence.

[**100**] I would also examine the question whether the claim has no real f prospect of succeeding at the outset from a totally neutral standpoint. By that I mean that I would not make any assumptions either one way or the other about the competence or integrity of the Bank or its officials as a prelude to examining the available evidence. I accept that conduct amounting to misfeasance in public office is not to be inferred lightly. That is true as a general proposition, whatever may be the task or status of the impugned public officer. But I think that it would g be to risk pre-judging the case to attempt to evaluate the action's prospects of success by considering at this stage, before hearing evidence, whether the claimants' case against the Bank as regulator is inherently implausible or scarcely credible. These factors, taken as a whole, seem to me to point clearly against giving a summary judgment in the Bank's favour under CPR Pt 24. h

[**101**] I turn then to the state of the evidence. I shall deal with this matter briefly. It is clear, as my noble and learned friend Lord Steyn has indicated, that the facts must be left to the trial judge if the case is to go to trial. As I said in my introduction (section (1)(a)), the history can conveniently be divided up into four periods: (a) prior to the grant of the licence in June 1980, (b) June 1980 to j December 1986, (c) December 1986 to April 1990, and (d) April 1990 to closure in July 1991.

[**102**] In regard to the period prior to the grant of the licence in June 1980 the majority in the Court of Appeal said that they agreed with Clarke J that there was material from which it could be said to be at least arguable that the Bank must have known that the Luxembourg regulators were not regulating BCCI SA properly

a and did not have the resources to do so. They were against the claimants on the question whether there was an arguable case on foresight of loss during this period ([2000] 2 WLR 15 at 92). Clarke J said, in his third judgment, that it seemed to him to offend common sense to conclude that it actually knew, believed or suspected that if it licensed BCCI SA it would, or even might, collapse. By April 1990, however, the picture had, in their view, entirely changed. The majority in the b Court of Appeal said (at 99) that the Price Waterhouse report to the board of BCCI Holdings of 18 April 1990 was highly significant, as it marked a date after which it would be impossible in their judgment to contend that there was no arguable case that the Bank was aware of a very serious and very immediate threat to depositors of BCCI SA. Clarke J said that it is plain that the Bank appreciated that in the absence of remedial steps BCCI would probably collapse. c His conclusion, however, was that at no time between April 1990 and June 1991 did the Bank believe or suspect that the majority shareholders would probably not save the Bank. At this point therefore, as the majority in the Court of Appeal observed (at 99), the prospect of a rescue operation being promoted by the Abu Dhabi government, and the Bank's perception of the various possible d outcomes, assumes central importance. The majority said (at 101) that they agreed with the judge that the claimants had no arguable case that the Bank dishonestly failed to revoke the authorisation of BCCI SA in circumstances when it knew, believed or suspected that the company would probably collapse without being rescued.

e **[103]** These views were, as can be seen from the judgments, heavily influenced by passages in the Bingham Report which I consider to be irrelevant to the question whether the claim should be struck out. I have examined the available material from a different standpoint. I have left those passages out of account. I have asked myself whether, in regard to each of the four periods, the available material can be taken to have been fully examined and tested at this f stage. The limitations which are inherent in this exercise are obvious. All we can do is read the material and compare it with the case that is being made in the new draft particulars. In a simple case this may be all that needs to be done in order to reach a clear view that the claim has no real prospect of succeeding. If one can reach that view, it follows as night follows day that all the usual fact-finding g exercises of discovery, interrogation and cross-examination of witnesses will achieve no purpose and the claim should be struck out. But I am not persuaded this exceptional case falls into that category.

[104] I agree that there is material in the documents that are already available to support the pleading in Sch 2 of the new draft particulars that the Bank knew h that before the grant of the full licence to BCCI SA that it was not entitled to rely on the Luxembourg regulator. Given that starting point, I cannot say that the claimants have no real prospect of proving that the Bank knew that their initial act in licensing BCCI SA was unlawful, that its licence and authorisation remained unlawful throughout the remaining three periods and that all subsequent j omissions to revoke the licence and authorisation were affected by the same illegality. I have more difficulty with the question whether there is material to support the pleading in Sch 3 that at the time of licensing the Bank knew that loss was probable or that it had the state of mind regarding loss to depositors and potential depositors that amounted to recklessness. There is no direct evidence of this in the available documents, and I am not confident that they contain any material which suggests that contemporary documentary evidence to this effect is likely to become available. At best for the claimants, it appears that is a matter which will have to be inferred from other evidence. a

[105] But it seems to me that, as events unfold, this part of the case gathers momentum and that the available material makes it clear that the Bank knew by April 1990 at the latest that, unless a rescue could be put in hand in time by the Abu Dhabi government, BCCI would collapse and that serious loss to depositors would then be inevitable. The pattern of events during this final period is b complicated, as the majority in the Court of Appeal recognised (at 100). For reasons already given I would leave out of account the fact, relied on by the majority (at 101), that the conclusion in the Bingham report was that rescue was feasible and collapse not inevitable. In my opinion the documents alone do not tell the full story, and the question whether the Bank knew that loss to depositors was probable or was reckless in the relevant sense cannot be answered satisfactorily c without hearing oral evidence.

[106] I agree with my noble and learned friend Lord Hobhouse that the overriding objective of dealing with cases justly includes dealing with them in a proportionate manner, expeditiously, fairly and without undue expense. As he says, each case is entitled only to an appropriate share of the court's resources. d Account has to be taken of the need to allot resources to other cases. But I do not believe that the course which I favour offends against these important principles. The most important principle of all is that which requires that each case be dealt with justly. It may well be that the claimants, on whom the onus lies, will face difficulties in presenting their case. They must face the fact that each and every allegation of bad faith will be examined rigorously. A trial in this case will be e lengthy and it will be expensive. There is only so much that astute case management can do to reduce the burdens on the parties and on the court. Nevertheless it would only be right for the claim to be struck out if it has no real prospect of succeeding at trial. I do not think that one should be influenced in the application of this test by the length or expense of the litigation that is in prospect. f Justice should be even-handed, whether the case be simple or whether it be complex. It is plain that the situation in which the claimants find themselves was not of their own making, nor are they to be blamed for the volume and complexity of the facts that must be investigated. I would hold that justice requires that the claimants be given an opportunity to present their case at trial so that its merits may be assessed in the light of the evidence. g

[107] I have taken one other factor into account. The decision which your Lordships are being asked by the Bank to take is to give summary judgment in its favour on the entire claim. It would only be right to strike out the whole claim if it could be said of every part of it that it has no real prospect of succeeding. That would mean that even the latest depositors who were entrusting their h money to BCCI SA up to the very end of the final period would be left without a remedy. I think that that is too big a step to take on the available material. Conversely, I consider that if one part of the claim is to go to trial it would be unreasonable to divide the history up and strike out other parts of it. A great deal of time and money has now been expended in the examination of the preliminary j issues, and I think that this exercise must now be brought to an end. I would reject the Bank's application for summary judgment.

(7) THE BANK'S CROSS-APPEAL

[108] The cross-appeal by the Bank is directed to the second and third of the three questions which in his order of 19 July 1995 Clarke J said should be tried as a preliminary issues. The first question was whether the Bank is capable of being liable to the claimants for the tort of misfeasance in public office. That is the question to which the main part of this judgment has been directed. For the reasons which I have given I consider that it cannot be answered until the facts have been established at trial. The second and third questions were whether the claimants' alleged losses were caused in law by the acts or omissions of the Bank, and b whether the claimants are entitled to recover for the tort of misfeasance in public office as existing or potential depositors. The Court of Appeal ([2000] 2 WLR 15 at 68–70) held that it would be premature to decide these points conclusively in the Bank's favour until the facts have been established. I respectfully agree. As I said earlier (at [34]), the Bank, while reserving the right to pursue the issue at trial, accepts that it is capable of being liable for the tort to potential depositors and c questions of fact are raised by the issue about causation which are unsuitable for summary determination at this stage.

(8) CONCLUSION AND FURTHER PROCEDURE

[109] For these reasons I would allow the appeal and I would dismiss the d cross-appeal. I would set aside the order that the reamended statement of claim be struck out, and I would give permission to the claimants to amend their particulars of claim in terms of the new draft particulars.

[110] The claimants invited your Lordships to direct the Bank to serve an amended defence within two months of the date of this order and the claimants to serve a reply, if so advised, within six weeks of service of the amended defence, e and to direct the parties to arrange a case management conference with the Commercial Court within four weeks of the date for service of the reply with a view to determining further progress of this action and establishing all necessary timetables and directions for bringing the case on for trial at the earliest date the Commercial Court considers feasible. These proposals seem to me to be entirely f reasonable. Like Lord Steyn, I anticipate that the court will wish to exercise its powers of case management with a view to bringing the case to trial with due despatch in accordance with the overriding objective and that further delay due to the hearing of interlocutory applications will now be kept to a minimum. But on balance I think that it is preferable to leave it to the commercial judge in charge of the case to make the appropriate directions.

g

LORD HUTTON. My Lords,

[111] I have had the advantage of reading in draft the speech of my noble and learned friend Lord Hope of Craighead and I gratefully adopt his account of the factual and statutory background to this appeal and of the course of the h proceedings in the High Court and the Court of Appeal. I am in general agreement with his conclusions and with the reasons which he gives for them, but because of the importance of the issues which have arisen for decision I propose to state the reasons which have led me to the conclusion that the plaintiffs' appeal should be allowed and that the action should not be struck out.

j **[112]** In his first judgment dated 1 April 1996 Clarke J ([1996] 3 All ER 558) stated the ingredients of the tort of misfeasance in public office. In his second judgment dated 10 May 1996 ([1996] 3 All ER 558 at 634) the learned judge held that the amended statement of claim as pleaded at that date did not allege the necessary knowledge of, or recklessness as to, the probability of loss, and that accordingly if that statement of claim were not further amended the plaintiffs' claim would fail and should be dismissed. But the judge gave leave to the plaintiffs to apply to amend further the statement of claim. The plaintiffs then brought an application before the judge for leave to reamend the statement of claim and by his third judgment dated 30 July 1997 (unreported) the judge held that even if all the proposed amendments to the statement of claim were permitted the plaintiffs' claim was bound to fail. The judge stated:

> 'I have reached the firm conclusion that on the material available at present the plaintiffs have no arguable case that the Bank dishonestly granted the licence to BCCI or dishonestly failed to revoke the licence or authorisation in circumstances when it knew, believed or suspected that BCCI would probably collapse. There is nothing in the Bingham report [*Inquiry into the Supervision of the Bank of Credit and Commerce International* (HC Paper 198 (1992–93))] or in the documents which I have seen to support such a conclusion and there is much to contradict it.'

Accordingly the judge ordered that the action be struck out, but the judge made it clear that, but for the conclusion which he had reached that the plaintiffs' action was bound to fail, it is likely that he would have allowed all, or almost all, the proposed amendments to the statement of claim.

[113] The Court of Appeal (Auld LJ dissenting) upheld the decision of Clarke J and, delivering the joint judgment of himself and Robert Walker LJ, Hirst LJ stated:

> 'The judge reached the firm conclusion, in his third judgment, that, on the material then available, the plaintiffs had no arguable case that the Bank dishonestly licensed B.C.C.I. S.A. or dishonestly failed to revoke the licence or authorisation in circumstances when it knew, believed or suspected that the company would probably collapse without being rescued. We agree with that conclusion. We also agree that, in all the circumstances of this extraordinary case, it is now for practical purposes inconceivable that new material would emerge of such significance as to alter that conclusion. The tort alleged is a tort of dishonesty, and the plaintiffs' claim must be rigorously assessed on their pleaded case and the evidential material shown to be available to support it.' (See [2000] 2 WLR 15 at 101.)

In his dissenting judgment, Auld LJ stated (at 180):

> 'As the authorities to which Hirst and Robert Walker L.JJ. have referred indicate, it is normally only in clear and obvious cases that a court should strike out a claim as incapable of proof at the interlocutory stage and before full discovery. In cases, such as this, of great legal and factual complexity, it requires a justified confidence that the plaintiffs' case is and will remain incapable of proof and most exceptional circumstances to justify stifling it at an early stage. For the reasons that I have given, I do not consider that the court can be confident that all the evidence material to Clark J.'s conclusion about the Bank's state of knowledge has been gathered in or, which is as important, properly tested.'

[114] In giving judgment on the legal issues relating to the nature of the tort of misfeasance in public office the House directed that the plaintiffs should prepare a new draft pleading ([2000] 3 All ER 1 at 13, [2000] 2 WLR 1220 at 1236) and accordingly the plaintiffs have prepared and served a new pleading consisting of particulars of claim which, with a few additions, largely contain the allegations a pleaded in the reamended statement of claim and in the re-reamendments which the plaintiffs sought leave to make from Clarke J.

[**115**] Before the House in the present hearing the plaintiffs submitted that the new particulars of claim disclosed a cause of action on which they were entitled to proceed to trial. The Bank of England (the Bank) advanced two main submissions. The first was that the plaintiffs' claim, whether as formulated in the b reamended statement of claim or in the re-reamendments which Clarke J considered in his third judgment, or as formulated in the new particulars of claim, disclosed no reasonable cause of action so that the action should remain struck out. The Bank's second submission was that the plaintiffs' claim, in whatever way it was formulated, was frivolous and vexatious and/or an abuse of process and on that ground also the action should remain struck out.

c [**116**] The issues which arose before Clarke J and the Court of Appeal as to whether the pleadings disclosed a reasonable cause of action and/or were frivolous and vexatious and/or an abuse of process were issues which were governed by RSC Ord 18, r 19(1)(a)(b) and (d). I think that in applications under the RSC a clear distinction was not always drawn between an application under Ord 18, d r 19(1)(a) to strike out a statement of claim on the ground that it disclosed no reasonable cause of action and an application under Ord 18, r 19(1)(b) and (d) to strike out a statement of claim on the ground that it was frivolous or vexatious and/or an abuse of the process of the court, and, in practice, there were cases where it was difficult to draw or give effect to this distinction. But in a complex e case such as the present one I think it is helpful to recognise the distinction.

[**117**] *The Supreme Court Practice 1999*, vol 1, para 18/19/10 stated with reference to r 19(1)(a):

> 'A reasonable cause of action means a cause of action with some chance of success when only the allegations in the pleading are considered (*per* Lord f Pearson in *Drummond-Jackson v. British Medical Association* ([1970] 1 All ER 1094, [1970] 1 WLR 688)). So long as the statement of claim or the particulars (*Davey v. Bentinck* ([1893] 1 QB 185)) disclose some cause of action, or raise some question fit to be decided by a Judge or a jury, the mere fact that the case is weak, and not likely to succeed, is no ground for striking it out (*Moore* g *v. Lawson* ((1915) 31 TLR 418); *Wenlock v Moloney* ([1965] 2 All ER 871, [1965] 1 WLR 1238)) …'

Therefore if a plaintiff would be entitled to judgment if he were successful in proving the matters alleged in his pleadings, the statement of claim could not be struck out under Ord 18, r 19(1)(a) on the ground that he had no prospect of h adducing evidence to prove the matters which he alleged. If a defendant wished to strike out a statement of claim and to obtain an order for the dismissal of the action on the ground that the plaintiff had no prospect of proving the case which he alleged in his statement of claim he had to do so under RSC Ord 18, r 19(1)(b) and/or (d). A case which illustrates this (although the application was to strike j out, not a statement of claim, but a plea of justification in a defence) was the application made in *McDonald's Corp v Steel* [1995] 3 All ER 615 where the Court of Appeal considered the correct approach to an application under Ord 18, r 19(d) to strike out a pleading for abuse of process and held (at 623) that the power to strike out was a draconian remedy which was to be employed only in clear and obvious cases where it is possible to say at an interlocutory stage and before full discovery that a particular allegation was incapable of being proved.

[118] In the present case when Clarke J struck out the action he did so on the ground that even with all the proposed re-reamendments the plaintiffs' claim was bound to fail and that in those circumstances it would be an abuse of the process or vexatious or oppressive to allow the action to proceed (paras 6 and 7 of his third judgment).

[119] The applications before Clarke J and the Court of Appeal were governed by the RSC but those rules have now been replaced by the Civil Procedure Rules 1998, SI 1998/3132. I think that r 3.4(2)(a) of the new rules corresponds in a broad way to RSC Ord 18, r 19(1)(a) and r 3.4(2)(b) and r 24.2(a)(i) correspond in a broad way to Ord 18, r 19(1)(b) and (d). CPR 3.4(2) provides:

> 'The court may strike out a statement of case if it appears to the court—(a) that the statement of case discloses no reasonable grounds for bringing or defending the claim; (b) that the statement of case is an abuse of the court's process or is otherwise likely to obstruct the just disposal of the proceedings …'

CPR 24.2(a)(i) provides:

> 'The court may give summary judgment against a claimant or defendant on the whole of a claim or on a particular issue if—(a) it considers that—(i) that claimant has no real prospect of succeeding on the claim or issue …'

[120] The new particulars of claim, served pursuant to the direction of the House, were served after the new CPR came into force, and therefore if Clarke J and the majority of the Court of Appeal erred in their approach to the application to strike out the action the question whether the action should remain struck out falls to be determined by the House under the wording of the new rules. In the present case I think it is desirable, as I have stated, to distinguish between the two grounds on which the Bank submits that the action should remain struck out. Using the terminology of the new rules one ground is that the statement of case (looking only at the pleadings themselves) discloses no reasonable ground for bringing the claim (which I shall term 'the attack on the pleadings point'), and the other ground is that, taking into account the evidence available to the plaintiffs to adduce at a trial, they have no real prospect of succeeding on the claim (which I shall term 'the no real prospect of success point').

The attack on the pleadings point

[121] My Lords, the essential ingredients of the tort of misfeasance in public office were stated in the judgment of the House following the previous hearing ([2000] 3 All ER 1 at 8–10, [2000] 2 WLR 1220 at 1230–1233) and I do not propose again to restate those elements with precision. But it is clear that a plaintiff must prove: (1) an abuse of the powers given to a public officer; (2) that the abuse was constituted by a deliberate act or deliberate omission by the public officer with knowledge that the act or omission was wrongful or with recklessness as to whether or not the act or omission was wrongful; (3) that the public officer acted in bad faith; and (4) that the public officer knew that his act or omission would probably injure the plaintiff or was reckless as to the risk of injury to the plaintiff. In addition the plaintiff must prove that the act or omission caused him loss, but issues of causation do not arise at this stage. As to the first and second matters to be proved, I consider that the particulars of claim sufficiently allege that the Bank deliberately abused its statutory powers in licensing BCCI and in failing to revoke the licence after it had been granted. Paragraph 33, for example, alleges:

a

'*No revocation of the licence under the 1979 Act* The Bank, knowingly, deliberately contrary to the statutory scheme or recklessly indifferent to whether it was acting in accordance with the statutory scheme or wilfully disregarding the risk that it was not acting in accordance with the statutory scheme and in bad faith:

33.1 purported to conclude that it was still entitled to rely upon assurances from the LBC/IML and/or that it had no discretion or power to revoke the full licence when the Bank knew or was recklessly indifferent as to whether or wilfully disregarded the risk that, as was the case:

b

33.1.1 the criteria under paragraphs 7 (fit and proper), 8 (four eyes) and 10 (prudent manner) of Schedule 2 to the 1979 Act had not been fulfilled at the time of the grant of the full licence and remained unfulfilled at all times thereafter;

c

33.1.2 BCCI SA was illegally calling itself a bank contrary to subsection 36(1) of the 1979 Act;

33.1.3 BCCI SA had conducted and continued to conduct its affairs in a way which threatened the interests of its depositors;

d

33.1.4 the Bank's continued reliance upon assurances from the LBC/IML as to BCCI SA's management and financial soundness was unlawful, and the Bank further knew that the likely consequences were that depositors and potential depositors would suffer losses or the Bank wilfully disregarded the risk of the consequences or was recklessly indifferent to the consequences; and/or …'

e

[122] Bad faith is an essential element in the tort of misfeasance. In accordance with a well-established rule it is necessary that bad faith (or dishonesty—the term used in some authorities) should be clearly pleaded. In *Davy v Garrett* (1878) 7 Ch D 473 at 489 Thesiger LJ said:

f

'There is another still stronger objection to this statement of claim. The Plaintiffs say that fraud is intended to be alleged, yet it contains no charge of fraud. In the Common Law Courts no rule was more clearly settled than that fraud must be distinctly alleged and as distinctly proved, and that it was not allowable to leave fraud to be inferred from the facts. It is said that a different rule prevailed in the Court of Chancery. I think that this cannot be correct. It may not be necessary in all cases to use the word "fraud"—indeed in one of the most ordinary cases it is not necessary. An allegation that the Defendant made to the Plaintiff representations on which he intended the Plaintiff to act, which representations were untrue, and known to the defendant to be untrue, is sufficient. The word "fraud" is not used, but two expressions are used pointing at the state of mind of the Defendant—that he intended the representations to be acted upon, and that he knew them to be untrue. It appears to me that a Plaintiff is bound to shew distinctly that he means to allege fraud. In the present case facts are alleged from which fraud might be inferred, but they are consistent with innocence. They were innocent acts in themselves, and it is not to be presumed that they were done with a fraudulent intention.'

g

h

j

I would observe that the last two sentences in this passage have to be read together with the sentence which immediately precedes them. In *Belmont Finance Corp Ltd v Williams Furniture Ltd* [1979] 1 All ER 118 at 130–131, [1979] Ch D 250 at 268 Buckley LJ stated:

'In the present case, do the facts alleged in the statement of claim suffice to bring home to the defendants or any of them a charge that (a) the object of the alleged conspiracy was a dishonest one; and (b) that they actually knew, or must be taken to have known, that it was so? An allegation of dishonesty must be pleaded clearly and with particularity. That is laid down by the rules and it is a well-recognised rule of practice. This does not import that the word "fraud" or the word "dishonesty" must necessarily be used: see *Davy v Garrett* (1878) 7 Ch D 473 at 489 ... per Thesiger LJ. The facts alleged may sufficiently demonstrate that dishonesty is allegedly involved, but where the facts are complicated this may not be so clear, and in such a case it is incumbent upon the pleader to make it clear when dishonesty is alleged. If he uses language which is equivocal, rendering it doubtful whether he is in fact relying on the alleged dishonesty of the transaction, this will be fatal; the allegation of its dishonest nature will not have been pleaded with sufficient clarity.'

[123] In the present case paras 36, 37 and 38 of the particulars of claim allege:

'36. *Failure to supervise* The Bank, knowingly, deliberately contrary to the statutory scheme or recklessly indifferent to whether it was acting in accordance with the statutory scheme or wilfully disregarding the risk that it was not acting in accordance with the statutory scheme and in bad faith failed in the respects set out in these particulars of claim to supervise either BCCI SA or BCCI Overseas when: (36.1) the Bank knew that it had a duty to supervise under the 1979 and 1987 Acts; (36.2) the Bank's motives in deliberately failing to supervise were those pleaded in paragraph 37; (36.3) the Bank knew that the consequences of BCCI SA and/or BCCI Overseas being unsupervised was that depositors and potential depositors would suffer losses or was recklessly indifferent to the consequences or wilfully disregarded the risk of the consequences. In support of these contentions the claimants will rely, prior to disclosure, on the facts and matters set out in Schedules 2 to 7.

THE BANK'S MOTIVES FOR BREACHING ITS STATUTORY DUTIES

37. The motives of the Bank in acting as pleaded above were improper and unlawful and in the premises the Bank acted in bad faith. The Bank's motives were: (37.1) to avoid having to comply with its duty to make, review and, if necessary revise its own express evaluation of the relevant statutory criteria in relation to BCCI SA, the Bank at all times knowing or suspecting that such criteria were not satisfied (as pleaded above); (37.2) to avoid having to become the lead supervisor in relation to BCCI or the consolidated supervisor of the BCCI Group, even though it knew that it was the only supervisor capable of performing those roles; (37.3) to avoid the risks attaching to the Bank from taking on responsibility for becoming lead supervisor or in undertaking consolidated supervision of the BCCI Group including: (37.3.1) the risk of blame; and (37.3.2) the risk of Her Majesty's Treasury having to act as a lender of last resort; (37.4) to avoid the substantial political and diplomatic problems which would have been generated by the refusal or revocation of BCCI SA's licence or authorisation and the closure of its 45 branches in the United Kingdom; (37.5) as to the use of a bank name by BCCI, to perpetuate a situation, which the Bank had favoured since as early as 1978, that regardless of any statutory requirements, BCCI SA should continue to be permitted to use the word "bank" as part of its corporate

a description in the United Kingdom; (37.6) to avoid having to comply with its statutory duty whereby it should have required BCCI Overseas forthwith to apply for and obtain a full licence under the 1979 Act or to cease trading in the United Kingdom.

38. The claimants' case is that in determining the Bank's motives the Bank must be considered in the round as the body made responsible by the 1979 b and 1987 Acts for providing the supervisory regime mandated by those Acts for banks. The motives attributed to the Bank pleaded above are a matter of inference from the primary facts pleaded in Schedules 2 to 7. Further particulars will be given following disclosure.'

[124] In *Armitage v Nurse* [1997] 2 All ER 705 at 715, [1998] Ch 241 at 256 Millett LJ c said:

> 'It is not necessary to use the word "fraud" or "dishonesty" if the facts which make the conduct complained of fraudulent are pleaded; but, if the facts pleaded are consistent with innocence, then it is not open to the court to find fraud.'

d Later in his judgment Millett LJ said:

> 'I am of opinion that, as at present drawn, the amended statement of claim does not allege dishonesty or any breach of trust for which the trustees are not absolved from liability by cl 15.' (See [1997] 2 All ER 705 at 718, [1998] e Ch 241 at 259.)

In *Taylor v Midland Bank Trust Co Ltd* [1999] CA Transcript 1200 Buxton LJ referred to the first observation of Millett LJ and said:

> 'That, however, was an observation about pleading, not about substance. If (unlike the pleader in our case) the claim does not expressly allege f dishonesty, but stands on facts alone, those facts on their face will meet the requirement of a specific allegation of dishonesty only if they can bear no other meaning.'

But in the present case, unlike in *Armitage*'s case, the pleader does expressly allege bad faith because para 37 pleads that 'the motives of the Bank in acting as pleaded g above were improper and unlawful and in the premises the Bank acted in bad faith' and the paragraph sets out particulars in support of that allegation. In my opinion those particulars are not consistent with mere negligence.

[125] I further consider that if a plaintiff clearly alleges dishonesty or bad faith and gives particulars, the statement of claim cannot be struck out under h CPR 3.4(2)(a) because the facts he pleads as giving rise to an inference of dishonesty or bad faith may at the trial, after a full investigation of the circumstances, be held not to constitute proof of that state of mind. If a defendant applies to strike out an action on the ground that the plaintiff has no prospect of adducing evidence at the trial to establish the case which he pleads the application j should be brought under CPR 3.4(2)(b) or CPR 24.2(a)(1).

[126] Mr Stadlen QC, for the Bank, submitted that the pleadings were defective because they did not allege that identified or identifiable bank officials took conscious decisions to do acts or to refrain from doing acts with the requisite guilty state of mind. I do not accept that submission. It is clear from the authorities that a plaintiff can allege misfeasance in public office against a body such as a local authority or a government ministry (see *Dunlop v Woollahra Municipal Council*

[1981] 1 All ER 1202, [1982] AC 158 and *Bourgoin SA v Ministry of Agriculture Fisheries and Food* [1985] 3 All ER 585, [1986] QB 716). Therefore I consider that the plaintiffs are entitled in their pleadings to allege in the manner they have done misfeasance in public office against the Bank without having to give particulars of the individual officials whose decisions and actions they claim combined to bring about the misfeasance alleged.

[127] The fourth element which the plaintiff must prove to establish the tort is that the public officer knew that his act or omission would probably injure the plaintiff or was reckless as to the risk of injury to the plaintiff. Mr Stadlen submitted that the judgments of the House after the earlier hearing established that to prove recklessness the plaintiff must not merely establish that the officer was aware that there was a risk of injury to the plaintiff but that he believed or suspected that his act or omission would probably injure the plaintiff and was recklessly indifferent to that probable injury. Mr Stadlen further submitted that in pleading recklessness in a number of places in the particulars of claim the plaintiffs had failed to plead that the Bank believed or suspected that its act or omissions would probably damage the plaintiffs and was recklessly indifferent to that injury and merely pleaded that the Bank 'wilfully disregarded the risk of the consequences or was recklessly indifferent to the consequences': see for example the last four lines of para 33.1 which I have set out above.

[128] Having expressly pleaded that 'the Bank further knew that the likely consequences were that depositors and potential depositors would suffer losses' the plaintiff then pleaded 'or the Bank wilfully disregarded the risk of the consequences or was recklessly indifferent to the consequences', and in my opinion the distinction between so pleading and pleading that the Bank believed or suspected that its acts or omissions would probably damage the plaintiffs and was recklessly indifferent to that probable injury is such a fine one that an argument based on the distinction cannot constitute a ground for a strike-out under r 3.4(2)(a). In *British Airways Pension Trustees Ltd v Sir Robert McAlpine & Sons Ltd* (1994) 45 Con LR 1 the plaintiffs' statement of claim alleged that defects in a development constructed by McAlpine and designed by Project Design Partnership had diminished its value. The defendants applied to strike out the statement of claim on the ground (inter alia) that it failed to identify which of the alleged defects had caused which part of the alleged diminution in value. In the Court of Appeal Saville LJ (at 4–5) stated:

> 'The various defects alleged by the plaintiffs might not all be attributable to all the defendants, the cost of remedying the individual defects was not given and no attempt was made to ascribe to each defect the amount by which it contributed to the alleged diminution in value. At the same time I have some difficulty in seeing how the defendants could fairly be said to be seriously prejudiced by these omissions. The pleading alleges that the defects respectively attributable to McAlpine and PDP each caused the alleged diminution in value. The alleged defects themselves were set out in some detail, McAlpine and PDP had been on site for a considerable time after practical completion and so had their own means of knowledge of the alleged defects. Thus it seems to me that it can hardly be said that these defendants were in any real fashion placed in a position where they were unable to know what case they had to meet or were facing an unfair hearing ... The basic purpose of pleadings is to enable the opposing party to know what case is being made in sufficient detail to enable that party properly to

a prepare to answer it. To my mind it seems that in recent years there has been a tendency to forget this basic purpose and to seek particularisation even when it is not really required. This is not only costly in itself, but is calculated to lead to delay and to interlocutory battles in which the parties and the court pore over endless pages of pleadings to see whether or not some particular point has or has not been raised or answered, when in truth each party b knows perfectly well what case is made by the other and is able properly to prepare to deal with it. Pleadings are not a game to be played at the expense of the litigants, nor an end in themselves, but a means to the end, and that end is to give each party a fair hearing.'

And in considering the purpose of pleadings under the CPR in *McPhilemy v Times* c *Newspapers Ltd* [1999] 3 All ER 775 at 793 Lord Woolf MR stated: 'What is important is that the pleadings should make clear the general nature of the case of the pleader. This is true both under the old rules and the new rules.'

[129] In the present case where the plaintiffs plead that the Bank knew that the likely consequences were that depositors and potential depositors would suffer loss and then, in the alternative, plead recklessness, I do not consider that the d omission to plead in the context of recklessness that the Bank believed or suspected that injury was likely could prejudice the Bank; and if the ultimate outcome of the trial were to depend on the precise elements necessary to constitute recklessness, I do not consider that the state of the pleadings would prejudice the Bank in advancing any arguments available to it.

e

The no real prospect of success point

[130] The decision by Clarke J, upheld by the majority of the Court of Appeal, that the action was bound to fail and therefore should be struck out was based on two principal conclusions. One was that there was before him all the evidence which was at that time available to the plaintiffs and that there was no reasonable f possibility of the plaintiffs obtaining more evidence in the future, whether by further investigation, discovery, cross-examination of the Bank's witnesses or otherwise which might enable them to succeed. The second conclusion was that on the basis of the evidence before him the plaintiff's claim was bound to fail (see Clarke J's third judgment).

g **[131]** It is apparent from the judgments of Clarke J and the majority of the Court of Appeal that in ruling that the plaintiffs' claim was bound to fail they took into account the findings and conclusions of Bingham LJ set out in his report. Thus in his third judgment Clarke J stated:

'Mr Stadlen submits that there is no support anywhere in the Bingham h report for the conclusion that the Bank acted dishonestly, or that it knew that it was acting unlawfully or that it suspected that its acts or omissions would probably cause loss to depositors or potential depositors. For the reasons already stated I shall focus only on the last of these, but I accept the submission that there is no statement in the report which gives any support j for the conclusion that at any stage the Bank suspected that depositors and potential depositors would probably suffer loss as a result of the Bank's action or inaction. Yet, as stated on page iii of the covering letter to which I have already referred, it is clear that Bingham LJ was considering the Bank's state of mind at every stage. In my judgment, if Bingham LJ had formed the view that at any stage the Bank suspected that its action or inaction would probably injure depositors or potential depositors he would have said so.

Thus, if he had thought that the Bank suspected that BCCI would probably collapse so that new depositors would probably lose their money at any stage of the story from 1979 to 1991 he would have said so. Yet, not only did he not say so, but his observations on the evidence are inconsistent with any such conclusion.'

There are other passages in his judgment where it is clear that Clarke J was influenced by findings or conclusions arrived at by Bingham LJ, and these have been referred to by my noble and learned friend Lord Hope in his speech.

[**132**] Bingham LJ is a judge of the greatest eminence and distinction and his report sets out the entire history of BCCI from its establishment in the United Kingdom until its liquidation and the Bank's relationship to it with the greatest clarity and with much detail. It was therefore inevitable that the plaintiffs would make use of the information contained in the report in drafting their statement of claim. However, notwithstanding the distinction of its author, it is clear that under well-established principles the findings and conclusions of Bingham LJ as to the actions and motives of the Bank would be inadmissible on the hearing of the action: it would be the duty and responsibility of the trial judge to decide for himself, on the evidence which he heard, what were the actions and motives of the Bank. And notwithstanding that it appears that both before Clarke J and the Court of Appeal the plaintiffs themselves sought to rely on certain passages of the Bingham report which they thought supported their case, I consider that it was also impermissible for the judge and the majority of the Court of Appeal in deciding at this interlocutory stage whether there was no real prospect of the action succeeding to be influenced by the findings and conclusions of Bingham LJ. Therefore I am in respectful agreement with the observation of Auld LJ ([2000] 2 WLR 15 at 180) in his dissenting judgment: 'In the circumstances, I am of the view that Clarke J was not entitled to treat Bingham LJ's report effectively as conclusive on the questions he, the judge, had to answer in this litigation …'

[**133**] Therefore I am of the opinion that by taking into account the findings and conclusions of Bingham LJ, Clarke J and the majority of the Court of Appeal erred in considering the issue whether the plaintiffs' claim was bound to fail and that accordingly the House must itself address its mind to the issue (using the terminology of CPR 24.2(a)(i)) whether the plaintiffs have no real prospect of succeeding in their claim.

[**134**] In *Swain v Hillman* [2001] 1 All ER 91 at 92 Lord Woolf MR said:

'The words "no real prospect of being successful or succeeding" do not need any amplification, they speak for themselves. The word "real" distinguishes fanciful prospects of success or, as Mr Bidder QC [counsel for the defendant] submits, they direct the court to the need to see whether there is a "realistic" as opposed to a "fanciful" prospect of success.'

And (at 95):

'Useful though the power is under Pt 24, it is important that it is kept to its proper role. It is not meant to dispense with the need for a trial where there are issues which should be investigated at the trial. As Mr Bidder put it in his submissions, the proper disposal of an issue under Pt 24 does not involve the judge conducting a mini-trial, that is not the object of the provisions; it is to enable cases, where there is no real prospect of success either way, to be disposed of summarily.'

a [135] Mr Stadlen submitted that an action should be struck out if it was apparent that at the trial the plaintiff could adduce no evidence to establish the case which he pleaded and he relied on the judgment of Neill LJ in *McDonald's Corp v Steel* [1995] 3 All ER 615 at 621:

'It is true that a pleader must not put a plea of justification (or indeed a plea of fraud) on the record lightly or without careful consideration of the evidence b available or likely to become available. But, as counsel for the plaintiffs recognised in the course of the argument, there will be cases where, provided a plea of justification is properly particularised, a defendant will be entitled to seek support for his case from documents revealed in the course of discovery or from answers to interrogatories. In recent times there has c been what I regard as a sensible development whereby pleadings in libel actions are treated in the same way as pleadings in other types of litigation. It is therefore instructive to refer to a short passage in the judgment of May LJ in *Steamship Mutual Underwriting Association Ltd v Trollope & Colls Ltd* (1986) 6 Con LR 11 at 27, where, on an application by a firm of structural engineers that the claim against them should be struck out, he said: "In my d opinion, to issue a writ against a party … when it is not intended to serve a statement of claim, and where one has no reasonable evidence or grounds on which to serve a statement of claim against that particular party, is an abuse of the process of the court." Actions for defamation take many forms. The allegations complained about may vary from the moderately serious to e the very grave. It may therefore be unwise to put forward a formula which will match all occasions. Nevertheless I am satisfied that before a plea of justification is included in a defence the following criteria should normally be satisfied: (a) the defendant should believe the words complained of to be true; (b) the defendant should intend to support the defence of justification at the trial; and (c) the defendant should have reasonable evidence to support f the plea or reasonable grounds for supposing that sufficient evidence to prove the allegations will be available at the trial.'

[136] Mr Stadlen submitted that in this case the plaintiffs have no reasonable evidence to support their allegations of deliberate abuse of power in bad faith g with knowledge of probable loss to the depositors or potential depositors, and he further submitted that the plaintiffs have no reasonable grounds for supposing that sufficient evidence to prove the allegations would be available at the trial. However, in considering this submission, it is necessary to take into account a later passage in the judgment of Neill LJ (at 622–623):

h 'It is to be remembered, however, that the evidence on which a defendant may be entitled to rely at trial may take a number of different forms. It may include: (a) his own evidence and the evidence of witnesses called on his behalf, (b) evidence contained in Civil Evidence Act statements, (c) evidence contained in his own documents or in documents produced by third parties on j subpoena, (d) evidence elicited from the plaintiff or the plaintiff's witnesses in the course of cross-examination, (e) answers to interrogatories and (f) evidence contained in documents disclosed by the plaintiff on discovery.

At the outset of the trial

I understand that it has become the practice in actions for defamation to consider at the outset of the trial whether some parts of the defence should be struck out on the basis that it has become apparent that some of the matters pleaded are not going to be supported by evidence. I can understand that in an appropriate case this is a sensible course which is likely to shorten the trial. On the other hand there may be cases where a defendant pleads some matter which he believes to be true but which he may still be unable to prove by admissible evidence otherwise than by eliciting an answer in cross-examination. Each case will have to be considered on its own facts.'

[137] Clarke J and the majority of the Court of Appeal were of the opinion that Bingham LJ had conducted such a thorough examination of the Bank's dealings with BCCI that it was unrealistic to think that any further material of relevance would emerge and that accordingly the question whether there was reasonable evidence to support the plaintiffs' case was to be determined on the basis of the evidence referred to in the Bingham report. Mr Stadlen submitted that Clarke J and the majority of the Court for Appeal were right to hold that that evidence provided no support for an allegation that the Bank had acted dishonestly or in bad faith or with knowledge of probable loss to depositors. I am unable to accept that submission. Both Clarke J and the majority of the Court of Appeal found that by April 1990 the Bank knew that BCCI would probably collapse with consequential loss to depositors and potential depositors in the absence of a rescue package. Clarke J, referring to April 1990, said in his third judgment:

'Bingham LJ concludes that he did not think that any informed reader of the report could have failed to read it as seriously impugning the honesty with which the group had been run. However, according to para 2.186, with the possible exception of Mr Beverly, no one did. Indeed in para 2.187 Bingham LJ concludes that in April 1990 and for a number of months afterwards the Governors, the Board of Banking Supervision, Mr Quinn and Mr Barnes were unaware of the serious doubts thrown by Price Waterhouse on the integrity of the Bank's most senior management. Sir Patrick submits that that conclusion is incredible. He submits that senior representatives of the Bank must have appreciated that that was the position. I see the force of that submission, but, for present purposes, the question is not whether the Bank appreciated that there had been fraud within BCCI but whether it suspected that BCCI would probably not be rescued and nevertheless dishonestly failed to revoke its authorisation. It is plain that the Bank appreciated that in the absence of remedial steps BCCI would indeed probably collapse.'

And in the judgment of the majority of the Court of Appeal Hirst LJ said ([2000] 2 WLR 15 at 99):

'The report of 18 April 1990 was not therefore a totally unheralded shock for the Bank. Nevertheless it is highly significant as marking a date after which it would be impossible, in our judgment, to contend that there was no arguable case that the Bank was aware of a very serious and very immediate threat to depositors of B.C.C.I. S.A. At this point, therefore, the prospect of a rescue operation being promoted by the Abu Dhabi ruling house, and the Bank's perception of the various possible outcomes, assumes central importance.'

And (at 101):

'Throughout the preceding four sections we have adopted the same approach as that taken by the judge, and asked ourselves whether the plaintiffs have an arguable case that the Bank actually foresaw B.C.C.I.'s a imminent collapse at each relevant stage. We have agreed with the judge's conclusion that all the evidence indicates that up to April 1990 it did not, and that thereafter it did, but properly relied on the prospect of a rescue. That is sufficient to dispose of the case in the Bank's favour.'

[138] In my opinion the Bank cannot validly contend that on the documentary evidence available to them the plaintiffs have no real prospect of succeeding in b establishing that the Bank knowingly and in a deliberate way abused its statutory powers in failing to revoke BCCI's licence after it had been granted. A memorandum dated 19 October 1983 from an official in the Bank's banking supervision division to a number of senior officials of the Bank states:

c 'This note reviews our approach to the supervision of BCCI, arguing that our present approach fails to satisfy the requirements of the Banking Act and recommending that we should press BCCI for local incorporation of UK operations … However, these problems are less serious than the present deficiencies in our supervisory approach in the light of the Banking Act's requirements. The problem with regard to the Section 36 contraventions is d more difficult, particularly with regard to the branches of BCCI SA, to which there seems no practicable alternative to turning a blind eye.'

And in a note of a meeting of Bank officials dated 17 December 1985, after a team from the Bank had visited the BCCI offices in Leadenhall Street, the following comment by an official is noted:

e

'There is no doubt in my mind that BCCI has centralised its management, control and operations in the City. This is a UK-based bank, with its White House encompassing two buildings fronting Leadenhall Street and three at the rear. There is absolutely no way that we should continue the pretence that Luxembourg are the prime supervisors. Luxembourg is prehistoric; f Grand Cayman is a tax haven; and it is the Bank of England who are the lender of last resort. If UK incorporation of the UK branch network means the movement of the Treasury Support Organisation from London to Abu Dhabi, the Bank must encourage Abedi all the way. This surely is the only route to effective supervision.'

g **[139]** I observed in my speech after the earlier hearing that I considered that, in the context of misfeasance, 'in bad faith' is a preferable term to 'dishonesty' (see [2000] 3 All ER 1 at 41–42, [2000] 2 WLR 1220 at 1266). In relation to the element of bad faith the plaintiffs plead in para 37 of the particulars of claim that the Bank's motives set out in that paragraph constitute bad faith. Lord Neill of Bladen QC, h for the plaintiffs, submitted that an inference can be drawn from a number of the Bank's documents that it was reluctant to face up to the difficulties and responsibilities involved in an adequate supervision of BCCI and that it placed its own interests before the discharge of its duty to protect depositors and that this constituted bad faith on its part. It is relevant to emphasise that this is the case made by the j plaintiffs. They do not make the case that the officials of the Bank were dishonest, in the sense that they acted improperly for their own financial gain. Therefore I consider, with respect, that the point that it is inherently improbable that in the absence of some financial incentive bank officials would act dishonestly does not assist the Bank's case.

[140] Lord Neill referred (inter alia) to a letter dated 8 April 1987 from a senior official of the Bank to a senior official of the Commissariat au Controle des Banques in Luxembourg written after the Bank had been informed that it was no longer possible for Luxembourg to carry out the consolidated supervisory role which it had accepted in the last few years. In the letter the official said:

'The precise formulation set out in your letter poses a particular problem for us. This is that having decided not to take a leading supervisory role, we believe that the incorporation of the 45 UK branches here, combined with the presence in London of a large part of BCCI's overall administration, is likely to draw us in practice into the position of lead supervisor which we seek to avoid. In those circumstances, our ability to do the job effectively would be even more restricted than if we had assumed the role officially from the outset. In any case we are not at all certain that we would feel able to grant a licence by applying the criteria under the UK Banking Act, to any part of the operation at this stage. This is because we have to be satisfied under our new legislation not only that an institution will be prudently run but that it will be run with integrity—and our experience with BCCI in the past make such a judgment difficult.'

[141] In respect of the need for the plaintiffs to show material to support their allegation that the Bank knew of probable loss to depositors or was reckless as to whether there would be loss to depositors, Lord Neill referred to certain paragraphs in the affidavit of a senior Bank official sworn in July 1991 in support of the Bank's petition to wind up BCCI. The official stated:

'20. The Bank is seriously concerned that BCCI has been managed and may still be being managed in a dishonest and fraudulent manner. The Bank is and continues to be concerned that the true financial position of BCCI has been and continues to be concealed by BCCI from the Bank and other regulatory authorities which are part of the "college". It appears from the Price Waterhouse report that the accounting records have completely failed and continue to fail to meet the standards required of institutions authorised under the Banking Act. It further appears that there is no proper or adequate system or controls for managing the business of BCCI. The management of BCCI have acted without integrity and with a lack of skill. Notwithstanding the fact that it might be said of some of the senior managers that they were not directly involved in the fraudulent activity described in the Price Waterhouse report, management have as a whole been involved in keeping that activity and its consequences concealed from the Bank and other regulatory authorities. As a result of the information provided to it, the Bank has no trust or confidence in the senior management of BCCI which is essential to the relationship between the regulator and the regulated bank.

21. As a supervisor of BCCI the Bank is concerned that the interest of depositors will be jeopardised if the affairs of BCCI are left in the hands of its managers and it has formed the view that the interest of depositors will be best served by the winding-up of BCCI. In these circumstances the Bank believes that it would be just and equitable to wind up BCCI ...

24. In April 1990 it became apparent that BCCI had a substantial portfolio of US $4 billion of problem loans. In the 1989 year-end accounts substantial provisions were first raised against a US $4 billion portfolio of problem loans in the Group, many of which were booked in BCCI. On 22 May 1991 a financial support arrangement was entered into by BCCI whereby these problem loans were transferred to new companies which were either owned

a directly by the Government of Abu Dhabi, or if not, largely guaranteed by the Government of Abu Dhabi. In return for the loan assets BCCI received promissory notes in US$ and UAE Dhirams equivalent in face value to US$3,061 million. However, from the report it appears that the loan assets can be reassigned to BCCI in the event of any breach of warranty that the loan assets do not involve any activity which is criminal or illegal and which, if revealed b might be expected to damage the international reputation of the Abu Dhabi Government. At a meeting held on 5 October 1990 the Abu Dhabi Government said that if fraud was detected there could be a serious problem about the continuation of the support of the Abu Dhabi Government. Whilst the Abu Dhabi Government has said that it has no present intention to reassign the loan assets, there must be a risk that it will do so. If it does, c the problem portfolio will revert to BCCI. In July 1991 the Abu Dhabi Government indicated to Price Waterhouse that it was not prepared to commit itself to providing further funds for BCCI to m[e]et all its liabilities on an unqualified basis. Given the present uncertainty surrounding BCCI's liabilities it is fair to conclude that there is no real prospect of sufficient funds d being made available within such time as the relevant regulators might require.'

[**142**] Lord Neill submitted that the concerns of the Bank set out in paras 20 and 21 had been known to the Bank for a number of years, as evidenced by the letter dated 8 April 1987 to the official in Luxembourg in which the senior official e of the Bank stated that the Bank had to be satisfied that BCCI would be run with integrity, 'and our experiences with BCCI in the past make such a judgment difficult'. Lord Neill also referred to a memorandum to the governors of the Bank dated 15 July 1983 from a senior official of the Bank in which he said that the Bank's officials had become increasingly concerned about the ineffectiveness of the present arrangements for the overall supervision of BCCI and that he f attached a note setting out possible ways of dealing with 'what has now become, in our view, an unacceptable position'. The note, which was headed 'WHY HAS BCCI BECOME A PROBLEM? WHY IS ACTION NOW URGENTLY REQUIRED?', stated that it was clear that the principal place of BCCI was not Luxembourg but was, administratively, the United Kingdom and that being so, and in the light of g the Luxembourg authorities' admission that their resources were no longer up to the task of supervising BCCI's operations, the Bank was in 'a vulnerable position'. The note further stated that the Bank's knowledge of the activities of BCCI in the United Kingdom and its limited knowledge of the BCCI group as a whole did not inspire confidence in the soundness of BCCI's worldwide operations. The note h went on to state:

'As noted, the present arrangements are wholly unsatisfactory and it is not therefore considered an option to sit back and do nothing. This leaves two basic choices:—(a) to try to have BCCI closed down, either worldwide or just the UK region; (b) to arrange for its supervision on a satisfactory basis.'

j

Lord Neill further referred to a paper of the Board of Banking Supervision dated 3 September 1987 which stated that at their last meeting they had expressed concern about whether the UK depositors with BCCI SA were receiving adequate protection from the supervisory regime in place, or in prospect. The board asked whether the UK depositors might not be better protected if BCCI were only permitted to take deposits in the UK via a UK subsidiary. They questioned whether the formation of such a subsidiary would increase the 'moral hazard' of the UK supervisors in relation to the whole BCCI group and whether, even if it did, the interests of the UK depositors should not be paramount. The paper went on to state that the cause of the concern did not stem from any obvious weakness in the BCCI group. The concern was rather one of scepticism towards a large, shadowy and swift-growing bank with no natural geographic base. The paper then stated:

> 'The BCCI group is frequently subject to rumours which suggest that it or its clients operate at the margin of legality. Many observers accordingly have developed a gut feeling that the bank might suddenly run into serious difficulties without warning. The fact that so much of the group's business is booked in centres where supervision is less professional, particularly in relation to the type of business which BCCI undertakes, makes the absence of warning all the more likely.'

Lord Neill submitted that in July 1983, in September 1987 and in April 1990 the Bank took no steps to arrange for supervision of BCCI on a satisfactory basis but was reckless as to the serious risk of loss to depositors.

[143] There are passages in the documents which support the Bank's case that whilst, prior to April 1990, it had concerns about the soundness of BCCI's operations, none the less it recognised that its overriding duty was to protect the interests of depositors and that its decisions and its conduct towards BCCI were intended to discharge that duty, so that the allegation of bad faith on its part cannot be established. Thus in the note sent to the governors of the Bank dated 15 July 1983 its author states:

> 'The closure route could only be pursued if it could be shown, with reasonable certainty, that the Group's operations were fundamentally unsound; and that continued existence posed a greater threat to depositors' money than a winding up. Without a very wide ranging investigation and the fullest co-operation of other supervisory authorities it would not be possible to state, categorically, that the Group's operations are unsound to the extent of endangering depositors.'

But at this stage in the proceedings a court is not concerned to try to assess which side will probably succeed if there is a trial: the question is whether there is material which shows that there are issues which should be investigated at a trial, and in my opinion the material does show this.

[144] As regards the prospect from April 1990 onwards of a rescue operation by the Abu Dhabi government I would not take the view that the plaintiffs have no real prospect of establishing that the Bank knew that it was probable, or was reckless as to the probability, that that government, notwithstanding its stated willingness to rescue BCCI, would not commit itself fully to meet all its liabilities as more information became available as to the extent of its liabilities and as to the dishonesty of its managers. In differing from the opinion of Clarke J and the majority of the Court of Appeal that the plaintiffs have no real prospect of success, I take into account two further considerations. One is that I think that it is reasonably possible that further material may become available to the plaintiffs before trial, and I am in respectful agreement with the view of Auld LJ of his judgment:

> 'In addition to the different function of Bingham L.J.'s inquiry from the more focused issues for determination in this litigation, there are several

a obvious disadvantages of his procedure when compared with the court's process for determining the truth of the matter and its legal significance. His was not a statutory inquiry, so he had no power to compel the attendance of witnesses or require the production of documents; he heard the evidence of some, but not all, relevant and important players in the story; there was no counsel to the inquiry and no opportunity for adversarial discovery, b interrogation or cross-examination of witnesses; and, as I have said, he acknowledged that most of his criticisms and a number of his factual conclusions were challenged, the validity of such challenges not capable of being tested on appeal. In the circumstances, I am of the view that Clarke J. was not entitled ... to conclude, as he did, that all the available material evidence on those questions had been gathered in. Given the greater c generality of the questions in the Bingham inquiry, the limitations of it as a fact-finding exercise when compared with litigation, his acknowledgement of a number of challenges to some of his factual conclusions and the emergence of additional material since the inquiry indicating the Bank's state of knowledge as to the Gokal unrecorded loans, I can see no basis for d Clarke J.'s confidence in this extraordinary and complex case for concluding that Bingham L.J. had seen and fully tested all the material evidence available or likely to become available on the issues confronting the court in this case.' (See [2000] 2 WLR 15 at 180.)

[145] Secondly, I consider that the material already available to the plaintiffs e provides reasonable grounds for thinking that they may be able to advance their case by the cross-examination of the Bank's officials.

[146] In the *McDonald's Corp* case Neill LJ recognised that the prospect of evidence emerging on cross-examination was a matter to be taken into consideration. Mr Stadlen relied on the judgment of Chadwick LJ in *Jarvis v f Hampshire CC* [2000] 2 FCR 310 at 338 where he said:

> '... it is an abuse of the process of the court to make allegations of [dishonesty and deliberate abuse of power] in circumstances in which they cannot be supported by particulars; no less so when they are inconsistent with the substantial documentary material which is available. It is not g enough to assert, as counsel for the claimant did assert before us, that—if the matter were allowed to go to trial—something might emerge through cross-examination. That is not a proper basis on which to make allegations of dishonesty. The judge was right to strike out those allegations.'

[147] But the assessment whether it is reasonable to take the view that h evidence may emerge in cross-examination depends on the particular facts of the case. In *Jarvis'* case it was clear that the allegations were groundless and could not be given any substance by the cross-examination of the defendant's witnesses. But in the present case, where there is an arguable case that the Bank had increasing concern about BCCI for a number of years prior to April 1990 and j knew from April 1990 onwards of the imminent collapse of BCCI unless there was a rescue, I think that justice requires that the plaintiffs, after discovery and interrogation, should have the opportunity to cross-examine the Bank's witnesses as to their concerns before 1990 and as to their belief from April 1990 onwards that there would be a rescue operation.

[148] The fact that a plaintiff does not have direct evidence as to the belief or foresight or motives of the defendant is not in itself a reason to strike out the action. In *Taylor v Midland Bank Trust Co Ltd* [1999] CA Transcript 1200 the plaintiff alleged dishonest breach of trust and the defendant applied for the dismissal of the claim without trial under r 24.2(a)(i). Upholding the decision of Carnwath J to dismiss the application, Buxton LJ stated:

> '[Counsel for the defendant] appeared at one stage to argue that the case must be made good by direct evidence, and could not rely, as it does, on inference. If that was the submission, I cannot agree with it. Where the motives or knowledge of a party is in issue, it may often be necessary to rely on inference rather than direct statements or admissions by that party. There is nothing objectionable in principle in that, however much an inference may be less cogent than an admission. Nor is it right that, in drawing inferences, a court can only infer this form of dishonesty if the primary evidence admits of no other explanation. That puts the test too high. The process of reasoning should be constrained only by the court's appreciation of the seriousness of the charge and the substantiality of the evidence therefore necessary to make it good.'

[**149**] In their judgment the majority of the Court of Appeal stated:

> 'Were officials of the Bank to give evidence which was fully tested by cross-examination in the adversarial process of a trial, it is not merely possible, but even likely, that a clearer and somewhat different picture would emerge as to the Bank's corporate state of mind from time to time, as constituted by the states of mind of a small number of its responsible officials. But we would agree that there is no realistic possibility that the picture which emerged would be fundamentally different. In that respect the Bingham report is, despite its relatively informal status, an invaluable aid to distinguishing between what is a practical possibility and what is fanciful or inconceivable.' (See [2000] 2 WLR 15 at 91.)

I am in full agreement with the first sentence of that passage, but I am, with respect, unable to agree with the last two sentences and I do not share the majority's confidence that though in cross-examination it is likely that a somewhat different picture would emerge, there is no realistic possibility that a fundamentally different picture would emerge.

[**150**] The Bank's application has been to strike out the entire action. The Bank's case that the plaintiffs have no reasonable prospect of success can be more strongly advanced in respect of the allegations relating to the earlier part of the history of the Bank's dealings with BCCI. But having regard to the extent to which the allegations in respect of the entire period from 1979 to 1991 are interwoven and interrelated I consider that it would not be appropriate to consider striking out certain parts of the claim and that the entire action should be permitted to proceed to trial.

[**151**] Because of the large number of documents which were referred to by counsel and the detailed and lengthy submissions which were advanced to the House I have thought it right to state my views at much greater length than is usual when an appellate court considers a strike-out application, particularly when the appellate court decides that the action should proceed to trial. But I wish to state my agreement with the observation of my noble and learned friend Lord Steyn as to the duty of the trial judge in para [8] of his speech. The judge will have to decide the case after the examination and cross-examination of witnesses on the evidence which he hears and he should not be influenced by any

a parts of the speeches of the House in this hearing which may appear to express any opinion on the facts of the case.

[152] Accordingly, for the reasons which I have given I would allow this appeal. I would dismiss the Bank's cross-appeal for the reasons given by my noble and learned friend Lord Hope and I would make the order proposed by him.

b **LORD HOBHOUSE OF WOODBOROUGH**. My Lords,

[153] It has been estimated that the trial of this action will occupy a whole year; I sincerely hope that this is too pessimistic. But, on any view, the continuation of the action will involve the application of very substantial resources both at the trial and in preparation for it by both of the parties and the c system of justice. The volume of paper, forensic and evidential, is already formidable and the events which will have to be trawled over extend over some 15 years. The investigation of those events gave rise to a report (*Inquiry into the Supervision of the Bank of Credit and Commerce International* (HC Paper 198 (1992–93))) (the Bingham report) which runs to 218 printed pages together with eight volumes of (unpublished) appendices recounting the history in greater detail. It d was thus understandable that it should have been thought right to examine whether such a trial and such proceedings were really appropriate and necessary in order to determine the just outcome to the parties' dispute. Indeed, under Pt 1 of the Civil Procedure Rules 1998, SI 1998/3132, now in force it is the overriding objective, and the duty of the courts and the parties, that cases should be dealt e with justly and that this includes dealing with cases in a proportionate manner, expeditiously and fairly, without undue expense and by allotting only an appropriate share of the court's resources while taking into account the need to allot resources to other cases. This represents an important shift in judicial philosophy from the traditional philosophy that previously dominated the administration of justice. Unless a party's conduct could be criticised as abusive f or vexatious, the party was treated as having a right to his day in court in the sense of proceeding to a full trial after having fully exhausted the interlocutory pre-trial procedures.

[154] There were limited exceptions to this traditional approach. One was the RSC Ord 14 procedure for summary judgment. This was not a procedure for g an informal trial; it was a procedure for enabling judgment to be entered for the plaintiff where there was no issue to be tried, in the words of the rule, no 'issue or question in dispute which ought to be tried' or 'other reason' why there ought to be a trial. It was to avoid delaying tactics on the part of a defendant and enable speedy judgment to be given for the plaintiff where that was appropriate and just notwithstanding that the defendant asserted that he had a defence. One of the h court's powers under Ord 14 was to order the defendant to pay money into court as a condition of being permitted to defend. Order 14 was available to the plaintiff alone; there was no equivalent procedure for summary judgment in favour of the defendant. This procedure was not the same as the striking out jurisdiction which had two aspects. One was the striking out of a party's pleading (or part of j it) because the conduct of the party was objectionable, i e abusive or vexatious. For this purpose evidence was relevant and admissible. The other was the demurrer procedure which had completely different origins and served a different purpose. It derived from the formal distinction between law and fact. It provided a mechanism for testing the propositions of law upon which the party (plaintiff or defendant) was relying; it was decided upon the pleadings alone and no evidence was admissible. The court could in its discretion deal with the issue of

law as a matter of striking out, or by directing the trial of a preliminary point of law, or by directing that the decision of the point of law should be left over to the full trial. In principle, though not always in practice, the striking out procedure should be used only where the point of law was not reasonably arguable. Warnings against the inappropriate use of the striking out procedure to decide arguable points of law were given by Lord Templeman and Lord Mackay of Clashfern in *Williams & Humbert Ltd v W & H Trade Marks (Jersey) Ltd* [1986] 1 All ER 129 at 139, 143, [1986] AC 368 at 435–436, 441; but the motive of simplifying procedures and saving costs was applauded and may, in the end, show that the procedure adopted was appropriate.

[155] Another exception in practice was the policy of the Commercial Court to assist the expeditious and efficient determination of disputes of commercial parties by adopting relatively informal procedures, usually at an early stage of the case, to identify the real points at issue and, by deciding them, enable the dispute to be resolved. Often this was an aspiration rather than a reality. Commercial disputes often involve lengthy and costly investigations and trials which defeat these aspirations. At times commercial litigation has been allowed to drift into over elaborate and drawn-out procedures which overlook any other priority than investigating every nook and cranny and ensuring that every angle receives the full forensic exposure. In *Ashmore v Corp of Lloyd's* [1992] 2 All ER 486 at 493, [1992] 1 WLR 446 at 453–454, Lord Templeman objected strenuously to the practice of taking 'every point conceivable and inconceivable without judgment and discrimination' and exhorted judges and appellate courts to control the conduct of proceedings. Lord Roskill agreed with him saying:

> 'The Court of Appeal appear to have taken the view that the plaintiffs were entitled of right to have their case tried to conclusion in such manner as they thought fit and if necessary after all the evidence on both sides had been adduced. With great respect, like my noble and learned friend, I emphatically disagree. In the Commercial Court and indeed in any trial court it is the trial judge who has control of the proceedings. It is part of his duty to identify the crucial issues and to see they are tried as expeditiously and as inexpensively as possible ... Litigants are not entitled to the uncontrolled use of a trial judge's time. Other litigants await their turn.' (See [1992] 2 All ER 486 at 488, [1992] 1 WLR 446 at 448.)

[156] There is always an exercise of judgment to be undertaken by the judge whether the perceived short-cut will turn out to have been beneficial and, inevitably, in a proportion of cases expectations will be confounded. Caution is required. But it is simplistic to suppose that in complex litigation the exercise should never be attempted. The volume of documentation and the complexity of the issues raised on the pleadings should be the subject of critical scrutiny and should not without more deter the judge from considering whether it is really necessary to commit the parties and the court to a lengthy trial and all the preparatory steps which that will involve. Indeed it can be submitted with force that those are just the sorts of case which most strongly cry out for the exclusion of anything that is unnecessary for the achievement of a just outcome for the parties.

[157] The present case illustrates these considerations. The commercial judge was faced with an action dependent upon a cause of action of which the parameters were not wholly certain and a statement of claim which may or may not have disclosed a case sufficient in law to enable the plaintiffs to succeed.

a He ordered the trial of preliminary questions of law. He was clearly right to do so even though the decision of those questions has led to appeals to your Lordships' House. However, difficulties then arose with the plaintiffs' pleadings. At each level the plaintiffs have re-pleaded their case to accommodate the fresh thinking about the elements of the tort of misfeasance in public office. Further, the courts at each level have been called on to adjudicate upon the proposed b revised pleading, your Lordships included. This has led to an unsatisfactory state of affairs. Any skilful pleader should be able to draft a pleading which sufficiently makes the minimum allegations to support the legal definition of the tort and I have detected no lack of skill in the lawyers acting for either side in this litigation. The question then becomes whether the particulars given provide realistic support for the primary allegations. This has in turn led to a detailed examination c both in the courts below and before your Lordships of these allegations. I will have to comment upon the suitability of that course in your Lordships' House. It was probably inevitable before the judge and may have been so before the Court of Appeal where questions of leave to amend were also debated. It was complicated in the Court of Appeal by the fact that Auld LJ did not agree with the d majority on the law. Before the judge and in the Court of Appeal the decision was given on the basis of the RSC not the CPR.

[158] This leads me back to the CPR. As previously noted, CPR Pt 1 adopts a philosophy similar to that enunciated in *Ashmore*'s case. It is followed through into the new version of RSC Ord 14. It is CPR Pt 24. It authorises the court to e decide a claim (or a particular issue) without a trial. Unlike Ord 14, it applies to both plaintiffs (claimants) and the defendants. It therefore can be used in cases such as the present where the application for judgment without trial is being made by the defendant. The court may exercise the power where it considers that the 'claimant has no real prospect of succeeding on the claim' and 'there is no other reason why the case or issue should be disposed of at a trial'. The concluding f phrase corresponds to the similar phrase used in RSC Ord 14, r.3(1) and has not been relied upon in the present case. The important words are 'no real prospect of succeeding'. It requires the judge to undertake an exercise of judgment. He must decide whether to exercise the power to decide the case without a trial and give a summary judgment. It is a 'discretionary' power, i e one where the choice g whether to exercise the power lies within the jurisdiction of the judge. Secondly, he must carry out the necessary exercise of assessing the prospects of success of the relevant party. If he concludes that there is 'no real prospect', he may decide the case accordingly. I stress this aspect because in the course of argument counsel referred to the relevant judgment of Clarke J as if he had made 'findings' h of fact. He did not do so. Under RSC Ord 14 as under CPR Pt 24, the judge is making an assessment not conducting a trial or fact-finding exercise. Whilst it must be remembered that the wood is composed of trees some of which may need to be looked at individually, it is the assessment of the whole that is called for. A measure of analysis may be necessary but the 'bottom line' is what ultimately j matters. CPR Pt 24 includes provisions covering various ancillary matters, at what stage the application can be made (r 24.4), the filing of evidence (r 24.5) and supplementary powers of the court (r 24.6). The practice direction which was originally appended (Practice Direction—The Summary Disposal of Claims) filled out some of what is in the rules:

> '4.2 Where a defendant applies for judgment in his favour on the claimant's claim, the court will give that judgment if either: (1) the claimant has failed

to show a case which, if unanswered, would entitle him to judgment, or (2) the defendant has shown that the claim would be bound to be dismissed at trial. *a*

4.3 Where it appears to the court possible that a claim or defence may succeed but improbable that it will do so, the court may make a conditional order as described below.'

The criterion which the judge has to apply under CPR Pt 24 is not one of probability; it is absence of reality. The majority in the Court of Appeal used the phrases 'no realistic possibility' and distinguished between a practical possibility and 'what is fanciful or inconceivable' ([2000] 2 WLR 15 at 91). Although used in a slightly different context these phrases appropriately express the same idea. CPR Pt 3 contains similar provisions in relation to the court's case management powers. These include explicit powers to strike out claims and defences on the ground, among others, that the statement of case discloses no reasonable ground for bringing or defending the claim. *b* *c*

[159] Before your Lordships it was accepted by counsel that this part of the appeal should be decided under CPR Pt 24 applying the criterion 'no real prospect of success'. An exchange of correspondence has confirmed this. (A similar criterion is also appropriate where there is an application for leave to amend to add a new case.) Recent statements in the Court of Appeal concerning CPR Pt 24 bear repetition: *d*

'The words "no real prospect of succeeding" do not need any amplification, they speak for themselves. The word "real" distinguishes fanciful prospects of success or, as [counsel] submits, they direct the court to the need to see whether there is a "realistic" as opposed to a "fanciful" prospect of success ... It is important that a judge in appropriate cases should make use of the powers contained in Pt 24. In doing so he or she gives effect to the overriding objectives contained in Pt 1. It saves expense; it achieves expedition; it avoids the court's resources being used up on cases where this serves no purpose and, I would add, generally, that it is in the interests of justice. If a claimant has a case which is bound to fail, then it is in the claimant's interests to know as soon as possible that that is the position.' (See *Swain v Hillman* [2001] 1 All ER 91 at 92, 94 per Lord Woolf MR.) *e* *f*

'The CPR are a procedural code with the overriding objective of enabling the court to deal with cases justly including saving expense and ensuring that it is dealt with expeditiously and fairly. The court must seek to give effect to the overriding objective when it exercises any power given to it or interprets any rule. I take this into account when considering the application under Part 24.2 ... [The language of Part 3.4] is very akin to that in the now extinct RSC Ords 18 and 19 and under which this application was commenced (and as good as succeeded) at the first hearing. This part includes "a claim which raises an unwinnable case where continuance of the proceedings is without any possible benefit to the respondent and would waste resources on both sides".' (See *Sinclair v Chief Constable of West Yorkshire* [2000] CA Transcript 2189 per Otton LJ, and see *Harris v Bolt Burdon* [2000] CPLR 9.) *g* *h* *j*

There is no point in allowing claims to proceed which have no real prospect of success, certainly not in proceeding beyond the stage where their hopelessness has clearly become apparent.

[160] The difficulty in the application of the criterion used by CPR Pt 24 is that it requires an assessment to be made in advance of a full trial as to what the outcome of such a trial would be. The pre-trial procedures give the claimant an opportunity to obtain additional evidence to support his case. The most obvious of these is discovery of documents but there is also the weapon of requesting particulars or interrogatories and the exchange of witness statements may provide a party with additional important material. Therefore the courts have in the present case recognised that they must have regard not only to the evidence presently available to the plaintiffs but also to any realistic prospect that that evidence would have been strengthened between now and the trial. Indeed, it was the submission of Mr Stadlen QC, for the defendants, that Clarke J had applied the right test when he said:

> 'In my judgment the question in the instant case is whether the bank has persuaded the court that the plaintiffs' case is bound to fail on the material at present available and that there is no reasonable possibility of evidence becoming available to the plaintiff, whether by further investigation, discovery, cross-examination or otherwise sufficiently to support their case and to give it some prospect of success. If the bank discharges that burden, it will follow that the plaintiffs' claim is bound to fail. In that event to allow the action to proceed would serve no useful purpose. It would only involve the expenditure of time and money—in this case a very great deal of both. Neither party would have any legitimate interest in such expenditure because it could not benefit either.'

It is possible that this test, in its reference to cross-examination, may be rather too favourable to the plaintiffs. It is derived from what was said in relation to a plea of justification by Neill LJ in *McDonald's Corp v Steel* [1995] 3 All ER 615, a defamation action. He included cross-examination no doubt because in a defamation action, although the burden of proving justification is upon the defendant, the publisher of the libel, it is normal for the plaintiff to call his evidence first; justification is a defence. Where an allegation of dishonesty is being made as part of the cause of action of the plaintiff, there is no reason why the rule should not apply that the plaintiff must have a proper basis for making an allegation of dishonesty in his pleading. The hope that something may turn up during the cross-examination of a witness at the trial does not suffice. It is of course different if the admissible material available discloses a reasonable prima facie case which the other party will have to answer at the trial.

[161] The judge's assessment has to start with the relevant party's pleaded case but the enquiry does not end there. The allegations may be legally adequate but may have no realistic chance of being proved. On the other hand, the limitations in the allegations pleaded and any lack of particularisation may show that the party's case is hopeless. The tort of misfeasance in public office is a tort which involves bad faith and in that sense dishonesty. It follows that to substantiate his claim in this tort, first in his pleading and then at the trial, a plaintiff must be able to allege and then prove this subjectively dishonest state of mind. The law quite rightly requires that questions of dishonesty be approached more rigorously than other questions of fault. The burden of proof remains the civil burden—the balance of probabilities—but the assessment of the evidence has to take account of the seriousness of the allegations and, if that be the case, any unlikelihood that the person accused of dishonesty would have acted in that way. Dishonesty is not to be inferred from evidence which is equally consistent with mere negligence. At the pleading stage the party making the allegation of dishonesty has to be prepared to particularise it and, if he is unable to do so, his allegation will be struck out. The allegation must be made upon the basis of evidence which will be admissible at the trial. This commonsense proposition has recently been re-emphasised by the Court of Appeal in *Medcalf v Mardell* (2001) Times, 2 January, in which Peter Gibson LJ said: 'The material evidence must be evidence which can be put before the court to make good the allegation.' Evidence which cannot be used in court cannot be relied upon to justify the making of the allegation of dishonesty. I mention this because it shows the principle to be applied and not because there is any suggestion in the present case that there is any inadmissible material which would support allegations of dishonesty in the present case. It is normally to be assumed that a party's pleaded case is the best case he can make (or wishes to make). Therefore, in the present case, the particulars given provide a true guide to the nature of the case being made by the plaintiffs (claimants).

[**162**] I agree with my noble and learned friend Lord Hope that in substance Clarke J asked himself the right questions and that, as he expressed it, he directed himself correctly as to the relevance of the Bingham report. My noble and learned friend and those who agree with him are, however, critical of the actual use made by Clarke J and the majority of the Court of Appeal of the report. I consider that with minor exceptions these criticisms are not fair to Clarke J nor to Hirst and Robert Walker LJJ. The relevant exercise was as I have said earlier not one of making findings of fact or comparable to a trial on admissible evidence. It was to make a predictive assessment. To use the report as an aid was clearly appropriate and proper. Further, as the plaintiffs themselves said, their pleading and its particularisation was substantially taken from the facts set out in the report. They were using the report to plead their case: 'With one principal exception, the statement of claim is pleaded on the basis of the Bingham report' (per Clarke J). It was therefore not only permissible but also pertinent to compare their selection from the history recounted in the report with the whole and the conclusions drawn in the report. If the plaintiffs seek to infer bad faith which Bingham LJ declined to infer or even contradicted, is it realistic to suppose that a judge will hereafter be persuaded to do so? The report is in reality at the present stage the context in which the plaintiffs' particulars must be read and their viability assessed. The approach of Clarke J was careful and fair to the plaintiffs. He distinguished between the presently available material and that which might become available in the future. He said:

> 'I have reached the firm conclusion that on the material available at present the plaintiffs have no arguable case that the Bank dishonestly granted the licence to BCCI or dishonestly failed to revoke the licence or authorisation in circumstances when it knew, believed or suspected that BCCI would probably collapse. There is nothing in the Bingham report or in the documents which I have seen to support such a conclusion and there is much to contradict it … There is nothing in [the report] which gives reasonable grounds for supposing that there might be other evidence which might in the future support the plaintiffs' case. In these circumstances I accept Mr Stadlen's further submission that there is no realistic possibility of more evidence becoming available, whether by further investigation, discovery, cross-examination or otherwise, which might throw light upon the state of mind of the Bank or any of its relevant officials during the period in which BCCI was operating.'

a He therefore concluded that the plaintiff's case would be bound to fail and that he could see no justification for allowing the action to continue: 'To do so would be to require an enormous expenditure of time and money to no avail.' For myself, I see nothing to criticise in this methodology or chain of reasoning. The critical matter is whether one agrees with his assessment of the inevitability of failure. Were this appeal simply about whether Clarke J had misdirected himself or acted b improperly in some way in the exercise of his discretion, I would regard it as improper to allow the appeal. But that is not the manner in which this appeal has been argued. The defendants have accepted that your Lordships' House should re-assess the decision to dismiss the plaintiffs' claim using CPR Pt 24 and it is to that that I now turn albeit with the apprehension that your Lordships may have been over-influenced by the plaintiffs' submissions about the relevance of the c Bingham report.

The cause of action

[**163**] This was the subject of the earlier hearing and decision of your Lordships ([2000] 3 All ER 1, [2000] 2 WLR 1220). It is easy to forget that the d reason why the plaintiffs have to rely upon the tort of misfeasance in public office is that they cannot allege that the defendants owed them a duty of care. If the plaintiffs were able to rely upon the tort of negligence, their claim would be easy to formulate and, whether or not it would ultimately succeed, would undoubtedly have to go to trial. But, in the present context, to formulate and sustain a claim e in the tort of misfeasance in public office is not straightforward, hence a need to have regard to its constituents.

[**164**] In the speeches of your Lordships, in which I joined, delivered in May of last year, the essential constituents of that tort were explained. The tort is exceptional in that it is necessary to prove the requisite subjective state of mind of the defendant in relation not only to his own conduct but also its effect on f others. That state of mind is one equivalent to dishonesty or bad faith and knowledge includes both direct knowledge and what is sometimes called 'blind eye' knowledge. ('Blind eye' knowledge has since been discussed in different contexts by your Lordships in *Manifest Shipping Co Ltd v Uni-Polaris Shipping Co Ltd* [2001] UKHL/1, [2001] 1 All ER 743, [2001] 2 WLR 170 and *White v White* g [2001] UKHL/9, [2001] 2 All ER 43, [2001] 1 WLR 481.) These features are referred to in the speeches.

> 'It involves bad faith inasmuch as the public officer does not have an honest belief that his act is lawful … [The nineteenth-century] decisions laid the h foundation of the modern tort; they established the two different forms of liability; and revealed the unifying element of conduct amounting to an abuse of power accompanied by subjective bad faith.' (See [2000] 3 All ER 1 at 8, [2000] 2 WLR 1220 at 1231 per Lord Steyn.)

> 'My Lords, I consider that dishonesty is a necessary ingredient of the tort, j and it is clear from the authorities that in this context dishonesty means acting in bad faith.' (See [2000] 3 All ER 1 at 41 , [2000] 2 WLR 1220 at 1266 per Lord Hutton.)

> 'The official concerned must be shown not to have had an honest belief that he was acting lawfully …' (See [2000] 3 All ER 1 at 44, [2000] 2 WLR 1220 at 1269 per Lord Hobhouse of Woodborough.)

'The policy underlying it is sound: reckless indifference to consequences is as blameworthy as deliberately seeking such consequences. It can therefore now be regarded as settled law that an act performed in reckless indifference as to the outcome is sufficient to ground the tort in its second form.' (See [2000] 3 All ER 1 at 9, [2000] 2 WLR 1220 at 1232 per Lord Steyn.)

'The official does the act intentionally being aware that it risks directly causing loss to the plaintiff or an identifiable class to which the plaintiff belongs and the official wilfully disregards that risk ... His recklessness arises because he chooses wilfully to disregard that risk ... Subjective recklessness comes into the formulation at the first and last stage because it is in law tantamount to knowledge and therefore gives rise to the same liability ...' (See [2000] 3 All ER 1 at 45, [2000] 2 WLR 1220 at 1270 per Lord Hobhouse.)

[165] Having carefully considered the submissions of the parties on both sides, the material which has been placed before us, what further material may reasonably be expected to become available to the plaintiffs before the time of the trial and the judgments of the courts below, I have come to the conclusion that the appeal should be dismissed. Like my noble and learned friend Lord Millett, my assessment is that the plaintiffs' claim does not have a real prospect of success. The majority of your Lordships are, however, of a different view and would allow the appeal and direct that the case proceed to a full trial on the alleged liability in tort. Under these circumstances, whilst it is my duty to state what my decision would have been and briefly give my reasons, it is inappropriate that I should say anything which will prejudge the conduct or outcome of that trial when it occurs. The outcome will be a matter for the trial judge in the light of the ruling which your Lordships have earlier given on the law, the evidence adduced at the trial and the submissions of the parties. It is the trial judge who will have to decide how the trial should be conducted and what findings of fact to make.

[166] To turn now to the reasons for my assessment of the prospects of the claim, I will structure what I say applying the law as stated last May and applying it to the facts in two periods, first, that period ending with the grant of the licence in June 1980, secondly, that from July 1980 to the collapse of BCCI in July 1991. The plaintiffs' complaint in these two periods is different. In the first period it is that the defendants wrongly licensed BCCI under s 3 of the Banking Act 1979 when they were forbidden by the statute from doing so. In the second period the complaint is that the defendants failed to supervise BCCI as they were required to do by the 1979 Act and its successor, the Banking Act 1987, and failed to perform an obligation under those Acts to revoke the licence. I will take the law as stated in my speech, not because it is materially different from what was said by Lord Steyn, but because its analysis is unifying and therefore easier to apply in the discussion of these two periods and was, indeed, the formulation primarily relied upon by the plaintiffs.

[167] The commission of the tort has two stages. The first is the act done by the defendant. The act must be an unlawful act, not in the sense that it is itself tortious but in the sense that it is contrary to the law for the defendant to have done what he did. In the case of a failure to act it must be a failure to do a specific act which it was the legal obligation of the defendant to do and which was therefore unlawful. In either case there must be unauthorised or forbidden conduct. The conduct must be accompanied by either actual or subjectively reckless, or 'blind eye', knowledge that it is unauthorised or forbidden. The second a stage is that which relates to the defendants' appreciation of the consequences of his conduct. This may arise from his purpose in doing what he did (my first 'limb', Lord Steyn's first form of the tort) or from his appreciation that the plaintiff will in the ordinary course be caused loss or his consciously and wilfully turning a blind eye to the possibility of such loss (my second and third 'limbs', Lord Steyn's second form of the tort). Therefore, in making the assessment required by this b appeal, one must apply this two-stage test to the plaintiffs' case for the two periods.

The first period

[168] The 1979 Act introduced a system of licensing for deposit-takers which was new. The task of the defendants was not easy since they were faced with c having to decide for the first time and within a relatively short time-scale whether to grant or refuse a licence to a substantial number of institutions which were already established businesses. The refusal of a licence would mean that the institution could no longer accept deposits and would have to go out of business (see s 1(1)). However, the defendants' statutory obligation was clearly stated. d In s 3(3)(b) and Sch 2, Pt II criteria are laid down which must be met unless sub-s (5) applies. In any other case the defendants were forbidden from granting the licence. The defendants purported to grant the licence under sub-s (5). For this to apply, the principal place of business of the institution must be in a country outside the United Kingdom *and* the supervisory authority in that country must have informed the defendants that they are satisfied with respect to the management of e the institution and its overall financial soundness *and* the defendants must be satisfied with the nature and scope of the supervision exercised by those authorities. I consider that the plaintiffs clearly have a fully arguable case that these criteria were not satisfied and that the officials acting for the defendants cannot have believed that these criteria were satisfied. Therefore the plaintiffs have an f arguable case on the first stage of the legal test. The courts below were of the same opinion and Mr Stadlen for the defendants only faintly argued the contrary.

[169] The plaintiffs failed in the courts below on the second stage. Clarke J said:

> g 'Both BCCI SA and the group appeared to be profitable, the shareholders appeared to be supportive and willing to supply more capital when asked, the auditors were giving unqualified opinions on the accounts and the LBC continued to give favourable opinions. [Bingham] also refers to the attitude of the Bank of America, to which I shall return. In these circumstances, it cannot fairly be said that at this stage the Bank suspected that BCCI would h probably collapse … In all the circumstances I have reached the clear conclusion that on the evidence available at present, either as referred to in the Bingham Report or as contained in the documents to which I have been referred, the plaintiffs' case that the Bank knew, believed or suspected that if it gave BCCI a licence it would probably collapse is bound to fail.'

> j 'I must say that, however critical one is of the Bank (and there is plenty of scope for criticism), it seems to me to offend common sense to conclude that before it licensed B.C.C.I. S.A. in 1980 it actually knew, believed or suspected that if it licensed B.C.C.I. S.A., B.C.C.I. S.A. would (or even might) subsequently collapse.' (Cited [2000] 2 WLR 15 at 91–92.)

In the Court of Appeal ([2000] 2 WLR 15 at 92), the majority agreed that there was no arguable case on foresight of loss. Auld LJ based his view on the application of a different view of the constituents of the tort, a view which has been held to be wrong by your Lordships.

a

[170] It is not suggested that the defendants granted the licence with the purpose of causing loss to any of the plaintiffs. The plaintiffs' case is, rather, that the officials consciously closed their eyes to what might be the consequences to present and future depositors of granting and not refusing the licence. There is no direct evidence to support this improbable allegation. The main evidence which is said to support the allegation is in part the self-evident proposition that the officials probably had in mind that one of the main purposes of the regime introduced by the 1979 Act was to protect depositors as is stated in the preamble of that Act plus the proposition that if the safeguards in the Act were not observed before granting a licence there must be a risk that depositors will not be effectively protected; and partly that the officials had already learnt some very disturbing facts about the conduct of the BCCI, for example, from the publicity surrounding the withdrawal of the Bank of America. But there is no evidence to support the appreciation of the officials of the risk they were running nor that, having appreciated it, they wilfully chose to disregard it and hazard the depositors. At the relevant time BCCI appeared to be a flourishing and successful, though to some extent controversial, institution with very many satisfied depositors. The evidence both at the time and subsequently is that the officials thought that they would look silly if they raised difficulties for the approval of BCCI and that if they did they would not have been supported if challenged on an appeal. The objective fact is that no depositor actually lost any money until many years later after much else had happened, including the passing of a new Act in 1987. Problems of proving legal causation will obviously also arise.

b

c

d

e

[171] There is simply no evidence of any contemplation at this stage that depositors with BCCI would lose their money. There is no evidence whatsoever, nor any allegation, of any corruption of any official of the defendants, either at this time or subsequently. The evidence of the requisite *subjective* state of mind is not there and there is no reasonable basis for believing that it ever will be. The case of the plaintiffs is in reality one in negligence supported by *objective* criteria and this does not suffice for the tort upon which they have to rely. This is as I see it an insuperable difficult for them on this part of the case.

f

The second period

g

[172] Here the difficulties which the plaintiffs have to overcome are more fundamental. The foundation of the tort is that the relevant person has done something (in the positive or negative sense) which is contrary to the law. The statutory provisions upon which the plaintiffs rely are ones which give the defendants powers in respect of licenced institutions. Their case is that they constitute a statutory scheme which included a duty to supervise the deposit-taker which the defendants failed to perform adequately. Their more specific case is that the defendants failed to make use of the statutory power given to them under s 11 of the 1987 Act to revoke the authorisation of BCCI, or to exercise one or more of the lesser powers given by sections such as s 12 (restriction of authorisation) or s 19 (directions) of that Act. The difficulty for the plaintiffs here is that they are unable to sue in the tort of negligence and that the failures of the defendants which they allege do not have the character of unlawfulness. They all involve the exercise of discretions and judgment. There is no allegation which the plaintiffs can make that the statute made it *unlawful* for the defendants not to take some particular step at any given time.

h

j

a [173] This ties in with the plaintiffs' next difficulty. There is no evidence that the defendants and their officials were doing anything other than their best to handle the developing situation in a responsible manner in accordance with the Act. The officials may have been out of their depth. They may have been more optimistic than was justified now that all the facts are known. But, particularly in the later stages, they were faced with a delicate situation where there were a b number of conflicting interests to be taken into account and where any overreaction would have caused BCCI to collapse without hope of rescue and with far greater losses to its creditors than ultimately occurred. It is easy to overlook the fact that the defendants' forbearance led to the injection in 1990 of substantial additional shareholder funds (how much these were and what happened to them is apparently questioned). The situation developed over the c years. In the earlier years, the problem was indiscipline without the anticipation of a threat of default. Later, that situation developed into one which included a growing threat of failure, at first remote, finally grave and imminent. But in all these situations the defendants had to exercise judgment. The wrong step on their part would only make things worse. In 1988 the 'College' was constituted d and an international approach adopted in which the defendants participated; the defendants would have been irresponsible not to have done so. The plaintiffs have sought to identify some four occasions when they submit that the defendants knew that they had grounds for exercising one or more of their statutory powers and decided not to. Their inaction may be open to criticism. It can be argued that they should have acted differently but that is not the same as e arguing that they acted unlawfully and, naturally, there is no evidence that they knew or even suspected that they might be acting unlawfully. The plaintiffs wish to present a case of dishonesty but they have not got the material to justify the allegation and have no realistic prospect of ever obtaining it. Instead, their case seeks to proceed from the proposition that the defendants were under a statutory f duty to supervise BCCI to an allegation that the defendants were aware that they were not exercising effective supervision and thence to the allegation that it was unlawful for the defendants not to have exercised one or more of certain powers given to them under the Act. This is a non sequitur. The powers remain discretionary. It does not follow from the proposition that it would have been lawful to exercise one or more of those powers that not to exercise them was g unlawful.

[174] The same applies to the second stage of the test. There is no evidence that the defendants were setting out to cause anyone loss. In the earlier stages they did not foresee the disaster that was to come. In the later stages they were striving to avoid disaster and, if it proved not possible to avoid it, to limit the h losses which would in that event inevitably be suffered. The officials had nothing to gain. All the evidence is that they were doing their best. Once they realised the scale of the problem with BCCI, they did not close their eyes to the consequences of a failure; they attempted to avoid precipitating that collapse which would clearly have been the consequence of the wrong kind of intervention. j One can illustrate the general point from the plaintiffs' own pleading (Sch 5, para 27(ii)): the decision not to revoke the full licence in October 1986 was taken because the officials concluded that 'there appeared to be no immediate danger to depositors and it seemed unlikely that there were grounds for revoking BCCI SA's licence outright'.

[175] The hearing before your Lordships has been concerned with whether the plaintiffs have a real prospect of success in the action. On any view they face

very serious difficulties in presenting and substantiating their case. The burden of proof is upon them. The tort upon which they must rely is one which requires the plaintiffs to prove serious allegations of actual bad faith—dishonesty—against the officials. It is an abuse of process to make the allegations unless the plaintiffs have material to support at least a prima facie case that the allegations are correct. They do not have that material. For the action to be allowed to proceed on the speculation, not backed up by any real expectation, that they may before trial find evidence to support their allegations is vexatious. It is also contrary to the procedural rules now in force. These rules are based upon sound principles of the administration of justice. Doing justice includes bringing to a conclusion highly expensive and long drawn-out litigation procedures, inevitably complex, which have no real prospect of success. The real grievance of the actual plaintiffs is that they believe that the law ought to allow actions in negligence against regulators but they accept through their counsel that it does not. I would dismiss the appeal.

LORD MILLETT. My Lords,

[176] The Bank of Credit and Commerce International SA (BCCI) was incorporated under the laws of Luxembourg and obtained a banking licence from the Luxembourg Banking Commission (the LBC) in 1972. In the years which followed it carried on a worldwide business as a bank and deposit-taking institution. Shortly after it received the licence from the LBC it established an office in London which eventually became its principal place of business. By 1979 it had 45 branches in the United Kingdom through which it offered a full range of banking services to members of the public.

[177] The Banking Act 1979 came into force in October 1979. That Act made the Bank of England (the Bank) formally responsible for supervising banks and other deposit-taking institutions in the United Kingdom and conferred wide regulatory powers upon the Bank to enable it to discharge its functions. For the first time authorisation was required for a banking or deposit-taking business to be carried on in the United Kingdom. The 1979 Act applied to companies like BCCI which was already carrying on an existing business in the United Kingdom as well as to those which wished to commence business here.

[178] In 1980 the Bank granted BCCI a licence to accept deposits. Withholding the licence would have compelled the closure of BCCI's business in the United Kingdom (and in all likelihood elsewhere), with virtually certain loss to depositors. In granting the licence the Bank relied on the judgment of the LBC and made no independent judgment of its own whether the statutory criteria for authorisation were satisfied. It was not entitled to do this because BCCI's principal place of business was in the United Kingdom. Thereafter BCCI continued to carry on business in the United Kingdom and elsewhere for a further 11 years before it was closed down in July 1991 by regulatory action taken by the Bank. Depositors, most of whom must have become depositors or increased their deposits after 1980, have suffered substantial losses. They blame the Bank for its supervisory failures and seek to hold it responsible for their losses. They believe that the Bank was grossly negligent in granting the licence in the first place and in failing to revoke it or take other regulatory action long before it did.

[179] Unfortunately for the depositors, a regulatory authority cannot be held liable in English law for negligence, however gross, in the exercise of its supervisory functions. So the depositors have been forced to base their claim on a very different cause of action. They allege that the Bank has been guilty of misfeasance in public office. This is an intentional tort. It involves deliberate or

a reckless wrongdoing. It cannot be committed negligently or inadvertently. Accordingly, it is not enough for the depositors to establish negligence, or even gross negligence, on the part of the Bank. They must establish some intentional or reckless impropriety. As your Lordships ruled unanimously at an earlier stage of these proceedings ([2000] 3 All ER 1, [2000] 2 WLR 1220), and in the absence of what has been described as 'targeted malice' (which is not alleged), the tort has b two elements. In the present case the depositors must prove: (i) not merely that the Bank acted unlawfully, that is to say in excess of its powers or for an improper purpose, but that it did so *knowingly* (or recklessly not caring whether it had the necessary power or not); and (ii) that the Bank *knew* that its actions would probably cause loss to depositors (or was recklessly indifferent to the consequences of its actions). Such conduct in a public official is grossly improper and equates to c dishonesty in a private individual.

[**180**] Seen in this light, the depositors' case is a most implausible one. A bank regulator has a very difficult task and one which may call for an exercise of judgment of some nicety, since it must seek to protect future depositors against the risk of loss without sacrificing the interests of existing depositors. No responsible d regulator would contemplate closing down a bank or other deposit-taking institution (or taking other action which risked a run on it) with inevitable loss to existing depositors unless there was no alternative, ie unless it considered that collapse was virtually inevitable. A regulator's task has often to be performed on incomplete information and is highly judgmental. Even an action based on e negligence would face formidable difficulties. But it is scarcely credible that, unless corrupt, public officials should have been guilty of intentional wrongdoing or have been indifferent to the consequences of their actions to the very people they were supposed to protect. It is not beyond the bounds of possibility, of course, but in the absence of any incentive to act in this way it is in the highest degree unlikely. Certainly such conduct cannot lightly be inferred.

f [**181**] But the present case goes far beyond this. The Bank was formally concerned with the supervision of BCCI for more than 11 years (and informally for a further eight years) and the supervisory attention which it paid to BCCI during this time was very great. The depositors are alleging deliberate or reckless wrongdoing on the part of a large number of officials at different levels of g seniority over a long period. This would involve wholesale wrongdoing on a spectacular scale in the public service. Absent any plausible motive for such conduct it is an extravagant allegation. It will require evidence of the most compelling kind to establish. As Lord Nicholls of Birkenhead observed in *Re H (minors) (sexual abuse: standard of proof)* [1996] 1 All ER 1 at 17, [1996] AC 563 at 586:

h > 'The more improbable the event, the stronger must be the evidence that it did occur before, on the balance of probability, its occurrence will be established. Ungoed-Thomas J expressed this neatly in *Re Dellow's Will Trusts, Lloyds Bank Ltd v Institute of Cancer Research* [1964] 1 All ER 771 at 773, [1964] 1 WLR 451 at 455: "The more serious the allegation, the more cogent j is the evidence required to overcome the unlikelihood of what is alleged and thus to prove it."'

In the absence of evidence to support the allegation, it would be an abuse of process to make it. It is not at all surprising that the depositors have striven hard to avoid pleading any such case until they were compelled to do so, preferring instead to argue that it was not necessary.

[**182**] In describing the depositors' case as 'implausible' or 'scarcely credible', I should not be taken as making any assumptions about the integrity of the Bank and its officials or as departing from the proper judicial stance of neutrality and impartiality. I do not take the view that the Bank can do no wrong or that public officials are incapable of acting in bad faith. But we are called upon to evaluate the action's prospects of success, and that exercise involves an impartial consideration of the inherent plausibility of the allegations and the strength of the evidence needed to establish them. The scales of justice must be evenly balanced at the commencement of such an operation; but they should not be incapable of movement while the operation is being undertaken. It is not unfair to observe that, in the absence of some financial or other incentive, a charge of dishonesty against professional men and public officials is possible but inherently improbable.

THE PLEADINGS: DEMURRER

[**183**] Having read and re-read the pleadings, I remain of opinion that they are demurrable and could be struck out on this ground. The rules which govern both pleading and proving a case of fraud are very strict. In *Jonesco v Beard* [1930] AC 298 at 300, [1930] All ER Rep 483 at 484 Lord Buckmaster, with whom the other members of the House concurred, said:

> 'It has long been the settled practice of the Court that the proper method of impeaching a completed judgment on the ground of fraud is by action in which, *as in any other action based on fraud, the particulars of the fraud must be exactly given and the allegation established by the strict proof such a charge requires.*' (My emphasis.)

[**184**] It is well established that fraud or dishonesty (and the same must go for the present tort) must be distinctly alleged and as distinctly proved; that it must be sufficiently particularised; and that it is not sufficiently particularised if the facts pleaded are consistent with innocence: see *Kerr on the Law of Fraud and Mistake* (7th edn, 1952) p 644, *Davy v Garrett* (1878) 7 Ch D 473 at 489, *Bullivant v A-G for Victoria* [1901] AC 196, [1900–3] All ER Rep 812, *Armitage v Nurse* [1997] 2 All ER 705 at 715, [1998] Ch 241 at 256. This means that a plaintiff who alleges dishonesty must plead the facts, matters and circumstances relied on to show that the defendant was dishonest and not merely negligent, and that facts, matters and circumstances which are consistent with negligence do not do so.

[**185**] It is important to appreciate that there are two principles in play. The first is a matter of pleading. The function of pleadings is to give the party opposite sufficient notice of the case which is being made against him. If the pleader means 'dishonestly' or 'fraudulently', it may not be enough to say 'wilfully' or 'recklessly'. Such language is equivocal. A similar requirement applies, in my opinion, in a case like the present, but the requirement is satisfied by the present pleadings. It is perfectly clear that the depositors are alleging an intentional tort.

[**186**] The second principle, which is quite distinct, is that an allegation of fraud or dishonesty must be sufficiently particularised, and that particulars of facts which are consistent with honesty are not sufficient. This is only partly a matter of pleading. It is also a matter of substance. As I have said, the defendant is entitled to know the case he has to meet. But since dishonesty is usually a matter of inference from primary facts, this involves knowing not only that he is alleged to have acted dishonestly, but also the primary facts which will be relied upon at trial to justify the inference. At trial the court will not normally allow proof of primary facts which have not been pleaded, and will not do so in a case of fraud.

a It is not open to the court to infer dishonesty from facts which have not been pleaded, or from facts which have been pleaded but are consistent with honesty. There must be *some* fact which tilts the balance and justifies an inference of dishonesty, and this fact must be both pleaded and proved.

[187] In *Davy v Garrett* Thesiger LJ in a well-known and frequently cited passage stated:

b

> 'In the present case facts are alleged from which fraud might be inferred, but they are consistent with innocence. They were innocent acts in themselves, and it is not to be presumed that they were done with a fraudulent intent.' (See (1878) 7 Ch D 473 at 489.)

c This is a clear statement of the second of the two principles to which I have referred.

[188] In *Armitage*'s case the plaintiff needed to prove that trustees had been guilty of fraudulent breach of trust. She pleaded that they had acted 'in reckless and wilful breach of trust'. This was equivocal. It did not make it clear that what was alleged was a dishonest breach of trust. But this was not fatal. If the d particulars had not been consistent with honesty, it would not have mattered. Indeed, leave to amend would almost certainly have been given as a matter of course, for such an amendment would have been a technical one; it would merely have clarified the pleading without allowing new material to be introduced. But the Court of Appeal struck out the allegation because the facts pleaded in support were consistent with honest incompetence: if proved, they e would have supported a finding of negligence, even of gross negligence, but not of fraud. Amending the pleadings by substituting an unequivocal allegation of dishonesty without giving further particulars would not have cured the defect. The defendants would still not have known why they were charged with dishonesty rather than with honest incompetence.

f [189] It is not, therefore, correct to say that *if there is no specific allegation of dishonesty* it is not open to the court to make a finding of dishonesty if the facts pleaded are consistent with honesty. If the particulars of dishonesty are insufficient, the defect cannot be cured by an unequivocal allegation of dishonesty. Such an allegation is effectively an unparticularised allegation of fraud. If the observations of Buxton LJ in *Taylor v Midland Bank Trust Co Ltd* [1999] CA Transcript 1200 are g to the contrary, I am unable to accept them.

[190] In the present case the depositors (save in one respect with which I shall deal later) make the allegations necessary to establish the tort, but the particulars pleaded in support are consistent with mere negligence. In my opinion, even if the depositors succeeded at the trial in establishing all the facts pleaded, it would h not be open to the court to draw the inferences necessary to find that the essential elements of the tort had been proved.

THE EVIDENTIAL MATERIAL: PROSPECTS OF SUCCESS

[191] But I prefer to decide this appeal on the broader and simpler ground that j the action has no real prospects of success. In reaching this conclusion I have not relied upon the Bingham report or its findings. My reasons are as follows.

1. *The grant of the licence*

(1) It is clear that the Bank was not entitled to grant the licence in reliance on the LBC. So the depositors can prove that the Bank acted unlawfully. However, it was not unlawful for the Bank to grant a licence, but only to do so without first

making its own independent inquiries. It must now be a matter of speculation whether the Bank would still have granted the licence if it had made its own inquiries, so there is a difficult (though I am willing to assume not insuperable) question of causation. The burden of proving this lies with the depositors.

(2) It is arguable that the Bank knew the facts which deprived it of the power to grant the licence in reliance upon the LBC and without making its own inquiries. But knowledge of facts which deprive a party of the power to take a particular course of action is not the same as knowledge that it is acting in excess of power. There is no reason to suppose, and not a shred of evidence to suggest, that any official of the Bank appreciated the position, or that any official suspected it but turned a blind eye. If the Bank had realised or suspected that it was not entitled to rely on the LBC, it would obviously have made its own inquiries. It had not the slightest reason not to do so. The facts pleaded, and all the evidence we have seen, are entirely consistent with an honest but (possibly) negligent failure to appreciate the legal consequences of the known facts. This is insufficient to sustain the claim, since the first element of the tort is lacking.

(3) Even if the depositors could establish the first element of the tort, they have no prospect of establishing the second. There is no case for supposing that in 1980 BCCI was in fact already insolvent or likely to collapse; and even if it was the Bank obviously had no knowledge or suspicion that it was. As Clarke J said: it defies common sense to suppose that regulators would licence a bank which they foresaw would probably (or be at all likely to) collapse.

2. *The failure to revoke the licence prior to 1990*

(1) The tort is concerned with the *abuse* of power by public officials who act in excess of their powers to the injury of the subject. It is not concerned with their failure to exercise the powers they do have, particularly when they have a discretion whether to exercise them or not.

(2) The Bank had a *power* to revoke the licence in certain circumstances. But it had no *duty* to do so unless the circumstances were such that (objectively) the discretion could only be exercised in favour of revocation. This was never the case, nor is it alleged that it was. Even if the Bank appreciated (after the event) that it had acted in excess of its powers when granting the licence, this did not impose a duty (as distinct from a power) to revoke the licence. It follows that the Bank never acted unlawfully in failing to exercise its power to revoke the licence.

(3) In any case, the Bank's internal documents show that it never believed that it had grounds to revoke the licence, and considered that even if it did revocation would not be justified. There is no reason to suppose (and there is nothing pleaded which would justify a finding) that these views were not honestly (even if erroneously) held. Accordingly, the first element of the tort is lacking.

(4) The real problem was that, as the Bank knew, BCCI was effectively unsupervised. The depositors laid considerable emphasis on this, and rightly so; but they did not face up to the consequences. It meant that the Bank did not know enough to justify either letting BCCI continue or closing it down. It was not unlawful to abstain from revoking the licence in these circumstances. The real charge against the Bank is that it never got to grips with the problem of supervision. This may have been negligent, but it did not amount to deliberate wrongdoing or bad faith.

(5) The right course may have been to impose restrictions. This never entered anyone's head. The failure to take a step which was never even considered may be negligent but cannot possibly amount to deliberate (or reckless) wrongdoing.

a 3. *The failure to revoke the licence: 1990–1991*

(1) By 1990 the Bank knew that BCCI was insolvent and fraudulently run. So it knew (for the first time) that there were grounds for closing it down. But it still had to consider whether this was in the interests of depositors, both present and future.

(2) No regulator would close down a bank in such circumstances while there b was any reasonable prospect of a rescue. The first question is whether, objectively and without the benefit of hindsight, there was a reasonable possibility of a rescue (with new funds and new management) until the s 41 report put paid to it. If so, the Bank was not acting unlawfully in exercising its discretion not to revoke the licence, and the first element of the tort would be lacking.

c (3) But even if the depositors satisfy the court that there was in fact no reasonable prospect of a rescue, this is not enough. The essential question is whether it was the Bank's honestly held view that there was. There is no reason to suppose and not a shred of evidence from which it could be inferred that the Bank did not honestly believe that a rescue was a reasonable possibility. All the documents we have seen show that this was why the Bank stayed its hand. There d is no hint of any other reason. As soon as it received the s 41 report, and realised that there would be no rescue, it moved to close the business down.

(4) The depositors do not even plead the necessary averment. They still plead only that (negatively) the Bank did not believe that there would probably be a rescue. This is remarkable given that Clarke J told them that what they needed e to allege and prove was that (positively) the Bank knew or suspected that there would probably *not* be a rescue. There can be only one reason for their failure to plead the necessary averment: it is because they know that they cannot. In the absence of the necessary pleading (supported by proper particulars), it is not open to the court to find that the Bank knew that depositors would probably suffer loss. The second element of the tort is lacking.

f (5) The depositors' case is that a regulator has a legal duty to close down an insolvent bank even if it believes that there is a reasonable prospect of a rescue, unless it also believes that a rescue is likely. It is only necessary to formulate the proposition to see that it must be rejected. Nothing could be more inimical to the interests of depositors than to place such a restriction on the regulator's power in g their interests to explore every alternative to closure. Not to do so would display the very reckless indifference to their interests of which the depositors in the present case complain.

CONCLUSION

[192] I agree with my noble and learned friend Lord Hope of Craighead that, h while cases should in principle be disposed of as expeditiously and cheaply as the circumstances permit, the most important principle of all is that justice should be done. But this does not mean justice to the plaintiff alone. It is not just to a plaintiff to strike out his claim without a trial unless it has no real prospect of success. It is not just to defendants to subject them to a lengthy and expensive j trial to defend their integrity when there is no foundation in the evidence for the attack upon it.

[193] In my opinion the depositors cannot establish the requisite elements of the tort in respect of any matter of complaint. They have either failed to make the necessary allegations, or where they have done so they have pleaded insufficient facts in support to entitle the court to draw the necessary inferences. They have produced no document which supports their case, and every document which they have produced and on which they have placed reliance is either neutral or more often contradictory of their case. When in addition regard is had to the seriousness and sheer improbability of their case and the cogency of the evidence required to prove it, the conclusion is inescapable that it has no real prospects of success.

a

[**194**] In agreement with my noble and learned friend Lord Hobhouse of Woodborough, I would dismiss the appeal and strike out the action.

Appeal allowed in part.

Dilys Tausz Barrister.

a

I v Director of Public Prosecutions
M v Director of Public Prosecutions
H v Director of Public Prosecutions

[2001] UKHL/10

b

HOUSE OF LORDS

LORD BINGHAM OF CORNHILL, LORD CLYDE, LORD HUTTON, LORD HOBHOUSE OF WOODBOROUGH AND LORD SCOTT OF FOSCOTE

29, 30 JANUARY, 8 MARCH 2001

c

Criminal law – Affray – Public place – Elements of offence – Threat of unlawful violence towards another – Whether overt possession of weapon capable of constituting threat of violence when not used or brandished in violent manner – Whether threat of violence having to be directed to person present at scene – Public Order Act 1986, s 3(1).

d

In response to an anonymous telephone call, a number of police officers were despatched to a block of flats in a marked police carrier. On arrival, the police saw a group of 40 to 50 youths outside the block. Eight or nine of them were carrying petrol bombs, but none of the fuses had been lit. When the carrier came into view, the group immediately dispersed and no violence was shown or threatened e towards the police officers. Nobody else was present at the scene. The police pursued some of the group and arrested the three defendants who, before capture, had thrown away the petrol bombs they had been holding. The defendants were charged with affray contrary to s 3(1)[a] of the Public Order Act 1986 which provided that a person was guilty of that offence if he used or f 'threatens unlawful violence towards another' and his conduct was such as would cause a person of reasonable firmness 'present at the scene' to fear for his personal safety. That provision had replaced the common law offence of affray, and had implemented a recommendation in a Law Commission report, subsequently accepted in a government White Paper. The defendants were convicted by a stipendiary magistrate, and they appealed by way of case stated. The Divisional g Court dismissed the appeals, holding (i) that the visible carrying in public of primed petrol bombs by a large number of youths 'obviously out for no good' was clearly capable of constituting a threat of unlawful violence; and (ii) that although there had to be someone at or in the vicinity towards whom the threat of violence could be said to be directed, in the special circumstances of the case h the overt carrying of petrol bombs, highly dangerous and untargeted in their effect if exploded, constituted a threat of violence to anyone in the vicinity, including the police on arrival at the scene. On the defendants' appeal to the House of Lords, two issues arose, namely (i) whether the overt possession of a weapon could constitute a threat of violence for the purpose of affray when it was j not used or brandished in a violent manner, and (ii) whether the threat of unlawful violence had to be towards a person or persons present at the scene.

Held – (1) For the purposes of s 3(1) of the1986 Act, the carrying of dangerous weapons such as petrol bombs by a group of persons could, in some circumstances,

a Section 3 is set out at [9], post

constitute a threat of violence without those weapons being waved or brandished. Such a conclusion was consistent with the ordinary and natural meaning of the words 'threatens unlawful violence'. It was also supported by the authorities which had dealt with what constituted a threat of violence for the purposes of the former common law offence of affray. It was permissible to have regard to those authorities since s 3 mirrored the common law alternatives of actual use and threatened use of violence. However, the mere possession of a weapon, without threatening circumstances, was not enough to constitute a threat of unlawful violence. Nor could the carrying of a concealed weapon itself be such a threat. In the instant case, the visible carrying in public of primed petrol bombs by a large number of what was obviously a gang out for no good was clearly capable of constituting a threat of unlawful violence. That was so whether it was characterised as a show of force or simply an obviously threatening spectacle, and regardless of the fact that the armed gang members were not yet throwing or brandishing their weapons. Accordingly, the Divisional Court's decision on the first issue had been correct (see [1], [2], [10], [11], [16], [29] and [30], post); *R v Sharp* [1957] 1 All ER 577 and *Taylor v DPP* [1973] 2 All ER 1108 considered.

(2) On the true construction of s 3(1) of the 1986 Act, the threat of unlawful violence had to be directed towards a person or persons present at the scene. Such a construction was supported by the Law Commission report which made it clear not only that s 3 was intended to penalise those who engaged in a fight—whether they were landing blows or attempting to land blows, or threatening to land blows—but also that in such circumstances the victim or victims were bound to be present with the offender or offenders. It followed that s 3(1) did not make guilty of an affray a person whose conduct constituted a threat of violence to persons who were not present. That conclusion also derived support from the requirement in s 3(1) that the conduct of the offender was such that it would cause a bystander 'present at the scene' to fear for his personal safety. The concept of presence at the scene suggested that the notional bystander would be in the presence of both the offender and the victim. It was also relevant to observe that there was no reported case of affray where the victim was not present at the scene where the accused had threatened violence. However, although the carrying of petrol bombs could constitute a threat of violence, it did not necessarily follow that there was a threat of violence towards a person merely because he was present at a location where a gang was carrying petrol bombs. Whether the carrying of a weapon or weapons constituted a threat of violence towards a person present at the scene depended on the facts of the actual case. That issue did not arise in the instant case since there was no one present at the scene apart from the police officers, and no threat was made towards them. Accordingly, on the second issue the Divisional Court had erred in its application of the law to the facts, and the appeals would therefore be allowed (see [1], [2], [22], [24] and [26]–[30], post).

Notes

For affray, see 11(1) *Halsbury's Laws* (4th edn reissue) para 151.

For the Public Order Act 1986, s 3, see 12 *Halsbury's Statutes* (4th edn) (1997 reissue) 951.

a

Cases referred to in opinions

Aswan Engineering Establishment Co v Lupdine Ltd (Thurgar Bolle Ltd, third party) [1987] 1 All ER 135, [1987] 1 WLR 1, CA.

Atkin v DPP (1989) 89 Cr App R 199.

R v Davison [1992] Crim LR 31, CA.

R v Dixon [1993] Crim LR 579, CA.

b *R v Robinson* [1993] Crim LR 581, CA.

R v Sanchez [1996] Crim LR 572, CA.

R v Sharp [1957] 1 All ER 577, [1957] 1 QB 552, [1957] 2 WLR 472, CCA.

R v Shivpuri [1986] 2 All ER 334, [1987] AC 1, [1986] 2 WLR 988, HL.

Swanston v DPP (1996) 161 JP 203.

Taylor v DPP [1973] 2 All ER 1108, [1973] AC 964, [1973] 3 WLR 140, HL.

c

Appeals

The defendants, I, M and H, three minors, appealed with leave of the Appeal Committee of the House of Lords given on 14 March 2000 from the order of the Divisional Court (Auld LJ and Hughes J) on 11 June 1999 ([2000] 1 Cr App R 251) d dismissing their appeals by way of case stated from their convictions for affray contrary to s 3(1) of the Public Order Act 1986 by the Metropolitan Stipendiary Magistrate (Justin Philips) at West London Youth Court on 22 July 1998. The Divisional Court certified that points law of general public importance, set out at [6], post, were involved in its decision. The facts are set out in the opinion of Lord Hutton.

e

Lady Kennedy of the Shaws QC and *Andrew Smiler* (instructed by *Sweetman Burke & Sinkler*) for I.

Michel Massih QC and *Mark Summers* (instructed by *McCauley Slowe*) for M.

Lady Kennedy of the Shaws QC and *Sanjay Lal* (instructed by *Alexander Johnson*) for H.

f *Bruce Houlder QC* and *Pamela Oon* (instructed by the *Crown Prosecution Service*) for the Crown.

Their Lordships took time for consideration.

g 8 March 2001. The following opinions were delivered.

LORD BINGHAM OF CORNHILL. My Lords,

[1] I have had the advantage of reading in draft the opinion of my noble and learned friend Lord Hutton. For the reasons which he gives, I would allow these appeals and respond to the certified questions as he proposes.

h

LORD CLYDE. My Lords,

[2] I have had the advantage of reading in draft the opinion of my noble and learned friend Lord Hutton. For the reasons which he gives, I would allow these appeals and respond to the certified questions as he proposes.

j

LORD HUTTON. My Lords,

[3] On the evening of 21 October 1997 the police received an anonymous telephone call that approximately 30 Asian youths armed with sticks were gathering together in Canon Street Road, London E1. A marked police carrier with seven police officers was despatched to Canon Street Road and on arrival there about 6.50 pm the police carrier turned into Bigland Street where there is a

block of residential flats called Luke House. The police in the carrier saw 40 to 50 Asian youths milling around in a group on a raised concourse outside Luke House, eight or nine of whom were carrying petrol bombs consisting of milk bottles containing petrol with a tissue wick in the mouth. When the police carrier came into view the group immediately dispersed and ran off and no violence was shown towards the police officers. The police pursued some of the group and the three appellants were captured and arrested close to Luke House. Before their capture the three appellants each threw away a petrol bomb which he had been carrying. The appellants were interviewed by the police and in the course of the interviews one of them said that he was a member of a gang called the 'Canon Street Boys' who were going to have a fight with another gang called the 'Barnado Boys', and the petrol bombs were going to be thrown in the fight.

[4] The appellants were charged with the statutory offence of affray contrary to s 3(1) of the Public Order Act 1986 and were convicted by Mr Justin Philips, a Metropolitan Stipendiary Magistrate, sitting at West London Youth Court on 22 July 1998. The appellants appealed to the Divisional Court by case stated. The three cases stated set out the facts found by the learned stipendiary magistrate in identical terms and two of the findings are of particular relevance to the present appeal:

> '... (f) As the police carrier came into view, the group dispersed immediately in all directions ... (k) Aside from the police no other persons, and in particular no member of any other gang, were shown to be present at the scene at 6.50pm.'

It is also appropriate to set out certain other findings:

> '... (e) Officers in the carrier thought that petrol bombs were being carried and PC Brown thought that there could be a disturbance ... (i) At no time was any fuse lit and when police came on the group there was no fighting, no shouting or throwing of any object. Nothing was said and no bottles were waved. (j) In the Bengali-populated East End, the street gangs are territorial and there is bad-blood between the various gangs.'

The stipendiary magistrate stated his opinion:

> 'I was of the opinion that in this part of London, with its agreed contemporary history of gang warfare, the presence of this group of youths (approximately a quarter of which was armed with petrol bombs) would threaten with violence any member of the public alighting upon the scene, whether that member of the public was a resident, a passer-by or a police officer; and although, with the exception of the officers in the carrier, there was no evidence of anyone to whom it could be said the threat was directed, the offence of affray in this instance was made out as the armed group had congregated in public and constituted a general threat to the public at large, and that a person of reasonable firmness present at the scene of this incident would have feared for his or her safety.'

The questions set out in the case stated for the opinion of the Divisional Court were:

> '1. Was I correct in deciding that a conviction for affray under Section 3(1) of the Public Order Act 1986 can be recorded without evidence being adduced that any person was or believed himself to have been subjected to

a or threatened with violence? 2. Was I correct in my ruling that a threat of violence towards a hypothetical person or persons or the public at large is sufficient to constitute a threat "towards another," and that this threat could be inferred from the evidence that police alighting on this scene thought that petrol bombs were being carried and one officer thought there could be a disturbance.'

b In his judgment in the Divisional Court ([2000] 1 Cr App R 251 at 254) Auld LJ reformulated the questions:

> '1. Whether the mere possession of petrol bombs in the circumstances was capable of amounting to a threat of unlawful violence? 2. If so, whether a threat of violence towards an unknown person or persons, or the public at c large, amounted to a threat of unlawful violence "towards another"? 3. And if so, whether such a threat could be inferred from the evidence of the police that they thought members of the group were carrying petrol bombs and that one officer thought there could be a disturbance?'

[5] The Divisional Court dismissed the appeals and held (1) that the visible d carrying in public of primed petrol bombs by a large number of youths 'obviously out for no good' was clearly capable of constituting a threat of unlawful violence and (2) that whilst there had to be someone at or in the vicinity towards whom the threat of violence could be said to be directed, in the special circumstances of this case the overt carrying of petrol bombs, highly dangerous and untargeted in e their effect if exploded, constituted a threat of violence to anyone in the vicinity, including the police on arrival on the scene.

[6] The questions certified by the Divisional Court as points of law of general public importance are:

> '(1) Whether the overt possession of a weapon may constitute a threat of f violence for the purpose of affray when it is not used or brandished in a violent manner. (2) Whether in order to constitute a threat for the purpose of affray it must be directed at a particular person or whether it is sufficient, providing that there is another or others present, that it is directed generally against anyone present. (3) Whether, in order to constitute a threat for the purposes of affray, the threat must be perceived as such by a person against g whom it is directed.'

[7] I consider that the second certified question is not apposite and that the point to which it relates should be reformulated:

> 'In order to constitute the statutory offence of affray does the threat of h unlawful violence have to be towards a person or persons present at the scene?'

[8] In its report in 1983 on *Offences Relating To Public Order* (Law Com No 123) the Law Commission recommended the abolition of the common law offences of affray, riot, unlawful assembly and rout and the replacement of the first three j by new statutory offences. In its Working Paper *Offences Against Public Order* (Law Com No 82 (1982)) which preceded its report the Law Commission stated:

> '4.3 The common law offence of affray is typically charged in cases of pitched street battles between rival gangs, spontaneous fights in public houses, clubs and at seaside resorts, and revenge attacks on individuals. The offence is apparently rarely resorted to in the context of demonstrations or

protests where disorder has broken out, although there is nothing in law to prevent a charge of affray being brought where serious fighting is involved in those circumstances.' a

[9] The long title of the 1986 Act states:

'An Act to abolish the common law offences of riot, rout, unlawful assembly and affray and certain statutory offences relating to public order; to create new offences relating to public order …' b

Section 1 creates the statutory offence of riot which is committed where 12 or more persons who are present together use or threaten unlawful violence for a common purpose and the conduct of them (taken together) is such as would cause a person of reasonable firmness present at the scene to fear for his personal safety. Section 2 creates the statutory offence of violent disorder which is committed where three or more persons who are present together use or threaten unlawful violence and the conduct of them (taken together) is such as would cause a person of reasonable firmness present at the scene to fear for his personal safety. Section 3 creates the statutory offence of affray and provides: c d

'(1) A person is guilty of affray if he uses or threatens unlawful violence towards another and his conduct is such as would cause a person of reasonable firmness present at the scene to fear for his personal safety.

(2) Where 2 or more persons use or threaten the unlawful violence, it is the conduct of them taken together that must be considered for the purposes of subsection (1). e

(3) For the purposes of this section a threat cannot be made by the use of words alone.

(4) No person of reasonable firmness need actually be, or be likely to be, present at the scene.

(5) Affray may be committed in private as well as in public places.' f

Section 4 creates the statutory offence of conduct intended or likely to cause fear or provoke violence and provides:

'(1) A person is guilty of an offence if he—(a) uses towards another person threatening, abusive or insulting words or behaviour, or (b) distributes or displays to another person any writing, sign or other visible representation which is threatening, abusive or insulting, with intent to cause that person to believe that immediate unlawful violence will be used against him or another by any person, or to provoke the immediate use of unlawful violence by that person or another, or whereby that person is likely to believe that such violence will be used or it is likely that such violence will be provoked. g h

(2) An offence under this section may be committed in a public or a private place …'

Section 6 provides:

'… (2) A person is guilty of violent disorder or affray only if he intends to use or threaten violence or is aware that his conduct may be violent or threaten violence.' j

Section 8 provides:

'In this Part … "violence" means any violent conduct, so that—(a) except in the context of affray, it includes violent conduct towards property as well a as violent conduct towards persons, and (b) it is not restricted to conduct causing or intended to cause injury or damage but includes any other violent conduct (for example, throwing at or towards a person a missile of a kind capable of causing injury which does not hit or falls short).'

Section 9 provides: '(1) The common law offences of riot, rout, unlawful assembly and affray are abolished.'

b

The first certified question

[10] My Lords, the issue which arises on the first certified question is whether, as a matter of law, the carrying of petrol bombs by a group of persons can constitute a threat of violence where those petrol bombs are not being waved or c brandished. I consider that, giving the words 'threatens unlawful violence' in s 3(1) their ordinary and natural meaning, the carrying of dangerous weapons, such as petrol bombs by a group of persons can, in some circumstances, constitute the threat of violence, without those weapons being waved or brandished.

[11] This view is supported by the authorities on the common law offence of d affray. Whilst as Taylor LJ observed in *Atkin v DPP* (1989) 89 Cr App R 199 at 204, a court is not assisted in construing words in a section creating a new offence by considering decisions of other courts in regard to the construction of an earlier section containing quite different words, s 3 of the 1986 Act did not create an entirely new offence but replaced the common law offence of affray and the Law Commission stated in para 3.1 of its report that it considered that the new e statutory offence 'should be similar to the common law offence with some clarification and narrowing of its elements'. Auld LJ rightly observed ([2000] 1 Cr App R 251 at 256) that where a statutory offence replaces a common law offence the courts should approach with care indications to be found in the earlier common law as to the elements of the offence. But he also observed that s 3 f mirrors the common law alternatives of actual use and threatened use of violence. Therefore I agree with Auld LJ that it is permissible in this case to take into account the common law decisions on what constitutes a threat of violence.

[12] In *R v Sharp* [1957] 1 All ER 577 at 579, [1957] 1 QB 552 at 559 Lord Goddard CJ in considering the offence of affray cited the institutional writers and said:

g

> 'The author who devotes most attention to the matter is Hawkins [*Pleas of the Crown* (1824)], Vol I, c 28. He lays down that there may be an affray when there is no actual violence, as when a man arms himself with dangerous and unusual weapons in such a manner as will naturally cause a terror to the h people. This, he says, was always an offence at common law and dealt with by many statutes. He then quotes in particular the Statute of Northampton, 2 Edw 3, c 3. Dealing with that statute he says that no wearing of arms is within the meaning of this statute unless it be accompanied with such circumstances as are apt to terrify the people. The wearing of unusual or dangerous weapons in public is only one species of affray and, in our opinion, j it is open to a jury to find that the circumstances amount to an affray although no person is actually called to say that he was put in terror. Just as the mere wearing of a sword in the days when this was a common accoutrement of the nobility and gentry would be no evidence of an affray while the carrying in public of a studded mace or battle axe might be …'

And Lord Goddard stated that an indictment for affray is one which alleges that—

> 'the circumstances involve a breach of the Sovereign's peace, that it was a real disturbance of the peace by two persons fighting each other in public instead of settling their differences in the royal courts, or endeavouring by a display of force though without necessarily using actual violence to overawe the public, which was what was aimed at by the Statute of Northampton.' (See [1957] 1 All ER 577 at 579, [1957] 1 QB 552 at 560.)

[13] In *Taylor v DPP* [1973] 2 All ER 1108 at 1112, [1973] AC 964 at 987, Lord Hailsham of St Marylebone LC stated:

> '... the extent to which the "display of force ... without actual violence" constitutes the offence of affray even where the element of terror is present is still not wholly clear. It seems that the brandishing of a fearful weapon does constitute the offence, and has always done so, though in most cases where this is done by an individual, a charge under the Prevention of Crime Act 1953 would now seem preferable. From the older authorities it seems plain enough that mere words, unaccompanied by the brandishing of a weapon or actual violence, are not enough. But all sorts of things are, arguably, a display of force. I am anxious that nothing in this case should be construed as necessarily implying that anything less than an unlawful participation in a violent breach of the peace will be enough to satisfy the requirement.'

Counsel for the appellants relied on the last sentence in this passage, but Lord Hailsham LC recognised that it can be contended that various types of conduct may constitute a display of force, and I consider that this passage in his judgment does not assist the appellants' case but provides support for the view that the carrying of dangerous weapons by a group of persons can constitute the threat of violence. Smith and Hogan in *Criminal Law* (4th edn, 1978) p 757, in their definition of the common law offence, also take the view that the display of force alone can constitute the commission of an affray:

> '(1) unlawful fighting or unlawful violence used by one or more persons against another or others; or an unlawful display of force by one or more persons without actual violence; (2) in a public place or, if on private premises, in the presence of at least one innocent person who was terrified; and (3) in such a manner that a bystander of reasonably firm character might reasonably be expected to be terrified.'

[14] Other more recent cases cited by the appellants' counsel do not, in my opinion, advance the appellants' case. In *R v Davison* [1992] Crim LR 31 the defendant was convicted of affray where he had 'swiped' a kitchen knife towards a police officer. In *R v Dixon* [1993] Crim LR 579 the defendant was convicted of affray where he and his Alsatian-type dog were pursued by two police officers and cornered in the driveway of a house and he repeated 'go on, go on' to the dog who ran forward and bit the police officers. No issue arose in either of those cases as to whether the carrying of a weapon could constitute a threat of violence.

[15] In *R v Robinson* [1993] Crim LR 581 the defendant was convicted of affray where he and his co-accused asked a motorist in an aggressive manner to drive them to a particular destination and threatened to take the car if he did not do so. Section 3(3) of the 1986 Act provides that on a charge of affray a threat cannot be made by the use of words alone, but at the trial counsel for the Crown argued that in addition to what was said there was conduct which created an aura of menace.

a The Court of Appeal allowed the appeal on the ground that the evidence was devoid of anything that went beyond the use of words alone. In *R v Sanchez* [1996] Crim LR 572 the defendant was convicted of an affray when she had lunged at her boyfriend with a knife in a car park. On appeal the Court of Appeal quashed the conviction because the trial judge had failed to direct the jury to consider whether a reasonable hypothetical bystander would have feared for his b personal safety. Again neither of these cases was concerned with the issue whether the carrying of dangerous weapons by a group of persons can constitute a threat of violence.

[16] Therefore I am of the opinion that as a matter of law the carrying of dangerous weapons such as petrol bombs by a group of persons can constitute a threat of violence within the meaning of s 3(1). Whether it does so in a particular c case is a matter for the tribunal of fact to decide having regard to the facts of the case. Accordingly I am in full agreement with that part of the judgment of Auld LJ where he said ([2000] 1 Cr App R 251 at 257):

> 'In my judgment, the visible carrying in public of primed petrol bombs by d a large number of what was obviously an East London gang out for no good was clearly capable of constituting a threat of unlawful violence. That is so whether it is characterised as a show of force or simply an obviously threatening spectacle, and regardless of the fact that the armed gang members were not yet throwing or brandishing their weapons. I stress, however, that mere possession of a weapon, without threatening circumstances e of the sort that I have mentioned, is not enough to constitute a threat of unlawful violence. So, for example, the mere carrying of a concealed weapon could not itself be such a threat.'

The second (reformulated) question

f **[17]** The offence of affray, both at common law and now under statute, was primarily intended to punish a person or persons who engaged in a face-to-face confrontation where violence was used or threatened and where reasonably firm-minded members of the public would be put in fear. As Lord Bingham of Cornhill CJ said in *R v Smith* [1997] 1 Cr App R 14 at 17:

g

> 'It typically involves a group of people who may well be shouting, struggling, threatening, waving weapons, throwing objects, exchanging and threatening blows and so on.'

[18] The appellants submit that the offence of affray requires three persons: a h person who uses or threatens unlawful violence, a person at whom he directs the violence or threat (the victim), and a hypothetical bystander of reasonable firmness. The appellants further submit that the victim must be present at the scene. In support of this submission they rely on the words 'towards another' in s 3(1). They contend that unlawful violence cannot be threatened towards j another unless that other person is present. They rely on the judgment of Taylor LJ in *Atkin v DPP* (1989) 89 Cr App R 199 at 204–205 where, in considering the words in s 4(1) of the 1986 Act, he said:

> 'The phrase "uses towards another person" means, in the context of section 4(1)(a) "uses in the presence of and in the direction of another person directly."'

[19] The Crown submits that where a person is in possession of a weapon, such as a bomb, which if it were detonated could cause injury to persons close to, but not present at, the location where the offender is holding the bomb, violence would be threatened towards those persons within the meaning of s 3(1).

[20] The Crown also submits that in this case the group of youths were congregated near a block of residential flats at a time when people would be returning to them from work and it could be inferred that members of the public were bound to be in the vicinity even if they were not present at the scene where the youths were gathered.

[21] The Crown further submits that the judgment of Taylor LJ in *Atkin*'s case on the meaning of the words 'uses towards another person threatening ... words' in s 4(1) of the 1986 Act does not assist in deciding the meaning of the different words in s 3(1) 'uses or threatens unlawful violence towards another'.

[22] If the point were to be determined by having regard only to the words of s 3(1), there would be some degree of force in the Crown's submissions, because I think that giving the words their ordinary meaning violence can be threatened towards another person even if that person is not present when the threatening conduct takes place. But s 3(1) was enacted to give effect to the recommendation of the Law Commission in its report and in para 3.15 of the White Paper *Review of Public Order Law* (1985) (Cmnd 9510), setting out its proposals for the reform of public order law, the government stated in relation to affray that it was 'content to accept the Law Commission's proposed statutory definition'. Therefore it is permissible, and indeed desirable, for the courts to have regard to the view of the Law Commission on this issue and to know the basis on which it recommended that threatening unlawful violence towards another, as well as using unlawful violence towards another, should constitute the offence of affray (see *R v Shivpuri* [1986] 2 All ER 334 at 343–344, [1987] AC 1 at 21 and *Aswan Engineering Establishment Co v Lupdine Ltd (Thurgar Bolle Ltd, third party)* [1987] 1 All ER 135 at 146–147, [1987] 1 WLR 1 at 14).

[23] In its report the Law Commission discussed the elements of the statutory offence of affray which it was recommending and explained why, contrary to its earlier view, it considered that threats of violence, without the actual use of violence, should also constitute the offence. It is desirable to set out the relevant paragraphs in full:

> '(a) *Using or threatening violence*
>
> 3.13 Common law affray requires the defendant to have engaged in unlawful fighting or violence, or a display of force without actual violence. All recent reported cases appear to have involved actual fighting or violence and, although the element of display of force is accepted as part of the law, precisely what this connotes is not clear: brandishing of a "fearful weapon" is probably sufficient, but not "mere words, unaccompanied by the brandishing of a weapon or actual violence".
>
> 3.14 Primarily because of the absence of reported cases in recent times relating to the element of display of force, we proposed in our Working Paper that mere threats or displays of violence should be excluded from any new offence replacing the common law. We pointed to the range of other offences capable of dealing with such threats, and noted that the scheme of offences in the Working Paper made provision for penalties to be imposed for serious threats or displays of force by a group under the terms of the proposed statutory offence of unlawful assembly. Nevertheless, we stressed

a that, were evidence presented to us of the need to include threats within the new offence, the issue would require reconsideration.

3.15 A substantial majority of those commenting on our Working Paper approved our proposed exclusion of threats or displays of force. Cogent evidence has, however, been presented to us by others which persuades us that our provisional proposal should be changed. In particular, it has been b urged on us that there is no reason of substance why, in this context, a punch thrown which misses should be distinguished from one which lands on another person; and, if there were insufficient evidence to show that any of those accused actually succeeded in hitting another, no-one, upon our provisional proposal, would have been guilty of the offence, and a person who punched but missed would not, therefore, have been liable for aiding c and abetting. And a person closely connected with an affray, such as an individual brandishing a razor, would if threats were excluded from the ambit of the offence, not be guilty of it. Some threats of violence might be met with charges of possessing an offensive weapon under the Prevention of Crime Act 1953; this, however, would only be the case if there were proof of d such possession, and in the case of, say, a mob terrifying shoppers in a shopping precinct there may be insuperable difficulties in proving which person had a particular weapon.

3.16 These examples of the difficulties which could arise on our provisional proposals have impressed us. Perhaps the most persuasive argument is that, e under those proposals, those engaged in what was in all respects one incident would have been capable of being prosecuted only be means of charges of different offences—affray and unlawful assembly—according to whether it appeared that they were hitting another or merely threatening to do so. In the context of street fighting such a distinction seems artificial: we believe, on reconsideration, that any offence which is aimed, in broad terms, at f unlawful fighting to the terror of the public should be capable of penalising all those concerned in a particular incident, whether the evidence is that—(i) in some cases blows actually landed on others, (ii) in others it is uncertain whether blows landed, or (iii) some defendants were merely threatening blows. Under our provisional proposals, only those falling g within (i) would have been liable to be penalised for affray. We now recommend that under any new offence persons in all three categories should be liable. This will enable the court to do justice on the whole of the evidence relating to a particular incident. It must be accepted, however, that a broadening of the categories of prohibited acts in this way would permit the offence to be charged when no-one was actually engaged in acts of h fighting. On the other hand, common law affray can at present be charged where the relevant conduct consists of threats alone, but we have no evidence that the offence is used in that way save where it is justified by quite exceptional circumstances. We would expect no change in prosecution practice under any new offence replacing the common law.'

j

[24] Therefore it is apparent that the Law Commission and Parliament intended that the offence set out in s 3 should penalise those who engage in a fight, whether they are landing blows, or attempting to land blows, or threatening to land blows, but it is also clear that in such circumstances the victim or victims are bound to be present with the offender or offenders. Accordingly I regard it as clear that the section does not make guilty of an affray a person whose conduct constitutes a threat of violence to persons who are not present. This conclusion also derives support from the requirement in sub-s (1) that the conduct of the offender is such that it would cause a bystander 'present at the scene' to fear for his personal safety. The concept of presence at the scene suggests that the notional bystander would be in the presence of both the offender and the victim. It is also relevant to observe that there is no reported case of affray where the victim was not present at the scene where the accused threatened violence.

[25] In the Divisional Court Auld LJ stated ([2000] 1 Cr App R 251 at 258–259):

> 'In my judgment, where there is a threat of violence taking the form of a gathering of armed persons in a public place, it is not necessary to prove that a person or persons present actually felt threatened … see *Swanston v. Director of Public Prosecutions* [(1996) 161 JP 203] … It is plain from the sight of an armed gathering in public that at least those openly displaying their weapons constitute a threat of violence to someone. That could be any local resident or other member of the public who happened to see them and also police officers called to the scene. The hypothetical bystander, for whose protection the offence of affray is primarily designed, is not to know precisely when and where and towards whom the threatened violence will occur. It is enough for him that there is such a threat to someone which puts him in fear. This is not introducing into the offence of affray a notional victim of threatened violence to join the notional bystander of reasonable firmness. There must have been someone at or in the vicinity towards whom the threat of violence can be said to have been directed. Often that can readily be inferred where such behaviour takes place in a public place, and, as I have said, may include police officers who attend, whether or not, when there, they perceive a threat of violence directed towards themselves. The circumstances of explosive devices such as those here would constitute a threat towards anyone in the immediate vicinity and in all directions, whatever their lack of connection with those charged or their role at the scene. Here, the obvious inference from the scene of a threat of violence by the group of armed youths towards someone other than themselves had as its background the magistrate's unchallenged finding that in that part of the East End of London there were street gangs who were territorially based and that there was bad blood between them. He was entitled also, in the special circumstances of this case, to find, as he did, that the diffuse threat of violence, inherent in the overt carrying of petrol bombs—highly dangerous and untargeted in their effect if exploded—constituted a threat of violence to anyone in the vicinity, including the police on arrival on the scene. The police officers' perception, or lack of it, of themselves as particular targets is immaterial. Accordingly, I would answer "yes" to the second question, that of whether a threat of violence towards an unknown person or persons or the public at large at the scene amounts to a threat of unlawful violence towards another. It follows from what I have said that it is not necessary to answer the third question, which goes in the main to the police witnesses' own perception of a threat of violence. The fact that they did not speak of a threat, in the form, say, of brandishing the petrol bombs either at others or themselves, and that one of them merely thought, whether before or on arrival at the scene, that there could be a disturbance, does not mean that there was no evidence, on the facts as found by the magistrate, of a threat of

a unlawful violence towards another or others. For the reasons he gave and which I have in substance and at greater length repeated, there plainly was.'

Hughes J stated (at 260–261):

'5. Affray does require the presence of a person threatened. The person of reasonable firmness who is referred to in section 3(1) is a hypothetical person. b He is often conveniently referred to as the "hypothetical bystander". He represents the standard by which the gravity of the behaviour is to be judged and he demonstrates that this public order offence is designed for the protection of the public. But although the bystander is hypothetical, the person threatened with unlawful violence is not. It seems to me possible that c the person who is threatened may be unaware of it, for example, if his back was turned. However, the person threatened must exist and he or she must be there.

6. Such person threatened may, however, be of unknown identity. Moreover, a threat may be made generally in a populous place to all about. In a case like the present, that might include the men, women and children d able to see from the windows of the flats, or those who were entering or leaving at a little short of 7 p.m. Even without the evidence of such a person being given to the court, a court is entitled in an appropriate case to conclude, as a matter of fact, that such persons were indeed threatened by the conduct of the defendant. Indeed, in the present case, someone telephoned e the police. However, in the present case, the magistrate has specifically found, as follows: "Aside from the police no other persons and in particular no member of any other gang was shown to be present at the scene at 6.50 pm". He has therefore not found, as he might perhaps have done, that others were there and were threatened. A finding that there was no one there to be threatened but anyone who might appear in the future would be likely to f be threatened is not sufficient.

7. That a police constable thinks that a disturbance might ensue is not by itself enough. If what he contemplates is no more than a future event, there is no present threat. Affray requires a threat rather than a risk of a future threat.

g 8. On the special facts of this case, for the reasons that have been fully explained by Auld L.J., the magistrate was entitled to conclude that, whether or not the police officers said that they felt threatened, the threat was a general one, and was in fact made towards them at a time when they were present.'

h **[26]** Therefore both Auld LJ and Hughes J recognised that the victim or victims towards whom the threat is directed must be present. But I consider, with respect, that they erred in applying this requirement to the facts as found by the stipendiary magistrate and set out in the case stated. It was not open to Auld LJ to find that the overt carrying of petrol bombs constituted a threat of j violence to anyone in the vicinity, including the police on arrival at the scene, because the magistrate found that no one other than the police was present at the scene, and he also found by clear implication that the group of youths constituted no threat towards the police as the group dispersed immediately the police carrier came into view. Similarly it was not open to Hughes J to find in para 8 of his judgment that there was a threat towards the police officers. In order to constitute an offence under s 3 there must be a threat of violence towards another person. Whilst the carrying of petrol bombs can constitute a threat of violence, it does not necessarily follow that because a person is present at a location where a gang are carrying petrol bombs there is a threat of violence towards that person. Whether there is a threat of violence towards a person present at the scene constituted by the carrying of a weapon or weapons will depend on the facts of the actual case, but that issue does not arise in the present case because, apart from the police officers towards whom there was no threat, no one was present at the scene.

[**27**] Accordingly I would answer Yes to the first certified question and Yes to the second (reformulated) question and would allow the appeals on the ground which I have stated in relation to the second question. I think that the third certified question was intended to relate to a situation where a person threatened was not present at the scene, and therefore it does not now arise for consideration.

[**28**] The appellants were clearly guilty of criminal conduct and it would have been open to the prosecuting authorities to have charged them with the carrying of an offensive weapon contrary to s 1 of the Prevention of Crime Act 1953 or with possession of explosives contrary to s 4 of the Explosive Substances Act 1883. It appears that there is an increasing tendency to charge the offence of affray and in the year 2000 there were 1,891 offences of affray charged in the Metropolitan Police area. The present case demonstrates that a person should not be charged with the offence unless he uses or threatens unlawful violence towards another person actually present at the scene and his conduct is such as would cause fear to a notional bystander of reasonable firmness.

LORD HOBHOUSE OF WOODBOROUGH. My Lords,

[**29**] For the reasons given by my noble and learned friend Lord Hutton, with whose speech I agree, I too would allow these appeals and answer the questions as he proposes.

LORD SCOTT OF FOSCOTE. My Lords,

[**30**] I have had the advantage of reading in draft the opinion of my noble and learned friend Lord Hutton. For the reasons which he gives, I, too, would allow these appeals and respond to the certified questions as he proposes.

Appeals allowed.

Dilys Tausz Barrister.

a

Eastbourne Town Radio Cars Association v Customs and Excise Commissioners

[2001] UKHL 19

b

HOUSE OF LORDS

LORD SLYNN OF HADLEY, LORD HOFFMANN, LORD COOKE OF THORNDON, LORD HOBHOUSE OF WOODBOROUGH AND LORD SCOTT OF FOSCOTE

6, 7 NOVEMBER 2000, 4 APRIL 2001

c

Value added tax – Club or association – Supply of services for consideration – Test for determining whether unincorporated body making taxable supplies to members – Value Added Tax Act 1994, s 94(2)(a).

The appellant association was an unincorporated body whose members were private hire car drivers. Members paid a joining fee and a proportion of the d association's expenses. Services, such as advertising and arranging jobs, were provided for the members through salaried employees. The association was registered for value added tax (VAT) on the basis that those services constituted a taxable supply in the course of the furtherance of a business carried on by it within the meaning of s 4(1)[a] of the Value Added Tax Act 1994. Under s 94(2)(a)[b], e 'the provision by a club, association, or organisation (for a subscription or other consideration) of the facilities or advantages available to its members' was deemed to be the carrying on of a business. In 1994 the association's constitution was revised, so that its objects included the employment by the members of persons to provide services to them, not, as previously stated, the employment by the association of such persons to provide services to the members. The f employees' contracts of employment also provided that the employees were employed by the members. The association applied for its VAT registration to be cancelled, contending that the sums paid by its members were not consideration for services supplied, but should be regarded as collective funding for the members' own employment of staff and for their obtaining other facilities. g That application was refused by the commissioners whose decision was upheld by the tribunal, set aside by the High Court and restored by the Court of Appeal. The association appealed to the House of Lords, relying on the changes to its constitution, the terms of the contracts of employment and the fact that the payment of subscriptions was on the basis of dividing the expenses of the association.

h

Held – Although s 94(2)(a) of the 1994 Act did not of itself mean that an association would automatically be making a taxable supply, it did mean that it was carrying on a business and could be within the scope of VAT. The intention of the Act was plainly that the activities of an association should not be excluded j from VAT merely because it was unincorporated and not a legal person. Such a body made a taxable supply to its members if two conditions were satisfied. First, it was necessary that there should be something which could be described as an association rather than a mere contractual arrangement for jointly obtaining

a Section 4, so far as material, is set out at [3], post

b Section 94 is set out at [6], post

goods and services and sharing their expense. An association would usually have a set of rules which constituted a mutually binding contract between the members, a statement of its objects and provisions for its governance by a committee or committees, the admission of members and the cessation of membership (giving the association a continuity beyond its original members) and provisions (or a rule-making power) for the terms and conditions upon which members could enjoy the benefits of membership. That list was not exhaustive, and it was perfectly possible for contractual arrangements to lack one or more of those features and yet still be regarded as constituting an association. The further, however, that the arrangements departed from those of the standard case, the less likely they were to be treated as an association for the purposes of the Act. Secondly, the facility or service in question had to be provided in accordance with the rules of the association and had to be in consideration of a payment into the funds of the association. That condition was to exclude arrangements which were not with members as such, but involved the association acting simply as an ordinary third party. In the instant case, both conditions were satisfied. There was an association and the right of any member to the services provided by the employees engaged for the purposes of the association was governed by the rules or byelaws made under the rules. He enjoyed those services in return for the payment of a subscription into the funds of the association. The factors relied upon by the association did not alter the character of the transaction as a supply by the association to the members. Accordingly, the appeal would be dismissed (see [18]–[25], [33]–[42], post).

Durham Aged Mineworkers' Homes Association v Customs and Excise Comrs [1994] STC 553 distinguished.

Notes

For the activities of clubs and associations in the context of value added tax, see 49(1) *Halsbury's Laws* (4th edn reissue) para 18.

For the Value Added Tax Act 1994, ss 4, 94, see 50 *Halsbury's Statutes* (4th edn) (2000 reissue) 33, 178.

Cases cited in opinions

Apple and Pear Development Council v Customs and Excise Comrs Case 102/86 [1988] 2 All ER 922, [1988] ECR 1443, ECJ.

Carlton Lodge Club v Customs and Excise Comrs [1974] 3 All ER 798, [1975] 1 WLR 66.

Customs and Excise Comrs v Reed Personnel Services Ltd [1995] STC 588.

Customs and Excise Comrs v Sinclair Collis Ltd [1999] STC 701, CA.

Durham Aged Mineworkers' Homes Association v Customs and Excise Comrs [1994] STC 553.

Glawe (H J) Spiel-und Unterhaltungsgeräte Aufstellungsgesellschaft mbH & Co KG v Finanzamt Hamburg-Barmbek-Uhlenhorst Case C-38/93 [1994] STC 543, [1994] ECR I-1679, ECJ.

IRC v Duke of Westminster [1936] AC 1, [1935] All ER Rep 259, HL.

Nell Gwynn House Maintenance Fund Trustees v Customs and Excise Comrs [1999] 1 All ER 385, [1999] 1 WLR 174, HL; *rvsg* [1996] STC 310, CA.

Appeal

Eastbourne Town Radio Cars Association (the Association) appealed with permission of the Appeal Committee of the House of Lords given on 14 July 1999 from the decision of the Court of Appeal (Simon Brown, Swinton Thomas and Potter LJJ) on a 7 May 1998 ([1998] STC 669) allowing an appeal by the respondent, the Commissioners of Customs and Excise, from the decision of Turner J on 18 October 1996 ([1996] STC 1469) allowing an appeal by the Association from the decision of the Value Added Tax and Duties Tribunal on 15 January 1996 ([1996] SWTI 664) dismissing its appeal from the decision of the commissioners on 18 November 1994, affirmed on 10 January 1995, refusing the Association's application to b de-register for the purposes of value added tax. The facts are set out in the opinion of Lord Slynn of Hadley.

Joe Smouha (instructed by *Brachers*, Maidstone) for the Association.

Melanie Hall and *Philippa Whipple* (instructed by the *Solicitor for the Customs and Excise*) for the commissioners.

c

Their Lordships took time for consideration.

4 April 2001. The following opinions were delivered.

d

LORD SLYNN OF HADLEY.

[1] My Lords, the Eastbourne Town Radio Cars Association (the Association) is an unincorporated body whose members are private hire car drivers in Eastbourne. They pay a joining fee and they pay each year a proportion of the Association's expenses. Through salaried employees services are provided for the e members such as advertising and arranging jobs by telephone or radio contact. The Association applied for registration and was registered with effect from 1 September 1991 for the purposes of value added tax (VAT). It was not disputed that the Association was making supplies for the purpose of VAT which exceeded the registration threshold.

f [2] In August 1994 the constitution of the Association was revised. The Association contended that thereafter it was not making supplies to its members and it applied for its registration to be cancelled under para 13(2) of Sch 1 to the Value Added Tax Act 1994 on the basis that it was no longer registerable. The commissioners refused the application and their decision was upheld by the London Value Added Tax Tribunal ([1996] SWTI 664), set aside by Turner J g ([1996] STC 1469) and restored by the Court of Appeal ([1998] STC 669). The question on this appeal is whether the Association does make taxable supplies to its members in view of the changes to its constitution.

[3] The Act provides that:

h

> '**4.**—(1) VAT shall be charged on any supply of … services made in the United Kingdom, where it is a taxable supply made by a taxable person in the course or furtherance of any business carried on by him.
>
> (2) A taxable supply is a supply of goods or services made in the United Kingdom other than an exempt supply.
>
> j **5.**—(1) Schedule 4 shall apply for determining what is, or is to be treated as, a supply of goods or a supply of services.
>
> (2) Subject to any provision made by that Schedule and to Treasury orders under subsections (3) to (6) … (a) "supply" in this Act includes all forms of supply, but not anything done otherwise than for a consideration; (b) anything which is not a supply of goods but is done for a consideration … is a supply of services.'

[4] There is no suggestion in this case that if the Association does make a supply for a consideration it is other than a supply of services.

[5] The Act has two other provisions which deal with the position of an association. Section 46 empowers the commissioners to make regulations determining by what persons anything required to be done under the Act is to be done—

> 'where a business is carried on in partnership or by a club, association or organisation the affairs of which are managed by its members or a committee or committees of its members.'

[6] Section 94 provides that:

> '(1) In this Act "business" includes any trade, profession or vocation.
>
> (2) Without prejudice to the generality of anything else in this Act, the following are deemed to be the carrying on of a business—(a) the provision by a club, association or organisation (for a subscription or other consideration) of the facilities or advantages available to its members ...'

[7] The 1994 version of the constitution of the Association provides for the management of the Association to be entrusted to an elected committee which is given power not only to deal with admissions to and expulsion from membership and to determine the contributions of members to the expenses of the Association but also to determine such matters as the number of employees required, to appoint subcommittees for special purposes and generally to manage 'the affairs' of the Association.

[8] Many of the articles of the 1994 constitution repeat what was in the 1991 constitution. But there are differences deliberately introduced with VAT liability in mind and which the Association submits are not only important but crucial. It is therefore necessary to consider these in some detail.

[9] Thus para 3 of the 1991 constitution provides that:

> 'The purposes for which the Association is established are the following:—(a) To provide for the members of the Association premises from which there shall be conducted the businesses of the members as independently contracting private car-hire drivers. (b) To provide by means of wireless telecommunications, telephone and such other means as may from time to time be deemed desirable, such communications network for the advancement of the members' business as may be appropriate. (c) To employ such manager, telephonist and other staff as may, from time to time, be desirable. (d) To conduct for and on behalf of the members from time to time, such negotiations and activities as may be deemed to be in the interests of the members in connection with their said businesses. (e) To do all other things as may from time to time, in the opinion of the Association, or of the committee of the Association be deemed desirable and opportune for the development of the business interests of the members.'

[10] The constitution further provides:

> '23. The Committee shall have power:—(a) Generally to manage the affairs of the Association in accordance with the rules and bye-laws; (b) To appoint from their number sub-committees for special purposes and to delegate to them any of the powers of the committee except those of electing and expelling and making, altering or revoking bye-laws ...

a 27. At the Annual General Meeting any member may propose a new rule or bye-law or alteration or deletion of any existing rule or bring before the meeting any subject or proposal which relates to the affairs of the Association, provided that by not less than seven days before the meeting he shall have given the Secretary notice thereof in writing.'

b **[11]** These were replaced in the 1994 constitution which contains the following paragraphs:

'3. The purposes for which the Association is established are the following: (a) The employment by the members of such manager, telephonist and other staff as may, from time to time, be desirable. (b) To facilitate the c supply by third parties to members as joint principals of the use of telephone equipment and such other services, goods and facilities as may be required by the members including (but not to the exclusion of any other services): (i) Advertising and promotion. (ii) Post and stationery. (iii) Insurance (but not insurance of vehicles belonging to members). (iv) Computers. (v) Radio facilities.

d 4. The Association shall carry out its activities upon a non-profit making basis.

5. The entire income and property of the Association shall be applied solely towards the promotion of the purposes set out in paragraph 3 above. No portion shall be paid or transferred to the persons who at any time are or e have been members of the Association or to any of them, or to any person claiming through any of them …

7 … (g) Each member shall contribute such weekly or other periodical sum as the committee shall from time to time resolve on account of his share of the expenses of the Association …

f 23. The Committee shall have power:—(a) Generally to manage the affairs of the Association as agents for the members in accordance with the rules and bye-laws; (b) To appoint from their number sub-committees for special purposes and to delegate to them any of the powers of the Committee except those of electing and expelling and making, altering or revoking bye-laws …

g 34. The Committee shall keep all proper and necessary records of all receipts and payments taken or made by them on behalf of the Association or its members and shall present an audited account thereof at the Annual General Meeting and the same shall be at the expense of the members of the Association. The total expenses of the Association thus ascertained will be divided equally among the members. Any member who has been a member h for only a part of the period covered by the account shall be allocated a rateable proportion of the total expenses computed on a time basis. At the same time every member will receive a statement of his account with the Association covering the same period in which he will be charged his share of the total expenses and credited with the contributions he has made in j accordance with clause 7(g) above. The balance of each member's account at the end of the period may be dealt with by reduction or increase or such member's future contribution or in any other manner at the discretion of the Committee including demand for immediate payment of any debit balance in the books of the Association. The Association shall obtain goods and services in accordance with this constitution as agent for the members jointly …

42. In the Driver's Rules attached to this Constitution the word "subscription" shall be read as if it referred to the contributions on account of expenses described in this Constitution under paragraph 7(g).' a

[12] Other changes may arguably point in the same direction of transferring the business from that of the Association to that of the members. Thus para 7(g) in 1991, 'Each member shall contribute such weekly or other periodical sum as the Committee shall from time to time resolve for the purposes of fulfilling the expenses of the Association', became in 1994, 'Each member shall contribute such weekly or other periodical sum as the Committee shall from time to time resolve on account of his share of the expenses of the Association.' I doubt however whether there is any real difference between them. b

[13] But Mr Smouha contends that the emphasis in the clauses to which I have referred on the members rather than on the Association fundamentally changes the position in regard to VAT. He further relies on the terms of the 'Statement of Conditions of Service' under the Employment Protection (Consolidation) Act 1978 which is given to employees who normally work 16 hours per week or more. In that document the employer is stated to be 'each of the members for the time being of Eastbourne Town Radio Cars Association'. c d

[14] The issue is thus whether that is enough to remove VAT liability from the Association, bearing in mind that:

'First, as I have already said, the concept of "supply" for the purposes of VAT is not identical with that of contractual obligation. Secondly, in consequence, it is perfectly possible that although the parties in any given situation may conclude their contractual arrangements in writing so as to define all their mutual rights and obligations arising in private law, their agreement may nevertheless leave open the question, what is the nature of the supplies made by A to B for the purposes of A's assessment of VAT. In many situations, of course, the contract will on the facts conclude any VAT issue, as where there is a simple agreement for the supply of goods or services with no third parties involved. In cases of that kind there is no space between the issue of supply for VAT purposes and the nature of the private law of contractual obligation. But that is a circumstance, not a rule. There may be cases, generally (perhaps always) where three or more parties are concerned, in which the contract's definition (however exhaustive) of the parties' private law obligations nevertheless neither caters for nor concludes the statutory question, what supplies are made by whom to whom. Nor should this be a matter for surprise: in principle, the incidence of VAT is obviously not by definition regulated by private agreement. Whether and to what extent the tax falls to be exacted depends, as with every tax, on the application of the taxing statute to the particular facts. Within those facts, the terms of contracts entered into by the taxpayer may or may not determine the right tax result. They do not necessarily do so.' (See *Customs and Excise Comrs v Reed Personnel Services Ltd* [1995] STC 588 at 595 per Laws J.) e f g h j

[15] It is also right to bear in mind the approach of Advocate General Jacobs in *H J Glawe Spiel-und Unterhaltungsgeräte Aufstellungsgesellschaft mbH & Co KG v Finanzamt Hamburg-Barmbek-Uhlenhorst* Case C-38/93 [1994] STC 543 at 547, [1994] ECR I-1679 at 1686 (para 18), where he said, in relation to a claim that tax

a was chargeable on the whole amount put into a gaming machine rather than on the net receipt after winnings had been taken:

> '... that view is inconsistent with the commercial reality of the transaction ... for all practical purposes the operator's turnover consists in the amounts he is able to remove from the machine, and not in the total amounts inserted b by players.'

[16] The importance of 'the commercial reality, and not straying outside the four corners of the contract' was also stressed in *Customs and Excise Comrs v Sinclair Collis Ltd* [1999] STC 701 at 708 (para 7).

[17] If the terms of the 1994 constitution and the statement are looked at only c as a matter of contract between the various drivers and the employees it may well be that since the Association is not a legal entity the employers would be the various drivers from time to time and the rights and obligations of the drivers would depend only on the contract between them. In such a case the Association would be acting as agent for the drivers; it would hold property in trust for the drivers d and the drivers would be individually or jointly liable to third parties for what they did or what was done on their behalf.

[18] In the context of liability to register for and to pay VAT, however, the starting point is the provision of s 94(2)(a) of the Act. When an association provides, for a subscription or other consideration, facilities or advantages e available to its members, such provision is 'deemed to be the carrying on of a business'. That does not of itself mean that the association is automatically making a taxable supply but it does mean that the association is carrying on a business and can be within the scope of VAT. The intention of the Act is plainly that the activities of an association should not be excluded from VAT merely because it was unincorporated and not a legal person.

f [19] It is plain that here there is an 'association' within the meaning of the Act. If there were any doubt about that it is at least an 'organisation'. The Association has members, a committee and a chairman. It has rules binding on the members which govern the activities of the Association and its members. There is provided an infrastructure for the provision of the various services. The Association g through its committee controls admissions and the discipline and removal of members. The Association is empowered to invest money. Only members of the Association are entitled to benefit from the activity of the Association. The members pay a joining subscription of £50 or such other fee as shall be fixed by the Association in general meeting and they also pay a periodical sum fixed by the h Association's committee on account of the members' share 'of the expenses of the Association' (para 7(g)). In the drivers' rules attached to the constitution the word 'subscription' is taken to refer to such contributions on account of expenses (para 42). The subscriptions are paid direct to the Association and they do not go to other members who are said to provide the employees. A member's share of j the expenses is not calculated on specific services rendered for him—eg in arranging a particular journey—but on the total expenses for the year divided amongst the members and—

> 'Any member who has been a member for only a part of the period covered by the account shall be allocated a rateable proportion of the total expenses computed on a time basis.' (Paragraph 34).

The subscription for 1994 included in each case a higher amount than the allocated share of expenses, the balance to be carried forward to the following year.

[**20**] It is to be noted that although the members are said in the statement of conditions of service to be the employer (which in itself creates difficulties of identification) the document is signed on behalf of the Association. Normal working hours are 'likely to be variable as agreed by yourself and the Association'; grievance and disciplinary procedures are to be carried out by committee members and members of the Association.

> 'The Association does not condone unnotified lateness or absenteeism. It puts undue pressure on other employees to cover duties, and expense to the Association if a driver has to be used instead.'

[**21**] It seems to me that the joining subscription and the share of expenses paid constitute consideration for what is done by the Association in engaging staff (whether as employees of the Association or the members) on the terms of the Association's constitution, in providing through the staff engaged the operation of a radio or telephone system to link customers to drivers, in advertising, procuring insurance and otherwise. The Association is reimbursed by the members for the services supplied and there is a direct link between the services and the payment as required by *Apple and Pear Development Council v Customs and Excise Comrs* Case 102/86 [1988] 2 All ER 922 at 935, 938, [1988] ECR 1443 at 1461, 1468.

[**22**] This is in my view so even though the sum is fixed annually and not by individual services specifically charged for. What is done thus constitutes the provision by an association for consideration of facilities or advantages available to members of the Association. It thus is deemed to be the carrying on of a business by the Association. In the course of its business the Association makes supplies of services to its members (see s 5(2)(b)). That supply is not an exempt supply. It is therefore a taxable supply (see s 4(2)). Since the quantity of such supplies exceeds the threshold figure for the payment of VAT (see Sch 1 to the Act) the Association is required to be registered; it is therefore a taxable person (see s 3(1)). The circle is thus complete—there is a taxable supply made by a taxable person in the course or furtherance of a business carried on by the Association. VAT is chargeable.

[**23**] It seems to me that this is not simply the provision of services by the Association as an administrative intermediary as the Association contends. Moreover, there is not simply a sharing of expenses between two bodies as in *Durham Aged Mineworkers' Homes Association v Customs and Excise Comrs* [1994] STC 553 upon which Mr Smouha strongly relied and the correctness of which decision on its own facts I do not doubt. Nor does this case raise the same issues as those decided by your Lordships' House in *Nell Gwynn House Maintenance Fund Trustees v Customs and Excise Comrs* [1999] 1 All ER 385, [1999] 1 WLR 174 which reversed the decision of the Court of Appeal ([1996] STC 310) to which the courts below referred.

[**24**] Such a conclusion is not contrary to what was said by Lord Russell of Killowen in *IRC v Duke of Westminster* [1936] AC 1 at 24, [1935] All ER Rep 259 at 270. On the contrary it is within the letter and spirit of the Act which implements the result intended in Council Directive (EEC) 77/388 (the Sixth VAT Directive). It also fully reflects the commercial reality whatever the drafting changes in the Association's constitution as to the providing of service for the drivers. It follows

a that in my opinion in this case the Court of Appeal reached the right conclusion. Whether an unincorporated association or group can in other circumstances achieve the result that VAT is not payable it is not necessary to consider. Each case has to be looked at on its own facts and circumstances.

[25] Accordingly, I would dismiss the appeal.

b **LORD HOFFMANN.**

[26] My Lords, the issue in this case is whether the Eastbourne Town Radio Cars Association (the Association) is for the purposes of value added tax (VAT) a taxable person making taxable supplies of services to its members, who are independent car hire drivers. The Association is unincorporated. It has a constitution which contains a statement of its objects (the employment by the members of a c manager, telephonist and other staff to provide a communications network for putting customers in contact with drivers and ancillary purposes), provisions for admission to membership, governance (by an elected committee) and subscriptions by periodic payments, subject to adjustment so as to divide the expenses among the members. The committee has power to make byelaws for the internal d management of the Association, including the terms and conditions on which members may avail themselves of the services provided by the Association.

[27] Section 4(1) of the Value Added Tax Act 1994 provides:

> 'VAT shall be charged on any supply of goods or services made in the United Kingdom, where it is a taxable supply made by a taxable person in e the course or furtherance of any business carried on by him.'

[28] So the issue divides into two. First, is the Association a taxable person? Secondly, is it making a taxable supply to its members in the course or furtherance of a business which it carries on?

[29] There is no doubt that the Association is a person. The term is not f defined in the Act but Sch 1 to the Interpretation Act 1978 provides that 'person' includes a body of persons corporate or unincorporate. For the purposes of VAT, the question is put beyond doubt by the terms of s 94(2)(a) of the Act, which provides:

> 'Without prejudice to the generality of anything else in this Act, the g following are deemed to be the carrying on of a business—(a) the provision by a club, association or organisation (for a subscription or other consideration) of the facilities or advantages available to its members ...'

[30] On its face, this provision does no more than deem certain activities to be the carrying on of a business when they might not otherwise be so regarded. It h enables a taxable supply made by a taxable person, which otherwise might have been thought to fall outside s 4(1) because it was not in the course or furtherance of a business, to be brought within it. It therefore obviously assumes that the provision of facilities by a club etc to its members can amount to a taxable supply by a taxable person. This confirms the construction which the 1978 Act gives to j 'person' in the term 'taxable person'.

[31] The next stage is to ask whether the Association is not only a person but a 'taxable person'. But this turns out to be linked with the second question about whether the Association is making taxable supplies to its members, because a taxable person is defined as a person who is, or is required to be, registered for VAT (s 3(1)) and a person is required to be registered (subject to a minimum turnover requirement and other immaterial qualifications) if he is making taxable

supplies (see Sch 1). So the critical question is whether the Association is making taxable supplies to its members. If so, it is a taxable person. In fact, the question may be even narrower, because Mr Smouha (who appeared for the Association) said that unless the facilities provided by the persons employed on behalf of the members of the Association were a taxable supply to its members, the consideration for the other facilities would be insufficient to bring the Association within the registration requirement. So the question is whether the Association is making a taxable supply by providing its members with the services of its employees or the right to avail themselves of those services.

[32] My Lords, an unincorporated association is, as I have said, not a legal entity. It is a number of legal persons having mutual rights and duties in accordance with rules which constitute the contract under which they have agreed to be associated. The property of the Association is owned by or on trust for the individual members and subject to the rules. The liability of the individual members for the debts incurred for the purposes of the association is governed by the ordinary law of contract and agency. The rights of the members, as against each other, to avail themselves of the common property and facilities are governed by their contract. Nevertheless, Parliament contemplated that such a body could be treated as making supplies to its members. What did it regard as the badges of such a supply?

[33] I think that there are two. First, it is necessary that there should be something which can be described as an association. Secondly, the facility or service in question must be provided in accordance with the rules of the association and must be in consideration of a payment into the funds of the association.

[34] The first condition is the existence of an association rather than simply a contractual arrangement for jointly obtaining goods and services and sharing their expense. *Durham Aged Mineworkers' Homes Association v Customs and Excise Comrs* [1994] STC 553, much relied upon by Mr Smouha, illustrates an arrangement in the second category. An association cannot be defined by the enumeration of a set of necessary and sufficient conditions. What can be done is to list features which are normally present in an association. So, for example, it will usually have a set of rules which constitute a mutually binding contract between the members, a statement of its objects and provisions for its governance by a committee or committees, the admission of members and the cessation of membership (giving the association a continuity beyond its original members) and provisions (or a rule-making power) for the terms and conditions upon which members may enjoy the benefits of membership. This list of the paradigm characteristics of an association is not intended to be exhaustive. Furthermore, it is perfectly possible for contractual arrangements to lack one or more of these features and still be regarded as constituting an association. But the further the arrangements depart from those of the standard case, the less likely they are to be treated as an association for the purposes of the Act.

[35] The second condition is to exclude arrangements which are not with members as such but involve the association acting simply as an ordinary third party. For example, if two members of a club ask the wine steward to buy them a case of wine as part of the club's next order, undertaking to reimburse the cost, there is no supply to the members by the club. It is simply acting as their purchasing agent. On the other hand, if the club, acting in accordance with its rules, supplies wine out of its own stock to a member in return for payment into the funds of the club, that is a supply by the club to the member (see *Carlton Lodge Club v Customs and Excise Comrs* [1974] 3 All ER 798, [1975] 1 WLR 66). And when I say, 'out of

a its own stock', I mean out of wine which is held for the purposes of the club in accordance with its rules. It does not matter how or from whom the wine was acquired.

[36] In my opinion, both conditions are satisfied in the present case. There is an association and the right of any member to the services provided by the employees engaged for the purposes of the association is governed by the rules b or byelaws made under the rules. He enjoys those services in return for the payment of a subscription into the funds of the association.

[37] Mr Smouha said that what made the difference in the present case was the terms upon which the employees had been engaged and certain features of the constitution. The contracts of employment stated that the employee was engaged, not on behalf of the Association, but on behalf of the members of the c Association for the time being. The objects of the Association were not the provision of the services of the employees to the members, but the employment by the members of persons to provide such services to them. And the payment of subscriptions was on the basis of simply dividing the expenses of the Association among the members pro rata in accordance with the time for which d they had been members.

[38] In my opinion these features do not alter the character of the transaction as a supply by the Association to the members. As between the Association and its employees, the employer may be a nominated person, the committee, the body of members as a whole. In the same way, a club's wine may have been bought by the wine steward, the committee or its chairman (who may or may not e be the member buying a glass at the bar). All that seems to me quite immaterial. What matters is that, as between the members, the provision of services to the members is governed by the rules and byelaws of the association. Whether or not a member is an employer in relation to an employee, he has no right to the services of that employee except such right as may be conferred by the rules and f byelaws. Likewise it seems to me immaterial that subscriptions are fixed pro rata by time of membership rather than by the occasions on which services are used or simply per capita or in any other way. What matters is that the consideration for the member's entitlement to services under the rules is a payment into the funds of the association in accordance with the rules.

[39] Mr Smouha submitted that it was surely conceptually possible for persons g in the position of the members of the Association to set up an arrangement which merely amounted to a joint purchase of services, with a central paymaster. If so, the only question was whether they had succeeded in doing so. My Lords, I would not like to engage in the question of whether it is conceptually possible. That question involves asking whether it can be done without interposing h between the employees and the members something which is treated in VAT law as an association and therefore a separate person making supplies to those who receive services by virtue of its rules. I do not wish to speculate upon whether complex arrangements for common provision of services can be created without involving an association of the recipients. It is sufficient that in my opinion the j present arrangements clearly do so. For these reasons, as well as those given by my noble and learned friend, Lord Slynn of Hadley, I would dismiss the appeal.

LORD COOKE OF THORNDON.

[40] My Lords, I have had the advantage of reading in draft the speeches of my noble and learned friends Lord Slynn of Hadley and Lord Hoffmann. I agree with them and for the reasons they give I would dismiss the appeal.

LORD HOBHOUSE OF WOODBOROUGH.

[41] My Lords, I agree that the appeal should be dismissed for the reasons which have been given by my noble and learned friends Lord Slynn of Hadley and Lord Hoffmann.

a

LORD SCOTT OF FOSCOTE.

[42] My Lords, I have had the advantage of reading in draft the speeches of my noble and learned friends Lord Slynn of Hadley and Lord Hoffmann. I agree with them and for the reasons they give I would dismiss the appeal.

b

Appeal dismissed.

Dilys Tausz Barrister.

a

R v Benjafield
R v Leal
R v Rezvi
R v Milford

b

COURT OF APPEAL, CRIMINAL DIVISION

LORD WOOLF CJ, JUDGE LJ AND COLLINS J

6, 7, 21 DECEMBER 2000

c

Human Rights – Compatibility of legislation with provisions of human rights convention – Duty of court to read and give effect to legislation in manner compatible with convention rights – Whether duty applying to appeals by defendants from orders made before implementation of human rights legislation in proceedings brought by or at
d *instigation of public authority – Human Rights Act 1998, ss 3(1), 6(1), 7(1)(b), 22(4).*

Sentence – Confiscation order – Burden of proof – Whether statutory provisions governing confiscation orders compatible with presumption of innocence and right to peaceful enjoyment of possessions under human rights convention – Criminal Justice Act 1988,
e *s 72AA – Drug Trafficking Act 1994, s 4 – Human Rights Act 1998, Sch 1, Pt I, art 6, Pt II, art 1.*

Conjoined appeals, which were otherwise unconnected, raised the question whether the provisions governing the making of confiscation orders under the Drug Trafficking Act 1994 and the Criminal Justice Act 1988, as amended by the
f Proceeds of Crime Act 1995, were compatible with the European Convention for the Protection of Human Rights and Fundamental Freedoms 1950 (as set out in Sch 1 to the Human Rights Act 1998). In two of the appeals, the appellants appealed from orders made against them under the 1994 Act, while the appellant in the third, R, appealed from an order made against him under the 1988 Act. In all three cases, the orders, which included substantial sentences of imprisonment
g in default, had been imposed before the implementation of the 1998 Act on 2 October 2000. Under the 1994 and 1988 Acts, proceedings for a confiscation order could only be brought once a person had been convicted of a relevant offence, but the order itself could be made in relation to the benefits of crime, irrespective of whether they could be proved to be linked to the original conviction or to any other
h specific or individual crime. The proceedings could be initiated either by the prosecutor or by the court if it considered that such proceedings were appropriate. Section 4[a] of the 1994 Act required, and s 72AA[b] of the 1988 Act empowered, the court to apply certain assumptions which had the effect of reversing the normal burden of proof by requiring the convicted person to explain the source of his
j assets, income and expenditure. Such an assumption, however, was not to be applied where there would be a serious risk of injustice in the defendant's case if the assumption were made. On the appeals, the issue arose whether the statutory assumptions were compatible with art 6(2)[c] of the convention which provided that

a Section 4, so far as material, is set out at p 618 *f* to *j*, post

b Section 72AA, so far as material, is set out at p 619 *g* to p 620 *e*, post

everyone charged with a criminal offence was to be presumed innocent until proved guilty. That in turn raised the question whether art 6(2) applied to the process involved in the making of a confiscation order. The Court of Appeal also considered the extent to which the statutory confiscation provisions were compatible with art 1[d] of the First Protocol to the convention, which provided that every person was entitled to the peaceful enjoyment of his possessions, and that no one was to be deprived of his possessions except in the public interest and subject to the conditions provided for by law and by the general principles of international law. A preliminary issue arose as to whether, in determining an appeal against a confiscation order, the court should apply the law as it was when the confiscation order was made or, assuming that the law had been modified by the 1998 Act, as it was in its modified form. That issue led the court to consider the interrelationship between four provisions of the 1998 Act: s 3(1)[e], which required the court, so far as possible, to read and give effect to legislation in a way which was compatible with convention rights; s 6(1)[f], which made it unlawful for a public authority to act in a way incompatible with a convention right; s 7(1)(b)[g], which provided that a person who claimed that a public authority had acted in a way made unlawful by s 6(1) could rely on the convention right or rights concerned in any legal proceedings; and s 22(4)[h], which provided that s 7(1)(b) applied to proceedings brought by or at the instigation of a public authority whenever the act in question took place, but did not otherwise apply to an act taking place before the coming into force of s 7. In the case of R, whose appeal was five months out of time, a further issue arose, namely whether an applicant should be granted leave to appeal out of time in reliance on rights secured from 2 October 2000 by the 1998 Act.

Held – (1) It was not usual to grant leave to appeal out of time where the grounds of appeal were based on post-trial changes in the law, and the court would not wish to do other than confirm the existing practice. However, the issues raised on R's behalf were of considerable general interest, and for that reason an extension of time would be granted (see p 633 *d e*, post).

(2) Section 3(1) of the 1998 Act had retrospective effect when ss 22(4) and 7(1)(b) applied. Moreover, where the original proceedings were brought by, or at the instigation of, a public authority, as was the case with a prosecution, an appeal by the defendant was part of the proceedings to which s 22(4) applied. Any other construction would mean that, in criminal cases, the Court of Appeal could not give the required protection to the individual (who would clearly be the victim of any unlawful act) so that there would be a need for otherwise unnecessary but time-consuming proceedings before the European Court of Human Rights. It would also mean that s 7(1)(b) would apply where appeal proceedings were brought by a public authority but not when the appeal was made by the defendant. It followed that in the instant cases the appellants were entitled to rely on ss 7(1)(b) and 22(4) (see p 624 *e j* to p 625 *a* to *e j*, post); dictum of Lord Steyn in *R v DPP, ex p Kebeline* [1999] 4 All ER 801 at 832 followed.

c Article 6, so far as material, is set out at p 621 *b* to *d*, post
d Article 1 is set out at p 621 *e f*, post
e Section 3(1) is set out at p 624 *h j*, post
f Section 6(1) is set out at p 624 *b*, post
g Section 7, so far as material, is set out at p 624 *c*, post
h Section 22(4) is set out at p 624 *d e*, post

a (3) The presumption of innocence in art 6(2) of the convention applied to the process involved in the making of a confiscation order. That provision was a specific example of the more general obligation contained in art 6(1) which provided, inter alia, that everyone was entitled to a fair and public hearing in the determination of any criminal charge against him. Article 6(1) would undoubtedly apply to the process leading up to the making of a confiscation order. Such an b order was penal, and had to be regarded for the purposes of art 6(1) as at least part of the determination of a criminal charge since there was no other option provided by art 6(1). That was underlined by the fact that a defendant who did not comply with a confiscation order, which might not be based on criminal conduct proved at the trial, could be ordered to serve a substantial sentence in c default. A defendant threatened with consequences of that nature would be expected to be entitled to protection equivalent to that provided by art 6(2) even if that provision did not exist under art 6(1), unless there was objective justification for not applying the presumption of innocence. It was true that, as a matter of domestic law, the way in which s 72AA of the 1988 Act and s 4 of the d 1994 Act were drafted meant that there was nothing in the nature of what in England would normally be regarded as a 'charge'. However, in determining whether art 6(2) could properly be applied to the confiscation process, it was the character of that process as a whole which was important, and it was a mistake to focus only on the word 'charge'. What was critical was that art 6(2) was a specific application of the broad principle contained in art 6(1). The proper approach in the e instant cases, therefore, was to examine the confiscation process on the basis that art 6 as a whole, including art 6(2), applied (see p 630 *c* to *g*, p 632 *f*, p 633 *j* and p 634 *a*, post); *Hoang v France* (1992) 16 EHRR 53 and *Brown v Stott (Procurator Fiscal, Dunfermline)* [2001] 2 All ER 97 considered.

(4) The provisions governing confiscation orders in the 1988 and 1994 Acts f were not incompatible with art 6 of the convention. Although the extent of the interference with the normal presumption of innocence was substantial, Parliament had clearly made efforts to balance the interest of the defendant against that of the public. It was only after the necessary convictions that any question of confiscation arose. That was significant since the trial which had resulted in the g convictions would be one where the usual burden and standard of proof rested upon the prosecution. Moreover, there was a discretion to be exercised in determining whether to bring confiscation proceedings, and the manner in which the discretion was exercised was capable of being reviewed by the Court of Appeal. Furthermore, the court could not make a confiscation order if it decided h that there was a serious risk of injustice. If those discretions were properly exercised, the solution adopted by Parliament was a reasonable and proportionate response to a substantial public interest, namely that those who had offended should not profit from their offending and should not use their criminal conduct to fund further offending. It was therefore justifiable, as was the interference with j the right under art 1 of the First Protocol. However, it was the application of art 6 to the facts of a particular case which was all important. In the first two appeals the application of the principles to the facts required further argument, but in R's case there was no reason to think that the order was other than appropriate and in accordance with art 6. Accordingly, his appeal would be dismissed (see p 634 *h* to p 635 *b j* to p 636 *b f j* and p 637 *d*, post).

Notes

For the presumption of innocence and the right to property, see 8(2) *Halsbury's Laws* (4th edn reissue) paras 142, 165, and for confiscation orders, see 11(2) *Halsbury's Laws* (4th edn reissue) paras 1284, 1305.

For the Criminal Justice Act 1988, s 72AA, see 12 *Halsbury's Statutes* (4th edn) (1997 reissue) 1028.

For the Drug Trafficking Act 1994, s 4, see 12 *Halsbury's Statutes* (4th edn) (1997 reissue) 1500.

For the Human Rights Act 1998, ss 3, 6, 7, 22, Sch 1, Pt I, art 6, Pt II, art 1, see 7 *Halsbury's Statutes* (4th edn) (1999 reissue) 502, 504, 505, 523, 525.

Cases referred to in judgment

Brown v Stott (Procurator Fiscal, Dunfermline) [2001] 2 All ER 97, [2001] 2 WLR 817, PC.
Deweer v Belgium (1980) 2 EHRR 439, ECt HR.
Eckle v Germany (1982) 5 EHRR 1, ECt HR.
Elton v UK App No 32344/96 (11 September 1997, unreported), E Com HR.
Foti v Italy (1983) 5 EHRR 313, ECt HR.
Hoang v France (1992) 16 EHRR 53, ECt HR.
McIntosh Petitioner 2001 JC 78, HC Just.
Minelli v Switzerland (1983) 5 EHRR 554, ECt HR.
Montgomery v HM Advocate, Coulter v HM Advocate [2001] 2 WLR 779, PC.
Phillips v UK App No 41087/98 (30 November 2000, unreported), ECt HR.
R v DPP, ex p Kebeline [1999] 4 All ER 801, [2000] 2 AC 326, [1999] 3 WLR 972, HL; *rvsg* [1999] 4 All ER 801, [2000] 2 AC 326, [1999] 3 WLR 175, DC.
R v Forbes [2001] 1 All ER 686, [2001] 2 WLR 1, HL.
R v Fulcher [1995] 2 Cr App R 251, CA.
R v Lambert, R v Ali, R v Jordan [2001] 1 All ER 1014, [2001] 2 WLR 211, CA.
R v Newton (1982) 2 Cr App R 13, CA.
R v Offen, R v McGilliard, R v McKeown, R v Okwuegbunam, R v S [2001] 2 All ER 154, [2001] 1 WLR 253, CA.
Raimondo v Italy (1994) 18 EHRR 237, ECt HR.
Salabiaku v France (1988) 13 EHRR 379, ECt HR.
Welch v UK (1995) 20 EHRR 247, ECt HR.

Appeals and application for leave to appeal

R v Benjafield

The appellant, Karl Robert Benjafield, appealed with leave of Scott Baker J granted on 5 October 1999 from a confiscation order in the sum of £327,971 imposed on him by Judge Downes at the Crown Court at Norwich on 1 July 1999 under the Drug Trafficking Act 1994. The facts are set out in the judgment of the court.

R v Leal

The appellant, Manoj Leal, appealed from a confiscation order in the sum of £1,908,605 imposed on him by Judge Freedman at the Crown Court at Harrow on 27 June 2000 under the Drug Trafficking Act 1994. The facts are set out in the judgment of the court.

R v Rezvi

a The appellant, Syed Rezvi, applied for leave to appeal from a confiscation order in the sum of £214,839 imposed on him by Judge Ader at the Crown Court at Snaresbrook on 10 April 2000 under the Criminal Justice Act 1988. The facts are set out in the judgment of the court.

b *R v Milford*

The appellant, David John Milford, appealed from a confiscation order in the sum of £13,342 imposed on him by Judge Nelligan at the Crown Court at Exeter on 21 January 2000 under the Drug Trafficking Act 1994 following his conviction on 27 October 1999, after a trial before the judge and a jury, for conspiracy to import a controlled drug. The appeal was adjourned pending the outcome of c Milford's appeal against conviction. On 21 December 2000, subsequent to the hearing of the appeal against the confiscation order, the Court of Appeal (Potter LJ, Bennett and Rafferty JJ) allowed Milford's appeal against his conviction, and the confiscation order fell with the conviction. Accordingly, the facts are not set out in the judgment.

d

Andrew Mitchell QC and *Kennedy Talbot* (instructed by the *Crown Prosecution Service*) for the Crown in all the appeals.

Charles Miskin QC and *Daniel Friedman* (instructed by *Stewarts*, Stowmarket) for Benjafield.

e *John Farmer* (instructed by the *Crown Prosecution Service*, Norwich) for the prosecution in Benjafield's appeal.

Maura McGowan (assigned by the *Registrar of Criminal Appeals*) for Leal.

Andrew Marshall (instructed by the *Crown Prosecution Service*) for the prosecution in Leal's appeal.

Tim Owen QC and *Gary Summers* (instructed by *Magrath & Co*) for Rezvi.

f *Stephen Winberg* (instructed by the *Crown Prosecution Service*) for the prosecution in Rezvi's appeal.

David Osborne (assigned by the *Registrar of Criminal Appeals*) for Milford.

Andrew Maitland (instructed by the *Solicitor for the Customs & Excise*) for the prosecution in Milford's appeal.

g *Cur adv vult*

21 December 2000. The following judgment of the court was delivered.

LORD WOOLF CJ.

h 1. These appeals, which are otherwise wholly unconnected, raise the stark question whether the statutory provisions which govern the making of confiscation orders under the Drug Trafficking Act 1994 and the Criminal Justice Act 1988, as amended by the Proceeds of Crime Act 1995, are compatible with the European Convention for the Protection of Human Rights and Fundamental j Freedoms (Rome, 4 November 1950; TS 71 (1953); Cmd 8969) (as set out in Sch 1 to the Human Rights Act 1998) (the convention).

2. A further appeal, *R v Milford*, which raised the same question, was also listed for hearing. However Milford appealed against his conviction. That appeal has now been decided. The appeal against sentence, and in particular the confiscation order made against him, had been adjourned. The adjournment serves to illustrate one critical aspect of the domestic statutory code, which is that without

a relevant conviction, there is nothing to trigger the confiscation process or to sustain a confiscation order. As Milford's appeal against conviction has now succeeded, the confiscation order against him cannot survive. *a*

3. The appeals also raise a number of distinct issues in relation to the individual confiscation orders made in each case. These will be dealt with in later hearings.

Karl Benjafield *b*

4. The essential facts are straightforward. In the summer of 1997, the appellant conducted a business in drugs from his home in Norfolk. He was at the centre of a conspiracy to bring large quantities of heroin, cocaine, ecstasy, cannabis resin and amphetamines into the area, and then to distribute them to dealers for onward supply. A group of associates carried out the purchase and sale of drugs on his behalf. Many of them were subsequently convicted of drug trafficking offences. The appellant never used drugs personally, profit was his only motive, and his profit from this conspiracy was considerable. *c*

5. On 8 September 1998, in the Crown Court at Norwich before Judge Downes, Benjafield pleaded guilty to one offence of conspiracy to supply class A controlled drugs and one offence of conspiracy to supply class B controlled drugs. The dates covered by the conspiracies were 6 May 1997 to 24 July 1997. On 9 October, Benjafield was sentenced to 14 years and five years imprisonment concurrent on the two counts. *d*

6. Confiscation proceedings under s 2 of the 1994 Act were postponed on more than one occasion. For present purposes, the precise circumstances of these postponements are irrelevant. Therefore dealing with the facts briefly, the prosecutor's statement dated 8 October 1998 noted that Benjafield had not been in remunerative employment nor taken up any statutory benefits since 1995. He had been living with his partner, Mandy Keable (who was convicted of conspiracy with him and received a suspended sentence), and their children at an address in Great Yarmouth which they bought on mortgage on 29 July 1996. *e* *f*

7. Shortly before that date, in May 1996, they had bought another residential but derelict bungalow in their joint names. In 1986 another property, 'The Bentleys', was bought in the appellant's sole name. This was lived in by his parents. The appellant's remaining property interests were found in two addresses in Cobholm, the first bought in June 1992 in his father's name, but run by the appellant who received and dealt with all the income from the property, and the second, 'Blackgates Farm', conveyed into the name of his mother in 1996, but again controlled by the appellant who obtained the necessary planning permission consents to erect a large building on the site. The appellant also held a property in Spain, originally purchased in 1987. The Crown alleged that this property was held in the joint names of the appellant and his mother, and also relied on a receipt in his name indicating payment for the property. *g* *h*

8. In addition to these properties, cash (approximately £10,000) and jewellery (valued at £35,000) was found at the appellant's home or the home of his 'mother-in-law', and there was evidence to show that he had spent considerable sums on living, and that he had made impressive loans, totalling some £30,000. *j*

9. The appellant had a number of bank accounts in joint names with Mandy Keable. Between 1991 and 1997, unidentified bankings totalling £52,355 were made into their account with Lloyds Bank, and between 1995 and 1997, £25,456 was deposited from unidentified sources into their account with the Halifax Building Society.

10. The total of the alleged benefit added up to £360,487. The traced realisable assets were calculated at £185,890.

11. The appellant sought to provide evidence to demonstrate that the inclusion of three of the properties in the calculation of his alleged benefit was erroneous. Dealing with the issues very briefly for present purposes, the property in Spain belonged to his father since 1987, but had been conveyed into his name for tax avoidance reasons. The person with the real interest in the Bentleys was his father and this property was bought in 1986. Tax, and health reasons, were given for the arrangement. Blackgates Farm belonged to his mother.

12. After a lengthy hearing into these issues, it was perfectly plain that the judge felt unable to accept the evidence of the appellant's father, and when the appellant eventually gave evidence, the appellant himself. The judge recorded his conclusion that the evidence of the appellant was 'something of a joke' and that he could not be relied on 'in any way whatever … He [was] quite incapable of belief'.

13. Accordingly, on 1 July 1999, making allowance for a shortfall which represented 'hidden assets', a confiscation order was made in the sum of £327,971, to be paid within two years, with a sentence of three years imprisonment in default to run consecutively to the sentence imposed on 9 October 1998.

Manoj Leal

14. Leal, and three co-defendants, were the subject of a National Crime Squad surveillance operation carried out on two particular dates, 1 and 10 December 1998. The Crown's case was that they were all involved in a major conspiracy to supply large quantities of controlled drugs to others. The appellant was the person in control of the enterprise. In due course the police seized drugs, including cannabis, cannabis resin, and cocaine, with a wholesale value approaching £1m, which formed the organisation's current stock in trade.

15. Leal was convicted on 28 July 1999 in the Crown Court at Harrow, before Judge Freedman and a jury, of a number of offences under the Misuse of Drugs Act 1971. On the following day, he was sentenced to a total of 12 years imprisonment which, on 12 June 2000, was reduced by the Court of Appeal to nine years imprisonment.

16. The prosecutor's statement was largely, and convincingly, based on an 'accounting' ledger. From this it was calculated that the 'take' from the sale of unlawful trafficking in drugs was £1,879,504. Expenditure on drugs was calculated at £984,268. With a number of additional items, this produced a total benefit of £2,892,873. The realisable assets which the police could trace amounted to £24,793, but the Crown argued, and the court subsequently concluded, that a good deal of money remained hidden and untraced which was 'awaiting the defendant's release from prison'.

17. On 27 June 2000, Judge Freedman considered the defendant's statement and his oral evidence, together with that of his common law wife, and unhesitatingly rejected it. In calculating the confiscation order, the judge deducted the expenditure on drugs (£984,268) which left a balance of £1,908,605. She made a confiscation order in that sum, to be paid within two years, with four years imprisonment consecutive in default.

Syed Rezvi

18. Rezvi was convicted of dishonesty, arising in the course of his employment as an assistant financial controller at a hotel in London. He worked there for

some nine years. By the time of his arrest, his annual salary was £23,000. In February 1999, the police were asked to investigate two thefts of £5,000 each from the hotel. When the appellant was arrested, he admitted stealing £10,000 by telling the cashiers to order two separate sums of £5,000 from the bank. The thefts took place on 2 and 12 February respectively. Security consultants were called in. They discovered that between April 1997 and February 1999 losses totalling approximately £283,000 had taken place at the hotel. These losses were attributed to transactions conducted by the appellant.

19. When Rezvi appeared on 11 October 1999 in the Crown Court at Snaresbrook, the indictment against him included 14 specimen counts, 11 of theft, and three of obtaining a money transfer by deception. The total sums involved in the 14 counts were £35,105. None of the individual sums specified in the individual counts exceeded £5,000. On arraignment, before Judge Izzard-Davies, the appellant pleaded guilty to the last two counts, which related to the thefts on 2 and 12 February 1999. He pleaded not guilty to the remaining counts. The Crown indicated that it would be seeking a trial of the remaining counts, and the case was accordingly adjourned for trial on 24 January 2000.

20. By notice dated 21 January 2000, the prosecutor informed the court that it was considered appropriate for the court to proceed with confiscation proceedings under s 71(1)(a) of the 1988 Act. The case was one in which, in the prosecutor's opinion, it would be appropriate for the court to make the statutory assumptions under s 72(AA)(4) of that Act in determining the appellant's benefit. The prosecutor's statement made under s 73(1A) of the 1988 Act identified benefits in excess of £622,000. The substantial proportion (£465,232) was based on the valuation of two properties, 19 Fell Walk and 1 Edgeworth Avenue, Hendon, which were respectively valued at £142,936 and £322,296.

21. It was alleged that 19 Fell Walk was originally purchased in December 1991, in the name of the appellant and his first wife. Title was transferred into his sole name in March 1995. Between January 1997 and his arrest in February 1999, mortgage repayments totalling £36,770 were paid in cash. On 28 November 1997, a lump cash sum of £30,000 was made.

22. Number 1 Edgeworth Avenue was bought in joint names with Ms Naqvi (the appellant's wife) in December 1998, with a down payment of £65,000. None of the appellant's bank accounts showed any debit which might be linked with this payment. Cash sums totalling £9,835 were made against this mortgage debt between December 1998 and the date when the appellant was charged.

23. The appellant held a number of bank and building society accounts in his sole name. Regular injections of cash were made into them from untraced resources, but no debits relating to mortgage repayments could be traced to the bank account into which the appellant's annual salary from his employment was made: similarly, with payments in cash to settle his credit card liabilities. The full details of all the cash payments made by the appellant between 1997 and the date of charge need no further analysis, with the exception of a series of refunds apparently made to his account from the hotel at which he worked. Between September 1997 and March 1998, these refunds amounted to £5,763.

24. The realisable assets were valued at £353,742, and the prosecutor's statement concluded that 'the court is in a position to make a confiscation order' in this sum.

25. On 24 January 2000, the case was re-listed before Judge Ader. Counsel for the Crown informed the judge that the appropriate notices under the 1988 Act had been served on the appellant, and that the Crown had decided not to proceed

a to trial on the outstanding counts. The Crown considered that in view of the appellant's pleas to counts 13 and 14, he fell within the confiscation provisions of the 1988 Act. The Crown, he said, 'are entitled to assert that there has been a benefit from criminal activities in a specified sum … It is for the defendant to show, putting it shortly, that those proceeds have not come to him from criminal activity'. He then indicated to the judge that having considered 'the whole b matter, questions of expense and so on and so forth … the Crown have decided to proceed with the matter in this way'. Counsel asked that the confiscation issue should be adjourned until 1 April.

26. Having heard counsel for the appellant, the judge ordered that counts 1 to 12 should lie on the file in the usual terms, that is, not to be proceeded with without leave of the court or the Court of Appeal, Criminal Division. He did not c enter verdicts of 'not guilty' under s 17 of the Criminal Justice Act 1967.

27. In due course the defence statement was served and the explanation for the apparent prosperity of the appellant, with his relatively modest earnings, and his wife, who had none, was that they were the fortunate recipients of considerable financial assistance from wealthy parents. They had also been d forced to dispose of valuable wedding gifts. The prosecution challenged this explanation.

28. On 10 April, Judge Ader conducted the hearing into the confiscation issue. Both sides were represented by counsel. Having heard the evidence given by the appellant and his wife 'in an attempt to rebut the assumptions made and evidence called by the prosecution', the judge considered that the defendant's evidence e was noteworthy for the absence of support which could easily have been forthcoming. He noted the appellant's account that many of his actions which involved him in responsibility for taking money from the hotel 'were in the main at the behest of his superior', and noted in particular that 'no explanation was ever forthcoming for refunds paid to [the appellant's] account from the hotel to f which he was not entitled'. He concluded that he was 'unable to accept the defendant's accounts where they are unsupported', but added that he found some support in the evidence of his wife, despite its variance from the appellant's evidence in some respects. He then applied the assumptions required by the legislation. He concluded that the total benefit should be assessed at £539,734, and the total realisable assets should be reduced to £214,839.

g 29. On 10 April 2000, the appellant was sentenced to 15 months imprisonment concurrent on each count to which he had pleaded guilty. A confiscation order was made under the 1988 Act in the sum of £214,839. The appellant was allowed six months in which to pay, with three years imprisonment, consecutive, in default.

h 30. Leave to appeal against the confiscation order was granted during the course of the hearing before us, some five months out of time.

31. We were persuaded that an important issue of considerable practical significance was raised in the application, and that in view of the decision in *McIntosh Petitioner* 2001 JC 78 in Scotland, it should be resolved as quickly as j possible in this jurisdiction, preferably together with the same issue of principle which arises in relation to drug trafficking offences.

Section 2 confiscation orders

32. The jurisdiction to make confiscation orders in this jurisdiction involves two separate statutory schemes. The 1994 Act represents the consolidated form of the Drug Trafficking Offences Act 1986, as amended by the Criminal Justice

Act 1993. The confiscation arrangements for offences other than drug trafficking offences as defined in s 1 of the 1994 Act, are governed by the 1988 Act, as amended by the 1993 Act, further amended by the Criminal Justice and Public Order Act 1994, and yet further amended by the Proceeds of Crime Act 1995.

33. Section 2 of the 1994 Act provides:

> '(1) Subject to subsection (7) below, where a defendant appears before the Crown Court to be sentenced in respect of one or more drug trafficking offences (and has not previously been sentenced or otherwise dealt with in respect of his conviction for the offence or, as the case may be, any of the offences concerned), then—(a) if the prosecutor asks the court to proceed under this section, or (b) if the court considers that, even though the prosecutor has not asked it to do so, it is appropriate for it to proceed under this section, it shall act as follows.
>
> (2) The court shall first determine whether the defendant has benefited from drug trafficking.
>
> (3) For the purposes of this Act, a person has benefited from drug trafficking if he has at any time (whether before or after the commencement of this Act) received any payment or other reward in connection with drug trafficking carried on by him or another person.
>
> (4) If the court determines that the defendant has so benefited, the court shall ... determine in accordance with section 5 of this Act the amount to be recovered in his case by virtue of this section ...
>
> (8) The standard of proof required to determine any question arising under this Act as to—(a) whether a person has benefited from drug trafficking, or (b) the amount to be recovered in his case by virtue of this section, shall be that applicable in civil proceedings.'

34. Section 4 of the 1994 Act provides for the assessment of the proceeds of drug trafficking:

> '... (2) Subject to subsections (4) and (5) below, the Crown Court shall, for the purpose—(a) of determining whether the defendant has benefited from drug trafficking, and (b) if he has, of assessing the value of his proceeds of drug trafficking, make the required assumptions.
>
> (3) The required assumptions are—(a) that any property appearing to the court—(i) to have been held by the defendant at any time since his conviction, or (ii) to have been transferred to him at any time since the beginning of the period of six years ending when the proceedings were instituted against him, was received by him, at the earliest time at which he appears to the court to have held it, as a payment or reward in connection with drug trafficking carried on by him; (b) that any expenditure of his since the beginning of that period was met out of payments received by him in connection with drug trafficking carried on by him; and (c) that, for the purpose of valuing any property received or assumed to have been received by him at any time as such a reward, he received the property free of any other interests in it.
>
> (4) The court shall not make any required assumption in relation to any particular property or expenditure if—(a) that assumption is shown to be incorrect in the defendant's case; or (b) the court is satisfied that there would be a serious risk of injustice in the defendant's case if the assumption were to be made; and where, by virtue of this subsection, the court does not make one or more of the required assumptions, it shall state its reasons.'

a 35. The making of confiscation orders other than in drug trafficking offences is governed by s 71 of the 1988 Act, which provides:

'(1) Where an offender is convicted, in any proceedings before the Crown Court or a magistrates' court, of any offence of a relevant description, it shall be the duty of the court—(a) if the prosecutor has given written notice to the court that he considers that it would be appropriate for the court to proceed
b under this section, or (b) if the court considers, even though it has not been given such notice, that is would be appropriate for it so to proceed, to act as follows before sentencing or otherwise dealing with the offender in respect of that offence or any other relevant criminal conduct.

(1A) The court shall first determine whether the offender has benefited
c from any relevant criminal conduct.

(1B) Subject to subsection (1C) below, if the court determines that the offender has benefited from any relevant criminal conduct, it shall then—(a) determine in accordance with subsection (6) below the amount to be recovered in his case by virtue of this section, and (b) make an order under this section ordering the offender to pay that amount …
d
(1D) In this part of this Act "relevant criminal conduct", in relation to a person convicted of an offence in any proceedings before a court, means (subject to section 72AA(6) below) that offence taken together with any other offences of a relevant description which are either—(a) offences of which he is convicted in the same proceedings, or (b) offences which the
e court will be taking into consideration in determining his sentence for the offence in question …

(4) For the purposes of this Part of this Act a person benefits from an offence if he obtains property as a result of or in connection with its commission and his benefit is the value of the property so obtained …

f (7A) The standard of proof required to determine any question arising under this Part of this Act as to—(a) whether a person has benefited from any offence; or … (c) the amount to be recovered in his case, shall be that applicable in civil proceedings.'

36. Section 72AA provides for confiscation proceedings arising from a 'course
g of criminal conduct':

'(1) This section applies in a case where an offender is convicted, in any proceedings before the Crown Court or a magistrates' court, of a qualifying offence which is an offence of a relevant description, if—(a) the prosecutor gives written notice for the purposes of subsection (1)(a) of section 71 …
h (b) that notice contains a declaration that it is the prosecutor's opinion that the case is one in which it is appropriate for the provisions of this section to be applied; and (c) the offender—(i) is convicted in those proceedings of at least two qualifying offences (including the offence in question); or (ii) has been convicted of a qualifying offence on at least one previous occasion
j during the relevant period.

(2) [Definition of 'qualifying offence' ie one to which Part VI of the Act applies, which was committed after the commencement of s 2 of the Proceeds of Crime Act 1995 and the court is satisfied that it is an offence from which the defendant has benefited.]

(3) When proceeding under section 71 … the court may, if it thinks fit, determine that (subject to subsection (5) below) the assumptions specified in

subsection (4) below are to be made for the purpose—(a) of determining whether the defendant has benefited from relevant criminal conduct; and (b) if he has, of assessing the value of the defendant's benefit from such conduct.

(4) Those assumptions are (a) that any property appearing to the court—(i) to be held by the defendant at the date of conviction or at any time in the period between that date and the determination in question, or (ii) to have been transferred to him at any time since the beginning of the relevant period, was received by him, at the earliest time when he appears to the court to have held it, as a result of or in connection with the commission of offences to which this Part of this Act applies; (b) that any expenditure of his since the beginning of the relevant period was met out of payments received by him as a result of or in connection with the commission of offences to which this Part of this Act applies; and (c) that, for the purposes of valuing any benefit which he had or which he is assumed to have had at any time, he received the benefit free of any other interests in it.

(5) Where the court has determined that the assumptions specified in subsection (4) above are to be made in any case it shall not in that case make any such assumption in relation to any particular property or expenditure if—(a) that assumption, so far as it relates to that property or expenditure, is shown to be incorrect in the defendant's case; (b) that assumption, so far as it so relates, is shown to be correct in relation to an offence the defendant's benefit from which has been the subject of a previous confiscation order; or (c) the court is satisfied that there would (for any other reason) be a serious risk of injustice in the defendant's case if the assumption were to be made in relation to that property or expenditure ...

(7) ["the relevant period" is defined as the period of six years ending when the proceedings in question were instituted against the defendant].'

37. Rule 25A of the Crown Court Rules 1982, SI 1982/1109, recently substituted by the Crown Court (Amendment) Rules 1995, SI 1995/2618, makes further provision relating to any statement tendered by the prosecution for the purpose of confiscation proceedings, whether arising under the 1994 Act or the 1988 Act:

'... (2) Any statement tendered to the Crown Court by the prosecutor under section 11(1) of the said Act of 1994 or section 73(1A) of the said Act of 1988 shall include the following particulars, namely—(a) the name of the defendant; (b) the name of the person by whom the statement is made and the date on which it was made; (c) where the statement is not tendered immediately after the defendant has been convicted, the date on which and the place where the relevant conviction occurred; (d) such information known to the prosecutor as is relevant to the determination as to whether or not the defendant has benefited from drug trafficking or relevant criminal conduct and to the assessment of the value of his proceeds of drug trafficking or, as the case may be, benefit from the relevant criminal conduct.'

38. Before turning to consider the convention, we must note the relevant statutory provisions in the 1998 Act:

'**3.**—(1) So far as it is possible to do so, primary legislation and subordinate legislation must be read and given effect in a way which is compatible with the Convention rights ...

a

4.—(1) Subsection (2) applies in any proceedings in which a court determines whether a provision of primary legislation is compatible with a Convention right.

(2) If the court is satisfied that the provision is incompatible with a Convention right, it may make a declaration of that incompatibility.'

b

39. Article 6 of the convention provides:

'1. In the determination of ... any criminal charge against him, everyone is entitled to a fair and public hearing within a reasonable time by an independent and impartial tribunal established by law. Judgment shall be pronounced publicly ...

c

2. Everyone charged with a criminal offence shall be presumed innocent until proved guilty according to law.

3. Everyone charged with a criminal offence has the following minimum rights: (a) to be informed promptly, in a language which he understands and in detail, of the nature and cause of the accusation against him; (b) to have adequate time and facilities for the preparation of his defence; (c) to defend himself in person or through legal assistance of his own choosing or, if he has not sufficient means to pay for legal assistance, to be given it free when the interests of justice so require; (d) to examine or have examined witnesses against him and to obtain the attendance and examination of witnesses on his behalf ... (e) to have the free assistance of an interpreter if he cannot understand or speak the language used in court.'

d

e

40. The First Protocol provides in art 1 that:

'Every natural or legal person is entitled to the peaceful enjoyment of his possessions. No one shall be deprived of his possession except in the public interest and subject to the conditions provided for by law and by the general principles of international law. The preceding provisions shall not, however, in any way impair the right of a State to enforce such laws as it deems necessary to control the use of property in accordance with the general interest or to secure the payment of taxes or other contributions or penalties.'

f

g

41. Examining the provisions of the 1988 Act and the 1994 Act, it is apparent that they have certain important features in common. These features are: (1) there have to be the relevant convictions before a confiscation order can be made. The convictions therefore provide a gateway to the confiscation process. Without a relevant conviction, there is nothing to trigger this process or to sustain a confiscation order. However, once the defendant has been convicted of the relevant offences, a confiscation order may be made in relation to the benefits of crime, irrespective of whether they can be proved to be linked to the original convictions or to any other specific or individual crime. Without these pre-conditions, a confiscation order cannot be made over the defendant's assets and property. (2) The standard of proof in determining whether a person has benefited from an offence, and for determining the amount in which a confiscation order is to be made, is that which is applicable to civil proceedings. (3) The confiscation process does not commence unless, following the relevant convictions, either the prosecutor has initiated the process or the court considers that the process would be *appropriate* (s 71(1) of the 1988 Act and s 2(1) of the 1994 Act). The language of the relevant provisions clearly confers a discretion initially on the prosecutor, and then on the court, as to whether to initiate the confiscation process. This

h

j

discretion will have to be exercised taking into account all relevant considerations, so as to avoid the risk of injustice. (4) In particular, while a defendant is required to show that an assumption in his case is incorrect, if he fails to do this, the court must still not apply an assumption where there would be a 'serious risk of injustice in the defendant's case if the assumption were to be made' (s 72AA(5) of the 1988 Act and s 4(4) of the 1994 Act). As to the weight that has to be given to the word 'serious', any real as opposed to a fanciful risk of injustice can be appropriately described as serious. The court, at the end of the confiscation process, has therefore a responsibility not to make a confiscation which could create injustice. (5) In addition, under s 72AA(3) of the 1988 Act, the court 'may, if it thinks fit' apply the assumptions, but it is not required to do so.

42. The statutory assumptions can very significantly increase the amount that a defendant is to be treated as having benefited from crime. A defendant does, however, have an additional protection against an order being made in an excessive sum. This arises from the distinction under both Acts between the benefits *received* to which the assumptions apply and benefits that can be *realised*. Although a defendant is unable or chooses not to rebut an assumption, he can still reduce his liability by showing that the amount which can be realised is less than the amount by which he is assumed to have benefited (see s 71(6) of the 1988 Act and s 5(3) of the 1994 Act).

43. The reason the legislation gives the courts the power to make confiscation orders and the reason why it creates statutory assumptions which interfere with the onus and burden of proof which normally exist in criminal proceedings is obvious and illustrated by the facts of these appeals. The provisions of the 1988 Act are aimed at depriving repeat offenders of the fruits of their crimes. The 1994 Act is aimed at achieving the same objective in relation to those who profit from drug trafficking. Both in the case of repeat offenders and drug traffickers, it is very much in the public interest that they are not able to profit from their crimes. If offenders are likely to lose their ill-gotten benefits, then this in itself will be a significant deterrent to the commission of further offences. In particular in relation to drug trafficking, justice requires that the profits made by the commission of those especially anti-social offences should be confiscated. Their profits are usually achieved at immense cost to those to whom the drugs are ultimately supplied. It is notoriously difficult to combat the traffickers' activities and the dangers that they create for society provide a justification for action out of the ordinary. In addition those at whom the legislation is aimed, whether repeat offenders or drug traffickers, are usually adept at concealing their profits and unless they are called upon to explain the source of their assets, it will be frequently difficult and often impossible to identify the proceeds of their crimes.

44. The 1988 Act only requires two offences of the specified description. It is argued by Mr Owen QC that you can commit two offences without being a repeat offender. However, in the case of Mr Rezvi (the only appellant to which the 1988 Act applies) there are substantial reasons for concluding that he has benefited substantially from crime. In cases where the position is not so clear, both the prosecution and the court should use the discretions to which reference has already been made to prevent s 72AA of the 1988 Act being misused. If there is a risk of injustice, the defendant is entitled to appeal against the confiscation order alone, without reference to any other aspect of the sentencing decision.

45. Mr Mitchell QC helpfully identifies six convention issues raised on this appeal. They are: (1) whether an appellant should be granted leave to appeal out

a of time in reliance on rights secured from 2 October 2000 by the 1998 Act; (2) whether in determining an appeal against a confiscation order the court should apply the law as it was when the confiscation order was made or, assuming the law has been modified by the 1998 Act, as it now is in its modified form; (3) whether a person against whom a confiscation order is sought under s 2 of the 1994 Act and s 71 of the 1988 Act is charged with a criminal offence within b the meaning of art 6 of the convention; (4) if such a person is charged with a criminal offence, whether the assumptions in s 4 of the 1994 Act and s 72AA of the 1988 Act are compatible with art 6(2) of the convention; (5) the extent to which the confiscation provisions of the 1994 Act and the 1988 Act are compatible with rights conferred by art 1 of the First Protocol of the convention; and (6) whether the provisions of s 11 of the 1994 Act (prosecutor's statements) are compatible c with art 6 of the convention.

We will consider these issues in turn.

Leave to appeal out of time

46. This is of importance to Mr Rezvi because his appeal was five months out d of time. It is desirable that the court should be in a position to deal with his grounds of appeal since the other appellants do not involve the 1988 Act. It is not usual to grant leave to appeal out of time where the grounds of appeal are based on post-trial changes in the law. This practice has been reaffirmed in relation to applications based on the coming into force of the 1998 Act (see *R v Lambert, R v Ali, R v Jordan* [2001] 1 All ER 1014, [2001] 2 WLR 211). The court would not wish in e this case to do other than confirm the existing practice. However, we are satisfied that the issues raised by Mr Owen on Mr Rezvi's behalf are of considerable general interest and for that reason we extend time.

Retrospectivity

f 47. Mr Mitchell has submitted that s 3(1) of the 1998 Act itself is not stated to be retrospective and so the normal rules of construction should apply and it should not be treated as retrospective. He submits that statutory provisions which were properly relied on at the time of the decision under appeal should not have their meaning changed retrospectively, because to do so would introduce g radical uncertainty into the legal system. It would, in an appropriate case, undermine the vires for subordinate legislation and might enable an appeal to succeed when there was no error of law at the trial. He has sought to pray in aid observations of the Attorney General in the House of Lords when resisting an attempt to include a specific provision in s 10 of the 1998 Act that it should not be retrospective; that the specific provision for retrospectivity in what became h s 22(4) of that Act implied 'that, in the absence of express provision to the contrary, the Bill should not have retrospective effect'. He also relies on observations of Lord Hobhouse of Woodborough in *R v DPP, ex p Kebeline* [1999] 4 All ER 801 at 858, [2000] 2 AC 326 at 397 where he said:

j 'Lord Lester submitted that once the 1998 Act comes into force, an additional and more potent principle of statutory construction will come into play … He submits that [s 3(1)] will enable s 16A [of the Terrorism (Temporary Provisions) Act 1989] to be construed so as not to impose any burden of proof upon the defendants. This, he submits, will retrospectively render invalid any conviction based upon a direction to the jury that s 16A(3) does impose such a burden and that any convictions would then have to be set aside. Whether this argument materially advances his submission is clearly open to contrary argument. Neither s 6 nor s 7 is retrospective; nor is, for that matter, s 3, as Lord Lester's argument recognises. It is therefore difficult to maintain that the prosecution and trial of the defendants in accordance with s 16A has involved any unlawful conduct or will do so or will provide them with any ground for having any convictions resulting from their trial quashed.'

48. Section 3(1) of the 1998 cannot be considered in isolation. Sections 6 and 7 of that Act are material. Section 6(1) provides: 'It is unlawful for a public authority to act in a way which is incompatible with a Convention right.' 'Public authority' includes both a court and the Director of Public Prosecutions (DPP) or the relevant Crown prosecutor (s 6(3)). The remedy for any action which is incompatible with a convention right lies in s 7 which, so far as material, provides:

> '(1) A person who claims that a public authority has acted (or proposes to act) in a way which is made unlawful by section 6(1) may ... (b) rely on the Convention right or rights concerned in any legal proceedings.'

Section 7(6) provides: 'In subsection (1)(b) "legal proceedings" includes—(a) proceedings brought by or at the instigation of a public authority; and (b) an appeal against the decision of a court or tribunal.' Finally, s 22(4) provides:

> 'Paragraph (b) of subsection (1) of section 7 applies to proceedings brought by or at the instigation of a public authority whenever the act in question took place; but otherwise that subsection does not apply to an act taking place before the coming into force of that section.'

49. Accordingly, and contrary to the general observations of Lord Hobhouse, the 1998 Act does provide for a limited retrospectivity. The prosecutions of all the appellants before us were clearly 'proceedings brought by or at the instigation of a public authority'. Indeed, the vast majority of criminal proceedings will be within s 22(4) of the 1998 Act. These considerations led Lord Bingham of Cornhill CJ to say in *Ex p Kebeline* in the Divisional Court:

> 'If, at the time of the appeal hearing, the central provisions of the 1998 Act had been brought into force, the applicants would on appeal be entitle to rely on ss 7(1)(b) and 22(4) of the 1998 Act and the convictions (on the hypothesis of inconsistency between s 16A and the convention) would in all probability be quashed, at some not inconsiderable cost to the public purse and no obvious advantage to the public ...' (See [1999] 4 All ER 801 at 812, [2000] 2 AC 326 at 341.)

Lord Bingham CJ did, however, at the end of his judgment, refer to s 3(1) of the 1998 Act in this way:

> 'I think it undesirable to express any opinion, authoritatively, on whether, if s 3 of the 1998 Act were in force, it would be possible to read and give effect to ss 16A and 16B in a way which is compatible with convention rights. This is a matter which in my view deserves attention, particularly in relation to s 16A.' (See [1999] 4 All ER 801 at 817, [2000] 2 AC 326 at 346.)

We do not understand Lord Bingham CJ to have been calling in question the Court of Appeal's power to apply s 3, but to have been referring to the question whether s 16A of the Terrorism (Temporary Provisions) Act 1989 could be a construed in accordance with s 3 of the 1998 Act so as to be compatible with the convention.

50. In the House of Lords, a majority (Lord Slynn of Hadley, Lord Steyn and Lord Cooke of Thorndon) accepted Lord Bingham CJ's views of the effect of ss 7(1)(b) and 22(4) of the 1998 Act. Lord Steyn specifically dealt with and rejected an argument put on behalf of the DPP that ss 7(1)(b) and 22(4) only applied to a b trial and not to an appeal. He said:

> 'On appeal to the House, but not in the Divisional Court, [counsel for the DPP, David Pannick QC] argued that s 22(4) read with s 7(1)(b), is apt only to extend to the trial. It was an argument of some technicality. The language of the statute does not compel its adoption and a construction which treats c the trial and the appeal as parts of one process is more in keeping with the purpose of the convention and the 1998 Act. It is the sensible and just construction. I would reject the argument advanced on behalf of the DPP on this point.' (See [1999] 4 All ER 801 at 832, [2000] 2 AC 326 at 368.)

51. While we have not been presented with an argument which raises the d technicalities which Mr Pannick developed before the House of Lords, we feel we should adopt Lord Steyn's approach, so the appellants are entitled to rely on s 7(1)(b) and s 22(4) of the 1998 Act in an appeal which takes place after 2 October 2000. In our judgment, where the original proceedings are brought by, or at the instigation of, a public authority, as is the case with a prosecution, an appeal by the defendant is part of the proceedings to which s 22(4) applies. There cannot e be a different position on an appeal from that of the trial so far as the issue of the retrospectivity of the 1998 Act is concerned. Any other construction would mean that in criminal cases, the Court of Appeal could not give the required protection to the individual (who would clearly be a victim of any unlawful act) so that there would be a need for an otherwise unnecessary but time-consuming and f expensive trip to Strasbourg. In addition, otherwise s 7(1)(b) of the 1998 Act will apply where appeal is by a public authority, but not when the appeal is made by the defendant.

52. In cases where primary legislation has not required the trial court to make a decision which is incompatible with a convention right, there is no difficulty. The Court of Appeal will be able to apply the convention and determine whether g any relief should result. But if the decision below was based on a provision of primary legislation, s 6(2)(a) of the 1998 Act will apply. This provides: 'Subsection (1) does not apply to an act if—(a) as the result of one or more provisions of primary legislation, the authority could not have acted differently.' This means that the prosecution and the court below, if unable to apply the approach required by h s 3(1) of the 1998 Act, would have been unable to decide differently, so that s 6(1) of that Act and consequently s 7 could not apply to them. But s 6(1) does apply to the Court of Appeal, and s 7(1) covers not only a past, but a proposed act.

53. It would, in those circumstances, be curious if the court were unable to apply s 3(1). Then, if satisfied that there was an incompatibility, the court would j be unable to remedy it by applying a compatible construction of the relevant provision. Furthermore, and equally importantly, the court would be unable to give the guidance needed for future application of the relevant provisions. This is not the position and s 3(1) has retrospective effect if ss 22(4) and 7(1)(b) of the 1998 Act apply.

54. Mr Mitchell deployed a further argument based on s 11(3) of the Criminal Appeal Act 1968. This enables the Court of Appeal to quash any sentence or order

which is the subject matter of the appeal and 'in place of it pass such sentence or make such order as they think appropriate for the case as the court below had power to pass or make when dealing with him for the offence'. It is submitted that where a statutory provision requires a particular sentence or order to be made, the Court of Appeal cannot intervene. That submission flies in the face of the decisions in a number of cases heard in this court (*R v Lambert* [2001] 1 All ER 1014, [2001] 2 WLR 211 (s 28 of the 1971 Act), *R v Fulcher* [1995] 2 Cr App R 251 (s 34 of the Criminal Justice and Public Order Act 1994) and *R v Offen, R v McGilliard, R v McKeown, R v Okwuegbunam, R v S* [2001] 2 All ER 154, [2001] 1 WLR 253 (mandatory life sentences)). In any event, in the instant cases the trial judges had power to make whatever order the Court of Appeal considers appropriate and so the argument could not apply to any of these cases.

55. Any legal system is entitled to impose time limits and, if reasonable, they can apply to disable an individual from alleging a breach of the convention.

Criminal charge

56. It is not in issue that art 6(2) of the convention applies to the trial of the offences which, if proved, provide the gateway for the confiscation orders. In general, the language of art 6(2) would be expected to apply to the trial process only and not generally to the sentencing process. (There is, however, the exceptional situation of a *Newton* hearing (see *R v Newton* (1982) 2 Cr App R 13) to which art 6(2) would apply.) In English domestic law, confiscation orders are part of the sentencing process which follow upon the conviction of the defendant of the criminal offences with which he is charged. There are, however, two arguments advanced on behalf of the appellants as to why art 6(2) should apply to the process involved in the making of a confiscation order. The first argument depends upon the mechanics involved in the making of a confiscation order. The order can and will usually be based upon benefits not directly attributable to the offences with which the defendant has been convicted. It is therefore argued that the confiscation procedure is in itself implicitly a trial of other offences to which the presumption of innocence should be applied. The second argument is that the confiscation process is so connected to the trial process that it should be considered part of that process.

57. In support of the first argument, strong reliance is placed upon the decision of the majority of the High Court of Justiciary in *McIntosh, Petitioner* 2001 JC 78. In that case, similar arguments were advanced to those that arise here but in relation to the Proceeds of Crime (Scotland) Act 1995. The 1995 Act contains similar provisions to s 72AA of the 1988 Act and s 4 of the 1994 Act. The relevant provisions of the 1995 Act are helpfully summarised by Lord Prosser (at 79–80) in the following terms:

> '[2] In terms of sec 1(5) of the Act, it is provided that the sum which a confiscation order requires an accused to pay in the case of a drug trafficking offence shall be an amount not exceeding what the court assesses to be "the value of the proceeds" of the person's "drug trafficking", subject to a limit related to what may be realised. The expression "drug trafficking" is defined in sec 49(2) of the Act as meaning, subject to subsecs (3) and (4) of the section, doing or being concerned in any of a list of activities, each of which would constitute a contravention of a statutory provision relating to controlled drugs. "Drug trafficking" is an expression which, in terms of the statutory definitions, is quite separate and distinct from a "drug trafficking offence".

a [3] Section 9(1) of the 1995 Act provides that where the prosecutor applies for the making of a confiscation order, he may lodge with the clerk of court a statement as to any matters relevant, in connection with a drug trafficking offence, to the assessment of the value of the accused's proceeds of drug trafficking. Such a statement was lodged: it concerns assets and expenditure, with no allegations of drug trafficking as such, but stating a figure for b proceeds of drug trafficking. Thereafter the petitioner lodged (and subsequently adjusted) answers to that statement. Section 9 contains a number of further provisions bearing upon the assessment of the value of the proceeds of drug trafficking when a statement has been lodged; but these give rise to no specific point in the present proceedings. Without prejudice to sec 9, however, in terms of sec 3(2) of the Act, "the court may, in making an c assessment as regards a person under sec 1(5) of this Act, make the following assumptions, except in so far as any of them may be shown to be incorrect in that person's case—(a) that any property appearing to the court—(i) to have been held by him at any time since his conviction; or, as the case may be, (ii) to have been transferred to him at any time since a date six years before d his being indicted, or being served with the complaint, was received by him, at the earliest time at which he appears to the court to have held it, as a payment or reward in connection with the drug trafficking carried on by him; (b) that any expenditure of his since the date mentioned in paragraph (a)(ii) above was met out of payments received by him in connection with drug trafficking carried on by him, and (c) that, for the purpose of valuing e any property received or assumed to have been received by him at any time as such a reward, he received the property free of any other interests in it." In terms of sec 3(1), a person's "proceeds of drug trafficking" are defined as any payments or other rewards received by him at any time in connection with drug trafficking carried on by him or another; and the value of these f proceeds of drug trafficking is the aggregate of the values of the payments or other awards. The figure for proceeds contained in the prosecutor's statement apparently derives from an application of these assumptions.'

58. Section 3(2) of the 1995 Act only states that the court 'may' make any of a g number of listed assumptions except in so far as any of them may be shown to be incorrect in the accused's case. To that extent, it is closer to s 72AA of the 1998 Act than s 4 of the 1994 Act. The 1995 Act does not, however, give the court a residual discretion to disapply the assumptions if there is a serious risk of injustice. However, the difference in the statutory provisions are not significant, having h regard to the approach adopted by Lord Prosser, with which Lord Allanbridge agreed.

59. Lord Prosser (at 81 (para 6)) referred to the decisions of the European Court of Human Rights in *Foti v Italy* (1983) 5 EHRR 313 at 325–326 (para 52) and *Eckle v Germany* (1982) 5 EHRR 1 at 27 (para 73). He cited, with apparent j approval, the statement in *Foti v Italy* that the charge 'may in some instances take the form of other measures which carry the implication of such an allegation and which likewise substantially affect the situation of the suspect'.

60. Lord Prosser indicated that both the petitioner and the advocate depute had asked the court to consider the essential nature of an application for a confiscation order, and the proceedings which followed such an application. As to this Lord Prosser said (2001 JC 78 at 81–82 (para 7)):

'They were triggered by the conviction and could be described as natural *sequelae* of conviction. While they were a part, they were not merely a part, of imposing sentence in respect of that conviction. Although they did not involve any new charge or new offence in terms of Scots law, and were part of the original proceedings, they also constituted, within that context, a separate identifiable process, which began with the application and statement, which were "measures" of the kind described in *Foti*, carrying the implication of an allegation that the petitioner had committed a criminal offence of the type envisaged in *Eckle*.'

61. Basing himself on these arguments, Lord Prosser went on to state (at 90–91 (para 29)):

'... even if one assumes for the moment that the application and statement are to be regarded as charging the petitioner with a criminal offence, in the appropriate Convention sense, I would make certain observations at this stage as to how, in my opinion, art 6(2) applies to the subsequent proceedings. Such proceedings are intended by the prosecutor to culminate in a confiscation order. It is true that the order is an order to pay a sum of money. It is also true, in my opinion, that such an order to pay a sum of money is a form of additional penalty for the offence of which the petitioner has been convicted. But I am not persuaded that it is only or merely an order to pay a sum of money, or that the various statutory provisions dealing with drug trafficking and its proceeds and their valuation are merely a mechanism for fixing a ceiling, casting no light upon the essential nature of the order to pay money. Such a proposition appears to me to fly in the face of the quite elaborate provisions of the statute dealing with these matters, as confirmed by the title of the Act. In particular, they fly in the face of the fact that if the assumptions are shown to be incorrect, and nothing has been resolved by evidence or admission, no confiscation order can be made. The court can make such an order only if, by one means or another, it has reached the position of being able to say that there are proceeds of drug trafficking. How it reaches that position—by making assumptions or otherwise—is another matter entirely. But the payment is a payment reflecting the value of the whole or part of proceeds of drug trafficking. The use of the word "confiscation" seems to me to be perfectly appropriate as a way of describing such an order; but whether it is so or not does not seem to me to matter. Nor does the fact that this is part of the sentencing process. The point is that such an order can only be made if there are, for this purpose, proceeds of drug trafficking, with an assessed value. Since that is a point which has to be reached, on a route towards the making of an order, the application is in my opinion properly to be seen as *inter alia* an assertion that there has been drug trafficking, and an invitation to the court to proceed on that basis. If an order is made, the petitioner will be significantly affected. And the requirements of *Eckle* and *Foti*, if one proceeds on the hypothesis that drug trafficking is criminal, will be met.'

62. Lord Prosser added (at 91 (para 30)):

'It is therefore asking the court to reach the stage of saying that he has trafficked in drugs. If that is criminal, that seems to me to be closely analogous to an actual charge of an actual crime under Scottish terms. There is of course no indictment or complaint, and no conviction. And the advocate a depute pointed out a further difference, that a Scottish complaint or indictment would have to be specific, and would require evidence, whereas this particular allegation was inspecific and based upon no evidence. But the suggestion that there is less need for a presumption of innocence in the latter situation appears to me to be somewhat Kafkaesque, and to portray a vice as a virtue. With no notice of what he is supposed to have done, or any basis b which there might be for treating him as having done it, the accused's need for the presumption of innocence is in my opinion all the greater.'

63. Lord Prosser continued (at 91–92 (para 31)) by indicating that he was not suggesting that draconian penalties were inappropriate in combating drug trafficking. Furthermore, he indicated that it was perfectly understandable and c appropriate for Parliament to incorporate in the law transfers of the burden of proof. In addition, he acknowledged 'without hesitation that such a burden could readily and properly be regarded as within reasonable limits' and indicated that it was his impression that if the section had only been slightly differently worded, the Crown could have achieved its objective. None the less, he was of the view that the assumptions could not be regarded as reasonable, apparently because d they could be 'baseless assumptions'.

64. Lord Kirkwood, on the other hand, considered (at 95 (para 6)) that a confiscation order is no more than an additional penalty 'which the court is given the power to impose in appropriate circumstances in respect of the drug trafficking offence of which the accused had already been convicted.' He added: e 'However, it is important to note that the confiscation order relates to the proceeds of drug trafficking, not the proceeds of drug trafficking offences.'

65. He therefore accepted the submission that 'drug trafficking' covered what could be called—

> 'a basket of different types of conduct, some of which would not be crimes f although others would. Accordingly, an allegation that an accused had been engaged in trafficking would not necessarily involve an allegation that he had committed a drug trafficking offence.'

66. We are not convinced that this last point is correct in the case of drug trafficking under the 1994 Act and we would refer to the definition of drug trafficking g in s 1 and the language of ss 49, 50 and 51 of that Act.

67. Turning to the alternative contention, Mr Owen relies strongly on *Minelli v Switzerland* (1983) 5 EHRR 554. In *Minelli*'s case, the European Court decided that art 6(2) of the convention could be contravened by making an order for costs when a private prosecution for criminal defamation was determined before h judgment on the ground that the limitation period had expired. This meant Minelli was never convicted of anything and the European Court upheld the contention of the defendant that an award of costs against him presumed his guilt in violation of the presumption of innocence required by art 6(2).

68. In its judgment the court stated (at 565 (para 30)): 'In the Court's opinion, Article 6(2) governs criminal proceedings in their entirety, irrespective of the j outcome of the prosecution, and not solely the examination of the merits of the charge.' Later (at 566 (para 35)) the European Court added the important point that:

> '... in conformity with its established *jurisprudence*, that in proceedings originating in an individual application, it has to confine itself, as far as possible, to an examination of the concrete case before it ... Accordingly, it

> has to give a ruling not on the Zürich legislation and practice *in abstracto* but solely on the manner in which they were applied to the applicant.'

The European Court concluded its opinion by stating (at 567 (para 37)):

> '... the presumption of innocence will be violated if, without the accused's having previously been proved guilty according to law and, notably, without his having had the opportunity of exercising his rights of defence, a judicial decision concerning him reflects an opinion that he is guilty. This may be so even in the absence of any formal findings; it suffices that there is some reasoning suggesting that the court regards the accused as guilty.'

69. Having carefully considered the judgments in *McIntosh*'s case and the arguments of the parties, we regard art 6(2) as being a specific example of the application of the more general obligations contained in art 6(1) which sets out the right to a fair trial. It is to be noted that art 6(1) commences by stating:

> 'In the determination of his civil rights and obligations or of any criminal *charge* against him, everyone is entitled to a fair and public hearing within a reasonable time by an independent and impartial tribunal established by law.' (My emphasis.)

70. English domestic law certainly does not regard a decision under the legislation we are considering as being a 'determination of' 'civil rights and obligations'. We would expect the European Court to take the same view. Yet undoubtedly, art 6(1) of the convention would apply to the process leading up to the making of a confiscation order. The confiscation order is made in criminal proceedings. It is accepted by all the parties that it is penal. It must therefore be regarded for the purposes of art 6(1) as at least part of the determination of a criminal charge since there is no other option for which art 6(1) provides. The fact that a defendant who does not comply with a confiscation order, which may not be based on criminal conduct proved at the trial, may be ordered to serve a substantial sentence in default underlines this fact. A defendant threatened with consequences of this nature would be expected to be entitled to protection equivalent to that provided by art 6(2) even if that paragraph did not exist under art 6(1), unless there was objective justification for not applying the presumption of innocence.

71. It is true that, as a matter of domestic law, the manner in which s 72AA of the 1988 Act and s 4 of the 1994 Act are drafted means that there is nothing in the nature of what in this jurisdiction would normally be regarded as a 'charge'. Using the term 'charge' in its domestic sense, it is the finding of a defendant guilty of the charge which renders him liable to a confiscation order. What is being confiscated is, however, either the proceeds of crime or trafficking in drugs. Under the legislation, if the defendant can show that the property is not the proceeds of crime then no confiscation order is made. The legislation is after all directed at a person who is alleged to have benefited from the proceeds of crime.

72. A decision of the European Court which explains our approach is *Hoang v France* (1992) 16 EHRR 53. In that case, a defendant charged and convicted under French drugs legislation with unlawful importation of narcotics and customs evasion complained that the Customs Code violated his right to a fair trial and his right to be presumed innocent until proved otherwise. In its judgment, the court stated (at 78–79 (para 33)):

a 'As was pointed out in the SALABIAKU judgment of 7 October 1988, (*Salabiaku v France* (1988) 13 EHRR 379), Article 6 requires States to confine presumptions of fact or of law provided for in their criminal law within reasonable limits which take into account the importance of what is at stake and maintain the rights of defence. However, the Court is not called upon to consider in the abstract whether ... the Customs Code conforms to the b Convention. Its task is to determine whether they were applied in the instant case in a manner compatible with the presumption of innocence and, more generally, with the concept of a fair trial.'

Later the court added (at 79–80 (para 36)):

c 'It therefore appears that the Court of Appeal duly weighed the evidence before it, assessed it carefully and based its finding of guilt on it. It refrained from any automatic reliance on the presumptions created in the relevant provisions of the Customs Code and did not apply them in a manner incompatible with Articles 6(1) and (2) of the Convention.'

d 73. As these passages from the judgment illustrate, the court was not adopting a technical approach to very similar issues to those which arise here. It was adopting a broad approach which fully recognised the importance of justice being done not only to a defendant but also to the legitimate interests of society. This is, of course, subject to the defendant receiving a fair trial. That is essential e (see Lord Hope of Craighead's opinion in *Montgomery v HM Advocate, Coulter v HM Advocate* [2001] 2 WLR 779).

74. Since the decision in *McIntosh*'s case, the Privy Council has given its decision in *Brown v Stott (Procurator Fiscal, Dunfermline)* [2001] 2 All ER 97, [2001] 2 WLR 817. This was a case involving the presumption of innocence in different f circumstances from here. However, in giving their opinions, the members of the Privy Council provide very valuable guidance as to the correct approach to art 6 of the convention. Each of the opinions of their Lordships contain helpful statements of principle. Their collective approach is reflected in the following passages from the opinion of Lord Bingham:

g 'What a fair trial requires cannot, however, be the subject of a single, unvarying rule or collection of rules. It is proper to take account of the facts and circumstances of particular cases, as the European Court has consistently done. Before considering the right not to incriminate oneself with which this appeal is specifically concerned, it is helpful to review the way in which h the European Court has treated other rights held to be comprised within art 6.' (See [2001] 2 All ER 97 at 105, [2001] 2 WLR 817 at 825.)

The presumption of innocence

75. The right to be presumed innocent of a criminal offence until proved j guilty according to law is expressed in art 6(2) of the convention. This appears on its face to be an absolute requirement. But it has been held that it does not prohibit rules which transfer the burden to the accused to establish a defence, providing the overall burden of proof remains on the prosecution, nor does it necessarily prohibit presumptions of law or fact provided that these are within reasonable limits. In *Salabiaku v France* (1988) 13 EHRR 379 at 388 (para 28) the European Court held:

'Presumptions of fact or of law operate in every legal system. Clearly, the Convention does not prohibit such presumptions in principle. It does, however, require the Contracting States to remain within certain limits in this respect as regards criminal law … Article 6(2) does not therefore regard presumptions of fact or of law provided for in the criminal law with indifference. It requires States to confine them within reasonable limits which take into account the importance of what is at stake and maintain the rights of the defence. The Court proposes to consider whether such limits were exceeded to the detriment of Mr. Salabiaku.'

76. Towards the end of his opinion, in *Brown v Stott* Lord Bingham adds:

'The jurisprudence of the European Court very clearly establishes that while the overall fairness of a criminal trial cannot be compromised, the constituent rights comprised, whether expressed or implicitly, within art 6 are not themselves absolute. Limited qualification of these rights is acceptable if reasonably directed by national authorities towards a clear and proper public objective and if representing no greater qualification than the situation calls for. The general language of the convention could have led to the formulation of hard-edged and inflexible statements of principle from which no departure could be sanctioned whatever the background or the circumstances. But this approach has been consistently eschewed by the court throughout its history. The case law shows that the court has paid very close attention to the facts of particular cases coming before it, giving effect to factual differences and recognising differences of degree.' (See [2001] 2 All ER 97 at 115, [2001] 2 WLR 817 at 836.)

77. This broad and flexible approach emphasised in the various opinions in *Brown v Stott* has to be applied not only to the issue of whether art 6(1) of the convention has been complied with but also to the question of whether the various sub-paragraphs of art 6 apply here. When the importance of this approach is recognised, we conclude that the proper approach on the present appeals is to examine the confiscation process on the basis that art 6 as a whole including art 6(2) applies. This does not mean however that the 1988 Act or the 1994 Act are incompatible with art 6. This is a question which we will have to consider later.

78. Before we do so, it is necessary to refer shortly to additional arguments relied on by Mr Mitchell on behalf of the Crown. He prays in aid the decision of the European Court in *Welch v UK* (1995) 20 EHRR 247. The *Welch* decision was concerned with art 7 and not art 6 of the convention. Article 7(1) prevents a person being found guilty of a criminal offence which did not constitute a criminal offence under national or international law at the time when it was committed. It also prevents 'a heavier penalty' being imposed than that which was applicable at the time that the criminal offence was committed. The issue was therefore different from that which is being considered here. Welch had complained to the European Court that the Drug Trafficking Offences Act 1986 (the predecessor of the 1994 Act) constituted a retrospective criminal penalty contrary to art 7. This application was upheld. But art 6 was not in issue. As appears from the headnote (at 247), the European Court decided that:

'The concept of a penalty in Article 7(1) is like the notions of "civil rights and obligations" and "criminal charge" in Article 6(1), an *autonomous* Convention concept. To render the protection offered by Article 7 effective, the Court

> must remain free to go behind appearances and assess for itself whether a particular measure amounts in substance to a penalty within the meaning of this provision.' (My emphasis.) (See 261 (para 27).)

79. We regard our approach to the interpretation of art 6 as reflecting this approach of the European Court in *Welch v UK*. An additional illustration of this approach is provided by *Deweer v Belgium* (1980) 2 EHRR 439. In that case, the court recognised (at 458 (para 44)) that in deciding the nature of proceedings, 'The Court is compelled to look behind the appearances to investigate the realities of the procedure in question.' The court added (at 459 (para 46)) that in that case there existed—

> 'a combination of concordant factors conclusively demonstrating that the case has a criminal character under the Convention. The "charge" could, for the purposes of Article 6(1), be defined as the official notification given to an individual by the competent authority of an allegation that he has committed a criminal offence.'

80. These statements appear highly relevant here. Mr Mitchell however, relies on the comment of the European Court in *Welch v UK* (1995) 20 EHRR 247 at 263 (para 36) where the court stated:

> 'The Court would stress, however, that this conclusion concerns only the retrospective application of the relevant legislation and does not call into question in any respect the powers of confiscation conferred on the courts as a weapon in the fight against the scourge of drug trafficking.'

81. In *Elton v UK* App No 32344/96 (11 September 1997, unreported) the European Commission of Human Rights applied the decision in *Welch v UK* to an application which raised the issue as to whether s 2 of the 1986 Act was compatible with art 6(2) of the convention. The commission unanimously concluded that the application was manifestly ill-founded. Decisions of the commission are always entitled to respect, but the decision like that in *Welch v UK* did not relate to the 1994 Act but the less stringent provisions of its predecessor and we do not find its limited reasoning convincing. In addition, since the hearing, we have been referred to the decision in *Phillips v UK* App No 41087/98 (30 November 2000, unreported) involving the 1994 Act, where the European Court found an application based on a confiscation order being made in breach of art 6(2) of the convention admissible notwithstanding the United Kingdom government's arguments as to the absence of a charge.

82. We accept, as the Crown submits, that a confiscation order while penal, is not a penalty for the qualifying offence or offences in respect of which the defendant has already been charged and convicted. We also accept under English law that the confiscation order, while a penalty, does not involve a conviction for some additional unparticularised offence. The conviction only places the defendant at risk of being subject to a confiscation order. But this does not mean art 6(2) of the convention is not capable of applying to the confiscation process. In determining whether art 6(2) can properly be applied to that process, it is the character of that process as a whole which is important. It is a mistake to focus only on the word 'charge'. What is critical is that art 6(2) is a specific application of the broad principle contained in art 6(1) and, in the absence of any justification for a different approach, the process is one to which the presumption of innocence should apply.

83. Mr Mitchell also relies on certain United Kingdom authorities, but those authorities are not binding upon us. In our view, they take the situation no further. The courts did not have the benefit of full argument or the decision in *Brown v Stott*.

84. We would therefore summarise our conclusions by saying that the compatibility of the confiscation procedure has to be considered on the assumption that it is subject to the requirements of both art 6(1) and (2) taken together.

Compatibility with art 6

85. Under both the 1988 and the 1994 Acts, the confiscation proceedings include an express reversal of the onus of proof. In both cases, if the court makes the statutory assumptions, the process will involve a burden being imposed upon a defendant which, if he does not rebut it, will mean he will be at risk of having a confiscation order made against him. It is therefore necessary to consider whether, notwithstanding this, the statutory confiscation processes are capable of complying with art 6 of the convention and, if so, whether in any particular case the manner in which the statutory provisions have been applied complies with art 6.

86. When considering the first question, it is appropriate to show a degree of deference to the policy which the legislature considered was in the public interest. This is made clear by the Privy Council in *Brown v Stott*. Lord Steyn's opinion refers both to the speech of Lord Hope in *R v DPP, ex p Kebeline* [1999] 4 All ER 801, [2000] 2 AC 326 and Lester and Pannick *Human Rights Law and Practice* (1999) p 74. It is incontrovertible that both Acts deal with a serious social problem which should be addressed. It is also clear that while in the majority of situations, it will be difficult for the prosecution to establish that any particular assets of a defendant were the proceeds of crime or drug trafficking, it will be far easier for a defendant, in the majority of circumstances, to establish, on the balance of probabilities, that the assets in dispute have an innocent source. After all, usually a defendant will know what the origin of his assets is. He will also be likely to be aware of his financial obligations which have to be set against his assets.

87. The onus which is placed upon the defendant is not an evidential one but a persuasive one, so that the defendant will be required to discharge the burden of proof (see Lord Hope's third category of provisions in *Ex p Kebeline* [1999] 4 All ER 801 at 843, [2000] 2 AC 326 at 379). This is therefore a situation where it is necessary to carefully consider whether the public interest in being able to confiscate the ill-gotten gains of criminals justifies the interference with the normal presumption of innocence. While the extent of the interference is substantial, Parliament has clearly made efforts to balance the interest of the defendant against that of the public in the following respects. (a) It is only after the necessary convictions that any question of confiscation arises. This is of significance, because the trial which results in the conviction or convictions will be one where the usual burden and standard of proof rests upon the prosecution. In addition, a defendant who is convicted of the necessary offence or offences can be taken to be aware that if he committed the offences of which he has been convicted, he would not only be liable to imprisonment or another sentence, but he would also be liable to confiscation proceedings. (b) The prosecution has the responsibility for initiating the confiscation proceedings unless the court regards them as inappropriate. In both cases there is a discretion to be exercised and the manner in which the discretion is exercised is capable of being reviewed by this

a court. (c) There is also the responsibility placed upon the court not to make a confiscation order when there is a serious risk of injustice. As already indicated, this will involve the court, before it makes a confiscation order standing back and deciding whether there is a risk of injustice. If the court decides there is, then the confiscation order will not be made. (d) There is the role of this court on appeal to ensure there is no unfairness.

b 88. It is very much a matter of personal judgment as to whether a proper balance has been struck between the conflicting interests. Into the balance there must be placed the interests of the defendant as against the interests of the public, that those who have offended should not profit from their offending and should not use their criminal conduct to fund further offending. However, in our judgment, if the discretions which are given to the prosecution and the court are properly c exercised, the solution which Parliament has adopted is a reasonable and proportionate response to a substantial public interest, and therefore justifiable.

89. The appellants point to the fact that a new approach to confiscation is being contemplated by the government. This approach does not involve a criminal process. Instead it adopts a civil process. This was relied on by the appellants for d suggesting that an appropriate alternative to the present procedures is capable of being devised. If the civil procedure is introduced and is successful, this does not mean that the present procedure is unjustified. On the contrary the fact that the present procedures take place within the criminal context, may well provide additional protection to the defendant.

90. In the different context of art 1 of the First Protocol of the convention, the e European Court has itself been prepared to regard as justified very significant interference with art 6. For example, this has occurred in cases involving those who are merely alleged to be members of the mafia (see the case of *Raimondo v Italy* (1994) 18 EHRR 237).

91. The jurisprudence of the European Court makes clear that it is the f application of the statutory provisions to the facts in a particular case which will be critical to the court's determination as to whether art 6 has been contravened. The courts have been given the responsibility of not making orders if there is a serious risk of injustice. The courts will be astute to avoid injustice. In performing their responsibility, the court's will be mindful of the structure of the legislation. This does not require any direct connection between an offence of which a g defendant has been convicted and the resources of the defendant which are to be confiscated. However, the scale of the offending actually proved may be significant in the court determining whether it is safe to make the confiscation order. The court should be alert to make allowance for situations which make it impractical for a defendant to satisfy the burden of proof which the legislation h places upon him.

92. In *McIntosh, Petitioner* 2001 JC 78, the majority took a different view of the legislation there being considered. It is not any part of our task to review their decision. However, we would not apply their approach to the legislation with which we are concerned. We appreciate that we have the advantage of the opinions j given in *Brown v Stott* which were not available at the time that *McIntosh*'s case was decided. On the information before us, we reject the suggestions that either Acts are incompatible with art 6 of the convention.

Compatibility with art 1 of the First Protocol of the convention

93. We do not see any reason for our coming to a different conclusion as to art 1 of the First Protocol to that to which we have come to in relation to art 6 of

the convention. It appears to us that virtually the same considerations are in issue. We regard the legislation as being a proportionate response to the need to protect the public; the interference which confiscation involves with art 1 is therefore justified. The burden on the convicted person is not to prove his innocence of any particular charge but as a consequence of his conviction simply to explain the source of his assets, income and expenditure. Having regard to the scale of the threat to society constituted by drugs and other serious crimes, as to which the evidence placed before us is eloquent, we do not regard the results as being disproportionate. As the Vienna Convention on the Law of Treaties (Vienna, 23 May 1969; TS 58 (1980); Cmnd 7964) confirms, the need for states to take action is not confined to this country.

Whether the provisions of s 11 of the 1994 Act and s 73 of the 1988 Act are compatible with art 6

94. Mr Milford's conviction has subsequent to the hearing been quashed and a retrial ordered. This confiscation order is no longer relevant. This is an issue raised only in the appeal by Mr Milford. However, it appears to us that this ground of appeal, which was not canvassed in oral argument, is misconceived. We deal with it briefly. The statement provided does not constitute a contravention of art 6. In fact, it is an example of the legislation seeking to protect the position of a defendant. A statement serves the useful purpose of forewarning the defendant of the case of the prosecution which he will have to meet as to his assets. It should assist a defendant by making it clear the matters with which he has to be prepared to deal. It is right that, as the rules require, the prosecution should identify any information which would assist the defendant.

Conclusion

95. The judgment which we have given so far has focussed on the general principles raised by the appeal. We have held that, if the statutory provisions giving the courts the power to make confiscation orders are properly applied by courts, they will not contravene art 6. It is, however, the application of art 6 to the facts of a particular case which are all important. As the Appellate Committee in *R v Forbes* [2001] 1 All ER 686 at 697, [2001] 2 WLR 1 at 13 (para 24) stated:

> 'Reference was made in argument to the right to a fair trial guaranteed by art 6 of the European Convention for the Protection of Human Rights and Fundamental Freedoms (Rome, 4 November 1950; TS 71 (1953); Cmd 8969). That is an absolute right. But, as the Judicial Committee of the Privy Council has very recently held in *Brown v Stott (Procurator Fiscal, Dunfermline)* ([2001] 2 All ER 97, [2001] 2 WLR 817), the subsidiary rights comprised within that article are not absolute, and it is always necessary to consider all the facts and the whole history of the proceedings in a particular case to judge whether a defendant's right to a fair trial has been infringed or not. If on such consideration it is concluded that a defendant's right to a fair trial has been infringed, a conviction will be held to be unsafe within the meaning of s 2 of the Criminal Appeal Act 1968.'

96. Apart from the appeal by Mr Rezvi, the exercise of applying this judgment to the facts of the individual cases will be left to further arguments. In the case of Rezvi, the argument which was advanced by Mr Owen depended on the fact that apart from the two offences to which he pleaded guilty, the other offences were not proceeded with. Mr Owen submitted that the convictions could not justify

a the confiscation order which was made. He argues that the scale of the confiscation order indicates that Mr Rezvi was in effect being found guilty of offences for which he had not been tried because the counts had been ordered to lie on the file. This argument misapplies the statutory structure of the confiscation process. The confiscation order is not made in relation to the offences for which Mr Rezvi has not been tried. The counts on which he has been found guilty only b enable the investigation as to the extent to which he has benefited from his criminal conduct to take place. The order is in relation to the benefit which he has obtained in consequence of 'any relevant criminal conduct'. It is not necessary to connect the benefit to any specific crime. The court must however, exercise the discretions to which we have already made reference.

97. The number of convictions is all-important in determining the punishment c of a defendant. Under the legislation, the object of confiscation is not punishment but the forfeiture of an illicit profit. Clearly, the greater the number of convictions the greater the likelihood of benefit, but the statutory minimum of convictions is all that is required for the confiscation process to be put in motion. In the course of that process, the court can take into account the number of offences proved d because they are probative either of the likelihood of the defendant having benefited or not benefited from his offences.

98. There is on the facts of Mr Rezvi's case no reason to think that the conclusion which the court came to was other than appropriate and in accordance with art 6 of the convention. In his case, we would dismiss the appeal.

99. Arrangements will be made to hear further argument in the case of the e other appeals.

Benjafield's and Leal's appeals adjourned for further argument. Rezvi's application for leave to appeal granted, but appeal dismissed. Leave to appeal refused, but court certifying that the following point of law of general public importance was involved in its f *decision: 'Are the provisions of s 72AA of the Criminal Justice Act 1988 as amended and s 4 of the Drug Trafficking Act 1994 incompatible with art 6 of the European Convention on Human Rights and/or Protocol 1?'*

Kate O'Hanlon Barrister.

McIntosh v Lord Advocate and another

a

[2001] UKPC D1

PRIVY COUNCIL

LORD BINGHAM OF CORNHILL, LORD HOFFMANN, LORD HOPE OF CRAIGHEAD, LORD CLYDE AND LORD HUTTON

b

24, 25 JANUARY, 5 FEBRUARY 2001

Sentence – Confiscation order – Burden of proof – Whether assumptions made in assessing proceeds of drug trafficking compatible with presumption of innocence under human rights convention – Proceeds of Crime (Scotland) Act 1995, s 3(2) – Human Rights Act 1998, Sch 1, Pt I, art 6(2).

c

The respondent, M, pleaded guilty to being concerned in the supply of heroin. The prosecutor applied for the making of a confiscation order under the Proceeds of Crime (Scotland) Act 1995, and a prosecutor's statement was duly served on M. The prosecutor intended to rely on s 3(2)[a] of the 1995 Act which empowered the court to make certain assumptions in assessing the value of the proceeds of an accused's drug-trafficking. M lodged answers, contending, inter alia, that s 3(2) was incompatible with art 6(2)[b] of the European Convention for the Protection of Human Rights and Fundamental Freedoms 1950 (as set out in Sch 1 to the Human Rights Act 1998), which provided that everyone 'charged with a criminal offence' was to be presumed innocent until proved guilty. M's contentions were recognised as raising a devolution issue under the Scotland Act 1998. At a subsequent hearing, the judge refused to make a declarator that the Crown had no power to invite the court to make the assumptions set out in s 3(2) of the 1995 Act. His decision was reversed by the High Court of Justiciary which held that the respondent to an application for a confiscation order was a person 'charged with a criminal offence' within the meaning of art 6(2), that art 6(2) therefore applied to such an application and that s 3(2) was incompatible with art 6(2). The Lord Advocate and the Advocate General for Scotland appealed to the Privy Council.

d

e

f

g

Held – Article 6(2) of the convention had no application to a prosecutor's application for a confiscation order. A person against whom such an application was made was neither 'charged' nor accused of any 'criminal offence'. He faced a financial penalty, with a custodial penalty in default of payment, but it was a penalty imposed for the offence of drug trafficking of which he had been convicted and involved no accusation of any other offence. That did not, however, leave him unprotected. He was entitled to all the protection afforded by the right to a fair hearing in art 6(1) of the convention (which applied at all stages), by the common law of Scotland and by the language of the 1995 Act. If the court acceded to the application of a prosecutor for a confiscation order under s 1(1)[c] of the 1995 Act, it would order an accused to pay 'such a sum as the court thinks fit'. In making a confiscation order, the court had to act with scrupulous fairness in making its assessment to ensure that neither the accused nor any third person suffered any

h

j

a Section 3 is set out at [7], post

b Article 6, so far as material, is set out at [12], post

c Section 1, so far as material, is set out at [5], post

a injustice. Accordingly, the appeal would be allowed (see [14], [25], [28], [38], [39], [41], [43], [47] and [48], post); *R v Benjafield* [2001] 2 All ER 609 disapproved in part.

Per curiam. If art 6(2) does apply to confiscation proceedings under the 1995 Act, the s 3(2) assumptions are not incompatible with it. They are a reasonable and proportionate response to a substantial public interest (see [36]–[38], [40], [41], [45], [47] and [48], post); *R v Benjafield* [2001] 2 All ER 609 approved in part.

b

Notes

For the presumption of innocence and for assessing the proceeds of drug trafficking, see respectively 8(2) *Halsbury's Laws* (4th edn reissue) para 142 and 11(2) *Halsbury's Laws* (4th edn reissue) para 1306.

For the Human Rights Act 1998, Sch 1, Pt I, art 6, see 7 *Halsbury's Statutes* (4th c edn) (1999 reissue) 523.

Cases referred to in judgments

Brown v Stott (Procurator Fiscal, Dunfermline) [2001] 2 All ER 97, [2001] 2 WLR 817, PC.
Deweer v Belgium (1980) 2 EHRR 439, ECt HR.
d *Donnelly v HM Advocate* [1999] SCCR 508, HC of Just.
Eckle v Germany (1982) 5 EHRR 1, ECt HR.
Elton v UK App No 32344/96 (11 September 1997, unreported), E Com HR.
Engel v Netherlands (No 1) (1976) 1 EHRR 647, ECt HR.
Foti v Italy (1982) 5 EHRR 313, ECt HR.
HM Advocate v McSalley 2000 SLT 1235, HC of Just.
e *HM Advocate v Monaghan* (5 May 2000, unreported), HC of Just.
Hoang v France (1992) 16 EHRR 53, ECt HR.
Lutz v Germany (1987) 10 EHRR 182, ECt HR.
Minelli v Switzerland (1983) 5 EHRR 554, ECt HR.
Phillips v UK App No 41087/98 (30 November 2000, unreported), ECt HR.
f *R v Benjafield* [2001] 2 All ER 609, CA.
R v Delaney (14 May 1999, unreported), CA.
R v DPP, ex p Kebeline [1999] 4 All ER 801, [2000] 2 AC 326, [1999] 3 WLR 972, HL.
R v Hussein (20 April 1999, unreported), CA.
Raimondo v Italy (1994) 18 EHRR 237, ECt HR.
Ringeisen v Austria (No 1) (1971) 1 EHRR 455, Ect HR.
g *Salabiaku v France* (1988) 13 EHRR 379, ECt HR.
Sporrong v Sweden (1982) 5 EHRR 35, Ect HR.
State v Coetzee [1997] 2 LRC 593, SA Con Ct.
Taylor v UK App No 31209/96 (10 September 1997, unreported), E Com HR.
Welch v UK (1995) 20 EHRR 247, ECt HR.

h

Appeal

The Lord Advocate and the Advocate General for Scotland appealed from the decision of the High Court of Justiciary (Lord Prosser and Lord Allanbridge, Lord Kirkwood dissenting) on 13 October 2000 (2001 JC 78) allowing an appeal by the j respondent, Robert McIntosh, from the decision of Lord Marnoch dismissing his application for a declarator that the Crown had no power to invite the court to make the assumptions set out in s 3(2) of the Proceeds of Crime (Scotland) Act 1994. The facts are set out in the opinion of Lord Bingham of Cornhill.

The Solicitor General for Scotland (*Neil Davidson QC*) and *Michael Howlin* (instructed by the *Crown Office*, Edinburgh) for the Lord Advocate.

The Advocate General for Scotland (*Dr Lynda Clark QC*) and *Lawrence Murphy QC* (instructed by the *Office of the Solicitor to the Advocate General for Scotland*) for the Advocate General.

Edward Targowski QC, Christopher Shead and *Arthur Devlin* (instructed by *Bennett & Robertson*, Edinburgh) for the respondent.

Their Lordships took time for consideration.

5 February 2001. The following judgments were delivered.

LORD BINGHAM OF CORNHILL.

[1] The respondent (Robert McIntosh) was charged jointly with his co-habitee Isobel Black with being concerned in the supply of heroin in contravention of s 4(3)(b) of the Misuse of Drugs Act 1971. Ms Black pleaded not guilty to that charge on 30 June 1999 at the High Court of Justiciary in Paisley and her plea was accepted. On the same date the respondent pleaded guilty to the charge. On the respondent's conviction the prosecutor applied for the making of a confiscation order and a prosecutor's statement supported by detailed schedules was duly served on him at court. Proceedings on the confiscation application were adjourned to enable the respondent to lodge answers, which he did, putting the prosecutor to proof of the matters set out in the schedules and expressly challenging the prosecutor's assertion that certain funds held in the name of Ms Black were 'implicative gifts' by him to her. In adjusted answers by the respondent to the prosecutor's statement it was further contended on his behalf that s 3(2) of the Proceeds of Crime (Scotland) Act 1995, on which the prosecutor intended to rely, was incompatible with art 6(2) of the Convention for the Protection of Human Rights and Fundamental Freedoms (Rome, 4 November 1950; TS 71 (1953); Cmd 8969) and that under s 57(2) of the Scotland Act 1998 the Lord Advocate as prosecutor had no power to act incompatibly with the convention. These contentions were recognised to raise a devolution issue within the meaning of para 1(d) of Pt I of Sch 6 to the Scotland Act, and a diet of debate was fixed.

[2] At that diet the judge (Lord Marnoch) was asked to pronounce a declarator that the 'Crown has no power to invite the court to make the assumptions set out in s 3(2) of the Proceeds of Crime (Scotland) Act 1995'. He declined to make the declarator sought and the respondent raised a petition to the nobile officium for review of Lord Marnoch's decision. The Advocate General for Scotland exercised her right to take part in the proceedings. The petition was heard by Lord Prosser, Lord Kirkwood and Lord Allanbridge, who on 13 October 2000 (Lord Kirkwood dissenting) allowed the respondent's appeal and made the declarator sought: see 2001 JC 78. Leave to appeal to the Judicial Committee of the Privy Council was granted to the Lord Advocate and the Advocate General.

[3] The issue now before the committee is whether the prosecutor is or would be acting incompatibly with the respondent's rights under art 6(2) of the convention in inviting the court to rely on the assumptions set out in s 3(2) of the 1995 Act.

The legislation

[4] As applicable in Scotland, the criminal law relating to controlled drugs is largely found in two statutes. The first is the Misuse of Drugs Act 1971, which creates a number of offences relating (among other things) to the production, importation and supply of such drugs. The other is the 1995 Act (which governs the confiscation of assets of convicted persons and is not restricted to crimes

a related to drugs). This body of legislation rests (so far as it concerns drug trafficking offences) on a series of important premises: that the unlawful consumption of drugs, particularly class A drugs, is a very grave, far-reaching and destructive social evil; that persistence of this evil depends on the availability of an adequate supply of drugs for consumption; that the availability of an adequate supply of drugs in its turn depends on the activity of those who traffic in drugs by b manufacturing, importing, buying and re-selling them; that those who traffic in drugs reap rich rewards from their activity; that those who traffic in drugs go to great lengths to conceal their activities, cover their tracks and conceal their assets; that the evil consequences of drug trafficking are such as properly to engage the sanctions and procedures of the criminal law; that those convicted of trafficking in drugs should be liable to imprisonment for what may be very long periods, to c punish them, to prevent them offending again and to deter others from similar offending; and that it is desirable to deprive traffickers of their ill-gotten gains, so that the hope of profit is heavily outweighed by the fear of punishment. These premises are reflected in the United Nations Convention against Illicit Traffic in Narcotic Drugs and Psychotropic Substances (Vienna, 20 December 1988; TS 26 d (1992) Cm 1927), which the United Kingdom ratified in June 1991, and in the experience and practice of very many states all over the world.

[5] Part I of the 1995 Act is entitled 'Confiscation of the Proceeds of Crime'. Section 1, so far as it relates to drugs, is in these terms:

e '(1) Subject to the provisions of this Part, where in respect of any offence to which this Part applies—(a) the accused is convicted, whether in solemn or summary proceedings; or (b) in the case of summary proceedings (without proceeding to conviction) an order is made discharging him absolutely, the court, on the application of the prosecutor, may make an order (a "confiscation order") requiring the accused to pay such sum as the court thinks fit.

f (2) This Part applies to any offence which has been prosecuted—(a) on indictment; or (b) on summary complaint if the offence is punishable by a fine of an amount greater than the amount corresponding to level 5 on the standard scale or by imprisonment for a period longer than 3 months or by both such fine and imprisonment, but it does not apply to an offence under Part III of the 1989 Act (financial assistance for terrorism).

g (3) A confiscation order shall not be made unless the court orders some other disposal (including an absolute discharge) in respect of the accused ...

(5) The sum which a confiscation order requires an accused to pay in the case of a drug trafficking offence shall be an amount not exceeding—(a) subject to h paragraph (b) below, what the court assesses to be the value of the proceeds of the person's drug trafficking; or (b) if the court is satisfied that the amount that might be realised in terms of this Act at the time the confiscation order is made has a value less than that of the proceeds of the person's drug trafficking, what it assesses to be that amount ...

j (7) Any application under this section shall be made—(a) in proceedings on indictment, when the prosecutor moves for sentence or, if the accused is remitted for sentence under section 195 of the 1995 Act, before sentence is pronounced; and (b) in summary proceedings, following the conviction of the accused.

(8) For the purposes of any appeal or review, a confiscation order is a sentence.'

[6] A number of points on the construction of this section are noteworthy. (1) In proceedings on indictment the making of a confiscation order is dependent on conviction of the accused. (2) The conviction must be of a drug trafficking offence, as defined in s 49(5) of the 1995 Act to embrace offences of importing, producing and supplying controlled drugs. (3) The sum confiscated need not be the profit made from the drug trafficking offence of which the accused has been convicted (in contrast with the ordinary procedure in relation to other offences). (4) An order may be made only on the application of the prosecutor. (5) Where such application is made the court has a discretion whether to make an order or not. (6) The court is required to assess the value of the proceeds of the accused's drug trafficking. (7) 'Drug trafficking' has a meaning distinct from and wider than 'drug trafficking offence': it is defined in s 49(2), (3) and (4) of the 1995 Act so as to include conduct which would, but also conduct which would not, give rise to criminal offences under Scots law. (8) The assessment made by the court is not final, but may later be adjusted (under ss 11 and 12 of the 1995 Act) if new information comes to light. (9) A confiscation order is regarded as a sentence, and is subject to appeal like any other sentence.

[7] Section 2 of the 1995 Act is largely concerned with non-drug offences, but contains a definition in broad terms of 'property'. Section 3 lies at the heart of this appeal and provides:

> '(1) For the purposes of this Act—(a) any payments or other rewards received by a person at any time (whether before or after the commencement of this Act) in connection with drug trafficking carried on by him or another are his proceeds of drug trafficking, and (b) the value of his proceeds of drug trafficking is the aggregate of the values of the payments or other rewards.
>
> (2) Without prejudice to section 9 of this Act the court may, in making an assessment as regards a person under section 1(5) of this Act, make the following assumptions, except in so far as any of them may be shown to be incorrect in that person's case—(a) that any property appearing to the court—(i) to have been held by him at any time since his conviction; or, as the case may be, (ii) to have been transferred to him at any time since a date six years before his being indicted, or being served with the complaint, was received by him, at the earliest time at which he appears to the court to have held it, as a payment or reward in connection with drug trafficking carried on by him; (b) that any expenditure of his since the date mentioned in paragraph (a)(ii) above was met out of payments received by him in connection with drug trafficking carried on by him, and (c) that, for the purpose of valuing any property received or assumed to have been received by him at any time as such a reward, he received the property free of any other interests in it.
>
> (3) Subsection (2) above does not apply if the only offence by virtue of which the assessment is being made is an offence under section 14 of the Criminal Justice (International Co-operation) Act 1990 or section 37 or 38 of the Criminal Law (Consolidation) (Scotland) Act 1995.
>
> (4) The court shall, in making an assessment as regards a person under section 1(5) of this Act, leave out of account any of his proceeds of drug trafficking that are shown to the court to have been taken into account in a case where a confiscation order (whether under this Act or under and within the meaning of—(a) section 2 of the 1994 Act; or (b) any corresponding provision in Northern Ireland), has previously been made against him.'

a [8] A number of points are again noteworthy in the construction of this section. (1) The court has a discretion whether to make the statutory assumptions or not. (2) The assumptions are rebuttable by the accused, on a balance of probabilities. (3) The proceeds in question relate to drug trafficking and not the commission of drug trafficking offences. (4) The assumptions relate to property which appears to the court to meet the conditions specified and to expenditure of the accused b during the relevant period.

[9] Section 4 deals with the definition of 'realisable property'. Section 6 defines 'implicative' gifts in the following way:

> '(1) In this Act references to an "implicative gift" are references to a gift (whether made before or after the commencement of this Act)—(a) made c not more than six years before the date on which, in respect of a person suspected of, or charged with, a drug trafficking offence, the proceedings were commenced or a restraint order was made (whichever first occurs); or (b) made at any time if the gift was of property—(i) received by the giver in connection with drug trafficking carried on by him or another, or (ii) which, in whole or in part, directly or indirectly represented in the giver's hands d property received by him in that connection.'

The section provides a defence for a person in innocent receipt of an implicative gift and a right of appeal for the recipient of an implicative gift. Section 8 provides that the court shall make its decision on the application for a confiscation order before imposing any other financial penalty on the accused.

e [10] Section 9 governs the submission of a statement by the prosecutor:

> '(1) Where the prosecutor applies for the making of a confiscation order, the prosecutor may lodge with the clerk of court a statement as to any matters relevant—(a) in connection with a drug trafficking offence, to the assessment of the value of the accused's proceeds of drug trafficking ...'

f The section goes on to provide for the service of the statement on the accused, the making of a response to the statement by the accused and the acceptance of the statement if the accused fails to respond to it. The attention of the committee was drawn to sub-ss (7) and (8) of this section which provide:

> g '(7) Where the judge presiding at a hearing held under subsection (6) above is not the trial judge he may, on the application of either party, if he considers that it would be in the interests of justice to do so, adjourn the hearing to a date when the trial judge is available.
>
> (8) No acceptance by a person under this section that any payment or h other reward was received by him in connection with drug trafficking carried on by him or another shall be admissible in evidence in any proceedings, whether in Scotland or elsewhere, in respect of an offence.'

It is evident that, although no reliance may be placed on evidence given by an accused during confiscation proceedings in any prosecution for a drug trafficking j offence other than that of which he has just been convicted, there is no bar to a prosecution for such a drug trafficking offence which may have given rise to proceeds which form part of his assessed proceeds of drug trafficking. Section 10 permits the court to adjourn the confiscation proceedings for up to six months if it considers that it has received insufficient information.

[11] Where a confiscation order is made, a term of imprisonment in default may be imposed to ensure compliance (see ss 214–219 of the Criminal Procedure

(Scotland) Act 1995 as applied by s 14 of the Proceeds of Crime (Scotland) Act 1995). Any such term will run from the expiry of any other sentence imposed for the offence (see s 14(4) of the Proceeds of Crime (Scotland) Act 1995).

[**12**] Section 6 of the Human Rights Act 1998 makes it unlawful for a public authority to act incompatibly with a convention right. The expression 'public authority' is defined in terms which include the Lord Advocate, who by s 57(2) of the Scotland Act has no power to do any act which is incompatible with a convention right unless exempted by s 57(3). The convention right central to this appeal is art 6, the terms of which are very familiar and need not be quoted in full. Article 6(1) begins:

> 'In the determination of his civil rights and obligations or of any criminal charge against him, everyone is entitled to a fair and public hearing within a reasonable time by an independent and impartial tribunal established by law.'

Article 6(2), with which the making of assumptions under s 3(2) of the 1995 Act is said to be incompatible, provides: 'Everyone charged with a criminal offence shall be presumed innocent until proved guilty according to law.' Article 6(3) guarantees to 'Everyone charged with a criminal offence' certain specified minimum rights. Attention was also briefly drawn to art 1 of the First Protocol to the convention, entitled 'Protection of property', which provides:

> 'Every natural or legal person is entitled to the peaceful enjoyment of his possessions. No one shall be deprived of his possessions except in the public interest and subject to the conditions provided for by law and by the general principles of international law. The preceding provisions shall not, however, in any way impair the right of a State to enforce such laws as it deems necessary to control the use of property in accordance with the general interest or to secure the payment of taxes or other contributions or penalties.'

The first issue

[**13**] The first issue in the appeal is whether, in relation to the application made against him for a confiscation order, the respondent is a person 'charged with a criminal offence' within the meaning of art 6(2) of the convention and so a person entitled to rely on the presumption of innocence guaranteed by that provision.

[**14**] It was not contended on the respondent's behalf in the Court of Appeal that, in relation to an application for a confiscation order, he was a person charged with a criminal offence as that expression would be understood in Scots domestic law (see the judgment of Lord Prosser, 2001 JC 78 at 81 (para 6)). There are a number of compelling reasons why he would not be so regarded. (1) The application is not initiated by complaint or indictment and is not governed by the ordinary rules of criminal procedure. (2) The application may only be made if the accused is convicted, and cannot be pursued if he is acquitted. (3) The application forms part of the sentencing procedure. (4) The accused is at no time accused of committing any crime other than that which permits the application to be made. (5) When, as is standard procedure in anything other than the simplest case, the prosecutor lodges an application under s 9, that application (usually supported by detailed schedules) is an accounting record and not an accusation. (6) The sum ordered to be confiscated need not be the profit made from the drug trafficking offence of which the accused has been convicted, or any other drug trafficking offence. (7) If the accused fails to pay the sum he is ordered

a to pay under the order, the term of imprisonment which he will be ordered to serve in default is imposed not for the commission of any drug trafficking offence but on his failure to pay the sum ordered and to procure compliance. (8) The transactions of which account is taken in the confiscation proceedings may be the subject of a later prosecution, which would be repugnant to the rule against double jeopardy if the accused were charged with a criminal offence in the b confiscation proceedings. (9) The proceedings do not culminate in a verdict, which would (in proceedings on indictment) be a matter for the jury if the accused were charged with a criminal offence. It is of course true that if, following conviction of the accused and application by the prosecutor for a confiscation order, the court chooses to make the assumptions specified in s 3(2) of the 1995 Act or either of them, an assumption is made (unless displaced) that the accused c has been engaged in drug trafficking which, as defined in s 49(2), (3) and (4), may (but need not) have been criminal. But there is no assumption that he has been guilty of drug trafficking offences as defined in s 49(5). The process involves no inquiry into the commission of drug trafficking offences. Unless Strasbourg jurisprudence points towards a different result, I would not conclude that a person d against whom application for a confiscation order is made is, by virtue of that application, a person charged with a criminal offence.

[15] That is the view which courts in Scotland have consistently taken (see, for example, *HM Advocate v McSalley* 2000 SLT 1235 at 1240); *HM Advocate v Monaghan* (5 May 2000, unreported) at p 16) as have the courts in England (see, for example, *R v Hussein* (20 April 1999, unreported), para 29; *R v Delaney* (14 May 1999, e unreported), at p 20, the latter cases not being concerned with drugs). It is accordingly necessary to consider the Strasbourg case law.

[16] *Engel v Netherlands (No 1)* (1976) 1 EHRR 647 concerned a number of Dutch servicemen who had been penalised for breaches of military discipline. In some of the cases the breaches were more serious and the penalties more severe f than in others. The European Court of Human Rights considered (at 677–678 (paras 81–82)) the distinction between disciplinary and criminal offences, a question on which the decision of the European Court (rather than the classification of the delinquency in domestic law) will ultimately be determinative. Two of the applicants complained that the military proceedings against them infringed the presumption of innocence guaranteed by art 6(2), but this g contention was rejected. The court ruled (at 681 (para 90)):

> 'In reality, this clause does not have the scope ascribed to it by the two applicants. As its wording shows, it deals only with the proof of guilt and not with the kind or level of punishment. It thus does not prevent the national h judge, when deciding upon the penalty to impose on an accused lawfully convicted of the offence submitted to his adjudication, from having regard to factors relating to the individual's personality. Before the Supreme Military Court Mr. Dona and Mr. Schul were "proved guilty according to law" as concerns the offences there alleged against them ... It was for the sole purpose of determining their punishment in the light of their character and previous j record that the said court also took into consideration certain similar, established facts the truth of which they did not challenge. The court did not punish them for these facts in themselves.'

This statement of principle is plainly unhelpful to the respondent.

[17] In *Deweer v Belgium* (1980) 2 EHRR 439, a butcher said to have sold meat at an illegal profit complained of a prosecutor's order that his shop be provisionally

closed until either judgment was given against him in proposed criminal proceedings or he paid a substantial fine in settlement of the proceedings. The butcher paid the fine under protest but complained that his rights under art 6(1), (2) and (3) and art 1 of the First Protocol had been infringed. The court found a breach of art 6(1), and did not find it necessary to examine the other provisions. In reaching its conclusion the court paid attention (at 458 (para 44)) to the realities of the procedure in question and not to appearances and concluded (at 459 (para 46)) that the case had a criminal character: the official notification given to an individual 'that he has committed a criminal offence' is to be treated as the charge for purposes of art 6(1). In the present case no notification was given to the respondent, in connection with the confiscation proceedings, that he had committed a criminal offence.

[**18**] The complaint in *Eckle v Germany* (1982) 5 EHRR 1 was of unreasonable delay in prosecuting criminal proceedings, contrary to art 6(1). To investigate that complaint it was necessary to consider when the criminal proceedings began and the case focused on that issue. The court did, however, make the important and valuable ruling that art 6(1) does not cease to apply when a defendant is convicted, but continues during the imposition of sentence and any appeal. The court held (at 28 (para 76)):

> 'As regards the end of the "time", in criminal matters the period governed by Article 6 (1) covers the whole of the proceedings in issue, including appeal proceedings.'

The court continued (at 28–29 (para 77)):

> 'In the event of conviction, there is no "determination ... of any criminal charge", within the meaning of Article 6(1), as long as the sentence is not definitively fixed. Thus, in the *Ringeisen* judgment [*Ringeisen v Austria (No 1)* (1971) 1 EHRR 455 at 471, 496 (paras 48, 110)] the Court took as the close of the proceedings the date on which the trial court had decided, following appeal proceedings, that the entire period spent by the applicant in detention on remand should be reckoned as part of the sentence.'

It is thus plain that in the confiscation proceedings the respondent has the benefit of art 6(1), for anything it may add to his rights under the common law of Scotland, whether or not he has the benefit of art 6(2).

[**19**] *Foti v Italy* (1982) 5 EHRR 313 also concerned the reasonable time provision of art 6(1). The importance of the case is in recognising that on appropriate facts the proceedings may be held to begin, for purposes of art 6(1), at a date earlier than the official notification to the defendant that he is alleged to have committed a criminal offence.

[**20**] Proceedings for a road traffic offence had been brought against the applicant in *Lutz v Germany* (1987) 10 EHRR 182, and had been discontinued as time-barred, but he had been left to bear his own costs. He complained that the failure to reimburse him infringed his rights under art 6(2). The court held that art 6(2) applied in principle but that it had not been violated in that case. (A different result was reached in *Minelli v Switzerland* (1983) 5 EHRR 554 where a criminal prosecution against a defendant for defamation was terminated before judgment on the ground that the statutory limitation period had expired, and he was ordered to pay costs to the court and the prosecutor. He complained, successfully, that this outcome violated the presumption of innocence to which he was entitled under art 6(2). The court held (at 565 (para 30)) that art 6(2) governed

a criminal proceedings in their entirety, irrespective of the result of the prosecution, and not solely the examination of the merits of the charge. The good sense of this decision is obvious: to impose a burden of costs on a defendant against whom nothing has been proved is in effect to treat him as guilty despite his acquittal.)

[**21**] In *Raimondo v Italy* (1994) 18 EHRR 237 the applicant was charged with offences based on alleged association with the mafia, but was acquitted of those b charges. At the same time he was subject to special supervision as a preventive measure directed to restraining further offences. He complained that these measures violated the reasonable time provision of art 6(1) and an issue was raised whether that article applied at all. The court held that art 6 did not apply to the special supervision and said (at 264 (para 43)):

c 'The Court shares the view taken by the Government and the Commission that special supervision is not comparable to a criminal sanction because it is designed to prevent the commission of offences. It follows that proceedings concerning it did not involve "the determination ... of a criminal charge".'

[**22**] A confiscation order was made against the applicant in *Welch v UK* (1995) 20 d EHRR 247, and in due course he complained that his rights under art 6(1) and (2) and art 7 of the convention had been infringed. His art 6 complaints were held by the commission to be manifestly ill-founded and inadmissible. His complaint under art 7 in relation to the confiscation order was rejected by the commission but upheld by the court. It was clear that the confiscation order had been made retrospectively e (see 261 (para 26)) and the question was whether it amounted to a penalty within the meaning of art 7. The reasoning of the court (at 262) is illuminating:

'28. The wording of Article 7(1), second sentence, indicates that the starting point in any assessment of the existence of a penalty is whether the measure in question is imposed following conviction for a "criminal f offence". Other factors that may be taken into account as relevant in this connection are the nature and purpose of the measure in question; its characterisation under national law; the procedures involved in the making and implementation of the measure; and its severity.

29. As regards the connection with a criminal offence, it is to be observed that before an order can be made under the 1986 Act [the Drug Trafficking g Offences Act 1986] the accused must have been convicted of one or more drug trafficking offences. This link is in no way diminished by the fact that, due to the operation of the statutory presumptions concerning the extent to which the applicant has benefited from trafficking, the court order may affect proceeds or property which are not directly related to the facts underlying h the criminal conviction. While the reach of the measure may be necessary to the attainment of the aims of the 1986 Act, this does not alter the fact that its imposition is dependent on there having been a criminal conviction.

30. In assessing the nature and purpose of the measure, the Court has had regard to the background of the 1986 Act, which was introduced to overcome j the inadequacy of the existing powers of forfeiture and to confer on the courts the power to confiscate proceeds after they had been converted into other forms of assets. The preventive purpose of confiscating property that might be available for use in future drug trafficking operations as well as the purpose of ensuring that crime does not pay are evident from the ministerial statements that were made to Parliament at the time of the introduction of the legislation. However, it cannot be excluded that legislation which

confers such broad powers of confiscation on the courts also pursues the aim of punishing the offender. Indeed, the aims of prevention and reparation are consistent with a punitive purpose and may be seen as constituent elements of the very notion of punishment.'

a

[23] The court briefly considered other matters before continuing (at 263):

b

'33. However, there are several aspects of the making of an order under the 1986 Act which are in keeping with the idea of a penalty as it is commonly understood even though they may also be considered as essential to the preventive scheme inherent in the 1986 Act. The sweeping statutory assumptions in section 2(3) of the 1986 Act that all property passing through the offender's hands over a six-year period is the fruit of drug trafficking unless he can prove otherwise; the fact that the confiscation order is directed to the proceeds involved in drug dealing and is not limited to actual enrichment or profit; the discretion of the trial judge, in fixing the amount of the order, to take into consideration the degree of culpability of the accused; and the possibility of imprisonment in default of payment by the offender—are all elements which, when considered together, provide a strong indication of *inter alia* a regime of punishment.

c

d

34. Finally, looking behind appearances at the realities of the situation, whatever the characterisation of the measure of confiscation, the fact remains that the applicant faced more far-reaching detriment as a result of the order than that to which he was exposed at the time of the commission of the offences for which he was convicted.

e

35. Taking into consideration the combination of punitive elements outlined above, the confiscation order amounted, in the circumstances of the present case, to a penalty. Accordingly, there has been a breach of Article 7(1).

f

36. The Court would stress, however, that this conclusion concerns only the retrospective application of the relevant legislation and does not call into question in any respect the powers of confiscation conferred on the courts as a weapon in the fight against the scourge of drug trafficking.'

g

The court was not here considering whether a defendant was entitled to rely on the presumption of innocence guaranteed by art 6(2) when meeting an application for a confiscation order. But it is plain that the court considered in detail the provisions of the Drug Trafficking Offences Act 1986, applicable to England and Wales, which was in terms similar although not identical to the 1995 Act, and perceived no apparent incompatibility with art 6(2).

h

[24] A similar complaint of retrospectivity under art 7 was made in *Taylor v UK* App No 31209/96 (10 September 1997, unreported). He had been convicted of drug trafficking offences in 1986 and 1994. On the second occasion a confiscation order was made which included the trafficking between 1974 and 1979 which had been the subject of the earlier conviction. The complaint was held by the commission to be inadmissible. In *Elton v UK* App No 32344/96 (11 September 1997, unreported) complaint was made of a confiscation order as violating art 6(2) as well as art 7 of the convention, but both complaints were held to be inadmissible. The commission noted the assumptions which the court could make when making a confiscation order but observed:

j

a '... the commission cannot find that the making of the confiscation order against the applicant raises any issues regarding the principle of presumption of innocence guaranteed by art 6(2) of the convention.'

On 30 November 2000 the court held admissible a complaint made against a confiscation order under art 6(2) in *Phillips v UK* App No 41087/98 (30 November b 2000, unreported), observing that 'it raises a serious question under art 6(2) of such complexity that its determination should depend on an examination of the merits'. This application awaits final determination.

[**25**] None of these authorities, in my opinion, provides substantive support for the respondent's contention. He cannot overcome the problem of showing either that he is 'charged' or that he is accused of any 'criminal offence'. He faces c a financial penalty (with a custodial penalty in default of payment) but it is a penalty imposed for the offence of which he has been convicted and involves no accusation of any other offence.

[**26**] Lord Kirkwood, dissenting in the Court of Appeal, reached a similar conclusion. In his leading opinion for the majority, Lord Prosser (2001 JC 78 at d 92–93 (para 33)) gave a weight to the decisions in *Eckle*'s case and *Foti*'s case, summarised above, which in my view they will not bear. He was impressed (at 93 (para 35)) by the title of the 1995 Act, which is indeed directed to ensuring that crime does not pay, but it is still plain that to obtain a confiscation order the prosecutor makes no accusation of criminal conduct against an accused.

[**27**] Since the decision appealed against, the Court of Appeal, Criminal e Division (Lord Woolf CJ, Judge LJ and Collins J) in *R v Benjafield* [2001] 2 All ER 609, construing similar legislation applicable in England and Wales, has reached the same conclusion as the Court of Appeal on this point. It regarded (at 630 (para 69)) art 6(2) as a specific example of the more general obligations in art 6(1) and concluded (at 634 (para 84)) that the confiscation procedure 'has to be considered f on the assumption that it is subject to the requirements of both art 6(1) and (2) taken together'. I do not think this conclusion does justice to the language of art 6(2), nor does it reflect the reasoning of the European Court of Human Rights in the cases which have come before it so far.

[**28**] In concluding, as I do, that art 6(2) has no application to the prosecutor's application for a confiscation order, I would stress that the result is not to leave g the respondent unprotected. He is entitled to all the protection afforded to him by art 6(1), which applies at all stages, the common law of Scotland and the language of the statute. If the court accedes to the application of a prosecutor under s 1(1) of the 1995 Act, it will order an accused to pay 'such sum as the court thinks fit'. In making a confiscation order the court must act with scrupulous h fairness in making its assessment to ensure that neither the accused nor any third person suffers any injustice.

The second issue

[**29**] If the answer given above to the first issue is correct, the second does not j arise. But if it be assumed that art 6(2) applies to the application for a confiscation order following conviction, the issue arises whether reliance on the assumptions permitted under s 3(2) of the 1995 Act violates or would violate the respondent's rights guaranteed by that article.

[**30**] The European Court of Humn Rights has made clear its approach to art 6(2) and reversal of the onus of proof in *Salabiaku v France* (1988) 13 EHRR 379 and *Hoang v France* (1992) 16 EHRR 53, and the topic has been discussed at some

length by the House of Lords in *R v DPP, ex p Kebeline* [1999] 4 All ER 801, [2000] 2 AC 326 and by the Judicial Committee of the Privy Council in *Brown v Stott (Procurator Fiscal, Dunfermline)* [2001] 2 All ER 97, [2001] 2 WLR 817. It is unnecessary for present purposes to rehearse those authorities. It is plain that the right is not absolute but equally plain that encroachments on the presumption are not to be uncritically accepted. As the court put it in *Salabiaku*'s case (1988) 13 EHRR 379 at 388 (para 28):

> 'Article 6(2) does not therefore regard presumptions of fact or of law provided for in the criminal law with indifference. It requires States to confine them within reasonable limits which take into account the importance of what is at stake and maintain the rights of the defence.'

As Lord Hope of Craighead put it in *Ex p Kebeline* ([1999] 4 All ER 801 at 847, [2000] 2 AC 326 at 384):

> 'As a matter of general principle therefore a fair balance must be struck between the demands of the general interest of the community and the protection of the fundamental rights of the individual: see also *Sporrong v Sweden* (1982) 5 EHRR 35 at 52 (para 69).'

[31] The general interest of the community in suppressing crime, however important, will not justify a state in riding roughshod over the rights of a criminal defendant, as graphically pointed out by Sachs J in *State v Coetzee* [1997] 2 LRC 593 at 677 (para 220). But it is not irrelevant. Nor is the position of the defendant. In weighing the balance between the general interest of the community and the rights of the individual, it will be relevant to ask (as Lord Hope suggested in *Ex p Kebeline* [1999] 4 All ER 801 at 848, [2000] 2 AC 326 at 386) what public threat the provision is directed to address, what the prosecutor must prove to transfer the onus to the defendant and what difficulty the defendant may have in discharging the onus laid upon him. In some cases the acceptability of a reverse onus provision will turn not on consideration of the provision in the abstract but on its application in a particular case (*Hoang v France* (1992) 16 EHRR 53 at 78 (para 33)). The right to a fair trial, guaranteed by art 6(1), will ensure that any reverse onus provision is fairly applied in the given case.

[32] The nature of the public threat to which the 1971 Act and the 1995 Act are directed sufficiently appears from the factors listed in [4] above. It is significant that the United Nations Convention already referred to provides, in art 5(7):

> 'Each Party may consider ensuring that the onus of proof be reversed regarding the lawful origin of alleged proceeds or other property liable to confiscation, to the extent that such action is consistent with the principles of its domestic law and with the nature of the judicial or other proceedings.'

In a 1991 report on *The Confiscation of the Proceeds of Crime* (LRC 35 (1991)) the Irish Law Reform Commission recommended the adoption of such a presumption (see p 75 of the report; and, as made clear on p 55, para 32, it regarded the presumption of innocence as inapplicable following conviction).

[33] In seeking to justify the reasonableness and fairness of the assumptions which the court is permitted to make under s 3(2) the Solicitor General drew attention to a number of points.

a (1) The starting point of the confiscation order procedure is proof beyond reasonable doubt that the accused has committed a drug trafficking offence: s 1(1) of the 1995 Act.

(2) It is open to the accused to rebut the assumptions on a balance of probabilities.

(3) The facts upon which the accused will rely to rebut the assumptions b are peculiarly within his personal knowledge.

(4) The proceedings are fully adversarial and the accused has every opportunity to challenge evidence against him and call witnesses: s 9(6).

(5) It is necessary for the prosecutor to prove the possession of property by and the expenditure of the accused under s 3(2).

c (6) The court has a discretion whether to make an order and whether to make the assumptions and will order the accused to pay such sum as it thinks fit: ss 1(1), 3(2).

(7) The accused has a full right of appeal: s 1(8).

(8) The liability of the accused is limited to the sum which may be realised from him, which if over-estimated at first may be later reduced: s 12.

d (9) The answers of the accused in the confiscation order proceedings cannot be relied upon against him in any later prosecution: s 9(8).

[34] Mr Targowski QC for the respondent submitted that the statutory assumptions were impermissible in particular because there was no onus on the prosecutor to raise any ground even for suspecting that the accused had during e the relevant period engaged in drug trafficking. He placed strong reliance on *Donnelly v HM Advocate* [1999] SCCR 508 in which Lord Coulsfield giving the opinion of the Court of Appeal said (at 538):

'… there is, in our view, nothing in the legislation to suggest that it is necessary that the court should have some evidence, or ground of suspicion, f that the accused has profited from drug-dealing before it can make the order. There is nothing in the wording of section 1 to suggest such a requirement. Section 3(2) similarly provides that the court "may" make the assumptions there set out, but there is nothing in the wording of section 3 which suggests that the court must have evidence or some ground of suspicion that the g accused has profited from drug-dealing before it can make those assumptions, and the structure of the legislation suggests the contrary. The only preconditions for the making of the assumptions which can be found in the statute are that the court must be satisfied that the accused has received payments or incurred expenditure, or both.'

h Lord Coulsfield added (at 539):

'In all the circumstances, in our opinion, it is not necessary that there should be either evidence that the accused has benefited from drug dealing or grounds for suspicion that he has so profited before the court can make the assumptions set out in section 3(2), and we therefore reject the main j argument in principle advanced on behalf of the appellants.'

Lord Prosser and Lord Allanbridge accepted Mr Targowski's submission (see 2001 JC 78 at 91–92 (para 31), 98–99 (para 5) respectively). The Court of Appeal, Criminal Division in *R v Benjafield* reached a different conclusion.

[35] On this point also I respectfully differ from the Court of Appeal. The confiscation order procedure can only be initiated if the accused is convicted of a

drug trafficking offence. The court is therefore dealing with a proven drug trafficker. It is then incumbent on the prosecutor to prove, as best he can, the property held by the accused and his expenditure over the chosen period up to six years, including any implicative gifts relied on. In practice the prosecutor's statement lodged under s 9 will always particularise such of the accused's sources of income as are known to the prosecutor, and any source of income known to the prosecutor of any person to whom the accused is said to have made an implicative gift. The schedules served by the prosecutor in this case contained those details (whether accurately or not has not yet been determined) relating to the respondent and Ms Black, and had they not done so the court would inevitably have exercised its power under s 10 to enable further information to be obtained. It is only if a significant discrepancy is shown between the property and expenditure of the accused on the one hand and his known sources of income on the other that the court will think it right to make the s 3(2) assumptions, and unless the accounting details reveal such a discrepancy the prosecutor will not in practice apply for an order. It would be an obviously futile exercise to seek an order where the assets and expenditure of the accused are fully explained by his known sources of legitimate income. If a significant discrepancy is shown, and in the first instance it is for the prosecutor to show it, I do not for my part think it unreasonable or oppressive to call on the accused to proffer an explanation. He must know the source of his assets and what he has been living on. In the respondent's case (unlike Mr Donnelly's) the sums involved are relatively small, but it cannot be hard for the respondent to explain the source of his and Ms Black's assets and expenditure, matters very much within his knowledge.

[36] The statutory scheme contained in the 1995 Act is one approved by a democratically elected Parliament and should not be at all readily rejected. I would for my part endorse the conclusion of the Court of Appeal, Criminal Division in *R v Benjafield* [2001] 2 All ER 609 at 635 (para 88):

> 'It is very much a matter of personal judgment as to whether a proper balance has been struck between the conflicting interests. Into the balance there must be placed the interests of the defendant as against the interests of the public, that those who have offended should not profit from their offending and should not use their criminal conduct to fund further offending. However, in our judgment, if the discretions which are given to the prosecution and the court are properly exercised, the solution which Parliament has adopted is a reasonable and proportionate response to a substantial public interest, and therefore justifiable.'

[37] I discern no arguable breach of art 1 of the First Protocol to the convention.

[38] I would resolve this issue also against the respondent and accordingly allow the appeal.

The third issue

[39] The Solicitor General submitted that even if both the foregoing issues were resolved against him, the Lord Advocate none the less had power to act as he proposed. In the light of the foregoing judgment this issue does not arise.

LORD HOFFMANN.

[40] I have had the advantage of reading in draft the judgments of my noble and learned friends Lord Bingham of Cornhill and Lord Hope of Craighead. For the reasons which they give I too would allow this appeal.

LORD HOPE OF CRAIGHEAD.

[**41**] I have had the advantage of reading in draft the judgment which my noble and learned friend Lord Bingham of Cornhill has prepared. I agree with it, and for the reasons which he has given I too would allow the appeal and recall the interlocutor of 1 November 2000 which was pronounced by the High Court of Justiciary. I would however like to add these comments, as I am conscious that we are differing from the views expressed by the majority.

[**42**] The first question is whether the prosecutor's act in inviting the court to make the assumptions mentioned in s 3(2) of the Proceeds of Crime (Scotland) Act 1995 involves charging the respondent with a criminal offence within the meaning of art 6(2) of the European Convention for the Protection of Human Rights and Fundamental Freedoms (Rome, 4 November 1950; TS 71 (1953); Cmd 8969). Lord Prosser, with whom Lord Allanbridge agreed, said that it did. He said that the court could make the order sought by the prosecutor only if, by one means or another, it had reached the position of being able to say that there are proceeds of drug trafficking: 2001 JC 78 at 90–91 (para 29). As he saw it, this involved among other things an assertion by the prosecutor that there had been drug trafficking, an invitation made by him to the court to proceed on this basis and, if the court were to reach this point, the making of an order which would significantly affect the respondent. He said that, if one proceeds on the hypothesis that drug trafficking is criminal, the requirements of *Eckle v Germany* (1982) 5 EHRR 1 and *Foti v Italy* (1982) 5 EHRR 313 would be met.

[**43**] In my opinion this approach is inconsistent with the Strasbourg case law: see *Engel v Netherlands (No 1)* (1976) 1 EHRR 647 at 681 (para 90) and *Elton v UK* App No 32344/96 (11 September 1997, unreported), where the commission said at p 4 that it could not find that the making of a confiscation order raised any issues regarding the principle of the presumption of innocence guaranteed by art 6(2). It also overlooks the fact that the procedure on which the prosecutor is now engaged assumes that the accused has already been convicted of the offence with which he was charged: see s 1(1) of the 1995 Act. Article 6(2) provides that everyone charged with a criminal offence shall be presumed innocent until proved guilty according to law. That stage is now passed. The court is concerned only with confiscation of the kind which the law prescribes where the conviction is for a drug trafficking offence. The respondent is not now being charged with another offence, nor is he at risk in these proceedings of being sentenced again for the offence of which he has been convicted. The assumptions on which the court is being asked to proceed do not require the court to hold that he has been engaged in criminal conduct. They have much more to do with the civil process of tracing (a restitutionary remedy), especially where, as in this case, the court is asked to bring the value of implicative gifts into the assessment.

[**44**] The second question is whether, if the prosecutor's act does involve a presumption of guilt within the meaning of art 6(2), the assumptions which the court is asked to make are compatible with that article. Lord Prosser criticised these assumptions on the ground that they were, as he put it, in a quite literal sense baseless (see 2001 JC 78 at 91–92 (para 31)). His impression was that if s 3(2) had been in only slightly different terms they would have been within reasonable limits. But (at 92 (para 32)) he found it difficult to see how a reasonable judge could make the assumptions unless further grounds for suspicion were available.

[**45**] I agree that, in view of the answer which we have given to the first question, this point does not arise. But I also agree that, if it were necessary for an answer to be given to this question, it should be answered against the

respondent. I do not think that it is right to say that the assumptions which the court is asked to make are quite literally baseless. The 1995 Act provides that they can only be made where the accused has been convicted of a drug trafficking offence: see s 1(4). In order to embark on this process the court must first prove that the accused is guilty of such an offence. That is the threshold that first must be crossed. Then there is the nature of those offences which the 1995 Act defines as drug trafficking offences: see s 49(5). The essence of drug trafficking is dealing or trading in drugs. People engage in this activity to make money, and it is notorious that they hide what they are doing. Direct proof of the proceeds is often difficult, if not impossible. The nature of the activity and the harm it does to the community provide a sufficient basis for the making of these assumptions. They serve the legitimate aim in the public interest of combating that activity. They do so in a way that is proportionate. They relate to matters that ought to be within the accused's knowledge, and they are rebuttable by him at a hearing before a judge on the balance of probabilities. In my opinion a fair balance is struck between the legitimate aim and the rights of the accused.

[**46**] Lastly, I should mention that Mr Targowski QC for the respondent suggested that the questions which in *R v DPP, ex p Kebeline* [1999] 4 All ER 801 at 848, [2000] 2 AC 326 at 386 I said it might be useful to consider were in need of being reformulated as they did not precisely fit the circumstances of this case. That however would be to read too much into what I was saying. The questions were not presented as a set of rules. They were no more than an indication of an approach which it might be useful to adopt when the interests of the individual are being balanced against those of society. Each case will vary, and they may be more helpful in some cases than others. But I would resist the suggestion that they need to be reformulated.

LORD CLYDE.

[**47**] I have had the advantage of reading in draft the speech of my noble and learned friend Lord Bingham of Cornhill. For the reasons he has given, I too would allow this appeal.

LORD HUTTON.

[**48**] I have had the advantage of reading in draft the judgment of my noble and learned friend Lord Bingham of Cornhill. I agree with it, and for the reasons which he gives I too would allow this appeal.

Appeal allowed.

Kate O'Hanlon Barrister.

a

Attorney General v Punch Ltd and another

[2001] EWCA Civ 403

COURT OF APPEAL, CIVIL DIVISION

LORD PHILLIPS OF WORTH MATRAVERS MR, SIMON BROWN AND LONGMORE LJJ

b 5 FEBRUARY, 23 MARCH 2001

Contempt of court – Criminal contempt – Intention to interfere with course of justice – Breach of injunction by person not party to action – Attorney General bringing proceedings against former security service officer and newspaper group relating to c alleged misuse of Crown's confidential information – Court granting interlocutory injunctions restraining defendants from disclosing or publishing material obtained by officer in his employment – Officer publishing article in magazine containing information covered by injunction – Judge finding that magazine's editor guilty of contempt regardless of whether information already in public domain – Whether purpose of injunctions protection of national security or preservation of any d information obtained by security officer in his employment – Whether Attorney General's consent required before publication of any material covered by injunctions.

In 1997 the Attorney General brought proceedings against S, a former officer of the Security Service, and a newspaper group, relating to the alleged misuse of e confidential information belonging to the Crown. In the course of those proceedings, the Attorney General obtained an order restraining S from disclosing, until trial or further order, any information obtained by him in the course of, or as a result of his employment in and position as, a member of the service, which related to its activities or intelligence activities generally. He also obtained, by consent, an order against the newspaper group, restraining it, until f trial or further order, from publishing any such information, whether in relation to the work of security or intelligence services 'or otherwise'. Both orders were subject to a proviso excluding from their scope any information which the Attorney General stated in writing was not information whose publication the Crown sought to restrain. Subsequently, S started writing a regular column in a g magazine edited by the appellant. In July 2000 the editor, who was aware of the terms of the injunctions, informed the Treasury Solicitor's office of an article by S which he intended to publish in the next issue. The Attorney General asked for it to be amended, and stated that he would be prepared to consent to publication provided that all the amendments were made. However, the published article, which contained both new material and some that had already been published, h did not incorporate all of the amendments. The Attorney General subsequently brought proceedings for contempt of court against the editor and the publishers of the magazine, contending that publication of the article had interfered with the administration of justice by defeating the purpose for which the injunctions had been granted. At the hearing, the editor contended that that purpose was to j prevent the publication of material likely to damage national security, and that he had had no intention of publishing such material and had not foreseen that he was doing so. Relying, inter alia, on the words 'or otherwise' in the order against the newspaper group, the judge held that the purpose of the injunctions was the preservation of any information obtained by S in his employment, regardless of whether it was already in the public domain, and that the publication of the article had frustrated that purpose. He further held that the editor had known that publication of the article would be in breach of the injunctions, that he had intended to act in breach of them and that accordingly he had intended to interfere with the administration of justice. The judge therefore concluded that the editor and the publishers had been guilty of contempt, and fined them both. On the editor's appeal, the Court of Appeal considered (i) the purpose of an order restraining the publication of allegedly confidential information pending trial and (ii) whether, as the Attorney General contended, no newspaper could knowingly publish any matter that fell within the terms of the injunction against the newspaper group without first obtaining clearance from himself or the court.

Held – When a claimant brought an action to preserve an alleged right of confidentiality in information and the court made an order that the information was not to be published pending trial, the purpose of the order was to protect the confidentiality of the information pending trial. A third party who, with knowledge of the order, published the information and thereby destroyed its confidentiality would commit a contempt of court. The contempt was committed not because the third party was in breach of the order, which did not bind him, but because the purpose of the judge in making the order was intentionally frustrated with the consequence that the conduct of the trial was disrupted. Thus the actus reus was not the publication of material covered by an order, but the destruction of the confidentiality of the material which it had been the purpose of the injunction to preserve. The court could not render it a criminal offence for a newspaper to fail to obtain clearance from the Attorney General before publishing material to which there could manifestly not be the slightest ground of objection. A conclusion to the contrary would result in the imposition of a restriction on the freedom of the press that was disproportionate to any public interest and thus in breach of the right to freedom of expression in the European Convention for the Protection of Human Rights and Fundamental Freedoms 1950. It would also extend the law of contempt beyond the principle that it was an offence intentionally to interfere with the course of justice. In the instant case the purpose of the injunctions was to preserve until trial the confidentiality of material whose disclosure arguably posed a risk of damaging national security. Re-publication of material which had already entered the public domain did not offend against that purpose, but the publication of the new material did defeat it. The actus reus of contempt was therefore established. However (Simon Brown LJ dissenting), the finding of contempt would be set aside since the Attorney General had failed to establish the necessary mens rea, namely knowledge that the publication would interfere with the course of justice by defeating the purpose underlying the injunctions. It was not sufficient to establish that the editor had known that the publication was one which the defendants to the action were enjoined from making under the terms of the injunctions. The Attorney General could have proceeded against the magazine and the editor on the basis that they had aided and abetted a breach by S of the injunction against him, but he had chosen not to do so. Accordingly, the appeal would be allowed (see [87], [88], [97], [99], [100]–[102], [108]–[118], [125], [128], [129], [137], [138], post).

Attorney General v Times Newspapers Ltd [1991] 2 All ER 398 explained.

Notes

For publications intended to interfere with or impede the course of justice, see 9(1) *Halsbury's Laws* (4th edn reissue) paras 421–422.

a

Cases referred to in judgments

A-G v Guardian Newspapers Ltd [1987] 3 All ER 316, [1987] 1 WLR 1248, Ch D, CA and HL.

A-G v Guardian Newspapers Ltd (No 2) [1988] 3 All ER 545, [1990] 1 AC 109, [1988] 3 WLR 776, Ch D, CA and HL.

A-G v Jonathan Cape Ltd, A-G v Times Newspapers Ltd [1975] 3 All ER 484, [1976] QB

b 752, [1975] 3 WLR 606.

A-G v Leveller Magazine Ltd [1979] 1 All ER 745, [1979] AC 440, [1979] 2 WLR 247, HL.

A-G v Newspaper Publishing plc [1987] 3 All ER 276, [1988] Ch 333, [1987] 3 WLR 942, Ch D and CA.

A-G v Times Newspapers Ltd [1991] 2 All ER 398, [1992] 1 AC 191, [1992] 2 WLR

c 994, HL; *affg* sub nom *A-G v Newspaper Publishing plc* (1990) Times, 28 February, [1990] CA Transcript 171; *affg* (8 May 1989, unreported), Ch D.

Commonwealth of Australia v John Fairfax & Sons Ltd (1980) 147 CLR 39, Aust HC.

Harrow London BC v Johnstone [1997] 1 All ER 929, [1997] 1 WLR 459, HL.

Marengo v Daily Sketch and Sunday Graphic Ltd [1948] 1 All ER 406, HL.

Seaward v Paterson [1897] 1 Ch 545, [1895–9] All ER Rep 1127, CA.

d *Wellesley (Lord) v Earl of Mornington* (1848) 11 Beav 180, 50 ER 785; *subsequent proceedings* (1843) 11 Beav 181, 50 ER 786.

X CC v A [1985] 1 All ER 53, sub nom *Re X (a minor) (wardship: injunction)* [1984] 1 WLR 1422.

Z Ltd v A [1982] 1 All ER 556, [1982] QB 558, [1982] 2 WLR 288, CA.

e

Appeal

The second defendant, James Steen, the former editor of Punch magazine, appealed from the order of Silber J on 7 November 2000, giving effect to his judgment of 6 October 2000, fining him £5,000 for criminal contempt of court in respect of the publication of an article in the magazine in July 2000 which the judge held to

f have interfered with the administration of justice by defeating the purpose of interlocutory injunctions made by Hooper J on 4 September 1997 in proceedings for breach of confidence brought by the respondent, the Attorney General, against David Shayler, the author of the article, and Associated Newspapers Ltd. The first defendant, Punch Ltd, the publishers of the magazine, did not appeal

g from the fine of £20,000 imposed on them by the judge for the same contempt. The facts are set out in the judgment of Lord Phillips of Worth Matravers MR.

David Price, solicitor advocate (instructed by *Henry Hepworth*) for Mr Steen.
Jonathan Crow (instructed by the *Treasury Solicitor*) for the Attorney General.

h

Cur adv vult

23 March 2001. The following judgments were delivered.

LORD PHILLIPS OF WORTH MATRAVERS MR.

j [1] Mr Steen, the appellant, used to be the editor of Punch. Both he and the publishers of that magazine have been held to have been guilty of contempt of court. This was because of an article published in an issue of Punch at the end of July last year. Silber J, who made the finding of contempt, fined Mr Steen £5,000 and Punch £20,000. Mr Steen now appeals to us against the finding of contempt. He is funding his own appeal and, in the interests of economy, originally instructed Mr David Price, the solicitor, who has ably presented his appeal, to confine himself to a single ground of appeal which it was estimated would occupy the court for two hours. With the encouragement of the court and without objection from Mr Jonathan Crow, who appeared for the Attorney General, he added a second ground of appeal in the course of argument. The appeal requires consideration of the basis of the findings of contempt made by the House of Lords in *A-G v Times Newspapers Ltd* [1991] 2 All ER 398, [1992] 1 AC 191, the 'Spycatcher' case.

THE FACTS

[2] The primary facts are not in dispute and the following summary of these draws largely from the judgment below.

[3] From November 1991 until he resigned in October 1996, Mr David Shayler served as an officer in the security service (the service). His engagement was subject to express terms prohibiting him from publishing information which related to or might be construed as relating to the service or its membership or activities or to security or intelligence activities generally without prior written approval.

[4] It is alleged by the Attorney General that some time before his resignation, Mr Shayler removed from the offices of the service approximately 30 documents or copies taken by him (the confidential documents) which contained confidential information belonging to the Crown and included details of or reference to secret intelligence, intelligence sources, the assessment of secret intelligence from intelligence sources, intelligence targets, investigative techniques and operational matters, the identity and telegraphic address of a number of foreign intelligence and security agencies and to diplomatic exchanges between Her Majesty's government and a foreign government.

[5] The Attorney General contends that subsequently Mr Shayler provided to Associated Newspapers Ltd material derived from the confidential documents relating to the service, including confidential information belonging to the Crown that had come into his possession in the course of his employment with the service. This material was incorporated in articles that were published in late August 1997 in the Mail on Sunday and the Evening Standard. He further provided to Associated Newspapers information which was incorporated into articles that it was intended to publish in the Mail on Sunday on 31 August 1997.

[6] At this point, however, the Attorney General intervened. He commenced an action against Mr Shayler as first defendant and Associated Newspapers as second defendant and, on 30 August 1997, obtained from Keene J interlocutory injunctions restraining publication. On 4 September the action came before Hooper J. Neither Mr Shayler nor Associated Newspapers appeared, but solicitors for Associated Newspapers wrote a letter giving undertakings and consenting to the order that Hooper J subsequently made against them.

[7] Hooper J made the following order against Mr Shayler:

> 'The first defendant be restrained until trial or further order whether by himself his servants or agents or otherwise howsoever from disclosing, whether to any newspaper or other organ of the media or any other person otherwise howsoever any information obtained by him in the course of or by virtue of his employment in and position as a member of the security service (whether presented as fact or fiction) which relates to or which may be construed as relating to the security service or its membership or activities or to security or intelligence activities generally, provided that this order does not apply to: (1) any information in respect of which the plaintiff (whether at the request of the defendants or any of them, or any third party,

a or of his own motion) makes a statement in writing (either personally or by the Treasury Solicitor) that such information is not information in respect of which the Crown seeks to restrain publication; (2) the repetition of information disclosed in the Mail on Sunday on 24 August 1997.'

[8] The first paragraph of the order made against Associated Newspapers read as follows:

b

'The second defendant be restrained until further order whether by itself, its servants or agents or otherwise howsoever from publishing, to any person any information obtained by it from the first defendant and obtained by the first defendant in the course of or as a result of his employment in and position as a member of the security service, whether in relation to the work of, or in support of, security or intelligence services or otherwise …'

c

[9] In June or July 1998, Mr Steen in his capacity as editor of Punch met Mr Shayler in Paris and, prior to that meeting, his office had requested and received copies of the injunctions from the Treasury Solicitor. Mr Steen wished d to know what was covered by the injunctions. Mr Shayler subsequently started writing a regular column in Punch commencing with issue 89 (September 11–September 24 1999) and, from issue 90 onwards, the column carried his name on a by-line. By that time, Mr Shayler was well known as a warrant for his arrest had been issued and he had been arrested in Paris pending extradition proceedings, which were ultimately unsuccessful. In addition the book *Defending the Realm—* e *MI5 and the Shayler Affair* (1999) by journalists Mark Hollingsworth and Nick Fielding had been published which gave details of Mr Shayler's experiences at MI5 as well as his gradual disenchantment with the service and the reasons for that disenchantment.

[10] Mr Steen explained to the court in an affidavit that he thought that Mr Shayler f had important comments to make, which readers of Punch were entitled to know about and would find interesting, namely 'the error and incompetence of MI5, and its direct and often tragic consequences'. He also felt that Mr Shayler should have a platform from which to speak out and 'not be pushed to the literal and figurative margins by the Security Services'. Mr Shayler had worked on student newspapers at university and had had a rudimentary journalistic training at the g Sunday Times; therefore he was, according to Mr Steen, quite capable of writing an interesting column in journalistic style.

[11] According to Mr Steen:

'Mr Shayler's column was intended to criticise the performance of the security services, to expose its errors and inefficiencies and to show that its past incompetence had had serious and sometimes tragic results. Mr Shayler's status, his locus standi, so far as Punch's readers were concerned, was that he had been on the inside, that he knew what he was talking about, that he was able to comment about security and related matters.'

h

j [12] By a letter of the 23 December 1999, following Mr Shayler's eighth piece in the magazine, Mr Martin for the Treasury Solicitor wrote to Mr Steen reminding him of the existence of the orders and stating that he had been instructed that 'some of the material in the articles is damaging to national security'.

[13] Vigorous correspondence ensued between Mr Steen and Mr Martin, in the course of which Mr Martin urged Mr Steen to 'take advantage of the proviso to the injunction allowing the Crown to confirm that it does not object to the

publication of certain material'. To this Mr Steen responded that editorial steps were taken to ensure that the injunction was not breached nor reference made to material which might remotely be considered to be damaging to the national interest. He accused Mr Martin of attempting to force Punch to submit to government censorship. The correspondence ended on 21 January 2000 with a letter from Mr Martin which included a statement that 'the purpose of an injunction is not … to prevent criticism of the Security Service but is to prevent damage to national security'.

[14] There the matter rested until Friday, 21 July 2000 when Mr Martin received a telephone call from Mr Steen who said that he intended to publish an article by Mr Shayler in the following week's edition relating to the Bishopsgate bombing. While much of the article was not new and would not come as a surprise, it contained, in his words, 'a lot of MI5 jargon'.

[15] This letter led to a flurry of urgent communications between Mr Martin and Mr Steen. Mr Martin's clients needed time in order to comment on the proposed article, while Mr Steen was concerned about his printing deadline. Mr Martin stated in a telephone conversation that the article appeared to fall within the terms of the injunction as the article set out information obtained by Mr Shayler in the course of his employment. He followed this up with a letter on 24 July in which he stated 'my clients are satisfied that the publication of the article in its existing form would be in breach of the injunction'.

[16] At about 1.00 pm on the 25 July, Mr Martin was supplied with his client's amendments to the draft article and he duly sent details to Mr Steen under cover of a letter in which he said that his clients would be prepared to consent to publication of the information contained in the article provided that all the amendments were made. He added that if Mr Steen did not regard some of the changes as acceptable, he should let Mr Martin have an amended version of the text indicating what changes had been made so he could take further instructions. By that stage the article had been finalised and sent to the printers.

[17] He did not receive a reply to this letter and on 26 July the defendants' Punch magazine issue 111 went on sale, which was the edition which gave rise to the contempt proceedings. The cover of the magazine reproduced Mr Martin's letter to Mr Steen dated 24 July 2000 albeit in a slightly amended form and beneath the letter there appeared a headline stating 'Inside whistle-blower David Shayler tells the story MI5 does not want you to read'.

[18] The article had been amended from the draft version but did not reflect all the amendments which had been notified to the defendants.

[19] The basis on which the Attorney General alleged that the publication of this article amounted to a contempt of court, as stated in the claim form, was that the publication:

> '… had the effect of publishing material which this Honourable court intended, by means of the injunctions, not to be published pending the trial in the action against Mr Shayler and Associated Newspapers. The defendants' said action thereby impeded or interfered with the administration of justice by thwarting and/or undermining the intended effects of the injunction. The defendants intended their actions should have that effect.'

THE MAJOR ISSUES BEFORE SILBER J

[20] The contempt alleged by the Attorney General is not contempt under the Contempt of Court Act 1981, but contempt at common law. As such, it is subject to common law principles that govern the commission of a criminal offence.

a Both the 'actus reus' and the 'mens rea' must be demonstrated if the offence is to be made out. There was a dispute as to the nature of each of these elements of the alleged contempt.

[21] The starting point was common ground. The nature of the contempt alleged was interference with the administration of justice. The 'actus reus' was conduct which defeated the purpose of the court in ordering the injunctions. b The 'mens rea' was an intention to defeat that purpose. This did not mean that the Attorney General had to demonstrate that Mr Steen had wished to defeat the purpose of the court, merely that he had foreseen that this would be the consequence of his conduct. At this point agreement ended.

ACTUS REUS

c [22] Mr Steen's case was that the purpose of the injunctions ordered by Hooper J was to prevent the publication of matter that was likely to damage the national security. The Crown had no right in law to restrain publication unless it could demonstrate that publication would be harmful to the public interest. The purpose of the injunctions must have been to restrain publication that would d be unlawful, not to restrain publication of matter to which no lawful objection could be taken. The Attorney General had not demonstrated that the publication had been damaging to the national interest, therefore the 'actus reus' of the contempt had not been made out.

[23] The case for the Attorney General was that the purpose of the injunctions appeared clearly from their express terms. This was to prevent the publication of e the matter identified in the first paragraph of each order. Whether or not at the conclusion of the action this proved to be matter, publication of which the Crown was entitled to restrain, was not material. The purpose of the injunctions was to prevent publication of that matter until the court could rule on whether or not publication was lawful. By publishing matter which was clearly covered by the f terms of the injunction, Mr Steen had committed the 'actus reus' of contempt.

MENS REA

[24] The issue on 'mens rea' followed from that on 'actus reus'. Mr Steen argued that he believed that the purpose of the court in ordering the injunctions was to prevent the publication of matter that was likely to damage the national g security. He had had no intention of publishing such matter, nor had he foreseen that he was doing so. If, in fact, he was mistaken as to the object of the court in ordering the injunctions, this mistake was, of itself, enough to absolve him of the necessary 'mens rea'.

[25] The case for the Attorney General was that Mr Steen had express knowledge h of the terms of the injunctions. Thus he knew the conduct which the court intended to prevent by those injunctions. Preventing that conduct was manifestly the purpose of ordering the injunctions. By publishing matter that he knew the court had intended should not be published he demonstrated the intention that constituted the 'mens rea' of the contempt.

j THE JUDGMENT OF SILBER J

Facts

[26] The judge made a number of further findings of primary fact, which are not now disputed. (i) Some of the information in the Punch article had been published before. (ii) Three significant areas of information in the article had never been published before. (iii) The information published was information

covered by the express terms of the injunction. (iv) While the publication of the article caused damage no details of damage to national security were adduced in evidence. a

Actus reus

[27] The facts of this case closely parallel those of the 'Spycatcher' case, and Silber J founded largely on that decision in his conclusions. The following passage from his judgment contains the essence of his conclusions on 'actus reus': b

> 'The Attorney General contends that the purpose of the court in granting the injunction was not to protect national security but to make an order for "the preservation of the information obtained by the employee in his capacity as a member of the Security Service pending the trial" (*A-G v Newspaper Publishing plc* [1987] 3 All ER 276 at 296, [1988] Ch 333 at 365); in other words to ensure that until trial, there should be no disclosure of information obtained by Mr Shayler in his employment other than that disclosed in the Mail on Sunday on 24 August 1997 (the MOS exception) unless the Attorney General had approved. I believe this contention to be correct for four reasons, some of which overlap. First, it is noteworthy that the terms of the injunction against Associated Newspapers are clear and they merely prevent publication of any information obtained from Mr Shayler and obtained by Mr Shayler in the course of and as a result of his employment and position as a member of the security service. It covers information "in relation to the work of or in support of the security and intelligence services or otherwise". This shows that the information covered by that injunction goes beyond security and intelligence matters and has no limitation on the subject matter or the material covered by the injunction. Second, the injunction against Mr Shayler refers to the work of the security and intelligence services but does not have a requirement that the information covered must relate to national security and it is quite likely that the injunction covers matters other than those of national security. The injunction against him might, for example, cover well-known facts about the identity of past or present heads of the security service. Third, the "Spycatcher" injunctions were in a similar form to the injunctions in this case against Associated Newspapers and they were regarded as being "originally imposed in order to preserve the confidentiality of the then unpublished allegations" (*A-G v Guardian Newspapers Ltd* [1987] 3 All ER 316 at 374, [1987] 1 WLR 1248 at 1318 per Lord Oliver of Alymerton) or "the right of private and public authorities to seek and obtain the protection of the courts for confidential information which they claim to be their property" (*A-G v Newspaper Publishing plc* [1987] 3 All ER 276 at 293, [1988] Ch 333 at 361 per Donaldson MR). In a later case, Lord Mustill said the "Spycatcher" injunctions were "obviously intended to stop the publication by any medium of materials which would compromise the pending proceedings" (*Harrow London BC v Johnstone* [1997] 1 All ER 929 at 937, [1997] 1 WLR 459 at 468). I cannot see why the purpose of the injunctions in the Associated Newspapers case should be regarded as being different. Fourth, these injunctions are no more concerned primarily with national security than the similar order in the "Spycatcher" case. In para 32 above I quoted Donaldson MR as saying of that application for contempt against a third party in a similar position to the defendants in this case that: "… I should like to re-emphasise with all the power at my command that this case is not primarily
> c d e f g h j

a about national security or official secrets. It is about the right of private citizens and public authorities to seek and obtain the protection of the courts for confidential information which they claim to be their property." (See [1987] 3 All ER 293, [1988] Ch 333 at 361.) Similar reasoning applies to the injunctions here and supports the idea that the purpose of the injunction was to preserve information. So a third party who knowingly uses that b information before trial would be damaging or destroying the confidentiality which the court was seeking to protect and thus have a significant or adverse effect on the administration of justice, irrespective of national security considerations.'

[**28**] The judge went on to consider whether Mr Steen had committed the 'actus c reus' that he had identified. He held that inasmuch as the terms of the injunctions prohibited the publication of the specified matter, regardless of whether or not it had already been published, Mr Steen frustrated the purpose of the court by publishing such matter. Thus he held:

d '... the purpose of the court in granting the injunctions was to ensure that there should be no disclosure of any information obtained by Mr Shayler during his employment outside the MOS exception without the Attorney General's consent. All the material in the offending article to which the Attorney General objected fell within the ambit of the injunctions and was published in contravention of the purpose of the court in granting the e injunctions, namely to ensure that it was not published before trial. This is so even though some of the material might have been previously published, as significantly the proviso does not relate to any previously published material except that falling within the MOS exception (which is not relevant to the material under consideration) and that approved by the Attorney f General. If it had been the court's intention when granting the injunctions to exclude from the terms of the injunctions all material previously published, that exception would have been clearly specified in the same way as the MOS exception was but this was not done. So I conclude the fact that material was previously published (and outside the MOS exception) does not prevent it from being covered by the injunctions and so in respect of this g material, the court's intention in granting the injunctions was to ensure that it was not republished. Both Associated Newspapers and Mr Shayler must have appreciated this and did not object to the injunctions or later seek a variation to exclude it from the injunction.'

h [**29**] He went on to hold that he would have concluded that the 'actus reus' was established, even if all the material in the article had previously been published.

Mens rea

j [**30**] Silber J held that to prove the necessary mens rea the Attorney General had to establish: (i) that Mr Steen knew of the injunctions; (ii) that he intended that the publication of the article would contravene the injunctions; and (iii) that he intended that the publication should interfere with the administration of justice or the purpose of the court in granting the injunctions.

[**31**] The judge found that Mr Steen was aware of the terms of the injunctions. This was not and is not disputed.

[32] The judge found that Mr Steen knew that 'the publication of the article was a breach of the injunctions and ... intended to act in breach of it'. The judge then equated this intention with an intention to interfere with the administration of justice. He put the matter thus:

> 'An injunction is a court order made to assist in the administration of justice and any interference with it impedes the administration of justice. By the same token and for the factors set out above and which demonstrate his intention to break the injunction, the second defendant must have intended to impede the administration of justice. Second, the second defendant clearly knew from reading the injunctions, which he clearly did, that the purpose of the court in granting them was to prevent publication or disclosure of information falling within para 1 of the order but not covered by the provisos. The terms of the injunction make it clear that it prevents publication falling outside the provisos; that was the only purpose that the court could have had in granting the injunction as that was what Associated Newspapers were restrained from doing. In his communication with the second defendant, Mr Martin referred to the purpose of the injunction from the claimant's point of view as being "to prevent damage to national security" but the court's purpose was to prevent disclosure as the terms of the injunctions would have demonstrated on a cursory reading of it.'

[33] The judge stated in terms that he would have been satisfied of the intention to interfere with the administration of justice even if the Attorney General's application had related solely to material that had already been published.

Human rights

[34] Before Silber J, Mr Steen argued that the Attorney General's case was in conflict with the right to freedom of expression enshrined in art 10 of the European Convention for the Protection of Human Rights and Fundamental Freedoms (Rome, 4 November 1950; TS 71 (1953); Cmd 8969) (as set out in Sch 1 of the Human Rights Act 1998) (the convention). On his case, the grant of the injunction against Mr Shayler and Associated Newspapers had the result of imposing a significant restriction on the freedom of expression of the entire media. This was neither necessary in a democratic society nor proportionate to any legitimate aim. It did not fulfil 'a pressing social need'.

[35] Silber J held that the principle of English law that held Mr Steen in contempt was both necessary in a democratic society and proportionate to the legitimate aim of ensuring that the court's purpose was not subverted and the rights of those protected by the injunctions not undermined. He focused particularly on the fact that art 10(2) of the convention permits restriction on the freedom of expression in the interests of 'maintaining the authority ... of the judiciary'. He stressed that:

> '... the basis of my decision on this application is not national security but the need to preserve the integrity and value of injunctions, to protect those whose rights under the injunctions have been undermined and to punish those who interfere with the administration of justice by being actively involved in the disclosure of what the court ordered should not be disclosed until trial.'

a [**36**] The judge considered, of his own motion, the effect of s 12(4) of the 1998 Act and concluded that it posed no bar to the Attorney General's application as it was not in the public interest that the article complained of should have been published.

THE ISSUES ON THE APPEAL

b [**37**] When Mr Price opened the appeal he stated that, while Silber J's judgment was open to attack on a number of grounds, his instructions were to limit his attack to the issue of mens rea. For purposes of argument he was prepared to accept that the purpose of the court in granting the injunctions was to prevent publication of the matter covered by the injunctions and, consequently, that the actus reus of contempt was publishing such matter. He proposed to argue, c however, that the judge should have accepted Mr Steen's evidence that he believed that the purpose of the injunctions was to prevent the publication of matter that might be damaging to national security. Mistake as to the true purpose of the injunction meant that Mr Steen did not have the necessary mens rea when he acted in a way that defeated that purpose. Mr Steen's approach was d reflected in his written grounds of appeal.

[**38**] We expressed disquiet at proceeding on this narrow basis. A court may have more than one purpose in granting an interlocutory injunction. The immediate purpose of restraining named defendants from publishing specific material will necessarily be to ensure that those defendants do not publish the material. An ulterior e purpose may be to ensure that the material remains confidential until its status is determined at trial and the ultimate purpose may be to ensure that any parts of the material that are likely to damage the national interest remain permanently confidential. It seemed to us that Mr Steen's case raised the question of which purpose was the *relevant* purpose under the principles of the law of contempt developed in the 'Spycatcher' case. In the course of argument Mr Price received f instructions to apply to add to the grounds of appeal a contention that Silber J should have held that the purpose of the court in granting the injunctions had been to prevent the publication of matter likely to harm national security and that, accordingly, the actus reus of the alleged contempt was publishing matter that was likely to harm national security. We granted permission to add this g ground.

SPYCATCHER

[**39**] The jurisprudence in this area of the law is mainly to be found in the series of decisions relating to the book *Spycatcher* (1987). The author of this was Peter Wright, a former member of MI5 who had retired to Tasmania. There he wrote h an account of alleged improprieties carried on by members of MI5 during his time in the service. In breach of the duty of confidence owed to the Crown under the terms of his contract of service he proposed to publish this. The backdrop to the proceedings that then ensued in England consisted of attempts by the Crown to restrain publication in Australia and steps taken to outflank these by j publication in the United States and elsewhere. In the English proceedings the Crown attempted to prevent publication of extracts from *Spycatcher* in this country. There were two parallel sets of proceedings. In the first the Attorney General sought injunctions against newspapers that had published references to or extracts from the contents of the book. I shall call these 'the injunction proceedings'. In the second he sought to have punished for contempt of court other newspapers for publishing precisely what their colleagues had been forbidden to publish by

interlocutory orders in the injunction proceedings. I shall call these 'the contempt proceedings'. a

THE CAUSE OF ACTION IN THE 'SPYCATCHER' CASE

[**40**] The cause of action in the injunction proceedings was breach of confidence—the Crown alleged that anyone who received information knowing that it had emanated from Mr Wright in breach of his duty of confidence owed a duty in equity to treat the information as confidential. The courts held, however, that where the Crown sought to restrain the disclosure of information relating to government, special principles applied. Both in the Court of Appeal and in the House of Lords the following passage from the judgment of Mason J in *Commonwealth of Australia v John Fairfax & Sons Ltd* (1980) 147 CLR 39 at 51–52 was cited with approval: b c

> 'The equitable principle has been fashioned to protect the personal, private and proprietary interests of the citizen, not to protect the very different interests of the executive government. It acts, or is supposed to act, not according to standards of private interest, but in the public interest. This is not to say that equity will not protect information in the hands of the government, but it is to say that when equity protects government information it will look at the matter through different spectacles. It may be a sufficient detriment to the citizen that disclosure of information relating to this affair will expose his actions to public discussion and criticism. But it can scarcely be a relevant detriment to the government that publication of material concerning its actions will merely expose it to public discussion and criticism. It is unacceptable in our democratic society that there should be a restraint on the publication of information relating to government when the only vice of that information is that it enables the public to discuss, review and criticize government action. Accordingly, the court will determine the government's claim to confidentiality by reference to the public interest. Unless disclosure is likely to injure the public interest, it will not be protected. The court will not prevent the publication of information which merely throws light on the past working of government, even if it be not public property, so long as it does not prejudice the community in other respects. Then disclosure will itself serve the public interest in keeping the community informed and in promoting discussion of public affairs. If, however, it appears that disclosure will be inimical to the public interest because national security, relations with foreign countries or the ordinary business of government will be prejudiced, disclosure will be restrained. There will be cases in which the conflicting considerations will be finely balanced, where it is difficult to decide whether the public's interest in knowing and in expressing its opinion, outweighs the need to protect confidentiality.' d e f g h

[**41**] In the leading speech in the House of Lords Lord Keith of Kinkel put the matter as follows:

> 'The position of the Crown, as representing the continuing government of the country, may, however, be regarded as being special. In some instances disclosure of confidential information entrusted to a servant of the Crown may result in a financial loss to the public. In other instances such disclosure may tend to harm the public interest by impeding the efficient attainment of proper governmental ends, and the revelation of defence or intelligence secrets certainly falls into that category. The Crown, however, as representing j

a the nation as a whole, has no private life or personal feelings capable of being hurt by the disclosure of confidential information. In so far as the Crown acts to prevent such disclosure or to seek redress for it on confidentiality grounds, it must necessarily, in my opinion, be in a position to show that the disclosure is likely to damage or has damaged the public interest. How far the Crown has to go in order to show this must depend on the circumstances b of each case. In a question with a Crown servant himself, or others acting as his agents, the general public interest in the preservation of confidentiality, and in encouraging other Crown servants to preserve it, may suffice. But where the publication is proposed to be made by third parties unconnected with the particular confidant, the position may be different. The Crown's argument c in the present case would go to the length that in all circumstances where the original disclosure has been made by a Crown servant in breach of the obligation of confidence, any person to whose knowledge the information comes and who is aware of the breach comes under an equitable duty binding his conscience not to communicate the information to anyone else irrespective of the circumstances under which he acquired the knowledge. d In my opinion that general proposition is untenable and impracticable, in addition to being unsupported by any authority. The general rule is that anyone is entitled to communicate anything he pleases to anyone else, by speech or in writing or in any other way. That rule is limited by the law of defamation and other restrictions similar to these mentioned in art 10 of the e Convention for the Protection of Human Rights and Fundamental Freedoms (Rome, 4 November 1950; TS 71 (1953); Cmd 8969). All those restrictions are imposed in the light of considerations of public interest such as to countervail the public interest in freedom of expression. A communication about some aspect of government activity which does no harm to the interests f of the nation cannot, even where the original disclosure has been made in breach of confidence, be restrained on the ground of a nebulous equitable duty of conscience serving no useful practical purpose.' (See *A-G v Guardian Newspapers Ltd (No 2)* [1988] 3 All ER 545 at 640, [1990] 1 AC 109 at 256–257.)

[**42**] It is noteworthy that Lord Keith considered that the Crown might have g good cause to restrain publication by a Crown servant, or his agents, in circumstances where a newspaper would be under no legal restraint in publishing the same subject matter.

[**43**] In the injunction proceedings the courts recognised that the subject matter of the 'Spycatcher' case included matter that it was in the public interest h should remain confidential. Lord Keith said:

'In relation to Mr Wright, there can be no doubt whatever that had he sought to bring about the first publication of his book in this country, the Crown would have been entitled to an injunction restraining him. The work j of a member of MI5 and the information which he acquires in the course of that work must necessarily be secret and confidential and be kept secret and confidential by him. There is no room for discrimination between secrets of greater or lesser importance, nor any room for close examination of the precise manner in which revelation of any particular matter may prejudice the national interest. Any attempt to do so would lead to further damage.' (See [1988] 3 All ER 545 at 642, [1990] 1 AC 109 at 259.)

[44] The courts held, however, that once widespread worldwide publication had destroyed the confidentiality of the material, there was no ground for restraining publication in England. In the Court of Appeal Bingham LJ put the matter as follows:

> 'Of course there will be those in this country who are still unaware of the contents of *Spycatcher*. Some people are impermeable to information or wholly out of touch with the topical subjects of the day. But anyone with the slightest interest in the subject matter of *Spycatcher* is likely either to have read the book or to be aware of its contents. It is in my view a conclusive answer to this claim that the confidentiality the Attorney General seeks to protect, through no act of the newspapers, no longer exists. I do not accept that an action for breach of confidence against third parties can succeed in those circumstances, whatever the position as between confider and confidant. The same conclusion can be put another way. I do not think that the editors of these newspapers can be said to be subject to a duty in conscience not to publish material which is freely available in the marketplace and publishable by other newspaper editors the world over.' (See [1988] 3 All ER 545 at 631, [1990] 1 AC 109 at 224.)

[45] The speeches in the House of Lords were to the same effect.

[46] The position can be summarised as follows. The Crown has no right to restrain a newspaper from publishing information about government unless; (i) disclosure of the information will be contrary to the public interest, and (ii) the information has not already been disclosed. I now propose to consider the judgment below in the light of these principles.

THE IMPLICATIONS OF THE JUDGMENT BELOW

[47] Silber J observed, in a passage from his judgment from which I have already quoted, that there was no limitation on the subject matter of the material covered by the injunction against Associated Newspapers. He went on to note that the injunction against Mr Shayler probably covered matters other than those affecting national security, including 'well-known facts'. It follows that the terms of the interlocutory injunctions extended beyond the categories of information that the Crown was entitled to require should remain confidential.

[48] In particular, Silber J held that the terms of the injunctions prohibited Mr Shayler and Associated Newspapers from publishing matter that had previously been published, and that for other newspapers to do this in the knowledge of the terms of the injunctions was to commit contempt of court. If this is correct, by endorsing the terms of the injunction to which Associated Newspapers submitted by consent, the court in effect made it a criminal offence for newspapers to publish matter which they would otherwise have been lawfully entitled to publish. It is true that the Attorney General agreed with Associated Newspapers a mechanism whereby the draconian effect of the injunction would be mitigated. The Attorney General could release information from the scope of the injunction by stating in writing that the Crown did not seek to restrain publication of the information in question. Furthermore a newspaper could always apply to the court to be released from the restraint of the injunction in relation to any particular information. None the less, if the judgment below is correct, the effect of the injunctions granted by Hooper J was to place a significant fetter on the right which the press would otherwise have enjoyed to republish matter that was in the public domain. It is

a time to turn to the 'Spycatcher' contempt proceedings to see whether they lead to this result.

THE 'SPYCATCHER' CONTEMPT PROCEEDINGS

[49] The 'Spycatcher' contempt proceedings flowed from an interlocutory injunction ordered by Millett J in the injunction proceedings on 11 July 1986 b against the Observer and Guardian newspapers in the following terms:

> 'The defendants and each of them be restrained until trial or further order from doing whether by himself or itself or by his or its servants or agents or any of them or otherwise howsoever the following acts or any of them that is to say: (1) Disclosing or publishing or causing; or permitting to be c disclosed or published to any person any information obtained by Peter Maurice Wright in his capacity as a member of the British Security Service and which they know or have reasonable grounds to believe to have come or been obtained whether directly or indirectly from the said Peter Maurice Wright.'

d [50] On 27 April 1987 the Independent published articles which had been obtained from Mr Wright's manuscript of *Spycatcher*, which was at this point of time still unpublished anywhere in the world. Similar articles were published in the Evening Standard and the Daily News. The Attorney General moved to have the publishers and editors of these three newspapers committed for contempt.

[51] A preliminary point of law was argued before Browne-Wilkinson V-C in e the following terms:

> 'Whether a publication made in the knowledge of an outstanding Injunction against another party and which if made by that other party would be in breach thereof, constitutes a criminal contempt of Court upon the footing that it assaults or interferes with the process of Justice in relation f to the said Injunction.' (See *A-G v Newspaper Publishing plc* [1987] 3 All ER 276 at 281, [1988] Ch 333 at 340.)

[52] Browne-Wilkinson V-C answered this question in the negative. He said:

> 'I have reached the conclusion that it is not. So to hold would be to subvert g the basic principles of our civil law and introduce into it uncertainty and unfairness. English civil courts act in personam, that is to say they adjudicate upon disputes between the parties to an action and make orders against those parties only. In certain instances where the court has assumed the care and administration of a person or property, the court does make orders which, in one sense, operate in rem. Any interference with the person or the h property being administered constitutes a contempt of court: for example, acts in relation to a ward of court, a ship subject to attachment or property of which the court has appointed a receiver. But in other cases so far as I am aware injunctions can only properly be made to restrain a defendant to the proceedings, as opposed to a third party, from doing certain acts: see j *Marengo v Daily Sketch and Sunday Graphic Ltd* [1948] 1 All ER 406 and *X CC v A* ([1985] 1 All ER 53, sub nom *Re X (a minor) (wardship: injunction)* [1984] 1 WLR 142). Even a declaration made by a court is not binding on persons who are not parties to the suit. In my judgment this is the basis of the present state of the law that, for a third party, C, to be liable for contempt, the acts complained of must constitute a breach of the actual terms of the order. The Attorney General's contention, if correct, strikes at the root of this basic principle.

An order of the court would, in effect, operate in rem, ie be enforceable against everyone who had notice of it. The practical implications of this in ordinary civil litigation would be far reaching and in many cases unjust.' (See [1987] 3 All ER 276 at 286–287, [1988] Ch 333 at 347.)

[53] He went on, however, to express concern about this conclusion:

'There ought to be some sanction against the publication of matters which prejudice national security and the decision as to what does prejudice national security should not be left to the judgment of the editors of individual newspapers. I had assumed that the Official Secrets Act 1911 to 1936 provided the necessary sanction. If it does not, then it is for Parliament, if it thinks fit, to provide the necessary sanction by providing a public law remedy linked directly to the protection of public rights. Private rights should not be bolstered by a distortion of the law of contempt in an attempt to produce a judge-made public law protecting official secrets.' (See [1987] 3 All ER 276 at 288–289, [1988] Ch 333 at 349–350.)

[54] The Court of Appeal reversed this decision. Dealing with Browne-Wilkinson V-C's expression of concern, Donaldson MR said:

'Whilst I agree that there ought to be some sanction against the publication of matters which prejudice national security, I should like to re-emphasise with all the power at my command that this case is not primarily about national security or official secrets. It is about the right of private citizens and public authorities to seek and obtain the protection of the courts for confidential information which they claim to be their property.' (See [1987] 3 All ER 276 at 293, [1988] Ch 333 at 361.)

[55] The Court of Appeal held that the terms of the injunction granted in the injunction proceedings did not bind newspapers which were not party to those proceedings. None the less the injunctions were ordered for the purpose of administering justice in those proceedings and in order to preserve the confidentiality of the subject matter of those proceedings until trial. Disclosure of the matter that the court had intended should remain confidential was an interference in the administration of justice which destroyed the very subject matter of the proceedings. It was for that reason that it constituted a contempt of court.

[56] In the course of their judgments the Court of Appeal considered three decisions in which third parties had been held in contempt of court for committing acts which had been forbidden by an injunction ordered against the defendant in the action. These decisions featured more prominently in the judgments that were subsequently delivered by the House of Lords, and it is convenient to refer to them at this stage.

[57] In *Lord Wellesley v Earl of Mornington* (1848) 11 Beav 180, 50 ER 785, an injunction had been ordered restraining the Earl from cutting down certain trees. This was a final, not an interlocutory order. The Earl's land agent, a Mr Batley, cut down the trees. The plaintiff moved to commit Mr Batley for contempt for breach of the order. The motion failed on the ground that Mr Batley was not bound by the order. The plaintiff then brought a second motion ((1848) 11 Beav 181, 50 ER 786) seeking to commit Mr Batley for contempt in knowingly assisting in the breach of the order. Lord Langdale MR ruled that he was entitled to this relief, for Mr Batley was in contempt for—

a 'intermeddling in these matters ... *Batley* in the position in which he was, and knowing the duty of the Earl of *Mornington*, ought to have taken care not to do any acts, in violation of the order of the Court.' (See (1848) 11 Beav 181 at 183, 50 ER 786 at 787.)

[58] In *Seaward v Paterson* [1897] 1 Ch 545, [1895–9] All ER Rep 1127 the plaintiff obtained an injunction restraining the defendant, who was his tenant, b from interfering with the quiet enjoyment of the plaintiff and other tenants living in the vicinity of the demised premises. Once again the injunction was a permanent injunction. The plaintiff successfully moved to commit for contempt one Murray who had assisted in the holding of a boxing match on the premises. On appeal the order was upheld. The basis of Murray's liability was stated by c each of the judges to be the aiding and abetting of the breach of the injunction ([1897] 1 Ch 545 at 554, 557, 560, [1895–9] All ER Rep 1127 at 1130, 1132, 1135), but passages in the judgment of Lindley LJ suggested that there might be a wider principle in play. Thus he said:

'A motion to commit a man for breach of an injunction, which is d technically wrong unless he is bound by the injunction, is one thing; and a motion to commit a man for contempt of Court, not because he is bound by the injunction by being a party to the cause, but because he is conducting himself so as to obstruct the course of justice, is another and a totally different thing. The difference is very marked. In the one case the party who is bound by the injunction is proceeded against for the purpose of enforcing e the order of the Court for the benefit of the person who got it. In the other case the Court will not allow its process to be set at naught and treated with contempt.' (See [1897] 1 Ch 545 at 555–556, [1895–9] All ER Rep 1127 at 1131.)

[59] Finally, in *Z Ltd v A* [1982] 1 All ER 556, [1982] QB 558 the Court of Appeal had to consider the basis upon which a bank could be required to freeze the funds f of a defendant against whom a Mareva injunction had been ordered. Lord Denning MR answered the question:

'The juristic principle is therefore this. As soon as the bank is given notice of the Mareva injunction, it must freeze the defendant's bank account. It must not allow any drawings to be made on it, neither by cheques drawn before g the injunction nor by those drawn after it. The reason is because, if it allowed any such drawings, it would be obstructing the course of justice, as prescribed by the court which granted the injunction, and it would be guilty of a contempt of court. I have confined my observations to banks and bank accounts. But the same applies to any specific asset held by a bank for safe h custody on behalf of the defendant, be it jewellery, stamps, or anything else, and to any other person who holds any other asset of the defendants. If the asset is covered by the terms of Mareva injunction, that other person must not hand it over to the defendant or do anything to enable him to dispose of it. He must hold it pending further order.' (See [1982] 1 All ER 556 at 563, j [1982] QB 558 at 574.)

[60] Eveleigh LJ said:

'I think that the following propositions may be stated as to the consequences which ensue when there are acts or omissions which are contrary to the terms of an injunction. (1) The person against whom the order is made will be liable for contempt of court if he acts in breach of the order after having notice of it. (2) A third party will also be liable if he knowingly assists in the breach, that is to say if knowing the terms of the injunction he wilfully assists the person to whom it was directed to disobey it. This will be so whether or not the person enjoined has had notice of the injunction. The first proposition is clear enough. As to the second, however, it was submitted that until the defendant had notice of the injunction nothing done by the bank could amount to contempt of court. Also two opposing views were canvassed (I use this expression as the arguments were not strictly contentious) as to the extent to which mens rea was a necessary ingredient in determining the bank's responsibility to the court. I will give my reasons for the second proposition and take first the question of prior notice to the defendant. It was argued that the liability of a third party arose because he was treated as aiding and abetting the defendant (ie he was an accessory) and as the defendant could himself not be in breach unless he had notice it followed that there was no offence to which the third party could be an accessory. In my opinion this argument misunderstands the true nature of the liability of the third party. He is liable for contempt of court committed by himself. It is true that his conduct may very often be seen as possessing a dual character of contempt of court by himself and aiding and abetting the contempt by another, but the conduct will always amount to contempt of court by himself. It will be conduct which knowingly interferes with the administration of justice causing the order of the court to be thwarted.' (See [1982] 1 All ER 556 at 566–567, [1982] QB 558 at 578.)

[61] Kerr LJ ([1982] 1 All ER 556 at 572, [1982] QB 558 at 586) remarked that all third parties were bound by the terms of a Mareva injunction as soon as they had notice of it without exploring the jurisprudential basis for this.

[62] Returning to the 'Spycatcher' case, Donaldson MR (*A-G v Newspaper Publishing plc* [1987] 3 All ER 276 at 298, [1988] Ch 333 at 367) relied on *Lord Wellesley*'s case in support of the general proposition that those who interfere with the due administration of justice may be liable to be proceeded against on that account. Lloyd LJ ([1987] 3 All ER 276 at 305–306, [1988] Ch 333 at 377) thought all three cases 'decided, and decided only, that a person may be liable in contempt if, with knowledge of the order, he aids and abets a breach of the order by the person enjoined'. Balcombe LJ ([1987] 3 All ER 276 at 311–312, [1988] Ch 333 at 384–385) was of the same view. He added:

'There is no English authority which establishes that it is a contempt of court, in the sense of knowingly interfering with the course of justice, for a person who is not prohibited by an order to do something which is forbidden by the order, unless he is "aiding and abetting" the person named in the order.' (See [1987] 3 All ER 276 at 312, [1988] Ch 333 at 385.)

[63] It is clear from the judgments of all three members of the Court of Appeal that the reason why they found that a third party could be in contempt for publishing matter the subject of an interlocutory injunction was the very fact that the injunction was *interlocutory*. The gravamen of the offence was knowing interference with the manner in which the court had ordered that the trial process should be conducted.

[64] Thus Donaldson MR observed:

'Knowledge of how the court is administering, or intends to administer, justice is of the essence of the unlawfulness of conduct which interferes with a that administration, whether or not that conduct consists of disobedience to an order.' (See [1987] 3 All ER 276 at 300, [1988] Ch 333 at 370.)

[**65**] He added:

'Here the newspapers without doubt have interfered with the administration of justice by rendering the trial of the government's claim against the Guardian b and the Observer less effective.' (See [1987] 3 All ER 276 at 303, [1988] Ch 333 at 373.)

[**66**] He summarised his conclusions as follows:

'I can summarise the position very shortly. (1) Confidential information, c whatever its nature (personal, financial, technical or security) has one essential common characteristic. It is *irremediably* damaged in its confidential character by every publication and the more widespread the publication, the greater the damage. (2) If a prima facie claim to confidentiality can be established, but this is opposed by a claim of a right to publish, whether on grounds of the public interest or otherwise, these opposing and wholly d inconsistent claims must be evaluated and balanced the one against the other. (3) The public interest in ensuring that disputes are resolved justly and by due process of law may require a different balance to be struck at different stages. Thus, pending the trial of the action, the balance will normally come down in favour of preserving confidentiality, for the very e obvious reason that, if this is not done and publication is permitted, there will be nothing left to have a trial about. (4) It is for the courts, and not for either of the opposing parties, to decide where, in the public interest, that balance lies. (5) Third parties (strangers to the action) who know that the court has made orders or accepted undertakings designed to protect the confidentiality of the information pending the trial, commit a serious offence against justice f itself if they take action which will damage or destroy the confidentiality which the court is seeking to protect and so render the due process of law ineffectual. (6) If such third parties, having a legitimate interest in so doing, wish to contest the court's decision to protect the confidentiality of the information on any grounds, including in particular that they have special rights or interests of which account has not been taken, they should apply to g the court which will hear them and make any modification of its orders which may be appropriate. This is a well-established procedure which works speedily and well in the context of ex parte orders such as those made in the exercise of the Mareva and Anton Piller jurisdictions. Similarly they should apply to the court if they have doubts whether the action which they h contemplate taking is lawful. (7) It is for the courts, and not for third parties, to decide whether, balancing competing public and private interests including those of the third parties, confidentiality should continue to be preserved at any particular time.' (See [1987] 3 All ER 276 at 304, [1988] Ch 333 at 375; Donaldson MR's emphasis.)

j [**67**] Lloyd LJ held:

'But the question here is not whether a third party is bound by the injunction, but whether he can be liable for contempt even though he is *not* bound by the injunction. He cannot be liable in contempt for breach of an order to which he is not a party; nor, on the facts of the present case, could the respondents be liable for aiding and abetting a breach. But it does not follow that they may not be liable for interfering with the course of justice … I would accept that not all acts which are calculated to interfere with the course of justice will necessarily ground a charge of contempt. The act must be sufficiently serious and sufficiently closely connected with the particular proceedings. But in the present case the conduct relied on by the Attorney General is not marginal. It is not a mere pre-judging of the issue to be decided in the particular proceedings. It is not a mere usurpation of the court's function. It is the destruction, in whole or in part, of the subject matter of the action itself. The central issue in the *Observer/Guardian* action is whether the Guardian should be restrained from publishing confidential information attributable to Mr Wright. Once the information has been published by another newspaper, the confidentiality evaporates. The point of the action is gone. It is difficult to imagine a more obvious and more serious interference with the course of justice than to destroy the thing in dispute.' (See [1987] 3 All ER 276 at 306–307, [1988] Ch 333 at 378; Lloyd LJ's emphasis.)

[68] He added:

'If a third party with knowledge of such an order does something which disables the court from conducting the case in the intended manner, then I see no reason why that should not be regarded as an ordinary interference with the process of justice. The third party would be liable for contempt, subject to proof of mens rea, not because he is in breach of the order, but because he has prevented the court from conducting the proceedings in accordance with its intention.' (See [1987] 3 All ER 276 at 308, [1988] Ch 333 at 380.)

[69] Balcombe LJ, after referring to the preliminary point, as set out at [51] above, added:

'In the course of the argument before us this preliminary point was refined in two particular respects. (i) It was taken to relate only to a case where the injunction in question is designed to preserve the subject matter of the action (in this case confidential information) pending the trial, and the nature of the subject matter is such that, if the injunction is broken, the subject matter will have ceased to exist, thereby rendering any trial between the parties pointless. (ii) The question was modified so as to ask whether such a publication was capable of constituting a criminal contempt of court, it being accepted by the parties that even if the publication was capable of being contempt of court, it would not be such unless the necessary element of intent were present.' (See [1987] 3 All ER 276 at 310, [1988] Ch 333 at 383.)

[70] He expressed ([1987] 3 All ER 276 at 315, [1988] Ch 333 at 389) the view that the court had jurisdiction to grant an injunction binding the world at large in order to preserve the subject matter of an action pending trial.

[71] Leave to appeal to the House of Lords was refused on the ground that the facts should be established before the law received consideration by the House of Lords. Findings of contempt were, in due course made by Morritt J (8 May 1989, unreported) at first instance and by the Court of Appeal ((1990) Times, 28 February). The decision of the Court of Appeal is not reported, but is of significance in the present context because issues of 'actus reus' and 'mens rea' were canvassed in a manner that was not to be repeated in the House of Lords. Before turning to a those issues, however, I propose to move on to the decision of the House of Lords, for that was essentially concerned with an attack on the decision of the Court of Appeal on the preliminary point of law.

THE VITAL ISSUE

[72] When considering the speeches in the House of Lords it is important to b bear in mind the question that lies at the heart of this appeal. I would define that issue as follows.

[73] Where a court orders that specified material is not to be published, will a third party who, with knowledge of the order, publishes the specified material automatically commit a contempt of court, or will contempt only occur if the third party thereby knowingly defeats *the purpose* for which the order was made?

c [74] To answer that question it is necessary to identify the reason for the finding of contempt made by their Lordships.

THE DECISION OF THE HOUSE OF LORDS

[75] In the House of Lords (*A-G v Times Newspapers Ltd* [1991] 2 All ER 398, d [1992] 1 AC 191) the appellants conceded that they had had 'mens rea'. By this I understand that they conceded that they were aware that they were doing precisely what the injunctions had prohibited the defendants from doing, and thus were deemed to have intended that result. The issue was whether this action constituted the 'actus reus' of contempt. The appellants' argument rested, essentially, on the proposition that it was an established principle of English law e that an injunction did not affect a third party unless it could be shown that he had aided and abetted a breach of the injunction by the defendant who was enjoined.

[76] Lord Keith did not make an independent speech, but concurred in the speeches of the other members of the committee.

[77] Lord Brandon of Oakbrook founded his decision very largely on the cases f of *Lord Wellesley v Earl of Mornington* (1848) 11 Beav 180, 181, 50 ER 785, 786, *Seaward v Paterson* [1897] 1 Ch 545, [1895–9] All ER Rep 1127 and *Z Ltd v A* [1982] 1 All ER 556, [1982] QB 558. The conclusion that he drew from these cases appears:

> 'Suppose that there is an action between A and B in which B claims, but A disputes, that B is entitled to demolish A's house and that in that action the g court grants A an interlocutory injunction restraining B from demolishing A's house pending the trial of the action. Suppose further that C, of his own volition and in no way aiding or abetting B, himself demolishes A's house while the action between A and B is still pending. On those facts C would, in my opinion, be committing a contempt of court, because he would be knowingly impeding or interfering with the administration of justice by the h court in the action between A and B. These examples of case 2 show that the test for deciding whether C has committed a contempt of court is whether C has by his conduct knowingly impeded or interfered with the administration of justice by the court in the action between A and B. That was the test applied in each of the three authorities referred to above. It might perhaps j appear that, since each authority was concerned with C aiding and abetting the breach of an injunction granted against B in an action between A and B to which C was not a party, that such aiding and abetting by C is the only kind of conduct on his part which can constitute a contempt of court by him. In my opinion, however, that is not the right conclusion to be reached from those authorities. The ground of decision in each of them was that the knowing impedance of and interference by C with the administration of

justice by the court in the action between A and B, to which C was not a party, was a contempt of court. It was incidental only that the form of conduct which was held to constitute contempt in the three cases concerned was the aiding and abetting of breaches by B of an injunction obtained against him by A. It seems to me, as a matter of principle that, if C's conduct, in knowingly doing acts which would, if done by B, be a breach of the injunction against him, results in impedance to or interference with the administration of justice by the court in the action between A and B, then, so far as the question of C's conduct being a contempt of court is concerned, it cannot make any difference whether such conduct takes the form of aiding and abetting B on the one hand or acting solely of his own volition on the other.' (See [1991] 2 All ER 398 at 405, [1992] 1 AC 191 at 206.)

[78] I would observe that although Lord Brandon takes as his example an interlocutory injunction, his analysis would seem applicable in principle to the situation where a third party defeats the object of the litigation by doing that which the court has expressly forbidden by final injunction at the end of the action. Furthermore, two of the three cases upon which Lord Brandon relied were cases of final injunctions. Yet Lord Brandon ([1991] 2 All ER 398 at 405–406, [1992] 1 AC 191 at 207) went on to make it plain that the defendants had committed the act of contempt because they had, by making public that which the court had ordered should remain private, nullified the purpose of the ongoing trial.

[79] Lord Ackner ([1991] 2 All ER 398 at 410–411, [1992] 1 AC 191 at 212–214) also considered that both *Lord Wellesley*'s case and *Seaward v Paterson* were examples of contempt of court consisting of interference with the course of justice, rather than cases where liability lay simply for aiding and abetting the breach of an injunction by a third party. Lord Ackner in his turn made no reference to the fact that these were cases of final injunctions. He went on to place particular reliance on the *Z Ltd* case. It is implicit in his judgment, having particular regard to the following passage, that he also considered that it was interference with *pending* proceedings that was the essence of the contempt:

'On this brief statement of the essential facts it would seem to me to be a remarkable lacuna in the law of contempt of court, its very function being to prevent interference with the course of justice, if it provided no remedy to deal with the situation which I have described. Whatever would be the point of a court making an order designed to preserve the confidentiality of material, the subject matter of a dispute between A and B, pending the trial of the action, if at the whim of C, the protection afford by the court by its order could be totally dissipated? How then do the appellants seek to justify the existence of what would be a most anomalous situation?' (See [1991] 2 All ER 398 at 409, [1992] 1 AC 191 at 211.)

[80] While Lord Brandon adopted an example of a contempt that involved an interlocutory injunction, Lord Oliver of Alymerton ([1991] 2 All ER 398 at 416, [1992] 1 AC 191 at 219) chose as his example a situation that involved the frustration of a final order. He went on to cite as further examples of such contempt *Lord Wellesley*'s case, *Seaward v Paterson* and the *Z Ltd* case. He also made no reference to the fact that the first two of these cases involved final orders.

[81] Subsequently, however, Lord Oliver ([1991] 2 All ER 398 at 420, [1992] 1 AC 191 at 224) made it plain that, on the facts of the case, the act of contempt a consisted of conduct which prevented the issue between the plaintiff and the defendant being properly and fairly tried:

'If the court has taken into its hands the conduct of the matter to the extent of ordering the interim preservation of the interest of the plaintiff so that the issue between him and the defendant can be properly and fairly tried, it has to be accepted that that is what the court had determined that the interests b of justice require. The gratuitous intervention of a third party intended to result in that purpose being frustrated and the outcome of the trial prejudiced must manifestly interfere with and obstruct what the court has determined to be the interests of justice. Those interests are not dependent upon the scope of the order.'

c [**82**] Lord Jauncey of Tullichettle also referred to the triumvirate of cases mentioned above. He went on to say:

'My Lords, in none of these cases, nor in any other case cited by the appellants, is it stated that in relation to a court order a third party can only d be liable for contempt of court if he aids and abets a person named therein to breach it. In all these cases, however, it is made clear that a third party's liability depends upon the fact that he has interfered with the course of justice; indeed nowhere more clearly than by Lindley LJ in *Seaward v Paterson* [1897] 1 Ch 545, [1895–9] All ER Rep 1127. Given that interference with the course of justice is the basis of a third party's liability for contempt in the e foregoing circumstances I can see no reason in principle for distinguishing the position of a third party who aids and abets a breach of the order and one who intends to and does achieve a similar interference with or frustration of the order by means which do not involve assisting the person named therein to breach it. If a third party by such independent act renders nugatory a court f order of whose existence he is aware, why should he not be liable for contempt as he would be if he had actively assisted the named person to defeat the operation of the order? In both cases the third party has, with knowledge, interfered with the course of justice, and in both cases he should in my view by subject to the same liability.' (See [1991] 2 All ER 398 at 425, [1992] 1 AC 191 at 229–230.)

g [**83**] I can see no basis for restricting these observations, made about a case involving a final order, to the position where the court's order is interlocutory. In a passage, however, Lord Jauncey appeared to suggest that this type of contempt of court was restricted to the interlocutory situation:

h 'I turn to consider whether there is any reason why established principle should not be applied to the situation in this case. I do not accept the proposition that to apply established principles in the foregoing circumstances would effectively be to convert every injunction from an order in personam to an order contra mundum. That proposition ignores the distinction between j the breach of an order by the person named therein and interference with the course of justice resulting from a frustration of the order by the third party. Every injunction is capable of being frustrated by a third party stranger. For example, A obtains an injunction against B trespassing on his land. C's subsequent trespass on A's land, in knowledge of that order, in no way impairs the effect of the order against B. It can only be in a limited type of case that independent action by a third party will have the effect of interfering with the operation of an order to which he is not a party. Cases involving confidential information are obvious examples. If B is restrained pending the trial of an action by A from publishing or otherwise communicating information which is claimed by A to be confidential and his property, it is obvious that publication of the information by C before the trial is likely to render the restraining order nugatory and proceedings abhortive. While in some cases B or C might be members of the media, they might equally well be private individuals as, for example, in a case involving the disclosure of trade secrets by an employee, past or present, to his employer's trade rivals.' (See [1991] 2 All ER 398 at 426–427, [1992] 1 AC 191 at 231.)

WHAT IS THE RATIO?

[84] I asked Mr Crow whether the principle upon which he relied in this case was restricted to the publication of material which was subject to an interlocutory injunction, or whether it extended also to the situation where a court had granted a final injunction against publication. With a degree of hesitation he plumped for the latter. I am not surprised that he did. All too often in these cases, the claimant's object is achieved when an interlocutory injunction is granted and the stage of a substantive hearing is never reached. It seems to me that in ordering an interim injunction in a case such as this the primary object of the court is to prevent what will *arguably* constitute a legal wrong for which damages will not be an adequate remedy. The party against whom the injunction is granted will be in criminal contempt if he breaches the injunction. The effect and, so it seems to me, the primary purpose, of the third party contempt jurisdiction is to render it a criminal offence for any third party who is aware of the injunction to commit the *potential* wrong which the injunction is designed to prevent. That surely is the most serious aspect of the contempt, and the fact that it will at the same time render the litigation pointless is a subsidiary consideration.

[85] Some of the reasoning of the House of Lords might appear to support the following principle. Where the court makes an order prohibiting a defendant from infringing a right, or potential right, of the plaintiff on the ground that damages will not be an adequate remedy, the court thereby rules on the requirement of justice. Any third party who, with knowledge of the injunction, intentionally destroys the plaintiff's right, thereby interferes with the ends of justice and commits a contempt of court.

[86] That principle, however, would run foul of the established principle of English law that an injunction does not bind a third party, a principle acknowledged by both the Court of Appeal and the House of Lords in the 'Spycatcher' case. For this reason the House of Lords judgment cannot support a principle of that width.

[87] I have some difficulty with the reliance placed by the House of Lords on cases where contempt was established in relation to final orders. Notwithstanding these problems, I have reached the following conclusions in relation to the basis of the House of Lords' finding that contempt of court was established in the 'Spycatcher' case. (a) Intentional interference with the manner in which a judge is conducting a trial can amount to a contempt of court. (b) When in the course of a trial a judge makes an order with the purpose of furthering some aspect of the conduct of the trial, a third party who, with knowledge of that purpose, intentionally acts in such a way as to defeat that purpose can be in contempt of court. (c) When a plaintiff brings an action to preserve an alleged right of confidentiality in information and the court makes an order that the information is not to be published pending trial, the purpose of the order is to protect the a confidentiality of the information pending trial. A third party who, with knowledge of the order, publishes the information and thereby destroys its confidentiality will commit a contempt of court. The contempt is committed not because the third party is in breach of the order—the order does not bind the third party. The contempt is committed because the purpose of the judge in making the order is intentionally frustrated with the consequence that the conduct of the trial is disrupted.

b [**88**] The speeches of the House of Lords make it plain that the offence lies not simply in the commission of the act prohibited by the order, but in the effect that the act has of interfering with the conduct of the trial.

THE PURPOSE OF THE ORDER

c [**89**] In the course of his speech in *A-G v Times Newspapers Ltd* [1991] 2 All ER 398, [1992] 1 AC 191, Lord Oliver had this to say about the need to show interference with *the purpose* for which the court makes an order:

> 'For my part, I doubt the value of cataloguing a series of hypothetical circumstances which can do no more than serve as illustrations of conduct d which can or may fall on one side of the line or the other. I think that a more dependable guide is to be found in the way in which the gravamen of the offence is expressed in the respondent's case and which, I think, must be based upon the speeches in this House in the *Leveller Magazine* case (*A-G v Leveller Magazine Ltd* [1979] 1 All ER 745, [1979] AC 440): "The publication … frustrates, thwarts, or *subverts the purpose* of the court's order and thereby e interferes with the due administration of justice in the particular action." "Purpose", in this context, refers, of course, not to the litigant's purpose in obtaining the order or in fighting the action but to the purpose which, in seeking to administer justice between the parties in the particular litigation of which it had become seized, the court was intending to fulfil. Where there f is room for genuine doubt about what the court's purpose is, then the party charged with contempt is likely to escape liability, not because of failure to prove the actus reus but for want of the necessary mens rea, for an intention to frustrate the purpose of the court would be difficult to establish if the purpose itself was not either known or obvious.' (See [1991] 2 All ER 398 at 419–420, [1992] 1 AC 191 at 222–223; Lord Oliver's emphasis.)

g

[**90**] It was on these passages that Mr Price founded his arguments on the 'actus reus' and 'mens rea' of the offence in the present case. I can summarise his arguments as follows.

h THE APPELLANT'S CASE ON THE PURPOSE OF THE COURT'S ORDERS

[**91**] Mr Price argued that the Crown's right against Mr Shayler and Associated Newspapers was to restrain publication of information which was likely to damage national security. It followed that in seeking interlocutory injunctions the Crown's purpose was to prevent, pending the trial, the publication of j information which would be damaging to national security. This purpose must equally have been that of the court in granting the injunctions. The Attorney General had not established that the publication complained of had damaged national security. This meant that he had failed to prove that Mr Steen committed the 'actus reus' of the offence. Furthermore, it was the unchallenged evidence of Mr Steen that he had been anxious to publish nothing that would harm national security and that he had not believed that the publication in question would do so.

Thus the 'mens rea' of the offence was not made out. This argument was very similar to that advanced in the Court of Appeal in the 'Spycatcher' case. a

'ACTUS REUS' AND 'MENS REA' IN THE 'SPYCATCHER' CASE

[92] In the contempt proceedings in the Court of Appeal the appellants challenged the finding both that they had committed the actus reus of contempt and that they had had the mens rea. b

ACTUS REUS

[93] As to the actus reus, it was contended: (1) that the actus reus would not be committed unless, at the end of the day, the publications complained of had actually prejudiced the outcome of the trial; (2) (in the case of one appellant) the publication had no adverse effect because the matter published was already in c the public domain at the time of publication. Fox LJ held (*A-G v Newspaper Publishing plc* (1990) Times, 28 February) that the purpose of the interlocutory injunctions was 'to keep the Wright material out of the public domain pending trial' in order to prevent putting a fair trial *at risk*. He rejected, on the facts, the appellant's submission that the material had already entered the public domain d by the time that the offending publications took place.

[94] Ralph Gibson LJ agreed. He held that the actus reus consisted of the destruction, by publication, of the subject matter of the action, in whole or in part, because this affected the prima facie right of the claimant and interfered with the administration of justice. He made this important observation:

e

> 'It seems to me that the circumstances existing at the date of a third party's publication might be such that the court would hold that the publication could not have the effect of destroying the subject matter of the pending proceedings, in whole or in part, even though the publication consists of information of which publication was prohibited by the injunction. There might have been for example, such prior widespread publication in this f country of the whole of the relevant information that discharge of the injunction by the courts would be inevitable as soon as application to that effect could be got before the court.'

[95] Nicholls LJ held that the purpose of the injunctions was that the material to which they related should remain unpublished until trial. He added: g

> 'I accept that, if the *Spycatcher* book or extracts from it had already been made public by others, not acting in collusion with the Sunday Times, before 12 July to such an extent that the object of the Millett injunctions had already effectively been frustrated, then the Sunday Times publication on 12 July h would not have constituted a contempt. The alleged vice of the Sunday Times publication was that the extracts from *Spycatcher*, set out or summarised in the article, defeated, to that extent, the object of the Millett injunctions. But if the object sought to be achieved by the non-publication orders had already been thwarted by massive publication by others, the Sunday Times publication would have been free from that view.' j

[96] He held, however, that the subject matter of the publication had not entered the public domain at the time of publication, so that the actus reus of contempt was made out.

[97] These passages make it plain that the actus reus of contempt was not the publication of the material covered by the order, but the destruction of the

a confidentiality of the material which it had been the purpose of the injunction to preserve.

MENS REA

[98] Similar arguments were advanced on behalf of both appellants. They had not appreciated that they were affected by the orders that had been made. Nor had b they appreciated that their conduct might interfere with the administration of justice. Their only intention in making the publications in question had been to inform their readers of what Mr Wright was saying in his book. The Court of Appeal rejected these arguments. The appellants had been aware of the terms of the interlocutory injunctions. They must have appreciated that the purpose of those injunctions was to preserve the confidentiality of the Wright material c pending trial. They knew that their actions would defeat that purpose. This was enough, according to established principles of criminal law, to constitute the intention to produce that result. The intention to defeat the purpose that the court had had in granting the injunctions constituted mens rea.

THE NATURE OF THE CONTEMPT ALLEGED AGAINST THE APPELLANT

d [99] The publication that forms the subject matter of the present contempt was of material written specifically for publication in Punch by Mr Shayler. In these circumstances, it seemed to us that it would have been open to the Attorney General to proceed against Punch and Mr Steen on the basis that they had aided and abetted a breach by Mr Shayler of the injunction granted against him. e The Attorney General did not, however, adopt this approach. He relied upon the 'Spycatcher' principle and urged that Punch and Mr Steen had intentionally interfered with the course of justice by defeating the purpose for which the injunctions had been ordered.

THE PURPOSE OF THE INJUNCTIONS

f [100] It has never been disputed that the purpose of the Attorney General in commencing the substantive proceedings and obtaining the interlocutory injunctions was to prevent the publication of material that might be prejudicial to national security. I consider that it is proper to infer that Hooper J had the same ultimate purpose in granting the interlocutory injunctions. The basis of the Crown's claim was the right to restrain the publication of material that was g confidential and whose disclosure would be prejudicial to the national interest. I consider that one must proceed on the assumption that Hooper J intended to protect the Crown's legal entitlement. At the interlocutory stage I believe that the correct approach is to proceed on the basis that Hooper J's purpose in granting the injunctions was to prevent the disclosure of any matter that *arguably* h *risked* harming the national interest. The terms of the interlocutory injunction that he granted against Mr Shayler himself was appropriate for this purpose in that the restraint was restricted to—

> 'information obtained by him in the course of or by virtue of his employment ... which related to, or might be construed as relating to, the j Security Service or its membership or activities or to security or intelligence activities generally.'

[101] The terms of the injunction against Associated Newspapers, by virtue of the addition of the words 'or otherwise', extended the scope of the injunction beyond material that could even arguably be made the subject of a final injunction. I do not agree with Silber J that the purpose of this injunction extended to the

restraint of publication of material which could not possibly be detrimental to the national interest and, in particular, material that had been previously published. That conclusion overlooks the significance of the proviso that the injunction would not apply to: a

'Any information in respect of which the [Attorney General] (whether at the request of the Defendants or any of them or any third party, or of his own motion) makes a statement in writing (either personally or by the Treasury Solicitor) that such information is not information in respect of which the Crown seeks to restrain publication.' b

[102] It seems to me that this proviso to the injunction was intended to provide a mechanism which would distinguish between material disclosure of which would, or might, damage the national interest and material which would not. I can readily appreciate the attraction of such an arrangement as between the parties to an action but a critical issue raised by this appeal is the effect, if any, that such a mechanism has on third parties who are not subject to the order. c

[103] It is the Attorney General's case that the effect of the injunctions was that no newspaper could knowingly publish any matter that fell within the wide terms of the Associated Newspapers injunction without first obtaining clearance from himself or from the court. In my judgment there are a number of objections to this contention. d

[104] It subjects the press to the censorship of the Attorney General. I would comment at this point that the role of the Attorney General in the present proceedings is far from clear. In the 'Spycatcher' contempt proceedings (*A-G v Newspaper Publishing plc* [1987] 3 All ER 276, [1988] Ch 333), Donaldson MR observed that: e

'Although it happens to be the case that the conduct complained of here is said to impinge on the trial of an action in which the Attorney General, acting as a minister and on behalf of the Crown, is the plaintiff, he brings the present proceedings in a quite different capacity independently of the government of the day, namely in that which I have described as "guardian of the public interest in the due administration of justice". In the light of the fact that there has been a change in the holder of the office of Attorney General during the course of the proceedings, it should perhaps also be pointed out that they are brought not by an individual but by "the Attorney General". Consistently with acting in this capacity, the Attorney General's complaint is not that the respondent newspapers and their editors have breached or assisted in the breach of the orders which he obtained in the *Observer/Guardian* action, but that the conduct complained of "was intended or calculated to impede obstruct or prejudice the administration of justice".' (See [1987] 3 All ER 276 at 294–295, [1988] Ch 333 at 362.) f g h

[105] In the House of Lords, Lord Ackner (*A-G v Times Newspapers Ltd* [1991] 2 All ER 398 at 407, [1992] 1 AC 191 at 209), remarked that the Attorney General appeared as respondent 'in his capacity as guardian of the public interest in the due administration of justice'. Yet Lord Oliver remarked: j

'The respondent to this appeal is the Attorney General, but it has to be stressed as was emphasised in both the courts below, that in this case he was in no different position from any other private citizen entitled to preserve the a sanctity of confidential information.' (See [1991] 2 All ER 398 at 422, [1992] 1 AC 191 at 226.)

[106] I did not ask Mr Crow what hat the Attorney General was wearing in this case, but I suspect that he might have had some difficulty in answering that question.

[107] Whatever hat he was wearing, I have difficulty with the proposition that b it was open to the court to render it a criminal offence for a newspaper to fail to obtain clearance from him before publishing material to which there might manifestly be not be the slightest ground of objection.

[108] Such a proposition results in the imposition of a restriction on freedom of the press that is disproportionate to any public interest and thus in breach of c art 10 of the convention.

[109] Such a proposition cannot be reconciled with the duty imposed on the court by s 12(3) of the 1988 Act.

[110] Such a proposition extends the law of contempt beyond the principle that it is an offence intentionally to interfere with the course of justice. Publication of manifestly innocuous material without clearance from the Attorney General d would in no way interfere with the future conduct of the action.

[111] For these reasons I have reached the conclusion that Hooper J's orders did not have the effect that any newspaper which knowingly published anything that fell within the terms of the order and that had not been cleared by the Attorney General would be in contempt of court. Mr Steen and Punch published e a number of articles written by Mr Shayler that fell within the terms of the order. No objection was taken to them by the Attorney General. It must be doubted whether they posed any threat to national security or impediment to the future course of the proceedings between the Attorney General and the defendants to the actions. If they did not, I do not see how their publication can have placed Punch and Mr Steen in contempt of court.

f

ACTUS REUS

[112] When considering whether the publication complained of amounted to the actus reus of contempt of court, Silber J broke it down into two components. One consisted of material that had been previously published. As to this Silber J held that it was the actus reus of contempt of court to publish the material g because it was the purpose of the court in granting the injunction that such material should not be published. For the reasons that I have given, I do not agree with this conclusion. Re-publication of material which had already entered the public domain did not offend against the purpose of the court when granting the injunction. Such re-publication was not the actus reus of contempt of court.

h [113] The more difficult question relates to—

> 'three significant areas in which the claimants contend that there had been no prior publication and this claim does not appear to be disputed. They related first to the identity of the two suspects in relation to the Bishopsgate bombing, second to further information about one of the suspects and third to j the way in which the Security Service surveillance operated.'

[114] Silber J found that publication of this material caused damage and that the Attorney General would not have consented to its publication. He also found that it was noteworthy that no evidence was adduced which showed that national security was in fact damaged by the publication. In my judgment, having regard to these findings, Silber J properly found, under the 'Spycatcher' principle,

that publication of this material constituted the actus reus of contempt of court. It defeated the purpose of the injunction which was to preserve until trial the confidentiality of material whose disclosure *arguably posed a risk* of damaging national security.

MENS REA

[115] It was Mr Steen's evidence that he was anxious not to publish any material which would harm national security and that he did not believe that the material which he published carried the risk of causing such harm. In my judgment this evidence focused on the correct issue of fact so far as mens rea was concerned. To establish contempt, the Attorney General needed to demonstrate knowledge that the publication would interfere with the course of justice by defeating the purpose underlying the injunctions. The Attorney General did not, however, set out to establish this. He set out simply to prove that Mr Steen knew that the publication was one which the defendants to the action were enjoined from making under the terms of the injunctions. For the reasons that I have given, this did not go far enough. When dealing with mens rea, the judge identified 'six factors' that satisfied him that Mr Steen 'knew that the publication of the article was a breach of the injunctions and that he intended to act in breach' of them. The fifth of these was as follows:

> 'Fifth, the second defendant must have appreciated that the disclosure of the three matters, which had not been published before, was a breach of the injunctions. These matters set out in para 58 above and relating to the identity of the two suspects responsible for the Bishopsgate bombing, further information about one of them and the way in which the security service operated were clearly within the injunction and potentially damaging. I cannot accept that that the second defendant did not appreciate and foresee that by publishing this material, he would be in breach of the injunctions.'

[116] I have considered the transcript of the cross-examination of Mr Steen to see whether it lays the ground for a finding that Mr Steen must have appreciated that these three matters had not been published before and that publication of them might arguably be a threat to national security. In my judgment it did not. Mr Steen said that he thought that the Treasury Solicitor was delaying his approval of the publication in order to stifle an article that would be embarrassing to the Security Services. He complained that he had not been told that there was objection to the publication of the names of the two suspects. It was not established to what extent Mr Steen knew that the article contained information not previously published. Indeed, the cross-examination included the following passage:

> '*Q.* But, Mr Steen, if these issues had been canvassed in the press over the previous seven years how can you really have thought that the Treasury Solicitor was trying to stifle the entire article? *A.* Because I was submitting an article that would be published within days of embarrassing publicity for the security services and for the Treasury Solicitor.
>
> *Q.* Re-published is all. The Express had written a very similar article in April of the same year, hadn't it? *A.* Yes.
>
> *Q.* So you were simply rehashing material that had already been out in the public? *A.* Well, sorry, I don't see the point.
>
> *Q.* What I'm asking you, Mr Steen, is why you thought it was necessary to publish on 26th without having received an answer from the Treasury

a Solicitor? There was no urgency for you to publish was there? *A.* I was led to believe that they would be coming back to me on Monday morning anyway, but if you're asking me if it was a stifling exercise, yes, I did consider it was.'

[117] The judge, in the passage from his judgment quoted above, did not expressly state that Mr Steen knew that the three matters referred to were b unpublished and potentially damaging. In so far as that finding is implicit in his comments, I do not consider that the evidence justified the finding.

[118] In summary I accept Mr Price's submission that the Attorney General failed to prove the element of mens rea necessary to establish that Mr Steen was in contempt of court, and for this reason I would allow this appeal.

c

WHERE DOES THIS LEAVE THE LAW?

[119] The principle applied by the House of Lords when finding that contempt of court was established in the 'Spycatcher' case was a broad one. Yet I am not aware that that principle has been invoked since then in any case other than one involving an injunction restraining a threatened breach of confidence. d More particularly the 'Spycatcher' jurisdiction has been invoked where the national security is alleged to be at risk.

[120] In the 'Spycatcher' injunction proceedings (*A-G v Guardian Newspapers Ltd (No 2)* [1988] 3 All ER 545, [1990] 1 AC 109) Scott J observed:

'It is, in my judgment, unacceptable that newspapers and their editors e should be judges in their own cause of the restraints on freedom of the press that the national security may require. It is equally unacceptable that the government's assertion of what national security requires should suffice to decide the limitations that must be imposed on freedom of speech or of the press. I repeat that, in my judgment, there is a balance to be struck and the courts must strike it.' (See [1988] 3 All ER 545 at 570, [1990] 1 AC 109 at 144.)

f

[121] Donaldson MR added this comment:

'Finally, I would agree with Lord Widgery CJ in *A-G v Jonathan Cape Ltd* (*A-G v Jonathan Cape Ltd, A-G v Times Newspapers Ltd* [1975] 3 All ER 484 at 495, [1976] QB 752 at 769) that "the court must have power to deal with g publication which threatens national security". In other words, the Crown, as the embodiment of the nation as a whole, has an enforceable right to the maintenance of confidentiality arising out of the very nature of such information and the consequences of its disclosure without regard to any contract binding the confidant to any relationship between him and the h Crown or to the Official Secrets Act 1911 or any other legislative provision. This special right in the Crown is not relied on in the present proceedings, but it is right that it should be noted and affirmed.' (See [1988] 3 All ER 545 at 595, [1990] 1 AC 109 at 177.)

[122] It may be that where national security is at risk it should be open to the j Crown to obtain an injunction binding on all the world. Balcombe LJ expressed a view to this effect. That is for future debate. It seems to me, however, that the well-established liability in contempt for aiding and abetting breach of an injunction by a defendant goes a long way towards meeting the needs of national security in a case such as the present.

[123] Where someone who has served in the security service threatens to disclose confidential information that is damaging to national security, an

injunction can be obtained against that person restraining the disclosure of such information. If a third party assists the confidant to breach the injunction by publishing information supplied by the confidant, whether directly or indirectly, the third party will be in contempt of court for aiding and abetting the breach of the court order by the confidant. It will not be often that a third party comes into possession of information that has emanated from the confidant and has not yet entered the public domain, but where publication is not one to which the confidant is party.

[124] This appeal demonstrates the limitations of the 'Spycatcher' jurisdiction. It is not easy to draft an interlocutory injunction in terms that go no wider than is necessary to restrain the publication of material in respect of which the claimant has an arguable claim to confidentiality. It is, however, necessary to do this if the terms of the injunction are to equate with the purpose for which the injunction is ordered, namely the preservation of the confidentiality of the material in question. Even then that purpose may be destroyed if, with the passage of time, the information in question is brought within the public domain. Third parties are not directly bound by the terms of such an injunction. If they are to be held liable for the contempt of interfering with the course of justice it must be demonstrated that the disclosure made by them defeated, in whole or in part, the court's purpose in granting the injunction and that they appreciated that it would do so. This will be particularly difficult to demonstrate if the court adopts the approach of ordering injunctions in wide terms, but delegating to the claimant the role of determining what is and what is not to be restrained from publication.

[125] For the reasons that I have given, I would allow this appeal.

SIMON BROWN LJ.

[126] I have read and re-read Lord Phillips of Worth Matravers MR's draft judgment with growing admiration and a recognition of the great contribution it makes to this important and difficult area of our jurisprudence. With much of my Lord's analysis I respectfully agree. Alas, however, I have the misfortune to disagree with his final conclusion on the present appeal. As I understand my Lord's judgment, he regards Mr Steen as plainly guilty of contempt for having aided and abetted Mr Shayler's breach of the injunction against him—a contempt not in fact alleged—but not guilty of the 'Spycatcher' form of contempt which *was* alleged. Whilst I entirely agree that the simpler and better course here would have been to allege contempt on an aiding and abetting basis, I for my part believe that Silber J was correct to hold Mr Steen in contempt on the basis alleged, albeit I would have rested that conclusion on a somewhat narrower basis than did the judge below.

[127] I gratefully take the facts and arguments as set out in my Lord's judgment and can accordingly indicate the basis of my own limited dissent really very shortly. First let me briefly summarise those of Lord Phillips MR's central conclusions with which I respectfully agree. First, I agree with his analysis (at [87] above) of the ratio to be derived from their Lordships' speeches in the House of Lords in *A-G v Times Newspapers Ltd* [1991] 2 All ER 398, [1992] 1 AC 191 (the 'Spycatcher' case) of the finding of contempt of court against the Sunday Times: the contemnors' mens rea consisted of their intention to frustrate the court's purpose in making the interlocutory order forbidding publication of the relevant information pending trial, namely the interim protection of its confidentiality. Whether or not the ratio must logically stretch to encompass final orders too (as a appears implicit in certain of the speeches) can be left over for decision in another case: the present injunctions were interlocutory.

[128] Secondly, I agree with my Lord's conclusion (at [112] above) that re-publication of material in the present case which had already entered the public domain did not offend the court's purpose when granting the injunction and did not, therefore, constitute the actus reus of contempt. I would note only b that, for the material to have entered the public domain, it would have had to be subject to extensive and not merely cursory publication—see the judgments of the Court of Appeal in the 'Spycatcher' contempt proceedings (*A-G v Newspaper Publishing plc* (1990) Times, 28 February), referred to in [94] and [95] above.

[129] Third, I agree with my Lord's conclusion (at [100] and [114] above) that the publication complained of constituted the actus reus of contempt, namely the c defeat of the court's purpose in having granted these injunctions which was to preserve until trial the confidentiality of material whose disclosure 'arguably posed a risk of damaging national security'.

[130] The critical question, therefore, with regard to mens rea was whether Mr Steen knew that such had been the court's purpose in granting the injunctions d and that his publication would defeat it. My Lord concludes that that was something the Attorney General never even set out to establish and that he instead contented himself merely with proving that Mr Steen knew the publication to be one which Associated Newspapers Ltd for their part were enjoined from making. This is the narrow but ultimately critical point at which I depart from my Lord's reasoning. As my Lord's judgment notes (at [23] above), the e Attorney General's case was not only that the purpose of the injunctions was to prevent publication until the court could rule on whether or not publication was lawful (which I take to include preserving until trial the confidentiality of material whose disclosure arguably threatened national security) but also that such purpose 'appeared clearly from their express terms'. The object of the first f proviso to these injunctions—the provision for written clearance by the Attorney General in respect of any particular information upon anyone's application—must surely have been obvious. It was a mechanism whereby national security could be safeguarded consistently with the tempering of an otherwise absolute pre-trial ban on publication. I accept that the Attorney General could not properly have withheld consent to the publication of 'manifestly innocuous material' (at [110] g above) unless perhaps he had sought to justify this on the basis that no one should be permitted to aid and abet a Crown servant breach his personal obligation of confidentiality (see Lord Keith of Kinkel's speech in the 'Spycatcher' case, cited at [41] above, with regard to the position arising where the third party is *not* 'unconnected with the particular confidant').

h **[131]** I cannot accept, however, that a provision of this character is intrinsically objectionable, nor that the Attorney General could not properly have refused his consent to the three specific aspects of this publication identified in [113] of my Lord's judgment (citing para 58 of the judgment below) as at the very least putting national security at risk. True it may well be, as Mr Steen protests, j that he had no *intention* of endangering national security and did not think he was doing so. That, however, is not the point. As he himself candidly admitted, he was not qualified to make that kind of judgment. If, as I would hold, he cannot have failed to appreciate that it was for this very reason that, pending a trial at which the court could have ruled on the substantive question, there was a bar on publication unless only the Attorney General consented to it, then he was guilty of the contempt alleged against him: he intended to take upon himself the responsibility for determining whether national security was risked and thereby he thwarted the court's intention. *a*

[132] I would have dismissed the appeal.

LONGMORE LJ.

[133] It has long been the law that if an order of the court is made in proceedings between two parties, a third party who aids or assists either party in the breach of such an order will be liable for contempt of court. It is, on the face of it, not so obvious that a person can be in contempt of court if, apart from any aiding and abetting, he intentionally does an act which frustrates, thwarts or subverts the purpose of an order of the court made in proceedings between two other parties. *A-G v Times Newspapers Ltd* [1991] 2 All ER 398, [1992] 1 AC 191 did, however, hold that a third party can be in contempt of court in such a case if he knowingly does an act which subverts the purpose of such an order. *b* *c*

[134] For the Attorney General to invoke this jurisdiction he must prove not only actual subversion of the purpose of the court's order but an intention to subvert that purpose. That presupposes that the third party must know what the purpose of the court order is. As Lord Oliver of Aylmerton observed: *d*

> 'Where there is room for genuine doubt about what the court's purpose is, then the party charged with contempt is likely to escape liability, not because of failure to prove the actus reus but for want of the necessary mens rea, for an intention to frustrate the purpose of the court would be difficult to establish if the purpose itself was not either known or obvious.' (See [1991] 2 All ER 398 at 420, [1992] 1 AC 191 at 223.) *e*

[135] In the present case the order made by Hooper J against Associated Newspapers Ltd by consent was that they were to be restrained until further order from publishing any information obtained by David Shayler in the course of or as a result of his employment as a member of the security service, whether in relation to the work of or in support of security or intelligence services or otherwise. *f*

[136] Both this order and the order made by Hooper J against Mr Shayler had a proviso that it did not apply to any information in respect of which the Attorney General made a statement in writing that such information was not information in respect of which the Crown sought to restrain publication. *g*

[137] It is not easy to say whether the purpose of the order of Hooper J was to restrain until trial the publication of any information originating from Mr Shayler or only to restrain information which endangered national security. It is agreed that any final order could only restrain the latter information but it is argued that the purpose of the interim order pending trial was to prevent publication of any information derived from Mr Shayler until the trial had taken place. I have come to the conclusion that the purpose of the order was to prevent publication, before trial, of any information derived from Mr Shayler which was not already in the public domain. *h*

[138] In these circumstances I agree with Lord Phillips of Worth Matravers MR that the actus reus of the contempt of court has been committed by Mr Steen but I am not satisfied he had the necessary mens rea. Mr Steen contended that he thought the purpose of the court order was to restrain publication of material dangerous to national security and that he had no intention to publish any such information. In the light of the inclusion of the proviso in the order made against Mr Shayler, I can well understand that Mr Steen might have thought that the *j*

a purpose of the order was to restrain material dangerous to national security and I do not consider the Attorney General has, therefore, established the necessary mens rea in this case. I too would allow the appeal.

Appeal allowed.

Kate O'Hanlon Barrister.

R v City of Westminster Housing Benefit Review Board, ex parte Mehanne

[2001] UKHL/11

HOUSE OF LORDS

LORD BINGHAM OF CORNHILL, LORD BROWNE-WILKINSON, LORD HOPE OF CRAIGHEAD, LORD HUTTON AND LORD HOBHOUSE OF WOODBOROUGH

1 FEBRUARY, 8 MARCH 2001

Social security – Housing benefit – Assessment – Assessment of amount by which eligible rent to be reduced when rent payable by claimant unreasonably high in comparison with suitable alternative accommodation – Whether claimant's personal circumstances relevant in assessing amount of reduction – Housing Benefit (General) Regulations 1987, reg 11(2).

In December 1995 M and his wife, who was then in the very early stages of pregnancy, moved into a flat on an assured shorthold tenancy at a weekly rent of £174·51. M, who was an asylum seeker, applied to the local authority for housing benefit. Under reg 11(2)[a] of the Housing Benefit (General) Regulations 1987 (as in force on 1 January 1996), an authority was required to consider whether the rent payable by a claimant for his dwelling was unreasonably high by comparison with rent payable in respect of suitable alternative accommodation elsewhere. Reg 11(2) further provided that where it appeared to the authority that the rent was unreasonably high, it 'shall ... treat the claimant's eligible rent as reduced by such amount as it considered appropriate having regard in particular to the cost of suitable alternative accommodation elsewhere'. The authority concluded that the rent was unreasonably high in comparison with rent payable for suitable alternative accommodation, and issued a determination under reg 11(2) that the eligible rent should be treated as reduced to £150. M challenged that determination before the review board, seeking to rely on his wife's pregnancy; the reduced rate of income support receivable by him as an asylum seeker; his greater vulnerability to eviction attributable to his having falsely represented, when obtaining his tenancy, that he was not dependent on housing benefit; and the authority's obligation to house him if the shortfall in housing benefit resulted in his eviction and he was unable to obtain suitable accommodation elsewhere. The review board concluded that £150 per week represented a fair approximation of the rent payable for suitable alternative accommodation, and that it was not entitled to take account of the features relied upon by M when considering the appropriate amount by which to treat the eligible rent as reduced. It therefore affirmed the authority's decision, and M applied for judicial review. The deputy judge dismissed the application, holding that a claimant's personal circumstances were not relevant when considering the amount of the reduction. The Court of Appeal allowed M's appeal, and the review board appealed to the House of Lords.

Held – When considering, under reg 11(2) of the 1987 regulations, the amount by which it was appropriate to treat the eligible rent as reduced, a local authority or review board could take account of the claimant's personal circumstances (so

a Regulation 11, so far as material, is set out at [4], post a far as relevant to his housing situation). The amount of the reduction was not automatic or mandatory: it was by such amount as was considered 'appropriate'. That was the language of discretion rather than of an obligation always to make a reduction in the eligible rent by the full amount of the difference between the rent and the cost of suitable alternative accommodation. Nor did the use of the expression 'in particular' limit the range of circumstances to be considered in b determining the amount of reduction in the eligible rent or exclude all consideration of factors other than the factor particularly identified, namely the cost of suitable alternative accommodation. That factor was singled out for special mention and was thereby given the status of a mandatory consideration which carried most weight in making a decision on the amount of the recommendation. However, other factors could be taken into account in c determining the amount of the reduction, so long as they were reasonably (or properly) regarded as relevant. It was for the decision making body to decide how much importance to attach, or how much weight to give, to each of the other factors. In the instant case, the review board could take into account the pregnancy of M's wife, M's difficulty in finding other accommodation and the consequences d of having to move as a result of the reduction in the eligible rent. Those factors were not irrelevant personal or financial circumstances of M. They were all relevant to his housing situation rather than, for example, to his ability to pay the rent. Accordingly, the appeal would be dismissed and the matter remitted to a differently constituted review board for reconsideration (see [10], [13]–[15] and [27]–[30], post).

e Decision of the Court of Appeal [1999] 2 All ER 317 affirmed.

Notes

For housing benefit in general, see 22 *Halsbury's Laws* (4th edn reissue) para 134.

For the Housing Benefit (General) Regulations 1987, reg 11, see 10 *Halsbury's Statutory Instruments* (1998 issue) 141.

f

Cases referred to in opinions

R v Brent London BC, ex p Connery [1990] 2 All ER 353.

R v Housing Benefit Review Board for East Devon DC, ex p Gibson (1993) 25 HLR 487, CA.

R v Waltham Forest London BC, ex p Holder (1996) 29 HLR 71.

g

Appeal

The Housing Benefit Review Board for the City of Westminster appealed with permission of the Appeal Committee of the House of Lords given on 7 December 1999 from the decision of the Court of Appeal (Stuart-Smith, Thorpe and h Mummery LJJ) on 21 December 1998 ([1999] 2 All ER 317, [2000] 1 WLR 16) allowing an appeal by the respondent, Fadi Mehanne, from the decision of Gerald Moriarty QC, sitting as a deputy judge of the High Court on 11 December 1997, dismissing his application for judicial review of the review board's decision on 12 December 1996 confirming the decision of Westminster City Council on 8 March 1996 to restrict his eligible rent for housing benefit purposes to £150 per week j rather than the sum of £174·51 claimed. The facts are set out in the opinion of Lord Bingham of Cornhill.

John McDonnell QC and *Clive Jones* (instructed by *Colin Wilson*) for the review board.

Richard Drabble QC and *Simon Cox* (instructed by *Moss, Beachley, Mullem & Coleman*) for Mr Mehanne.

Their Lordships took time for consideration. a

8 March 2001. The following opinions were delivered.

LORD BINGHAM OF CORNHILL.

[1] My Lords, the issue in this appeal concerns the correct construction of reg 11 of the Housing Benefit (General) Regulations 1987, SI 1987/1971 as in b force on 1 January 1996. This regulation had been the subject of several amendments before that date, and was to be the subject of radical amendment thereafter. This opinion is directed only to that version of the regulation. The question for decision by the House may be expressed in this way: where it appears to a local authority (or a review board) that the rent payable by a claimant c for housing benefit for a dwelling which he occupies is unreasonably high by comparison with the rent payable in respect of suitable alternative accommodation elsewhere, and the authority (or the review board) is required to treat the claimant's eligible rent as reduced by such amount as it considers appropriate, may the authority (or the review board) take account of the claimant's personal circumstances (so far as relevant to his housing situation) when considering the d amount by which it is appropriate to treat his eligible rent as reduced? The deputy judge (Gerald Moriarty QC) gave a negative answer to that question in his judgment (11 December 1997, unreported), which the appellant review board contends was correct. The Court of Appeal (Stuart-Smith, Thorpe and Mummery LJJ) gave an affirmative answer (see [1999] 2 All ER 317, [2000] 1 WLR e 16), which the respondent (Mr Mehanne) seeks to uphold.

[2] At the end of July 1994 Mr Mehanne with his wife arrived in the United Kingdom from Lebanon and claimed asylum. Just under three years later he was recognised as a refugee.

[3] In early December 1995 Mr Mehanne accepted an assured shorthold tenancy of a one-bedroom flat in London W2 at a rent of £174·51 per week. His f wife was in the very early stages of pregnancy with their first child. Mr Mehanne applied for housing benefit from Westminster City Council, the relevant authority. On 10 January 1996 the rent officer determined that the rent Mr Mehanne had agreed to pay was not significantly above a market rent when compared with other properties in London W2. Ten days later the authority's g housing benefit officer determined under reg 11(2) of the 1987 regulations that for the period December 1995 to June 1996 Mr Mehanne's eligible rent should be treated as reduced to £150 per week for the calculation of housing benefit. This determination was made on the basis that the rent was unreasonably high by comparison with the rent payable for suitable alternative accommodation in less h favoured parts of Westminster. Mr Mehanne pursued his rights of review under regs 79(2) and 81 of the 1987 regulations, but without success: on 29 July 1996 a review board considered Mr Mehanne's application and in due course confirmed the authority's decision that his eligible rent should be treated as reduced by £24·51 per week. The decision of the review board was the subject of a written note signed by the chairman dated 15 September 1996, later corrected. The j review board held that £150 per week represented a fair approximation of the rent payable for suitable alternative accommodation in the northern area of Westminster. In reaching its decision the board regarded itself as bound by reg 11(2) to treat Mr Mehanne's eligible rent as reduced and, in considering the appropriate amount by which to treat the eligible rent as reduced, regarded itself as precluded from paying attention to features of his personal circumstances on

a which he sought to rely. Those features were: the pregnancy of Mrs Mehanne; the reduced rate of income support receivable by Mr Mehanne as an asylum seeker; his greater vulnerability to eviction attributable to his having falsely represented, when obtaining his tenancy, that he was not dependent on housing benefit; and the obligation on the local authority to house Mr Mehanne if the shortfall in housing benefit resulted in his eviction and he was unable to obtain b suitable accommodation elsewhere.

[4] Housing benefit is an income-related benefit currently provided under Pt VII of the Social Security Contributions and Benefits Act 1992. Entitlement to benefit is subject to conditions set out in s 130. Under s 134 of the Social Security Administration Act 1992 housing benefit may be granted in the form of a rent c allowance funded and administered by the local authority in whose area the dwelling in question is situated. Under reg 61 of the 1987 regulations the maximum housing benefit may be the full amount of a claimant's eligible rent. A claimant's 'eligible rent' is determined under reg 11, the regulation with which this appeal is concerned. At 1 January 1996, the date material for this appeal, reg 11 (so far as relevant) provided:

d

> '(2) The appropriate authority shall consider—(a) whether by reference to a determination or re-determination made by a rent officer in exercise of a function conferred on him by an order under section 121 of the Housing Act 1988 or, as the case may be, section 70 of the Housing (Scotland) Act 1988, e or otherwise, whether a claimant occupies a dwelling larger than is reasonably required by him and others who also occupy that dwelling (including any non-dependants of his and any person paying rent to him) having regard in particular to suitable alternative accommodation occupied by a household of the same size; or … (c) whether by reference to a determination or re-determination made by a rent officer in exercise of a f function conferred on him by an order under section 121 of the Housing Act 1988 or, as the case may be, section 70 of the Housing (Scotland) Act 1988, or otherwise, whether the rent payable for his dwelling is unreasonably high by comparison with the rent payable in respect of suitable alternative accommodation elsewhere, and, where it appears to the authority that the g dwelling is larger than is reasonably required or that the rent is unreasonably high, the authority shall, subject to paragraphs (3) to (4), treat the claimant's eligible rent, as reduced by such amount as it considers appropriate having regard in particular to the cost of suitable alternative accommodation elsewhere and the claimant's maximum housing benefit shall be calculated h by reference to the eligible rent as so reduced.
>
> (3) If any person to whom paragraph (7) applies—(a) is aged 60 or over; or (b) is incapable of work for the purposes of one or more of the provisions of the Social Security Act, or Part I of the Social Security and Housing Benefit Act 1982 or Part II of the Act; or (bb) is treated as capable of work in j accordance with regulations made under section 171E of the Contributions and Benefits Act; or (c) is a member of the same household as a child or young person for whom he or his partner is responsible, no deduction shall be made under paragraph (2) unless suitable cheaper alternative accommodation is available and the authority considers that, taking into account the relevant factors, it is reasonable to expect the claimant to move from his present accommodation …

(6) For the purposes of this regulation—(a) in deciding what is suitable alternative accommodation, the appropriate authority shall take account of the nature of the alternative accommodation and the facilities provided having regard to the age and state of health of all the persons to whom paragraph (7) applies and, in particular, where a claimant's present dwelling is occupied with security of tenure, accommodation shall not be treated as suitable alternative accommodation unless that accommodation will be occupied on terms which will afford security of tenure reasonably equivalent to that presently enjoyed by the claimant; and (b) the relevant factors in paragraph (3) are the effects of a move to alternative accommodation on—(i) the claimant's prospects of retaining his employment; and (ii) the education of any child or young person referred to in paragraph (3)(c) if such a move were to result in a change of school.

(7) This paragraph applies to the following persons—(a) the claimant; (b) any member of his family …'

[5] Two points emerge clearly from this brief reference to the housing benefit regime. First, it is directed to the humane objective of assisting those of modest means to provide themselves with a roof over their heads. This is, after all, one of the most basic of human needs, and it is not surprisingly accepted as a proper object of public expenditure. But, secondly, such expenditure must be directed to meeting real needs. Thus expenditure may be restricted if a claimant is housed more expensively than necessary, whether because his accommodation is unnecessarily large, or because he is paying more than the market rate for the area in which he lives, or because he could be housed adequately but more economically in similar accommodation in an accessible but less expensive quarter. Special consideration is, however, given to those who are elderly, or unable to work, or who are responsible for a child or young person living with them.

[6] For present purposes it is convenient to describe a rent payable for a dwelling larger than is reasonably required under reg 11(2)(a) or a rent which is unreasonably high under reg 11(2)(c) as 'excess rent'. Mr Mehanne's case was covered by reg 11(2)(c) and his excess rent was the weekly rent of £174·51 which he contracted to pay for his flat in London W2. It is convenient also to describe the cost of suitable accommodation elsewhere as the 'alternative rent'. In Mr Mehanne's case his alternative rent was £150.

[7] There was much common ground between the parties on the construction of reg 11. (1) It was agreed that in a case where reg 11(2) applied and reg 11(3) did not, the local authority was obliged to treat the claimant's eligible rent as reduced. This conclusion was inevitable given the language of para (2)(c): 'the authority shall … treat the claimant's eligible rent, as reduced'. An earlier version of the provision had read: 'the authority may treat the claimant's … eligible rent, as reduced'. The effect of the change was plainly to transmute a permissive power into a mandatory obligation. In the terminology used above, the local authority was required to treat the claimant's excess rent as reduced. (2) It was agreed that where any of the factual conditions in reg 11(3) applied, the local authority might not treat the claimant's excess rent as reduced unless—(a) suitable cheaper alternative accommodation was available, and (b) the authority considered that, taking into account the relevant factors specified in para (6)(b), it was reasonable to expect the claimant to move from his existing accommodation. At the time relevant to this appeal Mr Mehanne did not meet any of the factual conditions in para (3), and he was accordingly unprotected by this paragraph. I

a understood it to be common ground between the parties, as held in *R v Housing Benefit Review Board for East Devon DC, ex p Gibson* (1993) 25 HLR 487 and *R v Waltham Forest London BC, ex p Holder* (1996) 29 HLR 71, that the availability of suitable alternative accommodation to the particular claimant was a relevant consideration under para (3) but not under para (2). (3) It was agreed that in a case where para (2) applied and the local authority was required to treat the b claimant's excess rent as reduced, it might not treat it as reduced to a level below the alternative rent. Schiemann J so held in *R v Brent London BC, ex p Connery* [1990] 2 All ER 353, and this conclusion was not challenged. It would indeed be disturbing if a local authority had power to treat a claimant's eligible rent as reduced below the level of rent payable for suitable alternative accommodation elsewhere. (4) It was agreed that in a case to which para (2) applied the local c authority was not required to determine the claimant's eligible rent by simply reducing his excess rent to his alternative rent. The paragraph could with the utmost simplicity have been drafted so as to have that effect, but such was not the course adopted. The obligation on the local authority was to—

d
> 'treat the claimant's eligible rent, as reduced by such amount as it considers appropriate having regard in particular to the cost of suitable alternative accommodation elsewhere ...'

Thus the duty of the local authority, following ascertainment of the excess rent and the alternative rent, was not to perform the merely mechanical task of e treating the former as reduced to the level of the latter. Instead, the local authority was to exercise a judgment, or, as it is often called, a discretion. The local authority was to treat the excess rent as reduced by some amount, but not to a level below the alternative rent.

[**8**] At that point the common ground between the parties ended and the issue between them arose: in making the judgment required under para (2), to what f matters could the local authority (if it thought it right) have regard other than the cost of suitable alternative accommodation elsewhere (namely the alternative rent, as I have defined it)?

[**9**] The review board's answer, taken from its printed case, was put in these terms:

g
> 'The relevant factors to which an authority may have regard in a [case governed by reg 11 as it stood on 1 January 1996] when determining the amount by which to reduce a claimant's eligible rent ... can only include: (a) factors to which reg 11 itself requires the authority to have regard, that is to say, the cost of suitable alternative accommodation elsewhere and the h sub-factors of which the authority is required by para (6)(a) to take account in deciding what is suitable alternative accommodation and by para (6)(b) to take account when deciding whether it is reasonable to expect a para (3) claimant to move, (b) factors which a local authority is always entitled or required to take into account when considering whether to exercise a j statutory power (like the financial effect of exercising the power on the authority itself—compare the case of *R v Brent London BC, ex p Connery* [1990] 2 All ER 353) and (c) any other factors which may affect the achievement of the objects for which the power has evidently been conferred, namely the prevention of subsidy being wasted either because the claimant is occupying property which is too valuable or because of overcharging and the provision for eligible claimants of rent allowances based on reasonable rents ...'

[10] The first factor mentioned in (a) is expressly referred to as a matter to which regard must be had by the local authority, and it is not controversial. I would also accept that in identifying what alternative accommodation would be suitable for Mr Mehanne some account could be taken of his wife's pregnancy: alternative accommodation elsewhere, otherwise suitable, might for example be regarded as unsuitable if situated at the top of a tall block with no lift. But para (3) did not apply to Mr Mehanne at the relevant time and the question whether it was reasonable to expect him to move was one which would have arisen under para (3) and not expressly under para (2). Mr Drabble QC for Mr Mehanne submitted that the effect of eviction on Mr Mehanne and his wife at that juncture, the difficulty he would experience in paying the alternative rent and the implications for Mr Mehanne and his wife and the local authority of housing them in accommodation for the homeless were all aspects of Mr Mehanne's housing situation to which the local authority could properly have regard, in addition to the alternative rent, when considering by what amount it was appropriate to treat his excess rent as reduced. This submission the review board challenged. Those matters (it was said) had no effect on the level of rent payable and were matters to which no regard could be paid.

[11] The review board's factor (b) in the passage quoted above was not controversial. In *Ex p Connery* Schiemann J held that the state of a local authority's own finances was a relevant matter for the authority to consider when exercising its judgment under para (2), then drafted to confer a permissive power and not to impose a mandatory obligation. Counsel for Mr Mehanne did not contend that this was not a proper matter to consider, only that it was not the only matter which could properly be considered.

[12] The review board's factor (c) adds nothing. It has already been pointed out, and it is obvious, that reg 11 is directed to preventing the waste of public money.

[13] In my opinion the argument advanced on behalf of Mr Mehanne is correct, for essentially the reasons given by Mummery LJ in his judgment:

> '(1) The substitution of "shall" for "may" did not deprive the review board of a discretion as to the *amount* of a reduction in the eligible rent. The amount of the reduction is not automatic or mandatory: it is by such amount "as it considers appropriate". That is the language of discretion rather than of an obligation always to make a reduction in the eligible rent by the full amount of the difference between the rent and the cost of suitable alternative accommodation.
>
> (2) The use of the expression "in particular" does not limit the range of circumstances to be considered in determining the amount of reduction in the eligible rent or exclude all consideration of factors other than the factor particularly identified (ie the cost of suitable alternative accommodation). That factor is singled out for special mention and is thereby given the status of a mandatory consideration which carries the most weight in making a decision on the amount of any reduction in the eligible rent.
>
> (3) Other factors may be taken into account in determining the amount of the reduction, so long as they are reasonably relevant to that decision. It is for the decision-making body to decide how much importance to attach, or how much weight to give, to each of the other factors.
>
> (4) As to the other factors relied on by the applicant in this case the review board may take account of the following relevant factors which were all

a present during the relevant benefit period before the review board: the pregnancy of the applicant's wife, which was known to the review board; the difficulty of the applicant in finding other accommodation and the consequences of having to move from this accommodation as a result of the reduction in the eligible rent (eg duty of the authority to rehouse the homeless). In my view, these are not irrelevant individual, personal or b financial circumstances of the applicant. They are all reasonably relevant to the housing situation of the applicant rather than, for example, to his inability to pay the rent.' (Mummery LJ's emphasis.) (See [1999] 2 All ER 317 at 324–325, [2000] 1 WLR 16 at 24.)

Criticism was made of the expression 'reasonably relevant' but it is obvious that c Mummery LJ meant 'reasonably (or properly) regarded as relevant' and that is the correct test. In the absence of clear language I would be very reluctant to conclude that the local authority or the review board were precluded from considering matters which could affect the mind of a reasonable and fair-minded person when deciding on the level to which a claimant's eligible rent should be d treated as reduced, and the very general language of para (2) gives no ground for inferring that such a constraint was intended.

[14] I would dismiss the appeal. The decision of the review board dated 15 September 1996 (as corrected) should be quashed and the review board should be directed to consider afresh and according to law (by a differently constituted board) Mr Mehanne's request of 26 March 1996 for a further review of the e determination of the City of Westminster dated 8 March 1996. I would order the review board to pay the costs before the House.

LORD BROWNE-WILKINSON.

[15] My Lords, I have had the advantage of reading in draft the speech f prepared by my noble and learned friend Lord Bingham of Cornhill. For the reasons which he gives, I too would dismiss the appeal.

LORD HOPE OF CRAIGHEAD.

[16] My Lords, this appeal is concerned with the amount of the housing benefit to which the respondent, Mr Mehanne, was entitled from December 1995 g to June 1996 for the rent of the one-bedroom flat which he was occupying as his home. Housing benefit is one of the income-related benefits currently provided under Pt VII of the Social Security Contributions and Benefits Act 1992. The detailed provisions affecting entitlement to housing benefit are set out in Pt II of the Housing Benefit (General) Regulations 1987, SI 1987/1971. These regulations h were made under an earlier statute, but they remain in force—albeit subject frequently to amendment. The issue which is raised in this appeal is concerned with reg 11 of the 1987 regulations in the form it was in when Mr Mehanne applied for housing benefit on 8 December 1995.

[17] Regulation 10(1)(a) of the 1987 regulations provides that housing benefit j in the form of a rent allowance is payable in respect of the periodical payments which a person is liable to make in respect of the dwelling which he occupies as his home including payments of rent. Mr Mehanne was occupying his flat under an assured shorthold tenancy, and the rent was £174·51 per week. The rent officer determined that this was not significantly above the market rent for the flat, so the rent which he had to pay was fixed at that amount. This was the claimant's eligible rent for housing benefit purposes. But the local authority's

housing benefit officer was of the opinion that the rent which he had to pay for his flat was unreasonably high by comparison with the rent payable in respect of suitable alternative accommodation elsewhere. That being so, reg 11(2) of the 1987 regulations came into play.

[**18**] Regulation 11(2) provides that where it appears to the authority that the rent payable for the claimant's dwelling is unreasonably high—

> 'the authority shall, subject to paragraphs (3) to (4), treat the claimant's eligible rent, as reduced by such amount as it considers appropriate having regard in particular to the cost of suitable alternative accommodation elsewhere and the claimant's maximum housing benefit shall be calculated by reference to the eligible rent as so reduced.'

[**19**] The word 'shall' in reg 11(2) indicates that, if it appears to the authority that the rent is unreasonably high, the authority must make a deduction from the eligible rent in order to arrive at the amount by reference to which the claimant's maximum housing benefit is to be calculated. It has no discretion in the matter as to whether or not a deduction is to be made. But it does have a discretion as to the amount of that deduction. This is because the rent is to be reduced 'by such amount as it considers appropriate'. The question is, what factors can the authority take into account when deciding the amount by which the rent should be reduced? The answer to this question must be found in the words used by the regulation, read in the light of the purpose for which it was made.

[**20**] The direction which is contained in reg 11(2) is subject to para (3) to (4) of the 1987 regulations. Paragraph (3) applies where the claimant, any member of his family or any member of his extended family as described in para (7) is aged 60 or over, is incapable of work or is a member of the same household as a child or young person for whom he or his partner is responsible. In these cases, to which it is convenient to refer as 'the priority cases', the authority is directed that no deduction shall be made under para (2) unless suitable cheaper alternative accommodation is available and the authority considers that, taking into account the relevant factors mentioned in para (6)(b), it is reasonable to expect the claimant to move from his present accommodation. The relevant factors mentioned in para (6)(b) are the effects of a move to alternative accommodation on the claimant's prospects of retaining his employment and the effects on the education of any child or young person who is a member of the same household if such a move were to result in a change of school.

[**21**] These provisions recognise the hardship that could result if a claimant whose case fell within one of these priority cases were to be forced out of his present accommodation by reason of the fact that the housing benefit which he received was insufficient to enable him to pay the rent. In the priority cases the authority is required by reg 11(3) to eliminate the gap between the claimant's eligible rent and the cost of suitable alternative accommodation elsewhere.

[**22**] Mr McDonnell QC for the authority submitted that the discretion which was given to the authority by reg 11(2) was a limited one, as the only factors which were relevant to the amount of the reduction were: the cost of suitable accommodation elsewhere, which was a factor to which the authority was required by regulation to have regard; those factors which a local authority is always entitled to have regard or to take into account when considering whether or not to exercise a statutory power, such as the financial effect on the authority of doing so; and any other factors which might effect the object for which the power had been conferred, which was to prevent the subsidy being wasted

a because the claimant was occupying property which was too valuable or was being overcharged for it. He said that it was not open to the authority to take into account factors such as those mentioned in reg 11(3) or any other factors which might be said to be, in the words of Mummery LJ in the Court of Appeal, 'reasonably relevant to the housing situation of the applicant' (see [1999] 2 All ER 317 at 325, [2000] 1 WLR 16 at 24).

b [**23**] I confess that I was at first attracted by this argument. Prior to its amendment by the Housing Benefit (General) Amendment Regulations 1991, SI 1991/235 the word used in reg 11(2) was 'may' not 'shall'. The discretion which was previously available to the authority to eliminate the gap by making no deduction at all from the eligible rent has been removed. It seemed to me that, c if it had been the intention to retain the authority's discretion to close the gap in non-priority cases, the logical thing to do would have been to leave it open to the authority, if it thought that this was appropriate, to close the gap entirely as it is required to do in the priority cases by reg 11(3). As it is, the effect of the amendment is that all it can now do is reduce the gap. It seemed to me that there was, perhaps, an indication here that the purpose of the amendment was to alter d the function of reg 11(2) so that the authority could no longer use it to avoid hardship to claimants who fell outside the list of priority cases in reg 11(3). The effect of the amendment would thus be to confine the authority's attention to the effect of the claim on public funds.

[**24**] I have come to be of the opinion, however, that this would be to take too e narrow a view of reg 11(2). I think that the key to the matter lies in the nature of the benefit with which we are concerned in this case and the context in which it is being made available. The benefit is closely related to the functions of the authority under the Housing Acts as the local housing authority. One of the functions of a local housing authority is to secure that advice and information about homelessness and the prevention of homelessness is available free of f charge to any person in its district and to give assistance to those who are homeless or threatened with homelessness (see s 179 of the Housing Act 1996). In *R v Housing Benefit Review Board for East Devon DC, ex p Gibson* (1993) 25 HLR 487 at 493 Bingham MR drew attention to the relevance of this point to the system which has been laid down for housing benefit:

g

> 'It is, as I have already suggested, plain that the procedure is designed to protect the public purse. But it is fair, I think, to infer that the procedure is not designed to produce homelessness, which would be the result if a beneficiary's rent were restricted, so that he could not afford to stay where he was but was unable to find any other accommodation to which he could h be expected to move at the level of rent payable.'

[**25**] As to the wording of the regulation, the extent of the discretion which the authority continues to have under reg 11(2) is indicated by the prohibition in reg 11(3). As Mr Drabble QC for the claimant pointed out, one would expect that j the factors which reg 11(3) says cannot be taken into account in the cases to which it refers would be factors which could be taken into account in reg 11(2) cases. There is nothing in the wording of reg 11(2) which prohibits this approach. And if the reg 11(3) factors can be taken into account, there would seem to be no good reason for excluding other factors which would enable the authority to take account of an individual claimant's housing requirements. This approach would enable the authority to balance the risk of hardship due to homelessness against

undue demands on the public purse resulting from over-generous payments of housing benefit. a

[26] I would also attach importance to the fact that the risk of hardship due to homelessness is inherent in the nature of the exercise which the authority is required by reg 11(2) to carry out. In order to avoid unreasonable demands on the public purse, the authority is required to make a reduction from the eligible rent if the dwelling which the claimant occupies is larger than is reasonably b required or the rent is unreasonably high by comparison with that payable for suitable accommodation elsewhere. The claimant who is subject to this reduction is then faced with a choice. Either he must move to suitable accommodation which is available elsewhere for letting at a rent which will be covered by the amount of his housing benefit, or he must accept the fact that the housing benefit which he receives will fall short of what he needs to pay the rent. c Some claimants will be able to make this choice. Others may not. For them, this may be a choice that cannot be made at all. Suitable alternative accommodation elsewhere may not be available in their area. A move to suitable accommodation in another area may bring with it loss of employment or other forms of very real hardship. And the margin between the rent that has to be paid and the housing d benefit may be such that claimants will find themselves at risk of being evicted because they are genuinely unable to pay the rent when it falls due.

[27] The authority has a statutory duty to rehouse claimants who become homeless. There are likely to be cases where all that is needed to prevent homelessness is a reduction in the gap between the eligible rent and the e alternative rent fixed by the housing benefit officer. Reducing the gap may be enough to enable claimants to meet their obligations and remain in the accommodation which they occupy. An interpretation of reg 11(2) which would disable an authority from reducing the gap between the eligible rent and the housing benefit in cases where to do this would prevent homelessness would seem to be contrary to good sense. It would also, I think, be contrary to the f overall purpose of the 1987 regulations. I would hold that there is nothing in the wording of reg 11(2) which drives one to the conclusion that the authority is so restricted in the discretion which it can exercise.

[28] For these reasons, and those given by my noble and learned friend Lord Bingham of Cornhill, whose speech I have had the advantage of reading in draft g and with which I agree, I too would dismiss the appeal.

LORD HUTTON.

[29] My Lords, I have had the advantage of reading in draft the speech prepared by my noble and learned friend Lord Bingham of Cornhill. For the h reasons which he gives, I too would dismiss the appeal.

LORD HOBHOUSE OF WOODBOROUGH.

[30] My Lords, this appeal has concerned a question of the construction of the Housing Benefit (General) Regulations 1987, SI 1987/1971. Your Lordships are j of the opinion that the review board misconstrued the regulations. Accordingly, I agree that the appeal should be dismissed.

Appeal dismissed.

Celia Fox Barrister.

a

Practice Note

COURT OF APPEAL, CIVIL DIVISION

LORD PHILLIPS OF WORTH MATRAVERS MR

20 FEBRUARY 2001

b

Court of Appeal – Practice – Civil Division – Listing – Short warned list procedure – Introduction of special fixtures list.

LORD PHILLIPS OF WORTH MATRAVERS MR gave the following direction at the sitting of the court.

c

1. This practice note supplements paras 15.7 to 15.9 of the Practice Direction supporting CPR Pt 52 (Practice Direction—Appeals). It sets out the procedure to be adopted in relation to the short warned list and introduces a new subdivision of the Civil Appeals List, namely 'the special fixtures list'.

d

The short warned list

2. As part of its case management functions the court will assign suitable appeals to the short warned list. It will do so where it considers that an appeal can be mastered by an advocate with no previous knowledge of the case, on half a day's notice, or such longer period as the court may direct, for the purpose of listing under para 5.

e

3. Where an appeal has been assigned to the short warned list the parties' solicitors will be notified in writing by the Civil Appeals Office and the time for filing any outstanding bundles may be abridged. It is the duty of solicitors to inform both their advocate and their client that the appeal has been assigned to the short warned list, as soon as such notification is received.

f

4. Any application for the appeal to be removed from the short warned list must be made in writing within 14 days of notification. A supervising Lord Justice, or the master, will consider any such application, which will be granted only for the most compelling reasons.

g

Short warned list appeals to be placed 'on call'

5. From time to time the Civil Appeals listing officer will place appeals from the short warned list, 'on call', from a given date, and the parties' advocate will be informed accordingly. An appeal which is 'on call' may be listed for hearing on half a days notice, or such longer period as the court may direct, as and when gaps in the list occur.

h

6. Where any party's advocate of the first choice is not available a substitute advocate must be instructed immediately. Paragraph 15.9 of the Practice Direction provides that once an appeal is listed, under these arrangements, it becomes the immediate professional duty of the advocate instructed in the appeal, if he is unable to appear at the hearing, to take all practical measures to ensure that his lay client is represented at the hearing, by an advocate who is fully instructed and able to argue the appeal.

j

The special fixtures list

7. The special fixtures list will be created as a subdivision of the 'fixtures list' and will be used to deal with cases that may require special listing arrangements,

such as the need to list a number of cases before the same constitution, in a particular order, during a particular period or at a given location. *a*

8. Where cases are assigned to the special fixtures list the parties' representatives, or the parties if acting in person, will be notified of the particular arrangements that will apply. This notice will give details of the specific period during which a case is scheduled to be heard. Directions may also be given, as necessary, in relation to the filing of any outstanding documents. *b*

9. The listing officer will notify the parties' representatives of the precise hearing date as soon as practicable. While every effort will be made to accommodate counsel's availability, where such special arrangements are engaged, the requirements of the court will necessarily prevail.

Kate O'Hanlon Barrister.

a

Practice Note

SUPREME COURT

LORD WOOLF CJ

12 FEBRUARY 2001

b

Crown Court – Distribution of court business – Classification of offences – Allocation of business within Crown Court – Supplementary directions.

LORD WOOLF CJ gave the following direction at the sitting of the court.

With the concurrence of the Lord Chancellor and pursuant to ss 75(1) and (2) of
c the Supreme Court Act 1981, the directions given on 26 May 1995 in *Practice Note (Crown Court: allocation of court business)* [1995] 2 All ER 900, [1995] 1 WLR 1083 as amended on 30 June 1998 by *Practice Note (Crown Court: allocation of court business: committals for trial)* [1998] 3 All ER 384, [1998] 1 WLR 1244 and further amended on 10 January 2000 by *Practice Direction (Crown Court: allocation of business)* [2000]
d 1 All ER 380, [2000] 1 WLR 203 are hereby amended.

1. Paragraphs 3 and 4 of the section headed 'Allocation of business within the Crown Court' are amended as follows:

> '3. Cases in class 3 may be tried by a High Court judge or, in accordance with general or particular directions given by a presiding judge, by a circuit
> e judge or by a recorder who has attended a Judicial Studies Board Continuation Seminar and has been duly authorised by a presiding judge.
>
> 4. Cases in class 4 may be tried by a High Court judge, a circuit judge or a recorder (including a recorder who has not attended a Continuation Seminar as referred to in para 3 above). A case in class 4 shall not be listed for trial by a High Court judge except with the consent of that judge or of a presiding
> f judge.'

2. These amendments shall take effect immediately.

Kate O'Hanlon Barrister.

Practice Direction

a

FAMILY DIVISION

Practice – Family proceedings – Committal applications – Procedure.

b

1. As from the date of this direction, the Practice Direction—Committal Applications supplemental to RSC Ord 52 (Sch 1 to the CPR) and CCR Ord 29 (Sch 2 to the CPR) (the CPR direction), shall apply to all applications in family proceedings for an order of committal in the same manner and to the same extent as it applies to proceedings governed by the CPR but subject to: (a) the provisions of the Family Proceedings Rules 1991, SI 1991/1247 (the FPR) and the rules applied by those rules namely, the RSC and the CCR in force immediately before 26 April 1999, and (b) the appropriate modifications consequent upon the limited application of the CPR to family proceedings.

c

1.1. In particular, the following modifications apply. (a) Where the alleged contempt is in connection with existing proceedings (other than contempt in the face of the court) or with an order made or an undertaking given in existing proceedings, the committal application shall be made in those proceedings. (b) As required by the FPR, r 7.2, committal applications in the High Court are to be made by summons. In county court proceedings applications are to be made in the manner prescribed by CCR Ord 29. References in the CPR direction to 'claim form' and 'application notice' are to be read accordingly. (c) In instances where the CPR direction requires more information to be provided than is required to be provided under the RSC and the CCR, the court will expect the former to be observed. (d) Having regard to the periods specified in RSC Ord 52, r 3, Ord 32, r 3(2)(a) and CCR Ord 13, r 1(2), the time specified in para 4.2 of the CPR direction shall not apply. Nevertheless, the court will ensure that adequate time is afforded to the respondent for the preparation of his defence. (e) Paragraph 9 of the CPR direction is to be read with para 3 of each of the directions issued on 17 December 1997, entitled *Practice Direction (interim care order: exclusion requirement: arrest)* [1998] 2 All ER 928, [1998] 1 WLR 475 and *Practice Direction (domestic violence: injunction: arrest)* [1998] 2 All ER 927, [1998] 1 WLR 476.

d

e

f

g

2. In any family proceedings (not falling within para 1 above), in which a committal order may be made, including proceedings for the enforcement of an existing order by way of judgment summons or other process, full effect will be given to the Human Rights Act 1998 and to the rights afforded under that Act. In particular, art 6 of the European Convention for the Protection of Human Rights and Fundamental Freedoms (Rome, 4 November 1950; TS 71 (1953); Cmd 8969) (as set out in Sch 1 to the 1998 Act) is fully applicable to such proceedings. Those involved must ensure that in the conduct of the proceedings there is due observance of the 1998 Act in the same manner as if the proceedings fell within the CPR direction.

h

j

3. As with all family proceedings, the CPR costs provisions apply to all committal proceedings.

4. Issued with the approval and concurrence of the Lord Chancellor.

DAME ELIZABETH BUTLER-SLOSS P

16 March 2001

a

R (on the application of McCormick) v Liverpool City Magistrates' Court

R (on the application of L) v Liverpool City Magistrates' Court

b

QUEEN'S BENCH DIVISION, DIVISIONAL COURT

ROSE LJ AND ELIAS J

1, 2 NOVEMBER 2000

c

Criminal law – Costs – Award out of central funds – Defendant acquitted – Whether payment to be made out of central funds only in respect of costs actually paid by defendant – Prosecution of Offences Act 1985, ss 16(6), 20 – Costs in Criminal Cases (General) Regulations 1986, reg 6(2).

d In the first of two cases raising issues on defendant's costs orders under s 16[a] of the Prosecution of Offences Act 1985, the applicant, M, was accused of various criminal offences. He approached a solicitor in May 1998 and signed an agreement on the firm's standard terms which stated that he was responsible for its costs of advising and representing him in any criminal proceedings. He was charged in e October 1998, and applied for legal aid two months later. Subsequently, M was acquitted by the magistrates, and a defendant's costs order was made in his favour. Under s 16(6) of the 1985 Act, such an order was for the payment out of central funds of such amount as the court considered 'reasonably sufficient' to compensate him for any expenses 'properly incurred' by him in the proceedings. M's solicitors applied to recover the costs incurred before the grant of legal aid, f but the clerk to the justices concluded that M had incurred no liability to pay the costs since he had known, when entering into the contract, that he could not make, and would not be expected to make, any payment not covered by public funds. Accordingly, the clerk refused to meet the claim, and M applied for judicial review.

g In the second case, the applicant, L, was also awarded a defendant's costs order after being acquitted of criminal charges. The clerk to the justices refused to make the payment claimed by L's solicitors on the ground that a client was required to have actually paid for the work in question by the Costs in Criminal Cases (General) Regulations 1986, made by the Lord Chancellor under s 20[b] of the 1985 h Act (which gave him the power to make provision for the circumstances in which, and the conditions under which, costs payable out of central funds might be allowed and paid). The clerk derived that conclusion from reg 6(2)[c] which provided that a claim for costs was to be accompanied by 'receipts or other evidence of the applicant's payment of the costs claimed'. Those words had been inserted by amendment into reg 6(2). Prior to the amendment, reg 6(2) had j merely provided that the claim was to be submitted to the appropriate authority in such form and manner as they might direct, and that it was to be accompanied by any receipt or other documents in support of any disbursement claimed.

a Section 16, so far as material, is set out at p 708 *j* to p 709 *c*, post

b Section 20, so far as material, is set out at p 709 *e f*, post

c Regulation 6(2) is set out at p 710 *b*, post

L applied for judicial review, contending that reg 6(2) was ultra vires the 1985 Act if it had the effect of requiring costs to have been paid, not simply incurred. The Lord Chancellor, who was given permission to intervene, contended that the amended version of reg 6(2) had just that effect, and that it was consistent with s 16(6) of the 1985 Act. In particular, he contended that it was his duty to fund only what was reasonably sufficient to meet the costs incurred, and that accordingly it was legitimate to withdraw support from those who had not in fact been required to meet the costs in question. He also contended that, in framing the 1986 regulations, he was entitled to take the view that costs were not 'properly' incurred by a defendant if he had no realistic prospect of meeting them in practice.

Held – (1) In determining whether costs had been properly incurred within the meaning of s 16(6) of the 1985 Act, the sole question was whether there was a contractual liability to pay. If there was such a liability, and there was no agreement that the defendant would not have to pay whatever happened, costs had been incurred. That was so even though there might be little prospect of any payment actually being recovered. Liability to pay was incurred if there was a contractual obligation to make the payment, not merely if it was likely that the sum would have to be paid. In M's case, the clerk had erred in law, either by assuming that a contractual liability was insufficient to amount to incurring the costs, or through wrongly taking the view that there was no such liability by approaching the question improperly. Accordingly, M's application would be allowed (see p 713 *j* to p 714 *c* and p 718 *g*, post); *R v Miller (Raymond)* [1983] 3 All ER 186 and *Hazlett v Sefton Metropolitan BC* [2000] 4 All ER 887 applied.

(2) On its true construction, reg 6(2) of the 1986 regulations, as amended, did not mean that a defendant could obtain reimbursement only if he had made a payment. Rather, it simply meant that, where a defendant had made such a payment, he should send in receipts or other evidence of it. Such a construction gave a more natural meaning to the amendment in its context since it was not to be expected that a fundamental change, disentitling a whole class of persons from the right to take the benefit of the defendant's costs order, would be heralded by an apparently minor amendment to a procedural rule. If that was wrong, however, and the amendment did have such an effect, it would be outside the Lord Chancellor's powers. Section 16(6) of the 1985 Act clearly required the central funds to meet, to some extent, costs which had been properly incurred by any individual defendant in receipt of a costs order. Although that was not a full indemnity, and the compensation need only be to the extent of reasonable sufficiency, that did not entitle the Lord Chancellor to make no payment at all to a class of persons who had incurred the costs, provided that they had otherwise met the conditions for payment. Nil compensation could not constitute 'reasonably sufficient' compensation within the meaning of the section. Moreover, the statutory concept of costs being 'properly incurred' did not include a consideration of whether the defendant could afford to meet the costs at the time when they were incurred. Nor was it open to the executive to adopt and impose through regulations its own different construction. That concept was not capable of having a variety of meanings, some of which had regard to the defendant's ability to pay and some of which did not. If Parliament had intended the right to reimbursement to depend on actual payment, it would have been very easy for it to have said so. Accordingly, reg 6(2) could not have the effect relied upon by the Lord Chancellor. It followed that L's application would also be allowed, although it was not necessary to strike down

a reg 6(2) since, on its proper construction, it was capable of taking effect lawfully (see p 715 *h* to p 716 *a c f g h*, p 717 *g j* to p 718 *b* to *f*, post).

Notes

For the award of defence costs out of central funds, see 11(2) *Halsbury's Laws* (4th edn reissue) para 1527.

b For the Prosecution of Offences Act 1985, ss 16, 20, see 12 *Halsbury's Statutes* (4th edn) (1997 reissue) 910, 917.

For the Costs in Criminal Cases (General) Regulations 1986, reg 6, see 6 *Halsbury's Statutory Instruments* (2000 issue) 98.

Cases referred to in judgments

c *Adams v London Improved Motor Coach Builders Ltd* [1921] 1 KB 495, [1920] All ER Rep 340, CA.

British Waterways Board v Norman (1993) 26 HLR 232, DC.

Gundry v Sainsbury [1910] 1 KB 645, CA.

Hazlett v Sefton BC [2000] 4 All ER 887, DC.

d *Hughes v Kingston upon Hull City Council* [1999] 2 All ER 49, [1999] QB 1193, [1999] 2 WLR 1229, DC.

R v Hereford Magistrates' Court, ex p Farrell (23 November 1999, unreported), DC.

R v Lord Chancellor, ex p Witham [1997] 2 All ER 779, [1998] QB 575, [1998] 2 WLR 849, DC.

R v Miller (Raymond) [1983] 3 All ER 186, [1983] 1 WLR 1056.

e *Thai Trading Co (a firm) v Taylor* [1998] 3 All ER 65, [1998] QB 781, [1998] 2 WLR 893, CA.

Applications for judicial review

f *R (on the application of McCormick) v Liverpool City Magistrates' Court*

Austin McCormick applied for judicial review of the decision of the respondent, the clerk to the Liverpool City Justices, embodied in letters dated 19 August and 9 September 1999, refusing a claim, made by his solicitors pursuant to a defendant's costs order awarded to Mr McCormick under s 16 of the Prosecution of Offences Act 1985, for the payment of costs incurred by him before the grant of legal aid g in respect of criminal charges of which he was subsequently acquitted. The facts are set out in the judgment of Elias J.

R (on the application of L) v Liverpool City Magistrates' Court

The applicant, L, applied for judicial review of the decision of the respondent, the h clerk to the Liverpool City Justices, refusing a claim, made by his solicitors pursuant to a defendant's costs order awarded to him under s 16 of the Prosecution of Offences Act 1985, for the payment of costs incurred by him before the grant of legal aid in respect of criminal charges of which he was subsequently acquitted. The Lord Chancellor was given permission to intervene j in the proceedings. The facts are set out in the judgment of Elias J.

Martin Westgate (instructed by *R M Broudie & Co*, Liverpool) for the applicants.
Rabinder Singh (instructed by the *Treasury Solicitor*) for the Lord Chancellor.

ROSE LJ.

1. Elias J will give the first judgment.

ELIAS J.

a

2. In this case there are two applications for judicial review which have been heard together. Each of these cases concerns the interpretation of certain regulations made under the Prosecution of Offences Act 1985. In each case the applicant was acquitted of criminal charges and was awarded a defendant's costs order. In each case there was a refusal by the justices' clerk to pay the applicant costs relating to work done, on the grounds that a condition precedent to payment had not been met. b In each case the same solicitor's firm was involved. Indeed, the substance as opposed to the form of the proceedings is that the applicant is the solicitor. It is the firm, rather than the individual applicants, who will benefit from any successful outcome to this application.

3. The respondents were not represented before the court. However, the validity c of certain regulations made by the Lord Chancellor, pursuant to the 1985 Act, were in issue. He sought to intervene and be represented, and the court agreed to that course being taken. Accordingly, we have benefited from helpful submissions by Mr Rabinder Singh.

d

The legislation

4. Before looking at the detail, it is helpful to set out the context of this legislation. Publicly funded defence work is currently regulated by the Legal Aid Act 1988 and regulations made thereunder. (It is anticipated that this will change as from April 2001, when the system of funding is replaced by the Criminal Defence Service, established under the Access to Justice Act 1999.) However, a criminal legal aid e order can only be granted once a person has been charged or summonsed, because legal aid is only available under the 1988 Act once proceedings have commenced in the relevant court.

5. There are a variety of ways in which public funds may be made available for work done prior to this time. First, reg 44(7) of the Legal Aid in Criminal and f Care Proceedings (General) Regulations 1989, SI 1989/344, specifies that a legal aid order may be deemed to include certain work done before the legal aid order was granted. Second, certain advice given by a lawyer, when someone is being questioned in a police station, may be paid for pursuant to the Legal Advice and Assistance at Police Stations (Remuneration) Regulations 1989, SI 1989/342 (the 1989 regulations). Third, certain advice may be given under the 1989 regulations. g

6. If, subsequently, a defendant's costs order is made, then work which predated the order and is not covered by a claim made under any of these other provisions may be recovered. The circumstances in which this may be done are defined by the 1985 Act and regulations made thereunder. The basic scheme is as follows. By s 16(1) of the 1985 Act, where a prosecution is determined in favour of the accused h then the court 'may make an order in favour of the accused for a payment to be made out of central funds in respect of his costs'.

7. Although the power is discretionary, it will in practice be exercised in the defendant's favour, unless he has in some way brought the prosecution on himself, or has led the prosecution to believe that the strength of the case against him is, j in some way, stronger than it actually is.

8. Section 16(6) is an important provision in this case and it provides as follows:

'A defendant's costs order shall, subject to the following provisions of this section, be for the payment out of central funds, to the person in whose favour the order is made, of such amount as the court considers reasonably a sufficient to compensate him for any expenses properly incurred by him in the proceedings.'

9. Section 16(7) empowers the court to make a partial award of costs. It is as follows:

> 'Where a court makes a defendant's costs order but is of the opinion that b there are circumstances which make it inappropriate that the person in whose favour the order is made should recover the full amount mentioned in subsection (6) above, the court shall—(a) assess what amount would, in its opinion, be just and reasonable; and (b) specify that amount in the order.'

10. By s 16(9), it is provided as follows:

> c 'Subject to subsection (7) above, the amount to be paid out of central funds in pursuance of a defendant's costs order shall—(a) be specified in the order, in any case where the court considers it appropriate for the amount to be so specified and the person in whose favour the order is made agrees the amount; and (b) in any other case, be determined in accordance with d regulations made by the Lord Chancellor for the purposes of this section.'

11. As this subsection indicates, there are therefore two regimes. One is where costs are awarded by the court itself, in which event the regulations are not applicable, and the other is where the assessment is made other than in court, when the regulations do apply.

e 12. The Lord Chancellor is empowered to make the regulations pursuant to s 20 of the 1985 Act. This, in so far as is material, provides as follows:

> '(1) The Lord Chancellor may make regulations for carrying this Part into effect and the regulations may, in particular, make provision as to—(a) the scales or rates of payments of any costs payable out of central funds in f pursuance of any costs order, the circumstances in which and conditions under which such costs may be allowed and paid and the expenses which may be included in such costs ... and any provision made by or under this Part enabling any sum to be paid out of central funds shall have effect subject to any such regulations.'

g 13. The current regulations are the Costs in Criminal Cases (General) Regulations 1986, SI 1986/1335. By reg 7(1), it is provided that:

> 'The appropriate authority shall consider the claim, any further particulars, information or documents submitted by the applicant under regulation 6 and shall allow such costs in respect of—(a) such work as appears to it to h have been actually and reasonably done; and (b) such disbursements as appear to it to have been actually and reasonably incurred, as it considers reasonably sufficient to compensate the applicant for any expenses properly incurred by him in the proceedings.'

14. By reg 5 of the 1986 regulations, the appropriate authority for cases before j the justices is the justices' clerk, although that officer, in turn, has power to delegate under reg 5(3) to other officers. These are described as 'determining officers' in the regulations.

15. Regulation 7(3) of the 1986 regulations provides as follows:

> 'When determining costs for the purpose of this regulation, there shall be allowed a reasonable amount in respect of all costs reasonably incurred and

> any doubts which the appropriate authority may have as to whether the costs were reasonably incurred or were reasonable in amount shall be resolved against the applicant.'

a

16. I pause to note here that the concept of 'costs incurred' is used in reg 7, and is the same concept as is found in s 16(6) of the 1985 Act.

17. Finally, reg 6(2) of the 1986 regulations provides as follows:

b

> 'Subject to paragraph (3), a claim for costs shall be submitted to the appropriate authority in such form and manner as it may direct and shall be accompanied by *receipts or other evidence of the applicant's payment of the costs claimed, and* any receipts or other documents in support of any disbursement claimed.'

c

18. The words emphasised were added by the Costs in Criminal Cases (General) (Amendment) Regulations 1999, SI 1999/2096, and took effect from 1 September 1999. They applied in the case of L, but not in the case of McCormick.

19. I pause to note that there are, potentially, two interpretations of the amended reg 6(2). First, the regulation could mean that unless the applicant has actually paid for the work done and produced relevant receipts, then he will not be able to recover anything. The second construction is that he must produce receipts and other documents but only if, and to the extent that, he has in fact personally made such payments. The first construction imposes a condition of personal payment before monies can be recovered, the second does not.

d

20. I now turn briefly to consider the facts of each of these cases.

e

McCormick

21. The applicant was accused of certain criminal offences of unlawfully taking a motor vehicle and burglary. He approached a solicitor in May 1998 and signed an agreement on the firm's standard terms. Mr Broudie, a partner in the firm, has produced a witness statement in these proceedings in which he has stated that all clients will sign the same agreement, whether or not they will be entitled to legal aid. Indeed, he said it will frequently not be clear at the time when the firm is instructed whether the client will be entitled to legal aid or not. We have seen a copy of the standard terms, the first paragraph of which says:

f

g

> 'Please note that you are of course responsible for our costs for advising you and representing you in connection with any criminal proceedings. You may be entitled to legal aid but the court will not consider any application for legal aid in criminal cases without documentary evidence in support.'

h

22. Mr Broudie accepted that often it would simply not be cost effective for the firm to proceed to seek to recover costs from the client if he was not in a position to pay them. But he said that the firm would reserve its position. It would certainly take steps to recover such monies if the client's financial position altered during the limitation period. McCormick was charged in early October 1998, which was the earliest time at which he could have made an application for legal aid. He in fact made that application in December. Mr Broudie explained that the reason for that was difficulties in obtaining relevant evidence and information to enable him properly to put in the application.

j

23. Subsequently, McCormick was acquitted of the charges before the Liverpool City Magistrates' Court and a costs order was made in his favour. The applicant's firm then applied to recover the costs which had been incurred prior to the legal

a aid order coming into effect, but the clerk to the justices refused to meet the claim. A detailed letter had been submitted, setting out the costs, but the justices' clerk, who was the determining officer, took the view that there was no liability incurred by the applicant to pay the costs. This was because McCormick knew when entering into the contract that he could not make, and would not be expected to make, any payment not covered by public funds, and that b accordingly he had incurred no liability within the meaning of reg 7(3) of the 1986 regulations.

24. I shall just refer to two letters which were sent from the clerk to the applicant's solicitors. In the first of these, dated 19 August 1999, the clerk said:

> 'Even if you can successfully argue that you have a contract between c yourselves and your client, and he would agree to it on your terms, how can he expect to pay towards his legal costs, when he has been assessed by the court as not being in a position to pay?'

25. Subsequently, in a further letter it was made plain that the clerk did not concede that there was a contract with the client, and he added:

d

> 'If there had been no prospect of Mr McCormick obtaining the benefit of a full legal aid order then I am pretty sure your client would not have agreed a contract where he was expected to pay [and then he sets out the fee] ... for your services, when clearly he would not be able to afford it, whether it is a fair rate or not.'

e

26. The applicant disputes the construction adopted by the clerk. The applicant says there was a legal liability to pay and that on the authorities that was sufficient to constitute the incurring of liability.

27. Mr Westgate, who appeared for the applicant in both these actions, submitted that liability had been incurred under s 16(6) of the 1985 Act and f reg 7(3) of the 1986 regulations, and he submitted that the respondent had erred in three ways in particular. Firstly, the clerk had assumed that even if there was a contractual obligation in place, there was a superadded requirement actually to pay for the services before costs could be recovered. Secondly, he submits that alternatively, the clerk assumed that if there was no expectation by the defendant that he would have to pay him back, then there could be no contractual liability; g and thirdly, he says that the clerk wrongly approached the question of whether or not there was a liability incurred.

28. He submits that the reason why the clerk erred was because he had identified what he perceived to be a problem in the way in which the current regulations operate, and sought to give effect to a construction which would h remove that defect. The alleged defect is the belief (which Mr Westgate said was not supported by evidence) that solicitors delay in seeking a legal aid order because they can recover costs at a more favourable rate under a defendant's costs order, than they would for the same work if it were done under legal aid.

29. Central to this application is the meaning of the phrase 'costs incurred'. I will j look first at that issue and will, at the same time, consider the question of how the determining, or assessing, officer should approach the question of deciding whether or not costs have been incurred, and more specifically whether there is a contractual obligation to pay.

30. The leading case on this matter is *R v Miller (Raymond)* [1983] 3 All ER 186, [1983] 1 WLR 1056. This case concerned a predecessor of the current regulations. The facts in that case were that the parties had been funded by their unions and

so they did not personally have to pay the costs. The question was whether that disentitled them from recovering under a defendant's costs order. The case was heard by Lloyd J, as he then was, sitting with assessors. He said:

> '... I reject the main argument of counsel for the Lord Chancellor that "costs incurred by" means "costs paid by". I would hold, following *Adams v London Improved Motor Coach Builders Ltd* ([1921] 1 KB 495, [1920] All ER Rep 340) and the other cases I have mentioned, that costs are incurred by a party if he is responsible or liable for those costs, even though they are in fact paid by a third party, whether an employer, insurance company, motoring organisation or trade union, and even though the third party is also liable for those costs. It is only if it has been agreed that the client shall in no circumstances be liable for the costs that they cease to be costs incurred by him, as happened in *Gundry v Sainsbury* ([1910] 1 KB 645).' (See [1983] 3 All ER 186 at 190, [1983] 1 WLR 1056 at 1061.)

31. Then a little later he said:

> 'There was also some discussion as to the burden of proof. The initial burden of proving that Richards Butler & Co were acting for Mr Glennie lay on Mr Glennie. But that burden could be discharged, as it was in the present case, by showing that Mr Glennie was the party to the proceedings, and Richards Butler & Co the solicitors on the record. Once it was shown, as is now conceded, that Mr Glennie was indeed the client, then a presumption arose that he was to be personally liable for the costs. That presumption could, however, be rebutted if it were established that there was an express or implied agreement, binding on the solicitors, that Mr Glennie would not have to pay those costs in any circumstances. In practice, of course, the taxing officer will have before him on the taxation the whole of the solicitor's file. If it appears to the taxing officer that there is doubt whether there was an express or implied agreement, binding on the solicitors, not to seek to recover the costs from the client, the taxing officer should ask for further evidence. It must then be for the taxing officer to come to a conclusion on the whole of the facts presented to him. Unless those facts establish a clear agreement, express or implied, that in no circumstances will the solicitors seek to obtain payment from their client, then the basic presumption stands, and reasonable costs must be allowed on a taxation out of central funds.' (See [1983] 3 All ER 186 at 190–191, [1983] 1 WLR 1056 at 1061–1062.)

32. Mr Westgate submitted that the premise of that case has then been applied in a number of decisions which have been made under the Environmental Protection Act 1990. He referred to *British Waterways Board v Norman* (1993) 26 HLR 232, *Hughes v Kingston upon Hull City Council* [1999] 2 All ER 49, [1999] QB 1193, and *Hazlett v Sefton BC* [2000] 4 All ER 887. In the last of these cases, the issue was, as in this case, which costs should be met under a costs order in circumstances where the legislation was similar but not the same. The relevant section was under the 1990 Act. The court hearing the case consisted of Lord Bingham of Cornhill CJ and Harrison J. Harrison J gave the decision of the court, and in the course of his judgment said (at 892–893):

> 'In our judgment, it is reasonable to assume in those circumstances that, where the complainant has a solicitor acting for him in pursuing his complaint, he will be liable to pay his solicitor's costs of doing so. In other words, there

a is normally a presumption that the complainant will be personally liable for his solicitor's costs and it should not normally be necessary for the complainant to have to adduce evidence to that effect. Such an approach would be consistent with that adopted in the case of *R v Miller (Raymond)* ([1983] 3 All ER 186, [1983] 1 WLR 1056) where, although the factual circumstances were different, the wording of the relevant statutory provisions in the 1973 Act b [the Costs in Criminal Cases Act 1973] is very similar to the wording of s 82(12) of the 1990 Act. The complainant will therefore be able to rely on the presumption that he is liable for his solicitor's costs where there is no effective challenge to it. Where, however, there is a genuine issue raised by the defendant as to whether the complainant has properly incurred costs in the proceedings, the position will be different. A defendant may, for instance, c have grounds for believing that the complainant will not be liable to pay his solicitor's costs, whether because he has entered into an unlawful and unenforceable conditional fee arrangement with his solicitor or for any other reason. In those circumstances, where the defendant has raised a genuine issue as to whether the complainant has properly incurred costs in the proceedings, d the complainant will be at risk if he continues to rely on the presumption that he is liable for his solicitor's costs. If he does not then adduce evidence to prove that he has properly incurred costs in the proceedings and the defendant can show by evidence or argument, that he has not, he would be most unlikely to succeed in recovering his costs.'

e 33. Mr Westgate also submitted that the authorities make it plain that there would be a liability to pay even, although there was no expectation that the defendant would be, in practice, able to pay. He referred to a passage in the judgment of Millett LJ, as he then was, in the case of *Thai Trading Co (a firm) v Taylor* [1998] 3 All ER 65, [1998] QB 781. It is not necessary to go into the facts of the case, but simply refer to part of the judgment:

f 'It is not uncommon for solicitors to take on a case for an impecunious client with a meritorious case, knowing that there is no realistic prospect of recovering their costs from the client if the case is lost, without thereby waiving their legal right to their fees in that event. As every debt collector knows, what is legally recoverable and what is recoverable in practice are not g the same.' (See [1998] 3 All ER 65 at 71, [1998] QB 781 at 788–789.)

34. Similarly, in the *British Waterways Board* case, to which I have already made reference, Tuckey J, as he then was, said:

h 'My Lord has referred to the professional standards which apply to solicitors on the subject of costs. If that procedure is followed in the way suggested by my Lord, so that it is made clear that the client is liable for costs irrespective of the outcome of proceedings, there can be no objection to the solicitor agreeing that such liability need not be discharged until the outcome of those proceedings, if any, is known. At that stage, provided it has j not formed the basis of the agreement with the client, it would be open to the solicitors, if the circumstances warranted it, to decide not to enforce their right to be paid, in the event that some or all of their costs were unrecovered from the other party to the proceedings.' (See (1993) 26 HLR 232 at 243.)

35. Mr Westgate submits that the sole question in the light of these authorities is merely whether there is a contractual liability to pay. If there is and there is no

agreement that whatever happens the defendant will not have to pay, then the costs have been incurred. This is so although there may be little prospect of any payment being recovered in fact.

a

36. I agree with that analysis and, in my view, it is precisely the position with this contract. I have no doubt that if the applicant were to win the lottery, for example, the firm would look to him for payment. The fact that they do not expect to be able to recover these costs, unless there is subsequently a defendant's costs order made in their favour, does not, in my opinion, prevent the liability being incurred by the applicant. Liability to pay is incurred if there is a contractual obligation to make the payment and not merely if it is likely that the sum will have to be paid.

b

37. Accordingly, I agree with Mr Westgate that in this case the justices' clerk erred in law. He either assumed that a contractual liability was insufficient to amount to incurring the costs, or wrongly took the view that there was no such liability by approaching the question improperly. Accordingly, in my judgment, this application should succeed and I would, if necessary, issue mandamus directing the clerk to assess and pay the amount due.

c

38. I turn to L's case.

d

L's case

39. The facts were essentially the same. As I have indicated, the same firm of solicitors was involved. In this case, however, the refusal to make the payment was on the ground that the amended regulations required the client actually to have paid the firm for the work concerned, and it is not disputed that he had not done so.

e

40. The central question in this case is whether the regulations now achieve, as a result of the amendment, what in the McCormick case the justices' clerk tried to secure by his interpretation of the unamended regulations. Mr Westgate submits that, in considering this question, it is necessary to bear in mind that there is no reason in principle to suppose that the provisions regulating the defendant's costs order should be read subject to, or in any way connected with, the rules regulating legal aid. He referred to a passage in the case of *R v Hereford Magistrates' Court, ex p Farrell* (23 November 1999, unreported). In that case, the justices' clerk had taken the view that they were not in a position to make a defendant's costs order, by virtue of a particular regulation, if legal aid had been granted. Turner J, sitting in the Divisional Court with Simon Brown LJ, said:

f

g

> 'It is fully understandable why, when a losing party has been in receipt of legal aid, a publicly funded service, provided because of the presumed impecuniosity of the person to whom legal aid has been granted, the solicitor or barrister who acts under a certificate should not receive additional payments beyond those which legal aid provides. The position where, as here, the costs are intended to be recovered from central funds is, in my judgment, essentially different. I can see no reason in principle why a solicitor or barrister should not receive payment for work properly done before legal aid was granted out of a source other than the legal aid fund where the proceedings have been determined in a defendant's favour. It is hard to see what reason there could be in those circumstances for depriving legal advisors of a right to remuneration and, thus, putting them in a position even more disadvantageous than if they had been acting for a privately funded client.'

h

j

a 41. Mr Westgate submitted that the regulations in this case were outwith the powers of the Lord Chancellor, broadly for two reasons. First, they were incompatible with the 1985 Act, and in particular, he submitted, they added a requirement to s 16(6) of that Act. He contended the effect of the regulations, as construed at least by the Lord Chancellor, was that they would require not merely that the costs should have been incurred, but also that they should have b been paid by the applicant. This, he submitted, involved a fundamental change to the scheme adopted by Parliament. In support of this ultra vires challenge, he also identified certain discriminatory consequences resulting from the amendment, to which I will return in due course.

42. The second principal challenge was that he submitted that the regulations infringed certain provisions of the European Convention for the Protection of c Human Rights and Fundamental Freedoms (Rome, 4 November 1950; TS 71 (1953); Cmd 8969) (as set out in Sch 1 to the Human Rights Act 1998) (the convention), and therefore could not stand for that reason either. I will first consider the ultra vires submission.

43. The principal question here, it seems to me, is whether the Lord Chancellor d has the power to make regulations of the kind that he has, and whether they are in fact in accordance with the provisions of s 16(6) of the 1985 Act. Mr Rabinder Singh has submitted that the Lord Chancellor was indeed empowered to make the amendment which he did. He reminded the court of the broad regulation-making power conferred by s 20 of the 1985 Act, to which I have made reference. He also drew the court's attention to a passage of the judgment of Laws J, giving e judgment in the Divisional Court, which consisted of Laws J and Rose LJ, in the case of *R v Lord Chancellor, ex p Witham* [1997] 2 All ER 779, [1998] QB 575, where Laws J said:

> 'Mr Richards submitted that it was for the Lord Chancellor's discretion to decide what litigation should be supported by taxpayers' money and what f should not. As regards the expenses of legal representation, I am sure that is right. Payment out of legal aid of lawyers' fees to conduct litigation is a subsidy by the state which in general is well within the power of the executive, subject to the relevant main legislation to regulate.' (See [1997] 2 All ER 779 at 788, [1998] QB 575 at 586.)

g

44. Mr Rabinder Singh then identified two distinct grounds, whereby the amendment could be justified as being consistent with s 16(6) of the 1985 Act in this case. First, he contended that it is the duty of the Lord Chancellor to fund only what is reasonably sufficient to meet the costs incurred. It is not necessary for the state to reimburse all the costs actually incurred, and accordingly it is h legitimate, he submitted, to withdraw support from a category of persons, namely those who have not personally in fact had to meet the costs in question.

45. I do not accept that argument. In my view s 16(6) of the 1985 Act clearly requires the central funds to meet, to some extent, costs which have been properly incurred by any individual defendant in receipt of a costs order. It is true j that it is not a full indemnity and the compensation need only be to the extent of reasonable sufficiency. But that would not, in my judgment, entitle the Lord Chancellor to make no payment at all to a class of persons who had incurred the costs, provided they have otherwise met the conditions for payment. I do not accept that the power of the Lord Chancellor to regulate the circumstances in which, and the conditions under which, the costs may be allowed, entitles him to provide that someone who has properly incurred costs should receive nothing. Nil

compensation cannot constitute reasonably sufficient compensation within the meaning of the section.

46. The second argument is that there is a duty to make a payment only if the expense is properly incurred, and that the Lord Chancellor in framing these regulations is entitled to form the view that, although incurred, they have not properly been incurred by a defendant if he has no realistic prospect, in practice, of meeting them.

47. I reject this argument also, for two interrelated reasons. First, in my view the concept of costs being incurred properly, within the meaning of the subsection, simply requires that they should be incurred for work which has been reasonably carried out in connection with the proceedings. This is indeed what reg 7(1) of the 1986 regulations envisages, which is the provision dealing with the assessment. In my judgment, the concept does not, properly construed, include a consideration of whether the defendant can afford to meet the costs at the time when they are incurred. The second and related point is that the construction of the statutory concept of 'properly incurred' is a matter for the court, and it is not open to the executive to adopt and impose through regulations its own different construction.

48. Mr Rabinder Singh accepts that in principle that is constitutionally correct. He also accepts that the concept of 'properly incurred' does not require that a court, or authorising body, should have regard to whether or not payment has actually been made. Indeed, if he were so to contend, then it would mean that money has for years been paid out to firms who should not have received it. What he does submit—as he has to if this argument can be sustained—is that the concept of 'properly incurred' is one which is sufficiently elastic to enable the Lord Chancellor to give it his own definition and limit it to payments actually paid. It is, he says, capable of having this meaning.

49. I do not accept this. In my opinion, the concept is not one which is capable of having a variety of meanings, some of which have regard to the defendant's ability to pay and some of which do not. Parliament has provided that there should be reimbursement, to a reasonable extent, of costs properly incurred. If it had intended the right to reimbursement to depend on actual payment, it would have been very easy for it to have said so.

50. Accordingly, I accept the applicant's submission that the effect of the amended regulation, if construed in the manner the Lord Chancellor suggests, would be inconsistent with the 1985 Act and, therefore, unlawful. Of course, I accept that whether or not any particular element of costs is properly incurred is a matter of fact and degree, and that more than one view may reasonably be adopted in any particular case about whether it has been incurred or not. But that does not permit different and equally valid opinions to be held and applied about the very principles to be adopted to determine whether costs have been reasonably incurred or not.

51. In my judgment, therefore, neither of these two routes of compatibility is open to the Lord Chancellor, and accordingly, the regulation as amended, if given the construction which he submits, is outside his powers.

52. Apart from those considerations, in my view, the effect of the change has certain very curious results and I would be loath to accept that they could possibly have been intended by Parliament.

53. First, as Mr Rabinder Singh accepted, their effect would be that some people who are not eligible for legal aid and yet were too impecunious to pay for a lawyer, or could only do so over a period of time, would also be prevented from

a being reimbursed under the regulations. The mischief which the amendment is allegedly designed to effect, namely to discourage delay in claiming criminal legal aid, would therefore, in the case of such persons, miss its mark since they cannot claim such legal aid. Yet it would mean that an obviously worthy recipient of state legal support would be denied it. Mr Rabinder Singh sought to meet this point by saying that they would not necessarily be denied legal aid since it would b be possible for the courts to make an assessment, under s 16(9) of the 1985 Act, and the courts could adopt a different meaning of the phrase 'reasonably incurred' than was done by the authorities applying the regulations. The courts, he submitted, could adopt the meaning which has been adopted up to now.

54. The idea that there would be two systems in place, applying wholly different tests for determining whether costs have been reasonably incurred or c not, strikes me as wholly bizarre. I cannot believe that the power to make regulations was intended to permit this consequence. Indeed, the logic of the argument seems to me that it would also be open to different courts to take different views as to what the meaning of the phrase was, depending upon their own particular inclination.

55. Second, and in any event, the effect of the regulation is that it does not d even necessarily disqualify only those who have improperly incurred liabilities, nor does it necessarily disqualify those who have. The reason is this. A party may have incurred the liability in circumstances where he or she could not afford it when it was incurred. It may be that by the time of the assessment, that person has come into money and can now make the payment. Accordingly, if he had made a payment by the date of assessment, then he would be entitled to recover e under the defendant's costs order. Conversely, of course, one can imagine a situation where an individual incurred the liability in the confident expectation of being able to pay, but for one reason or another fell on hard times. The difficulty here is that reg 7 of the 1986 regulations focuses on the time of assessment, rather than when the liability is incurred. Accordingly, the regulation will sometimes f adversely affect those who are outside the mischief and yet fail to achieve its objective in relation to some who are within it.

56. Thirdly, as I have already indicated, the effect of the regulation is that the courts and the legal aid authorities when applying the regulations could be applying a quite different test.

57. In my view, these considerations reinforce the conclusion that I have g already reached that the amendment is outside the powers of the Lord Chancellor. But even if I am wrong about that and even if, in principle, it is open to the Lord Chancellor to make this change, he does not, in my judgment, achieve his objective by the actual amendment made. I would not expect a change of such fundamental importance to be heralded by an apparently minor h amendment to a procedural rule. Regulation 6(2) of the 1986 regulations is solely concerned with providing evidence of the costs which have been incurred. Indeed, it is not even as if the amendment has been introduced into reg 7 of the 1986 regulations itself, yet that is the regulation which actually deals with the determination of costs. As Mr Westgate pointed out, that regulation would j appear to permit a claim to be allowed, even if some relevant documentation had not been provided. The only duty under that regulation appears to be to consider the information and documents submitted.

58. In my opinion, the amendment in the context in which it is found more naturally means that where the defendant has made a payment, he should send in receipts or other evidence of that payment, and not that he can only obtain a reimbursement if he has made such a payment. I accept that this gives little

significance to the amendment, since it is likely that such receipts would have had to have been provided even in the regulations' unamended form. But it could be said that the amendment puts the matter beyond doubt. In any event, I would be very reluctant to conclude that this change in the wording of this particular regulation, dealing with receipts, was intended to reflect a fundamental change in the terms on which the central fund would meet a claim for costs. To treat this amendment as disentitling a whole class of persons from the right to take the benefit of the defendant's costs order granted to them, would, in my view, be a classic case of the procedural tail wagging the substantive dog. I would give the regulation such a meaning, only if I felt that it was the only proper construction. I do not take that view.

59. In view of this conclusion, it is not necessary for me to consider Mr Westgate's other line of fire concerning provisions under the convention. We heard interesting submissions that the amended regulations infringed art 6; art 1, Protocol 1 of the convention, concerning the protection of the right to property; and art 13, relating to discrimination. The parties were at issue about whether the convention was applicable at all, given that the facts occurred prior to the 1998 Act coming into force. Also, they were in dispute about whether there was a breach and whether, at least in the case of art 1, Protocol 1 of the convention, any interference was justified and proportionate. As I have said, given my earlier conclusion, it is not necessary to resolve these issues in the application.

60. It follows, in my view, that the regulations cannot have the effect relied upon by the Lord Chancellor, and accordingly L's application succeeds also. However, I would not strike down the regulation since, as I have said, it is capable of taking effect lawfully, in what I consider to be its proper construction. My provisional view also is that it does not seem to me that a declaration is necessary, to the effect that the regulation does not mean what the Lord Chancellor has apparently understood it to mean, but I would, for my part, be willing to hear submissions about that matter.

61. For those reasons, these two applications succeed.

ROSE LJ.

62. I agree.

Applications allowed. Permission to appeal refused.

Dilys Tausz Barrister.

Re K (a child) (secure accommodation order: right to liberty)

COURT OF APPEAL, CIVIL DIVISION

DAME ELIZABETH BUTLER-SLOSS P, THORPE AND JUDGE LJJ

16–18 OCTOBER, 15 NOVEMBER 2000

Family proceedings – Orders in family proceedings – Secure accommodation order – Whether secure accommodation order a deprivation of liberty – Whether secure accommodation order incompatible with right to liberty under human rights convention – Children Act 1989, s 25 – Human Rights Act 1998, Sch 1, Pt I, art 5.

K, a 15-year old boy, suffered from learning difficulties. He also had serious behavioural problems, and had been assessed as posing a considerable risk to others as well as to himself. An interim order was made placing him in the care of the respondent local authority, and he had lived at a secure unit since December 1998 as a result of a series of secure accommodation orders made pursuant to s 25[a] of the Children Act 1989. K appealed against the most recent of those orders, seeking a declaration that s 25 of the 1989 Act was incompatible with art 5[b] of the European Convention for the Protection of Human Rights and Fundamental Freedoms 1950 (as set out in Sch 1 to the Human Rights Act 1998). Article 5(1) provided that everyone had the right to liberty and security of person, and that no one was to be deprived of his liberty save in certain specified cases and in accordance with a procedure prescribed by law. Those cases included, at para (d), the detention of a minor by lawful order for the purpose of educational supervision. On the appeal, the court considered whether a secure accommodation order constituted a deprivation of liberty and, if so, whether such a deprivation of liberty came within the exception in art 5(1)(d). K submitted that a s 25 order fell outside that exception since educational supervision did not form part of the criteria for making such an order.

Held – (1) (Thorpe LJ dissenting) A secure accommodation order under s 25 of the 1989 Act was a deprivation of liberty. The purpose of the section was to restrict the liberty of the child. Although it was a benign jurisdiction, protecting the child as well as others, it was restrictive none the less. That view was supported by the fact that a local authority was only authorised to detain a child in secure accommodation for 72 hours without a court order. It followed that a secure accommodation order would be incompatible with K's right to liberty under the convention unless such an order came within one of the exceptions in art 5(1) (see p 728 *j* to p 729 *c j* and p 745 *g* to p 746 *a*, post); *Nielsen v Denmark* (1988) 11 EHRR 175 and *Guzzardi v Italy* (1980) 3 EHRR 333 considered

(2) A secure accommodation order fell within the exception in art 5(1)(d) of the convention, and accordingly s 25 of the 1989 Act was not incompatible with the convention. It was not necessary for s 25 to refer to education since, by the provisions of the Education Act 1996, education was compulsory for any child under 16. Consequently, K's secure unit was under a statutory obligation to

---

a Section 25, so far as material, is set out at p 738 *c* and p 743 *g*, post

b Article 5, so far as material, is set out at p 725 *e* to *g*, post

provide him with education. In any event, the concept of 'educational supervision' went well beyond academic lessons in the classroom. In theory, there might be circumstances in which a s 25 order was made in respect of a child under the age of 18 where the words 'for the purpose of educational supervision' did not cover the facts of the particular case. However, that possibility did not render the section incompatible with art 5. A distinction had to be drawn between a complaint that a step taken by a local authority pursuant to a statutory power was in breach of an article of the convention, and a complaint that a statutory provision was itself incompatible with the article. The duty of the English courts under the 1998 Act was to attempt to find a compatible interpretation, and if such an interpretation could be found, there was no justification for a declaration of incompatibility. In each case where a secure accommodation order was sought, the court had to have the requirements of art 5(1)(d) in mind when considering the relevant criteria, and thereby ensure the compatibility of s 25 with the convention right. In the instant case, art 5(1)(d) covered the making of a secure accommodation order in respect of K, and accordingly the appeal would be dismissed (see p 730 *c* to *e*, p 731 *g* to p 732 *a h*, p 733 *a*, p 737 *a b*, p 738 *b*, p 746 *j* to p 747 *f*, p 748 *j* to p 749 *a* and p 751 *g*, post); *Koniarska v UK* App No 33670/96 (12 October 2000, unreported) applied; *Bouamar v Belgium* (1989) 11 EHRR 1 distinguished.

Notes

For secure accommodation and for the exception to the right to liberty in respect of minors, see respectively 5(2) *Halsbury's Laws* (4th edn reissue) paras 1248–1260 and 8(2) *Halsbury's Laws* (4th edn reissue) para 131.

For the Children Act 1989, s 25, see 6 *Halsbury's Statutes* (4th edn) (1999 reissue) 408.

For the Human Rights Act 1998, Sch 1, Pt I, art 5, see 7 *Halsbury's Statutes* (4th edn) (1999 reissue) 522.

Cases referred to in judgments

A (children) (conjoined twins: surgical separation), Re [2000] 4 All ER 961, [2001] 2 WLR 480, CA.
Bonham's Case (1610) 8 Co Rep 114a, 77 ER 646.
Bouamar v Belgium (1989) 11 EHRR 1, ECt HR.
Engel v Netherlands (No 1) (1976) 1 EHRR 647, ECt HR.
Family T v Austria (1990) 64 DR 176, E Com HR.
Guzzardi v Italy (1980) 3 EHRR 333, ECt HR.
Ireland v UK (1978) 2 EHRR 25, ECt HR.
Koniarska v UK App No 33670/96 (12 October 2000, unreported), ECt HR.
LM v Essex CC [1999] 1 FCR 673.
M (a minor) (secure accommodation order), Re [1995] 3 All ER 407, [1995] Fam 108, [1995] 2 WLR 302, CA.
Nielsen v Denmark (1988) 11 EHRR 175, ECt HR.
R v DPP, ex p Kebeline [1999] 4 All ER 801, [2000] 2 AC 326, [1999] 3 WLR 972, HL.
W (a minor) (secure accommodation), Re [1994] 3 FCR 248.

Cases also cited or referred to in skeleton arguments

A v UK (1998) 27 EHRR 611, ECt HR.
Abbott v UK (1990) 67 DR 290, E Com HR.
AK (secure accommodation order), Re [2000] 1 FLR 317.
AS (secure accommodation order), Re [1999] 1 FLR 103.
Ashingdane v UK (1985) 7 EHRR 528, ECt HR.

Benham v UK (1996) 22 EHRR 293, ECt HR.
Boulting v Association of Cinematograph Television and Allied Technicians [1963] 1 All ER 716, [1963] 2 QB 606, CA.
C (detention: medical treatment), Re [1997] 2 FLR 180.
Cast v Croydon College [1998] ICR 500, CA.
Curley v UK (28 March 2000, unreported), ECt HR.
Eastham v Newcastle United Football Club Ltd [1963] 3 All ER 139, [1964] Ch 413.
Eriksen v Norway (1997) 29 EHRR 328, ECt HR.
G (a child) (secure accommodation order), Re [2000] 2 FCR 385, CA.
Golder v UK (1975) 1 EHRR 524, ECt HR.
Håkansson v Sweden (1990) 13 EHRR 1, ECt HR.
K (ward: secure accommodation), Re [1985] 1 FLR 357.
Le Compte v Belgium (1981) 4 EHRR 1, ECt HR.
Litster v Forth Dry Dock and Engineering Co Ltd [1989] 1 All ER 1134, [1990] 1 AC 546, HL.
Muyldermans v Belgium (1991) 15 EHRR 204, ECt HR.
Owusu v London Fire & Civil Defence Authority [1995] IRLR 574, EAT.
R v Walsall Justices, ex p W (a minor) [1989] 3 All ER 460, [1990] 1 QB 253, DC.
Sougrin v Haringey Health Authority [1992] ICR 650, CA.
Wolverhampton Metropolitan BC v DB (a minor) (1996) 37 BMLR 172.

Appeal

By notice dated 4 October 2000 the appellant, K, appealed from the order of Judge Urquhart made at Liverpool County Court on 30 June 2000, pursuant to s 25 of the Children Act 1989, requiring him to remain in secure accommodation until 16 October 2000. The respondent local authority applied for a further secure accommodation order in respect of K. The Secretary of State for Health and the Lord Chancellor were joined as parties to K's appeal. The facts are set out in the judgment of Dame Elizabeth Butler-Sloss P.

Margaret de Haas QC and *Simon Crabtree* (instructed by *Herwald Seddon*, Salford) for K.
Ernest Ryder QC and *Clare Grundy* for the local authority.
Neil Garnham (instructed by the *Treasury Solicitor*) for the Secretary of State for Health.
Philip Sales and *Neil Garnham* (instructed by the *Treasury Solicitor*) for the Lord Chancellor.
The parents and the guardian ad litem did not appear and were not represented.

Cur adv vult

15 November 2000. The following judgments were delivered.

DAME ELIZABETH BUTLER-SLOSS P.

1. K is 15. He was born on 6 July 1985. His manifestly difficult problems come to be considered by the Court of Appeal in the context of an interim care order to the local authority and a series of secure accommodation orders as a result of which he has lived since 4 December 1998 at a secure unit. The appeal is brought by K through his own legal team against the most recent secure accommodation order made by Judge Urquhart on 30 June 2000. That order was made to run until 16 October 2000, the first day on which we began to hear this appeal. Miss de Haas QC for K raised on the appeal the issue that s 25 of the Children Act 1989

was incompatible with art 5 of the European Convention for the Protection of Human Rights and Fundamental Freedoms (Rome, 4 November 1950; TS 71 (1953); Cmd 8969) (the convention), made part of English domestic law by the Human Rights Act 1998. She sought a certificate of incompatibility under s 4(2). The Secretary of State for Health was, therefore, joined as a party under s 5(2). K also claimed damages under s 8 and the Lord Chancellor was joined under s 9(4). At short notice Mr Garnham attended on behalf of the Secretary of State and Mr Sales and Mr Garnham on behalf of the Lord Chancellor. We are very grateful to them for their written and oral arguments, largely without sight of the papers. The guardian ad litem was not represented but supported the local authority. The parents were not represented and did not attend, but by letter indicated their support for the local authority.

2. The second main issue before us was the application by the local authority for a new secure accommodation order, in order to keep K at his present secure unit beyond 16 October. This application had been before Wilson J in Manchester and very sensibly it was agreed that this court should decide the application after hearing the appeal. We gave K leave to appeal out of time; gave leave to the local authority to adduce further evidence and made a secure accommodation order to run until the end of the appeal. We reserved our decision.

The history

3. There is a long history of the difficulties experienced by K and by those looking after him starting long before he went to school. His parents married in 1983, separated in early 1996 and divorced in August 1996. He has an elder brother D, born in 1983, who was for some years in care. On K's first day at nursery in 1987, aged two, he was permanently excluded as a result of his destructive behaviour. He was referred to an educationalist at the age of four because of his aggressive behaviour and was described by the psychologist as being over-active to the point of being chaotic, deliberately destructive and using provocative and abusive language. He was assessed as having moderate learning difficulties and was admitted to a special school. The local authority became involved in 1991 as it became increasingly difficult for his parents to manage his behaviour. He was aggressive and physically and verbally abusive to staff and children. On occasions he damaged school property. From an early age he was fascinated by fire and behaved in a sexualised way. Respite care was arranged on a number of occasions to help his family.

4. In 1993, at the age of seven, he was reported as displaying sexualised behaviour towards a six-year-old girl. The same year he attempted to set fire to his home. He spent longer and longer periods accommodated by the local authority in residential care with the consent of his parents. His behaviour deteriorated and there were regular incidents of sexualised and aggressive behaviour. In 1994, at the age of eight, he went to a residential school and spent his holidays at home. In 1996 there was a marked deterioration in his behaviour. There were incidents of sexualised behaviour including masturbation and exposing himself in public. He was disruptive and in September 1996 he assaulted a female member of staff.

5. In December 1996 the Adolescent Forensic Service at hospital P carried out a psychiatric assessment. They considered that he did not have a mental illness or impairment as defined under the Mental Health Act 1983, but exhibited symptoms consistent with a diagnosis of Hyperkinetic Conduct Disorder. The report said that—

a 'we believe that [K] presents a serious risk to himself and others as is demonstrated by his recent offences, the continuation of his fire setting behaviour, the increasing aggressive behaviour coupled with his ability to target vulnerable members of staff and the inability to safely contain [K] despite intensive effort at his current placement. Our concern would include the current tendency for those caring for [K], both professional and personal b to minimise the risk he presents perhaps due to his young age and pre-pubertal nature. This risk is likely to increase with puberty, increasing physical size and strength.'

6. The report recommended a placement in secure accommodation. In January 1997, the local authority planning committee recommended a secure placement. c Since K was only 11 years old the approval of the Secretary of State was required. This was given in April 1997. Other residential placements were tried and his behaviour improved. A further psychiatric assessment was carried out in May 1998 which concluded that:

d 'At present he continues to present with all the risk behaviours identified at our initial assessment. These risks appear at present to be contained within his current placement. However our concern would be that as [K] develops in physical strength and size these behaviours will become more difficult to contain. Consideration must be given to constructing a longer term strategy to both recognise and react to this need.'

e 7. Between October and December 1998 there was a marked deterioration in K's behaviour. He was charged with two offences of indecent assault on a girl at his placement. He was moved and moved again. He was involved in two incidents of fire-setting. He assaulted two female members of staff and was charged with indecent assault. In November 1998 he was aggressive and assaulted f a male member of staff. This catalogue of incidents and K's general behaviour caused the local authority to place him in his present secure unit and apply, for the first time, for a secure accommodation order. A guardian ad litem was appointed. An interim order was made on 7 December 1998 for four weeks.

8. K had a further psychiatric assessment which concluded that he was not g suffering from a psychiatric illness. He did, however, have complex social and educational needs and mental health problems. He continued to present a significant risk to others through sexual aggression, even within a secure setting. K's father was unhappy for K to remain in secure accommodation and, with the possibility of withdrawal of consent by one parent, the local authority obtained an interim care order, as a precaution, on 4 January 1999. In February full h psychiatric assessment confirmed the earlier reports, including sexually inappropriate behaviour, sexual assaults, destructible and disorganised behaviour. It was thought that he needed a structured environment which could manage his violent and sexually aggressive behaviour and that his sexually inappropriate behaviour was likely to respond to a behavioural therapy programme. Further applications for j secure accommodation orders were not opposed by the guardian nor by either parent. K, however, appealed against the refusal of the family proceedings court to allow him to attend the s 25 hearing. Wall J allowed the appeal and, since the transfer of the case to the county court on 28 July 1999, K has attended the hearings. In the county court his case has been heard throughout by Judge Urquhart who has clearly taken a great deal of trouble over K. He held one hearing in the secure unit and went round the unit with K. He has seen and talked

to K at the court hearings and has established a rapport with him. K likes him and has confidence in him. I very much hope that, in due course, when the plans for K settle down, future applications concerning K will continue to be heard by Judge Urquhart.

9. A clinical psychologist assessed K in April 1999 when he was 13 years and 8 months old. He was assessed as having general, moderate learning difficulties with a cognitive age of approximately seven years. K continued to exhibit worrying behaviour which caused the principal of the secure unit to set out in a letter, dated 17 June 1999, his concerns about K's behaviour and sexual fantasies. He reported that K was acting out sexual fantasies even in the controlled and highly supervised environment in which he was placed. He posed a considerable risk to others. The principal of the unit then said:

> 'The identification of babies as victims, the anger he feels during abusive acts, the lack of victim sympathy and the impulsive urges to act out fantasies despite supervision only reinforces my professional opinion and that of my staff, that [K] is an extremely dangerous young man.'

He felt that K was likely to act upon his fantasies almost as soon as he had an opportunity to do so.

10. Inquiries were made last year throughout the country by the local authority to try to find a more specialist unit. Of those identified, none was suitable, or if suitable, willing to take him. He has, therefore, remained at the secure unit. He has received appropriate education and has made progress both in formal education and in his behaviour. His continued placement in the secure unit has been supported by both parents and the guardian ad litem. He was seen for a number of sessions by a senior therapist working with the Lucy Faithfull Foundation, which K chose to bring to an end. She expressed the view in two reports, in November 1999 and in January 2000, that it would be possible to work therapeutically with K and outside a closed environment. K was further assessed by an adolescent forensic psychiatrist, Dr D, who did not support a placement outside a secure unit. She confirmed the earlier psychiatric reports and said that if K was in an open environment he was at risk of absconding and, if so, would be at risk himself and would be a serious risk to others. She recommended that he should remain in secure accommodation. She also recommended a further psychological assessment of K to include speech and language. He was further assessed by a clinical psychologist in April 2000, when he was 14 years and 9 months old, as having verbal reasoning skills of around eight years. Further attempts were made by the local authority in April 2000 to find K another placement without success.

11. In August 2000 K described some of his sexual fantasies which gave rise to considerable concern to those caring for him in the secure unit. It had the effect of stopping the outside visits which had previously taken place and had been much enjoyed by K.

12. On 29 September 2000, the case was transferred to the High Court. On 16 October just before the hearing of the appeal, Dr D provided this court with two reports, the second one being based on an interview with K at the secure unit on 12 October. She expressed her concerns as to K's competence to understand and to take part in the court proceedings. She considered that he had made progress since she last saw him in February but that he continued to represent a risk to others and to be at risk from harm himself. She did not believe that his

a problems could be managed in any other description of accommodation and she considered that he continued to fulfil the criteria for detention under s 25.

13. It is worth noting that between August 1996 and April 1999, K appeared before a juvenile or youth court on four occasions and was, over that period, convicted of the following offences—arson, criminal damage, burglary, common assault, indecent assault and criminal damage caused by arson. He was also, over b the same period, cautioned for arson and criminal damage. It seems clear, from the reports of the clinical psychologist in April 2000 and the two reports of Dr D in October 2000, that K falls within the criteria for mental impairment and comes within the provisions of the 1983 Act. This conclusion will have, it seems to me, a significant effect upon any arrangements for K's long-term future. K has made it clear that he does not want to remain in a secure unit and wishes to be placed c in a normal children's home with a view to going eventually to live with his mother. This is the background to the appeal by K against the secure accommodation order made on 30 June 2000, the subject of this appeal.

The application for a declaration of incompatibility

d 14. Miss de Haas, for K, has sought a determination by this court that s 25 of the 1989 Act is incompatible with s 4(1) of the 1998 Act, and for a declaration of incompatibility under s 4(2). She relied upon art 5 of the convention. Article 5, 'Right to liberty and security', states:

> '1. Everyone has the right to liberty and security of person. No one shall e be deprived of his liberty save in the following cases and in accordance with a procedure prescribed by law ... (c) the lawful arrest or detention of a person effected for the purpose of bringing him before the competent legal authority on reasonable suspicion of having committed an offence or when it is reasonably considered necessary to prevent his committing an offence or f fleeing after having done so; (d) the detention of a minor by lawful order for the purpose of educational supervision or his lawful detention for the purpose of bringing him before the competent legal authority; (e) the lawful detention of persons for the prevention of the spreading of infectious diseases, of persons of unsound mind, alcoholics or drug addicts or vagrants ...
>
> 5. Everyone who has been the victim of arrest or detention in g contravention of the provisions of this Article shall have an enforceable right to compensation.'

15. Section 1 of the 1998 Act incorporates certain of the rights and fundamental freedoms set out in the convention into English domestic law. h Section 2 requires a court determining a question which has arisen in connection with a convention right to take into account the opinions of the Commission and decisions and judgments of the European Court of Human Rights. The English courts are, so far as it is possible to do so, required to read and give effect to English legislation in such a way as is compatible with the convention rights (see s 3(1)). It is clear from ss 3 and 4 that, if English legislation is found to be j incompatible with a convention right, that legislation is, none the less, to continue to be applied by the domestic court. Section 4(6) states:

> 'A declaration under this section ("a declaration of incompatibility")—(a) does not affect the validity, continuing operation or enforcement of the provision in respect of which it is given; and (b) is not binding on the parties to the proceedings in which it is made.'

It is a matter for the minister of the Crown to take the appropriate remedial action under s 10 (see *R v DPP, ex p Kebeline* [1999] 4 All ER 801 at 831, [2000] 2 AC 326 at 367 per Lord Steyn).

16. The effect of ss 3 and 4 is that, in the present case, it is the duty of this court to see if it is possible to read and give effect to s 25 of the 1989 Act in accordance with art 5 and, if it is not possible, then this court has the jurisdiction, by s 4(5), to make a declaration of incompatibility of s 25 with art 5. Such a declaration has, however, no immediate effect upon the position of K, and if the order of Judge Urquhart was correctly made, in accordance with the requirements of s 25, despite the application of Miss de Haas to the contrary, there can be no immediate challenge to the detention of K in the secure unit. Further, if the facts placed before this court demonstrate that K should remain in the secure unit, this court must consider whether to make a new order in accordance with our domestic law.

17. The argument on incompatibility of s 25 with the convention right of K under art 5 was in two parts: (1) whether a secure accommodation order was a deprivation of liberty and, if so; (2) whether such deprivation of liberty came within the permitted categories set out in art 5(1)(a) to (f).

18. Although some argument was addressed to us that the situation of K might come within either or both art 5(1)(c) and (e), those submissions were not pressed, and it is not necessary in the present appeal to express a view. If a secure accommodation order is a deprivation of liberty, for the purpose of this appeal, the justification for keeping K in a secure unit under s 25 comes within art 5(1)(d), or his detention is a breach of his convention right under art 5.

19. Section 25, 'Use of accommodation for restricting liberty', is as follows:

> '(1) Subject to the following provisions of this section, a child who is being looked after by a local authority may not be placed, and, if placed, may not be kept, in secure accommodation provided for the purpose of restricting liberty ("secure accommodation") unless it appears—(a) that—(i) he has a history of absconding and is likely to abscond from any other description of accommodation; and (ii) if he absconds, he is likely to suffer significant harm; or (b) that if he is kept in any other description of accommodation he is likely to injure himself or other persons ...
>
> (3) It shall be the duty of a court hearing an application under this section to determine whether any relevant criteria for keeping a child in secure accommodation are satisfied in his case.
>
> (4) If a court determines that any such criteria are satisfied, it shall make an order authorising the child to be kept in secure accommodation and specifying the maximum period for which he may be so kept.'

20. In the Children (Secure Accommodation) Regulations 1991, SI 1991/1505 secure accommodation is defined in para 2(1) as—

> 'accommodation which is provided for the purpose of restricting the liberty of children to whom section 25 of the Act (use of accommodation for restricting liberty) applies.'

21. The length of court orders is regulated by paras 11 and 12 of the 1991 regulations. The power of the local authority to keep a child in a secure unit for a maximum of 72 hours in any period of 28 days, in the absence of a court order, is to be found in para 10.

a *Deprivation of liberty*

22. Miss de Haas submitted that K's detention in a secure unit amounted to deprivation of his liberty. She recognised that every child was subject to a degree of control and deprivation of free movement. Examples were given such as—the child who was told by his mother that he cannot go out to the cinema because he had not completed his homework or—the child in boarding school with school b rules which deprived him of free movement outside the school grounds. She accepted that the right to liberty was not absolute and that some deprivation of liberty did not come within art 5. She argued, however, that it was a question of degree, and the point came at which the restrictions were so inhibiting that it became a breach of art 5. She submitted that in a secure unit, by its very nature, a child was deprived of his liberty. He could not leave the premises and was c locked in his room at night. The purpose of the section was to restrain children who would otherwise be likely to abscond. In order for a local authority to place the child in a secure unit, it had to obtain the authorisation of the court for any period exceeding 72 hours and the requirement to get the authorisation of the court was a good indication that a secure accommodation placement went d beyond the extent to which a parent could lawfully restrain a child. It was, therefore, a deprivation of liberty which required justification within the narrow exceptions set out in art 5(1)(a) to (f).

23. On the facts of this appeal, K was for many years accommodated voluntarily by the local authority under Pt III of the 1989 Act, s 20. The arrangements made for K by the local authority were with the consent of the parents who, until December e 1998, retained parental responsibility. From December 1998, when the first interim care order was made, parental responsibility was shared with the local authority. Mr Garnham pointed to the approach of the European Court of Human Rights that restrictions upon the liberty of a child need not amount to deprivation of liberty. He submitted that the placing of K in secure accommodation, particularly since it f was done with the consent of the parents, who still consented to him remaining there, was within the lawful application of parental responsibility and was not a deprivation of liberty within art 5. Further, by s 22(3)(a) of the 1989 Act, the local authority had a duty to safeguard and promote the welfare of the child and the restrictions upon the liberty of K were motivated by concerns for his welfare. This was a proper purpose for the exercise of parental responsibility and consistent g with the duties laid on the local authority by the 1989 Act. He relied upon the cases of *Nielsen v Denmark* (1988) 11 EHRR 175 and *Family T v Austria* (1990) 64 DR 176 in support of his submission that a secure accommodation order did not amount to a deprivation of liberty.

24. Mr Ryder QC, who was asked at a late stage to make a submission on this h issue, indicated that the local authority would not seek to argue that a secure accommodation order was not a deprivation of liberty. He accepted that it had to be justified under art 5(1)(d).

25. In approaching the words of art 5 of the convention I keep in mind the speech of Lord Hope of Craighead in *R v DPP, ex p Kebeline* [1999] 4 All ER 801 at j 839, [2000] 2 AC 326 at 375, in which he referred to the observations of Lord Woolf that a generous and purposive construction was to be given to that part of a constitution which protects and entrenches fundamental rights and freedoms to which all persons in the state are to be entitled. Lord Hope said:

> 'The same approach will now have to be applied in this country when issues are raised under the Human Rights Act 1998 about the compatibility

of domestic legislation and of acts of public authorities with the fundamental rights and freedoms which are enshrined in the convention.' a

26. Robert Walker LJ in *Re A (children) (conjoined twins: surgical separation)* [2000] 4 All ER 961 at 1068, [2001] 2 WLR 480 at 589 said: 'The convention is to be construed as an autonomous text, without regard to any special rules of English law ...'

27. It is clear that not every deprivation of liberty comes with the ambit of art 5. b Parents are given a wide measure of discretion in the upbringing of their children. This was recognised by the European Court in *Nielsen v Denmark* (1988) 11 EHRR 175, the case of a child committed to a psychiatric ward at the request of his mother. It said (at 191–192 (para 61)):

c

> 'It should be observed at the outset that family life in the Contracting States encompasses a broad range of parental rights and responsibilities in regard to care and custody of minor children. The care and upbringing of children normally and necessarily require that the parents or an only parent decide where the child must reside and also impose, or authorise others to impose, various restrictions on the child's liberty. Thus the children in a school or d other educational or recreational institution must abide by certain rules which limit their freedom of movement and their liberty in other respects. Likewise a child may have to be hospitalised for medical treatment. Family life in this sense, and especially the rights of parents to exercise parental authority over their children, having due regard to their corresponding e parental responsibilities, is recognised and protected by the Convention, in particular by Article 8. Indeed the exercise of parental rights constitutes a fundamental element of family life.'

(See also *Family T v Austria* (1990) 64 DR 176 at 180 following *Nielson*'s case.)

28. I recognise the force of the principles set out in the decisions in *Nielson*'s f case and *Family T*'s case. There is a point, however, at which one has to stand back and say—is this within ordinary acceptable parental restrictions upon the movements of a child or does it require justification? *In Guzzardi v Italy* (1980) 3 EHRR 333 at 362–363 the court said:

> '92. The Court recalls that in proclaiming the "right to liberty", g paragraph 1 of Article 5 is contemplating the physical liberty of the person; its aim is to ensure that no one should be dispossessed of this liberty in an arbitrary fashion ... In order to determine whether someone has been "deprived of his liberty" within the meaning of Article 5, the starting point must be his concrete situation and account must be taken of a whole range h of criteria such as the type, duration, effects and manner of implementation of the measure in question.
>
> 93. The difference between deprivation of and restriction upon liberty is nonetheless merely one of degree or intensity, and not one of nature or substance. Although the process of classification into one or other of these categories sometimes proves to be no easy task in that some borderline cases j are a matter of pure opinion, the Court cannot avoid making the selection upon which the applicability of Article 5 depends.'

29. Applying those principles to the application of a secure accommodation order upon a young person, it is clear that the purpose of s 25, as set out in the interpretation in the 1991 regulations dependent upon it, is to restrict the liberty

a of the child. The application of s 25 is not dependent upon the making of a care or interim care order. A child can be the subject of a secure accommodation order in circumstances in which the local authority does not share parental responsibility with the parents. It is a benign jurisdiction to protect the child as well as others (see *Re W (a minor) (secure accommodation)* [1994] 3 FCR 248 at 253 per Ewbank J), but it is none the less restrictive. If a parent exercised those b powers by detaining a child in a similar restrictive fashion and was challenged to justify such detention, for my part, I doubt whether the general rights and responsibilities of a parent would cover such an exercise of parental authority. It might be permissible for a few days but not for nearly two years. A court, under our domestic law, would be likely to intervene. The limit of 72 hours' detention c imposed by statute on a local authority without court authorisation, even in the most extreme case, is in my view significant support for the argument that this is a deprivation of liberty. The requirement for a court order, and for the court to find proved the relevant criteria before the authorisation to restrict the child's liberty beyond 72 hours can be made, underlines, in my view, that this is an extreme measure.

d 30. Miss de Haas drew our attention to the advice from the Department of Health on the use of s 25, that restricting the liberty of children is a serious step which must be taken only where there is no alternative, as a last resort, (see *The Children Act 1989: Guidance and Regulations (Court Orders)* vol 1, p 66, para 5.1). In *Re M (a minor) (secure accommodation order)* [1995] 3 All ER 407 at 412, [1995] e Fam 108 at 115, I referred to a decision by a local authority to restrict the liberty of a child as serious and draconian. Holman J held, in *LM v Essex CC* [1999] 1 FCR 673, that where the criteria which justified the making of a secure accommodation order ceased to exist, there was no justification for the local authority to continue to detain the child whom it had agreed was to be moved into non-secure f accommodation.

31. The Second Section of the European Court recently decided an application in respect of a secure accommodation order in *Koniarska v UK* (12 October 2000, unreported). The court declared inadmissible an application by a girl who was 17 at the time of the authorisation of the secure accommodation order. Although Mr Garnham argued with some force that the court may not have fully understood g the working of s 25, as seems evident from the judgment of the court, that does not seem to me to detract from its conclusion in the next paragraph:

> 'The next question is whether the applicant was "deprived of [her] liberty" within the meaning of art 5(1) of the convention. The court notes that the h aim of the orders under s 25 of the 1989 Act is to provide "secure" accommodation. No precise details have been furnished, but the applicant likens the security regime to that of a medium to high security prison for adult offenders, and this is not contested by the government. The court finds that the applicant was deprived of her liberty from 23 November 1995 until j 29 April 1996.'

32. In the light of the concession by the United Kingdom government, and for the reasons which I have set out above, for my part, I am satisfied that a secure accommodation order is a deprivation of liberty within the meaning of art 5 and requires, therefore, to come within one of the exceptions set out in art 5(1) so as not to be incompatible with K's right to liberty under the convention.

The exceptions under art 5

33. In *Engel v Netherlands (No 1)* (1976) 1 EHRR 647 at 669 (para 57) the European Court said 'the list of deprivations of liberty set out [in art 5] is exhaustive' (see also *Ireland v UK* (1978) 2 EHRR 25 at 87 (para 194)).

34. Miss de Haas submitted that K's deprivation of liberty did not fall within any of the exceptions within sub-paras (a) to (f) and was not therefore as a result of a lawful order. The European Court said in *Bouamar v Belgium* (1989) 11 EHRR 1 at 16 (para 50)):

> '"Lawfulness", however, also implies that the deprivation of liberty is in keeping with the purpose of the restrictions permissible under Article 5(1) of the Convention.'

The permissible exceptions are to be given a narrow interpretation (see *Guzzardi v Italy* (1980) 3 EHRR 333 at 366–367 (paras 98 and 100)).

35. Detention under the relevant part of the exception in art 5(1)(d) must be by lawful order and for the purpose of educational supervision. On the facts of this appeal K is receiving education which is carefully supervised, from which he is clearly benefiting, even though there is criticism of the lack of sufficient therapy. The submission advanced by Miss de Haas was not that the regime was in fact unsuitable, but that educational supervision did not form part of the relevant criteria in s 25 which, she submitted, had nothing to do with education and but were designed to restrict liberty. Since the criteria did not refer to education, the section was not in keeping with art 5(1)(d).

36. It is not necessary, in my judgment, for s 25 to refer to education since, by the provisions of the Education Act 1996, education is compulsory for any child under 16 (see s 7) and optional thereafter. Consequently at the secure unit to which K was sent in December 1998, there was a statutory obligation to provide him with education.

37. The decision in *Koniarska v UK* App No 33670/96 (12 October 2000, unreported) is helpful. The facts were that the applicant was 17 at the time of the secure accommodation order that was the subject of the application to the European Court. She had been diagnosed as suffering from a psychopathic disorder and there was a danger of her injuring herself or other persons. The court found that: 'There could thus be said to be both medical and social reasons for her detention.'

38. The court then considered the applicability of art 5(1)(d), and whether it covered her detention under a s 25 order. The court said that the only question was whether the detention was 'for the purpose of' educational supervision. It considered the decision in *Bouamar*'s case and noted that the orders were not isolated orders for detention but were made in the context of a long history of efforts to ensure the best possible upbringing of the applicant, and that the local authority considered that the applicant needed to be placed in secure accommodation. The court next noted that—

> 'the applicant had passed the school leaving age, and apart from the secure accommodation orders could not have been required to attend continuing education. However, the relevant parts of art 5(1)(d) of the convention are limited to the detention of "minors", and not to the detention of persons below the official school leaving age. The mere fact that the applicant aged 17, could no longer have been required to attend ordinary school does not taint her detention under a specific order, provided that the detention was

indeed "for the purposes of educational supervision". The applicant claims that the detention was not "for" the purpose of educational supervision, but that any education which was offered was purely incidental to the real reason for the detention, which was (in respect of the first order) "a need for protection and containment pending the actioning of her care plan". The court considers that, in the context of the detention of minors, the words "educational supervision" must not be equated rigidly with notions of classroom teaching. In particular, in the present context of a young person in local authority care, educational supervision must embrace many aspects of the exercise, by the local authority, of parental rights for the benefit and protection of the person concerned. The court has no doubt that the orders made by the magistrates' courts on 23 November 1995 and 23 February 1996, on the application of the local authority, were capable of constituting part of the "educational supervision" of the applicant. As to the reality of the educational provision in the present case, the court notes that Glenthorne, to which the applicant was sent, is a specialist residential facility for seriously disturbed young people. As part of its multi-disciplinary approach, it provides an educational programme in which young people are taught in groups of three or four, or sometimes on a one-to-one or one-to-two basis. Until January 1996 the applicant attended a full range of classes, and that even after an incident with another student she attended some classes and took part in life skills and social skills programmes. The fact that the number of classes attended by the applicant was limited because she chose not to go cannot affect the underlying position, which was that extensive educational provision was made, and the applicant benefited from it to a certain extent. The present case is therefore to be distinguished from the abovementioned *Bouamar*'s case, in which the applicant was detained "in a remand prison in conditions of virtual isolation and without the assistance of staff with educational training". The court therefore finds that the applicant's detention from 23 November 1995 until 29 April 1996 was justified under art 5(1)(d) of the convention as it was the detention of a minor "for the purpose of educational supervision". It follows therefore that this part of the application is manifestly ill-founded within the meaning of art 35(3) of the convention and it must be rejected pursuant to art 35(4).'

39. All the other grounds were rejected and the application was declared inadmissible. It is interesting to note that the court did not express any criticism of the statutory framework of a secure accommodation order. It found that the circumstances in which the secure accommodation order was made were covered by art 5(1)(d). Those circumstances bear in many ways a close resemblance to the facts of this appeal. In my view, the decision in *Koniarska*'s case is determinative of this part of the appeal and it is clear that art 5(1)(d) covers the making of a secure accommodation order in respect of K.

40. However, Miss de Haas submitted that a young person over 16 could be detained under s 25 without any requirement under English law that he should receive education. In a secure unit, which by its nature provides for those under 18, education is likely to be available. Miss Koniarska was 17 and was receiving educational supervision at her secure unit. Theoretically there might be circumstances in which a s 25 order was made in respect of a child under 18 where the words 'for the purpose of educational supervision' did not cover the facts of

that particular case. Miss de Haas argued that that possibility vitiated the entire section and made the section incompatible with art 5. a

41. I, however, reject that argument and agree with the submission of Mr Garnham that a distinction is to be drawn between a complaint that a step taken by a local authority pursuant to a power granted by statute is in breach of an article of the convention, and a complaint that the statutory provision is itself incompatible with the article. The duty of the English court under the 1998 Act b is to attempt to find a compatible interpretation. If a compatible interpretation can be found, there is no justification for a declaration of incompatibility. Mr Garnham referred us to an extra-judicial observation of Lord Cooke of Thorndon who said:

> 'Section 3(1) will require a very different approach to interpretation from c that to which the United Kingdom courts are accustomed. Traditionally, the search has been for the true meaning; now it will be for a possible meaning that would prevent the making of a declaration of incompatibility.' (See Lester and Pannick *Human Rights Law and Practice* (1999) p 23, footnote 2 to para 2.3.2.)

d

42. I respectfully agree with Lord Cooke. If the situation postulated by Miss de Haas did arise, it would be the application of a s 25 order to a situation that would be a breach of a convention right. That such a situation might arise is not in my judgment a reason for declaring that the section itself is incompatible with art 5(1)(d). In *Bouamar v Belgium* (1989) 11 EHRR 1 at 17 (para 52), the young e man (who was under 18) was placed on nine occasions for a total period of 119 days in a remand prison. He was placed in virtual isolation without the assistance of staff with educational training. The court pointed out that his confinement could not be regarded as furthering any educational aim. At the time there was, in that part of Belgium, no closed institution able to accommodate highly disturbed juveniles. The court found that there was a breach of art 5. The contrast between f the facts of that case and the present appeal is obvious. Having said that, it is interesting to see that in *Bouamar*'s case that the European Court also said (at 16 (para 50)):

> 'The Court notes that the confinement of a juvenile in a remand prison does not necessarily contravene sub-paragraph (d), even if it is not in itself g such as to provide for the person's "educational supervision". As is apparent from the words "for the purpose of" ("*pour*"), the "detention" referred to in the text is a means of ensuring that the person concerned is placed under "educational supervision", but the placement does not necessarily have to be an immediate one.'

h

43. In each case where a secure accommodation order is applied for, the English court, at any level, must have the requirements of art 5(1)(d) in mind when it is considering the relevant criteria, and thereby ensure the compatibility of the section with the convention right.

44. Miss de Haas raised issues in her written submissions under arts 3, 6 and 8 j but, rightly in my view, did not pursue them. It is not necessary for me to deal with any of them. I should, however, like to comment on the way in which the local authority gave K every opportunity to take part in these proceedings. Having been assessed as having a mental age of eight, one might raise an eyebrow at his ability to give instructions and his separate representation at various proceedings including before this court. But there is no doubt that it has been

a very beneficial for him to be allowed to play a part, and to have some understanding of the legal procedures which have the effect of depriving him of his liberty. I should like to commend the local authority for its careful, conscientious and sensitive approach to this very difficult case and to ensuring that K has been able to play such a full part in it. I would dismiss this appeal.

45. The issue of damages does not therefore arise but, for the reasons given in b the judgment of Judge LJ, which I have had an opportunity of reading in draft, I agree that there would be no basis for a claim in damages against either the court or the local authority.

Application for a new secure accommodation order

46. I turn now to the application by the local authority for a new secure c accommodation order. It is obvious from the wealth of evidence presented to us that, although K has made progress in the secure unit, he remains a serious risk to others and is at risk himself from others. It would be entirely wrong to expose others, especially young female children, to the danger that he would pose if he were in a non-secure environment and he would be unlikely to be able to manage d within the community without risk to himself. In the light of the evidence before this court, and for the reasons given in the judgment of Thorpe LJ, which I have had an opportunity of reading in draft, in my view, there should be a further secure accommodation order to run for four months from 16 October 2000.

47. I would therefore grant the application of the local authority for a secure accommodation order until 16 February 2001.

e

THORPE LJ.

Part I

48. In my judgment this appeal fails comprehensively. Despite Miss de f Haas QC's valiant efforts most of the arguments advanced in her skeleton argument, for instance her reliance on arts 3, 6 and 8 of the European Convention for the Protection of Human Rights and Fundamental Freedoms (Rome, 4 November 1950; TS 71 (1953); Cmd 8969) (the convention), crumbled at the first touch. In the end the only question for determination is whether the order of 30 June 2000 breached K's rights under art 5 of the convention on and after g 2 October.

49. On its facts this is an extreme case. The principal of the secure unit said on 26 September that K was the most dangerous young person he had come across in 23 years of experience. The problems of adolescent dangerousness confront all the states of Europe and, although solutions may vary, all necessitate the h deprivation of liberty in extreme cases. It would affront common sense to suggest that the human rights of those detained are thereby inevitably abused. The right to liberty cannot be absolute. It has a counterbalancing duty to refrain from behaviour that is both anti-social and criminal. In the case of minors decisions of the European Court of Human Rights make plain that the right is not j absolute but in certain circumstances qualified. Those circumstances are not confined to the exceptions defined in art 5(1)(a) to (f).

50. The first issue is therefore whether K has been deprived of his right to liberty guaranteed by art 5(1). As a matter of first impression the answer must be Yes. Secure accommodation is defined in s 25 of the Children Act 1989 itself as 'accommodation provided for the purpose of restricting liberty'. However, the order authorising the restriction of K's liberty was made on the ground that, if

kept in any other accommodation, he was likely to injure himself or other persons.

51. Thus the primary purpose of the restriction was protective, both of K and of others. The secondary purpose was corrective, to enable trained and skilled professionals to teach K to modify his anti-social tendencies. There is no punitive purpose or element. It is K's tragedy that he is profoundly disabled not only cognitively but in lacking the internal boundaries that safeguard the majority from anti-social behaviour.

52. Without the restriction of K's liberty there would be a disastrous reduction in the prospects of helping K during these most formative years to overcome or reduce his disability by the delivery of education in its broadest sense. In truth the restriction is vital for the promotion of his welfare which is in reality the court's paramount consideration. Protective regimes such as secure accommodation under the 1989 Act and guardianship under the Mental Health Act 1983 may be restrictive of liberties but are not necessarily so. Each case will depend on whether those applying the regime exercise proper responsibility in ensuring that statutory or common law safeguards are not breached and whether they remain faithful to the primary protective purpose of the regime. In the case of *Re W (a minor) (secure accommodation)* [1994] 3 FCR 248 it was submitted to Ewbank J by counsel for the child that a s 25 order was equivalent to a custodial order in a criminal court. Ewbank J rejected that argument saying (at 253):

> 'This jurisdiction is entirely different. It is, as the Official Solicitor said, a benign jurisdiction. It is to protect the child, sometimes from others and sometimes from itself, and in some cases it is necessary in order to protect the child and to act as a good parent would act to curtail the child's liberty for a time.'

53. This analysis emphasises that plainly not all restrictions placed on the liberty of children constitute deprivation. Obviously parents have a right and a responsibility to restrict the liberty of their children, not only for protective and corrective purposes, but also sometimes for a punitive purpose. So acting they only risk breaching a child's art 5(1) rights if they exceed reasonable bounds. Equally parents may delegate that right and responsibility to others. Every parent who sends a child to a boarding school delegates to the head teacher and his staff. A local authority may even send a child to a school that provides 52-week boarding facilities. Then restrictions on liberty imposed by the school do not amount to a breach of the pupil's rights under art 5(1) unless the school betrays its responsibilities to the family.

54. This reality is, it seems, well recognised in European-based law. As was said in *Nielsen v Denmark* (1988) 11 EHRR 175 at 191–192 (para 61):

> 'The care and upbringing of children normally and necessarily require that the parents or an only parent decide where the child must reside and also impose, or authorise others to impose, various restrictions on the child's liberty. Thus the children in a school or other educational or recreational institution must abide by certain rules which limit their freedom of movement and their liberty in other respects. Likewise a child may have to be hospitalised for medical treatment. Family life in this sense, and especially the rights of parents to exercise parental authority over their children, having due regard to their corresponding parental responsibilities, is recognised and

a protected by the Convention, in particular by Article 8. Indeed the exercise of parental rights constitutes a fundamental element of family life.'

55. Whilst *Nielsen v Denmark* was a hospitalisation case, in the following year in the case of *Family T v Austria* (1990) 64 DR 176 the European Commission of Human Rights considered a complaint against the accommodation of children in b a public children's home. In reliance on para 61 of the judgment in *Nielsen*'s case the complaint was rejected since the applicants had not shown that the conditions in the home deprived the children of their liberty.

56. The European authority most relevant to the determination of the question of whether secure accommodation in our jurisdiction necessarily curtails a deprivation of liberty is the recent decision of the court in the case of c *Koniarska v UK* App No 33670/96 (12 October 2000, unreported). The decision is on the admissibility of complaints brought by Lucy Koniarska following her accommodation at Glenthorne Centre authorised by secure accommodation orders under s 25. Her complaint under arts 5, 3 and 8 were all held to be inadmissible. However, her contention that she had suffered a deprivation of d liberty was not ruled inadmissible. Only because the deprivation was justified under art 5(1)(d) was that complaint ruled inadmissible. The court's reasoning is to be found where it is stated:

'The court recalls at the outset that in its *Nielsen v Denmark* judgment it found that art 5 was not applicable to the hospitalisation of the applicant as e that hospitalisation was a responsible exercise by the applicant's mother of her custodial rights in the interest of the child. That reasoning cannot be transposed to the present case as, although the local authority had custodial rights over the applicant by virtue of the care order which was still in force, the orders placing the applicant in secure accommodation were made by the f courts. There is no question of the respective courts having custodial rights over the applicant, and so art 5 applies in the present case.'

57. Mr Garnham emphasises that this finding for the applicant only took her across the threshold and that the government would have prevailed on any final determination since it would have convincingly demonstrated the fallacious g reasoning in the passage cited. I accept Mr Garnham's submission. As I will demonstrate when I come to the United Kingdom authorities, a secure accommodation order is created by the local authority in the exercise of its statutory duties. The role of the court is essentially supervisory, a role undoubtedly created by Parliament as a safeguard against unjustifiable or superfluous h detention.

58. From these European cases Mr Garnham develops his submission that in consequence of the interim care order of 1 January 1999 the local authority share parental responsibility with K's parents. The local authority is therefore in law doing no more in meeting K's needs by arranging for him to be cared for at the j secure unit (necessarily under the terms of a s 25 order) than does the parent of a less disabled 15-year-old who sends his child to a boarding school. I see considerable attraction in that argument but it does not seem to me to depend for successful foundation on the existence of an interim care order in this case. In a sense that is a fortuitous factor which results from the development that at one stage, although not now, the father seemed to contemplate exercising his parental right to remove K from secure accommodation.

59. Mr Garnham in his submissions emphasises that the making of the interim care order brings s 22(3)(a) of the 1989 Act into play. But K would equally be entitled to the protection of that subsection as an accommodated child. The interaction of ss 22 and 25, as well as the respective functions of the local authority and the court in the creation of a s 25 order, were very clearly explained by Hoffmann LJ in the case of *Re M (a minor) (secure accommodation order)* [1995] 3 All ER 407 at 415, [1995] Fam 108 at 118–119 when he said:

> 'The function of the court under s 25 is, in my view, to control the exercise of power by the local authority rather than to exercise an independent jurisdiction in the best interests of the child. What form should this control take? Subsection (3) says that the court's duty is to determine whether any relevant criteria are satisfied. What are the relevant criteria? ... In my judgment the criteria applied by the court must be the same as those applicable to an initial decision by the local authority. These include not only the question of whether para (a) or (b) of s 25(1) is satisfied, but also having regard to the local authority's general duty under s 22(3) to safeguard and promote the welfare of the child, subject to the important qualification in s 22(6): "If it appears to a local authority that it is necessary, for the purpose of protecting members of the public from serious injury, to exercise their powers with respect to a child whom they are looking after in a manner which may not be consistent with their duties under this section, they may do so." ... It seems to me that the question of whether a decision to keep the child in secure accommodation would be in accordance with these statutory duties imposed upon the local authority must be among the relevant criteria to be considered by the court under s 25(3). It is said that the mandatory language of sub-s (4)—if the court determines that the criteria are satisfied, it shall make an order—suggests that the criteria must involve giving a Yes or No answer to a question of fact rather than a flexible application of general principles. But the mandatory element in sub-s (4) is to some extent illusory. True, the court shall make an order, but the maximum period for which he may be kept is a matter for the court's discretion. Since there is in practice little difference between an order for a very brief period and no order at all, the use of the word "shall" does not seem to me to carry much weight. Thus I think that the duty of the court is to put itself in the position of a reasonable local authority and to ask, first, whether the conditions in sub-s (1) are satisfied and, secondly, whether it would be in accordance with the authority's duty to safeguard and promote the welfare of the child (but subject to the qualification in s 22(6)) for the child to be kept in secure accommodation and, if so, for how long.'

60. Thus I conclude that s 25 is to be categorised like s 34 as a section which gives the court a role to oversee the case management proposed by the local authority and only to sanction by order such proposals as fulfil the stated statutory criteria and are otherwise demonstrated to meet the welfare consideration. So the restriction on K's liberty is the consequence of a professional judgment as to what sort of accommodation best meets his needs, a judgment subsequently scrutinised and approved by a judge in accordance with the statutory requirement.

61. For these reasons I accept Mr Garnham's first and bold submission that the order of 30 June did not breach K's art 5-rights since the deprivation of liberty was a necessary consequence of an exercise of parental responsibility for the

a protection and promotion of his welfare. I am not deterred by Mr Ryder QC's skeleton: 'It is accepted that the purpose of secure accommodation is to restrict liberty' and his subsequent rejection of the opportunity to adopt Mr Garnham's submissions.

62. Fortunately my dissent from the opinion of Dame Elizabeth Butler-Sloss P and Judge LJ is of little moment since we are all very clear that if Mr Garnham b fails on his first submission his case in reliance on art 5(1)(d) must succeed. Indeed in my view it is unanswerable. The recent decision in *Koniarska*'s case, ruling that a contention indistinguishable from that advanced by Miss de Haas was inadmissible, confirms a conclusion that is already clear from the wide construction of the phrase 'educational provision'. In deciding that the contention was inadmissible the court in *Koniarska*'s case stated:

c

> 'In the context of the detention of minors, the words "educational supervision" must not be equated rigidly with notions of classroom teaching. In particular, in the present context of a young person in local authority care, educational supervision must embrace many aspects of the exercise, by the d local authority, of parental rights for the benefit and protection of the person concerned.'

63. A decision by the court that a complaint is inadmissible amounts to a decision that it is unarguable as art 35(3) makes plain:

> e 'The court shall declare inadmissible an individual application … which it considers incompatible with the provisions of the Convention … manifestly ill-founded, or an abuse of the right of application.'

64. Further I accept Mr Garnham's submission that education is unlikely to be and need not be demonstrated to be the sole purpose of the detention. f Article 5(1)(d) is satisfied if education is shown to be one of the purposes of detention as the case of *Bouamar v Belgium* (1989) 11 EHRR 1 demonstrates. Only when there is no present or reasonably imminent educational provision does the art 5(1)(d) defence fail. The relevant paragraph of the judgment in *Bouamar*'s case is para 50 (at 16–17) where it is stated:

> g 'The Court notes that the confinement of a juvenile in a remand prison does not necessarily contravene sub-paragraph (d), even if it is not in itself such as to provide for the person's "educational supervision". As is apparent from the words "for the purpose of" ("*pour*"), the "detention" referred to in the text is a means of ensuring that the person concerned is placed under "educational supervision", but the placement does not necessarily have to be h an immediate one. Just as Article 5(1) recognises—in sub-paragraphs (c) and (a)—the distinction between pre-trial detention and detention after conviction, so sub-paragraph (d) does not preclude an interim custody measure being used as a preliminary to a régime of supervised education, without itself involving any supervised education. In such circumstances, j however, the imprisonment must be speedily followed by actual application of such a régime in a setting (open or closed) designed and with sufficient resources for the purpose.'

65. Finally Mr Garnham rightly refers to the duty imposed on parents by s 7 of the Education Act 1996 to cause children of compulsory school age to receive suitable and sufficient full-time education. Since K is a child in care that statutory

duty falls on the local authority. No one has suggested the authority is in breach of that duty.

66. For all those reasons there can be no doubt in my mind that the art 5(1)(d) defence is well made. There is relatively clear evidence from Dr D to suggest that K's detention could equally be justified under art 5(1)(e) were the issue investigated and ventilated. On the same basis a second alternative defence appears to lie under art 5(1)(c).

67. Save in one area of disagreement I am in complete accord with the judgments of Dame Elizabeth Butler-Sloss P and Judge LJ which I have had the opportunity of reading in draft. I agree with the orders that Dame Elizabeth Butler-Sloss P proposes.

Part II

68. Section 25(8) of the 1989 Act provides:

> 'The giving of an authorisation under this section shall not prejudice any power of any court in England and Wales or Scotland to give directions relating to the child to whom the authorisation relates.'

69. The 'authorisation' is of course the secure accommodation order made under the terms of s 25(4). A secure accommodation order in respect of K was first made on 4 December 1998 and was swiftly followed by the first interim care order dated 4 January 1999. That interim care order has been regularly renewed in accordance with the local practice direction within the Liverpool County Court and this additional support for K's regime is likely to continue for the foreseeable future. The transcript of proceedings before Judge Urquhart on 30 June demonstrates its utility. Judge Urquhart inquired of Miss Hooper, who on that day represented K, whether she was content with a secure accommodation order then proposed to run until 27 October. There then followed this exchange:

> '*Miss Hooper*: Yes, K has indicated that he's happy with that. I have also explained to K that there are care proceedings running parallel to this and, if there are any problems, matters can be raised within the care proceedings.
>
> *Judge Urquhart*: Oh yes of course they can yes.
>
> *Miss Hooper*: I have told him he is to get in contact with the office if there's anything he has concerns about.'

70. This illustrates that whilst s 25 does not contemplate more than the secure accommodation order, once the court has determined the relevant criteria for keeping a child in secure accommodation are satisfied, there is room for ancillary directions to be made under the accompanying interim care order. It is therefore important to see whether the promotion of K's welfare requires any directions to supplement the secure accommodation order made under s 25(4).

71. In my opinion the answer to that question lies in a survey of the extent to which K's needs have been met and his welfare promoted under past secure accommodation orders. It is sufficient to confine this review to the current year.

72. The most hopeful feature of the current year is the extent to which K has progressed both educationally and behaviourally at the secure unit. This is a tribute to the dedication and professionalism of all concerned with his management, particularly the staff at the secure unit, Dr D and his social worker, KD, who K himself particularly commends.

73. Nevertheless there are a number of specific points in the recent history that give rise to real concern. For much of what follows I am indebted to the very

a helpful and detailed report extending to 52 pages submitted by the guardian ad litem for the purposes of this appeal. In para 39 he records that K was referred to Alix Brown, principal therapist of the Lucy Faithfull Foundation. She conducted nine sessions with K between October and December 1999. By her interim report of 26 November she stated: 'At this point it is clear that K is going to need long-term psychotherapy in order to address the trauma.'

b 74. Later in the report she said:

> 'I believe it is possible to work therapeutically with [K], but, as I have indicated, it is likely to be a lengthy process. His best chances lie in beginning the work early.'

75. Unfortunately their therapeutic relationship broke down in December c 1999 as K 'stated he found the sessions with Miss Brown too upsetting'. Nevertheless Alix Brown continued to advocate K's need for psychotherapy. At a hearing on 5 May she stated that therapeutic work needed to be undertaken with K as soon as possible and that that work would be required for a lengthy period, possibly for up to two years.

d 76. Although this was a free-standing opinion I suspect that it was not heeded because it accompanied an opinion that K should move to a less restrictive placement, an opinion opposed by all other professionals and rejected by the judge. Furthermore, there may have been some difference of professional opinion between Alix Brown and Dr D. Dr D in her letter to KD of 8 May stated:

e

> 'Finally it may be helpful to those working with [K] now and in the future to know that his intellectual ability is around that of an 8 year old child, thus it would be inappropriate to deliver therapeutic inputs to [K] if they would be unsuitable for an 8 year old child.'

77. Her stance is amplified by her report of 12 October in which she said:

f

> 'Thus any verbal therapies aimed at helping [K] with his sexually abusive experiences need to be pitched at the level of a six-eight year old child. Appropriate therapies for a child of that age, creative, such as art play therapy.' (Sic.)

78. A further factor seems undoubtedly to have been the absence of services g in the locality. At a meeting of 14 June attended by all the professionals including Dr D it was agreed that the best plan for K was to remain at the secure unit and for therapeutic work to be undertaken there by outside experts. At the hearing on 30 June Dr D expressed the hope that the closure of the Glenthorne Secure Treatment Unit would result in two staff members, Dr Jasper and Dr Eps, being h consequentially liberated to provide K with the therapy that he required. However, I note that Dr Jasper is a consultant adolescent forensic psychiatrist and Dr Eps a consultant clinical psychologist. In any event although Dr D's report of 12 October stated that their work had commenced on 10 October, during the hearing we were told that there had been some continuing delay. Mr Ryder told j us two other things. First, although an art therapist had been identified in the locality since 14 June, no arrangements had yet been made for her to meet K. Second I understood Mr Ryder to say that in the area there is only one consultant child psychotherapist in an NHS post with an existing case load that renders further referrals impossible.

79. From this review I draw the following conclusions. (i) There is an unresolved professional disagreement as to K's therapeutic needs. On the one hand

Alix Brown advised the immediate commencement of long-term psychotherapy. On the other hand Dr D favoured art or play therapy and/or the expertise of colleagues in forensic psychiatry. Dr D's additional view set out by Mr Ryder in his written response submitted to the court on the third day of the appeal: 'In [Dr D's] view psychotherapy commenced after [K] was expelled from nursery and has continued thereafter.' Whilst I understand that view in the sense that K has received extraordinary professional commitment in an endeavour to correct his behavioural problems, it was clearly not what Alix Brown contemplated in her advice to the court in May. (ii) Both in the locality of the secure unit and in the local authority's own area there is a dearth of consultant child psychotherapy appointments within the NHS. Therefore what K ideally requires may have to yield to what is available given that there is no other realistic placement for him at the present time. (iii) At least in this case there is no financial impediment to meeting K's needs. To their great credit the 'W' NHS Trust has agreed to bear the cost of whatever services have to be bought in to meet K's needs. (iv) This is as complex and as worrying a case as any that I have ever met. For K time is of the essence if he is to continue this year's progress to achieve any sort of adult independence. Every month within the formative years between his current age and his majority is a month of opportunity, the loss or waste of which may prove very damaging to his longer-term prospects. (v) It is a matter of concern that K has never been referred to a consultant child and adolescent psychiatrist for assessment and referral for treatment. (iv) It is imperative that K's case be referred to a national resource of ultimate expertise. During the course of argument it was agreed that the Tavistock and Portman NHS Trust was best qualified to advise as to what could be done as well as to what should be done. It does not seem to me necessary to direct such a referral since Mr Ryder on instructions confirmed his client's readiness to refer the case to the Tavistock/Portman. Whereas I was concerned to hear from Mr Ryder that Dr D is adamantly opposed to any further referral, I was relieved to hear that she herself regards the Portman Clinic as the centre of excellence in the treatment of perverted and aggressive sexual urges and fantasies. I would very much hope that the expertise of the Tavistock/Portman Clinic will foster collaboration between all the mental health professionals, particularly in the interests of a good outcome for K. In my opinion a letter of instruction to Dr Trowell at the Tavistock/Portman should be agreed by all parties and should be expedited. Whether the Tavistock/Portman will wish to assess K at the secure unit is entirely a matter for their discretion. Though the guardian and Dr D have expressed reservations at intrusive professional involvement, the court can be confident of Tavistock/Portman sensitivity in this area. Until their assessment is available the re-involvement of Dr Jasper and Dr Eps could be deferred as should the introduction of an art therapist. Equally there would be little point in a further meeting of professionals already involved to address therapy issues unless that meeting flowed from a request from the Tavistock/Portman.

80. The second major area of concern arising out of a review of the past nine months is the cessation of mobility visits. The records show that in May K had three days out from the secure unit, in June he had four days out, and in July he had six days out. On 5 August he visited the American working farm. However, on the following day K at the invitation of two members of staff spoke of his sexual thoughts and fantasies. What he then said caused understandable professional concern. The view of staff was that mobility visits must be suspended and Dr D's views should be sought on the implication of these disclosures. On

10 August KD discussed K's position with Dr D's team at hospital P. They did not feel that they possessed the necessary level of expertise to undertake therapeutic work with K. So throughout the remainder of the school holidays K was deprived of either home visits or day trips. His mother understandably felt that he was being punished for his openness.

81. I note that a visit to Birmingham's Sea World Centre on 15 April had raised concerns as a result of remarks made by K to his social worker after the visit. That led to an internal assessment of future mobility visits involving direct work with K during the course of which K made a variety of statements about his past exposure to or involvement in sexual activity. Despite these revelations in April, thereafter the mobility visits had not only continued but increased in frequency without any mishap.

82. Furthermore I note that on 26 September, during the course of a conversation with the guardian K said:

> 'I think the fantasies in sexualised behaviour are in the past … as I am growing up I am learning to grow out of it. I've said [K] you need to grow out of these things and you'll get somewhere with your life if you do.'

83. Equally in interview with Dr D on 12 October K said that as far as his sexual behaviour is concerned he feels that this is resolved because he has written it all down in a book and all he is thinking about now is schoolwork. I have not heard any explicit evaluation from the guardian or Dr D of these reassurances. However Dr D records that when she checked with the staff on 12 October they did not accept K's assertions although they accepted that he had learned to recognise when his behaviour is becoming sexualised and to seek their help to contain the onset.

84. From this review I conclude, of course with the advantage of hindsight, that there should have been greater urgency in the determination of whether and for how long K's words on 6 August required the suspension of outside visits. At least Mr Ryder was able to inform us that K had enjoyed a home visit on 8 October and that a further visit had been fixed for 29 October. There needs to be a firm foundation for any continuing withdrawal of occasional trips, to the shops and to the cinema for example, such as K enjoyed in July.

85. In reviewing the written reports covering the recent past I had an additional concern that genetic and hormone testing recommended by Dr D on 29 February had still not been carried out. However that concern was answered at the hearing by Mr Ryder's written response.

86. In summary, whilst I am completely persuaded that this court has no alternative but to make the secure accommodation order which Dame Elizabeth Butler-Sloss P proposes it is incumbent upon all who hold professional responsibility for K during its course to ensure that as well as protective it is also enhancing in order to ensure that it could not be interpreted by K or by anyone else as either punitive or stunting his potential for continuing progress. I am relieved that Dame Elizabeth Butler-Sloss P has made arrangements to ensure that at the end of the period prescribed by our order there will be a review by Wall J who will review with hindsight the months that we view prospectively and will with that advantage make such further orders under Pts III and IV of the Act as are best calculated to direct K's future progress.

JUDGE LJ.

87. The circumstances in which a secure accommodation order may be made under s 25 of the Children Act 1989 are prescribed by statute. Therefore to evaluate the sustained submission by Miss de Haas QC that such an order is incompatible with art 5 of the European Convention for the Protection of Human Rights and Fundamental Freedoms (Rome, 4 November 1950; TS 71 (1953); Cmd 8969) (the convention), the starting point is the relevant statutory framework.

88. Part III of the 1989 Act imposes substantial obligations on local authorities to provide support for children and their families. There is a duty under s 17(1)—

> '(a) to safeguard and promote the welfare of children within their area who are in need; and (b) so far as is consistent with that duty, to promote the upbringing of such children by their families, by providing a range and level of services appropriate to those children's needs.'

A child is 'in need' if—

> '(a) he is unlikely to achieve or maintain, or to have the opportunity of achieving or maintaining, a reasonable standard of health or development without the provision for him of services by a local authority ... (b) his health or development is likely to be significantly impaired, or further impaired, without the provision for him of such services ...' (See s 17(10).)

In this context 'health' refers both to physical and mental health, and 'development' is concerned with the child's 'physical, intellectual, emotional, social or behavioural development' (see s 31(9)).

89. The child 'in need' must be provided with accommodation if he has been lost or abandoned, or there is no one with parental responsibility for him, or when the person caring for him has been prevented from providing suitable accommodation or care (see s 20). The provision of such accommodation is not sustainable in the face of objection from a person with parental responsibility who is willing and able to provide accommodation, or arrange for it, and, unless a residence order or care order is made, the child may be removed from the accommodation. Provision must also be made by the local authority for the child who has been put under police protection or detained by the police. In such cases, too, the parental wishes cannot supervene.

90. Where the child is being 'looked after' by the local authority (see s 22), that is in the care of the local authority under s 31, or provided with accommodation, the focus remains the child's welfare, which must be safeguarded and promoted. Moreover, the authority must 'advise, assist and befriend him with a view to promoting his welfare when he ceases to be looked after by them' (see s 24(1)). Unfortunately as the public needs to be protected from some of the children who are being looked after by the local authority, for that purpose only, the welfare of the child may have to yield its priority to the need to protect the public from serious injury (see s 22(6)).

91. In addition to children who are being 'looked after' by the local authority, there are those for whom there is a responsibility much more akin to that of a parent. No doubt to reflect this increased responsibility, and the corresponding degree of interference in the life of a child, and perhaps also his parents, care and supervision orders under s 31 are not imposed on a child by the local authority. Any order is made by the court, which must be satisfied that—

a

> '(2)(a) … the child concerned is suffering, or is likely to suffer, significant harm; and (b) that the harm, or likelihood of harm, is attributable to—(i) the care given to the child, or likely to be given to him if the order were not made, not being what it would be reasonable to expect a parent to give to him; or (ii) the child's being beyond parental control.'

b Section 31(9) defines 'harm' as 'ill-treatment or the impairment of health or development' and health and development are defined in precisely the same wide terms as before.

92. In the present case K is subject to an interim care order.

93. These various strands in the arrangements for children who are being looked after by and subject to a care order culminates, where necessary, in the c provision of secure accommodation under s 25. For present purposes, the significant feature of such an order is that the liberty of the child will be restricted. That indeed is its express purpose, repeated in the Children (Secure Accommodation) Regulations 1991, SI 1991/1505, and confirmed in *The Children Act 1989: Guidance and Regulations* (*Court Orders*) vol 1, p 66, para 5.1. This is quite d unequivocal in its advice, emphasising as it does that a secure accommodation order is—

> 'a serious step which must be taken only when there is no genuine alternative which would be appropriate. It must be a "last resort" in the sense that all else must first have been comprehensively considered and e rejected—never because no other placement was available at the relevant time, because of inadequacies in staffing, because the child is simply being a nuisance or runs away from his accommodation and is not likely to suffer significant harm in doing so, and never as a form of punishment.'

The order creates additional control over the child, and extends both to the child f who is absconding, that is leaving accommodation as and when he wants to and so putting himself at risk of serious harm, and to the child in care because he is beyond parental control.

94. Even if it is faithfully applying the guidance, the local authority, again, cannot impose such an order on its own initiative. The child's liberty may only g be curtailed if the order is authorised by the court. The jurisdiction to make it depends on the local authority satisfying the court under s 25(1)—

> '(a) that—(i) he has a history of absconding and is likely to abscond from any other description of accommodation; and (ii) if he absconds, he is likely to suffer significant harm; or (b) that if he is kept in any other description of h accommodation he is likely to injure himself or other persons.'

In *Koniarska v UK* App No 33670/96 (12 October 2000, unreported), the language used in its judgment by the court suggests a misapprehension of this statutory position. The local authority's 'custodial rights' over the child continued j throughout, and the order made by the court authorised the use of secure accommodation. The court's involvement represented not an interference with the liberty of the child, but rather a safeguard against unacceptable and unjustified interference with it.

95. It is worth re-emphasising that it is a prerequisite to the order that the child is being 'looked after' by the local authority. There is therefore a continuing duty to safeguard and promote the welfare of the child. This point was emphasised by

Hoffmann LJ in *Re M (a minor) (secure accommodation order)* [1995] 3 All ER 407 at 415, [1995] Fam 108 at 119 where he said: a

> '... the duty of the court is to put itself in the position of a reasonable local authority and to ask, first, whether the conditions in sub-s (1) are satisfied and, secondly, whether it would be in accordance with the authority's duty to safeguard and promote the welfare of the child (but subject to the qualification in s 22(6)) for the child to be kept in secure accommodation and, if so, for how long.' b

The final consideration is that the child also needs, and must continue to be provided with education, in the formal sense. Where the local authority 'propose to provide accommodation ... in an establishment at which education is provided for children who are accommodated there' (see s 28(1)(b) of the 1989 Act), they must embark on a sensible consultation process with the appropriate local education authority. The statutory obligation to ensure that formal education continues (see s 7 of the Education Act 1996), at any rate until the child reaches the age of 16, survives the making of a secure accommodation order. c

96. The order cannot be made in respect of a child subject to 'punishment' imposed on conviction of major crimes (see s 53 of the Children and Young Persons Act 1933), or detained under formal procedures for the purposes of the Mental Health Act 1983. Unfortunately there is no avoiding the harsh reality that some children who have neither been convicted of very serious offences nor made subject to orders under the 1983 Act, are likely to injure themselves, or others, unless they are accommodated in secure premises. d e

97. In summary s 25 therefore forms part of the overall framework for the support and welfare of children who present particular difficulties and who for their own protection and that of others, and to ensure their continuing education, require that the accommodation in which they are being looked after should be secure. The necessary authorisation in domestic law, enabling the local authority to restrict the liberty of such children is provided by the court order. Although the maximum length of any order must be specified, the question whether this authorisation should be used, and if so for how long and in what degree, remains with the local authority. If and when the statutory conditions cease to apply, the order may no longer be enforced (see *LM v Essex CC* [1999] 1 FCR 673). f g

98. Miss de Haas argued that the order purporting to provide the legal justification for the restriction on K's liberty was deficient for this purpose, not because the statutory criteria were not established, nor the appropriate procedure followed, but because such an order, even when the statutory criteria are established, and proper procedures followed, contravenes art 5 of the convention, or more particularly, that the order falls outside the narrow ambit of the prescribed circumstances in which an individual may be deprived of his liberty. In short therefore the use of secure accommodation for the purposes of restricting liberty under s 25 is incompatible with art 5. Section 25, which purported to provide the justification for the restriction on K's liberty, should therefore be declared 'incompatible' with a convention right in accordance with s 4(2) of the Human Rights Act 1998, and indeed damages should be awarded for K's detention, in accordance with art 5(5). Article 5 provides: h j

> '1. Everyone has the right to liberty and security of person. No one shall be deprived of his liberty save in the following cases and in accordance with a procedure prescribed by the law: (a) the lawful detention of a person after

conviction by a competent court; (b) the lawful arrest or detention of a person for non-compliance with the lawful order of a court or in order to secure the fulfilment of any obligation prescribed by law; (c) the lawful arrest or detention of a person effected for the purpose of bringing him before the competent legal authority on reasonable suspicion of having committed an offence or when it is reasonably considered necessary to prevent his committing an offence or fleeing after having done so; (d) the detention of a minor by lawful order for the purpose of educational supervision or his lawful detention for the purpose of bringing him before the competent legal authority; (e) the lawful detention of persons for the prevention of the spreading of infectious diseases, of persons of unsound mind, alcoholics or drug addicts or vagrants; (f) the lawful arrest or detention of a person to prevent his effecting an unauthorised entry into the country or of a person against whom action is being taken with a view to deportation or extradition.'

99. Mr Garnham's first submission on behalf of the Secretary of State was that K had not been deprived of his liberty for the purposes of art 5. The local authority had simply exercised parental responsibility for him in his own best interests. There was some interesting discussion about the way in which parents restrict the movements of their children from time to time, by, for example, putting young children into bed when they would rather be up, or 'grounding' teenagers when they would prefer to be partying with their friends, or sending children to boarding schools, entrusting the schools with authority to restrict their movements. All this reflects the normal working of family life, in which parents are responsible for bringing up, teaching, enlightening and disciplining their children as necessary and appropriate, and into which the law and local authorities should only intervene when the parents' behaviour can fairly be stigmatised as cruel or abusive.

100. It is not necessary to deal with any argument that such parental behaviour might constitute an interference with a child's liberty or contravene his 'human rights'. No such absurdity was advanced. What however does arise for decision is whether what I have described as normal family life goes anywhere near what the local authority is empowered to do by a secure accommodation order.

101. By definition, the making of the order means that if accommodation less than adequate for the purpose of restricting liberty is provided, the child is likely to suffer significant harm because there is a history and continuing risk of absconding with a likelihood of significant harm or injury to himself or others. This means that he requires far more supervision and attention than any normal parent could reasonably provide or be expected to provide, and in accommodation which none of them have, that is accommodation provided for the very purpose of restricting a child's freedom. This is miles away from 'grounding' a teenager, or ensuring that a group of teenagers at a boarding school are all back within school bounds by a certain time each evening, or any other manifestation of normal parental control. If the restrictions necessarily imposed on K for his own safety and that of others were imposed on an ordinary boy of 15, who did not pose the problems requiring a secure accommodation order, in my view, there would be a strong case that his parents were ill-treating him. As it is, the local authority have been obliged, as a 'last resort', to seek authorisation to impose restrictions on the boy's liberty which would otherwise be unacceptable, whether imposed by his parents or anyone else. That, as it seems to me, is the

point of the unequivocal statutory language. The purpose is to restrict liberty, and there would be no point in such a restriction or the need for it to be authorised by the court, if it were not anticipated that much more was involved than ordinary parental control. It would have been enough to leave the local authority to exercise its parental responsibilities under s 33(3)(a) of the 1989 Act in relation to care, or to provide that the local authority should exercise such parental responsibilities in relation to children it was looking after, or to re-enact s 10(2) of the Child Care Act 1980, in a modified form, so that it would read something like:

> 'A local authority shall … have the same powers and duties with respect to a person who is being looked after by it … as his parents or guardian would have … and may … restrict his liberty to such extent as the authority considers appropriate.'

102. In short, although normal parental control over the movements of a child may be exercised by the local authority over a child in its care, the implementation of a secure accommodation order does not represent normal parental control.

103. This conclusion is reinforced by the further consideration that an order under s 25 may be made in respect of a child who is not subject to a care order under s 31. As already indicated, it is enough that the local authority is 'looking after' the child, and if it is doing so under s 22(1)(b) (provision of accommodation) rather than s 22(1)(a) (care) parental responsibilities are not in issue. In other words the secure accommodation order with its restrictions on liberty may be granted to the local authority in respect of children who are not in care and in relation to whom the local authority has no parental responsibility. This tends to confirm that s 25 is intended to reflect far wider restrictions on liberty than those which arise in a normal family situation.

104. In this case the evidence of the regime adopted for K demonstrates that after the order under s 25(4) was made he was deprived of his liberty.

105. Miss de Haas submitted that the purported justification, that is the order of the court under s 25, was outwith art 5(1)(a) to (f). For all the understandable emphasis she placed on the thrust of decisions of the European Court of Human Rights that art 5 itself provides a 'comprehensive' or an 'exhaustive' definition of the circumstances in which an individual may be deprived of his liberty (see, for example, *Ireland v UK* (1978) 2 EHRR 25), there is at least one critical respect in which the court itself accepted that the principle is not absolute:

> 'The care and upbringing of children normally and necessarily require that the parents or an only parent decide where the child must reside and also impose, or authorise others to impose, various restrictions on the child's liberty. Thus the children in a school or other educational or recreational institution must abide by certain rules which limit their freedom of movement and their liberty in other respects … Family life in this sense, and especially the rights of parents to exercise parental authority over their children, having due regard to their corresponding parental responsibilities, is recognised and protected by the Convention …" (See *Nielsen v Denmark* (1988) 11 EHRR 175 at 191 (para 61).)

106. It is therefore clear that, notwithstanding the absence of any express reference to the position of a parent in art 5, for the purposes of the convention the liberty of a child may be constrained by anyone with parental responsibilities

a for him, properly exercising 'custodial rights'. Subparagraph (d) is exclusively concerned with and limited to minors and although loosely described in conversation, or in oral argument as 'education', the permitted restriction is in much wider language, 'for the purpose of educational supervision'.

107. This goes far beyond school. It is not just about the restriction on liberty involved in requiring a reluctant child to remain at school for the school day. It b arises in the context of the responsibilities of parents which extend well beyond ensuring the child's attendance at school. So it involves education in the broad sense, similar, I would respectfully suggest, to the general development of the child's physical, intellectual, emotional, social and behavioural abilities, all of which have to be encouraged by responsible parents, as part of his upbringing and education, and for this purpose, an appropriate level of supervision of the child to c enhance his development, where necessary, by restricting his liberty is permitted. If less were involved than this, there would be no purpose in including 'educational supervision' as an express restriction on the right of a minor to liberty: the recognition of 'custodial rights' and parental responsibilities would have sufficed. It is, of course, quite unreal for anyone to decide in theory, or for d rigid guidelines to be laid down in advance, about the appropriate level of educational supervision which may be required by an individual child. The purpose of this order, and its implementation by the local authority, is to provide the best available environment to enable K's education, both in the narrow and broad senses, under the degree of supervision and control necessary to avoid harm or injury to himself, and to improve his prospects of avoiding both in the e long term as well as the immediate future. I should add, that if K were to cause injury to others which in the remotest degree corresponded to his fantasies, apart from any injury to them, the end result would be significant harm to him, with the major risk of conviction for a desperately serious crime, and a correspondingly severe sentence.

f 108. In summary, the normal standards of acceptable parental control are undiminished by, indeed consistent with the convention. Therefore the restriction in art 5(1)(d) is specifically directed to the situation of those minors who are beyond such normal control. Prosecution and punishment do not invariably present the most efficacious solution to the behavioural problems of children and young persons, and their long-term development, whether viewed entirely as a g matter of their own self-interest or the general benefit of the community as a whole. There is much to be gained if the underlying causes of the misbehaviour of a child or young person can be examined and addressed. Hence the need to allow restrictions on the liberty of minors with such problems, which goes beyond normal parental control and allows for the educational supervision. The h convention is not an appropriate instrument for spelling out precisely what form this may take or its limits. As Mr Garnham's helpful analysis of the differing procedures adopted in many of the countries adherent to the convention demonstrates, there are different traditions and regimes for dealing with troublesome as well as the criminal young. All these command respect, and the j convention is not an appropriate instrument for spelling out precisely what form this should take, and which particular regime is acceptable.

109. I have examined these conclusions by taking account of decisions from the European Court. Two features are of immediate significance. The first is that although the problems posed by children like K are plainly anticipated in most, and I would assume every other, European country, there are so few cases involving juveniles or minors in which these issues have been examined, and the

second is that where they have, they tend to confirm that the European Court would follow the same process of reasoning which I have endeavoured to explain. a

110. In *Bouamar v Belgium* (1989) 11 EHRR 1 the European Court was considering statutory provisions for the judicial protection of juveniles. The orders available to the domestic court culminated in the power to place the juvenile in a state reformatory. Such reformatories are divided between 'open' institutions, where the inmates live 'under a regime of semi-liberty', and 'closed' institutions—'for highly disturbed young people'—which presumably are entirely secure, certainly no less secure than the accommodation provided under a secure accommodation order. b

111. The judgment of the court included the following passage:

c

> 'The Court notes that the confinement of a juvenile in a remand prison does not necessarily contravene sub-paragraph (d), even if it is not in itself such as to provide for the person's "educational supervision". As is apparent from the words "for the purpose of" ("*pour*"), the "detention" referred to ... is a means of ensuring that the person concerned is placed under "educational supervision", but the placement does not necessarily have to be an immediate one ... however, the imprisonment must be speedily followed by actual application of such a régime in a setting (open or closed) designed and with sufficient resources for the purpose.' (See (1989) 11 EHRR 1 at 16–17 (para 50).) d

112. In short therefore, provided the inmate was receiving supervised education, the provision and use of closed institutions for very disturbed young people was not struck down. e

113. In the very recent decision of the court in *Koniarska v UK* App No 33670/96 (12 October 2000, unreported), s 25 itself was directly under consideration. The application was declared inadmissible. Significantly the court did not question or impugn the principle of a secure accommodation order. Moreover, although art 5(1)(e) might well have provided a proper justification for the restrictions on Koniarska's liberty, the court proceeded on the basis that the order fell within art 5(1)(d). f

114. The case was dismissed, in effect, as unarguable. The court observed:

g

> 'In the context of the detention of minors, the words "educational supervision" must not be equated rigidly with notions of classroom teaching. In particular, in the present context of a young person in local authority care, educational supervision must embrace many aspects of the exercise, by the local authority, of parental rights for the benefit and protection of the person concerned. The court has no doubt that the orders made ... on the application of the local authority, were capable of constituting part of the "educational supervision" of the applicant.' h

115. So far as this part of the judgment is concerned, I can see no sensible ground for distinguishing the decision in *Koniarska*'s case from the present case. j

116. Accordingly, in my judgment the principle is simply expressed: the concept of 'educational supervision' goes well beyond either normal parental control or academic lessons taught in the classroom, but, to the extent that the arrangements for the welfare of the child interfere with his liberty beyond the interference envisaged in normal parental control, and to avoid any arbitrary exercise of power by a local authority, judicial authorisation is required. That is

a provided by s 25(4). In this case the secure accommodation order was properly made. I can find no inconsistency or incompatibility between such an order under s 25 and the practical application of the convention rights under art 5. A declaration of incompatibility should be refused.

117. I should briefly note that in the papers prepared before the hearing it was suggested on behalf of K that his rights under arts 3, 6, and 8 had also been b infringed. The arguments were not pursued at the oral hearing, in my view, rightly. Beyond that I shall make no further observation, save to add that, again, at the hearing no argument was addressed to the question whether the restrictions on K's liberty may not have been justified under sub-paras (c) ('reasonably ... necessary to prevent his committing an offence') or (e) ('detention ... of persons of unsound mind').

c 118. This conclusion means that it is no longer essential to consider the consequences which would have arisen if s 25 had been declared incompatible with the convention. Miss de Haas suggested that the consequence of any such declaration would have been that K was entitled to damages in accordance with art 5(5). This provides:

d

> 'Everyone who has been the victim of arrest or detention in contravention of the provisions of this Article shall have an enforceable right to compensation.'

119. During the course of the argument I described the submission as 'stunning'. The time we have taken to reflect on our judgments has not e diminished my sense of astonishment. In fairness to Miss de Haas, I must briefly explain why.

120. If the argument were correct the implementation of the 1998 Act, on 2 October 2000, would have produced a constitutional earthquake. Parliament would have undermined the principle of Parliamentary sovereignty, and revived f Sir Edward Coke CJ's dictum in *Bonham's Case* (1610) 8 Co 114a at 118a, 77 ER 646 at 652 that 'the common law will controul Acts of Parliament and sometimes adjudge them to be utterly void', a principle identified by Coke in order to impose some fetter on the extravagant royal concept of the prerogative, a controversy eventually settled in this country by the revolution of 1688. And it would effectively 'set the judicial power above that of the legislature', emphatically g described in 1765 by Blackstone in the first edition of his *Commentaries*, some 150 years before universal adult suffrage was established, as 'subversive of all government' (see 1 Bl Com (1st edn) 91). (For a still vivid analysis of *Bonham's Case* in its historical context, the relationship of the legislature and the judiciary, and the development of divergent constitutional routes in this country and the h United States of America, see TFT Plucknett's article, first published in 1926 (40 Harv L Rev 30), '*Bonham's Case* and Judicial Review' in Plucknett *Studies in English legal history* (History Series 14, 1983).)

121. It may on another occasion be appropriate to examine whether the sovereignty of Parliament empowers it to dispense with or divest itself of its own j or any part of its sovereignty, but so far as the 1998 Act is concerned, this question simply does not arise. Neither this nor any other court is empowered to repeal or amend, ignore or act contrary to any single statute, or any part of any statute. To the contrary: the Act is carefully drafted to ensure that the court cannot and must not strike down or dispense with any single item of primary legislation.

122. The reason is simple. If satisfied that a statute is indeed incompatible with a convention right, the most that the 1998 Act empowers this court to do is to

make an appropriate declaration. The declaration gives no right by way of compensation. Section 4(6) is quite unequivocal: *a*

> 'A declaration under this section ("a declaration of incompatibility")—(a) does not affect the validity, continuing operation or enforcement of the provision in respect of which it is given; and (b) is not binding on the parties to the proceedings in which it is made.'

b

123. The effect of a declaration of incompatibility is that remedial action may be taken by a minister of the Crown to make whatever amendments to the primary legislation are thought necessary to remove the incompatibility. So, notwithstanding the declaration, the statutory provision continues in force until such time as it is amended, if indeed that ever happens. And until it does, the law which judges must apply includes the statutory provision which has been *c* declared to be incompatible.

124. In *R v DPP, ex p Kebeline* [1999] 4 All ER 801 at 831, [2000] 2 AC 326 at 367 Lord Steyn encapsulated the principle in unambiguous language:

> 'It is crystal clear that the carefully and subtlety drafted 1998 Act preserves the principle of parliamentary sovereignty. In a case of incompatibility ... *d* the courts may not disapply the legislation. The court may merely issue a declaration of incompatibility which then gives rise to a power to take remedial action ...'

125. Miss de Haas suggested that on the basis that K's detention under the secure accommodation order was incompatible with the convention, then *e* art 5(5) created an enforceable right to damages, certainly with effect from 2 October. From that date there would remain no sufficient justification for the regime in to which the local authority had detained K, or for the order itself. She referred to s 9(3):

> 'In proceedings under this Act in respect of a judicial act done in good faith, *f* damages may not be awarded otherwise than to compensate a person to the extent required by Article 5(5) of the Convention.'

126. From there she worked backwards through s 7(1) to s 6(1) which makes it 'unlawful for a public authority to act in a way which is incompatible with a Convention right'. *g*

127. The simple answer to this submission is that s 6(1) is expressly made subject to s 6(2), and any subsequent reference to s 6(1) in the Act is itself also subject to s 6(2). This provides:

> 'Subsection (1) does not apply to an Act if—(a) as the result of one or more *h* provisions of primary legislation, the authority could not have acted differently; or (b) in the case of one or more provisions of, or made under, primary legislation which cannot be read or given effect in a way which is compatible with the Convention rights, the authority was acting so as to give effect to or enforce those provisions.'

j

128. So far as domestic courts are concerned, even if s 25 were incompatible with K's convention rights, it would continue to protect both the court and the local authority from any claim under art 5(5).

129. It may just be worth touching on the practical consequences of Miss de Haas' submission in the day-to-day running of the judicial system. On this basis this court would have seen fit to make a declaration of incompatibility.

a Nevertheless s 25 would continue in force. Yet the right to damages under art 5(5) would arise every time such an order was made, while simultaneously, judges up and down the country, when satisfied that the conditions leading to a secure accommodation order were established, would remain under a continuing obligation to apply s 25. In some court buildings, one judge would be making an award of damages to a minor who had been deprived of his liberty on b the basis of a s 25 order: in the court next door, another judge would continue to make s 25 orders in relation to different children. Indeed it is not too fanciful in some of the smaller courts to foresee the same judge making an order under s 25 in relation to the first case in his list, and if Miss de Haas were right, in the afternoon case to assess damages for a child which had been made subject to a s 25 order on an earlier occasion. It would be nonsense for the local authority, or c the court, properly fulfilling the duties imposed on it by an unrepealed, unamended statute simultaneously to render itself liable to an order for damages in another domestic court on the basis of this convention right. The end result would be that the court, and the local authorities, would abdicate their statutory responsibilities and in practice dispense with or fail to apply s 25, while s 25 d remained on the statute book as the statutory scheme intended by Parliament to provide protection for children from injury and harm. The result would be, at best a constitutional mess, and at worst something of a constitutional crisis.

130. The 1998 Act does not create a system of justice which leaves the domestic court floundering between primary legislation and the convention and electing which is to be applied. Where incompatibility is found, generally e speaking at any rate, the court is required to declare it. Nevertheless the law which the court must enforce is the law as it is, even if it is incompatible with the convention.

131. Miss de Haas did not direct any argument to the consequences of a finding of incompatibility on the continued 'detention' of K in secure f accommodation. I have not examined the potential difficulties which would arise, if Miss de Haas were right, in the context of art 5(4). It is enough to record that they would be extreme. And, in view of the fact that a declaration of incompatibility would not be appropriate in this case, it has also been unnecessary to examine the additional arguments deployed by Mr Sales on this part of the case.

g 132. I agree both that the appeal should be dismissed, and that the application for a secure accommodation order should be granted.

Appeal dismissed. Local authority's application granted.

Kate O'Hanlon Barrister.

R v Inner London North Coroner, ex parte Touche

a

[2001] EWCA Civ 383

COURT OF APPEAL, CIVIL DIVISION

b

SIMON BROWN, ROBERT WALKER AND KEENE LJJ

21 FEBRUARY, 21 MARCH 2001

Coroner – Inquest – Duty to hold inquest – Unnatural death – Deceased dying from cerebral haemorrhage following caesarean section – Deceased's husband alleging that failure by hospital to provide appropriate post-operative care contributing to death – Husband obtaining medical reports supporting allegation but coroner refusing to order inquest – Whether coroner erring in concluding that there were no reasonable grounds to suspect that deceased's death 'unnatural' – Coroners Act 1988, s 8(1).

c

d

Costs – Order for costs – Discretion – Coroner – Court ordering coroner to pay costs incurred by applicant in successful challenge to his decision – Whether court having discretion to award costs against coroner in absence of misconduct – Coroners Act 1988, s 13.

T's wife gave birth to twins, delivered by caesarean section, at a London hospital. Following delivery, her blood pressure was noted to be within normal bounds and she was transferred to the postnatal ward. She was complaining of headache. The next note of her blood pressure was some two and a half hours later when it was recorded at an abnormal level. Only at that stage did treatment begin, and her blood pressure started to be taken regularly. By then, however, it was too late. Despite being transferred to a specialist neurosurgery hospital, she died eight days later from a cerebral haemorrhage. T subsequently asked the coroner to hold an inquest, referring to the two and a half hour period when it appeared that his wife's blood pressure had not been monitored and claiming that that failure had vitiated any opportunity to avoid the events which had led to her death. Those allegations were supported by three medical reports, obtained either by T or the coroner, including one which described the hospital's failure to monitor the deceased's blood pressure as 'astonishing' and its level of neglect as 'starkly apparent'. Under s 8(1)[a] of the Coroners Act 1988, the coroner was required to hold an inquest where there was reasonable cause to suspect that the deceased had died an 'unnatural death'. Although the coroner accepted that the post-operative monitoring appeared wholly inadequate, he concluded that the defects complained of did not put the case into the category of unnatural death. Accordingly, he refused to hold an inquest, and T applied for judicial review. The Divisional Court allowed the application, holding that a death was unnatural whenever it occurred in hospital and a failure to provide 'routine' treatment was a cause (even a secondary cause) of death. The court also ordered the coroner to pay T's costs. The coroner appealed, challenging both the decision on the substantive issue and the costs order. In relation to the costs order, the issue arose whether the court had jurisdiction to make such an order in the absence of misconduct by the coroner.

e

f

g

h

j

a Section 8(1) is set out at [13], post

a **Held** – (1) Where an inquest was sought into a person's death on the grounds that neglect by a hospital had contributed to it and the death was therefore unnatural, the critical questions were whether, on the available evidence, there was reason to suspect (i) that there was gross failure by the hospital to provide the deceased with basic medical attention, and (ii) that the deceased's need for such attention was obvious at the time. In the instant case, the coroner, on the b material presently available, could not properly have decided otherwise than that there was reasonable cause to suspect that the deceased's death was at least contributed to by neglect and thus unnatural, so that an inquest should be held. That conclusion did not mean, however, that the coroner or jury would be bound to qualify the inevitable verdict of death from natural causes by a reference c to 'neglect'. That would inevitably depend upon the evidence as it emerged and the coroner's or jury's evaluation of it in the light of appropriate legal directions or self-directions (see [29], [32], [36], [46], [60], [63], post); *R v North Humberside and Scunthorpe Coroner, ex p Jamieson* [1994] 3 All ER 972 applied.

(2) A costs order could be made against a coroner if he failed to defeat a d challenge to his decision, even when he had conducted himself impeccably. If a coroner were to win, he would certainly ask for and be awarded his costs. Furthermore, s 13[b] of the 1988 Act expressly provided that where the High Court, on an application brought with the Attorney General's fiat, was satisfied that the coroner had refused to hold an inquest which ought to be held, it could order the coroner to pay such costs of and incidental to the application as appeared just. e Given that express statutory discretion to award costs against a coroner whenever justice demanded—a discretion unqualified by any need to find misconduct on his part—there was no reason to subject its exercise to those cases where the coroner's conduct called for strong disapproval. It followed that in the instant case the Divisional Court had been correct to order the coroner to pay T's f costs, even though he had conducted himself impeccably (see [53]–[60], [63], post); *R v HM Coroner for Lincoln, ex p Hay* [2000] Lloyd's Med Rep 264 disapproved in part.

Per curiam. There are cases which fall outside the category of neglect and yet appear to call for an inquest, namely cases involving a wholly unexpected death g from natural causes which would not have occurred but for some culpable human failure. It is the combination of their unexpectedness and the culpable human failing that allows them to happen which makes such deaths unnatural. Although they are undoubtedly deaths by natural causes, they should plainly never have happened and in that sense are unnatural. An inquest will, of course, only be held h if the coroner has reasonable cause to suspect such a combination of circumstances, and he will not have to make detailed investigations into every hospital death (see [46], [47], [60]–[62], [64], [66]); *R v Poplar Coroner, ex p Thomas* [1993] 2 All ER 381 considered.

Notes

j For inquests and for the award of costs against coroners, see 9(2) *Halsbury's Laws* (4th edn reissue) paras 837–838, 972.

For the Coroners Act 1988, ss 8, 13, see 11 *Halsbury's Statutes* (4th edn) (2000 reissue) 662, 669.

---

b Section 13, so far as material, is set out at [57], post

Cases referred to in judgments

Alphacell Ltd v Woodward [1972] 2 All ER 475, [1972] AC 824, [1972] 2 WLR 1320, HL.
Associated Provincial Picture Houses Ltd v Wednesbury Corp [1947] 2 All ER 680, [1948] 1 KB 223, CA.
McGhee v National Coal Board [1972] 3 All ER 1008, [1973] 1 WLR 1, HL.
R v HM Coroner for Lincoln, ex p Hay [2000] Lloyd's Rep Med 264, DC.
R v HM Coroner for Western District of East Sussex, ex p Homberg (1994) 19 BMLR 11, DC.
R v Newcastle-under-Lyme Justices, ex p Massey [1995] 1 All ER 120, [1994] 1 WLR 1684, DC.
R v North Humberside and Scunthorpe Coroner, ex p Jamieson [1994] 3 All ER 972, [1995] QB 1, [1994] 3 WLR 82, CA.
R v Poplar Coroner, ex p Thomas [1993] 2 All ER 381, [1993] QB 610, [1993] 2 WLR 547, CA.
R v Southwark Coroner, ex p Hicks [1987] 2 All ER 140, [1987] 1 WLR 1624, DC.
Weld-Blundell v Stephens [1920] AC 956, [1920] All ER Rep 32, HL

Cases also cited or referred to in skeleton arguments

Brutus v Cozens [1972] 2 All ER 1297, [1973] AC 854, HL.
Steele Ford & Newton (a firm) v CPS [1993] 2 All ER 769, sub nom *Holden & Co (a firm) v CPS (No 2)* [1994] 1 AC 22, HL.
R v HM Coroner for Birmingham and Solihull, ex p Benton (1998) 162 JP 807.
R v HM Coroner for Birmingham and Solihull, ex p Cotton (1996) 160 JP 123, DC.
R v HM Coroner for Inner South London, ex p Epsom Health Care NHS Trust (1994) 158 JP 973, DC.

Appeal

The coroner for Inner London North appealed with permission of Laws LJ granted on 19 October 2000 from the order of the Divisional Court (Kennedy LJ and Morrison J) on 22 June 2000 ([2001] Lloyd's Rep Med 67) whereby, in allowing an application for judicial review by the respondent, Peter Francis Touche, the court quashed the coroner's decisions on 3 August and 30 September 1999 refusing to hold an inquest into the death of Mr Touche's wife, Laura Touche, and directed that an inquest be held. The facts are set out in the judgment of Simon Brown LJ.

Ian Burnett QC and *Ben Collins* (instructed by *Hempsons*, Harrogate) for the coroner.
Philip Havers QC and *Simon Taylor* (instructed by *Alexander Harris*) for Mr Touche.

Cur adv vult

21 March 2001. The following judgments were delivered.

SIMON BROWN LJ.

[1] On 6 February 1999 Laura Touche gave birth to twins, delivered by caesarean section. On 15 February 1999, tragically, she died. She was only 31. She died from a cerebral haemorrhage, the result of severe hypertension, possibly secondary to eclampsia. The medical evidence suggests that had her blood pressure been monitored in the immediate post-operative phase her death would probably have been avoided.

[2] The critical issue raised in these proceedings is whether such a death is natural or unnatural—whether, in particular, an inquest must be held into it

a pursuant to s 8(1) of the Coroner's Act 1988 which requires such an inquest 'Where ... there is reasonable cause to suspect that the deceased ... (a) has died ... an unnatural death ...'

[3] It is the coroner's contention that Mrs Touche died a natural death. Her husband contends the contrary. He is anxious for an inquest. The Divisional Court (Kennedy LJ and Morrison J) on 22 June 2000 ([2001] Lloyd's Rep Med 67) b accepted Mr Touche's argument and directed that an inquest be held. The coroner now appeals to this court.

[4] Perhaps not surprisingly the case has attracted some attention: the facts, after all, are heart-rending. The issue raised, however, is essentially one of law and its resolution cannot depend on sympathy.

c [5] With that brief introduction let me turn at once to set out such further facts as need be stated.

The facts

[6] The deceased was delivered of healthy twins at about 10.25 pm on 6 February 1999 by caesarean section under spinal anaesthetic at the Portland Hospital in d London. Her pregnancy and labour had been uncomplicated. Following delivery her blood pressure was noted to be 120/60 which was within normal bounds and at around 11 pm she was transferred to the postnatal ward. She was complaining of headache. The next note of her blood pressure was at 1.35 am when it was recorded to be 190/100. By then her headache was severe and she was clearly e unwell. Only at this stage did treatment begin and her blood pressure start to be taken regularly until finally it fell to normal limits. By then, however, it was too late. At 5.15 am she was suffering a left-sided hemiplegia. At 6.15 am she was transferred to the Middlesex Hospital and from there to the National Hospital for Neurology and Neurosurgery at Queen Square where eight days later, on 15 February, she died.

f [7] A hospital post-mortem examination, carried out by Professor Scaravilli on 18 February 1999, recorded the cause of death as:

> '1a. Brain swelling and tonsillar herniation
> b. Intra cerebral haemorrhage
> 2. Recent pregnancy'.

g

[8] It was some months before Mr Touche's investigations into the circumstances of his wife's death led him to seek an inquest. On 28 July 1999 he wrote to the coroner referring to the 2½-hour period between 11 pm and 1.30 am when it appeared that Mrs Touche's blood pressure had not been monitored. On h 26 August 1999 his solicitors wrote, alleging that—

> 'a basic, fundamental failure to record blood-pressure readings ... vitiated any opportunity to avoid the catastrophic events which lead to Mrs Touche's death.'

j On 15 September 1999 the solicitors wrote again saying:

> 'The Portland Hospital have already confirmed in writing to our client that a protocol does not exist to reflect the level of monitoring that should be given following a caesarean section. We have expert evidence to the effect that every NHS hospital in the country has a protocol in place for the care of patients in the post-operative phase in order to maintain standards within the

hospital and ensure an appropriate level of patient care. It is disturbing that a private hospital with this reputation chooses not to adopt such a protocol.' a

[9] On 31 August 1999 the solicitors obtained a report from Dr Bogod, an experienced consultant anaesthetist with a particular interest in obstetric anaesthesia. He was very critical of the lack of records relating to the periods during and after surgery. In particular he found the failure to monitor or record vital signs, including blood pressure, at a time when Mrs Touche was receiving pain relief b 'astonishing' and described the level of neglect as 'starkly apparent'.

[10] The coroner himself took the trouble to obtain a report from Professor Rubin whose particular interest is in the medical aspects of pregnancy. His report of 29 February 2000 pointed out that maternal death in the United Kingdom is now 'very rare' and described Mrs Touche's death as 'extraordinary' because he c has—

> 'looked after countless numbers of pregnant and post-partum women who have blood pressure in the range recorded in Mrs Touche [and] none has ever had a stroke.'

d

[11] The final report to which I must refer was obtained by Mr Touche's solicitors on 15 May 2000 by way of preliminary opinion from Dr Williams who runs a high-risk obstetrics service at the Chelsea and Westminster Hospital and who has a particular interest in pre-eclampsia. His essential conclusions were first that the failure to undertake blood-pressure readings during the post-operative e period involved 'sub-standard practice', and second that the deceased's severe hypertension was responsible for her cerebral haemorrhage and that 'it is likely that more prompt identification and treatment of her hypertension would have prevented her cerebral haemorrhage'.

[12] In short, the evidence as a whole provides clear grounds for suspecting that the Portland Hospital failed to monitor the deceased's blood pressure as it f should have done in the critical post-operative phase and that such failure was an effective cause of her death in that, but for it, she would probably (or at least possibly) not have suffered cerebral haemorrhage and died.

The 1988 Act g

[13] Section 8(1) provides:

> 'Where a coroner is informed that the body of a person ("the deceased") is lying within his district and there is reasonable cause to suspect that the deceased—(a) has died a violent or an unnatural death; (b) has died a sudden h death of which the cause is unknown; or (c) has died in prison or in such a place or in such circumstances as to require an inquest under any other Act, then, whether the cause of death arose within his district or not, the coroner shall as soon as practicable hold an inquest into the death of the deceased either with or, subject to subsection (3) below, without a jury.'

j

[14] Section 8(3) provides so far as relevant that the inquest must be held with a jury—

> 'If it appears to a coroner ... (d) that the death occurred in circumstances the continuance or possible recurrence of which is prejudicial to the health or safety of the public or any section of the public ...'

The issue arising

[**15**] The central question to address is whether, in the light of the facts already summarised, there is reasonable cause to suspect that Mrs Touche died an unnatural death. I pose it in the present tense (and earlier summarised the evidence as it now stands) because the coroner's stance has remained the same throughout: whilst he 'entirely accept[s] that … the post-operative monitoring would appear wholly inadequate', he does not regard the death as having been unnatural. He deposes as follows:

> 'I asked myself whether this was a case in which the defects and human fault complained of lifted the case out of the category of natural and into a category of unnatural death and, applying my common sense as a coroner, I concluded that it did not.'

[**16**] In the ordinary way, of course, it is for the coroner to decide whether there is reasonable cause to suspect that a particular death is unnatural, and his decision will not be challengeable unless it is *Wednesbury* unreasonable (see *Associated Provincial Picture Houses Ltd v Wednesbury Corp* [1947] 2 All ER 680, [1948] 1 KB 223) or involves a self-misdirection in law. The facts here having now substantially crystallised, however, the point has been reached where really there can only be one correct answer to the central question and that answer must necessarily depend on what is meant in s 8(1) by 'an unnatural death'. Clearly there is reasonable cause to suspect that the circumstances of Mrs Touche's death are those indicated by the evidence already summarised. Assuming they are, is it properly to be regarded as an unnatural death? If so, subject to a single qualification to which I shall shortly return, the coroner has no alternative but to hold an inquest. If, however, the death is not to be regarded as unnatural he has no power to hold an inquest.

The ruling authority

[**17**] The correct approach to take to the question whether there is reasonable cause to suspect that a deceased has died an unnatural death was decided by this court in *R v Poplar Coroner, ex p Thomas* [1993] 2 All ER 381, [1993] QB 610. The deceased in that case died aged 17 from a severe attack of asthma. The evidence suggested that she would not have died had the ambulance which was called arrived promptly rather than after a 33-minute delay. The late arrival of the ambulance notwithstanding, this court concluded that the coroner had been entitled to regard the death as natural and so not hold an inquest. The leading judgment was given by Dillon LJ who said:

> 'Whether Miss Thomas' death was natural or unnatural must therefore depend on what was the cause of death. At this point, I remind myself of the observation of Lord Salmon in *Alphacell Ltd v Woodward* [1972] 2 All ER 475 at 490, [1972] AC 824 at 847 where he said: "I consider … that what or who has caused a certain event to occur is essentially a practical question of fact which can best be answered by ordinary common sense rather than by abstract metaphysical theory."' Lord Salmon repeated what he had there said in his speech in *McGhee v National Coal Board* [1972] 3 All ER 1008 at 1017, [1973] 1 WLR 1 at 11 …' (See [1993] 2 All ER 381 at 386, [1993] QB 610 at 628.)

[**18**] Dillon LJ then considered five possible explanations for the delay including '(v) the ambulance came late because the ambulance crew were inefficient and the management was slack', and continued:

'I do not suggest that any of these scenarios actually fits the facts of Miss Thomas's case. I do not know what the cause of delay was. But in each of these scenarios common sense indicates that what caused the patient's death was, on Lord Salmon's test in *Alphacell Ltd v Woodward* [1972] 2 All ER 475 at 490, [1972] AC 824 at 847, the asthmatic attack not the congestion of the traffic, the bursting of the water main, the malfunction of the computer or the inefficiency of the ambulance service. But the asthmatic attack is a natural cause of death, and the death is not, in my judgment, turned into an unnatural death by any of the facts suggested in any of the alternative scenarios ... The coroner ... was saying that, even when all the other evidence is taken into account, the cause of death was still the asthmatic attack and the death was not an unnatural death. That is also my view, for the reasons I have endeavoured to give.' (See [1993] 2 All ER 381 at 386–387, [1993] QB 610 at 628.)

[19] Farquharson LJ agreed with Dillon LJ's reasoning.

[20] As the third member of the court, I agreed with the outcome but 'reach[ed] that conclusion with more hesitation than Dillon and Farquharson LJJ and by a rather different route'. I said:

'I agree ... that the question whether or not a death is natural or unnatural depends ultimately upon the view one takes as to the cause of death. But I do not find the question of causation in this context susceptible of quite the sort of robust approach as the House of Lords advocated in a very different context in cases such as *McGhee v National Coal Board* [1972] 3 All ER 1008, [1973] 1 WLR 1. The question arising there was: can the court properly infer, in the absence of a provable direct link, that one particular state of affairs caused or contributed to another. In those cases the possibility of there being more than one cause was immaterial ... The question posed in the present context is surely therefore different: given that all the important facts are known to the coroner, what view should he take of causes that may well be secondary but are not self-evidently irrelevant? As in litigation, why should he not sometimes find a death to be the result of two causes, either one of which could serve to make it unnatural.' (See [1993] 2 All ER 381 at 387–388, [1993] QB 610 at 630.)

[21] A little later I indicated that I for my part would have regarded the death as an unnatural one 'if the late arrival of the ambulance had constituted a more extreme failure of the service', adding that 'by "failure" I mean culpable human failure on the part of those responsible for providing a reasonably efficient emergency service' (see [1993] 2 All ER 381 at 388, [1993] QB 610 at 630–631). I concluded:

'... it seems to me necessary to recognise that cases may well arise in which human fault can and properly should be found to turn what would otherwise be a natural death into an unnatural one, and one into which, therefore, an inquest should be held.' (See [1993] 2 All ER 381 at 389, [1993] QB 610 at 631.)

The Divisional Court's judgment

[22] In their judgment below the Divisional Court said that they were 'unable to detect any conflict between' my judgment and that of the other two members of the court in *Ex p Thomas*, and that leading counsel appearing for the coroner before them (not Mr Burnett QC) had—

a 'realistically accepted that on occasions a coroner may have to find there was more than one cause of death. That possibility was simply not canvassed by Dillon LJ.' (See [2001] Lloyd's Rep Med 67 at 69.)

Then followed the first of two critical passages in the judgment:

b 'So where, as in this case, a patient is in hospital suffering from a condition which if not monitored and treated in a routine way will result in death, and, for whatever reason, the monitoring and treatment is omitted, then, as it seems to us, the coroner must hold an inquest unless he can say that there are no grounds for suspecting that the omission was an effective cause of death. That seems to us to be the conclusion to which one is led by a careful analysis of *Thomas*.'

c

[23] Later in the judgment, having reviewed the evidence, and set out the coroner's own conclusion, comes this passage (at 71):

'... we would prefer to see the coroner asking himself a question along the lines indicated earlier in this judgment, namely whether there are any d grounds for suspecting that the wholly inadequate post-operative monitoring and the consequential loss of the opportunity to provide timely treatment was an effective cause of death. If the coroner had approached the matter in that way it seems to us that his conclusion must have been different ... in dealing with the statutory test omission can be as important as commission, and that, as it seems to us, is what ... the coroner failed properly to recognise e and to evaluate.'

[24] There is one further paragraph in the judgment of the Divisional Court (at 71–72) to which I should refer before turning to the central arguments advanced on appeal. Under the heading '*Other matters*' appears this:

f 'Nothing in this judgment is concerned with what may in due course be the appropriate verdict, so we have not found it necessary to consider "lack of care" or two of the decisions to which we were referred (*R v Southwark Coroner, ex p Hicks* [1987] 2 All ER 140, [1987] 1 WLR 1624 and *R v North Humberside and Scunthorpe Coroner, ex p Jamieson* [1994] 3 All ER 972, [1995] QB 1).'

g *The arguments on appeal*

[25] Mr Burnett for the coroner submits, first, that the Divisional Court was wrong to have found no conflict between my judgment and that of the other Lords Justices in *R v Poplar Coroner, ex p Thomas* [1993] 2 All ER 381, [1993] QB 610 and wrong, therefore, to have applied my approach rather than that of Dillon LJ. h On Dillon LJ's approach, submits Mr Burnett, the coroner was clearly right, or at the very least entitled, to conclude that Mrs Touche died a natural death. Secondly he argues that the coroner in fact directed himself in accordance with my approach rather than the majority approach in *Ex p Thomas* and yet nevertheless properly came to the conclusion that this was a natural death. The j Divisional Court, in other words, went further even than I had gone in *Ex p Thomas*. On their judgment, submits Mr Burnett, there would have to be an inquest every time a death takes place in hospital which might have been avoided but for a failure to provide some routine monitoring or treatment. Indeed, he suggests, coroners in future will be required at the outset, when first notified of a hospital death, to embark upon a detailed examination of the facts to see what if any routine treatment should have been provided. The Divisional Court, he

suggests, has blurred the clear line established in *Ex p Thomas;* confusion and uncertainty now reign.

a

[**26**] Mr Havers QC for Mr Touche resists that argument at all points and submits that the judgment of the Divisional Court is correct for the reasons they gave. Alternatively he seeks to uphold the decision on the much narrower ground that it would be open to the coroner (or jury) in this case to return a verdict that the death was caused or contributed to by neglect, in which event, as is common ground, there would certainly have to be an inquest. The verdict which Mr Havers contemplates is that the deceased died from natural causes to which neglect contributed (see *R v North Humberside and Scunthorpe Coroner, ex p Jamieson* [1994] 3 All ER 972 at 991, [1995] QB 1 at 25). Such a verdict (which hereafter, for convenience, I shall call simply a 'neglect' verdict) is the preferred modern version of what in *R v Southwark Coroner, ex p Hicks* [1987] 2 All ER 140, [1987] 1 WLR 1624 was called 'lack of care'. Dillon LJ in *R v Poplar Coroner, ex p Thomas* [1993] 2 All ER 381 at 385, [1993] QB 610 at 627 expressly accepted that:

b

c

> 'Another instance of deaths which are unnatural but not violent is where persons die from "lack of care" in the narrow and somewhat technical sense in which that term was interpreted by the Divisional Court in [*Ex p Hicks*]'.

d

[**27**] As already noted, the Divisional Court in the present case expressly disavowed any such basis for their decision and this narrower argument was only introduced into the appeal at a late stage, a respondent's notice being settled for the purpose only during the hearing before us. It is nevertheless convenient to take it first.

e

Neglect

[**28**] Bingham MR, giving the judgment of the court in *Ex p Jamieson*, conducted a wide-ranging review of all relevant statutory and judicial authority (including not least a number of earlier cases concerned with lack of care verdicts) and stated 14 general conclusions as to the essential nature of the coroner's jurisdiction. It is a landmark decision in coronial law, given in the context of a prisoner who had hanged himself in a prison hospital cell. Mr Burnett usefully distilled such of those conclusions as affect the present appeal (in particular conclusions 7–12) into the following propositions: (1) self-neglect is a gross failure to take adequate nourishment or liquid or to obtain basic medical attention or adequate shelter or warmth; (2) neglect is the obverse of self-neglect; (3) neglect means a gross failure to provide or procure basic medical attention for someone in a dependent position (for example because of illness) who cannot provide it for himself; (4) the need for the basic medical attention must be obvious; (5) the crucial consideration is what the condition of the dependent person appeared to be; (6) neglect can rarely if ever be an appropriate verdict on its own but it may be factually accurate to say that it contributed to a death; (7) neither neglect nor self-neglect should ever form part of a verdict unless a clear and direct causal connection is established between the conduct so described and the cause of death. I did not understand Mr Havers to dissent from this analysis.

f

g

h

j

[**29**] It follows from this that the critical questions now to be asked under this head are whether, on the evidence presently available, there is reason to suspect, first, that there was a gross failure by the Portland Hospital to provide Mrs Touche (indisputably a dependant in their care) with basic medical attention, and, second, that her need for such attention was obvious at the time.

a [30] Mr Burnett submits that in addressing these questions the court is not concerned with considerations of fine judgment such as are generally in play in medical negligence actions. The concept of 'neglect' involves failure which is, as he puts it, plain as a pikestaff—note the words of emphasis in the *Ex p Jamieson* formulation: 'gross', 'basic', 'obvious'. The hospital's conduct here, he submits, cannot properly be stigmatised as involving a gross failure to meet an obvious b basic need.

[31] In submitting the contrary, Mr Havers relies in part on Dr Bogod's characterisation of the hospital's failure to monitor Mrs Touche's blood pressure as 'astonishing', and its level of neglect as 'starkly apparent'; in part on the coroner's own recognition that the post-operative monitoring was 'wholly inadequate'; and in part on the acknowledged rarity of maternal death in the United Kingdom. Such c a death is simply not to be expected nowadays and its very occurrence, submits Mr Havers, points strongly to a failure of care. There is, the evidence suggests, a basic need for routine blood-pressure monitoring in the immediate post-operative phase following a caesarean section under spinal anaesthetic. NHS hospitals apparently meet that need; the Portland Hospital does not.

d [32] I find Mr Havers' argument on this part of the case compelling. That, of course, is not to say that if an inquest is now held the coroner (or jury) will be bound to qualify the inevitable verdict of death from natural causes by a reference to 'neglect'. That would inevitably depend upon the evidence as it emerges and the coroner's (or jury's) evaluation of it in the light of appropriate legal directions (or self-directions) based on *Ex p Jamieson*. Still less, let me make plain at this e point, am I indicating any view upon the merits or prospects of success of a very substantial damages claim which apparently Mr Touche has outstanding against the Portland Hospital. Those proceedings are entirely separate from these and everything I have said is without prejudice to them. Who knows what evidence the hospital may have? Rather it is to conclude no more than that upon such f material as is presently available to the coroner he could not properly decide otherwise than that there is reasonable cause to suspect that Mrs Touche's death was (a) at least contributed to by 'neglect' (narrowly defined as by *Ex p Jamieson*) and thus (b) unnatural (as would necessarily follow from *R v Poplar Coroner, ex p Thomas* [1993] 2 All ER 381, [1993] QB 610).

g *The jurisdiction issue*

[33] Given this conclusion on the issue of 'neglect', an inquest would ordinarily be required. It is now that I come to the qualification I referred to in [16] above. The coroner's jurisdiction to hold an inquest under s 8 depends upon his being informed of the presence of a body within his district. The coroner in h the present case was so informed by his officer on 16 February 1999, the day following Mrs Touche's death. But the information then provided to him, from a doctor at the National Hospital at Queens Square, was that the deceased—

> 'Gave birth to twins by caesarean on 6.2.99 at Portland Hospital. Collapsed three hours later. Admitted to National Hospital on 7.2.99. Exam indicated j spontaneous brain haemorrhage unconnected with surgical procedure … No evidence of neglect nor complaint by family. No PM required.'

[34] Unsurprisingly in the light of that report, the coroner did not consider it appropriate to hold an inquest. The deceased in the event was cremated on 22 February, the procedures set out in the Regulations as to Cremations 1930, SR & O 1930/1016 being duly observed. These included the completion of a

series of prescribed forms by which Mr Touche as the applicant and two doctors acting respectively as the medical attendant and the medical referee certified amongst other things that they had no reasonable cause to suspect that the deceased died an unnatural death or from 'privation or neglect', and that there was no reason for any further inquiry or examination. Had the coroner, of course, decided at the outset to hold an inquest, the body would have remained in his charge.

[35] It was not until after the Divisional Court's judgment that the coroner became aware of Mrs Touche's cremation. The jurisdictional question, therefore, has arisen only in the course of this appeal. It arises because a coroner cannot decide to hold an inquest under s 8 unless at the time of his decision a body remains in existence. It presents, however, no insuperable problem. The solution lies in s 15 of the 1988 Act which, so far as material, provides:

> '(1) Where a coroner has reason to believe—(a) that a death has occurred in or near his district in such circumstances that an inquest ought to be held; and (b) that owing to the destruction of the body by fire or otherwise ... an inquest cannot be held except in pursuance of this section, he may report the facts to the Secretary of State.
>
> (2) Where a report is made under subsection (1) above, the Secretary of State may, if he considers it desirable to do so, direct a coroner ... to hold an inquest into the death.'

[36] Whilst it is clear that the coroner's original decision cannot be impugned, it seems to me that on the information subsequently brought to his attention he should have concluded that an inquest ought after all to be held. Mr Burnett has helpfully told us that if this is indeed the court's view, then the coroner will readily report the facts to the Secretary of State under the provisions of s 15 so that, whilst obviously we cannot dictate the Secretary of State's decision in the matter, an inquest appears likely to be directed.

The need for a jury

[37] Assuming there is now to be an inquest, will it be held with a jury? Although the point was not touched on by the Divisional Court nor addressed at length before us, Mr Burnett, I think, acknowledges that a jury would probably have to be summoned: it would seem difficult on the material presently available to regard this death as having occurred otherwise than 'in circumstances the continuance or possible recurrence of which is prejudicial to the health ... of ... [a] section of the public' within the meaning of s 8(3)(d) of the Act. The point needs no elaboration. On the authority of *Ex p Thomas*, however, this (perhaps somewhat surprisingly) cannot affect the question whether an inquest need be held at all (see [1993] 2 All ER 381 at 387, [1993] QB 610 at 629 per Dillon LJ).

The wider argument

[38] I have not thus far addressed the wider point which lies at the heart of this appeal: were the Divisional Court right to hold as they did that, whenever a death takes place in hospital and a failure to provide 'routine' treatment is a cause (even a secondary cause) of death, the death is unnatural? It is this holding which so concerns the coroner and, Mr Burnett says, other coroners too. It would result, he suggests, in a very significant increase in the number of inquests to be held. Had the Divisional Court founded their judgments simply on the possibility of a

a 'neglect' verdict, we are told, the coroner would probably not have appealed. Despite my conclusion on the issue of neglect, therefore, I must address the wider point.

[39] The first question arising, of course, is whether the Divisional Court's judgment is consistent with the Court of Appeal's judgment in *Ex p Thomas*, which in turn raises the question whether my judgment in that case was reconcilable with those of the majority. With regard to both these questions it is, I fear, necessary to b cite from another judgment of mine, this time in the Divisional Court in *R v Coroner for Western District of East Sussex, ex p Homberg* (1994) 19 BMLR 11 at 22:

> 'Although I myself would have been disposed to include within the proper scope of such a verdict [neglect] the death of someone seriously ill or injured who would have been saved by medical care but for wholly unreasonable c delay in the arrival of the emergency services, such a view is obviously inconsistent with the majority decision of the Court of Appeal in (*R v Poplar Coroner, ex p Thomas* [1993] 2 All ER 381, [1993] QB 610). That is not to say, however, that a lack of care verdict, whether freestanding or in terms of aggravating some other cause of death, would offend *ex p Thomas*. On the contrary, Dillon LJ's judgment clearly recognises the legitimate continuance d of such verdicts whenever properly founded on the facts. I would therefore accept Mr Fitzgerald's submission that *ex p Thomas* must be confined to the s 8(1)(a) context in which it arose; essentially it decides no more than that a broad common sense view must be taken when deciding the bald question whether a death is unnatural so as to determine whether to hold an inquest. e Whereas, however, for that purpose one shuts one's mind to all but the dominant cause of death, once an inquest is held, the duty to inquire into "how the deceased came by his death" requires one then to take a broader view and investigate not merely the dominant cause but also (in Jervis's language [Mathews and Foreman *Jervis on Coroners* (11th edn, 1993)]) any "acts or omissions which are directly responsible for the death".'

f

[40] A little later on (at 23) I referred to my own judgment in *Ex p Thomas* as 'not a dissenting judgment but clearly expressing a minority view'.

[41] As is plain from that passage, I was then regarding my view in *Ex p Thomas* as incompatible with the majority view. Revisiting the cases, I have to say that that remains my understanding. Subject only to 'neglect' cases (a category which I g suspect the majority in *Ex p Thomas* would have drawn even more narrowly than *Ex p Jamieson* does), Dillon LJ was, I believe, inviting the broadest view to be taken of causation so as simply to determine 'the dominant cause of death' as I called it in *Ex p Homberg*.

[42] I accordingly find it puzzling not merely that the Divisional Court in the h present case found no conflict within the *Ex p Thomas* judgments but also that the editors of both *Halsbury's Laws* and *Halsbury's Statutes* cite *Ex p Thomas* as authority for the proposition that—

> 'cases may well arise in which human fault can and properly should be found to turn what would otherwise be a natural death into an unnatural j one, and one into which therefore an inquest should be held',

a proposition of mine in which I had thought, and still think, I was differing from the majority view (see 9(2) *Halsbury's Laws* (4th edn reissue) para 837 n3 and 11 *Halsbury's Statutes* (4th edn) (2000 reissue) 664).

[43] How then ought this court now to proceed? The doctrine of precedent clearly suggests that the majority view in *Ex p Thomas* should be applied and the

Divisional Court's reasoning in the present case accordingly rejected. I nevertheless question whether many today would find the majority view in *Ex p Thomas* (certainly in the way I understand it) entirely satisfactory. Consider, for example, the very real doubt now thrown upon the usefulness of Lord Salmon's dictum in *Alphacell Ltd v Woodward* [1972] 2 All ER 475, [1972] AC 824—a dictum central to Dillon LJ's reasoning—as to causation being simply a matter of ordinary common sense, by Lord Hoffmann's illuminating lecture 'Common Sense and Causing Loss' (delivered to the Chancery Bar Association on 15 June 1999). As Lord Hoffmann explains, to get to the right answer on an issue of causation it is necessary first to identify the question and in formulating the question it is necessary to look at the rule of law which requires it to be asked. What policy underlies it? When deciding, therefore, whether or not for s 8(1)(a) purposes a death is unnatural, one should be considering why Parliament has included this category of deaths amongst those into which an inquest must be held. What is it about unnatural deaths that calls for an inquest? Is there not a powerful case for saying that an inquest should be held whenever a wholly unexpected death, albeit from natural causes, results from some culpable human failure? (Or, more strictly, whenever the coroner has reasonable grounds to suspect that such is the case.) Such deaths prompt understandable public concern and surely no small part of the coroner's function is to carry out an appropriate investigation to allay such concern.

[44] Is that not indeed the approach which the editors of the respective *Halsbury's* series appear to derive from *Ex p Thomas*? As we now learn, moreover, it appears consistent too with the approach coroners up and down the country take to certain rare deaths such as those from Legionnaires Disease. In *Ex p Thomas* we were given to understand that inquests are held into these deaths because 'it is regarded, on a broad view, as "unnatural" that a person should die of an extremely rare disease' (see [1993] 2 All ER 381 at 385, [1993] QB 610 at 627). Now we are told that such inquests are held because—

> 'the disease is caused by the mechanical spraying of infected water into the atmosphere. This act is unnatural and may be unlawful and the disease is seen as occurring unnaturally—unlike hypertension which occurs very naturally indeed. The holding of an inquest in such cases has nothing to do with the fact that the death may be rare.'

[45] 'The mechanical spraying of infected water into the atmosphere' I take to refer to the effect of inadequately maintained air-conditioning systems. Quite why that is said to be unnatural whereas inadequate monitoring which allows hypertension (itself, of course, 'very natural') to develop into death from cerebral haemorrhage is said to be natural, I have some difficulty in understanding.

[46] Given our conclusion on the narrow point—that inquests should in any event be held into cases like this because of the possibility of a 'neglect' verdict—the resolution of the wider point is clearly of less significance than it would otherwise be. Take, for example, the Divisional Court's example of Miss Thomas's attack having been relatively mild and the ambulance arriving quickly—

> 'but its journey to the hospital [having been] extended because the crew stopped for ten minutes at a public house, with the result that when she arrived at hospital her life could not be saved ...' (See [2001] Lloyd's Rep Med 67 at 69.)

I would regard such a case as falling comfortably into the 'neglect' category: Miss Thomas on that scenario would already have been a dependant of an a ambulance crew who then grossly failed in her care. But undoubtedly there will be cases which fall outside the category of 'neglect' and yet appear to call for an inquest on the basis already indicated, namely cases involving a wholly unexpected death from natural causes which would not have occurred but for some culpable human failure, a category of cases already perhaps recognised by the editors of *Halsbury's Laws* and *Halsbury's Statutes*. It is the combination of b their unexpectedness and the culpable human failing that allowed them to happen which to my mind makes such deaths unnatural. Deaths by natural causes though undoubtedly they are, they should plainly never have happened and in that sense are unnatural.

[47] An inquest will, of course, be held only if the coroner has reasonable cause to suspect such a combination of circumstances. That does not mean that c he will have to make detailed investigations into every hospital death. Mr Burnett's fears in this regard are to my mind misplaced. Nor would I expect such a view of the law to involve any substantial increase in the number of inquests now requiring to be held.

[48] I need hardly add that this approach must not be allowed to circumvent d the clear bar constituted by r 42 of the Coroners Rules 1984, SI 1984/552: the verdict must not appear to determine any question of criminal liability on the part of a named person or any question of civil liability.

[49] It follows from all this that I for my part would have upheld the judgment below even had I not concluded that an inquest was in any event required here e because of the possibility of a 'neglect' verdict (not itself a violation of r 42 (see *R v North Humberside and Scunthorpe Coroner, ex p Jamieson* [1994] 3 All ER 972, [1995] QB 1)).

The costs below

[50] The final issue arising on this appeal relates to the costs below which were f ordered to be paid by the coroner. The order was made apparently without argument to the contrary and certainly without reference to the Divisional Court's judgment in *R v HM Coroner for Lincoln, ex p Hay* [2000] Lloyd's Rep Med 264 at 278. Basing himself on *Ex p Hay*, Mr Burnett submits that the coroner ought not to have been required to pay Mr Touche's costs.

g [51] In *Ex p Hay* Brooke LJ reviewed a number of coroners' cases, noted Rose LJ's judgment in *R v Newcastle-under-Lyme Justices, ex p Massey* [1995] 1 All ER 120, [1994] 1 WLR 1684 as to magistrates, and continued:

> 'In my judgment, that situation [with regard to magistrates] is quite different from the situation here when a coroner is carrying out his h important statutory duty to conduct an inquest. In this context the relevant principle appears to be that if a coroner not only files an affidavit but also appears and contests the making of an adverse order in an inter partes adversarial mode, then he or she is at risk as to costs. If, on the other hand, the coroner, as is fitting for somebody holding judicial office, swears an j affidavit to assist the court and then appears in court, more in the role of an amicus than as a contesting party, then the court is likely to follow the normal rule set out in *Jervis* and make no order as to costs provided that it does not express strong disapproval of his or her conduct … It goes without saying that the court is greatly assisted by coroners who depose to what took place before them and then appear in court to assist the court in an amicus role.' (See [2000] Lloyd's Rep Med 264 at 279.)

[52] *Jervis*, I may perhaps note, states:

> 'If the coroner does appear at the hearing, and loses, then the court has a discretion whether to order the coroner to pay the successful applicant's costs, even though he acted reasonably. But such an order has only rarely been made; usually no order is made unless the coroner's behaviour called for strong disapproval. One additional factor against making a costs order is where the applicant is legally aided, and therefore it would only be the public paying the public.' (See Mathews and Foreman *Jervis on Coroners* (11th edn, 1993) pp 348–349.)

[53] No order for costs was made in favour of Mrs Hay. She, be it noted, was legally aided. Mr Touche is not. But nor, let it be made clear, has the coroner's behaviour attracted the least criticism. On the contrary he has conducted himself impeccably and, if a costs order is to be justified against him, that can only be because he failed in the event to defeat the challenge.

[54] I have, I confess, some difficulty with the approach in *Ex p Hay*. In the first place I can find no basis in earlier authority for the suggested distinction between the coroner's appearance on the one hand as 'a contesting party' ('contest[ing] the making of an adverse order in an inter partes adversarial mode', and on the other as 'an amicus'. Secondly, it seems to me difficult in practice to apply this distinction. How does one tell which role the coroner is playing? Both postulate that he will be resisting the challenge and arguing the relevant law. It can hardly be by reference to the force of his (or his counsel's) submissions. Amici curiae, indeed, play different roles according to the requirements for their assistance: sometimes they argue a case which otherwise would go by default, canvassing any arguments available, however unpromising; sometimes they address wider considerations or cover a particular interest not otherwise represented. What role, on the *Ex p Hay* approach, is this coroner playing? True, the point at issue is one of considerable importance. Yet, the point having been resolved against him at first instance, he then appealed. An amicus does not (cannot) appeal. Having appealed, as Mr Burnett recognises, the coroner is to be treated like any other appellant: if he wins, he recovers his costs; if he loses, he pays the respondent's costs. Why then should the position be different below? Indeed, had the coroner won below, he would certainly have asked for and, no doubt, been awarded his costs. Of course, as Brooke LJ observed, the court is greatly assisted by the coroner not merely swearing an affidavit but also appearing to argue the case—particularly in a case like the present which raises a true point of law of general application. But it would seem hard on the applicant that the more important the point, the less likely he will be to recover his costs—even though the point will obviously be of greater importance to coroners as a whole than to him as an individual.

[55] Naturally I recognise that if coroners who appear on the challenge and lose are regularly to be condemned in costs they may be more reluctant to be represented at the hearing, so that the court would be deprived of their assistance. That would be a pity. But it would always be open to the court to ask for an amicus and then at least the applicant's position as to costs would be fair: he would simply have to bear his own costs irrespective of the outcome. On Mr Burnett's argument, the applicant gets the worst of all possible worlds.

[56] Mr Burnett makes the additional point that Mr Touche's costs at first instance were probably no greater (or very little greater) than had the coroner chosen not to be represented: the application would still have had to be made and

a the hearing was in any event concluded within a day. Why then should the coroner have to pay the applicant's costs simply because he chose to appear? The answer seems to me to lie in the anomaly whereby a judicial officer (assuming only that he has done nothing calling for specific disapproval) can generally, by choosing not to appear, exempt himself from any costs liability even though his decision is found unlawful. In my judgment that anomaly ought not readily to b be extended.

[57] There is this further consideration. Section 13 of the 1988 Act expressly provides that where the High Court, on an application brought with the Attorney General's fiat, is satisfied, inter alia, that the coroner 'refuses … to hold an inquest which ought to be held' (s 13(1)(a)), it may, inter alia, 'order the coroner concerned to pay such costs of and incidental to the application as to the court c may appear just' (s 13(2)(b)). Indeed, this very challenge was brought before the court by way of a s 13 application as well as by judicial review. Given this express statutory discretion to award costs against the coroner whenever justice demands, a discretion unqualified by any need to find misconduct on his part (or even, I may observe, any reference to his appearance before the court), I see no d sufficient reason to subject its exercise to limitations as rigorous as those suggested by *Ex p Hay*.

[58] Coroners are, it is well known, funded as to their legal costs by the relevant local authority—here, we are told, by four London borough councils. There is no question of the coroner personally having to pay the applicant's costs. e Were it otherwise, indeed, he would hardly be appealing.

[59] In the result, given that Parliament has chosen not to heed repeated pleas by the court that there be power in this sort of case to order costs out of public funds, I would make the same order as to costs as the Divisional Court made below per incuriam the decision in *Ex p Hay*, and would accordingly dismiss the appeal on this issue too.

f

ROBERT WALKER LJ.

[60] I agree and I add a few words of my own on what Simon Brown LJ has called the wider argument. I agree with Simon Brown LJ that his judgment in *R v Poplar Coroner, ex p Thomas* [1993] 2 All ER 381, [1993] QB 610, although g concurring in the result, is in its reasoning significantly different from that of the other members of the court. I also respectfully agree that the majority view is not entirely satisfactory.

[61] The expression 'unnatural death' in s 8(1)(a) of the Coroners Act 1988 does not have a single clearly-defined meaning. (As Lord Sumner said in a h different context in *Weld-Blundell v Stephens* [1920] AC 956 at 983, [1920] All ER Rep 32 at 46, 'Everything that happens, happens in the order of nature and is therefore "natural".') Often 'unnatural' means little more than abnormal and unexpected, and that rather muted shade of meaning would appear to be consistent with the legislative purpose of the 1988 Act.

j [62] In particular, I doubt whether the naturalness or unnaturalness of a death should be determined exclusively in terms of causation, especially if that is seen as requiring a search for a single 'dominant cause of death'. That is the expression which Simon Brown LJ used in *R v HM Coroner for Western District of East Sussex, ex p Homberg* (1994) 19 BMLR 11 at 22 in summarising the majority view in *Ex p Thomas*. The better way forward is to look for a combination of circumstances rather than a single dominant cause.

KEENE LJ.

[**63**] I agree that, for the reasons given by Simon Brown LJ, there is reasonable cause to suspect that Mrs Touche's death was contributed to by 'neglect' in the sense used in *R v North Humberside and Scunthorpe Coroner, ex p Jamieson* [1994] 3 All ER 972, [1995] QB 1 and was for that reason alone 'unnatural' in terms of s 8(1)(a) of the Coroners Act 1988. That is sufficient to determine this appeal on the substantive issue. I also agree that the appeal on costs should be dismissed for the reasons given in Simon Brown LJ's judgment.

[**64**] On the 'wider point', as it has been described, I find myself arriving at the same conclusion as Simon Brown and Robert Walker LJJ, but by a somewhat different analysis of the judgments in the leading case of *R v Poplar Coroner, ex p Thomas* [1993] 2 All ER 381, [1993] QB 610. I do not discern any necessary conflict between the judgments of Dillon LJ and Farquharson LJ on the one hand and Simon Brown LJ on the other in that case. It is well established that there may be more than one cause of death in a given situation, and that is illustrated by the possibility of a verdict which incorporates a finding that neglect contributed to the death in question. *Ex p Jamieson* reflects that situation, as do a large number of other authorities. Simon Brown LJ's judgment in *Ex p Thomas* was dealing with the obvious possibility that a death may have more than one cause.

[**65**] But it is not the case that the judgments of the other members of the court in *Ex p Thomas* seek to deny that possibility. They did not deal with the possibility of there being more than one cause of death, but it cannot be that they took the view that, however complex the factual situation, it had to be forced onto the Procrustean bed of a single cause. Their judgments, properly read, amount to a finding that, on the facts of that particular case, there was only one cause. But there was no pronouncement that there has to be in all cases only a single cause of death. In short, I concur with the view expressed by the Divisional Court in the present case to the effect that they did not detect any conflict between the judgments in *Ex p Thomas*. They were right to say that the possibility of a coroner sometimes having to find more than one cause of death was not canvassed by Dillon LJ.

[**66**] I therefore do not find any difficulty in terms of precedent arising in this case. The approach spelt out by Simon Brown LJ on the wider issue in his judgment in the present case is not in conflict with the decision in *Ex p Thomas*, and it provides a practical, workable approach in this difficult area of law. For that reason also I would dismiss the substantive appeal.

Appeal dismissed.

Dilys Tausz Barrister.

a

Lister and others v Hesley Hall Ltd

[2001] UKHL 22

HOUSE OF LORDS

b LORD STEYN, LORD CLYDE, LORD HUTTON, LORD HOBHOUSE OF WOODBOROUGH AND LORD MILLETT

7, 8 MARCH, 3 MAY 2001

Vicarious liability – Master and servant – Authorised act done in improper manner – Defendants owning boarding school and employing warden to take care of boys – c *Warden sexually abusing boys in his care – Whether school owners vicariously liable for sexual abuse committed by employee – Test for determining whether employer vicariously liable for employee's wrongful act.*

Between 1979 and 1982 the claimants were resident at a school for boys with d emotional and behavioural difficulties, owned by the defendants. The latter employed G to take care of the boys as warden of the school's boarding annex. Unbeknown to his employers, G systematically sexually abused the claimants while they were resident at the school. He was eventually convicted of multiple offences involving sexual abuse. Subsequently, the claimants brought actions for e personal injury against the defendants, alleging, inter alia, that they were vicariously liable for the torts committed by their employee, G. The judge concluded, on the basis of binding Court of Appeal authority, that the defendants could not be vicariously liable for G's torts since sexual abuse was outside the course of his employment, not an improper mode of carrying out an act authorised by his employers. The judge nevertheless held that the defendants f were vicariously liable for G's breach of duty in failing to report his intentions and the acts of abuse. Accordingly, he gave judgment for the claimants on liability, and the defendants appealed. Like the judge, the Court of Appeal was bound by its earlier decision that an employer could not be vicariously liable for sexual abuse committed by a teacher against pupils in his care. Unlike the judge, it also g held that a failure to report wrong conduct could not be within the scope of employment, so as to make the employer vicariously liable for that failure, when it was not vicariously liable for the wrongful conduct itself. Accordingly, it allowed the defendants' appeal. On the claimants' appeal to the House of Lords, their Lordships considered the proper approach to determining whether an employee's wrongful act had been committed in the course of his employment, h and whether, on the proper approach, the defendants were vicariously liable for the sexual abuse itself.

Held – When determining whether an employer was vicariously liable for an employee's wrongful act, it was necessary to concentrate on the relative j closeness of the connection between the nature of the employment and the particular tort, taking a broad approach to the nature of the employment by asking what was the job on which the employee was engaged for his employer. If that approach to the nature of employment were adopted, it was not necessary to ask the simplistic question whether, in the instant case, the acts of sexual abuse were modes of doing authorised acts. Rather, it became possible to consider the question of vicarious liability on the basis that the defendants had undertaken to care for boys through the services of G and that there was a very close connection between his employment and his torts. They had been committed in the time and at the premises of the defendants while G was busy caring for the children in performance of his duties. In those circumstances, G's torts were so closely connected with his employment that it would be fair and just to hold the defendants vicariously liable. Accordingly, the appeal would be allowed (see [20], [23]–[25], [27], [28], [30], [37], [42], [43], [48]–[52], [59]–[61], [63], [69], [70], [80], [82] and [85], post).

Ilkiw v Samuels [1963] 2 All ER 879, *Morris v C W Martin & Sons Ltd* [1965] 2 All ER 725 and *Rose v Plenty* [1976] 1 All ER 97 applied.

Bazley v Curry (1999) 174 DLR (4th) 45 and *Jacobi v Griffiths* (1999) 174 DLR (4th) 71 adopted.

Trotman v North Yorkshire CC [1999] LGR 584 overruled.

Notes

For the liability of employers for torts committed by an employee in the course of his employment, see 45(2) *Halsbury's Laws* (4th edn reissue) paras 304, 819–820.

Cases referred to in opinions

Aldred v Nacanco [1987] IRLR 292, CA.

Barwick v English Joint Stock Bank (1867) LR 2 Exch 259, [1861–73] All ER Rep 194, Ex Ch.

Bazley v Curry (1999) 174 DLR (4th) 45, Can SC.

Canadian Pacific Rly Co v Lockhart [1942] 2 All ER 464, [1942] AC 591, PC.

Central Motors (Glasgow) Ltd v Cessnock Garage and Motor Co 1925 SC 796, Ct of Sess.

Century Insurance Co Ltd v Northern Ireland Road Transport Board [1942] 1 All ER 491, [1942] AC 509, HL.

Cheshire v Bailey [1905] 1 KB 237, CA.

Deatons Pty Ltd v Flew (1949) 79 CLR 370, Aust HC.

Dyer v Munday [1895] 1 QB 742, [1895–9] All ER Rep 1022, CA.

Foulkes v Metropolitan District Rly Co (1880) 5 CPD 157.

Gilchrist Watt & Sanderson Pty Ltd v York Products Pty Ltd [1970] 3 All ER 825, [1970] 1 WLR 1262, PC.

Heasmans v Clarity Cleaning Co Ltd [1987] ICR 949, CA.

Heiton & Co v M'Sweeney [1905] 2 IR 47, KBD.

Hooper v London and North Western Rly Co (1881) 50 LJQB 103.

Ilkiw v Samuels [1963] 2 All ER 879, [1963] 1 WLR 991, CA.

Imperial Chemical Industries Ltd v Shatwell [1964] 2 All ER 999, [1965] AC 656, [1964] 3 WLR 329, HL.

Irving v Post Office [1987] IRLR 289, CA.

Jacobi v Griffiths (1999) 174 DLR (4th) 71, Can SC.

Joel v Morison (1834) 6 C & P 501, 172 ER 1338.

Jones v Tower Boot Co Ltd [1997] 2 All ER 406, [1997] ICR 254, CA.

Kilboy v South Eastern Fire Area Joint Committee 1952 SC 280, Ct of Sess.

Kirby v National Coal Board 1958 SC 514, Ct of Sess.

Lloyd v Grace, Smith & Co [1912] AC 716, [1911–13] All ER Rep 51, HL.

Meux v Great Eastern Ry Co [1895] 2 QB 387, [1895–99] All ER Rep 710.

Morris v C W Martin & Sons Ltd [1965] 2 All ER 725, [1966] 1 QB 716, [1965] 3 WLR 276, CA.

Photo Production Ltd v Securicor Transport Ltd [1980] 1 All ER 556, [1980] AC 827, [1980] 2 WLR 283, HL.

a *Plumb v Cobden Flour Mills Co Ltd* [1914] AC 62, HL.
Port Swettenham Authority v T W Wu & Co (M) Sdn Bhd [1978] 3 All ER 337, [1979] AC 580, [1978] 3 WLR 530, PC.
Racz v Home Office [1994] 1 All ER 97, [1994] 2 AC 45, [1994] 2 WLR 23, HL.
Rose v Plenty [1976] 1 All ER 97, [1976] 1 WLR 141, CA.
Sanderson v Collins [1904] 1 KB 628, [1904–07] All ER Rep 561.
b *Staveley Iron and Chemcial Co Ltd v Jones* [1956] 1 All ER 403, [1956] AC 627, [1956] 2 WLR 479, HL.
Trotman v North Yorkshire CC [1999] LGR 584, CA.
Ward v Scotrail Rlys Ltd 1999 SC 255, Ct of Sess.
Warren v Henlys Ltd [1948] 2 All ER 935.
Williams v A & W Hemphill Ltd 1966 SC (HL) 31.
c

Appeal

The second and third plaintiffs, Steven Robert Bilcliff and Maurice Christopher Loaring, former residents of Axeholme House, the boarding annex of Wilsic Hall School, Wadsworth, Doncaster, appealed with permission of the Appeal d Committee of the House of Lords given on 16 May 2000 from the order of the Court of Appeal (Swinton Thomas, Waller LJJ and Jonathan Parker J) on 7 October 1999 allowing an appeal by the respondents, Hesley Hall Ltd, the owners of the school, from the order of Judge Walker at Dewsbury County Court on 21 January 1999, drawn up on 25 February 1999, giving judgment on liability for the first plaintiff, Konrad Maurice Lister, and the appellants in their actions against the e respondents for personal injury arising out of acts of sexual abuse committed on them between 1979 and 1982 by the person then employed by the respondents as the warden of the annex. Mr Lister did not appeal from the Court of Appeal's order. The facts are set out in the opinion of Lord Steyn.

f *Richard Maxwell QC* and *Rosalind Coe* (instructed by *Last Cawthra Feather*, Shipley) for the appellants.
Andrew Collender QC and *Andrew Miller* (instructed by *Beachcroft Wansbroughs*, Leeds) for the respondents.

Their Lordships took time for consideration.
g

3 May 2001. The following opinions were delivered.

LORD STEYN.

h (I) *The question*

[1] My Lords, the central question before the House is whether as a matter of legal principle the employers of the warden of a school boarding house, who sexually abused boys in his care, may depending on the particular circumstances be vicariously liable for the torts of their employee.

j

(II) *The sexual abuse*

[2] In 1979 Axeholme House, a boarding annex of Wilsic Hall School, Wadsworth, Doncaster, was opened. Between 1979 and 1982 the appellants were resident at Axeholme House. At that time the appellants were aged between 12 and 15 years. The school and boarding annex were owned and managed by Hesley Hall Ltd as a commercial enterprise. In the main children with emotional and behavioural difficulties were sent to the school by local authorities. Axeholme House is situated about two miles from the school. *a*

[3] The aim was that Axeholme House would provide care to enable the boys to adjust to normal living. It usually accommodated about 18 boys. The company employed Mr and Mrs Grain as warden and housekeeper to take care of the boys. The employers accept that at the material time they were aware of the opportunities of sexual abuse which may present themselves in a boarding school environment. *b*

[4] The warden was responsible for the day-to-day running of Axeholme House and for maintaining discipline. He lived there with his wife, who was disabled. On most days he and his wife were the only members of staff on the premises. He supervised the boys when they were not at school. His duties included making sure the boys went to bed at night, got up in the morning and got to and from school. He administered pocket money, organised weekend leave, evening activities, and supervised other staff. Axeholme House was intended to be a home for the boys and not an extension of the school environment. *c*

[5] The employers accept that, unbeknown to them, the warden systematically sexually abused the appellants in Axeholme House. The sexual abuse took the form of mutual masturbation, oral sex and sometimes buggery. The sexual abuse was preceded by 'grooming' being conduct on the part of the warden to establish control over the appellants. It involved unwarranted gifts, trips alone with the boys, undeserved leniency, allowing the watching of violent and X-rated videos, and so forth. What may initially have been regarded as signs of a relaxed approach to discipline gradually developed into blatant sexual abuse. Neither of the appellants made any complaint at the time. In 1982 the warden and his wife left the employ of the respondents. In the early 1990s a police investigation led to criminal charges in the Crown Court. Grain was sentenced to seven years' imprisonment for multiple offences involving sexual abuse. *d* *e*

[6] In 1997 the appellants brought claims for personal injury against the employers. *f*

(III) *The decision at first instance*

[7] The trial took place in January 1999. It is necessary to describe the shape of the case. There were then three claimants. Their claims were advanced on two separate grounds. First, it was alleged that the employers were negligent in their care, selection and control of the warden. Secondly, the plaintiffs alleged that the employers were vicariously liable for the torts committed by the warden. The case was heard before Judge Walker in the Dewsbury County Court. The evidence was adduced by witness statements and oral evidence. The judge was asked to give judgment on liability only. *g* *h*

[8] On 25 February 1999 the judge gave judgment. He dismissed the claim in negligence against the employers. That left the claim based on vicarious liability to be considered. This claim appeared to be ruled out by the *Salmond* test (*Salmond on Torts* (9th edn, 1936) p 95; *Salmond and Heuston on the Law of Torts* (21st edn, 1996) p 443) as interpreted and applied by the Court of Appeal in *Trotman v North Yorkshire CC* [1999] LGR 584. The following passage in the judgment of Butler-Sloss LJ (at 591) reveals the perceived difficulty: *j*

> '18. Having looked at some of the relevant decisions on each side of the line, it is useful to stand back and ask: applying general principles, in which category in the *Salmond* test would one expect these facts to fall? A deputy headmaster of a special school, charged with the responsibility of caring for

a a handicapped teenager on a foreign holiday, sexually assaults him. Is that in principle an improper mode of carrying out an authorised act on behalf of his employer, the council, or an independent act outside the course of his employment? His position of caring for the plaintiff by sharing a bedroom with him gave him the opportunity to carry out the sexual assaults. But availing himself of that opportunity seems to me to be far removed from an b unauthorised mode of carrying out a teacher's duties on behalf of his employer. Rather it is a negation of the duty of the council to look after children for whom it was responsible. Acts of physical assault may not be so easy to categorise, since they may range, for instance, from a brutal and unprovoked assault by a teacher to forceful attempts to defend another pupil or the teacher himself. But in the field of serious sexual misconduct, I find it c difficult to visualise circumstances in which an act of the teacher can be an unauthorised mode of carrying out an authorised act, although I would not wish to close the door on the possibility.'

Thorpe LJ agreed with this judgment and Chadwick LJ expressed himself in d materially similar terms. Not surprisingly, the judge felt compelled to conclude that the employers could not be held vicariously liable for the torts of the warden. On the other hand, the judge held that the employers were vicariously liable for the warden's failure to report to his employers his intentions (before the acts of sexual abuse) and the harmful consequences to the children (after acts of abuse). The judge explained his reasoning as follows:

e '1. The defendant admits it had a duty of care towards the plaintiffs. 2. That duty of care was to take all reasonable steps to safeguard the plaintiffs (and other pupils) in its physical, moral and educational development whilst at the school. 3. In carrying out that duty of care the defendant a limited company necessarily had to appoint a hierarchy of responsible agents … f 4. Mr Grain in particular was responsible for the boys while at Axeholme House … 5. He had a duty to report to the defendant … any harm which he perceived had come or might come to any of the boys in his care with a view to the defendant carrying out further its duty of care in taking remedial or preventative steps. 6. Failure by Mr Grain to report harm to the boys g would unquestionably be a failure to carry out a duty which he owed generally and specifically to each boy in his care. 7. The consequences of a report of abuse upon a boy would (I find) undoubtedly have resulted in the removal from the scene by the defendant of the source of the harm by the dismissal of Mr Grain and the report of the incident to the police. 8. The defendant is therefore vicariously liable for Mr Grain's failure to report the h acts of abuse.'

The judge entered judgment for the plaintiffs against the employers on liability, and ordered that damages be assessed. The judge gave leave to appeal to the Court of Appeal.

j

(IV) *The Court of Appeal decision*

[9] The employers appealed to the Court of Appeal. The plaintiffs did not cross-appeal the judge's decision that the employers were not negligent. The only remaining issue was therefore whether the employers were vicariously liable. But, like the judge, the Court of Appeal was bound by the previous Court of Appeal decision in *Trotman*'s case. In this situation counsel for the plaintiffs

found it difficult to argue that the employers were vicariously liable for the sexual acts of the warden. Instead counsel for the plaintiffs defended the judgment in favour of his clients on the basis of the warden's failure to report his own conduct. By judgments delivered on 7 October 1999 ((1999) Times, 13 October), the Court of Appeal dismissed this argument. The reasoning of the Court of Appeal is encapsulated in the following sentence in the judgment of Waller LJ:

> 'The simple point in this case is that if wrongful conduct is outside the course of employment, a failure to prevent or report that wrong conduct cannot be within the scope of employment so as to make the employer vicariously liable for that failure when the employer was not vicariously liable for the wrongful conduct itself.'

The Court of Appeal accordingly allowed the appeal. In due course the House of Lords granted leave to appeal. The appeal proceeded at the instance of two appellants only.

(V) *The issues before the House*

[10] Since the decision in the Court of Appeal the law reports of two landmark decisions in the Canadian Supreme Court, which deal with vicarious liability of employers for sexual abuse of children, have become available: *Bazley v Curry* (1999) 174 DLR (4th) 45 and *Jacobi v Griffiths* (1999) 174 DLR (4th) 71. Enunciating a principle of 'close connection' the Supreme Court unanimously held liability established in *Bazley*'s case and by a four to three majority came to the opposite conclusion in *Jacobi*'s case. The Supreme Court judgments examine in detail the circumstances in which, though an employer is not 'at fault', it may still be 'fair' that that it should bear responsibility for the tortious conduct of its employees. These decisions have been described as 'a genuine advance on the unauthorised conduct/unauthorised mode distinction': Peter Cane 'Vicarious Liability for Sexual Abuse' (2000) 116 LQR 21 at 24. Counsel for the appellants invited your Lordships to apply the test developed in *Bazley*'s case and in *Jacobi*'s case and to conclude that the employers are vicariously liable for the sexual torts of their employee.

[11] In another sense the approach to the appeals before the House differs from that adopted in the Court of Appeal. The House is not bound to follow the decision in *Trotman*'s case. On the contrary, quite apart from the high persuasive value of the two Canadian decisions, the first task of the House is to consider whether the decision in *Trotman*'s case, when examined from a perspective of legal principle, correctly states the position. On the principal point the present appeals therefore in reality challenge the law as stated by the Court of Appeal in *Trotman*'s case rather than in the cases under consideration.

[12] Only if the arguments of the appellants, which seek an overruling of *Trotman*'s case, fail will it become necessary to consider whether vicarious liability may nevertheless be based on the warden's failure to report his sexual intentions and misdeeds.

(VI) *The perspective of principle*

[13] It is right to acknowledge at once that *Trotman v North Yorkshire CC* is a carefully considered and reasoned decision. The leading judgment was given by Butler-Sloss LJ whose views are entitled to great weight. Nevertheless, our allegiance must be to legal principle. That is the subject to which I now turn.

a [14] Vicarious liability is legal responsibility imposed on an employer, although he is himself free from blame, for a tort committed by his employee in the course of his employment. Fleming observed that this formula represented—

> 'a compromise between two conflicting policies: on the one end, the social interest in furnishing an innocent tort victim with recourse against a financially responsible defendant; on the other, a hesitation to foist any b undue burden on business enterprise ...' (See *The Law of Torts* (9th edn, 1998) pp 409–410.)

[15] For nearly a century English judges have adopted Salmond's statement of the applicable test as correct. Salmond said that a wrongful act is deemed to be done by a 'servant' in the course of his employment if 'it is either (a) a wrongful c act authorised by the master, or (b) a wrongful and unauthorised *mode* of doing some act authorised by the master' (*Salmond on Torts* (1st edn, 1907) p 83 (author's emphasis) and *Salmond and Heuston on Torts* (21st edn, 1996) p 443). Situation (a) causes no problems. The difficulty arises in respect of cases under (b). Salmond did, however, offer an explanation which has sometimes been overlooked. He d said (*Salmond on Torts* (1st edn, 1907) pp 83–84) that 'a master ... is liable even for acts which he has not authorised, provided they are *so connected* with acts which he has authorised, that they may rightly *be regarded* as modes—although improper modes—of doing them' (my emphasis): see the citation of Salmond with approval in *Canadian Pacific Rly Co v Lockhart* [1942] 2 All ER 464 at 467, [1942] AC 591 at 599 (*Salmond on Torts* (9th edn, 1938) p 95) and in *Racz v Home Office* e [1994] 1 All ER 97 at 102, [1994] 2 AC 45 at 53 (*Salmond and Heuston on the Law of Tort* (19th edn, 1987) pp 521–522 (20th edn, 1992) p 457). Salmond's explanation is the germ of the close connection test adumbrated by the Canadian Supreme Court in *Bazley*'s case and *Jacobi*'s case.

[16] It is not necessary to embark on a detailed examination of the development f of the modern principle of vicarious liability. But it is necessary to face up to the way in which the law of vicarious liability sometimes may embrace intentional wrongdoing by an employee. If one mechanically applies *Salmond*'s test, the result might at first glance be thought to be that a bank is not liable to a customer where a bank employee defrauds a customer by giving him only half the foreign exchange which he paid for, the employee pocketing the difference. A preoccupation g with conceptualistic reasoning may lead to the absurd conclusion that there can only be vicarious liability if the bank carries on business in defrauding its customers. Ideas divorced from reality have never held much attraction for judges steeped in the tradition that their task is to deliver principled but practical justice. How the courts set the law on a sensible course is a matter to which I now h turn.

[17] It is easy to accept the idea that where an employee acts for the benefit of his employer, or intends to do so, that is strong evidence that he was acting in the course of his employment. But until the decision of the House of Lords in *Lloyd v Grace, Smith & Co* [1912] AC 716, [1911–13] All ER Rep 51 it was thought that j vicarious liability could only be established if such requirements were satisfied. This was an overly restrictive view and hardly in tune with the needs of society. In *Lloyd*'s case it was laid to rest by the House of Lords. A firm of solicitors were held liable for the dishonesty of their managing clerk who persuaded a client to transfer property to him and then disposed of it for his own advantage. The decisive factor was that the client had been invited by the firm to deal with their managing clerk. This decision was a breakthrough: it finally established that

vicarious liability is not necessarily defeated if the employee acted for his own benefit. On the other hand, an intense focus on the connection between the nature of the employment and the tort of the employee became necessary.

[**18**] A good illustration of the correct approach is provided by *Williams v A & W Hemphill Ltd* 1966 SC (HL) 31. Contrary to the instructions of his employers a driver of a lorry deviated substantially from his route. On the detour an accident occurred owing to the fault of the driver. The question arose whether the employers of the lorry driver were vicariously liable. In a speech assented to by all the members of the House Lord Pearson analysed the position as follows (at 46):

> 'Had the driver in the present case been driving a lorry which was empty or contained nothing of real importance, I think that so substantial a deviation might well have constituted a frolic of his own. The presence of passengers, however, whom the servant is charged *qua* servant to drive to their ultimate destination makes it impossible (at all events, provided that they are not all parties to the plans for deviation) to say that the deviation is entirely for the servant's purposes. Their presence and transport is a dominant purpose of the authorised journey, and, although they are transported deviously, continues to play an essential part. It was said in argument that there must be some limits to that contention and that one could not hold that, if the driver had gone to Inverness, he would still be acting on his master's business. No doubt there are such limits to the argument as common sense may set on the facts of each case. But when there are passengers whom the servants on his master's behalf has taken aboard for transport to Glasgow, their transport and safety does not cease at a certain stage of the journey to be the master's business, or part of his enterprise, merely because the servant has for his own purposes chosen some route which is contrary to his instructions. The more dominant are the current obligations of the master's business in connection with the lorry, the less weight is to be attached to disobedient navigational extravagances of the servant. In weighing up, therefore, the question of degree, whether the admittedly substantial deviation of the vehicle with its passengers and baggage was such as to make the lorry's progress a frolic of the servant unconnected with or in substitution for the master's business, the presence of the passengers is a decisive factor against regarding it as a mere frolic of the servant. In the present case the defenders remained liable, in spite of the deviation, for their driver's negligence.'

This was vicarious liability in the context of negligence. Nevertheless, the reasoning throws light on the problem under consideration.

[**19**] The classic example of vicarious liability for intentional wrong doing is *Morris v C W Martin & Sons Ltd* [1965] 2 All ER 725, [1966] 1 QB 716. A woman wanted her mink stole cleaned. With her permission it was delivered to the defendants for cleaning. An employee took charge of the fur and stole it. At first instance the judge held that the defendants were not liable because the theft was not committed in the course of employment. The Court of Appeal reversed the judge's decision and held the defendants liable. It is possible to read the case narrowly simply as a bailment case, the wrong being failure to re-deliver. But two of the judgments are authority for the proposition that the employee converted the fur in the course of his employment. Diplock LJ observed:

> 'If the principle laid down in *Lloyd v Grace, Smith & Co* is applied to the facts of the present case, the defendants cannot in my view escape liability for the

a conversion of the plaintiff's fur by their servant Morrissey. They accepted the fur as bailees for reward in order to clean it. They put Morrissey as their agent in their place to clean the fur and to take charge of it while doing so. The manner in which he conducted himself in doing that work was to convert it. What he was doing, albeit dishonestly, he was doing in the scope or course of his employment in the technical sense of that infelicitous but b time-honoured phrase. The defendants as his masters are responsible for his tortious act.' (See [1965] 2 All ER 725 at 738, [1966] 1 QB 716 at 736–737.)

Salmon LJ held ([1965] 2 All ER 725 at 739, [1966] 1 QB 716 at 738) that 'the defendants are liable for what amounted to negligence and conversion by their servant in the course of his employment'. The deciding factor was that the c employee had been given custody of the fur. *Morris'* case has consistently been regarded as high authority on the principles of vicarious liability. Atiyah *Vicarious Liability in the Law of Torts* (1967) p 271 described it as 'a striking and valuable extension of the law of vicarious liability'. Palmer *Bailment* (2nd edn, 1991) pp 424–425 treats *Morris'* case as an authority on vicarious liability beyond d bailment. He states that 'if a television repairman steals a television set he is called in to repair, his employers would be liable, for the loss occurred whilst he was performing one of the class of acts in respect of which their duty lay'. And that does not involve bailment. Moreover, in *Port Swettenham Authority v T W Wu & Co (M) Sdn Bhd* [1978] 3 All ER 337, [1979] AC 580 the Privy Council expressly approved *Morris'* case in respect of vicarious liability as explained by Diplock and e Salmon LJJ.

[**20**] Our law no longer struggles with the concept of vicarious liability for intentional wrongdoing. Thus the decision of the House of Lords in *Racz v Home Office* [1994] 1 All ER 97, [1994] 2 AC 45 is authority for the proposition that the Home Office may be vicariously liable for acts of police officers which amounted f to misfeasance in public office—and hence for liability in tort involving bad faith. It remains, however, to consider how vicarious liability for intentional wrongdoing fits in with Salmond's formulation. The answer is that it does not cope ideally with such cases. It must, however, be remembered that the great tort writer did not attempt to enunciate precise propositions of law on vicarious liability. At most he propounded a broad test which deems as within the course of g employment 'a wrongful and unauthorised mode of doing some *act* authorised by the master'. And he emphasised the connection between the authorised *acts* and the 'improper modes' of doing them. In reality it is simply a practical test serving as a dividing line between cases where it is or is not just to impose vicarious liability. The usefulness of the *Salmond* formulation is, however, h crucially dependent on focussing on the right act of the employee. This point was explored in *Rose v Plenty* [1976] 1 All ER 97, [1976] 1 WLR 141. The Court of Appeal held that a milkman who deliberately disobeyed his employers' order not to allow children to help on his rounds did not go beyond his course of employment in allowing a child to help him. The analysis in this decision shows how the pitfalls of terminology must be avoided. Scarman LJ said:

j

'The first defendant was, of course, employed at the time of the accident to do a whole number of operations. He was certainly not employed to give the plaintiff a lift, and if one confines one's analysis of the facts to the incident of injury to the plaintiff, then no doubt one would say that carrying the plaintiff on the float—giving him a lift—was not in the course of the first defendant's employment. But in *Ilkiw v Samuels* ([1963] 2 All ER 879 at 889,

> [1963] 1 WLR 991 at 1004) Diplock LJ indicated that the proper approach to the nature of the servant's employment is a broad one. He said: "As each of these nouns implies [he is referring to the nouns used to describe course of employment, sphere, scope and so forth] the matter must be looked at broadly, not dissecting the servant's task into its component activities—such as driving, loading, sheeting and the like—by asking: What was the job on which he was engaged for his employer? and answering that question as a jury would." Applying those words to the employment of the first defendant, I think it is clear from the evidence that he was employed as a roundsman to drive his float round his round and to deliver milk, to collect empties and to obtain payment. That was his job. He was under an express prohibition—a matter to which I shall refer later—not to enlist the help of anyone doing that work. And he was also under an express prohibition not to give lifts on the float to anyone. How did he choose to carry out the task which I have analysed? He chose to disregard the prohibition and to enlist the assistance of the plaintiff. As a matter of common sense, that does seem to me to be a mode, albeit a prohibited mode, of doing the job with which he was entrusted. Why was the plaintiff being carried on the float when the accident occurred? Because it was necessary to take him from point to point so that he could assist in delivering milk, collecting empties and, on occasions, obtaining payment.' (See [1976] 1 All ER 97 at 104, [1976] 1 WLR 141 at 147–148.)

If this approach to the nature of employment is adopted, it is not necessary to ask the simplistic question whether in the cases under consideration the acts of sexual abuse were modes of doing authorised acts. It becomes possible to consider the question of vicarious liability on the basis that the employer undertook to care for the boys through the services of the warden and that there is a very close connection between the torts of the warden and his employment. After all, they were committed in the time and on the premises of employers while the warden was also busy caring for the children.

(VII) *The correctness of Trotman's case*

[21] It is now opportune to take a closer look at the Court of Appeal decision in *Trotman v North Yorkshire CC* [1999] LGR 584. The appeal was from a decision on a preliminary issue arising on the pleadings. The pleaded facts were as follows (at 592):

> '(1) At all material times the [council] operated a school for mentally handicapped children ... whereat the plaintiff attended from about May 1990. (2) The [council's] servants or agents who were the staff at the school organised a holiday trip to Spain which took place on 28 May to 4 June 1991 and the plaintiff, with other pupils, went on the trip and was totally within the control, and subject to the care, of the [council's] said servants or agents, the staff at the said school. (3) Whilst on the holiday in Spain the plaintiff shared a bedroom with the deputy headmaster of the said school, the [council's] servant or agent, one [MS], and on several nights during the holiday the plaintiff was indecently assaulted by the said [MS].'

Accordingly, it was alleged, the council was vicariously responsible because the indecent assaults were committed by MS 'whilst carrying out his supervisory role a as a schoolmaster in charge of the plaintiff and responsible for his care'. No breach of duty by the council was alleged. Chadwick LJ further observed (at 594):

> 'There is no allegation in the particulars of claim that the council itself owed to the plaintiff a duty to ensure that he was free from harm during the Spanish holiday. No doubt there were thought to be good reasons for b pleading the case without alleging any duty owed by the council itself. I express no view on whether such an allegation could be made good. This court must decide this appeal on the basis that the preliminary issue is defined by the allegations which were before the judge. It would not be safe to proceed on the basis that the case might have been put in some other way which the plaintiff has not chosen to plead.'

c

Butler-Sloss LJ may have been influenced by similar considerations for at the end of her judgment she observed (at 592): '... on the basis of the case set out in the pleadings which is the only issue before this court, the blame for these events cannot be laid at the door of the council.' This was a rather restricted and technical view of the dispute. It would not have been overly bold to say that, d although the council was not itself in breach of any duty, it had undertaken to exercise reasonable care of the children on the Spanish holiday through the deputy headmaster. That would not have been the end of the matter but it would have facilitated a more realistic appraisal of the issue.

[**22**] The Court of Appeal treated the *Morris* line of authority as applicable only e in bailment cases. That was the Court of Appeal's answer to the argument that, in the context of vicarious liability, the law ought not to incur the reproach of showing greater zeal in protecting jewellery than in protecting children. My Lords, I trust that I have already shown that *Morris'* case cannot be so easily dismissed. It is only necessary to add that in *Photo Production Ltd v Securicor Transport Ltd* [1980] 1 All ER 556, [1980] AC 827 the House of Lords took the view f that the principles enunciated in *Morris'* case by Diplock and Salmon LJJ are of general application. The plaintiffs had contracted with the defendants for the provision of a night patrol service for their factory. The perils the parties had in mind were fire and theft. A patrol man deliberately lit a fire which burned down the factory. It was an unresolved issue whether the employee intended to cause g only a small fire or burn down the whole factory: see [1980] 1 All ER 556 at 559, [1980] AC 827 at 840. The question was whether Securicor was protected by an exemption clause. The basis of the prima facie liability of Securicor therefore had to be determined. Lord Wilberforce pointed out that it could be put on more than one basis. He said:

h

> '... it could be put on a vicarious responsibility for the wrongful act of Musgrove, viz, starting a fire on the premises; Securicor would be responsible for this on the principle stated in *Morris v C W Martin & Sons Ltd* ([1965] 2 All ER 725 at 739, [1966] 1 QB 716 at 739).' (See [1980] 1 All ER 556 at 564, [1980] AC 827 at 846.)

j

Lord Keith of Kinkel and Lord Scarman expressed agreement with Lord Wilberforce. In a separate speech Lord Salmon observed ([1980] 1 All ER 556 at 569, [1980] AC 827 at 852):

> 'There can be no doubt that, but for the clause in the contract which I have recited, Securicor would have been liable for the damage which was caused

> by their servant Musgrove whilst indubitably acting in the course of his employment: see *Morris v C W Martin & Sons Ltd*.'

It is therefore plain that the Court of Appeal in *Trotman*'s case erred in treating *Morris*' case as reflecting a special rule application in bailment cases only.

[**23**] But at the root of the reasoning of the Court of Appeal lay a terminological difficulty. Butler-Sloss LJ thought ([1999] LGR 584 at 591), that the sexual assaults were 'far removed from an unauthorised mode of carrying out a teacher's duties on behalf of his employer'. Chadwick LJ (at 592–593) found it—

> 'impossible to hold that the commission of acts of indecent assault can be regarded as a mode—albeit, an improper or unauthorised mode—of doing what … the deputy headmaster was employed by the council to do … Rather, it must be regarded as an independent act of self-indulgence or self-gratification.'

In giving the unanimous judgment of the Canadian Supreme Court in *Bazley v Curry* (1999) 174 DLR (4th) 45 McLachlin J criticised the decision in *Trotman*'s case in the following terms (at 57 (para 24)):

> '… the opinion's reasoning depends on the level of generality with which the sexual act is described. Instead of describing the act in terms of the employee's duties of supervising and caring for vulnerable students during a study trip abroad, the Court of Appeal cast it in terms unrelated to those duties. Important legal decisions should not turn on such semantics. As Atiyah points out [*Vicarious Liability in the Law of Torts*, p 263]: "conduct can be correctly described at varying levels of generality, and no one description of the 'act' on which the servant was engaged is necessarily more correct than any other".'

I am in respectful agreement with this comment.

[**24**] It is useful to consider an employer's potential liability for non-sexual assaults. If such assaults arise directly out of circumstances connected with the employment, vicarious liability may arise: see Rose 'Liability for an Employee's Assaults' (1977) 40 MLR 420 at 432–433. Butler-Sloss LJ considered this analogy. In the critical paragraph of her judgment, which I have already quoted in full, she stated ([1999] LGR 584 at 591):

> 'Acts of physical assault may not be so easy to categorise, since they may range, for instance, from a brutal and unprovoked assault by a teacher to forceful attempts to defend another pupil or the teacher himself. But in the field of serious sexual misconduct, I find it difficult to visualise circumstances in which an act of the teacher can be an unauthorised mode of carrying out an authorised act, although I would not wish to close the door on the possibility.'

If I correctly understand this passage, it appears to be indicating that there could not be vicarious liability by an employer for a brutal assault, or serious sexual misconduct whatever the circumstances. That appears to be a case of saying 'The greater the fault of the servant, the less the liability of the master' (see *Morris v C W Martin & Sons Ltd* [1965] 2 All ER 725 at 736, [1966] 1 QB 716 at 733 per Diplock LJ). A better approach is to concentrate on the relative closeness of the connection between the nature of the employment and the particular tort.

a [25] In my view the approach of the Court of Appeal in *Trotman*'s case was wrong. It resulted in the case being treated as one of the employment furnishing a mere opportunity to commit the sexual abuse. The reality was that the county council were responsible for the care of the vulnerable children and employed the deputy headmaster to carry out that duty on its behalf. And the sexual abuse took place while the employee was engaged in duties at the very time and place b demanded by his employment. The connection between the employment and the torts was very close. I would overrule *Trotman*'s case.

[26] It is not necessary to consider case law on the words 'in the course of his employment' which are to be found in s 32(1) of the Race Relations Act 1976 and s 41 of the Sex Discrimination Act 1975.

c (VII) *The application of the correct test*

[27] My Lords, I have been greatly assisted by the luminous and illuminating judgments of the Canadian Supreme Court in *Bazley*'s case and *Jacobi*'s case. Wherever such problems are considered in future in the common law world these judgments will be the starting point. On the other hand, it is unnecessary d to express views on the full range of policy considerations examined in those decisions.

[28] Employing the traditional methodology of English law, I am satisfied that in the case of the appeals under consideration the evidence showed that the employers entrusted the care of the children in Axeholme House to the warden. The question is whether the warden's torts were so closely connected with his e employment that it would be fair and just to hold the employers vicariously liable. On the facts of the case the answer is yes. After all, the sexual abuse was inextricably interwoven with the carrying out by the warden of his duties in Axeholme House. Matters of degree arise. But the present cases clearly fall on the side of vicarious liability.

f

(VIII) *The alternative argument*

[29] Having concluded that vicarious liability has been established on the appellants' primary case, it is not necessary to express a view on the alternative argument based on the employee's alleged breach of a duty to report his sexual intentions or the consequences of his misdeeds. Nevertheless, this line of g argument may require further consideration. For example, if the employee was aware of a physical injury sustained by a boy as a result of his conduct, it might be said to be part of his duties to report this fact to his employers. If that is so, why should the same not be true of psychological damage caused by his sexual abuse of a boy? In the present case those issues do not need to be decided. h Possibly they could arise in other cases, eg where otherwise a limitation issue may arise. I express no view on this aspect.

(IX) *The outcome*

[30] I would allow the appeal and order that judgment on liability be entered j in favour of the appellants. Damages are to be assessed.

LORD CLYDE.

[31] My Lords, Between 1979 and 1982 while the appellants were in their early teenage years they attended a school for maladjusted and vulnerable boys which was owned and managed by the respondents. During the course of that period they were the victims of repeated sexual and physical abuse by the warden of a

boarding house in which they were resident as students of the school. The warden was employed by the respondents to look after and care for the students resident in the house. The warden was later tried and convicted for a large number of offences against the appellants and other boys. The appellants have claimed damages from the respondents for personal injury. It is not now contended that the respondents had failed to take reasonable care in selecting or supervising the warden. The claims now rest on the basis that the respondents are vicariously liable for the acts of their employee.

[32] Before the Court of Appeal the case proceeded upon the proposition that the warden had failed in a duty to report his wrongful intentions and conduct to the respondents. In light of the decision in *Trotman v North Yorkshire CC* [1999] LGR 584 it was not open to the appellants either at first instance or in the Court of Appeal to present the case on the basis of a vicarious liability on the respondents for the acts of abuse themselves. In this House however that latter approach became the principal ground presented by the appellants. As regards the former proposition I would say nothing more than that it seems to be a somewhat artificial basis for the claim. But in light of the view which I am taking on the principal point there is no need to explore it in the present case. The critical question now is whether the respondents can and should be held vicariously liable for the acts of abuse committed by the warden on the appellants.

[33] Questions may arise in some cases whether the person who committed the tort was in such a relationship with another as to enable the concept of a vicarious liability on that other person to arise. In some circumstances difficult questions may occur in this regard. However that complication does not exist in the present case. The warden was plainly an employee and in a relationship of employment with the respondents. The situation is accepted to be one where a vicarious liability may arise. The question is whether there is a vicarious liability for the particular tortious, and indeed criminal, conduct complained of. In accordance with well-established law the question is whether that conduct fell within the scope of the employment.

[34] It is not useful to explore the historical origins of the vicarious liability of an employer in the hope of finding guidance in the principles of its modern application. In *Kilboy v South Eastern Fire Area Joint Committee* 1952 SC 280 at 285 the Lord President (Cooper) said of the rule respondeat superior: 'What was once presented as a legal principle has degenerated into a rule of expediency, imperfectly defined, and changing its shape before our eyes under the impact of changing social and political conditions.' Holmes (*The Common Law* (1888) ch 1, p 5 in the 44th printing of 1951), noting how rules may survive the customs or beliefs or needs which established them, described the situation more generally:

> 'The reason which gave rise to the rule has been forgotten, and ingenious minds set themselves to inquire how it is to be accounted for. Some ground of policy is thought of, which seems to explain it and to reconcile it with the present state of things; and then the rule adapts itself to the new reasons which have been found for it, and enters on a new career.'

[35] A variety of theories have been put forward to explain the rule. The expression 'respondeat superior' and the maxim 'qui facit per alium facit per se', while they may be convenient, do not assist in any analysis. Lord Reid observed in *Staveley Iron and Chemcial Co Ltd v Jones* [1956] 1 All ER 403 at 409, [1956] AC 627 at 643: 'The former merely states the rule baldly in two words, and the latter merely gives a fictional explanation of it.' Lord Pearce stated in *Imperial Chemical*

a *Industries Ltd v Shatwell* [1964] 2 All ER 999 at 1011–1012, [1965] AC 656 at 685: 'The doctrine of vicarious liability has not grown from any very clear, logical or legal principle but from social convenience and rough justice.' I am not persuaded that there is any reason of principle or policy which can be of substantial guidance in the resolution of the problem of applying the rule in any particular case. Theory may well justify the existence of the concept, but it is hard to find b guidance from any underlying principle which will weigh in the decision whether in a particular case a particular wrongful act by the employee should or should not be regarded as falling within the scope of the employment.

[**36**] A convenient starting point is the exposition which can be traced from the first edition of *Salmond on Torts* in 1907, p 83 to the 21st edition of *Salmond and Heuston on Torts* (1996) p 443. The passage was of course drafted before the c decision in *Lloyd v Grace, Smith & Co* [1912] AC 716, [1911–13] All ER Rep 51 which affirmed that vicarious liability could still arise where the fraud of the agent was committed solely for the benefit of the agent. But it has remained as a classic statement of the concept:

> d 'A master is not responsible for a wrongful act done by his servant unless it is done in the course of his employment. It is deemed to be so done if it is either (1) a wrongful act authorised by the master, or (2) a wrongful and unauthorised mode of doing some act authorised by the master.'

As regards the second of these two cases the text continues:

> e 'But a master, as opposed to the employer of an independent contractor, is liable even for acts which he has not authorised, provided they are so connected with acts which he has authorised that they may rightly be regarded as modes—although improper modes—of doing them.'

[**37**] That latter observation seems to me to be of particular importance. An f act of deliberate wrongdoing may not sit easily as a wrongful mode of doing an authorised act. But recognition should be given to the critical element in the observation, namely the necessary connection between the act and the employment. The point is made by Salmond even in the first edition, p 84, where he states:

> g 'On the other hand, if the unauthorised and wrongful act of the servant is not so connected with the authorised act as to be a mode of doing it, but is an independent act, the master is not responsible.'

What has essentially to be considered is the connection, if any, between the act in question and the employment. If there is a connection, then the closeness of h that connection has to be considered. The sufficiency of the connection may be gauged by asking whether the wrongful actings can be seen as ways of carrying out the work which the employer had authorised.

[**38**] In the first edition the statement which I quoted earlier is supported by reference to a passage in *Clerk and Lindsell on Torts* (4th edn, 1906) p 75 where the j same idea is expressed. On the previous page of that work the authors refer for the ascertainment of what constitutes scope of employment to *Sanderson v Collins* [1904] 1 KB 628, [1904–07] All ER Rep 561, and to *Heiton & Co v M'Sweeney* [1905] 2 IR 47, in which that decision was recognised and adopted. *Sanderson*'s case was a case of bailment. The defendant's coachman had taken out for his own purposes a dog-cart which belonged to the plaintiff and had been lent to the defendant. It was held that the defendant was not vicariously liable for the

coachman's actions. Collins MR observed ([1904] 1 KB 628 at 632, [1904–07] All ER Rep 561 at 563): 'If the servant in doing any act breaks the connection of service between himself and his master, the act done under those circumstances is not that of the master.'

[**39**] This area of the law is one where Scotland and England have each drawn on the other's jurisprudence and the importance of the existence of a sufficient connection has also been noticed in Scots law. In *Kirby v National Coal Board* 1958 SC 514 at 532–533, the Lord President (Clyde), in a passage part of which was quoted in this House by Lord Pearce in *Williams v A & W Hemphill Ltd* 1966 SC (HL) 31 at 44, observed that from the decisions—

> 'four different types of situation have been envisaged as guides to the solution of this problem. In the first place, if the master actually authorised the particular act, he is clearly liable for it. Secondly, where the workman does some work which he is appointed to do, but does it in a way which his master has not authorised and would not have authorised had he known of it, the master is nevertheless still responsible, for the servant's act is still within the scope of his employment. On the other hand, in the third place, if the servant is employed only to do a particular work or a particular class of work, and he does something outside the scope of that work, the master is not responsible for any mischief the servant may do to a third party. Lastly, if the servant uses his master's time or his master's place or his master's tools for his own purposes, the master is not responsible …'

The Lord President continued, under reference to the passage in *Salmond* to which I have already referred and to Lord Thankerton's approval of that passage in *Canadian Pacific Rly Co v Lockhart* [1942] 2 All ER 464 at 467, [1942] AC 591 at 599:

> 'It is often difficult in the particular case to distinguish between the second and the third of these situations, but the criterion is whether the act which is unauthorised is so connected with acts which have been authorised that it may be regarded as a mode—although an improper mode—of doing the authorised act, as distinct from constituting an independent act for which the master would not be liable …'

[**40**] Salmond refers to the 'course' of the employment and not the 'scope' of the employment. Both phrases are sometimes used interchangeably in the context of vicarious liability. In so far as the liability on the employer arises through the scope of the authority which the employer has expressly or impliedly delegated to the employee, the latter expression may be preferable. At the least the use of the word 'scope' may help to distinguish the present case from the various statutory occasions where the phrase 'in the course of has employment' or some such words have often been used. It may well be that some assistance may be found in the considerable case-law which has followed on the Workmen's Compensation Acts from 1897 to 1945 or the later social security legislation. Indeed some cross-fertilisation of ideas has occurred, for example in *Canadian Pacific Rly Co v Lockhart* [1942] 2 All ER 464 at 467, [1942] AC 591 at 599, where reference was made to the observation by Lord Dunedin in *Plumb v Cobden Flour Mills Co Ltd* [1914] AC 62 at 67, a case under the Workmen's Compensation Act 1906, that: '… there are prohibitions which limit the sphere of employment, and prohibitions which only deal with conduct within the sphere of employment.' But some caution has to be exercised in looking for assistance from cases where the court is engaged in an exercise of statutory construction. The language and

a the purpose of the provision may call for an approach and a solution which may not exactly accord with the application of the rule of vicarious liability. A particular statutory context may determine the extent of the application of the phrase and make the example an unsafe precedent to apply to vicarious liability. An example may be found in the context of legislation on sexual and racial discrimination in *Jones v Tower Boot Co Ltd* [1997] 2 All ER 406, [1997] ICR 254.

b [41] It was observed by the Lord President in *Kirby v National Coal Board* 1958 SC 514 at 532, that:

> 'It is probably not possible and it is certainly inadvisable to endeavour to lay down an exhaustive definition of what falls within the scope of the employment. Each case must depend to a considerable extent on its
> c particular facts.'

While, as has been seen, what is or is not included within the scope of the employment is very much a matter of fact, and very many of the reported cases are decisions which have turned essentially upon their own circumstances. Three matters however which are relevant to the present case deserve d consideration.

[42] The first is that in considering the scope of the employment a broad approach should be adopted. Where there is an express prohibition imposed on the employee the distinction mentioned by Lord Dunedin in *Plumb v Cobden Flour Mills Co Ltd* [1914] AC 62 at 67 to which I have already referred has to be drawn, namely, e whether it is a prohibition which limits the sphere of the employment or only one which deals with the conduct within the sphere of employment. In *Ilkiw v Samuels* [1963] 2 All ER 879 at 889, [1963] 1 WLR 991 at 1004 Diplock LJ said that:

> '... the decision into which of these two classes the prohibition falls seems to me to involve first determining what would have been the sphere, scope,
> f course (all these nouns are used) of the servant's employment if the prohibition had not been imposed. As each of these nouns implies, the matter must be looked at broadly, not dissecting the servant's task into its component activities—such as driving, loading, sheeting and the like—by asking: What was the job on which he was engaged for his employer? and
> g answering that question as a jury would.'

Thus in *Rose v Plenty* [1976] 1 All ER 97, [1976] 1 WLR 141 the employer was held liable where the prohibitions against the milk roundsman giving others lifts on his float and against employing others to help him in the delivery of the milk were regarded as prohibitions relating to the conduct of the work and not as limiting h the sphere of the employment.

[43] If a broad approach is adopted it becomes inappropriate to concentrate too closely upon the particular act complained of. Not only do the purpose and the nature of the act have to be considered but the context and the circumstances in which it occurred have to be taken into account. The particular act of lighting j a cigarette and throwing away the match, if viewed narrowly, may not in itself be an act which an employee was employed to do. But viewed more broadly it can be seen as incidental to and within the scope of his employment. Vicarious liability was thus established in *Century Insurance Co Ltd v Northern Ireland Road Transport Board* [1942] 1 All ER 491, [1942] AC 509 where the lighting of a match to light a cigarette and throwing it on the floor while transferring petrol from a lorry to a tank was held to be in the scope of employment. Both the negligent

quality of the act and the connection with the employment have to be assessed against the background of the particular circumstances.

[44] Secondly, while consideration of the time at which and the place at which the actings occurred will always be relevant, they may not be conclusive. That an act was committed outside the hours of employment may well point to it being outside the scope of the employment. But that the act was done during the hours of the employment does not necessarily mean that it was done within the scope of the employment. So also the fact that the act in question occurred during the time of the employment and in the place of the employment is not enough by itself. There can be cases where the place where the wrongful act was committed can be said to have been one where the employee was no longer to be treated as within the scope of his employment, such as *Kirby v National Coal Board* 1958 SC 514, where the mine worker retired from the working face to the waste and was no longer acting in the scope of his employment, or the various cases on travel, such as *Williams v A & W Hemphill Ltd* 1966 SC (HL) 31, where a deviation from an intended route may or may not take the employee outwith the scope of his employment. The acting may be so unconnected with the employment as to fall outside any vicarious liability. Where the employer's vehicle is used solely for a purpose unconnected with the employer's business, when, to use the language of Parke B in *Joel v Morison* (1834) 6 C & P 501 at 503, 172 ER 1338 at 1339, the driver is 'going on a frolic of his own', the employer will not be liable. Acts of passion and resentment (as in *Deatons Pty Ltd v Flew* (1949) 79 CLR 370) or of personal spite (as in *Irving v Post Office* [1987] IRLR 289) may fall outside the scope of the employment. While use of a handbasin at the end of the working day may be an authorised act, the pushing of the basin so as to cause it to move and startle a fellow-employee may be an independent act not sufficiently connected with the employment: *Aldred v Nacanco* [1987] IRLR 292.

[45] Thirdly, while the employment enables the employee to be present at a particular time at a particular place, the opportunity of being present at particular premises whereby the employee has been able to perform the act in question does not mean that the act is necessarily within the scope of the employment. In order to establish a vicarious liability there must be some greater connection between the tortious act of the employee and the circumstances of his employment than the mere opportunity to commit the act which has been provided by the access to the premises which the employment has afforded: *Heasmans v Clarity Cleaning Co Ltd* [1987] ICR 949.

[46] Among the multifarious kinds of employment one situation relevant to the present case is where the employer has been entrusted with the safekeeping or the care of some thing or some person and he delegates that duty to an employee. In this kind of case it may not be difficult to demonstrate a sufficient connection between the act of the employee, however wrong it may be, and the employment. One obvious example is *Morris v C W Martin & Sons Ltd* [1965] 2 All ER 725, [1966] 1 QB 716. There a fur had been entrusted to the defendants. They entrusted it to their employee. They were vicariously liable for his wrongdoing in converting it. In *Photo Production Ltd v Securicor Transport Ltd* [1980] 1 All ER 556, [1980] AC 827 the defendants had undertaken to provide a night patrol service for a factory. The factory was burned down by one of their employees who had started a fire on the premises while on duty patrol. But for the provisions of an exceptions clause in the contract for the night patrol service the defendants would have been liable in damages to the owners of the factory.

a [47] In *Central Motors (Glasgow) Ltd v Cessnock Garage and Motor Co* 1925 SC 796, a night watchman employed by garage proprietors to whom a car had been entrusted for safe keeping took the car out for his own purposes and damaged it in a collision with another vehicle. It was held that as the garage proprietors had delegated to their employee the duty of keeping the car safely secured in the garage they were liable to the owners of the car for the employee's failure in b performance. Lord Cullen, with whose opinion the Lord President (Clyde) expressly agreed, noted (at 802) the difficulty which can occur in deciding whether a particular act falls within the 'purely personal and independent sphere of life and action' which an employee may enjoy or within the sphere of service:

> 'The question is not to be answered merely by applying the test whether c the act in itself is one which the servant was employed or ordered or forbidden to do. The employer has to shoulder responsibility on a wider basis; and he may, and often does, become responsible to third parties for acts which he has expressly or impliedly forbidden the servant to do. A servant is not a mere machine continuously directed by his master's hand, d but is a person of independent volition and action, and the employer, when he delegates to him some duty which he himself is under obligation to discharge, must take the risk of the servant's action being misdirected, when he is, for the time, allowed to be beyond his master's control. It remains necessary to the master's responsibility that the servant's act be one done within the sphere of his service or the scope of his employment, but it may e have this character although it consists in doing something which is the very opposite of what the servant has been intended or ordered to do, and which he does for his own private ends. An honest master does not employ or authorise his servant to commit crimes of dishonesty towards third parties; but nevertheless he may incur liability for a crime of dishonesty committed by the servant if it was committed by him within the field of activities which f the employment assigned to him, and that although the crime was committed by the servant solely in pursuance of his own private advantage. The servant is a bad servant who has not faithfully served but has betrayed his master; still, *quoad* the third party injured, his dishonest act may fall to be regarded as an ill way of executing the work which has been assigned to him, g and which he has been left with power to do well or ill.'

[48] Cases which concern sexual harassment or sexual abuse committed by an employee should be approached in the same way as any other case where questions of vicarious liability arises. I can see no reason for putting them into any special category of their own. In the Scottish case *Ward v Scotrail Rlys Ltd* h 1999 SC 255 it appears to have been effectively conceded that the employee's conduct was not such as to attract a vicarious liability, but the judge held that in the circumstances the employee was indulging in an unrelated and independent venture of his own. In light of the particular facts of the case the concession seems to have been soundly made. The Canadian case of *Bazley v Curry* (1999) 174 DLR j (4th) 45 concerned vicarious liability for acts of sexual abuse carried out by an employee of a children's foundation who had been engaged to act as a parent-figure caring for emotionally troubled children in a children's home. The careful and comprehensive discussion of the problem by McLachlin J was presented in the context of policy considerations, but the essence of the decision seems to me to lie in the recognition of the existence of a sufficient connection between the acts of the employee and the employment. This in turn was

explored by reference to various factors by reference to which the strength of the connection can be established. In that case vicarious liability was held to exist. On the other hand in *Jacobi v Griffiths* (1999) 174 DLR (4th) 71 vicarious liability was not established. In that case the acts, with one minor exception, took place in the employee's home outside working hours and away from the club which was the principal place of employment. That the club had provided an opportunity to establish a friendship with the children did not constitute a sufficient connection. These two decisions seem to be consistent with the traditional approach recognised in this country.

[**49**] The Canadian cases were decided after the decision of the Court of Appeal in *Trotman v North Yorkshire CC* [1999] LGR 584. The Court of Appeal did not have the guidance which those cases afford in stressing the importance of finding a sufficient connection between the actings of the employee and the employment. The court proceeded upon the rather more narrow approach of looking to see if the conduct was an unauthorised way of carrying out a teacher's duties. That test, however, as I have already sought to explain, is not to be taken too precisely. Moreover in light of the way the case was pled the Court of Appeal felt that they were not able to take account of any duty which the employer might have had to take care of the children. Thus they were prevented from treating the case as comparable with the line of cases like *Morris'* case to which I have already referred. In my view the decision was unsound.

[**50**] I turn finally to the facts of the present case. It appears that the care and safekeeping of the boys had been entrusted to the respondents and they in turn had entrusted their care and safekeeping, so far as the running of the boarding house was concerned, to the warden. That gave him access to the premises, but the opportunity to be at the premises would not in itself constitute a sufficient connection between his wrongful actings and his employment. In addition to the opportunity which access gave him, his position as warden and the close contact with the boys which that work involved created a sufficient connection between the acts of abuse which he committed and the work which he had been employed to do. It appears that the respondents gave the warden a quite general authority in the supervision and running of the house as well as some particular responsibilities. His general duty was to look after and to care for, among others, the appellants. That function was one which the respondents had delegated to him. That he performed that function in a way which was an abuse of his position and an abnegation of his duty does not sever the connection with his employment. The particular acts which he carried out upon the boys have to be viewed not in isolation but in the context and the circumstances in which they occurred. Given that he had a general authority in the management of the house and in the care and supervision of the boys in it, the employers should be liable for the way in which he behaved towards them in his capacity as warden of the house. The respondents should then be vicariously liable to the appellants for the injury and damage which they suffered at the hands of the warden.

[**51**] I agree that the appeal should be allowed.

LORD HUTTON.

[**52**] My Lords, I have had the advantage of reading in draft the speech of my noble and learned friend Lord Steyn. I agree with it and for the reasons which he has given I, too, would allow this appeal.

a **LORD HOBHOUSE OF WOODBOROUGH.**

[53] My Lords, these appeals are described as raising a question of the vicarious liability for acts of sexual abuse by an employee. Indeed this is how the question has been described in articles (eg Peter Cane 'Vicarious Liability for Sexual Abuse' (2000) 116 LQR 21; Feldthusen 'Vicarious Liability for Sexual Torts' (see *Torts Tomorrow: A Tribute to John Fleming* (1998)) and in the leading Canadian b authority *Bazley v Curry* (1999) 174 DLR (4th) 45. It is true that sexual abuse is a particularly offensive and criminal act of personal gratification on the part of its perpetrator and can therefore be easily described as the paradigm of those acts which an employee could not conceivably be employed to do. It is thus argued that an employer should never be made vicariously liable for such acts; the employer should only be held liable where separate personal fault of the employer c has been proved. This argument succeeded in the Court of Appeal in *Trotman v North Yorkshire CC* [1999] LGR 584 which was binding upon the Court of Appeal in the present cases and was followed. Negligence in deciding to employ Mr Grain was not proved against the defendants. The argument that there was a vicarious liability for Mr Grain's failure to report what had happened to the d plaintiffs and to other boys whom he had abused was also rejected, a point to which I will have briefly to revert. Accordingly the Court of Appeal allowed the defendants' appeals and entered judgment for the defendants in the actions.

[54] What these cases and *Trotman's* case in truth illustrate is a situation where the employer has assumed a relationship to the plaintiff which imposes specific duties in tort upon the employer and the role of the employee (or servant) is that e he is the person to whom the employer has entrusted the performance of that duty. These cases are examples of that class where the employer, by reason of assuming a relationship to the plaintiff, owes to the plaintiff duties which are more extensive than those owed by the public at large and, accordingly, are to be contrasted with the situation where a defendant is simply in proximity to the f plaintiff so that it is foreseeable that his acts may injure the plaintiff or his property and a reasonable person would have taken care to avoid causing such injury. The category into which the present cases fall is recognised by the agreed facts and the useful summary of Judge Walker adopted by Swinton Thomas LJ:

> 'The defendant admits it had a duty of care towards the plaintiffs. That g duty of care was to take all reasonable steps to safeguard the plaintiffs (and other pupils) in their physical, moral and educational development whilst at the school. In carrying out that duty of care the defendant, a limited company, necessarily had to appoint a hierarchy of responsible agents … each of whom had either general or particular responsibilities which bore h upon this duty of care. Mr Grain in particular was responsible for the boys while at Axeholme House …'

The fact that sexual abuse was involved does not distinguish this case from any other involving the care of the young and vulnerable and the duty to protect them from the risk of harm.

j [55] The classes of persons or institutions that are in this type of special relationship to another human being include schools, prisons, hospitals and even, in relation to their visitors, occupiers of land. They are liable if they themselves fail to perform the duty which they consequently owe. If they entrust the performance of that duty to an employee and that employee fails to perform the duty, they are still liable. The employee, because he has, through his obligations to his employers, adopted the same relationship towards and come under the same duties to the plaintiff, is also liable to the plaintiff for his own breach of duty. The liability of the employers is a *vicarious* liability because the actual breach of duty is that of the employee. The employee is a tortfeasor. The employers are liable for the employee's tortious act or omission because it is to him that the employers have entrusted the performance of their duty. The employers' liability to the plaintiff is also that of a tortfeasor. I use the word 'entrusted' in preference to the word 'delegated' which is commonly, but perhaps less accurately, used. Vicarious liability is sometimes described as a 'strict' liability. The use of this term is misleading unless it is used just to explain that there has been no *actual* fault on the part of the employers. The liability of the employers derives from their voluntary assumption of the relationship towards the plaintiff and the duties that arise from that relationship and their choosing to entrust the performance of those duties to their servant. Where these conditions are satisfied, the motive of the employee and the fact that he is doing something expressly forbidden and is serving only his own ends does not negative the vicarious liability for his breach of the 'delegated' duty.

[**56**] The duty which I have described is also to be found in relation to the loss of or damage to goods. The leading case in this connection is *Morris v C W Martin & Sons Ltd* [1965] 2 All ER 725, [1966] 1 QB 716, a case upon the liability of a bailee, already referred to by my noble and learned friend Lord Steyn. A bailor is a person who entrusts the possession and care of goods to the bailee. It is a legal relationship giving rise to common law obligations owed by the bailee to the bailor. Diplock LJ analysed the law:

> 'Duties at common law are owed by one person to another only if there exists a relationship between them which the common law recognises as giving rise to such duty. One of such recognised relationships is created by the voluntary taking into custody of goods which are the property of another. By voluntarily accepting … the custody of a fur … they brought into existence between the plaintiff and themselves the relationship of bailor and bailee … One of the common law duties owed by a bailee of goods to his bailor is not to convert them, ie, not to do intentionally in relation to the goods an act inconsistent with the bailor's right of property therein … If the bailee in the present case had been a natural person and had converted the plaintiff's fur by stealing it himself, no one would have argued that he was not liable to her for its loss; but the defendant bailees are a corporate person. They could not perform their duties to the plaintiff to take reasonable care of the fur and not to convert it otherwise than vicariously by natural persons acting as their servants or agents. It was one of their servants, to whom they had entrusted the care and custody of the fur for the purpose of doing work on it, who converted it by stealing it. Why should they not be vicariously liable for this breach of their duty by the vicar whom they had chosen to perform it … They accepted the fur as bailees for reward in order to clean it. They put [their servant] as their agent in their place to clean the fur and to take charge of it while doing so. The manner in which he conducted himself in doing that work was to convert it. What he was doing, albeit dishonestly, he was doing in the scope or course of his employment in the technical sense of that infelicitous but time-honoured phrase. The defendants as his masters are responsible for his tortious act … I base my decision in this case on the ground that the fur was stolen by the very servant whom the defendants as

a bailees for reward had employed to take care of it and to clean it.' (See [1965] 2 All ER 725 at 734–738, [1966] 1 QB 716 at 731–737.)

Salmon LJ expressed himself similarly, referring to the duties of a bailee. He said ([1965] 2 All ER 725 at 739, [1966] 1 QB 716 at 738): '… the act of stealing the fur was a glaring breach of the duty to take reasonable care to keep it safe—and this b is negligence.' Doing the opposite of what it is your duty to do is still a breach of that duty. My Lords, I feel it necessary to mention this because one of the arguments which was advanced by the respondents (and which has found some favour) has been that it cannot be a breach of a duty to take care of a child to abuse him. It is an exemplary and egregious breach of the servant's duty both to his employer and to the child. The appreciation that there are duties involved is at c the heart of the analysis and the identification of the criteria for the existence or no of vicarious liability.

[57] The decision in *Morris'* case was reasoned applying the principles of vicarious liability. One of the cases followed was *Lloyd v Grace, Smith & Co* [1912] AC 716, [1911–13] All ER Rep 51, which also involved a special relationship d between the defendant solicitors and their client, the plaintiff. Another case which was followed was *Meux v Great Eastern Ry Co* [1895] 2 QB 387, [1895–99] All ER Rep 710 where the plaintiff was suing the railway company for carelessly damaging his goods but did not himself have a contract with the company. It is noteworthy that the conclusion that a duty was owed by the railway company towards the goods owner was based upon cases which had held that a railway e company owed a duty of care towards passengers injured by the carelessness of that company's employee even though the passenger had bought his ticket from another company. No distinction was drawn between an employee injuring the plaintiff and damaging or losing his property. Similar reasoning was adopted in the leading modern case on gratuitous bailments, *Gilchrist Watt & Sanderson Pty Ltd v York Products Pty Ltd* [1970] 3 All ER 825, [1970] 1 WLR 1262, in which f Lord Pearson giving the judgment of the Privy Council approved and followed *Morris'* case, citing cases on both personal injuries, *Foulkes v Metropolitan District Rly Co* (1880) 5 CPD 157, and the loss of or damage to goods, *Hooper v London and North Western Rly Co* (1881) 50 LJQB 103. Your Lordships have also been referred to statements to the same effect in *Photo Production Ltd v Securicor Transport Ltd* g [1980] 1 All ER 556, [1980] AC 827, a case of arson in relation to a building. All these cases illustrate the general proposition that, where the defendant has assumed a relationship to the plaintiff which carries with it a specific duty towards the plaintiff, the defendant is vicariously liable in tort if his servant, to whom the performance of that duty has been entrusted, breaches that duty.

h [58] In *Ilkiw v Samuels* [1963] 2 All ER 879, [1963] 1 WLR 991, Diplock LJ stated the law in similar terms to those he was later to use in *Morris'* case. It was a personal injuries case concerning an issue of vicarious liability for the careless manoeuvring of a lorry by the defendants' servant. Diplock LJ said:

j 'A person who makes use of a vehicle for the purposes of his business is under a duty in tort so to control it that it is driven with reasonable care while being used for that purpose. If he delegates the performance of the acts which give rise to this duty to his servant, he is vicariously liable if the servant fails to perform it. In this sense he may be said to delegate the duty though he cannot divest himself of it, as his continuing vicarious liability shows. The test whether the master has in this sense delegated the duty to his servant is whether the servant owes to the master a contractual duty to perform the

> master's duty owed to his neghbours ...' (See [1963] 2 All ER 879 at 889–890, [1963] 1 WLR 991 at 1005.) a

In the same case Diplock LJ encouraged a broad approach to what the duties of the employee were towards his employer and this approach was expressly approved by Scarman LJ in *Rose v Plenty* [1976] 1 All ER 97 at 104, [1976] 1 WLR 141 at 147–148. b

[59] The classic *Salmond* test for vicarious liability and scope of employment has two limbs. The first covers authorised acts which are tortious. These present no relevant problem and the present cases clearly do not fall within the first limb. The defendants did not authorise Mr Grain to abuse the children in his charge. The argument of the respondent (accepted by the Court of Appeal) is that Mr Grain's c acts of abuse did not come within the second limb either: abusing children cannot properly be described as a mode of caring for children. The answer to this argument is provided by the analysis which I have set out in the preceding paragraphs. Whether or not some act comes within the scope of the servant's employment depends upon an identification of what duty the servant was employed by his employer to perform (Diplock LJ supra). If the act of the servant which d gives rise to the servant's liability to the plaintiff amounted to a failure by the servant to perform that duty, the act comes within 'the scope of his employment' and the employer is vicariously liable. If, on the other hand, the servant's employment merely gave the servant the opportunity to do what he did without more, there will be no vicarious liability, hence the use by Salmond and in the e Scottish and some other authorities of the word 'connection' to indicate something which is not a casual coincidence but has the requisite relationship to the employment of the tortfeasor (servant) by his employer: *Kirby v National Coal Board* 1958 SC 514; *Williams v A & W Hemphill Ltd* 1966 SC (HL) 31.

[60] My Lords, the correct approach to answering the question whether the f tortious act of the servant falls within or without the scope of the servant's employment for the purposes of the principle of vicarious liability is to ask what was the duty of the servant towards the plaintiff which was broken by the servant and what was the contractual duty of the servant towards his employer. The second limb of the classic *Salmond* test is a convenient rule of thumb which provides the answer in very many cases but does not represent the fundamental g criterion which is the comparison of the duties respectively owed by the servant to the plaintiff and to his employer. Similarly, I do not believe that it is appropriate to follow the lead given by the Supreme Court of Canada in *Bazley v Curry* (1999) 174 DLR (4th) 45. The judgments contain a useful and impressive discussion of the social and economic reasons for having a principle of vicarious h liability as part of the law of tort which extends to embrace acts of child abuse. But an exposition of the policy reasons for a rule (or even a description) is not the same as defining the criteria for its application. Legal rules have to have a greater degree of clarity and definition than is provided by simply explaining the reasons for the existence of the rule and the social need for it, instructive though that may j be. In English law that clarity is provided by the application of the criterion to which I have referred derived from the English authorities.

[61] It follows that the reasoning of the Court of Appeal in *Trotman v North Yorkshire CC* [1999] LGR 584 and the present cases cannot be supported. On the undisputed facts, the present cases satisfy the criteria for demonstrating the vicarious liability of the defendants for the acts of Mr Grain.

[62] There remains for brief mention the point which was considered in the Court of Appeal and had formed the basis of the decision of Judge Walker. Faced with the binding decision in *Trotman*'s case, the plaintiffs had sought to rely upon a failure by Mr Grain to report to his employers what had happened and the psychological trauma being suffered by the plaintiffs (whom it must be remembered were already emotionally disturbed). This was an artificial argument because it was premised upon the assumption that Mr Grain's breaches of duty in abusing the plaintiffs were legally irrelevant. The Court of Appeal were unwilling to accept this artificiality given that they were not treating the abuse itself as coming within the scope of Mr Grain's employment. However, it was part of both the duty of the carers towards the plaintiffs and of Mr Grain towards his employers to report to them any incident which was relevant to the health and well-being of the plaintiffs: finding 5 in Judge Walker's list. It follows from this and what I have previously said about the nature of the duties owed to the plaintiffs and the principles governing the issue of vicarious liability that the Court of Appeal were mistaken in not attaching more validity to this way of putting the plaintiffs' case. In truth, there were a whole succession of breaches of the duty to care for the plaintiffs by Mr Grain. The fact that the defendants might not have been liable for some of them does not alter the fact that the defendants would have been liable for the others. All it does is to put the former class of acts into the same category as acts done by some third party but of which, or of the consequences of which, Mr Grain was aware. To take one of the hypothetical judge's examples, say, there might have been a groundsman at Axeholme House and he might have been the abusing party; Mr Grain might have discovered what had happened and the distress it had caused to the boy but did nothing about it and did not report the incident to the defendants. The defendants might not be liable for what the groundsman did; he was employed to look after the grounds, not to have anything to do with the boys. But the defendants would be liable for the breach of Mr Grain who was employed to care for the boys and their welfare. The liability of the defendants might not be so grave or extensive as if Mr Grain had been the abuser himself but it would in principle be capable of existing.

[63] Accordingly, for these reasons and for those given by my noble and learned friend Lord Steyn, I agree that these appeals should be allowed.

LORD MILLETT.

[64] My Lords, the question in this appeal is whether in principle the owner of a residential school for boys can, without fault on its part, be held vicariously liable for indecent assaults carried out by the warden of the school on the boys in his care. The facts are stated in the speech of my noble and learned friend Lord Steyn and I need not repeat them. The case calls for a reconsideration of the recent decision of the Court of Appeal in *Trotman v North Yorkshire CC* [1999] LGR 584. More generally it raises in a particularly stark form the question in what circumstances an employer may be vicariously liable for the deliberate and criminal wrongdoing of his employee, wrongdoing in which the employee indulged for his own purposes and which the employer must be taken to have expressly or at least impliedly prohibited.

[65] Vicarious liability is a species of strict liability. It is not premised on any culpable act or omission on the part of the employer; an employer who is not personally at fault is made legally answerable for the fault of his employee. It is best understood as a loss-distribution device: see Cane's edition of *Atiyah's Accidents, Compensation and the Law* (6th edn, 1999) p 85 and the articles cited by

Atiyah in his monograph on *Vicarious Liability in the Law of Torts* (1967) p 24. The theoretical underpinning of the doctrine is unclear. Glanville Williams wrote ('Vicarious Liability and the Master's Indemnity' (1957) 20 MLR 220 at 231):

> 'Vicarious liability is the creation of many judges who have had different ideas of its justification or social policy, or no idea at all. Some judges may have extended the rule more widely, or confined it more narrowly than its true rationale would allow; yet the rationale, if we can discover it, will remain valid so far as it extends.'

Fleming observed (*The Law of Torts* (9th edn, 1998) p 410) that the doctrine cannot parade as a deduction from legalistic premises. He indicated that it should be frankly recognised as having its basis in a combination of policy considerations, and continued:

> 'Most important of these is the belief that a person who employs others to advance his own economic interest should in fairness be placed under a corresponding liability for losses incurred in the course of the enterprise ...'

Atiyah *Vicarious Liability in the Law of Torts* wrote to the same effect. He suggested (at p 171): 'The master ought to be liable for all those torts which can fairly be regarded as reasonably incidental risks to the type of business he carries on.' These passages are not to be read as confining the doctrine to cases where the employer is carrying on business for profit. They are based on the more general idea that a person who employs another for his own ends inevitably creates a risk that the employee will commit a legal wrong. If the employer's objectives cannot be achieved without a serious risk of the employee committing the kind of wrong which he has in fact committed, the employer ought to be liable. The fact that his employment gave the employee the opportunity to commit the wrong is not enough to make the employer liable. He is liable only if the risk is one which experience shows is inherent in the nature of the business.

[66] While this proposition has never, so far as I am aware, been adopted in so many words as a test of vicarious liability in any of the decided cases, it does I think form the unspoken rationale of the principle that the employer's liability is confined to torts committed by an employee *in the course of his employment*. The problem is that, as Townshend-Smith has observed ((2000) 8 Tort Law Review 108 at 111), none of the various tests which have been proposed to determine this essentially factual question is either intellectually satisfying or effective to enable the outcome of a particular case to be predicted. The danger is that in borderline situations, and especially in cases of intentional wrongdoing, recourse to a rigid and possibly inappropriate formula as a test of liability may lead the court to abandon the search for legal principle.

[67] In the very first edition of his book on *Torts* (1907) p 83 Sir John Salmond wrote:

> '1. A master is not responsible for a wrongful act done by his servant unless it is done in the course of his employment. It is deemed to be so done if it is either (a) a wrongful act authorised by the master, or (b) a wrongful and unauthorised *mode* of doing some act authorised by the master.' (Author's emphasis.)

This passage has stood the test of time. It has survived unchanged for 21 editions, and has probably been cited more often than any other single passage in a legal textbook. Yet it is not without blemish. As has often been observed, the first of the two alternatives is not an example of vicarious liability at all. Its presence (and the word 'deemed') may be an echo of the discredited theory of implied authority. More pertinently, the second is not happily expressed if it is to serve as a test of vicarious liability for intentional wrongdoing.

[**68**] In the present case the warden was employed to look after the boys in his care and secure their welfare. It is stretching language to breaking-point to describe the series of deliberate sexual assaults on them on which he embarked as merely a wrongful and unauthorised mode of performing that duty. In *Trotman v North Yorkshire CC* [1999] LGR 584 the employee in question was the deputy headmaster of a special school run by the local council. He was charged with the responsibility of caring for a handicapped teenager on a foreign holiday, and he sexually assaulted the boy. Butler-Sloss LJ asked rhetorically whether that was in principle an improper mode of carrying out an authorised act on behalf of his employer or an independent act outside the course of his employment. She held that it fell into the latter category, because (at 591):

> 'His position of caring for the plaintiff by sharing a bedroom with him gave him the opportunity to carry out the sexual assaults. But availing himself of that opportunity seems to me to be far removed from an unauthorised mode of carrying out a teacher's duties on behalf of his employer. Rather it is a negation of the duty of the council to look after the children for whom it was responsible'.

In the same case Chadwick LJ agreed that the traditional test was not satisfied. He said (at 592–593):

> 'I find it impossible to hold that the commission of acts of indecent assault can be regarded as a mode—albeit, an improper and unauthorised mode—of doing what, on the case advanced, the deputy headmaster was employed by the council to do. In the circumstances alleged, [MS] was employed to supervise the plaintiff's welfare while on the holiday in Spain. The commission by him of acts of indecent assault on a pupil in his charge cannot be regarded as a way of doing that. *Rather, it must be regarded as an independent act of self-indulgence or self-gratification.*' (My emphasis.)

This antithesis lies at the heart of the present appeal.

[**69**] In a passage which is unfortunately less often cited, however, Sir John Salmond (*Salmond on Torts* (1st edn, 1907)) continued his exposition as follows (at pp 83–84):

> 'But a master, as opposed to the employer of an independent contractor, is liable even for acts which he has not authorised, provided they are so connected with acts which he has authorised, that they may rightly be regarded as modes—although improper modes—of doing them.'

This could, I think, usefully be elided to impose vicarious liability where the unauthorised acts of the employee are so connected with acts which the employer has authorised that they may properly be regarded as being within the scope of his employment. Such a formulation would have the advantage of dispensing with the awkward reference to 'improper modes' of carrying out the employee's duties; and by focussing attention on the connection between the employee's duties and his wrongdoing it would accord with the underlying rationale of the doctrine and be applicable without straining the language to accommodate cases of intentional wrongdoing.

[**70**] But the precise terminology is not critical. The *Salmond* test, in either formulation, is not a statutory definition of the circumstances which give rise to liability, but a guide to the principled application of the law to diverse factual situations. What is critical is that attention should be directed to the closeness of the connection between the employee's duties and his wrongdoing and not to verbal formulae. This is the principle on which the Supreme Court of Canada recently decided the important cases of *Bazley v Curry* (1999) 174 DLR (4th) 45 and *Jacobi v Griffiths* (1999) 174 DLR (4th) 71 which provide many helpful insights into this branch of the law and from which I have derived much assistance.

[**71**] Cases of intentional wrongdoing have always proved troublesome. At one time it was thought that the employer could not be held vicariously liable for his employee's deliberate wrongdoing. This view was not maintained, but even as late as the beginning of the twentieth century it was regarded as axiomatic that an employer could not be vicariously liable for his employee's dishonest acts unless they were committed for the benefit of his employer: see *Cheshire v Bailey* [1905] 1 KB 237 where the defendant was held not responsible for the theft of his customer's goods by his employee because the theft was outside the scope of his employment. As Salmon LJ explained in *Morris v C W Martin & Sons Ltd* [1965] 2 All ER 725 at 739, [1966] 1 QB 716 at 738–739, this view derived from a misunderstanding of what Willes J had said in *Barwick v English Joint Stock Bank* (1867) LR 2 Exch 259 at 265, [1861–73] All ER Rep 194 at 198. Observing that no sensible distinction could be drawn between the case of fraud and any other wrong, he had stated that the general rule was that—

> 'the master is answerable for every such wrong of the servant or agent as is committed in the course of the service *and for the master's benefit*, though no express command or privity of the master be proved.' (My emphasis.)

But this was very different, as Lord Macnaghten pointed out in *Lloyd v Grace, Smith & Co* [1912] AC 716 at 732, [1911–13] All ER Rep 51 at 57, from saying that a master cannot be liable for the fraud of his servant unless carried out for his benefit or with his privity. This may be a sufficient condition of liability, but it is not a necessary one.

[**72**] The heresy was not exposed until *Lloyd*'s case, and despite this has proved remarkably resilient. It took another 50 years until *Morris*' case for it to be recognised that *Cheshire*'s case was no longer good law; and regrettable traces of it appear in *Trotman*'s case. If the employer is to be absolved from liability in that case (or this) it cannot be because the acts complained of were 'independent acts of self-indulgence or self-gratification'.

[**73**] In *Lloyd*'s case a solicitor's managing clerk defrauded a client of the firm by obtaining her instructions to realise her property. He induced her to hand over the title deeds and to execute conveyances in his favour which he did not read over or explain to her. They enabled him to sell the property and pocket the proceeds. The firm was held liable for the fraud even though it was committed for the clerk's own benefit. In the course of argument before your Lordships in the present case it was accepted that the firm would not have been liable if the clerk had stolen the contents of his client's handbag. That is true, for the clerk would merely have been taking advantage of an opportunity which his employment gave him. But there was a much closer connection between the clerk's duties and his wrongdoing than that. The firm's liability arose from the fact that throughout the transaction the fraudulent clerk acted as the representative of the firm, and he

a received the custody of the documents of title with the consent of the client given because he was acting in that capacity.

[74] In the same year Laski (in 'The Basis of Vicarious Liability' (1916) 26 Yale Law Journal 105 at 130) had observed that there was no valid a priori reason why the doctrine of vicarious liability should cease to operate at that border where tort becomes crime. In England this had already been established: see *Dyer v Munday*
b [1895] 1 QB 742, [1895–9] All ER Rep 1022. Once this limitation on the operation of the doctrine is rejected, it is impossible to maintain the fiction that it is based on any kind of implied authority. An excessively literal application of the *Salmond* test must also be discarded. Stealing a client's property cannot sensibly be described as an unauthorised mode of dealing with it on her behalf. It is, as Butler-Sloss LJ put it in *Trotman v North Yorkshire CC* [1999] LGR 584 at 591, the
c negation of the employer's duty. Yet the employer may be liable none the less.

[75] In *Morris'* case a firm of cleaners was held vicariously liable to a customer whose fur was stolen by one of its employees. The firm was a sub-bailee for reward, but the decision was not based on the firm's own failure to take care of the fur and deliver it upon termination of the bailment. It was held vicariously
d liable for the conversion of the fur by its employee. Diplock LJ said, that he based his decision—

> 'on the ground that the fur was stolen *by the very servant* whom the defendants as bailees for reward had employed to take care of it and to clean it.' (See [1965] 2 All ER 725 at 738, [1966] 1 QB 716 at 737; my emphasis.)

e Salmon LJ too ([1965] 2 All ER 725 at 740, [1966] 1 QB 716 at 740), was anxious to make it plain that the conclusion which he had reached depended on the fact that the thief was 'the servant through whom the defendants chose to discharge their duty to take reasonable care of the plaintiff's fur'. He added that—

> f 'A bailee for reward is not answerable for a theft by any of his servants, but only for a theft by such of them as are deputed by him to discharge some part of his duty of taking reasonable care. A theft by any servant who is not employed to do anything in relation to the goods bailed is entirely outside the scope of his employment and cannot make the master liable.' (See [1965] 2 All ER 725 at 740, [1966] 1 QB 716 at 740–741.)

g The employee's position gave him the opportunity to steal the fur, but as Diplock LJ was at pains to make clear ([1965] 2 All ER 725 at 738, [1966] 1 QB 716 at 737), this was not enough to make his employer liable. What brought the theft within the scope of his employment and made the firm liable was that in the course of its business the firm had entrusted him with the care of the fur, and he
h stole it while it was in his custody as an employee of the firm.

[76] As my noble and learned friend Lord Steyn has observed, *Morris'* case has consistently been held to be an authority on vicarious liability generally and not confined to cases of bailment. The case was expressly approved by the Privy Council in *Port Swettenham Authority v T W Wu & Co (M) Sdn Bhd* [1978] 3 All ER 337
j at 341, [1979] AC 580 at 591, not altogether surprisingly as the opinion of the board was delivered by Lord Salmon. That was another case of bailment. But in *Photo Production Ltd v Securicor Transport Ltd* [1980] 1 All ER 556, [1980] AC 827, where a patrolman employed by a security firm deliberately set fire to the premises he was employed to protect, neither Lord Wilberforce nor Lord Salmon saw any difficulty in holding the employer vicariously liable on the principle stated in *Morris'* case. That was not a case of bailment. Yet the patrolman was said ([1980] 1 All ER 556 at 569,

[1980] AC 827 at 852 per Lord Salmon) to be 'indubitably acting in the course of his employment'. *a*

[77] Just as an employer may be vicariously liable for deliberate and criminal conduct on the part of his employee, so he may be vicariously liable for acts of the employee which he has expressly forbidden him to do. In *Ilkiw v Samuels* [1963] 2 All ER 879, [1963] 1 WLR 991 a lorry driver was under strict instructions from his employers not to allow anyone else to drive the lorry. He allowed a *b* third party, who was incompetent, to drive it without making any inquiry into his competence to do so. The employers were held vicariously liable for the resulting accident. Diplock LJ explained ([1963] 2 All ER 879 at 889, [1963] 1 WLR 991 at 1004) that some prohibitions limited the sphere of employment and others only dealt with conduct within the sphere of employment. In order to determine into which category a particular prohibition fell it was necessary to determine what would have *c* been the sphere, scope, or course (nouns which he considered to amount to the same thing) if the prohibition had not been imposed. In a passage which is of some importance in the present case, he added:

> 'As each of these nouns implies, the matter must be looked at broadly, not dissecting the servant's task into its component activities—such as driving, *d* loading, sheeting and the like—by asking: What was the job on which he was engaged for his employer? and answering that question as a jury would.' (See [1963] 2 All ER 879 at 889, [1963] 1 WLR 991 at 1004.)

He reasoned that the job which the driver was engaged to perform was to collect a load of sugar and transport it to its destination, using for that purpose his *e* employers' lorry, of which he was put in charge. He was expressly forbidden to permit anyone else to drive the lorry in the course of performing this job. That was not a prohibition which limited the scope of his employment, but one which dealt with his conduct within the sphere of his employment.

[78] The case was followed in *Rose v Plenty* [1976] 1 All ER 97, [1976] 1 WLR *f* 141 where despite strict instructions not to do so a milk roundsman employed a boy to help him deliver milk and let him accompany him on his float. The employer was held liable for injuries sustained by the boy when he fell off the float as a result of the roundsman's negligent driving. Scarman LJ agreed that the roundsman was certainly not employed to give the boy a lift, and that if one confined one's analysis of the facts to the incident which caused injury to the boy, *g* then it could be said that carrying the boy on the float was not in the course of his employment. But quoting with approval ([1976] 1 All ER 97 at 104, [1976] 1 WLR 141 at 147–148) the passage cited above from the judgment of Diplock LJ in *Ilkiw v Samuels* [1963] 2 All ER 879 at 889, [1963] 1 WLR 991 at 1004 he adopted a broad approach to the nature of the roundsman's employment. His job was to deliver *h* milk, collect empties, and obtain payment. Disregarding his instructions he enlisted the boy's assistance in carrying out his job. If one asked: why was the boy on the float the answer was that it was because he was assisting the roundsman to do his job.

[79] So it is no answer to say that the employee was guilty of intentional *j* wrongdoing, or that his act was not merely tortious but criminal, or that he was acting exclusively for his own benefit, or that he was acting contrary to express instructions, or that his conduct was the very negation of his employer's duty. The cases show that where an employer undertakes the care of a client's property and entrusts the task to an employee who steals the property, the employer is vicariously liable. This is not only in accordance with principle but with the

a underlying rationale if *Atiyah* has correctly identified it. Experience shows that the risk of theft by an employee is inherent in a business which involves entrusting the custody of a customer's property to employees. But the theft must be committed by the very employee to whom the custody of the property is entrusted. He does more than make the most of an opportunity presented by the fact of his employment. He takes advantage of the position in which the b employer has placed him to enable the purposes of the employer's business to be achieved. If the boys in the present case had been sacks of potatoes and the defendant, having been engaged to take care of them, had entrusted their care to one of its employees, it would have been vicariously liable for any criminal damage done to them by the employee in question, though not by any other employee. Given that the employer's liability does not arise from the law of c bailment, it is not immediately apparent that it should make any difference that the victims were boys, that the wrongdoing took the form of sexual abuse, and that it was committed for the personal gratification of the employee.

[80] Employers have long been held vicariously liable in appropriate circumstances for assaults committed by their employees. Clearly an employer d is liable where he has placed the employee in a situation where he may be expected on occasions to have to resort to personal violence: see *Dyer v Munday* [1895] 1 QB 742, [1895–9] All ER Rep 1022, where the employer was held vicariously liable for a criminal assault committed by his employee while attempting to repossess his employer's property. Equally clearly the employer is not liable for an assault by his employee on a customer merely because it was the result of a e quarrel arising out of his employment: see *Warren v Henlys Ltd* [1948] 2 All ER 935, where a petrol pump attendant assaulted a customer as a result of a dispute over payment. The case was decided partly on the ground that the customer had paid for the petrol and was driving away when he was assaulted, and partly on the ground that he was assaulted because he had threatened to report the attendant f to his employer. The reasoning has been criticised, and the better view may be that the employer was not liable because it was no part of the duties of the pump attendant to keep order. Attention must be concentrated on the closeness of the connection between the act of the employee and the duties he is engaged to perform broadly defined.

[81] In *Deatons Pty Ltd v Flew* (1949) 79 CLR 370 the owner of a hotel was held g not to be vicariously liable for an unprovoked assault by a barmaid who threw a glass of beer into a customer's face. The ground of decision was that the barmaid was not in charge of the bar—the publican was close at hand—and she did not throw the glass in the course of maintaining discipline or restoring order. In the words of Dixon J (at 381–382), it was—

h

> 'an act of passion and resentment done neither in furtherance of the master's interests nor under his express or implied authority *nor as an incident to or in consequence of anything the barmaid was employed to do*. It was a spontaneous act of retributive justice. The occasion for administering it and the form it took may have arisen from the fact that she was a barmaid but retribution j was not within the course of her employment as a barmaid.' (My emphasis.)

In other words, the barmaid's employment gave her the opportunity to wreak some personal vengeance of her own, but that was all; and it was not enough to make her employer liable. Had she been in charge of the bar and authorised to maintain order, the result might well have been different. It would not, in my opinion, have been enough in itself to exclude the employer's liability that she had been paying off a private score of her own. If so, then there is no a priori reason why an employer should not be vicariously liable for a sexual assault committed by his employee, though naturally such conduct will not normally be within the scope of his employment.

[**82**] In the present case the warden's duties provided him with the opportunity to commit indecent assaults on the boys for his own sexual gratification, but that in itself is not enough to make the school liable. The same would be true of the groundsman or the school porter. But there was far more to it than that. The school was responsible for the care and welfare of the boys. It entrusted that responsibility to the warden. He was employed to discharge the school's responsibility to the boys. For this purpose the school entrusted them to his care. He did not merely take advantage of the opportunity which employment at a residential school gave him. He abused the special position in which the school had placed him to enable it to discharge its own responsibilities, with the result that the assaults were committed by the very employee to whom the school had entrusted the care of the boys. It is not necessary to conduct the detailed dissection of the warden's duties of the kind on which the Supreme Court of Canada embarked in *Bazley*'s case and *Jacobi*'s case. I would hold the school liable.

[**83**] I would regard this as in accordance not only with ordinary principle deducible from the authorities but with the underlying rationale of vicarious liability. Experience shows that in the case of boarding schools, prisons, nursing homes, old people's homes, geriatric wards, and other residential homes for the young or vulnerable, there is an inherent risk that indecent assaults on the residents will be committed by those placed in authority over them, particularly if they are in close proximity to them and occupying a position of trust.

[**84**] I would hold the school vicariously liable for the warden's intentional assaults, not (as was suggested in argument) for his failure to perform his duty to take care of the boys. That is an artificial approach based on a misreading of *Morris*' case. The cleaners were vicariously liable for their employee's conversion of the fur, not for his negligence in failing to look after it. Similarly in the *Photo Production* case the security firm was vicariously liable for the patrolman's arson, not for his negligence. The law is mature enough to hold an employer vicariously liable for deliberate, criminal wrongdoing on the part of an employee without indulging in sophistry of this kind. I would also not base liability on the warden's failure to report his own wrongdoing to his employer, an approach which I regard as both artificial and unrealistic. Even if such a duty did exist, on which I prefer to express no opinion, I am inclined to think that it would be a duty owed exclusively to the employer and not a duty for breach of which the employer could be vicariously liable. The same reasoning would not, of course, necessarily apply to the duty to report the wrongdoing of fellow employees, but it is not necessary to decide this.

[**85**] I would overrule *Trotman*'s case and allow the appeal.

Appeal allowed.

Dilys Tausz Barrister.

a

Johnson v Unisys Ltd

[2001] UKHL/13

HOUSE OF LORDS

LORD BINGHAM OF CORNHILL, LORD NICHOLLS OF BIRKENHEAD, LORD STEYN, LORD
b HOFFMANN AND LORD MILLETT

5, 6 FEBRUARY, 22 MARCH 2001

Contract – Damages for breach – Wrongful dismissal – Employment tribunal upholding claimant's claim for unfair dismissal and awarding compensation – Claimant
c *subsequently bringing county court proceedings for financial loss arising from psychological injury caused by manner of dismissal – Whether employee having common law right of action to recover damages for financial loss arising from manner of dismissal.*

In 1994 the claimant, J, brought proceedings for unfair dismissal against the
d defendant employer after being summarily dismissed for an alleged irregularity. By decisions made the following year, the industrial tribunal upheld his complaint, holding that the employer had not given him a fair opportunity to defend himself and had not complied with its disciplinary procedure. The tribunal awarded him compensation of £11,691·88, subsequently reduced to the then
e statutory maximum of £11,000 (now £50,000). In 1997 J brought a county court action against the employer for breach of contract and negligence, seeking damages of £400,000 for loss of earnings allegedly resulting from the fact and manner of his dismissal which, he claimed, had caused him to suffer a nervous breakdown and had therefore made it impossible for him to find work. He relied, inter alia, on the implied term of mutual trust and confidence between employer
f and employee, contending that the employer had breached that term by failing to give him a fair hearing and by breaching its disciplinary procedure. Alternatively, J claimed that the employer, who had known that he was psychologically vulnerable, had owed him a duty of care in tort because it ought reasonably to have foreseen that the manner of his dismissal was likely to cause the injury suffered. The
g employer applied to have the particulars of claim struck out on the grounds that they disclosed no reasonable cause of action at common law. The judge granted that application, and his decision was affirmed by the Court of Appeal. On J's appeal to the House of Lords, the issue arose, inter alia, whether a common law right to recover financial loss resulting from the manner of a dismissal was consistent with the statutory regime on unfair dismissal, introduced in its original
h form by the Industrial Relations Act 1971 and currently in force under Pt X of the Employment Rights Act 1996.

Held – An employee (Lord Steyn dissenting) had no right of action at common law to recover financial losses arising from the unfair manner of his dismissal. A
j conclusion to the contrary would be inconsistent with the statutory system for dealing with unfair dismissals, established by Parliament in 1971 to remedy deficiencies in the law as it then stood. The remedy adopted by Parliament was not to build upon the common law by creating a statutory implied term that the power of dismissal should be exercised fairly or in good faith, leaving the courts to give a remedy on general principles of contractual damages. Instead, it had set up an entirely new system outside the ordinary courts, with tribunals staffed by

a majority of lay members, applying new statutory concepts and offering statutory remedies. Many of the new rules, such as the limit on the amount of the compensatory award, were not based upon any principle which it would have been open to the courts to apply. Rather, they were based upon policy and represented an attempt to balance fairness to employees against the general economic interests of the community. For the judiciary to construct a general common law remedy for unfair circumstances attending dismissal would be contrary to the evident intention of Parliament that there should be such a remedy, but that it should be limited in application and extent. The same reasoning was fatal to the claim based upon a duty of care. Although a duty of care could, of course, exist independently of the contractual relationship, the grounds which made it wrong to impose an implied contractual duty would make it equally wrong to achieve the same result by the imposition of a duty of care. Accordingly, (Lord Steyn concurring on other grounds) the appeal would be dismissed (see [1], [2], [29], [30], [54]–[58], [67] and [77]–[82], post).

Addis v Gramophone Co Ltd [1908–10] All ER Rep 1 and *Malik v Bank of Credit and Commerce International SA (in liq), Mahmud v Bank of Credit and Commerce International SA (in liq)* [1997] 3 All ER 1 considered.

Decision of the Court of Appeal [1999] 1 All ER 854 affirmed.

Notes

For damages for wrongful dismissal, see 16 *Halsbury's Laws* (4th edn reissue) paras 306–307.

Cases referred to in opinions

Addis v Gramophone Co Ltd [1909] AC 488, [1908–10] All ER Rep 1, HL.
Birmingham City Corp v West Midland Baptist (Trust) Association (Inc) [1969] 3 All ER 172, [1970] AC 874, [1969] 3 WLR 389, HL
Cassell & Co Ltd v Broome [1972] 1 All ER 801, [1972] AC 1027, [1972] 2 WLR 645, HL.
Foaminol Laboratories Ltd v British Artid Plastics Ltd [1941] 2 All ER 393.
Gogay v Hertfordshire CC [2000] IRLR 703, CA.
Goold (W A) (Pearmak) Ltd v McConnell [1995] IRLR 516, EAT.
Imperial Group Pension Trust Ltd v Imperial Tobacco Ltd [1991] 2 All ER 597, [1991] 1 WLR 589.
IRC v Dowdall O'Mahoney & Co Ltd [1952] 1 All ER 531, [1952] AC 401, HL.
Jarvis v Swan Tours Ltd [1973] 1 All ER 71, [1973] QB 233, [1972] 3 WLR 954, CA.
Malik v Bank of Credit and Commerce International SA (in liq), Mahmud v Bank of Credit and Commerce International SA (in liq) [1997] 3 All ER 1, [1998] AC 20, [1997] 3 WLR 95, HL.
Malloch v Aberdeen Corp [1971] 2 All ER 1278, [1971] 1 WLR 1578, HL.
Maw v Jones (1890) 25 QBD 107, DC.
McLoughlin v O'Brian [1982] 2 All ER 298, [1983] 1 AC 410, [1982] 2 WLR 982, HL.
Norton Tool Co Ltd v Tewson [1973] 1 All ER 183, [1973] 1 WLR 45, NIRC.
Ridge v Baldwin [1963] 2 All ER 66, [1964] AC 40, [1963] 2 WLR 935, HL.
Scally v Southern Health and Social Services Board (British Medical Association, third party) [1991] 4 All ER 563, [1992] 1 AC 294, [1991] 3 WLR 778, HL.
Spring v Guardian Assurance plc [1994] 3 All ER 129, [1995] 2 AC 296, [1994] 3 WLR 354, HL.
United Bank Ltd v Akhtar [1989] IRLR 507, EAT.
Walker v Northumberland CC [1995] 1 All ER 737.
Wallace v United Grain Growers Ltd (1997) 152 DLR (4th) 1, Can SC.

a *Wellman Alloys Ltd v Russell* [1973] ICR 616, NIRC.
White v Chief Constable of the South Yorkshire Police [1999] 1 All ER 1, [1999] 2 AC 455, [1998] 3 WLR 1509, HL.

Appeal
The claimant, Fenton Barry Johnson (the employee), appealed with permission b of the Appeal Committee of the House of Lords given on 3 November 1999 from the decision of the Court of Appeal (Lord Woolf MR, Hutchison and Tuckey LJJ) on 4 December 1998 ([1999] 1 All ER 854, [1999] ICR 809) dismissing his appeal from the decision of Judge Ansell at the Milton Keynes County Court on 26 June 1998 striking out his proceedings for wrongful dismissal and negligence against the defendant, Unisys Ltd (the employer), on the grounds that it disclosed no c reasonable cause of action. The facts are set out in the opinion of Lord Steyn.

Edward Faulks QC and *Oliver Wise* (instructed by *Sharpe Pritchard*) for the employee.
David Pannick QC and *Sam Neaman* (instructed by *Davies Lavery*) for the employer.

d Their Lordships took time for consideration.

22 March 2001. The following opinions were delivered.

LORD BINGHAM OF CORNHILL. My Lords,

[1] I have had the advantage of reading in draft the opinions of my noble and e learned friends Lord Hoffmann and Lord Millett. I agree with them both and would dismiss this appeal for the reasons which they give.

LORD NICHOLLS OF BIRKENHEAD. My Lords,

[2] On this appeal the appellant seeks damages for loss he claims he suffered f as a result of the manner in which he was dismissed. He uses as his legal foundation the decision of the House in *Malik v Bank of Credit and Commerce International SA (in liq), Mahmud v Bank of Credit and Commerce International SA (in liq)* [1997] 3 All ER 1, [1998] AC 20, although that was not a manner of dismissal case. In principle the appellant's argument has much to commend it. I said so, in my obiter observations in *Malik*'s case ([1997] 3 All ER 1 at 10, [1998] AC 20 at 39–40). g But there is an insuperable obstacle: the intervention of Parliament in the unfair dismissal legislation. Having heard full argument on the point, I am persuaded that a common law right embracing the manner in which an employee is dismissed cannot satisfactorily co-exist with the statutory right not to be unfairly dismissed. A newly developed common law right of this nature, covering the h same ground as the statutory right, would fly in the face of the limits Parliament has already prescribed on matters such as the classes of employees who have the benefit of the statutory right, the amount of compensation payable and the short time limits for making claims. It would also defeat the intention of Parliament that claims of this nature should be decided by specialist tribunals, not the j ordinary courts of law. I too would dismiss this appeal.

LORD STEYN. My Lords,

(I) *Addis v Gramophone Co Ltd*

[3] The headnote of the decision of the House of Lords in *Addis v Gramophone Co Ltd* [1909] AC 488, [1908–10] All ER Rep 1 purports to state the ratio decidendi

of that case as follows: where a servant is wrongfully dismissed from his employment the damages for the dismissal cannot include compensation for the manner of his dismissal, for his injured feelings, or for the loss he may sustain from the fact that the dismissal of itself makes it more difficult for him to obtain fresh employment. This statement of the law was based on an observation in the speech of Lord Loreburn LC. A majority of the Law Lords expressed agreement with this speech. On the other hand, only Lord Loreburn LC specifically referred to the unavailability of special damages for loss of employment prospects. The other Law Lords concentrated on the non-pecuniary aspects of the case. The headnote is arguably wrong insofar as it states that the House decided that a wrongfully dismissed employee can never sue for special damages for loss of employment prospects arising from the harsh and humiliating manner of the dismissal: see *MacGregor on Damages* (16th edn, 1997) p 810, para 1242. Nevertheless, the statement of the law encapsulated in the controversial headnote has exercised an influence over this corner of the law for more than 90 years. It has had a restrictive impact on the damages which an employee may recover for financial loss actually suffered as a result of the manner of wrongful dismissal.

[4] It is instructive to consider how this decision was viewed in 1909. Sir Frederic Pollock, the editor of the Law Quarterly Review, was not impressed. In a case note he contrasted 'an artificial rule or mere authority' to 'the rationale of the matter': (1910) 26 LQR 1. Citing cases contrary to what was perceived to be the *Addis* rule, and 'said to be exceptions', he plainly thought that as a matter of legal principle the decision was questionable. He said (at 2):

> 'In the case of wrongful dismissal, a harsh and humiliating way of doing it, by the imputation which such a dismissal conveys, may make it very difficult for the servant to obtain a new situation. That was how the Court looked at it in *Maw* v. *Jones* ((1890) 25 QBD 107); not as a mere personal slight or affront. So in *Addis* v. *Gramophone Co*. The plaintiff was dismissed summarily from an important post in India, and the whole management taken out of his hands in a way which could not but import obloquy among the commercial community of India, and as a result permanent loss. It was no mere rudeness or want of consideration. But the majority of the House of Lords thought the damages in question were really for defamation, and could be recovered only in a separate action.'

The supposed rule in *Addis*'s case has been controversial for a long time. When the first edition of Treitel's classic book on contract was published some 40 years ago the author described the exclusion of any claim by an employee for financial loss to reputation as hard to justify: *The Law of Contract* (1962) pp 606–607. In the tenth edition of the same work (1999) Sir Guenter Treitel QC remained of the same view and was able to cite further decisions in which damages were awarded for financial loss of employment prospects or for injury to reputation resulting from a breach of contract: see pp 921–924.

[5] During the course of the last century a fundamental alteration in the relationship between employer and employee has come about. And in the economic sphere that relationship has also drastically altered. This is the context in which the question of public importance now before the House is whether *Addis*'s case precludes the recovery by an employee of special damages for financial loss in respect of damage to his employment prospects resulting from the manner of a wrongful dismissal. It was on this basis that the Appeal Committee granted leave to appeal rather than the particular features of the claim under consideration.

a (II) *The background to the dispute*

[6] In outline the facts are as follows. The employee is now 52 years of age. With a gap of three years he was employed by the employers in the software computer industry from 1971 to 1994. In 1992 he became a director of the company. Over the years he suffered from work-related stress and the employers were aware of his particular psychological vulnerability. In January 1994 the b employers made allegations against him regarding his conduct. On 17 January 1994 he was asked to attend a meeting. No specific allegations were put to him. Later that day he was summarily dismissed. He lodged an internal appeal. On 3 March 1994 his dismissal was confirmed. Shortly thereafter he made a complaint of unfair dismissal to an industrial tribunal (now called an employment tribunal). By decisions made on 20 February 1995 and 26 July 1995 the tribunal upheld his c complaint and awarded him compensation, subject to a finding that he had contributed by 25% to his dismissal. Applying the statutory maximum the employee was awarded £11,691·88.

[7] It is agreed that as 'a result of the circumstances and the fact of his dismissal the [employee] suffered a major psychiatric illness, involving, inter alia, in-patient d treatment from March to August 1994'. In addition the employee had to undergo hypnotherapy every three weeks until January 1996; he was re-admitted twice in 1996 to hospital; thereafter he had to undergo intensive psychotherapy and visit a psychiatric nurse; and he had to take anti-depressant drugs for depression, mood swings and alcohol dependency. His health has remained severely affected. Despite repeated applications for jobs he remains unemployed. The main obstacles e facing him in seeking employment is the time he spent in hospital following his dismissal and the substantial period he has now been out of work in a rapidly developing industry.

(III) *The proceedings*

f [8] In August 1997 the employee instituted proceedings in the county court for breach of contract and negligence on the ground of the manner of his dismissal. He alleged that his employers never informed him of the complaints against him. He relied on an implied term of his contract that his employers would not without reasonable and proper cause conduct themselves in such a way so as to damage the relationship of trust and confidence between the parties. g The employee further alleged that the manner of his dismissal and the circumstances leading up to it had caused his mental breakdown and inability to find work, with the result that he would suffer a loss of earnings in excess of £400,000.

h (IV) *The decisions*

[9] The case came before a judge on an application to strike out the action. The judge viewed the case as in substance one seeking damages for unfair dismissal. He considered that the employee was seeking to circumvent the unfair dismissal legislation. He relied on the law as stated in the headnote in *Addis*'s case. j He held that an unfair dismissal could not by itself ground any action to recover financial loss caused by the manner of the employee's dismissal. He struck out the action.

[10] The employee appealed. The Court of Appeal gave him an opportunity to amend his particulars of claim. Re-amended particulars of claim were produced. The Court of Appeal indicated that, if the appeal was successful, leave to amend would be given. But Lord Woolf MR, with whom Hutchison and Tuckey LJJ

agreed, dismissed the appeal in a closely reasoned reserved judgment ([1999] 1 All ER 854). Lord Woolf MR expressed agreement with the views of the judge. Lord Woolf MR held that, despite the form of the re-cast pleading, the substance of the employee's complaint was as to the manner in which he had been dismissed. He proceeded on the basis that the headnote in *Addis*'s case correctly stated the effect of that decision. That is not surprising for the contrary was not argued in the Court of Appeal. He examined in detail the impact of the speeches in *Malik*'s case on the decision of the House in *Addis*'s case and concluded that the House had merely distinguished *Addis*'s case and had not departed from it. He observed (at 861) that *Addis*'s case precluded the recovery of damages for the manner of dismissal of an employee while *Malik*'s case was concerned with the recovery of damages for an anterior breach. He drew a distinction (at 859) between express and constructive dismissal. Applying the rule in *Addis*'s case, Lord Woolf MR held that the employee had no sustainable claim. Lord Woolf MR further held that, having regard to the circumstances, the prospects of the plaintiff overcoming the issue of remoteness were unreal (at 862).

(V) *The issues*

[11] It is necessary to explain the shape of the case. First, it must be assumed that as a result of the circumstances and fact of his dismissal the plaintiff suffered a major psychiatric illness, involving, inter alia, in-patient treatment in a mental hospital from March to August 1994; that subsequently he was hospitalised and treated as I have set out; and that in consequence he has been unable to find a job. Secondly, the claim is brought in contract and, alternatively, in tort. Thirdly, the claim in contract is based on a term implied in contracts of employment, namely that an employer shall not, without reasonable and proper cause, conduct himself in a manner calculated and likely to destroy or seriously damage the relationship of trust and confidence between employer and employee: see *Malik's* case ([1997] 3 All ER 1 at 15, [1998] AC 20 at 45). Fourthly, in the alternative, the re-amended particulars of claim put forward additional negative and positive implied terms. At the hearing of the appeal counsel for the employee explained that these implied terms were based on dicta in decided cases but he was content to regard these as instances of the application of the general obligation of mutual trust and confidence. The contractual claim is therefore squarely based on a breach of the implied obligation of mutual trust and confidence between employer and employee. The re-amended particulars of claim allege a breach of the implied obligation in that the employers failed—

> '(i) to put allegations to the plaintiff; (ii) to accord the plaintiff an opportunity to defend himself; (iii) to provide a full explanation of allegations against the plaintiff; (iv) to comply with the defendant's disciplinary procedures and the rules of natural justice ...'

The consequences of the breach allegedly involved the employee's mental breakdown and consequent total inability to find employment. Having regard to his previous earnings he claims a sum of the order of £400,000. Fifthly, it is important to note that the claim is solely for the recovery of special damages for financial loss. The separate question whether an employee may recover compensation for anxiety and mental stress arising from the manner of his dismissal was not raised before the judge or before the Court of Appeal. It is not an issue before the House and it would be wrong to express any view on it.

a [12] It will also be necessary to consider the issue of remoteness, namely whether the employee has any realistic prospect of establishing that his loss is not too remote.

[13] As I have explained the claim is framed in contract and tort. Having regard to the particular circumstances of this case, if the claim in contract is held to be unsustainable the fate of the claim in tort must inevitably be the same. I b propose therefore to concentrate on the potential sustainability of the claim in contract.

[14] It is convenient to start by examining the following issues. (1) What is the effect of the decision in *Addis*'s case? (2) Even if it is not part of the ratio decidendi of *Addis*'s case does the observation of Lord Loreburn LC (and the headnote) correctly state the law? (3) What was the impact of *Malik*'s case on c *Addis*'s case? Depending on the answer to these questions it will then be necessary to examine the further arguments in detail and to consider the impact of the conclusions on the disposal of the case.

(VI) *The effect of Addis's case*

d [15] It is necessary to examine what was decided in *Addis*'s case. The speeches in *Addis*'s case are not easy to understand. Two of their Lordships spoke in terms of exemplary damages: see Lord James of Hereford ([1909] AC 488 at 492) and Lord Collins, dissenting, ([1909] AC 488 at 497 and 500–501, [1908–10] All ER Rep 1 at 7–8). That could not have been an issue. In English law such damages have never and cannot be awarded for breach of any contract. That part of the e discussion in the speeches in *Addis*'s case can safely be put to one side. The context of the dispute has often been described. For my part it is sufficient to adopt the description of the case by Sir Frederic Pollock that the plaintiff—

> 'was dismissed summarily from an important post in India, and the whole management taken out of his hands in a way which could not but import f obloquy among the commercial community of India, and as a result permanent loss.'

The critical observation on the law of Lord Loreburn LC ([1909] AC 488 at 491, [1908–10] All ER Rep 1 at 3) was undeniably to the effect stated in the headnote. On the other hand, *MacGregor* p 810, para 1242 has argued that the other Law g Lords in the majority confined themselves to the non-pecuniary aspects of the case. Accordingly, it is said, the headnote may not reflect the ratio decidendi of the case. Lord James in his substantive reasons discussed the availability of general damages for injury to feelings. But he did say ([1909] AC 488 at 492) that he agreed with 'the entirety of the judgment delivered by my noble and learned h friend on the Woolsack'. In my view he endorsed the relevant part of the speech of Lord Loreburn LC. On the other hand, Lord Atkinson ([1909] AC 488 at 493, [1908–10] All ER Rep 1 at 4), Lord Gorrell ([1909] AC 488 at 502, [1908–10] All ER Rep 1 at 9) and Lord Shaw of Dunfermline ([1909] AC 488 at 505, [1908–10] All ER Rep 1 at 11) at most expressed general concurrence. In *Cassell & Co Ltd v* j *Broome* [1972] 1 All ER 801 at 837, [1972] AC 1027 at 1087 Lord Reid observed:

> 'Concurrence with the speech of a colleague does not mean acceptance of every word which he has said. If it did there would be far fewer concurrences than there are.'

When one turns to the substantive reasons given by Lord Atkinson, Lord Gorrell and Lord Shaw, one finds that they dealt exclusively with the non-pecuniary aspects of the case. Only one of the Law Lords who sat in the case can realistically be regarded as having evinced a clear endorsement of Lord Loreburn LC's observation so far as it ruled out special damages for loss of employment prospects flowing from the manner of a wrongful dismissal.

a

[**16**] Given the apparently harsh and humiliating manner of the dismissal, it is surprising that the other Law Lords did not consider this aspect. Indeed Lord Atkinson expressly said it was not 'necessary' to deal with it. The explanation may be the view taken of the pleadings: see Lord Atkinson's complaint ([1909] AC 488 at 493, [1908–10] All ER Rep 1 at 4) about the 'unscientific form' of the pleadings and 'the loose manner in which the proceeding's at trial were conducted'. Despite assumptions to the contrary (including in particular my assumption in *Malik*'s case ([1997] 3 All ER 1 at 20, [1998] AC 20 at 50–51) it is nevertheless tolerably clear that the ratio decidendi of *Addis*'s case does not preclude the recovery of special damages flowing from the manner of a wrongful dismissal.

b

c

(VII) *The correctness of the observation of Lord Loreburn LC*

d

[**17**] It is still necessary to consider whether the observation of Lord Loreburn LC, although not reflecting the ratio decidendi of *Addis*'s case, was nevertheless correct. This is so for two reasons. First, my interpretation of *Addis*'s case may not be correct. Secondly, the proposition of Lord Loreburn LC may be correct in all its constituent parts. As Sir Frederick Pollock explained in his case note in the Law Quarterly Review, Lord Loreburn LC enunciated a special and restrictive rule precluding the recovery of special damages in respect of financial loss flowing from the manner of wrongful dismissal. It was viewed as contrary to legal principle in 1909. In modern times it has been widely criticised as being in conflict with general principles of contract law. In *Malik*'s case Lord Nicholls of Birkenhead and I dealt with this point and it is unnecessary to cover the same ground again. But perhaps I may add that I am not aware of any modern academic writer, addressing the subject, who has tried to defend the relevant restrictive rule of Lord Loreburn LC. One is entitled to pose the question: why was the contract of employment singled out for a special rule to the disadvantage of employees?

e

f

g

[**18**] *Addis*'s case was decided in the heyday of a judicial philosophy of market individualism in respect of what was then called the law of master and servant. The idea that in the eyes of the law the position of a servant was a subordinate one seemed natural and inevitable. And in *Addis*'s case it may have been the background to the adoption of a special restrictive rule denying in all cases to employees the right to recover financial loss which naturally flowed from the manner of their wrongful dismissal. Since 1909 there has been a fundamental change in legal culture. A good illustration is the decision of the House in *Scally v Southern Health and Social Services Board (British Medical Association, third party)* [1991] 4 All ER 563, [1992] 1 AC 294. In *Scally*'s case a contract negotiated by trade unions conferred on an employee a valuable right contingent on him taking up the right in a prescribed manner. He was unaware of the right. The House of Lords held that there was an obligation implied by law as an incident of a contract of employment, as opposed to implied in fact, to bring the term to the notice of the employee. Such a decision would have been unthinkable at the time of *Addis*'s case. In *Spring v Guardian Assurance plc* [1994] 3 All ER 129 at 161, [1995] 2 AC 296 at 335, Lord Slynn of Hadley noted—

h

j

a 'the changes which have taken place in the employer/employee relationship, with far greater duties imposed on the employer than in the past, whether by statute or by judicial decision, to care for the physical, financial and even psychological welfare of the employee.'

One of the most important of those developments is the evolution since the b mid-seventies of the obligation of trust and confidence in contracts of employment and its unanimous and unequivocal endorsement in *Malik*'s case. The orthodox view is that this implied obligation may be displaced or qualified but only by express agreement or necessary implication: compare, however, a different view in Douglas Brodie 'Beyond Exchange: The New Contract of Employment' (1998) 27 ILJ 79 at 82–83.

c **[19]** Since 1909 our knowledge of the incidence of stress-related psychiatric and psychological problems of employees, albeit still imperfect, has greatly increased. What could in the early part of the last century dismissively be treated as mere 'injured feelings' is now sometimes accepted as a recognisable psychiatric illness. The outlines of the gradual development of the law in this area are well d known: see, for example, *McLoughlin v O'Brian* [1982] 2 All ER 298, [1983] 1 AC 410; *White v Chief Constable of the South Yorkshire Police* [1999] 1 All ER 1, [1999] 2 AC 455. Nowadays courts generally accept that they must act on the best medical insight of the day. Specifically, this realism has taken root in the field of employment law: *Walker v Northumberland CC* [1995] 1 All ER 737; *Gogay v Hertfordshire CC* [2000] IRLR 703. These considerations are testimony to the need for implied e terms in contracts of employment protecting employees from harsh and unacceptable employment practices. This is particularly important in the light of the greater pressures on employees due to the progressive deregulation of the labour market, the privatisation of public services, and the globalisation of product and financial markets: see Brendan J Burchell and others 'Job Insecurity f and Work Intensification' (1999), a report published for the Joseph Rowntree Foundation, at pp 60–61. This report documents a phenomenon during the last two decades 'of an extraordinary intensification of work pressures'. The report states as a major cause the fact that the 'quantity of work required of individuals has increased because of under-staffing so that hours of work have lengthened and, more importantly, the pace of work has intensified'. Inevitably, the g incidence of psychiatric injury due to excessive stress has increased. The need for protection of employees through their contractual rights, express and implied by law, is markedly greater than in the past.

[20] It is no longer right to equate a contract of employment with commercial contracts. One possible way of describing a contract of employment in modern h terms is as a relational contract. If (contrary to my view) the headnote of *Addis*'s case correctly states the ratio decidendi of *Addis*'s case I would now be willing to depart from it. That is not a particularly bold step. Indeed, in *Malik*'s case the House took that step.

j (VIII) *The impact of Malik's case on Addis's case*

[21] It is necessary to return to the analysis by Lord Woolf MR of the difference between *Addis*'s case and *Malik*'s case. Lord Woolf MR held that the relevant part of the rule in *Addis*'s case deals with the consequences of wrongful dismissal whereas *Malik*'s case concerned a breach of the obligation of mutual trust and confidence during the subsistence of a contract. It is noteworthy that the implied obligation of mutual trust and confidence was developed in a series of constructive dismissal cases: see Hepple and O'Higgins *Employment Law* (4th edn, 1981) pp 134–135, paras 291–292. It cannot therefore be confined to breaches during the subsistence of the contract. The development of the implied obligation of mutual trust and confidence as it has evolved was unanimously endorsed by the House as 'workable' and 'sound' in *Malik*'s case: see [1997] 3 All ER 1 at 5, [1998] AC 20 at 35 per Lord Nicholls, and in my speech ([1997] 3 All ER 1 at 15, [1998] AC 20 at 46). It was held in *Malik*'s case that the employees in that case would have been entitled to accept a breach of such an obligation as repudiatory and to claim damages ([1997] 3 All ER 1 at 8, [1998] AC 20 at 38 per Lord Nicholls, and my speech ([1997] 3 All ER 1 at 17, [1998] AC 20 at 48). If the employees had discovered the corrupt conduct of employers during the subsistence of the contract, they would on the law as stated in *Malik*'s case have been entitled to terminate the contract and sue for damages. Not only is this an inevitable result of the logic of the decision in *Malik*'s case but it had the express unanimous endorsement of the House. Pecuniary loss 'brought about by a loss of reputation caused by a breach of contract [does not] preclude the plaintiffs from recovering in respect of that pecuniary loss' (see *Foaminol Laboratories Ltd v British Artid Plastics Ltd* [1941] 2 All ER 393 at 400): [1997] 3 All ER 1 at 10, [1998] AC 20 at 40 per Lord Nicholls; and my speech ([1997] 3 All ER 1 at 21, [1998] AC 20 at 52). Damages for wrongful dismissal are governed not by a special rule applicable to employment contracts but by ordinary principles of contract law: see *Malik*'s case ([1997] 3 All ER 1 at 10, [1998] AC 20 at 39); and also informative comment in two major new publications, namely *English Private Law* (2000) vol 2, paras 18.60–18.61, per Professor Burrows; Butterworths Common Law Series *The Law of Contract* (1999) p 1259, para 8.59. The consequence is that '[c]ases previously regarded as exceptional can now be seen as examples of the general rule': *Anson's Law of Contract*, (27th edn, 1998) pp 562–563. In *Malik*'s case the House embarked on a process of synthesis. To this extent therefore the observation of Lord Loreburn LC, which rules out in all cases a claim for financial loss resulting from the manner of a wrongful dismissal, is qualified by the unanimous decision of the House in *Malik*'s case. In my respectful view the reasoning of the Court of Appeal is not correct.

(IX) *The contrary arguments of the employers*

[22] *The statutory dimension.* Counsel for the employers argued that *Addis*'s case has been a cornerstone of the law of employment for nearly a century. He submitted that the law as stated in *Addis*'s case was the background against which Parliament introduced the unfair dismissal legislation in its original form by the Industrial Relations Act 1971: see the Employment Protection Act 1975 and the Employment Rights Act 1996 for subsequent reforms of the system. In support of this submission he pointed to para 522 of the Report of the Royal Commission on Trade Unions and Employers Associations (1965–1968) (Cmnd 3623 (1968)), commonly described as the Donovan Report. It reads as follows:

> 'An employee has protection at common law against "wrongful" dismissal, but this protection is strictly limited; it means that if an employee is dismissed without due notice he can claim the payment of wages he would have earned for the period of notice. From this payment will be deducted any amount which he earned (or through his fault failed to earn) during the period of notice. Beyond this, the employee has no legal claim at common law, whatever hardship he suffers as a result of his dismissal. Even if the way

a in which he is dismissed constitutes an imputation on his honesty and his ability to get another job is correspondingly reduced he cannot—except through an action for defamation—obtain any redress (see the decision of the House of Lords in *Addis v Gramophone Co* [1909] AC 486).'

He argued further that, even if it would otherwise be right to depart from *Addis's* case in the respect under consideration, it would be wrong to do so in the face of b the elaborate statutory scheme governing unfair dismissal created by Parliament. In my opinion this argument ought not to prevail. In *Birmingham City Corp v West Midland Baptist (Trust) Association (Inc)* [1969] 3 All ER 172, [1970] AC 874, Lord Reid put such arguments in context. He said:

c 'But the mere fact that an enactment shows that Parliament must have thought that the law was one thing does not preclude the courts from deciding that the law was in fact something different. This has been stated in a number of cases including *Inland Revenue Comrs v Dowdall, O'Mahoney & Co Ltd*. No doubt the position would be different if the provisions of the enactment were such that they would only be workable if the law was as d Parliament supposed it to be.' (See [1969] 3 All ER 172 at 179–180, [1970] AC 874 at 898.)

It cannot be said that the unfair dismissal legislation would be unworkable if the House departs from *Addis's* case.

[**23**] The unfair dismissal legislation must be put in context. At the time of the e Donovan Report collective bargaining was seen as the main form of protection of individuals. It apparently covered about 83% of the workforce in 1980. It has, however, been contracting steadily. It fell to 35% in 1998. In the result individual legal rights have now become the main source of protection of employees: see Brown, Deakin, Nash and Oxenbridge 'The Employment Contract: From f Collective Procedures to Individual Rights' (2000) 38 British Journal of Industrial Relations 611 at 613–616. At the time of the Donovan Report reinstatement was envisaged as a major remedy: paras 551–552. In practice, however, only about three per cent of applicants are reinstated: see Davies and Friedland *Labour Legislation and Public Policy* (1993) p 210, citing statistics dating from 1987–1988. My understanding is that about three per cent still represents the reinstatement g figure. Not surprisingly, the award of compensation by a tribunal has to be the primary remedy. The 1971 Act in s 116 adopted the formula, which appears with minor changes in the current law, that the compensation should be—

h 'such amount as the … tribunal considers just and equitable in all the circumstances, having regard to the loss sustained by the aggrieved party in consequence of the matters to which the complaint relates, in so far as the loss was attributable to action taken by or on behalf of the party in default.'

Hugh Collins *Justice in Dismissal: The Law of Termination of Employment* (1992) pp 218–223 has shown how the award of compensation, by reason of artificial j limits, has markedly failed to meet the aim of corrective justice in accordance with the employee's contractual rights. One of those limits was the requirement of the unfair dismissal system that such cases had to be resolved in accordance with a very expeditious timetable. Initially, the claim had generally to be lodged within four weeks, that being a period within which the seriousness of damage to employment prospects would often not have become clear: see ss 22, 106(4) and (5) read with Sch 6, para 5 of the 1971 Act. Even now s 111(2) of the Employment Rights Act 1996 provides that such claims must generally be lodged within three months, that still being a period within which the seriousness of damage to employment prospects may not have become clear. More importantly, the low statutory limit on the award of compensation made the attainment of corrective justice impossible. At the inception of the statutory regime s 118(1) of the 1971 Act placed a limit on the maximum amount of compensation of two years' pay or £4,160 (whichever was the lesser). In 1975 the alternative way of expressing the limit was abolished. The monetary limit was from time to time increased. In April 1998 it reached £12,000. In October 1999 the maximum was increased to £50,000. It is now index-linked. It has been pointed out that allowing for inflation, £4,160 in 1971 is now worth about £50,000: HC Research Paper 98/99. The statutory system was therefore always only capable of meeting the requirements of cases at the lower end of seriousness. Manifestly, it was always incapable, for example, of affording any significant financial compensation to employees with substantial salaries and pension entitlements in cases where they suffered a serious loss of employment prospects due to the manner of their dismissal. In such cases, inter alia, the artificial statutory limits from the inception inhibited significant compensation. If Parliament is deemed to have been aware of the *Addis* decision, one must also deem Parliament to have been aware that the system it was creating was only capable of dealing effectively and justly with less serious cases where the threshold of a breach of contract was not necessarily established. Moreover, the changing nature of the relationship between employer and employee, and numerous judicial inroads in case law on *Addis*'s case were already well documented before 1971. The third edition of Treitel *The Law of Contract* was published in 1970. *Treitel* observed, at p 813, that 'the rule may be that *general* damages cannot be recovered for injury to reputation by a non-trader, but that *special* damages can be recovered for actual loss resulting from such injury' (author's emphasis). In my view the headnote in *Addis*'s case (and its recitation in the Donovan Report) in respect of special damages is based on a misconception. But at the very least the relevant part of the rule in *Addis*'s case was controversial. In all these circumstances it is unrealistic to say that Parliament would have assumed the common law as reflected in the headnote in *Addis*'s case to be set in stone and incapable of principled development. I would therefore reject this argument.

[24] *Conflict with express terms.* Counsel for the employers was asked to place the employment contract of the employee before the House. It was done. It revealed that either party was able to terminate the contract by giving four weeks' notice. This proved to be a platform for an argument for striking out the claim which was not considered by the judge or by the Court of Appeal. It was also not raised in the agreed statement of facts and issues or in the written cases. Nevertheless, relying on the notice provision, counsel for the employers submitted that to apply the implied obligation of mutual trust and confidence in relation to a dismissal is to bring it into conflict with the express terms of the contract. He said orthodox contract law does not permit such a result. His argument approached the matter as if one was dealing with the question whether a term can be implied *in fact* in the light of the express terms of the contract. This submission loses sight of the particular nature of the implied obligation of mutual trust and confidence. It is not a term implied in fact. It is an overarching obligation implied by law as an incident of the contract of employment. It can also be described as a legal duty imposed by law: Treitel *The Law of Contract* (10th edn, 1999) p 190. It requires at least express words or a necessary implication to displace it or to cut down its

a scope. Prima facie it must be read consistently with the express terms of the contract. This emerges from the seminal judgment of Sir Nicolas Browne-Wilkinson V-C in *Imperial Group Pension Trust Ltd v Imperial Tobacco Ltd* [1991] 2 All ER 597, [1991] 1 WLR 589. It related to an employer's express contractual right to refuse amendments under a pension scheme. The Vice-Chancellor held that the employer's express rights were subject to the implied obligation that they should b not be exercised so as to destroy or seriously damage the relationship of trust and confidence between the company and its employees and former employees. The employer's blanket refusal was unlawful. The decision did not involve trust law and the employer was not treated as a fiduciary. It was decided on principles of contract law. The Vice-Chancellor described the implied obligation of trust and confidence as 'the implied obligation of good faith'. It could also be described as c an employer's obligation of fair dealing. In the same way an employer's express right to transfer an employee may be qualified by the obligation of mutual trust and confidence: see *United Bank Ltd v Akhtar* [1989] IRLR 507, *Sweet and Maxwell's Encyclopaedia of Employment Law* (looseleaf edn) vol 1, pp 1456 and 1469, paras 1.5101 and 1.5107. The interaction of the implied obligation of trust and confidence and d express terms of the contract can be compared with the relationship between duties of good faith or fair dealing with the express terms of notice in a contract. They can live together. In any event, the argument of counsel for the employers misses the real point. The notice provision in the contract is valid and effective. Nobody suggests the contrary. On the other hand, the employer may become liable in damages if he acts in breach of the independent implied obligation by e dismissing the employee in a harsh and humiliating manner. There is no conflict between the express and implied terms. I would therefore dismiss this argument.

[25] *Unfair dismissal.* Counsel for the employers further argued that in substance the claim, based on a failure to follow disciplinary procedures, is one for unfair dismissal. This is a misdescription of the claim. It is not a claim for f unfair dismissal but one based on allegations of breach of the obligation of mutual trust and confidence. Counsel also said that a tribunal's award may include compensation for a breach in respect of the manner of a wrongful dismissal. That is so. But it is equally obvious that as at 1971, and afterwards, such amount would have been fairly nominal. Of course, an employee must not be allowed to recover the same damages twice. But such adjustments in common law damages g can be and are often made.

[26] *Inapplicability to termination.* Counsel for the employers also argued that the implied obligation of trust and confidence is restricted to unacceptable conduct by the employer during the relationship. It is a legalistic point. It ignores the purpose of the obligation. The implied obligation aims to ensure fair dealing h between employer and employee, and that is as important in respect of disciplinary proceedings, suspension of an employee and dismissal as at any other stage of the employment relationship. In my view this argument ought not to be accepted.

[27] *Floodgates.* Counsel for the employers further submitted that in virtually j every case there could be a claim based on the manner of dismissal. He said there would be an enormous proliferation of claims in the county court. These predictions are too alarmist. In *Malik*'s case it was held ([1997] 3 All ER 1 at 10, [1998] AC 20 at 39) that the mere fact of dismissal could not of itself handicap an employee in the labour market. On the other hand, if the employer acts in a harsh and oppressive manner that inflicts unnecessary and substantial financial damage on the employee there is no principled reason why an employee should

not put forward a claim for such loss. I would therefore reject the floodgates argument.

(X) *The cause of action*

[**28**] In my view the employee has a reasonable cause of action based on a breach of the implied obligation of trust and confidence.

(XI) *Remoteness*

[**29**] Leaving aside legal objections, there are formidable evidential difficulties in the way of the employee. It was suggested at the hearing that the claim would at trial inevitably fail on causation. The difficulty is real: how would the employee prove that his psychiatric condition was caused by the manner of his dismissal rather than the fact of his dismissal? On the facts, which must be assumed to be correct, I am however inclined to think that it would not be right to strike out the claim on this ground. But remoteness presents an even more formidable difficulty for the employee even at this stage. This issue must be judged at the date of the re-employment of the employee in 1990. The allegations of the knowledge of the employers before that date are set out in the pleadings as follows:

> '... during the plaintiff's posting to Paris and his work on a conference in Barcelona in 1985, the defendant's servant or agent, Keith Binks, was made aware that the plaintiff was under extreme stress and was at risk of suffering psychological injury. At the end of 1985 the plaintiff saw his GP who prescribed anti-depressants and wrote to the defendant requesting that the plaintiff be given time off work as a result of work-related stress. The defendant allowed the plaintiff some time off work as a result. The defendant's doctor was aware of the plaintiff's psychological condition as a result of a meeting with the plaintiff prior to his return to work in 1986. Further, in 1987 the defendant was aware of the plaintiff's special psychological needs, as was evidenced by its offering him one-to-one counselling because of his medical condition and impending redundancy.'

Taking into account what the employer is alleged to have known, as well as the lapse of time, I would not dissent from the view of Lord Woolf MR that there is no realistic prospect that the employee will be able to overcome this obstacle.

(XII) *Disposal*

[**30**] For the reasons I have given I would dismiss the appeal.

LORD HOFFMANN. My Lords,

[**31**] Mr Johnson has spent his working life in the computer industry. In 1971, at the age of 23, he started work for Unisys Ltd, a multinational software service company. In 1987 he was made redundant but in 1990 Unisys re-employed him. In January 1994, however, he was summarily dismissed for some alleged irregularity. The company paid him a month's salary in lieu of notice. He complained to an industrial tribunal of unfair dismissal and the tribunal upheld his claim. It found that the company had not given him a fair opportunity to defend himself and had not complied with its disciplinary procedure. On 26 July 1995 it ordered Unisys to pay him £11,691·88 compensation.

[**32**] On 11 August 1997 Mr Johnson commenced an action in the Milton Keynes County Court against Unisys for damages at common law. He claimed

a alternatively for breach of contract or negligence. In his re-amended particulars of claim, he alleged that his dismissal was in breach of various implied terms of his contract of employment. The main one was that the employer would not without reasonable cause conduct itself in a manner calculated and likely to destroy or seriously damage the relationship of trust and confidence between itself and the employee. The existence of this implied term in a contract of b employment has recently been affirmed by the House of Lords in *Malik v Bank of Credit and Commerce International SA (in liq), Mahmud v Bank of Credit and Commerce International SA (in liq)* [1997] 3 All ER 1, [1998] AC 20. It is commonly called the implied term of trust and confidence. He also pleaded various other implied terms; for example, that the company would not, without reasonable cause, do anything which would injure his physical or mental health, harm his professional c development and so forth. But the alleged breach of all these terms lies in the fact that he was dismissed without a fair hearing and in breach of the company's disciplinary procedure.

[33] Mr Johnson says that in consequence of the manner and the fact of his dismissal, he suffered a mental breakdown. He became depressed, attempted d suicide and started to drink heavily. In 1994 he spent five months in a mental hospital and since then has occasionally had to be re-admitted. His family life has suffered and despite over 100 applications, he has been unable to find work. He is 52 and considers it unlikely that he will find remunerated work again. He says that severe damage of this kind was reasonably foreseeable by Unisys because e during the period before his redundancy in 1987 it was known to persons whose knowledge should be attributed to the company that he was under stress and at risk of suffering psychological injury. The alternative claim in tort is based upon the allegation that Unisys owed him a duty of care because it ought reasonably to have foreseen that such injury was likely to result from dismissing him in the way it did.

f [34] Unisys applied to Judge Ansell in the Milton Keynes County Court to strike out the particulars of claim on the ground that the alleged facts disclosed no cause of action at common law. The judge did so. Mr Johnson appealed to the Court of Appeal (Lord Woolf MR, Hutchison and Tuckey LJJ) which affirmed the judge's decision. Mr Johnson now appeals to your Lordships' House.

g [35] My Lords, the first question is whether the implied term of trust and confidence upon which Mr Johnson relies, and about which in a general way there is no real dispute, or any of the other implied terms, applies to a dismissal. At common law the contract of employment was regarded by the courts as a contract like any other. The parties were free to negotiate whatever terms they h liked and no terms would be implied unless they satisfied the strict test of necessity applied to a commercial contract. Freedom of contract meant that the stronger party, usually the employer, was free to impose his terms upon the weaker. But over the last 30 years or so, the nature of the contract of employment has been transformed. It has been recognised that a person's j employment is usually one of the most important things in his or her life. It gives not only a livelihood but an occupation, an identity and a sense of self-esteem. The law has changed to recognise this social reality. Most of the changes have been made by Parliament. The Employment Rights Act 1996 consolidates numerous statutes which have conferred rights upon employees. European law has made a substantial contribution. And the common law has adapted itself to the new attitudes, proceeding sometimes by analogy with statutory rights.

[36] The contribution of the common law to the employment revolution has been by the evolution of implied terms in the contract of employment. The most far-reaching is the implied term of trust and confidence. But there have been others. For example, in *Goold (W A) (Pearmak) Ltd v McConnell* [1995] IRLR 516, Morison J (sitting in the Employment Appeal Tribunal) said that it was an implied term of the contract of employment that an employer would reasonably and promptly afford employees an opportunity to obtain redress of grievances. He inferred such a term from what is now s 3 of the 1996 Act, which requires that an employee be provided with a written statement of the particulars of his employment, including a note of how he may apply if he has any grievances. So statute and common law have proceeded hand in hand.

[37] The problem lies in extending or adapting any of these implied terms to dismissal. There are two reasons why dismissal presents special problems. The first is that any terms which the courts imply into a contract must be consistent with the express terms. Implied terms may supplement the express terms of the contract but cannot contradict them. Only Parliament may actually override what the parties have agreed. The second reason is that judges, in developing the law, must have regard to the policies expressed by Parliament in legislation. Employment law requires a balancing of the interests of employers and employees, with proper regard not only to the individual dignity and worth of the employees but also to the general economic interest. Subject to observance of fundamental human rights, the point at which this balance should be struck is a matter for democratic decision. The development of the common law by the judges plays a subsidiary role. Their traditional function is to adapt and modernise the common law. But such developments must be consistent with legislative policy as expressed in statutes. The courts may proceed in harmony with Parliament but there should be no discord.

[38] My Lords, I shall consider first the problem posed by the express terms of the contract. In developing the implied term of trust and confidence and other similar terms applicable to the continuing employment relationship, the courts were advancing across open country. No express provision that BCCI would be entitled to conduct a fraudulent business, or that the employer in the *Goold* case would have no grievance procedure, stood in their way. But the employer's right to dismiss the employee is strongly defended by the terms of the contract. In the present case, Mr Johnson's contract provided:

> 'If you decide to leave UNISYS you are required to give the company four weeks notice; equally, the company may terminate your employment on four weeks notice ... In the event of gross misconduct, the company may terminate your employment without notice.'

[39] The effect of such a provision at common law was stated with great clarity by McLachlin J of the Supreme Court of Canada in *Wallace v United Grain Growers Ltd* (1997) 152 DLR (4th) 1 at 39:

> 'The action for wrongful dismissal is based on an implied obligation in the employment contract to give reasonable notice of an intention to terminate the relationship (or pay in lieu thereof) in the absence of just cause for dismissal ... A "wrongful dismissal" action is not concerned with the wrongness or rightness of the dismissal itself. Far from making dismissal a wrong, the law entitles both employer and employee to terminate the employment relationship without cause. A wrong arises only if the employer

a breaches the contract by failing to give the dismissed employee reasonable notice of termination. The remedy for this breach of contract is an award of damages based on the period of notice which should have been given.'

[40] Likewise in *Malloch v Aberdeen Corp* [1971] 2 All ER 1278 at 1282, [1971] 1 WLR 1578 at 1581 Lord Reid said:

b 'At common law a master is not bound to hear his servant before he dismisses him. He can act unreasonably or capriciously if he so chooses but the dismissal is valid. The servant has no remedy unless the dismissal is in breach of contract and then the servant's only remedy is damages for breach of contract.'

c [41] The action for wrongful dismissal could therefore yield no more than the salary which should have been paid during the contractual period of notice. In the present case Mr Johnson's letter of engagement referred to terms and conditions of employment contained in the company's employee handbook, which stipulated expressly that 'The company reserves the right to make payment in d lieu of notice'. Unisys exercised that right.

[42] My Lords, in the face of this express provision that Unisys was entitled to terminate Mr Johnson's employment on four weeks' notice without any reason, I think it is very difficult to imply a term that the company should not do so except for some good cause and after giving him a reasonable opportunity to demonstrate that no such cause existed.

e [43] On the other hand, I do not say that there is nothing which, consistently with such an express term, judicial creativity could do to provide a remedy in a case like this. In *Wallace v United Grain Growers Ltd* (1997) 152 DLR (4th) 1 at 44–48, McLachlin J (in a minority judgment) said that the courts could imply an obligation to exercise the power of dismissal in good faith. That did not mean f that the employer could not dismiss without cause. The contract entitled him to do so. But in so doing, he should be honest with the employee and refrain from untruthful, unfair or insensitive conduct. He should recognise that an employee losing his or her job was exceptionally vulnerable and behave accordingly. For breach of this implied obligation, McLachlin J would have awarded the employee, who had been dismissed in brutal circumstances, damages for mental g distress and loss of reputation and prestige.

[44] My Lords, such an approach would in this country have to circumvent or overcome the obstacle of *Addis v Gramophone Co Ltd* [1909] AC 488, [1908–10] All ER Rep 1, in which it was decided that an employee cannot recover damages for injured feelings, mental distress or damage to his reputation, arising out of the h manner of his dismissal. Speaking for myself, I think that, if this task was one which I felt called upon to perform, I would be able to do so. In *Malik v Bank of Credit and Commerce International SA (in liq), Mahmud v Bank of Credit and Commerce International SA (in liq)* [1997] 3 All ER 1 at 19–20, [1998] AC 20 at 51 Lord Steyn said that the true ratio of *Addis*'s case was that damages were recoverable only for j loss caused by a breach of contract, not for loss caused by the manner of its breach. As McLachlin J said in the passage I have quoted, the only loss caused by a wrongful dismissal flows from a failure to give proper notice or make payment in lieu. Therefore, if wrongful dismissal is the only cause of action, nothing can be recovered for mental distress or damage to reputation. On the other hand, if such damage is loss flowing from a breach of another implied term of the contract, *Addis*'s case does not stand in the way. That is why in *Malik*'s case itself,

damages were recoverable for financial loss flowing from damage to reputation caused by a breach of the implied term of trust and confidence. a

[45] In this case, Mr Johnson says likewise that his psychiatric injury is a consequence of a breach of the implied term of trust and confidence, which required Unisys to treat him fairly in the procedures for dismissal. He says that implied term now fills the gap which Lord Shaw of Dunfermline perceived and regretted in *Addis*'s case ([1909] AC 488 at 504–505, [1908–10] All ER Rep 1 at 11) b by creating a breach of contract additional to the dismissal itself.

[46] It may be a matter of words, but I rather doubt whether the term of trust and confidence should be pressed so far. In the way it has always been formulated, it is concerned with preserving the continuing relationship which should subsist between employer and employee. So it does not seem altogether appropriate for use in connection with the way that relationship is terminated. If c one is looking for an implied term, I think a more elegant solution is McLachlin J's implication of a separate term that the power of dismissal will be exercised fairly and in good faith. But the result would be the same as that for which Mr Johnson contends by invoking the implied term of trust and confidence. As I have said, I think it would be possible to reach such a conclusion without contradicting d the express term that the employer is entitled to dismiss without cause.

[47] I must however make it clear that, although in my opinion it would be jurisprudentially possible to imply a term which gave a remedy in this case, I do not think that even if the courts were free of legislative constraint (a point to which I shall return in a moment) it would necessarily be wise to do so. It is not simply an incremental step from the duty of trust and confidence implied in e *Malik*'s case. The close association between the acts alleged to be in breach of the implied term and the irremovable and lawful fact of dismissal give rise to special problems. So, in *Wallace v United Grain Growers Ltd* (1997) 152 DLR (4th) 1, the majority rejected an implied duty to exercise the power of dismissal in good faith. Iacobucci J said (at 28) that such a step was better left to the legislature. It would f be 'overly intrusive and inconsistent with established principles of employment law'.

[48] Some of the potential problems can be illustrated by the facts of this case, in which Mr Johnson claims some £400,000 damages for the financial consequences of psychiatric damage. This form of damage notoriously gives rise at the best of times to extremely difficult questions of causation. But the difficulties are made g greater when the expert witnesses are required to perform the task of distinguishing between the psychiatric consequences of the fact of dismissal (for which no damages are recoverable) and the unfair circumstances in which the dismissal took place, which constituted a breach of the implied term. The agreed statement of facts records that for the purposes of this appeal against a strike-out h it is accepted that Mr Johnson's psychiatric illness was caused by 'the circumstances and the fact' of his dismissal. At a trial, however, it would be necessary to decide what was caused by what.

[49] Another difficulty is the open-ended nature of liability. Mr Johnson's case is that Unisys had knowledge of his psychological fragility by reason of facts j lodged in the corporate memory in 1985–1987 and therefore should have foreseen when he was engaged that a failure to comply with proper disciplinary procedures on dismissal might result in injury which deprived him of the ability ever to work again. On general common law principles it seems to me that if the necessary term is implied and these facts are made out, the claim should succeed. It may be that such liability would be grossly disproportionate to the employer's

a degree of fault. It may be likely to inhibit the future engagement of psychologically fragile personnel. But the common law decides cases according to principle and cannot impose arbitrary limitations on liability because of the circumstances of the particular case. Only statute can lay down limiting rules based upon policy rather than principle. In this connection it is interesting to notice that although the majority in *Wallace*'s case were unwilling to accept an implied term as to the b manner of dismissal, they treated it as relevant to the period of notice which should reasonably have been given. McLachlin J said that this was illogical and so perhaps it is. But one can understand a desire to place some limit upon the employer's potential liability under this head.

[50] It follows, my Lords, that if there was no relevant legislation in this area, I would regard the question of whether judges should develop the law by c implying a suitable term into the contract of employment as finely balanced. But now I must consider the statutory background against which your Lordships are invited to create such a cause of action.

[51] In 1968 the Royal Commission on Trade Unions and Employers' Associations under Lord Donovan recommended a statutory system of remedies d for unfair dismissal. The recommendation was accepted by the government and given effect in the Industrial Relations Act 1971. Unfair dismissal was a wholly new statutory concept with new statutory remedies. Exclusive jurisdiction to hear complaints and give remedies was conferred upon the newly created National Industrial Relations Court. Although the 1971 Act was repealed by the Trade Union and Labour Relations Act 1974, the unfair dismissal provisions were e re-enacted and, as subsequently amended, are consolidated in Pt X of the Employment Rights Act 1996. The jurisdiction is now exercised by employment tribunals and forms part of the fabric of English employment law.

[52] Section 94(1) of the 1996 Act provides that 'an employee has the right not to be unfairly dismissed by his employer'. The 1996 Act contains elaborate f provisions dealing with what counts as dismissal and with the concept of unfairness, which may relate to the substantive reason for dismissal or (as in this case) the procedure adopted. Over the past 30 years, the appellate courts have developed a substantial body of case law on these matters. Certain classes of employees are altogether excluded from the protection of the 1996 Act. Section 108 excludes those who have not had one year's continuous service and s 109 g excludes those over normal retiring age or 65. The tribunal may make an order for reinstatement, re-engagement or compensation. The latter consists of a basic award and a compensatory award. The basic award is related to the period of service but, by s 122(2), may be reduced by such amount as the tribunal considers just and equitable on account of the complainant's conduct before dismissal. A h compensatory award under s 123(1) shall be, subject to qualifications:

> '... such amount as the tribunal considers just and equitable in all the circumstances having regard to the loss sustained by the complainant in consequence of the dismissal in so far as that loss is attributable to action taken by the employer.'

j

[53] By sub-s (6), the tribunal may reduce the compensatory award by such amount as it considers just and equitable to take into account a finding that the complainant himself caused or contributed to his dismissal. These were the provisions applied by the tribunal in the present case to reduce Mr Johnson's award by 25%. Finally, s 124(1) limits a compensatory award to £50,000. This figure was substituted by s 34(4) of the Employment Relations Act 1999 with effect from 25 October 1999. Previously the maximum had been £12,000 and the applicable figure at the time of the award to Mr Johnson was £11,000. *a*

[54] My Lords, this statutory system for dealing with unfair dismissals was set up by Parliament to deal with the recognised deficiencies of the law as it stood at the time of *Malloch v Aberdeen Corp* [1971] 2 All ER 1278, [1971] 1 WLR 1578. The remedy adopted by Parliament was not to build upon the common law by creating a statutory implied term that the power of dismissal should be exercised *b* fairly or in good faith, leaving the courts to give a remedy on general principles of contractual damages. Instead, it set up an entirely new system outside the ordinary courts, with tribunals staffed by a majority of lay members, applying new statutory concepts and offering statutory remedies. Many of the new rules, such as the exclusion of certain classes of employees and the limit on the amount of the compensatory award, were not based upon any principle which it would *c* have been open to the courts to apply. They were based upon policy and represented an attempt to balance fairness to employees against the general economic interests of the community. And I should imagine that Parliament also had in mind the practical difficulties I have mentioned about causation and proportionality which would arise if the remedy was unlimited. So Parliament *d* adopted the practical solution of giving the tribunals a very broad jurisdiction to award what they considered just and equitable but subject to a limit on the amount.

[55] In my opinion, all the matters of which Mr Johnson complains in these proceedings were within the jurisdiction of the industrial tribunal. His most substantial complaint is of financial loss flowing from his psychiatric injury which *e* he says was a consequence of the unfair manner of his dismissal. Such loss is a consequence of the dismissal which may form the subject matter of a compensatory award. The only doubtful question is whether it would have been open to the tribunal to include a sum by way of compensation for his distress, damage to family life and similar matters. As the award, even reduced by 25%, *f* exceeded the statutory maximum and had to be reduced to £11,000, the point would have been academic. But perhaps I may be allowed a comment all the same. I know that in the early days of the National Industrial Relations Court it was laid down that only financial loss could be compensated: see *Norton Tool Co Ltd v Tewson* [1973] 1 All ER 183, [1973] 1 WLR 45; *Wellman Alloys Ltd v Russell* [1973] ICR 616. It was said that the word 'loss' can only mean financial loss. But *g* I think that is too narrow a construction. The emphasis is upon the tribunal awarding such compensation as it thinks just and equitable. So I see no reason why in an appropriate case it should not include compensation for distress, humiliation, damage to reputation in the community or to family life.

[56] Part X of the 1996 Act therefore gives a remedy for exactly the conduct of *h* which Mr Johnson complains. But Parliament had restricted that remedy to a maximum of £11,000, whereas Mr Johnson wants to claim a good deal more. The question is whether the courts should develop the common law to give a parallel remedy which is not subject to any such limit.

[57] My Lords, I do not think that it is a proper exercise of the judicial function *j* of the House to take such a step. Judge Ansell, to whose unreserved judgment I would pay respectful tribute, went in my opinion to the heart of the matter when he said:

> '... there is not one hint in the authorities that the ... tens of thousands of people that appear before the tribunals can have, as it were, a possible second

a bite in common law and I ask myself, if this is the situation, why on earth do we have this special statutory framework? What is the point of it if it can be circumvented in this way ... it would mean that effectively the statutory limit on compensation for unfair dismissal would disappear.'

[58] I can see no answer to these questions. For the judiciary to construct a b general common law remedy for unfair circumstances attending dismissal would be to go contrary to the evident intention of Parliament that there should be such a remedy but that it should be limited in application and extent.

[59] The same reason is in my opinion fatal to the claim based upon a duty of care. It is of course true that a duty of care can exist independently of the contractual relationship. But the grounds upon which I think it would be wrong c to impose an implied contractual duty would make it equally wrong to achieve the same result by the imposition of a duty of care.

[60] There is one further point. During the argument there was some discussion of whether the provisions for disciplinary hearings were express terms of Mr Johnson's contract and what the consequences would be if they were. No d such express terms were pleaded and Mr Faulks QC, who appeared for Mr Johnson, was not enthusiastic about doing so. Nevertheless, it may be useful to examine the matter in a little more detail.

[61] Section 1(1) of the 1996 Act provides that upon commencing employment, an employee shall be provided with 'a written statement of particulars of e employment'. This includes, but is not limited to, the 'terms and conditions' of employment concerning various matters, including 'the length of notice which the employee is obliged to give and entitled to receive to terminate his contract of employment' (s 1(4)(e)). Section 3(1) then provides that a statement under s 1 shall include a 'note ... specifying any disciplinary rules applicable to the employee or referring the employee to the provisions of a document specifying f such rules which is reasonably accessible to the employee'.

[62] Consistently with these provisions, Mr Johnson was written a letter of engagement which stated his salary and summarised the terms and conditions of his employment, including the notice period. Apart from the statement that in the event of gross misconduct, the company could terminate his employment g without notice, it made no reference to disciplinary matters. It was however accompanied by the employee handbook, which the letter of engagement said 'outlines all the terms and conditions of employment'. This was divided into various sections, the first being headed 'Employment terms and conditions'. These made no reference to the disciplinary procedure, which appeared in a h subsequent section under the heading 'Other procedures'. There one could find the various stages of the disciplinary procedure: formal verbal warning, written warning, final written warning, culminating in dismissal, as well as the separate procedure for summary dismissal in cases of serious misconduct.

[63] So did the disciplinary procedures constitute express terms of the contract j of employment? Perhaps for some purposes they did. But the employee handbook has to be construed against the relevant background and the background which fairly looms over the disciplinary procedure is Pt X of the 1996 Act. The whole disciplinary procedure is designed to ensure that an employee is not unfairly dismissed. So the question is whether the provisions about disciplinary procedure which (to use a neutral phrase) applied to Mr Johnson's employment were intended to operate within the scope of the law of unfair

dismissal or whether they were intended also to be actionable at common law, giving rise to claims for damages in the ordinary courts.

a

[**64**] Section 199(1) of the Trade Union and Labour Relations (Consolidation) Act 1992 gives the Advisory, Concilliation and Arbitration Service (ACAS) power to issue 'Codes of Practice containing such practical guidance as it thinks fit for the purpose of promoting the improvement of industrial relations'. By s 207, a failure to comply with any provision of a code is not in itself actionable but in any proceedings before an industrial tribunal 'any provision of the Code which appears ... relevant to any question arising in the proceedings shall be taken into account in determining that question.' In 1977 ACAS issued a code of practice entitled 'Disciplinary Practice and Procedures in Employment'. It explained why it was important to have disciplinary rules and procedures which were in writing and readily available to management and employees. It said in para 4:

b

c

> 'The importance of disciplinary rules and procedures has also been recognised by the law relating to dismissals, since the grounds for dismissal and the way in which the dismissal has been handled can be challenged before an industrial tribunal.'

d

[**65**] In para 10 it listed what disciplinary procedures should include. The Unisys procedures have clearly been framed with regard to the Code of Practice.

[**66**] My Lords, given this background to the disciplinary procedures, I find it impossible to believe that Parliament, when it provided in s 3(1) of the 1996 Act that the statement of particulars of employment was to contain a note of any applicable disciplinary rules, or the parties themselves, intended that the inclusion of those rules should give rise to a common law action in damages which would create the means of circumventing the restrictions and limits which Parliament had imposed on compensation for unfair dismissal. The whole of the reasoning which led me to the conclusion that the courts should not imply a term which has this result also in my opinion supports the view that the disciplinary procedures do not do so either. It is I suppose possible that they may have contractual effect in determining whether the employer can dismiss summarily in the sense of not having to give four weeks' notice or payment in lieu. But I do not think that they can have been intended to qualify the employer's common law power to dismiss without cause on giving such notice, or to create contractual duties which are independently actionable.

e

f

g

[**67**] I would dismiss the appeal.

LORD MILLETT. My Lords,

[**68**] I have had the advantage of reading in draft the speech of my noble and learned friend Lord Hoffmann, with which I am in full agreement. I add some words of my own in order to explain why I consider that the present is not an appropriate occasion in which to revisit the decision of your Lordships' House in *Addis v Gramophone Co Ltd* [1909] AC 488, [1908–10] All ER Rep 1.

h

[**69**] That case established the principle that damages are awarded for breach of contract and not for the manner of the breach; accordingly nothing can be recovered for mental distress, anxiety, injury to feelings or (so it is said) damage to reputation. The case was concerned with a contract of employment and the actual decision was that damages for wrongful dismissal are limited to compensation for the financial loss arising from the premature determination of the contract where proper notice of dismissal has not been given: they cannot include compensation for the employee's injured feelings because he has been

j

a dismissed in an offensive and humiliating manner. The principle, however, is not limited to contracts of employment but is of general application in the law of contract.

[**70**] The supposed rule that damages are not recoverable for financial loss arising from injury to reputation (or in a case of wrongful dismissal for making it more difficult for the plaintiff to find employment) is not easy to defend and may b no longer be the law after *Malik v Bank of Credit and Commerce International SA (in liq), Mahmud v Bank of Credit and Commerce International SA (in liq)* [1997] 3 All ER 1, [1998] AC 20. My noble and learned friend Lord Steyn has argued powerfully that it never was the law, being derived from a faulty headnote which misrepresented the true ratio decidendi of the case. Subject to this caveat, however, the general rule would seem to be a sound one, at least in relation to c ordinary commercial contracts entered into by both parties with a view of profit. In such cases non-pecuniary loss such as mental suffering consequent on breach is not within the contemplation of the parties and is accordingly too remote. The ordinary feelings of anxiety, frustration and disappointment caused by any breach of contract are also excluded, but seemingly for the opposite reason: they are so d commonly a consequence of a breach of contract that the parties must be regarded not only as having foreseen it but as having agreed to take the risk of its occurrence: see Treitel *The Law of Contract* (10th edn, 1999) p 923. Contracts which are not purely commercial but which have as their object the provision of enjoyment, comfort, peace of mind or other non-pecuniary personal or family benefits (as in *Jarvis v Swan Tours Ltd* [1973] 1 All ER 71, [1973] QB 233 and similar e cases) are usually treated as exceptions to the general rule, though in truth they would seem to fall outside its rationale. Such injury is not only within the contemplation of the parties but is the direct result of the breach itself and not the manner of the breach. Indeed the avoidance of just such non-pecuniary injury can be said to be a principal object of the contract.

f [**71**] In *Addis*'s case the House of Lords treated a contract of employment as an ordinary commercial contract terminable at will by either party provided only that sufficient notice was given in accordance with the terms of the contract. This was the classical approach to such contracts which the House of Lords was content to confirm more than half a century later. In *Ridge v Baldwin* [1963] 2 All ER 66 at 71, [1964] AC 40 at 65 Lord Reid observed that an employer can terminate g the contract of employment at any time and for any reason or for none. It follows that the question whether damages are recoverable does not depend on whether the employer had a good reason for dismissing the employee, or had heard him in his own defence, or had acted fairly towards him: it depends on whether the dismissal was in breach of contract. In *Malloch v Aberdeen Corp* [1971] 2 All ER h 1278 at 1282, [1971] 1 WLR 1578 at 1581 Lord Reid restated the position:

> 'At common law a master is not bound to hear his servant before he dismisses him. He can act unreasonably or capriciously if he so chooses but the dismissal is valid. The servant has no remedy unless the dismissal is in breach of contract and then the servant's only remedy is damages for breach j of contract.'

[**72**] The common law, which is premissed on party autonomy, treated the employer and the employee as free and equal parties to the contract of employment. Each had the right, granted by the contract itself, to bring the contract to an end in accordance with its terms. But by 1971 there was a widespread feeling, shared by both sides of industry, that the legal position was

unsatisfactory. In reality there was no comparison between the consequences for an employer if the employee terminated his employment and the consequences for an employee if he was dismissed. Many people build their lives round their jobs and plan their future in the expectation that they will continue. For many workers dismissal is a disaster. In 1964 the Government announced that it would discuss with representatives of employers and trade unions the provision of procedures to give employees effective safeguards against arbitrary dismissal. In 1968 the Royal Commission on Trade Unions and Employers' Associations under the chairmanship of Lord Donovan reported that it was urgently necessary for employees to be given better protection against unfair dismissal and recommended the establishment of statutory machinery to achieve this.

[73] The recommendations of the Royal Commission were given effect by the Industrial Relations Act 1971. This left the common law and the contract of employment itself unaffected. It did not import implied terms into the contract. Instead it created a new statutory right not to be unfairly dismissed, enforceable in the newly established National Industrial Relations Court. The 1971 Act was replaced by the Employment Protection Act 1975 and its provisions as amended are now contained in the Employment Rights Act 1996. The National Industrial Relations Court was short-lived and the jurisdiction in respect of unfair dismissal has for many years been exercised by industrial tribunals (now known as employment tribunals). These consist of a legally qualified chairman sitting with two lay members, one being a representative of the trade unions and the other of employers.

[74] For the first time the 1971 Act enabled an employee to challenge his employer's conduct in exercising his legal rights on the ground that it was unreasonable. The Act contained elaborate provisions which defined the concept and scope of unfair dismissal and provided for compensation to be awarded or reinstatement or re-engagement to be ordered. It set an upper limit to the amount of compensation which could be awarded, which has since been increased from time to time, and allowed the tribunal to reduce the amount of an award if it considered that the employee had caused or contributed to his own dismissal. It provided for an upper age limit and a qualifying period of employment (which has since been reduced but not abrogated) thereby excluding certain categories of employees from its scope altogether.

[75] During the past 30 years an extensive jurisprudence has been developed in relation to unfair dismissal. Employers have responded to the existence of the statutory right, as the Royal Commission intended that they should, by introducing elaborate procedures of complaint and warning before eventual dismissal which, whether or not contractually binding, are designed to ensure that employees are not unfairly dismissed. Since the right not to be unfairly dismissed is a statutory right which is not derived from contract, however, it is still open to an employee to claim that he has been unfairly dismissed even if his employer has faithfully complied with the contractual procedures.

[76] Section 205 of the 1996 Act provides that some claims under the Act (including a claim in respect of unfair dismissal) must be brought by way of complaint to an industrial tribunal and not otherwise. This is a new provision made necessary because the 1996 Act (unlike its predecessor) gives industrial tribunals a limited jurisdiction in respect of some common law claims. The 1971 Act did not expressly provide that the jurisdiction of the industrial tribunals was exclusive, but it did not need to. It was clearly predicated on the existing state of the law as established in *Addis*'s case and confirmed in *Malloch*'s case. There

a would have been no point (for example) in excluding certain categories of employee from obtaining compensation for unfair dismissal if they could obtain a remedy by way of damages at common law; or for enabling the industrial tribunal to reduce the amount of compensation by reference to the employee's own conduct if the employee could obtain damages at common law without any such reduction. Prior to 1996, therefore, the jurisdiction of the industrial tribunals b to award compensation for unfair dismissal was exclusive in practice, not because it was made so by statute, but because it was premissed on the absence of a corresponding remedy at common law.

[77] But the common law does not stand still. It is in a state of continuous judicial development in order to reflect the changing perceptions of the community. Contracts of employment are no longer regarded as purely commercial contracts c entered into between free and equal agents. It is generally recognised today that 'work is one of the defining features of people's lives'; that 'loss of one's job is always a traumatic event'; and that it can be 'especially devastating' when dismissal is accompanied by bad faith: see *Wallace v United Grain Growers Ltd* (1997) 152 DLR (4th) 1 at 33 per Iacobucci J. This change of perception is, of d course, partly due to the creation by Parliament of the statutory right not to be unfairly dismissed. If this right had not existed, however, it is possible that the courts would have fashioned a similar remedy at common law, though they would have proceeded by implying appropriate terms into the contract of employment. It would have been a major step to subject the employer's right to terminate the relationship on proper notice to an obligation not to exercise the e right in bad faith, and a still greater step to subject it to an obligation not to exercise it without reasonable cause (a difficult distinction, but one drawn by McLachlin J in *Wallace*'s case (at 44)). Even so, these are steps which, in the absence of the statutory right, the courts might have been prepared to take, though there would have been a powerful argument for leaving the reform to f Parliament. If the courts had taken the step themselves, they could have awarded common law damages for unfair dismissal consistently with *Addis*'s case, because such damages would be awarded for the breach of an implied but independently actionable term (as in *Malik*'s case) and not for wrongful dismissal. But the courts would have been faced with the difficult task of distinguishing between the mental distress and other non-pecuniary injury consequent upon the unfairness g of the dismissal (for which the employer would be liable) and the similar injury consequent upon the dismissal itself (for which he would not). In practice, they would probably have been reduced to awarding conventional sums by way of general damages much as the industrial tribunals do.

[78] I agree with Lord Hoffmann that it would not have been appropriate to h found the right on the implied term of trust and confidence which is now generally imported into the contract of employment. This is usually expressed as an obligation binding on both parties not to do anything which would damage or destroy the relationship of trust and confidence which should exist between them. But this is an inherent feature of the relationship of employer and j employee which does not survive the ending of the relationship. The implied obligation cannot sensibly be used to extend the relationship beyond its agreed duration. Moreover, manipulating it for such a purpose would be unrealistic. An employer who summarily dismisses an employee usually does so because, rightly or wrongly, he no longer has any trust or confidence in him, and the real issue is: whose fault is that? That is why reinstatement or re-engagement is effected in only a tiny proportion of the cases that come before the industrial tribunals.

[**79**] But the courts might well have developed the law in a different way by imposing a more general obligation upon an employer to treat his employee fairly even in the manner of his dismissal. They could not, of course, have overridden any express terms of the contract or have held the dismissal itself to be invalid. As in the case of the statutory right, employers would probably have responded by introducing their own procedures of complaint and warning before eventual dismissal. But there would have been this difference; they would surely have taken care to incorporate such procedures into the contract of employment so that an employee who was dismissed in accordance with the procedure laid down in his contract could not claim damages for breach of an implied term.

[**80**] But the creation of the statutory right has made any such development of the common law both unnecessary and undesirable. In the great majority of cases the new common law right would merely replicate the statutory right; and it is obviously unnecessary to imply a term into a contract to give one of the contracting parties a remedy which he already has without it. In other cases, where the common law would be giving a remedy in excess of the statutory limits or to excluded categories of employees, it would be inconsistent with the declared policy of Parliament. In all cases it would allow claims to be entertained by the ordinary courts when it was the policy of Parliament that they should be heard by specialist tribunals with members drawn from both sides of industry. And, even more importantly, the co-existence of two systems, overlapping but varying in matters of detail and heard by different tribunals, would be a recipe for chaos. All coherence in our employment laws would be lost.

[**81**] For these reasons it is a step which, for one, I am not prepared to take. For the same reasons I am satisfied that it would not be appropriate to attempt to achieve the same result by taking the novel course of subjecting the employer's contractual rights to a tortious duty of care.

[**82**] I would dismiss the appeal.

Appeal dismissed.

Kate O'Hanlon Barrister.

Peacock and another v Custins and another

COURT OF APPEAL, CIVIL DIVISION

SCHIEMANN, MANCE LJJ AND SMITH J

4 OCTOBER, 14 NOVEMBER 2000

Easement – Right of way – Extent – Claimants owning land with express right of way over defendants' land – Claimants owning another parcel of land adjacent to dominant tenement – Whether right of way could be used for purpose of cultivating land adjacent to dominant tenement.

The claimants owned a 15-acre parcel of land (the red land) which enjoyed the benefit of a right of way over a roadway owned by the defendants. That right, which had been granted in the conveyance of the red land to the claimants, was expressed to be 'at all times and for all purposes in connection with the use and enjoyment of the property hereby conveyed'. The claimants also owned another 10-acre parcel of land (the blue land) adjacent to the red land. The two parcels of land were farmed as one unit by the claimants' tenant, and he used the right of way for the purpose of farming both parcels. In proceedings brought by the claimants, the defendants counterclaimed for a declaration that the claimants were not entitled to use the right of way for the purpose of gaining access to the blue land. At the hearing, the claimants' tenant gave uncontested evidence that he needed to use the way about half a dozen times a year, and that farming the blue and red land required one or two more visits than would have been necessary if he had merely been farming the red land. The judge held that if the right of way was exercised for the purpose of farming the red land but at the same time opportunity was taken to enter the blue land from the red land as part of that farming activity, such a use of the right of way would not bring about an exceptional user or be in excess of the grant, provided that there was no significant additional user of the right of way. Applying that test, he refused to grant the declaration sought by the defendants. On appeal, the defendants did not press their entitlement to a declaration in the terms previously sought. Instead, they sought a declaration that the claimants were not entitled to use the right of way for the purpose of accessing the blue land in order to cultivate it, contending that such user was outside the scope of the grant and therefore constituted a trespass. The claimants contended that there would be no trespass unless either the use of the servient tenement was for the primary purpose of accessing the blue land or the use of the servient tenement for eventual access to the blue land increased the practical burden on it.

Held – The right to use a right of way was determined by the terms of the grant, specifying the dominant tenement for the purposes of which the right had been created, and trespass was whatever was not permitted by the grant. It was not a right to use a way for the purposes of benefiting any property provided that the total user did not exceed some notional maximum user which the beneficiary might have been entitled to make for the purposes of the dominant tenement. If that were the test, the beneficiary might in some circumstances use the way entirely for purposes other than those of the dominant tenement. The right was to use the way for the purposes of the dominant tenement only. The grant, when made, had a notional value, which would be identified by reference to those purposes and their likely impact. Use for other purposes would be likely to carry its own notional commercial value. Moreover, where the court was being asked to declare whether the right to use a way comprised a right to use it to facilitate the cultivation of land other than the dominant tenement, the court was not concerned with any comparison between the amount of use made or to be made of the servient tenement and the amount of use made or which might lawfully be made within the scope of the grant. Rather, it was concerned with declaring the scope of the grant, having regard to its purposes and the identity of the dominant tenement. Although the authorities indicated that the burden on the servient owner was not to be increased without his consent, burden in that context did not refer to the number of journeys or the weight of the vehicles. Any use of the way was, in contemplation of law, a burden, and it was necessary to ask whether the grantor agreed to the grantee making use of the way for that purpose. In the instant case, the claimants were claiming to use a way, granted for the limited purposes of the 15 acres of red land, for the extended or additional purpose of accessing and cultivating at the same time the further 10 acres of the blue land. That extended or additional use was of self-evident commercial value to the claimants, but any value attaching to it could not have been embraced in the notional value attached to the actual right of way for the benefit of the red land. Such use, which could not sensibly be described as ancillary to the cultivation of the red land, had clearly not been authorised by the grantor. Accordingly, the appeal would be allowed (see p 835 *f* to p 836 *g*, post).

Harris v Flower (1904) 74 LJ Ch 127 applied.

Notes

For limits on the use of the right of way by the dominant owner, see 14 *Halsbury's Laws* (4th edn reissue) para 147.

Cases referred to in judgment

Alvis v Harrison (1990) 62 P & CR 10, HL.
Harris v Flower & Sons (1904) 74 LJ Ch 127, CA.
Inverugie Investments Ltd v Hackett Ltd [1995] 3 All ER 841, [1995] 1 WLR 713, PC.
Jobson v Record [1998] 9 EG 148, CA.
Keefe v Amor [1964] 2 All ER 517, [1965] 1 QB 334, [1964] 3 WLR 183, CA.
Ladbroke Group plc v Bristol City Council [1988] 1 EGLR 126, CA.
Miller v Tipling (1918) 43 DLR 469, Ont SC.
Skull v Glenister (1864) 16 CB (NS) 81, 143 ER 1055.
Stoke-on-Trent City Council v W & J Wass Ltd [1988] 3 All ER 394, [1988] 1 WLR 1406, CA.
White v Richards (1993) 68 P & CR 105, CA.
Williams v James (1867) LR 2 CP 577.
Youell v Bland Welch & Co Ltd [1992] 2 Lloyd's Rep 127, CA.

Cases cited or referred to in skeleton arguments

Bracewell v Appleby [1975] 1 All ER 993, [1975] Ch 408.
National Trust for Places of Historic Interest or Natural Beauty v White [1987] 1 WLR 90.
Record v Bell [1991] 4 All ER 471, [1991] 1 WLR 853.

Appeal

Frank Custins and Teresa Mary Custins, the defendants to proceedings brought by the claimants, David Valentine John Peacock and Annie Sarah Jane Peacock, a appealed with permission of Mance LJ granted on 21 October 1999 from the order of Judge Sheerin made at Cambridge County Court on 2 July 1999, giving effect to his decision of 18 December 1998, dismissing the defendants' counterclaim for a declaration that the claimants were not entitled to use a right of way over the defendants' land for the purpose of gaining access to a parcel of land adjacent to the dominant tenement. The facts are set out in the judgment b of the court.

Timothy Morshead (instructed by *Birketts*, Ipswich) for the defendants.
Thomas Dumont (instructed by *Taylor Vintners*, Cambridge) for the claimants.

Cur adv vult

c

14 November 2000. The following judgment of the court was delivered.

SCHIEMANN LJ.

1. This is an appeal from the late Judge Sheerin which raises one point of d general significance in relation to the law of easements and a number of other points which are specific to the facts of the present case. The point of general significance is this: where the owner of a dominant tenement possesses a right of way for all purposes over a servient tenement, may he make any and if so what use of that right of way to access and cultivate (in conjunction with the dominant e tenement) other property of his which lies adjacent to the dominant tenement? The defendants, by their counterclaim, contend that this involves a trespass, on the basis that the purpose of accessing and cultivating the other property is outside the scope of the right of way granted. The claimants contend that there is no trespass in such a case unless either the use of the servient tenement is for the primary purpose of accessing the adjacent land or the use of servient f tenement for eventual access to the adjacent land increases the practical burden on the servient tenement.

2. For the purposes of the principal question the facts can be stated shortly. The defendants own a house, No 33 The Row, and a strip of land to the east, which we shall refer to as the yellow strip, which is the servient tenement. They g acquired title by deed on 25 January 1977. The property is described in the conveyance parcels as:

> 'All that piece or parcel of freehold land having a frontage to The Row, Sutton ... of 77 feet or thereabouts ... together with the dwelling house erected thereon and known as 33 The Row Sutton aforesaid all which said h property is shown edged green and yellow on the plan annexed hereto ... subject to a right of way at all times and for all purposes in favour of the owner or occupier for the time being of the property adjoining the rear of the property herein described all which said right of way is for the purpose of identification only edged yellow on the said plan annexed hereto.'

j

The plan annexed to that conveyance the judge referred to as plan 1 and again we shall do the same. The dominant tenement, namely 'the property adjoining the rear of the property' is in the ownership of the claimants and we shall refer to it as the red land.

3. The claimants had acquired title to the red land and to the easement by a conveyance dated 21 April 1976. The vendors conveyed:

> 'All those pieces or parcels of land situate in The Row Sutton in the county of Cambridgeshire containing 14.915 acres (more or less) all which said pieces or parcels of land are for the purpose of identification only delineated and edged red on the plan annexed hereto ... TOGETHER WITH the benefit of the right of way at all times and for all purposes in connection with the use and enjoyment of the property hereby conveyed ... over the roadway coloured yellow on the said plan ...'

a

b

The plan clearly identifies three rectangular plots adjacent to one another running north-south and having a total area of 14.915 acres. To the north of the most northern of those three plots is shown a rectangular strip coloured yellow running northwards until it meets The Row which runs east-west. To the west of the yellow strip is No 33 The Row. The plan attached to this conveyance dated 21 April 1976 was referred to throughout the trial as plan 2 and we shall do the same.

c

4. The claimants used to own a property, consisting of a house with land behind, known as No 39 The Row which lies further west than No 33. It consisted of a relatively small frontage to The Row and a long strip behind it which widened out. Once one moves away from The Row, where No 39 was separated from No 33 (by presumably Nos 35 and 37) one finds that the land behind the house standing on No 39 marches along the western edge of the red land. On plan 2 the whole of No 39 is shown edged blue. All of the land edged blue used to be accessed from The Row through No 39. In February 1997 the claimant sold part of No 39: the house and the four acres immediately behind it. He however failed to reserve any right of access by that route to the remainder of the land to which he retained title. We shall refer to the land over which he retained title as the blue land.

d

e

5. Thus it came about that the claimants owned the blue land and the red land. They are entitled to access the red land by means of the yellow strip. But are they ever entitled to use the yellow strip to gain access to the red land and thence to the blue land and, if so, in what circumstances? Those are the main points which fall for decision. In the action the defendants by counterclaim sought a declaration that the plaintiffs were not entitled to use the right of way over the yellow strip for the purpose of gaining access to the blue land. That declaration the judge refused to make and the defendants appeal that refusal. No other relief was sought by the counterclaim.

f

g

6. The judge found that the red land and the blue land were farmed as one unit. The red land was about 15 acres and the blue land ten acres more or less. The two fields were interconnected. The land was let to tenant farmer Mr Veale. He used the access for the purpose of farming both the red and the blue land. He did not claim to use the yellow roadway for the purpose of accessing the red land and then, as an incidental activity, picnic or stroll on the blue land. The defendants, rightly, do not contend that incidental activity of this nature would involve any excess of grant. But Mr Veale was using the access for the joint purpose of cultivating both properties, the red and the blue. His evidence was unchallenged that he might have to make one or two more visits with his tractor to farm the blue and red land than he would to farm merely the red land. The defendant accepted that so far Mr Veale had only used the access way on a couple of occasions and would appear to have need to use it on only about half a dozen times a year. The judge held that the actual use both at the present time and contemplated by Mr Veale was not excessive in quantitative terms. He stated

h

j

a that he was satisfied that access over the yellow roadway was never likely to be greatly increased by making access to the blue land as well as the red land. He concluded his judgment as follows:

> 'I accept and respectfully adopt the proposition of Romer LJ in *Harris v Flower & Sons* (1904) 74 LJ Ch 127 at 132: "If a right of way be granted for the enjoyment of Close A, the grantee, because he owns or requires Close B, b cannot use the way in substance for passing over the Close A to Close B." So in certain particular circumstances, which I am satisfied have not arisen here, the plaintiffs, or those authorised by them, would not be entitled to claim a right of way to the blue land over the yellow roadway. However, if the access over the right of way is exercised for the purpose of farming the red c land and at the same time the opportunity is taken to enter the blue land from the red land as part of that farming activity and there is no significant additional user of the right of way, such a use of the right of way would not bring about exceptional user, nor would it be in excess of the grant. The plaintiff would be wise to ensure that the blue and the red land are cropped in an identical way each year. I decline to make the declaration sought.'

d

7. The declaration sought by the defendants was a declaration that the claimants are not entitled to use the right of way over the yellow strip for the purpose of gaining access to the blue land.

8. The defendants, while not pressing their entitlement to a declaration in the absolute terms sought, submit that to use the yellow strip for the purpose of e accessing the blue land in order to cultivate the blue land, as well as the permitted red land, is to trespass on the yellow land and that they are entitled to a declaration that the claimants are not entitled to use the yellow land for that purpose. They submit that the identity of the dominant tenement for the benefit of which the easement was granted appears clearly from the grant and that it is f not permissible to use the servient land for the purpose of benefiting the blue land which was never land for the benefit of which the easement was granted. They submit that if indeed the use of the yellow strip for the purpose of gaining access to the blue land is not permitted by virtue of the easement then they would be entitled to damages not only on the basis of damage to the yellow land or to No 33 but also on a user basis. We recall that Nicholls LJ explained in g *Stoke-on-Trent City Council v W & J Wass Ltd* [1988] 3 All ER 394, [1988] 1 WLR 1406, in a passage in effect approved by the Privy Council in *Inverugie Investments Ltd v Hackett Ltd* [1995] 3 All ER 841, [1995] 1 WLR 713, that—

> 'It is an established principle concerning the assessment of damages that a h person who has wrongfully used another's property without causing the latter any pecuniary loss may still be liable to that other for more than nominal damages. In general, he is liable to pay, as damages, a reasonable sum for the wrongful use he has made of that other's property.' (See [1988] 3 All ER 394 at 402, [1988] 1 WLR 1406 at 1416.)

j 9. The defendants submit that in those circumstances the making of a declaration is in principle desirable and was wrongly refused by the judge.

The law

10. The present state of the law appears from an examination of the following cases. *Harris v Flower & Sons* (1904) 74 LJ Ch 127 was a case where the defendant had been granted a right of way over the claimant's land. That grant was to enable

him to access what was referred to as the pink land. At the time of the grant of the right of way the defendant's predecessor in title was already the owner of property adjoining the pink land, which adjoining property was referred to as the white land. The white land consisted of a public house with its own access and some land to the rear of the public house. The land at the rear of the public house adjoined the rear portion of the pink land. Years after the grant a factory was erected partly on the white land and partly on the pink and the licensed premises were completely severed from the land at the rear. The question arose whether the right of way could be used in order to access that factory including that portion of it which stood on the white land. Swinfen Eady J held that the defendant was entitled so to use it since he was using the access way bona fide for the purpose of accessing the pink land none the less so because a portion of the building on the pink land extended to the white land. This decision was reversed by this court.

11. In his judgment Vaughan Williams LJ cited with approval two earlier cases: *Skull v Glenister* (1864) 16 CB (NS) 81, 143 ER 1055, which shows that 'a mere colourable use' of a way for the purpose of entering the dominant land (when the real purpose was some other) will fall outside the grant; and *Williams v James* (1867) LR 2 CP 577.

12. *Williams v James* concerned a right of way over the plaintiff's land for the benefit of 'Nine acre field' in its ordinary use as a field. Hay grown on both Nine acre field and the adjoining 'Parrott's land' had been mowed and stored on Nine acre field in the summer of 1866, and in September 1866 its whole bulk was sold to the defendant who carted it away over the plaintiff's land to the highway. The jury held that the original storage on Nine acre field had been done honestly and not in order to gain the advantage of the right of way. The stacking and subsequent dealing with the hay must have been regarded by the jury as being in the ordinary and reasonable use of Nine acre field (see all three judgments (1867) LR 2 CP 577 at 581, 582, 583). The test identified in all three judgments was whether Nine acre field was being used for purposes others than those included in its ordinary and reasonable use, although Bovill CJ added that 'If no additional burthen was cast upon the servient tenement the jury might well find that there had been only the ordinary and reasonable use of the right of way'. This test is also reflected in the following passages quoted by Vaughan Williams LJ to explain the decision:

> 'The circumstances under which the hay was stacked, and the purpose and object of the defendant in carrying it away, are questions for the jury. As I read the finding of the jury, the stacking and the subsequent dealing with the hay were in the honest and reasonable use of Nine acre field.' (See *Harris'* case (1904) 74 LJ Ch 127 at 130.)

13. In view of the jury's findings the plaintiff's claim therefore failed.

14. Having cited those cases, Vaughan Williams LJ continued (at 132):

> 'I cannot help thinking that there not only may be, but there must be, many things to be done in respect of the buildings on the white land which cannot be said to be mere adjuncts to the honest user of the right of way for the purposes of the pink land. To begin with, the first thing he was doing before the completion of the building was to use the right of way for the purpose of carrying materials onto the white land so as to erect that part of the building, and I cannot doubt that as time goes on he will probably use this right of way for the purpose of doing repairs on the white land; and under these

a circumstances it seems to me that, notwithstanding the fact that the buildings on the white and on the pink lands are intended to be used jointly for one purpose, yet that consideration does not exclude the inference that the user of the way is for the purpose of giving access to land to which the right of way is not appurtenant. The reason of it is that a right of way of this sort restricts the owner of the dominant tenement to the legitimate user of his b right; and the Court will not allow that which is in its nature a burthen on the owner of the servient tenement to be increased without his consent and beyond the terms of the grant ... The burthen imposed on the servient tenement must not be increased by allowing the owner of the dominant tenement to make a use of the way in excess of the grant. There can be no doubt in the present case that, if this building is used as factory, a heavy and c frequent traffic will arise which has not arisen before. This particular burthen could not have arisen without the user of the white land as well as of the pink. It is not a mere case of user of the pink land, with some usual offices on the white land connected with the buildings on the pink land. The whole object of this scheme is to include the profitably user of the white land as well d as of the pink, and I think the access is to be used for the very purpose of enabling the white land to be used profitably as well as the pink, and I think we ought under these circumstances to restrain this user.'

15. Romer LJ said (at 132–133):

e 'I think that it is impossible to say that this large building is to be regarded as if wholly erected on the land coloured pink, nor can it be said that every user of the way for the purposes of the land coloured white is one for the proper enjoyment of the land coloured pink. I will take one instance. The defendant has used, and claims a right to use, this right of way for the purpose of carrying building materials for the part of his buildings on the f land coloured white. That, to my mind, is a user of the right of way for passage over the land coloured pink for the enjoyment of this land coloured white. It is impossible to say that by reason of one building being on both lands the defendant has made the right of way which was granted for the enjoyment of the one a right of way for the enjoyment of both, and that is g what the defendant is really doing. That would substantially enlarge the grant of the right of way. The servient tenement is not obliged to submit to the carrying of building materials for the purpose I have indicated; and other incidences might easily be given which would result in using the right of way for purposes of the land coloured white, and not for the true and proper enjoyment of the land to which the way was appurtenant.'

h

16. Cozens-Hardy LJ stated (at 133):

'It is a right of way for all purposes—that is, for all purposes with reference to the dominant tenement. The question is whether the defendant has not attempted, and is not attempting, to enlarge the area of the dominant j tenement. The land coloured white is entirely landlocked by the acts of the defendant. The only access is by the passage over the land coloured pink; and it is, in my judgment, impossible to use the right of way so as to enlarge the dominant tenement in that manner.'

17. In *Jobson v Record* [1998] 9 EG 148 a right of way was granted for all purposes connected with the use and enjoyment of the dominant tenement as agricultural

land. The dominant tenement was used for the purpose of storing timber felled on neighbouring land and the question was whether the right of way could be used for the purpose of removing that timber. *Harris'* case was followed and the question was answered in the negative. Morritt LJ (at 149) saying:

> 'If the storage was a separate operation it was not an agricultural use of [the dominant tenement]. If it was not an operation separate from the felling of the timber, then the use of the right of way for the removal of the timber felled at [the neighbouring tenement] was in substance for the accommodation of [the neighbouring tenement]. Either way, the use of the right of way was not authorised by the terms of the grant.'

18. Sir Brian Neil and Simon Brown LJ agreed. The court may have taken a more limited view of use 'as agricultural land' than that adopted by the jury in *Williams v James*, but that is neither here nor there.

19. *Alvis v Harrison* (1990) 62 P & CR 10 is a Scottish case but it is common ground that in this respect the law of Scotland is the same as that of England. The facts were unusual. The dominant tenement lay on either side of the servient tenement which was a driveway running north-south leading to the A73 highway. On the west of the driveway, on part of the dominant tenement, stood a house. The owner of the house wished to construct a new drive to run eastwards from the driveway and thence to join the highway further east than the place where the servient tenement joined it. The owner of the servient tenement sought to stop him from doing so. It was held that he could not. Lord Jauncey of Tullichettle (at 15–16) delivering the only substantive speech said:

> 'Before turning to the facts of this case it may be convenient to state certain general principles applicable to servitude rights of access and their use … Where a right of access is granted in general terms the owner of the dominant tenement is entitled to exercise that right not only for the purpose of the use to which the tenement is then being put but also for any other lawful purpose to which it may be put thereafter … The right must be exercised *civiliter,* that is to say, reasonably and in a manner least burdensome to the servient tenement … For the better enjoyment of his right the dominant owner may improve the ground over which the right extends provided that he does not substantially alter the nature of the road nor otherwise prejudice the servient tenement … A servitude right of access enures to the benefit of the dominant tenement and no other. Thus is cannot communicated for the benefit of other tenements contiguous thereto … What they may not do, however, is to use the way, or permit its use by others, to obtain access to subjects other than the dominant tenement, whether or not they happen to be heritable proprietors of those other subjects. They may not, in short, increase the scope of the right of access, and in particular they may not use the way for the purpose of securing access for persons or goods to subjects contiguous to the dominant tenement by using the dominant tenement merely as a bridge between the end of the lane and the non dominant subjects…'

20. Later in his judgment after dealing with facts Lord Jauncey (at 16–17) said:

> '… it is quite wrong to treat the A73 as though it were another tenement contiguous to the woodlands. The underlying reason for restricting the benefit of a servitude right of access to the dominant tenement alone is that

a to use it for the benefit of a second or third tenement is likely to generate more traffic and so increase the burden. In this case, the appellant already has a right of access to the A73 over the driveway. The new road merely provides a substitute means of access without altering the volume of traffic.'

21. We were also referred to *Miller v Tipling* (1918) 43 DLR 469 where Mulock CJ Ex said (at 475):

b

'The law is well-established that a right of way appurtenant to a particular close must not be used colourably for the real purpose of reaching a different adjoining close. This does not mean that where the way has been used in accordance with the terms of the grant for the benefit of the land to which it c is appurtenant, the party having thus used it must retrace his steps. Having lawfully reached the dominant tenement, he may proceed therefrom to adjoining premises to which the way is not appurtenant; but, if his object is merely to pass over the dominant tenement in order to reach other premises that would be an unlawful user of the way ...'

d 22. The law is clear at the extremes. To use the track for the sole purpose of accessing the blue land is outside the scope of the grant. However, in some circumstances a person who uses the way to access the dominant land but then goes off the dominant land, for instance to picnic on the neighbouring land, is not going outside the scope of the grant. The crucial question in the present case is whether those circumstances include a case where one of the essential purposes e of the use of the way is to cultivate land other than the dominant land for whose benefit the grant was made.

The present case

23. Mr Dumont for the claimants submits that the question to be asked is f whether the use of the yellow strip for the purpose of accessing both the red and the blue land involves a trespass on the yellow strip. He submits that it does not because it does not impose a significantly heavier practical burden on the owner of the servient tenement (the defendants) than they had willingly assumed. On one view, when the judge in the present case referred to the burden of use being 'not, or not significantly, increased', he was purporting to conclude that any additional g use resulting from the accessing and cultivation of the blue land with the red land was minimal. If that were the test, we would have to disagree with the judge's conclusion. Mr Veale's evidence that his likely use was about six times a year, and that this would involve one or two more visits than if he was farming the red land alone, would seem to us to disclose more than a minimal increase.

h 24. The right to use a right of way is determined by the terms of the grant, specifying the dominant tenement for the purposes of which the right is created. Trespass is whatever is not permitted by the grant. The right is not to use the way for the purposes of benefiting any property provided that the total user does not exceed some notional maximum user which the beneficiary might have been j entitled to make for the purposes of the dominant tenement. If that were the test, the beneficiary might in some circumstances use the way entirely for purposes other than those of the dominant tenement. The right is to use the way for the purposes of the dominant tenement only. The grant, when made, had a notional value which would be identified by reference to those purposes and their likely impact. Use for other purposes would be likely to carry its own notional commercial value. The claimants are claiming to use a way granted for the limited purposes of the 15 acres of red land for the extended or additional purpose of accessing and cultivating at the same time the further ten acres of the blue land. That extended or additional use is of self-evident commercial value to the claimants, but any value attaching to it cannot have been embraced in the notional value attached to the actual right of way for the benefit of the red land.

25. Considering the position as a matter of principle, we would consider that the defendants are entitled to the declaration that they seek. In our judgment the authorities to which we have referred, and in particular *Harris'* case, also confirm that, where a court is being asked to declare whether the right to use a way comprises a right to use it to facilitate the cultivation of land other than the dominant tenement, the court is not concerned with any comparison between the amount of use made or to be made of the servient tenement and the amount of use made or that might lawfully be made within the scope of the grant. It is concerned with declaring the scope of the grant, having regard to its purposes and the identity of the dominant tenement. The authorities indicate that the burden on the owner of the servient tenement is not to be increased without his consent. But burden in this context does not refer to the number of journeys or the weight of the vehicles. Any use of the way is, in contemplation of law, a burden and one must ask whether the grantor agreed to the grantee making use of the way for that purpose. Although in *Harris'* case Vaughan-Williams LJ mentioned the 'heavy and frequent traffic' arising from the factory which 'could not have arisen without the use of the white land as well as of the pink', the view we take of the reasoning in all three judgments in that case, as appears by the passages set out above, is that all three judges were addressing not the question of additional user, but the different question: whether the white land was being used for purposes which were not merely adjuncts to the honest use of the pink land (the dominant tenement); or, rephrasing the same question, whether the way was being used for the purposes of the white land as well as the dominant tenement.

26. Where there is a use in excess of that granted questions can arise as to whether an injunction should be granted or damages should be awarded. But such questions are not before us because neither relief was sought by the defendants. They wished to know what the legal position was.

27. It is in our judgment clear that the grantor did not authorise the use of the way for the purpose of cultivating the blue land. This can not sensibly be described as ancillary to the cultivation of the red land. We therefore allow the appeal and declare that the claimants are not entitled to use the yellow strip for the purpose of obtaining access to the blue land in order to cultivate it.

The size and location of the right of way

28. We turn to the issues relating to the size and location of the right of way. In his first judgment dated 18 December 1998, the judge concluded that the width of the right of way at its two extremities was 21 foot, and that in between it was limited by the physical existence of permanent obstruction and had a maximum width of 21 foot. In his second judgment dated 2 July 1999, he held that it would not reflect the intention of his first judgment to include a kink in the western side of this right of way, since the suggested kink reflected no more than the presence in 1976–1977 of outbuildings, which had since been removed; they were not part of the original house at No 33 and 'plainly were not permanent'.

29. The defendants submit that the judge erred, first of all, in treating the whole area coloured yellow as intended (subject to permanent obstructions) to be comprised in the right of way. In their submission the judgment should have

a had regard to the existing 'roadway' and, in that connection, to the presence and width of the gates and fences at each extremity. The result, they submit, should be to limit the northern entrance from the road to 15 foot (the width of the 3-foot and 12-foot gates) and the southern entrance to the field to 10 foot, the width of the dilapidated gate which there existed.

30. Mr Morshead points out that the 1976 conveyance gave the claimants no b more than 'a similar right of way over the roadway coloured yellow' on plan 2. The case was therefore, in his submission, in the same class as *White v Richards* (1993) 68 P & CR 105, where the right granted was to pass and repass over and along the track coloured brown; and it was in a different category to *Keefe v Amor* [1964] 2 All ER 517, [1965] 1 QB 334, where the right of way was simply 'over the land shown and coloured brown'. Accordingly, the first step in his submission c was to identify the existing roadway, and the right of way must be treated as limited to this. We of course accept, and *White*'s case shows, that the physical characteristics of the area at the time of the grant constitute potentially relevant background to any construction of the grant. But there was no evidence of any established roadway or use involving any particular route through or between d the gates. The general impression from photographs taken in 1998 is one of very flimsy structures at each end, and indeed we were told that the evidence was that any gate and fence which existed at the southern end in 1976–1977 was even more insubstantial or derelict.

31. Plan 2, which was actually attached to the conveyance, was small-scale and imprecise. It also carried the statement that 'This Plan is for identification e purposes Only and although believed to be correct its accuracy is in no way guaranteed'. It seems to me legitimate to look at other background for assistance as to what precisely was intended to be conveyed. The judge looked at the contract for sale (as well as a statement made by the auctioneer, which cannot in our view have been admissible). Both counsel were initially prepared to accept f that this was admissible background to the construction of the conveyance, although Mr Morshead later resiled from this after being referred to *Youell v Bland Welch & Co Ltd* [1992] 2 Lloyd's Rep 127. We were referred to *Ladbroke Group plc v Bristol City Council* [1988] 1 EGLR 126 at 129, where this court, when construing a lease, had regard to the terms of the building agreement pursuant to which, expressly, a lease was executed. In the present case, the recital in the conveyance g is less clear: it merely records that 'The Vendors have agreed with the Purchasers for the sale to them of the property hereinafter described'. But this statement confirms that the conveyance was designed to give effect to a specific agreement for sale of 'the property hereinafter described'. Indeed, the effect of the agreement had already been to transfer the equitable interest in that property h including its ancillary benefits such as the right of way. What is presently in issue is simply the precise scope of 'the right of way over the roadway coloured yellow', which was agreed to be sold and intended to be conveyed. We consider it permissible to look in these circumstances at the agreement which the conveyance was intended to implement. In condition 19 of the agreement the right of way is j identified as a right 'over the roadway as edged yellow on plan number one annexed hereto'.

32. Plan 1, in the judge's words, is 'meticulous and precise in its detail and leaves no doubt in the mind of anyone'. At the north and south ends of the yellow area, the dimensions are shown as 21 foot. There is no suggestion of any restriction or limitation by reference to any gate or gates at either end or any route between the two ends.

33. In these circumstances, the position seems to us clear. The background does not support any limitation of the right of way to any particular route between its two extremities or to any gate or part of its two extremities. The right of way extends to the full width of the yellow land shown on plans 1 and 2, subject only (on the judge's judgment) to permanent obstructions. But the claimants could not object to the presence of such restrictions as were imposed by the gates and fences, unless and until these substantially interfered with such use of the right of way as was reasonable from time to time (see *Keefe*'s case [1964] 2 All ER 517 at 521, [1965] 1 QB 334 at 347).

34. We turn to the question of the kink, shown on the large-scale and detailed plan 1, but not on the small-scale and imprecise plan 2. Plan 1 specifies this kink as starting 35 ft 2 in south of the road and running south at a slight easterly angle for 20 ft 10 in, before the western edge of the yellow coloured land resumes a southerly direction for its remaining 100 feet. The judge, in his original judgment, said that the right of way was precisely ascertainable from the location of the flank wall of No 33, the auctioneer's statement, plans 1 and 2 and the auction particulars. We have already indicated our view that the auctioneer's statement was not admissible. But plan 1, which shows no kink, is. Of plan 1, the judge said: 'The only deficiency in the plan is that the obtuse angle kink on the south western limit of width is not identified, nor are measurements given at that point.'

35. In his second judgment, however, he declared that the right of way was 21 foot wide at its ends and along its width, save where there were permanent obstructions and dismissed the outbuildings as impermanent. As to this, it does not follow from their subsequent demolition that the outbuildings would have been regarded as impermanent at the time, or that their owners would have been prepared to have them demolished or to forego their reconstruction. The kink appeared, because of them, in the very document which the judge accepted as 'meticulous and precise in its detail' and as 'leav[ing] no doubt in the mind of anyone'. Further, this is a document which is admissible, as we consider in common with the judge, on the issue whether the right of way was intended to extend to the whole of the yellow coloured area, or to be limited to some route or gates on that area. The judge's second judgment appears to us to ignore the clear effect of the very document which he elsewhere, rightly, found so helpful. We can see no basis for treating the right of way as having a 21-foot width along its whole length, regardless of the kink. Plan 1 shows that it was understood to have 21-foot width at each end, and to have kink in the middle, which must clearly reduce its width in the middle. To what width it there reduces must depend on a precise calculation based on an original and not a photocopy of plan 1.

36. The judge referred to permanent obstructions, and the plan annexed to his final order, which Mr Dumont defends, shows a telegraph pole on the east edge of the yellow area, near the road. It is 18 ft 6 in from the east flank wall of the defendants' house at No 33. We reject Mr Morshead's submission that this means that the judge has ordered a right of way impinging by 2 ft 6 in on the house at No 33. On the judge's judgment, the pole represents a permanent obstruction, and a necessary limitation on the right of way. Mr Dumont did not contend that the judge was wrong to qualify his judgment by reference to permanent obstructions to be found on or in the ground at the time of the sale in 1976–1977.

37. On the ground, the boundaries clearly intended to mark the yellow area appear to have been swivelled slightly on a central fulcrum, going eastwards at the south. The swivelling is reflected on the plan attached to the judge's order.

a The effect is that some 2 ft 9 in of the existing gate at the south-west end of the yellow area is shown as falling outside the yellow area and so outside any right of way. That is consistent neither with common sense nor with either party's case. In that respect also it seems to us that the plan attached to the order requires revision.

38. For these reasons, on the second issue, we vary the judge's order to b require the kink to be shown and also to reverse the swivelling of the yellow area. A revised plan will thus require to be drawn up and attached to the order of this court. A declaration along the lines of the first declaration made by the judge will be appropriate in relation to that revised plan. The second declaration made by the judge will require amendment in view of the kink. Paragraph 3 of the order under appeal still appears appropriate. Instead of para 4 of the order under appeal c we shall declare that the claimants are not entitled to use the yellow strip for the purpose of obtaining access to the blue land in order to cultivate it.

Appeal allowed.

Kate O'Hanlon Barrister.

Derby Specialist Fabrication Ltd v Burton

a

EMPLOYMENT APPEAL TRIBUNAL

KEENE J, LORD DAVIES OF COITY AND MR P PARKER

19 JULY, 28 SEPTEMBER 2000

b

Race relations – Discrimination – Employment – Discrimination on racial grounds – Statutory provision making it unlawful for employer to discriminate against employee on racial grounds by 'dismissing' him – Whether constructive dismissal falling within terms of provision – Race Relations Act 1976, s 4(2)(c).

c

Section 4(2)(c)[a] of the Race Relations Act 1976, which makes it unlawful for an employer to discriminate against an employee on racial grounds by 'dismissing' him, extends to constructive dismissal. Whether the employer deliberately dismisses the employee on racial grounds or he so acts to repudiate the contract by racially discriminating against him, which repudiation the employee accepts, the end result is the same, namely the loss of employment by the employee. d Accordingly, there was no reason to believe that Parliament had intended that 'dismissing' in s 4(2)(c) of the 1976 Act should have a restricted meaning (see p 844 *j* to p 845 *b h j*, post).

Harrold v Wiltshire Healthcare NHS Trust (16 March 1999, unreported) not followed.

e

Notes

For racial discrimination by employers, see 4(2) *Halsbury's Laws* (4th edn reissue) para 157.

For the Race Relations Act 1976, s 4, see 7 *Halsbury's Statutes* (4th edn) (1999 reissue) 121.

f

Cases referred to in judgment

Driskel v Peninsula Business Services Ltd [2000] IRLR 151, EAT.

Harrold v Wiltshire Healthcare NHS Trust (16 March 1999, unreported), EAT.

Hutchison v Westward Television Ltd [1977] ICR 279, EAT.

King v Great Britain-China Centre [1992] ICR 516, CA.

Owen & Briggs v James [1982] ICR 618, CA. g

Qureshi v Victoria University of Manchester (21 June 1996, unreported), EAT.

Reed v Stedman [1999] IRLR 299, EAT.

Sutcliffe v Hawker Siddeley Aviation Ltd [1973] ICR 560, NIRC.

Weathersfield Ltd v Sargeant [1998] ICR 198, EAT; *affd* [1999] ICR 425, CA.

Western Excavating (ECC) Ltd v Sharp [1978] 1 All ER 713, [1978] QB 761, [1978] 2 WLR 344, CA. h

Appeal

The appellant employer, Derby Specialist Fabrications Ltd, appealed from the decision of an employment tribunal at Nottingham, sent to the parties on 9 June 1999, j allowing a claim by the respondent employee, Joseph N Burton, that he had been unlawfully discriminated against by the appellant contrary to ss 1 and 4 of the Race Relations Act 1976, and awarding him compensation of £19,551·02 inclusive of interest. The facts are set out in the judgment of the tribunal.

---

a Section 4, so far as material, is set out at p 842 *j* to p 843 *a*, post

a *Richard Clayton* (instructed by *Engineering Employers' Federation*) for the appellant.
Heather Williams (instructed by *Bakewells*, Derby) for the respondent.

Cur adv vult

28 September 2000. The following judgment of the appeal tribunal was delivered.

b **KEENE J.** These are appeals first against a unanimous decision of an employment tribunal sitting at Nottingham that the respondent was unlawfully discriminated against, contrary to ss 1 and 4 of the Race Relations Act 1976, and secondly against the amount of compensation awarded. We shall deal with the liability appeal first.

1. The respondent, who is black, was employed by the appellant as a welder c between 1989 and May 1998. At some stage he was transferred from site construction to the tube shop. The employment tribunal found as a fact that:

> 'At all material times racial abuse was widespread throughout the tube shop. No action was taken by the respondent to check this. Indeed Mr Whalley, the personnel manager, did not appear to recognise the climate of racial abuse as d a problem. He failed to understand that it might be offensive for a black worker to be likened to a monkey and for another to be described as a "black bastard".'

2. The tribunal's findings also included the following:

> 'In or about April 1996 the applicant asked Mr Moore, then training school e instructor, why he had failed a test. Mr Moore said, "I am not having a jungle bunny working in the Welding Shop". The applicant was offended and upset by this incident ... In early 1998 the respondents were faced with a redundancy situation. Welders, including the applicant, were interviewed by an agency with a view to a possible transfer to another company. The agency told the applicant that there was no record that he did any welding work. f The applicant did not complain because he did not want to rock the boat. Unlike other welders, he did not get a second interview.'

3. In March 1998 there was a change of foreman. Mr Moore became the foreman. The tribunal found that:

> g 'The applicant reasonably believed that Mr Moore would participate in the redundancy selection process. On 1 May 1998 he resigned. If he had been told that he could take a less skilled job with protected salary, he would not have resigned.'

h 4. The tribunal went on to reject a submission that the claim was out of time, noting that the effective date of termination of employment was 1 May 1998 and the originating application was received on 31 July 1998. The tribunal stated:

> 'Accordingly, the applicant's application in respect of his claim that he was unlawfully discriminated against when constructively dismissed was clearly j within time, because it was presented within the statutory three-month period. The tribunal decided that the effect of Mr Moore's racial abuse was continuing and had a direct impact on the applicant's decision to resign. Therefore, the tribunal could properly consider the applicant's complaint with regard to this matter. However, if the tribunal was wrong in law, it decided that it was just and equitable to consider the complaint, pursuant to s 68(6) of the 1976 Act. In reaching that decision the tribunal took into account the applicant's medical

condition, his reliance on his union representatives and the advice given, and any prejudice to the respondent.' a

5. It then went on to consider the merits of the complaints, referring to *King v Great Britain-China Centre* [1992] ICR 516 and rejecting some of the complaints. But it decided that Mr Burton had established on the balance of probabilities that Mr Moore and Mr Harry Winfield had racially abused him. These incidents had occurred in a climate of racial abuse within the tube shop. The tribunal found that the appellant company was aware of this. It had been conceded that the company could not avail itself of the statutory defence in s 32(3) of the 1976 Act. The tribunal reminded itself of the test for constructive dismissal in *Western Excavating (ECC) Ltd v Sharp* [1978] 1 All ER 713, [1978] QB 761, including the fact that the employee must make up his mind soon after the conduct of which he complains. The respondent's representative, Mr Upton, had argued that there had been a continuing policy or practice of discrimination against the respondent up to 1 May 1998 when he resigned and Mr Upton had referred to the climate of racial abuse. The tribunal concluded in para 15 of its extended reasons as follows: b c

> 'The tribunal accepted Mr Upton's submissions. The [respondent] had been racially abused by Mr Moore. He reasonably believed that Mr Moore would be participating in the redundancy selection process and that he would not be favourably compared with other colleagues. He had been told by the agency that there was no record that he had done welding work. Unlike other welders, he did not receive a second interview. The [appellant] did not tell him that he might get a less skilled job with a protected salary. In all the circumstances the tribunal decided that the [appellant] had, without reasonable and proper cause, conducted itself in a manner calculated or likely to destroy or seriously damage the relationship of confidence and trust between the parties. The [respondent] was entitled to leave without notice and he had acted promptly. His dismissal amounted to unlawful direct discrimination contrary to ss 1(1)(a) and 4(2)(c) of the 1976 Act.' d e f

6. In its summary of its conclusions the tribunal found that one of the respondent's complaints of discrimination by racial harassment, namely by the trade union representative, Mr Harry Winfield, was out of time, though it had earlier found that Mr Winfield had at some time made a remark to the respondent about 'not running about after no black bastard'. The tribunal rejected complaints about racial harassment by the previous foreman, Mr North, and by the former manufacturing manager, Mr Bennett. But in separate conclusions it stated: g

> '(iii) the [respondent's] complaint that he was unlawfully discriminated against by the [appellant] contrary to ss 1 and 4 of the Race Relations Act 1976 when he was subjected to a detriment by Mr Wayne Paul Moore was well-founded; (iv) the [respondent's] complaint that he was unlawfully discriminated against contrary to ss 1 and 4 of the Race Relations Act when he resigned on 1 May 1998 was well-founded.' h

7. On behalf of the appellant Mr Clayton submits first that the complaint should have been held to be time-barred. He contends that constructive dismissal does not come within the term 'dismissal' as used in s 4(2)(c) of the 1976 Act. Section 4(2), in so far as material for present purposes, reads as follows: j

> 'It is unlawful for a person, in the case of a person employed by him at an establishment in Great Britain, to discriminate against that employee—(a) in the

a terms of employment which he affords him; or (b) in the way he affords him access to opportunities for promotion, transfer or training, or to any other benefits, facilities or services, or by refusing or deliberately omitting to afford him access to them; or (c) by dismissing him, or subjecting him to any other detriment.'

b 8. There is no definition of 'dismissing' or 'dismissal' in the 1976 Act. But reliance is placed by the appellant on the reasoning of the Employment Appeal Tribunal (EAT) in *Harrold v Wiltshire Healthcare NHS Trust* (16 March 1999, unreported), where it was pointed out that Parliament had chosen in the Sex Discrimination Act 1986 to amend the Sex Discrimination Act 1975 so as to include constructive dismissal expressly within the meaning of the term 'dismissal'. Its failure to do so c in respect of the 1976 Act was seen as significant and deliberate.

9. Therefore, contends Mr Clayton, the tribunal should have regarded the three-month period for a complaint as starting not from the date of resignation on 1 May 1998 but from the date of the act or acts of racial discrimination which, according to the tribunal, had given rise to the breach of the contract of d employment by the employer. In that context it is said that the only specific complaint of racial harassment upheld by the tribunal was that relating to Mr Moore in April 1996. Mr Clayton acknowledges that the appointment of Mr Moore as foreman of the tool shop in March 1998 could be seen as a further act leading to potential discrimination against the respondent, but even that would not be within a three-month period leading up to the originating application on 31 July 1998. All e the other specific allegations of racial abuse or harassment by named individuals were rejected by the tribunal.

10. The appellant submits that, beyond those factors, there was only the allegedly reasonable belief on the part of Mr Burton that Mr Moore would be involved in the redundancy selection process. At one point Mr Clayton accepted f that if Mr Moore had in fact been involved in the selection process, then that would have amounted to a continuing act when put together with his earlier racial remark, because it would have been inappropriate for him to have been involved in the selection process. But as Mr Moore was not so involved as a matter of fact, there was no continuing act of racial harassment and the respondent's reasonable belief that Mr Moore was so involved could not create g one. Subsequently, Mr Clayton conceded that if objectively the belief was a reasonable one, then that would suffice, even if it were mistaken. But he then argued that the tribunal failed to give adequate reasons for finding Mr Burton's belief to be a reasonable one. We shall consider that point after dealing with the time-bar issue.

h 11. So far as the tribunal's decision that, if necessary, it would extend time because it was 'just and equitable' to do so under s 68(6) of the 1976 Act, the appellant submits that that decision is flawed. Although the tribunal had a wide discretion, the reference to Mr Burton's medical condition concerned events back in 1996, two years before the claim became time-barred. The reference to his j reliance on his union representatives and the advice given is not based on any finding of fact in the decision that such advice had been given.

12. On these issues, Miss Williams for the respondent argues that constructive dismissal does come within the meaning of 'dismissal' in s 4(2)(c) of the 1976 Act. One should give the statutory wording a purposive construction and the natural meaning of the term 'dismissal' does not exclude constructive dismissal. Parliament can be taken to have known the common law position when enacting this statute.

Miss Williams draws our attention to *Weathersfield Ltd v Sargeant*, both in the EAT [1998] ICR 198 and in the Court of Appeal [1999] ICR 425, where the view was taken that constructive dismissal does fall within the meaning of 'dismissal' for these purposes.

13. Even if that is not so, then the respondent submits that the 'act complained of', which starts the three-month period, must be seen in the light of the tribunal's finding that the racial abuse and discrimination was a continuing act, as was the appellant's failure to do anything about it. By s 68(7) of the 1976 Act, an act extending over a period of time is to be treated as done at the end of that period. This was a case of an accumulation of acts and events demonstrating a repudiation by the appellant of the contract of employment and that accumulation should be seen as continuing until the time of the respondent's resignation. Miss Williams emphasises the tribunal's findings that at all material times racial abuse was widespread throughout the tube shop, that the appellant company knew about this climate of racial abuse, and that it took no action to check it. That, she submits, provides the context and the links between the individual incidents specifically referred to.

14. As for the tribunal's exercise of its discretion to extend time if necessary, the respondent contends that that was not a perverse decision. There was a factual basis for the matters referred to by the tribunal as justifying its decision on this aspect and its reasons are, it is said, sufficiently clear.

15. We note that in the *Weathersfield Ltd* case in the EAT, the tribunal's judgment given by Morison J, president, indicates that the tribunal there regarded the term 'dismissal' as being apt to cover a constructive dismissal case. The point was, however, conceded by counsel for the appellant. In the Court of Appeal, there was no dissent expressed from Morison J's views on this aspect, although it is fair to say that the court did not address the matter explicitly in the course of its judgments. In *Harrold*'s case, the EAT said:

> 'The Race Relations Act 1976 does not contain a definition of dismissal. That must be compared with the Sex Discrimination Act 1975 which, by an amendment contained in the Sex Discrimination Act 1986, designed to bring the Act into compliance with Community law, added s 82(1A) which extends dismissal for the purpose of that Act to include constructive dismissal and expiry of a fixed-term contract, as also provided for in s 95 of the Employment Rights Act 1996. The 1976 Act was not similarly amended and we must assume that it was Parliament's intention to do so deliberately.'

It later went on to observe:

> 'We think that the proper analysis is that the underlying racially discriminatory behaviour, leading an employee to resign in circumstances amounting to constructive dismissal for the purposes of unfair dismissal and sex discrimination legislation, amounts to some other detriment under s 4(2)(c) of the 1976. It is not a dismissal within the meaning of that provision.'

16. Given the fact that in constructive dismissal cases the employee must have acted with sufficient despatch as to avoid affirming the contract, it will not often matter in practice whether it is the resignation or the employer's conduct which is treated as the date of the 'act complained of' for the purposes of the three-month period prescribed by s 68 of the 1976 Act. We can see some force in the reasoning in *Harrold*'s case, but in the end we are not persuaded by it. There may be a number of reasons why Parliament chose to make an amendment to the

a 1975 Act, not least its wish to ensure that there could no doubt whatsoever about the Act's compliance with Community law, as the judgment in *Harrold*'s case indicates. It cannot be taken as an indication by Parliament that, in other legislation with which it was not dealing, 'dismissal' was to be given a restricted meaning. We emphasise that because, if one approaches the meaning of 'dismissal' in the 1976 Act without that extraneous influence, there is no reason b why it should be so construed as to exclude constructive dismissal. Whether the employer deliberately dismisses the employee on racial grounds or he so acts as to repudiate the contract by racially discriminatory conduct, which repudiation the employee accepts, the end result is the same, namely the loss of employment by the employee. Why should Parliament be taken to have distinguished between these two situations?

c 17. Somewhat similar reasoning to that employed in *Harrold*'s case was at one time advanced in the context of unfair dismissal, at a date when the industrial relations legislation did not include what is now s 95(1)(c) of the Employment Rights Act 1996, the current statutory provision which makes it clear that dismissal includes, for the purposes of unfair dismissal claims, constructive dismissal. d The Industrial Relations Act 1971 merely provided that dismissal of an employee arose if, but only if (s 23(2)):

> '(a) the contract under which he is employed by the employer is terminated by the employer, whether it is so terminated by notice or without notice, or (b) where under that contract he is employed for a fixed term, that term e expires without being renewed under the same contract.'

That contrasted with the Redundancy Payments Act 1965, s 3(1) where dismissal was defined so as to include not only (a) and (b) above but also (c): '... the employee terminates that contract without notice in circumstances ... such that he is entitled to terminate it by reason of the employer's conduct.' Consequently, in f *Sutcliffe v Hawker Siddeley Aviation Ltd* [1973] ICR 560, the argument was advanced that unfair dismissal did not embrace a constructive dismissal. That contention was rejected by the National Industrial Relations Court, Sir John Donaldson (at 564), president, saying:

> 'That comparison points, it is said, to Parliament having intended that g there should be no room for an "unfair constructive dismissal." We entirely reject that contention. We consider that the omission arose solely because the draftsman thought it unnecessary to include the subsection. We have no doubt that there can be constructive unfair dismissals and that any amendment of the Act of 1971 to include a subsection (c) equivalent to that h contained in the Act of 1965 would have no effect other than to dispose of a misconstruction of the Act.'

18. What that decision demonstrates is that there is no requirement as such for there to be an express statutory provision covering constructive dismissal for such to be included in the term 'dismissal'. It shows how case law established the j wider meaning of dismissal in advance of that meaning being incorporated into an express statutory provision. It is therefore a fallacy to believe that that wider meaning finds its origins in such a statutory provision. It does not. In the same way we conclude that there is no reason to give the word 'dismissal' in s 4(2)(c) of the 1976 Act the narrow meaning now contended for by the appellant. The tribunal below was right in law in the approach which it adopted. That is enough to dispose of the time-bar point.

19. However, in any event, it is clear that the employment tribunal found in this case that the discriminatory acts amounting to a fundamental breach of contract by the appellant continued up until the time of the respondent's resignation. That can be seen from its acceptance of the submissions of Mr Upton to that effect and from its express findings that *at all material times* racial abuse was widespread throughout the tube shop and that the effect of the racial abuse in April 1996 by the man who became his foreman in March 1998 was continuing. At no time did the company take any action to prevent the abuse. That failure was a continuing failure. There is no appeal against the finding that there was a climate of racial abuse in the tool shop or that the company was aware of this but did nothing about it. Those are not said to be perverse findings. To that had to be added what the tribunal found to be the reasonable belief in March 1998 and thereafter that the man who had racially abused him in 1996 was now to be involved in the selection process for redundancy.

20. In a case where the repudiation of the contract consists of an accumulation of events over a period of time, it would be wrong to seek to isolate individual incidents. The continuing conduct of the employer or its continuing failure to prevent racial abuse and discrimination constitutes what the EAT in *Harrold*'s case described as the underlying racially discriminatory behaviour, and would bring about the 'other detriment' within s 4(2)(c) of the 1976 Act. Section 68(7)(b) of that Act provides that any act extending over a period shall be treated as done at the end of that period for the purposes of the time limit provision. It follows that it makes no difference whether the three-month period is seen as commencing with the respondent's resignation because that was his acceptance of the repudiation of the contract and hence a constructive dismissal; or with the end of the period of racially discriminatory conduct amounting to repudiation. It makes no difference because it was only the respondent's resignation which brought that latter period to an end.

21. We conclude therefore that the employment tribunal was entitled to treat the complaints which it upheld as being made in time under s 68 of the 1976 Act. In any event it was prepared to extend time, should that have been necessary, because it saw that as being 'just and equitable' within s 68(6) of that Act. Those words give a tribunal a very broad discretion as was emphasised in *Hutchison v Westward Television Ltd* [1977] ICR 279. We do not accept that the tribunal failed to make adequate findings of fact on the matters it relied on in the respect of that exercise of discretion. The medical condition did indeed stem from events in 1996, as Mr Clayton has stressed, but the tribunal was none the less entitled to take it into account. The tribunal referred also to the respondent's reliance on his union representatives and the advice given. It is said that it is not clear what that is referring to. But that brief reference has to be seen in context, bearing in mind that these extended reasons are directed towards persons who are familiar with the case and with the evidence given. This factor would appear to relate back to the submissions recorded in para 8, where Mr Upton on behalf of Mr Burton was arguing that he had been unable 'to fully air his grievance and his union had not been helpful'. We bear in mind that Mr Burton's shop steward had been Mr Harry Winfield, who was found by the tribunal to have made the remark about 'not running about after no black bastard'. Put into that context, the tribunal's reference to Mr Burton's reliance on his union representatives and the advice given is sufficiently clear and understandable.

22. There is no other criticism levelled at the exercise of the tribunal's discretion to extend time. In our judgment it cannot be treated as perverse or open to

challenge. It follows that, for all these reasons, the tribunal had jurisdiction to deal with the respondent's complaints.

23. We turn to the substantive points made by the appellant about the tribunal's decision. There are two arguments which it advances.

24. First, it is submitted that the tribunal below erred in law in finding that Mr Burton had been constructively dismissed on grounds of race, when in certain instances there are no express findings that the appellant's acts were caused by race. Mr Clayton argues that if one looks at the matters taken into account by the tribunal in para 15 of its extended reasons, there is no finding that all of those were caused by race. While the racial abuse by Mr Moore and the respondent's reasonable belief that he would not be favourably compared with others in the redundancy selection process would seem to relate to race, there is no express finding that the absence of any record that Mr Burton had done welding work was so attributable nor is there any finding that the fact that he, unlike other welders, did not get a second interview was on grounds of race. There is no finding either that the failure to tell him that he could get a less skilled job with a protected salary was on such grounds.

25. It is clear that some of the individual acts of the employer which in total amounted to a repudiation of the contract of employment were based on racial grounds, as Mr Clayton accepts. It is true that the tribunal has not expressly said of each of the other matters in turn that they were based on racial grounds. However, it seems to us, when read in context, that this is what the tribunal was intending to convey. No doubt its extended reasons could have been worded with greater precision. But those reasons must be read as a whole. It had, before arriving at these conclusions in para 15, reminded itself of the guidance given by the Court of Appeal in *King v Great Britain-China Centre* [1992] ICR 516. If a tribunal finds a difference in treatment and finds also a difference in race, it should look to the employer for an explanation, and if one is not forthcoming, it can be inferred that the discrimination was on racial grounds. Here, the tribunal is recording differences in the treatment of Mr Burton—no record of him doing welding work, no second interview and no informing him of about a less skilled job with a protected salary—and it notes no reference to any explanation being proffered for those differences. It was clearly open to it to infer that they arose from racial grounds. Moreover, it seems that the tribunal did so infer because its overall finding was that his constructive dismissal amounted to unlawful direct discrimination under the 1976 Act.

26. In *Driskel v Peninsula Business Services Ltd* [2000] IRLR 151, this appeal tribunal emphasised that in discrimination cases based upon allegations of harassment (at 154):

> '... it is desirable not to include in this exercise judgments as to the discriminatory significance, if any, of individual incidents—judgment thus far should be limited to the finding of all facts that are prima facie relevant. If ad hoc assessments "discrimination or no" are made the result is a fragmented and discursive judgment; more importantly, there is the potential noted in *Reed and Bull* (*Reed v Stedman* [1999] IRLR 299) for ignoring the impact of totality of successive incidents, individually trivial.'

The EAT had referred earlier in that judgment to the case of *Qureshi v Victoria University of Manchester* (21 June 1996, unreported), where the EAT had criticised a tribunal for making judgments with respect to each incident, saying:

'It was not, however, necessary for the tribunal to ask itself, in relation to each such incident or item, whether it was itself explicable on "racial grounds" or on other grounds. That is a misapprehension about the nature and purpose of evidentiary facts. The function of the tribunal is to find the primary facts from which they will be asked to draw inferences and then for the tribunal to look at the totality of those facts (including the respondent's explanations) in order to see whether it is legitimate to infer that the acts or decisions complained of in the originating applications were on "racial grounds". The fragmented approach by the tribunal in this case would inevitably have the effect of diminishing any eloquence that the cumulative effect of the primary facts might have on the issue of racial grounds. The process of inference is itself a matter of applying common sense and judgment to the facts and assessing the probabilities on the issue whether racial grounds were an effective cause of the acts complained of or were not.'

27. We agree with that approach. An employment tribunal in such cases should have regard to the totality of a number of successive incidents, because there may well be a cumulative effect. If looking at them overall as a breach of contract they can be seen to be or inferred to be based on racial grounds, so that the complainant would have been treated differently but for his race, then the repudiation by the employer of the contract of employment is to be treated as racially discriminatory. Such racial grounds must, of course, amount to a substantial cause of the employer's actions or his inactions. They must be an important reason for them, but they need not be the sole reason (*Owen & Briggs v James* [1982] ICR 618).

28. The tribunal in this present case seems to have arrived at such an overall conclusion about the totality of the matters which it regarded as amounting to constructive dismissal. It was not required to make express findings of racial grounds for each of the individual acts. We cannot see that it went wrong in law in the approach which it adopted.

29. The second and final criticism made of the decision in this case, so far as liability is concerned, relates to the reference in the extended reasons to the respondent's 'reasonable belief' that Mr Moore would be involved in the redundancy selection process. As has already been indicated, the appellant's position on this changed during the course of argument. The initial challenge, later abandoned, was to the relevance of a reasonable belief on Mr Burton's part, it being suggested that what matters in cases of constructive dismissal on allegedly racial grounds is not what the employee believes, however reasonable in the circumstances, but whether the belief was true. Thus it was originally argued that this factor was of no relevance, because Mr Moore was not in fact involved in the selection process.

30. Mr Clayton accepted during the course of argument that this submission would not stand up to scrutiny. The crucial word in the tribunal's finding is 'reasonably', which implies that there were in existence facts which reasonably led to Mr Burton holding that belief. If an employer by its action or inactions leads an employee reasonably to believe that a discriminatory course of action is going to be followed, it matters not whether the employer intended that course to be followed or in most cases whether that course is in fact eventually followed. There would have been objectively good grounds for the employee's belief, and that is what is relevant when one is concerned with an alleged breach of the implied term of trust and confidence.

a 31. The appellant's eventual submission on this topic was that the tribunal had failed to give adequate reasons for concluding that the respondent's belief was reasonable. Mr Clayton contends that no explanation is given for this finding and thus the appellant does not know why it was arrived at.

32. As we have already said, it must be borne in mind that the extended reasons of an employment tribunal are directed towards parties who know in b detail the arguments and issues in the case. The tribunal's reasons do not need to be spelt out in the detail required were they to be directed towards a stranger to this dispute. In the present case, the tribunal first refers to Mr Burton's 'reasonable belief' at para (k) in its findings of fact. In the preceding paragraph it had found that in early 1998 a redundancy situation had arisen affecting the welders. We have been told that there was only one foreman in the tube shop, c and in March 1998 Mr Moore became that foreman. That event is referred to by the tribunal at the beginning of para (k). In those circumstances it seems to us that the tribunal's reasoning is sufficiently clear, namely that the foreman in charge of the tube shop would be in a position of responsibility and knowledge where he might reasonably be expected to be involved in a redundancy selection d process so far as welders were concerned.

33. It follows that there is no error of law by the tribunal in its decision that the respondent was unlawfully discriminated against by the appellant and the liability appeal will therefore be dismissed.

34. We turn to the appeal against the award of compensation. The employment tribunal ordered the appellant company to pay £19,551·02 compensation pursuant e to s 56(1)(b) of the 1976 Act. That was made up of a number of elements, including £5,000 for injury to feelings and £1,267·95 by way of interest on that particular element. It is the award of interest which is at issue in this appeal.

35. The tribunal, dealing with this matter in July 1999, in arriving at the appropriate award for injury to feelings decided that Mr Burton had suffered for f a period in the region of three years. It said: 'His condition had been moderate at first and had become more severe during May and June 1998. Although there had been some improvement, he was still suffering to some degree from injured feelings.'

36. When it considered the question of interest on this part of its award, its stated:

g 'The tribunal considered that it was appropriate to award interest from the date in which Mr Moore subjected [the respondent] to a detriment which was sometime in April 1996. From an assumed start date of 1 May 1996 to the date of the hearing was a period of three years and sixty two days.'

h It then did the calculation accordingly.

37. Regulation 6 of the Employment Tribunals (Interest on Awards in Discrimination Cases) Regulations 1996, SI 1996/2803, in so far as material for present purposes, reads as follows:

'(1) Subject to the following paragraphs of this regulation—(a) in the case of j any sum for injury to feelings, interest shall be for the period beginning on the date of the contravention or act of discrimination complained of and ending on the day of calculation; (b) in the case of all other sums of damages or compensation ... and all arrears of remuneration, interest shall be for the period beginning on the mid-point date and ending on the day of calculation ... (3) Where the tribunal considers that in the circumstances, whether relating to the case as a whole or a particular sum in an award, serious injustice would be caused if interest were to be awarded in respect of the period or periods in paragraphs (1) or (2), it may—(a) calculate interest, or as the case may be interest on the particular sum, for such different period, or (b) calculate interest for such different periods in respect of various sums in the award, as it considers appropriate in the circumstances, having regard to the provisions of these Regulations.'

38. It is contended by Mr Clayton that the tribunal has overcompensated the respondent by awarding interest on the £5,000 for the whole of the period during which injury to feelings had taken place. The £5,000 reflected acts of discrimination taking place after April 1996 and indeed injury to feelings which grew more severe in May and June 1998. Where a tribunal decides that there is a continuing discriminatory act (covering two years) the compensation it awards will reflect an assessment of the proper amount to be paid at the end of the period covered. Therefore, there is no justification for awarding interest calculated by reference to the beginning of the act. Consequently the appellant submits that the tribunal should have exercised its powers under reg 6(3) so as to award interest from the midpoint of the period between April 1996 and the date of the award. It is said that it was perverse of the tribunal not to have done so.

39. It is clear that Parliament intended that, unlike interest on other awards where the midpoint was to be taken, interest on an award for injury to feelings should normally be from the date of the discriminatory act. That must be taken to allow for the fact, of which Parliament cannot have been ignorant, that the injury to feelings is not a one-off event but something which will often persist over a period of time. So the mere fact that any award for such injury to feelings reflects injury occurring over a period of time cannot of itself justify a departure from the normal rule in reg 6(1)(a). Parliament has clearly chosen to depart from the normal approach to interest awards in personal injury cases involving pain, suffering and loss of amenity. Mr Clayton acknowledged this in the course of argument.

40. Thus the point becomes whether the tribunal's reference to the injury becoming more severe during May and June 1998, a factor presumably reflected in the £5,000, required the tribunal in its discretion under reg 6(3) to depart from the normal rule because serious injustice would result from doing otherwise. Had it stood alone, this argument might have succeeded. But the tribunal also found that the injury to feelings had diminished between then and its decision in July 1999. So the tribunal was faced with a variation first up and then down in the gravity of the injury to the respondent's feelings.

41. In those circumstances it must have been open to the tribunal to decline to find that serious injustice would be caused by adhering to the normal approach. It seems to have given consideration to whether or not it should exercise those powers, since it expressly uses the phrase 'it was appropriate to award interest'. The conclusion which it arrived at was not a perverse one and this tribunal is not justified in interfering with the award. This appeal will also be dismissed.

Appeal dismissed.

Ian Murphie Barrister.

a

R v Warrington Crown Court, ex parte RBNB (a company)

COURT OF APPEAL, CIVIL DIVISION

b OTTON, ROBERT WALKER LJJ AND SIR RONALD WATERHOUSE

24, 31 JULY 2000

Licensing – Licence – Transfer – Unlimited company owning public house – Shareholders not disclosing their identities – Company employee applying for transfer c *of licence – Application being refused because of failure to disclose shareholders' identities – Whether license could be refused merely because of refusal to disclose identities of shareholders – Licensing Act 1964, s 3(1).*

RBNB was an unlimited company which owned a number of public houses. The d identity of its directors was known, but not that of its shareholders. Such anonymity was permitted and protected by companies legislation. K, a manager employed by RBNB, applied to the licensing justices for the transfer of the licence in respect of one of the company's public houses. Under s 3(1)[a] of the Licensing Act 1964, the licensing justices could grant a licence to any such person as they thought 'fit and proper'. The police opposed K's application, contending that it was e impossible to be satisfied as to his fitness or propriety without knowing the identities of the shareholders. The licensing justices refused the application because of the shareholders' refusal to disclose their identities. On K's appeal, the Crown Court accepted that the shareholders left the day-to-day running of the business to their management team, and no objection was taken to K's fitness or propriety, f or to that of RBNB's managing director and area manager. Nevertheless, the court dismissed the appeal, relying partly on the licensing justices' published policy not to grant a licence in respect of premises which would be carried on for the benefit of another person who would himself be refused a licence because he was of bad character or otherwise unfit to hold a licence. In subsequent judicial g review proceedings, the judge held that that policy was unlawful and remitted the case to the Crown Court. Following the judge's decision, the justices made an amendment to their policy. Under that amendment, a licence would not be granted to a person who, though outwardly fit and proper himself, might be influenced or controlled in his management of the premises by others who h would be refused a licence on the ground of unfitness or impropriety. At the rehearing of the appeal, the Crown Court held that the continuing refusal to disclose the identities of the shareholders made it impossible for the court to be satisfied that they were fit and proper persons to exercise control and influence over the licensee and his management of the premises Accordingly, it again j dismissed the appeal, and once again its decision was challenged in judicial review proceedings. The judge allowed that challenge, and the chief constable appealed. He contended that it would be irresponsible and unreasonable for justices to exercise their discretion under s 3(1) in the absence of evidence of the identity of the shareholders.

---

a Section 3(1) is set out at p 855 *b*, post

Held – Licensing justices were not entitled to refuse to grant a licence to the manager of a public house under s 3(1) of the 1964 Act solely on the ground of a refusal to disclose the identity of shareholders in an unlimited company which owned that public house. Withholding information about shareholders of an unlimited company was not in itself indicative of the lack of fitness or bona fides of those shareholders. They were exercising a right which was given to them by virtue of the structure embodied in the Companies Acts. However, the court was entitled to draw a fair and proper inference from the withholding of information, provided there was some evidence other than the refusal from which it could properly reach its conclusions. Nevertheless, the court had to perform a balancing exercise by considering any non-disclosure against such factors as the known identity of the directors and the area manager and that there was no objection to their fitness and propriety; that the premises had previously been run properly in accordance with the terms of the licence; that the shareholders were not concerned in the day-to-day running of the business; the layers of management and whether the shareholders were insulated against any involvement in the business conducted at the premises; and the nature and characteristics and mechanisms for control of unlimited companies. In the instant case, there was no evidence from which it could be legitimately concluded that K was not a fit and proper person because he would have no proper control or would not be an effective licence holder, or that he could not operate the premises without infringing the law or that his relationship with the shareholders might render him indifferent as to whether he conducted the business properly. Moreover, the failure of the Crown Court to carry out the necessary balancing exercise constituted an error of law which flawed the decision. Accordingly, the appeal would be dismissed (see p 859 *j* to p 860 *a*, p 861 *d e j*, p 862 b to *f*, p 863 *j* and p 864 *a*, post).

Notes

For the general power of licensing justices to grant licences to such persons as they think fit and proper, see 26 *Halsbury's Laws* (4th edn reissue) para 35.

For the Licensing Act 1964, s 3, see 24 *Halsbury's Statutes* (4th edn) (1998 reissue) 355.

Cases referred to in judgments

Frome United Breweries Co Ltd v Bath JJ [1926] AC 586, [1926] All ER Rep 576, HL.
Keighley's Case (1609) 10 Co Rep 139a, 77 ER 1136.
Mellor v Lydiate [1914] 3 KB 1141, [1914–15] All ER Rep 762.
R v Crown Court at Manchester, ex p Dransfield Novelty Co Ltd (16 February 1981, unreported), DC.
R v Crown Court at Preston, ex p Cooper (22 November 1989, unreported), DC.
R v Holborn Licensing JJ, ex p Stratford Catering Co Ltd (1926) 136 LT 278, [1926] All ER Rep 279, DC.
R v Hyde JJ, ex p Atherton [1912] 1 KB 645, [1911–13] All ER Rep 713, DC.
Rooke's Case (1598) 5 Co Rep 99b, 77 ER 209.
Sharp v Wakefield [1891] AC 173, [1886–90] All ER Rep 651, HL.
White v South East Cornwall JJ [1989] COD 402.

Cases also cited or referred to in skeleton arguments

Lidster v Owen [1983] 1 All ER 1012, [1983] 1 WLR 516, CA.
Niemietz v Germany (1993) 16 EHRR 97, ECt HR.
R v Torquay Licensing JJ, ex p Brockman [1951] 2 All ER 656, [1951] 2 KB 784, DC.
R v Windsor Licensing JJ, ex p Hodes [1983] 2 All ER 551, [1983] 1 WLR 685, CA.

Appeal

By notice dated 3 February 2000, the Chief Constable of the Cheshire Constabulary appealed with permission of Newman J from his order on 15 December 1999 allowing an application by the respondent unlimited company, RBNB, for judicial review of the decision of the Crown Court at Warrington (Judge Clarke and licensing justices) on 9 October 1998 dismissing an appeal by Leslie Eric Kehoe, an employee of RBNB, from the decision of the Halton licensing justices sitting at Widnes Magistrates' Court on 5 March 1997 refusing his application for the transfer to him of the license of a public house known as the Weavers Hotel, South Parade, Weston Point, Runcorn. The facts are set out in the judgment of Otton LJ.

Lord Carlile of Berriew QC and *Peter Moss* (instructed by *Sarah Pimlott*, Chester) for the chief constable.

Roderick Cordara QC and *Paul Stanley* (instructed by *Finers Stephens Innocent*) for RBNB.

Cur adv vult

31 July 2000. The following judgments were delivered.

OTTON LJ.

1. This is an appeal from the decision of Newman J on 15 December 1999 whereby it was declared that the decision of the Warrington Crown Court made on 9 October 1998 was wrong in law. Permission to appeal was granted by the learned judge.

2. This appeal raises a question of general importance in licensing law. The proceedings have a long history and have now been in the Crown Office list on two previous occasions: first, before Sedley J who quashed the decision of the Warrington Crown Court refusing an appeal from the licensing justices and who ordered a rehearing of that appeal; the second before Newman J who granted declaratory relief in favour of the applicant (RBNB) for judicial review and from whose decision the respondent (the Chief Constable of Cheshire) now appeals.

3. RBNB is an unlimited company. It owns a number of public houses in the north of England, including the public house which led to this application, the Weavers Hotel, Runcorn, Cheshire. An associated company operates a brewery in Barnsley. Most of the public houses have been operated without any licensing difficulties. However, in relation to some of them, of which the Weavers Hotel is one, objections have been taken by the local police to the fact that the identity of the shareholders is unknown. In those cases the police have either opposed the transfer of licences to managers employed by RBNB (as is the case here), or have even sought the revocation of the licence. In each case the ground has been the same, namely that, without knowing who the shareholder(s) is or are, it is not possible to be satisfied as to the fitness or propriety of the proposed or existing licensee.

4. A number of appeals before the justices and to the Crown Court are pending. They have been stayed pending the determination of this appeal. The issue raised by this appeal is of significance for those appeals and hearings. The difficulty arises because RBNB, or more specifically their shareholders, choose to operate as an unlimited company. There was evidence from RBNB's managing director that the purpose of this arrangement is to protect the privacy of the shareholders who wish, so far as possible, to remain anonymous. The chief constable claims that the only information he has is that the shareholders are two in number, male and, by inference, rich. They guaranteed the loan to the

company by which the company effected the purchase of 38 public houses formerly owned by the Greenalls Group. a

5. However, in the case of each of the licensed premises, the identity of those who operate and control the premises on a day-to-day basis is known and their character has been investigated and found to be satisfactory. Thus, the identity of the directors of RBNB is known, in particular the managing director is Mr Neil Walsh. There is no objection to his fitness or propriety as is to be found in both b judgments of the Crown Court. Similarly, the identity of the area manager employed by RBNB is known; he is Mr Macken. There is no objection to his fitness and propriety. Obviously, the identity of the proposed manager licensee, Mr Kehoe, has been known throughout. It is an important feature in this case that there has never been any objection to his fitness or propriety. Unfortunately, because of the objectors' continuing attitude, Mr Kehoe has, since the second c Crown Court hearing, left RBNB's employment. This was the reason why the relief sought and granted by Newman J was in a declaratory form and, unlike the hearing before Sedley J, mandamus and certiorari did not issue.

6. On both occasions the matter has been before the Crown Court it has been satisfied that the shareholders are not 'concerned in the day-to-day running of the d business, the day-to-day nuts and bolts of the business, leaving that to their management team'. Mr John Fletcher, the divisional licensing officer employed by the chief constable to deal with licensing applications in the Runcorn area, told the Crown Court that he knew of no evidence that anyone other than Mr Walsh, Mr Macken and Mr Kehoe was involved in running the Weavers Hotel. e

7. The relevant employees all gave positive evidence that they were permitted to run the business at the Weavers Hotel without interference. It is to be noted that the Weavers Hotel had been operating in the three years prior to the objection in a satisfactory manner and had never caused any anxiety, either as to the suitability of the premises or the fitness and propriety of the licensee.

8. The matter has come before this court by the following route. In March f 1997 the Halton licensing justices originally refused the application to transfer the licence to Mr Kehoe because of the refusal to identify the shareholders. The Crown Court dismissed an appeal. In doing so, it relied partly on the published policy of the Halton licensing justices which provided:

> '4.1 No licence will be granted to an applicant of bad character or to anyone g who is otherwise unfit to hold a licence. Neither will a licence be granted where the premises would be managed by or carried on for the benefit of a person (other than the applicant) who would himself/herself be refused a licence on this ground.'

h

9. In April 1998, in an application for judicial review, Sedley J quashed this determination because he considered that the policy referred to went further than the law permitted and that the mere question of who will benefit from licensed activity could not be a legitimate inquiry for justices make. The case was remitted to the Crown Court for hearing.

10. The justices, following the decision of Sedley J, amended their policy to j read (I quote the relevant parts):

> 'Neither will a licence be granted to a person who, though outwardly fit and proper himself/herself, might be influenced or controlled by others in his/her management of the premises, where those others would be refused a licence on this ground.'

a 11. At the rehearing in November 1998 the Crown Court dismissed the appeal. In December 1999 Newman J granted the application for judicial review.

THE LAW

12. Section 3 of the Licensing Act 1964 provides:

> '(1) Licensing justices may grant a justices' licence to any such person, not
b disqualified under this or any other Act for holding a justices' licence, as they think fit and proper.'

13. The licensing jurisdiction has been in existence for more than a century. During this time a number of principles have emerged which are relevant to this appeal (see *Paterson's Licensing Acts* (108th edn, 2000) pp 347ff (para 2.464)).

c (1) The liquor licensing jurisdiction is a local jurisdiction. It focuses on particular premises and on particular local conditions.

(2) The purposes of the jurisdiction are: (a) for the protection of morality and public order at (inside and the immediate vicinity outside) licensed premises; (b) to ensure that the premises will be operated according to law; (c) to establish
d who is to be responsible for safety and good order at the premises.

(3) The licence is more often than not to be granted to the natural person who will in fact carry out the functions of licensee. Although in theory a company can be granted a proper licence, it is unusual and much less to shareholders (see *Mellor v Lydiate* [1914] 3 KB 1141, [1914–15] All ER Rep 762).

(4) In considering whether a person is a 'fit and proper' person to hold a licence,
e the justices are not confined to an inquiry as to his character; his health, temper and disposition may be considered (see *R v Hyde JJ, ex p Atherton* [1912] 1 KB 645, [1911–13] All ER Rep 713).

(5) Justices are not justified in attempting to regulate the terms upon which the licensee is to conduct his business so long as those terms do not in any proper sense affect his 'fitness'. However, justices may properly conclude that he is not
f a 'fit and proper' person if the terms on which he intends to carry on his business are such that the only legitimate inference from them is that he cannot carry on his business without infringing the law (see *Ex p Atherton*).

(6) On an application for a transfer, justices may consider the question of security of tenure as affecting the fitness of the proposed licence holder and that
g the justices might take into consideration the terms of the agreement with the proposed transferee and further that, if they came to the conclusion that those terms were such that the interest of the proposed transferee under that agreement might render him indifferent whether he conducted the business properly or not they might, upon that ground, refuse the transfer (see *R v Holborn Licensing JJ, ex p*
h *Stratford Catering Co Ltd* (1926) 136 LT 278, [1926] All ER Rep 279).

(7) Where a Crown Court found on dismissing an appeal against refusal that, behind an applicant for a new licence (who was an existing licensee), there lay a company which the court did 'not accept as law abiding and of the integrity required for this sort of venture', the Divisional Court refused to interfere (see *R v Crown Court at Preston, ex p Cooper* (22 November 1989, unreported)).

j (8) The discretion of licensing justices is unfettered by statutory restrictions:

> 'Although licensing justices are regarded as exercising a judicial function in the sense they are bound by the rules of natural justice, it has always been recognised that the licensed premises for the sale of intoxicating liquor inevitably involves a large element of administrative policy.' (See *Frome United Breweries Co Ltd v Bath JJ* [1926] AC 586, [1926] All ER Rep 576.)

(9) It is open to justices to rely upon local knowledge and to refuse an application on this ground even in the absence of objectors: see *R v Crown Court at Manchester, ex p Dransfield Novelty Co Ltd* (16 February 1981, unreported)). Although this was a decision under the Gaming Act 1968, Glidewell J's comments are pertinent to this appeal:

> 'The Crown Court on appeals must have some evidence before it on which it can properly reach its conclusion. It cannot decide on no evidence. It cannot properly guess or simply make assumptions not founded on evidence ... the nature of the evidence called or accepted in licensing matters generally is not of the nature of evidence called, for instance, in the criminal courts. Licensing courts and authorities dealing with licensing matters are not bound by the strict rules of evidence and they can, therefore, and properly do, accept hearsay evidence and unproved documents. Again, what weight they attach to such evidence is a matter for them to consider.'

(10) When justices have to exercise a discretion, it must be a judicial discretion and not a mere capricious act, regardless of the special circumstances of each application and where justices act capriciously, mandamus will lie. If justices come to a decision of fact, which there was no evidence to support, then they commit an error of law which the High Court will correct (per Roch J in *White v South East Cornwall JJ* [1989] COD 402).

THE DECISION OF SEDLEY J

14. When the matter came before Sedley J on 3 April 1998 his Lordship considered the legitimacy of asking for the identity of the shareholders. He concluded that, although it was not legitimate to inquire as to who would benefit from the licensed activity, it was legitimate to consider whether the identity of those who control the company which employs the licensee was such that he should not be granted a licence because of the control which others who cannot be trusted are in a position to exert over him. He stated:

> 'It is plain that there has never been an absolute bar on inquiries going wider than the personal character of the licensee. Equally it is clear that s 3 of the Licensing Act 1964 does not give licensing justices a roving commission to inquire into anything that arouses their curiosity. As Mr Duffy says, English law in various ways recognises a right to be left alone, save where some invasion is clearly warranted by the law itself ... I have reached the clear conclusion that while the mere question of who will benefit from licensed activity cannot be a legitimate inquiry for the purposes of s 3, it is perfectly legitimate for the justices to consider whether the identity of those who control the company which employs the licensee and owns the premises is such that they consider the licensee, in Bankes J's phrase, [in *R v Hyde JJ, ex p Atherton* [1912] 1 KB 645 at 665, [1911–13] All ER Rep 713 at 723] to be "such a man in such a position" that he is not a fit and proper person to hold the licence, or that, even if he himself is a fit and proper person, he should not be granted a licence because of the control which others who cannot be trusted are in a position to exert on him.'

15. Having considered the case of *Ex p Cooper* he stated:

> '... there is in my view no distinction of principle between that case and the present one. The justices may come to no similar conclusion here [ie a

a different]. But that does not disable them from embarking on the inquiry nor from drawing an adverse inference if they are met with silence.'

THE SECOND DECISION OF THE CROWN COURT

16. The Crown Court, presided over by Judge Clarke and licensing justices, stated:

b 'The issue before us is effectively this. Should the licence transfer be refused as a result of the failure of the appellants to disclose the principal shareholders of RBNB so that their identity cannot be discovered and thus the court being placed in a position whereby it cannot satisfy themselves as to the fitness of those capable of exercising ultimate influence or control upon the licensee, and is this a properly material consideration for the court c in the circumstances of this case to have regard to, or is it a matter to which the court should have no regard, it not being a legitimate consideration.'

17. The court set out in extended form their findings:

'(1) That the policy provision set out in para 4(1) of the policy as amended d on 2 September is a proper policy. (2) That we believe in the circumstances of this case that in the proper exercise of our discretion, the identity of those in a position to influence or control the management of the premises should be inquired into, so that we can be satisfied that they are people who would not be refused a licence as not being fit and proper. We find it difficult to e envisage a case where it would not be proper to make such inquiries. (3) We find that such inquiry into the identity of the principal shareholders in RBNB is a proper and legitimate inquiry because it is they who are the beneficial owners of the company, it is they who ultimately control the policy of the company, it is they who hire and fire the managing director. The company is in reality them. It is they who have refused to disclose their f identity to the court. (4) The court believes it is self-evident and transparent that those who hold the justices licence and that those who own the premises who are in a position to control and influence the premises should be fit and proper. It is legitimate for a court to be satisfied there is no question of the licensee being a stalking horse for others who might influence and control g the person in his management of the premises. (5) We find as a fact that a legitimate and proper inquiry does not cease at the managing director. It is not fanciful, we find, to say that the shareholders might seek to influence or control Mr Kehoe in his management of the premises. (6) There has been no proper inquiry in this case as to whether the shareholders can be called fit and proper other than the assertions of Mr Walsh … In the absence of h information by which the identity of the persons concerned can be discovered and proper inquiries made, the court would not be exercising its discretion judicially to declare itself satisfied as to the fitness and suitability of the persons concerned, that is in the present instance, the shareholders. (7) Accordingly, this court exercising its discretion judicially as it must, and j having regard to its responsibility as licensing justices to ensure that the licensing laws are properly observed, comes to the conclusion and seeking to exercise its discretion, it is proper for the court to inquire into the identity of the shareholders of RBNB so that the court can satisfy itself that the principal shareholders, in accordance with para 4(1) of the policy, are not people who would be refused a licence as being not fit and proper to hold a licence. The court cannot be properly satisfied that they are fit and proper persons to exercise control and influence over the licensee and his management of the premises. The court not being able to carry out such inquiry, such that it can be properly satisfied, and although Mr Kehoe himself is a fit and proper person, the court is not able to grant Mr Kehoe's application.' a

THE DECISION OF NEWMAN J

18. Newman J overturned the decision and rejected the reasoning of the Crown Court. He considered in detail the decision of *Ex p Atherton* and, in particular, two passages from the judgments, first of Lord Alverstone CJ: b

'I can conceive that cases might exist in which the terms of the tenancy were such that the licensee would have no proper control—would not really be the effective licence holder—and therefore might be a person who really ought not to have a licence granted to him. That would be a circumstance which the justices would be entitled to take into consideration.' (See [1912] 1 KB 645 at 657, [1911–13] All ER Rep 713 at 719.) c

19. The second citation is from the judgment of Bankes J:

'It may be that the circumstances are such that the only legitimate inference from a consideration of these terms is that the applicant cannot carry on his trade without infringing the law, and if the only legitimate conclusion from the terms arranged … is that in any ordinary business it would be impossible for the applicant to carry on his trade either without permitting drunkenness, or permitting gaming, or watering his beer, or some such infringement of the law, then I think the justices might legitimately come to the conclusion that such a man in such a position was not a fit and proper person to hold a licence.' (See [1912] 1 KB 645 at 665, [1911–13] All ER Rep 713 at 723.) d e

20. Newman J concluded: f

'I should not be understood as holding that if the evidence disclosed a risk that the premises could be a front for criminal activity that such a risk would be outside the justices' range of considerations. On the contrary, it would plainly be relevant. The excess of jurisdiction derives from it being a consideration in a case where there is no evidence to establish its existence.' g

21. There are other passages in the judgment which emphasise the necessity for evidence and the absence of it in the instant case.

THE APPEAL

Grounds one and two h

22. Lord Carlile of Berriew QC, on behalf of the chief constable, submitted that the learned judge erred in law in holding that the licensing justices and the Crown Court were not entitled to know the identity or the identities of the shareholders of the applicant company in considering how to exercise their discretion under s 3 of the 1964 Act, and therefore, in effect, that the same is not a material consideration for licensing purposes. He was also wrong to hold that the licensing justices were not entitled to force an answer to the question as to the identity or identities of the shareholders prior to exercising their discretion. j

23. In the appellant's skeleton argument it is contended that the real issue in the case is whether the justices were entitled to ask the question at all. That they were entitled to ask the question was settled by Sedley J. If they were entitled to

a ask it, it is submitted that they were entitled to an answer. In the absence of an answer, they were entitled to refuse the transfer of the licence as the applicant had deliberately failed to satisfy them as to something which they properly viewed as a material consideration and which they were entitled to treat as a prerequisite to the grant of any licence in their area.

24. I am not persuaded that the learned judge did hold that the justices and the b Crown Court were not entitled to know the identity of the shareholders. Sedley J (as he then was), correctly in my view, held that they were entitled to ask the question. In so stating, Sedley J was not departing from principle or creating new law. He was merely applying established principle. In *Ex p Cooper*, the court inquired beyond the characteristics of the proposed licensee to establish whether he was a fit and proper person. There was evidence to suggest that there were c persons behind the applicant who, by their existence and proximity to the applicant, might well have compromised the integrity of the applicant in the exercise of his control over the premises.

25. In the case of *Ex p Cooper*, Mann LJ, giving the decision of the Divisional Court, said:

d

> The point is a short and simple one. In the notes of the judgment of the Crown Court here is this to be found: "We find that this application has behind it a family firm which we do not accept as law abiding and of the integrity required for this sort of venture. Whatever has been done between the decision of the magistrates and our decision is what we call a paper e exercise." That is a conclusion reached without misdirection, the conclusion which this court, as a court of review and not an appellate court, should not call into question.'

26. I cannot accept the argument that in the absence of an answer the Crown Court was entitled to refuse the transfer of the licence on the ground that the f applicant had failed to satisfy them as to something they properly viewed as a material consideration. Sedley J did not so hold. He recognised that no distinction of principle arose between *Ex p Cooper* and the present case. The question was legitimate. He did not hold that silence or refusal to answer the question automatically disentitled the applicant to his licence. He stated that it was open to g them to 'draw an inference if they are met with silence', which is fundamentally different.

27. Lord Carlile submitted that the withholding of the information is in itself an index of the fitness and bona fides of those capable of exercising a degree of control or influence over the management of the company, which in turn employs h the particular proposed licensee. That is a material consideration in the context of the exercise of discretion under s 3(1) of the 1964 Act and it would be 'irresponsible and unreasonable' for the justices to grant the application in the absence of such evidence. To hold otherwise would be a rogues charter:

> 'For example, if told their identity the police might be able to establish by j evidence that the owners of the majority shareholding … were money launderers of large scale drug dealers, persons engaged in the evasion of custom duties on the importation of alcoholic drinks or the trustees of persons serving prison sentences for offences involving pornography.'

28. I do not accept the argument that withholding of the information is indicative of the lack of fitness or bona fides of the shareholders. They are

exercising a right which is given to them by virtue of the structure embodied in the Companies Acts in our domestic legislation.

29. Since the Companies Act 1967 unlimited companies have been relieved from the disclosure requirements in respect of the accounts that apply to limited companies (private or public). The members of an unlimited company are liable in a liquidation to contribute to the whole of the company's debts or obligations, however heavy they may be. An unlimited company must now be classified as a private company under the system of specification originally introduced by the Companies Act 1980. Unlimited companies may be registered either with or without a capital divided into shares. The memorandum of association must state: (1) the name of the proposed company; (2) whether the registered office of the company is to be situated in England or Scotland; and (3) the objects for which the company is to be established (see s 2(1) of the Companies Act 1985).

30. The memorandum must be accompanied by articles of association which must state the amount of the company's share capital, if any. As regards the powers of an unlimited company and its directors, the conduct of its business and proceedings, the alterations of its memorandum or articles of association and its winding up, the same considerations apply as in the case of a limited company. Returns required to be made by unlimited companies are the same as those by other companies, except that an unlimited company with no share capital is under no obligation to lodge a return of allotments. Unlimited companies are exempt from the obligation to file accounts. The advantage of secrecy can be obtained at the price of losing limited liability. The company's shareholding, together with that of associated companies has been structured in such a way that the shareholder's identity does not appear on any public register. Accordingly the law permits and protects the advantage of secrecy of the shareholders at the price of forfeiting limited liability (see *Gore-Browne on Companies* (44th edn, 1986)).

31. As Mr Roderick Cordara QC, on behalf of the company, pointed out, correctly, there exist mechanisms for investigating, controlling and dealing with the management of both limited and unlimited companies which eliminate, or significantly reduce, the opportunity to operate outside the law. He indicated, by way of example, investigation by DTI inspectors under s 432 of the 1985 Act; money laundering legislation, which requires banks and financial institutions to disclose suspect transactions, and which provides for forfeiture of the proceeds of crime; competition investigations pursuant to ss 25 to 30 of the Competition Act 1998; not least, the considerable powers of the police where there is suspicion that an offence has been committed. These methods include the power to require the beneficial ownership of shares to be disclosed. These powers are not conferred on licensing justices.

32. Accordingly I reject the notion that it would be irresponsible or unreasonable for the justices to grant the application in the absence of such evidence. The right to privacy in business affairs is not a rogue's charter.

33. It may be that the Crown Court, and maybe the justices, were not fully aware of the unique legal character of an unlimited company and the mechanisms which exist to control it. Consequently they may have been too ready to conclude, as they did, that—

> 'The court cannot be properly satisfied that they are fit and proper persons to exercise control and influence over the licensee and his management of the premises. The court not being able to carry out such inquiry, such that

a it can be properly satisfied, and although Mr Kehoe himself is a fit and proper person, the court is not able to grant Mr Kehoe's application.'

34. On the facts found by the Crown Court and the evidence adduced before it, an inquiry into the identity of the ultimate beneficial shareholders of RBNB was a legitimate inquiry for the purposes of deciding whether the licence should be transferred to Mr Kehoe.

b 35. The applicant, the directors of the company and the shareholders were entitled to decline to disclose the identity other than that RBNB is an unlimited company. Newman J said:

> c 'It is not easy to contemplate how an owner who intends, or who on the evidence is going to take day-to-day control, can remain anonymous, but assuming such a case, there must be evidence upon which the justices can conclude that the owner is not a fit and proper person before concluding that the applicant is not, because of the owner's control over him, and for that reason refusing a licence. The respondent has not submitted that a legitimate judicial inference from the mere refusal of the shareholders to identify d themselves justifies an inference that they are not fit and proper. There could be rational and respectable reasons for not being known as carrying on business in the licensed trade.'

36. In my judgment the Crown Court were not entitled, solely on the ground of refusal to disclose the identity of the shareholders of RBNB, to refuse the e application. They were not entitled to conclude that if there was any inability to carry out its inquiry completely or perfectly, it was incapable of being satisfied as to the fitness and propriety of Mr Kehoe and so refuse the application. However, the court was entitled to draw an inference from the withholding of the information. But before drawing any inference, adverse or otherwise, there had to f be some evidence, other than the refusal from which it could properly reach its conclusions.

37. As Glidewell J said in *R v Crown Court at Manchester, ex p Dransfield Novelty Co Ltd* (16 February 1981, unreported): 'It cannot decide on no evidence. It cannot properly guess or simply make assumptions not found on evidence …' The evidence must point towards the inference to be drawn. The evidence must g not be neutral or such that it would be equally fair to draw a favourable inference, for example, the existence of a right protected by law.

38. The court was not bound by the strict rules of evidence. They could properly have accepted hearsay evidence and unproved documents. For example, the divisional licensing officer might have said on oath that, from his inquiries, it was h his belief that the shareholders were parties to the laundering of drug proceeds and then subjected himself to cross-examination. If they do draw an inference, then it must be a fair and proper inference based on the whole of the evidence. The inference or conclusion must be clearly stated in open court.

39. In the instant case there was simply no evidence from which a legitimate j conclusion could be drawn that Mr Kehoe was not a fit and proper person because 'he would have no proper control or would not be an effective licence holder' or that he could not operate the premises 'without infringing the law', or that his relationship with the shareholders might render him 'indifferent' as to whether he conducted the business properly. As Roch J said in *White v South East Cornwall JJ* [1989] COD 402: 'If the justices came to decision of fact which there is no evidence to support, then they commit an error of law which the High Court will correct.'

The balancing exercise

40. Mr Cordara submitted before Newman J that, instead of refusing the grant on the ground that it did, the court should have gone on to perform a balancing exercise. The judge agreed. In the third ground of appeal Lord Carlile submitted that the judge was wrong in law to hold that the licensing justices were bound, in the absence of evidence of identity, to consider exercising their discretion in favour of the applicant. He posed the rhetorical question, 'What balancing exercise could they perform given they were deprived of a vital ingredient to place on the scales?' Where the identity of the owners is deliberately withheld, licensing justices could never acquire the evidence which might disclose that the premises were 'to be run as a front for criminal activity'.

41. On my analysis the justices were not entitled to withhold the licence in the absence of evidence of identity.The Crown Court should have gone on to exercise its discretion in a judicial manner. The non-disclosure, and any inference drawn, was a matter which could properly be taken into account. It had to be balanced against all the other relevant factors, which included: (1) the disclosed identity of the directors and the area manager and that there was no objection to their fitness and propriety; (2) that there was no objection to the fitness and propriety of Mr Kehoe, the licensee, as they found; (3) that the premises had previously been run properly in accordance with the terms of the licence; (4) their important finding of fact on both occasions that the shareholders are 'not concerned in the day-to-day running of the business, the day-to-day nuts and bolts of the business, leaving that to their management team'; (5) there were three layers of managers to insulate effectively the shareholders against any involvement in the business conducted at the premises; (6) the nature and characteristics and mechanisms for control of unlimited companies.

42. What weight was to be attached to these factors was entirely for the Crown Court.

43. The Crown Court did not perform the balancing exercise at all and accordingly fell into error. Newman J correctly decided that they had so erred and granted the declaration. I consider that this was an error of law which flawed the decision.

Ground four

44. Leading counsel contended that the judge erred in concluding that the licensing justices had wrongfully elevated to the level of a statutory requirement their entitlement to know the identity of those persons behind the licensing application. By their policy, they have made it a requirement in Halton that they do not want 'the Mafia, drugs dealers or persons disqualified from holding a justices licence owning controlling interests in public houses'. The policy does no more than to place an evidential hurdle in front of every applicant to satisfy the justices that the ultimate controllers of any given applicant are themselves fit and proper. If they refuse to satisfy the justices of that simple matter, then they have failed to discharge the onus upon them of satisfying the justices as to their fitness and propriety.

45. In my judgment, this ground adds little to what has gone before. It is understandable that the Halton justices do not want the 'mafia' or drug dealers, or launderers of drug proceeds, owning controlling interests in their public houses. Their policy may only place an evidential hurdle in front of every applicant. In order to avoid the perception that they are not applying their policy mechanistically, they must avoid the temptation to decide peremptorily on an automatic refusal when

a the shareholders of an unlimited company wish to retain their protected anonymity. They must then proceed to the balancing exercise. This is one of the factors that must be taken into account in the exercise of discretion.

46. The comments of *Paterson* at p 350 (para 2.464), dealing with the justices' discretion, are pertinent:

b '"Discretion is a science or understanding to discern between falsity and truth, between right and wrong, between shadows and substance, between equity and colourable glosses and pretences, not to do according to the will and private affections" (*Rooke's Case* ((1598) 5 Co Rep 99b, 77 ER 209), *Keighley's Case* ((1609) 10 Co Rep 139a, 77 ER 1136)). Discretion ought to be limited and bounded with the rules of reason, law, and justice (*Rooke's Case*, c supra; *Keighley's Case*, supra). "Discretion means, when it is said that something is to be done within the discretion of the authorities, that the something is to be done within the rules of reason and justice, and not according to private opinion; according to law and not humour. It is to be not arbitrary, vague and fanciful, but legal and regular" (per Lord Halsbury LC in *Sharp v Wakefield* d ([1891] AC 173 at 179, [1886–90] All ER Rep 651 at 653)).'

Ground five

47. This ground can be dealt with shortly. It is said that the judge erred in finding that in the exercise of their discretion the justices were restricted to e consider the question of infringements of the law which might arise *on* the premises. There was no issue either before the Crown Court or the judge as to whether the jurisdiction extended *outside* the premises. It was unnecessary for the judge to define the extent of the jurisdiction for the purposes of his decision. If his decision appears to restrict the jurisdiction to the interior of the premises, f which in my view it does not, then this would amount to an error of law, but about a matter which is immaterial to this appeal and which will not be sufficient to justify the interference by this court with the relief granted.

Ground six

g 48. In ground six Lord Carlile returns to his main theme. He submitted that the judge erred in concluding that the licensing justices were not entitled to refuse a licence to the applicant on the ground of its refusal to disclose the identity of its shareholder. By way of a rousing coda leading counsel exhorted us to consider the following:

h 'We live in a time when the nature and sophistication of criminal conduct is ever changing. The discretion bestowed by s 3 is wide and flexible. It is for local licensing committees to take the temperature of our society from time to time and to determine what is and what is not acceptable in the licensing arena in their local areas. They do this through the implementation and j variation of their policies from time to time and no doubt from area to area. It is to be observed that a morphine addict in 1912 would not have been guilty of criminal conduct and might well have been regarded as fit and proper.'

49. That may be so, but, for the reasons I have set out, I would dismiss this appeal.

ROBERT WALKER LJ.

50. I agree.

a

SIR RONALD WATERHOUSE.

51. I also agree.

Appeal dismissed. Permission to appeal to the House of Lords refused.

Dilys Tausz Barrister.

a

Bhai and another v Black Roof Community Housing Association Ltd

COURT OF APPEAL, CIVIL DIVISION

KENNEDY AND JONATHAN PARKER LJJ

b

2 NOVEMBER 2000

Housing – Housing association houses – Tenant's right to buy – Defendant mutual housing association letting flat to claimants – Mutual housing association not capable of satisfying 'landlord condition' for secure tenancy – Non-mutual association capable c *of satisfying 'landlord condition' until partial repeal of statutory provision relating to condition – Repeals not having effect in relation to tenancy while a housing association tenancy – Defendant ceasing to be mutual association and tenants claiming right to buy – Whether change of status of housing association converting tenancy into secure tenancy – Housing Act 1985, s 80 – Housing Act 1988, Sch 18, para 4.*

d

In 1985 the defendant housing association granted a periodic tenancy of a flat to the claimant tenants. At that time, the association was a fully mutual housing co-operative. Such an association could not satisfy the 'landlord condition' for the existence of a secure tenancy in s 80[a] of the Housing Act 1985. Accordingly, the claimants' tenancy was not a secure tenancy under that Act. It was, however, e a housing association tenancy as defined in Pt VI of the Rent Act 1977. Unlike mutual associations, non-mutual associations could satisfy the 'landlord condition', but they were eventually excluded from the list of prescribed landlords by Sch 18 of the Housing Act 1988 which partially repealed s 80 of the 1985 Act. From that point, therefore, neither mutual nor non-mutual associations were capable of f fulfilling the 'landlord condition'. However, Sch 18 contained a saving provision which provided, in para 4(a)[b], that the repeals in s 80 had effect in relation to any tenancy entered into before the coming into force of Pt I of the 1988 Act unless, immediately before that time, the landlord was a body which, in accordance with the repeals, would cease to be within s 80. Subsequently, the Local Government and Housing Act 1989 added a further subparagraph to para 4, sub-para (c), which g provided that the repeals in s 80 of the 1985 Act did not have effect 'in relation to a tenancy while it is a housing association tenancy'. In 1991 the housing association ceased to be fully mutual, and the tenants later claimed that they had the right to buy their flat under Pt V of the Housing Act 1985—a right that could only be exercised if the tenancy was a secure tenancy. In subsequent arbitration h proceedings, the arbitrator held that the tenancy was not a secure tenancy and that accordingly the tenants had no right to buy. That decision was affirmed on appeal by the judge who held that a pre-repeal non-secure tenancy could not subsequently be converted into a secure tenancy by a change in the status of the landlord. On a further appeal by the tenants, the Court of Appeal was required to determine whether para 4(c) of Sch 18 prevented the changes to s 80 from

j

a Section 80, prior to amendment, provides, so far as material: '(1) The landlord condition is that the interest of the landlord belongs to one of the following associations or bodies— … a housing association or housing co-operative to which this section applies.

(2) This section applies to—(a) a registered housing association other than a co-operative housing association … '

b Paragraph 4, so far as material, is set out at p 869 *c d*, post

applying to a housing association tenancy, whether it therefore created the possibility of the claimants' tenancy becoming a secure tenancy at some time in the future if the 'landlord condition' was satisfied, and whether that condition was satisfied when the housing association converted itself into a non-mutual association.

Held – On its true construction, para 4(c) of Sch 18 to the 1988 Act created the possibility of a housing association tenancy becoming a secure tenancy in the future if the landlord's interest became vested in a non-mutual association. The expression 'housing association tenancy' in that provision had the same meaning as in Pt VI of the 1977 Act. It followed that in the instant case the tenancy was a 'housing association tenancy' within the meaning of para 4(c), and that the repeals in the 1985 Act did not have effect in relation to it so long as it continued to fall within that definition. Accordingly, the 'landlord condition' in relation to the tenancy was the 'landlord condition' as it was immediately before the repeals took effect. Thus the relevant list of prescribed landlords in s 80 of the 1985 Act was the unamended list, which included non-mutual associations. It followed that when the association converted itself into a non-mutual association the 'landlord condition' was satisfied in relation to it, and the tenancy became a secure tenancy. Accordingly, the appeal would be allowed (see p 872 *c* to *g* and p 873 *a*, post).

Per curiam. On its true construction, para 4(a) of Sch 18 to the 1988 Act provides a saving for existing tenancies in respect of which, immediately prior to the commencement date, the 'landlord condition' was satisfied (so that they were secure tenancies), but in respect of which the 'landlord condition' would otherwise have ceased to be satisfied as from the commencement date, by virtue of the repeals, eg a tenancy where the landlord immediately before the commencement date was a non-mutual association. The saving is achieved by preserving the unamended 'landlord condition' in relation to such a tenancy, so that it will be a secure tenancy at any time in the future when the interest of the landlord belongs to an authority or body within the unamended s 80, eg a non-mutual association (see p 871 *j* to p 872 *a* and p 873 *a*, post).

Notes

For the landlord condition for secure tenancies and for the right to buy, see 27(2) *Halsbury's Laws* (4th edn reissue) paras 1125, 1635.

For the Housing Act 1985, s 80 (as amended), see 21 *Halsbury's Statutes* (4th edn) (1997 reissue) 116.

For the Housing Act 1988, Sch 18, para 4 (as amended), see 21 *Halsbury's Statutes* (4th edn) (1997 reissue) 726.

Cases referred to in judgments

Basingstoke and Deane BC v Paice (1995) 27 HLR 433, CA.

Pepper (Inspector of Taxes) v Hart [1993] 1 All ER 42, [1993] AC 593, [1992] 3 WLR 132, HL.

Appeal

Rizwan Ali Bhai and Cathy Cabare, the tenants of residential premises known as Flat 16, 97B Knatchbull Road, London SE5, appealed with permission of Judge Brian Knight from his order made at Central London County Court on 28 October 1999 dismissing their appeal from the decision of an arbitrator rejecting their claim that they had the right to buy the flat from the respondent landlord, Black Roof a Housing Association Ltd (the Association), under Pt V of the Housing Act 1985. The facts are set out in the judgment of Jonathan Parker LJ.

Jan Luba QC (instructed by *Thomas & Co*) for the appellants.
Stephen Knafler (instructed by *Evans Butler Wade*) for the Association.

b **JONATHAN PARKER LJ** (giving the first judgment at the invitation of Kennedy LJ).

Introduction

1. This is an appeal by the claimants in the proceedings, Rizwan Ali Bhai and Cathy Cabare, against an order made by Judge Brian Knight QC on 28 October 1999, c dismissing the appellants' appeal against a decision of an arbitrator appointed under the Independent Housing Ombudsman Scheme. The appeal to the judge was on a point of law, pursuant to s 69 of the Arbitration Act 1996. The appeal to this court is brought with the permission of the judge.

2. The defendant in the proceedings, and the opposing party in the arbitration, is a housing association now called Black Roof Community Housing Association Ltd d (the Association). The Association is the respondent to this appeal.

3. The issue before the arbitrator was whether the appellants, who are tenants of a residential property known as Flat 16, 97B Knatchbull Road, London SE5 (the flat) under a contractual periodic tenancy granted by the Association in 1985, have a right to buy the flat under Pt V of the Housing Act 1985.

e 4. It is common ground that the issue whether the appellants have a statutory right to buy the flat depends upon whether their tenancy is a secure tenancy for the purposes of the Housing Acts. If it is, then they have the right to buy.

5. The arbitrator decided that the tenancy was not a secure tenancy but an assured tenancy, and consequently that the appellants had no right to buy. However, neither party seeks to uphold the arbitrator's conclusion that the tenancy is an f assured tenancy.

6. Before the judge, the parties effectively repeated the arguments of law which they had addressed to the arbitrator. The judge, in a written judgment in which he reviewed the relevant statutory history (as set out below), held that the tenancy was not a secure tenancy and accordingly dismissed the appellants' appeal.

g *The factual background*

7. The factual background is non-controversial. On 9 December 1985 the Association (under its then name Black Roof Housing Co-operative Ltd) granted the appellants a periodic tenancy of the flat. At that time the Association was, as its then name suggested, a fully mutual housing co-operative; that is to say, its h membership was restricted to tenants or prospective tenants. As such, it was registered both with the Housing Corporation (under the Housing Acts) and with the Registrar of Friendly Societies (under the Industrial and Provident Societies Act 1965).

8. Since the grant of their tenancy the appellants have occupied the flat as their j home.

9. In or about December 1991 (the precise date is not material) the Association, by altering its rules, ceased to be fully mutual.

The statutory background

10. In considering the effect of the relevant statutory provisions in the instant case, it is necessary to keep in mind the distinction between a housing association

which is fully mutual, and one which is not. For convenience, I will refer hereafter to a fully mutual housing association (sometimes referred to as a housing co-operative) as a 'mutual association', and to a housing association which is not fully mutual as a 'non-mutual association'. As appears from the recital of the factual background, the Association was a mutual association at all material times prior to December 1991 or thereabouts, when it became a non-mutual association.

11. With that distinction in mind, I turn to the relevant statutory provisions.

12. When the appellants' tenancy was granted in 1985, it was neither a protected tenancy for the purposes of the Rent Act 1977 (see s 15 of that Act), nor was it a secure tenancy for the purposes of Ch II of the Housing Act 1980 (see s 49(2) of that Act). It was, however, subject to the fair rent regime contained in Pt VI of the 1977 Act, since it fell within the definition of the expression 'housing association tenancy' in Pt VI (see s 86 of the 1977 Act).

13. The Housing Act 1985 (which came into force on 1 April 1986) is a consolidating Act. It effectively replicates Ch II of the 1980 Act, albeit not in precisely the same terms. Section 79(1) of the 1985 Act provides that a tenancy under which a dwelling house is let as a separate dwelling is a secure tenancy at any time when the conditions described in ss 80 and 81 of that Act respectively as 'the landlord condition' and 'the tenant condition' are satisfied. (No issue arises in this case in relation to 'the tenant condition', and it is accordingly unnecessary to make further reference to it.)

14. As originally enacted, s 80(1) of the 1985 Act provided that 'the landlord condition' was that the interest of the landlord belonged to one of a list of specified authorities or bodies, including 'a housing association or housing co-operative to which this section applies', and sub-s (2)(a) provided that the section applied to a non-mutual association but not to a mutual one. Thus the appellants' tenancy continued to be a non-secure tenancy, since the Association was at that time a mutual association. In other words, so far as the appellants' tenancy is concerned, the 1985 Act had the same effect as the 1980 Act.

15. The Housing Act 1988 (which came into force on 15 January 1989) introduced the assured tenancy regime. Under the 1988 Act, most new housing association tenancies fall within that regime. But the regime did not apply to existing tenancies (see para 1 of Sch 1). Hence the appellants' tenancy did not become an assured tenancy (and, as noted earlier, it is common ground that the conclusion of the arbitrator to the contrary was wrong). However, the tenancy continued to be a 'housing association tenancy' (see para 13 of Sch 1).

16. The appellants' tenancy could only be or become a secure tenancy if and so long as the interest of the landlord belonged to an authority or body included in the list of prescribed landlords set out in s 80 of the 1985 Act (see para 14 above). However, s 80 of the 1985 Act was amended by the 1988 Act ('filleted' was the expression used by Mr Luba QC, for the appellants), so as to exclude non-mutual associations from that list. Thenceforth, subject to an immaterial exception, under s 80 as amended neither mutual nor non-mutual associations were capable of fulfilling 'the landlord condition' in relation to new tenancies.

17. Section 35 of the 1988 Act also had the effect of removing housing association tenancies from the protection of the fair rent regime contained in Pt V of the 1977 Act. In effect, there was to be no further rent protection for housing association tenancies, subject to a saving in relation to tenancies created before the commencement of the 1988 Act (see s 35(2)(a)). Hence the appellants' tenancy continued to be subject to the fair rent regime. Further, s 35(4) of the 1988 Act

a provides that a tenancy entered into after the commencement of that Act cannot be a secure tenancy unless certain specified conditions are fulfilled.

18. It is material to the arguments on this appeal to note s 35(5) of the 1988 Act provides that if, on or after the commencement of that Act, the interest of the landlord under a protected or statutory tenancy becomes held by a housing association, nothing in s 35 shall prevent it from being a housing association b tenancy or a secure tenancy and, accordingly: '… in such a case section 80 of the Housing Act 1985 … shall have effect without regard to the repeal of the provisions of that section effected by this Act.'

19. Thus, s 35(5) creates the possibility that a tenancy which is currently a non-secure tenancy may in the future become a secure tenancy.

20. Schedule 18 to the 1988 Act contains a list of the repeals effected by that c Act, including the partial repeal of s 80 of the 1985 Act (see above). Schedule 18 contains a saving provision in para 4. In its unamended form, para 4 is in the following terms (so far as material):

> 'The repeals in section 80 of the Housing Act 1985—(a) have effect (subject d to section 35(5) of this Act) in relation to any tenancy … entered into before the coming into force of Part I of this Act unless, immediately before that time, the landlord … is a body which, in accordance with the repeals, would cease to be within the said section 80; and (b) do not have effect in relation to a tenancy … entered into on or after the coming into force of Part I of this Act if the tenancy … falls within any of paragraphs (c) to (f) of subsection (4) e of section 35 of this Act.'

21. The Local Government and Housing Act 1989 (which came into force on 16 January 1990) added an additional subparagraph to para 4 of Sch 18 to the 1988 Act, prefaced by the word 'and'. The additional subparagraph is in the following terms: '(c) do not have effect in relation to a tenancy while it is a housing f association tenancy.'

22. The issue on this appeal turns entirely on the meaning of these added words. Mr Luba contends that they create the possibility of the appellants' tenancy becoming a secure tenancy at some time in the future if the 'landlord condition' in respect of that tenancy (ie the 'landlord condition' applied by g reference to the unamended list of prescribed landlords) is satisfied; and that in the instant case the 'landlord condition' was satisfied when the Association converted itself into a non-mutual association. Mr Stephen Knafler (for the Association) contends that the added words do not carry that meaning.

h *The judgment*

23. Having referred to the relevant statutory provisions much more succinctly than I have been able to do, and having summarised the arguments addressed to him, the judge expressed his conclusions as follows:

> 'If the tenancy in this case was not a secure tenancy when the repeals took j effect, then unless the case falls within one or other of the exceptions permitting the creation of a secure tenancy after 15 January 1989, I do not see how it can be converted into a secure tenancy after the date the repeals took effect. The tenancy in this case does not fall within any of the exceptions in section 35 of the 1988 Act. It would seem illogical therefore if a pre-repeal non-secure tenancy had the potential to become a secure tenancy in the event of a change of status of the landlord. In my view it does not get

Mr Luba very far to say that the repeal is ineffective in relation to a tenancy so long as it remains "a housing association tenancy" as defined in Part VI of the 1977 Act. The words in para 4(c) "... in relation to a tenancy while it is a housing association tenancy", I think must refer to a tenancy under which the landlord satisfied the landlord condition, otherwise it is difficult to see what relevance the provision has. If this is right, para 4(c) can have no application to this case because *at the date of the repeal the landlord did not satisfy the landlord's* [sic] *condition*. A contrary conclusion would be inconsistent with para 4(a). If, apart from the exceptions, a secure tenancy could not be created after 15 January 1989, I fail to see how a non-secure tenancy at that date could subsequently be converted into a secure tenancy. It may be that Mr Knafler's submission as to the purpose for the addition of para 4(c) is right, and that the addition of para 4(c) may have been simply to correct an omission from the original paragraph, as without it s 35(2) of the 1988 Act would appear to be purposeless. Whatever the true answer to this question is, it does not in my view have the result of creating a potential for the conversion of this tenancy into a secure tenancy. I therefore find in the landlord's favour, and dismiss the tenants' appeal.' (My emphasis.)

The arguments on this appeal

24. Mr Luba submits that in so far as he founded his decision on the (admitted) fact that '*at the date of the repeal the tenancy did not satisfy the landlord's condition*' the judge fell into error in that he failed to recognise that a tenancy may change from time to time from a secure tenancy to a non-secure tenancy and vice versa, according to whether the 'landlord condition' and the 'tenant condition' are for the time being satisfied in relation to that tenancy. This potential for change of status is, Mr Luba submits, inherent in the statutory code relating to secure tenancies. In support of this submission, he cites the decision of this court in *Basingstoke and Deane BC v Paice* (1995) 27 HLR 433, where Waite LJ said (at 437):

'The use of the term "at any time" in section 79(1) [of the 1985 Act] shows that the section is to have ambulatory effect. Occupiers, that is to say, may be liable to pass in and out of secure tenant status—depending upon whether their landlord for the time being is or is not a local authority; or upon changes in the tenant's own circumstances taking him in and out of the tenant condition.'

25. Mr Luba relies on s 35(5) of the 1988 Act as providing an example of a provision which envisages that a tenancy may in certain circumstances change in character from a non-secure to a secure tenancy.

26. Mr Luba also relies on the fact that the appellants' tenancy falls within the definition of 'housing association tenancy' for the purposes of Pt VI of the 1977 Act. He submits that on its true construction para 4(c) of Sch 18 to the 1988 Act gives the benefit of protection from the repeals to s 80 of the 1985 Act to tenants who held a 'housing association tenancy' so defined. On that footing, he contends that when the Association converted itself from a mutual association to a non-mutual association the appellants' tenancy became a secure tenancy, and that accordingly the appellants have the right to buy the flat.

27. Mr Knafler accepts the 'ambulatory' nature of the statutory code, but submits that the construction for which the appellants' contend would produce a result which would run contrary to the repeals themselves, in that the main change effected by the repeals was that non-mutual associations ceased thereafter

a to be capable of granting secure tenancies, attracting the right to buy, and that secure tenancies could thenceforth be granted only by a narrow band of landlords comprising local authorities and a few others. He stresses that these changes were of very considerable significance for housing associations, in allowing their housing stock to remain available to be rented out to persons in social need without being liable to be purchased at a substantial discount under the right to b buy scheme.

28. Mr Knafler refers us to s 35(4) of the 1988 Act as an example of a statutory provision which reinforces that view of the nature of the changes effected by the 1988 Act, by making it clear that new tenancies cannot be secure tenancies unless they are granted by a limited category of landlords or unless they are granted to tenants with existing secure tenancy rights.

c 29. As another example of this, Mr Knafler refers to para 4(a) in Sch 18 to the 1988 Act. He submits that the thrust of para 4(a) is essentially positive, emphasising that the repeals are to have effect in relation to tenancies entered into before the commencement date by landlords, such as the Association, who did not cease to be within s 80 of the 1985 Act by virtue of the repeals. This, he d submits, can only mean that tenancies granted before the commencement date by landlords who were not then on the s 80 list were subject to the repeals, so that if the landlord later changed its status the tenancy would only become secure if the landlord fell within s 80 as partially repealed.

30. Mr Knafler also relies on the fact that s 194 of the Local Government and Housing Act 1989 refers to Sch 11 to that Act (being the schedule which adds e sub-para (c) to para 4 in Sch 18 to the 1988 Act) as containing 'minor amendments and amendments consequential on the provisions of this Act'. He submits that in that context there is no warrant for construing para 4(c) as having effected the substantial change for which the appellants contend.

f *Conclusions*

31. I turn first to para 4(a) in Sch 18 to the 1988 Act. On even the most generous view, it is difficult to describe para 4(a) as a paradigm of clarity in statutory drafting. On the other hand it is clear (as I read it) that it is directed to the impact of the particular repeals (that is to say, the 'filleting' of the list of prescribed landlords in s 80 of the 1985 Act) on tenancies entered into prior to the g commencement date: ie on *existing* tenancies. In relation to such tenancies, I construe para 4(a) as meaning: (a) that where immediately before the commencement date the interest of the landlord belonged to an authority or body which remains on the s 80 of the 1985 Act list notwithstanding the repeals (ie which has not been 'filleted out'), the 'landlord condition' in relation to that tenancy is thereafter to be applied h by reference to the amended ('filleted') list; and (b) that, conversely, where before the commencement date the interest of the landlord belonged to an authority or body which has been removed from the list by the repeals (ie which has been 'filleted out'), the 'landlord condition' in relation to that tenancy is thereafter to be applied by reference to the unamended ('non-filleted') list.

j 32. Thus, on its true construction para 4(a) in my judgment provides a saving for existing tenancies in respect of which, immediately prior to the commencement date, the 'landlord condition' was satisfied (so that they were secure tenancies), but in respect of which the 'landlord condition' would otherwise have ceased to be satisfied as from the commencement date, by virtue of the repeals: eg a tenancy where the landlord immediately before the commencement date was a non-mutual association. The saving is achieved not by providing that such tenancies shall continue as secure tenancies until such time as the non-mutual association disposes of its interest to an authority or body which is not included in the amended list, for that would be inconsistent with the 'ambulatory' nature of the statutory code. Rather, the saving is achieved by preserving the unamended 'landlord condition' in relation to such a tenancy, so that it will be a secure tenancy at any time in the future when the interest of the landlord belongs to an authority or body within the unamended s 80 of the 1985 Act (eg a non-mutual association).

33. So construed, para 4(a) of Sch 18 to the 1988 Act does not impact upon the appellants' tenancy since immediately before the commencement date the landlord in respect of the appellants' tenancy was not an authority or body on the unamended s 80 list (the Association being at that stage a mutual association, not having as yet become a non-mutual association). Hence (as Mr Luba accepts) para 4(a) does not create the possibility of the appellants' tenancy becoming a secure tenancy in the future if the landlord's interest should become vested in a non-mutual association.

34. On the other hand, para 4(c) of Sch 18 to the 1988 Act, on its true construction, does in my judgment have that effect. The expression 'housing association tenancy' in sub-para (c) is not there defined, but it is in my judgment to be inferred that the relevant definition is to be found in Pt VI of the 1977 Act. This conclusion is reinforced by the fact that the expression 'housing association tenancy' is also to be found in s 35(5) of the 1988 Act—a subsection which is expressly referred to in para 4(a). Section 35(1) of the 1988 Act provides that in s 35 the expression 'housing association tenancy' has the same meaning as in Pt VI of the 1977 Act. It follows, in my judgment, that the appellants' tenancy is a 'housing association tenancy' within the meaning of sub-para (c), and that the repeals do not have effect in relation to it so long as it continues to fall within that definition.

35. That in turn means, in my judgment, that while it is a housing association tenancy for the purpose of Pt VI of the 1977 Act the 'landlord condition' in relation to the tenancy is the 'landlord condition' as it was immediately before the repeals took effect: ie that the relevant list of prescribed landlords in s 80 of the 1985 Act is the *unamended* list, which includes a non-mutual association.

36. It follows, in my judgment, that when the Association converted itself into a non-mutual association the 'landlord condition' was thereby satisfied in relation to it, and the appellants' tenancy thereupon became a secure tenancy.

37. For those reasons, I reach a contrary conclusion to that which the judge reached as to the true construction of para 4(c).

38. In a supplemental written skeleton argument Mr Knafler sought to pray in aid art 1 of Protocol 1 to the European Convention for the Protection of Human Rights and Fundamental Freedoms (Rome, 4 November 1950; TS 71 (1953); Cmd 8969), which provides as follows:

> 'Every natural or legal person is entitled to the peaceful enjoyment of his possessions. No one shall be deprived of his possessions except in the public interest and subject to the conditions provided for by law and by the general principles of international law.'

39. However, Mr Knafler did not elaborate on this alternative argument in his oral submissions, and in my judgment he was right not to do so. In my judgment, art 1 of Protocol 1 has no application to the issue which arises on this appeal, which is as to the true meaning and effect of a provision of the housing legislation.

40. I should also record that Mr Luba invited us, on the basis of the principles laid down by the House of Lords in *Pepper (Inspector of Taxes) v Hart* [1993] 1 All ER 42,

a [1993] AC 593, to refer to extracts from *Hansard* relating to the addition of para 4(c) should we think fit to do so. In the event we did not think fit to accept that invitation, regarding it as unnecessary to do so in order to resolve the issue arising on this appeal.

41. For the reasons which I have given, I would allow this appeal.

KENNEDY LJ.

42. I agree.

Appeal allowed.

Dilys Tausz Barrister.

R v Criminal Injuries Compensation Appeals Panel, ex parte August

R v Criminal Injuries Compensation Appeals Panel, ex parte Brown

COURT OF APPEAL, CIVIL DIVISION

PILL, BUXTON LJJ AND SIR ANTHONY EVANS

9, 10 NOVEMBER, 18 DECEMBER 2000

Compensation – Criminal injuries – Criminal act – Personal injury directly attributable to crime of violence – Crime of violence – Sexual offences being committed against claimants when children – Claimants bringing claims for compensation as victims of 'crime of violence' – Compensation appeal panel concluding that claimants had consented to sexual acts and that they were not victims of crimes of violence – Relevance of consent in determining whether crime was 'crime of violence' – Criminal Injuries Compensation Scheme, para 8(a).

In the first of two appeals raising similar issues, the appellant, A, had willingly performed, for money, an act of buggery on C, a 53-year-old man, when he was 13 or 14-years-old. C was subsequently convicted of sexual offences relating to A, including the act of buggery. A applied for compensation under the Criminal Injuries Compensation Scheme, contending that he had suffered personal injury directly attributable to a 'crime of violence' within the meaning of para 8(a)[a] of that scheme. His application was rejected by the Criminal Injuries Compensation Appeals Panel which concluded that C's crimes had not been crimes of violence towards A because he had consented to them. A's application for judicial review of that decision was dismissed, and he appealed to the Court of Appeal. He contended, inter alia, that the panel had been wrong to use consent as a disqualifying factor since current public policy required a child to be treated as a victim and not as a consenting participant.

In the second appeal, the respondent, B, also sought compensation under para 8(a) of the scheme, claiming that he had been subjected to non-consensual buggery by older boys when a 12-year-old pupil at an approved school in the 1960s. Taking account of the sexualised environment at the school, the panel concluded that any sexual conduct had probably been consensual, and that the crimes would not have been crimes of violence if B had consented. Accordingly, it rejected B's claim. B successfully applied for judicial review of that decision, and the panel appealed. In seeking to uphold the decision below, B contended that the panel had wrongly assumed that the crimes committed against him could not be crimes of violence if he had consented to them.

Held – Although consent was not a bar to a claim for physical injury under the scheme, it could be a real and important factor in assessing whether events constituted a crime of violence within the meaning of para 8(a). All relevant events should be considered, including whether consent was given and, if so, in what circumstances. There might be situations in sexual offences, such as buggery

a Paragraph 8, so far as material, is set out at p 877 *c d*, post

a and unlawful sexual intercourse, in which events could be classified as a crime of violence within the meaning of para 8, notwithstanding the giving of consent. In the case of unlawful sexual intercourse, for example, the degree of force might be such that a crime of violence had been committed within the meaning of the scheme. It would be necessary to weigh the degree and culpability of the conduct of the other party against the conduct of the claimant. In A's case, the panel had b not assumed that the presence of consent was conclusive as to whether the crime had been violent. Rather, it had correctly proceeded on the basis that consent was the only live issue, and had been entitled to conclude that A's consent or willing participation was highly relevant in deciding whether, as a matter of ordinary language, C's criminal acts had been violent towards him. Moreover, although the importance of society taking an active and sympathetic role in c protecting children in A's position should not be undervalued, the panel had to apply the scheme which did not award compensation for general failings on the part of society, but only for injuries caused by crimes of violence. None of the criticisms of the panel's conclusions were borne out, and accordingly A's appeal would be dismissed. In B's case, the panel had addressed itself not to buggery in d general, but to buggery in the particular context of the environment existing at the approved school. It was impossible to say that the panel had been irrational in concluding that the consensual acts were not crimes of violence. Accordingly, the panel's appeal would be allowed (see p 883 *g* to *j*, p 884 *e*, p 885 *j* to p 886 *a*, p 890 *e j*, p 891 *d e*, p 894 *f h*, p 896 j to p 897 *b d* and p 898 *j* to p 899 *a e* to *j*, post).

R v Criminal Injuries Compensation Board, ex p Warner [1986] 2 All ER 478 considered.

e

Notes

For qualifying conditions under the Criminal Injuries Compensation Scheme, see 11(2) *Halsbury's Laws* (4th edn reissue) paras 1505–1507.

Cases referred to in judgments

f *Gray v Criminal Injuries Compensation Board* 1999 SLT 425, Ct of Sess (2nd Div).

Lane v Holloway [1967] 3 All ER 129, [1968] 1 QB 379, [1967] 3 WLR 1003, CA.

R v Criminal Injuries Compensation Board, ex p Clowes [1977] 3 All ER 854, [1977] 1 WLR 1353, DC.

R v Criminal Injuries Compensation Board, ex p Moore (1999) Times, 14 May, [1999] CA Transcript 789.

g *R v Criminal Injuries Compensation Board, ex p Piercy* (14 April 1997, unreported), QBD.

R v Criminal Injuries Compensation Board, ex p Warner [1986] 2 All ER 478, sub nom *R v Criminal Injuries Compensation Board, ex p Webb* [1987] QB 74, [1986] 3 WLR 251, CA.

h **Cases also cited or referred to in skeleton arguments**

A v UK (1998) 5 BHRC 137, ECt HR.

Gillick v West Norfolk and Wisbech Area Health Authority [1985] 3 All ER 402, [1986] AC 112, HL.

R v Brown [1993] 2 All ER 75, [1994] 1 AC 212, HL.

j *R v Criminal Injuries Compensation Board, ex p Cook* [1996] 2 All ER 144, [1996] 1 WLR 1037, CA.

R v Criminal Injuries Compensation Board, ex p K (minors) [1999] QB 1131, [1999] 2 WLR 948.

R v Tyrrell [1894] 1 QB 710, [1891–4] All ER Rep 1215.

R v Whitehouse [1977] 3 All ER 737, [1977] QB 868, CA.

Stubbings v UK (1996) 1 BHRC 316, ECt HR.

Tinnelly & Sons Ltd v UK (1998) 4 BHRC 393, ECt HR.

Appeals

R v Criminal Injuries Compensation Appeals Panel, ex p August

The appellant, Carl Wade August, appealed with permission of Simon Brown LJ granted on 10 March 2000 from the decision of Owen J on 4 November 1999 dismissing his application for judicial review of the decision of the respondent, the Criminal Injuries Compensation Appeals Panel, on 3 November 1998 rejecting his claim for compensation under the Criminal Injuries Compensation Scheme on the grounds that the crimes committed against him had not been crimes of violence within the meaning of para 8(a) of the scheme. The facts are set out in the judgment of Buxton LJ.

R v Criminal Injuries Compensation Appeals Panel, ex p Brown

The Criminal Injuries Compensation Appeals Panel appealed with permission from the decision of Collins J on 30 June 2000 ((2000) Times, 1 August) allowing an application by the respondent, Andrew Brown, for judicial review of the panel's decision on 9 June 1999 rejecting his claim for compensation under the Criminal Injuries Compensation Scheme on the grounds that the crimes committed against him had not been crimes of violence within the meaning of para 8(a) of the scheme. The facts are set out in the judgment of Buxton LJ.

Allan Levy QC and *Carolyn Hamilton* (instructed by *Roach Pittis*, Newport, Isle of Wight) for Mr August.

Jonathan Crow and *Dinah Rose* (instructed by the *Treasury Solicitor*) for the panel as respondent in Mr August's case.

Jonathan Crow and *Hugo Keith* (instructed by the *Treasury Solicitor*) for the panel as appellant in Mr Brown's case.

James Guthrie QC and *William McCarthy* (instructed by *Hardwicks*, Chorley) for Mr Brown.

Cur adv vult

18 December 2000. The following judgments were delivered.

BUXTON LJ (giving the first judgment at the invitation of Pill LJ).

Introduction and summary

1. These appeals each raise a broadly similar question about the approach of the Criminal Injuries Compensation Appeals Panel to the construction of the expression 'crime of violence' as used in para 8 of the Criminal Injuries Compensation Scheme, the scheme having been made by the Secretary of State exercising his powers under s 1 of the Criminal Injuries Compensation Act 1995. The 1995 Act placed on a statutory basis what had previously been a scheme operated under the prerogative. It was not however suggested that in any respect relevant to these appeals the new vires had altered the position as it obtained before 1995. In particular, the concept of 'crime of violence' had simply been continued in the scheme from the earlier set of rules.

2. In both of the present cases the applicant was refused compensation by the panel on the ground that, while he had been the victim of a crime, he had not been the victim of a crime of violence. The central consideration in the panel's decision in both cases was that the applicant had consented to the criminal acts directed at him. In Mr August's case an application for judicial review of the

panel's decision was rejected by Owen J. Mr August appeals against that decision. In Mr Brown's case Collins J ((2000) Times, 1 August) quashed the panel's decision and remitted the matter for reconsideration. The panel appeals against that decision.

3. In the hope of avoiding undue repetition, it will be convenient to proceed as follows. First, I refer to the relevant terms of the scheme, and make some general comments on its structure. Second, at this stage purely as a matter of background, I set out the basic facts of the two cases. Third, I make some observations about the criminal law applying to the offences in issue in the two cases, since the argument was at some stages confused by misunderstanding on those points. Fourth, I indicate the extent of current authority on the proper approach in law to the construction of the expression 'crime of violence'. I then deal separately with the issues in each appeal.

The scheme

4. Compensation is only paid under the scheme to a person who has sustained a 'criminal injury'. That is defined in para 8 as a personal injury directly attributable to '(a) a crime of violence (including arson, fire-raising or an act of poisoning); or (b) an offence of trespass on a railway; or (c) [arresting or assisting in the arrest of an offender].'

5. Paragraph 13 indicates circumstances in which an award, although otherwise justified under the terms of the scheme, may be withheld or reduced. Those include, in para 13(e), the applicant's character; and in para 13(d) the conduct of the applicant before, during or after the incident giving rise to the application. Both of these provisions are potentially engaged in the present applications, but nothing arises in relation to them in the appeals before us.

6. Paragraph 9 of the scheme further defines 'personal injury' as including physical injury and mental injury, in the sense of a medically recognised psychiatric or psychological illness. Further provisions are however introduced limiting the circumstances in which compensation will be payable for mental injury. One aspect of these was discussed at some length in the appeal and it is necessary to make further reference to it.

7. One of the issues in these appeals is or was thought to be whether it was open to the panel to take into account the factual consent of the applicant to the acts causing his injury in determining whether he had been the victim of a crime of violence, even though that factual consent would in law not be effective to prevent the acts from being criminal. It was a prominent part of the appeal in Mr August's case to argue that since any consent given by Mr August to the acts done to him could not be effective in law to alter the criminality of those acts, the panel were by the same token precluded from taking the fact of his consent into account in deciding whether the crime that those acts constituted was a crime of violence. For reasons that I indicate in para 20 below, that argument was in any event based on a misconception of the law relating to the criminal offences of which Mr August complained. The argument did, however, draw attention to the terms of para 9(c) of the scheme, which includes amongst the circumstances in which compensation is payable for mental injury where the applicant 'was the non-consenting victim of a sexual offence (which does not include a victim who consented in fact but was deemed in law not to have consented)'.

8. It is important to see how para 9(c) fits into the structure of the scheme. Paragraph 8 limits compensation to personal injuries attributable to crimes of violence. Paragraph 9 adds the further limitation that personal injuries that are mental injuries will in any event not be compensatable (that is, even if they meet

the para 8(a) requirement of being directly attributable to a crime of violence) unless they have been caused in certain specifically defined circumstances. One of those circumstances is, by para 9(c), that the applicant was 'the non-consenting victim of a sexual offence'. In turn, however, the latter category excludes victims who consented in fact but were deemed in law not to consent: the category alleged to be in issue in Mr August's case. Such a person therefore cannot recover for mental injury, even though he is the victim of a crime of violence: because he is specifically said not to come within the otherwise eligible category of 'non-consenting' victim.

9. For two, separate, reasons, therefore, para 9(c) is of no assistance in the construction of the concept of 'crime of violence' in para 8(a). First, para 9 only arises once it is determined that a crime of violence does indeed exist as defined in para 8. It therefore cannot affect the issue of whether or not the consent of the victim is relevant to the construction of terms used in para 8. Second, nor is it of assistance even by way of analogy. Indeed, if analogy were to be sought, para 9(c) is contrary to the contentions advanced in Mr August's case, because it says that, irrespective of the effect of a victim's consent in law, a victim who consented in fact is not a 'non-consenting' victim. Mr Crow, counsel for the panel, sensibly declined to rely on any such argument, saying that it was dangerous to draw support for a construction of one part of a document that had evolved as had the scheme from other parts of that document. I agree. The short point however is that para 9(c) simply does not assist in deciding on the relevance of the victim's consent in applying the concept of crime of violence in para 8(a), because it is directed at the different and limited question of when compensation will be payable for mental injury attributable to such crime of violence.

10. *The facts*

11. A concise statement of the facts relevant to each appeal is not made easier by the claims of each applicant having been substantially disbelieved by the panel. However, it was, rightly, not suggested that the panel had erred in law in that part of its work, although in both appeals it was argued that there were further facts that should have been taken into account. For present purposes, therefore, I can confine myself to the facts as found by the panel.

12. Mr August was born in September 1976. He was placed in care in 1985, and was from a young age a psychologically seriously damaged child, who presented various manifestations of disturbed behaviour, including in particular sexual precocity. There is reason to think, though no proof, that he was sexually abused at an early stage of his life. In the early summer as it was thought to be (there was some uncertainty as to the exact date) of 1990 he met a man called Crow in some public lavatories. He was then aged 13 or 14, Crow was aged 53. Mr August had gone to the lavatories looking for homosexual congress, for which he expected to be paid. He found a willing co-operator in Crow. Eventually, Crow was convicted of three offences relating to Mr August. The first and most serious was an offence of buggery, which took the form of Mr August penetrating Crow. The second was gross indecency, which took the form of Crow and Mr August mutually committing fellatio on each other. The third was an offence of taking indecent photographs of Mr August.

13. Mr August gave evidence at Crow's trial, at the end of which Crow was sentenced to a total of seven years imprisonment, including an extended term under s 2(2)(b) of the Criminal Justice Act 1991. On appeal to the Court of Appeal (Criminal Division) the court accepted that the psychiatric evidence indicated that Crow was likely to commit sexual offences in the future which might cause

a serious harm, and that therefore an extended term was not only justified but inevitable; but it reduced the sentence from seven years to five. In so doing the court said (in the judgment of Lord Taylor of Gosforth CJ) that it was influenced by the fact that—

> b 'the only victim (if victim he was) of the conduct which brought the appellant before the court was a 13-year-old boy who was already corrupt, and who had gone to the public lavatory for the purpose of seeking out someone to obtain money from them for homosexual activity, and who was the active partner in the only act of buggery which took place.'

14. The panel concluded, having heard evidence not only from Mr August but also from Crow and from the officer in charge of Crow's prosecution, that the c crimes of which Crow had been convicted had not been crimes of violence towards Mr August, because of Mr August's consent to what had occurred. It rejected a claim by Mr August that in addition to the offences of which Crow had been convicted Crow had also buggered him. The panel found established only those matters in respect of which there had been convictions.

d 15. In Mr Brown's case the applicant had in the 1960s been a pupil at an approved school, where it was clear that a high level of sexual misconduct took place amongst the pupils, allegedly unchecked by the staff. He claimed that when he arrived at the school, at the age of about 12, he was 'raped' (that is, subjected to non-consensual buggery) on four specific occasions by larger and older boys; and also subjected against his will to various other sexual indignities in terms of e oral sex and masturbation which, if they had taken place, would have amounted to gross indecency. No prosecutions had been brought in respect of these events, and the panel accordingly had difficulty in deciding on the facts, particularly as it found the applicant himself to be a very unreliable witness. It appears to have accepted that the four incidents of buggery had taken place, but did not accept f that they were non-consensual on Mr Brown's part. Similarly, whilst doubtful about the very occurrence of the oral sex and masturbation, it concluded (in the words of the statement of Mr Lewer QC, chairman of the panel, the status of which I shall have to explore more fully below) that—

> g 'in the light of the ages of the other three boys he identified, which were similar to his own, it was more likely to have been consensual conduct between boys than something forced on him or which he had done through fear or because of assaults.'

16. The panel's conclusion was, therefore, in terms that are a matter of controversy in this appeal, and to which I shall have to return, that it was 'not h satisfied that any sexual activity between the applicant and any of the 3 boys he named was non-consensual and amounted to a crime of violence'.

17. *The law as to buggery and gross indecency*

18. It will be convenient to make some observations about the underlying criminal provisions, since they were the subject of some misunderstanding, at j least in the appeal in Mr August's case.

19. The offences are set out in ss 12 and 13 of the Sexual Offences Act 1956, which reproduce the common law. Contrary to the contentions advanced in Mr August's case, these offences were not created to protect children, or any other person involved in them. Rather, they seek to prevent what Parliament describes in terms, in the cross-note before s 12, as 'unnatural' behaviour. For that reason, first, both participants in any forbidden act are equally guilty of it, as

principals and not merely as aiders and abettors; and, second, consent is never a defence and is irrelevant to any issue of guilt. It was for that reason that Crow was convicted of buggery even though he had been the patient, not the agent; and even though the agent, Mr August, had, as the Court of Appeal concluded, been a willing and active partner in that act of buggery.

20. It follows from that that an act of buggery will not necessarily involve and entail an assault, as Parliament has confirmed in s 7(2)(c) of the Sexual Offences Act 1967, which in its provisions as to time limits for prosecutions distinguishes in terms between acts of buggery that do and do not amount to an assault. It also follows that, since the consent of either party is irrelevant to guilt, so the age of the participants is irrelevant: save when there apply the special provisions, not engaged in our case, introduced by s 1A of the 1956 Act to exempt from criminality acts of buggery done in private between consenting adults. The contention advanced on behalf of Mr August that 'Parliament has provided that a 13-year-old boy cannot give a valid consent in law to buggery' was therefore misconceived. Such a provision is to be found in relation to offences of *assault* in ss 14 and 15 of the 1956 Act. But it is not extended to ss 12 and 13 for the reason already indicated, that those sections are aimed at unnatural behaviour by both parties, rather than at the protection of the victim of an assault.

21. *Authority on the construction of 'crime of violence'*

22. The leading authority is the decision of this court in *R v Criminal Injuries Compensation Board, ex p Warner* [1986] 2 All ER 478, sub nom *R v Criminal Injuries Compensation Board, ex p Webb* [1987] QB 74. We were not shown any material derogating from the guidance given in that case. It has been approved and followed in later authorities, including most recently in Scotland in *Gray v Criminal Injuries Compensation Board* 1999 SLT 425. Nor was it suggested that the fact that *Ex p Warner* addressed the concept of 'crime of violence' as used in an earlier scheme made it any the less authoritative as a guide to the construction of those same words as used in our para 8(a) of the scheme.

23. All that said, however, two caveats must be entered. First, although the judgment in *Ex p Warner* does give guidance as to the meaning of 'crime of violence' in general terms, the actual case was addressing claims by persons caused mental illness by witnessing the death of trespassers on the railway. Such offence as those trespassers might have committed, under the provisions of s 34 of the Offences Against the Person Act 1861, was not a crime of violence. It will have been noted from para 4 above that that case is now specifically provided for, but as something other than a crime of violence, in para 8(b) of the scheme. Second, it necessarily follows from the circumstances of *Ex p Warner* that the specific issue in the present case, of the relevance of the victim's consent to whether the crime committed against him was a crime of violence, did not arise.

24. Mr Crow contended that six propositions of law could be drawn from *Ex p Warner*. I agree with him as to the first five of these. The sixth is a matter of more difficulty, a difficulty that has some bearing on the appeal in Mr Brown's case. The six propositions were: (a) The concept of 'crime of violence' is not a term of art. (b) The issue for the panel of whether a crime of violence has taken place is a jury question. As it was put in *Ex p Warner* [1986] 2 All ER 478 at 480, [1987] QB 74 at 78, it depends on 'a reasonable and literate man's understanding of the circumstances in which he could under the scheme be paid compensation for personal injury caused by a crime of violence'. (c) That question is not technical or complicated: as it was put in *Ex p Warner* [1986] 2 All ER 478 at 482,

a [1987] QB 74 at 80, the panel 'will recognise a crime of violence when they hear about it, even though as a matter of semantics it may be difficult to produce a definition which is not too narrow or so wide as to produce absurd consequences.' (d) The correct approach is not to classify particular offences, i e particular crimes such as 'buggery' or 'assault', as crimes of violence. Rather, the task of the panel is to decide whether the events that actually occurred were (i) a b crime; and (ii) a crime of violence. (e) In performing that task, the panel has to look at the nature, and not at the results, of the unlawful conduct. (f) A test (or possibly the test) for the existence of a crime of violence is whether there has been the infliction or threat of force or the doing of a hostile act.

25. All of these propositions are amply justified by *Ex p Warner* apart from the last of them. In that regard, what Lawton LJ said in *Ex p Warner*, was that—

c

> 'Most crimes of violence will involve the infliction or threat of force but some may not. I do not think it prudent to attempt a definition of words of ordinary usage in English which the [panel], as a fact finding body, have to apply to the case before them.' (See [1986] 2 All ER 478 at 482, [1987] QB 74 at 79–80.)

d

26. *The decision in Mr August's case*

27. In both cases before us the original decision was set out in brief (in Mr Brown's case, extremely brief) written form, the panel's reasoning however being further explained in these proceedings by witness statements by Mr Lewer. e Those statements were admitted without objection, and I shall therefore refer to them where appropriate. I understand that in his judgment Pill LJ is to make some further observations about this aspect of the procedure.

28. The reasons given at the end of the hearing were in the following terms:

> 'The applicant's history, his upbringing and his experiences before he met f Crow explain why, as a 14-year-old he was seeking sexual experiences with other men and doing so for money. But to explain and understand does not mean an applicant is entitled to an award within this scheme. On all the evidence, it is probable that Crow was one, though certainly not the first, in a series of men whom the applicant met and had sexual activity with. At 14, g he clearly needed help—but that does not mean he was not a consenting and willing partner to what he sought. Whether he can blame others is not a matter for us. We do not accept the submission that the cumulative sexual experiences he had were such as to nullify consent. We consider he did consent. On the issue of credibility, we are not satisfied that he was penetrated by Mr Crow, and we take note of the basis of the conviction as h explained to us by the police officer, whose evidence we accepted. However, this does not affect our decision on consent.'

29. In para 11 of his witness statement Mr Lewer gave some further background to the panel's decision:

j

> 'Submissions were made by the presenting officer, and by counsel for the applicant. The presenting officer submitted that there had been indecent assaults, or worse, and that the issue for the appeal panel was whether the applicant had in fact consented. Counsel for the applicant submitted that there was no dispute that the applicant had participated voluntarily, in that he was not forced. However, his consent had been vitiated by his earlier history and abusive experiences, and by the age of the assailant, who was 55.

The applicant had been sexualised by cumulative abuse by others, and was not responsible for his own actions.' a

30. It may be convenient to say that counsel referred to by Mr Lewer was neither Mr Levy QC nor Miss Hamilton who appeared for Mr August before us and in the court below. However, it was not suggested that Mr Lewer's account of the way in which the case had been put by Mr August's then representative b was inaccurate.

31. *The appeal in Mr August's case: preliminary*

32. It is tempting to say that the bare facts of Mr August's case render it impossible to say that a conclusion by the panel that there had been no crime of violence was irrational or contrary to law: which is what Mr August has to c establish in order to quash the panel's decision. He was the active and willing participant in an act of buggery in which he was the agent, not the patient. He was equally a willing participant in the acts of fellatio which, or something like them, he had positively gone in search of. The reasonable and literate man of *Ex p Warner* could not possibly be said to be clearly wrong in concluding that in the d ordinary understanding of language no 'violence' had been involved: however criminal and deplorable in other respects the conduct of Crow had been. However, Mr Levy, in a wide-ranging argument, said that that would be far too simplistic an approach to the matter. I hope that I do justice to that argument by summarising its main points as follows. (a) The panel had wrongly assumed that e the only issue as to whether a crime of violence had been committed was as to whether Mr August had consented to what had been done. (b) Even if that assumption were justified, the panel in acting on it was wrong as a matter of law to use consent as a disqualifying factor at all because (i) a child of 13 cannot as a matter of law consent to the acts committed in this case; and (ii) in any event, current public policy, perhaps more clearly than at the time of *Ex p Warner*, f requires such a child, and particularly one with the horrific background of Mr August, to be treated as a victim and not as a consenting participant. (c) The panel had ignored or misunderstood evidence that demonstrated that Mr August in any event had not consented in fact. (d) In so far as this was a different point from those set out above, the panel had wrongly assumed as a matter of principle g that, once consent was shown to exist, there could not be any question of the crime being one of violence. This complaint was only faintly discernible in the original argument, but it echoes the main, indeed in effect the only, complaint raised in resisting the appeal in Mr Brown's case.

33. Argument (b)(i) can be disposed of immediately, for the reasons set out in h para 20 above. The other contentions need further consideration.

34. *The issue before the panel in Mr August's case*

35. Mr Levy seized on the account of the hearing given by Mr Lewer as set out in para 29 above. The panel's own presenting officer had accepted that there had j been indecent assaults (Mr Levy would interpose, clearly a crime of violence) and that the only issue was whether the applicant had consented to them. 'Consent' was therefore presented as some sort of disqualifying factor, that (i) wrongly changed the nature of the offence; or (ii) was treated as a factor that conclusively determined the nature of the acts or offence. The panel had agreed with this analysis, as Mr Lewer's statement, and the statement of reasons given at the end of the hearing, clearly showed.

a 36. This argument takes too mechanistic an approach to what was said by the presenting officer, and ignores the way in which the case was presented on behalf of Mr August. I deal first with the suggestion that the case was one of indecent assault. In fact, as indicated above, it was not; and, in so far as the hearing officer said that it was, he either misunderstood the case (a misunderstanding plainly not shared by the panel, who proceeded on the basis of the offences actually b committed by Crow); or was speaking figuratively. But even if the case had been one of indecent assault, criminal because as set out in para 20 above the provisions of ss 14 and 15 of the 1956 Act render a child's consent ineffective, it would still be necessary to consider, on the basis that the applicant consented in fact, whether the crime had been one of violence. That was emphasised with his customary clarity by McCullough J in an indecent assault case, *R v Criminal* c *Injuries Compensation Board, ex p Piercy* (14 April 1997, unreported):

> 'Consent given by a girl under the age of 16 to unlawful sexual intercourse or indecent touching is not recognised by the law. It does not, however, follow that to commit either offence against a girl of that age involves the use of violence. Each case must be decided on its own facts. Not every application d of force is violent. Just as consensual sexual intercourse between a man and a woman would not normally be regarded as a violent act, so it is with a girl under the age of 16. [The offender's] admission that he had intercourse with the applicant did not amount to an admission that he had been violent towards her. The medical evidence did not negative her consent, and the e board clearly believed that she had not established that she did not consent. Not every indecent touching of a girl under the age of 16 involves violence.'

37. I respectfully agree with that analysis. Mr Levy indeed read us most of this passage, and declined an invitation from the court to say that it was wrong. He said, rather, that the facts of *Ex p Piercy* were very different from those in f Mr August's case. So they were, not least in the fact that in *Ex p Piercy* the applicant was the patient in the act of intercourse, whereas in our case he was the agent. I thus regard the reference to assault in the proceedings before the panel as at best a red herring.

38. I revert, therefore, to the nature of the case put before the panel by Mr August, as set out in para 29 above. It is plain that it was accepted on all sides g that consent was indeed the only issue, in the absence of any evidence of Mr August being forced to participate. The panel were clearly within the proper limits of their judgement, acting as the jury envisaged in *Ex p Warner*, to think that at least on the facts of Mr August's case the applicant's consent or willing participation was highly relevant to deciding whether, as a matter of ordinary h language, Crow's criminal acts had been violent towards him. And that was clearly also the view of Mr August's then counsel, both in his argument as reported by Mr Lewer and in the nature of the evidence that he adduced: to which I shall turn in more detail at a later stage of this judgment.

39. I therefore conclude that in the particular circumstances of Mr August's j case the panel were justified in thinking that (i) the issue of Mr August's consent was relevant to the construction and application of the concept of 'crime of violence'; and (ii) that issue was the only live issue before them at the panel hearing.

40. *Public policy and the child victim*

41. There were two strands to this argument. First, that the panel did not give sufficient consideration to the actual position of Mr August, and did not for

instance consider whether the whole history of his connection with the exploiter Crow demonstrated behaviour of a threatening nature on Crow's part. The presence of threats or intimidation, it was said, was indicated by Mr August's breaking off his connection with Crow in a state of fear, and reporting the events first to the social services and, when that produced no results, to the police. Second, that in any event the concept of 'crime of violence' as directed towards children should take account of recent thinking as to the need to protect and treat as victims children such as Mr August who had been sexually abused or entangled in prostitution. I consider those points in turn.

42. So far as the history is concerned, Mr Crow pointed to powerful reasons for doubting whether Mr August had, during the transactions with which the panel was concerned, been in the vulnerable position that Mr Levy urged. Amongst the matters to which he drew attention was the observation of the Court of Appeal (Criminal Division) which is cited in para 13 above. It is not necessary to descend into this dispute in detail, because I am quite satisfied on two points. First, this was not the basis on which the matter was put to the panel. Second, the argument overlooks the fact that the compensation claimed must be directly attributable to the commission of a crime. When the court asked what crime Crow had committed, during the alleged grooming and exploitation process, apart from the crimes upon which the panel proceeded, it was not surprised that no answer was forthcoming.

43. As to the second limb of this argument, I would certainly not undervalue the importance of society taking an active and sympathetic role in protecting those who find themselves in Mr August's position. The panel has, however, to apply the scheme, which does not award compensation for general failings on the part of society, such as may very well may have occurred in Mr August's case; but only for injuries caused by crimes of violence. This part of Mr Levy's argument was in truth a complaint that the scheme itself was inadequate in its terms and limitations. That complaint was at the bottom of the arguments relying on the European Convention for the Protection of Human Rights and Fundamental Freedoms (Rome, 4 November 1950; TS 71 (1953); Cmd 8969) (as set out in Sch 1 to the Human Rights Act 1998) that were ventilated at length in Mr August's skeleton argument, but in the event not pursued before us. I say no more about that than that I consider the latter decision to have been well-judged. But none of this has anything to do with the construction of the actual terms of the scheme, or its application by the panel. The panel cannot be criticised on this basis.

44. *The evidence before the panel*

45. Mr Levy complained that the panel had ignored or not given proper weight to reports from a clinical psychologist, Dr Gerrilyn Smith. These were prepared respectively on 22 December 1997, 2 July 1998 and 22 October 1999. The first two of them were before the panel. The last, as can be seen from its date, was prepared after the panel hearing and (presumably) for the purposes of these proceedings.

46. We have read all of these reports, and disturbing they indeed are in the account that they give of Mr August's problems and the lack of attention or inappropriate attention that they received in his childhood and early adolescence. Relevantly to this case, they are said to demonstrate that Mr August did not consent, or at least could not give informed consent, to his connections with Crow: so that as a matter of fact the panel was wrong to find that he had consented. The high- water mark of that conclusion is to be found in the concluding paragraph of Dr Smith's last report:

a

> 'It is debatable whether a psychologically well adjusted child connected to their family of origin could have made such an "informed choice". It would be highly improbable if not impossible for a grossly psychologically disturbed and damaged 13 year old boy living in the care system to do so. His life experiences and state of mind rendered him effectively incompetent in caring for himself in his long term best interest.'

b

47. Mr Levy very properly accepted that he could not use that report, which had not been before the panel, to criticise the panel's conclusions on the evidence that had been before it. He submitted, however, that those of Dr Smith's reports that had been before the panel were to the same effect. I fear that I cannot agree. The burden of the two earlier reports is not that Mr August was incapable of c consenting to what occurred or did not consent to what occurred, but rather that any such consent should not be regarded as diminishing the culpability of what had occurred. It will suffice to quote what I think to be a representative passage from para 3.12 of the first report:

d

> 'Carl's understanding of the legal situation regarding the episode with Mr Crow is somewhat confusing. However it is my opinion that adults must take responsibility for their behaviour. Carl was clearly below the age of consent, and the adult must therefore share a greater degree of responsibility for the sexual acts being committed. Children who have been sexually abused are often very sexualised, and will indeed make inappropriate e suggestions to adults in relation to sexual interactions. However, again the onus is on the adult to refuse to take part in such inappropriate activity, and the therapeutic imperative is to seek treatment to help the young person better understand themselves, including their sexual abuse experiences.'

f 48. It is instructive to read this and other passages in the light of the case as presented on behalf of Mr August before the panel, as set out in para 29 above, and the terms of the panel's ruling as set out in para 28 above. The case was not that Mr August had not consented, but rather that because of his psychological state and history his consent was 'vitiated': the view expressed by Dr Smith. It was that case that Mr Lewer was plainly addressing, without averting to it in g terms, in his written ruling. The panel's view was that while such considerations might excite sympathy for and understanding of Mr August's willing participation, they did not mean that he did not consent in fact. Such a conclusion was, on the evidence, plainly within the proper ambit of the panel's judgement.

h 49. *An assumption that the presence of consent was conclusive as to 'violence'?*

50. Such an assumption, if it were made, would in my view be inconsistent with the approach laid down in *R v Criminal Injuries Compensation Board, ex p Warner* [1986] 2 All ER 478, sub nom *R v Criminal Injuries Compensation Board, ex p Webb* [1987] QB 74, which requires all the circumstances of the case to be considered, j as a jury question, in deciding whether the crime as actually committed had been a crime of violence. The analysis of the panel's reasoning set out above demonstrates that no such assumption was made in this case; or, at least, that if such assumption was made it was not the basis on which the panel decided the case. Consent was regarded as the only live issue because, as the case developed and was presented, as described in paras 36–39 above, on the facts it was the only live issue.

51. *Conclusion in the case of Mr August*

52. None of the criticisms of the panel's conclusions are borne out. Owen J was right to reject them. I would dismiss this appeal.

53. *The decision in Mr Brown's case*

54. The written conclusion issued by the panel at the end of the hearing was in markedly shorter and less informative terms than that issued in Mr August's case. It has already been set out in para 16 above, but it bears repetition: 'The Panel was not satisfied that any sexual activity between the applicant and any of the 3 boys he named was non-consensual and amounted to a crime of violence.'

55. For greater understanding, therefore, it is necessary to turn to Mr Lewer's statement. Having indicated the (considerable) difficulties as to the applicant's credibility, he said (at paras 14–15):

> 'Given the sexualised environment, there were also likely to have been consensual sexual relationships and experimentation between boys of similar ages. The panel took the view that if what occurred was consensual, then it would not be a crime of violence, even if it still amounted to a criminal offence because of the ages of those concerned. The panel understood that this was also implicit in counsel's submission, though it notes that it is not how the case is now put in the "Grounds" [scil, of the application for judicial review, referred to in more detail in para 60 below] ... What we had to decide was first whether the applicant had been involved in 1966–67 in sexual activity of the kinds he described ... and secondly, if he had been involved in significant sexual activity of the nature he described, whether that was done consensually or was forced upon him (by fear or actual force) so as to amount to a crime of violence. If he participated consensually, the panel did not consider that he had been the victim of a crime of violence.'

56. The panel reviewed the evidence, such as it was, including a medical report that appeared to show that Mr Brown had in fact been subject to prolonged abuse, going beyond the four acts of non-consensual buggery on which he based his claim. It then expressed the conclusion that such crimes as had been committed had involved consensual acts and thus had not been crimes of violence as defined or analysed in para 55 above, and in Mr Lewer's statement as set out in para 15 above.

57. Having dealt with that issue Mr Lewer continued, in para 19 of his statement, in a passage cited here because it is strongly relied on by Mr Guthrie QC on behalf of Mr Brown, as it was relied on by Mr Keith on behalf of the panel before Collins J:

> 'The panel did not consider the claim under paragraph 13(d) of the scheme ... as no issue of conduct under that sub-paragraph had been raised or argued. Any reference to consensual conduct was to the conduct that the panel considered was an element that determined whether an act was or was not a crime of violence. Nor did the panel accept that anal intercourse cannot be seen as anything but an incident involving violence, as suggested. The panel considered that a person can consent in circumstances in which there may still be a crime but not a crime of violence.'

a 58. *The course of the proceedings in Mr Brown's case*

59. The short point relied on before us to uphold Collins J's judgment is that both the written statement of reasons and Mr Lewer's witness statement reveal that the panel wrongly assumed that, if the criminal acts directed at Mr Brown were consented to by him, then, for that reason alone, they could not have been crimes of violence. It was not, as I understood it, submitted that the panel could b not take the consent of the victim into account in deciding whether the crime had been one of violence. The complaint was rather that they had relied on that fact to the exclusion of all others. The panel thus had not reviewed all the facts and circumstances, as a jury, as the guidance in *Ex p Warner* required, but had applied a dogmatic and inappropriate policy. That approach revealed an error of public c law on familiar grounds of refusing to consider relevant facts or applying a policy or theory without proper regard for the instant case.

60. This complaint is not easy to extract from Mr Brown's Form 86A. The grounds expressed there were, first, that the panel's written reasons, as set out in para 54 above, were inadequate. That was said to be because it was unclear whether the reference in them to Mr Brown's consent indicated that the panel d thought that no crime had been committed; or whether, alternatively, it thought that, although a crime had been committed, Mr Brown should not recover in respect of it because of the provisions of para 13(d) of the scheme (see para 5 above). Form 86A then explored these two, hypothesised, alternatives, saying in respect of the first of them, at para 5(i) of Form 86A, that 'allegations of intercourse per e anum cannot be seen as anything but an incident involving violence'.

61. When I first saw the panel's written statement of reasons I was concerned at its brevity. I am not on reflection sure that that is a valid criticism. It has to be remembered that the statement is issued immediately after a full hearing, in this case a hearing at which Mr Brown was represented by counsel, and at which all f concerned may be expected to have identified the live issues: which, according to Mr Lewer's statement which has not been challenged, were principally related to the applicant's credibility. I also note that a judge as experienced in public law matters as Collins J was unimpressed by the complaint as to inadequacy of reasons.

62. However that may be, it was this complaint of ambiguity that elicited g Mr Lewer's statement in the judicial review proceedings, which I have already quoted from at length. If that statement, and in particular para 19 of it, extracted at para 57 above, is read in the context of the Form 86A it is clear that it is directly addressing the complaints there made. In particular, when addressing the complaint quoted in para 60 above Mr Lewer does not say (as he would be h expected to have said had the panel made the error complained of by the respondent to this appeal) that the submission *necessarily* failed in a case where consent was present. Rather, he appears to me to say that consent must be taken into account before concluding that an act of anal intercourse is an act of violence.

j 63. I make these points not to suggest that Mr Brown is in some way precluded by the history from advancing the case that he now asserts. Mr Crow rightly did not make any such submission. Rather, when reading the documents and statements in the case there is a danger that they may mislead unless the nature of the issues before the panel and as they were originally thought to be before the judge is kept in mind.

64. With those preliminary observations, I turn to the judgment of Collins J.

65. *The judgment of Collins J*

a

66. On the facts of Mr Brown's case there is no such easy answer as was suggested for Mr August in para 32 above. As Collins J ((2000) Times, 1 August) put it, in distinguishing Owen J's conclusion in Mr August's case:

> 'Here the applicant was buggered. He suffered direct physical injury. It was, as it seems to me, in the circumstances of a 12 or 13-year-old being buggered by others, inevitable that he would be injured. Consent apart, this would, in my judgment, undoubtedly have been regarded as a crime of violence.'

b

67. The issue as it finally took shape before Collins J was in narrow terms, and did not involve the extensive analysis that was adopted, at least before us, in Mr August's case. That issue is summarised in para 12 of his judgment. Mr Keith, then appearing for the panel, said that the proper construction of the panel's ruling, as shown by Mr Lewer's statement, was that it had concluded in all the circumstances of the case that Mr Brown's willing participation prevented what had been done to him, albeit that it was criminal, from being characterised as a crime of violence. That was a conclusion as to the nature of the actual offence committed, reached within the ambit of the panel's factual judgement as envisaged in *Ex p Warner*, and not open to criticism as having been irrational or entailing an error of law. That argument was advanced to meet the submission of Mr Guthrie (who appeared before Collins J and before us, but not before the panel) which I have summarised in para 59 above. Collins J recorded Mr Guthrie's submission in these terms:

c

d

e

> '... it is clear that the panel was effectively saying to itself "Because there was consent, there could be no crime of violence. Whatever may be thought of the offence of buggery in other circumstances, buggery where there is consent (albeit the victim's age does not prevent the crime from existing), it cannot be said to be a crime of violence."'

f

68. Mr Keith relied strongly on Mr Lewer's statement set out in para 57 above, that the panel had considered that consent was 'an' element, not the element, that determined whether an act was a crime of violence. That and other parts of Mr Lewer's statement showed that the panel had indeed addressed the particular facts of the applicant's case, without preconception as to the effect of the applicant's consent.

g

69. The judge did not accept Mr Keith's submission, but it is not wholly clear that he accepted the full force of Mr Guthrie's submission either. The judge said (at para 14 of his judgment):

h

> 'I find it difficult to read what Mr Lewer says in that narrow sense [as contended for by Mr Keith]. It seems to me that what the panel is saying is that, because this was an offence of buggery to which the victim consented (albeit as a matter of law the consent did not prevent the offence being committed), it could not be regarded as a crime of violence. It seems to me that the findings of fact that went only to whether or not there was consent shows that that is indeed the case. As I ventured to point out in argument, when dealing with what happened to a young lad aged 12 or 13, the reasons why he consented might well be thought to be material when considering whether he has been the victim of a crime of violence ... Was there in reality true consent which can properly be said to negate the element of violence that might otherwise be inherent in an act of buggery?'

j

a 70. The latter part of this observation would seem to indicate that the judge criticised the panel not because it had committed an error of public law by treating the presence of consent as conclusive of the, properly factual, issue of whether there had been a crime of violence; but rather because, in seeking to review the issue of consent, the panel had not considered that issue in sufficient depth. That that was the judge's concern is perhaps further demonstrated by the b fact that he went on from this part of the judgment to review the law applying to para 8 of the scheme; emphasised that he was bound by *Ex p Warner;* and then (at para 26 of his judgment) distinguished Owen J's judgment in Mr August's case by saying:

> 'Owen J said that it was for the appeals panel to consider all the evidence. c He was not prepared to say that on the evidence in that case the panel had reached a decision which was in any way flawed as a matter of law. Having regard to the facts found, that does not in the least surprise me because, as I repeat, there was no question in that case of the applicant being a victim of a crime of violence in the true sense of that word. He was not injured directly or physically as a result of the crime in question.'

d 71. There is no mention here of the real difference between Mr Brown's case and Mr August's case, if Mr Guthrie is right in saying that the judge accepted his argument: that the panel's decision in Mr Brown's case was flawed not because it made a wrong assessment of the facts, but because, by its assumption that the e presence of consent concluded the issue of violence, the panel precluded itself from making an assessment of the nature that *Ex p Warner* calls for at all.

72. The judge then went on to consider an example of a prize fighter claiming compensation for his injuries, and the suggestion that it would be open to the panel to decide that, because of the existence of consent, the assault occasioning actual bodily harm that he had suffered was not an offence of violence. The judge f continued (at paras 29–30):

> 'I venture to suggest that the "reasonable literate man" referred to by Lawton LJ in *R v Criminal Injuries Compensation Board, ex p Warner* [1986] 2 All ER 478, sub nom *R v Criminal Injuries Compensation Board, ex p Webb* [1987] QB 74 would be amazed that that was so. It seems to me in that sort of case g that consent cannot change the nature of the acts so as to render something which would otherwise have been a crime of violence not a crime of violence.'

73. He then said, in relation to the instant case:

> h 'What was done to the applicant? The answer is that he was buggered. It was inevitable from that that he would suffer some trauma. So much the doctor indicates. He did suffer trauma. As it seems to me, again the reasonable literate man would say to himself that the act of buggery by one person upon another who was aged 12 or 13 should be described as a "crime of violence" j against that 12 or 13-year-old. That being so, as it seems to me, the fact that there was consent (if there was) does not mean that it is not a crime of violence.'

It is difficult to read this passage as being anything other than the basis upon which the judge decided the case. It is notable that, in contrast to the example of the prize fighter, he did not feel able to say that on the facts of Mr Brown's case no reasonable literate man or panel acting as a jury could come to the conclusion that there had not been a crime of violence. Rather, he said that the juror looking at the facts of Mr Brown's case would say that violence had taken place, and the panel should not have been deflected from that conclusion by the presence of the victim's consent. That is a criticism different from that adumbrated in the passage cited in para 69 above, but it does seem to be the basis on which the judge proceeds. Mr Crow complains that if that was what the judge indeed did, he impermissibly substituted his judgment for that of panel, as the statutory decision-making body.

74. The issues in the appeal in Mr Brown's case are therefore as follows. (i) Did the panel fetter its discretion and thus fail to exercise its proper role as provided by *Ex p Warner* by assuming that the consent of the victim necessarily prevented the offence being one of violence? As already indicated, it is far from clear that that was the basis on which the judge proceeded, but if the panel did indeed commit that error the applicant is entitled to complain of it, as indeed he does, in resisting this appeal. (ii) If the answer to question (i) is no, is there any other basis on which the panel's conclusion can be attacked?

Question (i) requires further consideration of the terms in which the panel's decision was expressed.

75. *The panel's decision*

76. As has been demonstrated above, the original complaint was that the panel's reasons had not been sufficiently informative. The complaint now is that those reasons are all too informative, in that they reveal a clear error of law. The latter issue, one of construction, is not entirely easy to determine, but it is illuminated by reading Mr Lewer's witness statement against the background that has been set out above. Reading that statement as a whole, I do not think that it demonstrates the error contended for by Mr Guthrie. In particular, in para 19 of the statement (set out in para 57 above), where Mr Guthrie laid much stress on the use by Mr Lewer of the word 'determined', it seems to me that Mr Lewer is explaining the reference to consent in the written statement as an element in the decision as to whether the crime had been a crime of violence, and not as the only matter to be considered. I venture to repeat the observation about the relation of that part of the statement to the case as put in the Form 86A that I made in para 62 above.

77. It should also be borne in mind, as Mr Crow urged, that at the hearing before the panel consent would have been very much the central issue, because it was or appeared to be important or even crucial to Mr Brown's case that the crime committed against him must have been violent because he had not consented to it. Once that latter claim was disbelieved, it was understandable that the panel concluded that on the facts as they found them violence could not be said to have occurred; and it was open to them to reach that conclusion on the facts.

78. It was rightly not suggested to us that, once Mr Lewer's witness statement was admitted, it was to be regarded as unreliable or as a rationalisation. Nor indeed could it be the latter in any respect relevant to the issues in this appeal because, as we have seen, it was produced to meet a charge of lack of reasoning rather than a charge of irrationality. Reading it as a whole and in context, and for the reasons already given, I do not think that that charge of irrationality is made out.

79. That said, I should make plain that I do not accept the further submission advanced by Mr Crow, though without support from Mr Lewer's evidence as to its having been a ground of the panel's decision, that once Mr Brown's case of

a unwilling intercourse had been rejected there was no further material upon which a finding of violence could properly be based. That, as I understood it, was because in those circumstances the '*Warner* test' would not be met. The latter expression was used on a number of occasions during argument, and appears to refer to the test or principle set out in para 24(f) above: that for a crime to be one of violence there must be the infliction or threat of force or the doing of a hostile b act. For the reasons set out in para 25 above, that requirement, as a universal rule, cannot be extracted from *Ex p Warner*. A test in those dogmatic terms is inconsistent with Lawton LJ's emphasis on the issue being a jury question that turns on all the circumstances. As he said, while there will usually be the infliction or threat of force, that is not a universal requirement. Since however this was not the basis on which the panel proceeded it is unnecessary to pursue the issue further.

c

80. *Conclusion on the appeal in Mr Brown's case*

81. To the extent that the judge concluded that the panel had committed the error complained of by Mr Brown, for the reasons set out above I am unable to agree with him. To the extent that he proceeded on the basis tentatively d suggested in paras 72 and 73 above, then that is not a basis which Mr Guthrie sought to support in this court; and in any event would involve the judge's substituting his own judgment for that of the panel. Such a course cannot be justified in this case. Although the facts are not as straightforward as those in Mr August's case, it is in my view impossible to say that the panel were irrational in concluding that the acts committed, consensually, with Mr Brown were not e ones of violence.

82. *Disposal of the appeals*

83. I would dismiss the appeal in Mr August's case. I would allow the appeal in Mr Brown's case, set aside the judge's order, and substitute an order that the f application for judicial review be refused.

SIR ANTHONY EVANS.

84. The Criminal Injuries Compensation Scheme was introduced in 1964 on an ex gratia rather than a statutory basis, and was revised in 1969. The scheme provided for compensation for physical injury caused by a 'crime of violence'. g The meaning of that phrase was considered both by the Queen's Bench Divisional Court in *R v Criminal Injuries Compensation Board, ex p Clowes* [1977] 3 All ER 854, [1977] 1 WLR 1353 and by the Court of Appeal in *R v Criminal Injuries Compensation Board, ex p Warner* [1986] 2 All ER 478, sub nom *R v Criminal Injuries Compensation Board, ex p Webb* [1987] QB 74. In both cases it was h said that the phrase is not a term of art (*Ex p Clowes* [1977] 3 All ER 854 at 863, [1977] 1 WLR 1353 at 1364 per Lord Widgery CJ, *Ex p Warner* [1986] 2 All ER 478 at 480, [1987] QB 74 at 77 per Lawton LJ).

85. I can see no reason for doubting that the comment holds good when the meaning of the same phrase has to be considered, as it does here, in the context j of the statutory scheme, which was introduced by the Criminal Injuries Compensation Act 1995. The material provisions are as follows, under the heading 'Eligibility to apply for compensation':

> '6. Compensation may be paid in accordance with this Scheme: (a) to an applicant who has sustained a criminal injury on or after 1 August 1964 …
>
> 8. For the purposes of this Scheme, "criminal injury" means one or more personal injuries as described in the following paragraph, being … directly

attributable to: (a) a crime of violence (including arson, fire-raising or an act of poisoning) ... a

9. For the purposes of this Scheme, personal injury includes physical injury (including fatal injury), mental injury (that is, a medically recognised psychiatric or psychological illness) and disease (that is, a medically recognised illness or condition). Mental injury or disease may either result directly from the physical injury or occur without any physical injury, but b compensation will not be payable for mental injury alone unless the applicant: (a) was put in reasonable fear of immediate physical harm to his own person ... (c) was the non-consenting victim of a sexual offence (which does not include a victim who consented in fact but was deemed in law not to have consented ...'

c

86. In his judgment in *Ex p Clowes*, Lord Widgery CJ included this comment:

'What the meaning of "crime of violence" is in my opinion is very much a jury point. If the question arose in a case to be determined by a jury I should have thought the judge would have to leave the meaning of the phrase to the jury and would possibly interfere with their deliberations to the minimum.' d (See [1977] 3 All ER 854 at 863, [1977] 1 WLR 1353 at 1364.)

87. Mr Crow for the board adopted this as part of his submissions in this case. If it means no more than that the court should endeavour to give the phrase its natural and ordinary meaning, as it is required to do by the normal rules of statutory interpretation, then of course I do not demur. But I do not think that e treating the matter 'as a jury point' adds anything to this basic proposition. Even if the meaning was to be decided by a jury, it would be necessary for the judge to give a direction to that effect, and the search for the natural and ordinary meaning would be taken no further. In effect, the jury would have the same task as the judge does now.

f

88. The judgments in *Ex p Clowes* showed different approaches to the definition of 'crime of violence', but all were agreed that it was necessary to have regard to the context of the criminal injuries compensation scheme in which the words were found ([1977] 3 All ER 854 at 858, 861, 863, [1977] 1 WLR 1353 at 1358, 1361, 1364 per Eveleigh, Wien JJ and Lord Widgery CJ respectively). The inclusion of personal injury caused by arson and poisoning was regarded as g relevant ([1977] 3 All ER 854 at 839, 862, [1977] 1 WLR 1353 at 1359, 1362 per Eveleigh and Wien JJ). Whilst it was not necessary that 'actual physical force' was used in the commission of the crime ([1977] 3 All ER 854 at 858, [1977] 1 WLR 1353 at 1358 per Eveleigh J), nevertheless the crime had to be one which 'concerned' violence to the person, or at least one which involved the possibility h of violence to another person ([1977] 3 All ER 854 at 862, 863, [1977] 1 WLR 1353 at 1362, 1364 per Wien J and Lord Widgery CJ). Lord Widgery added ([1977] 3 All ER 854 at 864, [1977] 1 WLR 1353 at 1364) that a jury could be invited to consider 'whether violence in this context does not mean an unlawful use of force or threats directed at the person of another'.

j

89. The judgment of the court in *Ex p Warner* was given by Lawton LJ. He approved the submission made by Michael Wright QC (as he then was), counsel for the board, which is found at [1987] QB 74 at 76. The suggested definition was a crime 'which involved the infliction or threat of force to a victim' ([1986] 2 All ER 478 at 481, [1987] QB 74 at 79 per Lawton LJ), and 'what matters is the nature of the crime, not its likely consequences' ([1986] 2 All ER 478 at 482, [1987] QB 74 at 79). Lawton LJ added: 'Most crimes of violence will involve the

a infliction or threat of force, but some may not' ([1986] 2 All ER 478 at 482, [1987] QB 74 at 79–80). He contemplated, therefore, a 'crime of violence' for the purposes of the scheme where force was neither threatened nor used.

90. We were also referred to *R v Criminal Injuries Compensation Board, ex p Piercy* (14 April 1997, unreported) where the offence committed against the applicant was that of having unlawful sexual intercourse with a girl under the age of 16. b McCullough J held that in the circumstances of that case no 'crime of violence' was committed. There was evidence of a bruise on the middle of the girl's thigh but 'the medical evidence did not negate her consent, and the board clearly believed that she had not established that she did not consent'. The judge said: 'It does not, however, follow that to commit either offence against a girl of that age involves the use of violence. Each case must be decided on its own merits. c Not every application of force is violent.' The application was made under the 1990 scheme.

91. Coming to the 1995 statutory scheme, para 9 extends the definition of personal injury to include mental injury, but with the riders in sub-para (a) and following set out above.

d 92. The first question is whether para 9 is relevant to the meaning of 'crime of violence' in para 8 of the scheme. In my judgment, it is. It confirms that a crime of violence may be committed when there is no use of force, but the victim is put in reasonable fear of immediate physical harm (sub-para (a)). This reflects the observations of Lawton LJ in *Ex p Warner*. The profusion of negatives does not make sub-para (c) easy to follow, but at least it shows that the draftsman e recognised the distinction between non-consensual in fact and deemed lack of consent as a matter of law. It also suggests that a sexual offence is or may be regarded as a 'crime of violence' when the victim does not consent in fact.

93. There is, however, no express reference to another situation which may arise in sexual cases, where the victim submits to the sexual act but does not consent f voluntarily to it. Juries are directed that the victim of rape did not consent to intercourse unless the consent was 'real', freely and voluntarily given.

94. For these reasons, I would hold that the correct approach to determining whether or not a 'crime of violence' was committed for the purposes of the scheme is, first, to identify the crime that was committed, and then to consider whether in the circumstances of the particular case the crime can properly and g naturally be described as a crime of violence, taking account of the following factors in particular: (1) 'Crime of violence' includes personal injury caused by arson and by poisoning (I do not read these references as extending the scope of the statutory definition); (2) the statutory definition implies a non-consenting victim (cf *Ex p Piercy* which I would hold was rightly decided on the basis of h consent, rather than the minimal use of force); (3) it also implies a non-consenting victim in fact as distinct from any deemed lack of consent in law (cf para 9(c)); and (4) 'non-consenting' means the absence of 'real' consent, freely and voluntarily given.

95. The need to identify the crime that was committed makes it inevitable that there has been a tendency towards classifying certain crimes as crimes of violence, j and others not. Thus, Lord Widgery CJ in *Ex p Clowes* [1977] 3 All ER 854 at 864, [1977] 1 WLR 1353 at 1364 approved a submission that 'a crime of violence should mean a crime of which violence is an essential ingredient'. But Wien J ([1977] 3 All ER 854 at 862, [1977] 1 WLR 1353 at 1362) cautioned that 'One cannot categorise crimes of violence'. I would respectfully hold that the nature of the crime is relevant in deciding whether a 'crime of violence' was committed, but that other factors must be taken into account before reaching a final conclusion in the

particular case, principally the presence or absence of 'real' consent and to a lesser extent to the question whether force was threatened or used.

96. So, for example, the offence of rape negatives consent by the victim and I doubt whether rape could ever not be a 'crime of violence' committed towards her. Sexual intercourse is not an offence unless the girl is aged less than 16, and her consent is not relevant as a matter of law (except in certain circumstances when the defendant is aged less than 24). But I would not hold that it can never be a crime of violence against her, and in the absence of real consent freely and voluntarily given I would hold that it invariably is, notwithstanding that the offence of rape was not charged or proved.

97. As regards the offence of indecent assault and gross indecency, any assault implies the non-consensual threat or use of force, and in my view the inquiry should focus on the presence or absence of consent, rather than upon the precise amount of physical force that may have threatened or used.

98. The present cases are concerned with the crimes of buggery, indecent assault and gross indecency where a male person is the victim. The same approach should be adopted, in my judgment, as in heterosexual cases, which I have outlined above. By the same token, I doubt whether the victim of buggery could ever fail to establish that the offence was a 'crime of violence' towards him or her, unless the victim's 'real' consent was given, provided always that the applicant could properly be described as the victim of the offence in the circumstances of the particular case—a feature of one of the applications here.

99. Finally, I add one general comment in deference to Mr Levy's submission that a boy who becomes homosexually active and promiscuous with older men may himself be regarded as the victim of the sexual misconduct of others which caused him to develop in that way. I would not exclude the possibility that the boy could establish that he suffered non-physical injury amounting to actual bodily harm as the result of their activities, and therefore that he was the victim of 'crimes of violence' for the purposes of the scheme. However, this had not been explored in the present case.

Mr August's case

100. I agree that the appeal should be dismissed, substantially for the reasons given by Pill LJ. For myself, however, I would place greater emphasis on the fact that Mr August took the active part when the crime of buggery was committed, and therefore he cannot properly be described as the victim of that offence. There is no suggestion of duress or any other reason why it may be doubted that he gave his real consent.

Mr Brown's case

101. I find this case more difficult, but I conclude that the appeal should be allowed for the reasons given by Pill LJ. The board was entitled to reach the conclusion that it did, given the relevance and even the central importance, when the crime of buggery is concerned, of the issue of consent in fact.

Procedure

102. I agree with and would like to support the comments made by Pill LJ under this heading. The practical implications are such that this court ought not, in my view, to seek to lay down procedures for the board to follow. But in terms of principle, and as guidelines, I would suggest that some reasons ought to be given for the board's decisions, their nature and extent depending on the circumstances of the case, and that sufficient reasons should be prepared soon

a after the hearing, rather than many months later as occurred here, though apparently this has been the accepted practice to date.

PILL LJ.

103. These appeals raise questions on the construction of the Criminal Injuries Compensation Scheme made by the Secretary of State exercising his powers b under s 1 of the Criminal Injuries Compensation Act 1995. Paragraph 6 of the scheme provides that compensation may be paid in accordance with the scheme to an applicant who has sustained a criminal injury on or after 1 August 1964. Paragraph 8 provides that for the purposes of the scheme 'criminal injury' means one or more personal injuries 'as described in the following paragraph … and c directly attributable to (a) a crime of violence (including arson, fire raising or an act of poisoning)'. Personal injury is described in para 9 of the scheme so as to include physical injury (including fatal injury), and mental injury (that is, a medically recognised psychiatric or physiological illness). Later provisions of para 9 limit the circumstances in which compensation will be payable for mental injury alone.

d 104. The meaning of the expression 'crime of violence' was considered in this court in *R v Criminal Injuries Compensation Board, ex p Warner* [1986] 2 All ER 478, sub nom *R v Criminal Injuries Compensation Board, ex p Webb* [1987] QB 74. Having described the nature of the scheme, which at that time had not been put on a statutory basis, Lawton LJ stated ([1986] 2 All ER 478 at 480, [1987] QB 74 at 78) e that the court's task is to decided both 'what would be a reasonable and literate man's understanding of the circumstances in which he could under the scheme be paid compensation for personal injury caused by a crime of violence'. Lawton LJ ([1986] 2 All ER 478 at 482, [1987] QB 74 at 79) accepted that what matters is the nature of the crime and not its likely consequences and stated:

f 'I do not think it prudent to attempt a definition of words of ordinary usage in English which the board, as a fact finding body, have to apply to the case before them. They will recognise a crime of violence when they hear about it, even though as a matter of semantics it may be difficult to produce a definition which is not too narrow or so wide as to produce absurd g consequences …' (See [1986] 2 All ER 478 at 482, [1987] QB 74 at 80.)

105. The relevance of the applicant's consent to the relevant events was not considered in *Ex p Warner*. It is the central question in the present cases. Is consent to the relevant events a complete bar to their categorisation as a crime of violence? If not, what is the role of consent when deciding whether events constitute a h crime of violence? Buxton LJ has set out the relevant events in the cases of Mr August and Mr Brown. In each case, the Criminal Injuries Compensation Appeals Panel rejected a claim for compensation. Those were cases in which the consent of the applicant was, at least, a factor in the decision against the applicant. The court has to consider whether, in each case, the correct test was applied.

j

Mr August's case

106. In the case of Mr August, the panel decided on 3 November 1998 that there had not been a crime of violence. Reasons given orally at the hearing were reduced to writing on 18 January 1999. It was stated that 'we do not accept the submission that the cumulative sexual experiences he [Mr August] had were such as to nullify consent. We consider he did consent.' In a written statement dated

23 June 1999, Mr Michael Lewer QC, chairman of the panel elaborated on those reasons. He stated (at para 11):

> 'Submissions were made by the presenting officer, and by counsel for the applicant. The presenting officer submitted that there had been indecent assaults, or worse, and that the issue for the appeal panel was whether the applicant had in fact consented. Counsel for the applicant submitted that there was no dispute that the applicant had participated voluntarily, in that he was not forced. However, his consent had been vitiated by his earlier history and abusive experiences, and by the age of his assailant, who was 55. The applicant has been sexualised by cumulative abuse by others, and was not responsible for his own actions.'

107. The chairman referred to the earlier reasons and added (at para 12):

> 'The appeal was rejected under para 8(a) on the ground that the incidents complained of did not constitute a crime of violence. In summary, the appeal panel concluded that the applicant had consented to the sexual activity, and rejected the submission that his cumulative sexual experiences were such as to nullify consent. The panel did not accept the applicant's contention that he was the passive partner to buggery. In reaching its decision, the appeal panel acknowledged and fully took into account the applicant's history, his upbringing and his experiences before he met Mr Crow, which were fully set out in the evidence before it, including the evidence of previous sexual abuse and his history in institutional care.'

The applicant's consent to the sexual activity was plainly central to their conclusion that there had been no crime of violence.

108. For the appellant, Mr Levy QC submits that a boy of 12 or 13 cannot give a valid consent to acts of buggery. In any event, the appellant was a grossly psychologically disturbed and damaged 13-year-old boy living in the care system and was incapable of giving consent. Parliament recognised this by making acts of buggery involving persons under a certain age unlawful, irrespective of whether consent had been given. It made no difference that the appellant was the active rather than the passive partner in the buggery. Mr Levy submits that it was necessary to protect and treat as victims children such as the appellant even if it was they who initiated the conduct which led to the sexual activity and even if they were the active partners in it. The appellant was the victim of crimes of violence committed by Crow.

109. The only personal injury alleged in the case of Mr August was mental injury. Under para 9 of the scheme, compensation will not be payable for mental injury unless the applicant was 'a non-consenting victim of a sexual offence (which does not include a victim who consented in fact but was deemed in law not to have consented)'. From the chairman's statement, it would appear that the conclusion was reached upon a consideration of para 8(a) of the scheme without the need to refer to para 9. Upon their findings of fact, the same conclusion could have been reached upon a finding that there had been a crime of violence but, the personal injury involved being mental injury, the appellant had not satisfied the test of establishing that he was the non-consenting victim of a sexual offence under para 9(c). I refer later to that subparagraph.

110. Upon the facts in Mr August's case, and the way the case was argued before them, the panel were in my judgment entitled to treat consent as the only relevant issue. Upon those facts, the panel were entitled to conclude that, if there

a was consent by the appellant, there was no crime of violence. What is questioned in the case of Mr August is primarily the reality of the consent. The submission is made that there was no true consent. Mr Levy has argued that point forcefully and persuasively but in my judgment the panel were entitled on the evidence to reach the conclusion they did.

111. I agree with Buxton LJ that recent thinking as to the need to protect b children and treat them as victims did not require the panel to conclude that Mr August could not have consented for the purposes of the scheme and that he had not in fact consented. In considering whether there was a real consent, it was necessary to consider all the circumstances, including his age, background history and personality. It appears to me from the panel's statement of 18 January 1999 and the chairman's further statement of 23 June 1999 that the relevant c considerations were taken into account. I only add that when Mr Levy submitted that 'a 13 year old boy cannot give a valid consent in law to buggery' he was in my view correctly stating the law. Buggery with a boy of that age is a criminal offence and consent by the boy does not make it anything other than a criminal offence. The boy's consent or lack of consent is irrelevant to guilt. What does d not follow, however, is that his inability by his consent to render innocent an act of buggery in which he is involved means that for the purposes of the scheme he is incapable of consenting to an act of buggery.

112. I agree that the appeal in Mr August's case should be dismissed.

e *Mr Brown's case*

113. In Mr Brown's case, the only injury alleged was physical injury, a claim for psychological injury not being pursued. In this context, I should mention para 9(c) of the scheme, which is a part of the limitation upon the right to claim compensation for mental injury. Paragraph 9(c) provides that compensation will not be paid for mental injury alone unless the applicant was 'a non-consenting f victim of a sexual offence (which does not include a victim who consented in fact but was deemed in law not to have consented)'. It could be, but was not, argued that the presence of para 9(c) in the scheme assists physically injured appellants. The argument would be that by expressly barring a claim based on mental injury where consent has been given in sexual offences, it left open by g implication a claim for physical injury where consent had been given in such cases. In my judgment that argument would assist to defeat a suggestion that, in the case of physical injury, consent to events necessarily defeats a claim. It has not however been argued on behalf of the board that consent necessarily has that effect.

h 114. Collins J ((2000) Times, 1 August) appears to me to have allowed the appeal from the panel on the ground that he considered the panel had treated consent as a complete answer to a claim, by itself depriving relevant events of the quality of a crime of violence. Collins J stated (at para 30):

> 'As it seems to me, again the reasonable literate man would say to himself j that the act of buggery by one person upon another who was aged 12 or 13 should be described as a "crime of violence" against that 12 or 13-year-old. That being so, as it seems to me, the fact that there was consent (if there was) does not mean that it is not a crime of violence.'

115. Analysis of the findings of the panel, as set out in their brief reasoning of 8 June 1999 and the fuller reasoning provided in the chairman's statement of 3 February 2000 is necessary. In the earlier document, they stated that 'the panel was

not satisfied that the sexual activity between the applicant and any of the three boys he named was non-consensual and amounted to a crime of violence'. a

116. In para 14 of the later document it is stated that 'the panel considered the principal issue was the applicant's credibility'. Having considered the situation at Greystone Heath at the relevant time, the panel stated (at para 14):

> 'Given the sexualised environment, there were also likely to have been consensual sexual relationships and experimentation between boys of similar ages. The panel took the view that if what occurred was consensual, then it would not be a crime of violence, even if it still amounted to a criminal offence because of the ages of those concerned. The panel understood this was also implicit in counsel's submission, though it notes that it is not how the case is now put in the "Grounds".' b c

In para 15 the panel set out the second issue as whether—

> 'If he [Mr Brown] had been involved in significant sexual activity of the nature he described, whether that was done consensually or was forced upon him (by fear of actual force) so as to amount to a crime of violence. If he participated consensually, the panel did not consider that he had been the victim of a crime of violence.' d

In paras 16 and 17 the panel set out their reasons for concluding that the applicant was an unreliable witness. They concluded that any sexual conduct was 'more likely to have been consensual conduct between boys than something forced on him or which he had done through fear or because of assaults'. e

117. The panel's conclusions on the second issue are set out at paras 18 and 19:

> 'Because the extent of his sexual activities was not clear, the panel worded its decision by saying it was not satisfied that any sexual activity between the applicant and any of the 3 boys named was non-consensual and amounted to a crime of violence ... The panel did not consider the claim under para 13(d) of the scheme, as suggested in the Grounds, as no issue of conduct under that sub-paragraph had been raised or argued. Any reference to consensual conduct was to the conduct that the panel considered was an element that determined whether an act was or was not a crime of violence. Nor did the panel accept that anal intercourse cannot be seen as anything but an incident involving violence, as suggested. The panel considered that a person can consent in circumstances in which there may still be a crime but not a crime of violence.' f g

h

(Paragraph 13(d) of the scheme provides that an award may be withheld or reduced when 'the conduct of the applicant before, during or after the incident giving rise to the application makes it inappropriate that a full award or any award at all be made'.)

118. I read the chairman's statement as indicating that the panel addressed themselves not to buggery in general but buggery in the particular context of the environment of the then existing situation at Greystone Heath, which was considered in detail. That was the factual context in which the relevance of consent was considered. Consent was stated to deprive the events of the quality of a crime of violence in that specific situation. In stating that consensual conduct was 'an element' in determining whether an act was or was not a crime of violence and in using the word 'circumstances' later in para 19, the panel j

a demonstrated that they were not making a general pronouncement about consent but considering its relevance to the facts of the case.

119. Before expressing my general conclusion I add that in my judgment Collins J has put the point about the prize fighter too strongly. I would not expect the reasonable literate man to be amazed at the suggestion that a prize fighter who claimed under the scheme might have to deal with the suggestion that his b consent to the unlawful activity might prevent his recovery under the scheme. Dealing with a situation in which a 64-year-old man, whose wife had been insulted, challenged a younger man to a fight, Lord Denning MR stated in *Lane v Holloway* [1967] 3 All ER 129 at 131, [1968] 1 QB 379 at 386:

> 'I agree that in an ordinary fight with fists there is no cause of action to c either of them for any injury suffered. The reason is that each of the participants in a fight voluntarily takes it on himself the risk of incidental injury to himself. Volenti non fit injuria.'

Lord Denning MR added however that such a man does not 'take on himself the risk of a savage blow out of all proportion to the occasion. The man who strikes d a blow of such severity is liable in damages unless he can prove accident or self-defence'. The reasonable, literate man of today might not be familiar with the Latin tag but would be likely to see the force of those observations.

120. The basis of liability in tort is of course something different from the right to recover under the scheme but I would expect the reasonable literate man to take into account the applicant's consent to events as an element in a e consideration of whether those events amount to a crime of violence. Parliament did not intend to replicate in that part of the scheme covering cases based on physical injury, the situation in the law of negligence in which consent is a complete defence. While not a bar to a claim, it may however be a real and important factor in an assessment whether events constitute a crime of violence. All relevant events f should be considered, including whether consent was given and, if so, in what circumstances. There may be situations in sexual offences such as buggery and unlawful sexual intercourse in which events may be classified as a crime of violence within the meaning of para 8 of the scheme, notwithstanding a consent given. In the case of unlawful sexual intercourse, for example, the degree of force may be such that, unlike in *Ex p Piercy*, a crime of violence has been committed g within the meaning of the scheme. It would be necessary to weigh the degree and culpability of the conduct of the other party against the conduct of the claimant.

121. In my judgment, the panel in Mr Brown's case did not fall into error. On the facts, they were entitled to approach the claimant's consent in the manner h they did and to reach the conclusion they did. I agree with Buxton LJ that the appeal in Mr Brown's case should be allowed.

Procedure

122. In Mr August's case, the decision of the panel was on 3 November 1998. Reasons were given in writing in a four paragraph statement dated 18 January 1999. j Following the grant of permission to appeal, the chairman made a nine-paragraph witness statement on 23 June 1999.

123. In Mr Brown's case, the hearing was on 2 June 1999 and was before the chairman and three members of the panel. A very brief statement of reasons was given on 8 June 1999 and the chairman's statement is dated 3 February 2000. That is very full and consists of 20 paragraphs. The reasoning is very detailed both on the issue of credibility and when dealing with consent.

124. Collins J noted that permission to apply for judicial review had been given largely on the basis that the reasons given by the panel were inadequate. He stated that the objection had been overtaken by the witness statement and the issue was now a narrow one. Counsel in neither case has objected to the admission of the chairman's statement. Indeed, on the contrary, reliance is placed, on behalf of each of the claimants, on the relevant statement. The panel's decision in Mr August's case could not now fail for want of reasoning.

125. However, I do express misgivings about the procedure followed. We were told of the heavy workload of the panel and I am very conscious of that when making these comments. It is hardly satisfactory that the statement of reasons, which is in effect the reasoned judgment of the panel, is given in one case seven and a half months and in the other eight months after the hearing. The desirability of the court giving written reasons in appropriate cases was stated by this court in *R v Criminal Injuries Compensation Board, ex p Moore* (1999) Times, 14 May, [1999] CA Transcript 789. I accept that in most cases the need for detailed written reasons will not arise.

126. In the case of Mr Brown, a four-member panel was convened, though it is not clear what role the other three members have had in preparing the chairman's statement. Nor does the date when the statement was prepared emerge, and, in the absence of explanation, I would assume it was shortly before the statement was dated.

127. It may be that legal complexities were contemplated in Mr Brown's case and a four-member panel was convened with that in mind. If that is so, it would have been better if something more than the three-line statement of reasons had been produced after the hearing. I do not regard the emergence of what is in effect a reasoned judgment eight months after the hearing as satisfactory. It would not normally be acceptable in judicial proceedings.

128. I would expect there to be cases where the need for written reasons ought to be contemplated and a reasoned statement prepared at the time of or shortly after the hearing. Its absence invites appeals for lack of reasons, as in the present cases. Moreover, an attempt to express reasons long after the event, especially when four members are involved, will, with respect, inevitably create difficulties when clarity is sought. It may well be that the differing judicial views which have emerged in the case of Mr Brown are, at least in part, attributable to that factor.

129. I did invite submissions on behalf of the panel on this question which counsel met only with the volume of work as the explanation for the procedure followed by the panel. It may be that a better explanation is available, but whether it is or not, I hope that consideration will be given to the points raised.

Mr August's appeal dismissed. The panel's appeal allowed.

Kate O'Hanlon Barrister.

a

Jephson Homes Housing Association v Moisejevs and another

COURT OF APPEAL, CIVIL DIVISION

b SIMON BROWN AND RIX LJJ

17, 18 OCTOBER, 1 NOVEMBER 2000

Housing – Housing association – Possession – Jurisdiction to set aside execution of warrant of possession – Housing association obtaining warrant for possession after secure tenant falling into arrears – Tenant paying off part of arrears and mistakenly c *believing she had done all that was necessary to avoid execution of warrant – Tenant not applying for order suspending execution of warrant and being evicted – Whether jurisdiction to set aside execution of warrant exercisable in absence of abuse of process or oppression – Whether High Court rule requiring tenant to be given notice of application for warrant of possession to be imported into county court rules – County* d *Courts Act 1984, s 76 – Housing Act 1985, s 85(2).*

The appellant, M, was a secure tenant of the respondent housing association. After M fell into arrears of rent, the association obtained a suspended order for possession, requiring her to pay the arrears of £540·84 plus costs in weekly instalments. The arrears increased, and the association applied for a warrant of possession, e certifying the amount then due—£1,223·64. Subsequently, the county court bailiff notified M that a warrant had been issued for possession of the property and that unless she vacated he would take possession without further notice, and distrain on any goods found at the premises. Following a letter from the association warning her of the date of the eviction and stating that the arrears f had risen to £1,280·64, M paid off £876. To avoid eviction at that stage, M had to make an application for a stay or suspension of the warrant under s 85(2)[a] of the Housing Act 1985. She failed to do so because she wrongly believed that she had done all that was required to avoid eviction. The eviction therefore went ahead. M subsequently applied to the county court for an order setting aside execution of the warrant for possession, but her application was refused. M appealed, invoking the g court's jurisdiction to set aside execution on the grounds that there had been an abuse of process or oppression in the execution of the warrant for possession. In doing so, she contended that it was not necessary to identify someone as having acted oppressively towards the tenant, and that it was sufficient to establish that the end result was 'manifestly unfair' from the tenant's point of view. h Alternatively, she contended that natural justice required the tenant to be put on notice of an application for a warrant for possession, that a provision to that effect was to be found in the High Court rules and that s 76[b] of the County Courts Act 1984 permitted the High Court practice to be applied in the county court. In response, the association contended that s 76 had no application to the present j county court rules (CPR Sch 2) since they were made under the Civil Procedure

a Section 85, so far as material, provides: ' ... (2) On the making of an order for possession ... or at any time before the execution of the order, the court may—(a) stay or suspend the execution of the order, or (b) postpone the date of possession ... '

b Section 76 provides: 'In any case not expressly provided for by or in pursuance of this Act, the general principles of practice in the High Court may be adopted and applied to proceedings in a county court.'

Act 1997, and that, in any event, s 76 could not apply in a case where the county court rules made express provision, but in different terms from the High Court rules.

Held – (1) The court would not set aside an execution in the absence of abuse of process or oppression. Nor would it regard an eviction as oppressive merely because of its sympathy towards the tenant's plight and its realisation that he would have been well advised to make an application under s 85(2) of the 1985 Act. There could not be oppression without the unfair use of court procedures and something more than the mere use of the eviction process—some action on someone's part which was open to criticism—would be required before the court's procedures could be said to have been unfairly used. It followed that a possession warrant obtained and executed without fault on anyone's part could not properly be set aside as oppressive (see p 909 *g* to p 910 *b d* and p 913 *e*, post); *Leicester City Council v Aldwinckle* (1991) 24 HLR 40 applied.

(2) Section 76 of the 1984 Act was expressly referred to in the new CCR Ord 1, r 6[c], had not been repealed, could still apply to the new rules on its most literal construction and, in any event, common sense dictated that it should still apply. Further, there was no express provision in the county court rules which would actually be inconsistent with an imported High Court rule as to notice. However, in the light of the evident reluctance of the rules committee to amend the county court rules, it was impossible to find a requirement in natural justice that the tenant be given notice of a request for the issue of a possession warrant in all cases, although cases might arise where the landlord could properly be held to have acted oppressively if a tenant was never to receive any notice whatever of his impending eviction. The instant case was plainly not such a case. It was not for want of notice that M had failed to make a s 85(2) application or otherwise avert her eviction. She knew full well when the bailiffs were due to arrive. Her problem was in misunderstanding what was required to cancel their attendance, and that misunderstanding could not sustain her claim for reinstatement. Accordingly, the appeal would be dismissed (see p 912 *f g j* to p 913 *c e*, post).

Per curiam. A letter from a landlord to a secure tenant, warning that a warrant for possession would be executed, should expressly advise the tenant of the right to make an application to the county court under s 85(2) of the 1985 Act. It would also be highly beneficial if the standard court form for suspended possession orders expressly referred not merely (as it does) to the landlord's power on breach to enforce the order by eviction, but also to the tenant's right to apply back to the court for relief (see p 910 *h j* and p 913 *e*, post).

Notes

For warrants of possession, see 10 *Halsbury's Laws* (4th edn) para 499.

For the County Courts Act 1984, s 76, see 11 *Halsbury's Statutes* (4th edn) (2000 reissue) 749.

For the Housing Act 1985, s 85, see 21 *Halsbury's Statutes* (4th edn) (1997 reissue) 122.

c Rule 6, so far as material, provides: 'Where by virtue of these rules or section 76 of the [County Courts Act 1984] or otherwise any provision of the RSC is applied in relation to proceedings in a county court, that provision shall have effect with the necessary modification ...'

Cases referred to in judgments

a *Barking and Dagenham London BC v Saint* (1998) 31 HLR 620, CA.
Beale v MacGregor (1886) 2 TLR 311, CA.
Bremer Vulkan Schiffbau und Maschinenfabrik v South India Shipping Corp [1981] 1 All ER 289, [1981] AC 909, [1981] 2 WLR 141, HL.
Camden London BC v Akanni (1997) 29 HLR 845, CA.
b *Fleet Mortgage and Investment Co Ltd v Lower Maisonette 46 Eaton Place Ltd, Lower Maisonette 46 Eaton Place Ltd v Crown Lodge (Belgravia) Ltd* [1972] 2 All ER 737, [1972] 1 WLR 765.
Hammersmith and Fulham London BC v Hill [1994] 2 EGLR 51, CA.
Hammersmith and Fulham London BC v Lemeh [2000] L & TR 423, CA.
Lambeth London BC v Hughes [2000] CA Transcript 1552.
c *Leicester City Council v Aldwinckle* (1991) 24 HLR 40, CA.
McHenry v Lewis (1883) 22 Ch D 397, CA.
Peachey Property Corp v Robinson [1966] 2 All ER 981, [1967] 2 QB 543, [1966] 2 WLR 1386, CA.
R v Bloomsbury and Marylebone County Court, ex p Villerwest Ltd [1976] 1 All ER 897,
d [1976] 1 WLR 362, CA.
Rolph v Zolan [1993] 4 All ER 202, [1993] 1 WLR 1305, CA.
Southwark London BC v Sarfo (1999) 32 HLR 602, CA.

Appeal

e The appellant, Ann-Marie Moisejevs, the secure tenant of a property known as 51 Burge Court, Cirencester, appealed with the permission of Tuckey LJ granted on 26 May 2000 from the decision of Judge McNaught at Swindon County Court on 13 April 2000 dismissing her application to set aside execution of a warrant of possession obtained by the respondents, Jephson Homes Housing Association, such execution having taken place on 30 March 2000. The facts are set out in the
f judgment of Simon Brown LJ.

Stephen Knafler (instructed by *Bobbetts Mackan*, Bristol) for the appellant.
Timothy Fancourt (instructed by *Burgess Salmon*, Bristol) for the respondents.

Cur adv vult

g

1 November 2000. The following judgments were delivered.

SIMON BROWN LJ.

1. On 30 March 2000 the appellant, Mrs Moisejevs, was evicted from her
h home at 51 Burge Court, Cirencester, where she had lived since 1977. She was previously a secure tenant, evicted by county court bailiffs under a warrant of possession. Her appeal to this court is against Judge McNaught's order in the Swindon County Court on 13 April 2000 refusing to set aside the execution of that warrant. The case, therefore, is another in the line of authorities stretching back
j to *Leicester City Council v Aldwinckle* (1991) 24 HLR 40 raising the perennial problem of when secure tenants can properly be reinstated following eviction. The appellant's case in a nutshell is that at the time of her eviction she was under the misapprehension that she had done all that was necessary to avoid the execution of the warrant, that but for her misapprehension she would have applied to the court with every expectation of success for a stay or suspension of the warrant under s 85(2) of the Housing Act 1985, that in all the circumstances it

is manifestly unfair not to reinstate her, and that the court can and should avoid such unfairness (a) consistently with the approach followed in the *Aldwinckle* line of cases, alternatively (b) under its inherent jurisdiction, alternatively (c) by application of s 76 of the County Courts Act 1984 to read into the County Court Rules (CCR) the requirement in the High Court rules that the tenant be put on notice of an application for a warrant of possession.

2. With that brief introduction let me turn at once to the facts of the case which I shall deal with as briefly as possible although they are before us in the greatest profusion and gave rise to a great deal of argument.

3. As stated, the appellant began living at 51 Burge Court in 1977. The tenancy was in her husband's name but, when he left her in 1994, she became the effective tenant. Her son (now 20) and daughter (now 16) continued to live with her. Arrears of rent built up and on 27 August 1999 a suspended possession order was made requiring her to pay the respondent housing association £660·84 (£540·84 for unpaid rent and £120 costs) by instalments of £2·60 per week in addition to the current rent of £51 per week. The order further stated:

> 'If you do not pay the money owed and costs by the dates given and the current rent, the claimant can ask the court bailiff to evict you and remove your goods to obtain payment. This is called "enforcing the order and money judgment."'

4. That was not, let it be said, the first such order to be made in respect of this tenancy. Previous suspended possession orders had been made respectively in 1978, 1981, and 1993.

5. On 9 March 2000 the respondents applied to the court for a warrant of possession. By that date the arrears had increased to £1,223·64. All payments had in fact ceased on 13 January 2000 when the appellant's housing benefit was stopped because of a query relating to her son. Pursuant to CCR Ord 26, r 17(3A), the respondents in their request to the court for the warrant duly certified that the sum of £1,223·64 was due.

6. On 14 March the county court bailiff notified the appellant that a warrant had been issued for possession of the property and that unless she vacated before 30 March they would take possession without further notice and distrain on any goods found at the premises. Given that the warrant was for money due as well as possession such warning notice (of not less than seven days before distraint) was required by CCR Ord 26, r 1(4) (a provision strengthened by amendment in 1990).

7. On receipt of the eviction notice the appellant on 16 March consulted the Citizens Advice Bureau (CAB) who telephoned the respondents on her behalf and prepared for her an application to the court under s 85(2) of the 1985 Act to suspend the possession order, an application which in the event was never issued. Whether the appellant also spoke to the respondents that day and if so what was said was hotly disputed.

8. On 17 March the respondents wrote to the appellant stating that the outstanding rent arrears were now £1,280·64 together with court costs of £80 and continued:

> 'The County Court has informed me that the bailiff will carry out your eviction on Thursday 30 March 2000 at 10.30 am as you have broken the conditions of the court order held against you ... I strongly advise you to use the time before your eviction to find suitable alternative accommodation.

a You should consider contacting your local council homelessness section who may give you help and advice. However, you may only get limited help as they may consider that by not paying your rent you have made yourself intentionally homeless. If you are in a position to pay this debt before we evict you, you should pay us by cash, bankers draft or building society cheque and tell your housing officer immediately so that they can make b arrangements to cancel your eviction.'

9. On 20 March the appellant paid £876 off her arrears and on 24 March, following a phone conversation with the respondents, she also paid the £80 court costs.

10. It is clear that on both 24 March and 28 March there were phone conversations between the appellant and the respondents in which her housing benefit entitlement c was discussed. It is clear too that the respondents were concerned to discover from the housing benefit authority (Cotswold District Council) what the position was and that the appellant (who was assuring the respondents that her housing benefit was 'all sorted out') was seeking the respondents' confirmation that they were cancelling the eviction. On 29 March, however, the respondents learned d from the district council that housing benefit was only to be paid from 20 March and that accordingly there would be a shortfall in payment of the arrears of £433·64. In the result the eviction went ahead on 30 March.

11. Immediately upon eviction the appellant went to the Fosseway Housing Association who the following day complained to the respondents on her behalf that she had been misled into believing that were she to pay £876 and to ensure e that her housing benefit was reinstated the eviction would be stopped.

12. On 2 May (after the hearing before Judge McNaught) the appellant through her solicitors offered to discharge the outstanding balance of £433·64 and that sum has since remained in their client account. The respondents for their part agreed to leave the premises vacant pending the outcome of this appeal.

f 13. The appellant's primary case before the judge was that the respondents had indeed told her that were she to pay £876 off the arrears (that sum representing almost exactly the amount by which she was in default under the terms of the suspended possession order) and ensure that her housing benefit was reinstated, they would cancel the eviction. Had she established this case on the facts, plainly she would have been entitled to set aside the execution. But she failed to g persuade the judge that she had been misled in this way and I for my part, after exhaustive consideration of the documents, the oral evidence and the probabilities, am wholly unsurprised at this. Accordingly, at an early stage of the appeal hearing we refused permission to appeal on that ground (a ground for which permission had not previously been sought or granted) and I say no more about it.

h 14. The appellant's secondary case, however, is more difficult. This is that, even if she was not actively misled, she had nevertheless genuinely come to believe that she had done all that was required of her to avoid eviction. This contention on the facts is certainly more persuasive than the first although here again there were powerful arguments available to the respondents as to why it should be rejected. j One of the problems, however, was that it was never expressly put to the appellant that she was lying as to her belief nor does the judge seem to have made a clear finding that she knew perfectly well that the eviction was to proceed unless only the arrears were paid off in full (whether in cash or by the backdating of her housing benefit entitlement). Although the point is not free from difficulty, I think the right thing to do in these circumstances is to give the appellant the benefit of the doubt and deal with the appeal on the footing that she was under a genuine misapprehension as to what was required of her to avoid eviction, a misapprehension, however, which was neither induced by the respondents nor known to them. a

15. I turn, therefore, to the first of the appellant's arguments which is that the court in these circumstances should set aside the warrant (or at least the execution of the warrant) on the principle established in *Aldwinckle*'s case.

16. The effect of *Aldwinckle*'s case itself was helpfully summarised by Nourse LJ in *Hammersmith and Fulham London BC v Hill* [1994] 2 EGLR 51 at 52–53, thus: b

> '... after a warrant for possession has been executed in this class of case it can only be suspended or set aside if either: (1) the order on which it is issued is itself set aside; (2) the warrant has been obtained by fraud; or (3) there has been an abuse of process or oppression in its execution.' c

17. It is, of course, the third limb of this formulation which the appellant seeks to invoke here and it seems to me helpful at once to see the terms in which the later cases have discussed the concept of 'abuse of process or oppression in its [the warrant's] execution'. I will postpone until later any consideration of their individual facts. d

18. In *Camden London BC v Akanni* (1997) 29 HLR 845 at 849, Brooke LJ said:

> 'The context in which the court is willing in a rare, but appropriate, case to intervene to nullify the execution of a warrant for possession goes back to the principles set out in the judgment of Bowen L.J. in this court in *McHenry v. Lewis* ((1883) 22 Ch D 397 at 408). He said: "I would much rather rest on the general principle that the Court can and will interfere whenever there is a vexation and oppression to prevent the administration of justice being perverted for an unjust end. I would rather do that than attempt to define what vexation and oppression mean; they must vary with the circumstances of each case."' e

f

19. In *Barking and Dagenham London BC v Saint* (1998) 31 HLR 620 at 626, Peter Gibson LJ, describing the passage I have just cited from Brooke LJ's judgment in *Akanni*'s case as 'plainly right', continued:

> 'The categories of oppression are not closed and the court must have the power to intervene in the interests of justice in an appropriate case to correct the position where its procedures have been used unfairly to the oppression of a party.' g

20. Peter Gibson LJ (at 630) then concluded on the facts of that case that 'the result which Barking has achieved through the court process can properly be characterised as manifestly unfair and its conduct can properly be said to amount to oppression'. h

21. In *Southwark London BC v Sarfo* (1999) 32 HLR 602 at 609, Roch LJ concluded that 'the enforcement of the execution of this warrant was a use of an order made by the county court in a way which was manifestly unfair'.

22. In *Hammersmith and Fulham London BC v Lemeh* [2000] L & TR 423 at 426, Nourse LJ, having noted that there was no reported case in which it had actually been decided 'that oppression can include oppression caused by misleading information given by the court office', continued: j

> 'In principle, I am unable to see why oppression of that kind should not be included. The way in which that ground is usually stated is "oppression in the

a execution of the warrant". Once the warrant has been obtained, its execution is a matter between the court and the tenant. It is the officer of the court who executes the warrant and the landlord has no part in that process. Moreover, there seems to be no reason why oppression should be confined to oppressive conduct on the part of the landlord or some other person. It ought to include any state of affairs which is oppressive to the tenant.'

b 23. Finally, in *Lambeth London BC v Hughes* [2000] CA Transcript 1552, a case where the tenant was misled both by the respondent council and by the court, Waller LJ said:

> 'Mr Hughes has made out a case that he received misleading advice from the court. He has also made out a case that he was misled as to the procedures that were available to him i e a procedure available under s 85(2). In those circumstances, he has made out a case of oppression …'

c

24. Arden LJ added:

> 'It is clear from the authorities that oppression includes oppressive conduct which effectively deprives a tenant of his opportunity to apply for a stay (see *Hammersmith and Fulham London BC v Hill* [1994] 2 EGLR 51). The position in this case is due to a combination of factors … There was first the local authority's letter and the conversation with the housing officer … both of which indicated that payment in full of all arrears was required to avoid eviction … [Mr Hughes] went to the court office where he was given inaccurate information. He was told that eviction papers had not been issued … The ingredients of oppression in a case such as this have not been defined by the court. The court has stressed that what amounts to oppression depends on the circumstances, but it seems clear to me that the lack of opportunity would not have occurred if Mr Hughes had not been wrongly advised by the court or if the local authority had not given the impression that he had to pay the arrears in full. I agree with Waller LJ that the result is unfair to Mr Hughes.'

d e f

25. In the light of those judgments, submits Mr Knafler, it is no longer necessary to identify someone as having acted oppressively towards the tenant. It is sufficient g to establish merely that the end result is from the tenant's point of view 'manifestly unfair' and that, he argues, is the position here given the appellant's misunderstanding and that but for it she would in all probability have made a successful s 85(2) application for the warrant to be suspended. In advancing this submission Mr Knafler relies principally upon the last two sentences of the h above cited passage from Nourse LJ's judgment in *Lemeh*'s case and upon the concept of an unfair result exemplified in the passage cited above from Arden LJ's judgment in *Hughes*' case.

26. Before addressing this argument it is necessary to touch briefly upon the facts of the earlier cases to note the particular context in which the concepts of j oppression and unfairness were being discussed.

27. *Aldwinckle*'s case itself concerned a tenant who was evicted while absent from the premises for some months through illness and who, following her breach of the suspended possession order, received no notice whatever either of the council's application for a warrant, or of the issue of the warrant and the date of its proposed execution. Leggatt LJ (with whom Neill and Stocker LJJ agreed), said:

'The court undoubtedly has inherent power to prevent abuse of proceedings and avoid oppression: *cf. Beale v MacGregor* ((1886) 2 TLR 311). But in my judgment, even though Miss Aldwinckle was not expecting execution to be levied against her possessions, the use of available process does not of itself constitute abuse nor amount to oppression; and the court would be interfering unjustifiably with the existing policy of Parliament were it to introduce its own requirements as to additional conditions that have to be satisfied before execution may issue.' (See (1991) 24 HLR 40 at 46.)

28. The tenant in *Hill*'s case swore an affidavit following eviction stating that she only had three days notice of the warrant execution date and 'I was then informed by a representative of the Plaintiffs that I would have no chance of suspending the Warrant unless I could find £1,000 within twenty four hours' ([1994] 2 EGLR 51 at 52); that this was impossible and that it was on that account that she did not apply for suspension of the warrant. This court (at 53) held 'that an arguable case on oppression has been disclosed and that it ought to be tried'.

29. The tenant in *Akanni*'s case, having failed to comply with the suspended possession order, was notified that the council were requesting a warrant for possession and was told ((1997) 29 HLR 845 at 847):

'You will be advised in due course of the eviction date, but please note that the eviction will only be cancelled if the entire debt is cleared. You are also advised that you can approach the county court to have the warrant set aside, but the council will resist any such application.'

30. The court held that there was no arguable case of oppression on the part of the council.

31. In *Saint*'s case the council requested the warrant to issue on the basis of certified arrears of £333 when in fact, as the Court of Appeal held, they were in breach of their statutory duty to assist the tenant in his claim for housing benefit and accordingly, save to the extent of £28, were relying on the product of their own wrongdoing. There were further irregularities too in the application for the warrant. Finding the council's conduct oppressive, the court further distinguished *Aldwinckle*'s case on the footing that whereas in that case it was far from clear that a s 85(2) application would have succeeded, in *Saint*'s case the likelihood of a suspension being ordered was conceded.

32. The tenant in *Sarfo*'s case would have succeeded in setting aside the execution of the possession warrant but for her delay in applying to the court and the fact that by then the premises had been demolished. The basis of her case was described at one point of Roch LJ's judgment as 'maladministration', and appears more fully from this paragraph:

'On February 20, 1996 the appellant went to see Mrs Kakada. She filled in yet further applications for housing benefit and council tax benefit. She was then interviewed by a housing benefit officer. He headed the form of interview that he completed "URGENT" and he wrote on that form "STOP PROCEEDINGS—PLEASE". It is quite clear from the evidence of the appellant (which the Recorder accepted) that it did not occur to the appellant that the respondent would take any further step in the county court or by way of enforcing the warrant for possession. In my judgment, the appellant was entitled to conclude that no further step would be taken until her application for housing benefit had been decided. She was entitled to believe that a decision on her housing benefit might well remove a large part of the arrears a that had accrued. There is no evidence that she was given any warning following February 20, 1996 until the telephone call late on the afternoon of March 5. It is the respondent's own practice to write a letter before eviction here; they did not do so. It is their practice to visit before eviction; again they did not do so. In those circumstances, in my judgment, there can be no doubt that whatever the respondent's motives may have been, and I would b be prepared to accept that this was muddled and not deliberate behaviour, the enforcement of the execution of this warrant was a use of an order made by the county court in a way which was manifestly unfair.' (See (1999) 32 HLR 602 at 609.)

33. In *Lemeh*'s case [2000] L & TR 423, a case which Nourse LJ (at 424) c expressly said depended on its own 'very special' facts and would not have 'a wide effect on other comparable cases', the tenant had attended the county court saying that he was to be evicted the next day and been sent away by a member of the court staff who mistakenly understood from her own inquiries that no warrant had been issued. This court (at 426) thought it 'entirely clear ... that, if she [the member of court staff] had not unwittingly given him misleading d information, the defendant would have made the application there and then'.

34. *Hughes*' case involved both misleading advice from the court (once again mistaken information that no warrant had been issued but in addition advice that the tenant should await the bailiffs' letter, which in the event arrived too late to enable a s 85(2) application to be made), and misleading communications from e the council indicating that payment in full of all arrears was required to avoid eviction, in particular a letter notifying the tenant of the time of the bailiffs' intended arrival and continuing:

> 'If you want to stop the eviction you must pay all of your rent arrears by the day before the eviction. You can only pay in cash or by banker's draft. It f would be too late for us to clear a cheque. You must show proof of the payment to this office on or before the eviction date. These terms cannot be changed.'

35. It seems to me plain from that comparatively brief survey of the facts of those cases that in none of them did the tenant succeed unless he or she g demonstrated some clear fault on the part either of the landlord or of the court. In two of the cases (*Hill* and *Hughes*) the landlord was open to criticism for having suggested to the tenant that he had no prospect of escaping eviction save by payment of the full arrears, i e for implying (in contrast to the position in *Akanni*'s case) that there was no possibility of making a s 85(2) application to the court. h In two of the cases (*Saint* and *Sarfo*) the landlord was at fault in various respects in connection with the tenant's housing benefit entitlement and in the latter case also by more generalised 'maladministration'. In two of the cases (*Lemeh* and *Hughes*) the court was at fault in having misled the tenant as to the existence of a warrant and having deflected him from making a s 85(2) application which j otherwise he would have made. In all of them, therefore, the tenant was found in one way or another to have been misled or obstructed (even if inadvertently) in the exercise of his rights and it seems to me plain that it was for that reason that the court held the execution of the warrant to have been oppressive.

36. True it is that the result of the execution in these cases was invariably said to be 'unfair' or 'manifestly unfair', but in each case that expression was directly referable to the use of the court's 'process' (or 'order' or 'procedures') and, moreover,

to the use of that process in a way which was open to criticism. None of the cases on their facts lend the least support to the proposition that the court will set aside the execution absent abuse or oppression of the process or that the court will regard an eviction as oppressive merely because of its sympathy towards the tenant in his plight and its realisation that he would have been well advised to make a s 85(2) application.

37. I would therefore reject Mr Knafler's first and main argument and hold that a possession warrant obtained and executed without fault on anyone's part cannot properly be set aside as oppressive within the *Aldwinckle* principle. I am not, I confess, entirely clear what Nourse LJ meant when he said in *Lemeh*'s case that oppression ought to include 'any state of affairs which is oppressive to the tenant'. Either, however, he was meaning no more than that the giving of unintentionally misleading information by the court office, even if not 'oppressive conduct' on anyone's part, is nevertheless 'oppressive to the tenant' within the *Aldwinckle* principle (with which I would entirely agree), or the two sentences relied upon were obiter and, insofar as they may suggest that a tenant can be oppressively evicted without any fault on anyone's part, to my mind wrong. I accept, of course, that 'the categories of oppression are not closed', but in my judgment there cannot be oppression without the unfair use of court procedures; and something more than the mere use of the eviction process (some action on someone's part which is open to criticism) will be required before the court's procedures can be said to have been unfairly used.

38. Before turning to Mr Knafler's second and third arguments, there is one further aspect of the *Aldwinckle* line of cases I must deal with. This is the holding in *Hughes*' case that the council's letter to the tenant was misleading in implying that, to avoid eviction, he had no option but to pay the arrears in full, i e there was no alternative of applying to the court.

39. Mr Knafler submits that the letter of 17 March 2000 sent to the appellant here was in similarly objectionable terms and that her case of oppression is accordingly made out at least on this basis. The difficulty with that argument, however, is that on the facts of this case it is absolutely plain that the appellant was *not* misled by that letter. In the first place she says that despite it she continued to believe that the respondents were in fact requiring her to pay no more than the £876 arrears and £80 costs which she subsequently did pay. Secondly, and no less fatally to her argument, she undoubtedly did know of her right to make a s 85(2) application: the CAB had, indeed, drafted just such an application for her before ever the letter was written. There was accordingly no connection whatever between the letter and the appellant's failure to apply to the court. She was not misled or obstructed in the exercise of her rights.

40. That said, I would join with Waller LJ in deprecating this form of letter. Ideally such a letter should, as in *Akanni*'s case, expressly advise the tenant of the right to make an application to the county court. Certainly it should not imply, as did the letter in *Hughes*' case and, strongly arguably, the letter here, that there is no such right. It would also, I think, be highly beneficial if the standard court form for suspended possession orders (such as that made here on 27 August 1999 quoted above) itself expressly referred not merely (as it does) to the landlord's power on breach to enforce the order by eviction, but also to the tenant's right to apply back to the court for relief. As stated, however, these are not considerations which can avail the appellant in the circumstances of the present case.

41. I pass to Mr Knafler's second argument which is that the court can and should set aside this appellant's eviction under its inherent jurisdiction. This argument I

a can deal with very shortly. I accept, of course, that the court has an inherent power to prevent abuse of its procedures. Our jurisprudence is replete with examples of this principle in play. Amongst the authorities shown to us were *McHenry v Lewis* (1883) 22 Ch D 397, *Beale v MacGregor* (1886) 2 TLR 311, *R v Bloomsbury and Marylebone County Court, ex p Villerwest Ltd* [1976] 1 All ER 897, [1976] 1 WLR 362 and *Bremer Vulkan Schiffbau und Maschinenfabrik v South India* b *Shipping Corp* [1981] 1 All ER 289 at 295, [1981] AC 909 at 977. We also had the benefit of reading the essay 'The Inherent Jurisdiction of the Court' by Master Jacob (now Professor Sir Jack Jacob QC) in (1970) 23 Current Legal Problems 23. In my judgment, however, it is precisely this jurisdiction and no other which the court is exercising when applying the *Ardwinckle* principle. The court's inherent power is to prevent the oppressive use of its own processes; it is not to act as c Robin Hood and cure all perceived injustices. The court could not, for example, prevent a defendant from relying on the Statute of Limitations to defeat a claim which, as a result of an uninduced misunderstanding, was brought too late. No more, in my judgment, can the court here set aside this eviction merely on the footing that the appellant misunderstood her position and thereby lost her opportunity d to have the warrant stayed.

42. In short, once it is concluded that there is no oppression, it necessarily follows that there is no inherent power in the court to set aside the eviction. Lest, however, that be thought a needlessly restrictive view of the court's powers, I would add that in my judgment such an eviction will not in any event result in unfairness, let alone manifest unfairness (if in truth that be a different concept). e By definition no one but the tenant will have been in any way materially at fault in the eviction process (otherwise a case of oppression would arise). It will, therefore, be the tenant's own fault that he or she has been evicted, at least in the sense that the tenant will have breached a conditional possession order and have failed to apply to the court for relief under s 85(2) of the 1985 Act (albeit a failure f in the present case through the appellant's misunderstanding of her situation). The landlord for his part will be beyond criticism and, having finally obtained possession, ought to be allowed to benefit from it. It is surely one thing to say, in a case where, for example, the court staff are at fault, that the landlord risks the tenant being reinstated; quite another to say that a tenant can assert against her landlord her own uninduced misapprehension—a contention, incidentally, which g is not readily amenable to objective adjudication.

43. I turn finally to Mr Knafler's third and last argument, that a requirement that the tenant be put on notice of a possession warrant application should routinely be imported from the High Court rules into the CCR.

44. Although I for my part find the effect of RSC Ord 45, r 3(2) and (3)(a) and h Ord 46, r 2(1)(d) somewhat obscure, it was decided in *Fleet Mortgage and Investment Co Ltd v Lower Maisonette 46 Eaton Place Ltd, Lower Maisonette 46 Eaton Place Ltd v Crown Lodge (Belgravia) Ltd* [1972] 2 All ER 737, [1972] 1 WLR 765 that natural justice required the High Court rules to be construed as requiring the tenant to be given notice of the landlord's application for leave to issue a writ of j execution following an alleged breach of a conditional possession order. There is, of course, no such requirement in the CCR. In four of the cases already discussed (*Leicester City Council v Aldwinckle* (1991) 24 HLR 40, *Hammersmith and Fulham London BC v Hill* [1994] 2 EGLR 51, *Barking and Dagenham London BC v Saint* (1998) 31 HLR 620 and *Lambeth London BC v Hughes* [2000] CA Transcript 1552) this court touched upon the anomaly. The court in *Aldwinckle*'s case suggested that the Rules Committee should consider the matter. The court in *Saint*'s case wondered

whether s 76 of the 1984 Act could be invoked to distinguish *Aldwinckle*'s case but found it unnecessary to decide the point. Arden LJ in *Hughes*' case again invited the Civil Procedure Rules Committee to consider the discrepancy between the two sets of rules. *a*

45. Mr Knafler submits to us in the light of these authorities, first that natural justice plainly requires the tenant to be given notice of an application for a possession warrant (see the *Fleet Mortgage* case), and second, as suggested by Peter Gibson LJ in *Saint*'s case, that s 76 of the 1984 Act allows this High Court practice to be applied also in the county court. *b*

46. Mr Fancourt for the respondents advances a series of arguments in response. First he submits that on their true construction the High Court rules do not in fact require the tenant (or at any rate the head tenant) to be put on notice in all cases. Second, that s 76 of the 1984 Act has no application to the CCR in their present form (CPR Sch 2), made as these are under s 2 of the Civil Procedure Act 1997. Third, that even if s 76 of the 1984 Act otherwise applies, it cannot apply in a case like this where the CCR make express provision but in different terms to the High Court rules (see *Rolph v Zolan* [1993] 4 All ER 202, [1993] 1 WLR 1305). Fourth, that there are in truth good reasons for the two sets of rules to be different (not least because the High Court, unlike the county court, may initially have given a default judgment for possession), and it must be remembered that since this difference was first pointed out (as long ago as in *Peachey Property Corp v Robinson* [1966] 2 All ER 981, [1967] 2 QB 543) there have been two new sets of CCR (respectively in 1981 and now again in the CPR) quite apart from other relevant changes such as that to CCR Ord 26, r 1(4) (referred to at para 6 above), without it being thought necessary or appropriate to change Ord 26, r 17. *c* *d* *e*

47. For my part I would reject the first three of those arguments. The *Fleet Mortgage* case seems to me for present purposes conclusive on the first point. As for s 76 of the 1984 Act, (a) it is expressly referred to in the new CCR Ord 1, r 6, (b) unlike s 75 of the 1984 Act (under which the earlier CCR were made) it has not been repealed, (c) on its most literal construction it can still apply to the new rules, and (d) common sense in any event dictates that it should still apply. As to the third argument, there is to my mind no express provision in the CCR which would actually be inconsistent with an imported High Court rule as to notice. *f*

48. Mr Fancourt's fourth argument, however, seems to me to have much greater force. Certainly I find it impossible, in the light of the evident continuing reluctance of the Rules Committee to amend the CCR, to find, as Mr Knafler must necessarily contend for, a requirement in natural justice that the tenant be given notice of a request for the issue of a possession warrant in all cases. *g*

49. As a number of the cases make plain, the tenant will almost invariably be given notice at least of the date and time when the bailiff intends to execute the warrant. Assuming the tenant knows of his right to apply to the court under s 85(2) of the 1985 Act, that gives time enough for its exercise. If, of course, he is ignorant of his s 85(2) right, no notice whatever will alert him to it. *h*

50. I recognise, of course, that a case could occur when the tenant comes to be evicted without ever having been put on notice at all. *Aldwinckle*'s case, indeed, was such a case. The tenant would, of course, know of his breach of the suspended possession order. But, as in *Aldwinckle*'s case, he might not know that the landlord was requesting a possession warrant or that the bailiff was proposing to execute it. As *Aldwinckle*'s case decided, however, that of itself will not be regarded as oppressive. I can well imagine a case, unlike *Aldwinckle*'s case, in which it *would* *j*

a be oppressive for the landlord not to give notice to the tenant—where for example, following breach of the suspended order, the tenant has been progressively reducing the arrears—perhaps substantially beyond the point required by the suspended order—and where it would plainly be wrong suddenly to spring an eviction upon him.

51. In short, whilst I would reject the argument that a requirement for notice b must in all cases be introduced into the CCR, whether by way of natural justice and/or s 76 of the 1984 Act, I would accept that cases may arise when the landlord could properly be held to have acted oppressively if the tenant were never to receive any notice whatever of his impending eviction.

52. This, however, is plainly not such a case. It was not for want of notice that the appellant failed to make a s 85(2) application or otherwise avert her eviction. c She knew full well when the bailiffs were due to arrive. Her problem was in misunderstanding what was required to cancel their attendance. And this, as I have earlier explained, cannot sustain her claim for reinstatement.

53. It follows that I would reject all three of Mr Knafler's arguments and, sympathetic though I am to the appellant in her plight, dismiss her appeal.

d 54. I note by way of postscript that European Convention of Human Rights' contentions too were advanced in Mr Knafler's skeleton argument. These, however, although introducing very real difficulties as to the application of the convention to a housing association, added nothing of substance to the appellant's case on the merits. I accordingly say no more about them.

e **RIX LJ.**

55. I agree.

Appeal dismissed.

Dilys Tausz Barrister.

BHP Petroleum Great Britain Ltd v Chesterfield Properties Ltd and another

CHANCERY DIVISION

LIGHTMAN J

14, 15, 27 FEBRUARY 2001

Landlord and tenant – Covenant – Release – Assignment of lease – Statutory provisions providing mechanism for release of 'landlord covenants' and 'tenant covenants' on assignment – Whether personal covenants capable of being released under statutory provisions – Landlord and Tenant (Covenants) Act 1995, ss 3, 5, 6, 8, 15, 28.

Under an agreement for a lease executed in April 1997, the first defendant, CPL, agreed to grant a lease of part of a building to the claimant tenant on the completion of works of refurbishment. That agreement constituted a collateral agreement for the purposes of the Landlord and Tenant (Covenants) Act 1995. In cl 12.2 of the agreement, CPL gave a personal covenant to remedy or procure the remedy of any 'Building Works Defect' of which it had been notified by the tenant. Such a defect was defined in cl 1.1.8 as any physical damage to the demised premises manifesting itself during a period of six years commencing on the completion of the lease or any defect in the premises which would result in such damage manifesting itself during that period. In July 1997, following completion of the works of refurbishment, the parties duly executed the lease. Under cl 5.19 of the lease, the tenant gave covenants to comply with the provisions of all 'Legal Requirements' relating to the demised premises (cl 5.19.1), and not to omit on or about those premises any act or thing by reason of which the landlord might under any legal requirement incur or have imposed upon it or become liable to pay any charges or expenses (cl 5.19.2). The tenant also covenanted to indemnify the landlord against such liability. 'Legal Requirements' were defined as, inter alia, all orders, requirements and directions issued by any competent authority exercising powers under statute. In July 1999 CPL transferred the freehold reversion of the demised premises to the second defendant (the transferee). Subsequently, CPL served a notice on the tenant under s 8[a] of the 1995 Act seeking its release from the 'landlord covenants' of the tenancy as provided for in s 6[b] of the Act. Although the notice made no specific reference to the agreement, the definition of 'covenant' in s 28[c] of the Act included a covenant contained in a collateral agreement. Section 28 further provided that '"landlord covenant", in relation to a tenancy' meant a covenant falling to be complied with by the landlord of premises demised by the tenancy. 'Landlord' was defined as the person entitled to the reversion expectant on the term of the tenancy. 'Tenant' was defined as the person 'so entitled' to that term, while a 'tenant covenant' (which could be released under s 5[d] of the Act) was defined as one falling to be complied with by the tenant of premises demised by the tenancy. Under s 8, a release of the landlord covenants took effect if the tenant did not

a Section 8 is set out at [18], post
b Section 6, so far as material, is set out at [17], post
c Section 28, so far as material, is set out at [19], post
d Section 5, so far as material, is set out at [15], post

serve a notice objecting to the release within four weeks of service of the s 8 notice. The tenant served no such counternotice on CPL. The exterior of the building was largely clad in toughened glass, and in September 1999 two of the glass units fractured. In April 2000 a further unit fractured and fell out of its fixings. According to the tenant, the reason for those events was a defect in the premises, namely the use of the wrong and insufficiently tested glass. In May 2000 the local authority served a statutory dangerous structure notice, requiring works to be carried out to the glass units. In subsequent proceedings, the tenant sought to rely on CPL's personal obligation to remedy building work defects in cl 12.2 of the agreement, contending that that obligation was not confined to replacing the windows, but extended to remedying the underlying defect. CPL challenged that contention, but submitted that, in any event, 'landlord covenant' and 'tenant covenant' included a personal covenant, and that accordingly the cl 12.2 covenant had been released. In so contending, it relied on ss 3(6)[e] and 15(5)[f] of the 1995 Act which provided that nothing in ss 3 and 15 (the sections concerned with the transmission of the benefit and burden of covenants and their enforcement) operated to make a covenant expressed to be personal to any person enforceable by or against any other person. The issue also arose as to whether the transferee could recover from the tenant, under cl 5.19 of the lease, the costs of complying with the dangerous structure notice. The tenant contended that cl 5.19.1 did not apply in respect of the public duty created by the service of that notice because it implicitly limited the duty of compliance to 'Legal Requirements' imposing a duty on the tenant rather than the landlord.

Held – For the purposes of the 1995 Act, the only covenant that could constitute a landlord or tenant covenant was one which was capable of subsisting (in the language of s 3) as a transmissible covenant, and accordingly a personal covenant could not qualify. Such a construction was consistent with the policy of the legislation which was designed to substitute the transferee of the reversion or tenancy as obligor under transmissible covenants for the transferor, not to eliminate (as a windfall) the obligation of a landlord or tenant when it was personal and not to be transferred to a transferee. It was also supported by the words 'for the time being' in the definition of 'landlord'. Those words connoted not merely that the covenant fell to be complied with by the landlord at any particular point in time, but that it fell to be complied with by the person who might from time to time be entitled to the reversion. Similarly, the tenant covenant was likewise defined as a covenant falling to be complied with by the person 'so' (i e like the landlord in the case of the landlord covenant) for the time being entitled to the tenancy. As regards ss 3(6) and 15(5), they did not elevate, or reflect any intention to elevate, personal into landlord or tenant covenants. Rather, they were cautionary provisions, designed to prevent any question arising as to whether the sections might have the unexpected and unintended result referred to therein. They therefore provided no contra-indications to the correct construction. It followed in the instant case that CPL's personal

---

e Section 3, so far as material, provides: '(6) Nothing in this section shall operate—(a) in the case of a covenant which (in whatever terms) is expressed to be personal to any person, to make the covenant enforceable by or (as the case may be) against any other person …'

f Section 15, so far as material, provides: '(5) Nothing in this section shall operate—(a) in the case of a covenant which (in whatever terms) is expressed to be personal to any person, to make the covenant enforceable by or (as the case may be) against any other person …'

obligations under the agreement, including the covenant in cl 12.2, survived and were unaffected by its s 8 notice. However, the tenant could not require CPL to remedy the alleged defect under cl 12.2. Under that provision, the situation had to be viewed as at the date of the tenant's notification of the defect, and he could not then have said that further physical damage would result from the defect. Rather, he could only have said that the defect gave rise to a significant risk of further damage. Moreover, it was plain that the 'public duty' to carry out the required works under the dangerous structure notice fell within the definition of 'Legal Requirements', and that cl 5.19.1 embraced that notice. Accordingly, the tenant had, under that clause, assumed the primary contractual obligation to procure compliance at its own cost with the notice and had agreed, under cl 5.19.2, to indemnify the transferee in respect of the costs of its compliance (see [22]–[31], post).

Notes

For the release of landlord and tenant from covenants on assignment of interest, see Supp to 27(1) *Halsbury's Laws* (4th edn reissue) para 466B.

For the Landlord and Tenant (Covenants) Act 1995, ss 3, 5, 6, 8, 15, 28, see 23 *Halsbury's Statutes* (4th edn) (1997 reissue) 717, 720, 722, 725, 733, 750.

Case referred to in judgment

Monro v Lord Burghclere [1918] 1 KB 291.

Case also cited or referred to in skeleton arguments

Lehmann v Herman [1993] 1 EGLR 172.

Applications for summary judgment

The claimant, BHP Petroleum Great Britain Ltd, the tenant of premises at 1 Neathouse Place, London SW1, applied for summary judgment on an issue concerning the effect of the Landlord and Tenant (Covenants) Act 1995, which arose in its claim that the first defendant, Chesterfield Properties Ltd, the former landlord of the premises, was liable, under cl 12 of an agreement for a lease dated 30 April 1997, to undertake works to prevent the fracturing of glass units in which the premises were clad. The first defendant applied for the summary dismissal of that claim, while the second defendant, Chesterfield (Neathouse) Ltd, the landlord of the premises, applied for summary judgment on its claim that the tenant was liable under cl 5.19 of the lease of the premises, granted on 1 July 1997, for the cost of compliance by the second defendant with a dangerous structure notice, served by Westminster City Council on 5 May 2000 under s 62 of the London Building Acts (Amendment) Act 1939, requiring works to secure part of the external glazing of the premises which were shattered, fallen, insecure or otherwise defective. The facts are set out in the judgment.

Michael Barnes QC and *Joanne Wicks* (instructed by *Herbert Smith*) for the tenant.

Simon Berry QC and *Andrew Walker* (instructed by *Dechert*) for the defendants.

Cur adv vult

a 27 February 2001. The following judgment was delivered.

LIGHTMAN J.

Introduction

[1] I have before me applications for summary judgment which raise (besides b two questions of construction of two specific documents) a fundamental question under the Landlord and Tenant (Covenants) Act 1995. Section 6 of the Act makes provision for a landlord who has assigned his reversion upon a tenancy to apply in accordance with the procedure laid down in s 8 of the Act to be released from the landlord covenants in the tenancy or a collateral agreement. Section 8 provides that the landlord shall serve on the tenant notice of the assignment and c a request for the covenant to be released, and that if the tenant does not within four weeks thereafter serve a notice of objection the covenant is released to the extent mentioned in the notice. The question raised is whether such landlord's notice seeking release from all his covenants under the tenancy (in absence of a tenant's notice of objection) is effective to secure the release of the landlord from d a personal covenant imposed on the landlord and whether this is so even if the personal covenant is imposed by a collateral agreement, though the notice makes no specific reference to that collateral agreement.

Facts

[2] The facts relevant to the applications before me can be stated quite shortly. e By an agreement for a lease dated 30 April 1997 (the Agreement) made between the first defendant, Chesterfield Properties Ltd (D1), and the claimant, BHP Petroleum Great Britain Ltd (the Tenant), D1 agreed to undertake refurbishment works to a substantial building at 1 Neathouse Place, London SW1 (the Property).

[3] The Agreement provided that the Tenant should be entitled to occupy and f use by far the greater part of the Property as soon as it was practicable for the Tenant to carry out the Tenant's works (as there defined) which the Tenant undertook to carry out, from which date he would pay a licence fee at a rate equal to the initial rent payable of £3,113,846 pa. It went on to provide that five working days after the date of practical completion of what were referred to as the Podium Works, D1 should grant to the Tenant a lease of that part of the g Property for a term of 20 years commencing on 24 June 1997. For convenience I shall refer to the part demised (as well as the whole) as the Property, save where it is relevant to distinguish the part demised from the part retained by D1.

[4] Clause 12 of the Agreement contains the personal covenant on the part of D1 on which the applications primarily centre. The material parts of this clause h provide as follows:

> '12.2 *Building Works Defects*
>
> If on one or more occasions during the Defects Period a Building Works Defect manifests itself the following provisions shall apply.
>
> j 12.2.1 the Tenant shall notify the Landlord in writing of such Building Works Defect as soon as reasonably practicable and supply to the Landlord such details of the Building Works Defect as are in the possession of or under the control of the Tenant …
>
> 12.2.3.2 the Landlord shall with the minimum practical inconvenience to the Tenant and as economically as reasonably practicable remedy or procure

the remedying of each Building Works Defect as quickly as reasonably practicable ... *a*

12.2.4 If at any time during the Defects Period the Demised Premises or any part of the Demised Premises are rendered incapable of beneficial use and occupation by reason solely or principally of a Building Works Defect then the following provisions shall apply:-

12.2.4.1 if at the date upon which the Demised Premises or the relevant *b* part of the Demised Premises cease to be capable of beneficial use and occupation and for so long thereafter as the reversion immediately expectant on the determination of the term of the Lease remains vested in the Landlord then the yearly rent stated in clause 4.1.1 of the Lease or a fair proportion thereof according to the extent to which the Demised Premises are incapable of beneficial use and occupation ... *c*

12.3 *General*

12.3.1 The Landlord shall carry out any remedial works in relation to a Building Works Defect:-

12.3.1.1 in a good and workmanlike manner;

12.3.1.2 with good quality materials; *d*

12.3.1.3 in accordance with the Necessary Consents for such works and the requirements of any competent authority.

12.3.2 The Landlord shall obtain the approval of the Tenant (such approval not to be unreasonably withheld) to the contractors and professional advisers (and the terms of their appointment including any warranties to be given by them) instructed by the Landlord in relation to any *e* remedial works undertaken in relation to ...

12.4.2.2 if as at the date upon which the Demised Premises or relevant part of the Demised Premises cease to be capable of beneficial use and occupation the reversion immediately expectant on the determination of the term of the Lease is not vested in the Landlord then the Landlord shall pay to the Tenant *f* quarterly in advance an amount equal to the rent reserved by clause 4.1.1. of the Lease or a fair proportion thereof according to the extent to which the Demised Premises are incapable of beneficial use and occupation ... plus any VAT chargeable thereon on the usual quarter days and so in proportion for any part of a quarter in respect of the period during which the Demised Premises or relevant part of the Demised Premises are incapable of beneficial *g* use and occupation.

12.4.3 The provisions of clauses ... 12.4.2.1 shall cease to apply on and with effect from the date ("the Disposal Date") upon which the reversion immediately expectant on the determination of the Lease ceases to be vested in the Landlord and the provisions contained in clauses or 12.4.2.2 (if *h* appropriate) shall apply on and with effect from the Disposal Date ...

12.5 *General Provisions*

12.5.1 For the avoidance of doubt:-

12.5.1.1 the Tenant acknowledges that the obligations on the part of the Landlord contained in this clause 12 are personal obligations of Chesterfield *j* Properties Plc and the Tenant acknowledges and confirms that the Tenant shall have no claim of any nature whatsoever against the Landlords successors in title to the Demised Premises arising out of or otherwise in connection with the obligations on the part of the Landlord contained in this clause 12;

a

12.5.1.2 the benefit of the provisions contained in this clause 12 shall enure for the Tenants successors in title and the Tenant and the Tenants successors in title shall be entitled to assign the benefit of the provisions contained in this clause 12 to each subsequent assignee of the Lease but not otherwise.'

[5] 'Building Works Defect' is defined in cl 1.1.8 as—

b

'any physical damage to the Demised Premises manifesting itself during the Defects Period or any defect in the Demised Premises which will result in physical damage to the Demised Premises manifesting itself during the Defects Period and in either case:-

1.1.8.1 which is caused by defective design materials or workmanship in the construction of the Building Works and …

c

1.1.8.3 the cost of remedying which will in each such case exceed £50,000 (excluding VAT) …'

The 'Defects Period' is defined in cl 1.1.15 as—

d

'the period of six years commencing on and including the date of actual completion of the Lease or if completion of the Lease is delayed otherwise than by reason of the default of the Landlord the period commencing on and including the date upon which the Lease should have been completed pursuant to the provisions of this agreement.'

e

[6] D1 completed the refurbishment works and the Tenant completed the Tenant's works and on 1 July 1997 the parties duly executed the Lease (the Lease).

[7] The Lease contained the following relevant covenants by the Tenant:

'5.19 *Compliance with statutes, etc.*

5.19.1 To comply in all respects with the provisions of all Legal Requirements for the time being in force relating to the Demised Premises.

f

5.19.2 Not to … omit on or about the Demised Premises any act or thing by reason of which the Landlord may under any Legal Requirement incur or have imposed upon it or become liable to pay any levy, penalty, damages, compensation, costs, charges or expenses and so far as the law allows to indemnify the Landlord against all such liability and in particular (but without prejudice to the generality of the foregoing) against any liability under the Factories Act 1961 …

g

5.25 *Indemnity*

To keep the Landlord indemnified from and against all expenses, demands, costs, loss and claims recoverable at law (including without limitation diminution in value of the Demises Premises and damages for the loss of amenity of the Demised Premises) arising from:-

h

5.25.1 any breach of any of the Tenant's covenants contained in this lease;

5.25.2 the use of the Demised Premises;

5.25.3 any works carried out during the term to the Demised Premises … or …

j

5.25.5 any act, neglect or default by the Tenant, any subtenant or their respective servants or agents or any person on the Demises Premises or the Landlord's Development with the actual or implied authority of any of them.'

[8] 'Legal Requirements' was defined in cl 1.1.11 as—

'all statutes, regulations and orders and all requirements, directions, codes of practice, circulars and guidance notes of or issued by any competent authority exercising powers under statute or Royal Charter and all directly applicable EC law and case law …'

[**9**] On 9 July 1999 D1 transferred the reversion to the second defendant, an associate company, Chesterfield (Neathouse) Ltd (D2). On 30 July 1999 D1 served a notice on the Tenant under s 8 of the Act (the Landlord's Notice) which was in Form 5 prescribed by the Landlord and Tenant (Covenants) Act 1995 (Notices) Regulations 1995, SI 1995/2964. So far as material it read as follows:

'Landlord and Tenant (Covenants) Act 1995 (Notices) Regulations 1995.

Form 5

LANDLORD AND TENANT (COVENANTS) ACT 1995

Sections 7 and 8

Former Landlord's Notice Applying for Release from Landlord Covenants of a Tenancy

To BHP Petroleum Great Britain Public Limited Company of One Neathouse Place London SW1

1. This notice is given under section 8 of the Landlord and Tenant (Covenants) Act 1995

2. It relates to One Neathouse Place London SW1 let under a lease dated 1st July 1997 and made between (1) Chesterfield Properties Plc and (2) BHP Petroleum Great Britain Public Limited Company of which you are the tenant.

3. We were formerly landlord of the property of which you are tenant and remained bound by the landlord's obligations under the tenancy after transferring the landlord's interest. The landlord's interest, was transferred on 9th July 1999 to Chesterfield (Neathouse) Limited

[We] wish to be released from [our] obligations with effect from the date of that transfer.

4. If you consider that it is reasonable for [us] to be released, you do not need to do anything, but it would help [us] if you notify [us] using Part II of this Form.

5. If you do not consider it reasonable for [us] to be released, you must notify [us] of your objection, using Part II of this Form, within the period of four weeks beginning with the serving of this notice, or [we] will be released in any event. You may withdraw your objection at any time by notifying [us] in writing.'

The Tenant served no counternotice.

[**10**] The exterior of the Property is largely clad in toughened glass. In September 1999 two glass units fractured, but they did not fall out of their fixings. In April 2000 a further glass unit fractured and did fall out of its fixings. The Tenant says that a further glass unit fractured in August 2000. According to the Tenant (and as I must accept for the purpose of these applications) the reason for these events was a defect in the Property, namely the use of the wrong and insufficiently tested glass.

[**11**] On 5 May 2000 Westminster City Council (the council) served a dangerous structure notice (the DSN) pursuant to s 62 of the London Building Acts (Amendment) Act 1939 requiring works to be carried out to the glass units to

a 'secure' the Property. For the purposes only of the applications before me D2 accepts that the DSN was valid, was validly served on D2 and imposes on D2 alone the public legal duty to carry out the required works.

[12] The issues raised on this application are threefold: (i) whether the personal obligation assumed by D1 under the Agreement to remedy building work defects was extinguished upon the expiration of the four-week period after b service of the Landlord's Notice; (ii) (assuming that the obligation was not so discharged) as a matter of construction of the Agreement, the extent of the duty of D1 to remedy building work defects; and (iii) as a matter of construction of the Lease, the obligation of the Tenant to reimburse D2 for the cost of the remedial works required to be undertaken by the DSN.

c

The 1995 Act and personal covenants

[13] The 1995 Act introduced substantial changes in the law relating to covenants in leases and collateral agreements entered into on or after 1 January 1996, and in most particular their transmission and their release. The 1995 Act had its origins in the report of the Law Commission on *Landlord and Tenant Law,* d *Privity of Contract and Estate* published in 1988 (Law Com no 174) (the report). In Pt IV of the report, the Commission set out their proposals for reform, the material part of which reads as follows:

'REFORM PROPOSALS

e **Basis**

4.1 Our proposals for reform recognise the importance of two principles: First, a landlord or a tenant of property should not continue to enjoy rights nor be under any obligation arising from a lease once he has parted with all interest in the property. Secondly, all the terms of the lease should be regarded as a single bargain for letting the property. When the interest of f one of the parties changes hands the successor should fully take his predecessor's place as landlord or tenant, without distinguishing between different categories of covenant.

4.2 The majority of those who responded to the Working Paper believed that the effect of transferring property which has been leased should be the g "clean break" which results from applying the two principles. Nevertheless, the consultation convinced us that there are cases in which, for good reason, landlords can only agree to a proposed assignment if they are assured that their existing tenant will continue to be responsible for complying with the lease terms. We are therefore proposing a scheme based on the general h abrogation of the privity of contract principle, but which stops short of abolishing it in all cases.

Outline

4.3 We propose a general rule that the liability of the original tenant, and his entitlement to benefits under the lease, should not survive an assignment j of the lease. For this purpose, we propose that all the covenants in a lease should be treated in the same way, whether or not at present they touch and concern the land. Nevertheless, it would be possible for the landlord, when granting consent to the assignment, to impose a condition that the tenant will be liable to guarantee the performance of some or all of the lease covenants by his immediate successor.

4.4 The Landlord and Tenant Act 1988 implements our recommendations generally to impose a duty on landlords not unreasonably to withhold consent. The effect would be that in cases where the landlord is not entitled to withhold his consent to assign, he would only be able to impose a condition that the tenant has continuing liability where it was reasonable to do so. a

4.5 For landlords, we propose a rule that when they part with their interest in the property let by a lease they will escape further responsibility for the lease obligations if, but only if, they comply with prescribed conditions. These will involve their giving notice to the tenant and his being able to withhold consent if it is reasonable for him to do so. Again, the benefits of being landlord, so far as they can enure to an owner who has parted with the property, would only continue for a former landlord who had continuing liability … b c

Assignment of whole property by landlords

4.16 In relation to the liability of landlords, we should have preferred our proposals to have mirrored precisely our recommendations for tenants' covenants. However, that is not possible because tenants rarely, if ever, have a right to give or withhold consent to dispositions by their landlord. They would therefore not be in a position to require continuing liability after an assignment of the reversion and to block an assignment if the condition is not agreed. Moreover, there is less need here for radical change. In most leases, the landlord undertakes far fewer obligations than the tenant and landlords may not be troubled by the prospect of continuing responsibility. d e

4.17 For these reasons, we do not propose that an assignment of the landlord's reversionary interest should automatically affect his continuing liability. Rather, we recommend that an assigning landlord should have an option to operate a procedure which could end his liability, and his entitlement to benefits, under the lease. A landlord who wished to escape further responsibility would have to give the tenant notice of his proposal to assign. In the notice the landlord would propose that after the assignment he should no longer have any liability under the lease. It would give the tenant four weeks in which to reply.' f

[**14**] There were significant intermediate stages between the report and the enactment of the 1995 Act which are conveniently referred to in *Megarry & Wade: The Law of Real Property* (6th edn, 2000) p 975, para 15-064. It is accordingly not possible to assume that the 1995 Act gave unqualified effect to the recommendations in the report. There were modifications and additions. But I can find no indication in *Hansard* or elsewhere of any intention to qualify the adoption of the principle that the release of a landlord or tenant from a covenant was intended to be sequential upon, and only sequential upon, a parting by the landlord or tenant with his interest in the property let and the successor taking his predecessor's place as the party responsible for complying with that covenant. g h

[**15**] Section 5 of the 1995 Act applies where a tenant assigns premises demised to him under a tenancy. Section 5(2) (so far as material) reads as follows: j

'If the tenant assigns the whole of the premises demised to him, he—(a) is released from the tenant covenants of the tenancy, and (b) ceases to be entitled to the benefit of the landlord covenants of the tenancy, as from the assignment.'

a [16] The assignment by a tenant unless in breach of covenant (as to which see s 11) accordingly operates automatically to release him from liability under the tenant covenants of the tenancy (though s 24 spells out that this does not release him from liability for any prior breach).

[17] Section 6 applies where a landlord assigns the reversion in premises of which he is the landlord under a tenancy. Section 6(2) (so far as material) b provides as follows:

> 'If the landlord assigns the reversion in the whole of the premises of which he is the landlord—(a) he may apply to be released from the landlord covenants of the tenancy in accordance with section 8; and (b) if he is so released from all those covenants, he ceases to be entitled to the benefit of c the tenant covenants of the tenancy as from the assignment.'

[18] Section 8 lays down the procedure for seeking a release under s 6. It provides as follows:

> '(1) For the purposes of section 6 or 7 an application for the release of a d covenant to any extent is made by serving on the tenant, either before or within the period of four weeks beginning with the date of the assignment in question, a notice informing him of—(a) the proposed assignment or (as the case may be) the fact that the assignment has taken place, and (b) the request for the covenant to be released to that extent.
>
> (2) Where an application for the release of a covenant is made in e accordance with subsection (1), the covenant is released to the extent mentioned in the notice if—(a) the tenant does not, within the period of four weeks beginning with the day on which the notice is served, serve on the landlord or former landlord a notice in writing objecting to the release, or (b) the tenant does so serve such a notice but the court, on the application of f the landlord or former landlord, makes a declaration that it is reasonable for the covenant to be so released, or (c) the tenant serves on the landlord or former landlord a notice in writing consenting to the release and, if he has previously served a notice objecting to it, stating that that notice is withdrawn.
>
> (3) Any release from a covenant in accordance with this section shall be g regarded as occurring at the time when the assignment in question takes place.
>
> (4) In this section—(a) "the tenant" means the tenant of the premises comprised in the assignment in question (or, if different parts of those premises are held under the tenancy by different tenants, each of those h tenants); (b) any reference to the landlord or the former landlord is a reference to the landlord referred to in section 6 or the former landlord referred to in section 7, as the case may be; and (c) "the court" means a county court.'

[19] Section 28 is the interpretation section and includes the following critical definitions:

j

> '(1) In this Act (unless the context otherwise requires)—... "collateral agreement", in relation to a tenancy, means any agreement collateral to the tenancy, whether made before or after its creation ... "covenant" includes term, condition and obligation, and references to a covenant (or any description of covenant) of a tenancy include a covenant (or a covenant of

that description) contained in a collateral agreement; "landlord" and "tenant", in relation to a tenancy, mean the person for the time being entitled to the reversion expectant on the term of the tenancy and the person so entitled to that term respectively; "landlord covenant", in relation to a tenancy, means a covenant falling to be complied with by the landlord of premises demised by the tenancy ... "tenant covenant", in relation to a tenancy, means a covenant falling to be complied with by the tenant of premises demised by the tenancy.'

a

b

[20] Section 27 provides that the form of notice to be served for the purposes of s 8(1) should be prescribed by regulations made by statutory instrument and that any notice purporting to be served for the purposes of s 8(1) which is not in the prescribed form or in a form substantially to the same effect shall be ineffective for that purpose. The Landlord's Notice is in such prescribed form.

c

[21] The first question to be resolved is whether the personal covenant given by D1 in the Agreement was capable of being released by the operation of ss 6 and 8; and the second is whether (assuming that the answer to the first question is in the affirmative) such release was triggered by the Landlord's Notice.

d

[22] I turn to the first question. The rival contentions by the parties put the issue into perspective. Mr Berry QC for D1 submits any form of obligation on the part of a landlord in a tenancy or collateral agreement, whatever its character or topic, constitutes a landlord covenant and likewise any form of obligation on the part of a tenant constitutes a tenant covenant. On the other hand Mr Barnes QC for the Tenant submits that the obligation in either case must be capable of being annexed to the premises demised by the tenancy and the reversion and accordingly transmissible under s 3 of the Act, and that this excludes personal covenants. It is common ground that the Agreement is a 'collateral agreement' in relation to the Lease. It is sufficient to say the Agreement is an agreement 'running side by side' and 'parallel to' the Lease (see the definition of 'collateral' in *The Oxford English Dictionary* (2nd edn)). (It is unnecessary for this purpose, though it may be sufficient, that the Agreement constitutes the species of contract known as a collateral contract.) It is clear that the personal covenant, since it is 'a covenant in a collateral agreement', is for the purposes of the 1995 Act (in accordance with the definition of the term 'covenant') a covenant of the Lease. The critical question is whether that covenant falls within the definition in s 28 of a landlord covenant. For this purpose it must be a covenant 'falling to be complied with by the landlord of premises demised by the tenancy', and the landlord for this purpose means 'the person for the time being entitled to the reversion expectant on the term of the tenancy'. Focus, as it seems to me, must be placed on the words 'for the time being'. These words to my mind connote, not merely that the covenant falls to be complied with by the landlord at any particular point in time (as submitted by Mr Berry for D1), but that it falls to be complied with by the person who may from time to time be entitled to the reversion. It may be noted that a tenant covenant is likewise defined as a covenant falling to be complied with by the person 'so' (i e like the landlord in the case of the landlord covenant) for the time being entitled to the tenancy. In short the only covenant that can constitute a landlord or tenant covenant is a covenant which is capable of subsisting (in the language of s 3 of the Act) as a transmissible covenant and accordingly a personal covenant cannot qualify.

e

f

g

h

j

a [23] Mr Berry submitted that this construction could not stand with the two specific references in the 1995 Act to personal covenants. Section 3(6) provides that nothing in s 3 (which is concerned with the transmission of the benefit and burden of covenants) shall operate to make a covenant expressed to be personal to any person enforceable by or (as the case may be) against any other person; and s 15(5) again provides that nothing in that section (which is concerned with b enforcement of covenants) shall operate to make a covenant expressed to be personal to any person enforceable by or (as the case may be) against any other person. I do not find any contra-indication to the construction which I have adopted in either of those provisions. They are cautionary provisions designed to prevent any question arising whether the sections might have the unexpected and unintended result there referred to. They do not elevate, or reflect any c intention to elevate, personal into landlord or tenant covenants.

[24] I should add that I am relieved to reach this construction for a number of reasons. First the policy of the legislation (as the report makes clear) was to substitute the transferee of the reversion or tenancy as obligor under transmissible covenants for the transferor: it was not to eliminate (as a windfall) the obligation d of a landlord or tenant when it was personal and not to be transferred to a transferee. Second the consequences of the contention put forward by D1 would be remarkable. For it means that on any assignment by a landlord or tenant any obligation (whatever its character) which happened to be found for any reason in the Lease or collateral agreement would fall to be extinguished on a transfer. Thus, for example, if under an agreement for lease the prospective tenant agreed e to pay a premium (of say £10m) for the lease by 10 annual instalments of £1m over the 10-year period of the lease, on an assignment of the lease the whole liability for the balance of the purchase price would be extinguished. In the same way there will be extinguished any obligation imposed on a tenant although totally unrelated to the letting which for any reason happens to be included in any f collateral agreement. It will be remembered that the release of the tenant is automatic on his effecting a (lawful) assignment. I fully appreciate that a landlord may be able to protect himself against this risk by imposing a covenant against assignment, and in case of a non-residential lease (taking advantage of the provision of s 19(1B) of the Landlord and Tenant Act 1927 as inserted by s 22 of the 1995 Act) to make provision for a refusal of consent unless the landlord is duly g protected in this regard; and that a tenant can protect himself by refusing consent to the landlord's request for a release. Whilst measures may be taken in this way to limit the mischief which this construction would engender, I still think that Parliament should be expected to have made it plain (and certainly more plain than it is) if it had intended a release to be capable of having such a striking and h potentially inequitable consequence.

[25] Alarmed at the disturbing consequences of the construction advanced by Mr Berry flowing from the apparently innocuous terms of the Landlord's Notice, in the course of the hearing I raised the question whether the Landlord's Notice sufficiently gave notice of the intention to obtain a release of the j (personal) covenants in the Agreement when it refers only to the obligations under the Lease. Section 8 requires the landlord in his notice to identify from which of the landlord covenants he seeks his release. He may choose only to seek a release from some, but not all. He may do so for any of a number of reasons, for example, because he knows that the tenant will only agree to some and will vigorously oppose others in the county court. Hence it is important to examine

carefully the terms of the notice for this purpose. I was concerned that the Landlord's Notice did not identify any covenants in the Agreement or put the Tenant on notice that D1 was requesting to have extinguished the personal covenant in question, a request for which (if appreciated) would obviously have been refused. My concern is to a large degree allayed by the construction which I have arrived at that the reach of the 1995 Act does not extend to personal covenants. I am troubled that the form of notice makes no reference to the 'collateral agreement', and that a notice may for this reason mislead a lay tenant unfamiliar with the provisions of the 1995 Act, but I am satisfied that as a matter of law the Landlord's Notice would have been effective to achieve the release sought if the covenants in question had not been personal. For (as I have already said) the statutory form of notice prescribed by the 1995 regulations must be interpreted as one with the 1995 Act, and accordingly the reference in the Landlord's Notice, as in the 1995 Act, to the landlord covenants of the tenancy includes within it the covenants in any collateral agreement.

[26] I therefore hold that the personal obligations of D1 under the Agreement for Lease survive and are unaffected by the Landlord's Notice.

Extent of the duty of D1 to remedy

[27] The obligation of D1 to remedy accordingly survives the Landlord's Notice and the question I have to consider is the ambit of that obligation.

[28] The Tenant maintains that under cl 12.2.3.2 of the Agreement he is entitled to require D1 to remedy, not merely the physical damage that has occurred by reason of the building work defect (ie replace the windows if the total cost exceeds £50,000) but also the underlying defect, namely the use of the wrong and untested glass. This claim turns on the definition of Building Work Defect in cl 1.1.8, namely—

> 'any physical damage to the Demised Premises manifesting itself during the Defects Period or any defect in the Demised Premises which will result in physical damage to the Demised Premises manifesting itself during the Defects Period.'

The Tenant cannot say that further physical damage will result from this defect, nor could he say that further physical damage would result when the Tenant gave notice of the defect between the date of the resultant damage to the second and third window. All he can say now is, and all he could say then was, that the defect gives rise now and gave rise then to a significant risk of further damage. But Mr Barnes for the Tenant submits that the issue whether there is a defect which will cause damage (and accordingly requires remedying) must be looked at as at the date of the Agreement: looked at from that viewpoint it can now be seen and said that the defect would result in physical damage. It is, however, clear (most particularly from cl 12.2 of the Agreement) that the situation must be looked at as at the date of the Tenant's notification of the defect. Accordingly, the Tenant cannot require D1 to remedy the alleged defect: he can only require remedy of the accrued physical damage and then only if the cost of the remedy exceeds £50,000. Any complaint about this on the part of the Tenant must be in respect of the negotiation or drafting of this term of the Agreement.

The extent of the obligation of the Tenant to indemnify D2

[29] The DSN requires 'the Owner' of the Property—

a 'forthwith to take down, repair or otherwise secure parts of the external glazing where shattered, part fallen, insecure or otherwise defective and to carry out any further work found necessary by reason of the foregoing.'

The question raised is whether the costs occasioned to D2 in complying with the DSN are to be paid by the Tenant by reason of the provisions of the Lease. For b the purpose of this application only, D2 concedes (as contended by the Tenant) that the DSN is valid, and validly served on D2 and that the public law duty of compliance is imposed on D2 alone.

[**30**] In my view it is plain that the 'public duty' to carry out the required works falls within the definition of 'Legal Requirements'. The Tenant, however, argues that cl 5.19.1 does not bite in respect of the public duty created by service of the c DSN because cl 5.19.1 implicitly limits the duty of compliance to Legal Requirements imposing a duty on the Tenant and not on the landlord. I can see no justification for any such implicit limitation. The language of cl 5.19.1 is expressed in perfectly general terms. It could have been drafted in terms referring to Legal Requirements 'whether imposed on the Landlord or the Tenant' or it d could have been drafted in terms referring to Legal Requirements 'imposed on the Tenant'. But it was drafted in neither of these forms. I must take the clause as it is embracing any Legal Requirement relating to the Demised Premises and accordingly as embracing the DSN. The Tenant submitted that it is inapposite to read the clause as requiring the Tenant to comply with a duty imposed on someone else and in particular where compliance by the Tenant might prove e impracticable. For example (he said) it might involve work requiring access to use of parts of the Property not demised to the Tenant. I can see no substance in this submission. There is no reason why the Tenant should not oblige himself to secure compliance with an obligation of the landlord; and if in any particular respect compliance proves impracticable (and the Tenant's argument in this f regard is purely theoretical) that may excuse non-compliance in that respect alone, but not otherwise. Likewise, as it seems to me, cl 5.19.2 throws the cost of compliance with the DSN on the Tenant, for the Tenant has 'omitted' to carry out the necessary works to obviate the service of the DSN or the need for D2 to comply with it. Again the word 'omit' is perfectly general. It does not connote any breach of duty on the part of the Tenant (as suggested by the Tenant): the g mere omission (whether or not knowing or blameworthy) throws on the Tenant the obligation to indemnify D2 from the cost of making good that omission. (It may be noted that clearly the clause picks up situations where the landlord incurs costs and expenses where they are not occasioned by any breach of duty on the part of the Tenant (see cl 5.15.2 (not reproduced)).) In respect of both clauses the h Tenant took points that the construction which I have preferred is open to objection because it throws an onerous burden on the Tenant: the burden may be onerous for whichever party has to bear it, and it is necessary on a fair reading of the Lease to determine on whom (as part of the bargain between the parties) they agreed that the burden should be imposed.

j [**31**] I therefore hold that the Tenant has under cl 5.19.1 assumed the primary contractual obligation to procure compliance at his own cost with the DSN and further by cl 5.19.2 agreed to indemnify D2 in respect of the cost of compliance by D2. Mr Barnes referred me to s 107(1) of the 1939 Act which gives the county court jurisdiction to apportion the expenses of compliance with a DSN in accordance with what is just and equitable in the circumstances, and no order or declaration by me can operate to preclude an application to the county court to exercise this jurisdiction. But on the material before me, in view of the terms of the Lease, which cover the situation which has arisen, I cannot see how the county court could exercise this jurisdiction otherwise than to reflect and give effect to the provisions of the Lease to which I have referred (see *Monro v Lord Burghclere* [1918] 1 KB 291).

a

Order accordingly.

Celia Fox Barrister.

a

R (on the application of Alconbury Developments Ltd) v Secretary of State for the Environment, Transport and the Regions and other cases

b

[2001] UKHL 23

QUEEN'S BENCH DIVISION, DIVISIONAL COURT

TUCKEY LJ AND HARRISON J

c 29, 30 NOVEMBER, 1, 4, 5, 13 DECEMBER 2000

HOUSE OF LORDS

LORD SLYNN OF HADLEY, LORD NOLAN, LORD HOFFMANN, LORD CLYDE AND LORD HUTTON

26–28 FEBRUARY, 1, 5 MARCH, 9 MAY 2001

d

Human Rights – Right to a fair hearing – Impartial and independent tribunal – Whether Secretary of State's powers to call in applications for planning permission and recover appeals against refusal of permission incompatible with right to fair hearing by independent and impartial tribunal – Highways Act 1980, ss 14(3)(a), 16(5)(a), 18(3)(a), 125, Sch 1, Pt I, paras 1, 7, 8 – Acquisition of Land Act 1981, s 2(3), Sch 1, para 4 – e *Town and Country Planning Act 1990, ss 77, 78, 79, Sch 6, paras 3, 4 – Transport and Works Act 1992, ss 1, 3 and 23(4) – Human Rights Act 1998, Sch 1, Pt I, art 6(1).*

In a number of conjoined applications for judicial review, it was contended that certain statutory powers of the Secretary of State in relation to planning matters, f compulsory purchase, railways and highways were incompatible with art 6(1)[a] of the European Convention for the Protection of Human Rights and Fundamental Freedoms 1950 (as set out in Sch 1 to the Human Rights Act 1998). Under art 6(1), everyone was entitled, in the determination of his civil rights and obligations, to a fair and public hearing by an impartial and independent tribunal. The impugned powers were the processes by which the Secretary of State called in applications g for planning permission under s 77 of the Town and Country Planning Act 1990; recovered appeals against refusals of planning permission under ss 78 and 79 of, and paras 3 and 4 of Sch 6 to, the 1990 Act; and made orders under ss 1, 3 and 23(4) of the Transport and Works Act 1992, ss 14(3)(a), 16(5)(a), 18(3)(a) and 125 of, and paras 1, 7 and 8 of Pt I of Sch 1 to, the Highways Act 1980, and s 2(3) of, and para 4 h of Sch 1 to, the Acquisition of Land Act 1981. Decisions made under those processes were subject to judicial review or a statutory appeal to the High Court based on similar principles, but there was no provision for an appeal on the facts or the merits. In each case, the essential complaint was that, when a decision was taken by the Secretary of State himself rather than by an inspector appointed by him, j the Secretary of State's role in the making of policy meant that he had such an interest in the decision that he could not be regarded as an independent and impartial tribunal. The Divisional Court upheld the complaints, holding that the availability of judicial review proceedings was not sufficient to render the impugned provisions compatible with art 6(1). Accordingly, it granted declarations

a Article 6, so far as material, is set out at p 934 c, post

of incompatibility under the 1998 Act in respect of those provisions. The Secretary of State appealed directly to the House of Lords. a

Held – The impugned powers of the Secretary of State under the 1990, 1992, 1980 and 1981 Acts were not in breach of, or incompatible with, art 6(1) of the convention. Such a conclusion was consistent with the jurisprudence of the European Court of Human Rights. That court recognised that some administrative decisions b affecting civil rights were taken by ministers answerable to elected bodies, and that where such decisions were subject to review by a court regard had to be paid to both stages of the process. Thus although the Secretary of State was not himself an independent and impartial tribunal when dealing with called in or recovered matters, the crucial question was whether there was sufficient judicial control to ensure determination by such a tribunal subsequently. The European c Court's jurisprudence did not require such control to constitute a rehearing on an application by an appeal on the merits. Such a requirement would be surprising in view of the difference of function between the minister exercising his statutory powers—for the policy of which he was answerable to the legislature and ultimately the electorate—and that of the court. What was required of the latter d was that there should be a sufficient review of the legality of the decisions and the procedures followed. The judicial review jurisdiction of the High Court constituted such a review. Accordingly, the appeal would be allowed (see [29], [43], [44], [49], [54], [56], [58], [61], [63], [76], [100], [116], [117], [122], [128]–[130], [136], [153], [154], [159], [160]–[162], [169], [171], [172], [189], [196], [198], post).

Albert v Belgium (1983) 5 EHRR 533, *Bryan v UK* (1995) 21 EHRR 342 and *Chapman v* e *UK* (2001) 10 BHRC 48 applied.

Notes

For independent and impartial tribunal in the context of the right to a fair hearing, see 8(2) *Halsbury's Laws* (4th edn reissue) para 140, and for the Secretary of State's f powers to determine planning decisions and appeals, see 46 *Halsbury's Laws* (4th edn reissue) paras 419, 849.

For the Highways Act 1980, ss 14, 16, 18, 125, Sch 1, Pt I, paras 1, 7, 8, see 20 *Halsbury's Statutes* (4th edn) (1999 reissue) 88, 90, 92, 217, 400, 401, 402.

For the Acquisition of Land Act 1981, s 2, Sch 1, para 4, see 9 *Halsbury's Statutes* (4th edn) (2000 reissue) 363, 391. g

For the Town and Country Planning Act 1990, ss 77, 78, 79, Sch 6, paras 3, 4, see 46 *Halsbury's Statutes* (4th edn) (1998 reissue) 592, 593, 595, 890.

For the Transport and Works Act 1992, ss 1, 3 and 23, see 36 *Halsbury's Statutes* (4th edn) (1994 reissue) 554, 555, 571.

For the Human Rights Act 1998, Sch 1, Pt I, art 6, see 7 *Halsbury's Statutes* (4th h edn) (1999 reissue) 523.

Cases referred to in judgments and opinions

Albert v Belgium (1983) 5 EHRR 533, ECt HR.

Ashbridge Investments Ltd v Minister of Housing and Local Government [1965] 3 All ER 371, j [1965] 1 WLR 1320, CA.

Ashingdane v UK (1985) 7 EHRR 528, ECt HR.

Associated Provincial Picture Houses Ltd v Wednesbury Corp [1947] 2 All ER 680, [1948] 1 KB 223, CA.

Balmer-Schafroth v Switzerland (1997) 25 EHRR 598, ECt HR.

Belilos v Switzerland (1988) 10 EHRR 466, ECt HR.

a *Benthem v Netherlands* (1985) 8 EHRR 1, ECt HR.
Boden v Sweden (1988) 10 EHRR 367, ECt HR.
Brown v Stott (Procurator Fiscal, Dunfermline) [2001] 2 All ER 97, [2001] 2 WLR 817, PC.
Bryan v UK (1995) 21 EHRR 342, E Com HR and ECt HR.
Bushell v Secretary of State for the Environment [1980] 2 All ER 608, [1981] AC 75,
b [1980] 3 WLR 22, HL.
Chapman v UK (2001) 10 BHRC 48, ECt HR.
County Properties Ltd v Scottish Ministers 2000 SLT 965, Ct of Sess.
De Cubber v Belgium (1984) 7 EHRR 236, ECt HR.
Edwards (Inspector of Taxes) v Bairstow [1955] 3 All ER 48, [1956] AC 14, [1955] 3 WLR 410, HL.
c *Ettl v Austria* (1987) 10 EHRR 255, ECt HR.
Findlay v UK (1997) 24 EHRR 221, ECt HR.
Francis v Yiewsley and West Drayton UDC [1957] 3 All ER 529, [1958] 1 QB 478, [1957] 3 WLR 919, CA.
Fredin v Sweden (1991) 13 EHRR 784, ECt HR.
d *Golder v UK* (1975) 1 EHRR 524, ECt HR.
Gransden (EC) & Co Ltd v Secretary of State for the Environment [1986] JPL 519; *affd* (1987) 54 P & CR 361, CA.
H v France (1989) 12 EHRR 74, ECt HR.
Howard v UK (1987) 52 DR 215, E Com HR.
ISKCON v UK (1994) 76A DR 90, E Com HR.
e *Jacobsson v Sweden* (1989) 12 EHRR 56, ECt HR.
James v UK (1986) 8 EHRR 123, ECt HR.
Johnson (B) & Co (Builders) Ltd v Minister of Health [1947] 2 All ER 395, CA.
Kaplan v UK (1980) 4 EHRR 64, E Com HR.
Kingsley v UK (2001) Times, 9 January, ECt HR.
f *König v Germany* (1978) 2 EHRR 170, ECt HR.
Kraska v Switzerland (1993) 18 EHRR 188, ECt HR.
Le Compte v Belgium (1981) 4 EHRR 1, ECt HR.
McGonnell v UK [2000] 2 PLR 69, ECt HR.
Moreira de Azevedo v Portugal (1990) 13 EHRR 721, ECt HR.
Obermeier v Austria (1990) 13 EHRR 290, ECt HR.
g *Piersack v Belgium* (1982) 5 EHRR 169, ECt HR.
Procola v Luxembourg (1995) 22 EHRR 193, ECt HR.
Pudas v Sweden (1987) 10 EHRR 380, ECt HR.
R (Mahmood) v Secretary of State for the Home Dept [2001] 1 WLR 840, CA.
R v Criminal Injuries Compensation Board, ex p A [1999] 2 AC 330, [1999] 2 WLR 974, HL.
h *R v Gough* [1993] 2 All ER 724, [1993] AC 646, [1993] 2 WLR 883, HL.
R v Hereford and Worcester CC, ex p Wellington Parish Council [1996] JPL 573.
R v Secretary of State for Education and Employment, ex p Begbie [2000] 1 WLR 1115, CA.
R v Secretary of State for the Home Dept, ex p Turgut [2001] 1 All ER 719, CA.
R v Wicks [1997] 2 All ER 801, [1998] AC 92, [1997] 2 WLR 876, HL.
j *Reid v Secretary of State for Scotland* [1999] 1 All ER 481, [1999] 2 AC 512, [1999] 2 WLR 28, HL.
Ringeisen v Austria (No 1) (1971) 1 EHRR 455, ECt HR.
Secretary of State for Education and Science v Tameside Metropolitan Borough [1976] 3 All ER 665, [1977] AC 1014, [1976] 3 WLR 641, CA and HL.
Skärby v Sweden (1990) 13 EHRR 90, ECt HR.
Sporrong v Sweden (1982) 5 EHRR 35, ECt HR.

Sramek v Austria (1985) 7 EHRR 351, ECt HR. a
Stefan v UK (1998) 25 EHRR CD 131, ECt HR.
Stringer v Minister of Housing and Local Government [1971] 1 All ER 65, [1970] 1 WLR 1281.
Tesco Stores Ltd v Secretary of State for the Environment [1995] 2 All ER 636, [1995] 1 WLR 759, HL.
Tinnelly & Sons Ltd v UK, McElduff & Sons Ltd v UK (1998) 27 EHRR 249, ECt HR. b
Tre Traktörer Aktiebolag v Sweden (1989) 13 EHRR 309, ECt HR.
Varey v UK App No 26662/95 (27 October 1999, unreported), E Com HR.
W v UK (1987) 10 EHRR 29, ECt HR.
Wycombe DC v Secretary of State for the Environment [1988] JPL 111.
X v UK (1982) 28 DR 177, E Com HR. c
X v UK (1998) 25 EHRR CD 88, E Com HR.
Zander v Sweden (1993) 18 EHRR 175, ECt HR.
Zumtobel v Austria (1993) 17 EHRR 116, ECt HR.

d

Applications for judicial review

R (on the application of Alconbury Developments Ltd) v Secretary of State for the Environment, Transport and the Regions

Alconbury Developments Ltd (ADL) applied for judicial review of (i) the decision e of the repondent, the Secretary of State for the Environment, Transport and the Regions, on 20 April 1999 to entertain and thereafter to retain jurisdiction to determine (a) an appeal against the refusal by Huntingdonshire District Council (HDC) of planning permission for Class B8 and associated development at Alconbury Airfield, (b) an appeal by ADL in respect of the failure of Cambridgeshire County Council (CCC) to determine an application for planning permission for a f temporary recycling department at Alconbury Airfield, (c) an application by ADL for an order pursuant to the provisions of the Transport and Works Act 1992 in respect of a proposed rail link between ADL's proposed development at Alconbury Airfield and the East Coast main line; and (ii) the Secretary of State's decision, originally made on 20 May 1999, to appoint an inspector to hear the appeals and g to consider the application at a public local inquiry and to report to him with recommendations in respect of the appeals and the application. HDC, CCC, the Highways Agency, the Nene Valley Association (NVA) and another group of local residents known as Huntingdonshire Says No to Alconbury Proposals (HUNTSNAP) participated in the proceedings as interested parties. The facts are h set out in the judgment of the court.

R (on the application of Holding & Barnes plc) v Secretary of State for the Environment, Transport and the Regions

Holding & Barnes plc (HB) applied for judicial review of the decision of the j respondent, the Secretary of State for the Environment, Transport and the Regions, notified by letter dated 25 July 2000, to call in for his own determination HB's planning application for the use of land at Haven Road, Canvey Island, Essex, for the parking and storage of damaged cars and their sale by auction and for the retention of the surfacing and bund walls. The facts are set out in the judgment of the court.

a *R (on the application of Premier Leisure (UK) Ltd) v Secretary of State for the Environment, Transport and the Regions*

Premier Leisure (UK) Ltd (PL) applied for judicial review of the decision of the respondent, the Secretary of State for the Environment, Transport and the Regions, notified by letter dated 22 May 2000, to call in for his own determination PL's application for planning permission for a health and fitness centre at 200 Rayleigh b Road, Thundersley, Essex. The facts are set out in the judgment of the court.

Secretary of State for the Environment, Transport and the Regions v Legal & General Assurance Society Ltd

The claimant, the Secretary of State for the Environment, Transport and the Regions, applied, at the invitation of the defendant, Legal & General Assurance c Society Ltd (LG), for declarations (i) that the Secretary of State's decision on 20 April 2000 to hold public local inquiries into objections to the making of (a) the A34 Trunk Road (A34/M4 Junction 13 Improvement) Side Roads Order 1993 (Variation) Order 200, (b) the A34 Trunk Road (A34/M4 Junction 13 Improvement) Side Roads (No 2) Order 1993 (Variation) Order 200, (c) the A34 Trunk Road d (A34/M4 Junction 13 Improvement) Side Roads (No 3) Order 1993 (Variation) Order 200, (d) the A34 Trunk Road (A34/M4 Junction 13 Improvement) Side Roads (No 4) Order 1993 (Variation) Order 200, and (e) the A34 Trunk Road (A34/M4 Junction 13 Improvement) Complusory Purchase Order were lawful and within the Secretary of State's powers; (ii) that that decision was not in breach of the Human Rights Act 1998; (iii) that it was compatible with the e provisions of the 1998 Act; (iv) that the Secretary of State's decision on 29 June 2000 to appoint an inspector to hold public local inquiries into the draft orders and thereafter report to the Secretary of State with his recommendations as to whether the orders should be made was within the Secretary of State's powers; (v) that that decision was not in breach of the 1998 Act; (vi) that it was compatible f with the provisions of that Act; (vii) that the Secretary of State's decision on 20 April 2000 in due course to determine whether the draft orders should be made was lawful and within the Secretary of State's power; (viii) that that decision was not in breach of the 1998 Act; and (ix) that it was compatible with the provisions of that Act. LG was not represented on the application. The facts are set out in the judgment of the court.

g

Martin Kingston QC and *Peter Goatley* (instructed by *Colin Meadowcroft*, Huntingdon) for HDC.

Paul Stanley and *Timothy Eicke* (instructed by *David Barney & Co*) for NVA and HUNTSNAP.

h *Stephen Hockman QC, Kevin Leigh* and *Gordon Nardell* (instructed by *Jennings Son & Ash*) for HB.

Kevin Leigh (instructed by *Denton Wilde Sapte*) for PL.

John Howell QC and *Rabinder Singh* (instructed by the *Treasury Solicitor*) as amici curiae in the LG case.

j *David Elvin QC, Philip Sales* and *James Maurici* (instructed by the *Treasury Solicitor*) for the Secretary of State.

Keith Lindblom QC, Craig Howell Williams and *Hereward Phillpot* (instructed by *Marrons*, Leicester) for ADL.

Gregory Jones and *Darren Abrahams* (instructed by *Richard Braun*, Cambridge) for CCC.

Jonathan Karas (instructed by the *Treasury Solicitor*) for the Highways Agency in the ADL case.

John Litton (instructed by the *Treasury Solicitor*) for the Highways Agency in the LG case. a

Cur adv vult

13 December 2000. The following judgment of the court was delivered.

b

TUCKEY LJ .

1. These four applications raise the very important question whether the processes by which the Secretary of State for the Environment, Transport and the Regions makes decisions under the Town and Country Planning Act 1990 and orders under the Transport and Works Act 1992, the Highways Act 1980 and the c Acquisition of Land Act 1981 are compatible with art 6(1) of the European Convention for the Protection of Human Rights and Fundamental Freedoms (Rome, 4 November 1950; TS 71 (1953); Cmd 8969) (set out in Sch 1 to the Human Rights Act 1998). This article says: 'In the determination of his civil rights and obligations … everyone is entitled to a fair and public hearing … by an d independent and impartial tribunal established by law.'

2. It is common ground that such decisions and orders do affect civil rights and obligations. In the present cases the Secretary of State does not argue that he is himself an independent and impartial tribunal but contends that the decision making process as a whole including the right of appeal to and the reviewing role of the High Court does comply with art 6. Whether he is right about this is the e central question we have to decide. If he is not, the Secretary of State's alternative submission is that this court should expand its role to review his decisions consistently with ss 3 and 6 of the 1998 Act so as to make the processes compliant. These sections say:

> '**3.**—(1) So far as it is possible to do so, primary legislation and subordinate f legislation must be read and given effect in a way which is compatible with the Convention rights …
>
> **6.**—(1) It is unlawful for a public authority to act in a way which is incompatible with a Convention right.
>
> (2) Subsection (1) does not apply to an act if—(a) as the result of one or g more provisions of primary legislation, the authority could not have acted differently; or (b) in the case of one or more provisions of, or made under, primary legislation which cannot be read or given effect in a way which is compatible with the Convention rights, the authority was acting so as to give effect to or enforce those provisions. h
>
> (3) In this section "public authority" includes—(a) a court …'

If the processes are not compliant and cannot be made so, the Secretary of State contends that s 6(2) of the 1998 Act applies to them so s 6(1), which would otherwise make his acts unlawful, does not apply. Such a finding would enable us to make declarations of incompatibility under s 4 of the 1998 Act which says: j

> '(1) Subsection (2) applies in any proceedings in which a court determines whether a provision of primary legislation is compatible with a Convention right.
>
> (2) If the court is satisfied that the provision is incompatible with a Convention right, it may make a declaration of that incompatibility.'

a 3. Two of the cases (Holding & Barnes plc (HB) and Premier Leisure (PL)) involve decisions by the Secretary of State to call in their applications for planning permission under s 77 of the 1990 Act. As well as the art 6 challenge to the process as a whole HB contends that the decision to call in should be quashed on conventional judicial review grounds. The third case (Alconbury Developments Ltd (ADL)) involves 'recovered' appeals against refusals of planning permission b under ss 78 and 79 of the 1990 Act and proposed orders under s 1 of the 1992 Act relating to the construction and operation of a railway in connection with the proposed redevelopment of RAF Alconbury. The fourth case (Legal & General (LG)) involves proposed highway orders and related compulsory purchase orders (CPO) in connection with a scheme to improve the A34/M4 junction. It is the Secretary of State's acts in calling in or recovering planning decisions and c proposing to make the 1992 Act, 1980 Act or CPO orders which are alleged to be unlawful under s 6(1) of the 1998 Act because they do not comply with art 6.

4. In the PL case a public inquiry has been held but no decision has yet been made. In the ADL and LG cases public inquiries have started but are now adjourned to await the decision of this court. We have been told that a number of other d important public inquiries have been adjourned for the same reason. For these reasons the hearing before us was arranged at short notice and we are extremely grateful to all involved for the huge amount of work which has gone into its preparation and the presentation of the argument. In the interests of producing a judgment quickly we intend to summarise the material put before us (about e 2,500 pages of evidence, 200 authorities and nearly five days of submissions from ten counsel) as shortly as possible.

5. In view of the fact that the Secretary of State does not argue that he is an independent and impartial tribunal it may be thought that it is unnecessary to consider the way in which he acts in any detail and that the focus of our enquiry should be upon the effectiveness of the High Court's powers. But this is incorrect. f We shall come to the decisions of the European Court of Human Rights in due course. But they make it clear that in considering whether determinations made in the field of administrative law comply with art 6 the whole process must be looked at. Put shortly there would be nothing objectionable about the Secretary of State acting as he does, providing his decisions were subject to control by a g judicial body which has 'full jurisdiction'. What is meant by 'full jurisdiction' will be affected by the extent to which the statutory process is quasi-judicial in character and contains safeguards of the kind required by art 6. So the involvement of the Secretary of State and the way in which he comes to make his decisions does have to be considered.

h 6. What we propose to do first is to amplify the facts of the four cases, set out the relevant primary and secondary legislation and summarise the evidence about the involvement of the executive and the decision-making process filed on behalf of the Secretary of State. We shall then turn to the central and other issues to which we have already briefly referred.

j

THE FACTS

HB's application

7. HB is engaged in motor vehicle salvage on behalf of contracted insurance companies. It is presently based at Charfleet Industrial Estate on Canvey Island where it operates pursuant to a planning permission which was granted on appeal

by an inspector in March 1997. On that occasion the Secretary of State did not recover jurisdiction from his inspector, nor did he direct a call-in.

8. HB wishes to relocate its operation to Haven Road on Canvey Island, and the local planning authority, Castle Point Borough Council, accept there would be benefits for the area if that were to happen. In November 1999 HB made an application for planning permission for the use of land at Haven Road, Canvey Island for the parking and storage of damaged cars and their sale by auction, and for the retention of the surfacing and bund walls.

9. The Health and Safety Executive (HSE) was consulted on the application by the local planning authority. It advised in principle against allowing the development due to the proximity of gas storage on some neighbouring sites. However, it indicated that it would be prepared to withdraw its objection if the application were modified to keep members of the public out of the new site. HB agreed to restrict entry to the site to trade members for the purposes of attending auctions. The HSE made it clear, however, that it intended to attend the inquiry and to submit evidence in support of its objection unless directed to the contrary by the Secretary of State.

10. On 2 May 2000 the local planning authority resolved that it was minded to approve the planning application subject to completion of a s 106 agreement, the director of development having advised that he did not consider the proposal to be a major departure from the development plan warranting referral to the Secretary of State for his determination. Before the local planning authority could finally determine the application, the local Member of Parliament requested the Secretary of State to call in the application, drawing attention to concerns about the safety of local residents in the vicinity of the application site and the effect of the proposed development on the highway network.

11. On 25 July the Secretary of State made a direction under s 77 of the 1990 Act that the application should be referred to him instead of being dealt with by the council. In other words, he called in the application for his own decision. He gave three reasons for doing so: (1) the nature of the proposed use, (2) the impact it could have on the future economic prosperity of Canvey Island and (3) the site's location close to hazardous installations.

12. In his call-in letter the Secretary of State specified five matters about which he particularly wished to be informed. They were: (1) the extent to which the proposal accords with the policies in the adopted and emerging structure plan and the adopted local plan; (2) the suitability of the site for the proposed use given its proximity to two hazardous installations and its location within the cordon sanitaire, and the extent of any threat to public safety arising therefrom; (3) the effect of the proposal on the surrounding road network and the amenity of local residents, and its impact on the appearance and character of the area; (4) bearing in mind the inclusion of Castle Point in the extended Thames Gateway in the draft regional planning guidance, the effect of the proposal on the prospect of enhancing the environment of the area and attracting new investment and job-creating development to Canvey Island; and (5) the extent and value of any planning gain, particularly any benefit for the Charfleet Industrial estate and the provision of the Roscommon Way extension.

13. HB now seek judicial review of the Secretary of State's decision to call in their application on the grounds that it is contrary to art 6 and on domestic law grounds as well.

a *PL's application*

14. On 4 February 2000 PL applied to the local planning authority, Castle Point Borough Council, for planning permission for a health and fitness centre at 200 Rayleigh Road, Thundersley, Essex. The site lies in the Green Belt. On 3 March the local Member of Parliament wrote to the local planning authority and to the Secretary of State objecting on behalf of some third parties. On 4 April the local b planning authority resolved conditionally to approve the planning application subject to the completion of a s 106 agreement. On 22 May 2000 the Secretary of State decided to call in the application for his determination. The reason that he gave for doing so was 'because of the possible conflict with national policy guidance contained in Planning Policy Guidance Note No. 2 (PPG2) on "Green Belts" relating to inappropriate development in the Metropolitan Green Belt'. c In the letter of 22 May he set out the matters about which he particularly wanted to be informed. They included such matters as compatibility with green belt policies in the development plan, whether there were very special circumstances to outweigh the inappropriateness of the development in the green belt, the impact on residential amenity, landscape and wildlife, consistency with PPG17 on d 'Sport and Recreation' and consistency with PPG13 dealing with the need to reduce travel by private car.

15. A local public inquiry into the proposal was held between 10 and 13 October, and the Secretary of State's decision following the inquiry is awaited. However, in these proceedings PL seek judicial review of the Secretary of State's decision to e call in the application on the ground that it is contrary to art 6.

16. In making their application, PL point to the planning history of the site. In 1983 outline planning permission was granted on appeal by the Secretary of State for a sports and leisure complex on the site. In granting that permission the Secretary of State considered that there were circumstances justifying an exception to Green Belt policies. That consent subsequently lapsed.

f 17. In 1988 there was a similar application which was granted permission on appeal by an inspector appointed by the Secretary of State on the ground that there were very special circumstances justifying an exception to Green Belt policy. That consent was implemented to the extent of site clearance, the construction of drainage and site access and a car park. However, the development has never been g completed, although it could be. In 1995 the Secretary of State determined an application for a sports and leisure complex on the site, including a tenpin bowling alley, which he had called in for his own decision. Although he concluded that the 1988 consent was a very special circumstance and that the proposed leisure and sports facility did not constitute a greater threat to the Green Belt than h the 1988 consent, he refused the application on the ground that the tenpin bowling alley would harm residential amenity.

18. All of those matters were no doubt relied upon by PL at the recent public inquiry but, as we have said, they are also relied upon by PL in these proceedings.

j *ADL's application*

19. Alconbury Airfield is a redundant airfield which was vacated by the United States Air Force in 1995. It covers an area in excess of 1000 acres and is owned by the Ministry of Defence. It is located about 5 kilometres to the north-west of Huntingdon. It lies close to the A1 and the A14 trunk roads with direct access via slip roads to both those trunk roads. The east coast main line railway from London to Edinburgh lies about 500 metres to the east of the site.

20. ADL wish to develop the site into a distribution centre of national significance consisting of up to 650,300 square metres of warehousing and distribution floorspace. They have entered into a development agreement with the Ministry of Defence whereby the Ministry of Defence will receive a pecuniary benefit from ADL if planning permission is granted for development, together with a profit sharing agreement thereafter if the land is developed.

21. In October 1997 ADL made a number of planning applications to Huntingdonshire District Council (HDC), which is the local planning authority. There was one overarching outline application for warehousing, with ancillary offices and additional floorspace, leisure and administrative facilities with access and landscaping, plus approach infrastructure including road and rail sidings. There were also a number of individual outline applications for the separate components of the scheme. There was an individual outline application for a commercial airfreight operation which proved to be very controversial. A local residents group called HUNTSNAP (Huntingdonshire Says No to Alconbury Proposals) was formed to object to the proposals. The application for the air freight operation was withdrawn in March 1998. There was also an application for planning permission made to Cambridgeshire County Council (CCC), as the waste disposal authority, for a temporary recycling depot on part of the site. Later, in December 1999, ADL applied to the Secretary of State for an order under s 1 of the 1992 Act which, if made, would confer powers on ADL for the construction and use of a rail connection between the airfield and the east coast main line. It involves proposed compulsory purchase powers for the land required for the works and it includes a request to the Secretary of State for a direction deeming the grant of planning permission for the construction of the railway connection and accommodation works, together with the construction of railway sidings within the airfield in order to provide the railfreight facilities.

22. On 4 August 1998 the Secretary of State refused a request to call in the planning applications. On 17 February 1999 HDC resolved to refuse the overarching outline application. On 1 April 1999 ADL lodged an appeal against HDC's refusal of the overarching outline application and they also lodged an appeal against the failure of CCC to determine the application relating to the recycling depot within the requisite period. On 11 May 1999 the Secretary of State directed, in exercise of his powers under para 3 of Sch 6 to the 1990 Act, that the appeals would be determined by him instead of by his inspector. In other words, he recovered jurisdiction for both of the planning appeals. The reason that he gave for doing so was because 'the appeals relate to proposals for development of major importance having more than local significance.' An inspector, Mr Boyland, was appointed to hold the inquiry which was adjourned on a number of occasions for various reasons, one of them being the decision of the Secretary of State to hold a concurrent inquiry into ADL's 1992 Act application. Amongst the objectors to ADL's proposals are HUNTSNAP, the Nene Valley Association (NVA), which is an association of residents in the Nene Valley in East Northamptonshire, and Abbots Ripton Parish Council.

23. The Highways Agency, which is an executive agency of the Secretary of State, does not object to the proposed development provided that specific conditions are imposed on any planning permission that may be granted in order to protect the trunk road network. English Nature, which is a statutory body funded by the Department of the Environment, Transport and the Regions (DETR), object to the proposal due to the impact of the rail link to the east coast main line which affects a site of special scientific interest.

24. On 3 October 2000 the inspector opened the inquiry, whereupon submissions, which were handed to the inspector in written form, were made on behalf of HUNTSNAP and the NVA to the effect that the proceedings were contrary to art 6. As a result of those submissions, ADL decided to apply to this court for a number of declarations to resolve the position. The inquiry was formally adjourned on 7 November to await the outcome of these proceedings. ADL seek a number of declarations to the effect that the Secretary of State's decisions to entertain and retain jurisdiction over the planning appeals and the 1992 Act application, and to appoint the inspector to hold the public inquiry into them, are lawful and not in breach of, or incompatible with, the 1998 Act. Their application is supported by CCC but opposed by HDC, both of whom were represented by the counsel at the hearing before us.

Secretary of State's application: A34/M4 Junction 13 Improvement Scheme

25. The Secretary of State made this application at the invitation of the defendant, LG. Subsequently, LG decided not to be legally represented. The Attorney General therefore appointed Mr John Howell QC together with Mr Rabinder Singh as amici curiae. The application relates to the A34/M4 Junction 13 Improvement Scheme. Under that scheme, the Secretary of State proposes to provide a dual two-lane carriageway all-purpose road for A34 through-traffic under the M4 about 100 metres to the west of the existing Junction 13. New slip roads would link the A34 to Junction 13. Access to a service area, a hotel and the local road network south of Junction 13 would be provided by two new linked roundabouts connected by new slip roads to the A34 slip roads. North of Junction 13, new connecting side roads would replace the existing roads and Graces Lane south-facing slip roads.

26. This is a scheme which has a history. Put briefly, the relevant orders were first published back in 1992. An inquiry into objections was held during that year. Following the inquiry, the orders were confirmed and made in August 1993. However, one of the objectors, Mr Ian Ellison, successfully applied to the court to quash part of a side-road order. Subsequently, the government reviewed the scheme as part of its roads review. Mr Ellison's suggested alternative slip road proposal was considered by the minister responsible for trunk roads, but it was not adopted.

27. On 17 February 2000 various new draft orders were published to replace that part of the previous order that had been quashed and to vary other orders which had been made, in order to take account of the newly constructed Newbury by-pass and alterations that had been made to the Junction 13 roundabout since 1992. In addition to those 1980 Act orders, a draft CPO for the whole scheme was published on 24 February.

28. A number of objections to the draft orders were received, including an objection from Mr Ellison and an objection from LG who own land which is the subject of the draft CPO. The Secretary of State decided to hold a public inquiry into the draft orders. On 29 June the Secretary of State appointed an inspector to hold the public inquiry into the draft orders. On 26 July there was a pre-inquiry meeting at which the inspector identified the matters which were outside the scope of the inquiry. They included government policy, including methodologies and design standards adopted by the government, nationally-determined economic assumptions and forecasts of traffic growth to the extent that they had been adopted by the Secretary of State. The inspector, however, accepted that the application of national forecasts to local situations did come within the scope of the inquiry.

29. The public inquiry commenced on 19 September and sat for 11 days, after which it was adjourned until 23 October. Before the resumption of the inquiry, solicitors acting for LG wrote to the Secretary of State inviting him to seek declarations from the court to determine the compatibility of the proceedings with the convention. On 23 October, at the request of the Secretary of State, the inspector adjourned the inquiry for six months to enable the Secretary of State to seek declarations from the court. By these proceedings the Secretary of State seeks a number of declarations to the effect that his decisions to hold a public inquiry into the draft orders and to appoint the inspector to hold the inquiry were lawful and not in breach of, or incompatible with, the 1998 Act.

PRIMARY AND SECONDARY LEGISLATION

Town and country planning

30. The relevant primary legislation is to be found in the 1990 Act. Under s 57 planning permission is required for the carrying out of any development of land. Section 55 defines development of land as being the carrying out of building, engineering, mining or other operations in, on, over or under land or the making of any material change of use of any buildings or other land. Section 54A provides that where, in making any determination under the planning Acts, regard is to be had to the development plan, the determination shall be made in accordance with the plan unless material considerations indicate otherwise. Under s 70 a local planning authority can grant planning permission, either unconditionally or subject to such conditions as they think fit, or they can refuse planning permission. In dealing with an application, the authority shall have regard to the development plan, so far as material to the application, and to any other material considerations. Section 78 provides for a right of appeal to the Secretary of State against a refusal of planning permission, against a conditional grant of permission or against a failure to decide an application within the prescribed period. Section 79 provides that, before determining such an appeal, the Secretary of State shall, if the appellant or the local planning authority so wish, give them an opportunity of appearing before and being heard by a person appointed by him, following which he can allow or dismiss the appeal.

31. Paragraph 1 of Sch 6 to the 1990 Act empowers the Secretary of State to prescribe by regulations the classes of appeals under s 78 which may be determined by a person appointed by him rather than by the Secretary of State himself. Under the Town and Country Planning (Determination of Appeals by Appointed Persons) (Prescribed Classes) Regulations 1997, SI 1997/420, save for an exception relating to statutory undertakers, all s 78 appeals are transferred for determination to inspectors appointed by the Secretary of State. By virtue of para 2 of Sch 6, where an appeal is determined by an inspector appointed by the Secretary of State the appellant and the local planning authority must be given an opportunity to appear before and be heard by the inspector if either of them so wish. The procedure before the inspector is governed by the Town and Country Planning Appeals (Determination by Inspectors) (Inquiries Procedure) (England) Rules 2000, SI 2000/1625 which replaced the Town and Country Planning Appeals (Determination by Inspectors) (Inquiries Procedure) Rules 1992, SI 1992/2039 as from 1 August 2000. Under those rules the appellant and the local planning authority and certain other bodies have a right to appear at the inquiry and the inspector can permit any other person to appear at the inquiry, such permission not to be unreasonably withheld. The procedure at the public inquiry is

a determined by the inspector but it involves the calling of witnesses to give oral evidence, cross-examination of witnesses and the making of representations. Following the inquiry the parties are notified of the inspector's decision, and his reasons for it, by being sent a copy of the decision letter.

32. Although the vast majority of s 78 appeals are decided by inspectors pursuant to the 1997 regulations, para 3(1) of Sch 6 to the 1990 Act gives the b Secretary of State power to recover jurisdiction in s 78 appeals by directing that an appeal which would otherwise be determined by an inspector appointed by him shall instead be determined by him. Under para 3(2) of Sch 6, he must state his reasons for making such a direction.

33. The procedure for a public inquiry on an appeal under s 78 which has been recovered by the Secretary of State for his determination pursuant to para 3 of c Sch 6 is governed by the Town and Country Planning (Inquiries Procedure) (England) Rules 2000, SI 2000/1624, which replaced the Town and Country Planning (Inquiries Procedure) Rules 1992, SI 1992/2038 as from 1 August 2000. The procedure under the rules is the same as that for an appeal which is determined by an inspector, save that in this case the inspector makes a written report to the d Secretary of State containing his conclusions and recommendations. Rule 17(5) provides:

> 'If, after the close of an inquiry, the Secretary of State—(a) differs from the inspector on any matter of fact mentioned in, or appearing to him to be material to, a conclusion reached by the inspector; or (b) takes into consideration any e new evidence or new matter of fact (not being a matter of government policy), and is for that reason disposed to disagree with a recommendation made by the inspector, he shall not come to a decision which is at variance with that recommendation without first notifying the persons entitled to appear at the inquiry who appeared at it of his disagreement and the reasons for it; and affording them an opportunity of making written representations f to him or (if the Secretary of State has taken into consideration any new evidence or new matter of fact, not being a matter of government policy) of asking for the re-opening of the inquiry.'

Rule 17(7) provides that the Secretary of State shall reopen the inquiry in those circumstances if asked to do so by the applicant or the local planning authority, g otherwise he has a discretion whether to re-open the inquiry.

34. Besides the ability to determine a s 78 appeal by recovering jurisdiction pursuant to para 3 of Sch 6, the Secretary of State is also given the power under s 77 of the 1990 Act to call in an application for his own decision. Section 77(1) and (5) provide:

h

> '(1) The Secretary of State may give directions requiring applications for planning permission ... to be referred to him instead of being dealt with by local planning authorities ...
>
> (5) Before determining an application referred to him under this section, the Secretary of State shall, if either the applicant or the local planning j authority wish, give each of them an opportunity of appearing before, and being heard by, a person appointed by the Secretary of State for the purpose.'

The Town and Country Planning (Inquiries Procedure) (England) Rules 2000 also apply to a public inquiry in respect of an application called in by the Secretary of State for his own determination. The same rules, therefore, apply to the procedure at the inquiry, the inspector's report and the Secretary of State's consideration of the inspector's report as apply in the case of an appeal recovered by the Secretary of State for his own determination. a

35. The validity of a decision made by the Secretary of State on a called in application or an appeal recovered by him under para 3 of Sch 6 can, by virtue of s 284 of the 1990 Act only be questioned by an aggrieved person by way of an application to the High Court made under s 288 of the 1990 Act. The grounds upon which a person aggrieved by such a decision can apply to the High Court b are that it was not within the powers of the 1990 Act or that any of the relevant requirements have not been complied with in relation to the decision. Section 288(5) provides that the High Court, if it is satisfied that the decision is not within the powers of the 1990 Act, or that the interests of the applicant have been substantially prejudiced by a failure to comply with any of the relevant requirements in relation to it, may quash the decision. c

36. There is no statutory right of appeal against a decision by the Secretary of State to call in a planning application for his own decision under s 77 of the 1990 Act. Such a decision can only be challenged by judicial review in accordance with the normal principles of administrative law.

d

Transport and works

37. The 1992 Act provides a mechanism for the Secretary of State to grant statutory authority, by way of an order, for matters which were previously authorised by the promotion of a private bill in Parliament. The procedure is invoked by an application being made to the Secretary of State under s 6 for an order under s 1 or 3 of the 1992 Act. Section 1 empowers the Secretary of State e to make an order relating to the construction or operation of, inter alia, a railway. By virtue of Sch 1, such an order can include the power to acquire land compulsorily. An applicant may, when applying for a 1992 Act order, ask the Secretary of State to direct that planning permission be deemed for all or some of the development covered by the order. Section 16 of the 1992 Act inserts a new s 90(2A) into the f 1990 Act enabling the Secretary of State to make such direction. A request for such a direction is considered alongside the application for the 1992 Act order and a decision on both matters is taken at the same time.

38. The procedure for making 1992 Act applications and objections thereto is governed by the Transport and Works (Applications and Objections Procedure) Rules 1992, SI 1992/2902 for applications made before 16 October 2000. For g applications made after that date it is governed by the Transport and Works (Applications and Objections Procedure) (England and Wales) Rules 2000, SI 1992/2190. Where an objection is made by a statutorily-qualified objector (which will include local authorities and landowners whose land would be compulsorily acquired) the Secretary of State is obliged by s 11 of the 1992 Act to h hold a public inquiry if the objector so wishes.

39. The rules governing the public inquiry are the Transport and Works (Inquiries Procedure) Rules 1992, SI 1992/2817. The procedure at the inquiry is determined by the inspector but it is much the same as for planning appeals and called-in planning applications. Witnesses are called and cross-examined j and representations can be made. Thereafter, the inspector makes a written report to the Secretary of State containing his conclusions and recommendations. Rule 17(4) contains a similar procedural rule as r 17(5) of the Town and Country Planning (Inquiries Procedure) (England) Rules 2000.

40. Under s 13 the Secretary of State can either make the order with or without modifications or not make the order. The validity of an order made by the

a Secretary of State can only be questioned by an application under s 22, which is in similar form to s 288 of the 1990 Act.

41. Section 23 enables the Secretary of State to make regulations prescribing the classes of application which are to be dealt with by an inspector rather than by him, but no such regulations have been made by the Secretary of State. Even if they were made, any such order made by an inspector could not, by virtue of b s 23(4), authorise the compulsory acquisition of land or the compulsory creation or extinguishment of rights over land.

42. Finally, where a 1992 Act order is linked or related to a development which does not come within the provision of the 1992 Act, it is usual practice for the inquiries into the 1992 Act order and the planning appeal to be held concurrently before the same inspector so that he can consider all the related issues.

c

Highways orders

43. The primary legislation governing highways orders is the 1980 Act. Under s 1, the Secretary of State is the highway authority for any highway which is a trunk road. Section 10 places a duty on the Secretary of State to keep the trunk road d network under review and it gives him authority to make orders in relation to existing or proposed highways. Under s 14, provision may be made by an order to authorise a highway authority for a trunk road to improve and stop up highways that may be affected by the construction or improvement of the road and to construct new highways for purposes connected with any such alteration. Such an order may also, by virtue of s 125, deal with the stopping up of, and e provision of, new means of access to private premises adjoining the road.

44. Orders under the relevant empowering provisions must be made by the Secretary of State. The procedure for making the orders is governed by Pts I and III of Sch 1 to the 1980 Act. Paragraph 7 deals with the circumstances in which a local inquiry has to be held.

f 45. Any such inquiry is governed by the Highways (Inquiries Procedure) Rules 1994, SI 1994/3263. Under r 2, an inspector is defined as a person appointed by the Secretary of State to hold an inquiry, although in fact the inspector is nominated by the Lord Chancellor. After the close of the inquiry, the inspector is required by r 26(1) to make a report in writing to the Secretary of State which includes his conclusions and recommendations. Rule 26(4) contains a similar g procedural rule as in r 17(5) of the Town and Country Planning (Inquiries Procedure) (England) Rules 2000.

46. Having considered the inspector's report, the Secretary of State is empowered, under para 8 of Sch 1 to the 1980 Act, to make the order either with or without modification. The statutory right under Sch 2 to the 1980 Act to challenge h a highways order made by the Secretary of State is in similar form to that in s 288 of the 1990 Act.

Compulsory purchase

47. The 1980 Act gives the Secretary of State power to acquire land compulsorily j in certain circumstances when exercising his highways powers. Section 239 gives him power to acquire land compulsorily for the construction of a trunk road, for the carrying out of works authorised by an order under s 14 and for improvement to highways which he is authorised by the 1980 Act to carry out. He is also empowered under s 246 to acquire land compulsorily for the purpose of mitigating any adverse effect which the existence or use of an existing, improved or proposed highway may have on the surroundings.

48. Section 247 provides that the 1981 Act shall apply to the compulsory acquisition of land under those powers. The 1981 Act sets out the general scheme and procedures for the compulsory acquisition of land. Paragraphs 1 to 3 of Sch 1 to the 1981 Act make provision for the publication of the draft compulsory purchase order and its service on the owner, lessee and occupier of any land comprised in the order. Paragraph 4 of Sch 1 provides that a public local inquiry shall be held if any objection is duly made by any such owner, lessee or occupier and not withdrawn.

49. The rules governing such an inquiry are the Compulsory Purchase by Ministers (Inquiry Procedure) Rules 1994, SI 1994/3264. Rule 11 provides that the minister may be legally represented at the inquiry. It also provides that a representative of the minister shall be available to give evidence and be cross-examined, except on the merits of government policy. Rule 13 provides that every statutory objector is entitled to appear at the inquiry, and the inspector can permit any other person to appear, such permission not to be unreasonably withheld.

50. The procedure at the inquiry is determined by the inspector. Witnesses are called and cross-examined and representations can be made. Rule 17 provides that, after the close of the inquiry, the inspector shall make a written report to the minister, containing his conclusions and recommendations. Rule 17(4) contains a similar procedural rule as r 17(5) of the Town and Country Planning (Inquiries Procedure) (England) Rules 2000.

51. Under para 4 of Sch 1 to the 1981 Act the minister may make the CPO either with or without modification. There is no power for the Secretary of State to delegate to an inspector the power to make the decision whether or not the CPO should be made. Section 25 of the 1981 Act provides that the validity of the order can only be questioned by an application to the High Court under s 23. The grounds on which the validity of the order can be questioned on an application under s 23 are very similar to those under s 288 of the 1990 Act.

52. Finally, s 257 of the 1981 Act provides that, where a compulsory purchase order is proposed to be made in the exercise of highway acquisition powers for enabling a relevant highways order to be implemented, the proceedings required may be taken concurrently with the proceedings required under the 1981 Act.

The Secretary of State's evidence

53. The DETR is one of the largest departments of state. It has over 15,000 staff of which about 4,000 are in its central offices, 10,000 in executive agencies which include the Planning Inspectorate (PINS) and the Highways Agency and 1,000 in Government Offices for the Regions (GOs). Below the Secretary of State in the ministerial team there are four Ministers of State, each with a Parliamentary Under Secretary and different areas of responsibility. Planning and transport are the responsibility of different Ministers of State.

54. One of the most important functions of the DETR is the formulation and promotion of policy. Our planning system is described by Mr Bowden, the divisional manager in charge of the Development Control Division of the DETR, as one of the most sophisticated in the world. This system provides strategic direction for the use of land and control over individual development with the aim of securing the most efficient and effective use of land in the public interest. This is self-evidently reflected in the legislation to which we have already referred. The policy is promoted by national guidance issued centrally and regional guidance issued by the GOs. Local planning authorities are required to work within this wider policy framework when formulating detailed development plans for their areas.

a Wide requirements of public participation and consultation are built into the system to ensure that the formulation of policy at every level is democratic. The position is similar for transport policy. The Highways Agency has the responsibility for implementing national transport policy in so far as it affects the trunk road and motorway network although it is clear that with major developments such as Alconbury they have an input into the formulation of policy as well.

b 55. Given the executive's role in making and implementing planning and transport policy it must inevitably have an interest in decisions of the kind with which we are concerned. Thus, in the HB and PL cases its interest is in implementing its policies for a development which may have more than local implications, or is in the green belt. But the interest may be more direct as in the ADL case where, as well as implementing policies for the area, the land in question is owned by c the state and the proposed development will produce financial reward for government if permission is granted. In the LG case, as in all such cases, it is the executive itself which is promoting the 1980 Act and CPO orders.

56. So what safeguards are there against the executive acting simply in its own self-interest when making the decisions in question?

d 57. Ministerial decisions are made in the name of the Secretary of State but in practice are often taken by the relevant Minister of State or his or her Under Secretary. Detailed Propriety Guidance is issued to all ministers about their decision-making role. Recognising that ministers making decisions on planning and transport matters of the kind with which we are concerned are acting in a quasi-judicial role, the guidance makes it clear that ministers should act and be e seen to act fairly and even-handedly by bringing an unbiased, properly-directed and independent mind to consideration of the matter. The guidance recognises the need for natural justice. The guidance dealing with road proposals is the most detailed. It says:

> '**The Inquiry**
>
> f 4. The purpose of the inquiry is to enable the Inspector to advise the Secretary of State on the weight and nature of objections to a road proposal. In essence the Inspector acts as the Secretary of State's "eyes and ears" for hearing evidence and arguments and inspecting the site of the road proposal. The inquiry provides an open public forum for the arguments on both sides g to be brought to a head. The Rules ensure that everybody hears everybody else's arguments and has an opportunity to put counter-arguments. Having heard all the arguments the Inspector makes his report to the Secretary of State and recommends whether or not the draft schemes or orders should be made or confirmed.
>
> h **The Decision**
>
> 5. Having received the report the Secretary of State must then decide whether the schemes or orders should be made or confirmed in the light of the Inspector's recommendations. The period between the close of the inquiry and the announcement of the decision is particularly sensitive and Ministers need to avoid even giving the impression that the decision may have been j influenced by private representations or factors which were not put before the inquiry.'

58. All civil servants, whose task is to serve the duly constituted government of the United Kingdom, are required to follow a code of conduct which requires them to do so with integrity, honesty, impartiality and objectivity. They owe their loyalty to the administration in which they serve, whose lawful policies they

are obliged to carry out. But their public functions must be performed reasonably and according to law and the advice they give ministers must be honest, impartial and without fear or favour.

59. One of the obvious safeguards is the public inquiry. We have already referred to the secondary legislation under which such inquiries take place. The appointment of inspectors is the responsibility of PINS. This agency's 1998 framework document describes its duties as follows:

> '2.1 The Agency serves the Secretary of State on appeal and other casework under planning, housing, environmental and other allied legislation.
>
> 2.2 The Agency's duty is to decide appeals and process casework efficiently and effectively, embracing the principles of openness, fairness and impartiality ...
>
> 2.7 The Agency is responsible for the recruitment, training, development and management of a panel of independent Inspectors to hold public inquiries and report on matters on highways, harbours and other transport legislation in England and Wales and to be available for nomination by the Lord Chancellor to conduct enquiries into motorways and trunk roads schemes.
>
> 2.8 The processes of decision making on appeals and other casework are governed by common law, acts of parliament and statutory instruments which are interpreted by the court and developed by practice and convention. When inspectors are instructed to hold inquiries on behalf of the Secretary of State or appointed to decide appeals they have the same regard to the Secretary of State's policies as does the Secretary of State.
>
> 2.9 The Agency's work is subject to the scrutiny of the courts, the Parliamentary Commission for Administration and the Council on Tribunals. Each inspector must exercise independent judgment and must not be subject to any improper influence, nor must it appear that the inspector may be subject to such influence.'

60. Inspectors are recruited by open competition. Most inspectors are employed full time by PINS but the Lord Chancellor maintains a separate panel of inspectors who are employed on a case by case basis to conduct inquiries into motorway and trunk road schemes.

61. To give some indication as to how the system works in practice the planning statistics are as follows. There are about 500,000 planning applications each year of which about 130 are called in. There are about 13,000 appeals to the Secretary of State of which about 100 are recovered so the vast majority of appeals are decided by inspectors. Of the called-in decisions and recovered appeals the Secretary of State follows the recommendation of the inspector in about 95% of cases.

62. The focus of the submissions of those who criticise the process has been on the time between receipt of the inspector's report and the Secretary of State's decision. We have already referred to the rules which require the Secretary of State to refer back to the parties and reopen the inquiry in certain circumstances. The position is summarised in Mr Bowden's statement as follows:

> '7.2.9 At post-report stage in particular, the objective is to ensure that the Secretary of State has possession of all material considerations needed to reach an informed, fair, unbiased and reasonable decision in each case as quickly as practicable in all circumstances. To this end: the relevant government office receives the inspector's report—which contains conclusions

a and recommendations; advice is sought by the government office on particular points of legal or policy elucidation from the appropriate legal or policy officials to put to the Secretary of State with the report; the minister may wish to refer back to the parties in some circumstances (and in other circumstances must do so)—eg. to seek more information, before a decision is made.

b 7.2.10 All decisions on called in cases and recovered appeals are taken by ministers, whether the Secretary of State or, more usually, the Minister of State for Housing, Planning and Construction or the Parliamentary Under Secretary of State, in accordance with the advice contained in the Guidance on Propriety Issues in the handling of planning casework in DETR. Decisions are allocated to ministers on the basis of responsibility for c particular regions. The geographical split is determined so as to avoid ministers taking decisions in regions where they have a constituency or other interest. In the [ADL] case the decision will be taken by the Parliamentary Under Secretary of State, Beverley Hughes, who has no knowledge of the previous exchanges of correspondence referred to in the witness statement d by Caroline Bowdler.'

63. Caroline Bowdler is the director of the Planning and Transport Division (PTD) of GO East which is responsible for the ADL, HB and PL cases. She has been particularly involved with Alconbury and the formulation of regional planning guidance which, until recently at least, identified Alconbury as a e strategic site for substantial development. For this reason she will not be involved in the decision-making process. The evidence shows that after the steps described in para 7.2.9 of Mr Bowden's statement 'GO draft decision letter and prepare submission to ministers'. This is done by a decision officer whose role Mrs Bowdler describes as follows:

f '17. PTD also has an Appeals Decision Officer ("the Decision Officer"), an individual senior executive officer grade located (for line management purposes only) in the Bedfordshire, Hertfordshire and Essex casework team. The Decision Officer deals with all recovered appeals under s 78 of the 1990 Act and on occasions with other planning decisions within GO East's geographical area. The Decision Officer is usually only involved with g called-in applications where work loads or propriety make this necessary. The Decision Officer deals with these matters exclusively and has no other function within PTD, or GO East more generally. In exercising his functions, the Decision Officer works separately from the casework team of which he is nominally a part, does not discuss the merits of the planning decisions h before him with an individual either within or without GO East, is not copied into or involved in the preparation of the Regional Planning Guidance (RPG) or the exercise of any of the Secretary of State's powers of intervention under the 1990 Act, and only has before him the information which the inspector would have had at the inquiry into the particular appeal j or called-in application, together with any representation made after the close of the inquiries (all relevant parties are given the opportunity to comment on any such representations where they are material or raise new matters).

18. So far as the Alconbury decision is concerned I have made inquiries and confirmed that the Decision Officer has had no involvement with any of my officers who have been involved with Alconbury or with the discussions

which have taken place previously with regard to the planning of Alconbury. I can also confirm that it will be the Decision Officer who will write the relevant submission to the minister and sign the relevant decision letter, subject to the decision of the court.' *a*

64. Similar arrangements exist for handling inspector's reports and decision-making following inquiries into proposed 1992 Act, 1980 Act and CPO orders. These are dealt with by specialist units within DETR central which do not have any conflicting policy responsibilities for promoting or financing the scheme involved. *b*

APPROACH

65. To determine our approach we think it is helpful to start by considering the decision of the European Court of Human Rights which is closest to the situation in the cases before us and which both sides say support their arguments. This is *Bryan v UK* (1995) 21 EHRR 342. Mr Bryan was served with an enforcement notice which required him to demolish buildings which he had erected. The 1990 Act (s 174(2)) gave him a right of appeal to the Secretary of State on grounds which included (a) planning permission should be granted, (b) no planning permission was required and (g) demolition was unnecessary. The appeal to the Secretary of State was determined by an inspector who upheld the enforcement notice. Mr Bryan appealed to the High Court under s 289 of the 1990 Act which is in broadly similar terms to s 288 (para 35 above). Ground (b) was not pursued because (according to evidence put before the European Court of Human Rights) of the limited jurisdiction of the court. The question was whether the buildings were by their appearance and layout agricultural, in which case permission was not required. But this was a matter of planning judgment based on findings of fact which the court was not able to review. The appeal was however pursued and dismissed on grounds (a) and (g). Mr Bryan's complaint to the European Court of Human Rights was that the process involved a breach of art 6(1) because the inspector was not independent and impartial and the High Court's powers to review his decision were limited. The commission admitted the complaint but subsequently concluded that there had been no breach of art 6. In its judgment the court accepted that the proceedings before the inspector ensured the applicant a fair hearing for the purposes of art 6(1) but it still had to consider whether the inspector was an independent and impartial tribunal. It said (at 358–359): *c* *d* *e* *f* *g*

'37. In order to establish whether a body can be considered "independent", regard must be had, *inter alia*, to the manner of appointment of its members and to their term of office, to the existence of guarantees against outside pressures and to the question whether the body presents an appearance of independence. *h*

38. It is true that the inspector was required to decide the applicant's planning appeal in a quasi-judicial, independent and impartial, as well as fair, manner. However, as pointed out by the Commission in its report, the Secretary of State can at any time, even during the course of proceedings which are in progress, issue a direction to revoke the power of an inspector to decide an appeal. In the context of planning appeals the very existence of this power available to the Executive, whose own policies may be in issue, is enough to deprive the inspector of the requisite appearance of independence, notwithstanding the limited exercise of the power in practice as described by *j*

a the government and irrespective of whether its exercise was or could have been at issue in the present case. For this reason alone, the review by the inspector does not of itself satisfy the requirements of Article 6 of the Convention, despite the existence of various safeguards customarily associated with an "independent and impartial tribunal".'

b It then went on to consider review by the High Court recognising (at 359) that—

> 'even where an adjudicatory body determining disputes over "civil rights and obligations" does not comply with Article 6(1) in some respect, no violation of the Convention can be found if the proccedings before that body are "subject to subsequent control by a judicial body that has full jurisdiction and does provide the guarantees of Article 6(1)".'

c For this proposition it relied on the decision in *Albert v Belgium* (1983) 5 EHRR 533. The court's conclusions in *Bryan*'s case were as follows ((1995) 21 EHRR 342 at 360–361):

> '44. The Court notes that the appeal to the High Court, being on "points d of law", was not capable of embracing all aspects of the inspector's decision concerning the enforcement notice served on Mr Bryan. In particular, as is not infrequently the case in relation to administrative law appeals in the Council of Europe Member States, there was no rehearing as such of the original complaints submitted to the inspector; the High Court could not substitute its own decision on the merits for that of the inspector; and its e jurisdiction over the facts was limited. However, apart from the classic grounds of unlawfulness under English law (going to such issues as fairness, procedural propriety, independence and impartiality), the inspector's decision could have been quashed by the High Court if it had been made by reference to irrelevant factors or without regard to relevant factors; or if the f evidence relied on by the inspector was not capable of supporting a finding of fact; or if the decision was based on an inference from facts which was perverse or irrational in the sense that no inspector properly directing himself would have drawn such an inference.
>
> 45. Furthermore, in assessing the sufficiency of the review available to g Mr Bryan on appeal to the High Court, it is necessary to have regard to matters such as the subject matter of the decision appealed against, the manner in which that decision was arrived at, and the content of the dispute, including the desired and actual grounds of appeal.
>
> 46. In this connection the Court would once more refer to uncontested safeguards attending the procedure before the inspector; the quasi-judicial h character of the decision-making process; the duty incumbent on each inspector to exercise independent judgement; the requirement that inspectors must not be subject to any improper influence; the stated mission of the Inspectorate to uphold the principles of openness, fairness and impartiality. Further, any alleged shortcoming in relation to these safeguards could have j been subject to review by the High Court.
>
> 47. In the present case there was no dispute as to the primary facts. Nor was any challenge made at the hearing in the High Court to the factual inferences drawn by the inspector, following the abandonment by the applicant of his objection to the inspector's reasoning under ground (b). The High Court had jurisdiction to entertain the remaining grounds of the applicant's appeal, and his submissions were adequately dealt with point by point. These submissions,

as the Commission noted, went essentially to questions involving "a panoply of policy matters such as development plans, and the fact that the property was situated in a Green Belt and a Conservation Area". Furthermore, even if the applicant had sought to pursue his appeal under ground (b), the Court notes that, while the High Court could not have substituted its own findings of fact for those of the inspector, it would have had the power to satisfy itself that the inspector's findings of fact or the inferences based on them were neither perverse nor irrational. Such an approach by an appeal tribunal on questions of fact can reasonably be expected in specialised areas of the law such as the one at issue, particularly where the facts have already been established in the course of a quasi-judicial procedure governed by many of the safeguards required by Article 6(1). It is also frequently a feature in the systems of judicial control of administrative decisions found throughout the Council of Europe Member States. Indeed, in the instant case, the subject matter of the contested decision by the inspector was a typical example of the exercise of discretionary judgment in the regulation of citizens' conduct in the sphere of town and country planning. The scope of review of the High Court was therefore sufficient to comply with Article 6(1).'

66. The Secretary of State submits that the instant cases are within the principles set out in *Bryan*'s case. The other side say that they are not. In support of this submission they rely on the decision of the Scottish Outer House in *County Properties Ltd v Scottish Ministers* 2000 SLT 965. That case concerned a called-in application for listed building consent under Scottish planning legislation similar to the 1990 Act. The Scottish Ministers admitted that they were not independent and impartial but, relying on *Bryan*'s case, argued that the process as a whole, which included a public inquiry before an inspector (reporter) and a right of appeal to the High Court, complied with art 6. The judge disagreed. He distinguished *Bryan*'s case because (1) the decision was to be made by the ministers and not by the inspector, and (2) involved deciding an issue between the petitioner and Historic Scotland (who opposed the application), their own executive agency and (3) would depend largely upon matters of aesthetic and planning judgment which could not be challenged on appeal. This decision is being appealed to the Inner House and the Secretary of State submits that it is wrongly decided.

67. The Court in *Bryan*'s case and the judge in the *County Properties* case accepted and applied the principle in *Albert*'s case (1983) 5 EHRR 533 at 542 (para 29) that—

'the Convention calls for one of the two following systems: either the jurisdictional organs themselves comply with the requirements of Article 6(1), or they do not so comply but are subject to control by a judicial body which has full jurisdiction and does provide the guarantees of Article 6(1).'

68. This principle was not in issue before us. It was also accepted that the requirement for a judicial body with full jurisdiction did not mean jurisdiction to decide all issues of law and fact whenever the administrative decision-maker was not independent and impartial. This is clear from *Bryan*'s case, particularly the concurring opinion of Mr Bratza, then a member of the commission, who said ((1995) 21 EHRR 342 at 354):

'It appears to me that the requirement that a court or tribunal should have "full jurisdiction" cannot be mechanically applied with the result that, in all a circumstances and whatever the subject matter of the dispute, the court or tribunal must have full power to substitute its own findings of fact, and its own inferences from those facts, for that of the administrative authority concerned.'

He then identified the matters referred to in para 45 of the court's judgment (at 360) b as being relevant to whether the power of judicial review was sufficiently wide to satisfy the requirements of art 6.

69. There are other cases which support this view. (See *Zumtobel v Austria* (1993) 17 EHRR 116 at 132–133 (paras 30–32)—expropriation of land; *ISKCON v UK* (1994) 76A DR 90—another enforcement notice case; *Ortenberg v Austria* (1994) 19 EHRR 524 at 532 (para 33)—objection to development plan; *Stefan v* c *UK* (1998) 25 EHRR CD 131 at 134, 135—proceedings before GMC; and *X v UK* (1998) 25 EHRR CD 88). In the last case which concerned a determination by the Secretary of State that the applicant was not a fit and proper person to be the chief executive of an insurance company, the commission said (at 97):

d 'It is common ground that the power of review of the Court of Session was not capable of embracing all aspects of the decision of the Secretary of State. In particular, as is not infrequently the case in relation to administrative law appeals in the Member States of the Council of Europe, the Court of Session could not substitute its own view for that of the Secretary of State as to the fitness of the applicant. On the other hand, the Court of Session could have e quashed the decision of the Secretary of State if, *inter alia*, the decision was irrational, in the sense that it was a decision that no reasonable minister properly directing himself could have reached on the basis of the material before him, or if the decision was reached by reference to irrelevant factors or without regard to relevant factors or in a procedurally unfair manner. In [*Bryan v UK* (1995) 21 EHRR 342 at 360 (para 45)], the European Court of f Human Rights gave examples of the matters which were relevant to assessing the adequacy of the review on a point of law in that case: "the subject-matter of the decision appealed against, the manner in which that decision was arrived at, and the content of the dispute, including the desired and actual grounds of appeal" ... The subject-matter of the decision appealed g against in the present case was a classic exercise of administrative discretion. The legislature had charged the Secretary of State with the express function of insuring, in the public interest, that only appropriate persons would become chief executive of certain insurance companies, and the contested decision in the present case was the exercise of that discretion.'

h After analysing the manner in which the decision had been reached and the content of the dispute the commission held that the scope of review of the Court of Session was sufficient to comply with art 6(1).

70. Following this analysis the argument before us has been that there is such a lack of independence and impartiality in the processes involved in the instant j cases that the limited scope of review by the High Court is insufficient for compliance with art 6. Consideration of this argument firstly involves looking at what art 6 requires in terms of independence and impartiality and how the processes involved in the instant cases measure up to these requirements and then in the light of this assessment, whether the powers of review of the High Court are sufficient so that the whole process complies with art 6. In order to perform the second stage of this exercise we need to consider the extent of the

review available in the High Court since it is suggested that it is somewhat wider than the court put it in *Bryan*'s case (1995) 21 EHRR 342 at 360 (para 44). a

INDEPENDENCE AND IMPARTIALITY

71. It is common ground that the independence required by art 6(1) is independence from the executive and from the parties.

72. The Secretary of State is part of the executive as are all or any of his b ministerial team or the civil servants involved in the decision-making process. The contrary is, we think, unarguable which no doubt explains the Secretary of State's stance in these proceedings. Just how exacting is the requirement for independence from the executive is illustrated by *Bryan*'s case where the largely theoretical possibility that the inspector's appointment could be revoked by the Secretary of State meant that he was not an independent tribunal. c

73. Impartiality is the same or very similar to independence from the parties. This requires the absence of prejudice or bias. It is tested subjectively and objectively. Subjective personal impartiality is assumed until there is proof to the contrary. This is not alleged in the instant cases. Objectively the question is whether the tribunal offers guarantees sufficient to exclude any legitimate doubts d about its impartiality. Whilst appearances are important they are not decisive since misgivings must be capable of being held to be objectively justified (*Kraska v Sweden* (1993) 18 EHRR 188 at 201 (para 32)).

74. So much is common ground but Mr Elvin QC, for the Secretary of State, made a number of submissions which are very much in issue.

75. First, Mr Elvin submitted that the court could look beyond the statutory e framework when considering whether a person or body could be regarded as impartial in a particular case. It did not matter that the DETR had incompatible functions which would deprive it as a whole of impartiality, provided the individuals involved in discharging such functions are not identical. Since a government department is not a monolithic entity, different individuals could f always be found to discharge the incompatible functions and guarantees had been given that this would happen in these cases.

76. Mr Elvin supported these arguments by reference to domestic law. In this field of administrative law apparent bias cannot be shown unless the individual involved in the decision-making process has not kept an open mind. If such bias is shown, the law provides an adequate remedy by way of judicial review. This, he g submitted, is the same as the requirement for objective impartiality under art 6. Further, Mr Elvin submits that domestic law in this field does not recognise institutional or structural bias because that is built into the legislative scheme and cannot therefore be avoided.

77. These arguments met the objection that the Secretary of State's policies h were involved in the decisions which had to be taken and that he promoted highways and CPO orders. Mr Elvin admitted, however, that the fact that the Ministry of Defence had a financial interest in the Alconbury development did not mean that ministers discharging their planning functions in a different department of state should not be regarded as impartial. Niceties of constitutional j theory should not come into it. It would be quite unrealistic to imbue the Secretary of State with the knowledge and predispositions of ministers in other departments and all civil servants. The interest of the Ministry of Defence was in any event a public as opposed to a private financial interest.

78. Finally, Mr Elvin submitted, the fact that the HSE supported the objection to permission being granted in the HB case did not affect the Secretary of State's

a impartiality. Unlike Historic Scotland, the HSE was not an executive agency but a separate corporate entity.

79. In support of his argument that the court should look at how and by whom the decisions in these cases will be made, Mr Elvin referred to a number of Strasbourg cases which he submitted showed that the court was primarily concerned to see whether individuals were impartial rather than the body as a b whole of which they were part. He referred us to *Piersack v Belgium* (1983) 5 EHRR 169—criminal trial presided over by judge who had previously been in charge of department which decided to prosecute the applicant; *De Cubber v Belgium* (1984) 7 EHRR 236—criminal trial presided over by judge who had previously been investigating judge; *Procola v Luxembourg* (1995) 22 EHRR 193—four of the five members of judicial committee of Conseil D'Etat had previously taken c part in Conseil D'Etat's advisory opinion on the challenged legislation; *McGonnell v UK* [2000] 2 PLR 69—judge previously presided over legislative body which adopted the challenged legislation.

80. We have considered these and a number of other cases relied on by Mr Elvin but can find no support in them for the general proposition which he d advances. They do show, as one would expect, that the court will look for lack of objective impartiality on the part of individuals who form part of the tribunal in question, but they give no support for the proposition that the court is not also concerned with institutional or structural impartiality. Indeed, there are a number of cases which suggest that the court is concerned about this. Thus, in *Sramek v Austria* (1985) 7 EHRR 351, one of the parties to a hearing before the e regional authority deciding whether to approve the applicant's purchase of land was a senior civil servant who was the superior of three civil servants who were members of the authority. Their independence was guaranteed by statute but the court held (at 364 (para 42)):

> f 'Where, as in the present cases, a tribunal's members include a person who is in a subordinate position, in terms of his duties in the organisation of his service, viz-a-viz one of the parties, litigants may entertain a legitimate doubt about that person's independence. Such a situation seriously affects the confidence which the courts must inspire in a democratic society.

g 81. Similarly, in *Findlay v UK* (1997) 24 EHRR 221 the court held that the organisation of a court martial did not offer adequate guarantees of impartiality where the members of the court had been appointed by the convening officer. He played a significant role at the hearing and the members were subordinate in rank to him and fell within his chain of command. In *Belilos v Switzerland* (1988) h 10 EHRR 466 the applicant complained that the Police Board which convicted her of fraud was not impartial. The appointed member to the board was a municipal servant who was not subject to orders in the exercise of his judicial powers and took a different oath from the one taken by police. However, the court said (at 489 (para 67)):

> j 'Nonetheless, a number of considerations relating to the functions exercised and to internal organisation are relevant too; even appearances may be important. In Lausanne the member of the Police Board is a senior civil servant who is liable to return to other departmental duties. The ordinary citizen will tend to see him as a member of the police force subordinate to his superiors and loyal to his colleagues. A situation of this kind may undermine the confidence which must be inspired by the courts in a democratic

> society. In short, the applicant could legitimately have doubts as to the independence and organisational impartiality of the Police Board which accordingly did not satisfy the requirements of Article 6(1) in this respect.' *a*

82. However, we think there are more fundamental objections to this part of Mr Elvin's argument. Firstly, although the legislation vests all the relevant functions in the Secretary of State, the argument requires one to assume that there is no one entity involved, only a multiplicity of officials capable of acting, as necessary, independently and impartially of one another. This is not the position under domestic law. In *Bushell v Secretary of State for the Environment* [1980] 2 All ER 608 at 613, [1981] AC 75 at 95, where the making of certain highway orders was challenged, Lord Diplock said: *b*

> 'What is fair procedure is to be judged not in the light of constitutional fictions as to the relationship between the minister and the other servants of the Crown who serve in the government department of which he is the head but in the light of the practical realities as to the way in which administrative decisions involving forming judgments based on technical considerations are reached. To treat the minister in his decision making capacity as someone separate and distinct from the department of government of which he is the political head and for whose actions he alone in constitutional theory is accountable to Parliament is to ignore not only practical realities but also Parliament's intention.' *c* *d*

83. There are also immense practical difficulties in Mr Elvin's approach. How is one to identify within the department those who are impartial and those who are not? By definition none of them is independent. How in practice does any individual offer guarantees sufficient to exclude legitimate doubt in this respect when his superiors including the Secretary of State himself are not impartial? Ministers and civil servants may change over the period under review. Such a review might require the court to consider detailed evidence about the workings of the department on a case by case basis. The only sensible conclusion we think is to treat the DETR and the Secretary of State in the way in which Lord Diplock did in *Bushell*'s case. *e* *f*

84. There is no dispute about the position under domestic law. It is well stated in passages from Supperstone and Goudie *Judicial Review* (2nd edn, 1997) p 9.21: *g*

> 'In many administrative situations the possibility of bias is built into the system. Proposers of the scheme may have strong and carefully thought out views on the subject, and yet may have to hear and rule on objections to it. Administrators may have guidelines to help them in their day to day application of legislation. In such situations the concept of a fair trial may be impossible and indeed undesirable to achieve. It has been pointed out ... that the more indifferent to the aim in view the less efficient is a Minister or civil servant likely to be. After all, it is his job to get things done. So, while the obvious pre-judgment of an issue is not allowed, a challenge to a decision on the grounds of departmental bias is unlikely to succeed. It is a Minister's job to have a policy and to support it in public.' *h* *j*

and De Smith, Woolf and Jowell *Judicial Review of Administrative Action* (5th edn, 1995) pp 546–548 (paras 12-042–12-050):

> 'Closely related to the doctrine of necessity is that which permits public officials to exhibit certain kinds of bias in the exercise of their judgment or

a discretion on matters of public policy ... The normal standards of impartiality implied in the adjudicative setting cannot meaningfully be applied to a body entitled to initiate a proposal and then to decide whether to proceed with it in the face of objections. What standards should be imposed on the Secretary of State for the Environment when he has to decide whether or not to confirm a compulsory purchase order or clearance order made by a local b authority ... or to allow an appeal against a refusal of planning permission? It would be inappropriate for the courts to insist on his maintaining the lofty detachment required of a judicial officer determining a *lis inter partes*. The Secretary of State's decisions can seldom be wrenched entirely from their context and viewed in isolation from the governmental responsibilities.'

c These passages are supported by a number of authorities including *R v Hereford and Worcester CC, ex p Wellington Parish Council* [1996] JPL 573, where Harrison J held that the '*Gough*' test (real danger of bias) (see *R v Gough* [1993] 2 All ER 724, [1993] AC 646) had no application in such a case. All that was required was that the authority did not approach its task with a closed mind.

d 85. But the question we have to answer is whether the position under domestic law can withstand the unqualified procedural right conferred by art 6. We do not think it can. The common law approach has inevitably been determined by the constraints imposed by legislation. The logic is that if legislation vests a decision in a person who is biased or provides for a decision to be taken in a manner which is not compatible with the requirements of independence and impartiality, e no breach of the requirements of fairness can be found. Such requirements of fairness as there may be must be accommodated to the relevant statutory scheme. But the question now is not how art 6 can best be accommodated in the interests of fairness given the existing statutory scheme, but rather whether the scheme itself complies with art 6. To accept that the possibility of common law f bias is inherent in the system and mandated by Parliament is merely to admit that the system involves structural bias and requires determinations to be made by a person who is not impartial.

86. It must follow from these conclusions that the Secretary of State is not impartial in the manner required by art 6 because in each case his policy is in issue. This is not of course to say that there is anything wrong with his role as a g policy maker. What is objectionable in terms of art 6 is that he should be the judge in his own cause where his policy is in play. In other words he cannot be both policy maker and decision taker. In the ADL case there is the added factor of the financial interest of the government. In the LG case, as we think in any case where the Secretary of State through the Highways Agency promotes 1980 Act h and CPO orders, it cannot possibly be said that as a decision maker the Secretary of State is objectively impartial. He is a party to the cause in which he is also the judge. Where the Highways Agency is simply a party at the inquiry as in the ADL case the same may also be said. The point has less force in the case of the HSE.

j *High Court's powers of review*

87. Earlier in this judgment we identified the grounds of statutory challenge to decisions made under the legislative provisions relevant to these four cases—namely, the grounds under s 288 of the 1990 Act, s 22 of the 1992 Act, para 2 of Sch 2 to the 1980 Act and s 23 of the 1981 Act. All of those grounds are in broadly similar form. Put shortly, they are that the decision was outside the powers of the relevant Act or that there was a failure to comply with a relevant

requirement. Those grounds involve consideration of the same principles of review as are involved in judicial review under what is now CPR Pt 54. In other words, the scope of review by the High Court in all these cases involves consideration of the normal principles of judicial review that have now become well established.

88. The conventional grounds of challenge were stated by Lord Denning MR in *Ashbridge Investments Ltd v Minister of Housing and Local Government* [1965] 3 All ER 371 at 374, [1965] 1 WLR 1320 at 1326 in the following terms:

> '... it seems to me that the court can interfere with the Minister's decision if he has acted on no evidence; or if he has come to a conclusion to which, on the evidence, he could not reasonably come; or if he has given a wrong interpretation to the words of the statute; or if he has taken into consideration matters which he ought not to have taken into account, or vice versa; or has otherwise gone wrong in law. It is identical with the position when the court has power to interfere with the decision of a lower tribunal which has erred in point of law.'

89. The courts have made it clear on a number of occasions that they are only concerned with the legality of the decision, not with the merits of the case. The following two examples illustrate the position. Firstly, in *Tesco Stores Ltd v Secretary of State for the Environment* [1995] 2 All ER 636 at 657, [1995] 1 WLR 759 at 780 Lord Hoffmann stated:

> 'The law has always made a clear distinction between the question of whether something is a material consideration and the weight which it should be given. The former is a question of law and the latter is a question of planning judgment, which is entirely a matter for the planning authority. Provided that the planning authority has regard to all material considerations, it is at liberty (provided that it does not lapse into *Wednesbury* irrationality) to give them whatever weight the planning authority thinks fit or no weight at all. The fact that the law regards something as a material consideration therefore involves no view about the part, if any, which it should play in the decision-making process. This distinction between whether something is a material consideration and the weight which it should be given is only one aspect of a fundamental principle of British planning law, namely that the courts are concerned only with the legality of the decision-making process and not with the merits of the decision. If there is one principle of planning law more firmly settled than any other, it is that matters of planning judgment are within the exclusive province of the local planning authority or the Secretary of State.'

Secondly, in *Reid v Secretary of State for Scotland* [1999] 1 All ER 481 at 506, [1999] 2 AC 512 at 541 Lord Clyde put it in this way:

> 'Judicial review involves a challenge to the legal validity of the decision. It does not allow the court of review to examine the evidence with a view to forming its own view about the substantial merits of the case. It may be that the tribunal whose decision is being challenged has done something which it had no lawful authority to do. It may have abused or misused the authority which it had. It may have departed from the procedures which either by statute or at common law as matter of fairness it ought to have observed. As regards the decision itself it may be found to be perverse, or irrational, or

a grossly disproportionate to what was required. Or the decision may be found to be erroneous in respect of a legal deficiency, as for example, through the absence of evidence, or of sufficient evidence, to support it, or through account being taken of irrelevant matter, or through a failure for any reason to take account of a relevant matter, or through some misconstruction of the terms of the statutory provision which the decision-b maker is required to apply. But while the evidence may have to be explored in order to see if the decision is vitiated by such legal deficiencies it is perfectly clear that in a case of review, as distinct from an ordinary appeal, the court may not set about forming its own preferred view of the evidence.'

90. The extent to which the court may have regard to material errors of fact c was touched upon by Lord Slynn in *R v Criminal Injuries Compensation Board, ex p A* [1999] 2 AC 330 at 344–345, [1999] 2 WLR 974 at 982 when he said:

'Your Lordships have been asked to say that there is jurisdiction to quash the board's decision because that decision was reached on a material error of d fact. Reference has been made to *Wade & Forsyth, Administrative Law,* 7th ed. (1994), pp. 316–318 in which it is said: "Mere factual mistake has become a ground of judicial review, described as 'misunderstanding or ignorance of an established and relevant fact,' [*Secretary of State for Education and Science v Tameside Metropolitan Borough* [1976] 3 All ER 665 at 675, [1977] AC 1014 at 1030], or acting 'upon an incorrect basis of fact' ... This ground of review has e long been familiar in French law and it has been adopted by statute in Australia. It is no less needed in this country, since decisions based upon wrong facts are a cause of injustice which the courts should be able to remedy. If a 'wrong factual basis' doctrine should become established, it would apparently be a new branch of the ultra vires doctrine, analogous to finding facts based upon no evidence or acting upon a misapprehension of f law." *de Smith, Woolf and Jowell, Judicial Review of Adminstrative Action,* 5th ed. (1995), p. 288: "The taking into account of a mistaken fact can just as easily be absorbed into a traditional legal ground of review by referring to the taking into account of an irrelevant consideration, or the failure to provide reasons that are adequate or intelligible, or the failure to base the decision on g any evidence. In this limited context material error of fact has always been a recognised ground for judicial intervention." For my part, I would accept that there is jurisdiction to quash on that ground in this case, but I prefer to decide the matter on the alternative basis argued, namely that what happened in these proceedings was a breach of the rules of natural justice and constituted unfairness.'

h

91. So far as planning policy is concerned, the courts have made it clear that, if the determining authority is going to depart from its policy, it has to give its reasons for doing so but that the weight to be attached to the policy is a matter for the determining authority alone (see *EC Gransden & Co Ltd v Secretary of State for* j *the Environment* [1986] JPL 519 and *Wycombe DC v Secretary of State for the Environment* [1988] JPL 111). As we have already said, the court also has a restricted power to review decisions on the ground of alleged bias. When exercising its reviewing function the court does have power to hear oral evidence although that power is rarely exercised.

92. The scope of the High Court to review the kind of decisions involved in these four cases is, therefore, restricted in the way we have described above. It is

only concerned with the legality of the decision and it is not allowed to examine the evidence to form its own view about the substantial merits of the case. The merits of the case and questions of planning judgment are for the determining authority, not for the court. It seems to us that in *Bryan*'s case (1995) 21 EHRR 342 at 360 (para 44) the European Court of Human Rights gave a fair summary of the nature of the scope of the review of the High Court in the kind of cases with which we are concerned.

Are the processes involved in these cases saved by the High Court's powers of review?

93. This is the crucial question which we have to answer having regard to 'matters such as the subject matter of the decision appealed against, the manner in which that decision was arrived at, and the content of the dispute, including the desired and actual grounds of appeal' (*Bryan*'s case (at 360 (para 45)). We know of course what the subject matter of the decisions in question is (planning permission, 1992 Act, 1980 Act and CPO orders) and the manner in which those decisions will be arrived at. We know broadly the content of the dispute in each case. But at this stage we cannot know anything about desired or actual grounds of appeal. This led to the suggestion by Mr Stanley, for the NVA and HUNTSNAP, that these applications were premature. The same point was made in *County Properties Ltd v Scottish Ministers* 2000 SLT 965. The judge rejected it saying (at 975):

> 'The suggestion that the adequacy of the right of appeal cannot be judged until the grounds on which the petitioners seek to bring the respondents' decision under review are identified is in my view not only unsound in principle but also thoroughly impractical. As … counsel … submitted, it would be unreasonable to require the petitioners to defer their challenge to the validity of the call-in decision until after the inquiry process had run its course, a decision had been made, and it was possible to say for certain whether in the circumstances the statutory appeal afforded an adequate review to comply with art 6(1). Considerations of both time and expense make that approach unattractive.'

We find this reasoning compelling. All other parties to these applications supported it.

94. We have already said why we think the Secretary of State is not independent or impartial. This must be balanced against the safeguards inherent in the process, the most important of which is the public inquiry. The rules under which such inquiries are held are designed to and do, we think, give the parties a fair and public hearing at which all issues of fact and law can be ventilated. If the decision was for the inspector we have no doubt, as in *Bryan*'s case, that this would justify a restricted right of review by the High Court. But that is not the case. The inspector reaches conclusions and makes recommendations at the end of the inquiry and the Secretary of State cannot disagree with his material findings of fact without giving the parties the opportunity to make written representations. But having complied with this requirement of natural justice he is free to make his own decision and does so after taking account of internal legal and policy 'elucidation' and the recommendation of the decision officer (paras 62–64 above) which are not seen by the parties.

95. We do not think this process contains sufficient safeguards to justify the High Court's restricted power of review. In terms of art 6 the decision on the merits, which usually involves findings of fact and planning judgment, has not been

a determined by an independent and impartial tribunal or anyone approaching this, but by someone who is obviously not independent and impartial.

96. We have to say that we are not pleased to reach this conclusion which will obviously have far-reaching consequences. The system has generally worked well and we should like to think that it was fair. But art 6 does require us to think again and we do not think we can avoid the conclusions we have reached. If one asks b the question 'would those whose civil rights and obligations are at issue in these cases have them determined on the merits by a tribunal which was, or was largely, independent and impartial', the answer must be 'no'. Our attention has been drawn to the Privy Council's decision in *Brown v Stott (Procurator Fiscal, Dunfermline)* [2001] 2 All ER 97 at 115, [2001] 2 WLR 817 at 836 where Lord Bingham said:

c

> 'The general language of the convention could have led to the formulation of hard-edged and inflexible statements of principle from which no departure could be sanctioned whatever the background or the circumstances. But that approach has been consistently eschewed by the court throughout its history. d The case law shows that the court has paid very close attention to the facts of particular cases coming before it, giving effect to factual differences and recognising differences of degree.'

We hope we have recognised this in our judgment. But however flexible and friendly one makes art 6(1) we do not think one can escape from the conclusion e that the processes in issue in these cases are not compatible with it. To hold otherwise would substantially impair the right.

97. In support of his submissions Mr Elvin urged that the convention was concerned to maintain and promote the ideas and values of a democratic society. Planning and transport policy and decisions were often sensitive political issues f for which governments are held responsible in democratic societies. Because judges were not accountable in this way, it was desirable for such decisions to be made by government without interference from the courts, provided they were made lawfully.

98. We agree with much of what Mr Elvin says. It is not for us to decide how the system needs to be changed in the light of our decision, although it is obvious g that government has been considering the options for some time. Our decision should not be interpreted as a bid for more judge power. This is a specialist field in which most judges would be unqualified to make value judgments of the kind which have to be made. Most judges would not want to do so. With PINS the Secretary of State already has at hand a cadre of sufficiently independent h specialists well equipped to make such decisions. As with the decisions they now make, they would be required to have regard to government policy.

Should the scope of the court's powers of review be enlarged?

99. Here the Secretary of State's argument is that the court as a public j authority must not act in a way which is incompatible with the convention (s 6 of the 1998 Act) and so it must, if it can, read and give effect to the relevant legislation (s 3(1) of the 1998 Act) and/or enlarge its own powers by way of judicial review so as to save the processes in issue. In support of this argument Mr Elvin obviously contemplated that the court would undertake a more intensive review of findings of fact, but submitted that it would not be necessary to review matters of planning judgment.

100. There are principled and practical objections to these arguments. The first objection in principle is that it is not possible to read and give effect to the legislation which quite plainly precludes 'full' appeals or appeals against findings of fact to accommodate any enlarged power of review and it would not be right to do so by the back door of judicial review. Judicial review is a review and not a full appeal. The court's powers to review findings of fact are circumscribed by the nature of the process. Secondly, the court's powers under the legislation and on judicial review are limited to quashing the decision in question. If the court quashed the 1992 Act, 1980 Act or CPO orders made in these cases because the process did not comply with art 6, the cases could only go back for re-decision by the Secretary of State, so the court would not have provided an effective remedy. That would be a breach of art 6 (see *Kingsley v UK* (2001) Times, 9 January) where the European Court of Human Rights held that there was a breach of art 6 because the English court could only quash the decision in question which meant that the matter would have to go back for decision by the same authority which was not impartial). The practical objection is that if the court was to consider extending its powers it should not do so other than on a case by case basis or at least where it had a set of facts to consider. Here, the exercise we are being asked to perform is entirely hypothetical. We decline to do so.

Section 6 of the 1998 Act

101. It is common ground that if the 1992 Act, 1980 Act and 1981 Act processes do not comply with art 6 and cannot be made to do so (as we have found), this is because the primary legislation requires the Secretary of State to take the relevant decisions and so he cannot act differently (s 6(2)(a)). His acts are not therefore unlawful under s 6(1). This enables us to make a declaration of incompatibility under s 4, but we have said we will hear argument about this and any other relief after handing down this judgment.

102. There are however s 6 issues about the planning processes. In the call-in cases HB and PL argue that s 6(2) does not apply because no question arises as to whether s 77 of the 1990 Act can be given effect in a way which is compatible (s 6(2)(b)) with art 6, alternatively, if such a question does arise, s 77 can be given such effect. In the case of recovered appeals, ADL, supported by the amicus and others, argue that the relevant provisions can be given effect because they give the Secretary of State a discretion as to whether to recover the appeal or not. So the provisions can be given effect by choosing not to recover.

103. We deal with s 77 of the 1990 Act first. Mr Hockman QC, for HB, submitted that the court was only concerned with the call in decisions in these cases and so it did not need to speculate about whether it was possible for other call-ins to be made which would not involve a breach of art 6. But if one had to speculate, there were cases, such as where a local planning authority had to give itself permission, where there would not be a breach of art 6 because the local planning authority had no convention rights. Alternatively, s 77 could be read down even to the extent that the Secretary of State could never call in.

104. We do not accept these submissions. It seems to us that where the point is raised (as it is) the court is bound to consider whether the provision in question can ever be given effect to in a way which is compatible with convention rights. Once a planning application is called in, the legislation requires the Secretary of State to decide it. As all such cases involve the use of land, in practice there are unlikely to be any cases in which the civil rights or obligations of persons eligible to take proceedings under s 7 of the 1998 Act are not affected. The fact that a local

a planning authority may not be so eligible (s 7(7) of the 1998 Act and art 34 of the convention) does not mean that the authority, which is not the government (ie a High Contracting Party), has no rights under art 6. We do not think it is legitimate to read down a legislative provision so as to extinguish it. It follows that we think s 6(2)(b) of the 1998 Act applies to s 77 of the 1990 Act and so the Secretary of State's acts are not and will not be unlawful under s 6(1) in the HB b and PL cases.

105. It is argued that the position is different for recovered appeals. Here, the provisions of the legislation in question (ss 78 and 79 and paras 1 and 3 of Sch 6 to the 1990 Act) give the Secretary of State two powers: a power to delegate his decision to an inspector and a power to recall a decision to himself. These provisions c can be given effect in a way which is compatible with art 6 by not exercising the power to recover. The fact that this does away with the power to recover and converts the power to delegate into a duty to do so is irrelevant. A public authority does not fail to give effect to a statute if it invariably uses one of two powers conferred on it, if that is the only way of achieving compatibility with the convention.

d 106. We have not found this an easy issue to resolve. On analysis we think the answer depends upon what is meant by 'one or more provisions' in s 6(2)(b). If it refers to the whole statutory scheme by which appeals under s 78 are to be decided, we think the submissions which we have set out above are correct. On the other hand, if it refers simply to the provision by which the Secretary of State can e recover appeals under para 3 of Sch 6, then we think that s 6(2)(b) does apply for the same reasons that it applies to s 77. In other words *this* provision cannot be given effect in a way which is compatible with art 6. On balance we prefer the latter view. Looking at the matter more generally, ss 78 and 79 cast the primary duty of deciding appeals on the Secretary of State. We have held that he cannot f do so in a way which is compatible with art 6. It would be somewhat anomolous if the case did not fall within s 6(2). It follows that we think that s 6(2)(b) also applies to recovered appeals and so the Secretary of State's acts are not and will not be unlawful under s 6(1) in the ADL case.

DOMESTIC LAW CHALLENGE

g 107. HB's main complaint is that the Secretary of State has not given any reasons to make it clear whether he was treating the application as coming within his call-in policy and, if so, why, or whether he was departing from the policy and, if so, why.

108. The Secretary of State's call-in policy is contained in para D7 of Annex D h to Planning Policy Guidance Note (PPG1). It states:

> 'The Secretary of State may require applications to be referred to him for decision but this call-in power has in recent years only been exercised in around 130 cases each year. The policy of the Secretary of State is to be very j selective about calling in planning applications, and such action is generally taken only if planning issues of more than local importance are involved. Examples are applications which raise significant architectural and urban design issues, which could have wide effects beyond their immediate locality, which give rise to substantial national or regional controversy, which may conflict with national policy on important matters, or where the interests of foreign governments may be involved.'

109. The site to which HB's application relates lies within an area allocated for oil storage in the local plan. The application therefore involved a departure from the development plan. In his report to the town planning committee, the council's director of planning stated that, for reasons set out in his report, he did not consider the application to be a major departure warranting referral to the Secretary of State for his determination pursuant to the Town and Country Planning (Development Plans and Consultation) (Departures) Directions 1999 (Circular 7/99).

110. Mr Hockman submitted that there was nothing in the reasons given by the Secretary of State in his call-in letter (see para 12 above) to suggest that the application was of more than local importance so that, under the Secretary of State's call-in policy, it would not normally be called in for his determination. HB's 1997 application for its present site on the Charfleet Industrial Estate, which was ultimately determined by an inspector on appeal, had not been called in, and comparison was made with the Alconbury proposal which was of significantly greater importance but which had not been called in by the Secretary of State. It was therefore submitted that the Secretary of State's decision to call in the application was arbitrary as well as inadequately reasoned.

111. In support of his contention of arbitrariness Mr Hockman relied on a passage in the judgment of Sedley LJ in *R v Secretary of State for Education and Employment, ex p Begbie* [2000] 1 WLR 1115, which was an education case. When dealing with the principles relating to the exercise of discretion in relation to the policy relevant in that case, Sedley LJ said (at 1132):

> 'Thirdly, it must not be exercised arbitrarily or inconsistently as between one pupil and another … Everything therefore depends on there being adequate factual reasons for either agreeing or deciding to depart from a policy.'

In support of his reasons challenge, Mr Hockman relied on *EC Gransden & Co Ltd v Secretary of State for the Environment* [1986] JPL 519 where Woolf J, as he then was, said that if a body is going to depart from its policy it had to give clear reasons for doing so.

112. In our view, it is important to bear in mind that, under s 77 of the 1990 Act, the Secretary of State is given a very wide discretion whether or not to call in an application for his own decision. Furthermore, there is no statutory requirement for him to give reasons for his decision whether or not to call in an application. In fact, he has given his reasons in this case although he was not statutorily obliged to do so. Those reasons are now relied on by HB as giving rise to the need for further reasons as to whether or not he has treated the application as coming within his policy. In our judgment, it was not incumbent on the Secretary of State to give the further reasons suggested. The call-in policy contained in para D7 of Annex D of PPG1 is not an exclusive policy as is made clear by the word 'generally' in the policy. The Secretary of State was not, in our view, under any duty to explain whether or not he considered the application to come within the generality of the policy in the sense of involving issues of more than local importance. He gave clear reasons why he had decided to call in the application and there was no need for him to go any further than that.

113. Whilst we can understand HB's disappointment in having their application called in, the Secretary of State has a wide discretion whether or not to call in an application which he has to exercise on a case by case basis. We do not consider that it can be said that his decision to call in HB's application was arbitrary, nor can it be said to be perverse or irrational. In those circumstances, we do not

a accept the submission that the decision should be quashed on domestic law grounds.

CONCLUSIONS

114. The processes involved in these four cases are not compatible with art 6(1) of the convention, but the Secretary of State has not and will not act b unlawfully under s 6(1) of the 1998 Act because s 6(2) applies. We will hear argument whether we should make declarations of incompatibility in respect of these processes.

115. HB's domestic law challenge fails.

Declarations of incompatibility under s 4 of the Human Rights Act 1998 granted in respect c *of (i) the Town and Country Planning Act 1990, ss 77, 78, 79 (excluding the words inserted into s 79(4) by para 19 of Sch 7 to the Planning and Compensation Act 1991), Sch 6, paras 3 and 4 (in so far as it applied to s 79); (ii) the Transport and Works Act 1992, ss 1, 3 and 23(4); (iii)* the *Highways Act 1980, ss 14(3)(a), 16(5)(a), 18(3)(a), 125, Sch 1, Pt I, paras 1, 7 and 8; and (iv) the Acquisition of Land Act 1981, s 2(3), Sch 1,* d *para 4.*

Dilys Tausz Barrister

Appeal

The Secretary of State appealed to the House of Lords in the ADL, HB and LG e cases pursuant to s 12 of the Administration of Justice Act 1969. The Appeal Committee gave permission to appeal on 25 January 2001. The Lord Advocate intervened in support of the Secretary of State.

Jonathan Sumption QC, David Elvin QC, Philip Sales and *James Maurici* (instructed by f the *Treasury Solicitor*) for the Secretary of State.

Roderick Macdonald QC and *Andrew Webster* (both of the Scottish Bar) (instructed by the *Treasury Solicitor*) for the Lord Advocate.

Keith Lindblom QC, Craig Howell Williams and *Hereward Phillpot* (instructed by *Marrons*, Leicester) for ADL.

Gregory Jones and *Paul Hardy* (instructed by *Richard Braun*, Cambridge) for CCC.

g *Martin Kingston QC* and *Peter Goatley* (instructed by *Sharpe Pritchard*, agents for *Colin Meadowcroft*, Huntingdon) for HDC.

Paul Stanley and *Tim Eicke* (instructed by *David Barney & Co*, Stevenage) for NVA and HUNTSNAP.

Stephen Hockman QC, Kevin Leigh and *Gordon Nardell* (instructed by *Jennings Son &* h *Ash*) for HB.

John Howell QC and *Rabinder Singh* (instructed by the *Treasury Solicitor*) as amici curiae in the LG case.

Their Lordships took time for consideration.

j

9 May 2001. The following opinions were delivered.

LORD SLYNN OF HADLEY.

[1] My Lords, these three appeals come direct to the House pursuant to s 12 of the Administration of Justice Act 1969 from decisions of the Divisional Court (Tuckey LJ and Harrison J) in a judgment given on 13 December 2000. Although

there are differences between the three cases they raise broadly the same question as to whether certain decision-making processes of the Secretary of State for the Environment, Transport and the Regions are compatible with art 6(1) of the European Convention for the Protection of Human Rights and Fundamental Freedoms (Rome, 4 November 1950; TS 71 (1953); Cmd 8969) (the convention) as incorporated in the Human Rights Act 1998. There was a consequential question as to whether if these processes are not compatible there should be a declaration under s 4 of the 1998 Act.

[2] The Divisional Court held that the following statutory provisions were incompatible with art 6 and accordingly made a declaration of incompatibility under s 4 of the 1998 Act. (a) The Town and Country Planning Act 1990 (i) s 77; (ii) ss 78 and 79 (excluding the words inserted into s 79(4) by para 19 of Sch 7 to the Planning and Compensation Act 1991); and (iii) paras 3 and 4 of Sch 6 (in so far as it applied to s 79). (b) The Transport and Works Act 1992, ss 1, 3 and 23(4). (c) The Highways Act 1980, ss 14(3)(a), 16(5)(a), 18(3)(a) and 125 and paras 1, 7 and 8 of Pt 1 of Sch 1. (d) The Acquisition of Land Act 1981, s 2(3) and para 4 of Sch 1.

[3] The Secretary of State appeals against all these decisions and declarations. Since a related question had arisen in Scotland in *County Properties Ltd v Scottish Ministers* 2000 SLT 965, the Lord Advocate has intervened in support of the application that the decision of the Divisional Court be reversed on the basis that art 6(1) does not apply to the decision-making processes under review and on the basis that they are not in any event incompatible with a convention right. The role of other parties to the proceedings will appear in a brief summary of facts to which I turn. I summarise briefly because the facts are more fully set out in the judgment of the Divisional Court to which reference can be made and which it is not helpful to repeat

Alconbury Developments Ltd

[4] Alconbury Developments Ltd (ADL) has agreed with the Ministry of Defence, the owner of a disused airfield at Alconbury, that if planning permission is given ADL will redevelop the site into a national distribution centre in return for financial payments to the ministry. ADL applied to Huntingdonshire District Council (HDC) for planning permission for the overall scheme with adjunct facilities and approach road and rail sidings. It also applied under various individual applications for planning permission for parts of the scheme. There were related applications (1) to Cambridgeshire County Council (CCC) as the waste disposal authority for planning permission to construct a temporary recycling depot on part of the site; (2) to HDC for permission to set up a commercial air freight operation though this was opposed by a group of local residents (HUNTSNAP) and the application was withdrawn in March 1998; (3) to the Secretary of State under s 1 of the 1992 Act for permission to build a rail connection between the airfield and the east coast rail line together with railway sidings within the airfield.

[5] On 4 August 1998 the Secretary of State refused a request to call in the planning application to be determined by him but after HDC dismissed the overall application for planning permission and CCC failed to determine the application for the waste recycling depot within the prescribed period, ADL's appeals were 'recovered' by the Secretary of State for determination by him under para 3 of Sch 6 to the 1990 Act rather than by an inspector appointed by the Secretary of State. This was done on the basis that 'the appeals relate to proposals for development of major importance, having more than local significance'.

a [6] An inspector was appointed to hold an inquiry at which for various reasons HUNTSNAP and an association of Nene Valley residents (NVA) together with English Nature, a statutory body, appeared. HUNTSNAP and NVA contended that the proceedings were contrary to art 6. ADL accordingly applied for judicial review of the Secretary of State's decision in order to clarify the position, contending that the Secretary of State's decisions to take jurisdiction over the b planning appeals and the 1992 Act applications were lawful. CCC supported ADL; HDC, HUNTSNAP and NVA opposed it. On the present appeal ADL and CCC support the Secretary of State. HDC and NVA contend that the Divisional Court were right in holding that there was a breach of s 6(1) but wrong in its decision on s 6(2). The Secretary of State was bound to act so as to avoid incompatibility with the convention and therefore to permit the appeal to be determined by an c independent inspector.

Holding & Barnes plc

[7] Holding & Barnes plc (HB) applied for planning permission to use land at Canvey Island for the storage and sale of damaged cars. The Health and Safety d Executive objected because the development was near to gas storage on some neighbouring sites but the executive was willing to reconsider the position if modifications to the proposal could be made. The local planning authority on 2 May 2000 resolved that it was minded to grant permission. On 25 July 2000 the Secretary of State directed, pursuant to s 77 of the 1990 Act, that the application should be referred to him because of (a) the nature of the proposed use, (b) the e impact it could have on the future economic prosperity of Canvey Island and (c) the site's location close to hazardous installations. It is that direction which HB challenged on an application for judicial review.

Legal & General Assurance Society Ltd

f [8] These proceedings are brought by the Secretary of State at the invitation of Legal & General Assurance Society Ltd (LG). The issue relates to an improvement scheme at Junction 13 of the A34/M4 proposed by the Secretary of State through the Highways Agency. There are complex details of a dual two-lane carriageway all-purpose road, 100 metres to the west of the existing Junction 13, together with connected slip and side roads. In August 1993 following an inquiry, orders were g confirmed for the work to go ahead. The court quashed part of one of the side road orders and new draft orders were published on 17 February 2000 followed by a draft compulsory purchase order on 24 February 2000. Following objections the Secretary of State appointed an inspector to hold a public inquiry into the draft order. LG which own some land the subject of the draft compulsory purchase h order invited the Secretary of State to seek a ruling of the court as to the compatibility of the proceedings with the convention. LG decided not to be represented in the proceedings and the Attorney General appointed counsel as amici curiae in that case both before the Divisional Court and before the House.

[9] The Divisional Court set out with clarity the details of the legislation j relevant to these cases. I gratefully adopt their account in paras 30 to 52 of the judgment (pp 940–944, ante) and accordingly I only summarise the essential characteristics with which these appeals are concerned.

[10] It is important to make clear that these appeals are not concerned directly with issues which affect the vast majority of applications for planning permission. Those applications are dealt with by elected local authorities and not by the Secretary of State even though local authorities have to take into account the development

plan for their area which does reflect national policies, guidance and instructions given by the Secretary of State. Nor are the present appeals concerned with the majority of appeals from such local authority decisions which are decided by inspectors on the Secretary of State's behalf even though those inspectors may be full-time officials of the Planning Inspectorate and even though they must have regard to the Secretary of States' policies and the framework document setting out their functions. The present appeals under the 1990 Act are concerned only with applications which are 'called in' by the Secretary of State under s 77 of the Act and those appeals which are 'recovered' by the Secretary of State under para 3 of Sch 6 to the Act. The Divisional Court found that of some 500,000 planning applications each year about 130 were 'called in' by the Secretary of State and of some 13,000 appeals to the Secretary of State each year about 100 were 'recovered' by the Secretary of State. In both types of case the Secretary of State followed to a large extent the recommendations of the inspectors. These figures of 130 and 100 are not insignificant and they concern important questions, important both to the individual and to the nation, but the figures do show the limits of the question raised on the appeals.

[11] It is therefore important to see what are the statutory powers under these various sections.

[12] Under s 77 of the 1990 Act the Secretary of State may (1) give directions requiring applications for planning permission to be referred to him instead of being dealt with by local planning authorities:

> '(5) Before determining an application referred to him under this section, the Secretary of State shall, if either the applicant or the local planning authority wish, give each of them an opportunity of appearing before, and being heard by, a person appointed by the Secretary of State for the purpose.'

[13] By the Town and Country Planning (Inquiries Procedure) (England) Rules 2000, SI 2000/1624 the applicant and the local planning authority are entitled to appear before the inspector ('the person appointed') to call and cross-examine witnesses and to make representations.

[14] Section 78 of the 1990 Act provides for an applicant who has been refused planning permission or granted planning permission subject to conditions to appeal to the Secretary of State. Before determining an appeal, the Secretary of State is required by s 79(2), if the appellant or the local planning authority wish, to give them an opportunity to be heard by a person appointed by the Secretary of State. By para 1 of Sch 6 to the Act, the Secretary of State may prescribe classes of appeals to be determined by appointed persons rather than by the Secretary of State. By para 3(1) of Sch 6 the Secretary of State 'may, if he thinks fit, direct that an appeal which would otherwise fall to be determined by an appointed person shall instead be determined by the Secretary of State'. Such direction shall state the reasons for which it is given and it is to be served on the appellant, the local planning authority and any person who has made representations.

[15] The 2000 rules which replaced the Town and Country Planning Act (Inquiries Procedure) Rules 1992, SI 1992/2039 with effect from 1 August 2000, apply to any local inquiry ordered by the Secretary of State before he determines an application for planning permission referred to him under s 77 or an appeal to him under s 78 of the 1990 Act.

[16] When an inspector is holding an inquiry leading to an appeal which he will determine himself or when he is holding an inquiry before the Secretary of State decides an application for planning permission called in by him under s 77,

a or before the Secretary of State determines an appeal under s 78 'recovered' by him, the procedures are broadly the same until the inspector's final report. When an inspector takes a decision he must set out that decision with reasons and notify the parties. When, however, he is holding an inquiry before the Secretary of State takes a decision he must state his conclusions and make his recommendations. There is an important provision in r 17(5) of the 2000 rules:

b

> 'If, after the close of an inquiry, the Secretary of State—(a) differs from the inspector on any matter of fact mentioned in, or appearing to him to be material to, a conclusion reached by the inspector; or (b) takes into consideration any new evidence or new matter of fact (not being a matter of government policy), and is for that reason disposed to disagree with a
c recommendation made by the inspector, he shall not come to a decision which is at variance with that recommendation without first notifying the persons entitled to appear at the inquiry who appeared at it of his disagreement and the reasons for it: and affording them an opportunity of making written representations to him or (if the Secretary of State has taken
d into consideration any new evidence or new matter of fact, not being a matter of government policy) of asking for the re-opening of the inquiry …
>
> (7) The Secretary of State may, as he thinks fit, cause an inquiry to be re-opened, and he shall do so if asked by the applicant or the local planning authority in the circumstances mentioned in paragraph (5) and within the period mentioned in paragraph (6); and where an inquiry is re-opened
e (whether by the same or a different inspector)—(a) the Secretary of State shall send to the persons entitled to appear at the inquiry who appeared at it a written statement of the matters with respect to which further evidence is invited; and (b) paragraphs (3) to (8) of rule 10 shall apply as if the references to an inquiry were references to a re-opened inquiry.'

f

[**17**] In relation to applications made under the 1992 Act in relation to the construction and operation of a railway and to authorise the compulsory acquisition of land and to grant any necessary planning permission, under the 1992 Act, the decision is taken by the Secretary of State. Where an objection is received, a public inquiry must be held if the objector wishes. The provisions of
g the Transport and Works (Inquiries Procedure) Rules 1992, SI 1992/2817 are broadly similar to those found in the 2000 rules.

[**18**] The Highways Act 1980 gives to the Secretary of State power to make orders in relation to existing and proposed highways and to empower the highway authorities for trunk roads to stop up or improve highways in prescribed
h circumstances. If a local inquiry is held, the inspector appointed reports his conclusions and recommendations to the Secretary of State. The Highways (Inquiries Procedure) Rules 1994, SI 1994/3263 contain similar provision to those in the 2000 rules. The Secretary of State may make an order with or without modification but if he disagrees with his inspector's conclusions or recommendations
j the Secretary of State must follow a procedure similar to that in r 17(5) of the 2000 rules: see r 26(4) of the Highways (Inquiries Procedure) Rules 1994. When exercising his powers under the 1980 Act, the Secretary of State is given power to acquire land compulsorily. The Acquisition of Land Act 1981 and the Compulsory Purchase by Ministers (Inquiries Procedure) Rules 1994, SI 1994/3264 provide for a public local inquiry to be held if an objection is received. The inspector makes his conclusions and recommendations to the Secretary of State. If the latter

disagrees he is required once again to follow a procedure similar to that in r 17(5) of the 2000 rules.

a

[19] The various statutes provide for judicial review rather than for an appeal on the facts or the merits of the decision. Thus in s 288 of the 1990 Act:

> '**288.** *Proceedings for questioning the validity of other orders, decisions and directions.*—(1) If any person—(a) is aggrieved by any order to which this section applies and wishes to question the validity of that order on the grounds—(i) that the order is not within the powers of this Act, or (ii) that any of the relevant requirements have not been complied with in relation to that order; or (b) is aggrieved by any action on the part of the Secretary of State to which this section applies and wishes to question the validity of that action on the grounds—(i) that the action is not within the powers of this Act, or (ii) that any of the relevant requirements have not been complied with in relation to that action, he may make an application to the High Court under this section.'

b

c

[20] Section 22 of the 1992 Act, the provisions for challenge set out in para 2 of Sch 2 to the 1980 Act and s 23 of the 1981 Act are similar.

d

[21] The essence of the complaints in all these cases is that there is a violation of art 6 of the convention incorporated in Sch 1 to the Human Rights Act 1998. Article 6 provides as follows:

> '*Right to a Fair Trial*
>
> 1. In the determination of his civil rights and obligations or of any criminal charge against him, everyone is entitled to a fair and public hearing within a reasonable time by an independent and impartial tribunal established by law.'

e

[22] The second and third paragraphs of the article are concerned with criminal offences and are not relevant to the present appeal.

f

[23] The contention in these proceedings is that the processes which I have set out violate art 6. These are civil rights which are determined without a fair and public hearing by an independent and impartial tribunal established by law.

[24] There is really no complaint about the inquiry conducted by an inspector or about the safeguards laid down for evidence to be called and challenged and for representations and objections to be heard. It is not suggested that the inspector himself is not independent and impartial even though he is a member of eg the Planning Inspectorate in the case of planning appeals. The essential complaint is that when a decision is taken, not by such an inspector but by the Secretary of State or one of the Ministers of State or an Under Secretary on behalf of the Secretary of State there is such an interest in the decision that the person concerned cannot be regarded as an independent and impartial tribunal. The Secretary of State or his department, it is said, lays down policy and directs what he or the department considers to be the most efficient and effective use of land in what he sees to be the public interest. They issue guidance and framework directions which local authorities, inspectors and officials operating the planning system must follow. All of these are bound to affect the mind of the Secretary of State when he takes decisions on called-in applications or on appeals which he recovers, it is alleged. Moreover it is said that in the case of Alconbury there is a particular factor in that the land in question is owned by another government department, the Ministry of Defence.

g

h

j

a [**25**] Mr Kingston QC on behalf of HDC also criticised the correspondence and minutes relevant to the Alconbury project. He contends that the role of the officials involved at the Planning and Transport Division in the Government Office for the Region (GO) was such that there was a real connection not only with planning matters and planning ministers but also with transport ministers and officials and their policies. A site visit by the Parliamentary Under Secretary b for Transport may not have been prejudicial to the determination of the application before the matter was taken over by the Secretary of State. It was quite different once he took over the case for his own decision. As it was put in the case, even leaving aside the fact that the Secretary of State was carrying out his own policy 'it is quite clear that the structures in place in relation to cases where the Secretary of State has recovered jurisdiction do not preserve any c appearance of independence'.

[**26**] Your Lordships have been referred to many decisions of the European Court of Human Rights on art 6 of the convention. Although the 1998 Act does not provide that a national court is bound by these decisions it is obliged to take account of them so far as they are relevant. In the absence of some special d circumstances it seems to me that the court should follow any clear and constant jurisprudence of the European Court of Human Rights. If it does not do so there is at least a possibility that the case will go to that court which is likely in the ordinary case to follow its own constant jurisprudence.

[**27**] It is not necessary to refer to all these cases but some statements of principle by the European Court of Human Rights are important in guiding the e House in the present decisions. A preliminary question has arisen as to whether a dispute over administrative law matters of the present kind involved the determination of 'civil rights'. At first sight to a common lawyer there appears a difference and that difference might seem stronger to a lawyer in a civil law country. In *Ringeisen v Austria (No 1)* (1971) 1 EHRR 455 at 489–490 (para 94), f however, the court said:

> 'For Article 6 (1) to be applicable to a case ("contestation") it is not necessary that both parties to the proceedings should be private persons, which is the view of the majority of the Commission and of the government. The wording of Article 6 (1) is far wider; the French expression "*contestations* g *sur (des) droits et obligations de caractère civil*" covers all proceedings the result of which is decisive for private rights and obligations. The English text, "determination of ... civil rights and obligations", confirms this interpretation. The character of the legislation which governs how the matter is to be determined (civil, commercial, administrative law, etc.) and that of the h authority which is invested with jurisdiction in the matter (ordinary court, administrative body, etc.) are therefore of little consequence.'

See also *Kaplan v UK* (1980) 4 EHRR 64 at 85, *Jacobsson v Sweden* (1989) 12 EHRR 56.

[**28**] In *Fredin v Sweden* (1991) 13 EHRR 784, the court accepted that disputes under planning rules could affect civil rights to build on the applicant's land. j Despite the submissions of the Lord Advocate that a decision on a called-in application is not a 'contestation' on the basis of these and a number of other cases it seems to me plain that this dispute is one which involves the determination of 'civil rights' within the meaning of the convention.

[**29**] The European Court of Human Rights has, however, recognised from the beginning that some administrative law decisions which affect civil rights are taken by ministers answerable to elected bodies. Where there is a two-stage

process ie there is such an administrative decision which is subject to review by a court, there is a constant line of authority of the European Court of Human Rights that regard has to be paid to both stages of the process. Thus even where 'jurisdictional organs of professional associations' are set up:

> 'Nonetheless, in such circumstances the Convention calls at least for one of the two following systems: either the jurisdictional organs themselves comply with the requirements of article 6(1), or they do not so comply but are subject to subsequent control by a judicial body which has full jurisdiction and does provide the guarantees of article 6(1).' (See *Albert v Belgium* (1983) 5 EHRR 533 at 541–542 (para 29).)

See also *Le Compte v Belgium* (1981) 4 EHRR 1, *Golder v UK* (1975) 1 EHRR 524.

[**30**] In *Kaplan v UK* (1980) 4 EHRR 64 at 86 (para 150), the commission noted that—

> 'it is a feature of the administrative law of all the Contracting States that in numerous different fields public authorities are empowered by law to take various forms of action impinging on the private rights of citizens.'

The commission (at 87) referred to its earlier opinion in *Ringeisen*'s case where having referred to a number of examples of state regulation the commission had stated:

> 'These examples, to which numerous others could be added, seem to indicate that it is a normal feature of contemporary administrative law that the rights and obligations of the citizen, even in matters which relate very closely to his private property or his private activities, are determined by some public authority which does not fulfil the conditions laid down in Article 6 (1) with respect to independent and impartial tribunals.'

[**31**] The commission continued (at 89 (para 159)), in relation to judicial review:

> 'It is also a common feature of their administrative law, and indeed almost a corollary of the grant of discretionary powers, that the scope of judicial review of the relevant decisions is limited.'

And (at 90 (para 161)):

> 'An interpretation of Article 6 (1) under which it was held to provide a right to a full appeal on the merits of every administrative decision affecting private rights would therefore lead to a result which was inconsistent with the existing, and long-standing, legal position in most of the Contracting States.'

[**32**] In *ISKCON v UK* (1994) 76A DR 90 (a decision of the commission) a local authority served an enforcement notice on ISKCON alleging a material change of use of the land. ISKCON appealed against the notice under s 174(2) of the 1990 Act and after a report by an inspector the Secretary of State largely confirmed the enforcement notice. The High Court and the Court of Appeal rejected ISKCON'S appeal. On a complaint under the convention the commission recalled that an appeal under s 289 of the 1990 Act lay only on a point of law but it took into account that the local authority could only take proceedings within the limits of s 174 of that Act and that in accordance with its own structure plans and the policy guidance laid down by the Secretary of State ISKCON could

a then seek a determination as to whether the legal requirements had been met. The commission concluded (at 110–111):

> 'The Commission recalls that the High Court dealt with each of ISKCON'S grounds of appeal on its merits, point by point, without ever having to decline jurisdiction. Moreover, it was open to ISKCON to contend in the High Court that findings of fact by the Inspector and/or the Secretary of b State were unsupported by evidence, as they could have argued that the administrative authorities failed to take into account an actual fact or did take into account an immaterial fact. Finally, the High Court could have interfered with the administrative authorities' decisions if those decisions had been irrational having regard to the facts established by the authorities. It is not c the role of Article 6 of the Convention to give access to a level of jurisdiction which can substitute its opinion for that of the administrative authorities on questions of expediency and where the courts do not refuse to examine any of the points raised; Article 6 gives a right to a court that has "full jurisdiction" (cf [*Zumtobel v Austria* (1993) 17 EHRR 116 at 133 (para 32)]).'

d [33] In *Bryan v UK* (1995) 21 EHRR 342, a case which it is necessary to refer to in some detail since it has been followed in later cases, an applicant was served with an enforcement notice requiring him to demolish buildings erected without planning permission. He complained that the inspector's decision did not satisfy art 6(1). The court and the commission described the role of the inspector and the e procedures to be followed under the 1990 Act including both his duty under the framework directive of the Secretary of State to exercise independent judgment and not to be or to be seen to be subject to any improper influence and to act fairly but at the same time to have regard to the policies promulgated by the Secretary of State on matters of planning. Both the commission and the court accepted that there had been a fair hearing before the inspector. Because however f the inspector's appointment to hear the appeal could be revoked in a situation where the executive's own policies may be in issue, the inspector did not satisfy the requirements of art 6 that there must be an independent and impartial tribunal.

[34] However, having set out the national court's powers of review the court g like the majority of the commission concluded that in that case the High Court's powers of review were sufficient to comply with art 6. The court noted (at 360 (para 44)) that an appeal to the High Court was only on points of law and therefore—

> 'not capable of embracing all aspects of the inspector's decision … In h particular, as is not infrequently the case in relation to administrative law appeals in the Council of Europe Member States, there was no rehearing as such of the original complaints submitted to the inspector; the High Court could not substitute its own decision on the merits for that of the inspector; and its jurisdiction over the facts was limited.'

j [35] The court continued (at 360–361) that in assessing the sufficiency of the review available before the High Court—

> '45. … it is necessary to have regard to matters such as the subject matter of the decision appealed against, the manner in which that decision was arrived at, and the content of the dispute, including the desired and actual grounds of appeal.

46. In this connection the Court would once more refer to the uncontested safeguards attending the procedure before the inspector: the quasi-judicial character of the decision-making process; the duty incumbent on each inspector to exercise independent judgment; the requirement that inspectors must not be subject to any improper influence; the stated mission of the Inspectorate to uphold the principles of openness, fairness and impartiality. Further, any alleged shortcoming in relation to these safeguards could have been subject to review by the High Court.

47. ... The High Court had jurisdiction to entertain the remaining grounds of the applicant's appeal [ie other than his contention that as a matter of fact and degree the buildings could from their appearance and layout be considered to have been designed for the purposes of agriculture] and his submissions were adequately dealt with point by point. These submissions, as the Commission noted, went essentially to questions involving "a panoply of policy matters such as development plans, and the fact that the property was situated in a Green Belt and a conversation area". Furthermore, even if the applicant had sought to pursue his appeal under ground (b), the Court notes that, while the High Court could not have substituted its own findings of fact for those of the inspector, it would have had the power to satisfy itself that the inspector's findings of fact or the inferences based on them were neither perverse nor irrational. Such an approach by an appeal tribunal on questions of fact can reasonably be expected in specialised areas of the law such as the one at issue, particularly where the facts have already been established in the course of a quasi-judicial procedure governed by many of the safeguards required by Article 6(1). It is also frequently a feature in the systems of judicial control of administrative decisions found throughout the Council of Europe Member States. Indeed, in the instant case, the subject matter of the contested decision by the inspector was a typical example of the exercise of discretionary judgement in the regulation of citizens' conduct in the sphere of town and country planning. The scope of review of the High Court was therefore sufficient to comply with Article 6(1).'

[**36**] The respondents contend that this judgment does not assist the Secretary of State since his decision-making process was not of a quasi-judicial nature; he did not have to exercise an independent judgment, there was no obligation to uphold the principles of openness, fairness and impartiality.

[**37**] In *Chapman v UK* (2001) 10 BHRC 48, the question arose as to the refusal of planning permission and the service of an enforcement notice against Mrs Chapman who wished to place her caravan on a plot of land in the green belt. The refusal of planning permission and the enforcement notice were upheld by the inspector. The court like the majority of the commission held (at 76) that there had been no violation of art 6:

'124. The court recalls that in [*Bryan*'s case] it held that in the specialised area of town planning law full review of the facts may not be required by art 6 of the convention. It finds in this case that the scope of review of the High Court, which was available to the applicant after a public procedure before an inspector, was sufficient in this case to comply with art 6(1). It enabled a decision to be challenged on the basis that it was perverse, irrational, had no basis on the evidence or had been made with reference to irrelevant factors or without regard to relevant factors. This may be regarded as affording adequate judicial control of the administrative decisions in issue.'

a [38] It is also to be noted that in *Howard v UK* (1987) 52 DR 215, a submission that the power of appeal under s 23 of the 1981 Act did not provide an adequate remedy to challenge a compulsory purchase order so was not an effective remedy within the meaning of art 13 of the convention was rejected as inadmissible.

[39] In *Varey v UK* App No 26662/95 (27 October 1999, unreported) the commission concluded on the challenge to a planning decision that the fact that b an inspector's recommendation had been rejected by the Secretary of State did not mean that there had been a violation of art 6. The Secretary of State had given reasoned decisions on the basis of facts found by the inspectors:

> '... and the matters relied on by him in overruling their recommendations could be challenged on appropriate grounds before the High Court. c Consequently in these circumstances the commission is satisfied that the power of review of the process by the High Court ensures adequate judicial control of the administrative decisions in issue.' (See para 86.)

[40] The House has been referred to many other cases some involving other member states where the administrative provisions and the judicial control were d in different terms. I do not refer to these only because it seems to me that in the recent cases to which I have referred the court has given an indication of the principle to be followed sufficiently for the disposal of the present case.

[41] On the basis which I have accepted that the planning, compulsory purchase and other related decisions do affect civil rights even if the procedures e and decisions are of an administrative law nature rather than strictly civil law in nature, the first question is, therefore, whether the decision of the Secretary of State which effectively determined these rights in itself constitutes 'a fair and public hearing within a reasonable time by an independent and impartial tribunal established by law'.

[42] 'Independent' and 'impartial' may import different concepts but there is f clearly a link between them and both must be satisfied. It is not suggested that there is actual bias against particular individuals, on the part of the Secretary of State or the officials who report to him or who advise him. But it is contended that the Secretary of State is involved in laying down policy and in taking decisions on planning applications in accordance with that policy. He cannot g therefore be seen objectively to be independent or impartial. The position is said to be even more critical when roadworks and compulsory purchases are initiated by the Highways Agency or when as in the Alconbury case the land involved belongs to another ministry of the Crown.

[43] Before the House the Secretary of State did not contend that in dealing h with called-in or recovered matters he is acting as an independent tribunal. He accepts that the fact that he makes policy and applies that policy in particular cases is sufficient to prevent him from being an independent tribunal and for the same reasons he is not to be seen as an impartial tribunal for the purposes of art 6 of Pt 1 of Sch 1 to the 1998 Act.

[44] But the many decisions of the European Court of Human Rights make it j plain that one does not stop there. A choice was recognised as early as *Albert v Belgium* (1983) 5 EHRR 533 at 542 (para 29) that—

> 'either the jurisdictional organs themselves comply with the requirements of article 6(1), or they do not so comply but are subject to subsequent control by a judicial body that has full jurisdiction and does provide the guarantees of Article 6(1).'

[45] These judgements also show that the test whether there is a sufficient jurisdictional control is not a mechanical one. It depends on all the circumstances. *a*

[46] On the basis of these decisions it is in my view relevant as a starting point to have regard to such procedural safeguards as do exist in the decision-making process of the Secretary of State even if in the end, because he is applying his policy to which these controls do not apply, he cannot be seen as an impartial and independent tribunal. The fact that an inquiry by an inspector is ordered is *b* important. This gives the applicant and objectors the chance to put forward their views, to call and cross-examine witnesses. The inspector as an experienced professional makes a report, in which he finds the facts and in which he makes his recommendations. He has of course to take account of the policy which has been adopted in eg the development plan but he provides an important filter before the Secretary of State takes his decision and it is significant that in some 95% of *c* the type of cases with which the House is concerned, the Secretary of State accepts his recommendation. The Divisional Court had evidence, that other steps are taken to ensure that the contentions of the applicant and the objectors are adequately considered. Thus the Divisional Court quoted evidence in para 62 of their judgment (see pp 946–947, ante) as to the way in which it is sought to ensure *d* that all material considerations needed to reach an informed, fair, unbiased and reasonable decision could be arrived at as quickly as practicable. Decisions were taken by ministers who so far as possible had no connection with the area from which the case came and in respect of the decision officer who dealt with the case it was said, in para 63 (p 947, ante), that he—

e

> 'works separately from the casework team of which he is nominally a part, does not discuss the merits of the planning decisions before him with an individual either within or without GO East, is not copied into or involved in the preparation of the Regional Planning Guidance (RPG) or the exercise of any of the Secretary of State's powers of intervention under the 1990 Act, *f* and only has before him the information which the inspector would have had at the inquiry into the particular appeal or called-in application, together with any representation made after the close of the inquiries (all relevant parties are given the opportunity to comment on any such representations where they are material or raise new matters).'

g

[47] On the decision-making process I do not suggest that one can make artificial distinctions between different branches of a government department. I refer to what was said by Lord Diplock in *Bushell v Secretary of State for the Environment* [1980] 2 All ER 608 at 613, [1981] AC 75 at 95. But there is nothing unusual or sinister in the methods provided for planning decisions to be taken by *h* the executive in the United Kingdom. The European Court of Human Rights has recognised that in many European countries planning decisions are made by elected or appointed officers with a limited judicial review even though the extent of this may vary from state to state. In *B Johnson & Co (Builders) Ltd v Minister of Health* [1947] 2 All ER 395 at 399 Lord Greene MR recognised the importance of the administrative stage of the decision: *j*

> '... the raising of the objections to the order, the consideration of the matters so raised and the representations of the local authority and the objectors—is merely a stage in the process of arriving at an administrative decision. It is a stage which the courts have always said requires a certain method of approach and method of conduct, but it is not a *lis inter partes*, and for the

a simple reason that the local authority and the objectors are not parties to anything that resembles litigation. A moment's thought will show that any such conception of the relationship must be fallacious, because on the substantive matter, *viz.*, whether the order should be confirmed or not, there is a third party who is not present, *viz.*, the public, and it is the function of the Minister to consider the rights and the interests of the public ... It may well b be that, on considering the objections, the Minister may find that they are reasonable and that the facts alleged in them are true, but, nevertheless, he may decide that he will overrule them. His action in so deciding is a purely administrative action, based on his conceptions as to what public policy demands.'

c [**48**] The adoption of planning policy and its application to particular facts is quite different from the judicial function. It is for elected Members of Parliament and ministers to decide what are the objectives of planning policy, objectives which may be of national, environmental, social or political significance and for these objectives to be set out in legislation, primary and secondary, in ministerial d directions and in planning policy guidelines. Local authorities, inspectors and the Secretary of State are all required to have regard to policy in taking particular planning decisions and it is easy to overstate the difference between the application of a policy in decisions taken by the Secretary of State and his inspector. As to the making of policy, Wade and Forsyth *Administrative Law* (8th edn, 2000) p 464 says:

e 'It is self-evident that ministerial or departmental policy cannot be regarded as disqualifying bias. One of the commonest administrative mechanisms is to give a minister power to make or confirm an order after hearing objections to it. The procedure for the hearing of objections is subject to the rules of natural justice in so far as they require a fair hearing and fair procedure f generally. But the minister's decision cannot be impugned on the ground that he has advocated the scheme or that he is known to support it as a matter of policy. The whole object of putting the power into his hands is that he may exercise it according to government policy.'

g As Mr Gregory Jones for CCC put it pithily in argument, it is not right to say that a policy maker cannot be a decision maker or that the final decision maker cannot be a democratically elected person or body.

[**49**] Accepting this method of proceeding, the question as the European court has shown, is whether there is a sufficient judicial control to ensure a determination by an independent and impartial tribunal subsequently. The judgments to which h I have referred do not require that this should constitute a rehearing on an application by an appeal on the merits. It would be surprising if it had required this in view of the difference of function between the minister exercising his statutory powers, for the policy of which he is answerable to the legislature and ultimately to the electorate, and the court. What is required on the part of the j latter is that there should be a sufficient review of the legality of the decisions and of the procedures followed. The common law has developed specific grounds of review of administrative acts and these have been reflected in the statutory provisions for judicial review such as are provided for in the present cases. See, as relatively straightforward examples, *Ashbridge Investments Ltd v Minister of Housing and Local Government* [1965] 3 All ER 371, [1965] 1 WLR 1320 and *Stringer v Minister of Housing and Local Government* [1971] 1 All ER 65, [1970] 1 WLR 1281.

[50] It has long been established that if the Secretary of State misinterprets the legislation under which he purports to act, or if he takes into account matters irrelevant to his decision or refuses or fails to take account of matters relevant to his decision, or reaches a perverse decision, the court may set his decision aside. Even if he fails to follow necessary procedural steps—failing to give notice of a hearing or to allow an opportunity for evidence to be called or cross-examined, or for representations to be made or to take any step which fairness and natural justice requires, the court may interfere. The legality of the decision and the procedural steps must be subject to sufficient judicial control. But none of the judgments before the European Court of Human Rights requires that the court should have 'full jurisdiction' to review policy or the overall merits of a planning decision. This approach is reflected in the powers of the Court of Justice of the European Communities to review executive acts under art 230 of the European Community Treaty:

> 'It shall for this purpose have jurisdiction in actions brought by a Member State, the Council or the Commission on grounds of lack of competence, infringement of an essential procedural requirement, infringement of this Treaty or of any rule of law relating to its application, or misuse of powers.'

[51] The Court of Justice does of course apply the principle of proportionality when examining such acts and national judges must apply the same principle when dealing with Community law issues. There is a difference between that principle and the approach of the English courts in *Associated Provincial Picture Houses Ltd v Wednesbury Corp* [1947] 2 All ER 680, [1948] 1 KB 223. But the difference in practice is not as great as is sometimes supposed. The cautious approach of the Court of Justice in applying the principle is shown inter alia by the margin of appreciation it accords to the institutions of the community in making economic assessments. I consider that even without reference to the 1998 Act the time has come to recognise that this principle is part of English administrative law, not only when judges are dealing with community acts but also when they are dealing with acts subject to domestic law. Trying to keep the *Wednesbury* principle and proportionality in separate compartments seems to me to be unnecessary and confusing. Reference to the 1998 Act however makes it necessary that the court should ask whether what is done is compatible with convention rights. That will often require that the question should be asked whether the principle of proportionality has been satisfied: see *R v Secretary of State for the Home Dept, ex p Turgut* [2001] 1 All ER 719; *R (Mahmood) v Secretary of State for the Home Dept* [2001] 1 WLR 840.

[52] This principle does not go as far as to provide for a complete rehearing on the merits of the decision. Judicial control does not need to go so far. It should not do so unless Parliament specifically authorises it in particular areas.

[53] In *R v Criminal Injuries Compensation Board, ex p A* [1999] 2 AC 330 at 344–345, [1999] 2 WLR 974 at 982 I accepted that the court had jurisdiction to quash for a misunderstanding or ignorance of an established and relevant fact. I remain of that view which finds support in Wade and Forsyth *Administrative Law* (7th edn, 1994) pp 316–318. I said:

> 'Your Lordships have been asked to say that there is jurisdiction to quash the board's decision because that decision was reached on a material error of fact. Reference has been made to *Wade & Forsyth, Administrative Law,* 7th ed. (1994), pp. 316–318 in which it is said: "Mere factual mistake has become a

a ground of judicial review, described as 'misunderstanding or ignorance of an established and relevant fact,' [*Secretary of State for Education and Science v Tameside Metropolitan Borough* [1976] 3 All ER 665 at 675, [1977] AC 1014 at 1030], or acting 'upon an incorrect basis of fact' ... This ground of review has long been familiar in French law and it has been adopted by statute in Australia. It is no less needed in this country, since decisions based upon b wrong facts are a cause of injustice which the courts should be able to remedy. If a 'wrong factual basis' doctrine should become established, it would apparently be a new branch of the ultra vires doctrine, analogous to finding facts based upon no evidence or acting upon a misapprehension of law." *de Smith, Woolf and Jowell, Judicial Review of Adminstrative Action,* 5th ed. (1995), p. 288: "The taking into account of a mistaken fact can just as easily c be absorbed into a traditional legal ground of review by referring to the taking into account of an irrelevant consideration, or the failure to provide reasons that are adequate or intelligible, or the failure to base the decision on any evidence. In this limited context material error of fact has always been a recognised ground for judicial intervention."'

d [54] I accordingly hold that in relation to the judicial review of the Secretary of State's decision in a called-in application or a recovered appeal under the planning legislation and to a review of the decisions and orders under the other statutes concerned in the present appeals, there is in principle no violation of art 6 of the convention as set out in Sch 1 to the 1998 Act. The scope of review is e sufficient to comply with the standards set by the European Court of Human Rights. That is my view even if proportionality and the review of material errors of fact are left out of account: they do, however, make the case even stronger. It is open to the House to rule on that question of principle at this stage of the procedure in the various cases.

f [55] I do not consider that the financial interests of the Ministry of Defence automatically precludes a decision on planning grounds by the Secretary of State, or that the communication between government departments and site visits by ministers to which reference has been made in argument in principle vitiate the whole process. If of course specific breaches of the administrative law rules are established, as for example if the financial interests of the government were g wrongly taken into account by the Secretary of State, then, specific challenges on those grounds may be possible on judicial review.

[56] I would accordingly allow the appeals, dismiss the cross-appeals and set aside the declarations of the Divisional Court.

h **LORD NOLAN.**

[57] My Lords, I have had the advantage of reading in draft the speech delivered by my noble and learned friend Lord Slynn of Hadley. I gratefully adopt his account of the facts and of the issues raised in these appeals.

[58] I too would allow the appeals, and would declare that the impugned j decision-making procedures are not in breach of or incompatible with the Human Rights Act 1998. The case is one of great practical and constitutional importance for this country, and of importance also for the development of human rights law both in this country and abroad, and argument has ranged over a wide field. The central question, however, is the first of those raised in the agreed statement of facts and issues, namely whether the impugned procedures 'are compatible with art 6(1) of the convention as applied by the 1998 Act ... having regard to the

existence of statutory rights of appeal to the High Court and of supervision of the procedures by way of judicial review'. The alternative to these procedures would effectively involve the removal from the appellant Secretary of State of his discretion over the grant of planning permission and other matters related to the ownership and enjoyment of land in the rare and often controversial cases in which he exercises it at present, and its vesting in some other person or body which constitutes 'an independent and impartial tribunal' for the purposes of art 6(1). The precise nature of this alternative entity was not formulated by the respondents, but it would presumably be modelled on the Planning Inspectorate either in its present or in some modified form. Understandable, but, I think, also significant, was the absence of any suggestion that the discretion should be vested in the courts.

[**59**] My Lords, this brings me at once to my reasons for concluding that the decision of the Divisional Court cannot be allowed to stand. They can be shortly stated.

[**60**] The first, which reflects the obvious unsuitability of the courts as the arbiters in planning and related matters, is that the decision to be made, as explained by Lord Greene MR in *B Johnson & Co (Builders) Ltd v Minister of Health* [1947] 2 All ER 395 at 399, is an administrative and not a judicial decision. In the relatively small and populous island which we occupy, the decisions made by the Secretary of State will often have acute social, economic and environmental implications. A degree of central control is essential to the orderly use and development of town and country. Parliament has entrusted the requisite degree of control to the Secretary of State, and it is to Parliament which he must account for his exercise of it. To substitute for the Secretary of State an independent and impartial body with no central electoral accountability would not only be a recipe for chaos: it would be profoundly undemocratic.

[**61**] Electoral accountability alone is, of course, plainly insufficient to satisfy the rule of law. Are then the rights of the subject in planning and related matters adequately protected by the statutory provisions for appeal to the courts and by the process of judicial review? It is said that these remedies fail to meet the art 6(1) criterion because they do not permit a review of the decision of the Secretary of State on its merits. If this criticism is limited to the absence of a review of the decision on its *planning* merits it is indisputable. But a review of the merits of the *decision-making process* is fundamental to the courts' jurisdiction. The power of review may even extend to a decision on a question of fact. As long ago as 1955 your Lordships' House, in *Edwards (Inspector of Taxes) v Bairstow* [1955] 3 All ER 48, [1956] AC 14, a case in which an appeal (from general commissioners of income tax) could only be brought on a question of law, upheld the right and duty of the appellate court to reverse a finding of fact which had no justifiable basis.

[**62**] The reversal of a finding of fact in the field of planning would no doubt be highly unusual. I mention *Edwards'* case simply to illustrate the generosity with which the courts, including your Lordships' House, have interpreted their powers to review questions of law. A similarly broad and generous approach has been adopted in the development of judicial review extending as it does not only to points of law in the strict and narrow sense but to such matters as the rationality of the decision and the fairness of the decision-making process. One possibility canvassed in argument was that the powers of review as at present exercised by the courts might be enlarged in order to accommodate the requirements of the 1998 Act. For my part, at least in the context of the present case, I see no need for that.

a [63] My Lords, I have found it reassuring to read, in the judgments of the European Court of Human Rights and of the commission in the cases of *Bryan v UK* (1995) 21 EHRR 342, *ISKCON v UK* (1994) 76A DR 90, *Chapman v UK* (2001) 10 BHRC 48 and *Varey v UK* App No 26662/95 (27 October 1999, unreported) the expression of views which to my mind strongly support the contentions of the Secretary of State. If, as I understand to be the case, your Lordships are b unanimous in considering that the appeals should be allowed, I trust that the decision of your Lordships' House will be seen, not as in any way inconsistent with those decisions, but on the contrary as a contribution to the growth of convention jurisprudence.

[64] I would only add that the particular grounds of objection taken by some respondents to the role of the Secretary of State, such as the objection in the c Alconbury case based on the ground of his having a financial interest in the matter, might if appropriate be raised as objections to the ultimate decision itself. They are insufficient to disqualify him in limine.

LORD HOFFMANN.

d

The issue

[65] My Lords, the issue in these three appeals is whether it is compatible with the Human Rights Act 1998 for Parliament to confer upon the Secretary of State the power to make decisions which affect people's rights to the ownership, use or enjoyment of land. The Divisional Court has decided that art 6 of the European e Convention for the Protection of Human Rights and Fundamental Freedoms (Rome, 4 November 1950; TS 71 (1953); Cmd 8969) (set out in Sch 1 to the Human Rights Act 1998) requires such decisions to be made by independent and impartial tribunals. This would mean radical amendment to the system by which such decisions have been made for many years. In view of the importance of the case, f your Lordships have given leave for an appeal to be brought directly from the Divisional Court.

The facts

[66] Although the principle must be of general application, the contexts in which the question has arisen in these appeals are planning, highway improvement g and compulsory purchase. In the first appeal (the Alconbury case), a company has applied for planning permission to construct a distribution centre of national significance on a disused American air base near Huntingdon. It could generate 7,000 new jobs but would obviously affect the lives of many people living in the neighbourhood. In the second appeal (the Holding & Barnes case), the respondents h have applied for planning permission to use land at Canvey Island for the storage and sale of wrecked cars. Again, the activity will generate employment but the site is close to some gas storage installations and the Health and Safety Executive thinks that this would create a danger to people living in the area. In the third appeal (the Legal & General case), the respondent owns land near the j interchange between the M4 motorway and the A34 trunk road at Newbury. The Highways Agency, a branch of the department of the Environment, Transport and the Regions, has promoted a road improvement scheme which would involve taking the respondent's land.

[67] In each of these cases the statutory decision maker is the Secretary of State. In the first two, this is by virtue of his exercise of a statutory discretion. In the Alconbury case, the application for planning permission has been refused

by the Huntingdonshire District Council and the developer has appealed to the Secretary of State. The appeal could have been determined under Sch 6 to the Town and Country Planning Act 1990 by an inspector appointed to conduct a public inquiry, but the Secretary of State has exercised his discretion under para 3 of the Schedule to 'recover' the appeal and decide it himself. In the Holding & Barnes case, the local planning authority was minded to grant permission but the Secretary of State has exercised his power under s 77 of the 1990 Act to 'call in' the application and decide it himself. In the Legal & General case, the Secretary of State is the only statutory decision maker.

[68] All three cases involve general social and economic issues. They concern the rights of individuals to use, enjoy and own their land. But the number of persons potentially interested is very large and the decisions involve the consideration of questions of general welfare, such as the national or local economy, the preservation of the environment, the public safety, the convenience of the road network, all of which transcend the interests of any particular individual.

Democracy and the rule of law

[69] In a democratic country, decisions as to what the general interest requires are made by democratically elected bodies or persons accountable to them. Sometimes the subject matter is such that Parliament can itself lay down general rules for enforcement by the courts. Taxation is a good example: Parliament decides on grounds of general interest what taxation is required and the rules according to which it should be levied. The application of those rules, to determine the liability of a particular person, is then a matter for independent and impartial tribunals such as the general or special commissioners or the courts. On the other hand, sometimes one cannot formulate general rules and the question of what the general interest requires has to be determined on a case by case basis. Town and country planning or road construction, in which every decision is in some respects different, are archetypal examples. In such cases Parliament may delegate the decision-making power to local democratically elected bodies or to ministers of the Crown responsible to Parliament. In that way the democratic principle is preserved.

[70] There is no conflict between human rights and the democratic principle. Respect for human rights requires that certain basic rights of individuals should not be capable in any circumstances of being overridden by the majority, even if they think that the public interest so requires. Other rights should be capable of being overridden only in very restricted circumstances. These are rights which belong to individuals simply by virtue of their humanity, independently of any utilitarian calculation. The protection of these basic rights from majority decision requires that independent and impartial tribunals should have the power to decide whether legislation infringes them and either (as in the United States) to declare such legislation invalid or (as in the United Kingdom) to declare that it is incompatible with the governing human rights instrument. But outside these basic rights, there are many decisions which have to be made every day (for example, about the allocation of resources) in which the only fair method of decision is by some person or body accountable to the electorate.

[71] All democratic societies recognise that while there are certain basic rights which attach to the ownership of property, they are heavily qualified by considerations of the public interest. This is reflected in the terms of art 1 of Protocol 1 to the convention:

a 'Every natural or legal person is entitled to the peaceful enjoyment of his possessions. No one shall be deprived of his possessions except in the public interest and subject to the conditions provided for by law and by the general principles of international law.

The preceding provisions shall not, however, in any way impair the right of a State to enforce such laws as it deems necessary to control the use of b property in accordance with the general interest or to secure the payment of taxes or other contributions or penalties.'

[72] Thus, under the first paragraph, property may be taken by the state, on payment of compensation, if the public interest so requires. And, under the second paragraph, the use of property may be restricted without compensation c on similar grounds. Importantly, the question of what the public interest requires for the purpose of art 1 of Protocol 1 can, and in my opinion should, be determined according to the democratic principle—by elected local or central bodies or by ministers accountable to them. There is no principle of human rights which requires such decisions to be made by independent and impartial tribunals.

d [73] There is however another relevant principle which must exist in a democratic society. That is the rule of law. When ministers or officials make decisions affecting the rights of individuals, they must do so in accordance with the law. The legality of what they do must be subject to review by independent and impartial tribunals. This is reflected in the requirement in art 1 of Protocol 1 that a taking of property must be 'subject to the conditions provided for by law'. e The principles of judicial review give effect to the rule of law. They ensure that administrative decisions will be taken rationally, in accordance with a fair procedure and within the powers conferred by Parliament. But this is not the occasion upon which to discuss the limits of judicial review. The only issue in this case is whether the Secretary of State is disqualified as a decision-maker because f he will give effect to policies with which, ex hypothesi, the courts will not interfere.

The question of principle

[74] My Lords, these basic principles are the background to the interpretation of art 6(1):

g

'In the determination of his civil rights and obligations ... everyone is entitled to a fair and public hearing within a reasonable time by an independent and impartial tribunal established by law.'

Apart from authority, I would have said that a decision as to what the public h interest requires is not a 'determination' of civil rights and obligations. It may affect civil rights and obligations but it is not, and ought not to be, a judicial act such as art 6 has in contemplation. The reason is not simply that it involves the exercise of a discretion, taking many factors into account, which does not give any person affected by the decision the right to any particular outcome. There are j many such decisions made by courts (especially in family law) of which the same can be said. Such decisions may nevertheless be determinations of an individual's civil rights (such as access to his child: compare *W v UK* (1987) 10 EHRR 29) and should be made by independent and impartial tribunals. But a decision as to the public interest (what I shall call for short a 'policy decision') is quite different from a determination of right. The administrator may have a duty, in accordance with the rule of law, to behave fairly ('quasi-judicially') in the decision-making procedure. But the decision itself is not a judicial or quasi-judicial act. It does not involve deciding between the rights or interests of particular persons. It is the exercise of a power delegated by the people as a whole to decide what the public interest requires.

[75] The distinction between policy decisions and determinations of right was put with great clarity by Lord Greene MR in *B Johnson & Co (Builders) Ltd v Minister of Health* [1947] 2 All ER 395 at 398–399, when speaking of the decision to confirm a compulsory purchase order:

> '[T]he functions of the Minister in carrying these provisions into operation are fundamentally administrative … subject only to the qualification that, at a particular stage and for a particular and limited purpose, there is superimposed on his administrative character a character which is loosely described as "quasi-judicial." The language which has always been construed as giving rise to the obligations, whatever they may be, implied in the words "quasi-judicial" is to be found in the duty to consider the objections … The administrative character in which he acts reappears at a later stage because, after considering the objections, which may be regarded as the culminating point of his quasi-judicial functions, there follows something which again, in my view, is purely administrative, *viz.*, the decision whether or not to confirm the order. That decision must be an administrative decision, because it is not to be based purely on the view that he forms of the objections, *vis-a-vis* the desires of the local authority, but is to be guided by his view as to the policy which in the circumstances he ought to pursue … [O]n the substantive matter, *viz.*, whether the order should be confirmed or not, there is a third party who is not present, *viz.*, the public, and it is the function of the Minister to consider the rights and the interests of the public. That by itself shows that it is completely wrong to treat the controversy between objector and local authority as a controversy which covers the whole of the ground. It is in respect of the public interest that the discretion that Parliament has given to the Minister comes into operation … His views on that matter he must, if necessary, defend in Parliament, but he cannot be called on to defend them in the courts.'

[76] In principle, therefore, and apart from authority, I would say that art 6(1) conferred the right to an independent and impartial tribunal to decide whether a policy decision by an administrator such as the Secretary of State was lawful but not to a tribunal which could substitute its own view of what the public interest required. However, s 2(1) of the 1998 Act requires an English court, in determining a question which has arisen in connection with a convention right, to take into account the judgments of the European Court of Human Rights and the opinions of the commission. The House is not bound by the decisions of the European Court of Human Rights and, if I thought that the Divisional Court was right to hold that they compelled a conclusion fundamentally at odds with the distribution of powers under the British constitution, I would have considerable doubt as to whether they should be followed. But in my opinion the Divisional Court misunderstood the European jurisprudence. Although the route followed by the European Court of Human Rights has been a tortuous one and some of its statements require interpretation, I hope to demonstrate that it has never attempted to undermine the principle that policy decisions within the limits imposed by the principles of judicial review are a matter for democratically accountable institutions and not for the courts.

a *The European jurisprudence*

[77] The main European authorities are four decisions, two of the commission and two of the European Court of Human Rights, which deal specifically with the English planning system. But before I analyse these important cases, I must give a more general account of the development of the jurisprudence on the right to an independent and impartial tribunal.

b [78] As a matter of history it seems likely that the phrase 'civil rights and obligations' was intended by the framers of the convention to refer to rights created by private rather than by public law. In other words, it excluded even the right to a decision as to whether a public body had acted lawfully, which English law, with that lack of a clear distinction between public and private law which was noted by Dicey, would treat as part of the civil rights of the individual. c Sir Vincent Evans, in his dissenting judgment in *Le Compte v Belgium* (1981) 4 EHRR 1 at 36, said that an intention that the words should bear this narrow meaning appeared from the negotiating history of the convention. In his dissenting judgment in *König v Germany* (1978) 2 EHRR 170, Judge Matscher said that the primary purpose of art 6(1) was, by way of reaction against arbitrary punishments d under the Third Reich, to establish the right to an independent court in criminal proceedings. The framers extended that concept to cases which, according to the systems of the majority of contracting states, fell within the jurisdiction of the ordinary courts of civil law. But there was no intention to apply art 6(1) to public law, which was on the continent a matter for the administrative courts.

[79] These views of the meaning of 'civil rights and obligations' are only of e historical interest, because, as we shall see, the European Court of Human Rights has not restricted art 6(1) to the determination of rights in private law. The probable original meaning, which Judge Wiarda said, in *König's* case (1978) 2 EHRR 170 at 205 was the 'classical meaning' of the term 'civil rights' in a civilian system of law, is nevertheless important. It explains the process of reasoning, unfamiliar to an f English lawyer, by which the Strasbourg court has arrived at the conclusion that art 6(1) can have application to administrative decisions. The court has not simply said, as I have suggested one might say in English law, that one can have a 'civil right' to a lawful decision by an administrator. Instead, the court has accepted that 'civil rights' means only rights in private law and has applied art 6(1) to administrative decisions on the ground that they can determine or affect rights g in private law.

[80] The seminal case is *Ringeisen v Austria (No 1)* (1971) 1 EHRR 455. This concerned an Austrian statute which required transfers of agricultural land to be approved by a district land transactions commission with a right of appeal to a regional commission. In the absence of approval, the contract of sale was void. h The purpose of the law was to keep agricultural land in the hands of farmers of small and medium holdings and the district commission was required to refuse consent to a transfer which appeared to violate this policy. This was a classic regulatory power exercisable by an administrative body. The court nevertheless held that art 6(1) was applicable to its decision on the ground that it was 'decisive' j for the enforceability of the private law contract for the sale of land. Thus a decision on a question of public law by an administrative body could attract art 6(1) by virtue of its effect on private law rights. On the facts, the court held that art 6(1) had been satisfied because the regional commission was an independent and impartial tribunal.

[81] The full implications of *Ringeisen's* case were not examined by the court until some years later. It led in *König's* case to a sharp disagreement between those

members of the court who saw it as a means of enforcing minimum standards of judicial review of administrative and domestic tribunals and those who regarded it as a potential Pandora's box and wanted to confine it as narrowly as possible. Dr König was a surgeon charged with unprofessional conduct before a specialist medical tribunal attached to the Frankfurt Administrative Court. It withdrew his right to practice and run a clinic. He appealed to an administrative Court of Appeal and there followed lengthy and complicated proceedings. His complaint to the European Court of Human Rights under art 6(1) was that he had been denied the right to a decision 'within a reasonable time'. But this raised the question of whether, in principle, art 6(1) applied to disciplinary proceedings before an administrative court. By a majority, the court held that it did. On the *Ringeisen* principle, it affected private law rights such as his goodwill and his right to sell his services to members of the public.

[82] Judge Matscher delivered a powerful dissent, saying that it was unwise to try to apply the pure judicial model of art 6(1) to the decisions of administrative or domestic tribunals. They might share some characteristics with courts (eg requirements of fairness) but in other respects they were different. For example, one could not apply the imperative of a public hearing to a professional disciplinary body. A private hearing might be more in the public interest. If art 6(1) was going to be applied to administrative law, it would have to be substantially modified.

[83] The majority view which prevailed in *König*'s case has enabled the court to develop a jurisprudence by which it has imposed a requirement that all administrative decisions should be subject to some form of judicial review. Sweden, for example, has been held to be in breach of art 6(1) on a number of occasions because it lacked any procedure by which a government decision could be challenged in the courts: see *Sporrong v Sweden* (1982) 5 EHRR 35; *Boden v Sweden* (1988) 10 EHRR 367; *Tre Traktörer Aktiebolag v Sweden* (1989) 13 EHRR 309; *Jacobsson v Sweden* (1989) 12 EHRR 56; *Pudas v Sweden* (1987) 10 EHRR 380; *Zander v Sweden* (1993) 18 EHRR 175; *Skärby v Sweden* (1990) 13 EHRR 90. In *Benthem v Netherlands* (1985) 8 EHRR 1 the Netherlands was similarly held to be in breach because in constitutional theory the administrative court to which an appeal lay only tendered advice to the Crown which it was entitled to reject.

[84] But the dissent of Judge Matscher in *König*'s case has been vindicated in the sense that the application of art 6 to administrative decisions has required substantial modification of the full judicial model. The cases establish that art 6(1) requires that there should be the possibility of some form of judicial review of the lawfulness of an administrative decision. But the European Court of Human Rights, in deciding the *extent* to which such decisions should be open to review, has been in practice fairly circumspect. Its jurisprudence on this point has however been complicated by the apparent breadth of some statements in two cases concerning medical disciplinary proceedings in Belgium.

[85] In *Le Compte v Belgium* (1981) 4 EHRR 1 three doctors who had been suspended by a disciplinary tribunal sitting in private claimed that their right to a public hearing under art 6 had been infringed. They had a right of appeal to the Cour de Cassation, which did sit in public, but that was only on a point of law. The European Court of Human Rights said (at 19 (para 51)) that this was not good enough:

> 'Article 6(1) draws no distinction between questions of fact and questions of law. Both categories of question are equally crucial for the outcome of

a proceedings relating to "civil rights and obligations". Hence the "right to a court" and the right to a judicial determination of the dispute cover questions of fact just as much as questions of law. Yet the Court of Cassation does not have jurisdiction to rectify factual errors or to examine whether the sanction is proportionate to the fault. It follows that Article 6(1) was not satisfied …'

b [**86**] In the later case of *Albert v Belgium* (1983) 5 EHRR 533 at 542 (para 29), in which a similar situation arose, the court said, that although disciplinary jurisdiction could be conferred upon professional bodies which did not meet the requirements of art 6(1) (eg because they were not 'established by law' or did not sit in public)—

c 'Nonetheless, in such circumstances the Convention calls at least for one of the two following systems: either the jurisdictional organs themselves comply with the requirements of Article 6(1), or they do not so comply but are subject to subsequent control by a judicial body that has full jurisdiction and does provide the guarantees of Article 6(1).'

d [**87**] The reference to 'full jurisdiction' has been frequently cited in subsequent cases and sometimes relied upon in argument as if it were authority for saying that a policy decision affecting civil rights by an administrator who does not comply with art 6(1) has to be reviewable on its merits by an independent and impartial tribunal. It was certainly so relied upon by counsel for the respondents e in these appeals. But subsequent European authority shows that 'full jurisdiction' does not mean full decision-making power. It means full jurisdiction to deal with the case as the nature of the decision requires.

[**88**] This emerges most clearly from the decisions on the English planning cases, which I shall analyse later in some detail. But the leading European f authority for the proposition that it is not necessary to have a review of the merits of a policy decision is *Zumtobel v Austria* (1993) 17 EHRR 116. The Zumtobel partnership objected to the compulsory purchase of their farming land to build the L52 by-pass road in the Austrian Vorarlberg. The appropriate government committee heard their objections but confirmed the order. They appealed to an administrative court which said that the government had taken proper matters g into account and that it was not entitled to substitute its decision for that of the administrative authority. They complained to the commission and the European Court of Human Rights that, as the administrative court could not 'independently assess the merits and the facts of the case', it did not have 'full jurisdiction' within the meaning of the *Albert* formula. The European Court of Human Rights said h (at 133 (para 32)) that its jurisdiction was sufficient in the circumstances of the case, '[r]egard being had to the respect which must be accorded to decisions taken by the administrative authorities on grounds of expediency and to the nature of the complaints made by the Zumtobel partnership'.

j *Enforcement proceedings in English law*

[**89**] This background should make it easier to follow the reasoning of the commission and the European Court of Human Rights in the four cases in which they have specifically considered the English planning system. But before I examine these cases, it is necessary to say something more about certain aspects of English planning law. Since the appointed day under the Town and Country Planning Act 1947 (1 July 1948), planning permission has been required in respect

of any development of land: see s 12(1) of the 1947 Act and now s 57(1) of the 1990 Act. Development without planning permission is a 'breach of planning control': see s 171A of the 1990 Act as inserted by s 4 of the Planning and Compensation Act 1991. But a breach of planning control does not in itself give rise to any criminal or civil liability. It is necessary for the local planning authority to take enforcement proceedings in accordance with Pt VII of the 1990 Act.

[90] In applying the distinction between policy decisions and the determination of rights, one would expect that, while the question of whether planning permission should be granted was a matter of policy, the question of whether a breach of planning control had taken place would involve a determination of right. It is no different in principle from a determination as to whether a person has contravened any other rule. No questions of policy are involved in the decision as to whether there has been a breach of planning control or not. So prima facie one would think that enforcement proceedings should fall within the category of decisions in which one was entitled to the judgment of an independent and impartial tribunal.

[91] This was the view of Parliament when it enacted the 1947 Act. Section 23(1) provided that if it appeared to a local planning authority that there had been a breach of planning control, it could within a period of four years of the breach serve an 'enforcement notice' upon the owner and occupier of the land. The notice could require him to restore the land to its previous condition or discontinue any use of the land. The notice took effect after a specified period of not less than 28 days and if the owner nevertheless failed to restore the land to its previous condition, the local planning authority could enter, take the necessary steps and require him to pay the cost. If he did not comply with a notice requiring him to discontinue a use of land, he could be prosecuted before the magistrates and fined: see s 24(1) and (3).

[92] These enforcement provisions included a right for a person 'aggrieved' by an enforcement notice to appeal to the magistrates on various grounds, including the grounds that planning permission had been granted or that no planning permission was required. There was a further right of appeal to quarter sessions. In addition, a person prosecuted for failure to discontinue a use in accordance with an enforcement notice could challenge the validity of the notice before the criminal court on any ground whatever, including those upon which he could have appealed to the magistrates when it was served upon him: *Francis v Yiewsley and West Drayton UDC* [1957] 3 All ER 529, [1958] 1 QB 478.

[93] These provisions therefore made the question of whether there had been a breach of planning control entirely a matter for judicial decision. In addition, a person served with an enforcement notice could apply to the local planning authority for permission to retain or continue the offending structures or works, even if he had just applied and been refused. If he was refused (or again refused) by the local planning authority, he could appeal to the minister. An appeal against an enforcement notice (or resistance to a prosecution) proceeded in parallel with the application for planning permission, even though the quashing of the enforcement notice would make the planning application unnecessary and the grant of planning permission would invalidate the enforcement notice.

[94] Enforcement of planning control under the 1947 Act was therefore extremely complicated, time-consuming and expensive. As a result, the whole system was radically recast by Pt II of the Caravan Sites and Control of Development Act 1960. The appeal to the magistrates was abolished and instead, by s 33, a person served with an enforcement notice was given a right of appeal to the minister on a a number of grounds. These included '(a) that permission ought to be granted … for the development to which the enforcement notice relates … (b) that permission has been granted … (c) that no permission was required … (d) that what is assumed in the enforcement notice to be development did not constitute or involve development … (e) that the enforcement notice was not served on the owner or occupier of the land within the relevant period of four years' and some b other grounds. Section 33(8) then provided that the validity of an enforcement notice 'shall not be questioned in any proceedings whatsoever on any of the grounds specified in paragraphs (b), (c), (d) or (e) … except by way of an appeal under this part of this Act'. Section 34(1) gave a right of appeal from the minister's decision to the High Court, but only on a point of law. This right of appeal is now contained in s 289 of the 1990 Act.

c **[95]** My Lords, I draw attention to the significant changes made by the 1960 Act. First, it withdrew from the local planning authority the jurisdiction to deal with a planning application made in response to an enforcement notice. All such applications or deemed applications were to be treated as if they had been called in by the minister: s 33(2). Secondly, it withdrew the right to question an d enforcement notice before a court on the grounds that there had in fact been no breach of planning control, because permission (or a deemed permission under the general development order) had been granted or because no permission was required. It transferred the right to decide these questions to the minister. Thirdly, it removed the right of a defendant prosecuted for failure to comply with an enforcement notice to challenge the validity of the enforcement notice on e certain of the grounds which could have been raised by way of appeal to the minister. For present purposes, the second and third changes are the most important because they effectively vested in the minister, subject only to appeal on a point of law, the exclusive right to decide the question of whether there had been a breach of planning control for which the owner was ultimately, in the event f of non-compliance with the notice, liable to criminal sanctions. The changes also meant that the minister could now have the dual function of deciding in the same proceedings the policy question of whether planning permission should be granted and the factual question of whether there had been a breach of planning control.

[96] There have been further changes in the enforcement system since 1960 g but the essential features, as now contained in the 1990 Act, remain the same. The grounds for challenging the validity of the enforcement notice by an appeal to the Secretary of State under s 174 have been somewhat extended and the grounds for challenge in any other proceedings has been further restricted: see *R v Wicks* [1997] 2 All ER 801, [1998] AC 92.

h **[97]** The procedure for an appeal against an enforcement notice is prescribed by s 175 of the 1990 Act and Pt III of the Town and Country Planning (Enforcement Notices and Appeals) Regulations 1991, SI 1991/2804, as amended by the Town and Country Planning General Regulations 1992, SI 1992/1492. The appellant and the local planning authority have the right to appear and be j heard before an inspector, who makes his report and recommendations to the Secretary of State. If the Secretary of State is minded to disagree with the inspector on any material question of fact, he must notify the parties and give them the opportunity to make representations. Schedule 6 to the 1990 Act, which gives the Secretary of State power to confer power upon inspectors to hear and determine appeals (subject to recovery under para 3) also applies to enforcement notice appeals.

European cases on the English planning system

[98] My Lords, this background enables me to discuss the four cases to which your Lordships were referred in which the European Court of Human Rights or the commission have considered the English planning system. The first in time is *ISKCON v UK* (1994) 76A DR 90, a decision of the commission on admissibility. ISKCON was an Hindu religious organisation which owned a large manor house at Letchmore Heath in the Hertfordshire Green Belt near Watford. It entered into a planning agreement with the local planning authority by which it agreed not to allow more than 1,000 visitors on any one day without the consent of the authority, which was given for six festival days in the year. When an average of 1,500 people started coming every Sunday, the planning authority served an enforcement notice. ISKCON appealed to the Secretary of State on ground (a) (that planning permission should be granted) and other grounds which were later dropped. The inspector conducting the inquiry considered that the special needs of the organisation did not outweigh the policy of preserving the Green Belt and recommended that the appeal be dismissed. The Secretary of State accepted the recommendation. ISKCON appealed to the High Court under what is now s 289 of the 1990 Act. The points of law relied upon were that the inspector and Secretary of State failed to have regard to relevant considerations and had been under a misapprehension about various facts. The judge dismissed the appeal, saying that the Secretary of State 'was entitled to regard the inspector's conclusions as firmly founded'.

[99] ISKCON's complaint to the commission alleged the breach of various articles of the convention including art 6(1). The commission assumed that the Secretary of State was an 'administrative body' who did not himself comply with art 6 but held that the right of appeal on a point of law was sufficient. It recited the formula from *Albert*'s case (1983) 5 EHRR 533 at 542 (para 29) which required an appeal to 'judicial bodies with full jurisdiction', went on to describe the principles of judicial review by which the English High Court decided whether the Secretary of State had erred in law and concluded that this jurisdiction was wide enough to satisfy the *Albert* formula. It added ((1994) 76A DR 90 at 111):

> 'It is not the role of Article 6 of the Convention to give access to a level of jurisdiction which can substitute its opinion for that of the administrative authorities on questions of expediency and where the courts do not refuse to examine any of the points raised: Article 6 gives a right to a court that has "full jurisdiction" …'

[100] The *ISKCON* case is thus a decision that, at least when the ground of appeal against an enforcement notice is the policy ('expediency') question of whether planning permission should be granted, a decision by the Secretary of State subject to an appeal to the High Court satisfies art 6(1). It is fair to say that it does not address the question of whether this would also do for a decision on the factual question of whether there has been a breach of planning control. But the principle is sufficient for the purposes of the two planning appeals before your Lordships, which are both concerned solely with the question of whether planning permission should be granted.

[101] The next case, and the most important of the four, is *Bryan v UK* (1995) 21 EHRR 342. Mr Bryan was a farmer at Warrington in Cheshire. He built two brick buildings on land in a conservation area without planning permission and the planning authority served an enforcement notice which required them to be demolished. He appealed to the Secretary of State on grounds (a) (that planning permission should be granted), (b) (that there had been no breach of planning a control) and two other grounds. The Secretary of State appointed an inspector with power under Sch 6 to hear and determine the appeal. He rejected the appeal on ground (a) because the buildings did not enhance or preserve the appearance of the conservation area. On ground (b), Mr Bryan contended that the buildings were 'designed for the purpose of agriculture' and that planning permission for them was deemed to have been granted under art 3 of the Town and Country b Planning General Development Order 1988, SI 1988/1813. The planning authority said that they were not designed for the purpose of agriculture and drew attention to the fact that they looked like detached houses with Georgian windows and other domestic features. The inspector said that the question was one of fact and degree. He decided that the planning authority's view was correct and dismissed the appeal.

c **[102]** Mr Bryan appealed to the High Court under s 289. His notice of motion challenged the inspector's finding on ground (b) but the point was abandoned on the advice of counsel that, being a matter of fact and degree, it raised no arguable question of law. On ground (a) it was alleged that the inspector had failed to take into account a relevant factor, namely that Mr Bryan was entitled to erect d agricultural buildings of much the same size and appearance within the conservation area. The judge said that this was a matter of planning judgment for the inspector and dismissed the appeal.

[103] The complaint to the commission was on the ground that these procedures did not satisfy art 6(1). The commission held Mr Bryan's complaint admissible e but decided, by a majority of 11 to five, that there had been no breach of art 6(1). In order to understand the issues, it is convenient to start with the opinion of the minority (at 356). They were entirely concerned with whether art 6(1) had been satisfied in relation to the question of whether the building 'was indeed a barn designed and intended for agricultural use'. This, they emphasised, was not a question of 'expediency':

f

> 'In [*Zumtobel v Austria* (1993) 17 EHRR 116 at 132–133 (para 32)] the European Court of Human Rights referred to the "respect which must be accorded to decisions taken by administrative authorities on grounds of expediency". Whilst questions of expediency play a large role in matters g relating to, for example, the public interest involved if a particular development is permitted, the present case concerns, at least in part, the fundamental factual issue of whether the building erected by the applicant was, or was not, designed for the purposes of agriculture and so had deemed planning permission. This factual issue was in dispute and in the circumstances of this case the High Court judge was not able to provide a h "determination" of it. For us, this deprived the applicant of access to a "tribunal" to which article 6(1) of the Convention entitled him.'

[104] There is, if I may respectfully say so, considerable force in the reasoning of the minority and, as the history shows, it accords with the view which j Parliament took of the appropriate enforcement procedures in 1947. But the purity of the 1947 system had turned out in practice to be unworkable and it therefore had to be replaced with the impure system which we have today. For present purposes, the important point to notice is that the minority had no difficulty in accepting limited judicial review of the 'expediency' questions involved in deciding whether planning permission should be granted. There is nothing to suggest that they would have disagreed with the reasoning or decision in the *ISKCON* case.

[105] The majority said (at 353 (para 46)) that no complaint could be made about the limited right of appeal on ground (a) because it called for 'respect on the grounds of expediency' and referred to *Zumtobel*'s case. As for the ground (b) appeal, they accepted that it 'would have raised matters of a more factual nature' but said that as the point had not been argued, it was impossible to say whether judicial review would have been inadequate.

[106] Both the majority and minority judgements proceeded upon the assumption that the inspector was not an 'independent and impartial tribunal' and that the question was whether the High Court's jurisdiction under s 289 was a sufficiently 'full jurisdiction' to satisfy art 6(1). But the opinion of Mr Nicolas Bratza, concurring with the majority, needs some attention because it introduced a new and original element into the reasoning, which, as we shall see, influenced the judgment of the European Court.

[107] Mr Bratza started (at 353) by saying that the only ground of appeal which Mr Bryan had pursued in the High Court, namely (a), 'related to matters of planning policy' and that in accordance with the reasoning in *Zumtobel*'s case, art 6 did not require 'that a court should have the power to substitute its view for that of the administrative authorities on matters of planning policy or "expediency"'. On this point, therefore, all members of the commission were of the same mind. Mr Bratza then turned his attention to ground (b) and said that, in his view, the power of the High Court under s 289 was sufficient even for the purpose of fact-finding to amount to 'full jurisdiction'. He said (at 354):

> 'It appears to me that the requirement that a court or tribunal should have "full jurisdiction" cannot be mechanically applied with the result that, in all circumstances and whatever the subject matter of the dispute, the court or tribunal must have full power to substitute its own findings of fact, and its own inferences from those facts, for that of the administrative authority concerned. Whether the power of judicial review is sufficiently wide to satisfy the requirements of Article 6 must in my view depend on a number of considerations, including the subject matter of the dispute, the nature of the decision of the administrative authorities which is in question, the procedure, if any, which exists for review of the decision by a peron or body acting independently of the authority concerned and the scope of that power of review.'

[108] Mr Bratza pointed out (at 354–355) that an inspector hearing an appeal under s 174 acted in a quasi-judicial capacity and in accordance with prescribed procedures. Both parties were entitled to be heard and he gave a reasoned decision. It was true that for the purpose of applying policy, the inspectors could not be said to be independent. They were chosen from the salaried staff of the Planning Inspectorate, 'which serves the Secretary of State in the furtherance of his policies'. But for the purposes of finding and evaluating the facts, he was sufficiently independent:

> '... there is ... nothing to suggest that, in finding the primary facts and in drawing conclusions and inferences from those facts, an inspector acts anything other than independently, in the sense that he is in no sense connected with the parties to the dispute or subject to their influence or conrol; his findings and conclusions are based exclusively on the evidence and submissions before him.'

a [109] Mr Bratza then discussed the breadth of the High Court's judicial review powers and said that this power of review, 'combined with the statutory procedure for appealing against an enforcement notice', was sufficient to meet the requirement of 'full jurisdiction' inherent in art 6(1).

[110] Mr Bratza's particular insight, if I may respectfully say so, was to see that a tribunal may be more or less independent, depending upon the question b it is being called upon to decide. On matters of policy, the inspector was no more independent than the Secretary of State himself. But this was a matter on which independence was unnecessary—indeed, on democratic principles, undesirable—and in which the power of judicial review, paying full respect to the views of the inspector or Secretary of State on questions of policy or expediency, was sufficient to satisfy art 6(1). On the other hand, in deciding the questions of c primary fact or fact and degree which arose in enforcement notice appeals, the inspector was no mere bureaucrat. He was an expert tribunal acting in a quasi-judicial manner and therefore sufficiently independent to make it unnecessary that the High Court should have a broad jurisdiction to review his decisions on questions of fact.

d [111] I have spent some time on Mr Bratza's opinion because I think it is clear that it influenced and illuminates the reasoning of the European Court of Human Rights. The court said (at 359 (para 38)) that although the inspector was required to decide the appeal 'in a quasi-judicial, independent and impartial, as well as fair, manner', he was still the creature of the Secretary of State, whose own policies were in issue and who could remove him at any time. Therefore—

e

> 'the review by the inspector does not of itself satisfy the requirements of Article 6 of the Convention, despite the existence of various safeguards customarily associated with an "independent and impartial tribunal".'

f [112] The court noted (at 360 (para 44)) that—

> 'the appeal to the High Court, being on "points of law", was not capable of embracing all aspects of the inspector's decision ... In particular, as is not infrequently the case in relation to administrative law appeals in Council of Europe Member States, there was no rehearing as such of the original g complaints submitted to the inspector; the High Court could not substitute its own decision on the merits for that of the inspector; and its jurisdiction over the facts was limited.'

[113] The question was whether this limited jurisdiction was 'full jurisdiction' for the purposes of the *Albert* formula. The court considered grounds (a) and (b) h separately. On ground (a) it agreed (at 361 (para 47)) with the commission that the applicant's submissions 'went essentially to questions involving "a panoply of policy matters such as development plans, and the fact that the property was situated in a Green Belt and in a conservation area"'. Judicial review was, therefore, on the principle of *Zumtobel*'s case, a sufficiently full jurisdiction.

j [114] On ground (b), the European Court of Human Rights noted (at 360–361 (para 46)) what it described as:

> '... the uncontested safeguards attending the procedure before the inspector: the quasi-judicial character of the decision-making process; the duty incumbent on each inspector to exercise independent judgment; the requirement that inspectors must not be subject to any improper influence;

the stated mission of the Inspectorate to uphold the principles of openness, fairness and impartiality.' a

[115] It went on to say (at 361 (para 47)) that if Mr Bryan had pursued his appeal on ground (b), the High Court, while not being able to substitute its own findings of fact, 'had the power to satisfy itself that the inspector's findings of fact or the inferences based on them were neither perverse nor irrational'. This was enough to satisfy art 6: b

'Such an approach by an appeal tribunal on questions of fact can reasonably be expected in specialised areas of the law such as the one at issue, particularly where the facts have already been established in the course of a quasi-judicial procedure governed by many of the safeguards required by Article 6(1). It is also frequently a feature in the systems of judicial control of administrative decisions found throughout the Council of Europe Member States.' c

[116] My Lords, I have discussed *Bryan*'s case at length because the Divisional Court placed heavy reliance upon it and, in my view, seriously misunderstood it. The Divisional Court treated it as holding that *whatever the issues*, the 'safeguards' which the court enumerated (at 360–361 (para 46)) as attaching to the functions of the inspectors were necessary before the existence of an appeal on a point of law or judicial review would satisfy art 6. But this is the very opposite of what the court was at pains to emphasise. It said (at 360 (para 45)), in language echoing that of Mr Bratza's opinion: d e

'... in assessing the sufficiency of the review available to Mr Bryan on appeal to the High Court, it is necessary to have regard to matters such as the subject matter of the decision appealed against, the manner in which that decision was arrived at, and the content of the dispute, including the desired and actual grounds of appeal.' f

[117] If, therefore, the question is one of policy or expediency, the 'safeguards' are irrelevant. No one expects the inspector to be independent or impartial in applying the Secretary of State's policy and this was the reason why the court said that he was not for all purposes an independent or impatial tribunal. In this respect his position is no different from that of the Secretary of State himself. The reason why judicial review is sufficient in both cases to satisfy art 6 has nothing to do with the 'safeguards' but depends upon the *Zumtobel* principle of respect for the decision of an administrative authority on questions of expediency. It is only when one comes to findings of fact, or the evaluation of facts, such as arise on the question of whether there has been a breach of planning control, that the safeguards are essential for the acceptance of a limited review of fact by the appellate tribunal. g h

[118] My Lords, I can deal much more briefly with the other two cases. In *Varey v UK* App No 26662/95 (27 October 1999, unreported) the commission considered a complaint by gypsies against whom enforcement proceedings had been taken for stationing caravans on land without planning permission. They had applied three times for permission. On the first occasion, an appeal to the Secretary of State was dismissed. On the second occasion, the inspector said that there had been a change in circumstances and recommended that permission be granted but the Secretary of State disagreed. He said that the new circumstances were insufficient to justify overriding the green belt policy. On the third occasion j

a the inspector again recommended that permission be granted and for similar reasons the Secretary of State rejected his recommendation and dismissed the appeal. In no case did the applicants appeal to the High Court.

[119] The commission, following *Bryan*'s case, said that there had been no violation of art 6. The High Court's jurisdiction on appeal from the Secretary of State was sufficient. So the case adds little to *Bryan*'s case itself. I would only b comment that I find puzzling a remark of the commission (at para 78) that—

> 'the procedural protection afforded to the applicants' interests by the process of a public inquiry before a planning inspector, who had the benefit of inspecting the site and of receiving written and oral evidence and representations, must be regarded as considerably diminished by the rejection c on two occasions by the Secretary of State of the inspector's recommendations.'

[120] The Secretary of State does not appear to have differed from the inspector on any finding of fact or evaluation of the facts. He disagreed because he did not think that the inspector had given sufficient weight to the importance of maintaining the green belt. This is a pure question of administrative policy or d expediency. It has nothing to do with the issues on which it is essential for the inspector to be judicial and impartial. However, despite these remarks, the commission concluded that even though the safeguards had been diminished, the procedure still complied with art 6.

[121] Finally there is *Chapman v UK* (2001) 10 BHRC 48, a decision of the Grand Chamber of the European Court of Human Rights. This was another case e of enforcement proceedings against a gypsy. Her appeal on ground (a) was dismissed by an inspector exercising the power to determine the appeal under Sch 6. She did not appeal to the High Court and complained that the High Court would not have been entitled to determine the merits of her claim that she should have planning permission. The court stated briefly that, following *Bryan*'s case, f the scope of judicial review was sufficient to satisfy art 6.

[122] My Lords, I conclude from this examination of the European cases on our planning law that, despite some understandable doubts on the part of some members of the commission about the propriety of having the question of whether there has been a breach of planning control determined by anyone other than an independent and impartial tribunal, even this aspect of our planning g system has survived scrutiny. As for decisions on questions of policy or expediency such as arise in these appeals, whether made by an inspector or the Secretary of State, there has never been a single voice in the commission or the European Court of Human Rights to suggest that our provisions for judicial review are inadequate to satisfy art 6.

h

The judgment of the Divisional Court

[123] My Lords, I must now examine the reasoning of the Divisional Court. They considered the way in which decisions are made by the Secretary of State and came to the conclusion that he was not independent or impartial. Even though the j department has elaborate procedures to ensure that the decision-making process is not contaminated by reliance on facts which had not been found by the inspector or fairly put to the parties, the decision is bound to be influenced by the departmental view on policy. Mr Kingston, who appeared for the Huntingdonshire District Council, spent a good deal of time making this proposition good by examining the documents showing how the department was, at various levels, involved in the development of policy for Alconbury. But this was entirely what

I would have expected. It is the business of the Secretary of State, aided by his civil servants, to develop national planning policies and co-ordinate local policies. These policies are not airy abstractions. They are intended to be applied to actual cases. It would be absurd for the Secretary of State, in arriving at a decision in a particular case, to ignore his policies and start with a completely open mind.

[**124**] For these reasons, the Divisional Court said in para 86 of its judgment (p 955, ante) that the Secretary of State was not impartial in the manner required by art 6: 'What is objectionable in terms of article 6 is that he should be the judge in his own cause where his policy is in play'. I do not disagree with the conclusion that the Secretary of State is not an independent and impartial tribunal. He does not claim to be. But the question is not whether he should be a judge in his own cause. It is whether he should be a judge at all.

[**125**] The Divisional Court then considered whether the requirements of art 6 were satisfied by the right to have an application for judicial review determined by a court. This was rightly described by Tuckey LJ as the crucial question. The answer he gave was that the procedure by which the Secretary of State arrived at his decision did not contain 'sufficient safeguards to justify the High Court's restricted power of review'. The Secretary of State, having complied with the requirements of natural justice, was 'free to make his own decision' and to take account of legal and policy guidance and recommendations from within the department 'which are not seen by the parties'. Therefore, said Tuckey LJ (at para 95, p 958–959, ante):

> 'In terms of art 6 the decision on the merits, which usually involves findings of fact and planning judgment, has not been determined by an independent and impartial tribunal or anyone approaching this, but by someone who is obviously not independent and impartial.'

[**126**] There are three strands of reasoning here. First, there is the fact that the parties are not privy to the processes of decision-making which go on within the department. These contain, on the one hand, elaborate precautions to ensure that the decision-maker does not take into account any factual matters which have not been found by the inspector at the inquiry or put to the parties and, on the other hand, free communication within the department on questions of law and policy, with a view to preparing a recommendation for submission to the Secretary of State or one of the junior ministers to whom he has delegated the decision. The latter is standard civil service procedure and takes place, as Lord Greene MR said in *B Johnson & Co (Builders) Ltd v Minister of Health* [1947] 2 All ER 395, after the Secretary of State's quasi-judicial function has been concluded and when he is acting in his capacity as an administrator making a public policy decision. The constitutional relationship between the Secretary of State and his civil servants was analysed by Lord Diplock in *Bushell v Secretary of State for the Environment* [1980] 2 All ER 608 at 613, [1981] AC 75 at 95:

> 'To treat the minister in his decision-making capacity as someone separate and distinct from the department of government of which he is the political head and for whose actions he alone in constitutional theory is accountable to Parliament is to ignore not only practical realities but also Parliament's intention. Ministers come and go; departments, though their names may change from time to time, remain. Discretion in making administrative decisions is conferred on a minister not as an individual but as the holder of an office in which he will have available to him in arriving at his decision

a the collective knowledge, experience and expertise of all those who serve the Crown in the department of which, for the time being, he is the political head.'

[127] Thus the process of consultation within the department is simply the Secretary of State advising himself. If the Secretary of State was claiming to be, in his own person, an independent and impartial tribunal, the fact that he b received confidential advice and recommendations from civil servants in his department might throw some doubt upon his claim. But since he not only admits but avers that his constitutional role is to formulate and apply government policy, the fact that both formulation and application require the advice and assistance of his civil servants is no more than one would expect.

c [128] The second strand concerns the facts. These are found by the inspector and must be accepted by the Secretary of State unless he has first notified the parties and given them an opportunity to make representations in accordance with r 17(5) of the Town and Country Planning (Inquiries Procedure) (England) Rules 2000, SI 2000/1624. This is the point upon which, in my opinion, *Bryan*'s d case is authority for saying that the independent position of the inspector, together with the control of the fairness of the fact-finding procedure by the court in judicial review, is sufficient to satisfy the requirements of art 6.

[129] Finally, the third strand is that of planning judgment. In this area the principle in *Zumtobel*'s case, as applied in the *ISKCON* case and *Bryan*'s case to questions of policy, does not require that the court should be able to substitute its e decision for that of the administrative authority. Such a requirement would in my opinion not only be contrary to the jurisprudence of the European Court of Human Rights but would also be profoundly undemocratic. The 1998 Act was no doubt intended to strengthen the rule of law but not to inaugurate the rule of lawyers.

f [130] For these reasons I respectfully disagree with the Divisional Court's conclusion that decisions by the Secretary of State in planning cases are incompatible with convention rights. Equally, the fact that the Department of Transport has promoted the road improvement scheme in the Legal & General case does not mean that judicial review cannot satisfy art 6 unless the court can itself decide whether the scheme is a good idea. Nor do I think it makes any g difference that in the Alconbury case the Ministry of Defence, another emanation of the Crown, has a financial interest in the proposed development. Once again, this is something which might be significant if the Secretary of State was claiming to be an impartial tribunal. But as he is not, the remedy available by way of judicial review to quash a decision on the ground that the Secretary of State has h taken irrelevant matters into account is sufficient to satisfy art 6.

The Lord Advocate's intervention

[131] Your Lordships were referred to the decision of the Court of Session in *County Properties Ltd v Scottish Ministers* 2000 SLT 965 in which it was decided that j a decision on listed building consent by the Scottish ministers was inconsistent with art 6 because they were not, as they acknowledged, an independent and impartial tribunal, and a court could not substitute its own decision on the questions of planning and aesthetic judgment which were central to the decision. This decision is on appeal to the Inner House but the Lord Advocate intervened in the argument before your Lordships and appeared by counsel to put forward arguments as to why the case was wrongly decided.

[132] For the reasons I have already given, I would accept this submission. The very notion that such questions should be decided by a court or any other independent tribunal rather than by ministers accountable to the Scottish Parliament seems to me contrary to the democratic principle. I must however deal with a separate argument put forward by Mr Macdonald QC on behalf of the Lord Advocate, which he said provided a shorter route to the same answer.

[133] Mr Macdonald submitted that art 6 has no application to the decision by the Scottish Ministers (or the Secretary of State in England). Their decisions do not involve the determination of anyone's civil rights or obligations. They are simply the exercise of legal powers which affect, perhaps change, civil rights and obligations, but do not determine them within the meaning of art 6. The point at which rights or obligations are determined is in the proceedings by way of judicial review, which decide whether the exercise of power by the administrator was lawful or not. As that question is decided by a court which is undoubtedly independent and impartial, that is the end of the case. Mr Macdonald said that this analysis was supported by the opinion of the commission in *Kaplan v UK* (1980) 4 EHRR 64, which concerned a decision by the Secretary of State that the applicant was not a fit and proper person to be involved in running an insurance company. The commission said (at 88 (para 154)) that art 6 lays down—

> 'guarantees concerning the mode in which claims or disputes concerning legal rights and obligations (of a "civil" character) are to be resolved. A distinction must be drawn between the acts of a body which is engaged in the resolution of such a claim or dispute and the acts of an administrative or other body purporting merely to exercise or apply a legal power vested in it and not to resolve a legal claim or dispute. Article 6(1) would not, in the Commission's opinion, apply to the acts of the latter even if they do affect "civil rights". It could not be considered as being engaged in a process of "determination" of civil rights and obligations. Its function would not be to decide ("*décidera*") on a claim, dispute or "*contestation*". Its acts may, on the other hand, give rise to a claim, dispute or "*contestation*" and Article 6 may come into play in that way.'

[134] My Lords, this reasoning is in accordance with the way in which, at the outset of this speech, I suggested to your Lordships that, apart from European authority, the case ought to be decided. But it provides a short answer only if it assumed that art 6 requires no more than that judicial review proceedings be decided by an independent and impartial tribunal. If, however, art 6 is construed as going further and mandating some minimum content to the judicial review jurisdiction, then it is necessary to ask, as I have done at some length, whether the extent of the judicial review jurisdiction available in England and Scotland is sufficient to satisfy the requirements of the European Court of Human Rights jurisprudence. As appears from my analysis of that jurisprudence, there is no doubt that the European Court of Human Rights has construed art 6 as requiring certain minimum standards of judicial review. This appears most clearly from the Swedish cases to which I have referred.

[135] Once one accepts this construction, it makes little difference whether one says, as in *Kaplan*'s case, that the administrative act does not fall within art 6 at all and the question is concerned only with the adequacy and impartiality of the judicial review, or whether one says, as the European Court of Human Rights and commission have done in other cases, that the administrative act does in theory come within art 6 but the administrator's lack of impartiality can be cured

a by an adequate and impartial judicial review. The former seems to me a more elegant analysis, but the latter may be necessary in order to explain, in the context of civilian concepts, why the administrative process can be treated as involving at any stage a determination of civil rights and obligations. So, tempting as it is, I am unable accept Mr Macdonald's short cut.

b *Conclusion*

[136] I would therefore allow the appeals and declare that the impugned powers are not in breach of or incompatible with the 1998 Act.

LORD CLYDE.

[137] My Lords, by s 77 of the Town and Country Planning Act 1990 the c Secretary of State for the Environment, Transport and the Regions may give directions requiring applications for planning permission to be referred to him instead of being dealt with by local planning authorities. Section 78 provides for the making of appeals to the Secretary of State against planning decisions or the failure to take such decisions and s 79 provides for the opportunity of a hearing d before a person appointed by the Secretary of State for that purpose. By para 3 of Sch 6 to the 1990 Act the Secretary of State may direct that a planning appeal which would otherwise be determined by a person appointed by him shall instead be determined by the Secretary of State. By para 4 he may revoke such a direction. Provision is made in ss 14, 16, 18 and 125 of the Highways Act 1980 for the making of orders by the Secretary of State with regard to certain roadways e and by paras 1, 7 and 8 of Pt I of Sch I to that Act provision is made for the hearing of objections at a local inquiry and the subsequent making or confirmation of the order by the Secretary of State. Section 2(3) of the Acquisition of Land Act 1981 and para 4 of Sch 1 to that Act provide in relation to the making of a compulsory purchase order by a minister for the hearing of objections at a public local inquiry f and the subsequent making of the order by the minister. Under ss 1 and 3 of the Transport and Works Act 1992 the Secretary of State may make orders in relation to among other things railways and waterways and s 23(4) disentitles an inspector hearing objections into such orders from authorising compulsory acquisitions or the compulsory creation or extinguishment of rights over land. The Divisional Court has held that these provisions are incompatible with art 6(1) of the g European Convention for the Protection of Human Rights and Fundamental Freedoms (Rome, 4 November 1950; TS 71 (1953); Cmd 8969) (as set out in Sch 1 to the Human Rights Act 1998). That decision is challenged in the present appeals.

[138] At the heart of the challenge is the objection that the Secretary of State cannot compatibly with art 6(1) himself determine the various issues to which h these statutory provisions can give rise. No complaint is made where the decision is made by an inspector appointed by him. The objection is levelled against his taking upon himself the direct function of being the decision-maker.

The planning context

j **[139]** The general context in which this challenge is raised is that of planning and development. The functions of the Secretary of State in the context of planning may conveniently be referred to as 'administrative', in the sense that they are dealing with policy and expediency rather than with the regulation of rights. We are concerned with an administrative process and an administrative decision. Planning is a matter of the formation and application of policy. The policy is not matter for the courts but for the executive. Where decisions are required in the planning process they are not made by judges, but by members of the administration. Members of the administration may be required in some of their functions to act in a judicial manner in that they may have to observe procedural rules and the overarching principles of fairness. But while they may on some occasions be required to act like judges, they are not judges and their determinations on matters affecting civil rights and obligations are not to be seen as judicial decisions. Even although there may be stages in the procedure leading up to the decision where what used to be described as a quasi-judicial character is superadded to the administrative task, the eventual decision is an administrative one. As was long ago observed by Lord Greene MR in *B Johnson & Co (Builders) Ltd v Minister of Health* [1947] 2 All ER 395 at 399:

> 'That decision must be an administrative decision, because it is not to be based purely on the view that he forms of the objections, *vis-a-vis* the desires of the local authority, but is to be guided by his view as to the policy which in the circumstances he ought to pursue.'

Moreover the decision requires to take into account not just the facts of the case but very much wider issues of public interest, national priorities. Thus the function of the Secretary of State as a decision-maker in planning matters is not in a proper sense a judicial function, although certain qualities of a judicial kind are required of him.

[140] Planning and the development of land are matters which concern the community as a whole, not only the locality where the particular case arises. They involve wider social and economic interests, considerations which are properly to be subject to a central supervision. By means of a central authority some degree of coherence and consistency in the development of land can be secured. National planning guidance can be prepared and promulgated and that guidance will influence the local development plans and policies which the planning authorities will use in resolving their own local problems. As is explained in para I of the government's publication Planning Policy Guidance Notes, the need to take account of economic, environmental, social and other factors requires a framework which provides consistent, predictable and prompt decision-making. At the heart of that system are development plans. The guidance sets out the objectives and policies comprised in the framework within which the local authorities are required to draw up their development plans and in accordance with which their planning decisions should be made. One element which lies behind the framework is the policy of securing what is termed sustainable development, an objective which is essentially a matter of governmental strategy.

[141] Once it is recognised that there should be a national planning policy under a central supervision, it is consistent with democratic principle that the responsibility for that work should lie on the shoulders of a minister answerable to Parliament. The whole scheme of the planning legislation involves an allocation of various functions respectively between local authorities and the Secretary of State. In placing some functions upon the Secretary of State it is of course recognised that he will not personally attend to every case himself. The responsibility is given to his department and the power rests in the department with the Secretary of State as its head and responsible for the carrying out of its work. Within his department a minister may well take advice on law and policy (*Bushell v Secretary of State for the Environment* [1980] 2 All ER 608, [1981] AC 75) and the Secretary of State is entitled to seek elucidation on matters raised by the case which he has to decide, provided always that he observes the basic rules of a fairness. In particular he should in fairness give the parties an opportunity to comment if after a public inquiry some significant factual material of which the parties might not be aware comes to his notice through departmental inquiry.

[142] There may be various agencies which will advise him on particular aspects of planning, as for example an agency skilled in the conservation of historic buildings. But it is a false analysis to claim that there is a lis between a b developer and such an agency which will be heard and determined by the minister. As Lord Greene MR observed in the *Johnson* case [1947] 2 All ER 395 at 399, in relation to objections to a compulsory purchase order proposed by a local authority:

> '... it is not a *lis inter partes*, and for the simple reason that the local c authority and the objectors are not parties to anything that resembles litigation ... on the substantive matter, *viz.*, whether the order should be confirmed or not, there is a third party who is not present, *viz.*, the public, and it is the function of the Minister to consider the rights and interests of the public.'

d The minister is not bound to follow the view of any agency, nor is he bound to follow the desires or interests of any other government department. He is not bound to apply a particular policy if the circumstances seem to him inappropriate for its application. He is not independent. Indeed it is not suggested that he is. But that is not to say that in making the decisions on the matters in issue in the present appeals he is both judge and party. It does not seem to me correct to say e of the Secretary of State that he is judex in sua causa, at least in any strict sense of that expression. He is, as I have already sought to explain, not strictly a judge. Moreover the cause is not in any precise sense his own. No one is suggesting that he, or the officials in his department, have any personal financial or proprietary interest in these cases. The concern of the Secretary of State and his department f is to manage planning and development in accordance with the broad lines of policy which have been prepared in the national interest.

[143] One criticism which is levelled at the system is that the minister has the functions both of making planning policy and of applying the policies which he has made. But that combination of functions does not necessarily give rise to unfairness. The formulation of policies is a perfectly proper course for the g provision of guidance in the exercise of an administrative discretion. Indeed policies are an essential element in securing the coherent and consistent performance of administrative functions. There are advantages both to the public and the administrators in having such policies. Of course there are limits to be observed in the way policies are applied. Blanket decisions which leave no room for particular h circumstances may be unreasonable. What is crucial is that the policy must not fetter the exercise of the discretion. The particular circumstances always require to be considered. Provided that the policy is not regarded as binding and the authority still retains a free exercise of discretion the policy may serve the useful purpose of giving a reasonable guidance both to applicants and decision-makers. j Nor is this a point which can be made solely in relation to the Secretary of State. In a variety of administrative functions, in addition to planning, local authorities may devise and implement policies of their own.

[144] It is now argued that the planning process is flawed in so far as the decision-maker is the Secretary of State. It is said that where he is making the decision the case falls foul of art 6 of the convention. One possible solution which is proposed is that in the cases where at present the Secretary of State is himself the decision-

maker, cases for the most part which are likely to give rise to issues of widespread or even national concern, which may well have a wide impact on the lives of many and involve major issues of policy, the decision should be removed from the minister, who is answerable to Parliament, to an independent body, answerable to no one. That would be a somewhat startling proposition and it would be surprising if the convention which is rooted in the ideas of democracy and the rule of law should lead to such a result.

Applicability of the convention

[145] The first question is whether art 6 applies at all to decisions by planning authorities or by the Secretary of State. An attractive argument was presented on behalf of the Lord Advocate to the effect that art 6 was as regards civil matters concerned with the securing of justice in the resolution of a legal claim or dispute and not with the acts of an administrative body exercising a discretionary power. Article 6 would only come to affect matters of administrative discretionary decisions at the stage when a dispute arose on the grounds that the decision-maker had acted unlawfully, exceeding the parameters of his lawful discretion and erring in law. This argument looks to the whole terms of art 6(1) which can readily be seen as designed to cover judicial proceedings. Counsel pointed to the French text of the article and the use of the word 'contestations' which could be understood as relating to a dispute on civil rights and obligations and to litigation before a court of law. In support of this approach reference was made to a decision of the commission in *Kaplan v UK* (1980) 4 EHRR 64 at 88 (para 154) where, after referring to claims and disputes concerning legal rights and obligations of a civil character, the commission stated:

> 'A distinction must be drawn between the acts of a body which is engaged in the resolution of such a claim or dispute and the acts of an administrative or other body purporting merely to exercise or apply a legal power vested in it and not to resolve a legal claim or dispute. Article 6(1) would not, in the Commission's opinion, apply to the acts of the latter even if they do affect "civil rights". It could not be considered as being engaged in a process of "determination" of civil rights and obligations. Its function would not be to decide ("*décidera*") on a claim, dispute or "*contestation*". Its acts may, on the other hand, give rise to a claim, dispute or "*contestation*" and Article 6 may come into play in that way.'

[146] This approach provides a clean and simple solution to the present problem. But I do not consider that it is sound. The observations in *Kaplan*'s case on which the argument was supported have not been taken up by the court and reflect an earlier stage in the development of the jurisprudence on the scope and application of art 6(1). In the developing jurisprudence of the European Court of Human Rights it became recognised that a narrow view of the scope of art 6(1) was inappropriate. In *X v UK* (1982) 28 DR 177 at 186 the commission held that a compulsory purchase order affected the applicant's private rights of ownership, that these were 'civil rights', and that in challenging the making of the order she was entitled to the protection of art 6(1). Counsel recognised the difficulty which that decision presented for his argument and was constrained to contend that the decision was wrong. His proposition involves a narrow understanding of the scope of the article.

[147] In considering the scope of art 6(1) it is proper to take a broad approach to the language used and seek to give effect to the purpose of the provision.

a In *Ringeisen v Austria (No 1)* (1971) 1 EHRR 455 at 490 (para 94) the phrase was taken to cover 'all proceedings the result of which is decisive for private rights and obligations'. This included cases where the proceedings concerned a dispute between a private individual and a public authority. In *Golder v UK* (1975) 1 EHRR 524 at 532–533 (para 32) the court considered the French and English text of the article and concluded that the article covered a right of access to a court or b 'tribunal' without there being already proceedings pending. The court held (at 536 (para 36)) that 'Article 6(1) secures to everyone the right to have any claim relating to his civil rights and obligations brought before a court or tribunal'. These two cases pre-date the decision in *Kaplan*'s case. In *Le Compte v Belgium* (1981) 4 EHRR 1 at 16 (para 45) the court observed of the word 'contestation':

c 'Conformity with the spirit of the Convention requires that this word should not be construed too technically and that it should be given a substantive rather than a formal meaning besides, it has no counterpart in the English text of Article 6(1) …'

The court held that even if the use of the French word implied the existence of a d disagreement, the evidence showed that there was one in that case where there were allegations of professional misconduct which were denied. The reference to a determination reflects the necessity for there to be a dispute. But it does not require to be a dispute in any formal sense. In *Moreira de Azevedo v Portugal* (1990) 13 EHRR 721, the court followed the approach taken in *Le Compte*'s case and held that art 6(1) applied where the applicant had joined as an assistente in criminal e proceedings with a view to securing financial reparation for injuries which he claimed he had suffered at the hands of the accused but had not filed any claim in civil proceedings. The distinction noticed by the commission in *X v UK* (1998) 25 EHRR CD 88 at 96 is not to be overlooked, that is the distinction between—

f 'the acts of a body which is engaged in the resolution of a dispute ("contestation") and the acts of an administrative or other body purporting merely to exercise or apply a legal power vested in it and not to resolve a legal claim or dispute.'

But at least from the time when a power has been exercised and objection is taken to that exercise the existence of a dispute for the purpose of art 6(1) can be g identified.

[148] The scope of art 6 accordingly extends to administrative determinations as well as judicial determinations. But, putting aside criminal proceedings with which we are not here concerned, the article also requires that the determination should be of a person's civil rights and obligations. The concept of civil rights in h art 6(1) is an autonomous one (*König v Germany* (1978) 2 EHRR 170). In *H v France* (1989) 12 EHRR 74 at 87–88 (para 47) the court stated:

'It is clear from the Court's established case law that the concept of "civil rights and obligations" is not to be interpreted solely by reference to the respondent State's domestic law and that Article 6(1) applies irrespective of j the parties' status, be it public or private, and of the nature of the legislation which governs the manner in which the dispute is to be determined; it is sufficient that the outcome of the proceedings should be "decisive for private rights and obligations."'

It relates to rights and obligations 'which can be said, at least on arguable grounds, to be recognised under domestic law' (*James v UK* (1986) 8 EHRR 123 at 157 (para 81)). The rights with which the present appeals are concerned are the rights of property which are affected by development or acquisition. Those clearly fall within the scope of 'civil rights'. But there is no issue about the existence of these rights and no determination of the rights in any strict sense is raised.

[149] The opening words of art 6(1) are: 'In the determination of his civil rights and obligations or of any criminal charge against him ...' Here again a broad interpretation is called for. The decision need not formally be a decision on the rights. Article 6 will still apply if the effect of the decision is directly to affect civil rights and obligations. In *Le Compte v Belgium* (1981) 4 EHRR 1 at 17 (para 46) the court observed:

> '... it must be shown that the "contestation" (dispute) related to "civil rights and obligations", in other words that the "result of the proceedings" was "decisive" for such a right.'

The dispute may relate to the existence of a right, and the scope or manner in which it may be exercised (*Le Compte*'s case at 18 (para 49), also *Balmer-Schafroth v Switzerland* (1997) 25 EHRR 598). But it must have a direct effect of deciding rights or obligations. The court continued (at 17 (para 47):

> 'As regards the question whether the dispute related to the above-mentioned right, the Court considers that a tenuous connection or remote consequences do not suffice for Article 6(1) in either of its official versions ("*contestation sur*"; "determination of"): civil rights and obligations must be the object—or one of the objects—of the "*contestation*" (dispute): the result of the proceedings must be directly decisive for such a right.'

That case was followed in *Sporrong v Sweden* (1982) 5 EHRR 35 at 56 (para 80), where the court noted that art 6(1) extended to a dispute concerning 'an administrative measure taken by the competent body in the exercise of public authority'. It is also said that the dispute must be 'genuine and of a serious nature': *Benthem v Netherlands* (1985) 8 EHRR 1 at 8 (para 32). In that case a genuine and serious dispute was held to have arisen 'at least' from the date when the licence which the applicant had earlier obtained from the local municipality was cancelled by the Crown.

[150] It is thus clear that art 6(1) is engaged where the decision which is to be given is of an administrative character, that is to say one given in an exercise of a discretionary power, as well as a dispute in a court of law regarding the private rights of the citizen, provided that it directly affects civil rights and obligations and is of a genuine and serious nature. It applies then to the various exercises of discretion which are raised in the present appeals. But while the scope of the article extends to cover such discretionary decisions, the particular character of such decisions cannot be disregarded. And that particular factor has important consequences for the application of the article in such cases.

Compatibility with the convention

[151] If one was to take a narrow and literal view of the article, it would be easy to conclude that the respondents are correct and that the actions of the Secretary of State are incompatible with the article. It is accepted that he does not constitute an impartial and independent tribunal. In the context of a judicial proceeding that may well be fatal.

[152] The first point to be noticed here, however, is that the opening phrase in art 6(1), 'In the determination', refers not only to the particular process of the a making of the decision but extends more widely to the whole process which leads up to the final resolution. In *Zumtobel v Austria* (1993) 17 EHRR 116 at 125 (para 64) the commission under reference to *Ettl v Austria* (1987) 10 EHRR 255, recalled that:

> 'Article 6(1) of the Convention does not require that the procedure which determines civil rights and obligations is conducted at each of its stages
> b before tribunals meeting the requirements of this provision. An administrative procedure may thus precede the determination of civil rights by the tribunal envisaged in Article 6(1) of the Convention.'

It is possible that in some circumstances a breach in one respect can be overcome by the existence of a sufficient opportunity for appeal or review. While the failure
c to give reasons for a decision may in the context of some cases constitute a breach of the article, the existence of a right of appeal may provide a remedy in enabling a reasoned decision eventually to be given and so result in an overall compliance with the article. In the context of criminal cases art 6 will bite when a charge has been made, which could be long in advance of the trial or any subsequent appeal
d at which the actual resolution of the issue of guilt or innocence is made. In the civil context the whole process must be considered to see if the article has been breached. Not every stage need comply. If a global view is adopted one may then take into account not only the eventual opportunity for appeal or review to a court of law, but also the earlier processes and in particular the process of public inquiry at which essentially the facts can be explored in a quasi-judicial procedure
e and a determination on factual matters achieved.

[**153**] Next, account has to be taken of the context and circumstances of the decision. Here an important distinction has been made by the European Court of Human Rights. The distinction was explained in the context of medical disciplinary proceedings in *Albert v Belgium* (1983) 5 EHRR 533. The court observed
f (at 541–542 (para 29)):

> 'In many member States of the Council of Europe, the duty of adjudicating on disciplinary offences is conferred on jurisdictional organs of professional associations. Even in instances where Article 6(1) is applicable, conferring powers in this manner does not in itself infringe the Convention.
> g Nonetheless, in such circumstances the Convention calls at least for one of the two following systems: either the jurisdictional organs themselves comply with the requirements of Article 6(1), or they do not so comply but are subject to subsequent control by a judicial body that has full jurisdiction and does provide the guarantees of Article 6(1).'

h The court has recognised that planning decisions fall into a 'specialised area' (*Chapman v UK* (2001) 10 BHRC 48) and have applied this distinction in relation to such decisions.

[**154**] As regards the first of the two systems referred to in *Albert*'s case, where the 'jurisdictional organ' is the Secretary of State it cannot be said that the
j requirements of art 6(1) are met. So it is the second system which falls to be considered in the present context. In the first place consideration has to be given to the expression 'full jurisdiction'. At first sight the expression might seem to require in every case an exhaustive and comprehensive review of the decision including a thorough review of the facts as well as the law. If that were so a remedy by way of a statutory appeal or an application to the supervisory jurisdiction of the courts in judicial review would be inadequate. But it is evident

that this is not a correct understanding of the expression. Full jurisdiction means a full jurisdiction in the context of the case. As Mr N Bratza stated in his concurring opinion in the decision of the commission in *Bryan v UK* (1995) 21 EHRR 342 at 354:

> 'It appears to me that the requirement that a court or tribunal should have "full jurisdiction" cannot be mechanically applied with the result that, in all circumstances and whatever the subject matter of the dispute, the court or tribunal must have full power to substitute its own findings of fact, and its own inferences from those facts, for that of the administrative authority concerned.'

The nature and circumstances of the case have accordingly to be considered before one can determine what may comprise a 'full jurisdiction'. In the very different context of disciplinary proceedings a more exhaustive remedy may be required in order to satisfy art 6(1). In *Le Compte v Belgium* (1981) 4 EHRR 1, in the context of medical disciplinary proceedings, the court stated (at 19 (para 51)):

> 'For civil cases, just as for criminal charges, Article 6(1) draws no distinction between questions of fact and questions of law. Both categories of question are equally crucial for the outcome of proceedings relating to "civil rights and obligations". Hence, the "right to a court" and the right to a judicial determination of the dispute cover questions of fact just as much as questions of law.'

In that case the article was held not to be satisfied since the Court of Cassation had no jurisdiction to rectify factual errors or to examine whether the sanction was proportionate to the fault.

[155] I turn then next to consider whether in the circumstances of the present cases as they presently stand the opportunities for appeal and review are such as to constitute a full jurisdiction. Guidance here may be found in *Bryan v UK* (1995) 21 EHRR 342 where the court, echoing a passage from the opinion of Mr N Bratza in the commission (see 354) stated (at 360 (para 45)), that in assessing the sufficiency of the review available—

> 'it is necessary to have regard to matters such as the subject matter of the decision appealed against, the manner in which that decision was arrived at, and the content of the dispute, including the desired and actual grounds of appeal.'

These three matters may be considered separately.

[156] First, the subject matter of the decisions are in each case matters of planning determination in relation to proposed developments which are of some considerable public importance. As planning decisions, even if they were not of some size and importance, they fall within what the court has recognised as a specialised class of case (*Chapman v UK* (2001) 10 BHRC 48). The rights affected are principally rights to use land, which may be the subject of development or of compulsory acquisition. Moreover the right to use land is not an absolute right. It is under the domestic law subject to the controls of the planning regime, whereby permission may be required for the carrying out of a development or for the making of some change of use. Planning permission is not in general a matter of right.

[157] So far as the manner in which the decisions will be taken is concerned it is to be noticed that in each case there will be a public inquiry before an inspector.

a That will be an occasion for the exploration of the facts, including the need and desirability of the development. The inquiry will be regulated by rules whose broad intention is to secure fairness in the procedure. The eventual decision in the present cases is to be taken by the Secretary of State. A remedy by way of appeal or judicial review is available, and there may be opportunities for judicial review at earlier stages as indeed is demonstrated in the present appeals.

b **[158]** So far as the content of the dispute is concerned, the present point is that the Secretary of State should not be the decision-maker. The challenge is advanced substantially as one of principle, although in relation to the Huntingdonshire case a variety of particular points were raised regarding the interest or involvement in the Alconbury proposals on the part of various persons connected with the c department or the government. But I find it unnecessary to explore these in detail. The Secretary of State is admittedly not independent for the purposes of art 6(1). I do not consider that it can be decided at this stage whether the interest or involvement of these other persons is going to provide grounds for challenging the legality of the eventual decision. Grounds for challenge which are at present unpredictable may possibly arise in due course. As matters presently stand the d issue is whether art 6(1) is necessarily breached because the decision is to be taken by the Secretary of State with the assistance of his department. The challenge is directed not against the individual but against the office which he holds. The question which arises is whether the Secretary of State or some person altogether unconnected with the Secretary of State should make the decision.

e **[159]** As I indicated at the outset, Parliament, democratically elected, has entrusted the making of planning decisions to local authorities and to the Secretary of State with a general power of supervision and control in the latter. Thereby it is intended that some overall coherence and uniformity in national planning can be achieved in the public interest and that major decisions can be f taken by a minister answerable to Parliament. Planning matters are essentially matters of policy and expediency, not of law. They are primarily matters for the executive and not for the courts to determine. Moreover as matter of generality the right of access to a court is not absolute. Limitations may be imposed so long as they do not so restrict or reduce the access that the very essence of the right is impaired (*Tinnelly & Sons Ltd v UK, McElduff & Sons Ltd v UK* (1998) 27 EHRR 249 g at 271 (para 72)). Moreover the limitation must pursue a legitimate aim and the relationship between the means employed and the aim sought to be achieved must be reasonably proportionate (*Ashingdane v UK* (1985) 7 EHRR 528). In the context of the present cases the aim of reserving to a minister answerable to Parliament the determination of cases which will often be of very considerable h public interest and importance is plainly a legitimate one. In light of the considerations which I have already canvassed it seems to me that there exists a reasonable balance between the scope of matters left to his decision and the scope of the control possessed by the courts over the exercise of his discretionary power.

j **[160]** Accordingly as matters presently stand I find no evident incompatibility with art 6(1). That view seems to me to accord fully with the decisions of the European Court of Human Rights. A consideration of the cases on the specialised area of town and country planning to which I now turn suggests that the court has recognised the sufficiency of a limited appeal and the decisions fully support the view which I have expressed. It was correctly pointed out that the court is always careful to relate its decisions to the facts of the case before it. But that does not mean that the cases do not or cannot provide guidance by way of close precedent or principle. I turn first to *Bryan v UK* (1995) 21 EHRR 342.

[161] *Bryan*'s case concerned an enforcement notice for the demolition of two agricultural buildings which had the appearance of large detached houses. The scope of the appeal open to the applicant was on points of law. One ground of his complaints, referred to as ground (b), was on the decision as matter of fact and degree, whether the buildings could be considered to have been designed for the purposes of agriculture. That ground was not pursued before the High Court on appeal. It was a question of fact and degree. The European Court of Human Rights held that the other grounds had all been dealt with by the High Court, and continued (at 361 (para 47)):

> 'Furthermore, even if the applicant had sought to pursue his appeal under ground (b), the Court notes that, while the High Court could not have substituted its own findings of fact for those of the inspector, it would have had the power to satisfy itself that the inspector's findings of fact or the inferences based on them were neither perverse nor irrational.'

It is evident from this decision that where there was an inquiry before an inspector who could not be regarded as 'independent', but nevertheless with 'uncontested safeguards' attending the procedure which were open to review by the High Court, the limitations of the eventual remedy by way of appeal, limitations which equate with those attending a judicial review, did not mean that the requirements of art 6(1) were not satisfied.

[162] I do not consider that *Bryan*'s case can be put aside as distinguishable on its facts, nor that its importance is confined to its own particular circumstances. The Divisional Court made a distinction between a decision taken by an inspector and one taken by the Secretary of State. That appears to have been one of the three considerations which weighed with the Lord Ordinary (MacFadyen) in *County Properties Ltd v Scottish Ministers* 2000 SLT 965 in distinguishing the case. It seems to me that this difference is too slight to be of serious consequence. The Secretary of State is admittedly not independent. The inspector also lacks independence. As was pointed out by the commission in *Bryan*'s case (1995) 21 EHRR 342 at 359–360 (para 42), he was chosen for the staff of the Planning Inspectorate which served the Secretary of State in the furtherance of the Secretary of State's policies, he was making the decision on behalf of the Secretary of State, and the Secretary of State's policies could be at issue in the appeal. The court held (at 359 (para 38)) that the very existence of a power in the Secretary of State was 'enough to deprive the inspector of the requisite appearance of independence'. But that is not to say that the institutional link with the Secretary of State is not also of significance. The court in *Bryan*'s case noted (at 359 (para 42)) that a remedy would lie if the inspector showed some lack of independence of judgment, or had otherwise not acted fairly, or had been subjected to improper pressure. Those grounds should also apply to a review of a decision by the Secretary of State. In so far as the Divisional Court sought to distinguish *Bryan*'s case I am not persuaded that they were correct. But in any event the case does not stand on its own.

[163] In *ISKCON v UK* (1994) 76A DR 90, an enforcement notice had been served by the local authority on the grounds of an alleged change of use of land. Again the complaint was made by the applicant before the commission that the review by the High Court was limited to questions of law. The commission noted that the discretion of the local authority in taking enforcement proceedings was subject to certain statutory limitations, that the High Court had dealt with each a of ISKCON's grounds of appeal and that a challenge was available on the grounds that the findings of fact were unsupported by the evidence, that actual facts had not been taken into account, or that account had been taken of immaterial facts, or that the decision was irrational. The commission held that review by the High Court satisfied the requirements of art 6(1).

[164] The decision in *Bryan*'s case was followed in *Varey v UK* App No 26662/95 b (27 October 1999, unreported) where the Secretary of State had overruled recommendations made by inspectors after a public inquiry. Recalling *Bryan*'s case the commission (at para 86) had regard 'in particular to the court's finding that in the specialised area of town planning law full review of facts may not be required by art 6(1)' and held that the scope of review available in the High Court was sufficient to comply with that article. The commission stated:

c

> '… the Secretary of State gave reasoned decisions on the basis of the facts found by the inspectors, and the matters relied on by him in overruling their recommendations could be challenged on appropriate grounds before the High Court.'

d **[165]** The recent decision in *Chapman v UK* (2001) 10 BHRC 48 is of particular interest because the complaint there was expressly that the High Court could not review questions of fact, nor questions of the weight given to the needs of the applicant and her family. The court however held (at 76 (para 124)), following *Bryan*'s case, 'that in the specialised area of town planning law full review of the facts may not be required by art 6 of the convention' and that the opportunity to e challenge the decision 'on the basis that it was perverse, irrational, had no basis on the evidence or had been made with reference to irrelevant factors or without regard to relevant factors' afforded adequate judicial control of the administrative decisions in issue.

[166] Two other cases may be mentioned where the concern was about the f sufficiency of a remedy in the context of the compulsory acquisition of land. *Howard v UK* (1987) 52 DR 215 concerned the requirement in art 13 of the convention that everyone whose rights and freedoms are violated should have 'an effective remedy before a national authority'. The complaint was that in relation to a compulsory purchase order neither the statutory remedy nor judicial review extended to the content or substance of the decision, which g was the object of the attack. The commission took account of the opportunities which the applicants had of challenging the decision to make the order by way of judicial review, of making representations to an inspector at a public inquiry, and of making a statutory challenge to the confirmation of the order. They held that the limited review which was available satisfied the requirements of art 13.

h **[167]** *Zumtobel v Austria* (1993) 17 EHRR 116 concerned an order to expropriate land for the construction of a highway. The court held that the opportunity for challenge before the Constitutional Court was not sufficient to overcome the objection that the applicants had had no right to a fair and public hearing, because the jurisdiction of that court only extended to testing the constitutionality of the j order. But the opportunity to challenge the order before the Administrative Court was sufficient, because (in distinction from *Obermeier v Austria* (1990) 13 EHRR 290 at 306 (para 70)) that court could consider whether a statutory pre-condition for the validity of the order had been met and were able to meet and deal with all the points raised by the applicants in their challenge.

[168] It is also of significance that as matter of generality the state parties to the convention treat a limited review as an appropriate remedy in administrative matters. In *Kaplan v UK* (1980) 4 EHRR 64 the commission recognised that where an individual's right had been adversely affected by action taken by a public authority art 6(1) entitled him to access to a court for such remedy as the domestic law might allow. The question then arose whether the limited right of judicial review was sufficient. The commission noted that the limit to control of the lawfulness of the decision was fairly typical of many of the contracting states, and indeed the scope of protection afforded under art 173 of the Treaty of Rome was similarly limited. The commission observed (at 90 (para 161)):

> 'An interpretation of Article 6(1) under which it was held to provide a right to a full appeal on the merits of every administrative decision affecting private rights would therefore lead to a result which was inconsistent with the existing, and long-standing, legal position in most of the Contracting States.'

In *Bryan*'s case (1995) 21 EHRR 342 the court observed that while the High Court could not have substituted its own findings of fact for those of the inspector it was able to determine whether the findings or the inferences from them were perverse or irrational. The court continued (at 361 (para 47)):

> 'Such an approach by an appeal tribunal on questions of fact can reasonably be expected in specialised areas of the law such as the one at issue, particularly where the facts have already been established in the course of a quasi-judicial procedure governed by many of the safeguards required by Article 6(1). It is also frequently a feature in the systems of judicial control of administrative decisions found throughout the Council of Europe Member States.'

The scope of judicial review

[169] The suggestion was advanced that if the respondents were correct in their contention that the present proceedings are in breach of art 6(1), the scope of judicial review might somehow be enlarged so as to provide a complete remedy. The point in the event does not arise, but I consider that it might well be difficult to achieve a sufficient enlargement to meet the stated purpose without jeopardising the constitutional balance between the role of the courts and the role of the executive. The supervisory jurisdiction of the court as it has now developed seems to me adequate to deal with a wide range of complaints which can properly be seen as directed to the legality of a decision. It is sufficient to note the recognition of the idea of proportionality, or perhaps more accurately, disproportionality, and the extent to which the factual areas of a decision may be penetrated by a review of the account taken by a decision-maker of facts which are irrelevant or even mistaken (*R v Criminal Injuries Compensation Board, ex p A* [1999] 2 AC 330 at 344–345, [1999] 2 WLR 974 at 982). But consideration of the precise scope of the administrative remedies is not necessary for the purposes of the present appeals.

The Divisional Court

[170] The Divisional Court recognised that the Secretary of State could not disagree with the material findings of fact made by the inspector without giving the parties an opportunity of making representations. But what gave rise to concern (at para 94, p 958, ante), was the consideration that he was then 'free to make his own decision and does so after taking account of internal legal and policy "elucidation" and the recommendation of the decision officer ... which are a not seen by the parties'. It appears to be that consideration which led the Divisional Court to reach their conclusion. These matters bring me back to what I said at the outset of this speech. The Secretary of State is not entirely free to make his own decision. He cannot ignore what has passed at the inquiry. He cannot act in an arbitrary way. He has to proceed upon a reasonable assessment of the material before him. He has to respect the necessity to produce a decision b which is not open to attack on grounds of legality. Nor is there anything wrong in seeking or taking into account advice which he may obtain from within his department, at least where that advice is sought to clarify or elucidate law or policy. If his decision is materially affected by some error of law or misconstruction of policy that may be open to review. The precise mechanics of the decision-making process in a large department are necessarily more complex than the c process in which an inspector would engage if he was to make the actual decision. What is required is that there should be a decision with reasons. Provided that these set out clearly the grounds on which the decision has been reached it does not seem to me necessary that all the thinking which lies behind it should also be made available, whether the decision is made by an inspector or by the head of a d government department.

Prematurity

[171] The European Court of Human Rights tends to express its decisions in relation to a complete and concluded case. In the present appeals we are asked to form a view at a preliminary stage. It is not yet known what the decisions will e be. Far less is it known what grounds, if any, will emerge for dissatisfaction with the decision. But the practical advantages of testing the issue at this early stage are obvious. A very considerable expenditure of effort, time and money would have been spent in vain if the decision of the Divisional Court was correct. The Divisional Court followed the view taken by the Lord Ordinary in the f *County Properties* case that to wait until the eventual decision after the whole planning process has run its course would be unsound and impractical. That view seems to me to be correct. It can at least at this stage be affirmed that for the purposes of s 6(1) of the Human Rights Act 1998 it is not necessarily unlawful for the decisions in question to be made by the Secretary of State.

[172] I would accordingly allow the appeals. The cross-appeal which raised an g issue regarding the application of s 6(1) and (2)(b) of the 1998 Act does not then arise for determination.

LORD HUTTON.

[173] My Lords, in their applications to the Divisional Court the respondents h submitted that the respective procedures whereby the Secretary of State for the Environment, Transport and the Regions 'called in' and 'recovered' planning applications and decided whether to make a compulsory purchase order were not in compliance with art 6(1) of the European Convention for the Protection of Human Rights and Fundamental Freedoms (Rome, 4 November 1950; TS 71 (1953); j Cmd 8969) (as set out in Sch 1 to the Human Rights Act 1998) (the convention). This submission was accepted by the Divisional Court and the Secretary of State now appeals directly to this House pursuant to s 12 of the Administration of Justice Act 1969.

[174] Article 6(1) of the convention provides: 'In the determination of his civil rights and obligations … everyone is entitled to a fair and public hearing within a reasonable time by an independent and impartial tribunal established by law.'

[175] Prior to the incorporation of the convention into the law of England by the 1998 Act, the law in relation to the functions of a government minister in respect of planning applications and objections to compulsory purchase orders, as stated in the classic judgment of Lord Greene MR in *B Johnson & Co (Builders) Ltd v Minister of Health* [1947] 2 All ER 395, was clear. It was that whilst a quasi-judicial duty to consider objections was superimposed on the minister, the functions which he performed were essentially of an administrative nature and his decision would be arrived at on grounds of public policy. Thus Lord Greene stated (at 399):

> 'The administrative character in which he acts reappears at a later stage because, after considering the objections, which may be regarded as the culminating point of his quasi-judicial functions, there follows something which again, in my view, is purely administrative, *viz.*, the decision whether or not to confirm the order. That decision must be an administrative decision, because it is not to be based purely on the view that he forms of the objection *vis-a-vis* the desires of the local authority, but is to be guided by his view as to the policy which in the circumstances he ought to pursue.'

See also 397.

[176] Therefore the minister was entitled to overrule the objections of an individual citizen whose property was affected because of his views as to what the public interest required. But this did not mean that the citizen was subject to the decision of a minister which might be arbitrary and without oversight because, as Lord Greene observed (at 399), the minister was subject to the control of Parliament and he might have to defend his views and his decision in Parliament.

[177] The respondents' submissions to the Divisional Court were that when the Secretary of State made his decisions whether to uphold or reject their objections to a planning scheme and whether to make a compulsory purchase order, those decisions constituted determinations of their civil rights within the meaning of art 6(1). They further submitted that the Secretary of State was not an independent and impartial tribunal because he would come to his decisions in the light of the policy which he had formulated or adopted on behalf of the government and was duty bound to promote.

[178] The Divisional Court accepted these submissions. The reasoning of the court can be seen in the following passages of its judgment delivered by Tuckey LJ (see pp 980–981, 984–985, ante):

> '71. It is common ground that the independence required by art 6(1) is independence from the executive and from the parties.
>
> 72. The Secretary of State is part of the executive as are all or any of his ministerial team or the civil servants involved in the decision-making process. The contrary is, we think, unarguable which no doubt explains the Secretary of State's stance in these proceedings …
>
> 84. There is no dispute about the position under domestic law. It is well stated in passages from Supperstone and Goudie *Judicial Review* (2nd edn, 1997) p 9.21: "In many administrative situations the possibility of bias is built into the system. Proposers of the scheme may have strong and carefully thought out views on the subject, and yet may have to hear and rule on objections to it. Administrators may have guidelines to help them in their day to day application of legislation. In such situations the concept of a fair trial may be impossible and indeed undesirable to achieve. It has been

a pointed out … that the more indifferent to the aim in view the less efficient is a Minister or civil servant likely to be. After all, it is his job to get things done. So, while the obvious pre-judgment of an issue is not allowed, a challenge to a decision on the grounds of departmental bias is unlikely to succeed. It is a Minister's job to have a policy and to support it in public." …

85. But the question we have to answer is whether the position under b domestic law can withstand the unqualified procedural right conferred by art 6. We do not think it can. The common law approach has inevitably been determined by the constraints imposed by legislation. The logic is that if legislation vests a decision in a person who is biased or provides for a decision to be taken in a manner which is not compatible with the requirements of independence and impartiality, no breach of the requirements c of fairness can be found. Such requirements of fairness as there may be must be accommodated to the relevant statutory scheme. But the question now is not how art 6 can best be accommodated in the interests of fairness given the existing statutory scheme, but rather whether the scheme itself complies with art 6. To accept that the possibility of common law bias is inherent in d the system and mandated by Parliament is merely to admit that the system involves structural bias and requires determinations to be made by a person who is not impartial.

86. It must follow from these conclusions that the Secretary of State is not impartial in the manner required by art 6 because in each case his policy is in issue. This is not of course to say that there is anything wrong with his role e as a policy maker. What is objectionable in terms of art 6 is that he should be the judge in his own cause where his policy is in play. In other words he cannot be both policy maker and decision taker.'

[**179**] The Divisional Court then turned to consider whether the procedures involved in these cases were saved by the High Court's powers of review. It observed f at paras 87–95 of its judgment (see pp 985–987, ante) that decisions of this House have made it clear that the High Court is only concerned with the legality of the Secretary of State's decision; the merits of the case and questions of planning judgment are for the determining authority, not for the High Court. At para 94 the court drew a distinction between the decision of an inspector and the decision g of the Secretary of State, and referring to the process followed where the Secretary of State makes the decision, it said at para 95:

'We do not think this process contains sufficient safeguards to justify the High Court's restricted power of review. In terms of art 6 the decision on the merits, which usually involves findings of fact and planning judgment, h has not been determined by an independent and impartial tribunal or anyone approaching this, but by someone who is obviously not independent and impartial.'

[**180**] In arriving at its decision the Divisional Court found support in the judgment of the Court of Session in *County Properties Ltd v Scottish Ministers* 2000 j SLT 965 which had come to a similar decision in a case concerning a 'called-in' application for listed building consent under Scottish planning legislation similar to the Town and County Planning Act 1990. The Lord Ordinary (MacFadyen) stated (at 975 (para 26)):

'It is the petitioners' Convention right to have their civil rights determined by an independent and impartial tribunal. In my view the respondents' decision to call in the application for their own decision has brought about a situation in which the determination of the petitioners' civil rights will be made by the respondents, who are admittedly not independent and impartial, and against whose decision there is only a limited right of appeal to this court. The limitations on the right of appeal are such that it may well be impossible for this court, although indisputably an independent and impartial tribunal, to bring those qualities to bear on the real issues in the case.'

[181] Before this House Mr Sumption QC, for the Secretary of State, accepted that the determination of planning applications involved a 'determination of civil rights and obligations' within the meaning of art 6(1). Mr Roderick Macdonald QC, for the Lord Advocate, who intervened on behalf of the Scottish Ministers, submitted that art 6(1) only applied to claims or disputes concerning legal rights and obligations to be resolved by a judicial process, and not to the administrative process carried on by a minister when he decides a planning application. Viewed in the light of the common law there would have been obvious force in this submission. In addition there is support for the submission in some passages in the opinion of the European Commission of Human Rights in *Kaplan v UK* (1980) 4 EHRR 64, the commission stating (at 88 (para 154)):

'In the Commission's view the essential role of Article 6(1) in this sphere is to lay down guarantees concerning the mode in which claims or disputes concerning legal rights and obligations (of a "civil" character) are to be resolved. A distinction must be drawn between the acts of a body which is engaged in the resolution of such a claim or dispute and the acts of an administrative or other body purporting merely to exercise or apply a legal power vested in it and not to resolve a legal claim or dispute. Article 6(1) would not, in the Commission's opinion, apply to the acts of the latter even if they do affect "civil rights". It could not be considered as being engaged in a process of "determination" of civil rights and obligations. Its function would not be to decide (*"décidera"*) on a claim, dispute or *"contestation"*. Its acts may, on the other hand, give rise to a claim, dispute or *"contestation"* and article 6 may come into play in that way.'

See also 87–88 (paras 151–153).

[182] However I think it is clear that the commission and the European Court of Human Rights have departed from this view and have held in a number of subsequent cases that the determination of a planning application by an official or a minister falls within the ambit of art 6(1). In *Bryan v UK* (1995) 21 EHRR 342 in proceedings before the European Court of Human Rights the applicant complained that the review by the High Court of an inspector's decision upholding an enforcement notice was insufficient to comply with art 6(1). Before the commission the United Kingdom government had contended that the enforcement notice proceedings did not involve a determination of the applicant's 'civil rights', but this contention was rejected by the commission which stated (at 351 (para 38)):

'The Commission recalls that the right of property is clearly a "civil" right within the meaning of Article 6(1) of the Convention, and the enforcement notice issued by the local authority and the subsequent enforcement proceedings were directly concerned with the way in which the applicant a was entitled to use his land. Consequently, the proceedings in the present case determined a "civil right".'

[183] In its judgment the European Court of Human Rights stated (at 357 (para 31)):

> 'Before the Court the Government did not contest, as they had before the b Commission, that the impugned planning proceedings involved a determination of the applicant's "civil rights". On the basis of its established case law, the Court sees no reason to decide otherwise. Article 6(1) is accordingly applicable to the facts of the present case.'

[184] A similar view has been taken in *Chapman v UK* (2001) 10 BHRC 48 and c other decisions of the European Court and this view is now clearly established in the jurisprudence of the court.

[185] The decisions of the Divisional Court and the Court of Session that there would be non-compliance with art 6(1) in the proceedings which they were considering were largely influenced by the judgment of the European Court in d *Bryan*'s case and counsel for the respondents placed strong reliance on that judgment in their submissions to the House.

[186] The reasoning of the European Court of Human Rights in *Bryan*'s case (1995) 21 EHRR 342 contained a number of stages which I enumerate as follows. (1) Notwithstanding that the inspector was required to decide the applicant's planning appeal in a quasi-judicial, independent and impartial manner, the Secretary e of State could at any time revoke his power to decide the appeal. In the context of planning applications the very existence of this power available to the executive, whose own policies might be in issue, was enough to deprive the inspector of the requisite appearance of independence, and for this reason alone, the review by the inspector did not of itself satisfy the requirements of art 6(1) (see 359 f (para 38)). (2) The court then stated (at 359 (para 40)):

> 'As was explained in the Court's ... judgment [in *Albert v Belgium* (1983) 5 EHRR 533], even where an adjudicatory body determining disputes over "civil rights and obligations" does not comply with Article 6(1) in some respect, no violation of the Convention can be found if the proceedings g before that body are "subject to subsequent control by a judicial body that has full jurisdiction and does provide the guarantees of Article 6(1)". The issue in the present case is whether the High Court satisfied the requirements of Article 6(1) as far as the scope of its jurisdiction was concerned.'

(3) In paras 41–44 (at 359–360) the court noted that the appeal to the High Court, h being on 'points of law', was not capable of embracing all aspects of the inspector's decision concerning the enforcement notice served on Mr Bryan and, in particular—

> 'as is not infrequently the case in relation to administrative law appeals in the Council of Europe Member States, there was no rehearing as such of the j original complaints submitted to the inspector; the High Court could not substitute its own decision on the merits for that of the inspector; and its jurisdiction over the facts was limited.'

However the court then observed that in addition to the classic grounds of unlawfulness under English law the High Court had power to quash the inspector's decision if the inspector had taken into account irrelevant factors or had omitted to take into account relevant factors, or if the evidence was not capable of supporting a finding of fact or if the decision was perverse or irrational. (4) In paras 45 and 46 (at 360–361) the court stated that in assessing the sufficiency of the review available on appeal to the High Court, it was necessary to have regard to matters such as 'the subject matter of the decision appealed against' and the manner in which that decision was arrived at, and the court referred to the uncontested safeguards attending the procedure before the inspector designed to ensure that the inspector came to his decision in accordance with principles of openness, fairness and impartiality. (5) The court then stated (at 361 (para 47)):

> 'In the present case there was no dispute as to the primary facts. Nor was any challenge made at the hearing in the High Court to the factual inferences drawn by the inspector, following the abandonment by the applicant of his objection to the inspector's reasoning under ground (b). The High Court had jurisdiction to entertain the remaining grounds of the applicant's appeal, and his submissions were adequately dealt with point by point. These submissions, as the Commission noted, went essentially to questions involving "a panoply of policy matters such as development plans, and the fact that the property was situated in a Green Belt and a conservation area". Furthermore, even if the applicant had sought to pursue his appeal under ground (b), the Court notes that, while the High Court could not have substituted its own findings of fact for those of the inspector, it would have had the power to satisfy itself that the inspector's findings of fact or the inferences based on them were neither perverse nor irrational. Such an approach by an appeal tribunal on questions of fact can reasonably be expected in specialised areas of the law such as the one at issue, particularly where the facts have already been established in the course of a quasi-judicial procedure governed by many of the safeguards required by Article 6(1). It is also frequently a feature in the systems of judicial control of administrative decisions found throughout the Council of Europe Member States. Indeed, in the instant case, the subject matter of the contested decision by the inspector was a typical example of the exercise of discretionary judgment in the regulation of citizens' conduct in the sphere of town and country planning.'

The court therefore concluded that the scope of review by the High Court was sufficient to comply with art 6(1) and held that there had been no violation of that article.

[187] There were two strands in the reasoning of the European Court of Human Rights. One strand referred to the independent position of the inspector and to the procedure designed to ensure openness, fairness and impartiality on his part. The other strand laid emphasis on the consideration that it was a frequent feature throughout the Council of Europe member states that in specialised areas of the law such as judicial control of administrative decisions, the review by a court of law did not extend to a review of a decision on its merits.

[188] Counsel for the respondents submitted that the decision in *Bryan*'s case was distinguishable from the present case because in this case the Secretary of State lacked the independence of an inspector and his decision-making process did not have the safeguards which related to the decision-making process of an inspector. In relation to the decision-making process of the Secretary of State counsel pointed to the input of views and recommendations from civil servants a of which the objectors were unaware and to which they had no opportunity to reply. Counsel submitted that in *Bryan*'s case the European Court of Human Rights' reliance on the independence of the inspector was a crucial part of its reasoning and that, as the requisite independence did not exist when the Secretary of State made the decision, there would be non-compliance with art 6(1) in the present cases; the consideration that it was a common feature of b European systems of justice that a court did not review a planning decision on its merits was not sufficient to prevent a violation of art 6(1).

[189] Whilst there is some weight in these submissions I do not think that they are of sufficient force to distinguish *Bryan*'s case from the instant case. It is clear from para 47 of the judgment (at 361) that it was in relation to fact-finding that the European Court of Human Rights referred to the safeguards attaching to c the procedure before the inspector, and I consider that the second strand of the court's reasoning was the more important one. Moreover, the judgment cannot be viewed in isolation but must be considered in the light of other opinions of the commission and judgments of the European Court of Human Rights. I consider that the Strasbourg jurisprudence recognises that where an administrative d decision to be taken in the public interest constitutes a determination of a civil right within the meaning of art 6(1), a review of the decision by a court is sufficient to comply with art 6(1) notwithstanding that the review does not extend to the merits of the decision. Because it is a common feature of the judicial systems of the democratic member states of the Council of Europe that a court does not decide whether an administrative decision was well founded in e substance, the commission and the European Court of Human Rights have held that art 6(1) does not guarantee a right to a full review by a court of the merits of every administrative decision affecting private rights, but that there is compliance with the article where there is a right to judicial review of such a decision of the nature exercised by the High Court in England.

f **[190]** This approach is clearly set out and explained in the opinion of the commission in *Kaplan v UK* (1980) 4 EHRR 64 at 89–90:

> '159. The Commission has already noted that in the contracting States discretionary powers are frequently conferred on public authorities to take actions affecting private rights. It is also a common feature of their g administrative law, and indeed almost a corollary of the grant of discretionary powers, that the scope of judicial review of the relevant decisions is limited. In the RINGEISEN case the majority of the Commission drew attention to this. They observed as follows: "It is true that there is in all countries a legitimate concern to protect the citizen against arbitrary h administrative action. This concern may result in the adoption of legislative or other rules concerning administrative procedure. It may result in the introduction of judicial review of administrative action, and the States members of the Council of Europe have for historical and other reasons adopted widely divergent systems of such judicial review. One common feature, however, j seems to be that there are certain elements of administrative discretion which cannot be reviewed by the judge. If the administrative authority has acted properly and within the limits of the law, the judge can very rarely, if ever, decide whether or not the administrative decision was well-founded in substance. To that extent, there is no possibility of bringing the case before an independent and impartial tribunal, even if there is a dispute ('*contestation*') between the citizen and the public authority."

160. Following the court, the Commission does not conclude that Article 6 is therefore altogether inapplicable. However, this factor cannot be left out of account in considering the content or scope of the rights which Article 6 guarantees. The Commission also recalls that its minority in the same case considered that it guaranteed only a right to judicial control as to the "lawfulness" of administrative decisions affecting civil rights. It notes further that the limited scope of judicial review in many contracting states is also reflected in the scope of the jurisdiction afforded to the European Court of Justice under Article 173 of the Treaty establishing the European Economic Community. Under that provision the Court has jurisdiction to review the legality of acts of the Council and Commission of the European Communities only on grounds of "lack of competence, infringement of an essential procedural requirement, infringement of this Treaty or of any rule of law relating to its application, or misuse of powers". These limited grounds of action appear fairly typical of those existing in a number of the Contracting States.

161. An interpretation of Article 6(1) under which it was held to provide a right to a full appeal on the merits of every administrative decision affecting private rights would therefore lead to a result which was inconsistent with the existing, and long-standing, legal position in most of the Contracting States.'

[191] As I have observed in considering the submissions of Mr Macdonald, the commission in *Kaplan*'s case gave a narrower meaning to the words 'In the determination of his civil rights' than has been given in subsequent decisions, but the approach stated in *Kaplan*'s case (at 89 (paras 159–161)) has been adopted in a number of subsequent decisions, notwithstanding that those decisions have recognised that the administrative decisions of which the applicants complained involved the determination of civil rights within the meaning of art 6(1).

[192] In *X v UK* (1998) 25 EHRR CD 88 where the applicant complained of the decision of the Secretary of State that he was not a fit and proper person to be the chief executive of an insurance company, the commission held that the scope of judicial review by the Court of Session was sufficient to comply with art 6(1), and the commission stated (at 97):

'The subject-matter of the decision appealed against in the present case was a classic exercise of administrative discretion. The legislature had charged the Secretary of State with the express function of ensuring, in the public interest, that only appropriate persons would become chief executive of certain insurance companies, and the contested decision in the present case was the exercise of that discretion.'

[193] In *Varey v UK* App No 26662/95 (27 October 1999, unreported) the applicants appealed against refusals of planning permission and inspectors held public inquiries and recommended that the appeals be allowed, but the Secretary of State decided to dismiss the appeals. The applicants complained that the decisions of the Secretary of State overruling the inspectors' recommendations concerning their appeals disclosed a violation of art 6(1) as the High Court was unable to substitute its own decision on the merits for that of the Secretary of State. In its response the government relied on the decision in *Bryan*'s case as showing that the procedures complained of complied with the requirements of a art 6(1). The commission found that there had been no violation of art 6(1) and in para 86 of its opinion, after referring to the decision in *Bryan*'s case, it stated:

> 'While the applicants argue that the scope of review prevents examination of the merits of their claims, the commission notes that this does not contradict the position, as stated by the court, that the domestic courts will examine whether the Secretary of State had regard to all relevant factors. b It is true that the procedures by the inspectors do not themselves satisfy the requirements of art 6(1), the inspectors being appointed by the Secretary of State who retains the power of decision, and that the safeguards provided by their quasi-judicial role in the process have been diminished in this case by the Secretary of State's dismissal of the applicants' appeals notwithstanding c the inspectors' recommendations to the contrary (see para 78). However, the Secretary of State gave reasoned decisions on the basis of the facts found by the inspectors, and the matters relied on by him in overruling their recommendations could be challenged on appropriate grounds before the High Court. Consequently in these circumstances the commission is satisfied that the power of review of that process by the High Court ensures adequate d judicial control of the adminstrative decisions in issue. It finds that the applicants have not in the circumstances been deprived of a fair hearing by an independent and impartial tribunal in the determination of any of their civil rights and obligations. It would observe that matters concerning the compatibility of the subject matter of the planning decisions with the e requirements of the convention fall to be examined under its substantive provisions.'

[194] In *Chapman v UK* (2001) 10 BHRC 48 the applicant was refused planning permission and enforcement notices were issued against her. She appealed against the enforcement notices and after an inquiry an inspector dismissed her f appeal. She claimed that there had been a violation of art 6(1) on the ground that she had no access to a court to determine the merits of her claims. Before the European Court she argued that the court's case law did not support any general proposition that the right of appeal to the High Court on points of law caused planning procedures to be in compliance with art 6(1) and she submitted that *Bryan*'s case was decided on its particular facts.

g **[195]** The European Court did not accept the applicant's argument and held that there had been no violation of art 6(1) and stated (at 76 (para 124)):

> 'The court recalls that in the case of *Bryan v UK* … it held that in the specialised area of town planning law full review of the facts may not be h required by art 6 of the convention. It finds in this case that the scope of review of the High Court, which was available to the applicant after a public procedure before an inspector, was sufficient in this case to comply with art 6(1). It enabled a decision to be challenged on the basis that it was perverse, irrational, had no basis on the evidence or had been made with reference to irrelevant factors or without regard to relevant factors. This j may be regarded as affording adequate judicial control of the administrative decisions in issue.'

[196] A central element in the argument advanced on behalf of the respondents, which was supported by Mr Howell QC as amicus curiae, was that where there was the determination of a civil right within the meaning of art 6(1), the article required that the determination should be carried out (whether initially or on review by a court) by an independent and impartial tribunal which had power to consider the merits of the case, and that this requirement included discretionary matters to be decided by an official or a government minister and which involved matters of government policy. I am unable to accept that submission and I consider that the decisions of the commission and the European Court of Human Rights make clear that the ambit of the review required by art 6(1) does not extend to the merits of such decisions.

[197] I am further of opinion that the jurisdiction of the High Court by way of judicial review is sufficient to comply with art 6(1) in respect of any arguments that the Ministry of Defence has a financial interest in the Alconbury development and that the Department of Transport has promoted the road improvement scheme at Newbury.

[198] Therefore I consider, with respect, that the Divisional Court erred in concluding that art 6(1) prohibited the Secretary of State from being both a policy maker and a decision taker. In *B Johnson & Co (Builders) Ltd v Minister of Health* [1947] 2 All ER 395 Lord Greene MR recognised that in the democratic system of government in England a minister could properly perform both functions because he was answerable to Parliament as regards the policy aspects of his decision and answerable to the High Court as regards the lawfulness and fairness of his decision-making process. In my opinion the jurisprudence of Strasbourg also recognises that in a democracy, where the courts have jurisdiction to conduct a judicial review of the lawfulness and fairness of a decision, a government minister can be both a policy maker and a decision taker without there being a violation of art 6(1), and accordingly I would allow these appeals.

Appeal allowed.

Dilys Tausz Barrister.

a

Foenander v Bond Lewis & Co

[2001] EWCA Civ 759

COURT OF APPEAL, CIVIL DIVISION

BROOKE, SEDLEY AND DYSON LJJ

b 23 MAY 2001

Practice – Appeal – New provisions governing civil appeals in private law matters – Refusal by High Court judge to grant extension of time to appeal from decision of lower court – Whether refusal appealable to Court of Appeal – Access to Justice Act 1999, c *s 54(4).*

Section 54(4)[a] of the Access to Justice Act 1999, which prohibits an appeal against a decision of a court under that section to refuse permission to appeal, is based on the principle that if both a lower court and an appeal court at a lower level of the judicial hierarchy have decided that a proposed appeal has no real prospect of d success, and there is no other compelling reason why the appeal should be heard, that must be the end of the matter, and the issue cannot be relitigated higher up the judicial chain. That principle does not, however, apply to the order of a High Court judge refusing an application to extend time for an appeal from a decision of a lower court. Such an order can, with permission, be appealed to the Court e of Appeal as can any other order made by a High Court judge. If a circuit judge or a High Court judge sitting in an appeal court has the choice of disposing of a belated and unmeritorious appeal either by refusing to extend time for appealing or by refusing permission to appeal, he should bear in mind that taking the latter course will bring the appellate proceedings to an end. The adoption of the former course, on the other hand, may entail further expense and delay while a challenge f is launched at a higher appeal court against the decision not to extend time for appealing (see [16], [18], [19], [22], [23], post).

Per curiam. Under the CPR appellate regime, an appeal from a district judge on an assessment of damages in the High Court will ordinarily lie to a High Court judge, not a circuit judge (see [20]–[23], post); dictum of Brooke LJ in *Clark (Inspector* g *of Taxes) v Perks* [2000] 4 All ER 1 at 13 (para 54) corrected.

Cases referred to in judgments

Bokhari v Mahmood (1988) Times, 26 April, [1988] CA Transcript 323.

Clark (Inspector of Taxes) v Perks [2000] 4 All ER 1, [2001] 1 WLR 17, CA.

Lane v Esdaile [1891] AC 210, HL.

h *Podbery v Peak* [1981] 1 All ER 699, [1981] Ch 344, [1981] 2 WLR 686, CA.

R v Secretary of State for Trade and Industry, ex p Eastaway [2001] 1 All ER 27, [2000] 1 WLR 2222, HL.

Rickards v Rickards [1989] 3 All ER 193, [1990] Fam 194, [1989] 3 WLR 748, CA.

Tanfern Ltd v Cameron-MacDonald [2000] 2 All ER 801, [2000] 1 WLR 1311, CA.

j

Application

On an application by Johan Michael Richard Foenander, the Court of Appeal was required to determine whether it had jurisdiction under the CPR to entertain an

a Section 54, so far as material, provides: '(4) No appeal may be made against a decision of a court under this section to give or refuse permission ... '

appeal by him against the order of Astill J on 11 November 1999 refusing his application for permission to appeal out of time against the decision of Deputy Master Chism on 1 October 1999 striking out his action for professional negligence against the respondent, Bond Lewis & Co. The facts are set out in the judgment of Brooke LJ.

Mr Foenander appeared in person.
Alistair Craig (instructed by *Beachcroft Wansbroughs*) for the respondent.

BROOKE LJ.

[1] This application by a litigant in person raises an issue of general importance in relation to the new CPR appeals regime.

[2] In January 1995 Mr Foenander issued a writ against Bond Lewis & Co, who are a firm of solicitors, and against Mr Florence O'Donaghue of counsel, alleging professional negligence in the conduct of the matrimonial proceedings which followed the breakdown of his marriage. The action against the second defendant was dismissed in April 1995 on the grounds of forensic immunity. On 1 October 1999 Deputy Master Chism struck out the claim against the first defendant (the Chism order).

[3] Under the former appeals regime Mr Foenander could appeal to a judge against a master's order as of right provided his notice of appeal was given and served within five days (RSC Ord 58, r 1). In the event he delayed for about two weeks, and on 11 November 1999 Astill J refused to make an order extending his time for appealing (the Astill order). Mr Foenander then had the right to seek permission to appeal to this court against the Astill order, provided that this application was made within four weeks (RSC Ord 58, r 4). He did not exercise that right.

[4] On 2 May 2000 the new CPR appeals regime was introduced. This court has explained various aspects of the new regime on a number of occasions, and in particular in my judgments in *Tanfern Ltd v Cameron-MacDonald* [2000] 2 All ER 801, [2000] 1 WLR 1311 and *Clark (Inspector of Taxes) v Perks* [2000] 4 All ER 1, [2001] 1 WLR 17. The new appeals regime applies to all applications lodged at the appeal court on and after 2 May 2000 (see the *Tanfern* case [2000] 2 All ER 801 at 812, [2000] 1 WLR 1311 at 1320 (para 47)). Under the new regime there is no appeal as of right against a master's order (CPR 52.3(1)(a): for the definition of the word 'judge' see CPR 2.3(1)).

[5] On 14 February 2000 the first defendants sent Mr Foenander their bill relating to the costs payable to them pursuant to the Chism order and the Astill order. On 31 October 2000 they obtained a default costs certificate in the sum of £9,713·77, and on 7 December 2000 Deputy Costs Judge Thum made an order refusing to set aside this certificate (the Thum order). Mr Foenander's application for permission to appeal against the Thum order was dismissed on paper by McKinnon J on 11 January 2001 and in court by Owen J on 14 February 2001. Although he has sought to challenge the Thum order by a further application to this court, this court clearly has no jurisdiction to entertain this application under the new CPR appellate regime (s 54(4) of the Access to Justice Act 1999). On 6 March 2001 Deputy Master Joseph ruled, correctly, that there was no further right of appeal to the Court of Appeal against the Thum order because Owen J had refused permission to appeal.

[6] Within his notice of appeal against the Thum order Mr Foenander also sought an extension of time to lodge an application for permission to appeal out

a of time against the Chism order and the Astill order. The notice stated, among other things, that someone had impersonated Deputy Master Chism on 1 October 1999. Owen J rejected this allegation after seeing the original order which had been initialled that day, and after taking judicial notice of the practice whereby a master's signature is compared with the stock signatures held in the central office before the order is stamped.

b [7] McKinnon J dismissed this application on paper on the grounds that Mr Foenander had not sent out any explanation as to why he was now so many months out of time for appealing. On 19 January 2001 Mr Foenander purported to remedy this defect by swearing a long affidavit in which he described various features of the case going back to its inception. He attributed his failure to appeal against Astill J's order to the misconduct of solicitors he instructed 'to appeal this c case' on 15 October, nearly a month before Astill J made his order. On 14 February 2001 Owen J dismissed the application for an extension of time on the same grounds as McKinnon J, namely that there were no proper grounds on which an extension could be granted. He went on to say that he had no power to grant permission to appeal against his order because the practice direction to CPR Pt 52 d states (at para 4.8) that there is no appeal from a decision of an appeal court, made at an oral hearing, to allow or refuse permission to appeal to that court. This rule is of course derived from s 54(4) of the 1999 Act.

[8] Owen J's order, which was sealed on 20 February 2001, provides:

> '1. The application for permission to appeal from the Order of Deputy e Costs Judge Thum dated 7th December 2000 be and hereby is refused;
> 2. The application for an extension of time to appeal from: (1) the order of Deputy Master Chism dated 1st October 1999 and (2) the order of Mr Justice Astill dated 11th November 1999 be and hereby is refused.'

[9] I am not surprised that the proceedings in the court below took a peculiar f course, because as a lay litigant Mr Foenander had difficulty in identifying the appropriate procedure for the challenges he wished to make, but in fact neither McKinnon J nor Owen J had any power to extend the time for appealing against the Astill order. CPR 52.6(1) provides unequivocally that 'An application to vary the time limit for filing an appeal notice must be made to the appeal court'. g Needless to say, the attempt by Mr Foenander to obtain an extension of time for appealing against the Chism order was doomed because he had already sought and been refused this relief by Astill J.

[10] On 28 February 2001 Mr Foenander lodged with this court a notice of appeal against the order of Owen J. He maintained on the face of the notice that he did not need permission to appeal against para 2 of that order, and he set out h his grounds for appealing against para 1. The first of these contentions was clearly wrong (see CPR 52.3(1) which makes it obligatory to obtain permission to appeal against all decisions of a judge in the High Court, subject to exceptions which are irrelevant in the present case). I have already explained why this court would have no jurisdiction to entertain Mr Foenander's proposed challenge to j para 1 of Owen J's order (see [5] above).

[11] In these circumstances the Civil Appeals Office notified Mr Foenander that it accepted his notice of appeal in so far as it related to the Astill order on the basis that the court might need to consider whether it had jurisdiction to entertain this appeal as a preliminary issue. In due course I directed that his application should be heard in court. I gave him notice that the court would wish to consider the status of this application under the new CPR appeals regime.

Since the jurisdictional point was an important one, I elicited the assistance of a lawyer in the Civil Appeals Office who kindly prepared for Mr Foenander and for the court a bench memorandum explaining the legal issue we had to decide. We adopted the same technique in the *Tanfern* case (see [2000] 2 All ER 801 at 803, [2000] 1 WLR 1311 at 1312–1313 (para 4)). At the hearing today we also heard brief submissions from Mr Craig on behalf of the respondents.

[12] The short issue we have to decide is this. If Astill J had refused Mr Foenander permission to appeal against the Chism order, this court would have no jurisdiction to entertain an appeal against that refusal (s 54(4) of the 1999 Act). Is the position different because he decided to refuse an extension of time for appealing, so that he did not consider the application for permission to appeal against the Chism order on the merits?

[13] In the pre-CPR regime the answer to this question would have been very straightforward. In *Rickards v Rickards* [1989] 3 All ER 193, [1990] Fam 194 a party to matrimonial proceedings in a county court failed to file his notice of appeal from a decision of a registrar within the prescribed time limit. A circuit judge refused his application for leave to appeal out of time, but granted him leave to appeal to this court from his order refusing an extension of time. This court had held in the earlier case of *Podbery v Peak* [1981] 1 All ER 699, [1981] Ch 344 that it had no jurisdiction to entertain an appeal from a refusal to extend time for appealing. The court now held that that earlier decision had been made per incuriam. We are not concerned on this occasion with the reasons it gave for deciding that it was entitled not to follow the earlier case.

[14] Lord Donaldson of Lymington MR ([1989] 3 All ER 193 at 196–197, [1990] Fam 194 at 199–201) considered the effect of the decision of the House of Lords in *Lane v Esdaile* [1891] AC 210 on which the earlier decision has been based. He then said:

> 'In my judgment what *Lane v Esdaile* decided, and all that it decided, was that where it is provided that an appeal shall lie *by leave* of a particular court or courts neither the grant or refusal of leave is an appealable decision. Although the statute contained time limits, 21 days in the case of interlocutory orders and 12 months in the case of other orders, no court had any power to extend them, or, of course, was asked to do so. The effect of the expiry of those time limits was simply to attract a requirement for special leave to appeal. The grant or refusal of an application for leave to appeal is one thing. The grant or refusal of an application to extend the time limited for taking a step in proceedings, including but not limited to giving notice of appeal, is quite another. It arises in a multitude of contexts, none of which have even been held to be inherently unappealable, with the sole exception of an extension of time for appealing in *Podbery v Peak* ([1981] 1 All ER 699, [1981] Ch 344) and, following that decision, in *Bokhari v Mahmood* ((1988) Times, 26 April). Whilst it is true that a right of appeal may be barred either by a refusal of an extension of time or by a refusal of leave, the routes by which this result is achieved and the underlying concepts are essentially different. The husband did not need leave to appeal to the county court judge. He needed an extension of time. He did not need an extension of time for appealing to this court. He needed, and obtained, leave to appeal.' (See [1989] 3 All ER 193 at 197, [1990] Fam 194 at 201; Lord Donaldson MR's emphasis.)

[15] Lord Donaldson MR was making a distinction between the grant or refusal of an application for leave to appeal on the one hand and the grant or refusal a of an application to extend the time limited for taking a step in proceedings on the other. The former, he said, was governed by *Lane v Esdaile*: the latter was as appealable (subject to the necessity of obtaining permission to appeal) as any other decision made by a judge.

[16] The question we have to decide is whether this position has been affected by the introduction of the CPR regime. As I have already observed, s 54(4) of the b 1999 Act prescribes that no appeal may be made against a decision of a court under that section to give or refuse permission, but it is silent in relation to decisions of the kind with which we are concerned in the present case. Prima facie (subject to the need to obtain leave to appeal) an appeal lies to this court pursuant to s 16(1) of the Supreme Court Act 1981 (as amended) which provides:

c 'Subject as otherwise provided by this or any other Act ... or as provided by any order made by the Lord Chancellor under section 56(1) of the Access to Justice Act 1999, the Court of Appeal shall have jurisdiction to hear and determine appeals from any judgment or order of the High Court.'

d **[17]** Under the CPR appellate regime, an appeal from a decision of a High Court judge lies to this court, as I explained in para 15 of my judgment in the *Tanfern* case [2000] 2 All ER 801 at 805–806, [2000] 1 WLR 1311 at 1314–1315. The position is now set out clearly in para 2A.1 of the practice direction to CPR Pt 52. This is not a second appeal within the meaning of s 55(1) of the 1999 Act because the 'matter' on which Astill J gave judgment (viz whether to extend time for an e appeal against the Chism order) is different from the 'matter' on which Deputy Master Chism made his ruling (viz whether the action against the second defendants should be struck out).

[18] The principle which underlies the rule in *Lane v Esdaile* (which was recently reaffirmed by the House of Lords in *R v Secretary of State for Trade and* f *Industry, ex p Eastaway* [2001] 1 All ER 27, [2000] 1 WLR 2222) and in s 54(4) of the 1999 Act (in so far as it refers to the refusal of leave to appeal) is that if both a lower court and an appeal court at a lower level of the judicial hierarchy have decided that a proposed appeal has no real prospect of success, and that there is no other compelling reason why the appeal should be heard (see CPR 52.3(6)), that must be the end of the matter, and this issue cannot be relitigated higher up g the judicial chain. This principle does not, however, in my judgment apply to an order of the type made by Astill J on 11 November 1999. He decided, in the exercise of his discretion, not to extend time for an appeal from the deputy master's decision. Nobody else had considered, or had the power to consider (see CPR 52.6(1)) this exercise of discretion, and in those circumstances, provided that h permission to appeal is granted, Astill J's order is as appealable to this court as any other order made by a High Court judge.

[19] The logic of this decision is that if a circuit judge or a High Court judge sitting in an appeal court has the choice of disposing of a belated and unmeritorious appeal either by refusing to extend time for appealing or by j refusing permission to appeal, he/she should bear in mind that taking the latter course will bring the appellate proceedings to an end. The adoption of the former course, on the other hand, may entail further expense and delay while a challenge is launched at a higher appeal court against the decision not to extend time for appealing.

[20] Before I end this judgment, I would like to correct an error I made when describing the destination of appeals under the CPR appellate regime in para 54 of my judgment in *Clark (Inspector of Taxes) v Perks* [2000] 4 All ER 1 at 13, [2001] 1 WLR 17 at 30. I said: a

> 'It does not now matter whether a decision by a district judge on an assessment of damages was made in the county court or in the High Court. Appeal against such a decision will lie to a circuit judge unless the case was allocated to the multi-track in which case it will lie to this court.'

b

[21] It has been pointed out to me, correctly, that an appeal from a district judge on an assessment of damages in the High Court will ordinarily lie to a High Court judge, not a circuit judge. Paragraph 54 of that judgment must now be read subject to this gloss.

SEDLEY LJ. c

[22] I agree.

DYSON LJ.

[23] I agree.

Order accordingly.

Kate O'Hanlon Barrister.

End of Volume 2